*What they're saying about*

# The Complete Guide to Bed & Breakfasts, Inns & Guesthouses ...

*... all necessary information about facilities, prices, pets, children, amenities, credit cards and the like. Like France's Michelin ...*

— New York Times

*Definitive and worth the room in your reference library.*

— Los Angeles Times

*... innovative and useful ...*

—Washington Post

*A must for the adventurous ... who still like the Hobbity creature comforts.*

— St. Louis Post-Dispatch

*What has long been overdue: a list of the basic information of where, how much and what facilities are offered at the inns and guesthouses.*

— San Francisco Examiner

*Standing out from the crowd for its thoroughness and helpful cross-indexing ...*

—Chicago Sun Times

*A quaint, charming and economical way to travel—all in one book.*

— Waldenbooks (as seen in USA Today)

*Little descriptions provide all the essentials: romance, historical landmarks, golf/fishing, gourmet food, or, just as important, low prices. Take your pick!*

— National Motorist

*For those travelling by car, lodging is always a main concern ... The Complete Guide to Bed & Breakfasts, Inns & Guesthouses provides listings and descriptions of more than 2,500 inns.*

— Minneapolis Star & Tribune

*... the most complete compilation of bed and breakfast data ever published.*

—Denver Post

*Unique and delightful inns ...*

— Detroit Free Press

*. . . lists more than 260 places in California alone . . .*
— Oakland Tribune

*. . . I've got just the book for you . . . settle back and picture yourself lapping discount luxury.*
— Washington Times

*The book may give . . . readers everything they ever wanted to know . . .*
— Dallas Morning News

*A state-by-state and city-by-city guide . . . researched listings . . . an impressive number.*
— San Francisco Chronicle

*. . . comprehensive . . .*
— Atlanta Journal

*It is a good basic resource for inn fanciers.*
— ndianapolis Star

*. . . a worthwhile addition to libraries.*
— Library Journal

*. . . a concise guide. .thousands of hotels, inns & guesthouses . . .*
— Los Angeles Herald-Examiner

*. . . access to more than 10,000 private guesthouses . . .*
— Chicago Tribune

*. . . the best so far.*
— Whole Earth Review

*The joy of the Complete Guide to BBIG is that it compromises neither description nor practical info . . . an essential reference.*
— Midwest Book Review

*. . . excellent guide book.*
— Focus, Philadelphia, PA

*. . . well coded and full of practical information.*
— Diversion

# THE COMPLETE GUIDE TO
# BED &
# BREAKFASTS,
# INNS & GUESTHOUSES
## IN THE UNITED STATES, CANADA, & WORLDWIDE

## PAMELA LANIER

*Handwritten notes:*

NEW YORK

GROTTO AZURE (MUST HAVE TRANSPERTATION) BEFORE

8TH

SIT DOWNSTAIRS

WAREHOUSE DISTRI

*A Lanier Guide* ▲

*Other Books By Pamela Lanier*

| | |
|---|---|
| *All-Suite Hotel Guide* | (Lanier Publishing Int., Ltd.) |
| *Elegant Small Hotels* | (Lanier Publishing Int., Ltd.) |
| *Elegant Hotels—Pacific Rim* | (Lanier Publishing Int., Ltd.) |
| *Condo Vacations: The Complete Guide* | (Lanier Publishing Int., Ltd.) |
| *Family Travel Guide Online* | (Lanier Publishing Int., Ltd.) |
| *Golf Resorts: The Complete Guide* | (Lanier Publishing Int., Ltd.) |
| *Golf Resorts International* | (Lanier Publishing Int., Ltd.) |
| *22 Days in Alaska* | (Lanier Publishing Int., Ltd.) |
| *Cinnamon Mornings* | (Lanier Publishing Int., Ltd.) |
| *Bed & Breakfast Cookbook* | (Running Press) |

For further information, please contact:
   The Complete Guide to Bed & Breakfasts,
     Inns and Guesthouses
   Drawer D
   Petaluma, CA 94953

© 1997 by Lanier Publishing Int., Ltd.
All rights reserved. Published 1997

1997 edition. First printing

ISBN 0-89815-885-0

Distributed to the book trade by:
   Ten Speed Press
   P.O. Box 7123
   Berkeley, CA 94707

Cover by V. Ichioka

Design & Production by J.C. Wright

Typeset by Futura Graphics

Printed in Canada on recycled paper

In a nationwide survey of innkeepers conducted by *Innsider Magazine*

**For J.C. Dolphin Valdés**

# Acknowledgements

Corrine Rednour and George Lanier for your help, love, and support—thank you.

Assistant editor: Shannon Little.

To my friends who were so generous with their time and skills:

Venetia Young, Carol McBride, Marianne Barth, Vincent Yu, Madelyn Furze, Rus Quon, Terry Lacey, John Garrett, Chris Manley, Mary Kreuger, Mr. Wiley, Adele Novelli, Ruth Young, Mrs. Gieselman (the best English teacher ever), Mary Institute, Ingrid Head, Sumi Timberlake, Marvin Downey, Marguerite Tafoya, Peggy Dennis, Judy Jacobs, Derek Ng, Katherine Bertolucci, Margaret Callahan, Mary Ellen Callahan, Glenna Goulet, Mariposa Valdés, Hal Hershey, Leslie Chan, Jane Foster, Carolyn Strange .

Special thanks to Richard Paoli

To the great folks in the Chambers of Commerce, State and Regional Departments of Tourism, I am most grateful.

To the innkeepers themselves who are so busy, yet found the time to fill out our forms and provide us with all sorts of information, I wish you all great success.

*Lanier Publishing facilitates the planting of 9 trees for every tree used in the production of our guides.*

# Contents

# 1997 INN OF THE YEAR

## THE LEGACY OF WILLIAMSBURG B&B
## WILLIAMSBURG, VIRGINIA

Maryann Gist moved to Williamsburg in 1985 from Marion, Ohio where she had owned a restaurant. With her knowledge of 18th century America and her love of entertaining she decided to open a period inn, and what better location than Williamsburg, Virginia. With the help of Linson, a native from Beijing, China and former five star hotel chief concierge, Maryann delights in serving a grand breakfast each morning with special attention to guests' dietary restrictions.

The Inn is nestled in and surrounded by great pine, dogwood and holly trees, and the front is adorned with beautiful gardens that change with the seasons. There are many common areas of the house for guests to enjoy such as the tavern and billiard room complete with a pool table made in England and a fireplace. The grand living room and library, too, has a fireplace. In the "news room," guests can watch tapes about historic Colonial Williamsburg before they set out to tour the area. At the Legacy, you will walk over the threshold of time and fun-filled days of learning about America's humble beginnings.

---

### INNS OF THE YEAR     HONOR ROLL

| | | | |
|---|---|---|---|
| 1985 | Joshua Grindle Inn, Mendocino, CA | 1992 | The Lamplight Inn, Lake Luzerne, NY |
| 1986 | Carter House, Eureka, CA | 1993 | The Whalewalk Inn, Eastham, Cape Cod, MA |
| 1987 | Governor's Inn, Ludlow, VT | | |
| 1988 | Seacrest Manor, Rockport, MA | 1994 | The Captain Freeman Inn, Brewster, Cape Cod, MA |
| 1989 | Wedgewood Inn, New Hope, PA | | |
| 1990 | The Veranda, Senoia, GA | 1995 | The Williamsburg Sampler B&B, Williamsburg, VA |
| 1991 | Kedron Valley Inn, South Woodstock, VT | 1996 | Chicago Pike Inn B&B, Coldwater, MI |

# Introduction

There was a time, and it wasn't so long ago, when bed and breakfast inns were a rarity in the United States. Travelers made do at a hotel or motel; there was no alternative. The few bed and breakfast inns were scattered across the rural areas of New England and California. They were little known to most travelers; often their only advertisement was by word of mouth.

But in a few short years that has changed, and changed in a way that could only be called dramatic. There has been an explosion in the number of bed and breakfast inns. Today, inns can be found in every state, and often in cities; they have become true alternatives to a chain motel room or the city hotel with its hundreds of cubicles.

This sudden increase in bed and breakfast inns started less than two decades ago when Americans, faced with higher costs for foreign travel, began to explore the backroads and hidden communities of their own country.

Other factors have influenced the growth and popularity of bed and breakfast inns. Among them, the desire to get away from the daily routine and sameness of city life; the desire to be pampered for a few days; and also the desire to stay in a place with time to make new friends among the other guests.

The restored older homes that have become bed and breakfast inns answer those desires. The setting most often is rural; the innkeepers provide the service—not a staff with name tags—and the parlor is a gathering place for the handful of guests. They are a home away from home.

The proliferation of these inns as an alternative lodging has created some confusion. It's been difficult to find—in one place—up-to-date and thorough information about the great variety of inns.

Some books published in the past five or six years have tried to provide this information. But those books focused on one region of the country or named too few inns. While some earlier books gave detailed descriptions of the inns, few bothered to provide information about the type of breakfast served, whether there are rooms for non-smokers, and such things as whether the inn offered free use of bicycles or whether it had a hot tub.

An effort to collect as much information about as many inns as possible in one book has been overdue. Now that has been remedied. You hold a copy of the result in your hands.

*Richard Paoli,*
*Travel Editor*
*San Francisco Examiner*

# How to Use this Guide

## Organization

This book is organized alphabetically by state and, within a state, alphabetically by city or town. The inns appear first. More inns are listed after the featured inns. At the end of the listings you will find the World Wide Listings by country and within the country by the city. At the back of the guide are listings of the reservation service organizations serving each state and inns with special characteristics.

## Three Types of Accommodations

**Inn:** Webster's defines an inn as a "house built for the lodging and entertainment of travelers." All the inns in this book fulfill this description. Many also provide meals, at least breakfast, although a few do not. Most of these inns have under 30 guest rooms.

**Bed and Breakfast:** Can be anything from a home with three or more rooms to, more typically, a large house or mansion with eight or nine guest accommodations where breakfast is served in the morning.

**Guest House:** Private homes welcoming travelers, some of which may be contacted directly but most of which are reserved through a reservation service organization. A comprehensive list of RSOs appears toward the back of this guide.

## Breakfasts

We define a **full breakfast** as one being along English lines, including eggs and/or meat as well as the usual breads, toast, juice and coffee.

**Continental plus** is a breakfast of coffee, juice, and choice of several breads and pastry and possibly more.

**Continental** means coffee, juice, bread or pastry

If there is a charge for breakfast, then we note it as (fee).

## Meals

Bear in mind that inns that do not serve meals are usually located near a variety of restaurants.

## Can We Get a Drink?

Those inns without a license will generally chill your bottles and provide you with set-ups upon request.

## Prices

We include a price code to give you an idea of each inn's rates. Generally, the coded prices indicate a given lodging's lowest priced double room, double occupancy rate as follows:

$—under $50    $$—$50–$76    $$$—$76–$125    $$$$—more than $125

Appearing to the right of the price code is a code indicating the type of food services available:

**B&B:** Breakfast included in quoted rate

**EP** (European Plan): No meals

**MAP** (Modified American Plan): Includes breakfast and dinner

**AP** (American Plan): Includes all three meals

The World Wide Inns are listed by their country's currency.

All prices are subject to change. Please be sure to confirm rates and services when you make your reservations.

## Credit Cards and Checks

If an establishment accepts credit cards, it will be listed as VISA, MC, AmEx, or MostCC. Most inns will accept your personal check with proper identification, but be sure to confirm when you book.

## Ratings

One of the beauties of bed & breakfast travel is the individual nature of each inn. And innkeepers thrive on their independence! Some inns are members of their local, state or national inn association (most of which have membership requirements), and/or are members of or are rated by AAA, Mobil and others. Each of these rating systems relies upon different inspection protocol, membership and evaluative criteria. We use *Rated* in the listings to designate inns which have informed us that they have been rated by or are affiliated with any of these groups. If ratings are important to you, we suggest that you call and inquire of the specific inn for details. We continue to find, however, that some very good inns remain unrated, simply because of their size or idiosyncratic nature.

## Reservations

Reservations are essential at most inns, particularly during busy seasons, and are appreciated at other times. Be sure to reserve, even if only a few hours in advance, to avoid disappointment. When you book, feel free to discuss your requirements and confirm prices, services and other details. We have found innkeepers to be delightfully helpful.

Most inns will hold your reservation until 6 p.m. If you plan to arrive later, please phone ahead to let them know.

A deposit or advance payment is required at some inns.

## Children, Pets and Smoking

Children, pets, smoking and physical handicaps present special considerations for many inns. Whether or not they can be accommodated is generally noted as follows:

|  | Yes | Limited | No |
|---|---|---|---|
| Children | C-yes | C-ltd |  |
| Pets | P-yes | P-ltd | P-no |
| Smoking | S-yes | S-ltd | S-no |
| Handicapped | H-yes | H-ltd | H-no |

However, many inns with limited facilities for children will often have one or two rooms set aside for families. Be sure to inquire when you book your room.

## Accessibility for the Handicapped

Because many inns are housed in old buildings, access for handicapped persons in many cases is limited. Where this information is available, we have noted it as above. Be sure to confirm your exact requirements when you book.

## Big Cities

In many big cities there are very few small, intimate accommodations. We have searched out as many as possible. We strongly advise you to investigate the guest house alternative, which can provide you with anything from a penthouse in New York to your own quiet quarters with a private entrance in the suburbs. See our RSO listings at the back of the book.

## Farms

Many B&Bs are located in a rural environment, some on working farms. We have provided a partial list of farm vacation experiences. What a restorative for the city-weary. They can make a great family vacation—just be sure to keep a close eye on the kids around farm equipment.

## Bathrooms

Though shared baths are the norm in Europe, this is sometimes a touchy subject in the U.S.A. We list the number of private baths available directly next to the number of rooms. Bear in mind that those inns with shared baths generally have more than one.

## Manners

Please keep in mind when you go to an inn that innkeeping is a very hard job. It is amazing that innkeepers manage to maintain such a thoroughly cheerful and delightful presence despite long hours. Do feel free to ask your innkeepers for help or suggestions, but please don't expect them to be your personal servant. You may have to carry your own bags.

When in accommodations with shared baths, be sure to straighten the bathroom as a courtesy to your fellow guests. If you come in late, please do so on tiptoe, mindful of the other patrons visiting the inn for a little R&R.

## Special Offers

Many of our featured inns wish to make our readers special offers—discounts, bonuses, etc., which appear at the end of the inns' listing. To redeem the special offer be sure to confirm its availability—some are limited ("ltd.")— when you reserve your room and then you must present the Guide when you check in. And enjoy! with our compliments.

## Sample Bed & Breakfast Listing

Price and included meals
Numbers of rooms and private baths
Credit cards accepted
Name of inn
Street address and zip code   Travel agent commission  •
Phone number   Limitations:
Name of innkeeper       Children (C), Pets (P)
Dates of operation       Smoking (S), Handicapped Access (H)
    Foreign languages spoken

Name of city or town                                     Extra charge for breakfast

ANYPLACE
**Any Bed & Breakfast**   $$ B&B   Full breakfast (fee)
Any Street, ZIP code   8 rooms, 6 pb   Lunch, dinner
555-555-5555   Visa, MC •   sitting room
Tom & Jane Innkeeper   C-yes/S-ltd/P-no/H-ltd   library, bicycles
All year   French, Spanish   antiques

*Large Victorian country house in historic village. Hiking, swimming and golf nearby. Old-fashioned comfort with modern conveniences.* **Third night 50% off.**

Description given by the innkeeper about the   Meals and drinks   Special offer
original characteristics of his establishment   Amenities

## Ejemplo de una entrada para las posadas con cama & desayuno

Ciudad ó pueblo nombre

Nombre de la posada
Dirección
Teléfono
Fechas de temporada

Precio del alojamiento
Qué comidas van incluídas
Número de cuartos y número de cuartos
   con baño privado
Tarjetas de crédito aceptables
Agente de viaje comisión •
Limitaciones:
   niños (C); animales domésticos (P);
   prohibido fumar (S); entradas para
   minusválidos (H)
Se habla idiomas extranjeros

Comidas y bebidas

Entretenimientos

**ANYPLACE** —————————————————————————————

| | | |
|---|---|---|
| **Any Bed & Breakfast** | $$ B&B | Full breakfast (fee) |
| Any Street, ZIP code | 8 rooms, 6 pb | Lunch, dinner |
| 555-555-5555 | Visa, MC • | sitting room |
| Tom & Jane Innkeeper | C-yes /S-ltd/P-no/H-ltd | library, bicycles |
| All year | French, Spanish | antiques |

*Large Victorian country house in historic village. Hiking, swimming and golf nearby. Old-fashioned comfort with modern conveniences.* **Third night 50% off.**

Descripción proporcionada por el dueño de la
posada sobre las características especiales y
originales de establecimiento

Oferta especial

# Mode d'emploi

Prix des chambres Repas inclus
   ou non
Nombre de chambres et
   chambres avec salle de bain
   privées
Cartes de crédit acceptées

Nom de ville

Repas, boissons possibles

Commodités

**ANYPLACE** —————————————————————————————

| | | |
|---|---|---|
| **Any Bed & Breakfast** | $$ B&B | Full breakfast (fee) |
| Any Street, ZIP code | 8 rooms, 6 pb | Lunch, dinner |
| 555-555-5555 | Visa, MC • | sitting room |
| Tom & Jane Innkeeper | C-yes /S-ltd/P-no/H-ltd | library, bicycles |
| All year | French, Spanish | antiques |

*Large Victorian country house in historic village. Hiking, swimming and golf nearby. Old-fashioned comfort with modern conveniences.*

Nom de l'auberge
Addresse
Téléphone
Dates d'ouverture s'il n'y a
   pas de dates ouvert
   toute l'année

Restrictions—
   Enfants (C); Animaux (P);
   Fumeurs (S); Handicappés (H)
On parle les langues étrangères

L'aubergiste décrit ce qui rend
son auberge unique

# Erläuterung der Eintragungen der Unterkunfsstätte

Name der Stadt oder Ortschaft

Name der Unterkunft
Adresse
Telefon-Nummer
Zu welcher Jahreszeit offen?

Preis für die Unterkunft, und welche Mahlzeiten im Preis einbegriffen sind
Reisebüro-Kommission ●
Anzahl der Zimmer, und wieviel mit eigenem Badezimmer (=pb)
Beschränkungen in Bezug auf Kinder, Haustiere, Rauchen, oder für Behinderte geeignet (yes=ja; ltd=beschränkt; no=nicht zugelassen)
Man spricht Fremdsprachen

Was für ein Frühstück?
Andere Mahlzeiten und Bars

Was gibt's sonst noch?

**ANYPLACE**
**Any Bed & Breakfast**
Any Street, ZIP code
555-555-5555
Tom & Jane Innkeeper
All year

$$ B&B
8 rooms, 6 pb
Visa, MC ●
C-yes /S-ltd/P-no/H-ltd
French, Spanish

Full breakfast (fee)
Lunch, dinner
sitting room
library, bicycles
antiques

*Large Victorian country house in historic village. Hiking, swimming and golf nearby. Old-fashioned comfort with modern conveniences.*

Beschreibung des Gastwirts, was an diesem Gästehaus einmalig oder besonders bemerkenswert ist

都市又は町の名

旅館名
住所
電話番号
利用期間。

朝食のタイプ
その他の設備
昼食、夕食、アルコールのサービス

**ANYPLACE**
**Any Bed & Breakfast**
Any Street, ZIP code
555-555-5555
Tom & Jane Innkeeper
All year

$$ B&B
8 rooms, 6 pb
Visa, MC ●
C-yes /S-ltd/P-no/H-ltd
French, Spanish

Full breakfast (fee)
Lunch, dinner
sitting room
library, bicycles
antiques

*Large Victorian country house in historic village. Hiking, swimming and golf nearby. Old-fashioned comfort with modern conveniences.*

# Alabama

## ANNISTON

**Victoria, A Country Inn**
P.O. Box 2213, 36202
1604 Quintard
205-236-0503  Fax: 205-236-1138
800-260-8781
Fain & Beth Casey
All year

$$-B&B
60 rooms, 60 pb
AmEx, *Rated*, •
C-yes/S-ltd/P-no/H-yes

Continental plus bkfst.
Restaurant, bar service
Swimming pool
family friendly facility
gardens, gazebo

*This Southern estate is located midway between Atlanta & Birmingham & offers Victorian amenities from the antiques within the main house to the reproductions in the annex.*

## MENTONE

**Madaperca B&B**
5024 Al Hwy. 117, 35984
205-634-4792  Fax: 205-634-4792
Yvonne & Don Brock
All year

$$-B&B
4 rooms, 4 pb
Visa, MC, Disc., •
C-yes/S-no/P-no/H-no

Full breakfast
Snacks
Sitting room
river views
midst a bird sanctuary

*Riverside retreat atop Lookout Mountain. Mountain stone estate. Canoe Little River to Desoto Falls. Sleep to the sounds of a waterfall; wake to the smell of a country breakfast.*

## MONTGOMERY

**Red Bluff Cottage**
P.O. Box 1026, 36101
551 Clay St., 36104
334-264-0056  Fax: 334-262-1872
Mark & Anne Waldo
All year

$$-B&B
4 rooms, 4 pb
Most CC, *Rated*, •
C-yes/S-no/P-no/H-no

Full breakfast
Deep porches, gardens
gazebo, fenced play yard
family suite

*Two-story raised cottage in historic district. Panoramic view of river plain and state capitol. Family antiques, gazebo and gardens. Within blocks of I-65 & I-85*

## More Inns ...

| | |
|---|---|
| Alexander City | Mistletoe Bough, 497 Hillabee St., 35010,  205-329-3717 |
| Aliceville | Myrtlewood, 602 Broad St., 35442,  205-373-2121 |
| Aliceville | WillowBrooke, 501 Broad St., 35442,  205-373-6133 |
| Asheville | Roses & Lace Inn,  P.O. Box 852, 35953 |
| Citronelle | Citronella B&B Inn, 19055 S. Main St., 36522,  205-866-2849 |
| Decatur | Hearts and Treasures, 911 Seventh Ave., S.E., 35601,  205-353-9562 |
| Elba | Aunt B's B&B,  717 W. Davis St., 36323,  334-897-6918 |
| Eufaula | Kendal Manor, 534 W. Broad St., 36027,  334-687-8847 |
| Eufaula | St. Mary's B&B, 206 Rivers Ave., 36027,  205-687-7195 |
| Eutaw | Kirkwood Plantation, 111 Kirkwood Dr., 35462,  205-372-9009 |
| Fairhope | A Touch of Class, P.O. Box 1907, 36533,  334-928-7499 |
| Fairhope | Away At The Bay, 557 North Mobile St., 36532,  205-928-9725 |
| Fairhope | Barons on the Bay Inn, 701 S. Mobile Ave., 36532,  334-928-8000 |
| Fairhope | Church Street Inn, 51 S. Church St., 36532,  334-928-5144 |
| Fairhope | Doc & Dawn's Garden B&B, 314 De La Mare Ave., 36532,  205-928-0253 |
| Fairhope | Marcella's Tea Room & Inn, 114 Fairhope Ave., 36532,  334-990-8520 |
| Fairhope | Mershon Court B&B Inn, 203 Fairhope Ave., 36532,  205-928-7398 |
| Fayette | Rose House Inn, 325 - 2nd Ave. NW, 35555,  205-932-7673 |
| Florence | River View B&B,  Route 7, Box 123G, 35630,  205-757-8667 |
| Florence | Wood Avenue Inn, 658 N. Wood Ave., 35630,  205-766-8441 |
| Franklin | Rutherford Johnson House, P.O. Box 202, Main St., 36444,  205-282-4423 |
| Greensboro | Blue Shadows B&B, RR2, 35744,  334-624-3637 |
| Guntersville | Lake Guntersville, 2204 Scott St., 35976,  205-505-0133 |
| Huntsville | Nestled Amongst the Trees, 4117 Darby Court, 35442,  205-554-2577 |
| Huntsville | Wandlers Inn B&B, 101 Shawnee Dr. N.W., 35806,  205-895-0847 |
| Jasper | Victorian Riverbridge Inn, Rt 8, Box 621-C, 35510,  205-387-1761 |
| Jemison | The Jemison Inn, 212 Hwy. 191, 35085,  205-688-2055 |
| Lacey's Spring | Apple Jack's Inn, 127 Double Creek Rd., 35754,  205-778-7734 |
| Leesburg | The Secret, Rt. 1, Box 82, 35983,  205-523-3825 |

| Marion | Myrtle Hill, 303 W. Lafayette St., 36756, 334-683-9095 |
| Marion | Southern Tours, 110 W. Lafayette, 36756, 334-683-6100 |
| Mentone | Blossom Hill, P.O. Box 176, 35984, 205-634-4673 |
| Mentone | Mentone Inn B&B, P.O. Box 284, Hwy 117, 35984, 205-634-4836 |
| Mentone | Raven Haven, 651 Country Rd. 644, 35984, 205-634-4310 |
| Mentone | Valhalla, 672 Country Rd. 626, 35984, 205-634-4006 |
| Mobile | Malaga Inn, 359 Church St., 36602, 205-438-4701 |
| Mobile | Portman House Inn, 1615 Government St., 36604, 334-471-1703 |
| Montgomery | Lattice Inn, The, 1414 So. Hull St., 36104, 334-264-0075 |
| Mount Meigs | Colonel's Rest, 11091 Atlanta Hwy., 36117, 334-215-0380 |
| Munford | Cedars Plantation, 590 Cheaha Rd., 36268, 205-761-9090 |
| Opelika | Heritage House, 714 Second Ave., 36701, 334-705-0485 |
| Orange Beach | Original Romar House B&B, 23500 Perdido Beach Blv, 36561, 334-981-6156 |
| Pisgah | Lodge on Gorham's Bluff, 101 Gorham Dr., 35765, 205-451-3435 |
| Prattville | Plantation House, The, 752 Loder St., 36067, 334-361-0442 |
| Selma | Grace Hall, 506 Lauderdale St., 36701, 334-875-5744 |
| Talladega | Historic Oakwood B&B, 715 E. North St., 35160, 205-362-0662 |
| Talladega | Orangevale, 1400 Whiting Rd., 35160, 205-362-3052 |
| Talladega | The Governor's House, 500 Meadowlake Lane, 35160, 205-763-2186 |
| Talladega | Veranda, 416 Cherry St., 35160, 205-362-0548 |
| Talladega | Somerset House, 701 North St. E., 35160, 205-761-9251 |
| Troy | House of Dunn's, The, 204 S. Brundidge St., 36081, 205-566-9414 |
| Valley Head | Winston Place, 353 Railroad St., 35989, 205-635-6381 |
| Wetumpka | The Castle, 608 Company St., 36092, 334-567-9011 |

# Alaska

## ANCHORAGE

**Alaskan Frontier Gardens**
P.O. Box 241881, 99524
Hillside Dr. & Alatna
907-345-6556 Fax: 907-562-2923
Rita Gittins
All year

$$$-B&B
3 rooms, 2 pb
Visa, MC, AmEx, •
C-yes/S-no/P-no/H-no

Full breakfast
Sitting room, library
Sauna, laundry, jacuzzi
fireplace, hot tub

*Elegant Alaska hillside estate on peaceful scenic acres by Chugach State Park. Spacious luxury suites. Gourmet breakfast. Museum-like environment, Alaskan hospitality. **Weekly rate, Comp. wine or fruit.***

---

**Blackberry B&B**
6060 Blackberry Rd., 99502
907-243-0265 Fax: 907-243-2557
Stan & Dianna Hintze
May 15-Sept.30

$$$-B&B
3 rooms, 3 pb
Visa, MC,
C-yes/S-no/P-no/H-no

Full breakfast Mon-Sat
Continental on Sunday
Sitting room
family friendly
kitchen & laundry avail.

*Close to airport, trails, parks, shopping, restaurants & sightseeing, etc. Deck and much more.*

---

**Glacier Bear B&B**
4814 Malibu Rd., 99517
907-243-8818 Fax: 907-248-4532
K. & G. Taton, M. Brown
All year

$$$-B&B
5 rooms, 3 pb
MC, Visa, *Rated*, •
C-ltd/S-ltd/P-no/H-no

Full breakfast
Snacks
Hiking & biking trails
restaurants nearby
sitt. rm., 8 person spa

*First-class accommodations at reasonable rates. Our location: 1.2 mi. from airport, 3 miles to downtown. Airport pick-up. Bicycles available. **3rd night 50% off, ltd.***

## ANCHORAGE

**Lynn's Pine Point B&B**
3333 Creekside Dr., 99504
907-333-2244 Fax: 907-333-1043
Lynn & Rich Stouff
All year

$$$-B&B
3 rooms, 3 pb
MC, Visa, *Rated*, •
C-yes/S-no/P-no/H-yes

Full breakfast
Comp. wine, snacks
Sitting room, gazebo
VCR with 500 movies
laundry, family bedroom

*Lovely cedar retreat with all the comforts of home. Queen beds, private baths, VCRs. Complimentary cocktails and hors d'oeuvres. Views of mountain. Tour planning.*

**Walkabout Town B&B**
1610 "E" St., 99501
907-279-7808 Fax: 907-258-3657
Sandra & Stimson
April–October

$$-B&B
3 rooms,
•
C-yes/S-no/P-no/H-no

Full breakfast
Deck, cable TV
freezer, free laundry
parking, 4 in a room

*Downtown convenience with beautiful park and coastal trail. Hearty Alaskan breakfast of sourdough waffles, reindeer sausage.*

## FAIRBANKS

**7 Gables B&B**
P.O. Box 80488, 99708
4312 Birch Ln.
907-479-0751 Fax: 907-479-2229
Paul & Leicha Welton
All year

$$-B&B
11 rooms, 9 pb
MC, Visa, *Rated*, •
C-yes/S-ltd/P-ltd/H-yes
Spanish, German

Full gourmet breakfast
Comp. refreshments
Sitting room, library
Cable TV/VCR, phones
bikes, jacuzzis, canoes

*Spacious Tudor estate w/solarium entrance & waterfall. Each rm. follows a stained-glass icon theme. 4 apartments, conf./reception rm.* **Use boats, bikes, canoes, skis free; 10% off if book is mentioned.**

**Comfy 'n Cozy B&B**
928 Wood Way, 99709
907-474-0285 Fax: 907-479-7181
800-478-5570
Chuck & Carol Bean
All year

$$-B&B
2 rooms, 2 pb
Visa, MC, AmEx,
C-ltd/S-no/P-no/H-no

Full breakfast
Snacks
Fully equipped kitchen
sitting room

*Private entrance to spacious guest living area. Ideal for travelers seeking homelike comfort and relaxation. Enjoy original Alaskan sourdough pancakes.*

**Fox Creek B&B**
2498 Elliott Hwy., 99712
907-457-5494 Fax: 907-457-5464
Arna & Jeff Fay
All year

$$-B&B
2 rooms, 1 pb
*Rated*, •
C-yes/S-ltd/P-yes/H-no

Full breakfast
Sitting room
library, spacious rooms
family friendly facility

*Quiet, secluded setting in historic Fox, Alaska. Modern Alaskan style home. Lifelong Alaskan proprietors. Frequent aurora/wildlife sightings.* **10% discount 3rd night.**

## GUSTAVUS

**A Puffin's B&B Lodge**
P.O. Box 3, 99826
1/4 Mile Rink Creek Rd.
907-697-2260 Fax: 907-697-2258
800-478-2258
Chuck & Sandy Schroth
Mid-April–September

$$$-B&B
3 rooms, 3 pb
AmEx, MC, Visa,
*Rated*, •
C-yes/S-yes/P-yes/H-yes

Full breakfast
Dinner, coffee, tea
Separate lodge, bicycles
antiques, picnic area
travel service, TV/VCR

*Modern cabins with Alaskan art, quiet country atmosphere, hearty homestead breakfast. Fishing, wildlife, photography-charters, Glacier Bay tours.* **Free dessert in the cafe.**

## GUSTAVUS

**Glacier Bay Country Inn**
P.O. Box 5, 99826
Mile 1, Tong Rd.
907-697-2288 Fax: 907-697-2289
800-628-0912
Ponch & Sandi Marchbanks
All year

$$$$-AP
8 rooms, 7 pb
Visa, MC, AmEx,
*Rated*, •
C-yes/S-no/P-no/H-no

Full breakfast
All meals included
Library, sitting room
bicycles, hiking, walks
Glacier Bay yacht tours

*Idyllic homestead blends country living w/Alaskan wilderness. Yacht tours of Glacier Bay. A fisherman's dream, traveler's paradise, professional's retreat. $5.00 off cookbook.*

**Gustavus Inn**
P.O. Box 60, 99826
1 mile Gustavus Rd.
907-697-2254 Fax: 907-697-2255
800-649-5220
David & JoAnn Lesh
5/1–9/15

$$$$-AP
13 rooms,
*Rated*, •
C-yes/S-ltd/P-ltd/H-yes
French, Spanish

Full breakfast
Lunch & dinner included
Bar, tea, bicycles
fishing poles
courtesy van

*Original homestead, completely updated 1993. Garden & ocean harvest family-style dining. Glacier Bay boat tours, bicycling, charter & stream fishing, kayaking, whalewatching.*

## HAINES

**Bear Creek Camp**
P.O. Box 908, 99827
Small Tracts Rd.
907-766-2259 Fax: 907-766-3560
Brian & Laura Johnson
All year

$-EP
6 rooms, 6 pb
H-no

Sitting room, bikes
hot tubs
6 private family cabins

*Bald eagle capital. Spectacular scenery. Relaxed, friendly atmosphere. Clean, modern kitchen & bath facilites! Bike rentals. Rafting, kayaking, hiking, fishing nearby. $2.00 off hot tub rental.*

**Summer Inn B&B**
P.O. Box 1198, 99669
117 Second Ave.
907-766-2970 Fax: 907-766-2970
Mary Ellen & Bob Summer
All year

$$-B&B
5 rooms,
MC, Visa, •
C-yes/S-no/P-no/H-no
some Spanish

Full breakfast
Afternoon tea
Snacks
sitting room
library

*Historical house in beautiful coastal town; walking distance to downtown; near Eagle Preserve; full homemade breakfast. Be our guest in this unique Alaskan community. Eagle watching rates.*

## HOMER

**Tutka Bay Wilderness Lodge**
P.O. Box 960, 99603
Boat, Plane, Helicopter
907-235-3905 Fax: 907-235-3909
800-606-3909
Jon & Nelda Osgood
May-Sept

$$$$-AP
4 rooms, 4 pb
Most CC, •
C-yes/S-ltd/P-no/H-no

Full breakfast
Lunch, dinner
Sitting room, library
family friendly facility

*Discover Alaska's Kenai coast. Private, full service retreat. Fresh seafood. Nature trails, beach ecology, bird rookeries, sea otters, eagles. Packg. rate $275/person/night.*

## JUNEAU

**Mt. Juneau Inn B&B**
1801 Old Glacier Hwy., 99801
907-463-5855 Fax: 907-463-5423
Karen & Phil Greeney
All year

$$-B&B
8 rooms, 2 pb
Visa, MC, •
C-yes/S-no/P-no/H-no
Spanish

Full breakfast
Aftn. tea, comp. wine
Snacks, guest kitchen
library, bikes, robes
slippers, hair dryers

*Comfort & hospitality that makes you feel right at home from the warmth of a plush robe to the parlour filled with native art.* **10% disc't for Internet guest, mention site.**

**Pearson's Pond Luxury Inn**
4541 Sawa Circle, 99801
907-789-3772 Fax: 907-789-6722
Steve & Diane Mayer
Pearson
All year, 2 night min.

$$$-B&B
3 rooms, 3 pb
Most CC, *Rated*, •
C-ltd/S-no/P-no/H-no

Continental breakfast
Afternoon tea, snacks
Priv. baths & kitchens
dock, rowboats, library
bicycles, hot tubs

*Alaska charm at its best. Capture majestic glaciers as background to hot tub on pond. Suite retreat for privacy & quality. Ski packages, massages on site.* **3rd night 50%.**

## SELDOVIA

**Swan House South B&B**
P.O. Box 11, 99663
907-234-8888 Fax: 907-346-3535
800-921-1900
Judy Swanson    May-Sept.

$$$-B&B
5 rooms, 3 pb
Visa, MC, AmEx, Disc.,
•
C-ltd/S-no/P-ltd/H-no

Continental breakfast
Afternoon tea
Bicycles, library
halibut & salmon fishing
charters, hiking

*Waterfront hideaway with never ending views! Walking distance from airport, marina, and town. Fisherman's paradise, with King Salmon in sight from our deck.*

## SEWARD

**Falcon's Way B&B**
P.O. Box 2089, 99664
611 4th Ave.
907-224-5757 Fax: 907-224-5828
Clare Sullivan & Mike
Calhoon
All year

B&B
4 rooms, 1 pb
Visa, MC, Disc., •
C-ltd/S-no/P-no/H-no

Full breakfast
Afternoon tea, snacks
Sitting room

*In town bed & breakfast furnished with antiques & reproductions, charming Victorian home; easy walk to all sites and activities.* **H.O.G. Discount.**

## SITKA

**Alaska Ocean View B&B**
1101 Edgecumbe Dr., 99835
907-747-8310   Fax: 907-747-8310
800-687-0520
Carole & Bill Denkinger
All year

$$$-B&B
3 rooms, 3 pb
Visa, MC, AmEx,
*Rated*, •
C-yes/S-no/P-ltd/H-no

Full gourmet breakfast
Afternoon tea, snacks
Sitt. rm., slippers, VCR
cable TV, phones, lib.
hot tub, terry robes

*Executive home in gorgeous setting. Luxurious amenities, king beds; friendly, helpful hosts. Close to everything. "We've thought of everything."* **7th night 50% off, ltd.**

## ST PAUL ISLAND

**Lillian Capener's B&B**
PO Box 105,  99660
907-546-2334
Lillian L. Capener
All year

$$$-B&B
2 rooms,
S-no/P-no/H-no
Finnish

Full hearty breakfast
Can bring own supplies
Afternoon tea, snacks
sitting room, library
TV and some videos

*Plain from the outside—but most people seem to think "delightful & unique" inside. Old world charm, ornately decorated with jewels, as kings & queens, sculpted heads.*

## WASILLA ─────────────────────────

**Yukon Don's B&B Inn**
1830 E. Parks Hwy #386, 2221
Yukon Circle, 99654
907-376-7472 Fax: 907-376-6515
800-478-7472
"Yukon" Don & Kristan
Tanner   All year

$$$-B&B
7 rooms,
Most CC, *Rated*, •
C-yes/S-no/P-yes/H-no

Continental plus bkfst.
Restaurant nearby
Sitt. rm, library, deck
all-glass "view room"
exercise room, sauna

*Extraordinary mountain views; on the way to Denali Park; all rooms have Alaskan theme. AAA approved. King Salmon fishing.* **3rd night 50% off** .

## More Inns ...

| | |
|---|---|
| Anchorage | 42nd Avenue Annex, 410 W. 42nd Ave., 99503, 907-561-8895 |
| Anchorage | A Log Home B&B, 2440 Sprucewood St., 99508, 907-276-8527 |
| Anchorage | Adams House B&B, 700 W. 21st, #A, 99508, 907-274-1944 |
| Anchorage | All The Comforts of Home, 12531 Turk's Turn St., 99516, 907-345-4279 |
| Anchorage | Anchorage Eagle Nest Hotel, 4110 Spenard Rd. (BB), 99503, 907-243-3433 |
| Anchorage | Country Garden, 8210 Frank St., 99518, 907-344-0636 |
| Anchorage | Country Style B&B, P.O. Box 220986, 99522, 907-243-6746 |
| Anchorage | Darbyshire House B&B, 528 "N" St., 99501, 907-279-0703 |
| Anchorage | Denali Cabins Inc., 200 W. 34th. Ave. #362, 99503, 907-683-2643 |
| Anchorage | DreamCatcher B&B, 8640 Williwa Ave., 99504, 907-333-8530 |
| Anchorage | Fay's B&B, P.O. Box 2378, 99510, 907-243-0139 |
| Anchorage | Green Bough B&B, 3832 Young St., 99508, 907-562-4636 |
| Anchorage | Greens' Garden B&B, P.O. Box 142288, 99514, 907-333-7268 |
| Anchorage | Hillcrest Haven, 1455 Hillcrest Dr., 99503, 907-274-3086 |
| Anchorage | Pilot's Row B&B, 217 East 11th Ave., 99501, 907-274-3305 |
| Anchorage | Wright's Bed & Breakfast, 1411 Oxford, 99503, 907-561-1990 |
| Auke Bay | Adlersheim Lodge, P.O. Box 210447, 99821 |
| Bethel | Bentley's Porterhouse B&B, 62 First Ave. Box 529, 99559 |
| Big Lake | Jeanie's on Big Lake, Box 520598, 99652 |
| Chinak | Reed's End Lounge, Box 5629, Mile 42, 99615 |
| Chugiak | Peters Creek Inn B&B, P.O. Box 671487, 99567, 907-688-2776 |
| Denali | North Face Lodge, Denali National Park, 99755 |
| Douglas | Windsock Inn B&B, P.O. Box 240223, 99824 |
| Fairbanks | AAA Care B&B, 557 Fairbanks St., 99709, 907-479-2447 |
| Fairbanks | Beaver Bend B&B, 231 Iditarod, 99701, 907-452-3240 |
| Fairbanks | Blue Goose B&B, The, 4466 Dartmouth, 99709, 907-479-6973 |
| Fairbanks | Borealis Hotel, 700 Fairbanks St., 99709 |
| Fairbanks | Goldstream B&B, P.O. Box 80090, 99708, 907-455-6550 |
| Fairbanks | Iniakeek Lake Lodge, Box 80424, 99701, 907-479-6354 |
| Fairbanks | Minnie Street B&B, 345 Minnie St., 99701, 907-456-1802 |
| Fairbanks | Sophie Station Hotel, 1717 University Ave., 99701, 907-479-3650 |
| Gustavus | TRI B&B, P.O. Box 214, 99826 |
| Haines | Cache Inn Lodge, Box 441-VP, 99827, 907-766-2910 |
| Haines | Fort Seward B&B, House #1, Box 5, 99827, 907-766-2856 |
| Haines | Jotel Halsingland, P.O. Box 1589, 99827, 907-766-2000 |
| Homer | Brass Ring B&B, 987 Hillfair Court, 99603 |
| Homer | Driftwood Inn, 135 W. Bunnell Ave., 99603, 907-235-8019 |
| Homer | JP B&B, Box 2256, 99603 |
| Homer | Kachemak Bay Wilderness, Box 956-VP, 99603, 907-235-8910 |
| Homer | Lakewood Inn, 984 Ocean Dr., #1, 99608, 907-235-6144 |
| Homer | Magic Canyon Ranch, 40015 Waterman Rd., 99603, 907-235-6077 |
| Homer | Sadie Cove Wilderness Ldge, Box 2265-VP, 99603, 907-235-7766 |
| Homer | Seaside Farm, HCR 58335 East End Rd., 99603 |
| Homer | Sundmark's B&B, P.O. Box 375, 99603, 907-235-5188 |
| Homer | Wild Rose B&B, Box 665, 99603, 907-235-8780 |
| Juneau | A Channel View With A Rm., 1775 Diamond Drive, 99801 |
| Juneau | A Cozy Log B&B, 8668 Dudley St., 99801 |
| Juneau | Admiralty Inn, 9040 Glacier Hwy., 99801, 907-789-3263 |
| Juneau | Alaska B&B Association, 369 So. Franklin #200, 99801 |
| Juneau | Alaska House B&B, P.O. Box 21321, 99802 |
| Juneau | Alaskan Hotel, 167 S. Franklin, 99801, 800-327-9347 |
| Juneau | Blueberry Lodge on Tide., 9436 N. Douglas Hwy., 99801 |
| Juneau | Cashen Quarters B&B, 315 Gold St., 99801 |
| Juneau | Crondahls B&B, 626 5th St., 99801 |
| Juneau | Dawson's B&B, 1941 Glacier Hwy, 99801, 907-586-9708 |
| Juneau | Eagle's Nest B&B, P.O. Box 20537, 99802 |
| Juneau | Evergreen B&B, The, 300 W. 11th St. #3, 99801 |
| Juneau | Jan's View B&B, P.O. Box 32254, 99803 |
| Juneau | Juneau Hostel, 614 Harris St., 99801, 907-586-9559 |
| Juneau | Lost Chord, The, 2200 Fritz Cove Rd., 99801 |

| | |
|---|---|
| Juneau | Louie's Place-Elfin Cove, P.O. Box 020704, 99802,   907-586-2032 |
| Juneau | Lucia's Retreat,  6680 N. Douglas Rd., 99801 |
| Juneau | Mullins House, 526 Seward St., 99801,   907-586-2959 |
| Juneau | Pot Belly B&B,  5115 N. Douglas Rd., 99801 |
| Juneau | Sepel Hallow B&B,  10901 Mendenhall Loop, 99801 |
| Juneau | Silverbow Inn & Restaurant,  120 - 2nd St., 99801,   907-586-4146 |
| Juneau | Tenakee Inn,  167 S. Franklin, 99801,   907-586-1000 |
| Kodiak | Kalsin Inn Ranch,  Box 1696 VP, 99615 |
| Lake Louise | Evergreen Lodge, HC 1 Box 1709 GennAllen, 99588,   907-822-3250 |
| Petersburg | Beachcomber Inn,  Box 1027, 99833,   907-772-3888 |
| Petersburg | Heger Haus B&B,  P.O. Box 485, 99833,   907-772-4877 |
| Petersburg | Little Norway Inn B&B,  Box 192-BW, 99833 |
| Petersburg | Scandia House,  P.O. Box 689, 99833,   907-772-4281 |
| Port Graham | Fedora's B&B,  P.O. Box 5516, 99603,   907-284-2239 |
| Seal Bay | Afognak Wilderness Lodge,  99697,   907-486-6442 |
| Seldovia | Annie McKenzie's Boardwalk,  P.O. Box 72, 99663,   907-234-7816 |
| Seldovia | High Tide Originals, Main St., 99663,   907-234-7850 |
| Seldovia | Seldovia Rowing Club Inn, P.O. Box 41, Bay St., 99663,   907-234-7614 |
| Seward | Swiss Chalet B&B,  P.O. Box 1734, 99664,   907-224-3939 |
| Sitka | Helga's B&B, Box 1885, 99835 |
| Sitka | Karras B&B, 230 Kogwanton St., 99835,   907-747-3978 |
| Skagway | Golden North Hotel, P.O. Box 431, 99840,   907-983-2294 |
| Skagway | Irene's Inn, Box 538-VP, 99840,   907-983-2520 |
| Skagway | Sgt. Preston's Lodge, P.O. Box 538, 99840 |
| Skagway | Skagway Inn B&B, P.O. Box 500, 99840,   907-983-2289 |
| Skagway | Wind Valley Lodge, Box 354-VP, 99840,   907-983-2236 |
| Soldotna | Krog's Kamp, P.O. Box 3913, 99669,   907-262-2671 |
| Soldotna | Soldotna B&B Inn,  399 Lover's Ln., 99669,   907-262-4779 |
| Talkeetna | River Beauty B&B,  P.O. Box 525, 99676,   907-733-2741 |
| Talkeetna | Twister Creek Union, P.O. Box 525, 99676,   907-258-1717 |
| Tok | Stage Stop B&B, The,  P.O. Box 69, 99780,   907-883-5338 |
| Valdez | B&B—Valdez, Box 442, 99686,   907-835-4211 |
| Valdez | Johnson House, Box 364, 99686 |
| Valdez | Lake House, P.O. Box 1499, 99686,   907-835-4752 |
| Valdez | Rainbow Lodge,  Mile 4, Richardson Hwy., 99686 |
| Valdez | Totem Inn, P.O. Box 648 BB, 99686,   907-835-4443 |
| Willow | Willow Trading Post, P.O. Box 49, 99688 |
| Wrangell | Clarke B&B, Box 1020, 99686,   907-874-2125 |
| Wrangell | Harbor House Lodge, P.O. Box 2027, 99929,   907-874-3084 |

# Arizona

## AJO

**Guest House Inn**
3 Guest House Rd., 85321
520-387-6133
Norma Walker
All year

$$-B&B
4 rooms, 4 pb
Most CC, *Rated*,
C-yes/S-no/P-no/H-no
Spanish, French

Full breakfast
Sitting room, library
hiking trails
bird-watching

*Sonoran Desert retreat with excellent hiking, bird-watching, relaxation and spectacular desert vistas. Near Organ Pipe Cactus National Monument. Sumptuous breakfasts.*

## BISBEE

**Park Place B&B**
200 E. Vista, 85603
520-432-3054 Fax: 520-459-7603
800-388-4388
Bob & Janet Watkins
All year

$-B&B
4 rooms, 2 pb
Visa, MC, *Rated*,
C-ltd/S-ltd/P-no/H-no
Some Spanish

Full breakfast
Library, tennis court
spacious bedrooms
balconies, terraces.

*1920 vintage, 2 story Mediterranean style home with spacious bedrooms, balconies, library & sun room. 10 minutes to fascinating, quaint, Switzerland-like Bisbee District.*

## EUREKA SPRINGS

| **Cliff Cottage, A B&B Inn** | $$$-B&B | Bkfst. served in room |
|---|---|---|
| 42 Armstrong St., 72632 | 4 rooms, 4 pb | Lunch, dinner, aft. tea |
| 501-253-7409  800-799-7409 | Visa, MC, *Rated*, • | Refrig. in room, pool |
| Sandra CH Smith | C-ltd/S-ltd/P-no/H-no | library, tennis, golf |
| All year | French, Spanish, | boat, picnics, jacuzzis |
|  | German |  |

*Elegant Victorian suites/guestrooms in heart of Historic Downtown. Heirloom antiques, decadent bkfst, sunshine, laughter everywhere. Comp. champ./wine in room; 7th nite free.*

## FLAGSTAFF

| **Birch Tree Inn** | $$-B&B | Full breakfast |
|---|---|---|
| 824 W. Birch Ave., 86001 | 5 rooms, 3 pb | Afternoon tea, snacks |
| 520-774-1042  Fax: 520-774-8462 | MC, Visa, *Rated*, • | Sitting room, piano |
| 888-774-1042 | C-ltd/S-no/P-no/H-no | pool table, bicycles |
| The Pettingers, The Znetkos |  | tennis court nearby |
| All year |  |  |

*Comfortable, country charm; savory, down-home, hearty breakfasts. A four season retreat in the magnificent beauty of Northern Arizona. 7 nights for price of 6.*

| **Comfi Cottages, Flagstaff** | $$$-B&B | Full breakfast |
|---|---|---|
| 1612 N. Aztec St., 86001 | 5 rooms, 5 pb | Aftn. tea, snacks |
| 520-774-0731  Fax: 520-779-1008 | Visa, MC, Disc., • | Complimentary wine |
| 888-774-0731 | C-yes/S-no/P-no/H-ltd | sitt. rm., lib., bikes |
| Pat & Ed Wiebe  All year | French | fireplaces, cable TV |

*Arizona Republic's choice "Best Weekend Getaway." 5 charming cottages, all located near the heart of downtown. Fully equipped w/phones, cable TV, yard, fireplaces. Comp. wine/flowers for special occasions.*

| **Inn at 410 B&B** | $$$-B&B | Full breakfast |
|---|---|---|
| 410 N. Leroux St., 86001 | 9 rooms, 9 pb | Snacks |
| 520-774-0088  Fax: 520-774-6354 | Visa, MC, AmEx, | Sitting room |
| 800-774-2008 | *Rated*, • | lib., 5 rms. w/fireplace |
| Howard & Sally Krueger | C-ltd/S-no/P-no/H-yes | 2 rooms w/jacuzzi |
| All year |  |  |

*Charming 1907 home; antiques, stained glass, touches of the Southwest. Oven-fresh cookies, healthy breakfasts. Grand Canyon, Indian ruins, hiking, skiing nearby.*

## HEREFORD

| **Casa de San Pedro B&B** | $$$-B&B | Full gourmet breakfast |
|---|---|---|
| 8933 S. Yell Ln., 85615 | 10 rooms, 10 pb | Lunch & dinner available |
| 520-366-1300  Fax: 520-366-0701 | Visa, MC, | Sitting room, library |
| Chuck & Judy Wetzel | C-ltd/S-no/P-no/H-yes | courtyard, birdwatching |
| All year |  | small conference facil. |

*Territorial style inn with courtyard and fountain. Gourmet breakfast and fresh homemade pie. Peaceful and secluded environment.*

## MAYER

| **Serenity House B&B** | $$-B&B | Continental plus bkfst. |
|---|---|---|
| P.O. Box 1254, 86333 | 2 rooms, | Sitting room, TV room |
| 12701 Main St. | C-ltd/S-no/P-no/H-no | VCR with movie library |
| 520-632-4430  800-484-2366 |  | swimming pool |
| Sue Ward & Bob |  |  |
| Hetherington |  |  |
| All year |  |  |

*1905 country Victorian in small old mining town; 12 foot gabled ceilings; hardwood floors; porch swing; leaded glass; lace; pool. 3rd night 50% off.*

PEARCE ─────────────────────

| **Grapevine Canyon Ranch** | $$-AP | All meals included |
|---|---|---|
| P.O. Box 302, 85625 | 8 rooms, 8 pb | Sitting room, library |
| West End of Highland | Visa, MC, Disc., • | swimming pool, hot tub |
| 520-826-3185 Fax: 520-826-3636 | S-yes/P-no/H-no | conference facility |
| 800-245-9202 | | |
| All year | | |

*An intimate guest ranch providing first-class accommodations with emphasis on horse-back riding on 64,000 acres of spectacular mountain country. Game room, pool, golf.*

PHOENIX ─────────────────────

| **La Estancia B&B Inn** | $$$$-B&B | Full breakfast |
|---|---|---|
| 4979 E. Camelback Rd., 85018 | 5 rooms, 5 pb | Afternoon tea, snacks |
| 602-808-9924 Fax: 602-808-9925 | Most CC, *Rated*, • | Comp. wine, cappucino |
| 800-410-7655 | C-ltd/S-no/P-no/H-no | sitting room, library |
| Ruth & Richard Maloblock | | pool, hiking/golf nearby |
| Closed August | | |

*La Estancia-tranquil, elegantly renovated 1929 home on 2 acres in citrus grove, only B&B in Phoenix on Nat'l Historic Register, kingsize beds, whirlpool tubs, close to airport, museums, golf, etc.*

| **Maricopa Manor B&B Inn** | $$$-B&B | Continental plus bkfst. |
|---|---|---|
| 15 W. Pasadena Ave., 85013 | 5 rooms, 5 pb | Complimentary wine |
| 602-274-6302 Fax: 602-266-3904 | *Rated*, • | Sitting room, library |
| 800-292-6403 | C-yes/S-yes/H-yes | pool with fountains |
| Mary Ellen & Paul Kelley | | hot tubs |
| All year | | |

*Old World charm, elegant urban setting. Central and Camelback, close to everything. Luxury suites, secluded, gardens, patios, and palm trees.*

PRESCOTT ─────────────────────

| **Lynx Creek Farm B&B** | $$-B&B | Full gourmet breakfast |
|---|---|---|
| P.O. Box 4301, 86302 | 6 rooms, 6 pb | Comp. drinks, appetizers |
| Call for directions | Most CC, *Rated*, • | Private decks & hot tubs |
| 520-778-9573 | C-yes/S-ltd/P-yes/H-ltd | kitchenettes, BBQ, pool |
| Greg & Wendy Temple | Spanish | wood stoves, croquet |
| All year | | |

*Secluded, country setting on picturesque apple farm minutes from town. Log cabin rooms, coffee in rooms, quilts. Voted "Best B&B in Arizona" by The Arizona Republic 1994.*

| **Mt. Vernon Inn** | $$$-B&B | Full breakfast |
|---|---|---|
| 204 N. Mt. Vernon Ave., 86301 | 7 rooms, 7 pb | Aft. tea, snacks |
| 520-778-0886 Fax: 520-778-7305 | Visa, MC, Disc.*Rated*, | Sitting room, library |
| Michele & Jerry Neumann | • | TV |
| All year | C-ltd/S-ltd/P-no/H-yes | cottages |

*This 1900 home has charm of yesteryear & the amenities of today, in the largest Victorian neighborhood in Arizona. This inn is rated 3 diamonds by AAA.*

| **Prescott Pines Inn B&B** | $$-EP | Full breakfast (fee) |
|---|---|---|
| 901 White Spar Rd., 86303 | 13 rooms, 13 pb | Kitchenettes, patio BBQ |
| 520-445-7270 Fax: 520-778-3665 | MC, Visa, *Rated*, | Sitting room, library |
| 800-541-5374 | C-ltd/S-no/P-no/H-ltd | porches, ceiling fans |
| J. Wu, M. Action, B&M | | games, gardens |
| Sheldon | | |
| All year | | |

*Country-Victorian rooms in 4 guesthouses, including one chalet for up to 8 people, all under Ponderosa pines near National Forest. Gourmet breakfasts. Ideal 4-season climate.*

*A Touch of Sedona, Sedona, AZ*

## SCOTTSDALE

| | | |
|---|---|---|
| **Inn at the Citadel** | B&B | Continental plus |
| 8700 E. Pinnacle Peak, 85255 | 11 rooms, 11 pb | Lunch & Dinner (fee) |
| 602-585-6133 Fax: 602-585-3436 | Most CC, *Rated*, • | Restaurant |
| 800-927-8367 | S-no/P-yes/H-yes | Sitting room |
| All year | French | |

| | | |
|---|---|---|
| **Valley O' the Sun B&B** | $-B&B | Continental plus bkfst. |
| P.O. Box 2214, 85252 | 3 rooms, 1 pb | Full bkfst. on weekends |
| Tempe | • | Sitting room |
| 602-941-1281  800-689-1281 | | close to nearby |
| Kathleen Curtis | | attractions |
| All year | | |

*Valley O' the Sun B&B is more than just a place to stay. They are people-oriented and want to make your visit to the Great Southwest a memorable one.*

## SEDONA

| | | |
|---|---|---|
| **A Touch of Sedona** | $$$-B&B | Full gourmet breakfast |
| 595 Jordan Rd., 86339 | 5 rooms, 5 pb | Spec. diets accommodated |
| 520-282-6462 Fax: 520-282-1534 | MC, Visa, *Rated*, • | Deck & patio garden |
| 800-600-6462 | C-ltd/S-no/P-no/H-no | beautiful redrock views |
| Bill & Sharon Larsen | | near art galleries |
| All year | | |

*Eclectic elegance ... furnished with stained-glass lamps, antiques, but with a mix of contemporary. Just walking distance to uptown.* **3rd night free midweek, ltd.**

| | | |
|---|---|---|
| **B&B at Saddle Rock Ranch** | $$$-B&B | Full Breakfast |
| 255 Rock Ridge Dr., 86336 | 3 rooms, 3 pb | Comp. wine, snacks |
| 520-282-7640 Fax: 520-282-6829 | *Rated*, | Sitting room, library |
| Fran & Dan Bruno | C-ltd/S-no/P-no/H-no | Jacuzzi, pool, gardens |
| All year | Spanish, French, Italian | decks, hiking, wildlife |

*History. Romance. Elegance. Old West movie ranch. Antique-filled rooms feature native rock, adobe, timber beams, frplc. Remote control, color/cable TV in rooms.* **Comp. jeep tour for 2 w/a 5 night stay.**

SEDONA ───────────────────────────

| **Briar Patch Inn** | $$$$-B&B | Full breakfast |
| 3190 North Highway 89 A, | 16 rooms, 16 pb | Afternoon tea |
| Hwy 89A N., Oak Creek Cyn, | MC, Visa, *Rated*, • | Sitting room, library |
| 86336 | C-yes/S-ltd/P-no/H-ltd | fireplaces, kitchenettes |
| 520-282-2342 Fax: 520-282-2399 | Spanish, German | Breakfast by the creek |
| Jo Ann & Ike Olson | | |
| All year | | |

*One of the most beautiful spots in Arizona. Cottages nestled on 9 spectacular acres on sparkling Oak Creek. Warm, generous hospitality. A real gem! Fishing, bird watching, massage in your room. . .*

| **Canyon Villa B&B Inn** | $$$$-B&B | Full breakfast |
| 125 Canyon Circle Dr., 86351 | 11 rooms, 11 pb | Snacks |
| 520-284-1226 Fax: 520-284-2114 | Visa, MC *Rated*, • | Sitting room, library |
| 800-453-1166 | C-ltd/S-no/P-no/H-yes | swimming pool |
| Chuck & Marion Yadon | | golf & tennis nearby |
| All year | | |

*Southwest-style inn offers unmatched red rock views, exceptional guest accommodations with private patio or balcony, full bath, television, telephone.*

| **Canyon Wren - Cabins for 2** | $$$-B&B | Continental breakfast |
| 6425 N. Hwy. 89A, 86336 | 4 rooms, 4 pb | Easy access to the creek |
| 520-282-6900   800-437-9736 | MC, Visa, | hosts pleased to advise |
| Mike & Milena Pfeifer Smith | S-no/P-no/H-ltd | patios, hiking |
| | Slovenian | |

*In spectacular Oak Creek Canyon. Cabins have full kitchen, fireplace, whirlpool bath-tubs, decks. Most have open lofts. Romantic getaways are a Canyon Wren specialty. **7th night free.***

| **Casa Sedona, A B&B Inn** | $$$-B&B | Full breakfast |
| 55 Hozoni Dr., 86336 | 15 rooms, 15 pb | Afternoon appetizers |
| 520-282-2938 Fax: 520-282-2259 | Visa, MC, Disc, *Rated*, | Spa tubs |
| 800-525-3756 | • | fireplaces |
| John & Nancy True | C-ltd/S-no/P-no/H-yes | |
| All year | | |

*Casa Sedona offers fabulous red rock views from each of its spacious, luxurious, terraced rooms, individually appointed to please and pamper guests.*

| **Cozy Cactus B&B** | $$$-B&B | Full breakfast |
| 80 Canyon Circle Dr., 86351 | 5 rooms, 5 pb | Snacks |
| 520-284-0082 Fax: 520-284-4210 | MC, Visa, Disc. *Rated*, | Library, bicycles |
| 800-788-2082 | • | tennis, golf nearby |
| Lynne & Bob Gillman | C-yes/S-ltd/P-no/H-yes | hiking nearby, sitt. rm. |
| All year | Some Italian, Sign Lang. | |

*Cozy home furnished with heirlooms, theatrical memorabilia, fireplaces. Patios border national forest and spectacular Red Rock views. Old-fashioned hospitality.*

| **Ghost City Inn B&B** | $$-B&B | Full American breakfast |
| P.O. Box 1932, 86331 | 5 rooms, 1 pb | Afternoon tea, snacks |
| 541 N. Main St., Jerome | Visa, MC, AmEx, Disc., | Hot tubs, bicycles |
| 520-634-4678 Fax: 520-634-4678 | • | sitting room |
| Joy Beard | C-yes/S-no/P-no/H-no | family friendly facility |
| All year | | |

*Romantic get-a-way/pampered atmosphere. Exp. the elegance of days gone by. Magnificent views that rival the Grand Canyon-unforgettable memories. **Winter discounts when available.***

## SEDONA

| **Graham B&B Inn, The** | $$$-B&B | Full breakfast |
| 150 Canyon Circle Dr., 86351 | 6 rooms, 6 pb | Afternoon refreshments |
| 520-284-1425 Fax: 520-284-0767 | MC, Visa, *Rated*, | Sitting room, games |
| 800-228-1425 | C-yes/S-no/P-no/H-no | Golf nearby, TVs/VCRs |
| Roger & Carol Redenbaugh | | Hot tub & swimming pool |
| All year | | |

*Comfortable elegance; unmatched red rock views; fireplaces; jacuzzis. Choose South-west, antique, art deco, or contemporary room decor. AAA 4 Diamond Award.* **7th nite free, ltd.**

| **Lodge at Sedona, The** | $$$-B&B | Full gourmet breakfast |
| 125 Kallof Place, 86336 | 13 rooms, 13 pb | Afternoon refreshments |
| 520-204-1942 Fax: 520-204-2128 | Visa, MC, *Rated*, • | Sitting room, library |
| 800-619-4467 | C-ltd/S-no/P-no/H-yes | porch, one pvt. hot tub |
| Barb & Mark Dinunzio | | jacuzzi whirlpool tubs |
| All year | | |

*Voted "Arizona's best B&B,"—Arizona Republic newspaper, Sept. 93. Feel at home in our elegant, secluded inn. Enjoy our gourmet breakfast, appetaizers and desserts.*

| **Rose Tree Inn** | $$$-EP | Comp. wine/fruit basket |
| 376 Cedar St., 86336 | 5 rooms, 5 pb | In-room coffee & tea |
| 520-282-2065 Fax: 520-282-0083 | MC, Visa, *Rated*, • | Patios, library, jacuzzi |
| Gail & Stephen Hayter | C-ltd/S-yes/P-no/H-no | phones & TV/VCR in rms. |
| All year | | bicycles, kitchenettes |

*Sedona's "best-kept secret"! Quaint, quiet accommodations nestled in a gorgeous English garden environment close to "Old Town."* **Comp. bottle of wine or fruit basket.**

| **Southwest Inn at Sedona** | $$$-B&B | Continental plus bkfst. |
| 3250 W. Hwy. 89A, 86336 | 28 rooms, 28 pb | Refreshments |
| 520-282-3344 Fax: 520-282-0267 | Visa, MC, AmEx, | Hot tubs, swimming pool |
| 800-483-7422 | *Rated*, • | phones, 25" TVs |
| Joel & Sheila Gilguff | C-yes/S-no/P-no/H-yes | fireplaces |
| All year | Spanish | |

*Pampered is what you'll be at this combination B&B/Small Luxury Hotel. Concierge services, nature & adventure specialties. Privacy, cleanliness & outstanding customer service.* **Restaurnt Discounts, ask.**

| **Territorial House B&B** | $$$-B&B | Full breakfast |
| 65 Piki Dr., 86336 | 4 rooms, 4 pb | Aftn. tea, snacks |
| 520-204-2737 Fax: 520-204-2230 | Visa, MC, *Rated*, • | Sitting room, bicycles |
| 800-801-2737 | C-yes/S-ltd/P-no/H-no | whirlpool tub, fireplace |
| John & Linda Steele | | deck, outdoor hot tub |
| All year | | |

*Room decor depicts Sedona territorial days. Friendly, cozy, quiet, western hospitality.* **Jan.-Feb. & July-Aug. golf package with 2-night stay.**

## TUCSON

| **Adobe Rose Inn B&B** | $$-B&B | Full breakfast weekday |
| 940 N. Olsen Ave., 85719 | 5 rooms, 5 pb | Gourmet bkfst. weekend |
| 520-318-4644 Fax: 520-325-0055 | Most CC, *Rated*, • | Swimming pool, snacks |
| 800-328-4122 | C-ltd/S-ltd/P-no/H-no | afternoon tea |
| Diana Graham | | sitting room, library |
| All year | | |

*Cozy southwest adobe home near University. Pool, hot tub, five rooms, private backs, fireplaces. Gracious hospitality.*

TUCSON

**Casa Alegre B&B Inn**
316 E. Speedway Blvd., 85705
520-628-1800 Fax: 520-792-1880
800-628-5654
Phyllis Florek
All year

$$$-B&B
4 rooms, 4 pb
MC, Visa, *Rated*, •
C-ltd/S-no/P-no/H-no

Full breakfast
Afternoon tea, snacks
Sitting room, library
swimming pool, jacuzzi
public tennis courts

*Beautiful 1915 Craftsman bungalow near University of AZ, metropolitan Tucson, golf & mountain & desert attractions. Scrumptious breakfast, poolside refreshments.*

**Catalina Park Inn**
309 E. 1st St., 85705
520-792-4541 Fax: 520-792-0838
800-792-4885
Mark Hall, Paul Richard
All year

$$$-B&B
4 rooms, 4 pb
Visa, MC, *Rated*, •
C-ltd/S-ltd/P-no/H-no

Full breakfast
Afternoon tea, snacks
Sitting room
lush gardens
many amenities

*Stylish inn featuring beautifully decorated guestrooms & full range of amenities. Enjoy our lush perennial garden. Just 5 blocks to University of Arizona. **3rd night 50%, ltd.***

**El Presidio B&B Inn**
297 N. Main Ave., 85701
520-623-6151 Fax: 520-623-3860
800-359-6151
Patti Toci
All year except July

$$$-B&B
4 rooms, 4 pb
*Rated*, •
C-ltd/S-no/P-no/H-no

Full gourmet breakfast
Afternoon tea, snacks
Comp. wine, juice, soda
kitchenettes, phones, TV
nearby health club

*Historic Victorian adobe with Old-Mexico ambiance, courtyards, gardens, fountains. Antique decor. **Free bottle of wine; 5th night 50%.***

**Gable House, The**
2324 N. Madelyn Circle, 85712
520-326-1150   800-756-4846
Al & Phyllis Cummings
All year

$$-B&B
3 rooms, 2 pb
Visa, MC, AmEx, •
C-ltd/S-no/P-no/H-no

Continental plus bkfst.
Sitting room
hot tubs
non-smoking rooms

*Picturesque Sante Fe Pueblo style 1930 home w/Mexican influence. Home to actor Clark Gable in early 1940's. Smoke free. Bkfst. served in dining room or patio. **7th night free.***

**June's B&B**
3212 W. Holladay St., 85746
520-578-0857
June Henderson
All year

$-B&B
3 rooms,
C-ltd/S-no/P-no/H-no

Continental breakfast
Sitting room, piano
heated swimming pool
art studio, exercise rm.

*Mountainside home with pool. Majestic towering mountains. Hiking in the desert. Sparkling city lights. Beautiful backyard & patio. Owner's artwork for sale.*

**La Posada del Valle**
1640 N. Campbell Ave., 85719
520-795-3840 Fax: 520-795-3840
Karin Dennen
All year

$$$-B&B
5 rooms, 5 pb
MC, Visa, *Rated*, •
C-ltd/S-no/P-no/H-no
Spanish

Continental plus wkdays
Full breakfast (wkends)
Afternoon tea
library, sitting room
courtyard, patios

*Elegant 1920s inn nestled in the heart of the city, offering gourmet breakfast, afternoon tea; catering available for special functions. **Special summer rates.***

## 14  Arizona

TUCSON —————————————————————————————————

| | | |
|---|---|---|
| **Lodge on the Desert, The** | $$$-B&B/EP/MAP | Continental breakfast |
| 306 North Alvernon, 85711 | 40 rooms, 40 pb | Restaurant, bar |
| 520-325-3366 Fax: 520-327-5834 | Most CC, *Rated*, • | All meals available |
| 800-456-5634 | C-yes/S-yes/P-ltd/H-yes | sitting room, library |
| Schuyler W. Lininger | French | swimming pool, games |
| All year | | |

*A garden resort hotel established over fifty years ago, with the atmosphere of a Mexican ranch house. Relax! Lots of indoor & outdoor games.*

WILLIAMS —————————————————————————————————

| | | |
|---|---|---|
| **Red Garter Bed & Bakery** | $-B&B | Continental plus |
| P.O. Box 95, 86046 | 4 rooms, 4 pb | Afternoon tea, snacks |
| 137 W. Railroad Ave. | Most CC, • | Bakery, coffee shop |
| 520-635-1484  800-328-1484 | C-ltd/S-no/P-no/H-no | |
| John Holst | | |
| All year | | |

*Beautifully restored 1897 bordello in small mountain community next to Grand Canyon.*
*20% off Nov–March.*

## More Inns ...

| | |
|---|---|
| Ajo | Mine Managers House B&B,  One Greenway Rd., 85321,  602-387-6505 |
| Bisbee | Bisbee Grand Hotel B&B Inn,  P.O. Box 825, 85603,  602-432-5900 |
| Bisbee | Bisbee Inn, The, Box 1855, 85603,  602-432-5131 |
| Bisbee | Greenway House, The, 401 Cole Ave.,  85603,  520-432-7170 |
| Bisbee | Inn at Castle Rock,  P.O. Box 1161, 85603,  520-432-4449 |
| Bisbee | Judge Ross Home, 605 Shattuck St., 85605 |
| Bisbee | School House Inn B&B,  P.O. Box 32, 85603,  520-432-2996 |
| Chandler | Cone's Tourist Home,  2804 W. Warner Rd., 85224,  602-839-0369 |
| Chandler | La Casa Sevilla, 2545 W. Barrow Dr., 85224,  602-775-0815 |
| Cochise | Cochise Hotel, Box 27, 85606,  602-384-3156 |
| Flagstaff | Arizona Mountain Inn, 685 Lake Mary Rd., 86001,  602-774-8959 |
| Flagstaff | Cedar B&B, 425 W. Cedar, 86001,  602-774-1636 |
| Flagstaff | Dierker House B&B, 423 W. Cherry, 86001,  602-774-3249 |
| Flagstaff | Inn at Four Ten, The,  410 N. Lerous St., 86001,  602-774-0088 |
| Fountain Hills | Villa Galleria B&B, 16650 E. Hawk Dr., 85268,  602-837-1400 |
| Gold Canyon | Sinelli's B&B,  5605 South Sage Way, 85219,  602-983-3650 |
| Hereford | Ramsey Canyon Inn,  85 Ramsey Canyon Rd., 85615,  602-378-3010 |
| Jerome | Inn at Jerome,  P.O. Box 901, 86321,  520-634-5094 |
| Lakeside | Bartram's Bed & Breakfast,  Route 1, Box 1014, 85929 |
| Mesa | Casa Del Sol,  6951 E. Hobart, 85207,  602-985-5956 |
| Oracle | Triangle L Ranch B&B,  P.O. Box 900, 85623,  602-896-2804 |
| Oracle | Villa Cardinale,  P.O. Box 649, 85623,  602-896-2516 |
| Patagonia | Little House, The,  341 Sonoita Ave., 85624,  602-394-2493 |
| Phoenix | Gerry's B&B,  5150 37th Ave, 85019,  602-973-2542 |
| Prescott | Betsy's B&B,  1919 Rock Castle Dr., 86301,  602-445-0123 |
| Prescott | Marks House Inn, The,  203 E. Union, 86303,  602-778-4632 |
| Prescott | Prescott Country Inn,  503 S. Montezuma St., 86303,  602-445-7991 |
| Scottsdale | Azura East,  3703 N. 69th St., 85251 |
| Scottsdale | Valley 'O the Sun B&B,  P.O. Box 2214, 85252,  602-941-1281 |
| Sedona | Casa Lea Country Inn, A,  120 View Dr., 86336,  602-282-2833 |
| Sedona | Cathedral Rock Lodge,  SR 2, Box 836, Red Rock, 86336,  602-282-7608 |
| Sedona | Garland's Oak Creek Lodge,  P.O. Box 152, 86339,  520-282-3343 |
| Sedona | Kennedy House,  2075 Red Rock Loop Rd., 86336,  602-282-1624 |
| Sedona | L'Auberge de Sedona Resort,  P.O. Box B, 86336,  602-282-7131 |
| Sedona | Lantern Light Inn B&B, 3085 W. Hwy 89A, 86336,  602-282-3419 |
| Sedona | Moestly Wood B&B,  2085 Red Rock Loop Rd., 86336,  602-204-1461 |
| Sedona | Sipapu Lodge,  P.O. Box 552, 86339,  602-282-2833 |
| Sedona | Slide Rock Lodge,  Star Route 3, Box 1141, 86336,  602-282-3531 |
| Tempe | Mi Casa-Su Casa B&B,  P.O. Box 950, 85280,  602-990-0682 |
| Tombstone | Buford House B&B,  P.O. Box 38, 85638,  602-457-3168 |
| Tombstone | Tombstone Boarding House,  P.O. Box 906, 85638,  602-457-3716 |
| Tucson | Arizona Inn,  2200 E. Elm St., 85718,  602-325-1541 |
| Tucson | Bird In Hand B&B,  529 S. Meyer, 85701 |

*Casa Alegre,*
*Tucson, AZ*

| | |
|---|---|
| Tucson | Casa Suecia B&B, P.O. Box 36883, Ste 181, 85704 |
| Tucson | Casa Tierra, 11155 West Calle Pima, 85743, 602-578-3058 |
| Tucson | Copper Bell B&B, 25 N. Westmoreland Ave., 85745 |
| Tucson | Florence A. Ejrup, 941 W. Calle Dadivosa, 85704 |
| Tucson | Ford's B&B, 1202 N. Avenida Marlene, 85715, 602-885-1202 |
| Tucson | Hacienda del Sol Ranch, 5601 N Hacienda del Sol, 85718, 602-299-1501 |
| Tucson | Hideaway B&B, 4344 E. Poe St., 85711, 602-323-8067 |
| Tucson | Katy's Hacienda, 5841 E. 9th St., 85711, 602-745-5695 |
| Tucson | Mesquite Retreat, 3770 N. Melpomene Way, 85749, 602-749-4884 |
| Tucson | Natural B&B, 3150 E. Presidio Rd., 85716, 602-881-4582 |
| Tucson | Paz Entera Ranch B&B, 7501 N. Wade St., 85743, 602-744-2481 |
| Tucson | Peppertrees B&B Inn, 724 E. University Blvd., 85719, 620-622-7167 |
| Tucson | Quail Vista B&B, 826 E. Palisades Dr., 85737, 602-297-5980 |
| Tucson | Redbud House B&B, 7002 E. Redbud Rd., 85715, 602-721-0218 |
| Tucson | SunCatcher, 105 N. Avenida Javalina, 85748, 800-835-8012 |
| Tucson | Tanque Verde Ranch, 14301 E. Speedway, 85748, 602-296-6275 |
| Tucson | Tucson Old Pueblo, 4201 N. Saranac Dr., 85718 |
| Wickenburg | Kay El Bar Ranch, Box 2480, 85358, 602-684-7593 |
| Williams | Canyon Country Inn, 442 W. B. Williams Ave., 86046 |
| Williams | Johnstonian B&B, The, 321 W. Sheridan Ave., 86046, 602-635-2178 |
| Yuma | Casa de Osgood, 11620 Ironwood Dr., 85365, 602-342-0471 |

# Arkansas

## EUREKA SPRINGS

### 5 Ojo Inn B&B
| | | |
|---|---|---|
| 5 Ojo St., 72632 | $$-B&B | Full breakfast |
| 501-253-6734  800-656-6734 | 10 rooms, 10 pb | Dietary attention, snack |
| Paula Kirby Adkins | Visa, MC, Disc., • | Library, hot tub, gazebo |
| All year | C-ltd/S-ltd/P-no/H-ltd | jacuzzis, fireplaces |
| | | fresh flowers, deck |

*Award winning restoration of Victorian home says "stay here and revive." Historic District; 8-min. walk to shops and galleries.* **10% off 2nd & 3rd nights midweek.**

### Bonnybrooke Farm/Misty Mtn
| | | |
|---|---|---|
| Rt 2, Box 335A, 72632 | $$$-EP | Bread & fruit at arrival |
| 501-253-6903 | 5 rooms, 5 pb | Books & games, fireplace |
| Bonny & Josh | • | jacuzzi, glass showers |
| All year | S-no/P-no/H-no | basketball court |

*Sweet quiet & serenity atop Misty Mountain. Frplc., jacuzzi (for 2), shower under the stars in your glass shower. You're gonna love it! Mtn. views. 5 cottages. Very private.*

### Bridgeford House
| | | |
|---|---|---|
| 263 Spring St., 72632 | $$$-B&B | Full breakfast |
| 501-253-7853  Fax: 501-253-5497 | 4 rooms, 4 pb | Coffee in rooms |
| Denise & Michael McDonald | MC, Visa, *Rated*, • | Sitting room, garden |
| All year | C-yes/S-no/P-no/H-no | flowers in rooms, suite |
| | | 3 private porches |

*An 1884 antique-filled Victorian cottage located on a quiet tree-lined street in the historic district. Close to shops. Weddings, reunions, tours of town.* **3rd night 50% off.**

### Candlestick Cottage Inn
| | | |
|---|---|---|
| 6 Douglas, 72632 | $$-B&B | Full breakfast |
| 501-253-6813  800-835-5184 | 6 rooms, 6 pb | Reservations for local |
| Bill & Patsy Brooks | Most CC, *Rated*, • | restaurants/attractions |
| All year | C-ltd/S-no/P-no/H-no | Jacuzzi stes./queen beds |

*Located in historic district one block from downtown shops. Authentic Victorian-country setting. Breakfast served on treetop porch.* **3rd night, 20% off, ltd.**

## EUREKA SPRINGS

| **Crescent Cottage Inn** | $$-B&B | Full breakfast |
|---|---|---|
| 211 Spring St., 72632 | 4 rooms, 4 pb | Coffee |
| 501-253-6022 Fax: 501-253-6234 | Visa, MC, Disc.,*Rated*, | Historic district |
| Ralph & Phyllis Becker | • | 2 rms. w/double jacuzzis |
| All year | C-ltd/S-no/P-no/H-no | all queen-sized beds |

*Famous 1881 landmark Victorian home on National Register. Porches, gardens, and superb mountain views. Antiques throughout, warm ambience. Walk to town.* **3rd nite 20% off.**

| **Dairy Hollow House** | $$$$-B&B | Full breakfast to room |
|---|---|---|
| 515 Spring St., 72632 | 6 rooms, 6 pb | Restaurant, occ. dinner |
| 501-253-7444 Fax: 501-253-7223 | Most CC, *Rated*, • | Beverage upon check-in |
| 800-562-8650 | C-ltd/S-no/P-no/H-no | sitting room, hot tub |
| N. Shank, C. Dragonwagon | some French | fireplaces in rooms |
| Closed January | | |

*Restored Ozark farmhouse & late '40s bungalow. Full breakfast-in-a-basket, fireplaces, hot tub. 6-course "Nouveau 'Zarks" dinners offered 5-6 times/yr. Uncle Ben's Best Inn Awards, 1989-1991*

| **Dr. R. G. Floyd House** | $$$-B&B | Full breakfast |
|---|---|---|
| 246 Spring St., 72632 | 3 rooms, 3 pb | Comp. snacks & beverages |
| 501-253-7525 Fax: 501-253-2658 | Most CC, • | Sitting room, library |
| Georgia & Bill Rubley | S-ltd/P-no/H-no | bikes, CD players and |
| All year | | computers available |

*Authentically restored 1892 Queen Anne Victorian Mansion, quality antique furnishings. Limestone terrace gardens, balcony. Gourmet breakfast, room service. Historic District.*

| **Harvest House B&B** | $$-B&B | Full breakfast |
|---|---|---|
| 104 Wall St., 72632 | 4 rooms, 4 pb | Sitting room |
| 501-253-9363  800-293-5665 | • | Jacuzzi in 2 rooms |
| Bill & Patt Carmichael | S-ltd/P-yes/H-no | |
| All year | | |

*Nestled 100 years in Ozark mountains, this Victorian B&B displays antiques & delights with Arkansas' finest breakfast. Near walking trails & downtown.*

| **Heart of the Hills Inn** | $$$-B&B | Full gourmet breakfast |
|---|---|---|
| 5 Summit, 62 Business, 72632 | 4 rooms, 4 pb | Comp. beverage, dessert |
| 501-253-7468  800-253-7468 | MC, Visa, *Rated*, • | Sitting room, jacuzzi |
| Jan Jacobs Weber | C-ltd/S-no/P-no/H-no | suite w/double jacuzzi |
| All year | | cottage, crib, porches |

*Historic home furnished in genuine antiques; gourmet breakfast served on deck and porches. Gorgeous Victorian in a unique town. Trolley stops in front.* **3rd night 50% off, ltd.**

| **Heartstone Inn & Cottages** | $$-B&B | Full gourmet breakfast |
|---|---|---|
| 35 Kingshighway, 72632 | 9 rooms, 9 pb | Complimentary beverages |
| 501-253-8916 Fax: 501-253-6821 | MC, Visa, *Rated*, • | Sitting room, cable TVs |
| 800-494-4921 | C-ltd/S-yes/P-no/H-no | wedding gazebo, decks |
| Iris & Bill Simantel | | jacuzzi suite |
| February–mid December | | |

*Award-winning. Antique furniture, private baths & entrances, queen beds. Historic district by attractions. "Best breakfast in the Ozarks"-NY Times 1989.* **7th night free.**

*Singleton House B&B, Eureka Springs, AR*

## EUREKA SPRINGS

| **Hidden Valley Guest Ranch** | $$$-B&B | Continental plus bkfst. |
|---|---|---|
| 777 Hidden Vly. Ranch, 72632 | 2 rooms, 2 pb | Sitting room, hot tubs |
| 501-253-9777 888-HIDDEN-V | Visa, MC, Disc., • | TV/VCR, fireplaces |
| Jordan & Tandy Maxfield | C-yes/S-no/P-no/H-no | whirlpool for 2, horses |
| All year | Spanish | |

*Country at its best! Secluded cabins high on an Ozark's mountainside. Full amenities. 5 minutes from Eureka Springs.* **50% off Tues. with any other 2 nights.**

| **Kansas House, The** | $$$-B&B | Continental plus bkfst. |
|---|---|---|
| 2 Singleton, 72632 | 2 rooms, 2 pb | Snacks |
| 501-253-5558 Fax: 501-253-6649 | Visa, MC, | Sitting room |
| Larry & Kathy Harrison | C-ltd/S-ltd/P-no/H-no | walk to galleys and |
| All year | | restaurants, never drive |

*This 1881 home lovingly restored, nestled by Sweet Springs Park, in the heart of the Historic District. Relax on porches that wrap this 3 story comfortable haven.* **2nd night 20% off, 3rd night 25% off.**

| **Morningstar Retreat** | $$$-EP | Snacks |
|---|---|---|
| RT 1 Box 653, 72632 | 5 rooms, 5 pb | Library, hot tubs, river |
| 501-253-5995  800-298-5995 | Visa, MC, *Rated*, • | volleyball, trails |
| Janet & Michael Avenoso | C-ltd/S-no/P-no/H-no | croquet, horseshoes |
| All year | | |

*Secluded country resort 9 miles from romantic Eureka Springs. Beautifully decorated cottages on the King's River. Jacuzzis, woodstoves and king beds.* **Free cookbook, ltd.**

| **Singleton House B&B** | $$-B&B | Full breakfast |
|---|---|---|
| 11 Singleton, 72632 | 5 rooms, 5 pb | Jacuzzi w/priv. balcony |
| 501-253-9111  800-833-3394 | AmEx, MC, Visa, Disc., | Cottage, swing, rockers |
| Barbara Gavron | • | INNternship program |
| All year | C-yes/S-ltd/P-no/H-no | guest ice-box, microwave |
| | Spanish (some) | |

*1894 Victorian, antiques, folkart; breakfast balcony overlooks magical garden & fish pond. Vegetarian dining, bird house collection. Historic district; scenic 1 block walk to shops.* **Midweek discounts.**

### EUREKA SPRINGS

**Sunnyside Inn**
5 Ridgeway, 72632
501-253-6638   800-554-9499
Gladys Rose Foris
All year

$$$-B&B
6 rooms, 6 pb
•
C-yes/S-no/P-no/H-no

Full breakfast
Snacks
family friendly facility

*Enchanting Victorian Home on the National Register of Historic Homes. Queen size beds, private baths, antique furnishings, wilderness area, quiet serenity.* **3rd nite 50%.**

### HARDY

**Olde Stonehouse B&B Inn**
511 Main St., 72542
501-856-2983  Fax: 501-856-4036
800-856-2983
Peggy Johnson
All year

$$-B&B
9 rooms, 9 pb
MC, Visa, *Rated*, •
C-ltd/S-ltd/P-no/H-no

Full breakfast
Evening snack
Sitting room, library
A/C, ceiling fans
Bkfast in bed. TV, VCR

*Two-story native rock home with antiques. Two 2-rm. suites in separate bldg. Near quaint shops, Spring River, golf, water sports, antique auctions.* **3rd night 50% off ltd.**

### HEBER SPRINGS

**Anderson House Inn, The**
201 Main St., 72543
501-362-5266  Fax: 501-362-2326
800-264-5279
Jim & Susan Hildebrand
All year

$$-B&B
16 rooms, 16 pb
Most CC, *Rated*,
C-ltd/S-ltd/P-no/H-no
Some French

Full breakfast
Afternoon tea
Sitting room, hot tub
quilts, city park
with tennis courts

*Warm, comfortable country inn in the Ozark foothills; convenient to Grees Ferry Lake and world class fly fishing.* **Corporate rates available, Special Packages.**

### HELENA

**Edwardian Inn**
317 Biscoe, 72342
501-338-9155  Fax: 501-572-9105
800-598-4749
Margorie Hornbeck/Julie
Brown
All year

$$-B&B
12 rooms, 12 pb
Most CC, *Rated*,
C-yes/S-ltd/P-no/H-yes

Full breakfast
Wine & hors d'oeuvres
Sitting room, library
antiques, building
for long term guests

*The Edwardian Inn offers twelve antique guest rooms, private bath and continental breakfast. Elegance and romance from the turn of the century.* **Champagne for special occasions.**

---

**Foxglove B&B**
229 Beech St., 72342
501-338-9391  Fax: 501-338-9391
800-863-1926
John Butkiewicz   All year

$$-B&B
10 rooms, 9 pb
Visa, MC, AmEx, •
C-ltd/S-no/P-no/H-no

Full breakfast
Complimentary wine
Whirlpool tubs
sitting room
antiques

*Overlooks historic Helena and the Mississippi River. Stunning antiques, parqueted floors, stained glass, complimented by marble baths and whirlpool tubs.* **Free bottle of wine.**

### HOT SPRINGS

**Vintage Comfort B&B Inn**
303 Quapaw Ave., 71901
501-623-3258   800-608-4682
Helen R. Bartlett
All year

$$-B&B
4 rooms, 4 pb
MC, Visa, *Rated*, •
C-ltd/S-no/P-no/H-no

Full breakfast
Comp. tea & cookies
Sitting room
antique reed organ
weddings, receptions

*1903 Queen Anne home decorated with antiques, soft, light colors; featuring Southern hospitality. Romantic atmosphere ideal for weddings and honeymoons.*

*Vintage Comfort B&B Inn, Hot Springs, AR*

## HOT SPRINGS

**Williams House B&B Inn**
420 Quapaw Ave., 71901
501-624-4275
David & Kare Wiseman
All year

$$-B&B
6 rooms, 4 pb
Most CC, •
C-ltd/S-ltd/P-ltd/H-no

Full breakfast
Spring water, iced tea
Sitting rooms, fireplace
piano, picnic tables
BBQ, hiking trail maps

*Williams House shows Victorian flair for convenience and elegance. Your home away from home, nestled in Oachita Mountains. Romantic atmosphere. Mystery weekends.* **Free wine.**

## MOUNTAIN VIEW

**Wildflower B&B**
P.O. Box 72, 72560
100 Washington St.
501-269-4383  800-591-4879
Todd & Andrea Budy
All year, Nov-Mar res.

$-B&B
8 rooms, 6 pb
AmEx, *Rated*,
C-yes/S-no/P-no/H-no

Continental plus
Bakery on premises
Sitting room
Suite w/kitchenette
entertainment, porch

*Restored country inn on historic Courthouse Square; close to Ozark Folk Center & Blanchard Springs Caverns. Old-time music on our porch.* **Ask about "Frequent Sleeper" program.**

## More Inns ...

| | |
|---|---|
| Arkadelphia | Iron Mountain Lodge, 1 Marina Dr., 71923, 501-246-4310 |
| Brinkley | Great Southern Hotel, 127 W. Cedar, 72021, 501-734-4955 |
| Calico Rock | Arkansas and Ozarks B&B, HC 61, Box 72, 72519, 501-297-8221 |
| Des Arc | 5-B's, The, P.O. Box 364, 72040, 501-256-4789 |
| Eureka Springs | Bell Spring Cottage, Roiute 1, Box 981, 72632, 501-253-8581 |
| Eureka Springs | Brackenridge Lodge & Gifts, Rt. 4 Box 60, 72632 |
| Eureka Springs | Brownstone Inn, The, 75 Hillside Ave., 72632, 501-253-7505 |
| Eureka Springs | Cedarberry Cottage, 3 Kings Highway, 72632 |
| Eureka Springs | Coach House Inn, 140 S. Main, 72632, 501-253-8099 |
| Eureka Springs | Cobblestone Guest Cottage, 29 Ridgeway, 72632, 501-253-8105 |
| Eureka Springs | Crescent Moon, P.O. Box 429, 72632, 501-253-9463 |
| Eureka Springs | Enchanted Cottages, 18 Nut St., 72632, 501-253-6790 |
| Eureka Springs | Four Winds B&B, 3 Echols St., 72632, 501-253-9169 |
| Eureka Springs | Greenwood Hollow Ridge, 23 S. Greenwood Hollow, 72632, 501-253-5283 |
| Eureka Springs | Hillside Cottage B&B, 23 Hillside, 72632, 501-253-8688 |
| Eureka Springs | Lake Lucerne Resort, P.O. Box 441, 72632, 501-253-8085 |
| Eureka Springs | Lazee Daze, Route 1, Box 196, 72632, 501-253-7026 |
| Eureka Springs | Lookout Cottage, 12 Lookout Circle, 72632, 501-253-9545 |
| Eureka Springs | Maple Ridge, 2 First St., 72632, 501-253-5220 |
| Eureka Springs | Maplewood B&B, 4 Armstrong St., 72632, 501-253-8053 |
| Eureka Springs | New Orleans Hotel, 63 Spring St., 72632, 501-253-8630 |
| Eureka Springs | Old Homestead, The, 82 Armstrong, 72632, 501-253-7501 |

| | |
|---|---|
| Eureka Springs | Palace Hotel & Bathhouse, 135 Spring St., 72632, 501-253-7474 |
| Eureka Springs | Piedmont House B&B, 165 Spring St., 72632, 501-253-9258 |
| Eureka Springs | Primrose Place, 39 Steele St., 72632, 501-253-9818 |
| Eureka Springs | Queen Anne Mansion, 207 Kings Highway, 72632 |
| Eureka Springs | Red Bud Manor, 7 Kingshighway, 72632, 501-253-9649 |
| Eureka Springs | Red Bud Valley Resort, RR 1, Box 500, 72632, 501-253-9028 |
| Eureka Springs | Ridgeway House, 28 Ridgeway St., 72632, 501-253-6618 |
| Eureka Springs | Rock Cabins, 10 Eugenia, 72632, 501-253-8659 |
| Eureka Springs | Rosewood Guest Cottage, One Kings Highway, 72632, 501-253-7674 |
| Eureka Springs | Rustic Manor, Route 4, Box 66, 72632, 501-253-8128 |
| Eureka Springs | Scandia B&B Inn, 33 Avo, Hwy. 62 W., 72632, 501-253-8922 |
| Eureka Springs | Shady Rest Cottages, One Magnetic, 72632, 501-253-8793 |
| Eureka Springs | Spider Creek Resort, Route 2, Box 418, 72632, 501-253-9241 |
| Eureka Springs | Sweet Seasons Cottages, P.O. Box 642, 72632, 501-253-7603 |
| Eureka Springs | Tatman-Garret House, P.O. Box 171, 72632, 501-253-7617 |
| Eureka Springs | Tweedy House B&B, 16 Washington St., 72632, 501-253-5435 |
| Eureka Springs | Valais-Hi, 33 Van Buren, 72632, 501-253-5140 |
| Eureka Springs | White Flower Cottage, 62 Kings Hwy, 72632, 501-253-9636 |
| Eureka Springs | White River Oaks B&B, Rt. 2, Box 449, 72632, 501-253-9033 |
| Fayetteville | Eton House, 1485 Eton, 72703, 501-521-6344 |
| Fayetteville | North Forty, 40 N. Crossover Rd., 72101, 501-521-3739 |
| Fordyce | Wynne Phillips House, 412 W. Fourth St., 71742, 501-352-7202 |
| Gassville | Lithia Springs B&B Lodge, Rt. 1, Box 77-A, 72635, 501-435-6100 |
| Gilbert | Anna's House, P.O. Box 58, 72636, 501-439-2888 |
| Harrison | Mountain Pines Cabin, P.O. Box 1355, 72602, 501-420-3575 |
| Heber Springs | Oak Tree Inn, Vinegar Hill, 110 W., 72543, 501-362-6111 |
| Hot Springs | Dogwood Manor, 906 Malvern Ave., 71901, 501-624-0896 |
| Hot Springs | Gables Inn, The, 318 Quapaw Ave., 71901, 501-623-7576 |
| Hot Springs | Stillmeadow Farm, Route 1, Box 434-D, 71913, 501-525-9994 |
| Hot Springs | Stitt House, The, 824 Park Ave., 71901 |
| Hot Springs | Woodbine Place B&B, 213 Woodbine, 71901, 501-624-3646 |
| Hughes | Snowden House B&B, Hwy. 147, P.O. Box 486, 72348, 501-339-3414 |
| Jasper | Cliff House Inn, Scenic Ark., Highway 7, 72641, 501-446-2292 |
| Johnson | Johnson House 1882, P.O. Box 431, 72741, 501-756-1095 |
| Little Rock | Dr. Witt's Quapaw Inn, 1868 S. Gaines, 72206, 501-376-6873 |
| Little Rock | Hotze House, P.O. Box 164087, 72216 |
| Mountain View | Country Oaks B&B, HC 70, Box 63, Hwy 9, 72560, 800-455-2704 |
| Mountain View | Inn at Mountain View, The, P.O. Box 812, 72560, 800-535-1301 |
| Pine Bluff | Margland B&B, P.O. Box 8594, 71611, 501-536-6000 |
| Rogers | Coppermine Lodge, Rt. 6 Box 575, 72756 |
| Romance | Hammons Chapel Farm, 1 mile of Ark. 5, 72136, 501-849-2819 |
| Siloam Springs | Washington Street B&B, 1001 South Washington, 72761, 501-524-5669 |
| Wooster | Patton House B&B Inn, P.O. Box 61, 72181, 501-679-2975 |
| Yellville | Red Raven Inn, P.O. Box 1217, 72687, 501-449-5168 |

*[Handwritten:] HOT SPRINGS — MOUNTAIN THYME / 10860 SCENIC*

# California *[Handwritten:] BYWAY 1 NORTH JESSIEVILLE ARK. 71949 WWW.MOUNTAIN*

*[Handwritten:] $90 TO $125  501-984-5428 OR 1-888-820-3424*

## AHWAHNEE

| **The Homestead** | $$$-B&B | Continental breakfast |
|---|---|---|
| 41110 Road 600, 93601 | 5 rooms, 5 pb | Barbeque available |
| 209-683-0495 Fax: 209-683-8165 | Vias, MC, AmEx, | Equine layover avail. |
| Cindy Brooks & Larry Ends | *Rated*, • | near golf, antique shops |
| Closed January | C-ltd/S-no/P-no/H-ltd | and Miwok village site |
| | Spanish | |

*Romantic private cottages with kitchens on 160 wooded acres close to Yosemite, Gold Country, golf and restaurants. Equine layover available.*

| **Yosemite's Apple Blossom** | $$-B&B | Full breakfast |
|---|---|---|
| 44606 Silver Spur Trail, 93601 | 3 rooms, 2 pb | Afternoon tea, snacks |
| 209-642-2001 | Visa, Mc, AmEx, | Hot tubs, sitting room |
| Lance & Lynn Hays | *Rated*, • | game room w/woodburning |
| All year | C-yes/S-ltd/P-no/H-no | stove, trail walks, spa |

*Nestled in the midst of our apple farm; a special place to relax after a Yosemite sightseeing or stage coach ride! Beautiful views, quiet, romantic.* **Third night 50% off.**

**ALAMEDA** ───────────────────────────

| **Garratt Mansion** | $$$-B&B | Full breakfast |
|---|---|---|
| 900 Union St., 94501 | 7 rooms, 5 pb | Cookies, hot/cold drinks |
| 510-521-4779 Fax: 510-521-6796 | *Rated*, • | Sitting room, phones and |
| Royce & Betty Gladden | C-ltd/S-no/P-no/H-no | private baths in most |
| All year | | rooms, TV available |

*An elegant Victorian in a quiet island community just 20 minutes from downtown San Francisco, offering personalized attention. Meeting/wedding/party facilities.*

| **Webster House B&B Inn** | $$-B&B | Full breakfast |
|---|---|---|
| 1238 Versailles Ave, 94501 | 5 rooms, 3 pb | Restaurant on premises |
| 510-523-9697 | *Rated*, • | Snacks, public teahouse |
| Andrew & Susan | C-yes/S-ltd | deck, sun porch, library |
| McCormack | | waterfall, garden, games |
| All year | | |

*22nd City Historical Monument. Quaint, enchanting Gothic Revival Cottage is oldest house in Alameda. Walk to beach, shops, golf. San Francisco 20 min. away. **3rd night 50%**.*

**ALBION** ───────────────────────────

| **Fensalden Inn** | $$$-B&B | Full breakfast |
|---|---|---|
| P.O. Box 99, 95410 | 7 rooms, 7 pb | Wine & hors d'oeuvres |
| 33810 Navarro Ridge Rd. | MC, Visa, *Rated*, • | Sitting room |
| 707-937-4042 800-959-3850 | C-ltd/S-ltd/P-ltd/H-ltd | parlor, library |
| Frances & Scott Brazil | | library |
| All year | | |

*On 20 acres of Mendocino Coast. Historic country inn w/spectacular ocean views—only 10 min. from Mendocino village. 1 bungalow sleeps 4. **Free bottle of wine, 7th night free.***

**ANGWIN, NAPA VALLEY** ─────────────────

| **Forest Manor** | $$$-B&B | Full breakfast |
|---|---|---|
| 415 Cold Springs Rd., 94508 | 3 rooms, 3 pb | Comp. beverages & snacks |
| 707-965-3538 Fax: 707-965-3303 | MC, Visa, • | Jacuzzi, frig., limo |
| 800-788-0364 | C-ltd/S-ltd/P-no/H-no | sitting room, piano |
| Dr. Harold & Corlene | Thai, French | organ, 53' pool & spa |
| Lambeth All year | | |

*Beautiful, secluded 20-acre English Tudor forested estate & ostrich ranch in Napa Wine Country. Carved beams, fireplaces, decks, A/C, game rooms. **Various discounts, ask.***

**APTOS** ───────────────────────────

| **Apple Lane Inn** | $$$-B&B | Full breakfast |
|---|---|---|
| 6265 Soquel Dr., 95003 | 5 rooms, 3 pb | Comp. cookies & milk |
| 408-475-6868 Fax: 408-464-5790 | MC, Visa, *Rated*, • | Sitting room, library |
| 800-649-8988 | C-ltd/S-ltd/P-no/H-no | piano, new attic suite |
| Doug & Diana Groom | | Weddings to 175 people |
| All year | | |

*Victorian farmhouse furnished w/beautiful antiques offers country charm. Quiet, yet close to everything, incl. fine restaurants. Romantic Victorian gazebo. **3rd night 50% off.***

| **Bayview Hotel B&B Inn** | $$$-B&B | Full breakfast |
|---|---|---|
| 8048 Soquel Dr., 95003 | 8 rooms, 8 pb | Restaurant offering CA |
| 408-688-8654 Fax: 408-688-5128 | MC, Visa, *Rated*, • | Cuisine-bkfst./lun./din. |
| 800-4BAYVIEW | C-yes/S-no/P-no/H-no | sitting room |
| Gwen Burkard | French, Italian | 2-room suite available |
| All year | | |

*1878 California Victorian furnished with lovely antiques; near beaches, hiking trails, bicycle routes, golf, tennis, fishing, antique shops and restaurants. **10% off Sun.–Thur.***

APTOS —————————————————————————————————

| | | |
|---|---|---|
| **Mangels House B&B** | $$$-B&B | Full breakfast |
| P.O. Box 302, 95001 | 5 rooms, 5 pb | Comp. wine, piano |
| 570 Aptos Creek Rd. 95003 | MC, Visa, *Rated*, • | Sitting room, fireplace |
| 408-688-7982 | C-ltd/S-ltd/P-no/H-no | table tennis and darts |
| 800-320-7401 | French, Spanish | English garden, nursery |
| Jacqueline Fisher | | |
| All year exc. Christmas | | |

*Casual elegance in country setting, 5 min. drive to Hwy 1. 4 acres of lawn and woodland on edge of Redwood State Park. 1 mi. from beach, golf, Monterey Bay.* ***Discounts, ask.***

ARROYO GRANDE ———————————————————————

| | | |
|---|---|---|
| **Arroyo Village Inn** | $$$-B&B | Full breakfast |
| 407 El Camino Real, | 7 rooms, 7 pb | Picnic lunch w/notice |
| 818 Vista Brisa, 93420 | Visa, MC, AmEx, | Wine & hors d'oeuvres |
| 805-489-5926 | *Rated*, • | sitting room, library |
| Fax: 805-489-5926 800-563-7762 | C-ltd/S-no/P-no/H-no | large parlour, spa area |
| Gina Glass   All year | | |

*In the heart of California's scenic Central Coast. Convenient to golf, beach, wineries, Hearst Castle. Charming Laura Ashley decor.* ***3rd night 50%; 2nd night 50% Sun.–Thurs.***

AUBURN ———————————————————————————————

| | | |
|---|---|---|
| **Power's Mansion Inn** | $$$-B&B | Full breakfast |
| 164 Cleveland Ave., 95603 | 11 rooms, 11 pb | Deluxe amenities |
| 916-885-1166 | *Rated*, • | fireplaces, patios/decks |
| Arno & Jean Lejnieks | C-ltd/S-no/P-no/H-yes | terry robes |
| All year | Dut., Ger., Chi., Lat. | |

*1898 mansion built from gold-mining fortune. Has elegance of detailed restoration & antique furnishings with queen beds & central air & heat.* ***3+ nights 10% off.***

AVALON ———————————————————————————————

| | | |
|---|---|---|
| **Zane Grey Pueblo Hotel** | $$-B&B | Continental plus |
| P.O. Box 216, 90704 | 17 rooms, 17 pb | Sitting room, library |
| 199 Chimes Tower Rd. | Visa, MC, AmEx, • | pool, patios, hiking |
| 310-510-0966 | C-ltd/S-ltd/P-no/H-no | fishing, moutain views |
| Fax: 310-510-0639 | Spanish | |
| 800-378-8567 | | |
| Kevin Anderson & Karen | | |
| Baker   All year | | |

*Former private home of western novelist Zane Grey. Breathtaking view of Avalon Bay and the Pacific Ocean. Quiet, peaceful, clean.* ***10% discount, ask.***

BALLARD ———————————————————————————————

| | | |
|---|---|---|
| **Ballard Inn, The** | $$$$-B&B | Full breakfast |
| 2436 Baseline Ave., 93463 | 15 rooms, 15 pb | Aftn. tea, restaurant |
| 805-688-7770 800-638-2466 | Visa, MC, AmEx, | Sitting room |
| Kelly Robinson | *Rated*, • | library, comp. wine |
| Closed Christmas Day | C-ltd/S-no/P-no/H-yes | bicycles |
| | Spanish, French | |

*Comfortably elegant accommodations in the heart of Santa Barbara wine country. Dinner served Wednesday thru Sunday at the acclaimed Cafe Chardonnay.* ***Sun.–Thurs. room upgrade.***

## BAYWOOD PARK

| | | |
|---|---|---|
| **Baywood B&B Inn** | $$$-B&B | Full breakfast |
| 1370 Second St., 93402 | 15 rooms, 15 pb | Cafe, complimentary wine |
| 805-528-8888 Fax: 805-528-8887 | MC, Visa, *Rated*, • | Conferences for up to 14 |
| Tricia Chasse | C-yes/S-no/P-no/H-yes | sitting room, fireplaces |
| All year | British | 11 suites w/amenities |

*Bayfront Inn on South Morro Bay. Each room has its own personality. Near Hearst Castle, San Luis Obispo, Montano De Oro State Park.* **Wine & cheese hospitality hour.**

## BEN LOMOND

| | | |
|---|---|---|
| **Fairview Manor** | $$$-B&B | Full breakfast |
| P.O. Box 74, 95005 | 5 rooms, 5 pb | Comp.wine/hors d'ouevres |
| 245 Fairview Ave. | MC, Visa, *Rated*, • | Sitting room |
| 408-336-3355  800-553-8840 | C-ltd/S-yes/P-no/H-yes | bordered by river |
| Nancy Glasson | | weddings & meetings |

*Romantic country-styled redwood home, majestic stone fireplace, 2.5 wooded acres of Santa Cruz Mountains. Total privacy. Walk to town. Comp. Champagne.* **Comp. champagne.**

## BENICIA

| | | |
|---|---|---|
| **Painted Lady B&B, The** | $$-B&B | Full breakfast |
| 141 East F St., 94510 | 2 rooms, 2 pb | Snacks, comp. wine |
| 707-746-1646 | Visa, MC, • | Sitting room, library |
| Sally Watson | C-ltd/S-no/P-ltd/H-no | games & tapes of old |
| All year | | radio shows available |

*Cozy Victorian in Benicia's historic district - walk to shops, restaurants, Marina. Privacy, lovely garden, complimentary wine, antiques & breakfast.* **10% discount for 3+ nite.**

## BIG BEAR

| | | |
|---|---|---|
| **Gold Mountain Manor B&B** | $$-B&B | Full breakfast |
| P.O. Box 2027, 92314 | 7 rooms, 3 pb | Comp. beverages, snacks |
| 1117 Anita | *Rated*, • | Pool table, fireplaces |
| 909-585-6997 Fax: 909-585-0327 | C-ltd/S-ltd/P-ltd/H-no | veranda, hot tub |
| Robert, Jose, Gloria | French | parlor w/large fireplace |
| All year | | |

*Magnificent, historic & romantic 1920s log mansion featured in Ralph Lauren ads. Gourmet country breakfast. Near Nat'l Forest.* **2nd night 50% off, Sun.–Thurs.**

## BISHOP

| | | |
|---|---|---|
| **Chalfant House, The** | $$-B&B | Full breakfast |
| 213 Academy, 93514 | 7 rooms, 7 pb | Afternoon tea, snacks |
| 619-872-1790 | Most CC, *Rated*, | Library |
| Fred & Sally Manecke | C-ltd/S-no/P-no/H-no | sitting room, ice cream |
| All year | | sundeas every evening |

*Historical B&B furnished in antiques. In town, close to everything. Quiet; afternoon tea, Ice Cream Sundaes every evening 8-9. We love to pamper you.* **3rd night 50% off.**

## BLAIRSDEN

| | | |
|---|---|---|
| **Gray Eagle Lodge** | $$$$-MAP | Full breakfast |
| P.O. Box 38, 96103 | 17 rooms, 17 pb | Picnic lunch (fee) |
| 5000 Gold Lake Rd. | Visa, MC, *Rated*, | Bar service, lounge |
| 916-836-2511  800-635-8778 | C-yes/S-ltd/P-yes/H-ltd | book trade, hiking |
| Bret & Julia Smith | | swim hole w/waterfall |
| Mid May-Mid October | | |

*Rustic cabins nestled in the forest. Gourmet dining, daily maid service, hiking, fishing, mountain biking, wildflowers, golf and horseback riding nearby.*

BOONVILLE ─────────────────────────────────────

**Anderson Creek Inn**
P.O. Box 217, 95415
12050 Anderson Valley Way
707-895-3091 Fax: 707-895-2546
800-552-6260
Rod & Nancy Graham
All year

$$$-B&B
5 rooms, 4 pb
MC, Visa, *Rated*,
C-yes/S-no/P-ltd/H-yes

Full gourmet breakfast
Comp. wine, appetizers
Sitting room, bicycles
hiking trails, croquet
horseshoes, large pool

*Peaceful ranch home affords ultimate privacy, lush views. Guests treated to elegant full breakfast in bed or lounge. Llamas & sheep to enjoy. **Mid-week rates, ltd.***

BRIDGEPORT ───────────────────────────────────

**Cain House, The**
P.O. Box 454, 93517
340 Main St.
619-932-7040  800-433-CAIN
Chris & Marachal Gohlich
May 1 - Nov. 1

$$$-B&B
7 rooms, 7 pb
Most CC, *Rated*, •
C-ltd/S-no/P-no/H-no

Full breakfast
Comp. wine and cheese
Sitt. rm., tennis courts
6 rms. w/A/C, 2 w/priv.
entrance, all w/phones

*The grandeur of the eastern Sierras is the perfect setting for evening wine and cheese. Quiet, romantic, peaceful getaway.*

CALISTOGA ────────────────────────────────────

**Brannan Cottage Inn**
P.O. Box 81, 94515
109 Wapoo Ave.
707-942-4200
Dieter Back    All year

$$$-B&B
6 rooms, 6 pb
MC, Visa, *Rated*, •
C-ltd/S-no/P-no/H-no
Spanish, German

Full breakfast
Complimentary wine
Sitting room, A/C
library, fireplace
refrig., TV in 2 rooms

*Charming 1860 National Register cottage-style Victorian, original wildflower stencils, country furnishings, lovely grounds, close to famous spas, wineries.*

─────────────────────────────────────────────

**Calistoga Country Lodge**
2883 Foothill Blvd.,  94515
707-942-5555 Fax: 707-942-5864
Rae Ellen
February—December

$$$-B&B
6 rooms, 4 pb
Most CC, *Rated*, •
C-ltd/S-no/P-no/H-no

Continental plus buffet
Snacks, Comp. wine
Sitting room, new pool
jacuzzi spa, gardens
10 years of hospitality

*1917 ranch house restored in Southwest style offering country solitude, spacious common area, views of valley & open land. 1 mile from Calistoga spas. Small parties to 35 people. **10% discount,ltd.***

─────────────────────────────────────────────

**Calistoga Wayside Inn**
1523 Foothill Blvd.,  94515
707-942-0645 Fax: 707-942-4169
800-845-3632
Cora Freitas & Jan Balcer
All year

$$$-B&B
3 rooms, 3 pb
Most CC, •
C-yes/S-no/P-no

Full breakfast
Afternoon tea
Comp. wine & cheese
parlor, library
fireplace, sherry

*1920s Spanish-style home w/fountains & fish pond. Gourmet bkfst. served on patio in the summer. Close to wineries & spas. Good for small weddings. **15% off 3 night stay in 1 week.***

─────────────────────────────────────────────

**Culver's, A Country Inn**
1805 Foothill Blvd  94515
707-942-4535
Meg & Tony Wheatley
Exc. Nov.-Feb.

$$$$-B&B
6 rooms, 6 pb
MC, Visa, *Rated*, •
C-ltd/S-ltd/P-no/H-yes

Full country breakfast
Comp. sherry, beverages
Fruit, hors d'oeuvres
living room w/fireplace
pool, hot tub

*Comfortable, elegant Victorian home circa 1875, restored historical landmark in Napa. Easy access to wineries, spas, gliding, ballooning, restaurants*

CALISTOGA ─────────────────────────────────

**Elms B&B, The**
1300 Cedar St., 94515
707-942-9476 Fax: 707-942-9476
800-235-4316
Stephen & Karla Wyle
All year

$$$-B&B
7 rooms, 7 pb
Most CC, *Rated*, •
S-no/P-no/H-yes

Full gourmet breakfast
Snacks, comp. wine
Sitting room, bicycles
Wine & cheese in p.m.
choclates at bedtime

*Step into the past where life was quieter and the pace relaxed. Enjoy the romance and intimacy of this 1871 French Victorian.*

───────────────────────────────────────────

**Foothill House B&B Inn**
3037 Foothill Blvd., 94515
707-942-6933 Fax: 707-942-5692
800-942-6933
Doris & Gus Beckert
All year

$$$$-B&B
4 rooms, 4 pb
MC, Visa, AmEx,
*Rated*, •
C-ltd/S-no/P-no/H-no

Full breakfast
Comp. wine & cheese
Turndown service: sherry
3 rooms w/jacuzzi tub
sitting room, AC

*In a country setting, Foothill House offers 3 spacious rooms individually decorated with antiques, each with private bath, entrance & fireplace. Separate elegant cottage.*

───────────────────────────────────────────

**Scarlett's Country Inn**
3918 Silverado Trail, 94515
707-942-6669 Fax: 707-942-6669
Scarlett Dwyer
All year

$$$-B&B
3 rooms, 3 pb
•
C-yes/S-no/P-no/H-no
Spanish

Full breakfast
Comp. wine & cheese
Sitting room, A/C, TV's
microwaves & frigdes
coffee makers, pool

*Secluded French country farmhouse overlooking vineyards in famed Napa Valley. Breakfast served by woodland swimming pool. Close to spas and wineries. **3rd night 50% off.***

───────────────────────────────────────────

**Trailside Inn**
4201 Silverado Trail, 94515
707-942-4106 Fax: 707-942-4702
Randy & Lani Gray
All year

$$$-B&B
3 rooms, 3 pb
Visa, MC, AmEx, Disc.,
•
C-ltd/S-ltd/P-no/H-no

Continental plus bkfst.
Complimentary wine,
Mineral water, fireplace
kitchens, library, A/C
spa, private deck

*1930s farmhouse comfortably decorated with quilts and antiques. Each suite has private entrance, 3 rooms plus bath. Two suites sleep party of four. Family suite.*

───────────────────────────────────────────

**Zinfandel House**
1253 Summit Dr., 94515
707-942-0733 Fax: 707-942-4618
Bette & George Starke
All year

$$$-B&B
3 rooms, 2 pb
Visa, MC,
C-ltd/S-no/P-no/H-no

Full breakfast
Complimentary wine
Library
sitting room
hot tub

*Beautiful home situated on wooded hillside overlooking vineyards and mountains. Lovely breakfast served on outside deck or in dining room.*

CAMBRIA ─────────────────────────────────

**Beach House B&B, The**
6360 Moonstone Beach Dr,
   93428
805-927-3136 Fax: 805-927-3260
Penny Hitch
All year

$$$-B&B
7 rooms, 7 pb
MC, Visa, *Rated*, •
C-ltd/S-no/P-no/H-no

Full breakfast
Aftn. tea, comp. wine
Sitting room, fireplace
patios, 3 outside decks
mountain bikes

*Oceanfront home with antique oak furniture, queen and king-size beds, ocean views. Visit Hearst Castle, beach, wineries, shops. Rural atmosphere, gorgeous sunsets.*

## CAMBRIA

**Cambria Landing Inn**
6530 Moonstone Beach Dr,
  93428
805-927-1619  800-549-6789
Joan Apathy & Kern
MacKinnon
All year

$$$-B&B
26 rooms, 26 pb
Visa, MC, Disc. *Rated*,
•
C-ltd/S-yes/P-no/H-yes

Continental breakfast
Comp. wine/champagne
Hot tubs, jacuzzis for 2
oceanfront jacuz. suites
refrigs., VCR, bicycles

*Romantic country inn set on ocean bluff near rocky beaches. Oceanfront rooms w/TV, private decks/patios, frplcs. & "breakfast in bed." $10 off room rate w/mention of this ad.*

---

**Olallieberry Inn, The**
2476 Main St., 4435 Highland
Dr Carlsbad,  93428
805-927-3222 Fax: 805-927-0202
888-927-3222
Peter & Carol Ann Irsfeld
All year

$$$-B&B
6 rooms, 6 pb
Visa, MC, *Rated*, •
C-ltd/S-no/P-no/H-yes

Full gourmet breakfast
Comp. wine & appetizers
Parlor, gathering room
antiques, special diets
tennis & swimming priv.

*Pamper yourself where time stands still. Full gourmet breakfast; complimentary afternoon wine & hor'douvres; an endless supply of home baked cookies.*

---

**Pickford House B&B, The**
2555 MacLeod Way,  93428
805-927-8619
Anna Larsen
All year

$$$-B&B
8 rooms, 8 pb
MC, Visa, *Rated*,
C-ltd/S-ltd/P-no/H-yes

Full breakfast
Wine, fruit & bread
Hors d'oeuvres, cookies
sitting room, fireplaces
TV in all rms., antiques

*All rooms named after silent film-era stars and furnished with genuine antiques. All rooms have showers, TV and tubs. 7 miles to Hearst Castle. Extra person, $20.*

---

**Squibb House, The**
4063 Burton Dr.,  93428
805-927-9600
Martha Carolyn
All year

$$$-B&B
5 rooms, 5 pb
Visa, MC, *Rated*, •
C-ltd/S-no/P-no/H-no

Continental plus bkfst.
Restaurant steps away
Comp. wine tasting
sitting room

*Restored 1877 Victorian in the heart of Cambria. Within steps of galleries, shops and fine restaurants. Near Hearst Castle and wine country. Gift shop in 1885 Carpentry Shop.*

## CARLSBAD

**Pelican Cove B&B Inn**
320 Walnut Ave.,  92008
619-434-5995
Nancy & Kris Nayudu
All year

$$$-B&B
8 rooms, 8 pb
MC, Visa, *Rated*, •
C-ltd/S-no/H-yes

Full breakfast
Comp. sherry
Beach nearby
beach chairs, towels
picnic baskets

*Feather beds/fireplaces in every room. Jacuzzis in 2 rooms. Private tiled baths, private entries, fruit, flowers, candy in every room. Comp. Amtrak pickup. 3rd night 50% off.*

## CARMEL

**Carriage House Inn**
P.O. Box 1900, 93921
Junipero btwn 7th & 8th
408-625-2585 Fax: 408-626-6974
800-433-4732
Cathy Lewis
All year

$$$$-B&B
13 rooms, 13 pb
Most CC, *Rated*, •
C-ltd/S-yes/P-no/H-no

Continental plus bkfst.
Wine, hors d'oeuvres
Sitting room, library
some rooms w/Jacuzzi tub

*Intimate, romantic. King-size beds, down comforters, fireplaces, some sunken tubs. Within walking distance of shops, galleries, restaurants, & white beaches. Lanier rate, ask.*

CARMEL ─────────────────────────────────────

**Cobblestone Inn**
P.O. Box 3185, 93921
Junipero btwn 7th & 8th
408-625-5222 Fax: 408-625-0478
800-833-8836
Suzi Russo
All year

$$$-B&B
24 rooms, 24 pb
AmEx, MC, Visa,
*Rated*, •
C-yes/S-no/P-no/H-no

Full country breakfast
Wine & hors d'oeuvres
Sitting room w/fireplace
patio, bicycles
picnics avail.

*Charming country inn in English garden setting. Rooms have fireplace and country decor, turndown service, beverages and morning paper. Breakfast in bed. A Four Sisters Inn.*

**Cypress Inn**
P.O. Box Y, Lincoln & 7th Sts.,
  93921
408-624-3871 Fax: 408-624-8216
800-443-7443
D. Day, D. Levett, T. Melcher
All year

$$$-B&B
34 rooms, 34 pb
Most CC, *Rated*, •
C-ltd/S-ltd/P-yes/H-ltd

Continental breakfast
Aftn. tea, bar service
Fruit basket, sherry
daily paper
fresh flowers

*Charming Spanish-Mediterranean style, built in 1929. In the heart of the village within walking distance to shops, restaurants and galleries.*

**Happy Landing Inn**
P.O. Box 2619, 93921
Monte Verde bet. 5th/ 6th
408-624-7917
Robert Ballard & Dick
Stewart     All year

$$$-B&B
7 rooms, 7 pb
MC, Visa, *Rated*,
C-ltd/S-no/P-no/H-yes

Continental plus bkfst.
Comp. sherry
Sitting room
Gazebo, gardens, pond
Honeymoon cottage avail.

*Hansel & Gretel cottages in the heart of Carmel, like something from a Beatrix Potter book. Surrounds a central flowering garden; breakfast is served in your room.*

**Holiday House**
P.O. Box 782, 93921
Camino Real at 7th Ave.
408-624-6267
Dieter & Ruth Back
All year

$$$-B&B
6 rooms, 4 pb
*Rated*, •
C-ltd/S-ltd/P-no/H-no
German

Full breakfast
Afternoon sherry
Colorful garden
sitting room, library

*Lovely inn personifying Carmel charm, in quiet residential area. A short walk to beautiful Carmel beaches, quaint shops, restaurants. Ocean views, beautiful garden.*

**Homestead, The**
P.O. Box 1285, 93921
8th & Lincoln Sts.
408-624-4119
Betty Colletto
All year

$$-EP
12 rooms, 12 pb
*Rated*,
C-yes/S-yes

Comp. coffee in rooms
4 cottages w/kitchens
2 cottages w/fireplaces

*A unique inn nestled in the heart of Carmel. Rooms and cottages with private baths, some kitchens & fireplaces. Reasonably priced and close to town.*

**Lincoln Green Inn**
P.O. Box 2747, 93921
Carmelo btwn 15th & 16th
408-624-1880 Fax: 408-626-1243
800-262-1262
Honey Spence
All year

$$$$-EP
4 rooms, 4 pb
AmEx, MC, Visa, •
C-yes/S-yes/P-yes/H-yes

Complimentyary tea
English garden

*Four charming English country-style cottages set in a formal English garden behind a white picket fence; nestled in a quaint residential area near ocean.*

CARMEL ─────────────────────────────────────

| **San Antonio House** | $$$-B&B | Continental plus bkfst. |
|---|---|---|
| P.O. Box 3683, 93921 | 4 rooms, 4 pb | Complimentary tea |
| San Antonio @ Ocean & 7th | AmEx, MC, Visa, • | Sitting room, fireplaces |
| 408-624-4334 | C-ltd/S-no/P-no/H-no | flower gardens, patios |
| Sarah Lee, Brenda Bell | | private entrances |
| All year | | |

*Private 2- & 3-rm suites decorated w/antiques & art. One block from famous Carmel Beach. Sounds of surf & sense of yesteryear dissolve tensions. $10 off with mention of Guide.*

| **Sea View Inn** | $$$-B&B | Continental plus bkfst. |
|---|---|---|
| P.O. Box 4138, 93921 | 8 rooms, 6 pb | Afternoon tea & coffee |
| Camino Real @ 11th & 12th | MC, Visa, *Rated*, • | Comp. evening wine |
| 408-624-8778 Fax: 408-625-5901 | C-ltd/S-no/P-no/H-no | sitting room |
| Marshall & Diane Hydorn | | library, garden |
| All year | | |

*Small, intimate, cozy Victorian, near village and beach. Enjoy breakfast and evening wine served by the fireside, or relax in secluded garden. 3rd night 50%, ltd.*

| **Vagabond's House Inn** | $$$-B&B | Continental plus bkfst. |
|---|---|---|
| P.O. Box 2747, 93921 | 11 rooms, 11 pb | Sitting rm. w/fireplace |
| 4th & Dolores | MC, Visa, • | library, courtyard |
| 408-624-7738 Fax: 408-626-1243 | C-ltd/S-yes/P-yes/H-no | 2 blocks to downtown |
| 800-262-1262 | French | |
| Honey Spence   All year | | |

*Antique clocks and pictures, quilted bedspreads, fresh flowers, plants, shelves filled with old books. Sherry by the fireplace; breakfast served in your room.*

CARMEL BY-THE-SEA ─────────────────────────

| **Sandpiper Inn-at-the-Beach** | $$$-B&B | Continental plus bkfst. |
|---|---|---|
| 2408 Bay View Ave., 93923 | 16 rooms, 16 pb | Coffee, tea, sherry |
| 408-624-6433 Fax: 408-624-5964 | Most CC, *Rated*, • | Library, flowers |
| 800-633-6433 | C-ltd/S-ltd/P-no/H-no | fireplace lounge |
| Michelle Higgins | French, German | tennis, golf, bicycles |
| All year | | |

*Fifty yards from Carmel Beach. European-style country inn, filled with antiques & fresh flowers. Ocean views, fireplaces, garden. Mobil 2-star rating. Comp. bottle of wine.*

CARMEL VALLEY ────────────────────────────

| **Robles del Rio Lodge** | $$$-B&B | Continental plus bkfst. |
|---|---|---|
| 200 Punta Del Monte, 93924 | 31 rooms, 31 pb | French restaurant |
| 408-659-3705  800-833-0843 | MC, Visa, *Rated*, • | Sitting room, hot tub |
| Glen Gurries | C-yes/S-yes/P-no/H-yes | sauna, swimming pool |
| All year | Spanish, French | tennis courts |

*A charming country hideaway high atop a mountain. Breathtaking view of the beautiful Carmel Valley. Newly renovated. From $69 per room, per night, Sun.–Thur. + breakfast buffet for 2.*

| **Valley Lodge** | $$$-B&B | Continental plus |
|---|---|---|
| P.O. Box 93, 93924 | 35 rooms, 35 pb | Library, hot tub, sauna |
| Ford Road | Most CC, *Rated*, • | pool, fitness center, TV |
| 408-659-2261 Fax: 408-659-4558 | C-yes/S-yes/P-yes/H-yes | conf. fac., comp. paper |
| 800-641-4646 | French, Spanish | |
| Peter & Sherry Coakley | | |
| All year | | |

*Quiet, lovely spot. Romantic setting for lovers of privacy, nature, hiking, golf, tennis, swimming, riding & just plain lovers. Cozy fireplace cottages. 20% off Sunday-Thurs.*

## CAZADERO

| **Cazanoma Lodge** | $$-B&B | Continental plus bkfst. |
|---|---|---|
| P.O. Box 37, 95421 | 5 rooms, 5 pb | Bar, complimentary wine, |
| 1000 Kidd Creek Rd. | AmEx, MC, Visa, • | cheese & crackers |
| 707-632-5255 Fax: 707-635-5256 | C-yes/S-yes/P-ltd/H-yes | entertainment, swimming |
| Randy Neuman | | hiking trails, spa room |
| March–November | | |

*Secluded lodge on 147 acres of redwood forest w/creeks, trout pond & waterfall. Near the ocean & beautiful Russian River. 2 night stay 25% off, Sun.–Thur.*

## CHESTER

| **Bidwell House, The** | $$-B&B | Full Gourmet breakfast |
|---|---|---|
| P.O. Box 1790, 96020 | 14 rooms, 12 pb | Afternoon tea, snacks |
| #1 Main St. | Visa, MC, *Rated*, • | Sitting room, library |
| 916-258-3338  Fax: 916-258-3187 | C-yes/S-ltd/P-no/H-yes | hot tubs in rooms |
| Kim & Ian James | | Jacuzzis, fireplaces |
| All year | | |

*Historical Inn on the edge of Lassen National Park, beautiful lake Almanor and next to the Feather River; gourmet breakfast; hikers, golfers, and skier of both kinds paradise!*

## CHICO

| **Music Express Inn** | $$-B&B | Full breakfast |
|---|---|---|
| 1091 El Monte Ave., 95928 | 9 rooms, 9 pb | Library |
| 916-345-8376 Fax: 916-893-8521 | Most CC, *Rated*, | close to Chico State U. |
| Barney & Irene Cobeen | C-yes/S-ltd/P-no/H-yes | golf nearby |
| All year | | |

*Beautiful country inn with king size beds on 3 acres. Close to Bidwell Park, CSUC Chico. Your home away from home!*

## CLOVERDALE

| **Abrams House Inn** | $$ | Full breakfast |
|---|---|---|
| 314 N. Main St., 95425 | 4 rooms, 2 pb | Snacks, comp. wine |
| 707-894-2412 Fax: 707-894-4476 | AmEx, MC, Visa, | Afternoon Appetizers |
| 800-764-4466 | *Rated*, • | sitting room, library |
| P. Robarts & B. Fitz-Gerald | C-ltd/S-no/P-no/H-no | hot tub, evening sweets |
| All year | | |

*1870s Victorian home. Antiques, garden, gazebo, hot tub, near wineries, lake and river. Small weddings and seminars, pre-arrange meals, boat ride. Complimentary bottle of wine.*

| **Vintage Towers Inn** | $$-B&B | Full breakfast |
|---|---|---|
| 302 N. Main St., 95425 | 8 rooms, 6 pb | Afternoon snacks |
| 707-894-4535888-886-9377 | Visa, MC, AmEx, Disc., | 3 sitting rms., piano |
| Cindy & Gus Wolter | • | bicycles, gazebo, TV |
| All year | C-ltd/S-ltd/P-ltd/H-yes | veranda & gardens |

*A towered mansion on the national register, on a quiet tree-lined street in a wine country town. Walk to river, wineries and fine dining. 10% discount when you mention Lanier guide.*

## COLOMA

| **Coloma Country Inn, The** | $$$-B&B | Full breakfast |
|---|---|---|
| P.O. Box 502, 95613 | 7 rooms, 3 pb | Comp. wine, beverages |
| 345 High St. | • | Sitting room, bicycles |
| 916-622-6919 | C-yes/S-no/P-no/H-no | Victorian tea, rafting |
| Alan & Cindi Ehrgott | Spanish, French | 2 new suites, canoeing |
| All year | | |

*Country Victorian built in 1856, set among rose and flower gardens and pond on 5 acres. Half a block to Sutter's Mill and American River. Balloon flights nearby.*

## COLUMBIA

| **Columbia City Hotel** | $$-B&B | Full breakfast |
|---|---|---|
| P.O. Box 1870, 95310 | 10 rooms, 10 pb | French restaurant |
| Columbia State Park | AmEx, MC, Visa, | Sitting room, piano |
| 209-532-1479 Fax: 209-532-7027 | *Rated*, • | Anchor Steam beer on |
| Tom Bender    All year | C-yes/S-ltd/P-no/H-no | draft in saloon |

*Historical location in a state-preserved Gold Rush town; 9 antique-appointed rooms; small elegant dining room and authentic saloon. Goldpanning nearby, wine tasting events.*

| **Fallon Hotel** | $$-B&B | Continental plus bkfst. |
|---|---|---|
| P.O. Box 1870, 95310 | 14 rooms, 14 pb | Sitting rm., rose garden |
| 11575 Washington St. | MC, Visa, *Rated*, • | live theater, gold |
| 209-532-1470 Fax: 209-532-7027 | C-yes/S-ltd/P-no/H-yes | panning nearby, fishing |
| Tom Bender    All year | | |

*Restored Victorian hotel, full of antiques in state-preserved Gold Rush town. Elegant and intimate. Near Yosemite. Many historic family fun events throughout the year.*

## CORONADO

| **Coronado Village Inn** | $$-B&B | Continental breakfast |
|---|---|---|
| 1017 Park Pl.,   92118 | 14 rooms, 14 pb | Afternoon tea |
| 619-435-9318 | AmEx, MC, Visa, • | Sitting room, library |
| Elizabeth A. Bogh | C-yes/S-yes/P-no/H-no | bicycles, DD phones, TV |
| All year | | airport shuttle |

*A delightful small "European" hotel heart of village. One half block to fine dining & shopping. One block to large, sandy beach on Pacific Ocean. **7th day free.***

## DANA POINT

| **Blue Lantern Inn, The** | $$$$-B&B | Full country breakfast |
|---|---|---|
| 34343 Blue Lantern St., | 29 rooms, 29 pb | Wine, hor d'oeuvres |
|    92629 | AmEx, MC, Visa, | Library with fireplace |
| 714-661-1304 Fax: 714-496-1483 | *Rated*, • | bicycles, exercise room |
| 800-950-1236 | C-ltd/S-no/P-no/H-yes | hot tub in rooms |
| Lin McManon    All year | | |

*Cape Cod inn with a dramatic location overlooking the Pacific Ocean. Rooms have fireplaces, jacuzzi, decks and are individually decorated. Breakfast in bed. A Four Sisters Inn.*

## DAVENPORT

| **Davenport B&B Inn** | $$-B&B | Full breakfast |
|---|---|---|
| P.O. Box J, 31 | 12 rooms, 12 pb | Full breakfast (fee) |
| Davenport Ave.,   95017 | AmEx, MC, Visa, | Restaurant, gift shop |
| 408-425-1818 Fax: 408-423-1160 | *Rated*, | champagne on arrival |
| 800-870-1817 | C-ltd/S-no/P-no/H-yes | sitting room, gallery |
| Bruce & Marcia McDougal | | |
| All year | | |

*Charming ocean-view rooms decorated with antiques, handcrafts & ethnic treasures. Comp. champagne. Artist/owners. Beach access. **50% off 2nd night/whale watching special, ltd.***

## DAVIS

| **University Inn B&B** | $$-B&B | Continental plus bkfst. |
|---|---|---|
| 340 "A" St.,   95616 | 4 rooms, 4 pb | Comp. beverages |
| 916-756-8648  800-756-8648 | Most CC, *Rated*, • | Microwave |
| Lynda & Ross Yancher/M. | C-yes/S-no/P-no/H-yes | bicycles |
| Ramos | | airport shuttle |
| All year | | |

*A great taste of Davis, ten steps from the University. Quiet location. Rooms w/private phone, cable TV, refrigerator, microwave. **Special rates for University business.***

## DULZURA

**Brookside Farm B&B Inn**
1373 Marron Valley Rd., 91917
619-468-3043
Edd & Sally Guishard
All year

$$$-B&B
11 rooms, 8 pb
MC, Visa *Rated*, •
C-ltd/S-ltd/P-no/H-ltd

Full breakfast
4-course dinner by RSVP
Hot tub, piano
terraces, gardens
rm. w/2-sided frplc.

*Quaint farmhouse nestled in mountain setting w/stream. Handmande quilts and rugs, fireplace and farm animals. Gourmet dinners on weekends.* **Comp. soup/salad @ 6:30 Sun.-Thurs.**

## DUNSMUIR

**Dunsmuir Inn**
5423 Dunsmuir Ave., 96025
916-235-4543 Fax: 916-235-4154
888-DUNSMUIR
Julie & Jerry Iskra All year

$$-B&B
4 rooms, 4 pb
Most CC, •
C-yes/S-no/P-no/H-no

Full breakfast
Lunch, snacks
Vegetarian bkfst. avail.
sitting room, BBQ
fishing close by

*Year round recreation; skiing, fishing, golfing, hiking; northern California country inn; relax for one day or one week.* **Buy 1 night, get 1 free, Oct.-April.**

## ELK

**Elk Cove Inn, The**
PO Box 367, 6300 S. Hwy. 1,
   95432
707-877-3321 Fax: 707-877-1808
800-275-2967
Elaine Bryant & Jim Carr
All year

$$$-B&B
13 rooms, 13 pb
Visa, AmEx, MC,
*Rated*, •
C-ltd/S-no/P-no/H-ltd
German, Spanish

Full gourmet breakfast
Berr & wine pub
Comp. sherry
sitting room, deck
library, stereo, fishing

*1883 Victorian mansion on the Ocean. Dramatic views, private steps to beach, organic gardens, romantic gazebo. Cozy fireplace cottages and antique filled rooms. 10% off midweek, ask*

---

**Harbor House by the Sea**
P.O. Box 369, 95432
5600 S. Highway 1
707-877-3203
Helen & Dean Turner
All year

$$$$-MAP
10 rooms, 10 pb
*Rated*,
C-ltd/S-ltd/P-no/H-no
French, Spanish

Full breakfast
Full dinner, wine list
Sitting room, piano
fireplace, parlor stove
gardens, private beach

*Spectacular north coast vistas of the sea. Renowned country gourmet cuisine. Wine lover's pradise. Rooms include original artwork, fireplaces or parlor stoves, and decks.*

---

**Sandpiper House Inn**
P.O. Box 149, 95432
5520 S. Hwy 1
707-877-3587
Richard & Claire Melrose
All year

$$$-B&B
5 rooms, 5 pb
Most CC, *Rated*,
C-ltd/S-no/P-no/H-no

Full breakfast
Aftn. tea, snacks
Comp. sherry
breakfast in dining rm.
living room for guests

*Seaside country inn built in 1916. Rich redwood paneling, European charm, lush perennial gardens, stunning ocean views, private beach access. Massage studio on premises.* **Weekday rates Mon.-Thurs.**

## ESCONDIDO

**Castle Creek Inn & Spa**
29850 Circle "R" Way, 92026
619-751-8800 Fax: 619-751-8787
800-253-5341
All year

$$$-B&B
30 rooms, 30 pb
Visa, MC, AmEx, •
C-yes/S-yes/P-no/H-yes
Sp., Ar., Fr.

Continental plus bkfst.
Lunch & dinner (fee)
Sitting room, bikes
tennis courts, hot tubs
sauna, pool

*Nestled in the foothills of North San Diego County. One of California's "Best Kept Secrets." Antiques from King Ludwig's Castle in Bavaria, Germany.* **50% off 2nd night, ltd.**

EUREKA ────────────────────────────────────

| **Carter House Victorians** | $$$-B&B | Full breakfast |
|---|---|---|
| 301 L St., 1033 3rd St.,  95501 | 8 rooms, 8 pb | Dinner (by reservation) |
| 800-444-8062    Fax: 707-444- | Most CC, *Rated*,  • | Whirpools, fireplaces |
| 8067 800-404-1390 | C-yes/S-no/P-no/H-no | sitt rms, jacuzzis, TV/ |
| Mark & Christi Carter | | VCR/CD/stereo, gardens |
| All year | | |

*New Victorian. Enjoy wines & appetizers before dinner, cordials or teas & cookies @ bedtime. Warm hospitality; award-winning breakfasts. Bell cottage. OUR 1986 INN OF THE YEAR.* **10% off, ltd.**

| **Daly Inn, The** | $$$-B&B | Full breakfast |
|---|---|---|
| 1125 H St.,  91311 | 5 rooms, 3 pb | Wine, Hors D'oeuvres |
| 707-445-3638 Fax: 707-444-3636 | Most CC, *Rated*,  • | Comp. wine, snacks |
| 800-321-9656 | C-ltd/S-ltd/P-no/H-no | sitting room, library |
| Sue & Gene Clinesmith | | Victorian gardens, pond |
| All year | | |

*A beautifully restored turn-of-the-century mansion, one of Eureka's finest. 1 room w/twin beds, 4 rooms w/queen beds. Victorian gardens, fish pond. Weddings.* **3rd night 25% off.**

| **Elegant Victorian Mansion** | $$$-B&B | Full gourmet breakfast |
|---|---|---|
| 1406 "C" St., at 14th. St., | 3 rooms, 2 pb | Comp. ice cream sodas |
| 95501 | MC, Visa, *Rated*,  • | Sauna, massage, croquet |
| 707-444-3144 Fax: 707-442-5594 | C-ltd/S-no/P-no/H-no | parlors, cable TV, bikes |
| 800-386-1888 | French, Dutch, German | antique autos, bay views |
| Doug & Lily Vieyra | | |
| All year | | |

*1888 National Historic Landmark "House-Museum" for the discriminating connoisseur of authentic Victorian decor, who has a passion for quality, service and the extra-ordinary.*

| **Old Town B&B Inn** | $$-B&B | Full country breakfast |
|---|---|---|
| 1521 Third St.,  95501 | 6 rooms, 4 pb | Afternoon refreshments |
| 707-445-3951 Fax: 707-268-0231 | Most CC, *Rated*,  • | Comp. wine, phones |
| 800-331-5098 | C-ltd/S-no/P-no/H-no | sitting room w/fireplace |
| Leigh & Diane Benson | | feather beds, cable TV |
| All year | | |

*Historic 1871 home, graciously decorated w/antiques. Historical landmark. Original home of the Williams Carson family. Close to Old Town. Teak hot tub.* **Discounts, ask.**

FERNDALE ────────────────────────────────────

| **Gingerbread Mansion Inn** | $$$$-B&B | Full breakfast |
|---|---|---|
| P.O. Box 40, 95536 | 10 rooms, 10 pb | Afternoon tea & cake |
| 400 Berding St. | MC, Visa, *Rated*,  • | 5 guest parlors |
| 707-786-4000 Fax: 707-786-4381 | C-ltd/S-no/P-no/H-no | library w/fireplace |
| 800-952-4136 | Port., Sp., Fr., Jap. | English gardens, bikes |
| Ken Torbert    All year | | |

*Northern California's most photographed inn! Perfect getaway in quiet Victorian village ("his & her bubble baths"). Turndown w/chocolate.* **3rd nite 50%, ltd.**

| **Shaw House B&B** | $$-B&B | Full breakfast |
|---|---|---|
| P.O. Box 1125, 95536 | 6 rooms, 6 pb | Comp. beverages/cookies |
| 703 Main St. | *Rated*,  • | Sitting room, library |
| 707-786-9958 Fax: 707-786-9958 | C-ltd/S-ltd/P-no/H-no | gazebo, yard |
| 800-557-SHAW | | |
| Norma & Ken Bessingpas | | |
| All year | | |

*Ferndale's elegant inn—first house built in Ferndale (1854). Antiques, fresh flowers; join other guests in library, parlor.* **Discounts to returning guests.**

## FISH CAMP

**Narrow Gauge Inn**
48571 Hwy. 41,  93623
209-683-7720 Fax: 209-683-2139
April–December

$$$-EP
27 rooms, 27 pb
Most CC, *Rated*,  •
C-ltd/S-yes/P-no/H-yes
Spanish, French,
German

Restaurant
Sitting room
hot tubs, pool
historic locomotive

*Charming turn-of-the-century country inn, nestled at 5,000 feet in the Sierra Nevadas, just 4 miles from Yosemite National Park. Spa, walking trails, historic train rides.*

## FORT BRAGG

**Avalon House**
561 Stewart St.,  95437
707-964-5555  800-964-5556
Anne Sorrells
All year

$$-B&B
6 rooms, 6 pb
Most CC,  •
C-yes/S-no/P-no/H-no

Full breakfast
Comp. sherry/port
Fireplaces in rooms
whirlpool tubs in rooms

*1905 Craftsman house in a quiet neighborhood close to ocean and Skunk Train Depot. Fireplaces. Romantic Mendocino Coast retreat.* **20% discount, Mon.–Thurs., except holidays.**

---

**Glass Beach B&B Inn**
726 N. Main St.,  95437
707-964-6774
Richard & Nancy
All year

$$$-B&B
9 rooms, 9 pb
MC, Visa,  •
C-yes/S-yes/P-no/H-yes

Full breakfast
Snacks
Sitting room
hot tubs

*Glass Beach is a small, gracious guest house where we offer you elegance, relaxation, and the comforts of home.* **3rd night 50%, ltd.**

---

**Grey Whale Inn**
615 N. Main St.,  95437
707-964-0640 Fax: 707-964-4408
800-382-7244
John & Colette Bailey
All year

$$$-B&B
14 rooms, 14 pb
Most CC, *Rated*,  •
C-ltd/S-no/P-no/H-yes

Full buffet breakfast
Aft. tea, fresh fruit
Parlor, TV-VCR, fireplc.
in room phones, upgrades
gift shop, art gallery

*Mendocino coast landmark since 1915. Spacious rooms; ocean, town or garden views. Honeymoon suite w/jacuzzi & pvt. sundeck. Stroll to beach, shopping & dining.* **Winter rates.**

---

**Lodge at Noyo River, The**
500 Casa del Noyo Dr.,  95437
707-964-8045  800-628-1126
Sam Dillon
All year

$$$-B&B
16 rooms, 16 pb
Visa, MC, AmEx,
*Rated*,  •
C-ltd/S-ltd/P-no/H-ltd

Full breakfast
Snacks
Sitting room, hiking
golf, charter fishing &
charter whale watch

*Secluded country inn overlooks river and harbor. "Mendocino coast's best kept secret." 12 rooms cable TV, fireplaces; wildlife abounds off of back deck.*

---

**Pudding Creek Inn**
700 N. Main St.,  95437
707-964-9529 Fax: 707-961-0282
800-227-9529
Garry & Carole Anloff
All year

$$-B&B
10 rooms, 10 pb
AmEx, MC, Visa,
*Rated*,  •
C-ltd/S-no/P-no/H-no

Full buffet breakfast
Afternoon refreshments
Victorian parlor
lush garden
TV and game room

*1884 Victorian built by Russian Count. Enclosed garden court, walk to Glass Beach, Skunk Train and restaurants.* **15% off mid-week, ltd.**

## GARDEN GROVE

**Hidden Village B&B**
9582 Halekulani Dr., 92641
714-636-8312
Dick & Linda O'Berg
All year

$$-B&B
4 rooms, 2 pb
*Rated*, •
C-ltd/S-no/P-no/H-no

Full breakfast
Aftn. tea, comp. wine
Picnic baskets avail.
Sitting room, bicycles
garden setting

*Large Colonial home furnished in genuine antiques. spacious rooms with king and queen beds, master king with private patio and fireplace.* **Group discounts.**

## GEORGETOWN

**American River Hotel**
P.O. Box 43, 95634
Main & Orleans St.
916-333-4499  800-245-6566
Will & Maria Collin
All year

$$$-B&B
18 rooms, 12 pb
AmEx, MC, Visa,
*Rated*, •
C-ltd/P-no/H-yes

Full breakfast
Evening refreshments
Barbecue, games, aviary
player piano, bicycles
hot tubs, swimming pool

*An enchanting setting for weddings, honeymoons, anniversaries, corporate getaways or just a weekend away from the world. Putting green, mini-driving range.* **25% off 3rd night of 3 night stay.**

## GEYSERVILLE

**Campbell Ranch Inn**
1475 Canyon Rd., 95441
707-857-3476  Fax: 707-857-3239
800-959-3878
Mary Jane & Jerry Campbell
All year

$$$-B&B
5 rooms, 5 pb
Most CC, *Rated*, •
C-ltd/S-no/P-no/H-no

Full breakfast from menu
Evening dessert
Living room, A/C
family rm w/TV, VCR
hilltop views, gardens

*35-acre rural setting in heart of Sonoma County's wine country with tennis court, swimming pool & spa. Private cottage unit. Fresh flowers, evening dessert, and homemade pie.*

**Hope-Merrill/Hope-
Bosworth**
P.O. Box 42, 95441
21253/38 Geyserville Ave.
707-857-3356  Fax: 707-857-4673
800-857-4233
Rosalie Hope    All year

$$$-B&B
12 rooms, 12 pb
AmEx, MC, Visa,
*Rated*, •
C-yes/H-ltd

Full country breakfast
Picnic lunches, pool
Beer & wine license
sitting room, library
large Sterling Suite

*Victorians in Sonoma County's wine country. Old-fashioned hospitality. Stage-A-Picnic in the vineyards. Award-winning restoration.* **3rd night, 50%.**

## GILROY, SAN MARTIN

**Country Rose Inn B&B**
P.O. Box 2500, 95021
455 Fitzgerald Ave. #E
408-842-0441 Fax: 408-842-6646
Rose Hernandez
All year

$$$-B&B
5 rooms, 5 pb
MC, Visa, *Rated*, •
C-ltd/S-no/P-no/H-no
Spanish

Full breakfast
Snacks
Library, sitting room
suite with jet tub
Free t-shirt w/2 nights.

*A gracious farm house located in the heart of California's pastoral central coast. The coast is a scenic drive away. Unexpected. Serene. Debbie Reynolds has stayed here.*

## GRASS VALLEY

**Murphy's Inn**
318 Neal St., 95945
916-273-6873  Fax: 916-273-6873
800-895-2488
Nancy & Ted Daus
All year

$$$-B&B
8 rooms, 8 pb
AmEx, MC, Visa,
*Rated*, •
C-ltd/S-no/P-no/H-yes

Full breakfast
Beverages, snacks
2 sitting rooms
600 foot deck
house for families

*Victorian estate of gold baron. Walk to restaurants, historic district. Golf, ski, hike or pan for gold. Delicious breakfasts.* **10% discount to seniors & AAA members, ltd.**

GROVELAND ───────────────────────────────────────

| **Groveland Hotel, The** | $$$-B&B | Full breakfast |
| P.O. Box 289, 95321 | 17 rooms, 17 pb | Restaurant-lunch/dinner |
| 18767 Main St. | AmEx, MC, Visa, | Conf. fac., comp. wine |
| 209-962-4000 Fax: 209-962-6674 | *Rated*, • | bar service, sitting rm. |
| 800-273-3314 | C-yes/S-ltd/P-ltd/H-yes | library, hot tubs |
| Peggy A. Mosley | AT&T interpreter | |
| All year | service | |

*Beautiful, restored historic Gold Rush hotel. Gourmet dining in Victorian garden. Near Yosemite. Fly fishing and wilderness survival schools. Off-season, midwk specials.*

| **Inn at Sugar Pine Ranch** | $$$-B&B | Full breakfast |
| 21250 Hwy. 120,  95321 | 12 rooms, 12 pb | Afternoon tea |
| 209-962-7823 Fax: 209-962-7823 | Visa, MC, • | Sitting room, library |
| Elaine & Craig Maxwell | S-no/P-no/H-yes | swimming pool |
| All year | | family friendly facility |

*Situated on 60 acres, our home and cottages are a place for all seasons, just 22 miles from Yosemite's gate.*

GUALALA ───────────────────────────────────────

| **Gualala Hotel** | $-EP | Dinner |
| P.O. Box 675, 95445 | 19 rooms, 5 pb | Sitting room |
| 39301 S. Hwy. 1 | Most CC, *Rated*, | piano, bicycles |
| 707-884-3441 Fax: 707-884-3908 | C-yes/S-yes/P-no/H-no | golf, beaches, river |
| Howard E. Curtis & Staff | | |
| All year | | |

*Historic 1903 hotel, overlooking the ocean, furnished with original antiques. Extensive wine shop, family-style meals. Canoeing and kayaking.*

| **North Coast Country Inn** | $$$$-B&B | Full breakfast to room |
| 34591 S. Highway 1,  95445 | 4 rooms, 4 pb | Wet bar in all rooms |
| 707-884-4537  800-959-4537 | AmEx, MC, Visa, | Hot tub, library, gazebo |
| Loren & Nancy Flanagan | *Rated*, • | antique shop, fireplaces |
| All year | C-ltd/S-no/P-no/H-no | beach access |

*A cluster of weathered redwood buildings on a forested hillside overlooking the Pacific Ocean. Close to golf, tennis and riding facilities. Senior citizen discount, ask.*

GUERNEVILLE ───────────────────────────────────────

| **Ridenhour Ranch House** | $$$-B&B | Full gourmet breakfast |
| **Inn** | 8 rooms, 8 pb | Dinner weekends (fee) |
| 12850 River Rd.,  95446 | MC, Visa, *Rated*, • | Comp. port or sherry |
| 707-887-1033 Fax: 707-869-2967 | C-ltd/S-ltd/P-no/H-yes | picnic lunches, hot tub |
| Diane & Fritz Rechberger | | sitting room, fireplace |
| Exc. January & February | | |

*Country inn on the Russian River in the heart of the lush and lovely Sonoma wine country. Adjacent to historic Korbel Champagne Cellars. Fresh flowers.*

| **Willows, The** | $$-B&B | Continental plus bkfst. |
| 15905 River Rd.,  95446 | 13 rooms, 9 pb | Afternoon tea |
| 707-869-2824  800-953-2828 | Most CC, • | Sitting room, library |
| Rick Reese | S-no/P-no/H-no | hot tubs, sauna |
| All year | | riverside dock w/canoes |

*Five acre riverside park-like setting on Russian River. Old fashion country lodge, cozy rooms, antiques, near ocean and redwoods. $10 off Sunday–Thursday.*

## HALF MOON BAY

**Mill Rose Inn**
615 Mill St., 94019
415-726-8750  Fax: 415-726-3031
800-900-7673
Eve & Terry Baldwin
all year

$$$$-B&B
6 rooms, 6 pb
Most CC, *Rated*, •
C-ltd/S-no/P-no/H-no
French, Spanish,
German

Full breakfast
Complimentary tea, wine
Sitting room, cable TV
frplc. & spa w/rms. golf
VCR & phones, beach, spa

*Exquisitely appointed flower-filled rooms and suites with private bath, entrance. English country rose garden by the sea. Oriental rugs, European antiques. Horseback riding.*

**Old Thyme Inn, The**
779 Main St., 94019
415-726-1616  Fax: 415-712-0805
George & Marcia Dempsey
All year

$$$-B&B
7 rooms, 7 pb
Most CC, *Rated*, •
C-ltd/S-ltd/P-yes/H-no
French

Full breakfast
Complimentary wine
Library
sitting room
herb garden

*1890 Victorian with herb garden on historic Main Street. Some private baths with large whirlpool tubs, fireplaces. Great breakfasts.* **Comp. book on Growing Herbs, ask.**

**San Benito House**
356 Main St., 94019
415-726-3425  Fax: 415-726-9507
Greg Regan
All year

$$-B&B
12 rooms, 9 pb
Most CC, *Rated*, •
S-yes/P-no/H-no
Portuguese

Hearty continental bkfst
Lunch, dinner, bar (fee)
Sauna, sun deck
croquet, gardens

*A romantic bed and breakfast just south of San Francisco. Historic inn, gourmet restaurant, western-style saloon and garden-deli cafe.* **10% disc't . for guests at restaurant.**

**Zaballa House**
324 Main St., 94019
415-726-9123  Fax: 415-726-3921
800-77-BNB4U
Kerry Pendercast & S.
Lowings
All year

$$-B&B
9 rooms, 9 pb
Most CC, *Rated*, •
C-ltd/S-no/P-ltd/H-no

"All-you-can-eat" bkfst.
Full breakfast
Comp. wine and beverages
sitting room, gardens
near fine restaurants

*First house built in town (1859). Garden setting by creek. Fireplaces, whirlpool baths. Friendly, knowledgeable innkeepers. Conference facilities.*

## HANFORD

**Irwin Street Inn, The**
522 N. Irwin St., 93230
209-583-8000 Fax: 209-583-8793
888-583-8080
Michael Block
All year

$$$-B&B
30 rooms, 30 pb
Most CC, *Rated*, •
C-yes/S-yes/P-yes/H-yes

Full breakfast
Restaurant
Small pool
stroll to shops, art,
crafts, antiques

*Charming Victorian-style inn furnished with antiques and stained glass. Surrounded by beautiful grounds. Perfect for business, romance, or relaxation.* **3rd night, 50%.**

## HEALDSBURG

**Camellia Inn**
211 North St., 95448
707-433-8182 Fax: 707-433-8130
800-727-8182
Ray, Del & Lucy Lewand
All year

$$-B&B
9 rooms, 9 pb
MC, Visa, *Rated*, •
C-ltd/S-ltd/P-no/H-ltd

Full breakfast
Comp. beverage & snacks
Sitting room
swimming pool in summer
4 rms. w/whirlpool tub

*Elegant Italianate Victorian built in 1869, near Sonoma's finest wineries—beautifully restored and furnished with antiques, oriental rugs.* **Special gift.**

## HEALDSBURG

**Grape Leaf Inn**
539 Johnson St., 95448
707-433-8140
Karen & Terry Sweet
All year

$$$-B&B
7 rooms, 7 pb
MC, Visa, *Rated*, •
C-ltd/S-no/P-no/H-no

Full country breakfast
Complimentary wine 5-8
Jacuzzi tub/showers for
two in five guest rooms

*Victorian elegance amidst Sonoma County's finest wineries. Generous full breakfast, complimentary premium wines, all private baths, and more!*

**Healdsburg Inn @ the Plaza**
P.O. Box 1196, 95448
110 Matheson St.
707-433-6991 Fax: 707-433-9513
800-431-8663
Genny Jenkins & LeRoy
Steck      All year

$$$-B&B
10 rooms, 10 pb
MC, Visa, *Rated*, •
C-ltd/S-no/P-no/H-no

Full healthy breakfast
Aftn. tea on weekends
Champagne brunch
(wkend)
gallery, gift shops, A/C
frplcs., open balconies

*Individually appointed Victorian rooms with antiques. Whirlpool tub for 2. Centrally located overlooking old town plaza. Breakfast served in solarium tha overlooks town village.*

**Honor Mansion, The**
14891 Grove St., 95448
707-433-4277 Fax: 707-431-7173
800-554-4667
Cathi Fowler   All year

$$$-B&B
6 rooms, 6 pb
Visa, MC, *Rated*, •
C-ltd/S-no/P-no/H-ltd

Full breakfast
Afternoon tea, snacks
Sitting room
swimming pool

**Madrona Manor**
P.O. Box 818, 95448
1001 Westside Rd.
707-433-4231 Fax: 707-433-0703
800-258-4003
John & Carol Muir
All year

$$$$-B&B
21 rooms, 21 pb
Most CC, *Rated*, •
C-ltd/S-yes/P-ltd/H-yes
Spanish

Full breakfast
Gourmet restaurant
Music room, robes
antique rosewood piano
swimming pool, billiards

*Circa 1881, furnished with antiques. Carriage house. Wine country, canoeing, bicycling, historical points of interest. February "daffodil" month. **Champagne for birthdays or anniversaries.***

**Raford House B&B, The**
10630 Wohler Rd., 95448
707-887-9573 Fax: 707-887-9597
800-887-9503
Carole & Jack Vore
All year

$$$-B&B
7 rooms, 5 pb
Most CC, *Rated*, •
C-ltd/S-ltd/P-no/H-ltd

Full breakfast
Complimentary wine
Porch, vineyards, patio
some fireplaces, roses

*Victorian farmhouse overlooks vineyards of Sonoma County. Beautiful country setting is just 1½ hours from San Francisco. County historical landmark. **Special rate 3rd nite.***

## HOMEWOOD

**Rockwood Lodge**
P.O. Box 226, 96141
5295 W. Lake Blvd.
916-525-5273 Fax: 916-525-5949
800-LE-TAHOE
L. Reinkens & C. Stevens
All year

$$$-B&B
5 rooms, 3 pb
MC, Visa, •
C-ltd/S-no/P-no/H-no

Full breakfast
Comp. cordials & sweets
Wine
Sitting room
game room

*"Old Tahoe" estate nestled in pine forest; Lake Tahoe within 100 feet. Breakfast served in guest rooms. Many fine appointments.*

## HOPE VALLEY

**Sorensen's Resort**
14255 Hwy 88, 96120
916-694-2203 800-423-9949
John & Patty Brissenden
All year

$$-EP/B&B
23 rooms, 23 pb
MC, Visa, •
C-ltd/S-no/P-ltd/H-ltd

Full breakfast (fee)
Comp. coffee, tea, cocoa
Sitting room, bicycles
hot tub, sauna, gazebo
hiking, fishing

*Cozy creekside cabins nestled in Alps of California. Close to Tahoe & Kirkwood, cross-country skiing. Full-moon river rafting. Water color, fly tying & rod building courses.*

## IDYLLWILD

**Strawberry Creek Inn**
P.O. Box 1818, 92549
26370 State Hwy 243
909-659-3202 Fax: 909-659-4707
800-262-8969
Diana Dugan & Jim Goff
All year

$$$-B&B
9 rooms, 7 pb
MC, Visa, *Rated*,
C-ltd/S-no/P-no/H-ltd

Full breakfast
Afternoon wine
Library, fireplaces
sitting room
refrigerators

*Country inn located in the pines where comfort mixes with nostalgia in a uniquely decorated home. Cottage with spas. Many hiking trails, quiet walks along the creek.*

**Wilkum Inn B&B**
P.O. Box 1115, 92549
26770 Hwy. 243
909-659-4087 800-659-4086
A. Chambers & B. Jones
All year

$$-B&B
5 rooms, 3 pb
*Rated*, •
C-ltd/S-no/P-no/H-yes
Basic Sign Language

Continental plus
Aft./evening snacks
Guest frig/microwave
common room, fireplace
Max. 2 persons per room

*Warm hospitality enhanced by handmade quilts, antiques and collectibles. Shop, hike and relax in a pine-forested mountain village. **Discount 2+ nights.***

## INVERNESS

**Dancing Coyote Beach**
P.O. Box 98, 94937
27974 Sir Francis Drake
415-669-7200
Sherry King & Bobbi Stumpf
All year

$$$-B&B
3 rooms, 3 pb
MC, Visa,
C-ltd/P-no/H-no

Continental plus bkfst.
Coffee & tea
Popcorn poppers
fireplace, kitchen, deck
living room, library

*The best of both worlds ... Privacy while being catered to. 3 lovely, fully equipped cottages nestled among pines on secluded beach. **Complimentary bottle of champagne.***

**Fairwinds Farm B&B**
**Cottage**
P.O. Box 581, 94937
82 Drake's Summit
415-663-9454
Joyce H. Goldfield
All year

$$$$-B&B
2 rooms, 2 pb
*Rated*,
C-yes/S-no/P-no/H-no
Sign language

Full breakfast
Desserts, snacks
Full kitchen, library
TV, VCR and movies
hot tubs, fireplace

*Large cottages sleep 6. Ridge-top cottage adjoins 68,000-acre Nat'l Seashore. Ocean view from hot tub. Garden w/ponds & swing. Barnyard animals. **7th night free in cottage.***

**Rosemary Cottage**
Box 273, 94937
75 Balboa Ave.
415-663-9338 800-808-9338
Suzanne Storch
All year

$$$-B&B
1 rooms, 1 pb
*Rated*, •
C-yes/S-yes/P-yes/H-no

Full breakfast
Comp. tea, coffee
Kitchen, fireplace
decks, secluded
hot tub in garden

*Charming, romantic French country cottage nestled in secluded garden w/dramatic forest views. Close to beaches; families welcome. **20% discount, ltd.***

## INVERNESS PARK

| | | |
|---|---|---|
| **Blackthorne Inn** | $$$-B&B | Full breakfast |
| P.O. Box 712, 94937 | 5 rooms, 2 pb | Comp. tea, dessert |
| 266 Vallejo Ave. | MC, Visa, *Rated*, • | Wet bar sink area |
| 415-663-8621 | C-ltd/S-ltd/P-no/H-no | sitting room w/fireplace |
| Susan Wigert | | hot tub |
| All year | | |

*Sunset Magazine (April 1983) describes the Blackthorne Inn as "a carpenter's fantasy, with decks, hot tub, fireman's pole, and spiral staircase." 3rd. night 50%, ltd. ask.*

## INVERNESS, PT. REYES STA.

| | | |
|---|---|---|
| **Marsh Cottage B&B** | $$$-B&B | Continental plus bkfst. |
| P.O. Box 1121, 94956 | 1 rooms, 1 pb | Comp. coffee/tea/wine |
| 12642 Sir Francis Drake | C-yes/S-no/P-no/H-no | Kitchen, library |
| 415-669-7168 | | sitting room, fireplace |
| Wendy Schwartz | | porch, sun deck |
| All year | | |

*Cheerful, carefully appointed private cottage along bay. Kitchen, fireplace, queen bed, desk; extraordinary setting for romantics and naturalists. Free bottle of wine, ltd.*

## IONE

| | | |
|---|---|---|
| **Heirloom B&B Inn, The** | $$-B&B | Full gourmet breakfast |
| P.O. Box 322, 95640 | 6 rooms, 4 pb | Comp. wine/beverages |
| 214 Shakeley Ln. | Visa, MC, AmEx, | Weddings, hammock |
| 209-274-4468 | *Rated*, • | 18 hole champ. golf |
| Pat Cross, Melisande Hubbs | C-ltd/S-no/P-no/H-yes | garden, glider, gazebo |
| All year | | |

*Petite 1863 colonial mansion—spacious English romantic garden private setting, heirloom antiques, comfort, gracious hospitality. Private dinners. Local dicount shopping card.*

## JACKSON

| | | |
|---|---|---|
| **Wedgewood Inn, The** | $$$-B&B | Full gourmet breakfast |
| 11941 Narcissus Rd., 95642 | 6 rooms, 6 pb | Beverages, popcorn |
| 209-296-4300 Fax: 209-296-4301 | MC, Visa, *Rated*, • | Sitting room, porch |
| 800-WEDGEWD | C-ltd/S-no/P-no/H-no | 2 person jacuzzi in |
| Vic & Jeannine Beltz | | Carriage suite. |
| All year | | |

*Charming replica Victorian on wooded acreage. Antique decor, queen-size beds, wood stoves. InnTimes readers' Top 50 Inns 1991. Restaurant 2 for 1 discounts, ltd.*

## JAMESTOWN

| | | |
|---|---|---|
| **Palm Hotel B&B** | $$-B&B | Full breakfast |
| 10382 Willow St., 95327 | 9 rooms, 5 pb | Sitting room |
| 209-984-3429 Fax: 209-984-4929 | Visa, MC, AmEx, | near steam railroad |
| Rick & Sandy Allen | *Rated*, • | train & gold panning |
| All year | C-yes/S-no/P-no/H-yes | |

*Victorian mansion offering grace of the past with addition of modern comforts. Near restaurants, antique shops & champ. golf course. Near Yosemite and Columbia State Park.*

| | | |
|---|---|---|
| **Royal Hotel** | $-B&B | Continental plus bkfst. |
| P.O. Box 219, 95327 | 19 rooms, 12 pb | Lost of good restaurants |
| 18239 Main St. | AmEx, MC, Visa, • | Sitting room, steam |
| 209-984-5271 Fax: 209-984-1675 | C-yes/S-yes/P-no/H-yes | train, gold panning, old |
| 888-894-5271 | | time movies, balconies |
| Robert & Nancy Bosich | | |
| All year | | |

*Historic Victorian gold country hotel in second oldest gold town in U.S. Steam powered train rides, antiquing and great restaurants. Mid-week specials.*

## 40  California

JENNER ───────────────────────────────

**Jenner Inn & Cottages**
P.O. Box 69, 95450
10400 Coast Hwy 1
707-865-2377 Fax: 707-865-0829
800-732-2377
R. & S. Murphy, J. Carroll
All year

$$$-B&B
13 rooms, 13 pb
AmEx, MC, Visa, •
C-yes/S-no/P-no/H-yes

Continental plus bkfst.
Comp. teas & aperitifs
Port & sherry available
sitting room
private cottages

*Coastal retreat inn—antiques, lots of character, peaceful, romantic, river and ocean views. Sunset weddings by the sea, wineries, redwoods nearby, 8 beautiful sandy beaches.*

JULIAN ───────────────────────────────

**Julian Gold Rush Hotel**
P.O. Box 1856
2032 Main,   92036
619-765-0201  800-734-5854
Steve & Gig Ballinger
All year

$$-B&B
14 rooms, 14 pb
AmEx, MC, Visa,
*Rated*, •
C-yes/S-yes/P-no/H-no

Full breakfast
Afternoon tea
Sitting room, library
piano, cottage
family rates

*Surviving 1897 hotel in southern Mother Lode of CA, restored to full glory w/American antiques. Nat'l Register. "CA Point of Historical Interest."* **3rd night 50% off, ltd.**

**Lake Cuyamaca B&B**
P.O. Box 1887, 92036
34755 Yuma Rd.
619-765-2922 Fax: 619-765-2922
Janet Harris     All year

$$$-B&B
1 rooms, 1 pb
Visa, MC, AmEx, •
C-ltd/S-no/P-no/H-no

Full breakfast
Aftn. tea, snacks, bev.
Sitting room
hot tubs
family friendly facility

*Romance & privacy assured in 1940s lakeview cabin, filled with antiques. Private fireplace, jacuzzi under stars, luxurious amenities, gourmet breakfast.* **Complimentary bottle of champagne.**

**Orchard Hill Country Inn**
P.O. Box 425, 92036
2502 Washington St.
619-765-1700  Fax: 619-765-0290
D. & Pat Straube   All year

$$$$-B&B
19 rooms, 19 pb
Visa, MC, AmEx,
*Rated*, •
C-yes/S-no/P-no/H-yes

Full breakfast
Snacks, afternoon tea
Comp. wine, tub, wet bar
sitting room, snacks
library, restaurant

*Casually elegant inn, heart of Julian historic district. Deluxe suites w/frplc., whirlpool, wet bar & more. Full breakfast, afternoon refreshments.* **Midweek rates available.**

KERNVILLE ───────────────────────────

**Kern River Inn B&B**
P.O. Box 1725, 93238
119 Kern River Dr.
619-376-6750 Fax: 619-376-6643
800-986-4382
Jack & Carita Prestwich
All year

$$$-B&B
6 rooms, 6 pb
MC, Visa *Rated*,
C-yes/S-no/P-no/H-yes

Full breakfast
Afternoon tea
Park across street
riverviews, fireplaces
whirlpool tubs, TV, park

*New country inn on the Kern River. Fishing, golf, antique shops, giant redwoods. Outdoor activities, whitewater rafting, skiing. AAA 3-diamonds. AAA, senior discounts.*

KLAMATH ───────────────────────────

**Requa Inn**
451 Requa Rd.,   95548
707-482-8205
Paul & Donna Hamby
March—October

$$-B&B
15 rooms, 15 pb
AmEx, MC, Visa,
C-ltd/S-no/P-no/H-no

Full breakfast
Restaurant, dinner
Afternoon tea
sitting room

*Located on majestic Klamath River in Redwood National Park. A relaxing, romantic retreat. Stroll through woods, swim, boat, or fish. Wonderful dining.* **7th night free; $10 off any room Jan. 2–May 20.**

## LA JOLLA

**Prospect Park Inn**
1110 Prospect St., 92037
619-454-0133  800-433-1609
Jean A. Beazley
All year

$$$-B&B
25 rooms, 25 pb
AmEx, MC, Visa,
*Rated*, •
C-yes/S-no/P-no/H-no

Continental breakfast
Afternoon tea
Library, sun deck
color TV & A/C in rooms
small conference fac.

*Contemporary furnishings face balconies with sweeping ocean views, yet the charm of Europe prevails. In the heart of La Jolla, "The Jewel" of Southern California. AAA 2 stars.*

## LAGUNA BEACH

**Casa Laguna Inn**
2510 Coast Hwy, 92651
714-494-2996  Fax: 714-494-5009
800-233-0449
Kathleen Flint   All year

$$-B&B
21 rooms, 21 pb
Most CC, *Rated*, •
C-yes/S-yes/P-yes/H-no
Spanish

Continental plus bkfst.
Sitting room, library
swimming pool
family friendly facility

*Romantic country inn terraced hillside overlooking ocean. Decorated w/antiques, collectibles. Kitchen suites & cottages for families. 3rd night free, Sun.–Thurs.*

## LAKE ARROWHEAD

**Carriage House B&B, The**
P.O. Box 982, 92352
472 Emerald Dr.
909-336-1400  800-526-5070
Lee & Johan Karstens
All year

$$$-B&B
3 rooms, 3 pb
Most CC, *Rated*, •
C-ltd/S-no/P-no/H-no
Dutch

Full gourmet breakfast
Comp. wine, snacks
Sitting rm, deck w/swing
all rooms have lake view
room w/private balcony

*Our home is furnished in French country style, very warm & cozy. Walk to lake. Featherbeds w/down comforters. A perfect romantic retreat. Midweek 10% discount 2 nights or more.*

**Chateau Du Lac**
P.O. Box 1098, 92352
911 Hospital Rd.
909-337-6488  Fax: 909-337-6746
Jody & Oscar Wilson
All year

$$$-B&B
6 rooms, 4 pb
AmEx, MC, Visa, •
C-ltd/S-no/P-no/H-no

Full breakfast
Comp. wine, tea, snacks
Dinner by appointment
sitting room, library
hot tubs in room

*The Chateau du Lac overlooks a beautiful view of Lake Arrowhead. A warm and friendly place to stay. We do weddings, showers, and birthday parties. 10% discount for 3+ nights.*

**Prophet's Paradise B&B Inn**
P.O. Box 2116, 92352
26845 Modoc Lane
909-336-1969  800-987-2231
LaVerne & Tom Prophet
All year

$$$-B&B
3 rooms, 3 pb
MC, Visa, *Rated*,
C-ltd/S-no/P-yes/H-no

Full breakfast
Snacks, comp. wine
Bicycles, 1 hot tub
gym/billiard room
2 rooms with TV/VCR

*Multi-level home exudes country charm with stained glass, antiques, film memorabilia, warm colors. Two suites. Shopping, dining, restaurants nearby.*

## LAKEPORT

**Forbestown Inn**
825 N. Forbes St., 95453
707-263-7858  Fax: 707-263-7878
Jack & Nancy Dunne
All year

$$$-B&B
5 rooms, 1 pb
AmEx, MC, Visa,
*Rated*, •
C-ltd/S-no/P-no/H-no

Full breakfast
Pool, spa, veranda
free ride to airport
corporate rates

*1869 quaint Victorian inn. Country breakfast, refreshments, gardens, pool, spa, robes, bicycles, close to the lake, water sports, restaurants, wineries. 3rd night 50%.*

### LEMON COVE

**Mesa Verde Plantation B&B**
33038 Sierra Hwy. 198,  93244
209-597-2555 Fax: 209-597-2551
800-240-1466
Scott & Marie Munger
All year

$$-B&B
9 rooms, 7 pb
MC, Visa, *Rated*, •
C-ltd/S-ltd/P-no/H-no
Spanish

Full plantation bkfst.
Comp. beverages & snacks
Pool, spa, gazebos
verandas, courtyard

*Plantation home nestled in the foothills of the Sierra Nevada Mountains. Close to Sequoia National Park and beautiful mountain lake.*

### LITTLE RIVER

**Victorian Farmhouse**
P.O. Box 357, 95456
7001 N. Hwy 1
707-937-0697  800-264-4723
Carole Molnar
All year

$$$-B&B
10 rooms, 7 pb
AmEx, MC, Visa,
*Rated*, •
C-yes/S-no/P-no/H-no
Hungarian

Full breakfast
Comp. wine & sherry
Social hour
sitting room
7 rooms w/fireplaces

*Built in 1877; short walk to the ocean. Enjoy deer, flower gardens, creek, or sitting in our small orchard. Quiet atmosphere.* **2 for 1 night, Oct.–June 30, ltd.**

### LONG BEACH

**Lord Mayor's Inn B&B**
435 Cedar Ave.,  90802
310-436-0324 Fax: 310-436-0324
Laura & Reuben Brasser
All year

$$$-B&B
5 rooms, 5 pb
AmEx, MC, Visa,
*Rated*, •
C-yes/S-no/P-no/H-no
Dutch, Danish

Full breakfast
Special luncheons/dinner
Library, sitting room
croquet, sundecks
IBM PC on request

*Award-winning restored 1904 Edwardian home of Long Beach's first mayor. Spacious rooms with antiques, library, gardens, porches, parking. Guided walking tours, mystery nights.*

### LOS OLIVOS

**Los Olivos Grand Hotel**
2860 Grand Ave.,  93441
805-688-7788 Fax: 805-688-1942
800-446-2455
Ken Mortensen
All year

$$$$-B&B
21 rooms, 21 pb
Most CC, *Rated*, •
C-yes/S-no/P-no/H-yes
Spanish

Full country breakfast
Wine & hors d'oeuvres
Gourmet restaurant
fireplace rooms
some with spa tubs

*Luxury hideaway in the Santa Barbara wine country. Swimming pool, spa, bicycles. Award-winning restaurant, near art galleries and wineries. A Four Sisters Inn.*

### MAMMOTH LAKES

**Snow Goose Inn B&B**
P.O. Box 387, 93546
57 Forest Trail
619-934-2660  800-874-7368
Bob & Carol Roster
All year

$$-B&B
20 rooms, 20 pb
AmEx, MC, Visa,
*Rated*, •
C-yes/S-yes/P-no/H-no

Full breakfast
Comp. wine, appetizers
Sitting room
bicycles
hot tubs

*Winter ski resort/Sierra's summer getaway. European-style deluxe mountain bed and breakfast. Offering special ski packages midweek.*

**White Horse Inn**
P.O. Box 2326, 93546
2180 Old Mammoth Rd.
619-924-3656  800-982-5657
Lynn Criss   All year

$$$-B&B
4 rooms, 4 pb
Most CC, *Rated*, •
C-ltd/S-no/P-ltd/H-no

Full breakfast
Snacks, comp. wine
Pool table
sitting room
use of kitchen

*Private mountain hideaway, close to best Sierra skiing, Yosemite, golf, lakes, hiking trails, riding. Rooms beautifully decorated.* **Mid-week ski pkgs., lifts, lodging, breakfast.**

MARINA DEL REY ──────────────────────────────

**Mansion Inn**
327 Washington Blvd.,   90291
310-821-2557  Fax: 310-827-0287
800-828-0688
Richard Hunnicutt
All year

$$$-B&B
43 rooms, 43 pb
Most CC, *Rated*,  •
C-yes/S-yes/P-no/H-yes
Spanish

Continental plus bkfst.
Bicycle rentals nearby
tennis court nearby
walk to shops, cafes

*Comfortable French-style rooms, p/baths. Walk to Venice Beach. Continental breakfast served daily in cobblestone courtyard. Venice beach two blocks from inn.*

MARIPOSA ──────────────────────────────

**Finch Haven B&B**
4605 Triangle Rd.,   95338
209-966-4738
Bruce & Carol Fincham
All year

$$-B&B
2 rooms, 2 pb
•
C-yes/S-ltd/P-no/H-ltd
Spanish

Full breakfast
Nearby restaurant, bar
Library, tennis court
pool, rafting, rock
climbing, outdoor rec.

*Quiet country home with panoramic mt. views. Our 9 acres are a haven for wildlife. We are located in California Gold Rush Country near many historic attractions, Yosemite Park.* **3rd night 50%.**

**Meadow Creek Ranch B&B Inn**
2669 Triangle & Hwy 49S,
  95338
209-966-3843
Bob & Carol Shockley
All year

$$-B&B
3 rooms, 1 pb
AmEx, MC, Visa,
*Rated*,  •
C-ltd/S-ltd/P-no/H-no
Spanish

Full breakfast
Complimentary appetizers
Sitting room, antiques
airport pickup
country cottage

*Originally an 1858 stagecoach stop on the Golden Chain Highway. Front door to Yosemite National Park. Furnished with European and country antiques.* **3rd night, 50%.**

**Pelennor B&B, The**
3871 Hwy. 49 S.,   95338
209-966-2832
Dick & Gwen Foster
All year

$-B&B
4 rooms,
C-yes/S-ltd/P-ltd/H-ltd

Full breakfast
Kitchen
Sitting room
spa & lap pool, sauna
very economical

*Quiet country accommodations at economical rates. Enjoy the stars while listening to a tune on the bagpipes.* **Most economical B&B in Yosemite area.**

**Winsor Farms B&B**
5636 Whitlock Rd.,   95338
209-966-5592
Donald & Janice Haag
All year

$-B&B
2 rooms,
C-ltd/S-ltd/P-no/H-no

Continental plus bkfst.
Sitting room
picnic table, aid in
yosemite exploration

*Winsor Farms Bed & Breakfast is a one-story country home, a peaceful hilltop retreat among majestic pines and rugged oaks. Near Yosemite National Park.*

MENDOCINO ──────────────────────────────

**Agate Cove Inn B&B**
P.O. Box 1150, 95460
11201 Lansing St.
707-937-0551  Fax: 707-937-0550
800-527-3111
Scott & Betsy Buckwald
All year

$$$-B&B
10 rooms, 10 pb
AmEx, MC, Visa,
*Rated*,
C-ltd/S-ltd/P-no/H-ltd

Full country breakfast
Comp. sherry in room
Common room w/antiques
spectacular ocean views
whale watching Dec-Mar

*Romantic cottages w/fireplaces, spectacular ocean views. Full country breakfast served in 1860s farmhouse viewing ocean. Beautifully landscaped garden, stone walkways. Remodeled & redecorated.*

MENDOCINO ——————————————————————————————————

**Brewery Gulch Inn**
9350 Coast Highway 1,  95460
707-937-4752
Anne Saunders
All year

$$$-B&B
5 rooms, 4 pb
MC, Visa, *Rated*, •
C-ltd/S-no/P-no/H-ltd

Full country breakfast
Fireplaces, sitting room
down pillows
gardens

*Brewery Gulch is an unhurried authentic pre-Victorian farm surrounded by two acres of flowers & tree gardens. Full country breakfast. **Special winter rates.***

---

**Cypress Cove**
P.O. Box 303, 95460
45250 Chapman Dr.
707-937-1456  800-942-6300
Suzanne & Jim Hay
All year

$$$$-EP
2 rooms, 2 pb
S-no/P-no/H-no
German, French,
Spanish

Full breakfast
Kitchen, refrigerators
Fireplace, dramatic
oceanfront, soft robes
coffees, teas, brandy

*Luxurious, private, romantic getaway for two! On the ocean bluff w/spectacular view of Mendocino across the bay. Deluxe bathrooms w/jacuzzi for 2. **Off-season, midweek discount.***

---

**Headlands Inn, The**
P.O. Box 132, 95460
Howard St. at Albion St.
707-937-4431  Fax: 707-937-0421
800-354-4431
David & Sharon Hyman
All year

$$$-B&B
7 rooms, 7 pb
Most CC, *Rated*,
C-ltd/S-no/P-no/H-ltd

Gourmet breakfast to rm.
Aftn. tea, mineral water
Ocean views, fireplaces
feather beds, chocolates
parlor, English garden

*Romantic 1868 Victorian with lovely antiques in picturesque Mendocino Village. Quiet & peaceful. Breakfast served to each room. Ocean views, walk everywhere. **Special winter rates.***

---

**John Dougherty House**
P.O. Box 817, 95460
571 Ukiah St.
707-937-5266  800-486-2104
David & Marion Wells
All year

$$$-B&B
6 rooms, 6 pb
Visa, MC, *Rated*, •
C-ltd/S-no/P-no/H-no

Full breakfast
Complimentary wine
Sitting room, verandas
ocean views, near tennis
antiques, English garden

*Historic 1867 house in Village center. Large verandas w/ocean views; quiet peaceful nights; walk to shops & dining. Woodburning stoves in 5 rooms. **3 nights for price of 2, ltd.***

---

**Joshua Grindle Inn**
P.O. Box 647, 95460
44800 Little Lake Rd.
707-937-4143  800-474-6353
Arlene & Jim Moorehead
All year

$$$-B&B
10 rooms, 10 pb
*Rated*, •
C-ltd/S-no/P-no/H-yes

Full gourmet breakfast
Comp. sherry, min. water
Sitting room, Parlor
ocean views, fireplaces
off street parking

*Historic country charm on 2 beautiful acres with gardens. Complete remodel of 5 baths in Main House, 2 deep-soak tubs. Our best room has whirlpool tub w/separate shower.*

---

**MacCallum House Inn**
P.O. Box 206, 95460
45020 Albion St.
707-937-0289
Joe & Melanie Reding
All year

$$$-B&B
20 rooms, 8 pb
MC, Visa, •
C-ltd/S-yes/P-no/H-no

Continental breakfast
Restaurant, bar
Sitting room
Children welcome in
most rooms

*The MacCallum House provides friendly, personal attention to guests in a handsome, authentically restored Victorian home in the village of Mendocino. **3rd night, 50% off.***

MENDOCINO ————————————————————————————————

**Sea Rock B&B Inn**
P.O. Box 906, 95460
11101 Lansing St.
707-937-0926  800-906-0926
Susie & Andy Plocher
All year

$$$-B&B
14 rooms, 14 pb
Most CC,
C-yes/S-no/P-no/H-no

Continental plus
Sitting room, gardens
lawns, spectacular ocean
views

*Country cottages on a hillside overlooking the ocean. Spectacular ocean views, fireplaces, featherbeds, TV/VCR, relaxing, private get-away.* **Midwk discount 20%, ltd.**

**Seafoam Lodge**
PO Box 68, 6751 N. Coast
Hway One,  95460
707-937-1827  Fax: 707-937-0744
800-606-1827
Kathy Smith  All year

$$$-B&B
C-yes/S-yes/P-yes

Continental breakfast
Hot tubs, refrigarators
fantastic ocean views
VCR

*The Seafoam Lodge has panoramic ocean views and breathtaking sunsets. We are on six and a half acres of coastal gardens and pine trees above Buckhorn Cove.*

**Stanford Inn by the Sea**
P.O. Box 487, 95460
Hwy 1, Comptche-Ukiah Rd.
707-937-5615  Fax: 707-937-0305
800-331-8884
Joan & Jeff Stanford  All yr

$$$$-B&B
25 rooms, 25 pb
Most CC, *Rated*,
C-yes/S-yes/P-yes/H-yes
French, Spanish

Full breakfast
Wine, organic vegetables
Indoor pool, hot tub,
decks, nurseries, llamas
bicycles, canoe rentals

*A truly elegant country inn in a pastoral setting. All accommodations with ocean views, fireplaces, decks, antiques, four-posters and TVs. Organic gardens.*

**Stevenswood Lodge**
P.O. Box 170, 95460
8211 N. Hwy 1, 95456
707-937-2810  800-421-2810
Robert Zimmer  All year

$$$-B&B
10 rooms, 10 pb
MC, Visa, *Rated*, •
C-yes/S-no/P-no/H-yes

Full gourmet breakfast
Bar service, comp. wine
Coffee, snacks
sitting room, library
lounge, conference room

*Distinctive ocean view suites in "old growth" forest. Beach access, fireplaces, fine art decor, gallery. AAA 4 diamond rating.* **3 nights for price of 2, Sunday-Thursday, ltd.**

**Whitegate Inn**
P.O. Box 150, 95460
499 Howard St.
707-937-4892  Fax: 707-937-1131
800-531-7282
Carol & George Bechtloff
All year

$$$-B&B
7 rooms, 7 pb
Visa, MC, AmEx,
*Rated*, •
C-ltd/S-no/P-no/H-no

Full breakfast
Complimentary wine
Sitting room, organ
fireplaces, TVs, gardens
deck, gazebo, gardens

*Located in historic Mendocino. All rms redecorated w/French or Victorian antiques. Sit-down breakfast in dining room. Ocean views. English & herb gardens.* **50% 2nd night, ltd.**

MENDOCINO, LITTLE RIVER ————————————————————

**Glendeven Inn & Gallery**
8221 N. Hwy 1,  95456
707-937-0083  Fax: 707-937-6108
800-822-2690
Jan & Janet DeVries  All year

$$$-B&B
10 rooms, 10 pb
*Rated*, •
C-ltd/S-ltd/P-no/H-no

Continental plus bkfst.
Sitting room
baby grand piano, tennis
conference facilities

*A special country inn with lovely gardens and bayviews near Mendocino village and adjacent to state park trails and beach.* **Complimentary bottle of wine to return guests.**

## MIDPINES

| **Pimentel's B&B** | $$-B&B | Full breakfast |
| P.O. Box 207, 95345 | 3 rooms, 3 pb | Afternoon tea |
| 6484 Hwy. 140 | Visa, MC, Disc., | Sitting room, verandah |
| 209-966-6847 Fax: 209-966-6847 | C-yes/S-no/P-no/H-no | family friendly facility |
| Tom & Nancy Pimentel | | 20 min. from Yosemite |
| All year | | |

*New Victorian style home with period furnishings & warm friendly atmosphere. 3 rooms w/guest living room, fireplace & T.V., large porch.* **3rd. night 50%.**

## MILL VALLEY

| **Mountain Home Inn** | $$$$-B&B | Full breakfast |
| 810 Panoramic Hwy, 94941 | 10 rooms, 10 pb | Lunch, dinner |
| 415-381-9000 Fax: 415-381-3615 | MC, Visa, *Rated*, • | Jacuzzis |
| Lynn M. Saggese | C-ltd/S-yes/P-no/H-yes | hiking trails |
| All year | | telephones in rooms |

*Two-and-a-half-million-dollar restored classic California luxury inn. Adjacent to parklands, Muir Woods. Panoramic S.F. Bay views; jacuzzis, fireplaces, terraces.*

## MONTARA, HALF MOON BAY

| **Goose & Turrets B&B** | $$$-B&B | Full 4-course breakfast |
| P.O. Box 937, 94037 | 5 rooms, 5 pb | Afternoon tea, snacks |
| 835 George St. | Most CC, *Rated*, • | Sitting room w/woodstove |
| 415-728-5451 Fax: 415-728-0141 | C-ltd/S-no/P-no | quiet garden, fireplaces |
| Raymond & Emily Hoche- | French spoken | local airport pickup |
| Mong All year | | |

*Solitude. Bonhomie. Cozy down comforters, towel warmers, and fantastic breakfasts. 30 minutes from San Francisco; 1/2-mile from Pacific Ocean.* **Midweek restaurant disc'ts.**

## MONTE RIO

| **Huckleberry Springs Inn** | $$-MAP | Full breakfast |
| P.O. Box 400, 95462 | 4 rooms, 4 pb | Picnic bskt, din. (fee) |
| 8105 Old Beedle Rd. | AmEx, MC, Visa | Sitting room, library |
| 707-865-2683 800-822-2683 | *Rated*, • | hot tubs, pool |
| Suzanne Greene | S-no/P-no/H-no | video library w/VCR |
| March–December | Spanish, Italian | |

*This small country inn offers comfort, privacy and excellent cuisine, hillside spa and pool, sixty acres, wine country and coastal access.*

## MONTEREY

| **Del Monte Beach Inn** | $-B&B | Continental plus bkfst. |
| 600 Martin St., 93940 | 18 rooms, 2 pb | Fresh fruit, cocoa, tea |
| 408-649-4410 Fax: 408-375-3818 | MC, Visa, • | Sitting room |
| Marjorie Purcell | C-yes/S-yes/P-no/H-no | |
| All year | Spanish | |

*Quaint English-style bed & breakfast ideally located near the heart of Monterey. Across the boulevard from beautiful Monterey Bay. Newly redecorated! .* **3rd night 50% off.**

| **Jabberwock, The** | $$$-B&B | Full breakfast |
| 598 Laine St., 93940 | 7 rooms, 3 pb | Sherry & hors d'ouevres |
| 408-372-4777 Fax: 408-655-2946 | *Rated*, | Sitting room |
| Jim & Barbara Allen | C-ltd/S-ltd/P-no/H-no | sun porch |
| All year | Spanish, French, Danish | conference facility |

*Once a convent, this Victorian home is above Cannery Row. Sherry on the sun porch overlooking Monterey Bay, gardens & waterfalls. Near Monterey Bay Aquarium.*

## MONTEREY

**Old Monterey Inn**
500 Martin St., 93940
408-375-8284 Fax: 408-375-6730
800-350-2344
Ann & Gene Swett
All year

$$$$-B&B
10 rooms, 10 pb
*Rated*, •
C-ltd/S-no/P-no/H-no

Full breakfast
Comp. beverages anytime
Sitting room

*An architectural gem in a forestlike setting, the recently redecorated inn is a charming English country house with a unique sense of history and romance.*

## MOUNT SHASTA

**Mount Shasta Ranch B&B**
1008 W.A. Barr Rd., 96067
916-926-3870 Fax: 916-926-6882
Mary & Bill Larsen
All year

$$-B&B
10 rooms, 4 pb
Most CC, *Rated*, •
C-ltd/S-no/P-yes/H-no

Full breakfast
Afternoon tea
Comp. wine, snacks
sitting room, hot tub
library, ping-pong

*Affordable elegance in historical setting; Main Lodge, Cottage and Carriage House. Nearby lake fishing, year-round golf and winter skiing. Pool tables, horseshoes.*

## MUIR BEACH

**Pelican Inn**
10 Pacific Way, 94965
415-383-6000 Fax: 415-383-3424
Barry Stock
Closed Christmas

$$$$-B&B
7 rooms, 7 pb
MC, Visa,
C-yes/S-yes/P-no/H-ltd

Full English breakfast
Complimentary sherry
Sitting room
restaurant
British pub/bar, darts

*Romantic English inn capturing the spirit of the 16th century. Between ocean & redwoods, surrounded by countryside. Hiking, cycling trails. 20 min. from Golden Gate Bridge.*

## MURPHYS

**Dunbar House, 1880**
P.O. Box 1375, 95247
271 Jones St.
209-728-2897 Fax: 209-728-1451
800-692-6006
Barbara & Bob Costa
All year

$$$-B&B
4 rooms, 4 pb
MC, Visa, *Rated*, •
C-ltd/S-no/P-no/H-no

Full country breakfast
Comp. bottle of wine
Sitting room, library
wood-burning stoves
clawfoot tubs, TVs, VCRs

*Restored 1880 home w/historical designation located in Murphys, Queen of the Sierra. 2-room suite w/double jacuzzi, champagne, towel warmer. Walking distance to Main Street.*

## NAPA

**The 1801 Inn**
1801 First St., 94559
707-224-3739 Fax: 707-224-3932
800-51801INN
Linda & Chris Craiker
All year

$$$-B&B
5 rooms, 5 pb
S-no/P-no/H-no
Spanish

Full breakfast
Iced tea in shade garden
Sitting room, sun room
shade garden, fountain
showers, spacious vanity

*A lovingly restored Queen Anne style Victorian home located at the gateway to the famous Napa Wine Country. Each suite is appointed with a king sized bed, fireplace & private bath.* **Free bottle of wine.**

**Beazley House**
1910 First St., 94559
707-257-1649 Fax: 707-257-1518
800-559-1649
Carol & Jim Beazley  All year

$$$-B&B
11 rooms, 11 pb
MC, Visa, *Rated*, •
C-ltd/S-ltd/P-no/H-yes

Full gourmet breakfast
Comp. wine, wine list
Private spas/fireplaces
entertainment, sunroom
sitting room, library

*The Beazley House is a Napa landmark. Relax in old-fashioned comfort. Breakfast, complimentary sherry. Personal wine tour orientation.* **1 bottle Korbel champagne.**

NAPA————————————————————————————————

| | | |
|---|---|---|
| **Blue Violet Mansion** | $$$$-B&B | Full breakfast |
| 443 Brown St.,   94559 | 14 rooms, 14 pb | Candlelight dinners |
| 707-253-2583  Fax: 707-257-8205 | AmEx, MC, Visa,  • | Comp. wine, sitting room |
| 800-799-2583 | C-ltd/S-no/P-no/H-no | bicycles, gazebo w/swing |
| Bob & Kathy Morris  All year | | grape-arbored deck, pool |

*Theme floor: Camelot Castle courtyard & rooms w/deluxe amenities. 2 person whirlpool spas, French lighted mirror, silver goblet, port in crystal; hot & cold beverage service.*

| | | |
|---|---|---|
| **Churchill Manor** | $$-B&B | Full breakfast |
| 485 Brown St.,   94559 | 10 rooms, 10 pb | Comp. wine, tea, snacks |
| 707-253-7733  Fax: 707-253-8836 | Most CC, *Rated*,  • | Sitting room, pianos |
| Joanna Guidotti, Brian | C-ltd/S-ltd/P-no/H-ltd | side garden |
| Jensen | | croquet, bicycles |
| All year exc. Christmas | | |

*Grand beyond compare, this 1889 mansion, filled with antiques & surprises. Listed in National Historic Register. Weddings, 2 tandem bikes.*

| | | |
|---|---|---|
| **Hennessey House B&B Inn** | $$$-B&B | Full breakfast |
| 1727 Main St.,   94559 | 10 rooms, 10 pb | Comp. wine |
| 707-226-3774  Fax: 707-226-2975 | Most CC, *Rated*,  • | Sitting room with TV |
| Andrea Lamar, Lauriann | C-yes/S-no/P-no/H-no | whirlpool tubs, sauna |
| Delay | | fireplaces |
| All year | | |

*1889 Queen Anne Victorian boasts original architectural details and a spectacular, hand-painted, tin ceiling in the dining room. Napa Valley Wine Train and golf packages.* **Free bottle of signature wine.**

| | | |
|---|---|---|
| **La Belle Epoque B&B** | $$$-B&B | Full gourmet breakfast |
| 1386 Calistoga Ave.,   94559 | 6 rooms, 6 pb | Comp. wine, snacks |
| 707-257-2161  Fax: 707-226-6314 | Most CC, *Rated*,  • | Sitt. rm., fplace, wine |
| 800-238-8070 | C-ltd/S-no/P-no/H-no | tasting room and cellar |
| Merlin & Claudia Wedepohl | | fully AC, TV + VCR |
| All year | | |

*Historic Victorian bejeweled in stained glass, antique furnishings, gourmet breakfasts by the fireside. Walk to wine train depot, restaurant and shops.* **3rd night 50%, ltd.**

| | | |
|---|---|---|
| **La Residence** | $$$$-B&B | Full breakfast |
| 4066 St. Helena Hwy.,   94558 | 20 rooms, 18 pb | Complimentary wine |
| 707-253-0337 | MC, Visa, *Rated*,  • | CD players, hair dryers |
| David Jackson, Craig | C-yes/S-no/P-no | new veranda, jacuzzi spa |
| Claussen | | garden setting, vineyard |
| All year | | |

*For the sophisticated traveler who enjoys elegant yet intimate style, La Residence is the only choice in Napa Valley. Two acres of landscaped grounds.* **2nd night 50% Dec.–Mar.,ltd.**

| | | |
|---|---|---|
| **Napa Inn, The** | $$$$-B&B | Full breakfast |
| 1137 Warren St.,   94559 | 6 rooms, 6 pb | Snacks, comp. wine, tea |
| 707-257-1444  800-435-1144 | Most CC, *Rated* | Sitting room, library |
| Ann & Denny Mahoney | S-no/P-no/H-no | family friendly facility |
| All year | | bicycles |

*Beautiful Queen Anne Victorian built in 1899 and furnished with antiques. Reminiscent of a bygone era where life was simpler and pace more relaxed.* **Sun.–Thurs. 10% discount.**

## NAPA

**Oak Knoll Inn**
2200 E. Oak Knoll Ave,
94558
707-255-2200 Fax: 707-255-2296
Barbara Passino
All year

$$$$-B&B
3 rooms, 3 pb
MC, Visa, *Rated*, •
C-ltd/S-no/P-no/H-no

Full breakfast
Afternoon tea, snacks
Complimentary wine
spa, swimming pool
fireplaces in all rooms

*Romantic, elegant stone country inn surrounded by vineyards. Spacious rooms with fireplaces. Sip wine watching the sunset over the mountains. Winemaker special tasting in the evening.*

---

**Old World Inn**
1301 Jefferson St., 94559
707-257-0112 800-966-6624
Diane Audette
All year

$$$-B&B
8 rooms, 8 pb
AmEx, MC, Visa,
*Rated*, •
C-ltd/S-no/P-no/H-no

Continental plus bkfst.
Comp. wine & cheese
Afternoon tea
evening dessert buffet
sitting room, jacuzzi

*Run with Old World hospitality by its English innkeepers, this Victorian inn is uniquely decorated throughout in bright Scandinavian colors. Outdoor spa.*

---

**Trubody Ranch B&B**
5444 St. Helena Hwy, 94558
707-255-5907 Fax: 707-255-7254
Jeff & Mary Page
Exc. Christmas & January

$$$-B&B
3 rooms, 3 pb
MC, Visa,
S-no/P-no/H-no

Continental plus bkfst.
Sitting room, fireplaces
air conditioned rooms
cottage w/two person tub

*1872 Victorian home, water tower, & cottage nestled in 120 acres of family-owned vineyard. Stunning views. All rooms have phones, music system.* **3rd night we give midweek rate.**

## NAPA VALLEY

**Crossroads Inn**
6380 Silverado Trail, 94558
707-944-0646
Nancy & Sam Scott
All year

$$$$-B&B
3 rooms, 3 pb
MC, Visa, •
C-ltd/S-no/P-no/H-no

Full breakfast
Comp. wine, host bar
Aftn. tea, eve. brandies
library, game room, deck
hot tubs, bikes, gardens

*Sweeping Napa Valley views. Custom 2-person spas; complete privacy. King-sized beds, wine bars and full baths complement each suite.*

---

**Stahlecker House B&B Inn**
1042 Easum Dr., 94558
707-257-1588 Fax: 707-224-7429
800-799-1588
Ron & Ethel Stahlecker
All year

$$$-B&B
4 rooms, 4 pb
AmEx, MC, Visa, •
C-ltd/S-ltd/P-no/H-no

Full candlelight bkfst.
Beverages & cookies
Sitting room, fireplaces
piano, antiques, sundeck
ping-pong, croquet, A/C

*Quiet country inn on 1.5 acres w/creek setting, lawns, gardens, fountains. Queen canopy beds, private baths, frplcs., color TV. Some rooms w/dual dual head showers, whirlpool.*

## NEVADA CITY

**Downey House B&B**
517 W. Broad St., 95959
916-265-2815 800-258-2815
Miriam Wright
All year

$$$-B&B
6 rooms, 6 pb
MC, Visa, *Rated*, •
C-ltd

Full breakfast
Comp. wine, soft drinks,
Coffee, cookies, fruit
common area, veranda
library, garden, A/C

*Light, comfortable view rooms. Lovely garden and terrace. Near restaurants, shops, theaters, galleries, museums & outdoor recreational facilities.* **10% off midweek.**

## NEVADA CITY

**Emma Nevada House**
528 E. Broad St., 95959
916-265-4415  Fax: 916-265-4416
800-916-EMMA
Ruth Ann Riese
All year

$$$-B&B
6 rooms, 6 pb
Most CC, *Rated*,  •
C-ltd/S-no/P-no

Full breakfast
Aftn. tea & cookies
Sun room
library, game room
two in-room Jacuzzis

*Elegantly restored & decorated Victorian in peaceful setting near historic district. Beautiful rooms, great food & service. AAA-3 diamonds; ABBA-excellent.*

**Flume's End B&B Inn**
317 S. Pine St., 95959
916-265-9665  800-991-8118
Terrianne Straw, Steve
Wilson
All year

$$$-B&B
6 rooms, 6 pb
MC, Visa, *Rated*,  •
C-ltd/S-no/P-no/H-no

Full breakfast
Snacks
Sitting room, library
two jacuzzis

*Charming Victorian on Gold Run Creek. Walk to shopping and restaurants. Gourmet breakfast in serene natural setting.* **Reservations for dinner, plays, carriage rides.**

**Red Castle Inn, The**
109 Prospect St., 95959
916-265-5135  800-761-4766
Conley and Mary Louise
Weaver
All year

$$-B&B
7 rooms, 7 pb
MC, Visa, *Rated*,  •
C-ltd/S-ltd/P-no/H-no

Full candlelight bkfst.
Comp. beverages/desserts
Afternoon tea & sweets
parlor, antique organ
flowers in every room

*State Historic Landmark 4-story brick mansion. Elegant, homey, lush grounds, a nature lover's dream. Vegetarian breakfasts and horse & buggy rides available. Dinner by res.*

**U.S. Hotel B&B**
233-B Broad St., 95959
916-265-7999  Fax: 916-265-7990
Renee & Jim Salyards
All year

$$$-B&B
7 rooms, 7 pb
Most CC,
C-yes/S-no/P-ltd/H-no

Continental plus bkfst.
Sitting room
TV's & phones
two rooms for families

*This newly renovated 1856 hotel located downtown in historic Nevada City offers warmth, charm and a feeling that you are stepping back in time.* **3rd night, 50%.**

## NIPTON

**Hotel Nipton**
HCI, Box 357, 92364
10733 Nipton Rd.
619-856-2335
Jerry & Roxanne Freeman
All year

$$-B&B
4 rooms,
MC, Visa, *Rated*,  •
C-yes/S-yes/P-no/H-no
Spanish

Continental breakfast
Lunch, dinner, snacks
Comp. brandy, BBQ
sitting room, hot tub
horse trail, picnic tbl.

*19th-century desert hideaway w/antiques. Home-cooked breakfast from our cafe. Located in Mojave National Preserve; horses stay free.* **10% disc't when renting all 4 rooms.**

## OAKLAND

**Washington Inn**
495 10th St., 94607
510-452-1776  Fax: 510-452-4436
800-464-1776
All year

$$$-B&B
45 rooms, 45 pb
Visa, MC, AmEx,  •
C-ltd/S-yes/P-no/H-yes

Full breakfast
Lunch (fee), bar service

*The historic hotel with modern conveniences, amenities and personalized service. Located in the center of Downtown Oakland.*

## OCCIDENTAL

**Inn at Occidental, The**
P.O. Box 857, 95465
3657 Church St.
707-874-1047  Fax: 707-874-1078
800-522-6324
Jack Bullard    All year

$$$-B&B
8 rooms, 8 pb
AmEx, MC, Visa,
*Rated*, •
C-ltd/S-no/P-no/H-yes
French

Full breakfast
Comp. evening wine
New fireplaces, spa tubs
enlarged rooms, hot tubs
bicycles & tennis nearby

*Renovated 1867 Victorian with European ambience. Antique furnishings, goose down comforters, sumptuous breakfasts. Co ference facility.* **Special rates for extended stays.**

## OLEMA

**Pt. Reyes Seashore Lodge**
P.O. Box 39, 94950
10021 Coastal Highway One
415-663-9000  Fax: 415-663-9030
Jean & Scott Taylor
All year

$$$-B&B
22 rooms, 22 pb
Most CC, *Rated*, •
C-yes/S-no/P-no/H-yes

Continental plus bkfst.
Snack baskets
Antique pool table
game & sitting room
whirlpool tubs, frplcs.

*Unique re-creation of a turn-of-the-century lodge. Next to Pt. Reyes National Seashore. "Casa Olema Retreat" available for weddings & conferences (up to 125 people).*

## ORANGE

**Country Comfort B&B**
5104 E. Valencia Dr.,   92869
714-532-2802  Fax: 714-997-1921
Geri Lopker & Joanne Angell
All year

$$-B&B
2 rooms, 2 pb
•
C-yes/S-no/P-no/H-yes
Sign Language

Full breakfast
Complimentary wine
Sitting room, library
hot tub, swimming pool
close to attractions

*A guest weary from a day of sightseeing will find the pool and spa just the spot in which to relax! Guests will find nicely furnished rooms decorated for their comfort and pleasure.* **5th night, 50%.**

## OROVILLE

**Jean's Riverside B&B**
P.O. Box 2334, 95965
45 Cabana Dr.
916-533-1413  Fax: 916-533-9465
Jean Pratt
All year

$$-B&B
17 rooms, 17 pb
MC, Visa, *Rated*, •
C-ltd/S-ltd/P-ltd/H-yes

Full breakfast
Complimentary wine
River waterfront w/dock
deck overlooking river
lawn games, golf, pool

*Romantic waterfront hideaway w/private jacuzzis, fishing, goldpanning, birdwatching, historical sites. Near hiking, Feather River Cyn, Oroville Dam, Sac.* **3+ nites 10% disc't.**

## PACIFIC GROVE

**Gatehouse Inn**
225 Central Ave.,   93950
408-649-8436      Fax: 408-648-
8044 800-753-1881
Susan Kuslis & Lewis Shaefer

$$$-B&B
8 rooms, 8 pb
AmEx, MC, Visa,
*Rated*, •
C-ltd/S-no/P-no/H-yes
Spanish

Full breakfast
Afternoon tea
Comp. wine & cheese
sitting room, binoculars
near ocean and downtown

*Historic 1884 seaside Victorian home, distinctive rooms, stunning views, private baths, fireplaces, delicious breakfasts, afternoon wine and cheese. Centrally located.* **40% discount, Sun.–Thurs., ltd.**

**Gosby House Inn**
643 Lighthouse Ave.,   93950
408-375-1287  Fax: 408-655-9621
800-527-8828
Tess Arthur
All year

$$$-B&B
22 rooms, 20 pb
AmEx, MC, Visa,
*Rated*, •
C-yes/S-ltd/P-no/H-no

Full gourmet breakfast
Wine and hors d'oeuvres
Sitting room
bicycles
turndown service

*Romantic Victorian mansion. Antique furniture, cheerful pastel fabrics & fireplaces abound. Turndown service, morning paper. A Four Sisters Inn.* **Breakfast in bed.**

## PACIFIC GROVE

**Grand View Inn**
555 Ocean View Blvd., 557
Ocean View Blvd.,  93950
408-372-4341
The Flatley Family & Staff
All year

$$$-B&B
10 rooms, 10 pb
Visa, MC,  •
C-ltd/S-no/P-no/H-ltd
German, Spanish

Full breakfast
Afternoon tea

*Newly restored 1910 seaside Edwardian mansion overlooking Lover's Point and Monterey Bay. Elegant appointments, marble bathrooms, wraparound ocean views.*

---

**Green Gables Inn**
104 Fifth St., 93950
408-375-2095 Fax: 408-375-5437
Emily Frew
All year

$$$-B&B
11 rooms, 7 pb
AmEx, MC, Visa,
*Rated*,  •
C-yes/S-no/P-no/H-no

Full country breakfast
Wine and hors d'oeuvres
Sitting room w/fireplace
bicycles, newspapers
turndown service

*Spectacular Victorian mansion on Monterey Bay. Individually decorated rooms with antiques and beautiful fabrics. A Four Sisters Inn. **Breakfast in bed.***

---

**Martine Inn, The**
255 Ocean View Blvd.,
93950
408-373-3388 Fax: 408-373-3896
800-852-5588
D. & M. Martine, T. Harris
All year

$$$$-B&B
19 rooms, 19 pb
AmEx, MC, Visa,
*Rated*,  •
C-yes/S-yes/P-no/H-yes
Italian, Russian, Sp.

Full breakfast
Picnic basket lunches
Comp.wine/hors d'oeuvres
sitting room, game room
bicycles, conf. room

*12,000-sq. ft. mansion on Monterey Bay. Elegant museum quality American antiques. Bkfst. served on old Sheffield silver, crystal, Victorian china, & lace. Rooms redecorated.*

---

**Old St. Angela Inn**
321 Central Ave.,  93950
408-372-3246 Fax: 408-372-8560
800-748-6306
Susan Kuslis & Lewis Shaefer
All year

$$$-B&B
8 rooms, 5 pb
AmEx, MC, Visa,
*Rated*,  •
C-ltd/S-no/P-no/H-no

Full breakfast
Comp. wine/port, cookies
Solarium, gardens
hot tub in garden

*Intimate Cape Cod elegance overlooking Monterey Bay; walking distance to ocean & beaches, aquarium, Cannery Row. Champagne breakfast. Restored church rectory. **40% discount, Sun.–Thurs., ltd.***

---

**Seven Gables Inn**
555 Ocean View Blvd.,  93950
408-372-4341
Flatley Family & Staff
All year

$$$-B&B
14 rooms, 14 pb
*Rated*,  •
C-ltd/S-no/P-no/H-no
French, Spanish

Full breakfast
High tea
Grand Victorian parlor
aquarium tickets
ocean views in rooms

*Elegant Victorian mansion at the very edge of Monterey Bay. Fine antique furnishings throughout. Incomparable ocean views from all rooms. 1 room w/fireplace. Newly refurbished & remodeled.*

## PALM DESERT

**Tres Palmas B&B**
P.O. Box 2115, 92261
73-135 Tumbleweed Ln.
619-773-9858  800-770-9858
Karen & Terry Bennett
All year

$$$-B&B
4 rooms, 4 pb
Visa, MC, Rated*,  •
C-ltd/S-no/P-no/H-no

Continental plus bkfst.
Snacks
Library, sitting room
hot tubs
swimming pool

*Enjoy our casual, southwest elegance indoors or our warm desert sun outdoors. Walk to fabulous shopping & dining on El Paseo! **20% discount for 7 nights or more.***

PALM SPRINGS ─────────────────────────────────────────

**Casa Cody B&B Country** | $$-B&B | Continental breakfast
**Inn** | 23 rooms, 23 pb | Library, bicycles
175 S. Cahuilla Rd.,   92262 | Most CC, *Rated*,  • | hot tubs, swimming pools
619-320-9346  Fax: 619-325-8610 | C-ltd/S-ltd/P-ltd/H-yes | hiking, horseback riding
800-231-CODY | French, Dutch, German |
Frank Tysen, Therese Hayes |
All year

*Romantic hideaway in heart of Palm Springs Village. One or two bedrooms w/kitchens &*
*wood-burning fireplace. Beautifully restored in Santa Fe style.* **3rd night 50% off, ltd.**

─────────────────────────────────────────────────────

**Villa Royale Inn** | $$-B&B | Continental breakfast
1620 Indian Trail,   92264 | 31 rooms, 31 pb | Restaurant, bar service
619-327-2314  Fax: 619-322-3794 | AmEx, MC, Visa, | Comp. wine on arrival
800-245-2314 | *Rated*,  • | full room service
Bob Lee | S-yes/P-no/H-yes | tennis courts, 2 pools
All year

*Rooms & villas decorated as different European countries on 3.5 acres of flowering*
*gardens. Private patios, spas, fireplaces, poolside gourmet dinners. Villas, hotel rooms.*

PALO ALTO ─────────────────────────────────────────

**Victorian on Lytton** | $$$-B&B | Continental breakfast
555 Lytton Ave.,   94301 | 10 rooms, 10 pb | Comp. appetizers, port
415-322-8555  Fax: 415-322-7141 | MC, Visa, *Rated*,  • | Complimentary sherry
Susan & Maxwell Hall | C-ltd/S-no/P-no/H-yes | occasional entertainment
All year | | computer modem ports, TV

*A lovely Victorian built in 1895 offering a combination of forgotten elegance with a touch*
*of European grace. Near Stanford University, charming shops, cafes.*

PESCADERO ─────────────────────────────────────────

**Old Saw Mill Lodge** | $$$-B&B | Full breakfast
P.O. Box 96, 94060 | 5 rooms, 5 pb | Snacks, comp. wine
700 Ranch Rd. W. | Visa, MC, AmEx,  • | Sitting room, hot tubs
415-879-0111   Fax: 415-879-0111 | C-ltd/S-no/P-no/H-yes | swimming pool
800-596-6455 | German | hiking on premise
Tom & Annie Hines |
All year

*Coastal retreat only 1 hour from San Francisco; tucked away on 60 wooded acres—a great*
*escape for relaxation and romance.*

PETALUMA ─────────────────────────────────────────

**Cavanagh Inn** | $$-B&B | Full gourmet breakfast
10 Keller St.,   94952 | 7 rooms, 5 pb | Afternoon wine
707-765-4657  Fax: 707-769-0466 | Visa, MC, AmEx,  • | Sitting room, parlor
888-765-4658 | C-ltd/S-no/P-no/H-no | lib., evening turn-down
Ray & Jeanne Farris | | within historic downtown
All year

*Elegant 1902 Victorian & 1912 Craftsman cottage. 20 antique stores within walking*
*distance. 32 miles N. of Golden Gate at the gateway to the wine country. Meetings.* **10%**
***off when you mention Guide when booking.***

PLACERVILLE ─────────────────────────────────────────

**Chichester-McKee House** | $$$-B&B | Special full breakfast
800 Spring St.,   95667 | 3 rooms, 3 pb | Comp. soft drinks, mixes
916-626-1882  800-831-4008 | Most CC, *Rated*,  • | "Doreen's brownies"
Doreen & Bill Thornhill | C-ltd/S-no/P-no/H-no | queen-size beds, parlor
All year | | gardens, porches,library

*Elegant 1892 Victorian home filled w/family antiques. Near wineries, Apple Hill, Rafting,*
*State gold discovery site.* **Free Gold Bug Mine tour w/2nd nite stay.**

*Cavanagh Inn, Petaluma, CA*

PLACERVILLE────────────────────────────────

**Combellack-Blair House**          $$$-B&B                    Full breakfast
3059 Cedar Ravine,  95667          2 rooms,                   Comp. tea, coffee
916-622-3764                       *Rated*,  •                Baked goods
Al & Rosalie McConnell             C-ltd/S-no/P-no/H-no        sitting room
All year

*Elaborate 1895 Queen Anne Victorian furnished in genuine antiques. Original stained glass windows and free-standing spiral staircase.*

PLAYA DEL REY ───────────────────────────────

**Inn at Playa del Rey**           $$$-B&B                    Full breakfast
435 Culver Blvd.,  90293           21 rooms,                  Aftn. tea, snacks, wine
310-574-1920  Fax: 310-574-9920    Visa, MC, AmEx,            Sitting room, library,
Susan Zolla                        *Rated*,  •                bikes, romance suites,
All year                           C-yes/S-ltd/P-no/H-yes     private garden w/hot tub
                                   French, Japanese

*Overlooks sailboats and 200 acre bird sanctuary-3 blocks to beach. Decks, fireplaces, tubs, romance-a seaside hideaway.*

PLEASANTON ───────────────────────────────

**Evergreen**                      $$$-B&B                    Continental plus bkfst.
9104 Longview Dr.,  94588          4 rooms, 4 pb              Snacks, comp. wine
510-426-0901  Fax: 510-426-9568    Visa, MC, AmEx,  •         Sitting room, library
Jane & Clay Cameron                S-no/P-no/H-no             hot tubs, hiking trails
All year                           German                    frplc, fridge, ea. room

*Secluded, peaceful hideaway only 40 minutes from S.F.! Individually decorated rooms & a hot tub complete the relaxing atmosphere. **Complimentary bottle wine or champagne***

POINT REYES STATION ──────────────────────────

| **Ferrando's Hideaway** | $$$-B&B | Full breakfast |
| P.O. Box 688, 94956 | 5 rooms, 5 pb | Afternoon tea |
| 12010 Hwy. 1 | *Rated*, ● | Sitting room, library |
| 415-663-1966  Fax: 415-663-1825 | C-yes/S-no/P-no/H-no | hot tub |
| 800-337-2636 | German | |
| Greg & Doris Ferrando | | |
| All year | | |

*European hospitality. Elegant Alberti cottage. Cozy garden cottage. Rooms w/private baths. TV-VCR, gardens.* **Nov 1st-March 31, 3 nights for the price of 2, ltd.**

---

| **Holly Tree Inn/Cottages** | $$$-B&B | Hearty country breakfast |
| P.O. Box 642, 94956 | 5 rooms, 5 pb | Comp. refreshments |
| 3 Silverhills Rd. | MC, Visa, *Rated*, ● | Sitting room |
| 415-663-1554  Fax: 415-663-8566 | C-ltd/S-ltd/P-no/H-no | fireplaces, massages |
| 800-286-4655 | | herb gardens, hot tub |
| Tom & Diane Balogh | | |
| All year | | |

*Romantic country inn in a coastal valley near San Francisco. Also a cottage in the woods near the waterfront.* **Complimentary bottle of spring water for hikers.**

---

| **Jasmine Cottage & Retreat** | $$$$-B&B | Full breakfast |
| P.O. Box 56, 94956 | 1 rooms, 1 pb | Comp. teas & coffee |
| 11559 Coast Route 1 | Visa, MC, *Rated*, ● | Large naturalist library |
| 415-663-1166  Fax: 415-663-1390 | C-yes/S-no/P-ltd/H-no | picnic area, patio |
| Karen Gray    All year | | garden hot tub, Cable TV |

*Secluded country cottage sleeps 4. Fully equipped kitchen, writing desk, library, wood-burning stove, queen-sized bed, sun room, patio, garden, laundry. Pets by arrangement.* **3rd night 50% off**

---

| **Thirty-Nine Cypress** | $$$-B&B | Full breakfast |
| P.O. Box 176, 94956 | 3 rooms, 3 pb | Hot tub w/great view |
| 39 Cypress Way | ● | 140 mi. of hiking trails |
| 415-663-1709  Fax: 415-663-1709 | C-ltd/S-no/P-ltd/H-yes | bicycles, sitting room |
| Julia Bartlett | French | |
| All year | | |

*Antiques, original art, oriental rugs, spectacular view! Close to beaches. Horseback riding arrangements available.* **3rd night 50% off Oct.–April, ltd.**

QUINCY ──────────────────────────────────

| **Feather Bed, The** | $$-B&B | Full breakfast |
| P.O. Box 3200, 95971 | 7 rooms, 7 pb | Sitting room, gazebo |
| 542 Jackson St. | AmEx, MC, Visa, | Victorian garden, bikes |
| 916-283-0102  800-696-8624 | *Rated*, ● | fountain, fireplcs., A/C |
| Bob & Jan Janowski | C-ltd/S-no/P-no/H-yes | |
| All year | | |

*Country Victorian in forested surroundings, relaxing is our specialty, antiques in individually decorated rooms, located on Heritage Walk. Recreation area.* **10% off 3+ nights.**

RED BLUFF ────────────────────────────────

| **Faulkner House, The** | $$-B&B | Full breakfast |
| 1029 Jefferson St.,  96080 | 4 rooms, 4 pb | Complimentary beverage |
| 916-529-0520  Fax: 916-527-4970 | AmEx, MC, Visa, | Sitting room |
| 800-549-6171 | *Rated*, ● | bicycles |
| Harvey & Mary Klingler | C-ltd/S-no/P-no/H-no | all rms. have priv. bath |
| All year | | |

*1890s Queen Anne Victorian furnished in antiques. Screened porch on quiet street, hiking and skiing nearby. Visit Ide Adobe, Victorian Museum, Sacramento River.*

## 56  California

### REDDING

**Palisades Paradise B&B**
1200 Palisades Ave., 96003
916-223-5305 Fax: 916-223-1200
Gail McDaniel Goetz
All year

$$-B&B
2 rooms,
MC, Visa, *Rated*, •
C-ltd/S-ltd/P-no/H-ltd

Continental plus bkfst.
Complimentary tea/coffee
Cable TV, fireplace
porch swing, garden spa
hot tub with great view

*Breathtaking view of Sacramento River, mtns., & city from secluded contemporary home in Redding. Gateway to Shasta-Cascade Wonderland. Excellent Bird-Watching. 10% off, ltd.*

### REEDLEY

**Reedley Country Inn B&B**
43137 Rd 52, 93654
209-638-2585 209-638-3445
George & Linda Penner
All year

$$-B&B
4 rooms, 4 pb
MC, Visa, *Rated*, •
C-ltd/S-no/P-no/H-yes

Full breakfast
Complimentary wine
Hot tub, bikes, rosebush
Additional house w/suite
2 rms., balcony, bath

*Reedley Country Inn is a working plum farm where guests will find a quiet and restful atmosphere. Ride bikes to King River, where innertubing is popular.*

### SACRAMENTO

**Abigail's B&B**
2120 "G" St., 95816
916-441-5007 Fax: 916-441-0621
800-858-1568
Ken & Susanne Ventura
All year

$$$-B&B
5 rooms, 5 pb
Most CC, *Rated*, •
C-ltd/S-no/P-no/H-no

Full breakfast
Comp. beverages
Secluded garden, piano
sitting rooms, fireplace
hot tub, games, phones

*Grand old mansion in the heart of the State Capitol. Large & comfortable, delicious breakfasts, A/C. Ideal for business travelers & romantic escapes. **Restaurant discounts.***

---

**Amber House B&B Inn**
1315 - 22nd St., 95816
916-444-8085 Fax: 916-552-6529
800-755-6526
Michael & Jane Richardson
All year

$$$-B&B
9 rooms, 9 pb
Most CC, *Rated*, •
C-ltd/S-ltd/P-no/H-no

Full gourmet breakfast
Comp. wine, tea, coffee
8 rms. w/jacuzzi for two
all w/marble bathrooms
tandem bicycle, phones

*Luxury rooms offer ultimate comfort for the business traveler and perfect setting for a romantic escape. Phones, cable TV, breakfasts in room. **2nd night 50%, ltd.***

---

**Hartley House Inn**
700 - 22nd St., 95816
916-447-7829 Fax: 916-447-1820
800-831-5806
Randy Hartley
All year

$$$-B&B
5 rooms, 5 pb
*Rated*, •
C-ltd/S-ltd/P-no/H-no
Spanish

Full gourmet breakfast
Complimentary beverages
Sitting room, piano
inroom phones, modems
fax, air conditioned

*Stunning turn-of-the-century mansion furnished w/antiques, fine art work & stained glass. Perfect for business & romantic travelers. **Restaurant discount, horse & carriage ride.***

### SAN DIEGO

**Blom House B&B, The**
1372 Minden Dr., 92111
619-467-0890 Fax: 619-467-0890
Bette Blom
All year

$$-B&B
2 rooms, 2 pb
*Rated*, •
C-yes/S-ltd/P-no/H-no
Dutch, Spanish

Full gourmet breakfast
Comp. cheese & soda
Fabulous view from deck
and spa, babysitting
available, crib/hi-chair

*A 2 bedroom family suite w/private bath. All rooms are A/C & have color TV/VCR. All attractions nearby. **Ask about discounts. Free bottle of wine or sparkling cider.***

## SACRAMENTO

**Carole's B&B Inn**
3227 Grim Ave., 92104
619-280-5258 Fax: 619-283-9558
C. Dugdale & M. O'Brien
All year

$$-B&B
8 rooms, 4 pb
*Rated*, •
C-ltd/S-yes/P-no/H-no

Continental plus bkfst.
Complimentary wine
Cheese, sitting room
swimming pool, spa
player piano, cable TV

*Historical house built in 1904, tastefully redecorated/antiques. Centrally located near zoo, Balboa Park. Friendly, congenial atmosphere.* **Restaurant discounts and coupons.**

---

**The Cottage**
3829 Albatross St, 92103
619-299-1564
Carol & Robert Emerick
All year

$$-B&B
2 rooms, 2 pb
MC, Visa, *Rated*, •
C-yes/S-no/P-no/H-no

Continental breakfast
Herb garden
restaurant discounts

*Relaxation in a garden setting with turn-of-the-century ambiance is offered in a residential downtown San Diego neighborhood.*

---

**Harbor Hill Guest House**
2330 Albatross St., 92101
619-233-0638
Dorothy A. Milbourn
All year

$$-B&B
5 rooms, 5 pb
Visa, MC, *Rated*, •
C-yes/S-ltd/P-no/H-no

Continental breakfast
Kitchens on each level
Large sun deck & garden
barbecue, TV, phones
rooms with harbor views

*Charming circa 1920 home; private entrances. Near Balboa Park, zoo, museums, Sea World, Old Town, harbor, shopping, theater. Families welcome.* **10% off 3+ nights.**

---

**Heritage Park B&B Inn**
2470 Heritage Park Row,
  92110
619-299-6832 Fax: 619-299-9465
800-995-2470
Nancy & Charles Helsper
All year

$$$-B&B
11 rooms, 11 pb
MC, Visa, AmEx,
*Rated*, •
C-ltd/S-no/P-no/H-yes
Spanish

Full breakfast
Picnics, dinners, tea
Sitting room, library
bicycles, vintage films
discount tickets to Zoo

*Restored 1889 Queen Anne mansion in historic Old Town. Tantalizing breakfasts. Film shows, antiques, romantic candlelight dinners. Walking distance to Old Town Trolley.*

---

**La Jolla Oasis B&B**
P.O. Box 99666, 92169
La Jolla
619-456-1776
Winifred Krause
All year

$$$-B&B
2 rooms, 2 pb
•
C-ltd/S-no/P-no/H-no

Full breakfast
Fresh fruit, snacks
Video library, bicycles
spa, swimming pool
Mascot—Joey, the poodle

*Best location. Private million-$ residence above La Jolla Village. Near all, very quiet. Luxurious accommodations, gourmet breakfast. Let us spoil you.* **4th night 50% off.**

---

**Sea Breeze B&B Inn**
121 N. Vulcan Ave., Encinitas,
  92024
619-944-0318
Kirsten Richter
All year

$$-B&B
5 rooms, 5 pb
*Rated*, •
C-yes/S-yes/P-no/H-no

Continental plus bkfst.
Comp. wine & cheese
Wet bar, kitchenette
sitting room
near beach and tennis

*N. San Diego quiet beach town. Contemporary B&B w/ocean view. Penthouse Boudoir w/private 8'hot tub. Intimate oceanview wedding grotto. Spa packages.* **Free champagne special.**

SACRAMENTO ─────────────────────────────

**Tecolote House**
5402 Via Aquario,  92111
619-268-0446
Karen Lucas
All year

$$-B&B
1 rooms, 1 pb
•
C-ltd/S-no/P-no/H-no

Continental plus bkfst.
Snacks, comp. wine

*Suburban home. Close to Mission Bay. Within 5 miles of ocean, airport, city, zoo. Near La Jolla, colleges, Seaworld.*

---

**Villa Serena B&B**
2164 Rosecrans St.,  92106
619-224-2103  Fax: 619-224-2103
Kae & Alex Schreiber
All year

$$$-B&B
3 rooms, 2 pb
Visa, MC, Disc.,  •
C-yes/S-no/P-no/H-no
Spanish

Full breakfast
Snacks
Sitting room, library
hot tubs, pool
children under 12-free

*A wonderful Mediterranean paradise, 5 minutes to Sea World. Comfortable rooms, spa, abundant breakfasts, friendly hosts can help with suggestions.* **Family packages.**

SAN FRANCISCO ─────────────────────────

**Alamo Square Inn**
719 Scott St.,  94117
415-922-2055  Fax: 415-931-1304
800-345-9888
Wayne Corn & Klaus May
All year

$$$-B&B
14 rooms, 14 pb
Most CC, *Rated*,  •
C-yes/S-ltd/P-no/H-no
German, French

Full breakfast
Complimentary tea/wine
Free off-st. parking
jacuzzi suite, views
Near S.F. attractions

*Fine restoration of 2 magnificent mansions. Graced by European furnishings, Oriental rugs, flowers, fireplaces. Hosts committed to excellence. Weddings & receptions.*

---

**Albion House Inn, The**
135 Gough St,  94102
415-621-0896  Fax: 415-621-3811
800-6-ALBION
Regina Pechkite
All year

$$$-B&B
8 rooms, 8 pb
AmEx, MC, Visa,
*Rated*,  •
C-ltd/S-yes/P-no/H-no
Spanish

Full breakfast
Complimentary wine
Sitting room
conference facilities

*An elegant city hideaway conveniently located near the Opera House, just moments away from Union Square & other tourist attractions.* **3rd night 50% weekdays only.**

---

**Andrews Hotel, The**
624 Post St., Between Jones &
Taylor,  94109
415-563-6877  Fax: 415-928-6919
800-926-3739
Harry Andrews
All year

$$$-B&B
48 rooms, 48 pb
AmEx, MC, Visa,
*Rated*,  •
C-yes/S-ltd/P-no/H-no
Some It., Fr., Sp.

Continental plus bkfst.
Restaurant, bar
Comp. wine, coffee, tea
small meetings

*European-style charm in the heart of Union Square shopping and theater district. Just two blocks from cable cars.*

---

**Archbishop's Mansion Inn**
1000 Fulton St.,  94117
415-563-7872  Fax: 415-885-3193
800-543-5820
Rick Janvier
All year

$$$$-B&B
15 rooms, 15 pb
AmEx, MC, Visa,
*Rated*,  •
C-yes/S-no/P-no/H-no

Continental plus bkfst.
Comp. wine, tea, coffee
Sitting room, piano
reception & conference
facilities, spa services

*Luxury lodging in "Belle Epoque" style. "Arguably the most elegant, in-city small hotel on the West Coast if not the USA"–USA TODAY. Getaway pkgs.* **Free bottle of champagne.**

SAN FRANCISCO ──────────────────────────────────────────

| **Art Center Wamsley B&B** | $$$-B&B | Continental plus bkfst. |
|---|---|---|
| 1902 Filbert at Laguna,  94123 | 5 rooms, 5 pb | Picnics, pastry, fruit |
| 415-567-1526 | MC, Visa, *Rated*,  • | Studio room, art gallery |
| Helvi & George Wamsley | C-yes/S-no/P-no/H-no | art classes, city tours |
| All year | Finnish | enclosed patio, gardens |

*Art shows, classes, garden art, workroom & art materials. We offer an Art Package—includes 3-days lodging, museum tour, buffet. Suites w/whirlpool & easels.* **Class discounts.**

| **Auberge des Artistes** | $$-B&B | Full breakfast, buffet |
|---|---|---|
| 827-829 Fillmore St.,  94117 | 5 rooms, 3 pb | Aftn. tea, snacks, wine |
| 415-776-2530  Fax: 415-441-8242 | Visa, MC, AmEx, | Lunch/dinner by request |
| David & Laura Novick | C-yes/S-no/P-no/H-no | cooking class packages |
| All year | French, Spanish | bikes, jacuzzis, patio |

*San Francisco's hip, affordable, gourmet choice. Let candlelight, fireplaces, panoramic views, romantic artwork and sumptuous dining start your perfect vacation.* **disc't, ltd.**

| **Bed & Breakfast Inn, The** | $$-B&B | Continental breakfast |
|---|---|---|
| 4 Charlton Court,  94123 | 11 rooms, 8 pb | Complimentary wine |
| 415-921-9784 | *Rated*, | Sitting room, library |
| R. & M. Kavanaugh, F. Stone | C-ltd/S-yes/P-no/H-no | private 2b/2b flat |
| All year | French, Italian | garden |

*San Francisco's first "country inn." Ten unique accommodations are romantic hideaways. Antiques and flowers. You're treated as a very special person by the owners and staff.*

| **Carol's Cow Hollow Inn** | $$$-B&B | Full breakfast |
|---|---|---|
| 2821 Steiner St.,  94123 | 3 rooms, 3 pb | Tea, complimentary wine |
| 415-775-8295  Fax: 415-775-8296 | Visa, MC,  • | Sitting room, library |
| 800-400-8295 | C-yes/S-ltd/P-no/H-no | TV, refrigerator, desks |
| Carol Blumefeld | Rus., Ger., Fr., Sp. | phones, suberb location |
| All year | | |

*Charm in the heart of Pacific Heights. Memorable views and cuisine, original art. Close to Victorian Union Street boutiques and restaurants.*

| **Casa Arguello B&B** | $$-B&B | Continental plus bkfst. |
|---|---|---|
| 225 Arguello Blvd.,  94118 | 5 rooms, 5 pb | Sitting room, TV |
| 415-752-9482  Fax: 415-681-1400 | *Rated*, | Suite w/one king & one |
| E. Baires, M. & P. McKenzie | C-yes/S-no/P-no/H-no | double bed available |
| All year | Spanish | |

*An elegant townhouse near Golden Gate Park, the Presidio, Golden Gate Bridge, 10 minutes to Union Square.*

| **Chateau Tivoli B&B, The** | $$$-B&B | Continental plus (wkday) |
|---|---|---|
| 1057 Steiner St.,  94115 | 7 rooms, 5 pb | Full breakfast (wkend) |
| 415-776-5462  800-228-1647 | AmEx, MC, Visa, | Comp. wine, aftn. tea |
| Rodney Karr, Willard | *Rated*,  • | double parlors, library |
| Gersbach | C-yes/S-ltd/P-no/H-no | new suite |
| All year | | |

*A stay at the Victorian townhouse, Chateau Tivoli, provides guests a time travel experience back to San Francisco's Golden Age of Opulence, the 1890s.* **3rd night free**

SAN FRANCISCO ─────────────────────────────────────────────

**Edward II Inn & Suites**　　$$-B&B　　　　　　Continental plus bkfst.
3155 Scott St., 94123　　31 rooms, 20 pb　　　Italian dinner, pub
415-922-3000 Fax: 415-931-5784　MC, Visa, •　　　Parlour, conference room
800-473-2846　　　　　　C-yes/S-no/P-no/H-no　luxury suites available
Bob & Denise Holland　　Spanish, Italian　　　phones & cable TV in rms
All year

*Perched atop a delightful Italian restaurant & old English-style pub. Fully refurbished 1914 European-style hotel in San Francisco's Marina district. 5 Jacuzzi suites. 4 apartment suites for families.*

───────────────────────────────────────────────────────────

**Garden Studio, The**　　　$$-EP　　　　　　　Coffee
1387 Sixth Ave., 94122　　1 rooms, 1 pb　　　　Restaurants nearby
415-753-3574 Fax: 415-753-5513　C-yes/S-no/P-no/H-no　Garden, private entrance
Alice & John Micklewright　French　　　　　　fully equipped kitchen
All year　　　　　　　　　　　　　　　　　　TV/VCR, telephone, radio

*On lower level of charming Edwardian home; 2 blocks from Golden Gate Park. Studio opens to garden, has private entrance, private bath, queen-sized bed. **7 nites for price of 6.***

───────────────────────────────────────────────────────────

**Glenwood Hotel**　　　　$$$-B&B　　　　　　Continental plus bkfst.
717 Sutter St., 94109　　30 rooms, 30 pb　　　Sitting room
415-673-0700 Fax: 415-440-4466　Visa, MC, AmEx, Disc.,
888-442-2020　　　　　　•
All year　　　　　　　　　S-no/P-no

*Downtown boutique hotel. City charm, close to everything. Complimentary coffee during the day. Valet laundry service.*

───────────────────────────────────────────────────────────

**Golden Gate Hotel, The**　$$-B&B　　　　　　Continental breakfast
775 Bush St., 94108　　23 rooms, 14 pb　　　Afternoon tea
415-392-3702 Fax: 415-392-6202　Most CC, *Rated*, •　Sitting room
800-835-1118　　　　　　C-yes/S-yes/P-ltd/H-no　sightseeing tours
John & Renate Kenaston　German, French
All year

*Charming turn-of-the-century hotel. Friendly atmosphere. Antique furnishings, fresh flowers. Ideal Nob Hill location. Corner cable car stop. Guest rooms newly restored.*

───────────────────────────────────────────────────────────

**Grove Inn, The**　　　　$$-B&B　　　　　　Continental breakfast
890 Grove St., 94117　　16 rooms, 9 pb　　　Sitting room
415-929-0780 Fax: 415-929-1037　AmEx, MC, Visa　bicycles
800-829-0780　　　　　　*Rated*, •　　　　laundry
Klaus & Rosetta　　　　C-yes/S-ltd/P-no/H-no
Zimmermann　　　　　Italian, German
All year

*Turn-of-the-century Victorian, fully restored, simply furnished. Community kitchen, refrigerator. Part of Alamo Square Historic district.*

───────────────────────────────────────────────────────────

**Inn at Union Square, The**　$$$-B&B　　　　　Continental plus bkfst.
440 Post St., 94102　　30 rooms, 30 pb　　　Comp. wine, afternoon
415-397-3510 Fax: 415-989-0529　AmEx, MC, Visa,　Tea, Hors d'oeuvres
800-288-4346　　　　　　*Rated*, •　　　　complimentary shoe shine
Brooks Bayly　　　　　C-ltd/S-no/P-no/H-yes　paper, turn-down service
All year　　　　　　　　French, Spanish

*Rooms are individually decorated with Georgian furniture and warm colorful fabrics by noted San Francisco interior designer Nan Rosenblatt. A non-tipping property.*

SAN FRANCISCO ───────────────────────────────

**Inn San Francisco, The**
943 S. Van Ness Ave., 94110
415-641-0188   Fax: 415-641-1701
800-359-0913
Marty & Connie Neely
All year

$$-B&B
22 rooms, 17 pb
AmEx, MC, Visa,
*Rated*, •
C-yes/S-yes/P-no/H-no

Full breakfast buffet
Sun deck, gazebo, garden
hot tub, phones, TV's
off-street parking

*A grand 27-room Italianate 1872 Victorian mansion furnished in 19th-century antiques. Garden room, hot tub, fresh flowers in rooms. Jacuzzi, fireplace available.*

---

**Moffatt House B&B**
431 Hugo St., 94122
415-661-6210   Fax: 415-564-2480
Ruth Moffatt
All year

$-B&B
4 rooms, 2 pb
*Rated*, •
C-yes/S-yes/P-yes/H-no
Spanish, French, Italian

Continental plus
Hot beverages, kitchen
Tennis, bicycles nearby
Japanese Tea Garden
runner's discount

*Walk to Golden Gate Park's major attractions from our Edwardian home. Safe location for active, independent guests. Excellent public transportation.* **Weekly discounts.**

---

**Monte Cristo, The**
600 Presidio Ave., 94115
415-931-1875   Fax: 415-931-6005
George
All year

$$-B&B
14 rooms, 12 pb
AmEx, MC, Visa, •
C-yes/S-yes/P-no/H-yes
French, Spanish

Continental plus buffet
Complimentary tea/wine
Parlor w/fireplace
phones, TV

*1875 hotel-saloon-bordello, furnished with antiques. Each room uniquely decorated— Georgian four-poster, Chinese wedding bed, spindle bed, etc.* **10% off 5 nights or more.**

---

**Petite Auberge**
863 Bush St., 94108
415-928-6000   Fax: 415-775-5717
800-365-3004
Brian Larsen
All year

$$$-B&B
26 rooms, 26 pb
AmEx, MC, Visa,
*Rated*, •
C-ltd/S-no/P-no/H-no

Full country breakfast
Wine and hors d'oeuvres
Sitting room, aftn. tea
near Cable Car line
fireplace rooms

*Romantic French country inn near Union Square in San Francisco. Turndown service, robes, afternoon tea. Honeymoon packages. A Four Sisters Inn. Breakfast in bed.*

---

**Spencer House**
1080 Haight St., 94117
415-626-9205   Fax: 415-626-9230
Jack & Barbara Chambers
All year

$$$-B&B
6 rooms, 6 pb
*Rated*, •
S-no/P-no/H-no

Full breakfast
Complimentary wine
Sitting rooms
All rooms have phones

*Elegant Queen Anne mansion near Golden Gate Park. Antique furnishings, feather mattresses, crystal and silver breakfast service. All private baths. Parking*

---

**Stanyan Park Hotel**
750 Stanyan St., 94117
415-751-1000   Fax: 415-668-5454
Brad Bihlmeyer
All year

$$$-B&B
36 rooms, 36 pb
Most CC, •
C-yes/S-yes/P-no/H-yes
Sp., Chi., Fil., Rus.

Continental plus bkfst.
Afternoon tea
Sitting room, bikes

*Beautifully restored turn of the century hotel on Golden Gate Park. Conveniently located within easy walking distance to UCSF & USF campuses, Aquarium, Planetarium, museums.*

## SAN FRANCISCO

| | | |
|---|---|---|
| **Union Street Inn** | $$$-B&B | Full breakfast |
| 2229 Union St., 94123 | 6 rooms, 6 pb | Comp. wine, cookies |
| 415-346-0424 Fax: 415-922-8046 | AmEx, MC, Visa, | Sitting room |
| Jane Bertorelli, David Coyle | *Rated*, • | jacuzzi |
| All year | C-yes/S-ltd/P-no/H-no | English garden |

*Charming, elegant inn located in lively shopping/entertainment area of San Francisco; romantic old-fashioned garden, private carriage house with jacuzzi. Recently refurbished.*

| | | |
|---|---|---|
| **Victorian Inn on the Park** | $$$-B&B | Continental plus bkfst. |
| 301 Lyon St., 94117 | 12 rooms, 12 pb | Complimentary wine |
| 415-931-1830 Fax: 415-931-1830 | Most CC, *Rated*, • | Homemade breads, cheeses |
| 800-435-1967 | C-yes/S-ltd/P-no/H-no | library, phones in rooms |
| Lisa & William Benau | | TV on request, parlor |
| All year | | |

*1897 Queen Anne Victorian near Golden Gate Park, downtown. Each rm. has antiques, flowers, beautiful comforters, down pillows, phones. Historic landmark.* **3rd night, 50%, ltd**

| | | |
|---|---|---|
| **White Swan Inn** | $$$$-B&B | Full breakfast |
| 845 Bush St., 94108 | 26 rooms, 26 pb | Hors d'oeuvres, tea |
| 415-775-1755 Fax: 415-775-5717 | AmEx, MC, Visa, | Library, sitting room |
| 800-999-9570 | *Rated*, • | English garden |
| Brian Larsen | C-ltd/S-no/P-no/H-no | near Cable Car line |
| All year | Fr., Cantonese, Tagalog | |

*English garden, in cosmopolitan San Francisco; built in 1908. Business conference facilities; country breakfast; afternoon tea. 3 honeymoon suites. Breakfast in bed. A Four Sisters Inn.*

## SAN GREGORIO

| | | |
|---|---|---|
| **Rancho San Gregorio** | $$$-B&B | Full country breakfast |
| Route 1, Box 54, 94074 | 5 rooms, 4 pb | Comp. beverages, snacks |
| Hwy 84, 5086 La Honda | Most CC, *Rated*, • | Sitting room, library |
| Rd.(Hwy 84) | C-ltd/S-ltd | antiques, gazebo, garden |
| 415-747-0810 Fax: 415-747-0184 | | orchards, conferences |
| Bud & Lee Raynor | | |
| All year | | |

*California Mission-style coastal retreat; serene; spectacular views of wooded hills; friendly hospitality; hearty breakfast; Near Ano Nuevo.* **Over 4 days 10% off.**

## SAN JOSE

| | | |
|---|---|---|
| **Briar Rose B&B Inn, The** | $$-B&B | Full breakfast |
| 897 E. Jackson St., 95112 | 5 rooms, 3 pb | Aftn. tea, sherry |
| 408-279-5999 | AmEx, MC, Visa, • | Porch, gardens |
| Tom & Path Worthy | C-ltd/S-ltd/P-no/H-no | sitting room, library |
| All year | | Period furnishings |

*An 1875 Victorian—once a flourishing walnut orchard—restored to its former grandeur. Rooms fabulously wallpapered with Bradbury & Bradbury papers.* **10% disc't for week or more stay, & retirees.**

| | | |
|---|---|---|
| **Hensley House, The** | $$$-B&B | Full gourmet breakfast |
| 456 N. 3rd St., 95112 | 5 rooms, 5 pb | Lunch/dinner by reserv. |
| 408-298-3537 Fax: 408-298-4676 | AmEx, MC, Visa, | Comp. wine, tea, snacks |
| 800-498-3537 | *Rated*, • | sitting room, library |
| Sharon Layne & Bill Priest | C-ltd/S-no/P-no/H-no | 2 rms w/whirlpool, patio |
| All year | | |

*Elegant Queen Anne Victorian, near everything. TV/VCR each room. Business services, Fax, phone, PC, conference, meetings, murder mysteries, airport service. Historic Register*

*Adobe Inn, San Luis Obispo, CA*

SAN LUIS OBISPO —————————————————————————————

| | | |
|---|---|---|
| **Adobe Inn** | $$-B&B | Full homemade breakfast |
| 1473 Monterey St., 93401 | 15 rooms, 15 pb | Coffeemaker, refriger. |
| 805-549-0321 Fax: 805-549-0383 | AmEx, MC, Visa, | Outdoor Patio, Cactus |
| 800-676-1588 | *Rated*, • | Garden, Getaway Packages |
| Ann & Michael Dinshaw | C-yes/S-ltd/P-no/H-yes | include spa, kayak, wine |
| All year | | |

*Cozy, comfortable, southwestern-style inn, in the heart of charming town. Suite w/fireplace & cozy sitting rm. Near Hearst Castle, beaches, restaurants. 25% off 3rd night, ltd.*

| | | |
|---|---|---|
| **Apple Farm Inn** | $$$$-EP | Restaurant |
| 2015 Monterey Street, 93401 | 69 rooms, 69 pb | All meals served (fee) |
| 800-255-2040 Fax: 805-546-9495 | Most CC, *Rated*, • | Swimming pool, spa |
| Katy & Bob Davis | C-yes/S-ltd/P-no/H-yes | gift shop, millhouse with |
| All year | | working waterwheel |

*Memorable lodging experience; uniquely appointed rooms—canopy beds, fireplaces, turrets, cozy window seats. Breakfast in bed, box lunches. Gardens, patio dining.*

| | | |
|---|---|---|
| **Garden Street Inn B&B** | $$$-B&B | Full breakfast |
| 1212 Garden St., 93401 | 13 rooms, 13 pb | Comp. wine, snacks |
| 805-545-9802 Fax: 805-781-7469 | AmEx, MC, Visa, | Sitting room, library |
| Dan & Kathy Smith, Mozart | *Rated*, • | fireplaces, board games |
| | C-ltd/S-ltd/P-no/H-yes | hot tubs, decks |

*1887 Victorian lovingly restored. Romantic get-away in the heart of an old-fashioned downtown. Antiques, jacuzzis, homemade breakfast. Special hospitality*

# 64 California

## SAN RAFAEL

**Gerstle Park Inn**
34 Grove St., 94901
415-721-7611  Fax: 415-721-7600
800-726-7600
Jim Dowling
All year

$$$-B&B
10 rooms, 10 pb
Visa, MC, AmEx, •
C-yes/S-no/P-no/H-ltd

Full breakfast
Complimentary wine
Sitting room, library
tennis court, hot tubs

*Warm, elegant century old estate in Marin. Centrally located-30 minutes to San Francisco, wine country or the coast.*

---

**Panama Hotel**
4 Bayview St., 94901
415-457-3993  Fax: 415-457-6240
800-899-3993
Daniel Miller
All year

$$-B&B
15 rooms, 9 pb
Most CC, *Rated*,
C-yes/S-no/P-no/H-yes

Continental plus bkfst.
Buffet brunch on Sunday
Dinner

*A landmark inn and restaurant for 60 years, between San Francisco and wine country. The Panama is celebrated for its eccentric charm.* **Free appetizer with dinner.**

## SANTA BARBARA

**Bath Street Inn**
1720 Bath St., 93101
805-682-9680  Fax: 805-569-1281
800-341-2284
Susan Brown
All year

$$$-B&B
12 rooms, 12 pb
AmEx, MC, Visa,
*Rated*, •
C-yes/S-no/P-no/H-no

Full breakfast
Evening refreshments
Sitting & dining rooms
TV room, library, spas
kitchen avail., bicycles

*Luxurious 3-story Victorian, panoramic views, balconies, brick courtyards, gardens. Country inn appeal; near downtown. Summerhouse w/2 rooms, fireplace.* **20% off rates, ltd.**

---

**Blue Dolphin Inn**
420 W. Montecito St., 93101
805-965-2333  Fax: 805-962-9470
Byria O'Hayon-Crosby
All year exc. Dec 24-25

$$$-B&B
9 rooms, 9 pb
AmEx, *Rated*, •
C-ltd/S-no/P-no/H-no

Full breakfast
Comp. wine, refreshments
Fireplaces, balconies
spa tubs, mountain views
TV, canopied beds

*Harbour Carriage House—An Inn by the Sea. Simply elegant country French atmosphere in the main house and carriage house. 2 blocks from beach.* **3rd night, 50%, restrictions.**

---

**Casa Del Mar Inn**
18 Bath St., 93101
805-963-4418  Fax: 805-966-4240
800-433-3097
Mike & Becky Montgomery
All year

$$-B&B
20 rooms, 22 pb
Most CC, *Rated*, •
C-yes/S-ltd/P-ltd/H-yes
Spanish & German

Continental plus bkfst.
Afternoon tea
Sitting room, hot tub
beach towels, umbrellas
Comp. wine & cheese

*Spanish-style villa, quiet, charming. One block from beach. Courtyard jacuzzi. Several units with fireplaces and kitchens.* **Comp. bottle of Santa Barbara Winery vintage.**

---

**Cheshire Cat Inn, The**
36 W. Valerio St., 93101
805-569-1610  Fax: 805-682-1876
Amy Taylor
All year

$$$$-B&B
14 rooms, 14 pb
MC, Visa, *Rated*, •
C-ltd/S-no/P-no/H-no

Full breakfast
Wine & hors d'oeuvres
Sitting room, library
library, TV/VCR, bikes
4 in-room spas

*Victorian elegance, uniquely decorated in Laura Ashley & English antiques; kitchenettes, private baths, Jacuzzis, balconies, fireplaces, gardens.* **3rd night 50%, ltd.**

SANTA BARBARA ─────────────────────────────

| **Eagle Inn, The** | $$-B&B | Continental breakfast |
|---|---|---|

**Eagle Inn, The**
232 Natoma Ave., 93101
805-965-3586 Fax: 805-966-1218
800-767-0030
Janet & Alan Bullock
All year

$$-B&B
20 rooms, 20 pb
Most CC, *Rated*, •
C-ltd/S-ltd/P-no/H-no

Continental breakfast
Kitchen in some rooms
Coffee makers, phones,
cable TV, refrigerators
in all rooms

*A fine example of Spanish Colonial architecture, an elegant retreat, just a few steps from the ocean, and the heart of Santa Barbara. No smoking rooms available.*

**Glenborough Inn B&B**
1327 Bath St., 93101
805-966-0589 Fax: 805-564-8610
800-962-0589
Michael, Steve, Ken
All year

$$$-B&B
11 rooms, 11 pb
Most CC, *Rated*, •
C-ltd/S-ltd/P-no/H-no

Full gourmet breakfast
Wine & hors d'oeuvres
Bedtime snacks, jacuzzi
parlor with fireplace
refrigerator available

*Lovely grounds, elegant antique-filled rooms. Breakfast in bed, 6 rooms have fireplaces & private entrances, 2 rooms have hot tubs, 2 w/jacuzzis.* **15% discount, ltd.**

**Goodfriend Inn, The**
1734 Bath St., 93101
805-898-9336 Fax: 805-898-9336
Rick Goodfriend
All year

$$-EP
3 rooms, 3 pb
Visa, MC, •
C-yes/S-no/P-no/H-no

Optional Continental
Breakfast
Kitchen in cottage
suite with kitchenette

*Inn consists of cottage/suite/rooms. Some have kitchens to save on restaurant bills. Near downtown/beaches. Extremely friendly & knowledgeable staff.* **$10 off 3rd night.**

**Long's Sea View B&B**
317 Piedmont Rd., 93105
805-687-2947
LaVerne M. Long
All year

$$-B&B
1 rooms, 1 pb
S-no/P-no/H-no

Full breakfast
King size bed
Gardens, patio
1.5 Miles from Hwy. 101

*Home with a lovely view, furnished with antiques. Quiet neighborhood. Full breakfast served on the patio. Homemade jams and fresh fruits.* **Wine upon arrival.**

**Mary May Inn**
111 W. Valerio St., 93101
805-569-3398
Kathleen & Mark
All year

$$$$-B&B
12 rooms, 12 pb
Visa, MC, AmEx,
*Rated*, •
C-yes/S-no/P-no/H-no

Continental plus bkfst.
Aftn. tea, snacks
Sitting room
romantic pleasures are
within easy reach

*Perhaps Santa Barbara's best kept secret! 2 historical properties dating back to the 1800s. Some rooms have canopied beds, woodburning fireplaces or Jacuzzi tubs.* **3rd night 50% off.**

**Ocean View House**
P.O. Box 3373, 93105
805-966-6659
Carolyn Canfield
All year

$$-B&B
2 rooms, 1 pb
*Rated*,
C-yes/S-ltd/P-ltd/H-no

Continental plus bkfst.
Stocked refrigerator
Beach towels & chairs
2 room suite available -
with den, private entry

*Breakfast on the patio while viewing sailboats & Channel Islands. Pvt. home in quiet neighborhood. By a Zoo, beaches, park, museums. Fruit trees in yard.* **Free bottle of wine.**

SANTA BARBARA ─────────────────────────────────

**Old Yacht Club Inn, The**
431 Corona Del Mar Dr.,
   93103
805-962-1277 Fax: 805-962-3989
800-676-1676
Nancy Donaldson &
Sandy Hunt      All year

$$$-B&B
9 rooms, 9 pb
Most CC, *Rated*, •
C-ltd/S-ltd/P-no/H-no
Spanish

Full breakfast
Dinner on Saturdays
Comp. evening beverage
beach chairs & towels
bicycles, 1 whirlpool

*1912 California classic. Beautifully decorated w/antiques. Gourmet breakfast. Dinner on weekends. Close to beautiful beach.* **3rd night free to readers.**

---

**Olive House Inn, The**
1604 Olive St.,   93101
805-962-4902 Fax: 805-899-2754
800-786-6422
Lois Gregg & Bharti Singh
All year

$$$-B&B
6 rooms, 6 pb
Most CC, *Rated*, •
C-ltd

Full breakfast
Afternoon refreshments
Sitting room, library
fireplace, FAX
hot tubs, telephones, TV

*Quiet comfort & gracious hospitality in lovingly restored CA craftsman pattern home with bay windows, fireplaces, grand piano, sundeck, ocean views, private decks & hot tubs.* **Midweek discounts.**

---

**Parsonage B&B**
1600 Olive St.,   93101
805-962-9336
Hilde Michelmore
All year

$$$-B&B
6 rooms, 6 pb
*Rated*, •
C-ltd/S-no/P-no/H-no
German

Full breakfast
Complimentary wine
Sitting room, sundeck
off-season discounts
weekly rates

*A beautifully restored Queen Anne victorian. An atmosphere of comfort, grace and elegance with ocean and mountain views. Close to shops, dining, sightseeing.*

---

**Secret Garden Inn**
1908 Bath St.,   93101
805-687-2300 Fax: 805-687-4576
800-676-1622
J. Greenwald & C. Dunstan
All year exc. Dec 24-25

$$$-B&B
10 rooms, 10 pb
AmEx, MC, Visa,
*Rated*, •
C-ltd/S-ltd/P-no/H-no

Scrumptious Full bkfast.
Cider, comp. wine
Evening sweets
sitting room, garden
brick patio, bicycles

*Guest rooms, suites & private cottages filled w/country charm in a delightfully quiet and relaxing country setting. 4 rooms w/outdoor private hot tubs.* **Midweek discount, ltd.**

---

**Simpson House Inn**
121 E. Arrellaga St.,   93101
805-963-7067 Fax: 805-564-4811
800-676-1280
Glyn & Linda Davies
All year

$$$$-B&B
14 rooms, 14 pb
Most CC, *Rated*, •
C-ltd/S-ltd/P-no/H-yes
Spanish

Full gourmet breakfast
Comp. wine, beverages
Sitt. rm, library, patio
veranda, garden, jacuzzi
bikes, fireplaces, VCRs

*1874 Victorian estate secluded on an acre of English garden. Cottages & barn suites. Elegant antiques, art. Delicious leisurely bkfst. on verandas. Walk to historic downtown.*

---

**Tiffany Inn**
1323 De La Vina,   93101
805-963-2283 Fax: 805-962-0994
800-999-5672
C. & L. MacDonald, G.
Brusby
All year

$$$-B&B
7 rooms, 7 pb
AmEx, MC, Visa,
*Rated*, •
C-ltd/S-no/P-no/H-no

Full breakfast
Complimentary wine
Spa in 2 rooms
fireplaces in 5 rooms

*Classic antiques & period furnishings welcome you througout this lovely restored 1898 Victorian. Stroll to shops, restaurants, galleries, theaters, museums.* **3rd night 50&%, Sept–June.**

## SANTA BARBARA

| **Upham Hotel & Cottages** | $$$-B&B | Continental plus bkfst. |
|---|---|---|
| 1404 De La Vina St.,  93101 | 50 rooms, 39 pb | Comp. wine, coffee, tea |
| 805-962-0058 Fax: 805-963-2825 | Most CC, *Rated*, • | Newspaper, lobby |
| 800-727-0876 | C-yes/S-yes/P-no/H-no | garden veranda, gardens |
| Jan Martin Winn | Spanish | valet laundry, phones |
| All year | | |

*California's oldest Victorian hotel. Cottage rooms with patios and fireplaces, lawn, flowers. Complimentary wine and cheese by the lobby fireplace. Corporate rates available.*

## SANTA CLARA

| **Madison Street Inn** | $$-B&B | Full breakfast |
|---|---|---|
| 1390 Madison St.,  95050 | 5 rooms, 3 pb | Lunch, dinner w/notice |
| 408-249-5541 Fax: 408-249-6676 | AmEx, MC, Visa, | Comp. wine & beverages |
| 800-491-5541 | *Rated*, • | library, sitting room |
| Theresa & Ralph Wigginton | C-yes/S-ltd/P-no/H-no | hot tub, bicycles, pool |
| All year | French | |

*Santa Clara's only inn! A beautiful Victorian; landscaped gardens. Eggs Benedict is a brkfast favorite. Near Winchester Mystery House. Wknd dinner package.* **10% off stay, ask.**

## SANTA CRUZ

| **Babbling Brook Inn** | $$$-B&B | Full buffet breakfast |
|---|---|---|
| 1025 Laurel St.,  95060 | 12 rooms, 12 pb | Comp. wine, refreshments |
| 408-427-2437 Fax: 408-427-2457 | Most CC, *Rated*, • | Picnic baskets |
| 800-866-1131 | C-ltd/S-ltd/P-no/H-ltd | phone & TV in rooms |
| Helen King | | romantic garden gazebo |
| All year | | |

*Secluded among waterfalls, gardens, Laurel Creek, pines & redwoods. Country French decor; 10 fireplaces. Jet tubs in 4 rooms. Historic waterwheel. Garden gazebo weddings.*

| **Chateau Victorian, B&B Inn** | $$$-B&B | Continental plus bkfst. |
|---|---|---|
| 118 First St.,  95060 | 7 rooms, 7 pb | Comp. wine & cheese |
| 408-458-9458 | AmEx, MC, Visa, | Sitting room |
| Alice June | *Rated*, | 2 decks, patio |
| All year | S-no/P-no/H-no | fireplaces in rooms |

*One block from the beach and the boardwalk, in the heart of the Santa Cruz fun area. All rooms have queen-size beds with private bathrooms.* **7th night free.**

| **Cliff Crest B&B Inn** | $$$-B&B | Full gourmet breakfast |
|---|---|---|
| 407 Cliff St.,  95060 | 5 rooms, 5 pb | Evening wine & tidbits |
| 408-427-2609 Fax: 408-427-2710 | AmEx, MC, Visa, | Sitting room, library |
| 800-427-2609 | *Rated*, • | king size bed available |
| Bruce & Sharon Taylor | C-ltd/S-no/P-no/H-yes | |
| All year | | |

*Romantic Victorian mansion. Five unique rooms w/private baths, fireplaces, solarium, belvedere, breakfast in bed. One block to beach, boardwalk.*

| **Darling House B&B, The** | $$$-B&B/MAP | Continental plus bkfst. |
|---|---|---|
| 314 W. Cliff Dr.,  95060 | 8 rooms, 2 pb | Comp. dinner-wknite pkg. |
| 408-458-1958 | AmEx, MC, Visa, | Beverage, orchids in rm. |
| Darrell & Karen Darling | *Rated*, • | library, hot tub spa |
| All year | C-ltd/S-ltd/P-no/H-ltd | double size bathtubs |

*1910 ocean side mansion with beveled glass, Tiffany lamps, Chippendale antiques, open hearths and hardwood interiors. Walk to beach.* **2 nites for the price of one, ltd.**

SANTA CRUZ ───────────────────────────────

| **Inn Laguna Creek** | $$$-B&B | Full breakfast |
| 2727 Smith Grade,  95060 | 3 rooms, 3 pb | Afternoon tea, snacks |
| 408-425-0692  800-730-5398 | Most CC, *Rated*, | Sitting room, library |
| Jim & Gay Holley | C-ltd/S-no/P-no/H-no | wet bar, CD player |
| All year | | VCR & movies, lawn |

*A distinctive redwood retreat surrounded by coastal redwoods, nestled beside babbling Laguna Creek and sheltered from the outside world. Vegetarian breakfast with notice.*

| **Pleasure Point Inn** | $$$-B&B | Continental plus bkfst. |
| 2-3665 East Cliff Dr.,  95062 | 3 rooms, 3 pb | Comp. wine/cheese |
| 408-475-4657 | MC, Visa, *Rated*, • | Frplcs., whirlpool tubs |
| Sal & Margaret Margo | C-yes | 2 suites, TV, phones |
| All year | | day cruises on yacht |

*On beach, overlooking beautiful Monterey Bay. Walk to beach & shopping village. Rooms include private bath, sitting room & deck. Motor yacht available for fishing or cruises.*

| **Valley View** | $$$$-B&B | Full breakfast |
| P.O. Box 67438, 95067 | 2 rooms, 2 pb | Aft. tea, snacks, wine |
| 600 Hacienda Dr. | Most CC, *Rated*, • | Sitting room, library |
| 415-321-5195   Fax: 415-325-5121 | C-ltd/S-no/P-no/H-no | bicycles, hot tubs |
| Tricia Young | German, Spanish | 10 minutes to beach |
| All year | | |

*Secluded, romantic getaway! Un-hosted, self-catered contemporary glass & redwood house in forest overlooking 20,000 acre redwoods. Hot tub, fireplace, TV/VCR.* **7th night free.**

SANTA CRUZ, BEN LOMOND ───────────────────────

| **Chateau des Fleurs** | $$$-B&B | Full breakfast |
| 7995 Hwy 9,  95005 | 3 rooms, 3 pb | Complimentary wine |
| 408-336-8943  800-257-3594 | Most CC, • | Sitting room, library |
| Lee & Laura Jonas | C-yes/S-no/P-no/H-no | antique piano, hiking, |
| All year | German | swimming, tennis nearby |

*A Victorian mansion once owned by the Bartlett (pear) family, this inn is spacious, special, sensational, historic, quiet, unforgettable, surrounded by evergreens & wineries.*

SANTA MONICA ─────────────────────────────

| **Channel Road Inn** | $$$-B&B | Full breakfast |
| 219 Channel Rd.,  90402 | 14 rooms, 14 pb | Aft. tea, comp. wine |
| 310-459-1920  Fax: 310-454-9920 | MC, Visa, *Rated*, • | Sitting room, library |
| Kathy Jensen | C-yes/S-yes/P-no/H-yes | bikes, hot tubs |
| All year | Spanish, French, | small suite w/fireplace |
| | German | |

*Elegant historic home converted to luxury inn. 1 block from sea & furnished in period antiques. Room with fireplace, deck & ocean view. Historic & intimate . . . so romantic.*

SANTA ROSA ───────────────────────────────

| **Gables Inn, The** | $$$-B&B | Full breakfast |
| 4257 Petaluma Hill Rd., | 8 rooms, 8 pb | Lunch, dinner, snacks |
|   95404 | AmEx, MC, Visa, | Sitting room, piano |
| 707-585-7777 Fax: 707-584-5634 | *Rated*, • | parking, fireplaces |
| 800-GABLESNN | C-ltd/S-no/P-ltd/H-yes | conferences, weddings |
| Mike & Judy Ogne | | |
| All year | | |

*Built in 1877, on Nat'l Register of Historic Places. Museum-quality restoration, European-Victorian decor. Gateway to wine country; elegant, rural location. Cottage w/jacuzzi.*

## SANTA ROSA

**Melitta Station Inn**
5850 Melita Rd., 95409
707-538-7712  800-504-3099
Diane & Vic
All year

$$-B&B
6 rooms, 4 pb
MC, Visa, *Rated*, •
C-ltd/S-ltd/P-no/H-no

Full breakfast
Complimentary wine
Sitting room

*Restored railroad station in a beautiful country setting across the road from parks. Wineries nearby. Elegant country breakfast.* **Midweek 10% discount, except holidays.**

**Pygmalion House B&B**
331 Orange St., 95401
707-526-3407  Fax: 707-526-3407
Caroline
All year

$$-B&B
5 rooms, 5 pb
*Rated*, •
C-ltd/S-ltd/P-no/H-no

Full breakfast
Sparkling cider & snacks
Sitting room, fireplace
TV in rooms, veranda
tree covered gardens

*Lovely antiques from Gypsy Rose Lee and Sally Stanford. Memorabilia from both - even Raymond Burr is represented. Antiques are for sale.*

**Vintners Inn**
4350 Barnes Rd., 95403
707-575-7350  Fax: 707-575-1426
800-421-2584
Cindy Duffy
All year

$$$$-B&B
44 rooms, 44 pb
Most CC, *Rated*, •
C-yes/S-yes/P-no/H-yes
Spanish

Continental plus bkfst.
Restaurant, bar
Sitting room
hot tubs, wine touring
nearby tennis, pool

*European-styled country inn surrounded by a 50-acre vineyard. Antique furniture, conference facilities. Home of John Ash & Co. Restaurant. AAA Four Diamond rating.*

## SAUSALITO

**Casa Madrona Hotel**
801 Bridgeway, 94965
415-332-0502  Fax: 415-533-2537
800-567-9524
John W. Mays
All year

$$$-B&B
34 rooms, 34 pb
AmEx, MC, Visa,
*Rated*, •
C-ltd/S-yes/P-no/H-ltd
German, French,
Spanish

Continental plus bkfst.
Restaurant
Wine & cheese hour
outdoor dining, spa
VCR in rooms/VCR library

*Casa Madrona offers the privacy and coziness of a European country inn with individually decorated rooms, spectacular views of S.F. Bay & yacht harbor. Pacific Rim cuisine.*

**Inn Above Tide, The**
30 El Portal, 94965
415-332-9535  Fax: 415-332-6714
800-893-8433
Verena Zurcher & M.
Flaherty
All year

$$$$-B&B
30 rooms, 30 pb
Visa, MC, AmEx, •
C-yes/S-no/P-no/H-yes
Spanish, German

Continental plus bkfst.
Comp. wine and cheese
Meeting room, massages
binoculars, spa services
data ports, hair dryers

*Guest rooms w/private balconies each with breathtaking, panoramic views of the San Francisco Bay & Skyline. Located in the heart of Sausalito. Most rooms have fireplaces.*

## SEAL BEACH

**Seal Beach Inn & Gardens**
212 - 5th St., 90704
310-493-2416  Fax: 310-799-0483
800-HIDEAWAY
M. Bettenhausen-Schmaehl
All year

$$$-B&B
23 rooms, 23 pb
AmEx, MC, Visa,
*Rated*, •
C-ltd/S-ltd/P-no/H-no

Lavish full breakfast
Comp. wine and cheese
Fruit, tea, coffee
sitting rooms, library
pool, jacuzzis, frplcs.

*Elegant historic So. CA Inn, 1 block from ocean beach in charming seaside town. Lush gardens, lovely estate appearance. Exquisite rooms & suites.* **Free gift at checkout.**

SEBASTOPOL ───────────────────────────────

| **Green Apple Inn** | $$$-B&B | Full breakfast |
|---|---|---|
| 520 Bohemian Hwy., 95472 | 4 rooms, 4 pb | Comp. wine |
| 707-874-2526 | MC, Visa, | Sitting room w/fireplace |
| Rogers & Rosemary Hoffman | C-ltd/H-yes | bicycles |
| All year | Spanish | |

*1860 farmhouse in a sunny meadow backed by redwoods. Located in a designated historic village near coast and wine country.* **3rd night 50% off.**

SODA SPRINGS ───────────────────────────────

| **Royal Gorge Rainbow** | $$$-B&B | Full breakfast |
|---|---|---|
| **Lodge** | 33 rooms, 10 pb | Restaurant, lunch |
| P.O. Box 1100, 95728 | MC, Visa, *Rated*, • | Dinner, snacks |
| 50080 Hampshire Rock Rd. | C-yes/S-yes/P-no/H-yes | bar service, library |
| 916-426-3871  Fax: 916-426-9221 | | sitting room |
| 800-500-3871 | | |
| Jacqui James   All year | | |

*Cozy & romantic with Swiss-Italian cuisine. Enjoy a winter skiers paradise or summer serenity by the Yuba River. Hiking, biking, fishing areas.* **Comp. bottle of wine.**

SONOMA ───────────────────────────────

| **Cottage, The** | $$$-B&B | Continental plus bkfst. |
|---|---|---|
| 302 First St. E., 95476 | 3 rooms, 3 pb | Private courtyard |
| 707-996-0719  Fax: 707-939-7913 | C-ltd/S-ltd/P-no/H-ltd | fireplaces, hot tubs |
| Robert Behrens/Marga | | seating in each room |
| Friberg | | |
| All year | | |

*Luxury accommodations, garden entries & private gardens, fireplaces & cathedral ceilings, a short stroll from the Plaza, shops & restaurants.*

---

| **Sonoma Chalet B&B** | $$$-B&B | Continental plus bkfst. |
|---|---|---|
| 18935 Fifth St. W., 95476 | 7 rooms, 4 pb | Comp. sherry, tea/coffee |
| 707-938-3129  800-938-3129 | AmEx, MC, Visa, | Sitting room, fireplaces |
| Joe Leese | *Rated*, • | wood burning stoves |
| All year exc. Christmas | C-ltd/S-ltd/P-ltd/H-no | garden, spa, bicycles |

*Swiss-style chalet & country cottages located in the beautiful Sonoma Valley. Romantic, antique filled rooms. Wonderful country farm setting near historic plaza and wineries.*

---

| **Sonoma Hotel** | $$-B&B | Continental breakfast |
|---|---|---|
| 110 W. Spain St., 95476 | 17 rooms, 5 pb | Comp. wine, snacks |
| 707-996-2996  Fax: 707-996-7014 | AmEx, MC, Visa, | Restaurant, bar |
| 800-468-6016 | *Rated*, • | lunch, dinner (fee) |
| Dorene & John Musilli | C-yes/S-yes | garden patio |
| All year | | |

*Nationally acclaimed vintage hotel w/bed & breakfast ambiance, exceptional dining amidst antiques or on the garden patio. Sunday brunch.* **Winter packages available.**

---

| **Trojan Horse Inn** | $$$-B&B | Full breakfast |
|---|---|---|
| 19455 Sonoma Hway, 95476 | 6 rooms, 6 pb | Complimentary wine |
| 707-996-2430  Fax: 707-996-9185 | Visa, MC, *Rated*, • | Hors d'oeuvres |
| 800-899-1925 | C-ltd/S-no/P-no/H-yes | outside jacuzzi, bikes |
| John & Doris Leonard | | |
| All year | | |

*Beautifully decorated 1887 Victorian, 6 rooms, private baths, full breakfast. Spa, bicycles, complimentary hors d'oevres with wine and wine country hospitality.*

SONOMA ─────────────────────────

**Victorian Garden Inn**
316 E. Napa St., 95476
707-996-5339 Fax: 707-996-1689
800-543-5339
Donna Lewis
All year

$$$-B&B
4 rooms, 3 pb
AmEx, MC, Visa,
*Rated*, •
C-ltd/S-ltd/P-no/H-no
Spanish

Continental plus bkfst.
Sitting room
piano, therapuetic spa
swimming pool

*Secluded, large 1870 Greek revival farmhouse. Antiques, private entrances, fireplaces, Victorian rose gardens, winding paths, near plaza. Gracious hospitality.*

SONORA ─────────────────────────

**Barretta Gardens B&B Inn**
700 S. Barretta St., 95370
209-532-6039 Fax: 209-532-8257
800-206-3333
Nancy & Mike Brandt
All year

$$$-B&B
5 rooms, 5 pb
AmEx, MC, Visa,
*Rated*, •
C-ltd/S-ltd/P-no/H-no

Full breakfast
Comp. beverages
Sitting rooms, library
firelplace, solarium
1 & 2 bedroom suites

*Our turn-of-the-century Victorian overlooks Sonora & Sierra Foothill sunsets. Antique furnishings, terraced gardens, whirlpool bath for 2. Near Yosemite. Theatre & golf packages. **3rd night 30% off.***

───────────────────────────────

**Hammons House Inn B&B**
22963 Robertson Ranch,
  95370
209-532-7921
Linda Hammons
All year

$$-EP
4 rooms, 3 pb
Visa, MC, AmEx,
C-yes/S-ltd/P-no

Full breakfast
Snacks, diet specials
Sitting room, pool
TV, VCR, phones
new Platinum Suite-ask!

*Where time slows down, tranquillity abounds. Enjoy panoramic views from the main inn or private, 2-story bungalow w/frplc. New suite w/frplc. & 2 person jacuzzi. **3rd. nite 50%.***

───────────────────────────────

**Lavender Hill B&B**
683 S. Barretta St., 95370
209-532-9024
Jean & Charlie Marinelli
All year

$$-B&B
4 rooms, 4 pb
Most CC *Rated*, •
C-yes/S-ltd/P-no/H-no
Italian

Full breakfast
Comp. coffee or tea
Sitting rm., porch swing
phone & TV available
one room w/king bed

*Restored Victorian in historic Gold Country. Antique furnishings, lovely grounds, porch swing & unmatched hospitality. Walk to town. Near Yosemite. Small conferences. **Dinner & theatre packages***

───────────────────────────────

**Ryan House, 1855**
153 S. Shepherd St., 95370
209-533-3445  800-831-4897
Nancy & Guy Hoffman
All year

$$$-B&B
3 rooms, 3 pb
MC, Visa, *Rated*, •
C-ltd/S-no/P-no/H-no

Full breakfast
Aftn. tea, comp. wine
Sitting room, 2 parlors
newly decorated dining
room w/antique oak table

*Gold Rush romance in historic Mother Lode, nearby fine dining & antique shops. Suite available w/parlor, 2 person bathtub. **Comp. bottle of local wine, 3rd night.***

───────────────────────────────

**Serenity - A B&B Inn**
15305 Bear Cub Dr., 95370
209-533-1441  800-426-1441
Fred & Charlotte Hoover
All year

$$$-B&B
4 rooms, 4 pb
Most CC, *Rated*, •
C-ltd/S-ltd/P-no/H-no

Full breakfast
Comp. tea/wine/lemonade
Sitting room, library
queen/twin beds, veranda
beautiful grounds

*Enjoy relaxed elegance in 19th-century-styled home. Large rooms, library, veranda, and 6 acres of wooded grounds with pines, wildflowers and wildlife. Fireplaces in 2 rooms.*

*The Artists' Inn, South Pasadena, CA*

## SONORA, TUOLUMNE

| | | |
|---|---|---|
| **Oak Hill Ranch B&B** | $$-B&B | Full gourmet breakfast |
| P.O. Box 307, 95379 | 5 rooms, 3 pb | Comp. tea, coffee |
| 18550 Connally Ln. | *Rated*, | Gazebos, gardens |
| 209-928-4717 | C-ltd/S-no/P-no/H-yes | player piano, organ |
| Sanford & Jane Grover | | sitting room, fireplaces |
| All year | | |

*"For a perfect sojourn into the past," spacious rural Victorian on 56 acres, near three state parks and Yosemite in California Gold Country. Hiking, horseback riding nearby. **One-on-one discounts.***

## SOUTH PASADENA

| | | |
|---|---|---|
| **Artists' Inn** | $$$-B&B | Full breakfast |
| 1038 Magnolia St.,  91030 | Visa, MC, AmEx | Aftn.tea, Teas for 20-30 |
| 818-799-5668  Fax: 818-799-3678 | *Rated*, • | Events, Sitting room |
| 888-799-5668 | C-yes/S-no/P-no/H-no | front porch, wicker |
| Lisa Carroll    All year | | rose garden, canopy beds |

*Delightful 100-year-old Victorian farmhouse in charming South Pasadena - antiques, fresh flowers in rms. Large porch for gourmet breakfasts & aftn tea. **2 nites, 2 dinners, 1 lunch, champagne for $299.***

| | | |
|---|---|---|
| **Bissell House B&B** | $$$ | Cont. plus bkfst. wkdays |
| 201 Orange Grove Ave., | 3 rooms, 3 pb | Full breakfast weekends |
|  91030 | Visa, MC, AmEx, | Snacks, comp. wine |
| 818-441-3535  Fax: 818-441-3671 | *Rated*, • | sitting room, library |
| 800-441-3530 | C-ltd/S-ltd/P-no/H-no | hot tubs, jacuzzi tub |
| Russell & Leonore Butcher | Spanish | |
| All year | | |

*1887 Victorian beautifully decorated with antiques. Twelve minutes and 100 years from downtown L.A. Walk to Old Town Pasadena. Business and vacation travelers welcome.*

SPRINGVILLE ───────────────────────────────

| **Annie's B&B** | $$$-B&B | Full breakfast |
|---|---|---|
| 33024 Globe Dr., 93265 | 3 rooms, 3 pb | Dinner, afternoon tea |
| 209-539-3827 | Most CC, *Rated*, • | Snacks, comp. wine, pool |
| Annie & John Bozanich | C-ltd/S-no/P-no/H-no | sitting room, hot tubs |
| All year | | Cancellation policy |

*Quiet, beautifully furnished w/antiques, on 5 acres in the Sierra foothills. Full breakfast cooked on a wood stove. Relax on deck overlooking pool/spa. 3rd night 10% off.*

ST. HELENA ───────────────────────────────

| **Bartels Ranch/Country Inn** | $$$$-B&B | Full breakfast |
|---|---|---|
| 1200 Conn Valley Rd., 94574 | 4 rooms, 4 pb | Catered lunch & dinner |
| 707-963-4001  Fax: 707-963-5100 | Most CC, *Rated*, • | Comp. wine/fruit/cheese |
| 800-932-4002 | C-ltd/S-yes/P-no/H-yes | library, sauna, jacuzzi |
| Jami E. Bartels | Spanish, German | darts, horseshoes, golf |
| All year | | |

*Elegant, secluded wine country estate; ideal for honeymoon. 10,000-acre view, frplc., billiards, bicycles, TV/VCR & phones in all rooms. Champagne under stars. 3rd night 50%, ltd; Free bottle of wine.*

| **Bylund House B&B** | $$$-B&B | Continental plus bkfst. |
|---|---|---|
| 2000 Howell Mtn. Rd., 94574 | 2 rooms, 2 pb | Wine & hors d'oeuvres |
| 707-963-9073 | *Rated*, • | Sitting rm. w/fireplace |
| Bill & Diane | S-ltd/P-no/H-no | swimming pool, bicycles |
| All year | | spa with deck |

*Wine country villa designed by owner-architect in secluded valley with sweeping views. 2 private rooms with views, balconies and European feather beds. 3rd night, 50% off.*

| **Chestelson House B&B** | $$$-B&B | Full breakfast |
|---|---|---|
| 1417 Kearney St., 94574 | 3 rooms, 3 pb | Snacks |
| 707-963-2238  800-959-4505 | Visa, MC, *Rated*, • | One room with whirlpool |
| Jackie Sweet | C-ltd/S-ltd/P-no/H-no | |
| All year | | |

*Warm hospitality with individual attention to making your trip a wonderful experience of sampling restaurants and wineries. Gourmet breakfast.*

| **Cinnamon Bear B&B** | $$$-B&B | Full breakfast |
|---|---|---|
| 1407 Kearney St., 94574 | 3 rooms, 3 pb | Comp. snacks |
| 707-963-4653  Fax: 707-963-0251 | MC, Visa, *Rated*, • | Sitting room, games |
| Cathye Ranieri | C-ltd/S-no/P-no/H-no | fireplace, piano |
| All year | | classical music or swing |

*Homesick for a visit to your favorite aunt's house? Bring your teddy and come to the Napa Valley wine country. Midweek rates discounted, ltd.*

| **Deer Run Inn** | $$$$-B&B | Full breakfast |
|---|---|---|
| P.O. Box 311, 94574 | 3 rooms, 3 pb | Complimentary wine |
| 3995 Spring Mtn. Rd. | Visa, MC, AmEx, • | Library, pool, Ping Pong |
| 707-963-3794  Fax: 707-963-9026 | C-ltd/S-no/P-no/H-no | horseshoes, featherbeds |
| 800-843-3408 | | frplcs., priv. entrances |
| Tom & Carol Wilson | | |
| All year | | |

*Romantic, cozy country hideaway, furnished in antiques, wrapped in treed deckings on four acres of forest. Situated in the heart of the Napa Valley wine country.*

ST. HELENA ───────────────────────────────────

| **Erika's-Hillside** | $$$-B&B | Continental breakfast |
|---|---|---|
| 285 Fawn Park,   94574 | 3 rooms, 2 pb | Comp. sparkling water |
| 707-963-2887 | *Rated*, ● | Sitting room |
| Erika Cunningham | C-yes/S-ltd/P-no/H-no | |
| All year | German | |

*Enjoy a peaceful & romantic retreat nestled on a hillside overlooking the Silverado Trail with inspiring views of the Napa Valley and its vineyards.* **3rd weekday night free, Nov.–May.**

| **Hilltop House B&B** | $$$-B&B | Full breakfast |
|---|---|---|
| P.O. Box 726, 94574 | 3 rooms, 3 pb | Comp sherry after dinner |
| 9550 St. Helena Rd. | MC, Visa, *Rated*, ● | Guest refrigerator |
| 707-944-0880 Fax: 707-571-0263 | C-yes/S-no/P-no/H-yes | sitting room, hot tub |
| Annette Gevarter | | hiking trails |
| All year | | |

*Secluded mountain hideaway in romantic setting on 135 acres of unspoiled wilderness, offers a hang glider's view of Mayacamas Mountains. Spa on deck.* **10% off stay, ask.**

| **Shady Oaks Country Inn** | $$$$-B&B | Full gourmet w/champagne |
|---|---|---|
| 399 Zinfandel Ln.,   94574 | 4 rooms, 4 pb | Picnic basket |
| 707-963-1190 | *Rated*, ● | Wine & hors d'oeuvres |
| John & Lisa Wild-Runnells | C-ltd/S-no/P-no/H-yes | horseshoes, croquet |
| All year | | sightseeing tips, garden |

*Romantic, secluded on 2 acres among finest wineries in Napa Valley. Elegant ambience; country comfort; antiques; warm hospitality.* **Off-season midweek rates available.**

| **Villa St. Helena** | $$$$-B&B | Continental plus bkfst. |
|---|---|---|
| 2727 Sulphur Springs Av, | 3 rooms, 3 pb | Complimentary wine |
| 94574 | AmEx, MC, Visa, | Swimming pool |
| 707-963-2514 Fax: 707-963-2624 | *Rated*, ● | library, hiking |
| Ralph & Carolyn Cotton | C-ltd/S-ltd/P-no/H-no | walking trails |
| All year | | |

*Secluded hilltop Mediterranean villa overlooking Napa Valley. Romantic antique-filled rooms, fireplaces, private entrances; elaborate bkfst. Country elegance.* **4th nite free.**

STINSON BEACH ───────────────────────────────

| **Casa Del Mar** | $$$-B&B | Full breakfast |
|---|---|---|
| P.O. Box 238,   94970 | 5 rooms, 5 pb | Comp. wine, juice |
| 415-868-2124 Fax: 415-868-2305 | AmEx, MC, Visa, | Hors d'oeuvres |
| 800-552-2124 | *Rated*, ● | sitting room, library |
| Rick Klein | C-ltd/S-no/P-no/H-no | garden, near ocean |
| All year | | |

*Romantic ocean views, historic garden, delicious breakfasts, colorful artwork, and you can hear the waves break all day long.* **10% discount Monday-Thursday, excl. holidays.**

SUMMERLAND ───────────────────────────────────

| **Inn on Summer Hill** | $$$$-B&B | Full gourmet breakfast |
|---|---|---|
| P.O. Box 376, 93067 | 16 rooms, 16 pb | Afternoon tea & wine |
| 2520 Lillie Ave. | AmEx, MC, Visa, | Sitting room, library |
| 805-969-9998 Fax: 805-565-9946 | *Rated*, ● | room service, jacuzzi |
| 800-845-5566 | C-ltd/S-no/P-no/H-yes | fireplaces, canopy beds |
| Verlinda Richardson | Spanish | |
| All year | | |

*Elegant, romantic European inn. Decks & balcony overlooking Pacific, spa, antiques. One of Country Inn magazine's top 12 inns for 1993. ABBA top rated inn.* **3rd night 50%, Mon-Thur, ltd.**

SUTTER CREEK ─────────────────────────────────────────────

**Gold Quartz Inn, The**
15 Bryson Dr., 95685
209-267-9155  Fax: 209-267-9170
800-752-8738
Wendy Woolrich
All year

$$$-B&B
24 rooms, 24 pb
MC, Visa, •
S-no/P-no/H-yes

Full breakfast
Afternoon tea, beverages
Food catered for groups
porch, picnics, A/C
TV in rm./conference rm.

*Tucked away in charming Gold Country town. Step back 100 years. Rooms are decorated with antique furniture, prints and charming small touches, and have private porches.*

---

**Hanford House B&B Inn**
P.O. Box 1450, 95685
61 Hanford St., Hwy. 49
209-267-0747  Fax: 209-267-1825
800-871-5839
Bob & Karen Tierno
All year

$$$-B&B
10 rooms, 10 pb
MC, Visa, *Rated*, •
C-ltd/S-no/P-no/H-yes
American Sign
Language

Full breakfast
Complimentary wine
Sitting room
gift boutique

*A country inn in historic Sutter Creek. Spacious rooms, queen-sized beds, air-conditioned, private baths. Large deck, parlor and patio. Suite w/Jacuzzi tub. Room w/fireplace.* **15% disc't Sun.–Fri.**

---

**Sutter Creek Inn**
P.O. Box 385, 95685
75 Main St.
209-267-5606  Fax: 209-267-9287
Jane Way
All year

$$-B&B
18 rooms, 18 pb
•
C-ltd/S-ltd/P-no/H-no

Full breakfast
Comp. refreshments
Sitting room, piano
library, A/C, fishing
reflexology, graphology

*Lovely country inn known for swinging beds & fireplaces. Beautiful grounds w/hammocks & chaise lounges. Professional massage & handwriting analysis. 2 rooms have hot tub for 2, frplc., & queen bed.*

TAHOE CITY ─────────────────────────────────────────────

**Chaney House**
P.O. Box 7852, 96145
4725 W. Lake Blvd.
916-525-7333  Fax: 916-525-4413
Gary & Lori Chaney
All year

$$$-B&B
4 rooms, 4 pb
Visa, MC, *Rated*, •
C-ltd/S-no/P-no/H-no

Full breakfast
Sitting room, bicycles
private beach and pier

*Unique stone lakefront home. Gourmet breakfast on patios overlooking the lake in season. Private beach and pier. Close to ski areas.*

---

**Mayfield House B&B**
P.O. Box 5999, 96145
236 Grove St.
916-583-1001
Bruce & Cynthia Knauss
All year

$$-B&B
6 rooms, 3 pb
MC, Visa, *Rated*, •
C-ltd/S-ltd/P-no/H-yes

Full breakfast
Comp. wine, brandy
Cheese & crackers

*Within walking distance to shops and restaurants. Each room individually decorated— "spit-spat" clean. Convenient shuttle to skiing.* **10% discount for 5+ nights.**

---

**River Ranch Lodge**
P.O. Box 197, 96145
2285 River Rd.
916-583-4264  Fax: 916-583-7237
800-535-9900
Pete Friedrichsen    All year

$-B&B
22 rooms, 22 pb
AmEx, MC, Visa,
*Rated*, •
C-yes/S-yes/P-yes/H-no

Continental breakfast
Dinner, bar
Close to skiing, hiking
river rafting, fishing
horesback riding

*High Sierra lodge furnished with antiques, on the banks of the Truckee River. One mile from Squaw Valley's famous ski slopes. Wild game & steak restaurant.*

### TAHOE VISTA

**Shore House at Lake Tahoe**
P.O. Box 343, 96148
7170 North Lake Blvd.
916-546-7270  Fax: 916-546-7130
800-207-5160
Marty & Barb Cohen
All year

$$$-B&B
9 rooms, 9 pb
Visa, MC, *Rated*, •
C-ltd/S-no/P-no/H-no

Full gourmet breakfast
Afternoon tea, snacks
Complimentary wine
Sitting room, hot tubs
Skiing, hiking, biking

*Romantic lakefront hideaway, custom log beds, down comforters, feather beds. Gourmet breakfast in lakefront dining room or at lakefront lawns and gardens.*

### TEMECULA

**Loma Vista B&B**
33350 La Serena Way,  92591
909-676-7047  Fax: 909-676-0077
Betty & Dick Ryan
All year

$$$-B&B
6 rooms, 6 pb
Visa, MC, *Rated*, •
C-yes/S-no/P-no/H-no
Spanish

Full champagne bkfst.
Complimentary wine/snack
Sitting room, library
bicycles
hot tubs, firepit

*Mission style home, built as a B&B, located in the heart of the So. California wine country, surrounded by lush citrus groves and premium vineyards. Special weekday rate/pkgs.*

### TEMPLETON

**Country House Inn**
91 Main St.,  93465
805-434-1598  800-362-6032
Dianne Garth
All year

$$$-B&B
5 rooms, 5 pb
*Rated*, •
C-ltd/S-no/P-no/H-no

Full breakfast
Comp. refreshments
Picnic lunches w/notice
dining & sitting room
room with fireplace

*Home built in 1886 by founder of Templeton. Spacious bedrooms, antiques, fresh flowers, beautiful gardens. Near 28 wineries, Hearst Castle, restaurants. 3rd night 50% Off.*

### TRINIDAD

**Lost Whale Inn, The**
3452 Patrick's Pt. Dr.,  95570
707-677-3425  800-677-7859
Susanne Lakin & Lee Miller
All year

$$$-B&B
8 rooms, 8 pb
Visa, MC, Disc, *Rated*,
•
C-yes/S-no/P-no/H-no

Full gourmet breakfast
Afternoon tea, snacks
Complimentary wine/soda
sitting room, hot tubs
full playground, garden

*The only B&B in CA with a private beach. Spectacular ocean view, sea lions, greenhouse, gardens, decks, jacuzzi, and huge breakfast. Newly remodeled. 10% discount, ask.*

**Trinidad Bay B&B**
P.O. Box 849, 95570
560 Edwards St.
707-677-0840
Paul & Carol Kirk
All year

$$$-B&B
4 rooms, 4 pb
Visa, MC, Disc.,
C-ltd/S-no/P-no

Full breakfast
Comp. beverages & snacks
Sitting rooms, walk to
beaches and redwoods
ocean views all rooms

*Sitting high above the rugged North Coast, this Cape Cod house provides the most picturesque view of the Pacific to be seen anywhere! Minutes to Redwook National Park.*

### TRUCKEE

**Richardson House**
P.O. Box 2011, 96160
10154 High St.
916-587-5388  Fax: 916-587-0927
Jeannine Karnofsky
All year

$$$-B&B
6 rooms, 1 pb
MC, Visa, •
C-yes/S-no/P-no/H-no

Continental plus bkfst.
Wine & cheese
Sitting room,
bicycles, raft
cats in residence

*Restored 1880s Victorian with period furnishings in historic Truckee; walk to Amtrak or bus service, minutes to Tahoe north shore skiing. Room for small groups & weddings.*

UKIAH ————————————————————————————

| **Vichy Hot Springs Resort** | $$$$-B&B | Full breakfast |
| 2605 Vichy Springs Rd., | 14 rooms, 14 pb | Restaurant, lunch/dinner |
| 95482 | Most CC, *Rated*, • | Sitting room, library |
| 707-462-9515  Fax: 707-462-9516 | C-yes/S-no/P-no/H-yes | mineral baths, pool |
| Gilbert & Marjorie Ashoff | Spanish | sauna, 700-acre ranch |
| All year | | |

*A true historic country inn—quiet, elegant, and charming. The baths are incomparable memories for a lifetime. Swedish massage.* **2nd night free January–March, ltd.**

VALLEY FORD ————————————————————————

| **Inn at Valley Ford** | $$-B&B | Full breakfast |
| P.O. Box 439, 94972 | 4 rooms, | Complimentary tea |
| 14395 Hwy 1 | MC, Visa, *Rated*, • | Hot tub, spas, bikes |
| 707-876-3182 | C-ltd/S-ltd/P-no/H-ltd | conference facilities |
| N. Balashov, S. Nicholls | French | sitting room, fishing |
| All year | | |

*Comfortable Victorian farmhouse furnished with antiques, books and flowers. Located in rolling, pastoral hills, minutes from the Pacific & Sonoma Wine Country.*

VENTURA ————————————————————————————

| **Bella Maggiore Inn** | $$-B&B | Full breakfast |
| 67 S. California St., 93001 | 24 rooms, 24 pb | Comp. wine, snacks |
| 805-652-0277  800-523-8479 | AmEx, MC, Visa, | Sitting room, lobby |
| Thomas J. Wood | *Rated*, • | spas in some rooms |
| All year | C-yes/S-yes/P-no/H-ltd | sundeck, conference room |

*Enjoy European elegance—garden courtyard, chandeliers, antiques, original artwork, grand piano in lobby & downstairs shops.* **Business rates; Comp. champagne for honeymoon/anniversaries.**

| **La Mer B&B** | $$$-B&B | Bavarian full breakfast |
| 411 Poli St., 93001 | 5 rooms, 5 pb | Comp. wine or champagne |
| 805-643-3600  Fax: 805-653-7329 | MC, Visa, AmEx, | Picnic baskets, library |
| Gisela Baida | *Rated*, • | therapeutic massages |
| All year | C-ltd/S-no/P-no/H-no | antique carriage rides |
| | German, Spanish | |

*Authentic European style in old Victorian. Ocean view, three blocks to beach. Private entrances. Special packages available.* **20% off Monday thru Thursday nights.**

VOLCANO ————————————————————————————

| **St. George Hotel** | $$-EP/MAP | Full breakfast |
| P.O. Box 9, 95689 | 20 rooms, 6 pb | Dinner included, bar |
| 16104 Pine Grove | C-ltd/S-no/P-ltd/H-ltd | Sitting room, pianos |
| 209-296-4458 Fax: 209-296-4458 | | new porches & deck |
| Marlene & Chuck Inman | | meeting facilities |
| Wed-Sun, mid-Feb—Dec | | |

*Elegant Mother Lode hotel built in 1862. Maintains a timeless quality. On Nat'l Resistry of Historic Places. Back-to-1862 porches and balausters.* **2nd night, 50%.**

WESTPORT ————————————————————————————

| **Howard Creek Ranch** | $$-B&B | Full ranch breakfast |
| P.O. Box 121, 95488 | 10 rooms, 8 pb | Complimentary tea |
| 40501 N. Hwy 1 | MC, Visa, AmEx, | Piano, hot tub, cabins |
| 707-964-6725 | *Rated*, • | sauna, massage by resv. |
| Charles & Sally Grigg | C-ltd/S-ltd/P-ltd/H-ltd | heated swimming pool |
| All year | German, Italian, Dutch | |

*Historic farmhouse filled with collectibles, antiques & memorabilia, unique health spa with privacy and dramatic views adjoining a wide beach. Award-winning flower garden.*

## WINDSOR

**Country Meadow Inn**
11360 Old Redwood Hwy,
   95492
707-431-1276  800-238-1728
Susan Hardesty
All year

$$$-B&B
5 rooms, 5 pb
MC, Visa *Rated*, •
C-ltd/S-ltd/P-no/H-yes

Full breakfast
Refreshments, wet bar
Sitting room, library
games, hot tubs in room
pool, Victorian garden

*Romantic & comfortable. Fireplaces, whirlpool tubs, decks, flower gardens, tennis court, swimming & a freshness that extends to the abundant gourmet breakfast. **10% off wkdays.***

## YOSEMITE NAT'L PARK

**Waldschloss B&B**
7486 Henness Circle,
Yosemite West,   95389
209-372-4958
John & Betty Clark
Closed Dec.-Feb.

$$$-B&B
2 rooms, 2 pb
Visa, MC, *Rated*, •
C-ltd/S-no/P-no/H-no
Some German

Full breakfast
Afternoon tea, snacks
Sitting room

*Minutes to wonders of Yosemite National Park. Starry nights, old toys, home cooked breakfasts and hospitality await guests. Single nights OK. **3rd night 50% Off.***

## YOSEMITE NATIONAL PARK

**Yosemite Peregrine B&B**
7509 Henness Circle,  95389
209-372-8517  Fax: 209-372-4241
800-396-3639
Kay & Don Pitts   All year

$$$-B&B
3 rooms, 3 pb
Visa, MC, *Rated*, •
C-ltd/S-no/P-no/H-no

Full breakfast
Snacks, comp. wine
Sitting room, hot tubs
fireplace in each room
view decks

*In Yosemite - away from the crowds. New mountain home filled with original art & furniture. Hike and ski from front door.*

## YOSEMITE(INSIDE PARK)

**Yosemite West High Sierra**
7460 Henness Ridge Rd.,
   95389
209-372-4808
Bob & Karen
All year

$$$-B&B
3 rooms, 2 pb
Visa, MC, AmEx
*Rated*, •
C-ltd/S-no/P-no/H-no

Full breakfast
Afternoon tea
Sitting room
one room with whirlpool

*Large, new mountain home at 6000-ft. elevation, quiet, wooded. Inside Yosemite Park, 15 miles from Yosemite Valley. Experience magnificent sunsets from our large decks.*

## YOSEMITE/OAKHURST

**Chateau du Sureau**
P.O. Box 577, 93644
48688 Victoria Ln.
209-683-6860
E. Kubin-Clanin & R. Clanin
All year

$$$$-B&B
9 rooms, 9 pb
Most CC, *Rated*, •
C-ltd/S-no/P-no/H-yes
German, French, Italian

Full breakfast
Lunch, dinner, aft. tea
Snacks, comp. wine, bar
sitting room, library
pool, outdoor chess

*At our "Estate by the Elderberries" you'll take a step back in time into a world of gracious service & romance. Erna's Elderberry House Restaurant.*

## YOUNTVILLE

**Burgundy House**
P.O. Box 3156, 94599
6711 Washington St.
707-944-0889
Deanna Roque
All year

$$$-B&B
5 rooms, 5 pb
*Rated*, •
C-ltd/S-no/P-no/H-no
French, German

Full breakfast
Comp. wine
Air conditioned
Mobil 4-star rated

*1870 rustic country French stone house with Old World appeal. Furnished with country antiques. Perfect location in beautiful Napa Valley.*

## YOUNTVILLE

| **Maison Fleurie** | $$$-B&B | Full country breakfast |
|---|---|---|
| 6529 Yount St., 94599 | 13 rooms, 13 pb | Wine & hors d'oeuvres |
| 707-944-2056 Fax: 707-944-9342 | Visa, MC, AmEx, | Fireplace rooms |
| 800-788-0369 | *Rated*, • | bicycles |
| Roger Asbill   All year | C-yes/S-no/P-no/H-no | pool & spa |

*Romantic Napa Valley French country inn with terra cotta tiles, exposed brick and hand painted touches throughout. Rooms with fireplaces and spa tubs. Breakfast in bed. A Four Sisters Inn.*

| **Oleander House** | $$$-B&B | Full breakfast |
|---|---|---|
| P.O. Box 2937, 94599 | 4 rooms, 4 pb | Comp. soft drinks |
| 7433 St. Helena Hwy | MC, Visa, *Rated*, • | Sitting room, spa, patio |
| 707-944-8315 Fax: 707-944-4448 | S-no/P-no/H-no | near ballooning, tennis, |
| 800-778-0357 | Spanish | golf, dining, shops |
| John & Louise Packard | | |
| All year | | |

*Country French charm. Antiques. Spacious rooms with brass beds, private decks, fireplaces, central A/C, and Laura Ashley fabrics and wallpapers. Beautiful rose garden.*

## More Inns . . .

| | |
|---|---|
| Albion | Albion Ridge Huckleberry, 29381 Albion Ridge Rd., 95410,  707-937-2374 |
| Albion | Huckleberry House, 29381 Albion Ridge Rd., 95410,  707-937-2374 |
| Albion | Wool Loft, 32751 Navarro Ridge Rd., 95410,  707-937-0377 |
| Alleghany | Kenton Mine Lodge, P.O. Box 942, 95910,  916-287-3212 |
| Alpine | Cedar Creek Inn, P.O. Box 1466, 92001,  619-445-9605 |
| Alturas | Dorris House B&B, P.O. Box 1655, 96101,  916-233-3786 |
| Amador City | Imperial Hotel, P.O. Box 195, 95601 |
| Amador City | Mine House Inn, P.O. Box 245, 95601,  209-267-5900 |
| Angels Camp | Cooper House B&B Inn, P.O. Box 1388, 95222,  209-736-2145 |
| Arcata | Lady Anne Victorian Inn,  902 - 14th St., 95521,  707-822-2797 |
| Arnold | Lodge at Manuel Mill, P.O. Box 998, 95223,  209-795-2622 |
| Arroyo Grande | Crystal Rose Inn, 789 Valley Rd., 93420,  805-481-1854 |
| Arroyo Grande | Guest House, 120 Hart Ln., 93420,  805-481-9304 |
| Atascadero | Lakeview B&B, 9065 Lakeview Dr., 93422,  805-466-5665 |
| Auburn | Lincoln House B&B Inn, The,  191 Lincoln Way, 95603,  916-885-8880 |
| Auburn | Victoria Inn, P.O. Box 9097, 95603 |
| Auburn | Victorian Manor, P.O. Box 959, 95658,  916-663-3009 |
| Avalon | Catalina Is. Seacrest Inn, P.O. 128, 90704,  310-510-0800 |
| Avalon | Gull House, P.O. Box 1381, 90704,  310-510-2547 |
| Avalon | Hotel Monterey,  108 Summer Ave., 90704 |
| Avalon | Hotel Villa Portofino, P.O. Box 127, 90704,  310-510-0555 |
| Avalon | Inn at Mt. Ada, P.O. Box 2560, 90704,  213-510-2030 |
| Avalon | Mavilla Inn, P.O. Box 2607, 90704,  213-510-1651 |
| Avalon | Seacrest Inn, P.O. Box 128, 90704,  213-510-0196 |
| Avila Beach | San Luis Bay Inn,  Box 188, 93424,  805-595-2333 |
| Bakersfield | Helen K Inn,  2105 - 19th St., 93301,  805-325-5451 |
| Balboa Peninsula | Balboa Inn,  105 Main St., 92663,  714-675-3412 |
| Bass Lake | Ducey's on the Lake, P.O. Box 109, 93604,  800-350-7463 |
| Baywood Park | Bayview House,  1070 Santa Lucia Ave., 93402,  805-528-3098 |
| Benicia | Captain Walsh House,  235 East L St., 94510,  707-747-5653 |
| Benicia | Union Hotel & Gardens,  401 First St., 94510,  707-746-0100 |
| Berkeley | B&B Accomm. in Berkeley,  2235 Carleton St., 94704,  510-548-7556 |
| Berkeley | Bancroft Club Hotel,  2680 Bancroft Way, 94704,  510-549-1000 |
| Berkeley | Delphinus B&B,  Berkeley Marina, 94530,  510-527-9622 |
| Berkeley | Elmwood House B&B,  2609 College Ave., 94705,  510-540-5123 |
| Berkeley | French Hotel,  1538 Shattuck Ave., 94709,  510-548-9930 |
| Berkeley | Gramma's Rose Garden Inn,  2740 Telegraph Ave., 94705,  510-549-2145 |
| Berkeley | Hillegass House,  2834 Hillegass Ave., 94705 |
| Berkeley | Mary Joes Guest House,  801 Channing Way, 94710,  510-622-8391 |
| Beverly Hills | Ray Abrams c/o Heitman Prp,  9601 Wilshire Blvd. 200, 90210 |
| Big Bear Lake | Janet Kay's, P.O. Box 3874, 92315,  800-243-7031 |
| Big Bear Lake | Knickerbocker Mansion,  Box 3661, 92315,  714-866-8221 |
| Big Bear Lake | Moonridge Manor, P.O. Box 6599, 92315 |
| Big Sur | Deetjen's Big Sur Inn,  Hwy 1, 93920,  408-667-2377 |
| Big Sur | Lucia Lodge,  93920,  408-667-2391 |
| Big Sur | Post Ranch Inn, P.O. Box 219, Hwy 1, 93920 |
| Big Sur | River Inn,  Pheneger Creek, 93920 |
| Bishop | Matlick House B&B, The, P.O. Box 744, 93515,  619-873-3133 |

| | |
|---|---|
| Blue Jay | Arrowhead Summit, P.O. Box 2357, 92317, 909-337-5077 |
| Bodega | Bodega Vista Inn, P.O. Box 362, 94922, 707-876-3300 |
| Bodega | School House Inn, 17699 Hwy.1, Box 255, 94922 |
| Bodega Bay | Holiday Inn - Bodega Bay, P.O. Box 55, 94923, 707-875-2217 |
| Bolinas | Elfriede's Haus, 59 Brighton Ave., 94924, 415-868-9778 |
| Bolinas | One Fifty-Five Pine B&B, Box 62, 94924, 415-868-0263 |
| Bolinas | Star Route Inn, 825 Olema-Bolinas Rd., 94924, 415-868-2502 |
| Bolinas | Thomas' White House Inn, 118 Kale Rd., 94924, 415-868-0279 |
| Boonville | Boonville Hotel, P.O. Box 326, 95415, 707-895-2210 |
| Boonville | Colfax's Guest House, Redwood Ridge Rd., 95415, 707-895-3241 |
| Boonville | Toll House Restaurant/Inn, P.O. Box 268, 95415, 707-895-3630 |
| Borrego Springs | Le Petit Chateau, P.O. Box 2524, 92004 |
| Brentwood | Diablo Vista B&B, 2191 Empire Ave., 94513, 510-634-2396 |
| Bridgeport | Bridgeport Hotel, Main St., 93517, 619-932-7380 |
| Burlingame | Burlingame B&B, 1021 Balboa Ave., 94010, 415-344-5815 |
| Burlingame | Cora Harschel, 8 Mariposa Ct., 94010, 415-697-5560 |
| Burnt Ranch | Madrone Lane B&B, HCR #34, 95527, 916-629-3642 |
| Calistoga | Brannan's Loft, P.O. Box 561, 94515, 707-963-2181 |
| Calistoga | Calistoga Inn, 1250 Lincoln Av., 94515, 707-942-4101 |
| Calistoga | Calistoga Wishing Well Inn, 2653 Foothill Blvd., 94515, 707-942-5534 |
| Calistoga | Carlin Country Cottages, 1623 Lake St., 94515, 707-942-9102 |
| Calistoga | Christopher's Inn, 1010 Foothill Blvd., 94515, 707-942-5755 |
| Calistoga | Comfort Inn, 1865 Lincoln Ave., 94515, 707-942-9400 |
| Calistoga | Falcon's Nest, 471 Kortum Canyon Rd., 94515, 707-942-0758 |
| Calistoga | Golden Haven Hot Springs, 1713 Lake St., 94515, 707-942-6793 |
| Calistoga | Hideaway Cottages, 1412 Fairway, 94515, 707-942-4108 |
| Calistoga | Hillcrest B&B, 3225 Lake County Hwy., 94515, 707-942-6334 |
| Calistoga | La Chaumiere, 1301 Cedar St., 94515, 707-942-5139 |
| Calistoga | Larkmead Country Inn, 1103 Larkmead Ln., 94515, 707-942-5360 |
| Calistoga | Le Spa Francais, 1880 Lincoln Ave., 94515, 707-942-4636 |
| Calistoga | Meadowlark Country House, 601 Petrified Forest Rd, 94515, 707-942-5651 |
| Calistoga | Mount View Hotel, 1457 Lincoln Ave., 94515, 707-942-6877 |
| Calistoga | Mountain Home Ranch, 3400 Mountain Home, 94515, 707-942-6616 |
| Calistoga | Old Toll Road Inn, 3875 Old Toll Rd., 94515 |
| Calistoga | Pine Street Inn, 1202 Pine St., 94515, 707-942-6829 |
| Calistoga | Pink Mansion, The, 1415 Foothill Blvd., 94515, 707-942-0558 |
| Calistoga | Quail Mountain B&B Inn, 4455 N. St. Helena Hwy, 94515, 707-942-0316 |
| Calistoga | Scott Courtyard, 1443 2nd St., 94515, 800-942-1515 |
| Calistoga | Silver Rose Inn, 351 Rosedale Rd., 94515, 707-942-9581 |
| Calistoga | Village Inn & Spa, 1880 Lincoln Ave., 94515, 707-942-0991 |
| Calistoga | Washington Street Lodging, 1605 Washington St., 94515, 707-942-6968 |
| Calistoga | Wine Away Inn, 1019 Foothill Blvd., 94515, 707-942-0680 |
| Calistoga | Wine Way Inn, 1019 Foothill Blvd., 94515, 707-942-0680 |
| Cambria | Blue Whale Inn, The, 6736 Moonstone Beach Dr, 93428, 805-927-4647 |
| Cambria | Sylvia's Rigdon Hall Inn, 4022 Burton Dr., 93428, 805-927-5125 |
| Camino | Camino Hotel, P.O. Box 1197, 95709, 916-644-7740 |
| Capistrano | Country Inn, 34862 S. Coast Hwy, 92624, 714-496-6656 |
| Capitola | Inn at Depot Hill, The, P.O. Box 1934, 95010, 408-462-3376 |
| Capitola | Monarch Cove Inn, 620 El Salto Dr., 95010 |
| Cardiff | Cardiff by the Sea B&B, 1487 San Elijo, 92007 |
| Carmel | Candle Light Inn, P.O. Box 1900, 93921, 408-624-6451 |
| Carmel | Carmel Garden Court Inn, P.O. Box 6226, 93921, 408-624-6926 |
| Carmel | Colonial Terrace Inn, P.O. Box 1375, 93921, 408-624-2741 |
| Carmel | Dolphin Inn, P.O. Box 1900, 93921, 408-624-5356 |
| Carmel | Green Lantern Inn, P.O. Box 2619, 93921, 408-624-4392 |
| Carmel | Hofsas House, 3rd & San Carlos,Box 11, 93921 |
| Carmel | Mission Ranch, 26270 Dolores, 93923, 408-624-6436 |
| Carmel | Monte Verde Inn, P.O. Box 3373, 93921, 408-624-6046 |
| Carmel | Sandpiper Inn, The, 2408 Bay View Dr., 93923, 408-624-6433 |
| Carmel | Stonehouse Inn, P.O. Box 2517, 93921, 408-624-4569 |
| Carmel | Stonepine, 150 East Carmel Valley , 93924 |
| Carmel | Sundial Lodge, P.O. Box J, 93921, 408-624-8578 |
| Carmel | Svends Gaards Inn, P.O. Box 1900, 93921, 408-624-1511 |
| Carmel | Tally Ho Inn, P.O. Box 3726, 93921, 408-624-2232 |
| Carmel | Wayside Inn, P.O. Box 1900, 93921, 408-624-5336 |
| Carpinteria | Prufrock's Garden Inn, 600 Linden Ave., 93013, 805-566-9696 |
| Castro Valley | Lore's Haus, 22051 Betlen Way, 94546, 510-881-1533 |
| Cathey | Chibchas Inn, P.O. Box 127, 95306 |
| Cathey | Rancho Bernardo, 2617 Old Hwy. South, 95306 |
| Cazadero | Ten Aker Wood, P.O. Box 208, 95421, 707-632-5328 |
| Cazadero | Timberhill Ranch Resort, 35755 Hauser Bridge Rd., 95421, 707-847-3258 |

*The Shore House at Lake Tahoe, Tahoe City, CA*

| | |
|---|---|
| Chester | Drakesbad Guest Ranch, Warner Valley Rd., 96020, 916 Drakes |
| Chico | Bullard House B&B Inn, 256 E. 1st Ave., 95926, 916-342-5912 |
| Chico | Esplanade B&B, The, 620 The Esplanade, 95926, 916-345-8084 |
| Chico | Johnson's Country Inn, 3935 Morehead Ave., 95928, 916-345-STAY |
| Chico | O'Flaherty House, 1462 Arcadian, 95926 |
| Clearlake | Muktip Manor, 12540 Lakeshore Dr., 95422, 707-994-9571 |
| Clearlake Park | Inn Oz, P.O. Box 1046, 95424, 707-995-0853 |
| Clio | White Sulphur Springs B&B, P.O. Box 136, 96106, 916-836-2387 |
| Cloverdale | Ye Olde' Shelford House, 100 Oakbrook Ln., 95425, 707-894-5956 |
| Cobb | Brookhill, Box 1019, 17655 Hwy 17S, 95426, 707-928-5029 |
| Colusa | O'Rourke Mansion, 1765 Lurline Rd., 95932, 916-458-5625 |
| Coronado | Coronado Victorian House, 1000 Eighth St., 92118, 619-435-2200 |
| Crescent City | Fernbrook Inn, 4650 N. Bank Rd., 95531, 707-458-3202 |
| Crowley Lake | Rainbow Tarns, Rt 1, P.O. Box 1097, 93546, 619-935-4556 |
| Davis | Davis Bed 'N Breakfast Inn, 422 A St., 95616 |
| Davis | Partridge Inn, 521 First St., 95616, 916-753-1211 |
| Del Mar | Blue Door, The, 13707 Durango Dr., 92014, 619-755-3819 |
| Del Mar | Gulls Nest, 12930 Via Esperia, 92014, 619-259-4863 |
| Del Mar | Rock Haus Inn, 410 - 15th St., 92014, 619-481-3764 |
| Desert Hot Springs | Travelers Repose, P.O. Box 655, 92240 |
| Dillon Beach | Windmist Cottage, P.O. Box 291, 94929, 707-878-2465 |
| Dinuba | Country Living B&B, 40068 Rd. 88, 93618, 209-591-6617 |
| Dorrington | Dorrington Hotel, P.O. Box 4307, 95223, 209-795-5800 |
| Dorris | Hospitality Inn, 200 S. California St., 96023 |
| Downieville | Sierra Shangri-La, P.O. 285, Route 49, 95936, 916-289-3455 |
| El Cajon | Lion's Head Guest House, Box 21203, 92021, 619-463-4271 |
| El Dorado Hills | Mission San Francisco, 1518 Planeta Way, 95762, 916-933-0370 |
| Elk | Green Dolphin Inn, P.O. Box 132, 95432, 707-877-3342 |
| Elk | Greenwood Pier Inn, P.O. Box 36, 95432, 707-877-9997 |
| Elk | Griffin House at Greenwood, P.O. Box 172, 95432, 707-877-3422 |
| Elkcreek | Stony Creek Retreat B&B, P.O. Box 205, 95939, 916-968-5178 |
| Encinitas | Sea Breeze B&B, 121 N. Vulcan, 92024, 619-944-0318 |
| Escondido | Halbig's Hacienda, 432 S. Citrus Ave., 92026, 619-745-1296 |
| Eureka | A Weaver's Inn, 1440 "B" St., 95501, 707-443-8119 |
| Eureka | Campton House B&B, 305 M St., 95501, 707-443-1601 |
| Eureka | Eagle House Victorian Inn, 139 2nd St., 95501, 707-442-2334 |
| Eureka | Heuer's Victorian Inn, 1302 "E" St., 95501, 707-445-7334 |
| Eureka | Hollander House, 2436 E. St., 95501, 707-443-2419 |
| Eureka | Iris Inn, 1134 "H" St., 95501, 707-445-0307 |
| Fawnskin | Inn at Fawnskin, P.O. Box 378, 92333 |
| Felton | Inn at Felton Crest, The, 780 El Solyo Hghts. Dr., 95018 |
| Ferndale | Ferndale Inn, P.O. Box 887, 95536, 707-786-4307 |
| Fish Camp | Apple Tree Inn, P.O. Box 41, 93623, 209-683-5111 |
| Fish Camp | Karen's B&B Yosemite Inn, P.O. Box 8, 93623, 209-683-4550 |
| Folsom | Folsom Hotel, 703 Sutter St., 95630 |
| Folsom | Plum Tree Inn, 307 Leidesdorff St., 95630, 916-351-1541 |
| Forestville | Farmhouse Inn, 7871 River Rd., 95436, 707-887-3300 |
| Fort Bidwell | Fort Bidwell Hotel, Main & Garrison, 96112 |
| Fort Bragg | Blue Rose Inn, 520 N. Main St., 95437, 707-964-3477 |
| Fort Bragg | Cleone Lodge, 24600 N Hwy. #1, 95437, 707-964-2788 |
| Fort Bragg | Colonial Inn, P.O. Box 565, 95437, 707-964-9979 |
| Fort Bragg | Jughandle Beach Country I, 32980 Gibney Ln., 95437, 707-964-1415 |
| Fort Bragg | Oceanview Lodge, 1141 N. Main St., 95437, 707-964-1951 |
| Fort Bragg | Pine Beach Inn, P.O. Box 1173, 95437, 707-964-5603 |
| Fort Bragg | Roundhedge Inn, 159 N. Whipple St., 95437, 707-964-9605 |
| Fremont | Lord Bradley's Inn, 43344 Mission Blvd., 94539, 510-490-0520 |
| Galeta | Circle Bar B Guest Ranch, 1800 Refugio Rd., 93117, 805-968-1113 |
| Garberville | Benbow Inn, 445 Lake Benbow Dr., 95542, 707-923-2124 |
| Garberville | Ranch House, The, 2906 Alderpoint Rd., 95542, 707-923-3441 |
| Garden Valley | Mountainside B&B, 5821 Spanish Flat Rd., 95633, 916-626-1119 |
| Geyserville | Isis Oasis Lodge, 20889 Geyserville Ave., 95441, 707-857-3524 |
| Glen Ellen | Beltane Ranch, P.O. Box 395, 95442 |
| Glen Ellen | Gaige House Inn, 13540 Arnold Dr., 95442, 707-935-0237 |
| Glen Ellen | Glenelly Inn, 5131 Warm Springs Rd., 95442, 707-996-6720 |
| Glen Ellen | Jack London Lodge, P.O. Box 300, 95442, 707-938-8510 |
| Glen Ellen | Stonetree Ranch, 7910 Sonoma Mt. Rd., 95442, 707-996-8173 |
| Glen Ellen | Tanglewood House, 250 Bonnie Way, 95442, 707-996-5021 |
| Graeagle | Feather River Inn, P.O. Box 67, 96103, 916-836-2623 |
| Grass Valley | Annie Horan's B&B, 415 W. Main St., 95945, 916-272-2418 |
| Grass Valley | Golden Ore House B&B, 448 S. Auburn St., 95945, 916-272-6872 |
| Grass Valley | Holbrooke Hotl/Purcell Hse, 212 W. Main St., 95945, 916-273-1353 |
| Grass Valley | Swan-Levine House, 328 S. Church St., 95945, 916-272-1873 |
| Green Valley | Lodge, The, 33655 Green Valley Lake, 92341, 909-867-5410 |
| Gridley | McCracken's B&B Inn, 1835 Sycamore Ln., 95948, 916-846-2108 |
| Groveland | Berkshire Inn, P.O. Box 207, 95321, 209-962-6744 |
| Groveland | Lee's Middle Fork Resort, 11399 Cherry Oil Rd., 95321 |

| | |
|---|---|
| Gualala | Old Milano Hotel, The, 38300 Hwy 1, 95445, 707-884-3256 |
| Gualala | Saint Orres, P.O. Box 523, 95445, 707-884-3303 |
| Gualala | Whale Watch Inn by the Sea, 35100 Hwy 1, 95445, 707-884-3667 |
| Guerneville | Applewood Inn, 13555 Hwy 116, 95446, 707-869-9093 |
| Guerneville | Camelot Resort, P.O. Box 467 4th & Mill, 95446, 707-869-2538 |
| Guerneville | Creekside Inn & Resort, P.O. Box 2185, 95446, 707-869-3623 |
| Guerneville | Fern Grove Inn, 16650 River Rd., 95446, 707-869-9083 |
| Guerneville | Santa Nella House, 12130 Hwy. 116, 95446, 707-869-9488 |
| Half Moon Bay | Cypress Inn—Miramar Beach, 407 Mirada Rd., 94019, 415-726-6002 |
| Healdsburg | All Seasons Suites, 226 Healdsburg Ave., 95448, 707-433-4215 |
| Healdsburg | Belle de Jour Inn, 16276 Healdsburg Ave., 95448, 707-433-7892 |
| Healdsburg | Calderwood Victorian Inn, P.O. Box 967, 95448, 707-431-1110 |
| Healdsburg | Calistoga Silver Rose Inn, P.O. Box 1376, 95448, 707-942-9581 |
| Healdsburg | Frampton House B&B, 489 Powell Ave., 95448, 707-433-5084 |
| Healdsburg | George Alexander House, 423 Matheson St., 95448, 707-433-1358 |
| Healdsburg | L'Auberge du Sans-Souci, 25 W. Grant St., 95448, 707-431-1110 |
| Healdsburg | Villa Messina, 316 Burgundy Rd., 95448 |
| Homeland | Rancho Kaeru, 28140 Juniper Flats Rd., 92548 |
| Homewood | Palmer House at Lake Tahoe, P.O. Box 717, 96141, 800-726-1308 |
| Homewood | Tahoma Medows B&B, P.O. Box 810, 96141, 916-525-1553 |
| Hopland | Hopland House, P.O. Box 310, 95449, 707-744-1404 |
| Hopland | Thatcher Inn, P.O. Box 660, 95449, 707-744-1890 |
| Independence | Winnedumah Hotel, P.O. Box 147, 93526, 619-878-2040 |
| Indio | Palm Shadow Inn, 80-761 Hwy. 111, 92201, 619-347-3476 |
| Inverness | Ark, The, P.O. Box 273, 94937, 415-663-9338 |
| Inverness | Hickman House, P.O. Box 235, 94937, 415-669-7428 |
| Inverness | Hotel Inverness, P.O. Box 780, 94937, 415-669-7393 |
| Inverness | Inverness Lodge, P.O. Box 1110, 94937, 415-669-1034 |
| Inverness | Laurel Ridge Cottage Inn, P.O. Box 38, 94937, 415-633-1286 |
| Inverness | Laurels, The, P.O. Box 394, 94937 |
| Inverness | MacLean House, P.O. Box 651, 94937, 415-669-7392 |
| Inverness | Sandy Cove Inn, P.O. Box 869, 94937, 415-669-2683 |
| Inverness | Ten Inverness Way B&B, P.O. Box 63, 94937, 415-669-1648 |
| Isleton | Delta Daze Inn, 179 Oxbow Marina Dr., 95641, 916-777-4667 |
| Jackson | Ann Marie's Country Inn, 1 Raggio Rd., 95642, 209-223-1452 |
| Jackson | Court Street Inn, 215 Court St., 95642, 209-223-0416 |
| Jackson | Gate House Inn, 1330 Jackson Gate Rd., 95642, 209-223-3500 |
| Jackson | Windrose Inn, 1407 Jackson Gate Rd., 95642, 209-223-3650 |
| Jamestown | Historic National Hotel, 77 Main St., 95327, 209-984-3446 |
| Jamestown | Jamestown Hotel, P.O. Box 539, 95327, 209-984-3902 |
| Jamestown | National Hotel, The, P.O. Box 502, 95327, 209-984-3446 |
| Jenner | River's End, No. Coast Hwy 1, 95450 |
| Jenner | Salt Point Lodge, 23255 Coast Hwy 1, 95450, 707-847-3234 |
| Jenner | Sea Coast Hideaways, 21350 N. Coast Hwy 1, 95450, 707-847-3278 |
| Jenner | Stillwater Cove Ranch, 22555 Coast Hwy. 1, 95450, 707-847-3227 |
| Jenner | Timber Cove Inn, 21780 North Coast Hwy, 95450 |
| Julian | Julian Lodge, P.O. Box 1930, 92036, 619-765-1420 |
| Julian | Julian White House, P.O. Box 824, 92036, 619-765-1764 |
| Julian | Pine Hills Lodge, P.O. Box 701, 92036, 619-765-1100 |
| Julian | Pinecroft Manor, P.O. Box 665, 92036, 619-765-1611 |
| Kenwood | Kenwood Inn, 10400 Sonoma Hwy., 95452, 707-833-1293 |
| Kernville | Neill House, The, P.O. Box 377, 93238 |
| Kernville | Whispering Pines Lodge B&B, Rt. 1, Box 41, 93238, 619-376-2237 |
| Kings Canyon | Montecito-Sequoia Inn, Box 858, Grant Grove, 93633, 209-565-3388 |
| Kingsburg | Kingsburg's Swedish Inn, 401 Conejo St., 93631, 209-897-1022 |
| La Habra Heights | Fran's Around a Corner B&B, 1584 N. Cypress St., 90631, 310-690-6422 |
| La Jolla | B&B Inn at La Jolla, The, 7753 Draper Ave., 92037, 619-456-2066 |
| La Jolla | Irish Cottage, 5623 Taft Ave., 92037, 619-454-6075 |
| La Jolla | Scripps Inn, 555 Coast Blvd. S., 92037, 619-454-3391 |
| La Jolla | Sea Lodge, 8110 Camino Del Oro, 92037 |
| Laguna Beach | Carriage House B&B, The, 1322 Catalina St., 92651, 714-494-8945 |
| Laguna Beach | Eiler's Inn, 2891 Chateau Way, 92651, 714-494-3004 |
| Laguna Beach | Hotel San Maarten, 696 S. Coast Hwy, 92651, 714-494-9436 |
| Laguna Beach | Spray Cliff, P.O. Box 403, 92677, 714-499-4022 |
| Lake Almanor | Lake Almanor Inn, 3965 Hwy. A-13, 96137, 916-596-3910 |
| Lake Arrowhead | Bracken Fern Manor, 815 Arrowhead Villas Rd, 92352, 909-337-8557 |
| Lake Arrowhead | Eagles Landing B&B, P.O. Box 1510, 92317, 909-336-2642 |
| Lake Arrowhead | Romantique Lakeview Lodge, P.O. Box 128, 92352, 909-337-6633 |
| Lake Arrowhead | Saddleback Inn, 300 S. State Hwy 173, 92352, 714-336-3571 |
| Lake Arrowhead | Storybook Inn, P.O. Box 352, 92385, 909-336-1483 |
| Lake Arrowhead | Windermere Manor, P.O. Box 2177, 92352, 909-336-3292 |
| Lakeport | Wooden Bridge B&B, 1441 Oakwood Ct., 95453, 707-263-9125 |
| Leggett | Bell Glen Eel River Inn, 70400 Highway 101, 95455, 707-925-6425 |
| Leggett | Sky Canyon Ranch, P.O. Box 98, 95585, 707-925-6415 |
| Lewiston | Lewiston B&B, P.O. Box 688, 96052, 916-778-3385 |
| Little River | Fools Rush Inn, 7533 N. Highway 1, 95456, 707-937-5339 |
| Lodi | Wine & Roses Country Inn, 2505 W. Turner Rd., 95242, 209-334-6988 |
| Long Beach | Appleton Place B&B Inn, 935 Cedar Ave., 90813, 310-432-2312 |
| Long Beach | Crane's Nest, 319 W. 12th St., 90813, 310-435-4084 |

| | |
|---|---|
| Los Alamos | Union Hotel, P.O. Box 616, 93440, 805-344-2744 |
| Los Angeles | Casablanca Villa, 449 N. Detroit St., 90036, 213-938-4794 |
| Los Angeles | Inn at 657, The, 657 W. 23rd St., 90007, 800-347-7512 |
| Los Angeles | Norja-B&B, 1139 Tremaine Ave., 90019, 213-933-3652 |
| Los Angeles | Salisbury House B&B, 2273 W. 20th St., 90018, 213-737-7817 |
| Los Angeles | Secret Garden B&B, The, 8039 Selma Ave., 90046 |
| Los Angeles | Suzanne Multout, 449 N. Detroit St., 90036, 213-938-4794 |
| Los Angeles | Terrace Manor, 1353 Alvarado Terrace, 90006, 213-381-1478 |
| Los Gatos | Courtside, 14675 Winchester Blvd., 95030, 408-395-7111 |
| Los Gatos | La Hacienda Inn, 18840 Los Gatos Rd., 95030, 408-354-9230 |
| Los Olivos | Red Rooster Ranch, P.O. Box 554, 93441, 805-688-8050 |
| Los Olivos | Zaca Lake, P.O. Box 187, 93441, 805-688-4891 |
| Los Osos | Geralda's B&B, 1056 Bay Oaks Dr., 93402, 805-528-3973 |
| Lotus | Golden Lotus B&B Inn, P.O. Box 830, 95651, 916-621-4562 |
| Lower Lake | Big Canyon Inn, P.O. Box 1311, 95457, 707-928-5631 |
| Lucerne | Kristalberg B&B, P.O. Box 1629, 95458, 707-274-8009 |
| Magalia | J & J's B&B, P.O. Box 1059, 95954, 916-873-4782 |
| Malibu | Malibu Beach Inn, 22878 Pacific Coast Hwy, 90265, 213-456-6444 |
| Mammoth Lakes | Tamarack Lodge Resort, P.O. Box 69, 93546, 619-934-2442 |
| Mammoth Lakes | Wildasinn House, The, 26 Lupin St., Box 8026, 93546, 619-934-3851 |
| Manchester | Blueroses, P.O. Box 338, 95459, 707-882-2240 |
| Manchester | Victorian Gardens, 14409 S. Hwy. 1, 95459, 707-882-3606 |
| Mariposa | 5th Street Inn, P.O. Box 1917, 95338, 209-966-6048 |
| Mariposa | Boulder Creek, 4572 Ben Hur Rd., 95338, 209-742-7729 |
| Mariposa | Chalet on the Mount, 4960 Usona Rd., 95338, 209-966-5115 |
| Mariposa | Chubb's, The, P.O. Box 1060, 95338, 209-966-5085 |
| Mariposa | Dubord Restful Nest B&B, 4274 Buckeye Creek Rd., 95338, 209-742-7127 |
| Mariposa | Dubord's Restful Nest, 4274 Buckeye Creek Rd., 95338, 209-742-7127 |
| Mariposa | Eagle's Nest, 6308 Jerseydale Rd., 95338, 209-966-3737 |
| Mariposa | Granny's Garden B&B, 7333 Hwy. 49 N., 95338, 209-377-8342 |
| Mariposa | Guest House, The, 4962 Triangle Rd., 95338, 209-742-6869 |
| Mariposa | Ken and Flo's B&B, P.O. Box 2141, 95338, 209-966-7677 |
| Mariposa | Little Valley Inn, 3483 Brooks Rd., 95338, 209-742-6204 |
| Mariposa | Mariposa Hotel Inn, P.O. Box 745, 95338, 209-966-4676 |
| Mariposa | Oak Meadows, too B&B, P.O. Box 619, 95338, 209-742-6161 |
| Mariposa | Poppy Hill B&B, 5218 Crystal Aire Dr., 95338, 209-742-6273 |
| Mariposa | Restful Nest Resort, 4274 Buckeye Creek Rd., 95338, 209-742-7127 |
| Mariposa | Rock & Rill, P.O. Box 1036, 95338, 209-742-4494 |
| Mariposa | Schlageter House, P.O. Box 1202, 95338, 209-966-2471 |
| Mariposa | Shangri-La, 6316 Jerseydale, 95338, 209-966-2653 |
| Mariposa | Shiloh, 3265 Triangle Park Rd., 95338, 209-742-7200 |
| Mariposa | Shirl's B&B, P.O. Box 1293, 95338, 209-966-2514 |
| Mariposa | Sky View Village, P.O. Box 1482, 95338, 209-966-6972 |
| Mariposa | Twelve Oaks Carriage House, 4877 Wildwood, 95338, 209-966-3231 |
| Mariposa | Villa Monti, P.O. Box 1888, 95338, 209-966-2439 |
| Mariposa | Vista Grande B&B, 4160 Vista Grande Way, 95338, 209-742-6206 |
| Mariposa | Yosemite-Mariposa Townhse, P.O. Box 1947, 95338 |
| Marshall | Inn at Tomales Bay, 22555 Highway 1, 94940, 415-663-9002 |
| McCloud | Joanie's B&B, P.O. Box 924, 96057, 916-964-3106 |
| McCloud | McCloud Guest House, The, P.O. Box 1510, 96057, 916-964-3160 |
| McCloud | Stoney Brook Inn, P.O. Box 1860, 96057, 916-964-2300 |
| Mendocino | 1021 Main St. Guest House, P.O. Box 803, 95460, 707-937-5150 |
| Mendocino | Blackberry Inn, 44951 Larkin Rd., 95460, 707-937-5281 |
| Mendocino | Captain's Cove Inn, P.O. Box 803, 95460, 707-937-5150 |
| Mendocino | Hill House Inn, P.O. Box 625, 95410, 707-937-0554 |
| Mendocino | Mendocino Farmhouse, P.O. Box 247, 95460, 707-937-0241 |
| Mendocino | Mendocino Hotel, P.O. Box 587, 95460, 707-937-0511 |
| Mendocino | Mendocino Tennis Club/Ldge, 43250 Little Lake Rd., 95460, 707-937-0007 |
| Mendocino | Mendocino Village Inn, P.O. Box 626, 95460, 707-937-0246 |
| Mendocino | Rachel's Inn, Box 134, 95460, 707-937-0088 |
| Mendocino | Sea Gull Inn, P.O. Box 317, 95460, 707-937-5204 |
| Mendocino | Sears House Inn, Main St., P.O. Box 844, 95460, 707-937-4076 |
| Middletown | Harbin Hot Springs Retreat, P.O. Box 782, 95461, 707-987-2477 |
| Midpines | Happy Medium, P.O. Box 10, Midpine, 95345, 209-742-6366 |
| Midpines | Homestead Guest Ranch B&B, P.O. Box 13, 95345, 209-966-2820 |
| Mill Creek | St. Bernard Lodge, Rt. 5, Box 550, 96061 |
| Mill Valley | Mill Valley Inn, 165 Throckmorton Ave., 94941, 415-389-6608 |
| Mill Valley | Sycamore House, 99 Sycamore Ave., 94941, 415-383-0612 |
| Mokelumne Hill | Hotel Leger, P.O. Box 50, 95245, 209-286-1401 |
| Monte Rio | House of a 1000 Flowers, P.O. Box 369, 95421, 707-632-5571 |
| Monte Rio | Rio Villa Beach Resort, 20292 Hwy 116, 95462, 707-865-1143 |

*The Goose & Turrets B&B, Montara, CA*

| | |
|---|---|
| Monte Rio | Village Inn, P.O. Box 850, 95462, 707-865-2304 |
| Monterey | Carter Art Galleries B&B, 44 Sierra Vista Dr., 93940 |
| Monterey | Charlaine's Bay View B&B, 44 Sierra Vista Dr., 93940, 408-655-0177 |
| Monterey | Merritt House, 386 Pacific St., 93940, 408-646-9686 |
| Monterey | Monterey, The, 406 Alvarado St., 93940, 408-375-3184 |
| Moss Beach | Seal Cove Inn, 221 Cypress Ave., 94038, 415-728-4114 |
| Murphys | Redbud Inn, 402 Main St., 95247 |
| Murphys | Trade Carriage House, P.O. Box 2429, 95247 |
| Napa | Arbor Guest House, 1436 G St., 94559, 707-252-8144 |
| Napa | Candlelight Inn, 1045 Easum Dr., 94558, 707-257-3717 |
| Napa | Cedar Gables Inn, 486 Coombs St., 94559, 707-224-7969 |
| Napa | Chateau, The, 4195 Solano Ave., 94558, 707-253-9300 |
| Napa | Coombs Residence Inn, 720 Seminary St., 94559, 707-257-0789 |
| Napa | Country Garden Inn, 1815 Silverado Trail, 94558, 707-255-1197 |
| Napa | Crystal Rose Victorian Inn, 7564 St. Helena Hwy, 94558, 707-944-8185 |
| Napa | Elm House, 800 California, 94559, 707-255-1831 |
| Napa | Hillview Country Inn, 1205 Hillview Ln., 94558, 707-224-5004 |
| Napa | Inn on Randolph, 411 Randolph St., 94559, 707-257-2886 |
| Napa | John Muir Inn, The, 1998 Trower Ave, 94558, 707-257-7220 |
| Napa | Rockhaven, 7774 Silverado Trail, 94558, 707-944-2041 |
| Napa | Tall Timber Chalets, 1012 Darms Ln., 94558, 707-252-7810 |
| Napa | Yesterhouse Inn, 643 Third St., 94559, 707-257-0550 |
| National City | Dickinson/Boal Mansion, 1433 E. 24th St., 92050 |
| Needles | Old Trails Inn, 304 Broadway, 92363, 619-326-3523 |
| Nevada City | Deer Creek Inn, The, 116 Nevada St., 95959, 916-265-0363 |
| Nevada City | Grandmere's Inn, 449 Broad St., 95959, 916-265-4660 |
| Nevada City | Kendall House, The, 534 Spring St., 95959, 916-265-0405 |
| Nevada City | National Hotel, 211 Broad St., 95959, 916-265-4551 |
| Nevada City | Piety Hill Inn, 523 Sacramento St., 95959, 916-265-2245 |
| Newcastle | Victorian Manor, 482 Main St., 95658 |
| Newport Beach | Doryman's Inn, 2102 W. Oceanfront, 92663, 714-675-7300 |
| Newport Beach | Island Cottage B&B, 1305 Park Ave., 92662, 714-723-1125 |
| Newport Beach | Little Inn on the Bay, 617 Lido Park Dr., 92663, 714-673-8800 |
| Newport Beach | Newport Channel Inn, 6030 W. Coast Hwy., 92663, 714-642-3030 |
| Newport Beach | Newport Classic Inn, 2300 W. Coast Hwy., 92663 |
| Newport Beach | Portofino Beach Hotel, 2306 W. Oceanfront, 92663, 714-673-7030 |
| Nipomo | Kaleidoscope Inn, 130 E. Daha St., 93444, 805-929-5444 |
| Norden | Norden House, Box 94, 95724, 916-426-3326 |
| North Fork | Ye Olde South Fork Inn, P.O. Box 731, 93643, 209-877-7025 |
| North Hollywood | La Maida House, 11154 La Maida St., 91601, 818-769-3857 |
| Oakland | Bayside Boat & Breakfast, 49 Jack London Square, 94607, 510-444-5858 |
| Oakland | Dockside Boat & Bed, 77 Jack London Square, 94607, 415-392-5526 |
| Ojai | Ojai B&B, 921 Patricia Ct., 93023, 805-646-8337 |
| Ojai | Theodore Woolsey House, 1484 E. Ojai Ave., 93023, 805-646-9779 |
| Olema | Bear Valley Inn, P.O. Box 33, 94950, 415-663-1777 |
| Olema | Olema Inn, P.O. Box 37, 94950, 415-663-9559 |
| Olema | Rounstone Farm B&B, P.O. Box 217, 94950, 415-663-1020 |
| Olympic Valley | Christy Hill Inn, Box 2449, 95730, 916-583-8551 |
| Ontario | Red Lion Inn, 222 N. Vineyard Rd., 91764, 714-983-0909 |
| Orland | Inn at Shallow Creek Farm, 4712 Road DD, 95963, 916-865-4093 |
| Orosi | Valley View Citrus Ranch, 14801 Ave. 428, 93647, 209-528-2275 |
| Oroville | Lake Oroville B&B, 240 Sunday Dr., 95916, 916-589-0700 |
| Oroville | Montgomery Inn, 1400 Montgomery St., 95965, 916-532-1400 |
| Pacific Grove | Andril Fireplace Cottages, 569 Asilomar Blvd., 93950, 408-375-0994 |
| Pacific Grove | Centrella Hotel, 612 Central Ave., 93950, 408-372-3372 |
| Pacific Grove | Lighthouse Lodge Suites, 1249 Lighthouse Ave., 93950, 408-655-2111 |
| Pacific Grove | Maison Bleue French B&B, P.O. Box 51371, 93950, 408-373-2993 |
| Palm Desert | Korakia Pensione, 257 So. Patencio Rd., 92255 |
| Palm Springs | Casa de los Ninos D'Amor, P.O. Box 8453, 92263, 619-323-4733 |
| Palm Springs | Ingleside Inn, 200 W. Ramon Rd., 92262, 619-325-0046 |
| Palm Springs | Monte Vista, 414 N. Palm Canyon Dr., 92262, 619-325-5641 |
| Palm Springs | Orchid Tree Inn, 261 S. Belardo Rd., 92262, 619-325-2791 |
| Palm Springs | Raffles Palm Springs Hotel, 280 Mel Ave., 92262, 619-320-3949 |
| Palo Alto | Cowper Inn, 705 Cowper St., 94301, 415-327-4475 |
| Palomar Mountain | Patricia Mendenhall B&B, P.O. Box 236, 92060 |
| Paso Robles | Arbor Inn, The, P.O. Box 3260, 93447 |
| Paso Robles | Just Inn, 11680 Chimney Rock Rd., 93446 |
| Paso Robles | Roseleith Bed & Breakfast, 1415 Vine St., 93446 |
| Pescadero | Ocean View Farms B&B, 515 Bean Hollow Rd., 94060, 415-879-0698 |
| Petaluma | Flower Garden B&B, 517 Petaluma Blvd. S, 94952, 707-622-7837 |
| Philo | Anderson Valley Inn, 8480 Hwy. 128, 95466, 707-895-3325 |
| Philo | Philo Pottery Inn, P.O. Box 166, 95466, 707-895-3069 |
| Pismo Beach | Pismo Landmark B&B, 701 Price St, 93449, 805-773-5566 |
| Placerville | Fleming Jones Homestead, 3170 Newtown Rd., 95667, 916-626-5840 |
| Placerville | James Blair House, 2985 Clay St., 95667, 916-626-6136 |
| Placerville | River Rock Inn, 1756 Georgetown Dr., 95667, 916-622-7640 |
| Placerville | Vineyard House, 4204 Woodland Ct., 95667, 916-622-2217 |
| Plymouth | Amador Harvest Inn, 12455 Steiner Rd., 95664, 209-245-5512 |

| | |
|---|---|
| Plymouth | Shenandoah Inn, 17674 Village Dr., 95669,   209-245-4491 |
| Pocket Canyon | Estate, The,  13555 Hwy 116, 95446,   707-869-9093 |
| Point Arena | Coast Guard House,  695 Arena Cove, 95468,   707-882-2442 |
| Point Arena | Point Arena Lighthouse,  Box 11, 95468,   707-882-2777 |
| Point Arena | WharfMaster's Inn,  P.O. Box 674, 95468,   707-882-3171 |
| Pope Valley | James Creek Ranch B&B,  2249 James Crk., 94567 |
| Portola | Pullman House,  256 Commercial St., 96122,   916-832-0107 |
| Portola | Upper Feather B&B,  256 Commercial St., 96122 |
| Posey | Road's End at Paso Creek,  RR #1, Box 450, 93260,   805-536-8668 |
| Pt. Reyes Stat. | Casa Mexicana,  P.O. Box 365, 94956,   415-663-8313 |
| Pt. Reyes Stat. | Country House, The,  P.O. Box 98, 94956,   415-663-1627 |
| Pt. Reyes Stat. | Cricket Cottage,  P.O. Box 627, 94956,   415-663-9139 |
| Pt. Reyes Stat. | Eureka House,  P.O. Box 660, 94956 |
| Pt. Reyes Stat. | Gallery Cottage,  P.O. Box 118, 94956 |
| Pt. Reyes Stat. | Horseshoe Farm Cottage,  P.O. Box 332, 94956,   415-663-9401 |
| Pt. Reyes Stat. | Knob Hill,  P.O. Box 1108, 94956,   415-663-1784 |
| Pt. Reyes Stat. | Neon Rose,  P.O. Box 632, 94956,   800-358-8346 |
| Pt. Reyes Stat. | Roundstone Farm,  P.O. Box 217, 94950,   415-663-1020 |
| Pt. Reyes Stat. | Sea Star Cottage,  Box 642, 94956,   415-663-1554 |
| Pt. Reyes Stat. | Terris Homestay,  P.O. Box 113, 94956 |
| Pt. Reyes Stat. | Tree House Bed & Breakfast,  P.O. Box 1075, 94956,   415-663-8720 |
| Pt. Reyes Stat. | Windsong Cottage,  P.O. Box 84, 94956,   415-663-9695 |
| Pt. Richmond | East Brother Light Station,  117 Park Place, 94801,   510-233-2385 |
| Pt. Richmond | Quinta Quetzalcoati,  P.O. Box 27, 94807,   415-235-2050 |
| Quincy | New England Ranch,  2571 Quincy Junction Rd, 95971 |
| Ramona | Lake Sutherland B&B,  24901 Dam Oaks Dr., 92065,   800-789-6483 |
| Rancho Cucamonga | Christmas House B&B Inn,  9240 Archibald Ave., 91730,   714-980-6450 |
| Redding | Redding's Bed & Breakfast,  1094 Palisades Ave., 96003 |
| Redding | Tiffany House B&B Inn,  1510 Barbara Rd., 96003,   916-244-3225 |
| Redlands | Morey Mansion B&B Inn,  190 Terracina Blvd., 92373,   909-793-7970 |
| Redondo Beach | Ocean Breeze Inn,  122 S. Juanita Ave., 90277,   310-316-5123 |
| Redondo Beach | Sea Breeze B&B,  122 S. Juanita, 90277,   310-316-5123 |
| Redwood Valley | Olson Farmhouse B&B,  3620 Road B, 95470,   707-485-7523 |
| Reedley | Fairweather Inn,  259 South Reed, 93654,   209-638-1918 |
| Reedley | Hotel Burgess,  1726 11th St., 93654 |
| Running Springs | Spring Oaks B&B,  P.O. Box 2918, 92382,   714-867-9636 |
| Rutherford | Auberge du Soleil,  180 Rutherford Hill Rd., 94573,   707-963-1211 |
| Rutherford | Rancho Caymus Inn,  P.O. Box 78, 94573,   707-963-1777 |
| S. Lake Tahoe | Christiana Inn,  Box 18298, 95706,   916-544-7337 |
| S. Lake Tahoe | Richardson's Resort,  P.O. Box 9028, 96158,   800-544-1801 |
| Sacramento | Inn at Parkside,  2116 6th St., 95818,   916-658-1818 |
| Sacramento | Moon River Inn,  8201 Freeport Blvd., 95832,   916-665-6550 |
| Sacramento | Riverboat Delta King,  1000 Front St., 95814 |
| Sacramento | Savoyard,  3322 H St., 95816,   916-442-6709 |
| Sacramento | Sterling Hotel,  1300 "H" St., 95814 |
| Sacramento | Vizcaya B&B,  2019 21st St., 95818,   916-455-5243 |
| San Andreas | Courtyard B&B,  334 W. St. Charles, 95249,   209-754-1518 |
| San Andreas | Robin's Nest, The,  P.O. Box 1408, 95249,   209-754-1076 |
| San Andreas | Thorn Mansion,  P.O. Box 1437, 95249,   209-754-1027 |
| San Clemente | Casa Tropicana,  610 Avenida Victoria, 92672,   714-492-1234 |
| San Clemente | Casa de Flores B&B,  184 Ave. La Cuesta, 92672 |
| San Clemente | San Clemente Hideaway,  323 Cazador Ln., 92672,   714-498-2219 |
| San Diego | Balboa Park Inn,  3402 Park Blvd., 92103,   619-298-0823 |
| San Diego | Burley B&B,  6500 San Miguel Rd., 92002,   619-479-9839 |
| San Diego | Crones Cobblestone Cottage,  1302 Washington Place, 92103,   619-295-4765 |
| San Diego | Hotel Churchill,  827 C St., 92101 |
| San Diego | Keating House Inn,  2331 Second Ave., 92101,   619-239-8585 |
| San Diego | Monets Garden,  7039 Casa Ln., 91945,   619-464-8296 |
| San Diego | Quince St. Trolley B&B,  P.O. Box 7654, 92167,   619-226-8454 |
| San Diego | Skyview II,  2156 Becky Place, 92104,   619-584-1548 |
| San Diego | Vera's Cozy Corner,  2810 Albatross St., 92103,   619-296-1938 |
| San Francisco | 1818 California,  1818 California St., 94109 |
| San Francisco | Adelaide Inn,  5 Adelaide Place, 94102,   415-441-2261 |
| San Francisco | Alexander Inn,  415 O'Farrell St., 94102 |
| San Francisco | American Family Inn,  P.O. Box 420009, 94142,   415-479-1913 |
| San Francisco | Amsterdam Hotel, The,  749 Taylor St., 94108,   415-673-3277 |
| San Francisco | Anna's Three Bears,  114 Divisadero St., 94117,   415-255-3167 |
| San Francisco | Ansonia-Cambridge Hotel,  711 Post St., 94109,   415-673-2670 |
| San Francisco | Aurora Manor,  1328 16th Ave., 94122,   415-564-2480 |
| San Francisco | Bock's B&B,  1448 Willard St., 94117,   415-664-6842 |
| San Francisco | Casita Blanca,  330 Edgehill Way, 94127,   415-564-9339 |
| San Francisco | Clementina's Bay Brick,  1190 Folsom St., 94103,   415-431-8334 |
| San Francisco | Commodore International,  825 Sutter St. at Jones, 94109,   415-885-2464 |
| San Francisco | Dolores Park Inn,  3641 - 17th St., 94114,   415-621-0482 |
| San Francisco | Fay Mansion Inn,  834 Grove St., 94117,   415-921-1816 |
| San Francisco | Haus Kleebauer a B&B,  225 Clipper St., 94114,   415-821-3866 |
| San Francisco | Hotel David B&B,  480 Geary St., 94102,   415-771-1600 |
| San Francisco | Hotel Louise,  845 Bush St., 94108,   415-775-1755 |

| | |
|---|---|
| San Francisco | Hyde Park Suites, 2655 Hyde St., 94123 |
| San Francisco | Inn at the Opera, 333 Fulton St., 94102, 415-863-8400 |
| San Francisco | Inn on Castro, 321 Castro St., 94114, 415-861-0321 |
| San Francisco | Jackson Court, 2198 Jackson St., 94115, 415-929-7670 |
| San Francisco | Lyon Street B&B, 120 Lyon St., 94117, 415-552-4773 |
| San Francisco | Majestic, The, 1500 Sutter St., 94109, 415-441-1100 |
| San Francisco | Mansions Hotel, The, 2220 Sacramento St., 94115, 415-929-9444 |
| San Francisco | Marina Inn, 3110 Octavia St., 94123, 415-928-1000 |
| San Francisco | Millefiori Inn, 444 Columbus, 94133, 415-433-9111 |
| San Francisco | No Name Victorian B&B, P.O. Box 420009, 94142, 415-479-1913 |
| San Francisco | Pacific Bay Inn, 520 Jones St., 94102, 800-445-2631 |
| San Francisco | Pension San Francisco, 1668 Market St., 94102, 415-864-1271 |
| San Francisco | Queen Anne Hotel, The, 1590 Sutter St., 94109, 415-441-2828 |
| San Francisco | Red Victorian Peace Center, 1665 Haight St., 94117, 415-864-1978 |
| San Francisco | Subleties/Cow Hollow Inn, 2821 Steiner St., 94123, 415-775-8295 |
| San Francisco | Washington Square Inn, The, 1660 Stockton St., 94133, 415-981-4220 |
| San Francisco | Willows B&B Inn, 710 - 14th St., 94114, 415-431-4770 |
| San Juan Bautista | B&B San Juan, P.O. Box 613, 95045, 408-623-4101 |
| San Juan Capistrano | Forster Mansion Inn, 27182 Ortega Hwy., 92675, 714-240-7414 |
| San Luis Obispo | Heritage Inn, 978 Olive St., 93401, 805-544-2878 |
| San Miguel | Darken Downs Equestre-Inn, Star Route Box 4562, 93451, 805-467-3589 |
| San Miguel | Ranch B&B, R.R. Box 3653, 93451 |
| San Rafael | Casa Soldavini, 531 "C" St., 94901, 415-454-3140 |
| Santa Barbara | B&B at Valli's View, 340 N. Sierra Vista Rd., 93108, 805-969-1272 |
| Santa Barbara | Bayberry Inn B&B, The, 111 W. Valerio St., 93101, 805-682-3199 |
| Santa Barbara | Inn at Two Twenty Two, 222 W. Valerio, 93101, 805-687-7216 |
| Santa Barbara | Villa Rosa, 15 Chapala St., 93101, 805-966-0851 |
| Santa Barbara | Villa d'Italia, 780 Mission Canyon Rd., 93105, 805-687-6933 |
| Santa Cruz | Blue Spruce Inn, 2815 Main St., 95073, 408-464-1137 |
| Santa Cruz | Hanna's Guest House, 780 El Solyo Heights Dr, 95018, 408-335-4011 |
| Santa Cruz | Jasmine Cottage, 731 Riverside Ave., 95060, 408-429-1415 |
| Santa Cruz | La Casa de Espritas, 2817 Smith Grade, 95060, 408-423-0181 |
| Santa Cruz | Sea and Sand Inn, 201 W. Cliff Dr., 95060, 408-427-3400 |
| Santa Maria | Santa Maria Inn, 801 S. Broadway, 93454, 805-928-7777 |
| Santa Monica | Shutters On The Beach, 1 Pico Blvd., 90405, 800-334-9000 |
| Santa Paula | Fern Oaks Inn, The, 1025 Ojai Rd., 93060, 805-933-5000 |
| Santa Paula | White Gables Inn, The, 715 E. Santa Paula St., 93060 |
| Santa Rosa | Belvedere Inn, 727 Mendocino Ave., 95401, 707-575-1857 |
| Santa Rosa | Cooper's Grove Ranch, 5763 Sonoma Mountain Rd, 95404, 707-571-1928 |
| Saratoga | Eden Valley Place, 22490 Mt. Eden Rd., 95070, 408-867-1785 |
| Saratoga | Inn at Saratoga, 20645 Fourth St., 95070 |
| Sausalito | Alta Mira Continental Htl, P.O. Box 706, 94966, 415-332-1350 |
| Sausalito | Butterfly Tree, P.O. Box 790, 94966, 415-383-8447 |
| Scotia | Scotia Inn, P.O. Box 248, 95565, 707-764-5683 |
| Sea Ranch | Sea Ranch Lodge, P.O. Box 44, 95497, 707-785-2371 |
| Sebastopol | O'Hagin's Guest House, P.O. Box 126, 95472, 707-823-4771 |
| Shelter Cove | Shelter Cove B&B, 148 Dolphin, 95589, 707-986-7161 |
| Sherman Oaks | El Camino Real B&B, P.O. Box 5598, 91403, 818-785-8351 |
| Sierra City | Busch & Heringlake Inn, P.O. Box 68, 96125 |
| Sierra City | High Country Inn, HCR 2, Box 7, 96125 |
| Soda Springs | Serene Lakes Lodge, P.O. Box 164, 95728, 916-426-9001 |
| Solvang | Danish Country Inn, 1455 Mission Dr., 93463, 805-688-2018 |
| Solvang | Storybook Inn, 409 First St., 93463, 805-668-1703 |
| Somerset | Fitzpatrick Winery Lodge, 7740 Fairplay Rd., 95684, 209-245-3248 |
| Somerset | Seven Up Bar Guest Ranch, 8060 Fairplay Rd., 95684, 209-245-5450 |
| Somis | Ranch at Somis, 6441 La Cumbre Rd., 93066, 805-987-8455 |
| Sonoma | Au Relais Inn, 681 Broadway, 95476, 707-996-1031 |
| Sonoma | Country Cottage, 291 1st St. East, 95476, 707-938-2479 |
| Sonoma | El Dorado Inn, 405 First St. W., 95476, 707-996-3030 |
| Sonoma | Hidden Oak, 214 E. Napa St., 95476, 707-996-9863 |
| Sonoma | Kate Murphy's Cottage, 43 France St., 95476, 707-996-4359 |
| Sonoma | Magliulo's Pensione, 691 Broadway, 95476 |
| Sonoma | Thistle Dew Inn, 171 W. Spain St., 95476, 707-938-2909 |
| Sonora | Eller House B&B, P.O. Box 4056, 95370, 209-532-0420 |
| Sonora | Lulu Belle's B&B, 85 Gold St., 95370, 209-533-3455 |
| Sonora | Mountain View B&B, 12980 Mtn. View Rd., 95370, 209-533-0628 |
| St. Helena | Ambrose Bierce House, 1515 Main St., 94574, 707-963-3003 |
| St. Helena | Bale Mill Inn, 3431 N St. Helena Hwy., 94574, 707-963-4545 |
| St. Helena | Bell Creek B&B, 3220 Silverado Tr., 94574, 707-963-2383 |
| St. Helena | Creekside Inn, 945 Main St., 94574, 707-963-7244 |
| St. Helena | Creekwood, 850 Conn Valley Rd., 94574, 707-963-3590 |
| St. Helena | Elsie's Conn Valley Inn, 726 Rossi Rd., 94574, 707-963-4614 |
| St. Helena | Glass Mountain Inn, 3100 Silverado Trail, 94574, 707-963-3512 |
| St. Helena | Harvest Inn, One Main St., 94574, 707-963-9463 |
| St. Helena | Hotel St. Helena, 1309 Main St., 94574, 707-963-4388 |
| St. Helena | Ink House B&B, The, 1575 St. Helena Hwy., 94574, 707-963-3890 |
| St. Helena | Judy's Ranch House, 701 Rossi Rd., 94574, 707-963-3081 |
| St. Helena | Meadowood Resort, 900 Meadowood Ln., 94574, 707-963-3646 |

| | |
|---|---|
| St. Helena | Oliver House Country Inn, 2970 Silverado Tr., 94574, 707-963-4089 |
| St. Helena | Prager Winery B&B, 1281 Lewelling Ln., 94574, 707-963-3713 |
| St. Helena | Spanish Villa Inn, 474 Glass Mtn. Rd., 94574, 707-963-7483 |
| St. Helena | Toller's Guest Cottage, 917 Charter Oak, 94574 |
| St. Helena | Vineyard Country Inn, 201 Main St., 94574, 707-963-1000 |
| St. Helena | White Ranch, 707 White Ln., 94574, 707-963-4635 |
| St. Helena | Wine Country Inn, The, 1152 Lodi Lane, 94574, 707-963-7077 |
| St. Helena | Zinfandel Inn, The, 800 Zinfandel Ln., 94574, 707-963-3512 |
| Stockton | Old Victorian Inn, 207 W. Acacia St., 95203, 209-462-1613 |
| Studio City | Figs Cottage, 3935 Rhodes Ave., 91604, 818-769-2662 |
| Summerland | Summerland Inn, 2161 Ortega Hill Rd,B12, 93067, 805-969-5225 |
| Sunset Beach | Sunset B&B Inn, P.O. Box 1202, 90742, 213-592-1666 |
| Susanville | Roseberry House, 609 North St., 96130 |
| Sutter Creek | Foxes in Sutter Creek, 77 Main St., 95685, 209-267-5882 |
| Sutter Creek | Grey Gables B&B Inn, P.O. Box 1687, 95685 |
| Sutter Creek | Nancy & Bob's Inn, P.O. Box 386, 95685, 209-267-0342 |
| Sutter Creek | Picturerock Inn, P.O. Box 395, 95685 |
| Tahoe City | Chateau Place, P.O. Box 5254, 96145, 800-773-0313 |
| Tahoe City | Cottage Inn at Lake Tahoe, P.O. Box 66, 95730, 916-581-4073 |
| Tahoma | Norfolk Woods Inn, P.O. Box 262, 96142, 916-525-5000 |
| Three Rivers | Cort Cottage, P.O. Box 245, 93271, 209-561-4671 |
| Tomales | Tomales Country Inn, P.O. Box 376, 94971, 707-878-2041 |
| Torrance | White's House, The, 17122 Faysmith Ave., 90504, 310-324-6164 |
| Trinity Center | Carrville Inn, Star Rt. 2, Box 3536, 96091 |
| Twain Harte | Twain Harte's B&B, P.O. Box 1718, 95383, 209-586-3311 |
| Ukiah | Sanford House, 306 S. Pine, 95482, 707-462-1653 |
| Universal City | E. Daday, P.O. Box 8774, 91608 |
| Upper Lake | Narrows Lodge, 5670 Blue Lake Rd., 95485, 707-275-2718 |
| Valley Ford | Llamas Loft B&B Cottage, 14430 Coast Hwy. 1, 94972, 707-795-5726 |
| Valley Ford | Valley Ford Hotel, 14415 Coast Hwy. One, 94972 |
| Venice | Rose Inn, The, 2435 Lincoln Blvd, 90291 |
| Venice | Venice Beach House, The, 15 30th Ave., 90291, 310-823-1966 |
| Ventura | Baker Inn, 1093 Poli St., 93001, 805-652-0143 |
| Ventura | Clocktower Inn, The, 181 E. Santa Clara St., 93001, 805-652-0141 |
| Ventura | Pierpont Inn by the Sea, 550 Sanjon Rd., 93001, 805-643-6144 |
| Ventura | Roseholm, 51 Sulphur Mt. Rd., 93001, 805-649-4014 |
| Visalia | Ben Maddox House, 601 N. Encina St., 93291, 209-739-0721 |
| Visalia | Spalding House, 631 E. Encine, 93291 |
| Volcano | Volcano Inn, P.O. Box 4, 95689, 209-296-4959 |
| Walnut Creek | Gasthaus zum Baren, 2113 Blackstone Dr., 94598, 510-934-8119 |
| Walnut Creek | Mansion at Lakewood, The, 1056 Hacienda Dr., 94598, 510-945-3600 |
| Warner Springs | Warner Springs Ranch, Box 10, 92086, 619-782-4219 |
| Watsonville | Knighttime B&B, 890 Calabasas Rd., 95076, 408-684-0528 |
| Weaverville | Granny's House, P.O. Box 31, 96093, 916-623-2756 |
| West Covina | Hendrick Inn, 2124 E. Merced Ave., 91791, 818-919-2125 |
| Westport | Bowen's Pelican Lodge, P.O. Box 35, 95488, 707-964-5588 |
| Westport | DeHaven Valley Farm, 39247 N. Highway One, 95488, 707-961-1660 |
| Westport | Westport Inn B&B, Box 145, 95488, 707-964-5135 |
| Whittier | Coleen's California Casa, P.O. Box 9302, 90608, 310-699-8427 |
| Williams | Wilbur Hot Springs, Star Route, 95987, 916-473-2306 |
| Yosemite W. | Rockwood Gardens, 5155 Tip Top Rd., 95389 |
| Yountville | Napa Valley Railway Inn, 6503 Washington St., 94559, 707-944-2000 |
| Yountville | Sybron House, P.O. Box 3449, 94599, 707-944-2785 |
| Yountville | Webber Place, 6610 Webber St., 94599, 707-944-8384 |
| Yuba City | Harkey House B&B, 212 C St., 95991, 916-674-1942 |
| Yuba City | Moore Mansion Inn, 560 Cooper Ave., 95991, 916-674-8559 |
| Yuba City | Wick's, 560 Cooper Ave., 95991, 916-674-7951 |

# Colorado

## ALAMOSA

**Cottonwood Inn B&B**
123 San Juan Ave., 81101
719-589-3882 800-955-2623
Julie Ann Mordecai
All year

$$-B&B
7 rooms, 7 pb
MC, Visa, *Rated*, •
C-yes/S-ltd
Spanish

Full gourmet breakfast
Library, carriage house
Neutrogena soaps/creams
turn-down service

*Charming inn adorned with artwork & antiques. Biking, hiking, dune walking, fishing, bird-watching, skiing. Historically furnished dining room. 3rd night 50% Nov.–Feb.*

## ASPEN

| **Hearthstone House** | $$$-B&B | Full breakfast |
|---|---|---|
| 134 E. Hyman St., 81611 | 17 rooms, 17 pb • | Afternoon tea, cookies |
| 970-925-7632 Fax: 970-920-4450 | AmEx, MC, Visa, • | Hot tub, bed turndown |
| Irma Prodinger | C-ltd/S-ltd/P-no/H-no | service, sitting room, |
| Summer & winter | French, German | fireplace, herbal bath |

*The preferred place to stay! Distinctive lodge with the hospitality and services in the finest tradition of European luxury inns.* **Complimentary chocolates.**

| **Innsbruck Inn** | $$-B&B | Cont. bkfst. (summer) |
|---|---|---|
| 233 W. Main St., 81611 | 30 rooms, 30 pb | Full bkfst. (winter) |
| 970-925-2980 | Most CC, *Rated*, • | Afternoon tea (winter) |
| Heinz & Karen Coordes | C-yes/S-yes/P-no/H-no | sitt. rm, hot tub, sauna |
| 6/1–10/15, 11/23–4/15 | German | heated outdoor pool |

*Tyrolean charm and decor; located at ski shuttle stop, 4 blocks from malls. Sunny breakfast room, generous breakfast buffet, apres-ski refreshments, fireside lobby.*

| **Snow Queen Victorian B&B** | $$-B&B | Continental plus bkfst. |
|---|---|---|
| 124 E. Cooper St., 81611 | 7 rooms, 7 pb | Weekly party in winter |
| 970-925-8455 Fax: 970-925-7391 | AmEx, MC, Visa, • | Parlor w/fireplace, TV |
| Norma Dolle, L. Ledingham | C-yes/S-yes/P-no/H-no | outdoor hot tub, skiing |
| All year | Spanish | 2 kitchen units |

*Quaint, family-oriented Victorian lodge built in 1880s. Parlor w/fireplace & color TV. Walk to restaurants, shops & ski area. Most rooms have TV & phone.* **Weekly discounts, ltd.**

## BASALT

| **Altamira Ranch B&B** | $$-B&B | Full breakfast |
|---|---|---|
| P.O. Box 875, 81621 | 2 rooms, | Sitting room, river fun |
| 23484 Hwy 82 | Visa, MC, • | gold medal trout stream |
| 970-927-3309 | C-ltd/S-no/P-no/H-no | by Glenwood Hot Springs |
| Martha Waterman | | |
| All year | | |

*Beautiful ranch house situated on 180 acres bordering the Roaring Fork River. Quiet, peaceful, country atmosphere only 15 min. from Aspen. Close to skiing, hiking & biking.*

| **Shenandoah Inn** | $$-B&B | Full breakfast |
|---|---|---|
| P.O. Box 560, 81621 | 4 rooms, 2 pb | Snacks, wine |
| 0600 Frying Pan Rd. | *Rated*, • | Sitting room, hot tub |
| 970-927-4991 Fax: 970-927-4990 | C-ltd/S-ltd/P-no/H-no | bicycles, skiing, rafts, |
| 800-804-5520 | French, Spanish | golf, tennis, fishing |
| Bob & Terri Ziets | | |
| All year | | |

*Contemporary Colorado B&B, situated on 2 riverfront acres on premier gold-medal trout stream. 20 min. to Aspen. Warm, friendly atmosphere, exceptional cuisine. New log cabin.*

## BOULDER

| **Boulder Victoria, The** | $$$-B&B | Continental plus bkfst. |
|---|---|---|
| 1305 Pine St., 80302 | 7 rooms, 7 pb | Afternoon tea, snacks |
| 303-938-1300 | AmEx, MC, Visa, | Sitting room, patio |
| Kristen Peterson & Zoe | *Rated*, • | deck, steam showers |
| Kircos | C-ltd/S-no/P-no/H-ltd | 2 new guest houses |
| All year | | |

*Victorian grandeur in downtown Boulder. Brass beds with down comforters; fine period antiques; evening desserts & cappucino served in elegant parlor after a night on the town.*

## BOULDER

**Briar Rose B&B Inn**
2151 Arapahoe Ave., 80302
303-442-3007 Fax: 303-786-8440
Margaret & Bob Weisenbach
All year

$$$-B&B
9 rooms, 9 pb
Most CC, *Rated*, •
C-ltd/S-no/P-no/H-no
Spanish

Continental plus bkfst.
Afternoon tea & cookies
Comp. sherry & lemonade
bicycles, A/C, renovated
AAA rated 3 diamonds

*Entering the Briar Rose is like entering another time when hospitality was an art & the place for dreams was a feather bed. Three rooms w/fireplaces.* **10% disc't for 5 nights.**

---

**Earl House Historic Inn**
2429 Broadway, 80304
303-938-1400 Fax: 303-938-9710
Zoe Kircos, Meredith
Lederer     All year

$$$-B&B
6 rooms, 6 pb
Visa, MC, AmEx,
*Rated*, •
C-ltd/S-no/P-no/H-ltd

Continental plus bkfst.
Aftn. tea, comp. wine
Sitting room
sauna
Jacuzzis in some rooms

*Indulge in the luxury of Victorian grandeur. Enjoy beautifully renovated rooms with steam showers or Jacuzzis, gourmet breakfast, afternoon tea. Downtown location.*

## BRECKENRIDGE

**Allaire Timbers Inn**
P.O. Box 4653, 80424
9511 Hwy #9/So. Main St.
970-453-7530 Fax: 970-453-8699
800-624-4904
Jack & Kathy Gumph
All year

$$$$-B&B
10 rooms, 10 pb
AmEx, MC, Visa,
*Rated*, •
C-ltd/S-no/P-no/H-yes

Full breakfast
Winter full breakfast
Snacks, comp. wine
Sitting room, fireplaces
hot tubs, in-room phones

*Newly constructed log and stone Inn; suites with private hot tub and fireplace; spectacular mountain views; quiet luxury; personalized hospitality.*

---

**Hunt Placer Inn**
P.O. Box 4898, 80424
275 Ski Hill Rd.
970-453-7573 Fax: 970-453-2355
800-472-1430
Carl & Gwen Ray
All year

$$$-B&B
8 rooms, 8 pb
Most CC, *Rated*, •
C-ltd/S-no/P-no/H-yes
German

Full breakfast
Afternoon tea
Sitting room, library
guest area fireplaces
private balconies avail.

*New European-style chalet, surrounded by Spruce, Pine, & Aspen, with private balconies. In-town seclusion with marvelous breakfasts. Elevator for wheelchair access.*

---

**Swan Mountain Inn**
16172 Hwy. 9, 80435
970-453-7903  800-578-3687
Steve Gessner
All year

$-B&B
4 rooms, 3 pb
Visa, MC, Disc., •
C-yes/S-no/P-no/H-yes

Full gourmet breakfast
Afternoon tea
Restaurant, bar service
Sitting room, hot tubs
Glassed sun porch

*A log inn creating a cozy, warm atmposhere of beauty and luxury; combining an elegant, cathedral dining room, 2 cozy fireside bars, & romantic rooms.* **Glass of wine w/dinner.**

---

**Williams House B&B, c.1885**
P.O. Box 2454, 80424
303 N. Main St.
970-453-2975  800-795-2975
Diane Jaynes, Fred Kinat
All year exc. May & Oct

$$$-B&B
6 rooms, 6 pb
AmEx, *Rated*, •
C-ltd/S-no/P-no/H-no

Full breakfast—winter
Continental plus—summer
Fireplace, hot tub
Front porch swing
Victorian Cottage c1880

*Step back in time to gold fever Breckenridge. Restored historic mining home furnished w/ antiques. 2 romantic fireplaced parlours. Separate cottage, great for honeymoons.*

## BUENA VISTA

| **Adobe Inn, The** | $$-B&B | Full breakfast |
| P.O. Box 1560, 81211 | 5 rooms, 5 pb | Complimentary beverages |
| 303 N. Hwy 24 | MC, Visa, *Rated*, | Restaurant, sitting room |
| 719-395-6340 | C-ltd/S-no/P-no/H-no | library, piano, solarium |
| Paul, Marjorie & Michael | some Spanish | 2 suites, jacuzzi |
| Knox   All year | | |

*Santa Fe-style adobe hacienda. Indian, Mexican, antique, wicker & Mediterranean rooms. Indian fireplaces. Jacuzzi. Majestic mountains. Gourmet Mexican restaurant.*

## CARBONDALE

| **Mt. Sopris Inn** | $$$-B&B | Full breakfast |
| P.O. Box 126, 81623 | 23 rooms, 23 pb | Snacks |
| 0165 Mr. Sopris Ranch Rd. | Visa, MC, *Rated*, • | Sitting room, library |
| 970-963-2209 Fax: 970-963-8975 | C-ltd/S-no/P-no/H-yes | hot tub, swimming pool |
| 800-437-8675 | | pool table, game room |
| Barbara Fasching   All year | | |

*Country elegance-central to Aspen. Professionally decorated for the discriminating guest who appreciates the opportunity to relax & enjoy. 18 hole golf course adjacent to Inn.*

## COLORADO SPRINGS

| **Cheyenne Canon Inn** | $$-B&B | Full breakfast |
| 2030 W. Cheyenne Rd., | 7 rooms, 7 pb | Snacks |
| 80906 | Most CC, *Rated*, • | Sitting room (2) |
| 719-633-0625  Fax: 719-633-8826 | C-ltd/S-no/P-no/H-no | hot tubs, great room |
| 800-633-0625 | French | porch, library |
| John, Barbara & Josh Starr | | |
| All year | | |

*Historic 10,000-sq.-ft. Arts & Crafts mansion secluded in Cheyenne Canyon. Luxury honeymoon/VIP cottage with kink-sized bed, marble bath with 2 person shower, fireplace & more*

| **Holden House—1902 B&B** | $$$-B&B | Full gourmet breakfast |
| 1102 W. Pikes Peak Ave., | 6 rooms, 6 pb | Comp. coffee, tea, snack |
| 80904 | Most CC, *Rated*, • | Parlor w/TV, living room |
| 719-471-3980 | S-no/P-no/H-yes | suite w/disabled access |
| Sallie & Welling Clark | | "Tubs for Two," veranda |
| All year | | |

*Charming 1902 storybook Victorian home filled w/antiques & family heirlooms in Historic District. Suites w/fireplaces & phones. Conveniently located. Friendly resident cats.*

| **Painted Lady B&B Inn** | $$-B&B | Full breakfast |
| 1318 W. Colorado Ave., | 4 rooms, 4 pb | Comp. coffee/tea, snacks |
| 80904 | Most CC, *Rated*, • | Parlor w/TV, living room |
| 719-473-3165  Fax: 719-635-1396 | C-ltd/S-no/P-no/H-no | wraparound porch, frplc. |
| Valerie & Zan Maslowski | | outdoor hot tub & deck |
| All year | 800-370-3165 | |

*1894 Victorian home nestled in historic Old Colorado City. Guest rooms feature Victorian furnishings. Hearty, healthy breakfasts begin your day. Friendly resident cat.*

| **Room @ the Inn, Victorian** | $$$-B&B | Full breakfast |
| 618 N. Nevada Ave.,   80903 | 7 rooms, 7 pb | Afternoon tea, snacks |
| 719-442-1896 Fax: 719-442-6302 | Most CC, *Rated*, • | Sitting room, library |
| 800-579-4621 | C-ltd/S-no/P-no/H-yes | hot tubs, library |
| Chick & Jan McCormick | | museums, city parks |
| All year | | |

*Experience the charm, elegance and hospitality of an 1896 Victorian home. A romantic retreat in the heart of the city.* **3rd night, 30% off.**

## COLORADO SPRINGS/CASCADE

| | | |
|---|---|---|
| **Eastholme in the Rockies** | $$-B&B | Full gourmet breakfast |
| P.O. Box 98, 80809 | 8 rooms, 5 pb | Sitting room |
| 4445 Haggerman Ave. | Visa, MC, • | library, guest kitchen |
| 719-684-9901 800-672-9901 | C-ltd/S-no/P-no/H-no | hiking trails nearby |
| Terry Thompson All year | | |

*Quiet mountain getaway, spectacular setting, gracious Victorian atmosphere with large antique-filled rooms. Gourmet breakfast. Convenient to many scenic areas.*

## CONEJOS

| | | |
|---|---|---|
| **Conejos River Guest Ranch** | $$-B&B | Full breakfast |
| P.O. Box 175, 81129 | 8 rooms, 8 pb | Boxed lunch/dinner (fee) |
| 25390 Hwy 17 | Visa, MC, • | Restaurant, bar service |
| 719-376-2464 | C-yes/S-yes/P-yes/H-ltd | sitting room, library |
| Ms. Shorty Fry | Spanish | bikes, fishing |
| Mid May-Jan 2nd | | |

*The traveller's choice in south central Colorado; twelve park-like acres with mile of river frontage; fabulous food; hospitality extraordinaire; relax-revive-renew.*

## CRESTED BUTTE

| | | |
|---|---|---|
| **Cristiana Guesthaus B&B** | $$-B&B | Continental plus bkfst. |
| P.O. Box 427, 81224 | 21 rooms, 21 pb | Comp. hot beverages |
| 621 Maroon Ave. | Most CC, • | Sitting room |
| 970-349-5326 Fax: 970-349-1962 | C-yes/S-ltd/P-no/H-no | hot tub, sauna |
| 800-824-7899 | | |
| Rosie & Martin Catmur | | |
| All year | | |

*Close to historic downtown. Relaxed, friendly atmosphere. Enjoy the hot tub, sauna, sun deck, and homebaked breakfast served in our cozy lobby. Superb mountain views.*

| | | |
|---|---|---|
| **Purple Mountain Lodge** | $$-B&B | Full breakfast |
| P.O. Box 547, 81224 | 5 rooms, 3 pb | Sitting room, hot tub |
| 714 Gothic Ave. | Most CC, • | aftn. apres ski daily |
| 970-349-5888 800-286-3574 | C-ltd/S-no/P-no/H-no | close to downtown, shops |
| Paul & Marilyn Caldwell | Swiss | |
| Summer & winter | | |

*Newly remodeled and redecorated Victorian home in historic town. Relax by the massive stone fireplace in the living room; breakfast with view of Mt. Crested Butte.* **Disc't on 3+ nights.**

## DENVER

| | | |
|---|---|---|
| **Capitol Hill Mansion** | $$$-B&B | Full breakfast |
| 1207 Pennsylvania St., 80203 | 8 rooms, 8 pb | Snacks, comp. wine, frig |
| 303-839-5221 Fax: 303-839-9046 | Most CC, *Rated*, • | Sitting room, hot tub |
| 800-839-9329 | C-ltd/S-no/P-no/H-yes | A/C, cable TV, phones |
| Kathy Robbins All year | | heirlooms, original art |

*Colorado's most luxurious inn! Downtown Denver in historic mansion, perfect for business travelers but also designed for perfect romance. Historic Register. 2 rooms w/king beds, 1 w/king or 2 twins.*

| | | |
|---|---|---|
| **Castle Marne—Urban Inn** | $$$-B&B | Full gourmet breakfast |
| 1572 Race St., 80206 | 9 rooms, 9 pb | Afternoon tea |
| 303-331-0621 Fax: 303-331-0623 | AmEx, MC, Visa, | Library, gift shop |
| 800-92-MARNE | *Rated*, • | game room w/pool table |
| The Peiker Family & Staff | C-ltd/S-no/P-no/H-no | computer, Fax, copier |
| All year | Spanish, Hungarian | |

*Luxury urban inn. Minutes from convention center, business district, shopping, fine dining. Local & Nat'l Historic Structure. 3 rooms w/private balconies & hot tubs for two.*

## DENVER

**Haus Berlin B&B**
1651 Emerson St., 80128
303-837-9527 Fax: 303-837-9527
800-659-0253
Christiana Brown
All year

$$$-B&B
4 rooms, 4 pb
AmEx, MC, Visa,
*Rated*, •
S-no/P-no/H-no
German

Full breakfast
Complimentary wine
Sitting room
library

*Beds are dressed in luxurious European linens. Urban, conveniently located uptown for tourists and business travelers. 10% discount on 3+ nights.*

**Queen Anne B&B Inn**
2147 Tremont Pl., Clements
Historic Dist., 80205
303-296-6666 Fax: 303-296-2151
800-432-INNS
Tom & Chris King    All year

$$$-B&B
14 rooms, 14 pb
Most CC, *Rated*, •
C-yes/S-no/P-no/H-ltd

Full breakfast
Afternoon wine
Fresh flowers, phones
7 rooms w/special tubs
flower garden,patio, A/C

*Award winning Victorian Inn. Facing downtown park. Walk to 16th St. Mall, shops, museums, convention center/business district. On National Historic Register. Airport shuttle.*

**Victoria Oaks Inn**
1575 Race St., 80206
303-355-1818 Fax: 303-331-1095
800-662-6257
Clyde & Ric
All year

$$-B&B
9 rooms, 7 pb
Most CC, *Rated*, •
S-yes/P-no/H-no

Continental plus bkfst.
Complimentary wine
Sitting room

*Located 1 mile east of downtown Denver in the Wymans Historic District; convenient to restaurants, museums, shopping, zoo, parks, theater & sports. 2 nights free on 7.*

## DIVIDE

**Silver Wood B&B at Divide**
463 Country Rd. 512, 80814
719-687-6784 Fax: 719-687-1009
800-753-5592
Bess & Larry Oliver
All year

$$-B&B
2 rooms, 2 pb
Most CC, *Rated*, •
C-yes/S-no/P-no/H-no

Full breakfast
Snacks
Sitting room, library
friendly resident cats

*Perfect get-away with glorious views from private decks. Nature trails abound. Enjoy a country/gourmet breakfast and outstanding hospitality.*

## DURANGO

**Apple Orchard Inn**
7758 Country Rd. 203, 81301
970-247-0751 800-426-0751
Celeste & John Gardiner
All year

$$$-B&B
10 rooms, 10 pb
Most CC, *Rated*, •
C-ltd/S-ltd/P-no/H-yes
Portuguese & Italian

Full breakfast, snacks
Aftn. tea, comp. wine
Lunch, dinner
Sitting room
Airport Shuttle

*Charming, spacious rooms and cottages with featherbeds, fireplaces, Jacuzzi tubs, and private patios. Beautiful gardens. Convenient to town, golf, skiing. 10% disc't., ltd.*

**Country Sunshine B&B**
35130 Hwy. 550 N., 81301
970-247-2853 Fax: 970-247-1203
800-383-2853
Beanie & Gary Archie
All year

$$$-B&B
6 rooms, 6 pb
Most CC, *Rated*, •
C-ltd/S-no/P-no/H-yes

Full country breakfast
Afternoon tea
Comp. wine, beer, snacks
sitting room
library, hot tub

*Spacious ranch-style house on 3 acres of Pine Oak forest. Abundant wildlife, skiing, fishing, golf, mountain biking, hot tub. Package ski offer, ask.*

DURANGO ─────────────────────────────────

| **Leland House/Rochester** | $$$-B&B | Full gourmet breakfast |
| **Htl** | 25 rooms, 25 pb | Afternoon tea, library |
| 721 E. Second Ave.,  81301 | Most CC, *Rated*,  • | Sitting room |
| 970-385-1920  Fax: 970-385-1967 | C-ltd/S-no/P-ltd/H-yes | |
| 800-664-1920 | Spanish | |
| The Komicks    All year | | |

*Historic downtown location–walk to unique shops, restaurants, Durango-Silverton RR. Cowboy Victorianna decor inspired by movies made in the area.* **7th night free, ltd.**

─────────────────────────────────

| **Lightner Creek Inn** | $$$-B&B | Full breakfast |
| 999 CR 207,  81301 | 8 rooms, 5 pb | Afternoon tea, snacks |
| 970-259-1226  Fax: 970-259-0732 | Visa, MC, Disc.,*Rated*, | Sitting room, cross-country |
| The Houston | • | skiing, hiking, mountain |
| All year | C-ltd/S-no/P-no/H-yes | biking, llama hikes, town 4 mi. |

*Romantic country retreat amid wildlife refuge on 20 acres. Breakfast in sunroom over-looking pond, stream & llama pasture. Cozy, luxurious rooms.* **10% off 6 or more nights.**

─────────────────────────────────

| **Logwood B&B** | $$-B&B | Full country breakfast |
| 35060 Hwy. 550N,  81301 | 6 rooms, 6 pb | Aftn. tea, snacks |
| 970-259-4396  Fax: 970-259-7812 | MC, Visa, *Rated*,  • | Lunch box by request |
| 800-369-4082 | C-ltd/S-no/P-no/H-no | sitting room, library |
| Greg & Debby Verheyden | | swimming pool nearby |
| All year | | |

*Luxurious, 3-story log home w/wrap-around porch on 15 acres—animals, river valley, San Juan Mtns. Award-winning desserts.* **10% off 2+ nights during winter, 3+ nights in summer.**

─────────────────────────────────

| **River House B&B** | $$-B&B | Full gourmet breakfast |
| 495 Animas View Dr.,  81301 | 6 rooms, 6 pb | Comp. wine, juice/snacks |
| 970-247-4775  Fax: 970-259-1465 | Visa, MC. Disc. *Rated*, | Massage & hypnosis sess. |
| 800-254-4775 | • | exercise rm, hot springs |
| C. Carroll, K. & L. Enggren | C-yes/S-no/P-no/H-no | fish pond, hot tub |
| Exc. Oct 15–Nov 15, Apr | | |

*Dine in skylighted atrium. View the Animas River Valley. Hear the whistle of narrow-gauge train. Vegetarian meals avail. Cottage w/kitchen, bedroom.* **10% off 3 or more nights.**

DURANGO, HESPERUS ─────────────────────────────────

| **Blue Lake Ranch** | $$$-B&B | Full European breakfast |
| 16000 State Hwy 140,  81326 | 8 rooms, 8 pb | Afternoon tea |
| 970-385-4537  Fax: 970-385-4088 | *Rated*,  • | Sitt. room, sauna, lake |
| Shirley & David Alford | C-yes/S-no/P-no/H-no | extraordinary gardens |
| All year | | Cabin avail., bikes |

*Victorian farmhouse surrounded by gardens of flowers/vegetables/herbs. Spectacular lake & mountain views, trout-stocked lake, meals of homegrown ingredients.* **10% off 7+ nights.**

ESTES PARK ─────────────────────────────────

| **Anniversary Inn B&B, The** | $$$-B&B | Full gourmet breakfast |
| 1060 Mary's Lake Rd, | 4 rooms, 4 pb | Snacks |
| Moraine Route,  80517 | MC, Visa, *Rated*,  • | Sitting room, library |
| 970-586-6200  Norma & Harry | C-ltd/S-no/P-no/H-ltd | "Sweetheart" cottage |
| Menke      All year | | 3 rms w/jacuzzi tubs |

*Cozy, turn-of-the-century log home one mile from Rocky Mountain National Park. Come and be pampered. Member of BBCI and PAII. Special chocolate basket by request & payment.*

## ESTES PARK

| **Aspen Lodge at Estes Park** | $$$-B&B | Full breakfast |
| 6120 Hwy. 7,   80517 | 21 rooms, 21 pb | Lunch, dinner, bar |
| 970-586-8133  Fax: 970-586-8133 | *Rated*, • | Swimming pool |
| 800-332-6867 | C-yes/S-yes/P-no/H-no | entertainment |
| Tom & Jill Hall | | horseback riding, skiing |
| All year | | |

*Beautiful cozy lodge with magnificent view of Long's Peak & Rocky Mountain National Park. Exceptional meals and fine wine list.*

| **Black Dog Inn B&B** | $$-B&B | Full gourmet breakfast |
| P.O. Box 4659, 80517 | 4 rooms, 4 pb | Afternoon tea, snacks |
| 650 S. St. Vrain Ave. | MC, Visa, *Rated*, • | Jacuzzi tub for 2 |
| 970-586-0374 | C-ltd/S-no/P-no/H-no | sitt. room, lib., piano |
| Pete & Jane Princehorn | | 2 suites with fireplaces |
| All year | | |

*1910 Rambling mountain home snuggled among towering aspen & pine. View, antiques, cozy frplc. Western hospitality makes stay memorable. Honeymoon suite w/Jacuzzi for two.* **Free bottle of wine.**

| **Eagle Cliff B&B** | $$$-B&B | Full breakfast |
| Box 4312, 80517 | 3 rooms, 3 pb | Comp. wine, snacks |
| 2383 Hwy. 66 | • | Hot tubs |
| 970-586-5425 | C-yes/S-no/P-no/H-no | golf, tennis, horseback, |
| Nancy & Michael Conrin | Some Spanish | hiking, cross-country skiing- |
| All year | | near |

*Enjoy our cozy and quaint B&B and join us for one of our favorite hikes. New Jacuzzi tub in cottage. Our backyard is the Rocky Mountain National Park!*

## EVERGREEN

| **Bears R Inn** | $$$-B&B | Continental breakfast |
| 27425 Spruce Ln,   80439 | 12 rooms, 12 pb | Afternoon tea, snacks |
| 303-670-1205  Fax: 303-670-8542 | S-no/P-no/H-no | Sitting room |
| 800-863-1205 | | |
| Billie & Bob Lewis | | |
| All year | | |

*Secluded mountain country inn with great views of the Continental Divide. Full country breakfast served from May 15-Sep.15. Golfing, hiking, bicycling, fishing and horseback riding locally*

| **Highland Haven Creekside** | $$$-B&B | Continental plus |
| 4395 Independence Trail, | 16 rooms, 16 pb | Afternoon tea, snacks |
| 80439 | Most CC, *Rated*, • | Sitting room, library |
| 303-674-3577  Fax: 303-674-9088 | C-yes/S-no/P-no/H-no | bicycles, tennis courts |
| 800-459-2406 | | hot tubs, sauna, pool |
| Gail Riley & Tom Statzell | | |
| All year | | |

*Mountain hideaway with exquisite views of mountains, streams, towering pines and gardens. Stroll to quaint shops and fine dining on Main Street Evergreen.*

## FORT COLLINS

| **West Mulberry Street B&B** | $$$-B&B | Full breakfast |
| 616 W. Mulberry St.,   80521 | 4 rooms, 4 pb | Beverage table |
| 970-221-1917  Fax: 970-490-2810 | Most CC, | Sitting room |
| Michael & Rebecca Martin | C-ltd/S-no/P-no/H-no | bicycles |
| All year | | |

*This lovely turn of the century four square style home built in 1905 offers charming, traditional style bed & breakfast accommodations.*

FRASER ───────────────────────────────

| **Anna Leah a B&B, The** | $$-B&B | Full breakfast |
| PO Box 305,   80442 | 5 rooms, 5 pb | Afternoon snacks, tea |
| 970-726-4414  800-237-9913 | Visa, MC, • | Sitting room, library |
| Patricia Handel | C-ltd/S-no/P-no/H-yes | 3 fireplaces, skiing |
| All year | Spanish | private balconies |

*New home furnished in antiques on 25 acres overlooking the Continental Divide in the heart of the Rocky Mts. A few miles from Winter Park. Hiking and biking nearby.*

FRISCO ───────────────────────────────

| **Galena St. Mountain Inn** | $$-B&B | Full breakfast (winter) |
| P.O. Box 417, 80443 | 14 rooms, 14 pb | Cont. Plus bkfst. (sum.) |
| 106 Galena St. | Most CC, *Rated*, • | Aftn. tea, sitting room |
| 970-668-3224  Fax: 970-668-1569 | C-yes/S-no/P-no/H-yes | library, hot tubs |
| Brenda McDonnell | | sauna, meeting rooms |
| All year | | |

*Striking Neo-mission-style furnishing, down comforters, windowseats, mountain views. Located minutes from Breckenridge, Keystone, Copper Mountain. **3rd night free, May & Oct. 1997, ltd.***

| **Mar Dei's B&B** | $-B&B | Full breakfast |
| P.O. Box 1767, 80443 | 5 rooms, 2 pb | Afternoon tea, snacks |
| 221 S. 4th Ave. | C-yes/S-no/P-no | Complimentary wine |
| 970-668-5337 | | sitting room, library |
| Mike & Amy Wolach/All year | | outdoor hot tub |

*Mar Dei's is a cozy European-style B&B, surrounded by 80 pines. Enjoy outside hot tub, bike path. 2 blocks to boat dock. **7th night free.***

GEORGETOWN ───────────────────────────────

| **Hardy House B&B Inn** | $$-B&B | Full breakfast |
| P.O. Box 156, 80444 | 4 rooms, 4 pb | Dinner on request, tea |
| 605 Brownell | Visa, MC dep. only, • | Sitting room, hot tub |
| 303-569-3388  800-490-4802 | C-ltd/S-no/P-no/H-no | sleigh rides, decks |
| Carla & Mike Wagner | | carriage, tandem bicycle |
| All year | | |

*Rocky Mountain Victorian 50 minutes from Denver. Candlelight breakfast of fresh baked goods. Shopping, hiking, skiing, fishing, cycling, carriage rides.*

GLENWOOD SPRINGS ───────────────────────────────

| **The B&B on Mitchell Creek** | $$$-B&B | Full breakfast |
| 1686 Mitchell Creek Rd., | 1 rooms, 1 pb | Dinner, snacks |
|  81601 | Visa, | Hiking trails, golf |
| 970-945-4002 | C-yes/S-no/P-ltd/H-no | horseback riding |
| Carole & Stan Rachesky | Some Spanish | river rafting |
| All year | | |

*Located in mountain setting, one private warm romantic suite; full breakfast served on deck overlooking rushing creek. Romantic dinners on request.*

GOLDEN ───────────────────────────────

| **Dove Inn, The** | $$-B&B | Full breakfast |
| 711 - 14th St.,   80401 | 6 rooms, 6 pb | Rooms have A/C, desks, |
| 303-278-2209  Fax: 303-273-5272 | Most CC, *Rated*, | phones and TVs |
| Connie & Tim Sheffield | C-yes/S-no/P-no/H-no | Golden West Shuttle |
| All year | | |

*Built prior to 1873, lots of country charm in the West Denver foothills. All Denver attractions and Rocky Mountains are nearby. **10% discount for 7 or more days.***

*Leroux Creek Inn, Hotchkiss, CO*

## GRAND JUNCTION

**Cider House B&B, The** | $-B&B | Full breakfast
1126 Grand Ave., 81501 | 5 rooms, 1 pb | Lunch, dinner (fee)
970-242-9087 | Visa, MC, AmEx, | Sitting room
Helen Mills   All year | C-yes/S-ltd/P-no/H-n | family friendly facility

*Victorian B&B close to downtown shopping, swimming, golf, tennis. Hearty breakfasts which you'll remember.*

## GRAND LAKE

**Columbine Creek Ranch** | $$-B&B | Full breakfast
P.O. Box 1675, 80447 | 11 rooms, 5 pb | Coffee & snacks
14814 US Hwy. 34 | Visa, MC, | Boat rental, fishing,
970-627-2429 Fax: 970-627-2429 | C-yes/S-no/P-ltd/H-ltd | golf, horseback riding
Tami & Jim Wold | | nearby, hot tubs
All year

*We offer quaint & charming surroundings. Built in the 1920s. 7 rooms, 1 with private bath; 6 share 2 baths. Family style breakfast. Sitting room w/fireplaces, big screen t.v.*

## GUNNISON

**Mary Lawrence Inn, The** | $$-B&B | Full breakfast
601 N. Taylor, 81230 | 5 rooms, 5 pb | Sack lunch (fee)
970-641-3343 Fax: 970-641-6719 | MC, Visa, *Rated*, • | Two suites
Pat & Jim Kennedy | C-ltd/S-no/P-no/H-no | sitting room, many books
All year | | tandem bicycles

*Our renovated home is inviting and comfortable; delectable breakfasts. Gunnison country offers marvelous outdoor adventures. Special diets accomodated.*

## HESPERUS

**La Plata Vista Ranch B&B** | $$-B&B | Full breakfast
13400 Country Rd. 120, | 3 rooms, 3 pb | Complimentary wine
81326 | Visa, MC, *Rated*, • | Close to river rafting,
970-247-9062 Fax: 970-247-5056 | C-yes/S-ltd/P-ltd/H-no | shopping, San Juan Nat'l
Kathy & John   All year | Korean | Forest & Mesa Verde Park

*Spectacular view of La Plata Mountains. Perfect for sky watchers dream. Private and quiet. 3rd night forward, 15% off.*

## HOTCHKISS

**Leroux Creek Inn, B&B** | $$-B&B | Full breakfast
P.O. Box 310, 81419 | 4 rooms, 4 pb | Snacks, comp. wine
1220-3100 Rd. | Visa, MC, • | Sitting room, library
970-872-4746 Fax: 970-872-4745 | C-ltd/S-no/P-no/H-yes | bicycles
Tom Leach   All year

*Adobe house on 80 scenic acres; views of mountains, mesas, desert canyons; quiet for renewal of body and spirit.*

## INDIAN HILLS

| | | |
|---|---|---|
| **Mountain View B&B** | $$-B&B | Full breakfast |
| P.O. Box 631, 80454 | 4 rooms, 4 pb | Afternoon tea |
| 4754 Picutis Rd. | Visa, MC, • | Sitting room |
| 303-697-6896 | C-ltd/S-no/P-no/H-no | breathtaking view of |
| Graham & Ortrud | German | Rockies |
| Richardson | | |
| All year | | |

*Large 1920s mountain home with warm, homey atmosphere. Easy access to mountain parks. Elegant English tea and gourmet breakfast. 3rd night, 50% off.*

## KEYSTONE

| | | |
|---|---|---|
| **Ski Tip Lodge** | $$$-B&B | Full breakfast |
| Box 38, 0764 Old Montezuma | 11 rooms, 9 pb | Restaurant, bar service |
| Rd., 80435 | Most CC, • | Cross-country skiing |
| 303-468-4202  800-222-0188 | C-ltd/S-no/P-no/H-no | tennis courts, library |
| Erin E. Clark | | sitting room |
| All year | | |

*Furnished in rustic style, no television or telephones. Ski Tip is perfect for seclusion and serenity. Guests get 25% off the entire dinner bill at Ski Tip.*

## LEADVILLE

| | | |
|---|---|---|
| **Apple Blossom Inn, The** | $$-B&B | Full breakfast |
| 120 W. 4th St., 80461 | 6 rooms, 2 pb | Lunch, dinner, snacks |
| 719-486-2141  800-982-9279 | MC, Visa, *Rated*, • | Sitting room |
| Maggie Senn | C-ltd/S-no/P-no/H-no | games provided |
| All year | | |

*Elegant and comforatable 1879 renovated banker's home. Beautiful and charming guest rooms in historic Leadville. Fabulous breakfast.*

| | | |
|---|---|---|
| **Delaware Hotel, THe** | $$-B&B | Full breakfast |
| 700 Harrison Ave., 80461 | 36 rooms, 36 pb | Lunch, dinner |
| 719-486-1418  800-748-2004 | Most CC, *Rated*, • | Restaurant, bar service |
| Susan & Scott Brackett | S-ltd/P-no/H-ltd | sitting room, library |
| All year | | hot tubs |

*"Award Winning" Historic Hotel. Period antiques, heirloom quilts, elegant Victorian lobby. Fine dining at Callaway's. Experience the charm of this 1860s Victorian mining town. 3rd night, 50% discount.*

| | | |
|---|---|---|
| **Ice Palace Inn, The** | $$$-B&B | Full breakfast |
| 813 Spruce St., 80461 | 3 rooms, 3 pb | Afternoon tea, snacks |
| 719-486-8272 | Most CC, • | Sitting room, library |
| Giles & Kami Kolakowski | C-ltd/S-no/P-no/H-no | antique shop, biking |
| All year | | hiking, tennis, fishing |

*Our inn's name, theme and location is based on Leadville's famous Ice Palace built in 1896. Come hear the story! 3rd night 50% off.*

| | | |
|---|---|---|
| **Wood Haven Manor B&B** | $$-B&B | Full breakfast |
| P.O. Box 1291, 80461 | 8 rooms, 7 pb | Afternoon tea, snacks |
| 809 Spruce | Most CC, *Rated*, • | Sitting room, library |
| 719-486-0109  Fax: 719-486-0210 | C-ltd/S-no/P-no/H-no | whirlpool, ski packages |
| 800-748-2570 | | family retreats |
| Jolene & Bobby Wood | | |
| All year | | |

*1890s Victorian home, spacious & comfortable living room w/massive carved wood fireplace, cable TV & VCR. Each room furnished w/antiques. 3rd night 50% off, Honeymoon Baskets.*

### LIMON

**Midwest Country Inn**
PO Box 550, 795 Main St.,
  80828
719-775-2373
Harold & Vivian Lowe
All year

$-EP
32 rooms, 32 pb
Most CC, *Rated*, •
C-yes/S-yes/P-no/H-no

Coffee & tea available
Restaurant—1 block
Sitting room, gift shop
"listening" waterfall
and "watching" fountain

*Beautiful rooms, oak antiques, stained glass, elegant wallpapered bathrooms. Quilts & antiques in rooms. Near I-70, 1.5 hours from Denver and Colorado Springs. Train rides available Saturday evenings.*

### LOVELAND

**Cattail Creek Inn**
2665 Abarr Dr.,  80538
970-667-7600 Fax: 970-667-8968
800-572-2466
Sue & Harold Buchman
All year

$$$-B&B
8 rooms, 8 pb
Most CC, •
C-ltd/S-no/P-no/H-yes

Full breakfast
Complimentary wine
Sitting room, bicycles
snacks, golf, trails
near art galeries

*Designed and built to be a luxury inn, mountain views, golf course location, gourmet breakfasts, bronze scuplture and orginal art work.*

**Derby Hill Inn B&B**
2502 Courtney Dr.,  80537
970-667-3193  Fax: 970-667-3193
800-498-8086
Beverly J. McCue
All year

$$-B&B
2 rooms, 2 pb
Visa, MC, AmEx, •
S-no/P-no/H-no
German

Full breakfast
Comp. soft drinks
Early morning coffee
sitting room

*Awake from luxurious accommodations to the aroma of freshly brewed coffee and gourmet breakfast. Four star golf packages available.* **10% disc't for 5+ days; 10% senior discount.**

### MANCOS

**Lost Canyon Lodge**
15472 Country Rd. 35.3,
  81328
  800-992-1098
Beth Newman
All year

$$-B&B
5 rooms, 5 pb
Visa, MC, *Rated*, •
C-yes/S-no/P-no/H-no

Full breakfast
Snacks
Sitting room, library
hot tubs, we host mtngs
renunions and weddings

*Contemporary log home nestled in the tall pines overlooking Lost Canyon Lake. Country breakfast. 5 guestrooms w/private baths. Personalized pampering.*

**Riversbend B&B**
42505 Hwy. 160,  81328
970-533-7353  800-699-8994
Gaye & Jack Curran
All year

$$-B&B
4 rooms,
Visa, MC, Disc., •
C-ltd/S-no/P-no/H-no

Full breakfast
Snacks, comp. wine
Sitting room, hot tubs

*7 miles from Mesa Verde National park. Log inn on Mancos River. Antiques. Hot Tub. Porch swings.*

### MANITOU SPRINGS

**Red Crags B&B Inn**
302 El Paso Blvd.,  80829
719-685-1920 Fax: 719-685-1073
800-721-2248
Howard & Lynda Lerner
All year

$$-B&B
6 rooms, 6 pb
Most CC, *Rated*, •
C-ltd/S-no/P-no/H-no

Full gourmet breakfast
Afternoon tea, dessert
Complimentary wine
parlor/sun rm., hot tub
murder mistery weekends

*Historic 1870s Victorian mansion—a romantic hideaway. Lose yourself somwhere in time. Extensive herb & flower gardens. A favorite of Teddy Roosevelt.*

MANITOU SPRINGS ─────────────────────────────────

| **Two Sisters Inn-a B&B** | $$-B&B | Full gourmet breakfast |
|---|---|---|
| Ten Otoe Place,   80829 | 5 rooms, 3 pb | Comp. beverages, incl. |
| 719-685-9684 | MC, Visa *Rated*, • | Manitou Mineral Water |
| 800-2-SISINN | C-ltd/S-no/P-no/H-no | living room w/fireplace |
| Sharon Smith, Wendy | | parlor with 1896 piano |
| Goldstein | | |
| All year | | |

*Award-winning gracious Victorian nestled at base of Pike's Peak in historic district. Garden honeymoon cottage. Mineral springs, hiking, art galleries, shops, restaurants.*

MINTURN ─────────────────────────────────────────

| **Eagle River Inn** | $$$-B&B | Full breakfast |
|---|---|---|
| P.O. Box 100, 81645 | 12 rooms, 12 pb | Comp. wine & cheese |
| 145 N. Main St. | AmEx, MC, Visa, | Sitting room, patio |
| 970-827-5761 | *Rated*, • | hot tub, backyard, bikes |
| Fax: 970-827-4020 | C-ltd/S-no/P-no/H-no | conference/banquet room |
| 800-344-1750 | | |
| Patty Bidez | | |
| Exc. May & mid-October | | |

*Quiet romantic mountain inn nestled alongside the Eagle River minutes from Vail Ski Resort. Furnished in southwest decor. Hot tub, snowshoes in winter, mountain bikes in summer. Perfect for couples.*

| **Minturn Inn, The** | $$-B&B | Full breakfast |
|---|---|---|
| P.O. Box 186, 81645 | 7 rooms, 5 pb | Complimentary wine |
| 442 Main St. | Visa, MC, AmEx, • | Sitting room, sauna |
| 970-827-9647 | C-ltd/S-no/P-no/H-no | Fantastic starting point |
| Fax: 970-827-5590 | | for all activities |
| 800-646-8874 | | |
| T & C Sullivan, M. Kelly | | |
| All year | | |

*Ideally located between Vail & Beaver Creek resorts. A 1915 historic home featuring custom made log beds, antler chandeliers, hardwood floors and a river rock fireplace.*

MONTROSE ────────────────────────────────────────

| **Uncompahgre B&B, The** | $$-B&B | Full breakfast |
|---|---|---|
| 21049 Uncompahgre Rd., | 8 rooms, 8 pb | Afternoon tea |
|   81401 | Visa, MC, AmEx, Disc., | Complimentary wine |
| 970-240-4000  800-318-8127 | • | sitting room |
| Barb & Rich Helm | C-yes/S-no/P-yes/H-yes | |
| All year | | |

*Historic lodge in lush valley; views of Cimarrons & San Juan Mtns. Central to SW Colorado attractions. Elegant decor, spacious.* **3rd night, 50%.**

OURAY ────────────────────────────────────────────

| **China Clipper B&B** | $$-B&B | Delicious full breakfast |
|---|---|---|
| P.O. Box 801, 81427 | 11 rooms, 11 pb | Afternoon wine, snacks |
| 525 Second St. | Visa, MC, *Rated*, • | Sitting room, library |
| 970-325-0565  Fax: 970-325-4190 | C-ltd/S-no/P-no/H-yes | hot tubs |
| 800-315-0565 | | Champagne w/2 nights. |
| Elaine & Earl Yarbrough | | |
| All year | | |

*Elegant, romantic, comfortable inn centrally located in Switzerland of America. In-room tubs for two, fireplaces, garden hot tub. Pampering, utter relaxation guaranteed.*

## OURAY

**St. Elmo Hotel**
P.O. Box 667, 81427
426 Main St.
970-325-4951  Fax: 970-325-0348
Dan & Sandy Lingenfelter
All year

$$-B&B
9 rooms, 9 pb
MC, Visa, *Rated*, •
C-yes/S-ltd/P-no/H-no

Full breakfast
Restaurant
Comp. wine, coffee, tea
piano, outdoor hot tub
sauna, meeting room

*Hotel & Bon Ton Restaurant surrounded by beautiful, rugged 14,000-ft. peaks. Furnished with antiques, stained glass & brass; honeymoon suite. Hot springs, jeeping, cross-country skiing.*

## PAGOSA SPRINGS

**Endaba Wilderness Retreat**
P.O. Box 1211, 81147
1197A Perry Dr.
970-731-4310  Fax: 970-731-4888
Bill & Lyn Gullette
All year

$-B&B
8 rooms, 2 pb
Visa, MC, •
C-yes/S-no/P-no/H-no
German, Spanish, Sign

Full breakfast
Sitting room, library
hot tubs, barbeques
game rooms, lake fishing

*Comfortable, secluded mountain lodge overlooking small lake, beautiful scenery and wildlife. Full breakfast. Back country skiing, hiking, biking, fishing, birding.*

## PUEBLO

**Abriendo Inn**
300 W. Abriendo Ave.,   81004
719-544-2703  Fax: 719-542-6544
Kerrelyn Trent
All year

$$-B&B
10 rooms, 10 pb
Most CC, *Rated*, •
C-ltd/S-no/P-no/H-no

Full breakfast
24 hr. snacks/beverages
All rooms have TV/phones
rooms w/double whirlpool
park-like grounds

*Classic B&B on the Nat'l Register of Historic Places. Comfortable elegance & luxury of the past. Tempting breakfasts. Near attractions & recreation. **3rd night 15% off & ski season offer, ask.***

## SALIDA

**Century House B&B, The**
401 E. 1st St.,   81201
719-539-7064
Ruth Fisher    All year

$$-B&B
4 rooms, 2 pb
Visa, MC,
C-ltd/S-no/P-no/H-no

Full breakfast
Afternoon tea
Snacks

*1890s Victorian now a "Painted Lady." Painted grain woodwork, brass hardware and lighting. Antiques abound. Adjacent to downtown historic district.*

**River Run Inn B&B**
8495 C.R. 160,   81201
719-539-3818  Fax: 719-539-3818
800-385-6975
Virginia Nemmers    All year

$$-B&B
7 rooms, 3 pb
MC, Visa, *Rated*,
C-ltd/S-ltd/P-no/H-no

Full country breakfast
Comp. tea, coffee, cider
Library, fishing, dorm
room available, reunions
stocked trout pond, view

*Secluded area on Arkansas River. Turn of the century home, antiques. Special dinners for groups, meetings, events. Enjoy the four seasons. **Mention this guide & receive free champagne in your room.***

**Tudor Rose, The**
P.O. Box 89, 81201
6720 Paradise Rd.
719-539-2002  Fax: 719-530-0345
800-379-0889
Jon & Terre' Terrell
All year

$$-B&B
6 rooms, 4 pb
Visa, MC, AmEx,
*Rated*, •
C-yes/S-ltd/P-ltd/H-no

Full breakfast
Lunch (fee)
Sitting room, library
hot tubs
horse & dog facilities

*Stately country manor on 37 acre mountain paradise. Elegant comfort. Min. from town, skiing, rafting. Horses welcome. **3-7 nights 10% off, 8+ nights 20% off.***

## SNOWMASS

| **Starry Pines B&B** | $$$-B&B | Continental plus |
| 2262 Snowmass Creek Rd., | 3 rooms, 3 pb | Fireplace, VCR movies |
| 81654 | *Rated*, • | hot tub under stars |
| 970-927-4202  Fax: 970-927-9134 | C-ltd/S-no/P-no/H-no | horses boarded, picnic |
| 800-527-4202 | | |
| Shelley Burke  All year | | |

*Enjoy contemporary comfort on 70 acres w/trout stream and panoramic views. 25 minutes to Aspen's year-round activities. Fishing in our own trout stream. **7th night free.***

## STEAMBOAT SPRINGS

| **Sky Valley Lodge** | $$-B&B | Continental, summer |
| P.O. Box 3132, 80477 | 24 rooms, 24 pb | Full breakfast, winter |
| 31490 E. U.S. Hwy 40 | AmEx, MC, Visa, | Restaurant, bar, library |
| 970-879-7749  Fax: 970-879-7752 | *Rated*, • | sitting room, hot tub |
| 800-449-4759 | C-yes/S-yes/P-yes/H-no | sauna, shuttle in winter |
| Steve & Rita Myler  All year | | |

*Nestled in the side of the mountains, this English country manor-style lodge affords a sweeping view of the valley below. Nearby skiing, dining, shopping, hiking. **50% off, ltd.***

## TELLURIDE

| **Alpine Inn B&B** | $$-B&B | Full breakfast |
| P.O. Box 2398, 81435 | 8 rooms, | Afternoon tea—winter |
| 440 W. Colorado Ave. | Visa, MC, *Rated*, • | Comp. wine—winter |
| 970-728-6282  Fax: 970-728-3424 | C-ltd/S-no/P-no/H-no | sitting room, library |
| 800-707-3344 | | hot tub |
| Denise & John Weaver | | |
| All year | | |

*Charming downtown Victorian. Enjoy a full breakfast in the sunroom. Relax in the hot tub with sunset views. Walk to slopes and hiking trails.*

| **Johnstone Inn** | $$-B&B | Full breakfast |
| P.O. Box 546, 81435 | 8 rooms, 8 pb | Comp. refreshments |
| 403 W. Colorado | AmEx, MC, Visa, • | In ski season |
| 970-728-3316  Fax: 970-728-0724 | C-ltd/S-no/P-no/H-no | sitting room w/fireplace |
| 800-752-1901 | | games, outdoor hot tub |
| Bill Schiffbauer | | |
| Ski season & summer | | |

*Restored historic Victorian boarding house in center of Telluride. Walk to lifts, shops, and everything else. A warm, comfortable inn in a friendly mountain town.*

| **New Sheridan Hotel** | $$-B&B | Full country breakfast |
| P.O. Box 980, 81435 | 32 rooms, | Wine & hor d'oeuvres |
| 231 W. Colorado | AmEx, MC, Visa, | Gourmet restaurant |
| 970-728-4351  Fax: 970-728-5024 | *Rated*, • | fitness room |
| 800-200-1871 | C-yes/S-no/P-no/H-no | rooftop Jacuzzi |
| Tom Taylor  All year | Spanish, French | |

*Elegant Victorian Inn offering history and romance in the heart of Telluride-a national historic landmark. Steps from shopping, dining & lifts. A Four Sisters Inn.*

## VAIL

| **Intermountain B&B** | $$-B&B | Continental plus bkfst. |
| 2754 Basingdale Blvd.,  81657 | 2 rooms, 2 pb | Snacks |
| 970-476-4935  Fax: 970-476-7926 | • | Hot tubs |
| Kay & Sepp Cheney | C-ltd/S-no/P-no/H-no | sitting room |
| All year | German | cable TV |

*Contemporary home two miles from ski lifts on free bus route. Delicious home-baked pastries, fresh fruit and gourmet coffees.*

## WINTER PARK

**Alpen Rose B&B**
P.O. Box 769, 80482
244 Forest Trail
970-726-5039 800-531-1333
Robin & Rupert Sommerauer
Closed October-Nov 15

$$-B&B
6 rooms, 6 pb
Most CC, •
C-ltd/S-no/P-no/H-no
German

Full breakfast
Afternoon tea, snacks
Sitting room, library
hot tubs
Fax: 970-726-0993

*Rocky Mountain hideaway with breathtaking views of The Continental Divide. Close to everything, but hidden away, with Austrian decor and hospitality.* **3rd night 50%.**

## WOODLAND PARK

**Pikes Peak Paradise**
236 Pinecrest Rd., 80863
719-687-6656 Fax: 719-687-9008
800-728-8282
Priscilla Arthur
All year

$$$-B&B
2 rooms,
Most CC, •
C-ltd

Full breakfast
Picnic lunches avail.
Comp. sherry, cheese
fresh flowers
sitting room

*Relaxation was never better! A spectacular view of Pikes Peak, wildlife, birds. Fresh flowers. Breakfast buffet offered with a smile. Fireplaces, hot tubs in rooms.* **Ask for weekday discounts.**

## More Inns . . .

| | |
|---|---|
| Allenspark | Allenspark Lodge, P.O. Box 247, 80510, 303-747-2552 |
| Allenspark | Lazy H Ranch, Box 248, 80510, 303-747-2532 |
| Arriba | Tarado Mansion, Route 1, Box 53, 80804, 719-768-3468 |
| Arvada | On Golden Pond B&B, 7831 Eldridge, 80005, 303-424-2296 |
| Arvada | Tree House, The, 6650 Simms, 80004, 303-431-6352 |
| Aspen | Aspen Ski Lodge, 101 W. Main St., 81611, 970-925-3434 |
| Aspen | Crestahaus Lodge, 1301 E. Cooper Ave., 81611, 970-925-7081 |
| Aspen | Hotel Lenado, 200 S. Aspen St., 81611, 970-925-6246 |
| Aspen | Inn at Aspen, The, 38750 Highway 82, 81611 |
| Aspen | Little Red Ski Haus, 118 E. Cooper Ave., 81611, 970-925-3333 |
| Aspen | Mountain House B&B, 905 East Hopkins, 81611, 970-920-2550 |
| Aspen | Sardy House, 128 E. Main St., 81611, 970-920-2525 |
| Aspen | Tipple Inn, 747 S. Galena St., 81611, 800-321-7025 |
| Aspen | Ullr Lodge, 520 W. Main St., 81611, 970-925-7696 |
| Ault | Eastridge Farms, 38634B Weld Cty. Rd# 39, 80610, 303-834-2617 |
| Avon | Just Relax Inn, P.O. Box 2753, 81620, 970-845-8885 |
| Bellvue | Raindrop B&B, 6901 McMurry Ranch Rd., 80512, 303-493-0799 |
| Bethoud | Berthoud B&B, 444 1st St., 80513 |
| Boulder | Alps, The, 38619 Boulder Canyon Dr, 80302, 303-444-5445 |
| Boulder | Coburn Hotel, 2040 16th St., 80302, 303-545-5200 |
| Boulder | Gunbarrel Inn, 6901 Lookout Rd., 80301 |
| Boulder | Magpie Inn, The, 1001 Spruce St., 80302, 303-449-6528 |
| Boulder | Pearl Street Inn, 1820 Pearl St., 80302, 303-444-5584 |
| Boulder | Salina House, 365 Gold Run, 80302, 303-442-1494 |
| Breckenridge | Cotten House B&B, P.O. Box 387, 80424, 970-453-5509 |
| Breckenridge | Fireside Inn, P.O. Box 2252, 80424, 970-453-6456 |
| Breckenridge | Little Mountain Lodge, P.O. Box 2479, 80424, 970-453-1969 |
| Breckenridge | Ridge Street Inn, P.O. Box 2854, 80424, 970-453-4680 |
| Breckenridge | Swiss Inn, The, P.O. Box 556, 80424, 970-453-6489 |
| Breckenridge | Wellington Inn, The, P.O. Box 5890, 80424, 970-453-9464 |
| Brighton | Country Gardens, 1619 E. 136th Ave., 80601, 303-451-1724 |
| Buena Vista | Blue Sky Inn, 719 Arizona St., 81211, 303-395-8865 |
| Buena Vista | Trout City Inn, Box 431, 81211, 719-495-0348 |
| Carbondale | Ambiance Inn B&B, 66 N. 2nd Street, 81623, 970-963-3597 |
| Carbondale | Van Horn House-Lions Ridge, 0318 Lions Ridge Rd., 81623, 970-963-3605 |
| Cascade | Black Bear Inn, 5250 Pikes Peak Hwy., 80809, 719-684-0151 |
| Cascade | Sue's Guest House, P.O. Box 483, 80809, 303-684-2111 |
| Cedaredge | Cedar' Edge Llamas B&B, 2169 Hwy. 65, 81413, 303-856-6836 |
| Cedaredge | Timberline B&B, 2457 U50 Rd., 81413, 303-856-7379 |
| Central City | Winfield Scott GuestQrtrs., P.O. Box 369, 80427, 303-582-3433 |
| Clark | Home Ranch, Box 822, 80428, 303-879-1780 |
| Clark | Inn at Hahn's Peak, Box 867, 80486 |
| Clifton | Mt. Garfield B&B, 3355 F Road, 81520, 970-434-8120 |
| Colorado Springs | Alpine Chalet Country Inn, 11685 Howells Rd., 80908 |
| Colorado Springs | Black Forest B&B, 11170 Black Forest Rd., 80908, 719-495-4208 |
| Colorado Springs | Hearthstone Inn, The, 506 N. Cascade Ave., 80903, 719-473-4413 |

| | |
|---|---|
| Colorado Springs | Hughes Hacienda, 12060 Calle Corvo, 80926 |
| Colorado Springs | Our Hearts Inn, 2215 W. Colorado Ave., 80904 |
| Colorado Springs | Twilight Canyon Inn, 2275 Twilight Canyon, 80866, 719-576-7707 |
| Colorado Springs | Wedgewood Cottage B&B, 1111 W. Pikes Peak Ave., 80904, 719-636-1829 |
| Crested Butte | Alpine Lace Inc. B&B, P.O. Box 2183, 81224, 970-349-9857 |
| Crested Butte | Claim Jumper, 704 Whiterock, Box 1181, 81224, 970-349-6471 |
| Crested Butte | Crested Beauty, The, P.O. Box 1204, 81224, 970-349-1201 |
| Crested Butte | Crystal Inn B&B, P.O. Box 125, 81224 |
| Crested Butte | Elizabeth Anne B&B, The, P.O. Box 1051, 81224, 970-349-0147 |
| Crested Butte | Forest Queen Hotel, Box 127, 2nd & Elk Ave., 81224, 970-349-5336 |

*Queen Anne Bed & Breakfast,*
*Denver, CO*

| | |
|---|---|
| Crested Butte | Great Escape B&B, The, P.O. Box 1204, 81224 |
| Crested Butte | Nordic Inn, P.O. Box 939, 81224, 970-349-5542 |
| Cripple Creek | Imperial Casino Hotel, P.O. Box 869, 80813, 719-689-7777 |
| Delta | Delta-Escalante Ranch, 701-650 Rd., 81416, 303-874-4121 |
| Delta | Escalante Ranch, 701-650 Rd., 81416, 303-874-4121 |
| Denver | Cambridge Club Hotel, 1560 Sherman, 80203, 303-831-1252 |
| Denver | Lumber Baron Inn, 2555 West 37th Ave., 80211 |
| Denver | Merritt House B&B, 941 E. 17th Ave., 80218, 303-861-5230 |
| Dillon | Annabelle's B&B, 276 Snowberry Way, 80435, 970-468-8667 |
| Dillon | Paradox Lodge, 35 Montezuma Rd., 80435, 970-468-9445 |
| Dolores | Little Southfork B&B, 15247 County Rd. 22, 81323, 303-882-4259 |
| Durango | Edgemont Ranch, 281 Silver Queen, 81301, 970-247-2713 |
| Durango | Gable House, The, 805 E. Fifth Ave., 81301, 970-247-4982 |
| Durango | Leland House B&B, 721 E. Second Ave., 81301, 970-385-1920 |
| Durango | Pennys Place, 1041 County Rd. 307, 81301, 970-247-8928 |
| Durango | Scrubby Oaks B&B Inn, P.O. Box 1047, 81302, 970-247-2176 |
| Durango | Vagabond Inn B&B, P.O. Box 2141, 81302, 970-259-5901 |
| Durango | Waterfall B&B, 4138 Country Rd. 203, 81301 |
| Edwards | Lazy Ranch B&B, Cowboy Art, P.O. Box 404, 81632, 970-926-3876 |
| Edwards | Lodge at Cordillera, P.O. Box 1110, 81632, 970-926-2200 |
| Edwards | Mountain Weavery, The, P.O. Box 1016, 81632 |
| Empire | Mad Creek B&B, P.O. Box 404, 80438, 303-569-2003 |
| Estes Park | Baldpate Inn, P.O. Box 4445, 80517, 970-586-6151 |
| Estes Park | Big Horn Guest House, P.O. Box 4486, 80517, 970-586-4175 |
| Estes Park | Cottenwood House, P.O. Box 1208, 80517, 970-586-5104 |
| Estes Park | Emerald Manor, P.O. Box 3592, 80517, 970-586-8050 |
| Estes Park | Romantic RiverSong, P.O. Box 1910, 80517, 970-586-4666 |
| Estes Park | Wind River Ranch, P.O. Box 3410, 80517, 970-586-4212 |
| Florence | Wilson House, The, 104 Lock Ave., 81226 |
| Fort Collins | Edwards House B&B, 402 West Mountain Ave., 80521, 970-493-9191 |
| Fort Collins | Elizabeth St. Guest House, 202 E. Elizabeth St., 80524, 303-493-2337 |
| Fort Collins | Helmshire Inn, 1204 S. College, 80524, 303-493-4683 |
| Frisco | Creekside Inn, P.O. Box 4835, 80443, 800-668-7320 |
| Frisco | Lark B&B, P.O. Box 1646, 80443, 970-668-5237 |
| Frisco | Twilight Inn, P.O. Box 397, 80443, 970-668-5009 |
| Fruita | Stonehaven B&B, 798 North Mesa St., 81521 |
| Georgetown | Alpine Hideaway B&B, The, P.O. Box 788, 80444, 303-569-2800 |
| Georgetown | Kip on the Creek Inn, P.O. Box 754, 80444 |
| Glenwood Springs | Back in Time, 927 Cooper, 81601 |
| Glenwood Springs | Kaiser House, The, 928 Cooper Ave., 81601, 970-945-8827 |
| Golden | Antique Rose B&B, 1422 Washingtin Ave., 80401, 303-277-1893 |
| Golden | Jameson Inn, The, 1704 Illinois St., 80401, 303-278-2209 |
| Golden | Royal Scot B&B, 30500 US Hwy 40, 80401, 303-526-2411 |
| Granby | Drowsy Water Ranch, Box 147A, 80446, 303-725-3456 |
| Grand Junction | Gatehouse B&B, The, 2502 N. First St., 81501, 970-242-6105 |
| Grand Junction | Junction Country Inn B&B, 861 Grand Ave., 81501, 970-241-2817 |
| Grand Lake | Spirit Mountain Ranch, P.O. Box 942, 80447, 970-887-3551 |
| Grand Lake | Winding River Resort, P.O. Box 629, 80447, 970-627-3215 |
| Grant | Tumbling River Ranch, 80448, 303-838-5981 |
| Greeley | Sterling House B&B Inn, 818 12th St., 80631, 303-351-8805 |
| Green Mt. Falls | Lakeview Terrace Hotel, Box 115, 80819, 719-684-9119 |
| Green Mt. Falls | Outlook Lodge B&B, P.O. Box 5, 80819, 719-684-2303 |
| Grover | West Pawnee Ranch B&B, 29451 WCR 130, 80729 |
| Gunnison | Waunita Hot Springs Ranch, 8007 Country Rd. 877, 81230, 970-641-1266 |
| Gypsum | 7-W Guest Ranch, 3412 County Rd. 151, 81637, 303-524-9328 |
| Gypsum | Sweetwater Creek Ranch, 2650 Sweetwater Rd., 81637, 303-524-7949 |
| Hesperus | Sunflower B&B, 10829 Country Rd. 141, 81326 |

| | |
|---|---|
| Hotchkiss | Ye Ole Oasis, 3142 "J" Rd., Box 609, 81419, 970-872-3794 |
| Howard | Robin's Nest B&B, 9134 Highway 50, 81233 |
| Idaho Springs | St. Mary's Glacier B&B, 336 Crest Dr., 80452 |
| Ignacio | Kelsall's Ute Creek Ranch, 2192 County Rd. 334, 81137, 303-563-4464 |
| Keystone | Ski Tip Lodge, Box 38, 80435, 303-468-4202 |
| La Junta | Jane Ellen Inn, 722 Colorado Ave., 81050 |
| La Junta | My Wife's Inn B&B, 801 Colorado Ave., 81050 |
| La Veta | 1899 Inn, 314 S. Main, 81055, 303-742-3576 |
| Lake City | Alpine Loop B&B, P.O. Box 955, 81235 |
| Lake City | Cinnamon Inn B&B, The, 426 Gunnison Ave., 81235, 970-944-2641 |
| Lake City | Crystal Lodge, 81235, 970-944-2201 |
| Lake City | Moncrief Mountain Ranch, Slumgullion Pass, 81235, 970-944-2796 |
| Lake City | Moss Rose B&B, P.O. Box 910, 81235, 970-366-4069 |
| Lake City | Old Carson Inn, P.O. Box 144, 81235, 970-944-2511 |
| Lake City | Ryan's Roost, P.O. Box 218, 81235, 970-944-2339 |
| Lake George | Stuart House, 120 Broken Arrow Path, 80929 |
| Lakewood | Gourmet B&B, The, 2020 Brentwood, 80215, 303-237-8395 |
| Leadville | Leadville Country Inn, 127 E. 8th St, Box 1989, 80461, 719-486-2354 |
| Limon | Midwest Country Inn, P.O. Box 550, 80828, 719-775-2373 |
| Loveland | Apple Avenue B&B, 3321 Apple Ave., 80538 |
| Loveland | Lovelander B&B Inn, The, 217 W. 4th St., 80537, 970-669-0798 |
| Loveland | Wild Lane B&B Inn, 5445 Wild Lane, 80538 |
| Lyons | Benam B&B, P.O. Box 577, 80540 |
| Mancos | Bauer House B&B, P.O. Box 1049, 81328, 970-533-9707 |
| Mancos | Gingerbread Inn, The, 41478 Highway 184, 81328, 970-533-7892 |
| Manitou Springs | Frontier's Rest, 341 Ruxton Ave., 80829, 719-685-0588 |
| Manitou Springs | Gray's Avenue Hotel, 711 Manitou Ave., 80829, 719-685-1277 |
| Manitou Springs | On a Ledge, 336 El Paso Blvd., 80829 |
| Manitou Springs | Red Eagle Mountain B&B, 616 Ruxton Ave., 80829, 719-685-4541 |
| Manitou Springs | Spring House, 13 Pawnee Ave., 80827 |
| Manitou Springs | Sunnymede B&B, 106 Spencer Ave., 80829, 719-685-4619 |
| Marble | Inn At Raspberry Ridge, 5580 Country Rd. 3, 81623, 303-963-3025 |
| Meredith | Diamond J Guest Ranch, 26604 Frying Pan Rd., 81642, 303-927-3222 |
| Meredith | Frying Pan River Ranch, 32042 Frying Pan Rd., 81642, 800-352-0980 |
| Montezuma | Granny's B&B, 5435 Montezuma Rd., 80435 |
| Monument | Cross Keys Inn B&B, 20450 Beacon Lite Rd., 80132, 719-481-2772 |
| Morrison | Cliff House Lodge B&B, 121 Stone St., 80465, 303-697-9732 |
| Mosca | Great Sand Dunes Inn, 5303 Hwy 150, 81146, 719-378-2356 |
| Nathrop | Claveau's Streamside B&B, 18820 C.R. 162, 81236, 719-395-2553 |
| Nathrop | Deer Valley Ranch, Box Y, 81236, 303-395-2353 |
| Northglenn | Country Gardens B&B, P.O. Box 33765, 80233 |
| Ouray | Ouray 1898 House, P.O. Box 641, 81427, 970-325-4871 |
| Ouray | Weisbaden Spa & Lodge, Box 349, 81427, 970-325-4347 |
| Pagosa Springs | Davidson's Country Inn B&B, Box 87, 81147, 970-264-5863 |
| Pagosa Springs | Echo Manor Inn, 3366 Hwy 84, 81147, 970-264-5646 |
| Pagosa Springs | TLC's, A B&B, P.O. Box 3337, 81147 |
| Palisade | Garden House B&B, 3587 G Rd., 81526 |
| Palisade | Orchard House, The, 3573 E-1/2 Rd., 81526, 303-464-0529 |
| Parshall | Aspen Canyon Ranch, 13206 Country Rd. #3, 80468, 303-725-3518 |
| Parshall | Bar Lazy J Guest Ranch, Box N, 80468, 303-725-3437 |
| Pine | Meadow Creek B&B Inn, 13438 US Hwy 285, 80470, 303-838-4167 |
| Poncha Springs | Jackson Hotel, 220 S. Main St., 81242, 303-539-3122 |
| Red Cliff | Pilgrim's Inn, The, P.O. Box 151, 81649, 303-827-5333 |
| Redstone | Avalanche Ranch, 12863 Hwy 133, 81623, 970-963-2846 |
| Redstone | Cleveholm Manor, 0058 Redstone Blvd., 81623, 970-963-3463 |
| Redstone | Crystal Dreams B&B, 0475 Redstone Blvd., 81623 |
| Redstone | Historic Redstone Inn, 82 Redstone Blvd., 81623, 303-963-2526 |
| Ridgway | Chipeta Sun Lodge B&B, P.O. Box 2013, 81432 |
| Ridgway | MacTiernan's San Juan, 2882 Highway 23, 81432, 970-626-5360 |
| Rifle | Coulter Lake Guest Ranch, P.O. Box 906, 81650, 303-625-1473 |
| Salida | Gazebo Country Inn, The, 507 E. Third, 81201, 719-539-7806 |
| Salida | Pinon & Sage B&B, 803 F St., 81201 |
| Salida | Thomas House B&B, 307 East 1st St., 81201 |
| Shawnee | North Fork Ranch, Box B, 80475, 303-838-9873 |
| Silver Plume | Brewery Inn B&B, Box 473, 80476, 303-674-5565 |
| Silverthorne | Alpen Hutte, 471 Rainbow Dr., Box 91, 80498, 303-468-6336 |
| Silverthorne | Mountain Vista B&B, P.O. Box 1398, 80498, 303-468-7700 |
| Silverton | Alma House Hotel, P.O. Box 359, 81433, 970-387-5336 |
| Silverton | Christopher House B&B, 821 Empire St., Box 241, 81433, 970-387-5857 |
| Silverton | Teller House Hotel, P.O. Box 2, 81433, 970-387-5423 |
| Silverton | Wingate House, P.O. Box 2, 81433 |
| Silverton | Wyman Hotel & Inn, P.O. Box 789, 81433, 970-387-5372 |
| Steamboat Springs | Alpine Rose B&B Inn, The, P.O. Box 775602, 80477, 970-879-1528 |
| Steamboat Springs | Country Inn at Stmbt Ranch, 46915 County Rd. 129, 80487, 970-879-5767 |
| Steamboat Springs | Crawford House, Box 775062, 80477, 970-879-1859 |
| Steamboat Springs | Harbor Hotel, P.O. Box 4109, 80477, 800-543-8888 |
| Steamboat Springs | House on the Hill, P.O. Box 770598, 80477, 970-879-1650 |
| Steamboat Springs | Log Cabin B&B, 47890 Country Road 129, 80487, 970-879-5837 |

| | |
|---|---|
| Steamboat Springs | Steamboat B&B, Box 772058, 80477,  970-879-5724 |
| Steamboat Springs | Steamboat Llama Ranch, 46915 County Rd. 129, 80487,  970-879-5767 |
| Steamboat Springs | Steamboat Valley Guest Hse, P.O. Box 773815, 80477,  970-870-9017 |
| Steamboat Springs | Vista Verde Guest Ranch,  Box 465, 80477,  970-879-3858 |
| Sterling | Crest House, 516 S. Division St., 80751,  303-522-3753 |
| Stoneham | Elk Echo Ranch Country B&B,  47490 WCR 155, 80754 |
| Telluride | Bear Creek Inn, P.O. Box 1797, 81423,  970-728-6681 |
| Telluride | Dahl Haus B&B,  122 S. Oak St., Box 695, 81435,  970-728-4158 |
| Telluride | Pennington's Mountain Inn, P.O. Box 2428, 81435,  800-543-1437 |
| Telluride | San Sophia,  330 W. Pacific Ave., 81435,  970-728-3001 |
| Telluride | Skyline Guest Ranch, 7214 Highway 145, 81435,  970-728-3757 |
| Twin Lakes | Mount Elbert Lodge,  P.O. Box 40, 81251 |
| Twin Lakes | Twin Lakes Mtn. Retreat, P.O. Box 175, 81251,  719-486-2593 |
| Vail | Black Bear Inn of Vail, 2405 Elliot Rd., 81657,  970-476-1304 |
| Victor | Portland Inn,  412 W. Portland, Box 32, 80860,  719-689-2102 |
| Walsenburg | Grape Garden, 24857 Hwy. 160, 81089 |
| Westcliffe | Purnell's Rainbow Inn,  P.O. Box 578, 81252 |
| Westcliffe | Rainbow Inn,  104 Main, P.O. Box 578, 81252,  719-783-2313 |
| Westminister | Victorian Lady, The,  4199 W. 76th Ave., 80030,  303-428-9829 |
| Windsor | Porter House B&B, 530 Main St., 80550,  970-686-5793 |
| Winter Park | Angelmark B&B, 50 Little Pierre Ave., 80482,  970-726-5354 |
| Winter Park | Beau West B&B,  P.O. Box 587, 80482,  970-726-5145 |
| Winter Park | Engelmann Pines, P.O. Box 1305, 80482,  970-726-4632 |
| Winter Park | Outpost Inn,  P.O. Box 41, 80482,  970-726-5346 |
| Winter Park | Pines Inn, The,  P.O. Box 15, 80482 |
| Winter Park | Something Special, P.O. Box 800, 80482,  970-726-5346 |
| Woodland Park | Hackman House B&B, Box 6902, 80866,  719-687-9851 |
| Woodland Park | Woodland Hills Lodge, P.O. Box 276, 80863,  800-621-8386 |
| Woodland Park | Woodland Inn B&B,  159 Trull Rd., 80863,  719-687-8209 |
| Yellowjacket | Wilson's Pinto Bean Farm,  House No. 21434 Rd. 16, 81335 |

# Connecticut

## BARKHAMSTED

**Rose & Thistle, The**
24 Woodland Acres, 24
Woodland, Collinsville,
06022
860-379-4744
Lorraine Longmoor
All year

$$$-B&B
4 rooms, 4 pb
C-ltd/S-ltd/P-ltd/H-yes

Full breakfast
10 acres, trout pond
swimming, paddleboat
skating, hikes, skiing

*Breathe new life from garden & woods. Capture timelessness in a half-timbered English Cottage high on the edge of secluded valley. Gameroom with Inglenook fireplace & kitchen.*

## BRISTOL

**Chimney Crest Manor B&B**
5 Founders Dr.,   06010
860-582-4219 Fax: 860-584-5903
Dan & Cynthia Cimadamore
All year

$$$-B&B
4 rooms, 4 pb
MC, Visa, *Rated*,  •
C-ltd/S-no/P-no/H-no

Full breakfast
Sitting room, piano
2 suites with fireplaces
1 suite with thermal spa

*32-rm Tudor mansion on National Historic Register. 20 minutes from Hartford & Litchfield. Walking distance to Carousel Museum. Mobil 3-star rating.* **1 Rose & Champagne split.**

## BROOKLYN

**Friendship Valley B&B Inn**
P.O. Box 845, 06234
60 Pomfret Rd. (Rt. 169)
860-779-9696 Fax: 860-779-9844
"Rusty" and Beverly Yates
All year

$$$-B&B
5 rooms, 5 pb
•
C-ltd/S-no/P-no/H-no

Full breakfast
Afternoon tea
Sitting room, library
TV room, screened porch

*An inn grows in Brooklyn—Connecticut! Antiques, frplcs., hearty breakfasts, stone walls & picket fences welcome discerning guests to this 1795 country house.* **3rd night 50%, Free glass of wine at restaurant.**

## CHESTER

**Inn at Chester, The**
318 W. Main St.,   06412
860-526-9541 Fax: 860-526-4387
800-949-7829
Deborah L. Moore
All year

$$$-B&B
48 rooms, 48 pb
AmEx, MC, Visa,
*Rated*, •
C-yes/S-yes/P-ltd/H-yes

Continental plus bkfst.
Lunch, dinner, tavern
Bicycles, tennis, sauna
sitting room, library,
piano, entertainment

*The inn, on 15 acres centered around a 1776 farmhouse, abounds with fireplaces, antiques, and public areas for resting, reading, refreshment.* **10% discount, ask.**

## CLINTON

**Captain Dibbell House**
21 Commerce St.,   06413
860-669-1646 Fax: 860-669-2300
Helen & Ellis Adams
Closed Jan.-March (call)

$$-B&B
4 rooms, 4 pb
MC, Visa, *Rated*, •
C-ltd/S-ltd/P-no/H-no

Full breakfast
Comp. refreshments & mug
Sitting room, gazebo
bicycles, horseshoes
beach chairs & towels

*Our 1866 sea captain's Victorian offers comfortable lodging and home-baked savories to guests while they discover the charms of our coastal towns. A/C in summer months.*

## COVENTRY

**Maple Hill Farm B&B**
365 Goose Ln.,   06238
860-742-0635  800-742-0635
T. Felice & M.B. Gorke-Felice
All year

$$-B&B
4 rooms, 1 pb
MC, Visa, *Rated*, •
C-yes/S-no/P-no/H-no
Spanish

Full breakfast
Dinners cook open hearth
Hot tubs, herb garden
pool, picnic areas
hammocks, horses

*A warm friendly home circa 1731 filled with antiques. Unique mixture of old and new. Room for relaxation or recreation. Amish wedding buggy.* **Discount after 4 nights.**

## DEEP RIVER

**Riverwind Inn**
209 Main St.,   06417
860-526-2014
Barbara Barlow, Bob
Bucknall
All year

$$$-B&B
8 rooms, 8 pb
MC, Visa, *Rated*,
C-ltd/S-yes/P-no/H-no

Full breakfast
Comp. sherry
8 common rooms
piano, classic British
limousine service

*Furnished in country antiques. Smithfield ham with breakfast, fireplace in dining room. New England charm and southern hospitality.*

## EAST HADDAM

**Bishopsgate Inn**
P.O. Box 290, 06423
7 Norwich Rd.
860-873-1677 Fax: 860-873-3898
The Kagel Family
All year

$$$-B&B
6 rooms, 6 pb
Visa, MC, *Rated*,
C-yes/S-no/P-no/H-yes

Full breakfast
Afternoon tea, snacks
Lunch, dinner (fee)
sitting room, library
sauna

*1818 historic Colonial amid formal gardens. Rooms w/open frplcs., private baths furnished in antiques & reproductions. Walk to shops, the Goodspeed Opera House & the Connecticut River.* **Seasonal pkgs.**

## ESSEX

**Griswold Inn, The**
36 Main St., 06426
860-767-1776 Fax: 860-767-0481
Greg, Douglas & Geoffrey
Paul
All year

$$$-B&B
28 rooms, 28 pb
AmEx, MC, Visa,
*Rated*,
C-yes/S-yes/P-ltd/H-yes

Continental breakfast
Restaurant, bar service
Lunch & dinner available
sitting room, library
Suite overlooking garden

*Located in center of historic Essex. Renowned marine art collection. Entertainment nightly from Griswold Inn Banjo Band to Cliff Haslem's Sea Chantys.*

## GLASTONBURY

**Butternut Farm**
1654 Main St., 06033
860-633-7197 Fax: 860-659-1758
Don Reid
All year

$$-B&B
5 rooms, 5 pb
AmEx, *Rated*,
C-yes/S-ltd/P-no/H-no

Full breakfast
Comp. wine, chocolates
Piano, 8 fireplaces
sitting rooms, library
bicycle

*An 18th-century jewel furnished with period antiques. Attractive grounds with herb gardens and ancient trees, dairy goats and prize chickens. 10 minutes from Hartford.*

## GREENWICH

**Homestead Inn**
420 Field Point Rd., 06830
203-869-7500 Fax: 203-869-7500
Lessie Davison, Nancy Smith
All year

$$$$-B&B
23 rooms, 23 pb
Most CC, •
C-yes/S-yes/P-no/H-ltd
Sp., Fr., It., Ger., Ch.

Continental breakfast
Lunch, dinner, bar
Sitting room, patio
turn-down service
meeting rms. up to 25

*Sophisticated country inn, built in 1799, completely restored. 45 min. from NYC. Superb French cuisine for lunch and dinner; full breakfast available.* **3rd night 50%.**

## GROTON LONG POINT

**Shore Inne**
54 E. Shore Rd., 06340
203-536-1180
Helen Ellison
April–October

$$$-B&B
5 rooms, 5 pb
MC, Visa,
C-yes/S-ltd/P-no/H-no

Continental plus bkfst.
Living room, sunroom
dining room, swimming
biking, tennis, beach

*Unique location on the water with splendid views. Residential area. 3.5 miles from Mystic. Private beaches, fishing, tennis, nature trails in conservation area.*

## IVORYTON

**Copper Beech Inn, The**
46 Main St., 06442
860-767-0330 Fax: 860-767-7840
Sally & Eldon Senner
Closed Tuesdays Jan-Mar

$$$-B&B
13 rooms, 13 pb
Most CC, *Rated*,
C-ltd/S-no/P-no/H-ltd

Continental plus bkfst.
French country dining
TV, Jacuzzi, meeting rm.
lovely gardens & grounds
Victorian conservatory

*A hostelry where even a short visit is a celebration of good living. One of few 4-star restaurants in Connecticut. The feel of country elegance.* **Week night upgrades.**

## MADISON

**Madison Beach Hotel**
P.O. Box 546, 06443
94 West Wharf Rd.
203-245-1404 Fax: 203-245-0410
Roben & Kathy Bagdasarian
April–December

$$$-B&B
32 rooms, 32 pb
Most CC, •
C-yes/S-ltd/P-no/H-ltd

Continental plus bkfst.
Lunch, dinner, bar
Sitting room, conference
facilities,entertainment
beach with swimming

*Victorian beach hotel furnished with oak and wicker antiques. Seafood tops the menu at the attached restaurant. Weekend entertainment. Conference facilities.*

MADISON ───────────────────────────────

| | | |
|---|---|---|
| **Tidewater Inn** | $$$-B&B | Full breakfast |
| 949 Boston Post Rd.,   06443 | 9 rooms, 9 pb | Complimentary wine |
| 203-245-8457  Fax: 203-318-0265 | Visa, MC, AmEx, | Sitting room |
| Jean Foy & Rich Evans | C-ltd/S-no/P-no/H-no | Fireplaces, antiques |
| All year | | |

*Explore coastal Connecticut. Elegant, cozy inn, circa 1880. Antiques and estate furnishings. Fireplaces, canopy beds, English garden. Beaches 1 mile.*

MIDDLEBURY ───────────────────────────

| | | |
|---|---|---|
| **Tucker Hill Inn** | $$-B&B | Full breakfast |
| 96 Tucker Hill Rd.,   06762 | 4 rooms, 2 pb | Tea & coffee served |
| 203-758-8334  Fax: 203-598-0652 | MC, Visa, *Rated*,  • | Sitting room, library |
| Susan & Richard Cebelenski | C-yes/S-ltd/P-no/H-no | TV & VCR, A/C |
| All year | | conference facilities |

*Large colonial-style inn near Village Green. Large, spacious period rooms. Hearty breakfast. Near sights & sports. **3rd night 50% off.***

MYSTIC ───────────────────────────────

| | | |
|---|---|---|
| **Adams House, The** | $$$-B&B | Full breakfast |
| 382 Cow Hill Rd.,   06355 | 7 rooms, 7 pb | Sitting room |
| 203-572-9551 | MC, Visa, *Rated*, | fireplaces |
| Gregory & Mary Lou Peck | C-ltd/S-no/P-no/H-no | garden cottage |
| All year | | |

*Historic 1750s home located 1 1/2 miles from downtown Mystic; close to seaport & aquarium. Surrounded by lush greenery and flower beds. **3rd night 50% Sun.–Thurs.***

| | | |
|---|---|---|
| **Comolli's Guest House** | $$-B&B | Continental breakfast |
| 36 Bruggeman Place,   06355 | 2 rooms, 1 pb | Kitchen privileges |
| 860-536-8723 | C-ltd/S-no/P-no/H-no | TV in rooms |
| Dorothy M. Comolli | | nearby many activities |
| All year | | |

*Immaculate home, situated on a quiet hill overlooking the Mystic Seaport complex; convenient to Olde Mistick Village & the Acquarium. Sightseeing & restaurant info. provided.*

| | | |
|---|---|---|
| **Harbour Inne & Cottage** | $$-EP | Kitchen privileges |
| 15 Edgemont St.,   06355 | 5 rooms, 5 pb | Sitting room, A/C |
| 203-572-9253 | • | canoe & boats, cable TV |
| Charles Lecouras, Jr. | C-yes/S-yes/P-yes/H-no | Fireplaces, hot tub |
| All year | Greek | |

*Small inn plus 3-room cottage on Mystic River. Walk to seaport & all attractions. Waterfront tables, canoeing and boating. Cottage with fireplace. Waterfront gazebo.*

| | | |
|---|---|---|
| **Pequot Hotel B&B** | $$$-B&B | Full country breakfast |
| 711 Cow Hill Rd.,   06355 | 3 rooms, 3 pb | Complimentary beverages |
| 860-572-0390  Fax: 860-536-3380 | Visa, MC,  • | Picnic lunch |
| Nancy Mitchell | C-ltd/S-no/P-no/H-no | 2 sitting rooms, library |
| All year | | A/C, whirlpool tubs |

*Authentically restored 1840s stagecoach stop; friendly, casual elegance amongst period antiques. Relaxing parlors, romantic fireplaces, & a welcoming screened porch.*

## MYSTIC

| **Red Brook Inn** | $$$-B&B | Full country breakfast |
|---|---|---|
| P.O. Box 237, 06372 | 9 rooms, 9 pb | Comp. wine, tea, cider |
| 2750 Gold Star Hwy | MC, Visa, *Rated*, | Sitting room, library |
| 860-572-0349 | C-yes/S-no/P-no/H-no | bicycles, patio, A/C |
| Ruth Keyes | | whirlpool, gardens |
| All year | | |

*The inn strikes a nice balance between authentic handsome furnishings & comfort. Surrounded by wooded acres, convenient to old New England sights.* **Midweek 3rd night 50% off.**

| **Steamboat Inn** | $$$-B&B | Continental plus bkfst. |
|---|---|---|
| 73 Steamboat Wharf, 06355 | 10 rooms, 10 pb | Restaurant |
| 860-536-8300 Fax: 860-536-9528 | Most CC, *Rated*, • | Sitting room |
| Diana Stedtmiller | C-ltd/S-no/P-no/H-yes | sailing trips |
| All year | | |

*Elegant and intimate, on the waterfront in historic downtown Mystic. Shopping, restaurants and seaport within walking distance.*

## MYSTIC, NOANK

| **Palmer Inn, The** | $$$-B&B | Continental plus bkfst. |
|---|---|---|
| 25 Church St., 06340 | 6 rooms, 6 pb | Comp. sherry, tea |
| 860-572-9000 | MC, Visa, AmEx, | Sitting rooms, fireplace |
| Patricia Ann White | *Rated*, | games, flowers, fans & |
| All year | C-ltd/S-ltd/P-no/H-no | A/C in all rooms |

*Elegant 1907 mansion with antique furnishings. Quiet charm of New England fishing village, near historic Mystic. Sailing lessons.* **20% off for reservations of 3 or more nights Mon.–Thur.**

## NEW LONDON

| **Queen Anne Inn, The** | $$$-B&B | Full breakfast |
|---|---|---|
| 265 Williams St., 06320 | 10 rooms, 8 pb | Comp. tea, refreshments |
| 860-447-2600 800-347-8818 | Most CC, *Rated*, • | Sitting room |
| Janet Moody & Ed Boncich | C-ltd/S-no/P-no/H-no | sauna, hot tub |
| All year | | |

*Award winning renovation, genuine antiques, near historically rich Mystic-Groton-New London waterfront resort area, close to Foxwoods Casino & Long/Block Island ferries.*

## NEW PRESTON

| **Boulders Inn** | $$$$-EP | Full breakfast |
|---|---|---|
| East Shore Road, Rte 45, | 17 rooms, 17 pb | Restaurant, bar, dinner |
| 06777 | AmEx, MC, Visa, • | Sitting room, bicycles |
| 860-868-0541 Fax: 860-868-1925 | C-ltd/S-yes/P-no/H-yes | tennis, private beach |
| 800-552-6853 | German, Dutch, French | boats, hiking trail |
| Kees & Ulla Adema | | |
| All year | | |

*Exquisitely furnished country inn in spectacular location, viewing Lake Waramaug. Lakeview dining inside or on terrace.* **4th. night 50% off, 7th. night free.**

## NORFOLK

| **Angel Hill B&B** | $$$-B&B | Full gourmet breakfast |
|---|---|---|
| P.O. Box 504, 06058 | 5 rooms, 5 pb | Comp. beverages, treats |
| 54 Greenwoods Rd. East | • | Sitting room, library |
| 860-542-5920 | C-ltd/S-no/P-no/H-no | jacuzzi, A/C, antiques |
| Donna & Del Gritman | | separate Carriage House |
| All year | | |

*Romantic 1880 Victorian with English country personality, just steps from the Village Green. Welcoming porches, enchanting guest suites with Jacuzzis, fireplaces, canopy beds.* **2+ nights mdwk discount.**

NORFOLK ──────────────────────────────

| Greenwoods Gate B&B Inn | $$$$-B&B | Full gourmet breakfast |
|---|---|---|
| P.O. Box 491, 06058 | 4 rooms, 3 pb | Comp. wine |
| 105 Greenwoods Rd. E. | AmEx, • | Sitting room, library |
| 203-542-5439 | C-ltd/S-yes/P-no/H-no | fireplaces, antiques |
| George E. Schumaker | | tennis nearby, bicycles |
| All year | | |

*Warm hospitality greets you in this beautifully restored 1797 colonial home. 4 exquisitely appointed guest suites (each w/private bath), 1 w/Jacuzzi. Sumptuous breakfasts.*

| Manor House | $$$-B&B | Full breakfast (to room) |
|---|---|---|
| P.O. Box 447, 06058 | 9 rooms, 9 pb | Comp. tea, coffee, cocoa |
| 69 Maple Ave. | MC, Visa, *Rated*, • | Weddings, massages |
| 860-542-5690 Fax: 860-542-5690 | C-ltd/S-ltd/P-no/H-ltd | piano, sun porch, gazebo |
| Hank & Diane Tremblay | French | bicycles, gardens, lake |
| All year | | |

*Historic Victorian mansion furnished with genuine antiques, on 5 acres. Romantic, elegant bedrooms. Sleigh/carriage rides. Concert series.* **3rd night 50%, ltd.**

NORWALK ──────────────────────────────

| Silvermine Tavern | $$$-B&B | Continental breakfast |
|---|---|---|
| 194 Perry Ave, 06850 | 12 rooms, 12 pb | Restaurant, bar |
| 203-847-4558  Fax: 203-847- | Most CC, *Rated*, • | Lunch, dinner |
| 9191 | C-yes/S-yes/P-no/H-no | sitting room |
| Frank Whitman, Jr. | | weddings and conferences |
| All year | | |

*Charming 225-year-old country inn only an hour from New York City. Decorated with hundreds of antiques. Overlooking the Tranquil Millpond. AAA 3-Diamond. Mobil 3-Star.*

OLD LYME ──────────────────────────────

| Bee and Thistle Inn | $$$-EP | Lunch, dinner, bar |
|---|---|---|
| 100 Lyme St., 06371 | 11 rooms, 9 pb | Bicycles, phone in room |
| 800-434-1667  Fax: 860-434- | Most CC, *Rated*, • | 2 parlors, piano |
| 3402 800-622-4946 | C-ltd/S-yes/P-no/H-no | harpist Saturdays |
| Bob, Penny, Lori, Jeff Nelson | | |
| All year | | |

*An inn on 5.5 acres in historic district. On the Lieutenant River set back amidst majestic trees. Sophisticated country cuisine.* **3rd night 50% off (no holidays, weekends).**

| Old Lyme Inn | $$$-B&B | Continental breakfast |
|---|---|---|
| P.O. Box 787, 06371 | 13 rooms, 13 pb | Lunch, dinner |
| 85 Lyme St. | Most CC, *Rated*, • | Sitt. rm., TV, phones |
| 860-434-2600 Fax: 860-434-5352 | C-yes/S-yes/P-ltd/H-yes | clock radios, porch |
| 800-434-5352 | | teddy bear in the rooms |
| Diana Field Atwood | | |
| All year | | |

*An 1850 Victorian inn in Old Lyme's historic district. 3-star restaurant (New York Times, 3 times). Empire and Victorian furnishings.* **25% off midweek, ltd.**

PLAINFIELD ──────────────────────────────

| French Renaissance House | $$-B&B | Full breakfast |
|---|---|---|
| 550 Norwich Rd., Route 12, | 4 rooms, 3 pb | Comp. wine & beverages |
| 06374 | Most CC, • | Sitting room |
| 680-564-3277 | C-yes/S-no | near antique shops and |
| Lucile Melber   All year | | restaurants, large rooms |

*1871 Victorian French Renaissance Second Empire architecture; in Historic District. Round arched windows; high ceilings; charming atmosphere.* **Discount after 3 nights, (winter rates).**

*Bee and Thistle Inn, Old Lyme, CT*

PLYMOUTH ──────────────────────────────────────

| | | |
|---|---|---|
| **Shelton House B&B** | $$-B&B | Full breakfast |
| 663 Main St. Rt. 6,  06782 | 4 rooms, 2 pb | Afternoon tea |
| 860-283-4616  Fax: 860-283-4616 | C-ltd/S-no/P-no/H-no | Large guest parlor with |
| Pat & Bill Doherty | | fireplace |
| All year | | perennial garden |

*Historic 1825 Greek Revival in scenic Litchfield Hills. Beautiful grounds; fountain; antiques. Convenient to I-84 and Route 8.*

POMFRET CENTER ──────────────────────────────────

| | | |
|---|---|---|
| **Clark Cottage, Wintergreen** | $$-B&B | Full breakfast |
| Box 94, 06259 | 5 rooms, 3 pb | Restaurant nearby |
| Rt. 44 & 169, 354 Pomfret St. | MC, Visa, • | Aftn. tea, comp. wine |
| 860-928-5741  Fax: 860-928-1591 | C-yes/S-no/P-no/H-no | sitting room, library |
| Doris & Stan Geary | | screened porch, bicycles |
| All year | | |

*1890 cottage 4 acres of lawn, extensive flower, rose gardens. Vegetable garden overlooking undeveloped valley. Magnificent when the leaves turn. **3rd night half price.***

RIDGEFIELD ──────────────────────────────────────

| | | |
|---|---|---|
| **West Lane Inn** | $$$-B&B | Continental breakfast |
| 22 West Ln.,  06877 | 20 rooms, 20 pb | Full breakfast (fee) |
| 203-438-7323 Fax: 203-438-7325 | Most CC, *Rated*, • | Comp. whiskey or julep |
| Maureen M. Mayer | C-yes/S-yes/P-no | bicycles, tennis nearby |
| All year | Spanish | cable TV, voice mail |

*Colonial elegance framed by majestic old maples and flowering shrubs. Breakfast served on the veranda. Always a relaxing atmosphere. Newly decorated lobbies & rooms.*

SIMSBURY —————————————————————————————————————————

**Simsbury 1820 House**
731 Hopmeadow St., Rte. 10
& 202,   06070
860-658-7658 Fax: 860-651-0724
800-TRY-1820
Wayne Bursey   All year

$$$-B&B
34 rooms, 34 pb
Most CC, *Rated*, •
C-yes/S-yes/P-no/H-yes

Continental plus bkfst.
Lunch, dinner
Restaurant, bar
sitting rm., meeting rm.
private dining facil.

*A graciously restored 34-room, 19th-century mansion in period decor, with 20th-century amenities. Noted dining room serves daily. Brochure available. **Restaurant discount 10%.***

TOLLAND —————————————————————————————————————————

**Tolland Inn, The**
P.O. Box 717, 06084
63 Tolland Green
860-872-0800 Fax: 860-870-7958
Susan & Stephen Beeching
All year

$$-B&B
7 rooms, 7 pb
AmEx, MC, Visa,
*Rated*, •
C-ltd/S-no/P-no/H-no

Full breakfast
Comp. wine, aftn. tea
Winter/summer sunporch
sitting rm., bridal room
guest room w/fireplace

*Seven guest rooms, all with private baths. Two suites, one with kitchen, one with fireplace. All antique handmade furnishings. Excellent location, Brimfield antique shows.*

TORRINGTON ————————————————————————————————————————

**Yankee Pedlar Inn/Rest.**
93 Main St,   06790
203-489-9226
Christopher J. Bolan
All year

$$$-EP
60 rooms, 60 pb
Most CC, *Rated*, •
C-yes/S-yes/P-no/H-ltd

Full breakfast (fee)
Restaurant, bar
Comp. drink/chocolates
bicycles, pool
comp. passes to YMCA

*100-year-old hotel in the heart of Litchfield and Berkshire Foothills. Old fashioned country charm surrounded by skiing, golf, antiques and breathtaking scenery.*

WESTPORT —————————————————————————————————————————

**Cotswold Inn**
76 Mrytle Ave.,   06880
203-226-3766 Fax: 203-221-0098
Lorna & Richard Montanaro
All year

$$$$-B&B
4 rooms, 4 pb
AmEx, MC, Visa, •
C-ltd/S-ltd/P-no/H-no

Continental plus bkfst.
Snacks, comp. wine
Comp. brandy, sitting rm
bicycles, land
some canopy beds

*Authentic, private country charm in cheerful, pleasant new inn. Walking distance to Westport's fine restaurants, shops, theatres, recreational facilities.*

WETHERSFIELD ————————————————————————————————————————

**Chester Bulkley House
B&B**
184 Main St.,   06109
860-563-4236 Fax: 860-257-8266
Frank & Sophie Bottaro
All year

$$-B&B
5 rooms, 3 pb
*Rated*, •
C-yes/S-no/P-no/H-no

Full breakfast
Snacks
Sitting room
Family friendly facility

*Nestled in the historic village of old Wethersfield, Frank & Sophie provide a warm and gracious New England welcome to the vacationer, traveler & business person. **3rd night, 50%.***

WINDSOR —————————————————————————————————————————

**Charles R. Hart House**
1046 Windsor Ave.,   06095
860-688-5555 Fax: 860-687-1992
Bob & Dorothy McAllister
All year

$$$-B&B
4 rooms, 4 pb
•
C-ltd/S-no/P-no/H-no

Continental plus bkfst.
Or full breakfast
Sitting room

*Step back in time and enjoy this authentically restored & furnished Victorian "Painted Lady" w/surrounding gardens. Within minutes to Hartford or Bradley International airports. **15% off after 3rd day.***

# More Inns ...

| | |
|---|---|
| Bethlehem | Dutch Moccasin, The, 51 Still Hill Rd., 06751, 203-266-7364 |
| Bolton | Jared Cone House, 25 Hebron Rd., 06043, 203-643-8538 |
| Brooklyn | Barrett Hill Farm, 210 Barrett Hill Rd., 06234 |
| Brooklyn | Golden Lamb Buttery, Bush Hill Rd., 06234 |
| Brooklyn | Tannerbrook, 329 Pomfret Rd., 06234 |
| Centerbrook | Fine Bouche Inn, 23 Main St., Box 121, 06409 |
| Central Village | Issac Shepard House, 165 Shepard Hill, Bx503, 06322 |
| Colchester | Hayward House Inn, 35 Hayward Ave., 06415, 203-537-5772 |
| Cornwall Bridge | Cornwall Inn, The, Route 7, 06754, 203-672-6884 |
| Cornwell | College Hill Farm, College St., 06759, 203-672-6762 |
| Coventry | Birdin House, 2011 Main St., 06238, 203-742-0032 |
| Coventry | Mill Brook Farm, 110 Wall St., 06238 |
| Coventry | Special Joys B&B, 41 N. River Rd., 06238 |
| Danielson | Quiet Waters, 465 Cook Hill Rd., 06239 |
| East Haddam | Gelston House, Goodspeed Landing, 06423, 203-873-1411 |
| East Haddam | Mount Parnassus View, 122 Shanaghan Rd., 06423 |
| East Haddam | Whispering Winds Inn, 93 River Rd., 06423, 203-526-3055 |
| East Lyme | Island, The, 20 Island Dr., Box 2, 06333 |
| East Lyme | Red House, 365 Boston Post Rd., 06333 |
| East Windsor | Stephen Potwine House, The, 84 Scantic Rd., 06088, 203-623-8722 |
| Farmington | Barney House, 11 Mountain Spring Rd., 06032, 203-677-9735 |
| Goshen | Twelve Maples, 89 North St., 06756, 203-491-9316 |
| Kent | Chaucer House, 88 North Main St., 06757, 203-927-4858 |
| Kent | Constitution Oak Farm, Beardsley Rd., 06757, 203-354-6495 |
| Kent | Country Goose B&B, 211 Kent-Cornwall Rd., 06757 |
| Kent | Fife n' Drum Rest. & Inn, P.O. Box 188, 06757, 203-927-3509 |
| Kent | Flanders Arms, Box 393, Kent-Cornwall, 06757 |
| Kent | Mavis, 230 Kent Cronwall Rd., 06757, 203-927-4334 |
| Killingworth | B&B at Laharan Farm, 350 Route 81, 06417, 203-663-1706 |
| Killingworth | Killingworth Inn, 249 Rt. 81, 06417, 203-663-1103 |
| Lakeville | Wake Robin Inn, Route 41, 06039, 203-435-2515 |
| Ledyard | Applewood Farms Inn, 528 Col. Ledyard Hwy., 06355, 203-536-2022 |
| Litchfield | Litchfield Inn, The, P.O. Box 798, 06759, 203-567-4503 |
| Litchfield | Tollgate Hill Inn, P.O. Box 1339, 06759, 203-567-4545 |
| Madison | Dolly Madison Inn, 73 W. Wharf Rd., 06443, 203-245-7377 |
| Madison | Honeysuckle Hill B&B, 116 Yankee Peddler Path, 06443, 203-245-4574 |
| Moodus | Fowler House, P.O. Box 340, Plains Rd, 06469, 203-873-8906 |
| Mystic | Inn at Mystic, P.O. Box 100, 06355, 203-536-9604 |
| Mystic | Whaler's Inn, P.O. Box 488, 06355, 800-243-2588 |
| N. Grosvenordale | Corttis Inn, 235 Corttis Rd., 06255 |
| New Canaan | Maples Inn, 179 Oenoke Rd., 06840, 203-966-2927 |
| New Canaan | Roger Sherman Inn, 195 Oenoke Ridge Rt. 12, 06840, 203-966-4541 |
| New Haven | Inn at Chapel West, 1201 Chapel St., 06511, 203-777-1201 |
| New Milford | Heritage Inn, 34 Bridge St., 06776, 203-354-8883 |
| New Milford | Homestead Inn, The, 5 Elm St., 06776, 203-354-4080 |
| New Preston | Altha House B&B, P.O. Box 2015, 06777, 203-355-7387 |
| New Preston | Birches Inn, West Shore Rd., 06777, 203-868-0229 |
| New Preston | Hopkins Inn, Hopkins Rd., 06777, 203-868-7295 |
| New Preston | Inn on Lake Waramaug, The, 107 North Shore Rd., 06777, 203-868-2168 |
| Norfolk | Blackberry River Inn, Route 44, 06058, 203-542-5100 |
| Norfolk | Breezes B&B, The, P.O. Box 504, 06058, 203-542-5920 |
| Norfolk | Covered Bridge B&B, P.O. Box 447A, 06058, 203-542-5944 |
| Norfolk | Mountain View Inn, 67 Litchfield Rd, 06058, 860-542-5595 |
| Norfolk | Weaver's House, P.O. Box 336, Route 44, 06058, 203-542-5108 |
| North Stonington | Randall's Ordinary, P.O. Box 243, 06359, 203-599-4540 |
| Old Greenwich | Harbor House Inn, 165 Shore Rd., 06870, 203-637-0145 |
| Old Mystic | Old Mystic Inn, The, P.O. Box 634, 06372, 203-572-9422 |
| Old Saybrook | Castle Inn, 50 Hartlands Dr., 06475 |
| Old Saybrook | Saybrook Point Inn, 2 Bridge St., 06475, 800-243-0212 |
| Pomfret | Cobbscroft, Rts. 169 & 44, 06258 |
| Pomfret | Inn at Gwyn Careg, Route 44, Box 96, 06230 |
| Portland | Croft B&B, The, 7 Penny Corner Rd, 06480, 203-342-1856 |
| Putnam | Felshaw Tavern, The, Five Mile River Rd., 06260, 203-928-3467 |
| Putnam | Thurker House, 78 Liberty Way, 06260, 203-928-6776 |
| Putnam Heights | Thurber House, 78 Liberty Hwy., Rt. 21, 06260 |
| Quinebaug | Cpt.Parker's Inn/Quinebaug, 32 Walker Rd., 06262, 800-707-7303 |
| Ridgefield | Elms Inn, The, 500 Main St., 06877, 203-438-2541 |
| Ridgefield | Stonehenge Inn, P.O. Box 667, 06877, 203-438-6511 |
| Riverton | Old Riverton Inn, Box 6, Rt. 20, 06065, 203-379-8678 |
| Salisbury | Ragamont Inn, Main St., 06068 |
| Salisbury | Under Mountain Inn, 482 Under Mountain Rd., 06068, 203-435-0242 |
| Salisbury | White Hart, The, P.O. Box 385, 06068, 203-435-0030 |
| Scotland | Nathan Fuller House, 147 Plains Rd., Box 257, 06264 |
| Seymour | Inn at Villa Bianca, Rt. 34, 312 Roosevelt, 06483 |
| Sharon | 1890 Colonial B&B, Rte. 40, P.O. Box 25, 06069, 203-364-0436 |
| Sharon | Alexander's B&B, 17 Rhynus Rd., 06069, 800-727-7592 |

| | |
|---|---|
| Sherman | Barnes Hill Farm B&B, Route 37, 06784,  203-354-4404 |
| Somersville | Old Mill Inn, The, 63 Maple St., 06072,  203-763-1473 |
| South Windsor | Cumon Inn, 130 Buckland Rd., 06074,  860-644-8486 |
| South Woodstock | Inn at Woodstock Hill, P.O. Box 98, 06267,  203-928-0528 |
| Southington | Chaffee's, 28 Reussner Rd., 06489 |
| Staffordville | Winterbrook Farm, Beffa Rd., 06076,  203-684-2124 |
| Stonington Village | Lasbury's B&B, 24 Orchard St., 06378,  203-535-2681 |
| Storrs | Diesel Home, 92 East Rd., 06268 |
| Storrs | Farmhouse on the Hill, 418 Gurleyville Rd., 06268,  203-429-1400 |
| Storrs | Spring Gardens, 359 Spring Hill Rd., 06268 |
| Thompson | A Taste of Ireland B&B, P.O. Box 521, 06277,  203-923-2883 |
| Thompson | Hickory Ridge, 1084 Quaddick Tn.Fm.Rd., 06277,  203-928-9530 |
| Thompson | Lord Thompson Manor, Rt. 200, Box 428, 06277 |
| Thompson | Samuel Watson House, P.O. Box 86, 06277, 203-923-2491 |
| Tolland | Old Babcock Tavern B&B, 484 Mile Hill Rd, 06084,  203-875-1239 |
| Torrington | Yankee Pedlar Inn Hotel, 93 Main St., 06790,  203-489-9226 |
| Uncasville | 1851 House, 1851 Route 32, 06382 |
| Warren | Evie's Turning Point Farm, Rte 45, Cornwall Bridge, 06754,  203-868-7775 |
| Washington | Mayflower Inn, Route 47, 06793, 213-868-0515 |
| Waterbury | Boulevard B&B, 15 Columbia Blvd., 06710 |
| Waterbury | House on the Hill, 92 Woodlawn Terrace, 06710 |
| Watertown | Graham House, The, 1002 Middlebury Rd., 06795,  203-274-2647 |
| West Cornwall | Hilltop Haven, Rte 7 Dibble Hill Rd, 06796 |
| West Woodstock | Ebenezer Stoddard House, Rt. 171, Perrin Rd., 06281 |
| Westbrook | Captain Stannard House, 138 S. Main St., 06498,  203-399-4634 |
| Winsted | B&B by the Lake, 19 Dillon Beach Rd., 06098,  203-738-0230 |
| Winsted | Provincial House, 151 Main St., 06098,  203-379-1631 |
| Woodbury | Curtis House, Inc., 506 Main St. South, 06798,  203-263-2101 |
| Woodbury | Merryvale B&B, 1204 Main St. S., 06798,  203-266-0800 |
| Woodstock | Beaver Pond, 68 Cutler Hill Rd., 06281 |

# Delaware

## MILFORD

| | | |
|---|---|---|
| **Towers B&B Inn, The** | $$$-B&B | Full breakfast |
| 101 N.W. Front St.,   19963 | 6 rooms, 4 pb | Afternoon tea |
| 302-422-3814  800-366-3814 | MC, Visa,  • | Complimentary wine, pool |
| Daniel Bond | C-ltd/S-no/P-no/H-no | sitting room, library |
| Open only on weekends | Spanish | bikes, fireplaces |

*A whimsical Victorian dream. Unique Steamboat Gothic Victorian mansion. Suites with fireplaces, furnishings in the French Victorian manner. Rehoboth and beaches nearby.*

## NEW CASTLE

| | | |
|---|---|---|
| **Jefferson House B&B** | $$-B&B | Continental breakfast |
| 5 The Strand,   19720 | 3 rooms, 3 pb | Restaurant, lunch/dinner |
| 302-325-1025302-322-8944 | *Rated*,  • | Afternoon tea, jacuzzi |
| Brenda | C-yes/S-yes | room w/porch river view |
| All year | | kitchen. Nearby park |

*Charming 200-yr-old riverfront hotel, historic district center. Furnished w/antiques, country motif. Orig. wood floors/millwork. William Penn landed here.* **10% off 3+ nights.**

| | | |
|---|---|---|
| **William Penn Guest House** | $$-B&B | Continental breakfast |
| 206 Delaware St.,   19720 | 4 rooms, | Living room |
| 302-328-7736 | *Rated*, | |
| Irma & Richard Burwell | C-ltd/S-no/P-no/H-no | |
| All year | Italian | |

*This house was built about 1682, and William Penn stayed overnight! Restored and located in the center of the Square.*

REHOBOTH BEACH ────────────────────────────────

| **Corner Cupboard Inn, The** | $$$-MAP/B&B | Full breakfast |
| 50 Park Ave.,   19971 | 18 rooms, 18 pb | Dinner included, limited |
| 302-227-8553 | AmEx, MC, Visa, | Restaurant, golf |
| Fax: 302-226-9113 | *Rated*, | sitting room, piano |
| Elizabeth G. Hooper | C-yes/S-yes/P-yes/H-no | half block to beach |
| All year | | |

*The inn that was in before inns were in! Fifty years at 50 Park Ave. as a summer retreat for Baltimore and Washington. B&B mid-Sept. to Mem. Day, MAP otherwise.*

────────────────────────────────

| **Tembo B&B** | $$-B&B | Continental plus bkfst. |
| 100 Laurel St.,   19971 | 6 rooms, 1 pb | Use of kitchen |
| 302-227-3360 | *Rated*, | Sitting room w/fireplace |
| Don & Gerry Cooper | C-ltd/S-no/P-no/H-no | A/C, enclosed porch |
| All year | | refrigerators in rooms |

*Warm hospitality in cozy beach cottage furnished with antiques, fine art, braided rugs. Short walk to beach, quality shops, restaurants. Non-smoking.* **10% discount Sun.– Thurs.**

WILMINGTON ────────────────────────────────

| **Darley Manor Inn B&B** | $$-B&B | Full breakfast |
| 3701 Philadelphia Pike, | 5 rooms, 5 pb | Aftn. tea, comp. wine |
|    19703 | AmEx, MC, Visa, | Snacks, Library |
| 302-792-2127 | *Rated*, • | sitting rm., exercise rm |
| Fax: 302-798-6143 | C-ltd/S-ltd/P-no/H-no | TV/VCR, phones, AC |
| 800-824-4703 | | |
| Ray & Judith Hester | | |
| All year | | |

*Historic register, c-1790 colonial manor house, offering southern hospitality, first class amenities, and easy access to all Brandywine Valley attractions.*

────────────────────────────────

# More Inns ...

| Bethany Beach | Addy Sea, P.O. Box 275, 19930,  302-539-3707 |
| Bethany Beach | Homestead Guests, 721 Garfield Pkwy, 19930,  302-539-7244 |
| Claymont | Darley Manor Inn B&B, 3701 Philadelphia Pike, 19703,  302-792-2127 |
| Dagsboro | Becky's Country Inn,  401 Main St., 19939,  302-732-3953 |
| Dover | Biddles B&B, 101 Wyoming Ave., 19901,  302-736-1570 |
| Dover | Inn @ Meeting House Square,  305 S. Governors Ave., 19901,  302-678-1242 |
| Laurel | Spring Garden, RD 1, Box 283A, 19956,  302-875-7015 |
| Milton | Drawing Room, The,  6 Main Sail Dr., 19968,  302-684-0339 |
| New Castle | Terry House B&B, 130 Delaware St., 19720,  302-322-2505 |
| Odessa | Cantwell House B&B, 107 High st., 19730,  302-378-4179 |
| Rehoboth Beach | Beach House, The,  15 Hickman St., 19971,  302-227-7074 |
| Rehoboth Beach | Drift Inn, 16 Brooklyn Ave., 19971 |
| Rehoboth Beach | Lord & Hamilton Seaside In,  20 Brooklyn Ave., 19971,  302-227-6960 |
| Rehoboth Beach | Lord Baltimore Lodge, 16 Baltimore Ave., 19971,  302-227-2855 |
| Rehoboth Beach | Pleasant Inn Lodge, 31 Olive Ave. @ 1st St., 19971,  302-227-7311 |
| Selbyville | Victorian Rose B&B, 22 Church St, 19975,  302-436-2558 |
| Wilmington | Boulevard B&B, The, 1909 Baynard Blvd., 19802,  302-656-9700 |
| Wilmington | Creek View B&B, 2901 Faulkland Rd., 19808,  302-994-5924 |
| Wilmington | Pink Door, The,  8 Francis Ln., 19803 |

# District of Columbia

**A Capitol Place**            $$$-B&B                    Full breakfast
134 12th St. S.E.,  20003      1 rooms, 1 pb              Comp. evening wine
202-543-1020 Fax: 202-543-1734 C-ltd/S-no/P-no/H-no       Private cable TV
Jim & Mary Pellettieri                                    phone, A/C
All year                                                  shops & cafes nearby

*Private 5 room apartment in restored Victorian Townhouse on Capitol Hill. Quiet, tree lined residential street. 12 blocks from US Capitol, 7 blocks from metro. **10% off 7 consecutive nights.***

---

**Adams Inn**                  $$-B&B                     Continental plus bkfst.
1744 Lanier Pl. NW,  20009     11 rooms, 6 pb             Coffee, tea, donuts
202-745-3600 Fax: 202-319-7958 AmEx, MC, Visa, •          Sitting room, gardens
800-578-6807                   C-yes/S-no/P-no/H-no        library, TV lounge, deck
G. & N. Thompson                                          winter get-away packages
All year

*Restored Edwardian townhouse. Enjoy charm and quiet of residential street in the heart of the famous Adams-Morgan neighborhood. Shops and restaurants nearby. Walk to zoo.*

---

**Connecticut-Woodley**        $$-EP                      Reataurant nearby
**House**                      15 rooms, 7 pb             TV lounge, family rates
2647 Woodley Rd. NW,           C-yes/S-yes/P-no/H-no       laundry facilities, A/C
  20008                                                   convention center nearby
202-667-0218 Fax: 202-232-0082
Ray Knickel
All year

*Comfortable, convenient, and inexpensive accommodations. Walk to restaurants, shops, Metro, bus transportation, Smithsonian museums. Direct-dial phone in rooms.*

---

**Embassy Inn, The**           $$$-B&B                    Continental plus bkfst.
1627 16th St. NW,  20009       38 rooms, 38 pb            Complimentary sherry
202-234-7800 Fax: 202-234-3309 Most CC, *Rated*, •        Snacks, sitting room
800-423-9111                   C-yes/S-yes/P-no/H-no       cable TV & HBO
Jennifer Schroeder, S. Stiles  Spanish                    Near Metro & White House
All year

*Near Metro, White House, restaurants and shops; knowledgeable and helpful staff. Colonial style, in renovated 1920s boarding house. **10% off, ask; free mug.***

---

**Kalorama Guest House**       $$-B&B                     Continental breakfast
1854 Mintwood Place, NW,       19 rooms, 12 pb            Comp. wine, lemonade
Kalorama Park,  20009          Most CC, *Rated*,          Parlor, sun room
202-667-6369 Fax: 202-319-1262 C-yes/S-yes/P-no/H-no       24-hour message service
Tami, John & Carlotta                                    free local phone calls
All year

*Victorian townhouse decorated in period furnishings. Antique-filled, spacious rooms. Beautiful sun room for your morning breakfast. Charming, unique & inexpensive.*

WASHINGTON ─────────────────────────────

**Kalorama Guest House,**
**The**
2700 Cathedral Ave., NW,
Woodley Park,   20008
202-328-0860 Fax: 202-328-8730
Michael & Mary Anne
All year

$$-B&B
50 rooms, 50 pb
Most CC, *Rated*,  •
C-yes/S-no/P-no/H-no

Continental plus
Comp. wine, lemonade
Sitting room
conference room avail.
completely non-smoking

*Charming European-style bed & breakfast in six turn-of-the-century townhouses. Period art, furnishings, brass beds, plants, outdoor landscaped garden, and hospitality.*

**Morrison-Clark Inn**
Mass. Ave. & 11th St NW,
   20001
202-898-1200  Fax: 202-289-8576
800-332-7898
Bill Petrella
All year

$$$-B&B
54 rooms, 54 pb
AmEx, MC, Visa,
*Rated*,  •
C-yes/S-yes/P-no/H-yes
Spanish

Continental plus bkfst.
Award winning restaurant
Bar, sitting room
cable TV, weddings
fitness center

*The perfect urban oasis for visitors to downtown Washington. Victorian decor is alive in D.C.'s finest historic inn. All rooms have minibars, hairdryers, 2 phones & dataport.* **3rd night 50%, ltd.**

**Reeds, The**
P.O. Box 12011,   20005
202-328-3510  Fax: 202-332-3885
Charles & Jackie Reed
All year

$$$-B&B
6 rooms, 1 pb
*Rated*,  •
C-yes/S-yes/P-no/H-no
French, Spanish

Continental plus bkfst.
Sitting room, gardens
library, Victorian porch
piano, antiques

*Spacious rooms with wood-burning fireplaces and crystal chandeliers bring a bit of the Nineteenth Century to historic downtown Washington.*

**Swiss Inn**
1204 Massachusetts NW,
   20005
202-371-1816  800-955-7947
Kelley Carpenter
All year

$$-EP
8 rooms, 8 pb
AmEx, MC, Visa,  •
C-ltd/S-yes/P-yes/H-no
French, German,
Spanish

Kitchenettes
Library, color TV
Air conditioning
climate control

*Within walking distance to White House, FBI, Convention Center, Smithsonian Museum and the Mall. Suites have private baths and fully equipped kitchenettes.* **10% off stay, ask.**

**Windsor Inn, The**
1842 16th St., NW,   20009
202-667-0300 Fax: 202-667-4503
800-423-9111
Jennifer Schroeder, S. Stiles
All year

$$$-B&B
46 rooms, 46 pb
Most CC, *Rated*,  •
C-yes/S-yes/P-no/H-no
French, Spanish

Continental plus bkfst.
Comp. sherry & snacks
5-10 p.m. in lobby
cable TV & HBO in rooms
Renovated lobby

*Relaxing and charming haven in heart of nation's capitol. Art deco flair. Close to Metro and many restaurants. 11 blocks north of White House.* **10% off, ask; free mug.**

## More Inns ...

| | | |
|---|---|---|
| Washington | B&B Accom. of Washington, 3222 Davenport St. NW, 20008,  202-363-8909 | |
| Washington | Capitol Hill Guest House, 101 Fifth St. NE, 20002,  202-547-1050 | |
| Washington | Hereford House, 604 S. Carolina Ave, SE, 20003,  202-543-0102 | |
| Washington | Tabard Inn, 1739 N Street, N.W., 20036,  202-785-1277 | |

*Elizabeth Pointe Lodge, Amelia Island, FL*

# Florida

## AMELIA ISLAND

**Bailey House**
28 S. 7th St., 32034
904-261-5390 Fax: 904-321-0103
800-251-5390
Tom & Jenny Bishop
All year

$$-B&B
5 rooms, 5 pb
Most CC, *Rated*, •
C-ltd/S-no/P-no/H-yes

Continental plus bkfst.
Old pump organ, victrola
authentic antiques
A/C, heat, beach towels

*Elegant 1895 Queen Anne Victorian on National Register, in historic district. Walk to shopping, restaurants, marina, dining. Near state park beach, large rooms.*

---

**Elizabeth Pointe Lodge**
98 S. Fletcher Ave., 32034
904-277-4851 Fax: 904-227-6500
800-772-3359
David & Susan Caples
All year

$$$-B&B
25 rooms, 25 pb
AmEx, MC, Visa,
*Rated*, •
C-yes/S-yes/P-no/H-yes

Full breakfast
Complimentary wine/snack
Sitting room, library
bicycles, oceanfront
kids program, room serv.

*Reminiscent of a turn-of-the-century lodge; oceanfront on a small Florida barrier island; bike to historic seaport village nearby. Hearty breakfast, newspaper, fresh flowers.*

---

**Fairbanks House, The**
227 S. Seventh St., 32034
904-277-0500 Fax: 904-277-3103
800-261-4838
Mary & Nelson Smelker
All year

$$$-B&B
12 rooms, 12 pb
Most CC, •
C-yes/S-ltd/P-no/H-yes

Full breakfast
Complimentary wine
Sitting room, bicycles
swimming pool
conference faciliy

*Elegant 1885 Historic Register Italianate villa restored in 1994 with antiques and period pieces. Gourmet continental breakfast. Jacuzzis, suites, cottages available.*

AMELIA ISLAND ───────────────────────────

| **Florida House Inn** | $$-B&B | Full breakfast |
|---|---|---|

**Florida House Inn**
P.O. Box 688, 32034
22 S. Third St.
904-261-3300 Fax: 904-277-3831
800-258-3301
Bob & Karen Warner
All year

$$-B&B
12 rooms, 12 pb
AmEx, MC, Visa,
*Rated*, •
C-ltd/S-no/P-no/H-yes
some Spanish

Full breakfast
Restaurant, bar
Sitting room, library
bicycles, near beaches,
golf, tennis, fishing

*Florida's oldest continually operating tourist hotel, circa 1857, in 50-block historic district. Antiques, quilts, shady porches, crtyrd. with fountain & gazebo.* ***3rd night 50%, ltd.***

**Hoyt House B&B**
804 Atlantic Ave., 32034
904-277-4300 Fax: 904-277-9626
800-432-2085
Rita & John Kovacevich
All year

$$$-B&B
9 rooms, 9 pb
Most CC, *Rated*, •
C-yes/S-no/P-no/H-yes

Full breakfast
Tea, snacks, comp. wine
Sitting room, library
hot tubs, fam. friendly
by beaches, tennis, golf

*A historic Queen Anne. Each bed chamber beautifully decorated. Full gourmet breakfast, warm hospitality. Piano, gardens, gazebo, porch swing. Come enjoy!* ***Free bottle of wine.***

BARTOW ───────────────────────────

**Stanford Inn, The**
555 E. Stanford St., 33830
941-533-2393 Fax: 941-533-2393
Freddie Guess
All year

$$-B&B
6 rooms, 6 pb
Most CC, *Rated*,
C-ltd/S-ltd/P-ltd/H-yes

Full breakfast
Comp. wine, bar service
Sitting room, library
swimming pool, BBQ
weddings & receptions

*Victorian mansion in Florida's largest historic district. Spectacular art and antiques, spacious suites, pool. Close to Tampa and Orlando.* ***3rd night 50%.***

BAY HARBOR ISLAND ───────────────────────────

**Bay Harbor Inn**
9660 E. Bay Harbor Dr., 33154
305-868-4141 Fax: 305-868-4141
Lee Machette
All year

$$$-B&B
38 rooms, 38 pb
AmEx, MC, Visa,
*Rated*, •
C-yes/S-yes/P-yes/H-ltd
Spanish

Continental plus bkfst.
Lunch, dinner, snacks
Comp. wine, bar service
Asia Garden Restaurant
sitting room, pool

*Award-winning waterfront inn, adjacent to Bay Harbour shops. Beautiful tropical setting w/world famous Palm Restaurant & B.C. Chong's Seafood.* ***Frequent guest discounts.***

BIG PINE KEY ───────────────────────────

**Deer Run B&B**
P.O. Box 431, 33043
305-872-2015
Sue Abbott
All year

$$$-B&B
3 rooms, 3 pb
*Rated*, •
S-no/P-no/H-yes

Full breakfast
Comp. bottle of wine
Bicycles, beach
hot tubs, library
grill, hammocks

*Ocean front hideaway - quiet, serene. Breakfast is served on the veranda overlooking the ocean. 33 miles to Key West.* ***Free wine.***

BRADENTON BEACH ───────────────────────────

**Duncan House B&B**
1703 Gulf Dr., Anna Maria Island, 34217
941-778-6858 Fax: 941-778-3082
Joe & Becky Garbus
All year

$$$-B&B
4 rooms, 4 pb
AmEx, MC, Visa, •
C-ltd/S-no/P-no/H-no

Full breakfast
Complimentary wine
Sitting room
sun deck
hot tub, pool

*Turn-of-the-century Victorian. Located on beautiful Anna Maria Island. Steps away from white sandy beaches.* ***10% off week stay.***

### CEDAR KEY

| **Island Hotel** | $$-B&B | Full breakfast |
| P.O. Box 460, 32625 | 10 rooms, 6 pb | Full menu, cafe |
| 220 - Main St. | MC, Visa, AmEx, | Natural foods restaurant |
| 352-543-5111 | *Rated*, • | comp. wine, draft beer |
| Tom & Alison Sanders | C-ltd/S-no/P-no/H-ltd | sitting & dining room |
| All year | Spanish | |

*1850 Jamaican architecture in historic district. Antiques. Gourmet natural foods specializing in original recipes, seafood and vegetarian, poppy-seed bread.* **25% off weekdays.**

### DAYTONA BEACH

| **Captain's Quarters Inn** | $$-B&B | Full breakfast |
| 3711 S. Atlantic Ave., 32127 | 25 rooms, 25 pb | Lunch, comp. wine |
| 904-767-3119 Fax: 904-767-0883 | AmEx, MC, Visa, | Cheese, crackers |
| 800-332-3119 | *Rated*, • | All suites |
| Becky Sue Prince & Family | C-yes/S-yes/P-ltd/H-yes | heated pool, bicycles |
| All year | | |

*Daytona's first new B&B inn, directly on world's most famous beach. Old-fashioned coffee shop. Unique antique shoppe, all-suite inn, balconies. AAA "excellent.* **10% off stay.**

| **Live Oak Inn/Restaurant** | $$-B&B/MAP | Continental plus bkfst. |
| 444-448 South Beach St., 32114 | 15 rooms, 15 pb | Restaurant, bar service |
| 904-252-4667 Fax: 904-239-0098 | Visa, MC, Disc., • | Comp. wine, tea, snacks |
| Del & Jessie Glock    All year | S-no/P-ltd/H-yes | sitting room, library |
| | | jacuzzis, massage avail. |

*Daytona's only Historic Registry inn. Early Florida antiques. A Romantic setting: marina, river & garden views, fine dining. Close to airport, beach, speedway, pool, golf.*

### EVERGLADES CITY

| **Ivey House, The** | $$-B&B | Continental plus bkfst. |
| P.O. Box 5038, 33929 | 10 rooms, | Lunch, dinner, aft. tea |
| 107 Camellia St. | MC, Visa, | Snacks, sitting room |
| 941-695-3299 | C-yes/S-no/P-no/H-no | library, bicycles |
| David Harraden | French | canoes, kayaks |
| October 15 - May 1 | | |

*Located in a small crabbing village boardering the Everglades National Park. We offer friendship, charm, guided adventures, tiki-torch lit porches.* **10% off, ask.**

### FORT MYERS BEACH

| **Island Rover Sailing** | $$$-B&B | Continental breakfast |
| 11470 S. Cleveland Ave., Snug Harbor, 33907 | 5 rooms, 2 pb | Snacks, comp. wine |
| 941-691-7777 Fax: 941-936-7391 | Most CC, | Bar service (beer, wine) |
| Jessie Shepard & Jim Perkins | C-yes/S-yes/P-no/H-no | family friendly facility |
| All year | | sailing cruises |

*Newly remodeled 72 foot sailing ship. We anchor in the shallow waters of the Gulf of Mexico. Relax and sail with us.*

### FORT PIERCE

| **Mellon Patch Inn, The** | $$-B&B | Full breakfast |
| 3601 N. A-1-A, 34949 | 4 rooms, 4 pb | Afternoon tea |
| 407-461-5231 Fax: 407-464-6463 | Visa, MC, AmEx, • | Sitting room, sailing |
| 800-656-7824 | C-ltd/S-no/P-no/H-yes | tennis court, canoeing |
| Andrea & Arthur Mellon | | ocean swimming, fishing |
| All year | | |

*This new Florida-style B&B is across from a magnificent beach. All rooms have hand-painted furniture & water view. Enjoy a gourmet breakfast while your soul feasts on beauty.*

GAINESVILLE ───────────────────────────────────

| **Magnolia Plantation B&B** | $$-B&B | Full breakfast |
|---|---|---|
| 309 SE 7th St.,  32601 | 5 rooms, 5 pb | Lunch by res., snacks |
| 352-375-6653 Fax: 352-338-0303 | MC, Visa, AmEx, | Comp. beverages, library |
| 800-201-2379 | *Rated*, • | sitting room, bicycles |
| Joe & Cindy Montalto | C-ltd/S-no/P-ltd/H-no | 60-feet pond, gazebo |
| All year | | |

*Restored 1885 Victorian in downtown. Two miles from Univ. of Florida. Beautifully landscaped gardens, pond, waterfalls & gazebo. 1880s cottage 2 bedroom, 1 bath.*

| **Sweetwater Branch Inn** | $$-B&B | Full breakfast |
|---|---|---|
| 625 E. University Ave.,  32601 | 7 rooms, 7 pb | Dinner avail. comp. wine |
| 352-373-6760  Fax: 352-371-3771 | AmEx, MC, Visa | Afternoon tea, snacks |
| Cornelia Holbrook | *Rated*, • | sitting room, bicycles |
| All year | S-no/P-no/H-yes | airport/univ. transport |
| | Spanish, Italian, French | |

*Enjoy a piece of the past; restored 1880 Victorian with antiques, English garden/patio. Walk to historic district—fine dining, Hippodrome Theatre.* **Comp. glass of wine.**

HOLMES BEACH ───────────────────────────────────

| **Harrington House B&B** | $$$-B&B | Full gourmet breakfast |
|---|---|---|
| 5626 Gulf Dr.,  34217 | 8 rooms, | Comp. iced tea, popcorn |
| 941-778-5444 Fax: 941-778-0527 | MC, Visa, *Rated*, • | Sitting room |
| Jo & Frank Davis | C-ltd/S-no/P-no | bicycles |
| All year | | swimming pool |

*Charming restored 1920s home directly on Gulf of Mexico reflects "casual elegance." Antiques, balconies, great rooms, swimming pool, peace & quiet. Near major attractions.*

HOMESTEAD ───────────────────────────────────

| **Room at the Inn** | $$-B&B | Continental plus bkfst. |
|---|---|---|
| 15830 SW 240 St.,  33031 | 4 rooms, 3 pb | Great room w/fireplace |
| 305-246-0492 Fax: 305-246-0590 | *Rated*, | swimming pool with spa |
| Sally Robinson | C-ltd/S-no/P-ltd/H-no | |
| All year | | |

*A quiet retreat on a country estate. Furnished in period antiques. Convenient to southern Florida, Everglades National Park and Florida Keys.*

JACKSONVILLE ───────────────────────────────────

| **House on Cherry Street** | $$-B&B | Full breakfast |
|---|---|---|
| 1844 Cherry St.,  32205 | 4 rooms, 4 pb | Complimentary wine/snack |
| 904-384-1999 Fax: 904-981-2998 | MC, Visa, *Rated*, • | Sitting room, color TV |
| Carol Anderson | C-ltd/S-yes/P-no/H-no | air conditioned |
| All year | | porch, bicycles, Fax |

*In historic Riverside, a restored colonial house filled with period antiques, decoys, four poster beds and country collectibles. On beautiful St. John's River.*

| **Plantation Manor Inn** | $$$-B&B | Full breakfast |
|---|---|---|
| 1630 Copeland St.,  32204 | 9 rooms, 9 pb | Comp. refreshments |
| 904-384-4630 Fax: 904-387-0960 | AmEx, MC, Visa, | 3rd night free wine |
| Kathy & Jerry Ray | *Rated*, • | sitting room, spa |
| All year | C-ltd/S-yes/P-no/H-no | swimming pool |

*Restored 1905 Southern Mansion with antique furnishings and oriental carpets. 2 blocks from river, restaurants, antique shops. Convenient to Cummer Art Museum, downtown.*

KEY WEST —————————————————————————————————

| **Andrew's Inn** | $$$-B&B | Full breakfast |
|---|---|---|
| 0 Whalton Lane, 900 block of | 9 rooms, 9 pb | Aftn. tea, comp. wine |
| Duval St., 33040 | Most CC, • | Bar service |
| 305-294-7740 Fax: 305-294-0021 | C-ltd/S-yes/P-no/H-yes | swimming pool |
| 888-ANDREW-3 | Spanish, German, | |
| Ana & Bruno Wirz | French | |
| All year | | |

*No guesthouse embodies the spirit of Key West as much as Andrew's Inn. The inn shares a wall with the Hemingway Estate & the suites are named for locations in the author's books. Open bar all day*

| **Authors of Key West** | $$$-B&B | Continental plus bkfst. |
|---|---|---|
| 725 White St., 33040 | 10 rooms, 10 pb | Comp. wine in season |
| 305-294-7381 Fax: 305-294-0920 | Visa, MC, AmEx, Disc., | Sitting room, bicycles |
| 800-898-6909 | • | swimming pool, sundeck |
| Sam & Suzanne Langfitt | C-ltd/S-ltd/P-no/H-ltd | garden with hammock |
| All year | | |

*Get the feel of the real Key West of Hemingway and Tennessee Williams and other famous Authors of Key West. 5 new suites across street.* **Summer packages, 3–7 day.**

| **Blue Parrot Inn** | $$-B&B | Continental plus bkfst. |
|---|---|---|
| 916 Elizabeth St., 33040 | 10 rooms, 10 pb | Refrigerator, some rooms |
| 305-296-0033 Fax: 305-296-5697 | Most CC, *Rated*, • | Ceiling fan, cable TV |
| 800-231-BIRD | S-yes/P-no/H-ltd | swimming pool, phones |
| Frank & Larry | | A/C, private bath |
| All year | | |

*Classic Bahamian Conch house built in 1884 with major renovations in 1989. In the heart of Old Town Key West. Walk to beaches, shopping, restaurants, clubs.* **10% off, ask.**

| **Center Court Historic Inn** | $$$-B&B | Continental plus |
|---|---|---|
| 916 Center St., 33040 | 7 rooms, 7 pb | Free bottle of wine |
| 305-296-9292 Fax: 305-294-4104 | Most CC, *Rated*, • | Sitting room, library |
| 800-797-8787 | C-ltd/S-ltd/P-ltd/H-ltd | hot tubs, pool, exercise |
| Naomi Van Steelandt | | facilities |
| All year | | |

*Located in the heart of the historic Old Town, 1/2 block from Duval on quiet lane. Winner 2 Historic Preservation awards. We'll pamper you with Carribean charm.* **50% off, ltd.**

| **Conch House Heritage Inn** | $$$-B&B | Continental plus bkfst. |
|---|---|---|
| 625 Turman Ave., 33040 | 8 rooms, 8 pb | Swimming pool, phones |
| 305-293-0020 Fax: 305-293-8447 | Most CC, *Rated*, • | family friendly facility |
| 800-207-5806 | C-ltd/S-yes/P-no/H-yes | bicycles, porches |
| Sam Holland | Spanish | |
| All year | | |

*Victorian architecture w/Bahama influences. Family owned & operated over 100 years. Extremely large rooms, tropical cottages by pool/garden; walk to everything.* **10% discount.**

| **Cypress House** | $$$-B&B | Continental plus bkfst. |
|---|---|---|
| 601 Caroline St., 33040 | 16 rooms, 6 pb | Complimentary wine |
| 305-294-6969 Fax: 305-294-1174 | Most CC, • | Sitting room, library |
| 800-525-2488 | C-ltd/S-yes/P-no/H-no | swimming pool |
| Arthur Kelley | | an adult only inn |
| All year | | |

*1888 Bahamian Conch mansion. Private, tropical. Large rooms with A/C and ceiling fans. Walk to all historic sites, shopping, restaurants.* **10% disc't for stays of & nights.**

KEY WEST ───────────────────────────────────────

**Douglas House**
419 Amelia St.,   33040
305-294-5269 Fax: 305-292-7665
800-833-0372
Robert Marrero, Andrew
Davies
All year

$$$-B&B
15 rooms, 15 pb
Visa, MC, AmEx,  •
C-ltd/S-yes/P-yes/H-no
Spanish, French,
German

Continental breakfast
Afternoon tea
Bikes, hot tub
swimming pool

*Choose from 15 deluxe rooms & large suites. Imagine sitting on your own private porch as dusk turns into night and the warmth of the Caribbean Sea relaxes your entire body.*

**Duval House**
815 Duval St.,   33040
305-294-1666  Fax: 305-292-1701
800-22-Duval
Richard Kamradt
All year

$$$-B&B
27 rooms, 25 pb
Most CC, *Rated*,  •
C-ltd/S-yes

Continental plus bkfst.
2 apts. with kitchenette
Sitting room, TV lounge
Gazebo in nearby gardens
swimming pool, sun deck

*A restored guest house (circa 1885). Ideally located in historic Old Key West. Tropical gardens and a laid-back atmosphere. Walk to beaches, restaurants.* **10% off snorkeling.**

**Duval Suites**
524 Eaton St. #150,   33040
305-293-6600 Fax: 305-293-6629
800-648-3780
Ed Cox
All year

$$$$-EP
8 rooms, 8 pb
Most CC,  •
S-yes/P-no/H-yes

Hot tubs
bicycles

*Located on Upper Dural Street and new this year. Each suite has a balcony overlooking either Dural Street or our gardens.*

**Eden House, The**
1015 Fleming St.,   33040
305-296-6868 Fax: 305-294-1221
800-533-KEYS
Mike Eden
All year

$$-EP
41 rooms, 41 pb
MC, Visa,  •
C-yes/S-yes/P-no/H-no
Spanish, French,
German

Restaurant, cafe
Free happy hour
Swimming pool, jacuzzi
snorkeling, scuba diving
sailing & jet ski nearby

*In old Key West. Ceiling fans, white wicker. Sip a cool drink under a poolside gazebo, lounge on veranda, dine in garden cafe, join us on a sunset sail.* **Packages, wkly rates.**

**Heron House**
512 Simonton St.,   33040
305-294-9227 Fax: 305-292-8497
800-294-1644
Fred Geibelt
All year

$$$-B&B
23 rooms, 21 pb
AmEx, MC, Visa
*Rated*,  •
C-ltd/S-yes/P-no/H-yes

Continental breakfast
Orchid gardens, sun deck
gym, swimming pool
breakfast bar, phones

*Old island charm situated in location central to all the main tourist attractions. Pool, sun deck, gardens and gym. Continual renovation.* **Specials depending on occasion.**

**Key West B&B/Popular House**
415 William St.,   33040
305-296-7274 Fax: 305-293-0306
800-438-6155
Jody Carlson
All year

$$-B&B
8 rooms, 4 pb
Most CC, *Rated*,  •
C-ltd/S-ltd

Continental plus bkfst.
1 room with private deck
hot tubs, sauna
sun deck, sitting room

*In heart of Historic District, restored 100-yr-old Victorian. Breakfast at your leisure. Caribbean casual. Sun deck, sauna, Jacuzzi for your relaxation.* **10% off 3+ nights.**

KEY WEST ──────────────────────────────────────────────

**La Casa de Luces**
422 Amelia St.,   33040
305-296-3993 Fax: 305-293-7669
800-432-4849
Fred Salireno
All year

$$$-B&B
8 rooms, 6 pb
Visa, MC, AmEx,  •
C-yes/S-yes/P-ltd
Spanish

Continental breakfast
Hot tubs
inluces membership to
Marriot's Beach Resort

*Just off Duval Street, off street parking, guest membership to full-service resort.*

──────────────────────────────────────────────

**La Pensione Inn**
809 Truman Ave.,   33040
 Fax: 305-296-6509 800-893-1193
Monica Wiemer, Jane
Rodriguez
All year

$$$-B&B
7 rooms, 7 pb
Most CC, *Rated*,
C-ltd/S-yes/P-no/H-yes
Spanish, French,
German

Continental plus bkfst.
Swimming pool

*Old Victorian completely renovated with spacious, clean rooms simply furnished with private baths, A/C, pool, parking available. Close to all major attractions.*

──────────────────────────────────────────────

**Merlinn Guesthouse**
811 Simonton St.,   33040
305-296-3336 Fax: 305-296-3524
800-642-4753
Pat Hoffman
All year

$$-B&B
18 rooms, 18 pb
Most CC, *Rated*,  •
C-ltd/S-no/P-ltd/H-ltd

Full breakfast
Comp. rum punch, snacks
Sitting room, library
garden, swimming pool
Wheelch. to prvt. patio

*Tropical B&B in center of Historic District. Homemade breakfast served in pool garden. Rooms and apartments all non-smoking with A/C & TV, private baths.*

──────────────────────────────────────────────

**Nassau House**
1016 Fleming St.,   33040
305-296-8513 Fax: 305-293-8423
800-296-8513
D. Leard, B. Tracy
All year

$$-B&B
6 rooms, 6 pb
AmEx, MC, Visa,  •
C-ltd/S-yes/P-ltd/H-yes

Continental plus bkfst.
Full kitchens in units
Tropical lagoon pool
with waterfall, A/C
free bottle of wine

*Located in "Old Town." Six intimate units all fully renovated w/white wicker furniture, private baths, plants, color cable TV, private deck. Lagoon-style pool w/waterfall.*

──────────────────────────────────────────────

**Pilot House Guest House**
414 Simonton St.,   33040
305-294-8719 Fax: 305-294-9298
800-648-3780
Ed
All year

$$$$-EP
8 rooms, 8 pb
AmEx, MC, Visa,
*Rated*,  •
C-ltd/S-ltd/P-no/H-no

Fully equipped kitchens
Hot tubs, marble baths,
verandas, pool, garden
courtyard w/gas grill

*The 19th-century Victorian Guest House is conveniently located in the heart of Historic Old Town Key West. Suites have A/C, TV & phones. Spanish cabana guesthouse w/in room Jacuzzis.*

──────────────────────────────────────────────

**Seascape**
420 Olivia St.,   33040
305-296-7776 Fax: 305-296-7776
800-765-6438
Alan D. Melnick
All year

$$-B&B
5 rooms, 5 pb
AmEx, MC, Visa,  •
C-ltd/S-yes/P-no/H-no

Continental plus bkfst.
Sunset wine hr-seasonal
Heated pool-spa
sun decks, wicker
A/C, TVs, Bahama fans

*c. 1889, listed on National Historic Register. In tropical garden setting. Royal blue & white wicker motif. Center of Old Town Key West. Recommended by New York Times.*

KEY WEST ───────────────────────────────────

**White Street Inn**
905-907 White St.,  33040
305-295-9599 Fax: 305-295-9503
800-207-9767
C. Biscardi, G. & N. Pentz
All year

$$$-B&B
7 rooms, 7 pb
Most CC, *Rated*,  •
C-yes/S-yes/P-no/H-no
Italian, German

Continental plus bkfst.
Swimming pool
microwave, refrigerator

*Historic property surrounded by lush tropical garden & secluded pool. Newly renovated spacious rooms open out onto private deck/porches. Centrally located-marinas & beaches nearby.* **10% disc't 7+ nites.**

───────────────────────────────────

**William Anthony House**
P.O. Box 107, 33041
613 Caroline St., 33949
305-294-2887
Fax: 305-294-9209
800-613-2276
Tony Minore & Bill Beck
All year

$$$-B&B
8 rooms, 8 pb
Most CC,  •
C-ltd/S-no/P-no/H-yes
Spanish

Continental plus bkfst.
Snacks, bar service
Hot tubs

*Award winning historic inn with luxury suites and rooms. All with private baths, A/C, kitchenettes. Excellent quiet location. Complimentary breakfast & social hour.* **Complimentary champagne.**

KISSIMMEE ───────────────────────────────────

**Unicorn Inn, English B&B**
8 S. Orlando Ave.,  34741
407-846-1200
Fax: 407-846-1773
800-865-7212
Don & Fran Williamson
All year

$$-B&B
7 rooms, 5 pb
Visa, MC, *Rated*,  •
C-yes/S-ltd/P-no/H-no

Full breakfast
Comp. tea/coffee/wine
TV in all rooms, Cable
extended stay discounts
A/C in all rooms

*1901 Colonial house. Authentic English B&B. Antiques throughout; quiet & romantic. 25 min. to Disney, Sea World, Orlando airport. Health club & swimming nearby.*

LAKE BUENA VISTA,ORLANDO ───────────────────────

**PerriHouse B&B Inn**
P.O. Box 22005, 32830
10417 Centurion Ct.
407-876-4830  Fax: 407-876-0241
800-780-4830
Nick & Angi Perretti
All year

$$$-B&B
6 rooms, 6 pb
Most CC, *Rated*,  •
C-yes/S-ltd

Continental plus bkfst.
Private entrance to room
pool, A/C, TV, phones
bird sanctuary project

*A private & secluded country estate on 20 acres conveniently nestled adjacent to the Walt Disney World complex. 3 min. to Disney Village; 5 min. to EPCOT; 20 min. to airport.*

LAKE HELEN ───────────────────────────────────

**Clauser's Bed & Breakfast**
201 E. Kicklighter Rd.,  32744
904-228-0310 Fax: 904-228-2337
800-220-0310
Tom & Marge Clauser
All year

$$-B&B
8 rooms, 8 pb
MC, Visa, *Rated*,  •
C-ltd/S-no/P-no/H-no

Full breakfast
Comp. wine, snacks, tea
Sitting room, library
verandas, gardens
rockers, bicycles

*1880s Victorian home in tranquil country setting. Magnificent trees, heirlooms, quilts, linens and lace. "Everybody's grandmother's house."* **Ask about packages and events.**

*Chalet Sizanne Country Inn, Lake Wales, FL*

## LAKE WALES

| | | |
|---|---|---|
| **Chalet Suzanne Country Inn** | $$$$-B&B | Full breakfast |
| 3800 Chalet Suzanne Dr., 33853 | 30 rooms, 30 pb | Restaurant, lounge |
| | Most CC, *Rated*, • | Comp. sherry in room |
| 941-676-6011   Fax: 941-676-1814 | C-yes/S-yes/P-yes/H-yes | pool on lake, airstrip |
| 800-433-6011 | German, French | 4 rooms w/pvt. jacuzzi |
| Carl & Vita Hinshaw | | |
| All year | | |

*Unique country inn centrally located for Florida attractions. Gourmet meals; award-winning restaurant. Ranked one of 10 most romantic spots in Florida.* **10% discount, ltd.**

## MAITLAND

| | | |
|---|---|---|
| **Thurston House** | $$$-B&B | Continental plus bkfst. |
| 851 Lake Ave., 32751 | 4 rooms, 4 pb | Comp. wine, snacks |
| 407-539-1911   Fax: 407-539-0365 | MC, Visa, AmEx, | Sitting room |
| 800-843-2721 | *Rated*, • | screened porches |
| Carole & Joe Ballard | C-ltd/S-no/P-no/H-no | lake front |
| All year | | |

*Newly renovated 1885 Queen Anne Victorian home. Hidden away in a country setting but moments from downtown Orlando. Come experience the "old Florida.*

## FULMIAMI

| | | |
|---|---|---|
| **Miami River Inn** | $$$-B&B | Continental breakfast |
| 118 SW South River Dr., 33130 | 40 rooms, 39 pb | Complimentary wine |
| | Most CC, • | Sitting room, library |
| 305-325-0045  Fax: 305-325-9227 | C-yes/S-no/P-no/H-no | jacuzzi, pool, croquet |
| 800-HOTEL89 | Spanish | table games, telephone |
| Sallye G. Jude | | |
| All year | | |

*Make your vacation unforgettable at this tropical hideaway, within 15 minutes of everything. Miami's only B&B, across the Miami River from downtown. Conference facility.*

## MIAMI BEACH

| | | |
|---|---|---|
| **Brigham Gardens** | $$-EP | Coffee service all rooms |
| 1411 Collins Ave., 33139 | 18 rooms, 18 pb | Family friendly facility |
| 305-531-1331  Fax: 305-538-9898 | Visa, MC, AmEx, • | close to beach |
| Erika & Hillary Brigham | C-yes/S-yes/P-yes/H-no | |
| All year | Spanish, German | |

*Historical south beach guest house. Over 100 special plants and many tropical birds. Half a block to the beach. Kitchens available. Ten miles to Miami International Airport.*

MIAMI BEACH ─────────────────────────────

| **Sunshine Inn** | $$$-B&B | Continental breakfast |
|---|---|---|
| 800 West Ave,  33139 | 1 rooms, 1 pb | Sitting room |
| 305-672-9297 Fax: 305-672-0177 | C-ltd/S-ltd/P-no/H-yes | hot tub, sauna |
| Susan Schein | Spanish | swimming pool |
| All year | | |

*Exquisite sunset view on peaceful western side of South Miami Beach with many amenities and Art Deco furnishings*

| **White House on the Prairie** | $$$-B&B | Continental plus bkfst. |
|---|---|---|
| P.O. Box 402691, 33140 | 2 rooms, | Sitting room |
| 2146 Prairie Ave. | • | bicycles |
| 305-532-1366 Fax: 305-532-1366 | S-no/P-yes/H-no | |
| All year | | |

*Art Deco home on South Beach. Walk to the ocean, the convention center, shops and restaurants. Nine miles from Miami International Airport.*

MICANOPY ─────────────────────────────

| **Herlong Mansion** | $$-B&B | Full breakfast |
|---|---|---|
| P.O. Box 667, 32667 | 12 rooms, 12 pb | Afternoon tea |
| 402 N.E. Cholokka Blvd. | MC, Visa, *Rated*, • | Complimentary wine |
| 352-466-3322 Fax: 352-466-3322 | C-yes/S-no/P-no/H-yes | sitting room, library |
| 800-437-5664 | | Pump House w/jacuzzi |
| H.C. (Sonny) Howard, Jr. | | |
| All year | | |

*Twenty antique and craft shops one block away. Historic Greek Revival house, c.1845. Moss draped oaks, pecans and dogwoods. **2 nights 25%, 3rd night free, ltd.***

MOUNT DORA ─────────────────────────────

| **Emerald Hill Inn, The** | $$$-B&B | Continental plus bkfst. |
|---|---|---|
| 27751 Lake Jem Rd.,  32757 | 4 rooms, 4 pb | Vegetarian breakfasts |
| 352-383-2777 Fax: 352-383-6701 | Visa, MC, *Rated*, • | Overlooks Lake Victoria |
| Michael & Diane Wiseman | C-ltd/S-no/P-no/H-no | by Ocala National Forest |
| All year | | Disney Theme Parks near |

*Serene 1941 lakeside country estate. Rediscover romance. Moss-draped tall oaks, sweeping lawn, spectacular sunsets. Spacious designer rooms. Near Orlando.*

NAPLES ─────────────────────────────

| **Inn by the Sea** | $$$-B&B | Continental plus bkfst. |
|---|---|---|
| 287 - 11th Ave. S.,  34103 | 5 rooms, 5 pb | Bicycles, sitting room |
| 941-649-4124  800-584-1268 | MC, Visa, AmEx, | beach just 700 feet away |
| Peggy Cormier | *Rated*, • | 2 suites |
| All year | C-ltd/S-no/P-no/H-no | |

*Tropical beach house just 700 feet from beach. Walk to fabulous shopping, art galleries, restaurants. Located in Old Naples Historic District*

NEW SMYRNA BEACH ─────────────────────────────

| **Night Swan Int'coastal B&B** | $$-B&B | Full breakfast |
|---|---|---|
| 512 South Riverside Dr., | 12 rooms, 12 pb | Sitting room, 4 suites |
| 32168 | Visa, MC, AmEx, | Playground nearby |
| 904-423-4940 Fax: 904-427-2814 | *Rated*, • | 140 foot dock |
| 800-465-4261 | C-yes/S-no/P-no/H-yes | |
| Charles & Martha | | |
| Nighswonger | | |
| All year | | |

*Located in the Historic District on the Intracoastal Waterway between Daytona Beach and Kennedy Space Center; just one mile from the beach. **3rd night free, Sept.–Dec.***

ORANGE PARK ――――――――――――――――――――――――――

**Club Continental Suites**
P.O. Box 7059, 32073
2143 Astor St.
904-264-6070    Fax: 904-264-
4044 800-877-6070
K.M. Stevens, C. Massee
All year

$$-B&B
37 rooms, 37 pb
AmEx, MC, Visa,
*Rated*, •
C-yes/S-yes/P-ltd/H-yes

Continental breakfast
Lunch, dinner, bar serv.
Restaurant, sitting room
7 tennis courts, 2 pools
entertainment

*Florida riverfront inn with giant live oaks, gardens & fountains. Historical Palmolive Estate, superior suites, jacuzzis, tennis. 3rd night 50% off, excluding Fri. & Sat.*

ORLANDO, WINTER GARDEN ――――――――――――――――――

**Meadow Marsh B&B**
940 Tildenville School,
   34787
407-656-2064
Cavelle & John Pawlack
All year

$$$-B&B
4 rooms, 4 pb
Visa, MC, *Rated*,
C-ltd/S-no/P-no/H-ltd

Continental plus bkfst.
Lunch & dinner (fee)
Afternoon tea, snacks
Sitting room, library
nature abounds

*Experience true Florida. Built in 1877, beautiful 3-story Victorian takes you back to slower pace of yester-year. Romantic getaway. Close to Central Florida attractions.*

PALM BEACH ――――――――――――――――――――――――――

**Plaza Inn**
215 Brazilian Ave., 33480
561-832-8666 Fax: 561-835-8776
800-233-2632
Ajit Asrani
All year

$$$-B&B
50 rooms, 50 pb
AmEx, MC, Visa,
*Rated*, •
C-yes/S-yes/P-yes
Spanish, French

Full American breakfast
Bar service
Free parking, bikes
tennis close, pool, golf
Worth Ave. shopping

*Romantic, intimate hideaway. Boutique Hotel. Uniquely affordable w/European ambiance. Heated pool, Jacuzzi. Canopy & four-poster beds. One block to beach. Free bottle of wine.*

PALMETTO ―――――――――――――――――――――――――――

**Five Oaks Inn**
1102 Riverside Dr., 34221
941-723-1236 800-658-4167
Colorito & Kreissler Families
All year

$$-B&B
4 rooms, 4 pb
Most CC, *Rated*, •
S-ltd/P-no/H-no

Full breakfast
Aftn. tea, snacks
Comp. wine, bar service
sitting room, library
bicycles, tanning beach

*Magnificent Southern estate. River setting, a taste of Florida elegance & grace. Antiques, history & hospitality. Near shops, restaurants, beach.*

PENSACOLA ―――――――――――――――――――――――――――

**Gulf Beach Inn**
10655 Gulf Beach Hwy.,
   32507
904-492-4501
Fred & Lisa Krause   All year

$$-B&B
1 rooms, 1 pb
•
C-yes/S-yes/P-yes/H-yes
German

Full breakfast
Snacks
Library, private beach
fishing, waverunner
rental

*Beach front inn, private beach w/dock, close to Nat'l Seashore, Civil War forts, Naval Aviation Museum, historic Pensacola, great restaurants and golf courses. 3rd nite, 50%.*

RUSKIN ――――――――――――――――――――――――――――

**Ruskin House B&B**
120 Dickman Dr. S.W.,   33570
813-645-3842
Dr. Arthur M. Miller
All year

$-B&B
4 rooms, 2 pb
MC, Visa, •
C-ltd/S-ltd/P-ltd/H-yes
French, some Spanish

Continental plus bkfst.
Full breakfast (wkends)
Sitting room, library
health club nearby (fee)

*Gracious 1910 waterfront home with period (1860-1920) antiques, between Tampa & Sarasota on west coast. Three minutes from I-75. Friendly! 10% off 2nd night; 7th day free.*

## SANFORD

| **Higgins House, The** | $$-B&B | Continental plus bkfst. |
|---|---|---|
| 420 S. Oak Ave., 32771 | 3 rooms, 3 pb | Snacks, comp. wine |
| 407-324-9238  800-584-0014 | Most CC, *Rated*, • | Sitting room, bicycles |
| Roberta & Walter Padgett | C-ltd/S-no/P-no/H-no | outdoor hot tub, deck |
| All year | | gardens, tennis nearby |

*Romantic, elegant Victorian inn close to the St. Johns River and Lake Monroe in the Historic District. Cottage w/2 bdrm., 2 bath, living rm., kitchen.* **10% disc't Mon.–Thurs.**

## SEASIDE

| **Josephine's French Inn** | $$$$-B&B | Full gourmet breakfast |
|---|---|---|
| P.O. Box 4767, 32459 | 11 rooms, 11 pb | Dinner |
| 101 Seaside Ave. | Visa, MC, *Rated*, • | Sitting room, bicycles |
| 904-231-1940 Fax: 904-231-2446 | C-ltd/S-no/P-no/H-yes | tennis court |
| 800-848-1840 | | swimming pool |
| Jody, Judy, Bruce & Sean | | |
| All year | | |

*Eleven elegantly furnished and appointed rooms in the heart of nature's splendor. Your romantic hideaway on the Gulf of Mexico.* **Complimentary bottle of champagne.**

## ST. AUGUSTINE

| **Carriage Way B&B** | $$-B&B | Full breakfast |
|---|---|---|
| 70 Cuna St., 32084 | 9 rooms, 9 pb | Lunch/dinner/tea/snacks |
| 904-829-2467 Fax: 904-826-1461 | MC, Visa, AmEx, Disc., | Comp. wine & beverages |
| 800-908-9832 | • | picnics. Honeymoon |
| Bill & Diane Johnson | C-ltd/S-no/P-no/H-no | breakfast in bed |
| All year | French | |

*1883 Victorian home in heart of historic district; antiques & reproductions, clawfoot tubs, bicycles available. Casual, leisurely atmosphere.* **Midweek discounts, ask.**

| **Castle Garden B&B** | $$-B&B | Full breakfast |
|---|---|---|
| 15 Shenandoah St., 32084 | 7 rooms, 7 pb | Comp. wine & champagne |
| 904-829-3839 | Most CC, *Rated*, • | Picnic lunches |
| B. Kloeckner & K. Van | C-ltd/S-ltd/P-no/H-no | bicycles, fresh flowers |
| Kooten | | 3 bridal suites w/spas |
| All year | | |

*St. Augustine's only Moorish Revival dwelling, former Castle Warden Carriage House, built 1800s. Restored, beautiful gardens. Murder mystery tour midweek, honeymoon pkg.* **Senior & 2nd nite disc't, ltd.**

| **Cedar House Inn, The** | $$$-B&B | Full breakfast |
|---|---|---|
| 79 Cedar St., 32084 | 6 rooms, 6 pb | Din., aftn. tea, snacks |
| 904-829-0079 Fax: 904-825-0916 | Visa, MC, Disc. *Rated*, | Sitting room, library |
| 800-233-2746 | • | piano, porches, bikes |
| Russ & Nina Thomas | C-ltd/S-no/P-no/H-no | free walking tour guide |
| All year | | |

*Capture romantic moments in our antique filled 1893 Victorian home. Enjoy hospitality at its finest. Comp. beverages, snacks & bikes. Walk to all historic sites.* **Mon.–Thurs. discount.**

| **Kenwood Inn, The** | $$$-B&B | Continental breakfast |
|---|---|---|
| 38 Marine St., 32084 | 15 rooms, 15 pb | Sitting room, piano |
| 904-824-2116 Fax: 904-824-1689 | Visa, MC, Disc. *Rated*, | swimming pool |
| Mark and Kerrianne | C-ltd/S-ltd/P-no/H-no | walled in courtyard |
| Constant | | |
| All year | | |

*Lovely old 19th-century Victorian inn located in historic district of our nation's oldest city. Walk to attractions; beautiful beaches 5 minutes away.* **Sun–Thurs. 10% discount, ask.**

## ST. AUGUSTINE

| | | |
|---|---|---|
| **Old Powder House Inn, The** | $$$-B&B | Full gourmet breakfast |
| 38 Cordova St., 32084 | 8 rooms, 8 pb | Comp. wine, snacks, tea |
| 904-824-4149 Fax: 904-825-0143 | Most CC, *Rated*, • | Sitting room |
| 800-447-4149 | C-ltd/S-no/P-no/H-no | bicycles, hot tub |
| Al & Eunice Howes | | family friendly facility |
| All year | | |

*Romantic Victorian inn furnished with antiques, wraparound verandas, located in the heart of the Historic District, Special packages available.*

| | | |
|---|---|---|
| **Secret Garden Inn, The** | $$$-B&B | Continental plus bkfst. |
| 56½ Charlotte St., 32084 | 3 rooms, 3 pb | Kitchens, sitting rooms |
| 904-829-3678 | MC, Visa, • | Decks, patio, cable TV |
| Nancy Noloboff | C-ltd/S-no/P-no/H-no | private entrances |
| All year | | carriage rides nearby |

*Three very private suites in a garden setting. Secluded historic district hideaway—1 block from the Bay. Walk to restaurants, shops & attractions. $20 midweek discount, ask.*

| | | |
|---|---|---|
| **St. Francis Inn** | $$-B&B | Continental plus bkfst. |
| 279 St. George St., 32084 | 11 rooms, 11 pb | Iced tea & lemonade |
| 904-824-6068 Fax: 904-810-5525 | MC, Visa, *Rated*, • | Sunday aftn. music |
| 800-824-6068 | C-ltd/S-yes/P-no/H-no | fireplaces available |
| Joe Finnegan | | bicycles |
| All year | | |

*Built in 1791, located in Historic District, one block west of the "Oldest House in USA." Sev. rooms w/working fireplaces & Jacuzzi tubs. 3rd night 50%.*

| | | |
|---|---|---|
| **Westcott House** | $$$-B&B | Continental plus bkfst. |
| 146 Avenida Menendez, 32084 | 8 rooms, 8 pb | Comp. wine, brandy |
| 904-824-4301 Fax: 904-824-4301 | MC, Visa, *Rated*, • | Sitting room, courtyard |
| Janet & Tom Murray | C-ltd/S-ltd/P-no/H-no | 3 Victorian porches |
| All year | | Municipal Marina |

*Built in the late 1880s, example of fine vernacular architecture. St Augustine's most elegant B&B. Overlooks Matanzas Bay, exquisitely furnished rooms with king or queen beds.*

## ST. PETERSBURG

| | | |
|---|---|---|
| **Bayboro House B&B** | $$$-B&B | Continental plus bkfst. |
| 1719 Beach Dr. SE, 33701 | 4 rooms, 4 pb | Comp. wine/cocktails |
| 813-823-4955 Fax: 813-823-4955 | MC, Visa, *Rated*, • | Veranda, player piano |
| Gordon & Antonia Powers | S-ltd/P-no/H-no | voted 1 of 10 best by |
| All year | | Miami Herald (Ap. 1995) |

*Walk out the door to sunning and beachcombing from a turn-of-the-century Queen Anne house. 1991 St. Petersburg Historical Preservation Award. Romantic pkg. 10% discount, ltd.*

| | | |
|---|---|---|
| **Mansion House B&B** | $$$-B&B | Full American breakfast |
| 105 5th Ave. NE, 33701 | 6 rooms, 6 pb | Comp. wine, cheese, soda |
| 813-821-9391 Fax: 813-821-9391 | Mc, Visa, AmEx, | Sitting room, patio, VCR |
| 800-274-7520 | *Rated*, • | carriage room, library |
| Robert & Rose Marie Ray | C-ltd/S-no/P-no/H-no | cable TV, Jacuzzi |
| Jan-May, Jun-Dec | | |

*Turn-of-the-century Southern home; renowned American hospitality and hearty breakfast. Beaches, marina, baseball, festivals and many other attractions. American hospitality. 10% discount after 3rd night.*

## STUART

**Homeplace, The**
501 Akron,  34994
561-220-9148  Fax: 561-221-3265
800-251-5473
Suzanne & Michael Pescitelli
All year

$$$-B&B
4 rooms, 4 pb
MC, Visa,
C-ltd/S-ltd/P-no/H-no

Continental plus bkfst.
Comp. wine, fruit/cheese
Sitting room, library
bicycles, hot tubs, pool
city walking tour

*Welcomed back in time, to a period much softer. Guests enjoy the quiet hospitality & fresh-baked "old Florida" recipes. W/great location 12 min. to the beach.* **2nd night 50%; 3rd night free, ltd.**

## TAMPA

**Gram's Place B&B**
3109 Ola Avenue N.,  33603
813-221-0596  Fax: 813-221-0596
Mark Holland
All year

$$-EP/B&B
7 rooms, 4 pb
Visa, MC, AmEx,  •
C-ltd/S-yes/P-no/H-no

Continental breakfast
Courtyard w/BYOB bar
Sitting room, jacuzzi
2 waterfalls, sun deck
artists retreat

*European attitude. Music lovers paradise, shuttle serv. for ½ cab fare. If you like jazz, folk, country, blues, and/or rock, you'll love this place.* **7th night free.**

**Hyde Park Inn**
404 W. Kennedy,  33606
813-254-5834  Fax: 813-254-5834
800-347-5834
Melissa Peabody
All year

$$-B&B
11 rooms, 4 pb
Visa, MC, *Rated*,  •
C-yes/S-yes/P-no/H-no

Continental plus bkfst.
Afternoon tea, snacks
Sitting room
discounted deep-sea
fishing trips

*Tampa's Victorian B&B. Unique and romantic, est. 1908. Gourmet breakfast. Parks, museums, theaters & shopping within walking distance.* **Free gourmet dinner for 2 w/2 night stay.**

## TARPON SPRINGS

**Spring Bayou Inn**
32 W. Tarpon Ave.,  34689
813-938-9333  Fax: 813-938-9333
Sharon A. Birk
All year

$$-B&B
5 rooms, 3 pb
S-no/P-no/H-no

Continental plus bkfst.
Parlor, library
fireplace, front porch
baby grand piano

*Elegant Victorian with modern conveniences. Walk to shops, bayou, restaurants, sponge docks. Golf, beaches, tennis, and fishing nearby.* **10% discount.**

## VENICE

**Banyan House, The**
519 S. Harbor Dr.,  34285
813-484-1385  Fax: 813-484-8032
Ian & Suzie Maryan
All year

$$-B&B
9 rooms, 9 pb
Mc, Visa *Rated*,
C-ltd/S-no/P-no

Continental plus bkfst.
Sitting room, jacuzzi
bicycles, hot tubs
swimming pool

*Historic Mediterranean-style home. Enormous banyan tree shades courtyard, pool and spa. Centrally located to shopping, restaurants, beaches and golfing.*

## WEST PALM BEACH

**Hibiscus House B&B**
501 30th St.,  33407
561-863-5633  800-203-4927
Raleigh Hill
All year

$$$-B&B
6 rooms, 6 pb
•
C-yes/S-ltd/P-no/H-no

Full breakfast
Bar service
Sitting room
bicycles
swimming pool

*Elegant Florida '20s home. Antiques, 5 minutes to fabulous Palm Beach. Private baths, terraces. Full breakfast. Tropical pool area.*

## More Inns ...

| | |
|---|---|
| Apalachicola | Gibson Inn, The, P.O. Box 215, 32329, 904-653-2191 |
| Apalachicola | Pink Camellia Inn, The, 145 Ave. E, 32320, 904-653-2107 |
| Apollo Beach | B&B of Apollo Beach, 6350 Cocoa Lane, 33572, 813-645-2471 |
| Big Pine Key | B&B-on-the-Ocean Casa, P.O. Box 378, 33043, 305-872-2878 |
| Big Pine Key | Barnacle B&B, Route 1 Box 780A, 33043, 305-872-3298 |
| Big Pine Key | Canal Cottage B&B, P.O. Box 430266, 33043, 305-872-3881 |
| Big Pine Key | Vacation in Paradise, Route 1, Box 641, 33043, 305-872-9009 |
| Boca Grande | Barrier Island Marine B&B, P.O. Box 175, 33921, 813-964-2626 |
| Boca Grande | Gasparilla Inn, 33921, 813-964-2201 |
| Brandon | Mary Lee B&B, 717 Sunlit Court, 33511, 813-653-3807 |
| Bushnell | Cypress House B&B, 8545 C.R. 476B, 33513, 904-568-0909 |
| Cedar Key | Cedar Key B&B, P.O. Box 700, 32625, 904-543-9000 |
| Clewiston | Clewiston Inn, The, 108 Royal Palm Ave., 33440, 947-983-8151 |
| Coral Gables | Hotel Place St. Michel, 162 Alcazar Ave., 33134, 305-444-1666 |
| Crescent City | Sprague House Inn, 125 Central Ave., 32112, 904-698-2430 |
| Daytona Beach | Coquina Inn B&B, The, 544 S. Palmetto Ave., 32114, 904-254-4969 |
| De Funiak Springs | Mrs. W.L. Bishop, 401 Bay Ave., 32433 |
| De Funiak Springs | Sunbright Manor, 606 Live Oak, 32433, 904-892-0656 |
| DeLand | DeLand Country Inn, 228 W. Howry Ave., 32720, 904-736-4244 |
| Edgewater | Colonial House, The, 110 E. Yelkca Terr., 32132, 904-427-4570 |
| Englewood | Manasota Beach Club, 7660 Manasota Key Rd., 34223, 813-474-2614 |
| Everglades City | Rod & Gun Club, P.O. Box G, 33929, 813-695-2101 |
| Fernandina Beach | 1735 House, The, 584 S. Fletcher Ave., 32034, 904-261-4148 |
| Fernandina Beach | Greyfield Inn, P.O. Box 900, 32034, 904-261-6408 |
| Florida City | Grandma Newton's B&B, 40 N.W. 5th Ave., 33034, 305-247-4413 |
| Fort Lauderdale | Casa Alhambra B&B Inn, 3029 Alhambra St., 33304, 305-467-2262 |
| Fort Myers | Embe's Hobby House, 5570-4 Woodrose Ct., 33907, 813-936-6378 |
| Fort Myers | Windsong Garden, 5570-4 Woodrose Court, 33907, 813-936-6378 |
| Haines City | Holly Garden Inn, 106 First St. S., 33844, 813-421-9867 |
| Havana | Graver's B&B, 301 E. 6th Ave., 32333, 904-539-5611 |
| Hollywood | Maison Harrison House, 1504 Harrison St., 33020, 604-922-7319 |
| Homestead | Tropical Paradise, 19801 S.W. 318 St., 33030, 305-248-4592 |
| Indian Shores | Meeks B&B on the Gulf, 19418 Gulf Blvd. #407, 34635, 813-596-5424 |
| Inverness | Crown Hotel, 109 N. Seminole Ave., 32650, 904-344-5555 |
| Jacksonville | 1217 On the Bouelvard, 1217 Boulevard St., 32206, 904-354-6959 |
| Jupiter | Innisfail, 134 Timber Lane, 33458, 407-744-5905 |
| Key Biscayne | Hibiscus House, 345 W. Endid Dr., 33149, 305-361-2456 |
| Key West | Alexander's, 1118 Fleming St., 33040, 305-294-9919 |
| Key West | Ambrosia House, 615 Fleming St., 33040, 305-296-9838 |
| Key West | Angelina, 302 Angela St., 33040, 305-294-4480 |
| Key West | Artist House, 534 Easton St., 33040, 305-296-3977 |
| Key West | Banana's Foster, 537 Caroline St., 33040 |
| Key West | Bananas Foster B&B, 537 Caroline St., 33040, 305-294-9061 |
| Key West | Banyan Resort, The, 323 Whitehead St., 33040, 800-225-0639 |
| Key West | Big Ruby's Guesthouse, 409 Appelrouth Ln., 33040, 305-296-2323 |
| Key West | Brass Key Guesthouse, 412 Frances St., 33040, 305-296-4719 |
| Key West | Cade House, 1501 Truman Ave., 33040, 305-296-4724 |
| Key West | Casa Buena Honeymoon Cott., 317 Whitehead St., 33040 |
| Key West | Chelsea House, 707 Truman Ave., 33040, 305-296-2211 |
| Key West | Coconut Beach Resort, 1500 Alberta, 33040 |
| Key West | Coconut Grove Guest House, 817 Fleming St., 33040, 305-296-5107 |
| Key West | Coral Tree Inn, 822 Fleming St., 33040 |
| Key West | Cottages, 1512 Dennis St., 33040, 305-296-6003 |
| Key West | Courtney's Place, 720 Whitmarsh Ln., 33040, 305-294-3480 |
| Key West | Cuban Club Suites, The, 1108 Duval St., 33040 |
| Key West | Curry House, 806 Fleming St., 33040 |
| Key West | Curry Mansion Inn, 511 Caroline St., 33040, 305-294-5349 |
| Key West | Denoit's Cottage, 512 Angela St., 33040, 305-294-6324 |
| Key West | E.H. Gato Jr. Guesthouse, 1327 Duval St., 33040, 305-294-0715 |
| Key West | Eaton Lodge, 511 Eaton St., 33040, 305-292-2170 |
| Key West | Eaton Manor, 1024 Eaton St., 33040 |
| Key West | Eaton Square, 1031 Eaton St., 33040 |
| Key West | Fleming Street Inn, 618 Fleming St., 33040, 305-294-5181 |
| Key West | Fogarty House, 227 Duval St., 33040, 305-296-9592 |
| Key West | Frances Street Bottle Inn, 535 Frances St., 33040 |
| Key West | Garden House, 329 Elizabeth St., 33040, 305-296-5368 |
| Key West | Hollinsed House, 611 Southard St., 33040, 305-296-8031 |
| Key West | Incentra Carriage House, 729 Whitehead St., 33040, 305-296-5565 |
| Key West | Island City House Hotel, 411 William St., 33040, 305-294-5702 |
| Key West | Island Key Courts, 910 Simonton St., 33040 |
| Key West | Knowles House, The, 1004 Eaton St., 33040, 305-296-8132 |
| Key West | La Mer Hotel, 506 South St., 33040 |
| Key West | La Te Da, 1125 Duval St., 33040 |
| Key West | Lamp Post House, 309 Louisea St., 33040, 305-294-7709 |
| Key West | Lighthouse Court, 902 Whitehead St., 33040, 305-294-9588 |
| Key West | Marquesa Hotel & Cafe, 600 Fleming St., 33040, 305-292-1919 |

*The Magnolia Plantation, Gainesville, FL*

| | |
|---|---|
| Key West | Mermaid & Alligator, The, 729 Truman Ave., 33040, 305-294-1894 |
| Key West | Newton Street Station, 1414 Newton St., 33040 |
| Key West | Oasis Guest House, 823 Fleming St., 33040, 305-296-2131 |
| Key West | Old Customs House Inn, 124 Duval St., 33040 |
| Key West | Old Town Garden Villas, 921 Center St., 33040, 305-294-4427 |
| Key West | Orchid House, 1025 Whitehead St., 33040, 305-294-0102 |
| Key West | Palms Hotel, The, 820 White St., 33040, 305-294-3146 |
| Key West | Papa's Hideaway Guesthouse, 309 Louisa St., 33040, 305-294-7709 |
| Key West | Pines of Key West, 521 United St., 33040, 305-296-7467 |
| Key West | Potters Cottage, The, 1011 Whitehead St., 33040 |
| Key West | Rainbow House, 525 United St., 33040, 305-292-1450 |
| Key West | Sea Isle Resort, 915 Windsor Ln., 33040, 305-294-5188 |
| Key West | Simonton Court Inn, 320 Simonton St., 33040, 305-294-6386 |
| Key West | Southernmost Point, 1327 Duval St., 33040, 305-294-0715 |
| Key West | Speakeasy Inn, 1117 Duval St., 33040 |
| Key West | Sunrise Sea House B&B, 39 Bay Dr., Bay Point, 33040, 305-745-3525 |
| Key West | Sweet Caroline, 529 Caroline St., 33040, 305-296-5173 |
| Key West | Tilton Hilton, 511 Angela St., 33040, 305-294-8697 |
| Key West | Tradewind Guesthouse, 415 Julia St., 33040, 305-296-2212 |
| Key West | Travelers Palm, 815 Catherine St., 33040 |
| Key West | Treetop Inn Historic B&B, 806 Truman Ave., 33040, 305-293-0712 |
| Key West | Tropical Inn, 812 Duval St., 33040, 305-294-9977 |
| Key West | Walden House, 717 Caroline St., 33040, 305-296-7161 |
| Key West | Watson House, The, 525 Simonton St., 33040, 305-294-6712 |
| Key West | Westwinds, 914 Eaton St., 33040, 305-296-4440 |
| Key West | Whispers B&B Inn, 409 William St., 33040, 305-294-5969 |
| Key West | Wicker Guesthouse, 913 Duval St., 33040, 305-296-4275 |
| Key West | William House, The, 1317 Duval St., 33040 |
| Lake Wales | Noah's Ark, 312 Ridge Manor Dr., 33853, 941-676-1613 |
| Lauderdale | Breakaway Guest House, 4457 Poinciana, 33308, 305-771-6600 |
| Madeira Beach | Lighthouse B&B, 13555 2nd St. E., 33708, 813-391-0015 |
| Marathon | Hopp-Inn Guest House, 500 Sombrero Beach Rd., 33050, 305-743-4118 |
| Mayo | Jim Hollis River Rendevous, Route 2, Box 60, 32066, 904-294-2510 |
| Miami | Roberts Ranch, 6400 SW 120 Ave., 33183, 305-598-3257 |
| Miami Beach | Cavalier Hotel/Cabana Club, P.O. Box 1157, 33139, 305-534-2135 |
| Miami Beach | Essex House, 1001 Collins Ave., 33139, 305-534-2700 |
| Miami Beach | Penguin Hotel, 1418 Ocean Dr., 33139, 305-534-9334 |
| Mount Dora | Christopher's, 539 Liberty Ave., 32757, 904-383-2244 |
| Naples | Olde Naples Inn, The, 801 Third St. S., 33940, 941-262-5194 |
| Ocala | Neva's B&B, 520 Southeast 17th Pl., 32671, 904-732-4607 |
| Ocala | Seven Sisters Inn, 820 SE Fort King St., 34471, 904-867-1170 |
| Ocklawaha | Lake Weir Inn, Rt. 2, 12660 SE Hwy 25, 32179, 904-288-3723 |
| Orange Springs | Orange Springs, One Main St., Box 550, 32682, 904-546-2052 |
| Orlando | Alpen Gast Haus, 8328 Curry Ford Rd., 32822, 305-277-1811 |
| Orlando | Briercliff, 1523 Briercliff Dr., 32806 |
| Orlando | Courtyard at Lake Lucerne, 211 N. Lucerne Cir. E., 32801, 407-648-5188 |
| Orlando | Rinaldi House, 502 Lake Ave., 32801, 407-425-6549 |
| Orlando | Rio Pinar House, The, 532 Pinar Dr., 32825 |
| Orlando | Robin Dodson, 11754 Ruby Lake Rd., 32819, 305-239-0109 |
| Orlando | Spencer Home B&B, 313 Spencer St., 32809, 407-855-5603 |
| Palm Beach | Heron Cay, 15106 Palmwood Rd., 33410, 407-744-6315 |
| Palm Beach | Palm Beach Historic Inn, 365 S. Country Rd., 33480, 407-832-4009 |
| Palm Harbor | B&B of Tampa Bay, 126 Old Oak Circle, 34683, 813-785-2342 |
| Panama City | Gulf View Inn, 21722 Front Beach Rd., 32413, 904-234-6051 |
| Pensacola | Homestead Village, 7830 Pine Forest Rd., 32526, 904-944-4816 |
| Pensacola | New World Inn, 6000 South Palafox St., 32501, 904-432-4111 |
| Pensacola | North Hill Inn, 422 N. Baylen St., 32501, 904-432-9804 |
| Pensacola | Sunshine, 508 Decatur Ave., 32507, 904-455-6781 |
| Ramrod Key | Florida Keys House, 27441 W. Indies Dr., 33042, 800-833-9857 |
| Ramrod Key | Knightswood, Box 151 Summerland Key, 33042 |
| San Mateo | Ferncourt B&B, 150 Central Ave., 32187, 904-329-9755 |
| Sanibel Island | Sanibel's Seaside Inn, 541 E. Gulf Dr., 33957, 813-472-1400 |
| Sanibel Island | Song of the Sea/European, 863 E. Gulf Dr., 33957, 813-472-2220 |
| Sarasota | Gary Cooper, 6863 Old Ranch Rd., 34241 |
| Seaside | Dolphin Inn at Seaside, P.O. Box 4732, 32459, 904-231-5477 |
| Siesta Key | Crescent House, 459 Beach Rd., 33578 |
| St. Augustine | Casa de La Paz, 22 Avenida Menendez, 32084, 904-829-2915 |
| St. Augustine | Casa de Solana, B&B Inn, 21 Aviles St., 32084, 904-824-3555 |

*The Blue Parrot Inn, Key West, FL*

| | |
|---|---|
| St. Augustine | Old City House Inn & Rest., 115 Cordova St., 32084, 904-826-0113 |
| St. Augustine | Southern Wind B&B, 18 Cordova St., 32084, 904-825-3623 |
| St. Augustine | Victorian House B&B, 11 Cadiz St., 32084, 904-824-5214 |
| St. Petersburg | Bay Gables B&B, 136 4th Ave. N.E., 33701, 813-822-8855 |
| Summerland Key | Knightswood, P.O. Box 151, 33042, 305-872-2246 |
| Tarpon Springs | East Lake B&B, 421 Old East Lake Rd., 34689, 813-937-5487 |
| Tarpon Springs | Fiorito's B&B, 421 Old E. Lake Rd., 34689, 813-937-5487 |
| Tarpon Springs | Heartsease, 272 Old E. Lake Rd., 34689, 813-934-0994 |
| Tarpon Springs | Inn on the Bayou, P.O. Box 1545, 34688, 813-942-4468 |
| Tarpon Springs | Kathy Carbaugh Inn, 928 Bayshore Dr, 34689 |
| Wakulla Springs | Wakulla Springs Lodge, #1 Springs Dr., 32305, 904-224-5950 |
| Wellborn | 1909 McLeran House B&B, 12408 County Rd. 137, 32094, 904-963-4603 |
| West Palm Beach | West Palm Beach B&B, 419 32nd St., 33407, 800-736-4064 |
| Winter Garden | Casa Adobe, P.O. Box 770707, 34777, 407-876-5432 |
| Winter Park | Fortnightly Inn, 377 E. Fairbanks Ave., 32789, 407-645-4440 |
| Zolfo Springs | Double M Ranch B&B, Route 1, Box 292, 33890, 813-735-0266 |

# Georgia

## AMERICUS

**Pathway Inn, The**
501 S. Lee St., 31709
912-928-2078 800-889-1466
Sheila and David Judah
All year

$$
5 rooms, 5 pb
Most CC, *Rated*, •
C-yes/S-ltd/P-ltd/H-no

Full breakfast
Afternoon tea, snacks
Complimentary wine
sitting room

*Stay in pampered English Colonial Revival Victorian. Comfort oriented. Stroll historic district, shops, meet President Carter, Civil War Andersonville, candlelight, romance.*

## ATLANTA

**Beverly Hills Inn**
65 Sheridan Dr. N.E., 30305
404-233-8520 Fax: 404-233-8659
800-331-8520
Mit Amin
All year

$$$-B&B
18 rooms, 18 pb
Most CC, *Rated*, •
C-yes/S-yes/P-no/H-no

Continental plus bkfst.
Sitting room, library
piano, health club priv.
London taxi shuttle

*Charming city retreat, fine residential neighborhood. Close to Lenox Square, Historical Society and many art galleries. 15 min. to downtown.* **Fourth night free, ltd.**

**Gaslight Inn B&B, The**
1001 St. Charles Ave., 30306
404-875-1001 Fax: 404-876-1001
Jim Moss
All year

$$$-B&B
6 rooms, 6 pb
Most CC, *Rated*, •
C-ltd/S-no/P-no/H-ltd

Continental plus bkfst.
Sitting room, library
grand piano, bicycles
walk to 35 restaurants

*Featured in Better Homes & Gardens and Southern Homes magazines. Single rooms, suites, fireplaces, jacuzzi tubs, whirlpool baths, sauna & private gardens.* **10% off any suite.**

**Inman Park B&B**
100 Waverly Way, NE, 30307
404-688-9498 Fax: 404-524-9939
Eleanor Matthews
All year

$$$-B&B
3 rooms,
MC, Visa, AmEx, •
C-ltd/S-no/P-no/H-no

Continental plus bkfst.
Private garden
Screened porch
fireplaces

*Totally restored Victorian located in historic Inman Park. 1 block to subway, close to restaurants. 12-ft ceilings, heart-pine woodwork, antiques.*

## ATLANTA

**King-Keith House B&B**
889 Edgewood Ave., NE,
  30307
404-688-7330 Fax: 404-584-0730
Jan & Windell Keith
All year

$$-B&B
5 rooms, 5 pb
AmEx, MC, Visa, •
C-yes/S-no/P-no/H-no

Full breakfast
Snacks
Sitting room
upstairs porch
suite w/kitchen sleeps 4

*1890 Victorian loaded w/charm. Period furnishings. Close to downtown. Shops & restaurants nearby. 2 blocks to MARTA (subway). Small parties & meetings in drawing room.* **Special discount for 3+ nites.**

**Oakwood House B&B**
951 Edgewood Ave., N.E.,
  30307
404-521-9320 Fax: 404-688-6034
Robert & Judy Hotchkiss
All year

$$$-B&B
5 rooms, 5 pb
AmEx, MC, Visa,
*Rated*, •
C-yes/S-no/P-no/H-ltd

Continental plus bkfst.
Exercise bike, library
front porch, back deck
garden, one child free

*Comfortable Craftsman home. Privacy (owners next door), close to downtown. In historic distric, near subway. Garden romance room w/Japanese-style whirlpool.* **Summer discounts.**

**Shellmont B&B Lodge**
821 Piedmont Ave. NE,
  30308
404-872-9290 Fax: 404-872-5379
Ed & Debbie McCord
All year

$$$-B&B
5 rooms, 5 pb
AmEx, MC, Visa,
*Rated*, •
C-ltd/S-ltd/P-no/H-yes

Full breakfast
Beverages, chocolates
Sitting room, bicycles
fruit baskets
near restaurants

*Classic Victorian home; guest suites; verandas; authentic furnishings; magnificent woodwork. Located near historic district. National Register; City Of Atlanta Landmark.*

**Sugar Magnolia B&B**
804 Edgewood Ave., NE,
  30307
404-222-0226 Fax: 404-681-1067
Debi Starnes & Jim Emshoff
All year

$$-B&B
3 rooms, 3 pb
Visa, MC, *Rated*, •
C-ltd/S-no/P-no/H-no

Continental plus bkfst.
Afternoon tea, snacks
Bar service, sitting rm.
business center
roof deck, fireplaces

*Beautiful 1892 Queen Anne Victorian in historic in-town neighborhood near Atlanta's attractions. Garden room and cottage suite great for families. Step back in time and enjoy!*

## BARNESVILLE

**Rose Inn, The**
643 Greenwood St., 30204
770-358-6969  800-318-1633
Wayne & Rosalyn Curenton
All year

B&B
4 rooms, 4 pb
Visa, MC, •
C-ltd/S-no/P-no/H-no

Full breakfast
Snacks
Sitting room
library

*Built in 1859, this Civil War headquarters and college president's home has 8 fireplaces, a player piano, beautiful antiques and a theme of roses.*

## BRUNSWICK

**Brunswick Manor-Major Dwn.**
825 Egmont St., 31520
912-265-6889
Harry and Claudia Tzucanow
All year

$$-B&B
9 rooms, 8 pb
MC, Visa, *Rated*, •
C-ltd/S-ltd/P-ltd/H-ltd
some Spanish

Full gourmet breakfast
Comp. wine, high tea
Sitting room, library
bicycles, tennis courts
hot tub, airport pickup

*Elegant Olde Towne historic 1886 inn near Golden Isles. Gourmet breakfast; afternoon high tea. Boat chartering avail. Gracious hospitality.* **Flowers, Sherry, fruit and cheese.**

## CLAYTON

**English Manor Inns**
P.O. Box 1605, 30525
US Hwy 76 - East
706-782-5789 Fax: 706-782-5789
800-782-5780
Susan & English Thornwell
All year

$$-B&B/AP
70 rooms, 70 pb
•
C-yes/S-yes/P-yes
French, Spanish,
German

Full breakfast
We meet dietary needs
Dinner (fee), comp. wine
setups, pool, hot tubs
croquet, golf, tennis

*8 inns furnished in exquisite antiques, reflecting charm of an earlier era with all of today's amenities. 10 jacuzzis. White water rafting & skiing nearby,. 10% discount.*

## COMMERCE

**Magnolia Inn**
206 Cherry St., 30529
706-335-7257
Annette & Jerry Potter
All year

$$-B&B
4 rooms, 3 pb
Visa, MC,
C-ltd/S-no/P-no/H-yes

Full breakfast
Afternoon tea
Sitting rm., rose garden
wrap-around porch
Mystery Weekends

*Restored Victorian in downtown Historic Commerce. All guestrooms are furnished with antiques. Close to outlet malls and 20 minutes from U of GA. 3rd night, 50%.*

**Pittman House, The**
81 Homer Rd., 30529
706-335-3823
Tom & Dot Tomberlin
All year

$$-B&B
4 rooms, 2 pb
Visa, MC, Disc. *Rated*,
•
C-ltd/S-no/P-no/H-no

Full breakfast
Snacks
Sitting room, library
tennis court nearby

*The Pittman House is a restored 1890 Colonial with wrap-around rocking porch. Completely furnished with antiques. Great sports & shopping nearby. 10% off 3+ nights.*

## DAHLONEGA

**Mountain Top Lodge**
Rt 7, Box 150, 30533
706-864-5257 Fax: 706-864-8265
800-526-9754
Karen A. Lewan
All year

$$-B&B
13 rooms, 13 pb
Most CC,
C-ltd/S-ltd/P-no/H-ltd

Full breakfast
Sitting room, library
hot tubs, horseshoe pit

**Royal Guard Inn**
203 South Park St., 30533
706-864-1713
John & Farris Vanderhoff
All year

$$-B&B
5 rooms, 5 pb
MC, Visa, *Rated*, •
C-ltd/S-no/P-no/H-no

Full breakfast (limited)
Afternoon tea
Wine, cheese, sitting
room, reading material
large wrap-around porch

*Historic home in N.E. Georgia mountains. Site of the first gold rush! Complimentary gourmet breakfast, wine & cheese on wrap-around porch. Close to town.*

**Smith House, The**
202 S. Chestatee St., 30533
706-867-7000 Fax: 706-864-7564
800-852-9577
The Welch Family
All year

$$-B&B
16 rooms, 16 pb
Most CC, *Rated*,
C-yes/S-no/P-no/H-ltd

Continental breakfast
Restaurant family menus
sitt. room, gold panning
pool, close to shops

*All-you-can-eat family-style dining for over 50 years. Smith House Inn is of old-fashioned nostalgic character. Reservations made by hotel clerk. Located in historic district close to shops.*

## DARIEN

**Open Gates B&B**
Box 1526, 31305
Vernon Sq., Vernon Sq.
Historic Dist.
912-437-6985
Carolyn Hodges
All year

$$-B&B
5 rooms, 3 pb
•
C-ltd/S-no/P-no/H-no

Full breakfast
Boxed lunch, comp. wine
Library, Steinway piano
bicycles, pool, antiques
sailing, boat tours

*Timber baron's gracious home on oak-shaded historic square. Access to untrammeled barrier islands, including Sapelo and the Altamaha Delta rice culture.* **10% off 4+ nights.**

## EASTMAN

**Dodge Hill Inn, The**
105 Ninth Ave., 31023
912-374-2644
Ann Dobbs
All year

$$-B&B
5 rooms, 5 pb
Visa, MC, AmEx, •
C-ltd/S-ltd/P-no/H-ltd

Full breakfast
Snacks, rm. refrigerator
Sitting room, library
front porch w/swing
fireplaces, golf

*Gracious 1912 home furnished in antiques; business amenities; near downtown in a lazy Southern community; private candlelight suppers, executive luncheons & dinners, by prior arrangement.*

## FORT OGLETHORPE

**Captain's Quarters Inn**
13 Barnhardt Circle, 30742
706-858-0624 Fax: 706-861-4053
800-710-6816
Betty & Daniel McKenzie
All year

$$-B&B
7 rooms, 7 pb
Most CC, *Rated*, •
C-ltd/S-ltd/P-no/H-no

Full breakfast
Sitting room, library

*1902 officer's quarters filled with antiques. 3 course gourmet breakfast. 4 miles south of Chatanooga, TN. Next to Chickamauga Battlefield Park.*

## GAINESVILLE

**Dunlap House, The**
635 Green St., 30501
770-536-0200 Fax: 770-503-7857
Ann & Ben Ventress
All year

$$$-B&B
9 rooms, 9 pb
Most CC, *Rated*, •
C-yes/S-ltd/P-no/H-yes

Continental plus bkfst.
Comp. tea/refreshments
Wedding facilities
no-smoking inn

*Luxurious historic accommodations. Bkfast in bed or on veranda. Restaurant and lounge across the street. Lodging & dining excellence. AAA rating 3 diamonds.* **3rd night 50% off.**

## HELEN

**Dutch Cottage B&B**
P.O. Box 757, 30545
114 Ridge Rd.
706-878-3135
Bill & Jane Vander Werf
May - October

$$-B&B
4 rooms, 3 pb
C-ltd/S-ltd/P-no/H-no
Dutch - a little

Full breakfast buffet
Afternoon tea
Sitting room
hammock, walk to town
bird watching

*Tranquil waterfall. Ivy covered hillside. Idyllic wooded setting. Large rooms furnished with Dutch antiques. Also charming hillside chalet. Spring water.* **3rd night 10% off.**

**Hilltop Haus B&B**
P.O. Box 154, 30545
362 Chattahoochee St.
706-878-2388
Frankie Allen
All year

$$-B&B
2 rooms, 2 pb
C-ltd/S-ltd/P-no/H-yes

Continental plus bkfst.
Afternoon coffee
Bicycles
sitting rooms
with fireplaces

*Located within walking distance of alpine village, Helen. Country-style breakfast with buttermilk biscuits, Appalachian Trail nearby.* **10% off 4+ days off-season.**

## MACON

**1842 Inn**
353 College St., 31201
912-741-1842　Fax: 912-741-1842
800-336-1842
Phillip Jenkins
All year

$$$-B&B
22 rooms, 22 pb
AmEx, MC, Visa,
*Rated*, •
C-ltd/S-yes/H-yes

Continental plus bkfst.
Tea, coffee, bar service
Morning paper, whirlpool
turn-down/bedtime sweets
overnight shoeshines

*Antebellum mansion and Victorian cottage furnished with fine antiques. All rooms have private baths, A/C & color televisions. Access to country club. Conferences. **2nd night, 50% off if on Sunday.***

## SAUTEE

**Stovall House, The**
1526 Hwy. 255 N., 30571
706-878-3355
Ham Schwartz
All year

$$-B&B
6 rooms, 6 pb
*Rated*,
C-yes/S-yes/P-no/H-ltd
Spanish

Continental plus bkfst.
Restaurant
Lunch, dinner
sitting room
Historic Register

*Award-winning restoration of 1837 country farmhouse on 28 serene acres with beautiful mountain views. One of the top 50 restaurants in Georgia. Small meetings & receptions. **3rd night 50% off.***

## SAVANNAH

**East Bay Inn**
225 East Bay St., 31401
912-238-1225　Fax: 912-232-2109
800-500-1225
Jean R. Bearden
All year

$$$-B&B
28 rooms, 28 pb
Most CC, *Rated*, •
C-yes/S-yes/P-no/H-yes

Continental plus bkfst.
Lunch, dinner
Eve. wine & sherry
turn-down service

*Steps away from the bustling riverfront, shops and museums. Original flooring, brick walls, and cast iron columns add true charm to this restored 1853 warehouse.*

---

**Eliza Thompson House**
5 West Jones St., 31401
912-236-3620　Fax: 912-238-1920
800-348-9378
Carol & Steve Day
All year

$$$-B&B
25 rooms, 25 pb
Visa, MC, AmEx,
*Rated*, •
C-yes/S-ltd/P-no/H-yes

Continental plus bkfst.
Sherry on arrival
Evening cordials/sweets
small conference room
imported wine, concierge

*Regally refurbished home in the heart of the Historic District. Elegant parlor, updated furnishings, beautifully landscaped courtyard w/splashing fountains. **Free wine.***

---

**Forsyth Park Inn, The**
102 W. Hall St., 31401
912-233-6800
Hal & Virginia Sullivan
All year

$$$-B&B
10 rooms, 10 pb
AmEx, MC, Visa,
*Rated*,
C-yes/S-yes
Some French

Continental breakfast
Comp. wine
Sitting room, park near
tennis courts, hot tubs
piano music nightly

*An elegantly restored Victorian mansion in the historic district. Rooms feature fireplaces, whirlpool tubs, antiques and 16-foot ceilings.*

---

**Gaston Gallery B&B**
211 E. Gaston St., 31401
912-238-3294　Fax: 912-238-3294
LeVan C. Rogers
All year

$$$$-B&B
2 rooms, 2 pb
Most CC, *Rated*,
C-ltd/S-no/P-no/H-no

Continental plus bkfst.
Aftn. tea, comp. wine
Snacks

*Experience historical Savannah like you were visiting friends in an elegant 1876 Savannah Townhouse. Two suites with private baths.*

SAVANNAH ———————————————————————————————

**Gastonian, The**
220 E. Gaston St.,   31401
912-232-2869  Fax: 912-232-0710
800-322-6603
Hugh & Roberta Lineberger
All year

$$$-B&B
16 rooms, 16 pb
AmEx, MC, Visa,
*Rated*,  •
S-no/P-no/H-yes

Full Southern breakfast
Comp. wine & fruit
Twin parlors, elevator
fireplace in each room
hot tub, private parking

*1868 southern elegance! Completely furnished with antiques, Persian rugs, whirlpool baths. Hot tubs on the sun deck. Luxurious. Mobil 4-Star; AAA 4-Diamond.*

---

**Joan's on Jones B&B**
17 West Jones St.,   31401
912-234-3863  Fax: 912-234-1455
800-407-3863
Joan & Gary Levy
All year

$$$-B&B
2 rooms, 2 pb
*Rated*,
C-yes/S-no/P-ltd/H-yes

Continental breakfast
Complimentary wine
Sitting room
tennis nearby
golf, fishing by nearby

*Victorian townhouse with private entrance to each suite, secluded garden. Here are location, comfort and southern hospitality . . . amid period antiques.*

---

**Lion's Head Inn**
120 E. Gaston St.,   31401
912-232-4580  Fax: 912-232-7422
800-355-5466
Christy Dell'Orco
All year

$$$-B&B
5 rooms, 5 pb
AmEx, MC, Visa,
*Rated*,  •
C-yes/S-no/P-no/H-yes

Continental plus bkfst.
Aft. tea, comp. wine
Sitting room, library
bicycles, massage
babysitting available

*19th century mansion, proximity to Savannah's amenities, tastefully decorated with Federal furnishings, unique 19th century lighting, romantic ambiance.*

---

**Manor House, The**
201 West Liberty St.,   31401
912-233-9597  Fax: 912-236-4626
800-462-3595
Tim Hargus
All year

$$$$-B&B
20 rooms, 20 pb
AmEx, MC, Visa
*Rated*,  •
C-ltd/S-yes/P-no/H-yes

Continental plus bkfst.
Comp. sherry, cognac
Full service bar, parlor
elevator, VCRs, florist
courtyard, gift shop

*Closest B&B inn to the Savannah Riverfront. 1835 mansion with beautiful antiques and courtyard. Fireplaces, jacuzzis. Recommended by the New York Times, Gourmet, and Brides.*

---

**Olde Harbour Inn**
508 E. Factor's Walk,   31401
912-234-4100  Fax: 912-233-5979
800-553-6533
Jean R. Bearden
All year

$$$-B&B
24 rooms, 24 pb
AmEx, MC, Visa,
*Rated*,  •
C-yes/S-yes/P-no/H-ltd

Continental plus bkfst.
Comp. wine, cheese,
   crackers & ice cream
sitting room, library
kitchens in suites

*Our traditionally renovated inn, built in 1892, offers spacious suites complete with kitchens and river views in Savannah's Historical District.* **Carriage Tour for 2.**

---

**Presidents' Quarters**
225 E. President St.,   31401
912-233-1600  Fax: 912-238-0849
800-233-1776
Muril L. Broy
All year

$$$$-B&B
16 rooms, 16 pb
Most CC, *Rated*,  •
C-yes/S-ltd/P-no/H-yes

Continental plus bkfst.
Comp. wine, aftn. tea
Ltd. bar, sandwiches
sitting room, courtyard
jacuzzi, swimming pool

*Newly restored 1885 home in heart of Historic District: jacuzzi bathtubs, gas log fireplaces, period reproductions. Deluxe yet affordable.* **10% room tariff discount.**

## SAVANNAH

**Remshart-Brooks House**
106 W. Jones St., 31401
912-234-6928
Anne E. Barnett
All year

$$-B&B
1 rooms, 1 pb
•
C-ltd/S-yes/P-no/H-ltd

Continental breakfast
Sherry in room
Sitting room
terrace garden

*Experience the charm and hospitality of historic Savannah while being "at home" in the garden suite of Remshart-Brooks House—built in 1854.*

## SENOIA

**Culpepper House B&B**
35 Broad St., 30276
770-599-8182 Fax: 770-559-8182
Maggie & Barb
All year

$$$-B&B
3 rooms, 3 pb
Visa, MC, *Rated*, •
C-ltd/S-ltd/P-yes/H-no

Full gourmet breakfast
Comp. wine
Sitting room, porch
tandem bicycles
10% discounts, ask

*Enjoy romance as you step back 120 years to casual Victorian elegance. Share a special evening in a four-poster canopy bed next to a fireplace-wake to a gourmet bkfst.* **15% off when you mention ad.**

## SENOIA/ATLANTA

**Veranda, The**
P.O. Box 177, 30276
252 Seavy St.
770-599-3905 Fax: 770-599-0806
Jan & Bobby Boal
All year

$$$-B&B
9 rooms, 9 pb
Most CC, *Rated*, •
C-ltd/S-ltd/P-no/H-yes
German

Full breakfast
Lunch, dinner RSVP
Library, conference fac.
sitting rm., organ, Fax
tennis, fishing nearby

*Historic inn furnished w/antiques & fascinating Victorian memorabilia. Delicious meals served in beautiful Old South setting. 1990 INN OF THE YEAR.* **$10 certif. for gift shop.**

## ST. MARYS

**Goodbread B&B on Osborne**
209 Osborne St., 31558
912-882-7490
Betty & Alison Krauss
All year

$$-B&B
4 rooms, 4 pb
•
C-ltd/S-ltd/H-no

Full breakfast
Complimentary wine
Sitting room

*Victorian hideaway in quaint fishing village off I-95. Ferry to Cumberland National Seashore. Seated breakfast in cozy dining room.* **Third night half price.**

## ST. SIMONS ISLAND

**Little St. Simons Island**
P.O. Box 21078, 31522
912-638-7472 Fax: 912-634-1811
Kevin & Debbie McIntyre
All year

$$$$-AP
12 rooms, 12 pb
MC, Visa, •
C-ltd/S-yes/P-no/H-ltd

Full breakfast
Meals & activities incl.
Swimming pool
sitting room
bicycles, horses

*A 10,000-acre undeveloped barrier island with early 1900s lodge and guest cottages. Southern cuisine. Professional naturalists and activities included. Groups only June—Sept.*

## STATESBORO

**Statesboro Inn, Restaurant**
106 S. Main St., 30458
912-489-8628 Fax: 912-489-4785
800-846-9466
Garges Family
All year

$$-B&B
19 rooms, 19 pb
Visa, MC, AmEx,
*Rated*, •
C-yes/S-no/P-ltd/H-yes

Full breakfast
Complimentary wine
Dinner, restaurant
sitting room, hot tubs
family friendly facility

*Elegant country inn. Antiques, porches, rockers, fireplaces, cozy nooks and jetted tubs make this the place to leave home for.*

## THOMASVILLE

**Evans House B&B**
725 S. Hansell St.,   31792
912-226-1343 Fax: 912-226-0653
800-344-4717
Lee & John Puskar
All year

$$-B&B
4 rooms, 4 pb
*Rated*,  •
C-ltd/S-no/P-ltd/H-yes

Full breakfast
Comp. wine, snacks
Bicycles

*Restored Victorian home located in Parkfront historical district across from Paradise Park. Walking distance of historic downtown, tours, antique shops and restaurants.*

---

**Serendipity Cottage B&B**
339 E. Jefferson St.,   31792
912-226-8111   Fax: 912-226-2656
Kathy & Ed Middleton
Closed 1st 2 wks in Jan.

$$-B&B
3 rooms, 3 pb
•
C-ltd/S-no/P-no/H-no

Full breakfast
Snacks, comp. wine
Sitting room, bikes

*Lovely old house, welcoming porches, gourmet breakfast, caring accommodations, Southern hospitality, all located in a charming Victorian town.* **3rd night 50%, ltd.**

## THOMSON

**1810 West Inn**
254 No. Seymour Dr.,   30824
706-595-3156  800-515-1810
Virginia White
All year

$$-B&B
10 rooms, 10 pb
Most CC, *Rated*,  •
C-ltd/S-no/P-no/H-no

Continental plus
Afternoon tea, snacks
Sitting room, library
jogging trail, pond
peacocks, 11 acres

*Country charm, city amenities-restored historic plantation house c.1810 and adjoining folk houses on 14 landscaped acres. Convenient to I-20 and Augusta*

## TURNERVILLE

**Glen-Ella Springs**
1789 Bear Gap Rd., Rt 3 Box
3304 Clarksville,   30523
706-754-7295 Fax: 706-754-1560
Barrie & Bobby Aycock
All year

$$$-B&B
16 rooms, 16 pb
AmEx, MC, Visa,
*Rated*,  •
C-ltd/S-yes/P-no/H-yes

Full breakfast
Rest., dinner only, BYOB
Conf. room, pool
gardens, mountain creek
hiking trails

*100-year old inn on National Register, rustic rural setting near Tallulah Gorge, lovely views, genuine hospitality, outstanding food.*

## WARM SPRINGS

**Hotel Warm Springs B&B**
PO Box 351, 47 Broad St.,
31830
706-655-2114  Fax: 706-655-
2771 800-366-7616
Geraldine Thompson
All year

$$-B&B
18 rooms, 18 pb
Most CC, *Rated*,
C-yes/S-ltd/P-no/H-no

Full southern breakfast
Restaurant, Comp. wine
Sitting room, library
honeymoon suite, jacuzzi
conferences & weddings

*Pefect get-away in 1907 historic hotel, authentically restored, decorated w/Roosevelt furniture & family antiques. Southern breakfast on silver service.* **3rd night 50%.**

## VILLA RICA

**Ahava Plantation B&B**
2236 S. Van Wert Rd.,   30180
770-459-2836 Fax: 770-459-3339
800-858-3473
Larry & Diane Camp

$$-B&B
5 rooms, 3 pb
Most CC,  •
C-yes/S-no/P-ltd

Full breakfast
Afternoon tea, snacks
Sitting room, library
porch, yard area

*Step back into "Gone With the Wind" in this southern antebellum home located 30 minutes from most metro Atlanta functions.* **10% discount if you mention The Guide.**

## More Inns ...

| | |
|---|---|
| Adairsville | Old Home Place, 764 Union Grove Church, 30103, 404-625-3649 |
| Albany | Beggar's Bush-Cane Miller, 615 Mud Creek Rd., 31707, 912-432-9241 |
| Alto | Burns-Sutton House, 230 Crane Mill Rd., 30510, 706-754-5565 |
| Americus | Cottage Inn,The, Box 488, Hwy. 49N, 31709, 912-924-9316 |
| Americus | Lee Street 1884, 622 S. Lee St., 31709, 912-924-1290 |
| Americus | Morris Manor, The, 425 Timberlane Dr., 31709, 912-924-4884 |
| Andersonville | Place Away B&B, A, 110 Oglethorpe St., 31711, 912-924-2558 |
| Athens | Oakwood B&B, 4959 Barnett Shoals Rd., 30605, 706-546-7886 |
| Atlanta | Ansley Inn, 253 Fifteenth St. NE, 30309, 404-872-9000 |
| Atlanta | Halcyon B&B, 872 Euclid Ave., 30307, 404-688-4458 |
| Atlanta | Woodruff B&B Inn, The, 223 Ponce de Leon Ave., 30308, 404-875-9449 |
| Augusta | Oglethorpe Inn, 836 Greene St., 30901, 706-724-9774 |
| Bainbridge | White House B&B, The, 320 Washington St., 31717, 912-248-1703 |
| Blackshear | Pond View Inn, 4200 Grady St., 31516 |
| Blairsville | Maple Bend Inn, Rt. 7, Box 7332A, 30512 |
| Blairsville | Stonehenge B&B, Rt. 6, Box 6314, 30512 |
| Blakely | Layside B&B, 611 River St., 31723, 912-723-8932 |
| Blue Ridge | Harry & June's B&B, Box 1247, 30513, 404-632-8846 |
| Brunswick | Rose Manor Guest House, 1108 Richmond St., 31520, 912-267-6369 |
| Buena Vista | Jenny May & Sapp's B&B, 229 Broad St., 31803, 912-649-7307 |
| Calhoun | Stoneleigh B&B, 316 Fain St., 30701, 706-629-2093 |
| Cave Spring | Hearn Academy Inn, P.O. Box 715, 30124, 404-777-8865 |
| Cherokee Pt. | Standifer Inn, Rt. 4, 30114, 404-345-5805 |
| Chickamauga | Gordon-Lee Mansion, 217 Cove Rd., 30707, 404-375-4728 |
| Clarkesville | LaPrade's, Route 1, Hwy 197N, 30523, 404-947-3312 |
| Clarkesville | Spring Hill B&B, R. 5, Box 5450, 30523 |
| Clarksville | Charm House, The, P.O. Box 392, 30523, 706-754-9347 |
| Cleveland | Lodge at Windy Acres, The, Rt. 5, Hwy. 75, 30528 |
| Cleveland | RuSharon B&B, 177 Old Clarksville Rd., 30528, 706-865-5738 |
| Concord | Inn Scarlett's Footsteps, 40 Old Flat Shoals Rd., 30206, 770-884-9012 |
| Dahlonega | Forest Hills Mt. Resort, Route 3, 30533, 404-864-6456 |
| Dahlonega | Laurel Ridge, P.O. Box 338, 30533, 404-864-7817 |
| Dahlonega | Worley Homestead Inn, 410 W. Main St., 30533, 404-864-7002 |
| Danielsville | Honey Bear Hideaway Farm, Rt. 4, Box 4106, 30633, 706-789-2569 |
| Danville | Magnolia Plantation, U.S. 80, 31017, 912-962-3988 |
| Dawsonville | Blackburn Park, Route 3, Box 160, 30534 |
| Demorest | Herb Patch Inn, 115 Hwy. 441 Business N, 30534 |
| Dillard | Dillard House Inn, P.O. Box 10, 30537, 404-746-5349 |
| Dublin | VIP B&B, 501 N. Dr., 31021, 912-275-3739 |
| Eatonton | Crockett House, The, 671 Madison Rd., 31024, 706-485-2248 |
| Elberton | Grenoke B&B, 914 Lower Heard St., 30635 |
| Ellijay | Elderberry Inn B&B Home, 75 Dalton St., 30540, 404-635-2218 |
| Flowery Branch | Whitworth Inn, 6593 McEver Rd., 30542, 404-967-2386 |
| Forsyth | Country Place, Route 3, Box 290, 31029 |
| Fort Valley | Evans House, The, 206 Miller St., 31030, 912-922-6691 |
| Greensboro | Early Hill, 1580 Lick Skillet Rd., 30648, 404-453-7876 |
| Hamilton | Wedgwood B&B & Gifts, P.O. Box 115, 31811, 706-628-5659 |
| Hawkinsville | Black Swan Inn, 411 Progress Ave., 31036, 912-783-4466 |
| Helen | Habersham Hollow Inn, Route 6, Box 6208, 30523, 706-754-5147 |
| Helen | Helendorf Inn, P.O. Box 305, 30545, 404-878-2271 |
| Hoboken | Blueberry Hill, RR1, Box 256, 31542, 912-458-2605 |
| Homerville | Helmstead, The, P.O. Box 61, 31634, 912-487-2222 |
| Jesup | Trowell House B&B, 256 E. Cherry St., 31545, 912-530-6611 |
| Lakemont | Anapauo Farm, Star Route, Box 13C, 30522, 404-782-6442 |
| Lakemont | Barn Inn, Rt. 1, 30552 |
| Lakemont | Lake Rabun Inn, The, P.O. Box 10, 30552, 706-782-4946 |
| Lakemont | Southern Trace, The, 14 Baker St., 30553 |
| Lyons | Robert Toombs Inn, 101 South State St., 30436, 912-526-4489 |
| Macon | Stone-Conner House, 575 College St., 31302, 912-745-0258 |
| Madison | Boat House, 383 Porter St., 30650, 404-342-3061 |
| Madison | Brady Inn, The, 250 N. Second St., 30650, 706-342-4400 |
| Marietta | Arden Hall, 1052 Arden Dr. SW, 30060, 404-422-0780 |
| Marietta | Marlow House/Stanley House, 192 Church St., 30060, 404-426-1887 |
| Milledgeville | Revel Wylly Hoga, 167 Kenan Dr., 31061 |
| Moultrie | Pinefields Plantation, Rt. 2, Box 215, 31768, 912-985-2086 |
| Mountain City | York House, The, P.O. Box 126, 30562, 706-746-2068 |
| Newnan | Parrott-Camp-Soucy Home, 155 Greenville St., 30263, 404-253-4846 |
| Norman Park | Quailridge B&B, Box 155, 31771, 912-985-7262 |
| Parrott | 217 Huckaby, Box 115, 31777, 912-623-5545 |

*Glen Ella Springs,*
*Turnerville, GA*

| | |
|---|---|
| Perry | Swift Street Inn B&B, 1204 Swift St., 31069, 912-988-4477 |
| Pine Mountain | Mountain Top Inn, Box 147, 31822, 800-533-6376 |
| Plains | Plains B&B Inn, The, P.O. Box 217, 31780, 912-824-7252 |
| Ringgold | Buckley's Cedar House, Route 10, Box 161, 30736, 404-935-2619 |
| Sautee | Glen-Kenimer-Tucker House, Hwy. 17, 30571 |
| Sautee | Lumsden Homeplace, The, Guy Palmer Rd., 30571, 404-878-2813 |
| Sautee | Nacoochee Valley House, Box 249, Hwy. 17, 30571, 404-878-3830 |
| Savannah | 118 West, 118 W. Gaston St., 31401, 912-234-8557 |
| Savannah | 17 Hundred 90 Inn, 307 E. President St., 31401, 912-236-7122 |
| Savannah | Bed & Breakfast Inn, 117 W. Gordon St., 31401, 912-238-0518 |
| Savannah | Charlton Court, 403 Charlton St. E., 31401, 912-236-2895 |
| Savannah | Comer House, 2 East Taylor St., 31401, 912-234-2923 |
| Savannah | Foley House Inn, 14 W. Hull St., 31401, 912-232-6622 |
| Savannah | Habersham at York Inn, 130 Habersham St., 31401, 912-234-2499 |
| Savannah | Haslam-Fort House, 417 E. Charlton St., 31401, 912-233-6380 |
| Savannah | Jesse Mount House, 209 W. Jones St., 31401, 912-236-1774 |
| Savannah | Kehoe House, The, 123 Habersham St., 31401, 912-232-1020 |
| Savannah | Magnolia Place Inn, 503 Whitaker St., 31401, 912-236-7674 |
| Savannah | Mulberry, The, 601 E. Bay St., 31401, 912-238-1200 |
| Savannah | Planters Inn, 29 Abercorn St., 31499, 912-232-5678 |
| Savannah | River Street Inn, 115 E. River St., 31499, 912-234-6400 |
| Savannah | Royal Colony Inn, 29 Abercorn St., 31401, 912-232-5678 |
| Savannah | Timmons House, 407 E. Charlton St., 31401, 912-233-4456 |
| Savannah | Victoria Barie House, 321 E. Liberty St., 31499, 912-234-6446 |
| St. Marys | Riverview Hotel, 105 Osborne St., 31558, 912-882-3242 |
| St. Simons Island | Country Hearth Inn, 301 Main St., 31522, 800-673-6323 |
| St. Simons Island | King's on the March, 1776 Demere Rd., 31522, 912-638-1426 |
| Statesboro | Aldred's Trellis Gardens, 107 S. Main St., 30458 |
| Swainsboro | Coleman House, 323 N. Main St., 30401, 912-237-2822 |
| Swainsboro | Edenfield House Inn, Box 556, 30401, 912-237-3007 |
| Tate | Tate House Resort, P.O. Box 33, 30177, 404-735-3122 |
| Thomaston | Gordon Street Inn, 403 W. Gordon St., 30286, 404-647-5477 |
| Thomaston | Whitfield Inn, 327 W. Main St., 30286, 404-647-2482 |
| Thomaston | Woodall House, 324 W. Main St., 30286, 404-647-7044 |
| Thomasville | Deer Creek B&B, 1304 S. Broad St., 31792, 913-226-7294 |
| Thomasville | Quail Country B&B, 1104 Old Monticello Rd., 31792, 913-226-7218 |
| Thomasville | Susina Plantation Inn, Route 3 Box 1010, 31792, 912-377-9644 |
| Thomson | Four Chimneys B&B, 2316 Wire Rd., S.E., 30824, 706-597-0220 |
| Thomson | West Fields B&B, Rt. 3, Box 728, 30824, 404-595-3156 |
| Tifton | Myon B&B, 128 1st St., 31793, 912-382-0959 |
| Toccoa | Habersham Manor House, 326 W. Doyle St., 30577, 404-886-6496 |
| Tucker | Robert Toombs Inn, 3401 Lawrenceville Hwy, 30084 |
| Tybee Island | Hunter House B&B, 1701 Butler Ave., 31328, 912-786-7515 |
| Villa Rica | Twin Oaks B&B Cottages, 9565 E. Liberty Rd., 30180, 404-459-4374 |
| Washington | Blackmon B&B, 512 N. Alexander Ave., 30673, 404-678-2278 |
| Washington | Colley House B&B, The, 210 S. Alexander Ave., 30673, 404-678-7752 |
| Washington | Holly Ridge Country Inn, Rt. 2, Box 356, 30673, 404-285-2594 |
| Washington | Liberty B&B Inn, 108 W. Liberty St., 30673, 404-678-3107 |
| Washington | Olmstead B&B, Pembroke Dr., 30673, 404-678-1050 |
| Washington | Water Oak Cottage, 211 S. Jefferson St., 30673, 404-678-3605 |
| Watkinsville | Rivendell B&B, 3581 S. Barnett Shoals, 30677, 706-769-4522 |
| Waynesboro | Georgia's Guest B&B, 640 E. 7th St., 30830, 404-554-4863 |
| Winterville | Old Winterville Inn, 108 S. Main St., 30683, 404-742-7340 |
| Young Harris | Brasstown Valley Resort, 6321 U.S. Highway 76, 30582, 706-379-9900 |

# Hawaii

## ANAHOLA, KAUAI

| | | |
|---|---|---|
| **Mahina Kai** | $$$-B&B | Continental plus bkfst. |
| P.O. Box 699, 96703 | 4 rooms, 2 pb | Kitchenette facilities |
| 4933 Aliomanu Rd. | *Rated*, • | Sitting room, bicycles |
| 808-822-9451 Fax: 808-822-9451 | C-ltd/S-yes | library, art collection |
| 800-337-1134 | Italian, French | ideal place for retreats |
| Trindy Comba   All year | | |

*Asian-Pacific beach villa and tropical gardens overlooking secluded bay. Separate guest wing with ethnic art collected by artist/owner, conf. facilities. **Free bottle of wine.***

## HAIKU, MAUI

| **Haikuleana B&B** | $$$-B&B | Full bkfst. (2 courses) |
|---|---|---|
| **Plantation** | 4 rooms, 4 pb | Sitting room, library |
| 555 Haiku Rd., 96708 | • | hot tubs, swimming pool |
| 808-575-2890 Fax: 808-575-9177 | C-ltd/S-ltd/P-no/H-no | |
| Jeanne Elizabeth & Ralph | Rus., Fr., Ger., It., Sp | |
| Blum | | |
| All year | | |

*Hawaiian country life with waterfalls, beaches and quiet relaxation, built amongst pineapple fields and pine trees in the time of King Kamehameha.*

## HANA, MAUI

| **Kaia Ranch B&B** | $$-B&B | Continental in refrig. |
|---|---|---|
| P.O. Box 404, 96713 | 2 rooms, 2 pb | Coffee, tea, cocoa |
| Ulaino Rd. | • | Pick your own fruit |
| 808-248-7725 | S-no/P-no/H-no | private kitchens |
| John & JoLoyce Kaia | | queen-size beds, no alc. |
| All year | | |

*Located in a tropical botanical garden/ranch–the real Hawaii that few visitors see. Experience gardens, animals & friends you'll never forget. Hana is a unique experience!*

## HANALEI, KAUAI

| **Bed, Breakfast & Beach** | $$-B&B | Continental plus bkfst. |
|---|---|---|
| P.O. Box 748, 96714 | 4 rooms, 4 pb | Restaurant nearby |
| 5095 Opelu Rd. | • | Sitting room, library |
| 808-826-6111 | C-ltd/S-no/P-no/H-no | television, coolers & |
| Carolyn Barnes | | snorkel equip. available |
| All year | | |

*Beach on famous Hanalei Bay is 125 yards away. View of 1000-foot waterfalls. Antiques & rattan. Hike Na Pali, snorkel, golf, kayak, windsurf, fish & sail. Cottage with kitchen available.*

## HILO

| **Holmes' Sweet Home** | $$-B&B | Continental plus |
|---|---|---|
| 107 Koula St., 96720 | 2 rooms, 2 pb | Refrigerator, microwave |
| 808-961-9089 Fax: 808-961-9089 | • | Sitting room |
| John & Charlotte Holmes | C-ltd/S-no/P-no/H-yes | 15 minutes from airport |
| All year | | Hilo Bay, shopping |

*Cook, quiet, lush setting with sweeping view of Hilo Bay; 5 minutes from restaurants, shopping, ocean; 30 miles from Volcano*

| **Shipman House B&B Inn** | $$$$-B&B | Continental plus bkfst. |
|---|---|---|
| 131 Ka'iulani St., 96720 | 3 rooms, 3 pb | Afternoon tea, snacks |
| 808-934-8002 800-Map-This | Visa, MC, • | Sitting room, library |
| Barbara Ann & Gary | C-ltd/S-no/P-no/H-no | 2 units in 1910 house |
| Andersen | A little French | 1 unit in big house |
| All year | | |

*Enjoy exotic flowers, wide verandahs. Continental breakfast buffet on lanai overlooking fern-lined gorge. Renovated Victorian mansion and guesthouse. Exquisite!*

## KAILUA

| **Pillows in Paradise** | $$-B&B | Continental plus |
|---|---|---|
| 336 Awakea Rd., 96734 | 3 rooms, 3 pb | Swimming pool |
| 808-262-8540 Fax: 808-262-8540 | • | 3 blocks from Kailua |
| 800-952-4582 | C-yes/S-yes/P-no/H-yes | beach |
| Barbara High | | |
| All year | | |

*Palms swaying quietly by the pool, near Kailua's pristine white sand beaches. Come! Enjoy a breakfast of fruits and pastries.* **Discounts for weekly/monthly rates.**

## KAILUA

**Sheffield House**
131 Kuulei Rd., 96734
808-262-0721 Fax: 808-262-0721
Paul & Rachel Sheffield
All year

$$-EP
2 rooms, 2 pb
•
C-yes/S-ltd/H-yes

Continental plus bkfst.
Library
ceiling fans, coolers
beach chairs

*Picture yourself in small town residential Hawaii. 9 houses from the beach, rated #1 in the USA, no hotels in sight. If this is your dream, call us.* **1 night free w/week stay, ltd.**

## KAILUA, KONA

**Hale Kipa 'O Pele**
P.O. Box 5252, 96745
808-329-8676 800-528-2456
Scot Eastwood, Brent
Williams
All year

$$-B&B
3 rooms, 3 pb
Visa, MC, *Rated*, •
S-yes/P-no/H-no

Continental plus bkfst.
Snacks
Complimentary wine
garden jacuzzi
waterfalls, koi pond

*Plantation home on a lush tropical gated estate. Expansive central covered lanai & atrium. 5 miles to beach & all attractions.* **10% off for 7+ nites & airline/travel employees.**

**Kailua Plantation House**
75-5948 Alii Dr., 96740
808-329-3727 Fax: 808-326-7323
Danielle Berger
All year

$$$$-B&B
5 rooms, 5 pb
AmEx, MC, Visa, •
C-ltd/S-no/P-no/H-no
French

Continental plus bkfst.
Restaurants nearby
Sitting room,
dipping pool, hot tubs
private baths & lanais

*HI's most elegant oceanfront B&B. Situated atop a promontory of black lava rocks under 1 mi. from the quaint town, Kailua-Kona.*

## KEALAKEKUA, KONA

**Merryman's B&B**
P.O. Box 474, 96750
808-323-2276 Fax: 808-323-3749
800-545-4390
Don & Penny Merryman
All year

$$-B&B
3 rooms, 1 pb
*Rated*, •
C-yes/S-no/P-no/H-no

Full Hawaiian breakfast
Afternoon tea, snacks
Comp. wine
sitting room, jaccuzzi
beach supplies, snorkle

*Tropical country setting; beautiful home furnished with antiques and fresh flowers. Near shopping, restaurants and beaches with fantasy snorkling—gear supplied.*

## KIHEI, MAUI

**Aloha Pualani**
15 Wailana Place, 96753
808-874-9265 Fax: 808-874-9127
800-PUALANI
Keith & Marina Dinsmoor
All year

$$-B&B
5 rooms, 5 pb
Visa, MC, AmEx, •
C-yes/S-no/P-no/H-ltd

Continental plus bkfst.
Sitting room
swimming pool, beach
snorkel, sailing trips

*Cozy suites with full kitchens face pool and tropically landscaped courtyard only 100 feet from Maui's longest sandy beach. Sunsets!*

**Ann/Bob's Vacation Rental**
3371 Keha Dr., 96753
808-874-1166 Fax: 808-879-7906
800-824-6409
Ann & Bob Babson
All year

$$-B&B
4 rooms, 4 pb
Visa, MC,
C-ltd/S-ltd/P-no/H-no

Continental plus bkfst.
Sitting room
laundry facilities
easy access to beaches

*Enjoy panoramic ocean views/glorious sunsets/tropical setting in South Maui. Five minutes from snorkeling/scuba, beaches. B&B rooms/apartment/cottage.*

## KIHEI-WAILEA

**Whale Watch House**
726 Kumulani Dr., 96753
808-879-0570 Fax: 808-874-8102
Pat & Pat Lowry    All year

$$-B&B
4 rooms, 4 pb
•
C-ltd/S-no/P-no/H-yes

Continental plus bkfst.
Sitting room, library
swimming pool
spectacular views

*Spectacular B&B with wonderful views of ocean and islands, 5 minutes from the beach, large swimming pool in tropical garden on sunny side of Maui.* **10% discount for seniors.**

## KULA, MAUI

**Kula Cottage**
206 Puakea Place, 96790
808-878-2043 Fax: 808-871-9187
Cecilia Gilbert    All year

$$$-B&B
1 rooms, 1 pb
Travel checks ok, •
H-no     Spanish

Continental breakfast
Stylish retreat, gardens
woodburning stove, patio
washer, dryer, color TV

*Fully equipped luxury one bedroom cottage with private driveway. Fireplace, patio and much more. A quiet, romantic and cozy hideaway.*

## LAHAINA, MAUI

**Old Lahaina House B&B**
P.O. Box 10355, 96761
808-667-4663 Fax: 808-667-5615
800-847-0761
John & Sherry Barbier
All year

$$-B&B
5 rooms, 5 pb
Visa, MC, AmEx, •
C-yes/S-no/P-no

Continental breakfast
Swimming pool
bikes, TVs, phones, A/C
beach across street

*Air-conditioned privacy, tropical courtyard. Walk to historic Lahaina town w/museums, shops, restaurants & harbor. Your own bit of paradise!* **Activity & dining discounts.**

## LAWAI, KAUAI

**Victoria Place B&B**
P.O. Box 930, 96765
3459 Lawai Loa Ln.
808-332-9300 Fax: 808-332-9465
Edee Seymour    All year

$$$-B&B
4 rooms, 4 pb
•
C-ltd/S-no/H-yes

Continental plus bkfst.
Lunch & dinner nearby
Large library, pool
lanai overlooking mtns.
beach mats, snorkel gear

*Jungle & ocean views—all rooms open to pool—near beaches, golf course, tennis. We pamper: flowers, homemade muffins, popcorn machine, fridge, microwave at poolside, & aloha.*

## PAHOA, KEHENA BEACH

**Kalani Oceanside**
**EcoResort**
RR2, Box 4500, 96778
Hwy 137
808-965-7828  800-800-6886
Richard Koob    All year

$$-B&B/AP
32 rooms, 16 pb
AmEx, MC, Visa, •
C-ltd/S-ltd/P-no/H-yes
Fr., Ger., Sp., Japanese

Full breakfast
Lunch, dinner, coffee
Sitting room, library
hot tub, sauna, pool
tennis, snorkel equip.

*Only coastal lodging in Hawaii's largest conservation area: dolphin beach, thermal springs, Volcanos National Park. "Kalani makes you fall in love with Hawaii"—S.F. Chronicle.* **Extended stay discounts.**

## PRINCEVILLE, KAUAI

**Hale 'Aha in Princeville**
P.O. Box 3370, 96722
3875 Kamehameha
808-826-6733 Fax: 808-826-9052
800-826-6733
Herb & Ruth Bockelman
All year

$$$-B&B
4 rooms, 4 pb
Visa, MC, *Rated*, •
C-ltd/S-no/P-no/H-no

Continental plus bkfst.
Many restaurants nearby
Library, hot tubs
decks on golf course
tennis/pool nearby

*Peaceful resort w/ocean, mountains, waterfalls, lush hiking trails, hidden beaches, rivers. Helicopters, snorkeling, boating & luaus. 3-day min.* **7th day free, direct booking-golf discounts.**

## VOLCANO

| | | |
|---|---|---|
| **Kilauea Lodge &** | $$$-B&B | Full breakfast |
| **Restaurant** | 15 rooms, 15 pb | Restaurnat, dinner, bar |
| P.O. Box 116,  96785 | MC, Visa, *Rated*, | Sitting room |
| Old Volcano Rd. | C-yes/S-no/P-no | Two bedroom bungalow |
| 808-967-7366 Fax: 808-967-7367 | German | Volcanoes National Park |
| Albert & Lorna Jeyte | | |
| All year | | |

*Mountain lodge with full service restaurant. 6 rooms with fireplace. One mile from spectacular Volcanoes National Park. 28 miles from Hilo. Helicopters and golf nearby.*

## VOLCANO VILLAGE

| | | |
|---|---|---|
| **Chalet Kilauea** | $$$-B&B | Full 2-course breakfast |
| P.O. Box 998,  96785 | 11 rooms, 11 pb | Comp. afternoon tea |
| Wright Rd. & Laukapu Rd. | Most CC, *Rated*, • | Marble baths, jacuzzis |
| 808-967-7786 Fax: 808-967-8660 | C-ltd/S-no/P-no/H-no | TV/VCR, videos, wet bar |
| 800-937-7786 | Fr., Dutch, Sp. | bathrobes, hot tubs |
| Brian & Lisha Crawford | | |
| All year | | |

*Romantic inn featuring rooms w/international themes, Treehouse, Lace & Owners suites. A lush Hawaiian haven just minutes from Volcanoes Nat'l Park.* **10% off 3+ nights.**

## WAINIHA

| | | |
|---|---|---|
| **River Estate Guest House** | $$$-B&B | Continental breakfast |
| 5-6691 Kuhio Hwy.,  96714 | 2 rooms, 2 pb | Barbeque |
| 808-826-5118  Fax: 808-826-4616 | • | River, beach chairs |
| 800-484-3060 | C-yes/S-ltd/P-no/H-no | snorkle gear |
| Mark Barbanell | | complete homes |
| All year | | |

*River Estate is a deluxe private accommodation situated on the river 2 blocks from the beach. It is an ideal spot for honeymooners and families.* **Mention Lanier Publishing for discount.**

# More Inns ...

| | |
|---|---|
| Aiea | Alohaland Guest House, 98-1003 Oliwa St., 96701,  808-487-0482 |
| Captain Cook | Adriennes B&B Paradise, RR 1, Box 8E, 96704,  808-328-9726 |
| Captain Cook | Manago Hotel, Box 145, 96704,  808-323-2642 |
| Captain Hook | Rainbow Plantation, P.O. Box 122, 96704,  808-323-2393 |
| Haiku, Huelo | Halfway to Hana House, P.O. Box 675, 96708,  808-572-1176 |
| Haiku, Maui | Hamakualoa Tea House, P.O. Box 335, 96708 |
| Haiku, Maui | Pilialoha B&B Cottage, 2512 Kaupakalua Rd., 96708,  808-572-1440 |
| Hana Maui | Hana Plantation Houses, P.O. 249, 96713,  808-248-7867 |
| Hana, Maui | Heavenly Hana Inn, P.O. Box 146, 96713,  808-248-8442 |
| Hana, Maui | Hotel Hana-Maui, P.O. Box 8, 96713,  808-248-8211 |
| Hilo | Arnott's Lodge, 98 Apapane Rd., 96720,  808-969-7097 |
| Hilo | Hale Kai B&B, 111 Honolii Pali, 96720,  808-935-6330 |
| Holualoa | Holualoa Inn, P.O. Box 222-C, 96725 |
| Honaunau | Pomaika'i Farm B&B, P.O. Box 57, 96726,  808-328-2112 |
| Honokaa | Kalopa Orchard Hale B&B, P.O. Box 1463, 96727,  808-775-0568 |
| Honokaa | Waipio Wayside B&B Inn, P.O. Box 840, 96727,  808-775-0275 |
| Honolulu | B&B Manoa, 2651 Terrace Dr., 96822,  808-988-6333 |
| Honolulu | John Guild Inn, 2001 Vancouver Dr., 96822,  808-947-6019 |
| Honolulu, Oahu | Bev & Monty's B&B, 4571 Ukali St., 96818,  808-422-9873 |
| Honolulu, Oahu | Hale Plumeria B&B, 3044 Hollinger St., 96815,  808-732-7719 |
| Honolulu, Oahu | Manoa Valley Inn, 2001 Vancouver Dr., 96822,  808-947-6019 |
| Kailua | Akamai B&B, 172 Kuumele Pl., 96734,  808-261-2227 |
| Kailua | Hale Pau Kala, 33 Kalaka Pl., 96734,  808-261-3098 |
| Kailua | Homer & Mahina Maxey B&B, 1277 Mokulua Dr., 96734,  808-261-1059 |
| Kailua, Kona | Adrienne's Casa Del Sol, 77-6335 Alii Drive, 96740,  800-328-9726 |
| Kailua, Kona | Hale Maluhia B&B, 76-770 Hualalai Rd., 96740,  800-559-6627 |
| Kailua, Oahu | Ali'i B&B, 237 Awakea Rd., 96734,  800-262-9545 |
| Kailua, Oahu | Papaya Paradise B&B, 395 Auwinala Rd., 96734,  808-261-0316 |
| Kamuela | Villa Rosa B&B, P.O. Box 2126, 96743,  808-882-4422 |
| Kamuela | Waimea Gardens, P.O. Box 563, 96743,  808-885-4550 |
| Kanuakakai | Ka Hale Mala, P.O. Box 1582, 96748,  808-553-9009 |

| Kapaa | Paradise Inn B&B, 4540 Fernandes Rd., 96746,   808-822-4104 |
| Kapaa Kauai | Lampy's B&B, 6078 Kolopua St., 96746,   808-822-0478 |
| Kapaa, Kauai | Kay Barker's B&B, P.O. Box 740, 96746,   808-822-3073 |
| Kapaa, Kauai | Keapana B&B, 5620 Keapana Rd., 96746,   800-822-7968 |
| Kapaa, Kauai | Orchid Hut, The,  6402 Kaahele St., 96746,   808-822-7201 |
| Kapaa, Kauai | Randy Rosario, 6470 Kawaihau Rd., 96746,   808-822-1902 |
| Kapaau | Big Sky Ranch, Kohala G.C.,  P.O. Box 1468, N.Kohala, 96755,   808-889-0564 |
| Kaunakakai | Kamalo Plantation, Star Route, Box 128, 96748,   808-558-8236 |
| Kaunakakai | Pau Hana Inn, P.O. Box 546, 96748,   800-367-8047 |
| Keaau | Paradise Place, HCR 9558, 96749,   808-966-4600 |
| Keaau | Rainforest Retreat, HCR 1 Box 5655, 96749,   808-966-7712 |
| Kealakekua | Hale Honua Ranch, P.O. Box 347, 96750,   808-328-8282 |
| Kihei, Maui | Whaler's Way B&B,  541 Kupulau Dr, 96753,   808-879-7984 |
| Kilauea, Kauai | Hale Ho'o Maha, P.O. Box 422, 96754,   808-828-1341 |
| Koloa, Kauai | Hale Keoki B&B, P.O. Box 1508, 96756,   808-332-9094 |
| Koloa, Kauai | Island Home, 1707 Kelaukia St., 96756,   808-742-2839 |
| Koloa, Kaui | Halemanu, P.O. Box 72, 96756 |
| Koloa, Poipu | Gloria's Spouting Horn B&B,  4464 Lawai Beach Rd., 96756,   808-742-6995 |
| Kukuihaele | Hamakua Hideaway, P.O. Box 5104, 96727,   808-775-7425 |
| Kula | Kula View B&B, 140 Holopuni Rd., 96790,   808-878-6736 |
| Kula, Maui | Country Garden Cottage B&B, RR2 Box 224-A Kula Hwy., 96790,   808-878-2858 |
| Kula, Maui | Kula Lodge,  RR 1 Box 475, 96790,   808-878-2517 |
| Lahaina, Maui | Lahaina Inn, 127 Lahainaluna Rd., 96761,   808-661-0577 |
| Lahaina, Maui | Plantation Inn, The,  174 Lahainaluna Rd., 96761,   808-667-9225 |
| Lanai City | Hotel Lanai, P.O. Box A-119, 96763,   800-321-4666 |
| Naalehu | Becky's B&B, P.O. Box 673, 96772,   808-929-9690 |
| Napili, Maui | Coconut Inn, 181 Hui Rd. "F", 96761,   808-669-5712 |
| Paauilo | Suds Acres B&B, P.O. Box 277, 96776,   808-776-1611 |
| Pahoa | Al's Volcano Ranch, 13-3775 Kalapana Hwy., 96778,   808-965-8800 |
| Pahoa | Aloha B&B, 13-3591 Luana St., 96778,   808-965-7434 |
| Pahoa | Oloha B &B, 13-3591 Luana St., 96778,   808-965-9898 |
| Paia Maui | Spreckelsville B&B, 204 Kealakai Pl., 96779,   808-877-5749 |
| Poipu Beach | Poipu B&B Inn & Cottages, 2720 Hoonani Rd., 96756,   808-742-1146 |
| Volcano | Carson's Volcano Cottage,  P.O. Box 503, 96785,   808-967-7683 |
| Volcano | Guesthouse at Volcano, P.O. Box 6, 96785,   808-967-7775 |
| Volcano | Hale Kilauea,  P.O. Box 28, 96785,   808-967-7591 |
| Volcano | Lokahi Lodge,  P.O. Box 7, 96785,   808-985-8647 |
| Volcano | My Island B&B,  P.O. Box 100, 96785,   808-967-7110 |
| Volcano Village | Hale Ohia Cottages,  P.O. Box 758, 96785,   808-967-7986 |
| Wailua, Kauai | Fern Grotto Inn, 4561 Kuamoo Rd, 96746,   808-822-2560 |

# Idaho

## COEUR D'ALENE

**Berry Patch Inn B&B**
N. 1150 Four Wind Rd.,
   83814
208-765-4994 Fax: 208-664-0374
Lee M. Ray
All year

$$$-B&B
3 rooms, 3 pb
Visa, MC, *Rated*, •
S-no/P-no/H-no

Full breakfast
Snack, comp. night cap
Sitting room, library
Indian tepee, aft. tea
free herbal bath grains

*Secluded mountain chalet, low fat cookery-homemade conserves. Near lake, downtown, golf, skiing. Honeymoons-Pampering. Nordstroms recognition & Nat'l acclaim. **Free bath grains.***

## FISH HAVEN

**Bear Lake B&B**
500 Loveland Lane,  83287
208-945-2688
Esther Harrison
All year

$$-B&B
4 rooms, 1 pb
Visa, MC,
C-ltd/S-no/P-no/H-no

Full breakfast
Sitting room, TV room
hot tub

*Spacious, secluded log home between the forest and Turquoise Lake, country hospitality. Winter and summer activities. Delicious breakfasts.*

## MOSCOW

**Beau's Butte B&B** | $$-B&B | Full breakfast
702 Public Ave., 83843 | 2 rooms, 1 pb | Comp. beverage, snacks
208-882-4061 | MC, Visa, *Rated*, | Sitting room
Joyce & Duane Parr | C-ltd/S-no/P-no/H-no | fireplace, sun room
All year | | hot tub, TV, VCR

*Tranquil country setting, convenient to university. Locally crafted country decor; fantastic views; scrumptious breakfasts.* **Discount for repeat guests.**

## STANLEY

**Idaho Rocky Mtn. Ranch** | $$$$-MAP | Full breakfast
HC 64, Box 163, 83278 | 21 rooms, 21 pb | Dinner included in price
Hwy 75, 9 miles-Stanley | MC, Visa, *Rated*, | Restaurant, beer & wine
208-774-3544 | C-ltd/S-no/P-no/H-no | library, horses
Bill & Jeana Leavell | Spanish | natural hot springs pool
June–Sept, Nov–April

*Historic log lodge and cabins; spectacular mountain scenery; gourmet dining in rustic atmosphere; extensive outdoor activities. Washroom for guests'laundry. Weekly rates.*

## SUN VALLEY, KETCHUM

**Idaho Country Inn** | $$$$-B&B | Full breakfast
P.O. Box 2355, 83353 | 11 rooms, 11 pb | Comp. wine, snacks
134 Latigo Lane, 83340 | AmEx, MC, Visa, | Sitting room, patio
208-726-1019  Fax: 208-726-5718 | *Rated*, • | library, sun room, deck
800-250-8341 | C-ltd/S-no/P-no/H-no | large outdoor hot tub
Terry & Julie Heneghan
All year

*Rooms reflect the history of Idaho. Wonderful mountain views, log beams, Riverock fireplace, gourmet breakfast in sun room, modern amenities. World-famous Sun Valley.*

# More Inns ...

| | |
|---|---|
| Albion | Mountain Manor B&B, P.O. Box 128, 83311, 208-673-6642 |
| Almo | Old Homestead, P.O. Box 186, 83312, 208-824-5521 |
| Blackfoot | Alder Inn B&B, 384 Alder St., 83221, 208-785-6968 |
| Boise | Idaho Heritage Inn, 109 W. Idaho, 83702, 208-342-8066 |
| Boise | Idaho Heritage Inn, 109 W. Idaho, 83702, 208-342-8066 |
| Boise | Littletree Inn, 2717 Vista Ave., 83703 |
| Boise | Robin's Nest B&B, 2389 W. Boise, 83706, 208-336-9551 |
| Boise | Sunrise, 2730 Sunrise Rim Rd., 83705, 208-345-5260 |
| Boise | Victoria's White House, 10325 W. Victory Rd., 83709 |
| Bruneau | Pleasant Hill Country Inn, HC 85, Box 179A, 83604, 208-845-2018 |
| Cambridge | Cambridge House B&B, P.O. Box 313, 83610, 208-257-3325 |
| Cascade | Wapati Meadow Ranch, HC 72, Johnson Creek Rd, 83611 |
| Coeur d'Alene | Amor's Highwood House, 1206 Highwood Ln., 83814, 208-667-4735 |
| Coeur d'Alene | Ann & Mel's Log House, P.O. Box 2294, 83816, 208-667-8015 |
| Coeur d'Alene | Baragar House B&B, 316 Military Dr., 83814, 208-664-9125 |
| Coeur d'Alene | Blackwell House, 820 Sherman Ave., 83814, 208-664-0656 |
| Coeur d'Alene | Coeur d'Alene B&B, 906 Foster Ave., 83814, 208-667-7527 |
| Coeur d'Alene | Country Ranch B&B, 1495 S. Green Ferry Rd., 83814, 208-664-1189 |
| Coeur d'Alene | Cricket on the Hearth, 1521 Lakeside Ave., 83814, 208-664-6926 |
| Coeur d'Alene | Greenbriar B&B Inn, 315 Wallace, 83814, 208-667-9660 |
| Coeur d'Alene | Gregory's McFarland House, 601 Foster Ave., 83814, 208-667-1232 |
| Coeur d'Alene | Highwood House B&B, 1206 Highwood Ln., 83814, 208-667-4735 |
| Coeur d'Alene | Inn the First Place, 509 N. 15th St., 83814, 208-667-3346 |
| Coeur d'Alene | Katie's Wild Rose Inn, E. 5150 Lake Dr., 83814, 208-765-9474 |
| Coeur d'Alene | Roosevelt Inn B&B, 105 Wallace Ave., 83814, 208-765-5200 |
| Coeur d'Alene | Silver Beach House B&B, 1457 Silver Beach Loop, 83814, 208-667-5406 |
| Coeur d'Alene | Sleeping Place of Wheels, P.O. Box 5273, 83814 |
| Coeur d'Alene | Someday House B&B, 790 Kidd Island Rd., 83814, 208-664-6666 |
| Coeur d'Alene | Summer House by the Lake, 1535 Silver Beach Rd., 83814, 208-664-9395 |
| Coeur d'Alene | Warwick Inn B&B, 303 Military Dr., 83814, 208-765-6565 |
| Dixie | Lodgepole Pine Inn, P.O. Box 71, 83525, 208-842-2343 |
| Downey | Downata Hot Springs, P.O. Box 185, 83234, 208-897-5736 |
| Driggs | Teton Creek B&B, 41 S. Baseline Rd., 83422, 208-354-2584 |
| Elk City | Canterbury House Inn B&B, P.O. Box 276, 83525, 208-842-2366 |
| Fruitland | Elm Hollow B&B, 4900 Hwy. 95, 83619, 208-452-6491 |

| | |
|---|---|
| Garden Valley | Warm Springs Creek B&B, HC 76, Box 2540, 83622, 208-462-3516 |
| Gooding | Gooding Hotel B&B, 112 Main St., 83330, 208-934-4374 |
| Hagerman | Cary House, The, 17985 U.S. 30 North, 83332, 208-837-4848 |
| Hailey | Comfort Inn, Box 984, 83333, 208-788-2477 |
| Harrison | Peg's B&B Place, P.O. Box 144, 83833, 208-689-3525 |
| Hayden Lake | Clark House on Hayden Lake, E. 4550 S. Hayden Lake, 83835, 208-772-3470 |
| Horseshoe Bend | Riverside B&B, Highway 55, 83629, 208-793-2408 |
| Idaho City | Idaho City Hotel, P.O. Box 70, 83631, 208-392-4290 |
| Idaho City | One Step Away B&B, P.O. Box 55, 83631, 208-392-4938 |
| Idaho Falls | Swan Valley B&B, P.O. Box 115, 83402, 208-483-4663 |
| Indian Valley | Indian Valley Inn, P.O. Box 54, 83632 |
| Irwin | McBride's B&B Guesthouse, P.O. Box 56, 83428, 208-483-4221 |
| Kellogg | Inn at Silver Mountain, 305 S. Division, 83837, 208-786-2311 |
| Kellogg | McKinley Inn, 210 McKinley Ave., 83837, 208-786-7771 |
| Kellogg | Montgomery Inn B&B, 305 S. Division, 83837 |
| Kellogg | Patrick's Inn, P.O. Box 11, 83837, 208-786-2311 |
| Kellogg | Scott's Inn, 126 E. Mullan Ave., 83837, 208-786-8581 |
| Ketchum | Busterback Ranch, Star Rt., 83340, 208-774-2217 |
| Ketchum | Knob Hill Inn, P.O. Box 800, 83353, 208-726-8010 |
| Ketchum | Lift Haven Inn, Box 21, 100 Lloyd Dr., 83340, 208-726-5601 |
| Kooskia | Bear Hollow B&B, HC 75, Box 16, 83539, 208-926-7146 |
| Kooskia | Looking Glass Guest Ranch, HC-75, Box 32, 83539, 208-926-0855 |
| Kooskia | Three Rivers Resort, HC 75, Box 61, 83539, 208-926-4430 |
| Laclede | Mountain View Farm B&B, P.O. Box 0150, 83841, 208-265-5768 |
| Laclede | River Birch Farm B&B, P.O. Box 280, Hwy 2, 83841, 208-263-3705 |
| Lava Hot Springs | Lava Hot Springs Inn, P.O. Box 420, 83246, 208-776-5830 |
| Lava Hot Springs | Riverside Inn B&B, 255 Portneuf Ave., 83246, 208-776-5504 |
| Lava Hot Springs | Royal Hotel, 4 E. Main St., 83246 |
| Lewiston | Carriage House B&B, 611 - 5th St., 83501, 208-746-4506 |
| Lewiston | Shiloh Rose, 3414 Selway Dr., 83501, 208-743-2482 |
| Mackay | Martini's Mountainside B&B, P.O. Box 456, 83251, 208-588-2940 |
| McCall | 1920 House B&B, P.O. Box 1716, 83638, 208-634-4661 |
| McCall | Northwest Passage B&B, P.O. Box 4208, 83638, 208-634-5349 |
| McCall | The Chateau B&B, P.O. Box 1957, 83638, 208-634-4196 |
| Meridian | Home Place, 415 W Lake Hazel Rd., 83642, 208-888-3857 |
| Moscow | Cottage B&B, The, 318 N. Hayes, 83843, 208-882-0778 |
| Moscow | Pardise Ridge B&B, 3377 Blaine Rd., 83843, 208-882-5292 |
| Moscow | Peacock Hill, 1245 Joyce Rd., 83843, 208-882-1423 |
| Moscow | Twin Peaks Inn, 2455 W. Twin Rd., 83843, 208-882-3898 |
| Moscow | Van Buren House, The, 220 N. Van Buren, 83843, 208-882-8531 |
| Mountain Home | Rose Stone Inn, 495 N. 3 E., 83647, 208-587-8866 |
| Nampa | The Pink Tudor B&B, 1315 12th Ave. S., 83651, 208-465-3615 |
| New Meadows | Hartland Inn, Box 215, 83654 |
| North Fork | Cummings Lake Lodge, Box 810, 83466 |
| North Fork | Indian Creek Guest Ranch, HC 64 Box 105, 83466, 208-394-2126 |
| Oakley | Poulton's B&B, 200 E. Main St., 83346, 208-862-3649 |
| Pierce | Cedar Inn, P.O. Box 494, 83546, 208-464-2704 |
| Plummer | Bonnie's B&B, Box 258, 83851, 208-686-1165 |
| Plummer | Owl Chalet, Route 1, Box 96A, 83851 |
| Pocatello | Dan Schroeder, 1741 Satterfield, 83201 |
| Pocatello | Hales Half Acre B&B, Rt 2, Box 26, 83202, 208-237-7130 |
| Pocatello | Libery Inn Victorian B&B, 404 S. Garfield, 83204, 208-232-3825 |
| Post Falls | Abel & Oliver's B&B, W. 2225 Hwy. 53, 83854, 208-773-6925 |
| Post Falls | River Cove, P.O. Box 1862, 83854, 208-773-9190 |
| Potlatch | Rolling Hills B&B, Rt. 1, Box 157, 83855, 208-668-1126 |
| Priest Lake | Whispering Waters B&B, HRC 5, Box 125B, 83856, 208-443-3229 |
| Priest River | Linger Longer, Route 5, Box 203C, 83856 |
| Riggins | Lodge B&B, P.O. Box 498, 83549 |
| Salmon | Bilger's Place, 1026 Hwy. 93 N. #5, 83467, 208-756-2206 |
| Salmon | Greyhouse Inn B&B, HC 61, Box 16, 83467 |
| Salmon | Heritage Inn, 510 Lena St., 83467, 208-756-3174 |
| Salmon | Syringa Lodge, P.O. Box 583, 83467, 208-756-4424 |
| Sandpoint | Angel on the Lake B&B, 410 Railroad Ave., 83864, 208-263-0816 |
| Sandpoint | Coit House B&B, 502 N. Fourth St., 83864, 208-265-4035 |
| Sandpoint | Green Gables Lodge, P.O. Box 815, 83864, 208-263-0257 |
| Sandpoint | Osprey Cove B&B, 8680 Sunnyside Rd., 83864, 208-265-4200 |
| Sandpoint | Page House, 506 N. 2nd, 83864, 208-263-6584 |
| Sandpoint | Priest Lake B&B, Route 5, Box 150-2A, 83864 |
| Shoshone | Governor's Manion, P.O. Box 326, 83352, 208-886-2858 |
| St. Anthony | Riverview B&B, 155 E. 3rd S., 83445, 208-624-4323 |
| St. Maries | Knoll Hus, P.O. Box 572, 83861, 208-245-4137 |
| Stanley | Redfish Lake Lodge, P.O. Box 9, 83278, 208-774-3536 |
| Sun Valley | River Street Inn, The, P.O. Box 182, 83353, 208-726-3611 |
| Swan Valley | Swan Valley B&B, P.O. Box 115, 83449, 208-483-4663 |
| Tensed | Seven Springs Farm B&B, HCR 1, Box 310, 83870, 208-274-2470 |
| Wallace | Jameson B&B, 304 Sixth St., 83873, 208-556-1554 |
| Wallace | Pine Tree Inn, 177 King St., Box 1023, 83873, 208-752-4391 |
| Yellow Pine | Yellow Pine Lodge, P.O. Box 77, 83677 |

# Illinois

CHAMPAIGN ───────────────────────────────

| | | |
|---|---|---|
| **Golds B&B, The** | $-B&B | Continental plus bkfst. |
| 2065 Cty Rd. 525E,  61821 | 3 rooms, 1 pb | |
| 217-586-4345 | *Rated*, • | |
| Rita & Bob Gold | C-yes/S-no/P-no/H-no | |
| All year | | |

*Country charm & hospitality in 1874 farmhouse. Handy to interstate & university attractions. Furnished with antiques. Quiet & peaceful.*

CHICAGO ───────────────────────────────

| | | |
|---|---|---|
| **B&B Lincoln Park** | $$-B&B | Continental breakfast |
| 2022 N. Sheffield,  60614 | 6 rooms, 4 pb | Telephone, answering |
| 312-327-6546  Fax: 312-883-1170 | Visa, MC, Disc., • | machines & coffee makers |
| Elia Sandoval | C-yes/S-yes/P-no/H-no | each unit has cable TV |
| All year | Spanish | |

*Renovated Victorian building with self-contained apartments close to downtown, lake and DePaul University. Excellent transportation, fine neighborhood restaurants and shops.*

| | | |
|---|---|---|
| **Lake Shore Drive B&B** | $$-B&B | Continental plus bkfst. |
| P.O. Box 148643,  60614 | 1 rooms, 1 pb | Sitting room, A/C |
| 312-404-5500 | • | roof top garden, parking |
| Barbara Mark | C-ltd/S-no/P-no/H-no | cable TV, telephone |
| All year | Italian, Spanish | |

*SPECTACULAR wraparound lake, city views! Lovely, upscale neighborhood; 50+ fine restaurants, theatres, clubs, shops. Minutes to downtown, museums, McCormick Place. 3 night minimum.* **7th night free.**

| | | |
|---|---|---|
| **Old Town B&B** | $$$-B&B | Continental plus bkfst. |
| 1451 N. North Park Ave., | 2 rooms, | Afternoon tea |
| 60610 | Visa, MC, AmEx, • | A gentrified residential |
| 312-440-9268 | C-ltd/S-no/P-no/H-no | neighborhood village |
| All year | | surrounds |

*This modern house is splendidly furnished & decorated with art objects from three centuries. A walled garden, library with easy chairs & cherrywood sleighbeds invite rest & reflection.*

CHILLICOTHE ───────────────────────────────

| | | |
|---|---|---|
| **Glory Hill** | $$-B&B | Full breakfast |
| 18427 N. Old Galena Rd., | 2 rooms, 2 pb | Aftn. tea, snacks |
| 61523 | Visa, MC, *Rated*, | Sitting room, library |
| 309-274-4228  Fax: 309-691-3125 | C-ltd/S-ltd/P-no/H-no | swimming pool, color TV |
| Bonnie Russell | | 1 room has whirlpool |
| All year | | |

*1841 country estate, antique furnishings, verandah, porch, fireplace, gourmet breakfasts, elegant, relaxed, comfortable, romantic, scenic, warm, friendly, quiet seclusion.*

EVANSTON ——————————————————————————————————————

| **Homestead, The** | $$-EP | Complimentary coffee |
| 1625 Hinman Ave., 60201 | 35 rooms, 35 pb | French restaurant |
| 847-475-3300 Fax: 847-570-8100 | MC, Visa, AmEx, | |
| David T. Reynolds | C-ltd/S-yes/P-no/H-ltd | |
| All year | | |

*Historic residential neighborhood; two blocks from Lake Michigan & Northwestern Univ.; 30 minutes from downtown Chicago. Award winning restaurant.*

GALENA ——————————————————————————————————————

| **Avery Guest House B&B** | $$-B&B | Continental plus bkfst. |
| 606 S. Prospect St., 61036 | 4 rooms, | Afternoon tea or cider |
| 815-777-3883 | MC, Visa, | Library |
| Gerry & Armon Lamparelli | C-ltd/S-no/P-no/H-no | sitting room |
| All year | | porch swing |

*Enjoy historic Galena, scenic beauty, fine restaurants, antiques. Comfortable 1840s house, homey hospitality, porch swing, piano and sunny dining room.*

| **Pine Hollow Inn B&B** | $$-B&B | Continental plus bkfst. |
| 4700 N Council Hill Rd, | 5 rooms, 5 pb | Comp. wine, snacks |
| 61036 | MC, Visa, *Rated*, • | Afternoon tea |
| 815-777-1071 | C-ltd/S-no/P-no/H-no | cross-country skiing |
| Larry & Sally Priske | | whirlpool bath |
| All year | | |

*A secluded country inn located on 120 acres, surrounded by one hundred and twenty acres of woods. Nestle in front of your own cozy fireplace.* **3 nights for price of 2, ltd** .

| **Captain Gear Guesthouse** | $$$$-B&B | Full breakfast, formal |
| P.O. Box 1040, 61036 | 3 rooms, 3 pb | Historic house tour |
| 1000 South Bench St. | Visa, MC, Disc, *Rated*, | garden patio, whirlpool |
| 815-777-0222 Fax: 815-777-3210 | S-no/P-no/H-no | tub, VCR/TV in rooms |
| 800-794-5656 | | |
| Susan Pettey | | |
| All year | | |

*1855 Mansion, eight restored fireplaces, American antique furniture, on four secluded acres in the Galena National Register Historic District.*

| **Park Avenue Guest House** | $$-B&B | Continental plus bkfst. |
| 208 Park Ave., 61036 | 4 rooms, 4 pb | Aftn. tea, snacks |
| 815-777-1075 | Visa, MC. Disc. *Rated*, | Sitting room w/TV |
| John & Sharon Fallbacher | C-ltd/S-no/P-no/H-no | 2 parlours, gazebo, A/C |
| All year | | fireplaces in rooms |

*Elegant yet comfortable, in quiet residential area. Short walk to beautiful Grant Park, Galena River and Main St. shopping and restaurants.* **$10 off midweek, Ltd.**

GENEVA ——————————————————————————————————————

| **Oscar Swan Country Inn** | $$$-B&B | Full breakfast |
| 1800 W. State St., 60134 | 7 rooms, 4 pb | Comp. snacks & beverages |
| 630-232-0173 Fax: 630-232-1194 | MC, Visa, *Rated*, • | Sitting room, library |
| Hans & Nina Heymann | C-yes/S-no/P-no/H-no | tennis courts, pool |
| All year | German | cross-country skiing on 7 |
| | | acres |

*Country hideaway on 7 private acres. Fireplaces, cozy kitchen, hearty breakfast, wonderful River Town, antiques, bike paths. The New England of the Midwest.* **3rd night, 50%; 10% restaurant discount.**

## MAEYSTOWN

| | | |
|---|---|---|
| **Corner George Inn** | $$-B&B | Full breakfast |
| P.O. Box 103,  62256 | 7 rooms, 5 pb | Aft. tea, restaurant |
| 1101 Main St. | MC, Visa, *Rated*,  • | Sitting room, library |
| 618-458-6660  800-458-6020 | C-ltd/S-no/P-no/H-yes | bicycles, ice cream shop |
| David & Marcia Braswell | German | horse-drawn carriage |
| All year | | |

*Restored 1880s elegance in historic 19th-century German village, 45 minutes south of St. Louis, 45 minutes via ferry to Ste. Genevieve.*

## METROPOLIS

| | | |
|---|---|---|
| **Isle of View** | $$-B&B | Full gourmet breakfast |
| 205 Metropolis,  62960 | 5 rooms, 5 pb | Dinner (with notice) |
| 618-524-5838 | Most CC,  • | Sitting room, hot tubs |
| Gerald & Kim Offenburger | C-ltd/S-ltd/P-ltd/H-no | near antique/specialty |
| All year | | shops, restaurants |

*1889 Victorian mansion, 1 block from Riverboat Casino. Jacuzzi suites. Spacious, antique-appointed rooms; lots of romance. Rooms have color TV, remote control, cable.* **Stay 2 weekend nights for weekday rate.**

## MORRISON

| | | |
|---|---|---|
| **Hillendale B&B** | $$-B&B | Full breakfast |
| 600 Lincolnway West,  61270 | 10 rooms, 10 pb | Sitting room, fireplaces |
| 815-772-3454  Fax: 815-772-7023 | MC, Visa, *Rated*,  • | billiard & fitness rooms |
| 800-349-7702 | C-ltd/S-no/P-no/H-no | whirlpools for two |
| Barb & Mike Winandy | | |
| All year | | |

*Travel the world in rural America in our international theme rooms. Relax in the Japanese Teahouse while viewing the water gardens with its fish.* **10% off 2 night stay.**

## MOUNT CARMEL

| | | |
|---|---|---|
| **Poor Farm B&B, The** | $-B&B | Full country breakfast |
| Poor Farm Rd.,  62863 | 5 rooms, 5 pb | Lunch & dinner by reser. |
| 618-262-4663  Fax: 618-262-8199 | Most CC, *Rated*,  • | Sitt. room, library |
| 800-646-3276 | C-yes/S-ltd/P-no/H-yes | bike built for 2, player |
| Liz & John Stelzer | | piano, antique juke box |
| All year | | |

*The "Inn" place to stay! Old-time charm just minutes from golf, swimming, fishing, boating, parks. Full country breakfasts - private baths.* **10% off at gift shop; 7th night free.**

## RED BUD

| | | |
|---|---|---|
| **Magnolia Place** | $$-B&B | Full breakfast |
| 317 S. Main,  62278 | 4 rooms, 2 pb | Afternoon tea, snacks |
| 618-282-4141 | Visa, MC, AmEx, | Complimentary wine |
| Dolly Krallman | C-ltd/S-no/P-no/H-no | sitting room, bridal |
| All year | | suite, private parties |

*Elegant accommodations and gracious hospitality await you. We offer a unique setting for intimate garden weddings, special parties and receptions.* **15% corporate discount.**

## ROCK ISLAND

| | | |
|---|---|---|
| **Top O' The Morning B&B** | $$-B&B | Full breakfast |
| **Inn** | 3 rooms, 3 pb | Piano, tennis nearby |
| 1505 - 19th Ave.,  61201 | *Rated*, | hot tub, sitting room |
| 309-786-3513 | C-yes/S-ltd/P-no/H-no | A/C in all bedrooms |
| Sam & Peggy Doak | | |
| All year | | |

*Brick mansion on 3.5 acres in the center of town. Large porch, grand piano, formal dining. Irish hospitality. Champagne, flowers & breakfast in bridal suite for honeymoons.*

## ROCK ISLAND

**Victorian Inn B&B**
702-20 St.,  61201
309-788-7068  800-728-7068
David & Barbara Parker
All year

$$-B&B
6 rooms, 6 pb
Visa, MC, AmEx,
*Rated*,
C-ltd/S-no/P-no/H-no

Full gourmet breakfast
Aftn. beverages, snacks
Sitting room

*20 room mansion furnished with genuine antiques. Gourmet breakfast served on fine china, crystal and sterling silver—welcome to our home.*

## ST. CHARLES

**Cornfields "Grotto"**
3N698 Bittersweet Rd.,  60175
630-584-3376  Fax: 630-584-7000
Sally Golan
All year

$$$-B&B
1 rooms, 1 pb
Visa, MC, AmEx,
C-ltd/S-ltd/P-no/H-no

Continental breakfast
Snacks
Bikes & bike paths
cross-country skiing
screen house

*Secluded Grotto room; private entrance, whirlpool, kitchen. Breakfast basket in room. Cornhusk doll studio. For show dealers, we're near fairgrounds.* **Discount on Cornfields products.**

## WHEATON

**Wheaton Inn, The**
301 W. Roosevelt Rd.,  60187
630-690-2600  Fax: 630-690-2623
800-447-4667
Dennis Stevens
All year

$$$-B&B
16 rooms, 16 pb
Most CC, *Rated*,  •
C-yes/S-yes/P-ltd

Full breakfast
Bar Service (ltd)
Comp. wine, snacks
sitting room, library
near golf, tennis, etc.

*Elegant yet homey atmosphere in the Williamsburg tradition, 10 rooms with fireplaces, 6 with whirlpools. Weekend getaways or corporate traveler's delight.*

## WINNETKA

**Chateau des Fleurs**
552 Ridge Rd.,  60093
847-256-7272  Fax: 847-256-7272
Sally H. Ward
All year

$$$-B&B
3 rooms, 3 pb
*Rated*,  •
C-ltd/S-no/P-no/H-no

Full breakfast
Afternoon tea, snacks
Grand piano, 50" TV
VCR with movies, bikes
jacuzzis in 2 rms, pool

*Beautiful French country home furnished in rare antiques. Lovely views of magnificent trees, English gardens. Near train & private road for walking/jogging. 2 night minimum.*

# More Inns ...

| | |
|---|---|
| Alton | Haagen House B&B,  617 State St., 62002,  618-462-2419 |
| Anna | Goddard Place, The,  RR 2, P.O. Box 445G, 62906,  618-833-6256 |
| Arcola | Curley's Corner B&B,  425 E. Country Rd 200 N, 61910,  217-268-3352 |
| Arcola | Flower Patch, The,  225 E. Jefferson, 61910,  217-268-4876 |
| Arthur | Favorite Brother Inn, The,  106 E. Columbia, 61911,  217-543-2938 |
| Atwood | Harshbarger Homestead,  RR 1, P.O. Box 110, 61913,  217-578-2265 |
| Beardstown | Nostalgia Corner,  115 W. 7th, 62618,  217-323-5382 |
| Belle Rive | Enchanted Crest,  RR 1, P.O. Box 216, 62810,  618-736-2647 |
| Cairo | Windham,  2606 Washington Ave., 62914,  618-734-3247 |
| Carlyle | Country Haus B&B Inn,  1191 Franklin, 62231,  618-594-8313 |
| Carlyle | Victorian Inn B&B,  1111 Franklin St., 62231,  618-594-8506 |
| Carthage | Wright Farmhouse,  RR 3, 62321,  217-357-2421 |
| Champaign | Alice's Place,  1915 Winchester, 61821,  217-359-3332 |
| Champaign | Barb's B&B,  606 S. Russell, 61821,  217-356-0376 |
| Champaign | Glads B&B, The,  RR 3, Box 69, 61821,  217-586-4345 |
| Champaign | Grandma Joan's B&B,  2204 Brett Dr., 61820,  217-356-5828 |
| Chicago | Hyde Park House,  5210 S. Kenwood, 60615,  312-363-4595 |
| Chicago | Robert Ford,  1860 N. Maud, 60614 |
| Collinsville | Maggie's Bed & Breakfast,  2102 North Keebler Rd., 62234,  618-344-8283 |
| Dallas City | 1850's Guest House,  RR 1, P.O. Box 267, 62330,  217-852-3652 |
| Danforth | Fannie's House B&B,  P.O. Box 194, 60930,  815-269-2145 |
| Danville | Bookwalter House, The,  1701 N. Logan Ave., 68132,  217-443-5511 |
| Dixon | River View Guest House,  507 E. Everett, 61021,  815-288-5974 |
| Du Quoin | Francie's,  104 S. Line St., 62832,  618-542-6686 |

| | |
|---|---|
| Dwight | La Petite Voyageur B&B, 116 E. South St., 60420,  815-584-2239 |
| Eldred | Hobson's Bluffdale, Eldred-Hillview Rd, 62027,  217-983-2854 |
| Elizabeth | Locker Knoll Inn, 8833 S. Massbach Rd., 61028,  815-598-3150 |
| Elizabeth | Ridgeview B&B, 8833 S. Massbach Rd., 61028,  815-598-3150 |
| Elizabeth Town | River Rose Inn, 1 Main St., 62931,  618-287-8811 |
| Elsah | Corner Nest B&B, P.O. Box 220, 62028,  618-374-1892 |
| Elsah | Green Tree Inn, P.O. Box 96, 62028,  618-374-2821 |
| Elsah | Maple Leaf Cottage B&B, P.O. Box 156, 62028 |
| Evanston | Charles & Barbara Pollard, 2633 Poplar, 60201,  312-328-6162 |
| Evanston | Margarita European Inn, 1566 Oak Ave., 60201,  708-869-2273 |
| Freeburg | Westerfield House, The, RR #2, Box 34, 62243,  618-539-5643 |
| Galena | Aldrich Guest House, 900 Third St., 61036,  815-777-3323 |
| Galena | Bedford House, Route 20 West, 61036,  815-777-2043 |
| Galena | Belle Aire Mansion, 11410 Route 20 West, 61036,  815-777-0893 |
| Galena | Brierwreath Manor, 216 N. Beach St., 61036,  815-777-0608 |
| Galena | Country Gardens Guesthouse, 1000 Third St., 61036,  815-777-3062 |
| Galena | De Soto House Hotel, 230 S. Main St., 61036 |
| Galena | DeZoya House, 1203 Third St., 61036,  815-777-1203 |
| Galena | Early American Settlement, P.O. Box 250, 61036,  815-777-4200 |
| Galena | Farster's Executive Inn, 305 N. Main St., 61036,  815-777-9125 |
| Galena | Felt Manor Guest House, 125 S. Prospect St., 61036,  800-383-2830 |
| Galena | Gallery Guest Suite, 204-l/2 South Main St, 61036,  815-777-1222 |
| Galena | Goldmoor, The, 9001 Sand Hill Rd., 61036,  815-777-3925 |
| Galena | Grandview Guest Home, 113 S. Prospect St., 61036,  815-777-1387 |
| Galena | Hellman Guest House, 318 Hill St., 61036,  815-777-3638 |
| Galena | Main St. Inn, 404 S. Main St., 61036,  815-777-3454 |
| Galena | Mars Avenue Guest House, 515 Mars Ave., 61036,  815-777-2808 |
| Galena | Mother's Country Inn, 349 Spring St., 61036,  815-777-3153 |
| Galena | Queen Anne Guest House, 200 Park Ave., 61036,  815-777-3849 |
| Galena | Ryan Mansion Inn, Route 20 West, 61036,  815-777-2043 |
| Galena | Stillman's Country Inn, 513 Bouthillier, 61036,  815-777-0557 |
| Galena | Victorian Mansion, 301 High St., 61036,  815-777-0675 |
| Galesburg | Seacord House, 624 N. Cherry St., 61401,  309-342-4107 |
| Geneva | Herrington Inn, The,  17 No. First St., 60134 |
| Gibson City | Stolz Home, RR 2, Box 27, 60936,  217-784-4502 |
| Golconda | Mansion of Golconda, P.O. Box 339, 62938,  618-683-4400 |
| Goodfield | Brick House B&B, P.O. Box 301, 61742,  309-965-2545 |
| Grafton | Wildflower Inn B&B, P.O. Box 31, 62037,  618-465-3719 |
| Grand Detour | Colonial Rose Inn, The, 8230 S. Green St., 61021,  815-652-4422 |
| Grant Park | Bennett Curtis House, 302 W. Taylor, 60940,  815-465-6025 |
| Greenville | Prairie House Country Inn, RR 4, P.O. Box 47AA, 62246,  618-664-3003 |
| Gurnee | Sweet Basil Hill Farm, 15937 W. Washington St., 60031,  708-244-3333 |
| Harrisburg | White Lace Inn, 204 W. Poplar St., 62946,  618-252-7599 |
| Havana | McNutt Guest House, 409 W. Main St., 62644,  309-543-3295 |
| Hillsboro | Red Rooster Inn,  123 E. Seward St., 62049 |
| Huntley | Croaking Frog, The,  12618 W. Hensel Rd., 60142,  708-669-1555 |
| Jerseyville | Homeridge B&B, The,  1470 N. State St., 62052,  618-498-3442 |
| Kankakee | Norma's B&B, 429 So. Fourth Ave., 60901 |
| Lanark | Standish House B&B, 540 W. Carroll St., 61046,  815-493-2307 |
| Lena | Sugar Maple Inn,  607 Maple, 61048,  815-369-2786 |
| Lincoln | Prairie Fields Inn B&B, R.R. 3, Hwy. 121, 62656,  217-732-7696 |
| Macomb | Brockway House, The,  331 E. Carroll, 61455,  309-837-2375 |
| Macomb | Pineapple Inn, The,  204 W. Jefferson, 61455,  309-837-1914 |
| Marseilles | Annie Tique's Hotel, 378 Main St., 61341,  815-795-5848 |
| Mendota | Elizabeth's B&B, 1100 5th St., 61342,  815-539-5555 |
| Mendota | Lord Stocking's,  803 3rd Ave., 61342,  815-539-7905 |
| Momence | Surenaut B&B, 304 W. Second St., 60954,  815-472-3156 |
| Monticello | Linda's Country Loft B&B, R.R.1, Box 198A, 61856,  217-762-7316 |
| Mossville | Old Church House Inn,  1416 E. Mossvill Rd., 61552,  309-579-2300 |
| Mount Carmel | Living Legacy Homestead BB, Box 146A, RR #2, 62863,  618-298-2476 |
| Mount Pulaski | Dorsey's B&B,  318 North Belmont, 62548 |
| Mt. Carroll | Farm, The,  8239 Mill Rd., 61053,  815-244-9885 |
| Mt. Carroll | Prairie Path Guest House, 1002 N. Lowden Rd., 61053,  815-244-3462 |
| Mt. Morris | Kable House, Sunset Hill, 61054,  815-734-7297 |
| Mundelein | Round-Robin Guesthouse, 231 East Maple Ave., 60060,  312-566-7664 |
| Naperville | Die Blaue Gaus,  95265 Route 59, 60565,  312-355-0835 |
| Naperville | Harrison House B&B,  26 N. Eagle St., 60540,  708-420-1117 |
| Nauvoo | Ancient Pines B&B, The,  2015 Parkley St., 62354,  217-453-2767 |
| Nauvoo | Ancient Pines, The,  2015 Parley St., 62354,  217-453-2767 |
| Nauvoo | Hotel Nauvoo, Route 96, Town Center, 62354,  217-453-2211 |
| Nauvoo | Mississippi Memories B&B, Box 291, Riverview Hght, 62354,  217-453-2771 |
| Nauvoo | Parley Lane B&B,  Route 1, Box 220, 62354,  217-453-2277 |
| Oak Park | Cheney House, 520 N. E. Ave., 60302,  708-524-2067 |
| Oak Park | Toad Hall, 301 N. Scoville Ave., 60302,  708-386-8623 |
| Oak Park | Under The Ginkgo Tree, 300 N. Kenilworth Ave., 60302,  708-524-2327 |
| Oakland | Inn-on-the-Square, 3 Montgomery St., 61943,  217-346-2289 |
| Oakland | Johnson's Country Home B&B, 109 E. Main St., 61943,  217-346-3274 |
| Oblong | Welcome Inn, 506 W. Main St., 62449,  618-592-3301 |

| | |
|---|---|
| Oregon | Pinehill B&B, 400 Mix St., 61061, 815-732-2061 |
| Paris | Tiara manor, 403 W. Court St., 61944, 800-531-1865 |
| Pekin | Herget House, 420 Washington, 61554, 309-353-4025 |
| Peoria | Ruth's B&B, 1506 W. Alta Rd., 61615, 309-243-5971 |
| Petersburg | Bit of Country B&B, 122 W. Sheridan, 61615, 217-632-3771 |
| Petersburg | Oaks B&B, The, 510 W. Sheridan Rd., 61615, 217-632-4480 |
| Pinckneyville | Oxbow B&B, Rt. 1, P.O. Box 47, 62274, 618-357-9839 |
| Pleasant Hill | Pleasant Haven B&B, 201 E. Quincy, Box 51, 62366, 217-734-9357 |
| Plymouth | Plymouth Rock Resort, 201 W. Summer, 62367, 309-458-6444 |
| Port Byron | Olde Brick House, The, 502 No. High St., 61275, 309-523-3236 |
| Prairie Du Rocher | La Maison du Rocher Inn, 2 Duclos & Main, 62277, 618-284-3463 |
| Princeton | Yesterday's Memories, 303 East Peru St., 61359, 815-872-7753 |
| Quincy | Kaufmann House, The, 1641 Hampshire, 62301, 217-223-5202 |
| Rantoul | Better 'n Grandma's, 102 S. Meyers, 61866, 217-893-0469 |
| Robinson | Heath Inn, The, P.O. Box 175, 62454, 618-544-3410 |
| Rock Island | Potter House, The, 1906 - 7th Ave., 61201, 309-788-1906 |
| Rockford | Victoria's B&B, 201 N. Sixth St., 61107, 815-963-3232 |
| Sesser | Hill House, The, 503 S. Locust, 62884, 618-625-6064 |
| Springfield | Mischler House, 718 South 8th St., 62703, 217-523-5616 |
| St. Charles | Stage Coach Inn, 41 W. 278 Whitney Rd., 60174, 312-584-1263 |
| Stockton | Maple Lane, 3115 Rush Creek Rd., 61085, 815-947-3773 |
| Streator | Dicus House B&B, 609 E. Broadway St., 61364, 815-672-6700 |
| Sullivan | Little House OnThe Prairie, P.O. Box 525, 61951, 217-728-4727 |
| Sycamore | Country Charm Inn, 15165 Quigley Rd., 60178, 815-895-5386 |
| Sycamore | Stratford Inn, 355 W. State St., 60178, 815-895-6789 |
| Toulon | Rockwell Victorian B&B, 404 N. Washington, 61483, 309-286-5201 |
| Urbana | Shurts House In Urbana, 710 W. Oregon St., 61801, 217-367-8793 |
| Warren | Nonis Bed & Breakfast, 516 W. Main St., 61097 |
| Wenona | Hart of Wenona, 303 North Walnut, 61377, 815-853-4778 |
| West Dundee | Ironhedge Inn B&B, 305 Oregon, 60118, 708-426-7777 |
| West Salem | Thelma's Bed & Breakfast, 201 South Broadway, 62476, 618-456-8401 |
| Williamsville | Bed & Breakfast at Edie's, 233 E. Harpole, POB 351, 62693, 217-566-2538 |
| Yorkville | Silver Key B&B, The, 507 West Ridge, 60504, 800-246-3384 |

# Indiana

## BETHLEHEM

**Inn at Bethlehem**
101 Walnut St, Walnut &
Riverview,   47104
812-293-3975
C. & J. Browne, P. Webber
All year

$$$-B&B
6 rooms, 6 pb
Visa, •
S-no/P-no

Full breakfast
Lunch, dinner
Sitting room, bicycles
boat dock

*Federal, 160 year old home, newly renovated. In unique, country small town. Watch the Ohio River from your room or the beautiful patio. Stately and secluded in rolling hills.*

## BEVERLY SHORES

**Dunes Shore Inn**
P.O. Box 807,   46301
33 Lakeshore County Rd.
219-879-9029
Rosemary & Fred Braun
All year

$$-B&B
12 rooms,
MC, Visa, *Rated*,
C-ltd/S-ltd/P-no/H-no
German

Continental plus bkfst.
Fruit, cider & cookies
Library, sitting room
outdoor grill, tables
bicycles

*Located one block from Lake Michigan and surrounded by the National Lakeshore and Dunes State Parks, this inn is an oasis for nature lovers. One hour from Chicago.* **Request weekly rate.**

## BLOOMINGTON

**Grant Street Inn**
310 N. Grant St.,   47408
812-334-2353  Fax: 812-331-8673
800-328-4350
Bob Bohler
All year

$$$-B&B
24 rooms, 24 pb
Visa, MC, AmEx,
*Rated*,  •
S-ltd/P-no/H-yes

Full breakfast buffet
Snacks
Sitting room, library
TV's & phones in rooms

*The ambiance of the 1880s with the amenities of the 1990s. Suites have fireplaces and whirlpool Jacuzzis. Walk to downtown or Indiana University.*

## CHESTERTON

**Gray Goose Inn**
350 Indian Boundary Rd.,
   46304
219-926-5781  Fax: 219-926-4845
800-521-5127
Tim Wilk
All year

$$$-B&B
8 rooms, 8 pb
Most CC, *Rated*,  •
C-ltd/S-ltd/P-no/H-no

Full gourmet breakfast
Comp. beverages, snacks
Sitting & meeting rooms
telephone in rooms
bicycles, boats

*In Dunes Country. English country house on private wooded lake. Charming guest rooms, private baths, fireplaces, jacuzzis, sun porch. Near interstates. Dinner by reservation.*

## COLUMBUS

**Columbus Inn B&B, The**
445 5th St.,   47201
812-378-4289  Fax: 812-378-4289
Paul A. Staublin
All year

$$$-B&B
,
Most CC, *Rated*,
C-yes/P-no/H-yes
Spanish

Full breakfast
Aftn. tea, snacks
Sitting room, library
close to theatre, golf,
tennis, shopping, parks

*Restored 1895 City Hall-National Register. Elegance of a premium hotel. High tea available daily. Breakfast buffet. Downtown renowned architecture. **2 people, 2 nights, 2 dinners, $200.***

## CONNERSVILLE

**Maple Leaf Inn B&B**
831 N. Grand Ave.,   47331
317-825-7099
Jose Angel & Cindy Perez
All year

$$-B&B
4 rooms, 4 pb
MC, Visa, *Rated*,  •
C-yes/S-ltd/P-no/H-no

Continental plus bkfst.
Snacks
Sitting room
bicycles

*1860s home furnished with antiques; pictures by local artists; nearby are antique shops, state parks, nature trails, restored canal town.*

## CORYDON

**Kinter House Inn**
P.O. Box 95,   47112
201 S. Capitol Ave.
812-738-2020
Mary Jane Bridgwater
All year

$-B&B
15 rooms, 15 pb
Most CC, *Rated*,  •
C-ltd

Full breakfast
Comp. coffee, tea, cider
Tennis/swim nearby
golf arrangements
piano organ, TVs & VCRs

*National Historic Registry. Victorian & country decor, fireplaces. In downtown historic Corydon—walk to attractions. 2 miles south of I-64. **Free gift to honeymooners.***

## EVANSVILLE

**Cool Breeze Estate B&B**
1240 S.E. Second St.,   47713
812-422-9635
Kateline & David Hills
All year

$$-B&B
4 rooms, 4 pb
AmEx, Disc.,
C-yes/S-no/H-no

Full breakfast
Sitting room, library
family friendly facility

*Historic Graham-Ingleheart 1906 home near river, 1½ shady acres. Spacious rooms. Dining room mural also in White House. Home-made breads.*

## FISHERS, INDIANAPOLIS

**Frederick-Talbot Inn, The**
13805 Allisonville Rd., 46038
317-578-3600  Fax: 317-579-3600
800-566-2337
Susan Muller, Ann Irvine
All year

$$$-B&B
10 rooms, 10 pb
Most CC, *Rated*, •
C-ltd/S-ltd/P-yes/H-yes

Full breakfast
Snacks
Sitting room

*Upscale twelve room inn is housed in two restored farmhouses and furnished with English country decor. All with private baths, TV's, phones. **Special mid-week discount.***

## GOSHEN

**Checkerberry Inn, The**
62644 County Rt 37, 46526
219-642-4445
John/Susan Graff, S. Reed
All year exc. January

$$$$-B&B
12 rooms, 12 pb
AmEx, MC, Visa,
*Rated*, •
C-ltd/S-ltd/H-yes

Continental plus bkfst.
Lunch/dinner, restaurant
Sitting room, library
tennis court, pool
croquet court, 100 acres

*European-style country inn surrounded by Amish farmland, 100 acres of fields and woods. French country cuisine, luxuriously comfortable decor. Large summer room seating 35.*

## GREENCASTLE

**Walden Inn of Greencastle**
PO Box 490, 2 Seminary
Square, 46135
317-653-2761
Matthew O'Neill
All year exc. Christmas

$$$-EP
AmEx, MC, Visa,
*Rated*, •
C-yes/S-yes/P-no/H-yes

Full breakfast
Restaurant, pub, lunch
bicycles, pool, sauna
tennis, golf, canoeing
meeting facilities

*A warm and unpretentious atmosphere with distinctive cuisine and personalized service. Guest rooms comfortably furnished with Amish furniture. Near quaint shops, restaurants.*

## HUNTINGTON

**Purviance House B&B**
326 S. Jefferson, SR #5 &
U.S.224, 46750
219-356-4218  219-356-9215
Bob & Jean Gernand
All year

$$-B&B
3 rooms, 2 pb
•
C-yes/S-no/P-no/H-no

Full breakfast
Lunch & dinner by res.
Comp. wine, tea, snacks
sitting room, library
kitchen privileges

*Lovingly restored 1859 National Register house furnished w/antiques, offers warm hospitality & homey comforts. Near historic & recreational areas. **10% off 2nd consec. night**.*

## INDIANAPOLIS

**Hoffman House, The**
P.O. Box 906, 46202
545 E. 11th St.
317-635-1701  Fax: 317-635-1701
Laura A. Arnold
May - October

$$-B&B
2 rooms,
MC, Visa, *Rated*, •
C-ltd/S-no/P-no/H-no

Continental plus bkfst.
Library, sitting room
fax, copier, modem
laser printer

*Affordable elegance in 1903 homestay in the heart of downtown. Close to State Capitol, Hoosier Dome and Convention Center. **After 10 nights, 11th night is free.***

**Nuthatch B&B, The**
7161 Edgewater Place, 46240
317-257-2660  Fax: 317-257-2677
Joan H. Morris
All year

$$$-B&B
2 rooms, 2 pb
*Rated*, •
C-ltd/S-ltd/P-no/H-no

Full breakfast
Tea, cookies, snacks
Sitting room, deck
picnic table, swing
canoe rental nearby

*1920s country French architecture in resort river setting minutes from downtown Indianapolis. **Free cooking class if party of 4 rents 2 rooms/2 nights. Thai breakfast on request.***

**INDIANAPOLIS**

| **Tranquil Cherub, The** | $$-B&B | Full gourmet breakfast |
|---|---|---|
| 2164 N. Capitol Ave., 46202 | 4 rooms, 4 pb | Snacks |
| 317-923-9036 | Visa, MC, AmEx, | Airport pickup |
| Barbara & Thom Feit | *Rated*, • | library, sitting room |
| All year | C-ltd/S-ltd/P-no/H-no | transportation downtown |

*Exciting downtown Indianapolis, museums, zoo, theatre, shopping, antiques, and gourmet breakfasts are yours at The Tranquil Cherub.*

**KNIGHTSTOWN**

| **Main Street Victorian B&B** | $$-B&B | Full breakfast |
|---|---|---|
| 130 W. Main St, 46148 | 3 rooms, 3 pb | Dessert |
| 317-345-2299 | Trav. Cks., Check, Cash, | Gardens, sitt rm, swing |
| Don & Ginny Warnick | S-ltd/P-no/H-no | bicycles, golf, TV, loft |
| All year | | special occ. packages |

*1870 restored Victorian on Antique Alley, coppersmith, covered bridges. 2 resident dogs. Business traveler friendly. 3rd night 50% and/or 10% AARP discount*

| **Old Hoosier House B&B** | $$-B&B | Full gourmet breakfast |
|---|---|---|
| 7601 S. Greensboro Pike, 46148 | 4 rooms, 3 pb | Cheese, snacks, dessert |
| | *Rated*, • | Sitting room |
| 317-345-2969  800-775-5315 | C-yes/S-ltd/P-no/H-no | library, bicycles |
| Jean & Tom Lewis | | special golf rates |
| All year | | |

*1840 country home near Indianapolis in antique area. Comfortable homey atmosphere; delicious breakfast on patio with view of Royal Golf Club. **Senior 10% discount; multiple night discount.***

**LA GRANGE**

| **1886 Inn, The** | $$$-B&B | Continental plus bkfst. |
|---|---|---|
| P.O. Box 5, 46761 | 3 rooms, 3 pb | Sitting room |
| 212 W. Factory St. | MC, Visa, *Rated*, | bicycles |
| 219-463-4227 | C-ltd/S-no/P-no/H-no | |
| D. & G. Billman, K. Shank | | |
| April-November | | |

*The 1866 Inn is filled with historical charm & elegance. Every room aglow with old-fashioned beauty. Finest lodging area, yet affordable. 10 min. from Shipshewana Flea Market.*

**MADISON**

| **Schussler House B&B** | $$$-B&B | Full breakfast |
|---|---|---|
| 514 Jefferson St., 47250 | 3 rooms, 3 pb | Snacks |
| 812-273-2068  800-392-1931 | Visa, MC, Disc., • | Sitting room |
| Judy & Bill Gilbert | C-ltd/S-no/P-no/H-no | |
| All year | | |

*Gracious accommodations in the heart of the historic district; a sumptuous breakfast served in the formal dining room.*

**MCCALL**

| **Bear Creek Lodge** | $$$-MAP | Full buffet breakfast |
|---|---|---|
| P.O. Box 8, 83654 | 13 rooms, 13 pb | Dinner, snacks |
| 3492 Hwy. 55, Marker 149 | Most CC, *Rated*, • | Restaurant, bar service |
| 208-634-3551 Fax: 208-634-4299 | | Sitting room, library |
| Mike & Debra Dunn | | Hot tubs |
| All year | | |

*Unique lodge and restaurant located on 65 beautiful acres. Accommodations feature fireplaces, whirl jet tubs, plush robes and more. **3rd night, 50% off.***

## MICHIGAN CITY

| **Hutchinson Mansion Inn** | $$$-B&B | Full breakfast |
|---|---|---|
| 220 W. 10th St., 46360 | 10 rooms, 10 pb | Snacks |
| 219-879-1700 | MC, Visa, *Rated*, • | Sitting room, piano |
| Ben & Mary DuVal | C-ltd/S-ltd/P-no/H-ltd | whirlpools, FAX |
| All year | | tennis & golf nearby |

*Elegant Victorian mansion filled with antiques, stained glass, friezes. Near Nat'l Lakeshore, dunes, beaches, antique stores, shopping, orchards, wineries. **3rd night 50% off.***

## MIDDLEBURY

| **Bee Hive B&B** | $$-B&B | Full breakfast |
|---|---|---|
| P.O. Box 1191, 46540 | 3 rooms, 1 pb | Comp. refreshments |
| 51129 CR 35, Bristol | MC, Visa, *Rated*, | Sitting room |
| 219-825-5023 Fax: 219-825-5023 | C-yes/S-no/P-no | restaurant nearby |
| Herb & Treva Swarm | | guest cottage available |
| All year | | |

*A country home in a relaxing atmosphere. Located in Amish Country with plenty of local attractions. Ski trails nearby. Easy access to Indiana Toll Road. **3rd night 50% off.***

| **Country Victorian B&B, The** | $$-B&B | Full breakfast |
|---|---|---|
| 435 South Main St., 46540 | 5 rooms, 4 pb | Afternoon tea |
| 219-825-2568 Fax: 219-825-3411 | Visa, MC, Disc., • | Sitting room, bicycles |
| Mark & Becky Potterbaum | C-yes/S-no/P-no/H-no | tennis courts nearby |
| All year | | |

*Charming Victorian in Northern Indiana Amish Country. Wonderful hospitality. Located near Shipshewana. Expansive Flea Market, antique auction. **Weekend packages available.***

| **Patchwork Quilt Cntry. Inn** | $$-B&B | Full breakfast |
|---|---|---|
| 11748 CR 2, 46540 | 15 rooms, 15 pb | Lunch, dinner available |
| 219-825-2417 Fax: 219-825-5172 | *Rated*, | Sitting room |
| Ray & Rosetta Miller | C-ltd/S-no/P-no/H-no | piano, Amish tours |
| All year | | gift shop, buggy rides |

*Prepare to be pampered in gracious country home. In Amish country. Near Shipshewana Flea Auction. Closed Sundays. Conference facilities.*

| **Varns Guest House** | $$$-B&B | Continental plus |
|---|---|---|
| P.O. Box 125, 46540 | 5 rooms, 5 pb | Complimentary candy |
| 205 S. Main St. | MC, Visa, *Rated*, • | Whirlpool tub in 1 room |
| 219-825-9666 800-398-5424 | C-yes/S-no/P-no/H-no | wrap-around porch |
| Carl & Diane Eash | | swing, TV, golfing, A/C |
| All year | | |

*Beautifully restored turn-of-the-century home in Amish community features modern luxury. Many country shops and fine dining nearby. **Free box of home made candy.***

## MIDDLETOWN

| **Cornerstone Guest House** | $$-B&B | Full breakfast |
|---|---|---|
| 705 High St., 47356 | 2 rooms, 2 pb | Snacks |
| 800-792-6004 Fax: 317-354-6057 | Visa, MC, | Sitting room, library |
| Dave & Debbie Lively | C-ltd/S-ltd/P-no/H-no | bicycles, computer & fax |
| All year | | for business travellers |

*Experience Hoosier hospitality with a touch of elegance in this 1909 home. Close to Indianapolis, outlet shopping, golf and horse racing.*

MUNCIE ───────────────────────────────────────────

| **Ole Ball Inn B&B** | $$-B&B | Full breakfast |
| 1000 W. Wayne St.,  47304 | 4 rooms, 4 pb | Snacks |
| 317-281-0466  Fax: 317-281-6439 | Visa, MC, AmEx, | Sitting room, organ |
| Momma Kreps | *Rated*, | cable TV, A/C |
| All year | C-ltd/S-ltd/P-no/H-no | |

*Comfortable Victorian home, new queen size beds, private, refrigerators, close to strip with restaurants & shopping, plentiful parking, 2 blocks to Ball State University.* **50% off a month's stay.**

NASHVILLE ────────────────────────────────────────

| **Allison House Inn** | $$$-B&B | Full breakfast |
| P.O. Box 1625,  47448 | 5 rooms, 5 pb | Library |
| 90 S. Jefferson | *Rated*, | sitting room |
| 812-988-0814 | C-ltd/S-no/P-no/H-no | |
| Tammy Galm | | |
| All year | | |

*In the heart of Brown County, the center for the arts and craft colony. Coziness, comfort and charm.*

───────────────────────────────────────────────────

| **Story Inn** | $$-B&B | Full country breakfast |
| 6404 S. State Rd. 135,  47448 | 12 rooms, 12 pb | Lunch, dinner, aft. tea |
| 812-988-2273  Fax: 812-988-6516 | Most CC, *Rated*, | Restaurant, sitting room |
| Bob Haddix | C-ltd/S-no/P-ltd/H-no | larger units available |
| All year | | for 2-6 persons |

*Bed & Breakfast lodging and surrounding village cottages. Furnished with period antiques, private baths, designer decorated and air conditioned.*

NEW ALBANY ───────────────────────────────────────

| **Honeymoon Mansion B&B** | $$-B&B | Full country breakfast |
| 1014 E. Main St.,  47150 | 6 rooms, 6 pb | Afternoon tea |
| 812-945-0312  800-759-7270 | Visa, MC, *Rated*, • | Bedtime snacks |
| Franklin & Beverly Dennis | C-ltd/S-ltd/P-no/H-yes | 9 miles to casinos |
| All year | | Wedding chapel |

*A National Historic Register landmark. Six lovely suites; three marble jacuzzis. Gourmet breakfast. Finished in genuine antiques. State Park nearby.* **3rd night 50%, ltd.**

RICHMOND ─────────────────────────────────────────

| **Phillip W. Smith B&B** | $$-B&B | Full breakfast |
| 2039 E. Main St.,  47374 | 4 rooms, 4 pb | Afternoon tea, snacks |
| 317-966-8972  800-966-8972 | Visa, MC, *Rated*, | Library, 4 guest rooms |
| Chip & Chartley Bondurant | C-yes/S-ltd/P-no/H-no | with traditional decor |
| All year | | and comfortable seating |

*1890 Queen Anne Victorian on National Register of Historic Places. Stained glass and ornate wood throughout. Lovely gardens. Nearby parks, lakes, antiquing.*

ROCKVILLE ────────────────────────────────────────

| **"Suits Us" B&B** | $$-B&B | Continental breakfast |
| 514 N. College St,  47872 | 5 rooms, 5 pb | Full breakfast (weekend) |
| 317-569-5660 | *Rated*, | Sitting room, library |
| Bob & Ann McCullough | C-ltd/S-no/P-no/H-no | color TVs, books in rms |
| All year | | bicycles, tennis court |

*Classic plantation-style home w/beautiful spiral hanging staircase. Large porch w/wicker rockers. Close to Turkey Run State Park, Billie Creek Village & universities.*

## SOUTH BEND

| | | |
|---|---|---|
| **Book Inn B&B, The** | $$$-B&B | Continental plus bkfst. |
| 508 W. Washington St., 46601 | 5 rooms, 5 pb | Library, sitting room |
| 219-288-1990 | Visa, MC, AmEx, | quality used bookstore |
| Peggy & John Livingston | *Rated*, • | located downstairs |
| All year | C-ltd/S-no/P-no/H-no | |

*Designers Showcase Second Empire urban home. Twelve-foot ceilings, irreplaceable butternut woodwork, comfortable antiques & fresh flowers welcome you.* **3rd night, 50%.**

| | | |
|---|---|---|
| **Queen Anne Inn** | $$-B&B | Full breakfast |
| 420 W. Washington St., 46601 | 6 rooms, 6 pb | Snacks, tea on Thursdays |
| 219-234-5959 800-582-2379 | AmEx, MC, Visa, | Sitting room, library |
| Robert & Pauline Medhurst | *Rated*, • | phones, TV in rooms, FAX |
| All year | C-yes/S-ltd/P-no/H-no | conference room (15-25) |

*Relax in a charming 1893 Victorian home with Frank Lloyd Wright influence—near city center & many restaurants. Victorian getaway package w/carriage ride, dinner, museum.*

## SPENCER

| | | |
|---|---|---|
| **Canyon Inn** | $-EP | Restaurant |
| P.O. Box 71, 47460 | 76 rooms, 76 pb | Sitting room |
| McCormic's Ck., State Pk. | Most CC, | tennis court, pool |
| 812-829-4881 Fax: 812-829-1467 | C-yes/S-yes/P-no/H-yes | |
| All year | | |

*Country style inn located in McCormic's Creek State Park setting; outdoor recreation at its best; relaxed atmosphere; families and groups welcome.*

## SYRACUSE

| | | |
|---|---|---|
| **Anchor Inn B&B** | $$-B&B | Full breakfast |
| 11007 N. State Rd. 13, 46567 | 6 rooms, 4 pb | Comp. coffee and tea |
| 219-457-4714 888-347-7481 | MC, Visa, Disc. *Rated*, | Adjacent to golf course |
| Robert & Jean Kennedy | S-no/P-no/H-no | Across from Lake Wawasee |
| All year | | |

*Turn-of-the-century home filled with period furniture. Close to Amish communities & several antique shops. Many lakes in the area & adjacent to 18-hole public golf course.*

## VALPARAISO

| | | |
|---|---|---|
| **Inn at Aberdeen, The** | $$$-B&B | Full gourmet breakfast |
| 3158 S. State Rd. 2, 46383 | 11 rooms, 11 pb | Snacks, comp. wine |
| 219-465-3753 Fax: 219-465-0259 | Most CC, *Rated*, | Sitting room, library |
| S Simon, L & J Johnson | C-yes/S-no/P-no/H-yes | bikes, hot tubs |
| All year | | conference center |

*Travel back to the 1800s while enjoying your own jacuzzi, balcony, cozy fire and truly regal service and amenities. Free bottle of wine.*

## WARSAW

| | | |
|---|---|---|
| **White Hill Inn** | $$-B&B | Full breakfast |
| 2513 E. Center St., 46580 | 8 rooms, | Suite w/dbl jacuzzi |
| 219-269-6933 Fax: 219-268-1936 | Most CC, *Rated*, | Conference room |
| Carm & Zoyla Henderson | C-yes/S-ltd/P-no/H-yes | sitting room |
| All year | German | |

*Restored English Tudor mansion. 8 elegant rooms w/bath, TV, A/C. Adjacent to Wagon Wheel Theater, lake recreation, antique shops.* **2 night special, including dinner certificate.**

# More Inns . . .

| | |
|---|---|
| Albion | Pathfinder Country Inn, 3491 S. 200 W., 46701,  219-636-2888 |
| Alexandria | Country Gazebo Inn,  RR 1, Box 323, 46001,  317-754-8783 |
| Alexandria | Inter Urban Inn,  503 S. Harrison, 46001,  317-724-2001 |
| Angola | Potawatomi Inn,  6 Lane 100 A Lake James, 46703,  219-833-1077 |
| Angola | Sycamore Hill,  1245 S. Golden Lake Rd., 46703,  219-665-2690 |
| Attica | Apple Inn Museum B&B,  P.O. Box 145, 47918,  317-762-6574 |
| Auburn | Auburn Inn, 225 Touring Dr., 46707 |
| Auburn | Hill Top Country Inn,  1733 CR 28, 46706,  219-281-2529 |
| Austin | Morgan's Farm,  730 W. St. Rd. 256, 47102,  812-794-2536 |
| Berne | Hans Haus of Berne, 166 Columbia St., 46711,  219-589-3793 |
| Berne | Schug House Inn,  706 West Main St., 46711 |
| Bloomington | Bauer House, 4595 N. Maple Grove Rd., 47401 |
| Bloomington | Cartwright Home, 2927 N. Bankers Dr., 47401 |
| Bloomington | Quilt Haven B&B,  711 Dittemore Rd., 47404,  812-876-5802 |
| Bloomington | Scholars Inn, 801 N. Gollege, 47404,  800-765-3466 |
| Bluffton | Wisteria Manor,  411 W. Market St., 46714,  219-824-4619 |
| Bristol | Milburn House, 707 E. Vistula St., 46507,  219-848-4026 |
| Bristol | Open Hearth B&B, 56782 SR 15, 46507,  219-825-2417 |
| Bristol | Rust Hollar B&B,  55238 C.R. 31, 46507,  219-825-1111 |
| Bristol | Tyler's Place,  19562 S.R. 120, 46507,  219-848-7145 |
| Brookville | Duck Creek Farm B&B,  12246 SR 1, 47012,  317-647-4575 |
| Brookville | Sulina Farm,  10052 U.S. 52, 47012,  317-647-2955 |
| Cambridge City | Overbeck House,  520 E. Church, 47327 |
| Cannelton | Castlebury Inn,  615 Washinston, 47520,  812-547-4714 |
| Centerville | Historic Lantz House Inn,  214 National Road West, 47330,  317-855-2936 |
| Chesterton | Wingfield's Inn B&B,  526 Indian Oak Mall, 46304,  702-348-0766 |
| Churubusco | Sycamore Spring Farm,  Box 224, 46723,  219-693-3603 |
| Columbus | Lafayette Street B&B,  723 Lafayette St., 47201, 812-372-7245 |
| Corydon | Warren Cabin B&B,  1161 Church St., 47112,  812-738-2166 |
| Crawfordsville | Davis House,  1010 W. Wabash Ave., 47933,  317-364-0461 |
| Crawfordsville | Sugar Creek's Queen Anne,  P.O. Box 726, 47933,  800-392-6293 |
| Crawfordsville | Yount's Mill Inn, 3729 Old State Rd. 32 W, 47933,  317-362-5864 |
| Danville | Fairhavens,  320 W. Main St., 46122,  317-745-0417 |
| Danville | Marigold Manor,  368 W. Main St., 46122,  317-745-2347 |
| Decatur | Cragwood Inn B&B,  303 N. Second St., 46733,  219-728-2000 |
| Elkhart | Eby's B&B,  29168 CR 30, 46517 |
| Evansville | Brigadoon B&B Inn,  1240 SE 2nd St., 47713,  812-422-9635 |
| Fort Wayne | Carole Lombard House,  704 Rockhill St., 46802,  219-426-9896 |
| Fort Wayne | Union Chapel B&B,  6336 Union Chapel Rd., 46845,  219-627-5663 |
| Fowler | Pheasant Country B&B,  900 E. 5th St., 47944,  317-884-0908 |
| Franklin | Oak Haven,  4975 Hurricane Rd., 46131,  317-535-9491 |
| Goshen | B&B on the Farm,  26620 C.R. 40, 46526,  219-862-4600 |
| Goshen | Country B&B, 27727 CR 36, 46526,  219-862-2748 |
| Goshen | Flower Patch B&B,  16263 CR 22, 46526,  219-534-4207 |
| Goshen | Indian Creek B&B,  20300 Cr. 18, 46526 |
| Goshen | Ol' Barn B&B,  63469 C.R. 33, 46526,  219-642-3222 |
| Goshen | Royer's,  22781 C.R. 38, 46526,  219-533-1821 |
| Goshen | Spring View B&B,  63189 C.R. 31, 46526,  219-642-3997 |
| Goshen | Timberidge B&B,  16801 SR 4, 46526,  219-533-7133 |
| Goshen | Waterford B&B,  3004 S. Main St., 46526,  219-533-6044 |
| Goshen | Whippoorwill Valley Inn,  63608 C.R. 11, 46526,  219-875-5746 |
| Goshen | White Birch B&B,  17200 Institutional Dr., 46526,  219-533-3763 |
| Grandview | Grandview Guest House,  Box 311, 47615,  812-649-2817 |
| Grandview | River Belle B&B, The,  P.O. Box 669, 47615,  800-877-5165 |
| Granger | 1900 House, The,  50777 Ridgemoor Way, 46530,  219-277-7783 |
| Greenwood | Candlestick Inn,  402 Euclid Ave., 46142,  317-888-3905 |
| Hagerstown | Teetor House, The,  300 West Main St., 47346,  317-489-4422 |
| Hartford City | De'Coy's B&B,  1546 W. 100 N., 47348,  317-348-2164 |
| Howe | Lasata B&B,  702 Defiance St., 46746,  219-562-3655 |
| Huntington | Purviance House B&B,  326 S. Jefferson, 46750,  219-356-4218 |
| Idianapolis | Old Northside B&B,  1340 N. Alabama, 46202,  800-635-9127 |
| Indianapolis | Boone Docks on the River,  7159 Edgewater Pl., 46240,  317-257-3671 |
| Indianapolis | Friendliness With A Flair,  5214 E. 20th Place, 46218,  317-356-3149 |
| Indianapolis | Harney House Inn,  345 N. East St., 46202,  317-636-7527 |
| Indianapolis | Laura Arnold,  P.O. Box 906, 46206 |
| Indianapolis | Le Chateau Delaware,  1456 N. Delaware, 46202 |
| Indianapolis | Stonegate B&B,  8955 A Stonegate Rd., 46227,  317-887-9614 |
| Jamestown | Oakwood B&B,  9530 W. US Hwy. 136, 46147,  317-676-5114 |
| Jasper | Artist's Studio B&B,  429 W. Haysville, 47546 |
| Jasper | Powers Inn B&B,  325 W. 6th St., 47546,  812-482-3018 |
| Jeffersonville | 1877 House Country Inn,  1408 Utica-Sellersburg, 47130 |
| Kendallville | Olde McCray Mansion Inn,  703 E. Mitchell St., 46755,  219-347-3647 |
| Knightstown | Olde Country Club,  8544 S. County Rd., 46148,  317-345-5381 |
| Koontz Lake | Koontz House B&B,  7514 N. Hwy 23, 46574,  219-586-7090 |

| | |
|---|---|
| Ladoga | Vintage Reflections, 125 W. Main St., 47954, 317-942-1002 |
| Lagrange | Atwater Century Farm, 4240 W. US 20, 46761, 219-463-2743 |
| Lagrange | M & N B&B, 215 N. Detroit, 46761, 219-463-2699 |
| Lagrange | Weavers Country Oaks, RR 4, Box 193H, 46761, 219-768-7191 |
| Lagro | Celene Kandis, General Delivery, 46941 |
| Laotto | Tea Rose B&B, 7711 E. 500 S., 46763, 219-693-2884 |
| Lapel | Kati-Scarlett B&B, P.O. Box 756, 46051, 317-534-4937 |
| Laurel | Ferris Inn, P.O. Box 197, 47024, 317-698-2259 |
| Lawrenceburg | Folke Family Farm, P.O. Box 66, 47025 |
| Leavenworth | Ye Olde Scotts Inn, RR 1, Box 5, 47137, 812-739-4747 |
| Leesburg | Prairie House B&B, 495 E. 900 N., 46538, 219-658-9211 |
| Ligonier | Minuette, 210 S. Main St., 46767, 219-894-4494 |
| Ligonier | Solomon Mier Manor, 508 S. Cavin St., 46767, 219-894-3668 |
| Loogootee | Stone Ridge Manor B&B, 612 Kentucky Ave., 47553, 812-295-3382 |
| Madison | Autumnwood B&B, 165 Autumnwood Ln., 47250, 812-265-5262 |
| Madison | Cliff House B&B, 122 Fairmount Dr., 47250, 812-265-5272 |
| Madison | Clifty Inn, P.O. Box 387, 47250, 812-265-4135 |
| Madison | Main Street B&B, 739 W. Main St., 47250 |
| Madison | Millwood House, 512 West St., 47250, 812-265-6780 |
| Marshall | Turkey Run Inn, R.R. 1 Box 444, 47859, 317-597-2211 |
| Metamora | Gingerbread House, P.O. Box 28, 47030, 317-647-5518 |
| Metamora | Grapevine Inn, P.O.Box 207, 47030, 317-647-3738 |
| Metamora | Publick House, P.O. Box 202, 47030, 317-647-6729 |
| Metamora | Thorpe House, Clayborne St., 47030, 317-647-5425 |
| Michigan City | Creekwood Inn, Rt 20-35 at I-94, 46360, 219-872-8357 |
| Michigan City | Duneland Beach Inn, 3311 Potawatomi, 46360, 219-874-7729 |
| Middlebury | Auer House, 11584 C.R. 14, 46540, 219-825-5366 |
| Middlebury | Bittersweet Hill, P.O.Box 1147, 46540, 219-852-5953 |
| Middlebury | Bontreger Guest Rooms, 10766 C.R. 16, 46540, 219-825-2647 |
| Middlebury | Coneygar, 54835 C.R. 33, 46540, 219-825-5707 |
| Middlebury | Empty Nest B&B, 13347 C.R. 12, 46540, 219-825-1042 |
| Middlebury | Essenhaus Country Inn, 240 US 20, 46540, 219-825-9471 |
| Middlebury | Johnson's B&B, 56823 Oak Dale Dr., 46540 |
| Middlebury | Lookout Bed & Breakfast, 14544 CR-12, 46540 |
| Middlebury | Mary's Place, 305 Eugene Dr., PBx 428, 46540, 219-825-2429 |
| Middlebury | Mill Street B&B, P.O. Box 91, 46540, 219-825-5359 |
| Middlebury | The Tayler House, P.O. Box 1131, 46540, 219-825-7296 |
| Middlebury | Theora's B&B, 525 S. Wayne St., 46540, 800-528-4111 |
| Middlebury | Windmill Hideaway B&B, 11380 W. SR 120, 46540, 219-825-2939 |
| Middlebury | Yoder's Zimmer, P.O. Box 1396, 46540, 219-825-2378 |
| Middlebury | Zimmer Haus, 120 Orpha Dr., 46540 |
| Middletown | Country Rode B&B, 5098 N.Mechanicsburg Rd, 47356, 317-779-4501 |
| Middletown | Maple Hill B&B, 9909 N.C.R. 600W, 47356, 317-354-2580 |
| Millersburg | Big House in Little Woods, 4245 S. 1000 W, 46543, 219-593-9076 |
| Mishawaka | Beiger Mansion Inn, 317 Lincoln Way East, 46544, 219-256-0365 |
| Mishawaka | Kamm House, 617 Lincolnway W., 46544, 800-664-5790 |
| Mitchell | Spring Mill Inn, P.O. Box 68, 47446, 812-849-4081 |
| Monon | Bestemor's House B&B, 201 Market Box 205, 47959, 219-253-8351 |
| Monticello | 1887 Black Dog Inn, 2830 Untalulti, 47960, 219-583-8297 |
| Monticello | The Victoria B&B, 206 S. Bluff St., 47960, 219-583-3440 |
| Morgantown | Rock House Country Inn, P.O. Box 10, 46160, 812-597-5100 |
| Muncie | Spurgeon Inn, 1101 N. Wheeling Ave., 47303 |
| N. Manchester | Fruitt Basket Inn B&B, 116 W. Main St., 46962, 219-982-2443 |
| Nappanee | Bob & Arlene Mast, 26206 CR 50, 46550, 219-773-4714 |
| Nappanee | Homespun Country Inn, P.O. Box 369, 46550, 219-773-2034 |
| Nappanee | Indiana Amish Country B&B, 1600 W. Market St., 46550, 219-773-4188 |
| Nappanee | Market Street Guest House, 253 E. Market St., 46550, 219-773-2261 |
| Nappanee | Olde Buffalo Inn, 1061 Parkwood Dr., 46550, 800-272-2135 |
| Nappanee | Victorian Guest House, 302 E. Market, 46550, 219-773-4383 |
| Nashville | Abe Martin Lodge, P.O. Box 547, 47448, 812-988-4418 |
| Nashville | Chestnut Hill Log Home B&B, RR 4, Box 295, Hoover, 47448, 812-988-4995 |
| Nashville | Coffey House B&B, Route 4, Box 179, 47448 |
| Nashville | Fifth Generation Farm, 4564 N. Bear Wallow Rd., 47448, 812-988-7553 |
| Nashville | Mindheim's Inn, RR 5, Box 592, 47448 |
| Nashville | Plain & Fancy, SR 135 N., RR 3, Box 62, 47448, 812-988-4537 |
| Nashville | Seasons, P.O. Box 187, 47448, 812-988-2284 |
| Nashville | Victoria House, Route 4, Box 414, 47448, 812-988-6344 |
| Nashville | Wraylyn Knoll Inn, P.O. Box 481, 47448, 812-988-0733 |
| New Castle | Country Haven Inn, 395 N.C.R. 300 W, 47362, 317-533-6611 |
| New Harmony | Mrs. Bill Williams, Route 1, Box 167, 47631 |
| New Harmony | Raintree Inn, P.O. Box 566, 47631 |
| Newburgh | Phelps Mansion Inn, 208 State St., 47630, 812-853-7766 |
| Paoli | Big Locust Farms, 3295 W.C.R 25 S, 47454, 812-723-4856 |
| Paoli | Braxtan House Inn B&B, 210 N. Gospel St., 47454, 812-723-4677 |
| Peru | Rosewood Mansion Inn, 54 North Hood St., 46970, 317-472-7151 |
| Plymouth | Driftwood, P.O. Box 16, 46563, 219-546-2274 |

| Richland | Country Homestead Guest Ho, Route 1, Box 353, 47634, 812-359-4870 |
| Richmond | Norwich Lodge, 920 Earlham Dr., 47374, 317-983-1575 |
| Rising Sun | Jelley House Country Inn, 222 S. Walnut St., 47040, 812-438-2319 |
| Roanoke | James and Ann Crawford, 161 W. 4th St., 46783 |
| Rochester | Minnow Creek Farm, RR 3 Box 381, 46975 |
| Rockport | Rockport Inn, 130 S. Third St., 47635 |
| Rockville | "Suits Us" B&B, 514 N. College St., 47872, 317-569-5660 |
| Salem | Lanning House, 206 E. Poplar St., 47167, 812-883-3484 |
| Shipshewana | Country Inn, Route 1, Box 19, 46565 |
| Shipshewana | Green Meadow Ranch, 7905 W. 450 N., 46565, 219-768-4221 |
| Shipshewana | Morton Street B&B, 140 Morton St., Box 3, 46565 |
| Shoals | Brenda Rodgers, Route 3, Box 70B, 47581 |
| South Bend | Home B&B, 21166 Clover Hill Ct., 46614, 219-291-0535 |
| South Bend | Jamison Inn, 1404 N. Ivy Rd., 46637, 219-277-9682 |
| South Bend | Oliver Inn B&B, 630 W. Washington St., 46601, 219-232-4545 |
| Speedway | Speedway Inn B&B, 5223 W. 16th St., 46224, 317-487-6531 |
| Taswell | Victoria Bay B&B, Rt. 2 Box 22C, 46567, 812-338-3120 |
| Terre Haute | Deere Run B&B, 6218 N. 13th St., 47805 |
| Tippecanoe | Bessinger's Hillfarm B&B, 4588 SR 110, 46570, 219-223-3288 |
| Topeka | Four Woods B&B, 4800 South SR 5, 46571, 219-593-2021 |
| Unionville | Possum Trot B&B, 8310 N. Possum Trot Rd., 47468, 812-988-2694 |
| Valparaiso | Embassy B&B, P.O. Box 42, 46383 |
| Vincennes | The Harrison Inn, 902 Buntin St., 47591, 812-882-3243 |
| Wabash | Around Window Inn, 313 W. Hill St., 46992, 219-563-6901 |
| Wabash | Lamp-Post Inn, 261 W. Hill St., 46992, 219-563-3094 |
| Walkerton | Hesters Cabin B&B, 71880 S.R. 23, 46574, 219-568-2105 |
| Walkerton | Koontz House B&B, R.R. 3 Box 592, 46574, 219-586-7090 |
| Warsaw | Candlelight Inn, 503 E. Fort Wayne St., 46580, 219-267-2906 |
| Washington | Haven B&B, P.O. Box 798, 47501, 812-254-7770 |
| Washington | Mimi's House, 101 W. Maple St., 47501, 812-254-5562 |
| Westfield | Camel Lot, 4512 W. 131st St., 46074, 317-873-4370 |
| Westfield | Country Roads Guesthouse, 2731 West 146th St., 46074, 317-846-2376 |
| Winona Lake | Gunn Guest House, 904 Park Ave., 46590, 219-267-2023 |
| Zionsville | Brick Street Inn, 175 S. Main St., 46077, 317-873-5895 |

*The Queen Anne Inn,*
*South Bend, IN*

# Iowa

## ATLANTIC

**Chestnut Charm B&B**
1409 Chestnut St., 50022
712-243-5652
Barbara Stensvad
All year

$$-MAP
5 rooms, 5 pb
MC, Visa, *Rated*, •
S-no/P-no/H-no

Full breakfast
Dinner with reservation
Sitting room, piano
A/C, sun rooms, antiques
fountained patio, gazebo

*Enchanting 1898 Victorian mansion on large estate. Just a short drive to the famous bridges of Madison County. Gourmet dining. Experience beauty & fantasy w/someone special.*

## BURLINGTON

**Mississippi Manor**
809 N. 4th, 52601
309-753-2218
Michael Cline
All year

$$-B&B
4 rooms, 4 pb
Visa, MC, •
C-ltd/S-no/P-no/H-no

Continental breakfast
Full breakfast avail.
Lunch, dinner (fee)
sitting room, porch
bicycles

*Renovated Victorian Italianate home c.1877; along the Mississippi in charming river town; easy highway, rail and airplane access.*

*Juniper Hill Farm B&B, Dubuque, IA*

## DUBUQUE

| **Juniper Hill Farm B&B** | $$-B&B | Full breakfast |
| 15325 Budd Rd., 52002 | 3 rooms, 3 pb | Snacks |
| 319-582-4405 Fax: 319-583-6607 | Visa, MC, Disc., • | Sitt. rm., library, bike |
| 800-572-1449 | C-ltd/S-no/P-no/H-no | hot tubs, golf courses |
| Ruth & Bill McEllhiney | | pond fishing, skiing |
| All year | | |

*Enjoy warm hospitality & country elegance at this B&B in the beautiful Mississippi River hills. An inn for all seasons - bird watching, hikes. **Snacks & beverages in evening.***

| **Richards House, The** | $-B&B | Full breakfast |
| 1492 Locust St., 52001 | 5 rooms, 4 pb | Snacks |
| 319-557-1492 | Most CC, *Rated*, • | Sitting room, antiques |
| Michelle Delaney | C-yes/S-ltd/P-ltd/H-no | concealed TVs, phones |
| All year | | fireplaces |

*1883 Stick-style Victorian mansion with over 80 stained-glass windows. Seven varieties of woodwork and period furnishings. Working fireplaces in guest rooms.*

## FORT MADISON

| **Mississippi Rose & Thistle** | $$-B&B/MAP/AP | Full gourmet breakfast |
| 532 Avenue F, 52627 | 5 rooms, 5 pb | Lunch & dinner |
| 319-372-7044 | • | Snacks, comp. wine |
| Bill & Bonnie Saunders | C-ltd/S-no/P-no/H-ltd | sitting room, library |
| All year | | sauna, boating, fishing |

*Victorian Italianate mansion w/period antiques, located in the historic district, offering romance, sumptuous elegant feasts & graciousness. **10% discount November–April.***

## FT. MADISON

| **Kingsley Inn** | $$-B&B | Continental plus bkfst. |
| 707 Ave. H., 52627 | 14 rooms, 14 pb | Snacks, restaurant |
| 319-372-7074 Fax: 319-372-7096 | Most CC, *Rated*, • | Sitting room |
| 800-441-2327 | C-ltd/S-no/P-no/H-yes | hot tubs |
| N. Evans/F. Colbert/C. Click | | |
| All year | | |

*Historic inn on Mississippi River. Antique furnishings, all modern conveniences, museums, shops, riverboat, fifteen miles to Nauvoo, Illinois. **10% off room rate.***

## GREENFIELD

**Brass Lantern, The**　　　$$-B&B　　　Full breakfast
2446 State Hwy. 92, 50849　　2 rooms, 2 pb　　Wine & cheese social hr.
515-743-2031 Fax: 515-343-7500　C-yes/S-ltd/P-ltd　Indoor swimming pool
Terry & Margie Moore　　　　　　　　　　　　guest kitchen, library
All year　　　　　　　　　　　　　　　　　challenging golf course

*Spacious guestrooms open directly to indoor pool overlooking Iowa's countryside. Antique shops and tennis nearby. Whole house rental available. Near bridges of Madison County.* **3rd nite 50% off.**

## MAQUOKETA

**Squiers Manor B&B**　　　　$$-B&B　　　　Full gourmet breakfast
418 W. Pleasant St., 52060　　8 rooms, 8 pb　　Sitting room, library
319-652-6961　　　　　　　　MC, Visa, AmEx,　bridal suite available
Virl & Kathy Banowetz　　　　*Rated*,　　　　fireplaces, whirlpool
All year　　　　　　　　　　C-yes/S-ltd/P-no/H-no

*Experience Victorian elegance, ambiance & hospitality at its finest. Private whirlpool baths, fireplaces, antiques. Candlelight evening dessert. 1100 square foot suite avail.*

## MCGREGOR

**McGregor Manor**　　　　　$$-B&B　　　　Full breakfast
320 4th St., 52157　　　　　4 rooms, 4 pb　　Snacks, comp. wine
319-873-2600 Fax: 319-873-2218　Visa, MC, *Rated*,　Dinner (fee)
Carolyn & David Scott　　　　C-ltd/S-no/P-no/H-no　Sitting room, bicyles
All year

*Come share the warmth and hospitality of our home, one that will transport you back to an era of Victorian elegance and charm.* **Complimentary wine and cheese.**

## NEWTON

**LaCorsette Maison Inn**　　　$$-B&B　　　　Full breakfast
629 First Ave E, 50208　　　　7 rooms, 7 pb　　Gourmet dinner, Rest.
515-792-6833 Fax: 515-792-6597　MC, Visa AmEx,　Whirlpools, fireplaces
Kay Owen　　　　　　　　　*Rated*, •　　　sitting room. Near I-35.
All year　　　　　　　　　　C-ltd/S-no/P-ltd/H-no　Near Des Moines on I-80.

*Turn-of-the-century mission-style mansion. Charming French bedchambers, beckoning hearths. Gourmet Dining 4-1/2 star rating. One suite has double whirlpool.*

## PRINCETON

**Woodlands Inn B&B, The**　　$$-B&B　　　　Full breakfast
P.O. Box 127, 52768　　　　　2 rooms, 2 pb　　Lunch, dinner available
319-289-4661 800-257-3177　　MC, Visa, *Rated*, •　Snacks, sitt. rm., bikes
The Wallace Family　　　　　C-yes/S-ltd/P-yes/H-no　library, pool, hot tub
All year　　　　　　　　　　Sp., Norwegian, Port.　near Mississippi River

*A secluded woodland escape nestled among pines on 26 acres of forest & meadows. Elegant breakfast by pool/cozy fireplace. Skiing, fishing, golf, nature trails.* **3rd night 40% off.**

## SWEDESBURG

**Carlson House, The**　　　　$$-B&B　　　　Full breakfast
105 Park. St., 52652　　　　　2 rooms, 2 pb　　Afternoon tea, snacks
319-254-2451 Fax: 319-254-2451　C-ltd/S-no/P-no/H-no　Lunch, dinner (fee)
Ruth & Ned Ratekin　　　　　　　　　　　　sitting room, library
All year

*The stately Carlson House provides a Swedish accent in decor, foods and ambiance. Comfortable lounging in sitting rooms & porches. A rich supply of browsing materials, air conditioning , & gracious hosts.*

## TAMA

| | | |
|---|---|---|
| **Hummingbird Haven B&B** | $$-B&B | Full breakfast |
| 1201 Harding St.,   52339 | 2 rooms, | Afternoon tea, snacks |
| 515-484-2022 | Visa, MC, *Rated*, | Lunch & dinner (fee) |
| Bernita Thomsen | C-yes/S-no/P-no/H-no | central air |
| All year | | |

*Refurbished turn of the century home. Guest rooms decorated w/antiques. Fishing, golf and casino nearby. Within an hour of Cedar Rapids, Des Moines.* **3rd night, 50%.**

## VINTON

| | | |
|---|---|---|
| **Lion & The Lamb, The** | $$-B&B | Full breakfast |
| 913 2nd Ave.,   52349 | 3 rooms, 1 pb | Evening dessert |
| 319-472-5086  Fax: 319-472-9115 | Visa, MC, • | Sitting room, bicycles |
| 800-808-LAMB | C-yes/S-no/P-no/H-no | year round boutique |
| Richard & Rachel Waterbury | | many attractions nearby |
| All year | | |

*1892 Victorian mansion with seven fireplaces. Each guest room has a queen size bed, air conditioning, ceiling fan and TV.* **Business discount Sunday thru Thursday nights.**

## WATERLOO

| | | |
|---|---|---|
| **Wellington B&B** | $$-B&B | Gourmet full breakfast |
| 800 West Fourth St.,   50702 | 4 rooms, 4 pb | Whirlpools in suites |
| 319-234-2993 | Most CC, *Rated*, • | screened porches |
| Jim & Reatha Aronson | C-ltd/S-no/P-no/H-no | library, sitting rooms |
| All year | | |

*Nat'l. Registry Mansion. Business travelers/honeymooners enjoy gourmet bkfsts. in spacious priv. suites. Guests return for peaceful, gracious "old-time" living.* **5th night free.**

# More Inns . . .

| | |
|---|---|
| Adair | Lalley House, 701 5th St., 50002,  515-742-5541 |
| Adel | The Grey Goose B&B, 1740-290th, 50003,  515-833-2338 |
| Akron | Wildflower Log Cabin B&B, Box 1, RR 3, 51001,  712-568-2206 |
| Alta | Addie's Place B&B, 121 Cherokee St., 51002,  712-284-2509 |
| Ames | Green Belt B&B, RR 2, 50010,  515-232-1960 |
| Battle Creek | Inn at Battle Creek, The, 201 Maple St., 51006,  712-365-4949 |
| Bellevue | Mont Rest, 300 Spring St., 52031,  319-872-4220 |
| Bellevue | Spring Side Inn, P.O. Box 41, RR 2, 52031,  319-872-5452 |
| Boone | Barkley House B&B, 326 Boone St., 50036,  515-432-7885 |
| Brayton | Hallock House B&B, The, P.O. Box 9, 50042,  712-549-2449 |
| Brooklyn | Hotel Brooklyn, 154 Front St., 52211,  515-522-9229 |
| Buckingham | The ABC Country Inn, 2637 Hwy. D-65, 50612,  319-478-2321 |
| Calmar | Calmar Guesthouse B&B, 103 North St., 52132,  319-562-3851 |
| Cedar Falls | Carriage House Inn B&B, 3030 Grand Blvd., 50613,  319-277-6724 |
| Cedar Falls | Melody Acres Country B&B, 5829 N. Union Rd., 50613,  319-277-8206 |
| Cedar Rapids | Gwendolyn's B&B, 1809 Second Ave., S.E., 52403,  319-363-9731 |
| Cedar Rapids | Snoozie's B&B, 1570 Hwy. 30 East, 52403,  319-364-2134 |
| Centerville | One of a Kind, 314 W. State, 52544,  515-437-4540 |
| Clarinda | Colonial White House B&B, 400 N. 16th-Glen Miller, 51632,  712-542-5006 |
| Clarinda | Paiges of Thyme, 222 W. Washington, 51632,  712-542-5796 |
| Clarinda | Westcott House, 510 W. Main, 51632,  712-542-5323 |
| Clear Lake | Budget Inn, Box 102, 50428 |
| Clear Lake | Larch Pine Inn, 401 N. 3rd St., 50428,  515-357-7854 |
| Clear Lake | Norsk Hus By-The-Shore, 3611 N. Shore Dr., 50428,  515-357-8368 |
| Clear Lake | North Shore House, 1519 N. Shore Dr., 50428,  515-357-4443 |
| Clermont | Mill St. B&B, P.O. Box 34, 52135,  319-423-5531 |
| Colo | Martha's Vineyard, Box 247, 50056,  515-377-2586 |
| Council Bluffs | Terra Jane Country Inn, Rt 5, Box 69, 51503,  712-322-4200 |
| Davenport | Bishop's House Inn, 1597 Brady St., 52803,  319-324-2454 |
| Davenport | Fulton's Landing, 1206 E. River Dr., 52803,  319-322-4069 |
| Davenport | River Oaks Inn B&B, 1234 E. River Dr., 52803,  800-352-6016 |
| Decorah | Montgomery Mansion, 812 Maple Ave., 52101,  319-382-5088 |
| Decorah | Orval & Diane Bruvold, Route 1, 52101,  319-382-4729 |
| Denison | Conner's Corner B&B, 104 S. 15th St., 51442,  712-263-8826 |
| Denison | Queen Belle B&B, 1430 3rd Ave. S., 51442,  712-263-6777 |
| Des Moines | Carter House, 640 Twentieth St., 50314,  515-288-7850 |
| Des Moines | Jardin Suite, 6653 NW Timberline Dr., 50313,  515-289-2280 |

| | |
|---|---|
| Dubuque | Another World-Paradise, 16338 Paradise Valley, 52039,  319-552-1034 |
| Dubuque | Hancock House, 1105 Grove Terrace, 52001,  319-557-8989 |
| Dubuque | Mandolin Inn, The, 199 Loras Blvd., 52001,  319-556-0069 |
| Dubuque | Redstone Inn, The, 504 Bluff St., 52001,  319-582-1894 |
| Dunlap | Get-Away, The, Rt. 2, P.O. Box 109, 51529,  712-643-5584 |
| Elk Horn | Joy's Morning Glory B&B, 4308 Main St., 51531,  712-764-5631 |
| Elk Horn | Rainbow H. Lodging House, RR 1, Box 89, 51531,  712-764-8272 |
| Elk Horn | Travelling Companion, 4314 Main St., 51531,  712-764-8932 |
| Elkader | Elkader B&B, P.O. Box 887, 52043 |
| Elkader | Little House Vacations, 52043,  319-783-7774 |
| Emmetsburg | Queen Marie Victorian B&B, 707 Harrison St., 50536,  712-852-4700 |
| Fairfield | Polly's B&B, 201 E. Burlington Ave., 52556,  515-472-2517 |
| Forest City | 1897 Victorian House, 306 S. Clark St., 50436,  515-582-3613 |
| Fort Atkinson | LaVerne & Alice Hageman, Route 2, Box 104, 52144,  319-534-7545 |
| Fort Madison | Coffe House, 1020 Avenue D, 52627,  319-372-1656 |
| Fort Madison | Kountry Klassics, 2002 295th Ave., 52627,  319-372-5484 |
| Galva | Pioneer Farm B&B, RR1 Box 96, 51020 |
| Garner | Mrs. B's B&B, 920 Division St., 50438,  515-923-2390 |
| Grinnell | Carriage House B&B, 1133 Broad St., 50112,  515-236-7520 |
| Guttenberg | Old Brewery B&B, P.O. Box 217, 52052,  319-252-2094 |
| Hampton | Country Touch B&B, RR 2, 1034 Hwy. 3, 50441,  515-456-4585 |
| Hampton | Spring Valley B&B, RR 4, P.O. Box 47, 50441,  515-456-4437 |
| Hartley | Time Out B&B, 250 W. Maple Dr., 51346,  712-728-2213 |
| Homestead | Die Heimat Country Inn, Main St, Amana Colonies, 52236,  319-622-3937 |
| Independence | Riverside B&B, 506 2nd Ave. S.W., 50644,  319-334-4100 |
| Indianola | Summerset Inn, 1507 Fairfax, 50125,  515-961-3545 |
| Iowa City | Bella Vista Place, 2 Bella Vista Pl., 52245,  319-338-4129 |
| Iowa City | Golden Haug, The,  517 E. Washington, 52245,  319-338-6452 |
| Iowa City | Haverkamp Linn St Homestay,  619 N. Linn St., 52245,  319-337-4363 |
| Keokuk | Grand Anne B&B, The,  816 Grand Ave., 52632,  319-524-6310 |
| Keosauqua | Mansion Inn, 500 Henry, 52565,  319-293-2511 |
| Keosauqua | Mason House/Bentonsport, RR 2, Box 237, 52565,  319-592-3133 |
| Keota | Elmhurst,  Rt. 1 Box 3, 52248 |
| Knoxville | La Grande Victorian B&B,  802 E. Montgomery, 50138,  515-842-4653 |
| Lansing | FitzGerald's Inn B&B,  P.O. Box 157, 52151,  319-538-4872 |
| Lansing | Lansing House,  Box 97, 291 N. Front St, 52151,  319-538-4263 |
| LaPorte City | Brandt's Orchard Inn, RR 1, P.O. Box 224, 50651,  319-342-2912 |
| LeClaire | Country Inn,  22755 282 Ave., 52753 |
| LeClaire | Mississippi Sunrise B&B, 18950 Great River Rd., 52753,  319-332-9203 |
| LeClaire | Monarch, The,  303 Second St., 52753,  319-289-3011 |
| Leighton | Heritage House, RR 1, 50143,  515-626-3092 |
| Malcom | Pleasant Country B&B, R.R. #2, Box 23, 50157,  515-528-4925 |
| Marengo | Loy's B&B, RR 1, Box 82, 52301,  319-642-7787 |
| Massena | Evergreen Inn, RR 1, Box 65, 50853 |
| Maynard | Boedeker's Bungalow West, 125 7th St. N., 50655,  319-637-2711 |
| McGregor | Little Switzerland Inn, 126 Main St., 52157,  319-873-2057 |
| McGregor | River's Edge B&B, 112 Main St., 52157,  319-873-3501 |
| Middle | Dusk to Dawn B&B, Box 124, 52307 |
| Middle | Rettig House, 52307,  319-622-3386 |
| Mitchellville | Whitaker Farms, 11045 NE 82nd Ave., 50169,  515-967-3184 |
| Montezuma | English Valley B&B, RR 2, 50171,  515-623-3663 |
| Montpelier | Varner's Caboose, P.O. Box 10, 204 2 St., 52759,  319-381-3652 |
| Nevada | Queen Anne B&B, 1110 9th St., 50201,  515-382-6444 |
| Nichols | Townsend Nichols House B&B, P.O. Box 6, 52766,  319-723-4503 |
| Ottumwa | Guest House B&B, The,  645 North Court, 52501,  515-684-8893 |
| Pella | Strawtown Inn & Lodge, 1111 Washington St., 50219,  515-628-2681 |
| Postville | Old Shepherd House, 256 W.Tilden, Box 251, 52162,  319-864-3452 |
| Rockwell City | Pine Grove B&B, 2361 270th St., 50579,  712-297-7494 |
| Sabula | Castle B&B, The, 616 River St., 52070,  319-687-2714 |
| Sabula | The Castle B&B, 616 River St., 52070,  319-687-2714 |
| Sac City | Brick Bungalow B&B, 1012 Early St, 50583,  800-848-7656 |
| Sac City | Drewry Homestead, RR2, P.O. Box 98, 50583,  712-662-4416 |
| Sioux Rapids | Hansen House B&B, P.O. Box 448, 50585,  712-283-2179 |
| Siver City | Robin's Nest Inn B&B, P.O. Box 64, 51571,  712-323-1649 |
| South Amana | Babi's B&B, Route 1, Box 66, 52334,  319-662-4381 |
| Spencer | Hannah Marie Country Inn, RR 1, Hwy. 71 S., 51301,  712-262-1286 |
| Spillville | Old World Inn, The,  331 S. Main St., 52168,  319-562-3739 |
| Spillville | Taylor Made B&B, 330 S. Main, 52168,  319-562-3958 |
| Spirit Lake | Francis Hospitality Manor, 608 Lake St., 51360,  712-336-4345 |
| St. Ansgar | Blue Belle Inn, P.O. Box 205, 50472,  515-736-2225 |
| Stratford | Hook's Point Farmstead B&B, Rt. 1, P.O. Box 222, 50249,  515-838-2781 |
| Stratford | Valkommen House, The,  RR 1, P.O. Box 175, 50249,  515-838-2440 |
| Swedesburg | Carlson House, The,  105 Park ST., 52652 |
| Swisher | Terra Verde Farm, Route 1, Box 86, 52338,  319-846-2478 |
| Thurman | Plum Creek Inn, RR 1, P.O. Box 91, 51654,  712-628-2191 |
| Turin | The Country Homestead B&B, RR 1, Box 53, 51059,  712-353-6772 |
| Walnut | Walnut Creek Station B&B, P.O. Box 261, 51577,  712-784-3310 |
| Washington | Quiet Sleeping Room, 125 Green Meadow Dr., 52353 |

| Waterloo | Daisy Wilton Inn, The, 418 Walnut St., 50703, 319-232-0801 |
| Waverly | Villa Fairfield B&B, 401 2nd Ave. S.W., 50677, 319-352-0739 |
| Webster City | Centennial Farm B&B, 1091-220th St., 50595, 515-832-3050 |
| West Branch | Inn Nearby the Wapsinonoc, P.O. Box 209, 52358, 319-643-7484 |
| West Des Moines | Ellendale B&B, 5340 Ashworth Rd., 50265, 515-225-2219 |
| Whiting | Lighthouse Marina Inn, RR 1, P.O. Box 72, 51063, 712-458-2066 |
| Whittemore | Prairie Oasis, 5720 430th St., 50598, 515-887-4953 |
| Williamsburg | Lucille's Bett Und Brkfast, 2835 225th St., 52361, 319-668-1185 |

# Kansas

## COLUMBUS

**Meriwether House B&B**
322 W. Pine,   66725
316-429-2812  Fax: 316-429-1790
800-238-1957
Margaret Meriwether
All year

$-B&B
7 rooms, 4 pb
MC, Visa, *Rated*,
C-yes/S-no/P-no/H-ltd

Continental breakfast
Sitting room

*Cottage home close to downtown, furnished with antiques.*

## COTTONWOOD FALLS

**1874 Stonehouse, The**
RR1 Box 67A, Mulberry Hill,
  66845
316-273-8481  Fax: 316-273-8481
Dan & Carrie Riggs
All year

$$-B&B
3 rooms, 3 pb
Visa, MC,
C-ltd/S-ltd/P-yes/H-no

Full breakfast
Snacks, special diets
Sitting room
library
family friendly facility

*Set in the middle of Kansas Flint Hills. 121 year old limestone house filled with comfortable antiques. Surrounded by 120 acres of hiking trails, pond, river. 3rd night 50%.*

## COUNCIL GROVE

**Cottage House-Hotel, The**
25 N. Neosho,   66846
316-767-6828  800-727-7903
Connie & Don Essington
All year

$$-B&B
26 rooms,
Most CC, *Rated*, •
C-yes/S-yes/P-ltd/H-yes

Continental breakfast
Restaurant nearby
Sitting room, sauna room
6 rms. w/whirlpool tubs
near Hays House Restaur.

*Beautifully renovated Victorian hotel w/modern comforts & lovely antique furnishings-in historic "Birthplace of the Santa Fe Trail." 2 nights for 1, Sun.–Thur, ltd.*

## IOLA

**Northrup House B&B**
318 East St.,   66749
316-365-8025
Jody & Earl Gehrt
All year

$$
4 rooms, 4 pb
Visa, MC, •
C-ltd/S-no/P-no/H-no

Full breakfast
Afternoon tea, snacks
Sitting room
conservatory
a delightful get-away

*On the Register of Historic Places, one of Kansas' finest examples of Victoriana. Built in 1895, furnished w/authentic antiques, orginal stained glass windows, woodwork.*

## LEAVENWORTH

**Salt Creek Valley B&B**
16425 Fort Riley Rd.,   66048
913-651-2277  Fax: 913-682-4647
Ed & Mary Baldwin

$$-B&B
3 rooms, 3 pb
Most CC,
C-ltd/S-no/P-no/H-yes

Full breakfast
Lunch & dinner (fee)
Family friendly facility

*An historic stage coach stop to charm you along the Sante Fe Trail. Country splendor. Close to Kansas City.*

*Salt Creek Valley B&B, Leavenworth, KS*

NICKERSON ───────────────────────────────

**Hedrick's B&B Inn**
7910 N. Roy L Smith Rd.,
   67561
316-422-3245  Fax: 316-422-3355
800-618-9577
Joe & Sondra Hedrick
All year

$$-B&B
7 rooms, 7 pb
Visa, MC, Disc,
C-yes/S-no/P-no/H-yes

Full breakfast
Snacks
Sitting room
lake facilities
conference/banquet room

*Situated on an exotic animal farm. Get up close and personal with giraffe, zebra, kangaroo, camels and more. **50% off 3rd night, $5 off when you mention this Guide.***

TONGANOXIE ───────────────────────────────

**Almeda's B&B Inn**
220 S. Main,   66086
913-845-2295
Almeda & Richard Tinberg
All year

$-B&B
3 rooms, 2 pb
*Rated*,
C-ltd/S-ltd/P-no/H-no

Continental plus bkfst.
Complimentary cold drink
Sitting & TV room
organ, all rooms A/C
suite available

*Dedicated as historical site 1983; in '30s was the inspiration for the movie "Bus Stop." Decorated country style w/many antiques. Close to Opera house, golf courses & pool.*

VALLEY FALLS ───────────────────────────────

**Barn B&B Inn, The**
RR 2, Box 87,   66088
913-945-3225  Fax: 913-945-3326
800-869-7717
T. & M. Ryan, P. Ryan Miller
All year

$$-B&B
20 rooms, 20 pb
Visa, MC, AmEx,
*Rated*, •
C-yes/S-no/P-no/H-yes

Full breakfast
Supper day of arrival
Lunch & dinner avail.
sitting room, walking
fishing, hunting, pool

*A 93-year-old barn converted into a country inn. Offers peace, quiet and a very restful atmosphere. Come be a part of our family.*

WAKEENEY ───────────────────────────────

**Thistle Hill B&B**
Rt. 1, Box 93,   67672
913-743-2644
Dave & Mary Hendricks
All year

$$-B&B
4 rooms, 3 pb
*Rated*, •
C-yes/S-ltd/P-no/H-no

Full breakfast
Afternoon tea
Sitting room, library
flower & herb gardens
hiking, walking paths

*Nestled halfway between Kansas City & Denver along I-70. A peaceful, modern farm home surrounded by cedars, prairie, wildflowers & herbs. Hot tub, solarium.*

WICHITA ──────────────────────────────────────

| | | |
|---|---|---|
| **Inn at the Park** | $$$-B&B | Continental plus bkfst. |
| 3751 E. Douglas,  67218 | 12 rooms, 12 pb | Afternoon tea |
| 316-652-0500  Fax: 316-652-0610 | AmEx, MC, Visa, | Sitting room |
| 800-258-1951 | *Rated*,  • | library, hot tubs |
| Jan Lightner | C-yes/S-no/P-no/H-yes | tennis and pool nearby |
| All year | Spanish | |

*A 1910 mansion, nestled on the edge of a park. 12 uniquely decorated suites. Close to fine dining, theater, business, shopping. Ideal for vacationers and corporate travelers.*

| | | |
|---|---|---|
| **Inn at Willowbend, The** | $$$-B&B | Full breakfast |
| 3939 Comotara,  67226 | 23 rooms, 22 pb | Comp. wine |
| 316-636-4032  Fax: 316-634-2190 | Most CC, *Rated*,  • | Bar service |
| 800-553-5775 | C-yes/S-yes/P-no/H-yes | sitting room, library |
| Gary & Bernice Adamson | | hot tubs in suites |
| All year | | |

*A traditional bed and breakfast with modern conveniences located on a championship golf course.* **2 nights in suite, 50% 2nd. night, Fri.+Sat., Sat.+Sun.**

## More Inns . . .

| | |
|---|---|
| Abilene | Balfours' House B&B, Rt 2, Box 143 D, 67410,  913-263-4262 |
| Abilene | Dora Theay Ah's B&B, 210 N.W. 10th St., 67410,  913-263-0226 |
| Abilene | Spruce House,  604 N. Spruce, 67410,  913-263-3900 |
| Abilene | Windmill Inn,  1787 Rain Rd., 67431,  913-263-8755 |
| Alma | Stuewe Place,  617 Nebraska, 66401,  913-765-3636 |
| Ashland | Rolling Hills B&B,  204 E. 4th Ave., 67831,  316-635-2859 |
| Ashland | Slaton House, The,  319 W. 7th, 67831,  316-635-2290 |
| Ashland | Wallingford Inn B&B,  Box 799, 67831,  316-635-2129 |
| Atchison | Williams House, The,  526 N. 5th, 66002,  913-367-1757 |
| Atwood | Flower Patch,  610 Main, 67730,  913-626-3780 |
| Auburn | Lippincott's Fyshe House,  8720 W. 85th St., 66402 |
| Baldwin | Three Sisters Inn,  1035 Ames, 66006 |
| Baldwin City | Grove House,  807 Grove St., 66006 |
| Barnes | Gloria's B&B,  P.O. Box 84, 66933,  913-763-4569 |
| Basehor | Bedknobs & Biscuits B&B,  15202 Parallel, 66007,  913-724-1540 |
| Bern | Lear Acres-B&B on a Farm,  Rt. 1 Box 31, 66408,  913-336-3903 |
| Burlington | Victorian Memories,  314 N. 4th, 66839,  316-364-5752 |
| Caney | Caney B&B,  Hwy 75, 67333,  316-879-5478 |
| Cassoday | Sunbarger Guest House,  RR 1, 66842,  316-735-4499 |
| Cawker City | Oak Creek Lodge,  R.R. 2, 67430 |
| Cimarron | Cimarron Hotel & Restauran,  P.O. Box 633, 67835,  316-855-2244 |
| Clyde | Clyde Hotel,  420 Washington, 66938,  913-446-2231 |
| Concordia | Crystle's B&B,  508 W. 7th St., 66901,  913-243-2192 |
| Council Grove | Flint Hills B&B,  613 W. Main, 66846,  316-767-6655 |
| Dorrance | Country Inn, The,  HC 01, Box 59, 67634,  913-666-4468 |
| Dorrance | Dorrance—The Country Inn,  HC 01, Box 59, 67634,  913-666-4468 |
| Dover | Sage Inn,  P.O. Box 24, 66420 |
| Elk Falls | Sherman House, The,  P.O. Box 15, 67345 |
| Elkhart | Cimarron, The,  P.O. Box 741, 67950,  405-696-4672 |
| Ellis | Grape Vine Boarding House,  101 E. 12th, 67637 |
| Elmdale | Clover Cliff Ranch B&B,  Rt. 1 Box 30-1, 66850 |
| Emporia | Plumb House B&B,  628 Exchange, 66801,  316-342-6881 |
| Emporia | White Rose Inn B&B, The,  901 Merchant, 66801 |
| Enterprise | Ehrsam Place B&B,  103 S. Grant, 67441 |
| Eureka | 123 Mulberry St. B&B,  123 S. Mulberry St., 67045,  316-583-7515 |
| Fort Scott | Bennington House,  123 Crescent Dr., 66701,  316-223-1837 |
| Fort Scott | Chenault Mansion, The,  820 S. National Ave., 66701,  316-223-6800 |
| Fort Scott | Country Quarters,  Route 5, Box 80, 66701,  316-223-2889 |
| Fort Scott | Courtland B&B Inn, The,  121 East First, 66061 |
| Fort Scott | Huntington House,  324 S. Main, 66701,  316-223-3644 |
| Fort Scott | Lyons' House,  742 South National, 66701 |
| Fowler | Creek Side Farm B&B,  Rt. 1, Box 19, 67844,  316-646-5586 |
| Garnett | Kirk House,  145 W. 4th Ave., 66032,  913-448-5813 |
| Glasco | Rustic Rememberances B&B,  Rt. 1, Box 68, 67445,  913-546-2552 |
| Goodland | Heart Haven Inn,  2145 Rd. 64, 67735,  913-899-5171 |
| Great Bend | Peaceful Acres B&B,  Route 5, Box 153, 67530,  316-793-7527 |

| | |
|---|---|
| Great Bend | Walnut Brook B&B, R.R. 3, Box 304, 67530, 316-792-5900 |
| Halstead | Heritage Inn, 300 Main, 67056, 316-835-2118 |
| Halstead | Nee Murray Way, 220 W. 3rd., 67056, 316-835-2027 |
| Hays | Aurora Hill B&B, 898 W. Hwy 40, 67601 |
| Hiawatha | Pleasant Corner, R.R. 5, Box 222, 66434, 913-742-7877 |
| Highland | Meadowlark B&B & Tea Room, 207 S. Ives, 66035 |
| Hill City | Pheasant Run B&B, 609 N. 4th Ave., 67642, 913-674-2955 |
| Hill City | Pomeroy Inn, 67642, 913-674-2098 |
| Hillsboro | A Nostalgic B&B Place, 310 South Main, 67063, 316-947-3519 |
| Holton | Country Reflections, Inc., 20975 "R" Rd., 66436 |
| Holton | Dodds House B&B, Hwy 75S, 66436, 913-364-3172 |
| Holton | Hotel Josephine, 5th & Ohio, 66436, 913-364-3151 |
| Holyrood | Hollyrood House B&B, Route 1, Box 47, 67450, 913-252-3678 |
| Hutchinson | Rose Garden, The, 3815 East 56th, 67502 |
| Independence | Rose Wood B&B, 417 W. Myrtle, 67301, 316-331-2221 |
| Lakin | Country Pleasures B&B, 1107 S. Bridge St., 67860, 316-355-6982 |
| Lawrence | Halcyon House, 1000 Ohio, 66044, 913-841-0314 |
| Lenexa | Kansas City B&B, P.O. Box 14781, 66215, 913-888-3636 |
| Lenora | Barbeau House B&B, 210 E. Washington Ave., 67645 |
| Lincoln | Woody House B&B, Route 1, Box 156, 67455, 913-524-4744 |
| Lindsborg | Smoky Valley B&B, 2nd & State, 67456, 913-227-4460 |
| Lindsborg | Swedish Country Inn, 112 W. Lincoln, 67456, 913-227-2985 |
| Louisburg | Red Maple Inn, 201 S. 11th St., 66053 |
| Ludell | Holste Homestead, 67744, 913-626-3522 |
| Ludell | Pork Palace, 67744, 913-626-9223 |
| Lyons | Quivira House B&B, 400 E. Commercial St., 67554 |
| Manhattan | Kimble Cliff B&B, 6782 Anderson Ave., 66502, 913-539-3816 |
| Marienthal | Krause House, Route 1, Box 42, 67863, 316-379-4627 |
| Marion | Country Dreams, Rt. 3, Box 82, 66861, 316-382-2250 |
| Marquette | Rustic Remembrances, Box 458, 67464 |
| Melvern | School House Inn, 106 E. Beck, 66510, 913-549-3473 |
| Meriden | Village Inn, RR 2, Box 226D, 66512, 913-876-2835 |
| Moran | Hedge Apple Acres B&B, Rt. 2, Box 27, 66755, 316-237-4646 |
| Newton | Hawk House B&B Inn, 307 W. Broadway, 67114, 316-283-2045 |
| Osborne | Loft B&B, 67473, 913-346-5984 |
| Oskaloosa | Stone Crest B&B, P.O. Box 394, 66066, 913-863-2166 |
| Overbrook | Pinemoore Inn, The, R.R. 1, Box 44, 66524, 913-453-2304 |
| Paola | Victorian Lady B&B, The, 402 South Pearl, 66071 |
| Peabody | Jones Sheep Farm B&B, 66866, 316-983-2815 |
| Pleasanton | Cedar Crest, P.O. Box 387, Rt. 1, 66075, 913-352-6706 |
| Randolph | Shadow Springs Farm, 13170 Tuttle Creek Blvd, 66554 |
| Riley | Trix's Riley Roomer, 104 N. Hartner, 66531, 913-485-2654 |
| Rose Hill | Queen Anne's Lace B&B, 2617 Queen Anne's Lace, 67133, 316-733-4075 |
| Salina | Happy Trail B&B, 507 Montclair Dr., 67401 |
| Salina | Hunters Leigh B&B, 4109 E. North St., 67401, 913-823-6750 |
| Seneca | Stein House B&B, The, 314 N. 7th St., 66538 |
| Stafford | Henderson House B&B Inn, 518 W. Stafford, 67578, 316-234-6048 |
| Summerfield | Walnut Inn, 415 4th St., 66541 |
| Sylvan Grove | Spillman Creek Lodge, 67481, 913-277-3424 |
| Syracuse | Braddock Ames B&B, P.O. Box 892, 67878, 316-384-5218 |
| Tecumseh | Old Stone House, 6033 SE Hwy. 40, 66542 |
| Topeka | Brickyard Barn Inn, 4020 N.W. 25th St., 66618, 913-235-0057 |
| Topeka | Elderberry B&B, The, 1035 S.W. Fillmore St., 66604, 913-235-6309 |
| Topeka | Heritage House, 3535 SW Sixth Ave., 66606, 913-233-3800 |
| Topeka | Sunflower B&B, The, 915 SW Munsion Ave., 66604, 913-357-7509 |
| Ulysses | Fort's Cedar View, RR 3, Box 120B, 67880, 316-356-2570 |
| Wakefield | Rock House B&B, 201 Dogwood, 67487, 913-461-5732 |
| Wakefield | Wakefield Country B&B, 197 Sunflower Rd., 67487, 913-461-5533 |
| Wathena | Carousel B&B, Rt. 1 Box 124, 66090, 913-989-3537 |
| Wells | Traders Lodge, 1392 210th Rd., 67488 |
| Wichita | Castle Inn Riverside, The, 1155 N. River Blvd., 67203, 316-263-9300 |
| Wichita | Holiday House-Res. B&B, 8406 W. Maple, 67209, 316-721-1968 |
| Wichita | Vermilion Rose B&B, 1204 N Topeka Ave., 67214, 316-267-7636 |

# Kentucky

## BARDSTOWN

**Jailer's Inn**
111 W. Stephen Foster,  40004
502-348-5551 Fax: 502-348-1852
800-948-5551
Paul McCoy
March–December

$$-B&B
6 rooms, 6 pb
MC, Visa, *Rated*,  •
C-yes/S-ltd/H-yes

Continental plus bkfst.
Comp. wine & cheese
Sitting room, gazebo
landscaped courtyard
roses, 2 rm. w/jacuzzi

*Jailer's Inn was a jail (1819-74), then a jailer's residence (1874-1987), and is now completely remodeled, attractively decorated w/antiques & heirlooms.* **Comp. wine/lemonade.**

**Mansion B&B, The**
1003 N. Third St.,  40004
502-348-2586 800-399-2586
Joseph D. & Charmaine
Downs
All year

$$$-B&B
8 rooms, 8 pb
Most CC,  •
C-ltd/S-ltd/P-no/H-no

Continental plus bkfst.
Sitting room, piano
mimosa trees

*Bardstown's most elegant B&B. Greek revival mansion with beautiful period antiques. Seated breakfast using our silver, crystal and china.* **3rd night 50% off.**

## COVINGTON

**Licking Riverside Historic**
516 Garrard St.,  41011
606-291-0191 Fax: 606-291-0939
800-483-7822
Lynda L. Freeman
All year

$$$-B&B
2 rooms, 2 pb
AmEx,  •
C-ltd/S-no/P-no/H-no

Continental plus bkfst.
Snacks
Sitting room
jacuzzi

*Come and enjoy our historic bed and breakfast. We offer Southern hospitality in the beautiful Blue Grass state of Kentucky. Each room has private bath.* **10% senior discount; 3rd night 50%.**

## GEORGETOWN

**Pineapple Inn B&B**
645 S. Broadway,  40324
502-868-5453 Fax: 502-868-5453
Muriel & Les
All year

$$-B&B
4 rooms, 4 pb
Visa, MC, *Rated*,  •
C-ltd/S-ltd/P-no/H-no

Full breakfast
Snacks, comp. wine
Sitt. room, bar service
Heart of Bluegrass
horse country, spa avail

*Built in 1876 - on historical register - gourmet breakfast in country French dining room. Furnished with antiques. Close to many activities.* **3rd night 50% off.**

## LOUISVILLE

**Columbine B&B, The**
1707 S. Third St.,  40208
502-635-5000 800-635-5010
James & Carole Slattery
All year

$$-B&B
5 rooms, 5 pb
Most CC,  •
C-yes/S-ltd/P-no/H-ltd

Full breakfast
Snacks, comp. wine
Sitting room

*Genuine Victorian Inn, c1900, with beautiful wood, porches, dining room. Sumptuous breakfast and delightful evening goodies. Beautiful English garden.* **3rd night 50% off.**

## LOUISVILLE

**Old Louisville Inn**
1359 S. Third St.,   40208
502-635-1574  Fax: 502-637-5892
Marianne Lesher
All year

$$-B&B
11 rooms, 8 pb
MC, Visa, *Rated*,  •
C-yes/S-ltd/P-no/H-no

Continental plus bkfst.
Afternoon tea
Sitting room, library
bicycles, tennis, piano
hot tub, exercise room

*"Your home away from home." Wake up to the aroma of freshly baked breads and muffins and Southern hospitality. Children under 12 free.* **3rd night 50%, except at Kentucky Derby week.**

## MIDDLESBOROUGH

**RidgeRunner B&B, The**
208 Arthur Heights,   40965
606-248-4299
Sue Richards, Irma Gall
All year

$$-B&B
5 rooms, 2 pb
MC, Visa, *Rated*,
C-ltd/S-no/P-no/H-no

Full breakfast
Comp. tea, refreshments
Sitting room
library
porch

*Charming and lovingly restored Victorian mansion. Lovely woodwork, pocket doors, interesting windows, spacious porch. Breathtaking views of mountains. Antique furnishings.*

## MURRAY

**Diuguid House B&B**
603 Main St.,   42071
502-753-5470
Karen & George Chapman
All year

$-B&B
3 rooms,
MC, Visa, *Rated*,  •
C-yes/S-no/P-no/H-no

Full breakfast
Afternoon tea, snacks
Sitting room, porch
piano, TV, laundry
Children welcome

*Historic Queen Anne centrally located in beautiful university town; close to Kentucky Lake and many antique shops. Nice retirement area.* **7th night free.**

## NEW HAVEN

**Sherwood Inn**
P.O. Box 86,   40051
138 S. Main St.
502-549-3386 Fax: 502-549-5822
Errol P. & Cecilia M. Johnson
All year

$-B&B
5 rooms, 3 pb
Visa, MC, Disc.,
C-yes/P-no/H-no

Full breakfast
Dinner available
Complimentary wine
bar service

*Experience fine regional cuisine and the hospitality of one of the oldest country inns on the rail line. Listed on the National Historic Register.*

## PADUCAH

**1857's B&B**
P.O. Box 771,  42002
127 Market House Sq.
502-444-3960 Fax: 502-444-3960
Deborah Bohnert
All year

$$-B&B
3 rooms, 1 pb
Visa, MC,  •
C-ltd/H-no

Continental plus bkfst.
Snacks
Sitting room, library
hot tubs

*In historic downtown Paducah, with antique stores, carriage rides, quilt museum, restaurants & the Market House Cultural Center. 1 block from the Ohio River. Warm, friendly atmosphere.* **3rd night 50%.**

**Paducah Harbor Plaza B&B**
201 Broadway,  42001
502-442-2698  800-719-7799
Beverly McKinley
All year

$$-B&B
4 rooms,
AmEx, MC, Visa,
*Rated*,  •
C-yes/S-no/P-no/H-no

Continental plus bkfst.
Snacks, catered food
Sitting room
library
specialty quilting store

*Restored Victorian turn-of-the-century hotel. Lovely antique furnishings. Located in historic district. One block from American Quilter's Society Museum.* **3rd night 50%.**

## VERSAILLES

| | | |
|---|---|---|
| **B&B at Sills Inn** | $$$-B&B | Full gourmet breakfast |
| 270 Montgomery Ave., | 12 rooms, 12 pb | Complimentary snacks |
| 40383 | Most CC, *Rated*, • | Sitting room, library |
| 606-873-4478 Fax: 606-873-7099 | C-ltd/S-ltd/P-no/H-ltd | jacuzzi for two suites |
| 800-526-9801 | | hot tubs, meeting rooms |
| Tony Sills | | |
| All year | | |

*Restored Victorian in historic downtown. Antique shops, art studios, cafes & restaurants.*
*Individual decor for each room. The perfect romantic get-away. Near Shaker Village.*

## WEST POINT

| | | |
|---|---|---|
| **Ditto House Inn B&B, The** | $$-B&B | Full breakfast |
| 204 Elm St., 40177 | 4 rooms, 2 pb | Snacks |
| 502-922-4939 | Visa, MC, | Sitting room |
| Pete & Jody Bond | C-yes/S-no/P-ltd/H-no | family friendly facility |
| All year | | |

*Our 1841 Federal style home, furnished with antiques, is on the National Register of*
*Historic Places and overlooks the Ohio River.* **3rd night, 50% off.**

# More Inns ...

| | |
|---|---|
| Allensville | Pepper Place, P.O. Box 95, 42204, 502-265-9859 |
| Auburn | Auburn Guest House, 421 W. Main St., 42206, 502-542-6019 |
| Auburn | David Williams Guest House, 421 West Main St., 42206, 502-542-6019 |
| Augusta | Augusta White House Inn BB, 307 Main St., 41002, 606-756-2004 |
| Augusta | Lamplighter Inn, 103 W. 2nd St., 41002, 606-756-2603 |
| Bardstown | 1790 House, 110 E. Broadway, 40004, 502-348-7072 |
| Bardstown | Amber LeAnn B&B, 209 E. Stephen Foster, 40004, 800-828-3330 |
| Bardstown | Bruntwood Inn, 714 N. 3rd. St., 40004, 502-348-8218 |
| Bardstown | Coffee Tree Cabin, 980 McCubbin's Lane, 40004, 502-348-1151 |
| Bardstown | Talbot Tavern/McLean House, 107 W. Stephen Foster, 40004, 502-348-3494 |
| Bellevue | Weller Haus, 319 Poplar St., 41073, 606-431-6829 |
| Berea | Boone Tavern Hotel, CPO 2345, 40404, 606-986-9358 |
| Bloomfield | Vintage Rose, The, 118 Hwy. 62, 40008, 502-252-5042 |
| Bowling Green | Alpine Lodge, 5310 Morgantown Rd., 42101, 502-843-4846 |
| Bowling Green | Bowling Green B&B, 3313 Savannah Dr., 42104, 502-781-3861 |
| Brandenburg | Doe Run Inn, Route 2, 40108, 502-422-2982 |
| Brandenburg | East Hill Inn, 205 LaFayette St., 40108, 502-422-3047 |
| Cadiz | Round Oak Inn, P.O. Box 1331, 42211, 502-924-5850 |
| Campbellsville | Yellow Cottage, The, 400 N. Central, 42718, 502-789-2669 |
| Carrolton | P.J. Baker House B&B, The, 406 Highland Ave., 41008, 502-732-4210 |
| Covington | Amos Shinkle Townhouse B&B, 215 Garrard St., 41011, 606-431-2118 |
| Covington | Carneal House Inn, The, 405 E. 2nd St., 41011, 606-431-6130 |
| Covington | Sandford House B&B, 1026 Russell St., 41011, 606-291-9133 |
| Cynthiana | Broadwell B&B, Route 6, Box 58, 41031, 606-234-4255 |
| Cynthiana | Seldon Renaker Inn, 24 S. Walnut St., 41031, 606-234-3752 |
| Danville | Randolph House, 463 W. Lexington, 40422, 606-236-9594 |
| Danville | Twin Hollies Retreat, 406 Maple Ave., 40422, 606-236-8954 |
| E. Bardstown | Kenmore Farms, 1050 Bloomfield Rd., 40004, 502-348-8023 |
| Elizabethtown | Cabin Fever, 459 Sportsman Lake Rd., 42701, 502-737-8748 |
| Elizabethtown | Olde Bethlehem Academy, 42701, 502-862-9003 |
| Frankfort | Olde Kantucke B&B Inn, 210 E. Fourth St., 40601, 502-227-7389 |
| Frankfort | Taylor-Compton House, 419 Lewis St., 40601, 502-227-4368 |
| Franklin | College Street Inn, 223 South College, 42134, 502-586-9352 |
| Georgetown | Blackridge Hall B&B, 4055 Paris Pike, 40324, 800-768-9308 |
| Georgetown | Jordan Farm B&B, 4091 Newtown Pike, 40324, 502-863-1944 |
| Georgetown | Log Cabin B&B, 350 N. Broadway, 40324, 502-863-3514 |
| Ghent | Ghent House, P.O. Box 478, 41045, 502-347-5807 |
| Glasgow | B&B Country Cottage, 1609 Winn School Rd., 42141, 502-646-2940 |
| Glasgow | Four Seasons Country Inn, 4107 Scottsville Rd., 42141, 502-678-1000 |
| Glasgow | Hall Place, 313 S. Green, 42141, 502-651-3176 |
| Glendale | Petticoat Junction, P.O. Box 36, 42740, 502-369-8604 |
| Harrodsburg | Beaumont Inn, P.O. Box 158, 40330, 606-734-3381 |
| Harrodsburg | Canaan Land Farm B&B, 4355 Lexington Rd., 40330, 606-734-3984 |
| Harrodsburg | Shaker Village Pleas. Hill, 3501 Lexington Rd., 40330, 606-734-5411 |
| Hartford | Ranney Porch B&B, 3810 Hwy 231 North, 42347, 502-298-7972 |
| Hazel | Outback B&B, Box 4, 42049, 502-436-5858 |

| | |
|---|---|
| Hindman | Quilt Maker Inn, P.O. Box 973, 41822, 606-785-5622 |
| Hopkinsville | Oakland Manor, 9210 Newstead Rd., 42240, 502-885-6400 |
| Kuttawa | Davis House B&B, The, Rt 2, Box 21A1, 42055, 502-388-4468 |
| Lancaster | Perkins Place Farm, P.O. Box 553, 40444, 800-762-4145 |
| Lexington | Cherry Knoll Farm B&B, 3975 Lemons Mill Rd., 40511, 606-253-9800 |
| Lexington | Ms. Jesta Belle's, P.O. Box 8225, 40533, 606-734-7834 |
| Lexington | Sycamore Ridge, 6855 Mt. Horeb Rd., 40511 |
| Liberty | Liberty Greystone Manor, P.O. Box 329, 42539, 606-787-5444 |
| Louisville | Angelmelli Inn, 1342 S. 6th St., 40208, 800-245-9262 |
| Louisville | Ashton's Victorian Secret, 1132 South First St., 40203, 502-581-1914 |
| Louisville | Rose Blossum, 1353 S. 4th St., 40203, 502-636-0295 |
| Louisville | St. James Court, 1436 St. James Court, 40208, 502-636-1742 |
| Manchester | Blair's Country Living, RR #3, Box 865-B, 40962, 606-598-2854 |
| Marion | LaFayette Club House, 173 LaFayette Hts., 42064, 502-965-3889 |
| Morgantown | Helm House, 309 S. Tyler, 42261, 800-441-4786 |
| Mount Sterling | Trimble House, 321 N. Maysville, 40353, 606-498-6561 |
| Newport | Getaway B&B, 326 E. 6th St., 41071, 606-581-6447 |
| Nicholasville | Cedar Haven Farm, 2380 Bethel Rd., 40356, 606-858-3849 |
| Nicholasville | Sandusky House, 1626 Delaney Ferry Rd., 40356, 606-223-4730 |
| Old Kuttawa | Silver Cliff Inn, 1980 Lake Barkley Dr., 42055, 502-388-5858 |
| Owensboro | WeatherBerry B&B, 2731 W. Second St., 42301, 502-684-8760 |
| Paducah | Ehrhardts B&B, 285 Springwell Dr., 42001, 502-554-0644 |
| Perryville | Elmwood Inn, 205 East Fourth, 40468, 606-332-2400 |
| Richmond | Barnes Mill B&B, 1268 Barnes Mill Rd., 40475, 606-623-5509 |
| Russellville | Log House, 2139 Franklin St., 42276, 502-726-8483 |
| Sandy Hook | Charlene's Country Inn B&B, HC 75, Box 265, 41171, 606-738-5712 |
| Somerset | Osborne's of Cabin Hollow, 347B Elihu-Cabin Hollow, 42501, 606-382-5495 |
| Somerset | Shadwick House, 411 S Main St., 42501, 606-678-4675 |
| South Union | Shaker Tavern, P.O. Box 181, Hwy 73, 42283, 502-542-6801 |
| Springfield | Maple Hill Manor B&B, 2941 Perryville Rd., 40069, 606-366-3075 |
| Sterns | Marcum-Porter House, P.O. Box 369, 42647, 606-376-2242 |
| Taylorsville | Bowling's Villa, 1090 Stumps Lane, 40071, 502-477-2636 |
| Versailles | Bluegrass B&B, 2964 McCracken Pike, 40383, 606-873-3208 |
| Versailles | Rosehill Inn, 233 Rose Hill, 40383, 606-873-5957 |
| Versailles | Shepherd Place, 31 Heritage Rd., 40383, 606-873-7843 |
| Wilmore | Scott Station Inn, 305 E. Main, 40390, 606-858-0121 |
| Winchester | Windswept Farm B&B, 5952 Old Boonesboro Rd., 40391, 608-745-1245 |

*Diuguid House, Murray, Kentucky*

# Louisiana

## LAFITTE ─────────────────────────────

**Victoria Inn**
Box 545B Hwy 45,   70067
504-689-4757 Fax: 504-689-3399
800-689-4797
Dale & Roy Ross
All year

$$$-B&B
7 rooms, 7 pb
Visa, MC, AmEx,
*Rated*, •
C-yes/S-no/P-ltd/H-no
Spanish (with notice)

Full breakfast
Comp. refreshments
Sitting room, library
swim in lake, swamp tour
near National Park

*Experience Cajun living near bayous once haunted by the pirate, Jean Lafitte. A raised cottage on six acres of gardens overlooking a lake only 22 miles from New Orleans. Good birding.*

## LAKE CHARLES

**Ramsay-Curtis Mansion B&B**
626 Broad St.,  70601
318-439-3859  Fax: 318-439-3859
800-52-CHARM
Michael & Judy Curtis
All year

$$$-B&B
4 rooms, 4 pb
Most CC, •
C-ltd/S-no/P-no/H-no

Continental plus bkfst.
Snacks, comp. wine
Sitting room, library
close to downtown, mins.
from riverboat casinos

*This Queen Anne mansion (c.1885) offers elegant, yet comfortable rooms with private bath, TV and phones. National Historic Landmark.*

## NAPOLEONVILLE

**Madewood Plantation House**
4250 Hwy. 308,  70390
504-369-7151  Fax: 504-369-9848
800-375-7151
Keith & Millie Marshall
All year

$$$$-MAP
8 rooms, 8 pb
*Rated*, •
C-yes/S-ltd/P-ltd/H-no
some French

Full breakfast
Dinner included
Wine & cheese included
sitting room, piano
canopied beds

*Greek Revival mansion. Canopied beds, antiques, fresh flowers, wine and cheese, dinner by candlelight in formal family dining room. July & Aug., $100.00 second night.*

## NEW ORLEANS

**Annabelle's House B&B**
1716 Milan St.,  70115
504-899-0701  Fax: 504-899-0095
Randy & Ronna Griest
All year

$$$-B&B
5 rooms, 5 pb
Visa, MC, •
C-yes/S-no/P-yes/H-no

Continental plus bkfst.
Complimentary wine
Sitting room
family friendly facility

*Experience peaceful antique atmosphere with the luxury of every modern amenity. Elegant 1840s Greek Revival mansion in uptown. One block to street car. Open since 1984*

**Cornstalk Hotel, The**
915 Royal St.,  70116
504-523-1515  Fax: 504-522-5558
Debi & David Spencer
All year

$$-B&B
14 rooms, 14 pb
AmEx, MC, Visa,
C-yes/S-yes/P-no/H-no
French, German

Continental plus bkfst.
Comp. tea, wine, paper
Stained-glass windows
oriental rugs
fireplaces

*Small, elegant hotel in heart of French Quarter. All antique furnishings. Recent renovation. Complimentary wine/liqueurs upon check in.*

**Degas House**
2302 Esplanade Ave.,  70119
504-821-5009  Fax: 504-821-0870
All year

$$$-B&B
4 rooms, 4 pb
Visa, MC, AmEx,
*Rated*, •
C-yes/S-no/P-no/H-no

Continental plus bkfst.
Near French Quarter
tours of house

*America's premiere art B&B. Award-winning restored 1852 home of famous French painter. Memorable ambiance, modern amenities. Near French Quarter. 3rd night, 20% off, non-peak season.*

**Dusty Mansion, The**
2231 Gen. Pershing,  70115
504-895-4576  Fax: 504-891-0049
Cynthia Tomlin Riggs
All year

$$-B&B
4 rooms, 2 pb
Visa, MC, Disc., AmEx,
•
C-yes/S-yes/P-no/H-no
Spanish, French

Continental plus bkfst.
Sunday champagne brunch
Comp. wine, beverages
sitting room, hot tub
pool table, sun deck

*Charming turn-of-the-century home, spacious, comfortable. Near St. Charles Street Car; easy access to French Quarter. Southern hospitality! 3rd night 50% off.*

NEW ORLEANS ───────────────────────────────────

**Essem's House**
P.O. Box 8163,  70182
3660 Gentilly Blvd.
504-947-3401  Fax: 504-838-0140
888-240-0070
Sarah-Margaret Brown
All year

$$-B&B
3 rooms, 1 pb
Most CC, *Rated*,
C-ltd/S-no/P-no/H-yes

Continental plus bkfst.
Sitting room
New Orleans first B&B
Near zoo, aquarium, park

*Lovely brick home in convenient area of New Orleans, which is surrounded by pictur-
esque live oak trees. Guest enjoy solarium in summer and parlour fireplace in cooler
months.*

---

**Girod House, The**
1133 Chartres St., 835
Esplanade Ave.,  70116
504-522-5214  Fax: 504-522-7208
800-544-8808
Rodney & Frances Smith

$$$-B&B
6 rooms, 6 pb
C-yes

Southern Continental
Suites have kitchens and
1 or 1½ private baths
Built around courtyard

*A 6 suite guesthouse built in 1833 by New Orleans' first mayor, Nicholas Girod for his son.
Beautiful French Creole architecture. Renovated & custom decorated with antiques.*

---

**Lafitte Guest House**
1003 Bourbon St.,  70116
504-581-2678  Fax: 504-581-2678
800-331-7971
Robert Guyton & Bill Stuart
All year

$$$-B&B
14 rooms, 14 pb
AmEx, MC, Visa,
*Rated*, •
C-ltd/S-ltd/P-no/H-ltd

Continental plus bkfst.
Wine & hors d'oeuvres
Sitting room
balconies, courtyard
queen & king-size beds

*This fine French manor building greets you with elegance and tradition. Fine antique
pieces and reproductions. In the heart of the French Quarter and liveliness of Bourbon St.*

---

**Lamothe House**
621 Esplanade Ave.,  70116
504-947-1161  Fax: 504-943-6536
800-367-5858
Carol Chauppette
All year

$$$-B&B
20 rooms, 20 pb
AmEx, MC, Visa,
*Rated*, •
C-yes/S-yes/P-no/H-no

Continental breakfast
Pralines, comp. beverage
Sitting room, courtyard
newspaper, parking
AAA 4-Diamond rating

*An elegantly restored historic old mansion located on the eastern boundary of the French
Quarter. This old mansion surrounds a romantic courtyard.*

---

**Marigny Guest House**
621 Esplanade Ave., 617
Kerleree St.,  70116
504-944-9700 Fax: 504-943-6536
800-367-5858
Carol Chauppette
All year

$$$-B&B
3 rooms, 3 pb
*Rated*, •
C-ltd/S-ltd/P-no/H-no

Continental breakfast
Light refreshment avail.
Sitting room
front porch
courtyard sitting

*Famous restaurants, jazz clubs in riverboat cruises nearby. Charming historic property
on a quiet street at the French Quarter's edge.* **Discount to tours & sightseeing.**

---

**Marquette House**
2253 Carondelet St.,  70130
504-523-3014  Fax: 504-529-5933
Steve & Alma Cross
All year

$-EP
12 rooms, 12 pb
MC, Visa, •
C-yes/S-no/P-no/H-no

Kitchenettes
Sitting rooms, veranda
garden-patio, fountain
TV in some rms., laundry

*12 suites in a pre-1850 2 story brick & wrought iron balconied building. Additional
spacious now available in a pre-1880s 3 story Victorian style building as well.*

*Marigny Guest House, New Orleans, LA*

## NEW ORLEANS

**Nine-O-Five Royal Hotel**
905 Rue Royal St.,  70116
504-523-0219
J.M.
All year

$$$-EP
14 rooms, 14 pb
*Rated*,
C-yes/S-yes/P-no/H-no

Kitchens in all rooms
Daily maid service
three suite

*Quaint guest house built in the 1890s, located in the French Quarter. Nicely furnished, antiques, high ceilings. Kitchenettes and Southern charm.*

---

**Old World Inn**
1330 Prytania St.,  70130
504-566-1330
Jean & Charlie Matkin
All year

$-B&B
20 rooms, 10 pb
Visa, MC, •
C-ltd/S-yes/P-no/H-no
French, Spanish, Arabic

Continental plus bkfst.
Comp. wine, juice
Sitting room, library
common rm w/piano, chess
fireplaces, A/C

*French cafe style w/unique ambiance, excellent concierge. Hosts are professional broadcasters/musicians. Int'l clientele. Location, comfort, personality. **Upgrades when avail.***

---

**Soniat House Hotel, The**
1133 Chartres St.,  70116
504-522-0570 Fax: 504-522-7208
800-544-8808
Rodney & Frances Smith
All year

$$$$-EP
31 rooms, 31 pb
AmEx, MC, Visa,
*Rated*, •
C-ltd/S-yes/P-no/H-ltd
Spanish, French

Continental bkfst. (fee)
Bar service
Jacuzzis, balconies
suites available
small meeting rooms

*A private hotel in the residential area of the French Quarter, furnished in period antiques offering modern amenities. 1991 One of 10 Best Small Hotels in America—Traveler.*

## NEW ORLEANS

**Southern Nights**
1827 S. Carrollton Ave.,
70118
504-861-7187  Fax: 504-861-8615
Judy Garwood
All year

$$-B&B
5 rooms, 5 pb
Visa, MC, AmEx,
Checks, •
S-no/P-ltd/H-no
Spanish

Continental plus bkfst.
Snacks
Sitting room
bikes

*Savor the romance of Southern nights in the Big Easy. In the heart of things on the historic streetcar line.*

**St. Charles Guest House**
1748 Prytania St.,  70130
504-523-6556 Fax: 504-529-2952
Dennis & Joanne Hilton
All year

$-B&B
38 rooms, 26 pb
C-yes/S-ltd
Spanish

Continental breakfast
Afternoon tea, bakery
Swimming pool
library
family friendly facility

*Oldest running B&B, historic district, antiques, cozy, yet unpretentious. Eccentrically old New Orleans pensione; on trolley line, near everything.* **Spec. rates June–Sept; Dec.**

**Streetcar B&B**
S. Carrollton Ave.,  70118
601-435-0531  Fax: 504-835-1206
800-341-4665
Sheila Burke, Ronnie Kohler
All year

$$-B&B
3 rooms, 3 pb
Visa, MC, AmEx,
*Rated*, •
C-yes/S-ltd/P-no/H-no
Spanish, French

Continental breakfast
Lunch, dinner (fee)
Afternoon tea, snacks
restaurant, bar service
sitting room, library

*Unique location to all New Orleans jazz & music. Lots of gourmet restaurants within walking distance. Streetcar to all important old New Orleans locations just out front door.* **Stay 3 nights, 4 is free.**

**Sully Mansion-Garden Dist.**
2631 Prytania St.,  70130
504-891-0457 Fax: 504-899-7237
Maralee Prigmore
All year

$$$-B&B
7 rooms, 7 pb
Most CC, •
S-no/P-no/H-no

Continental plus bkfst.

*Circa 1890. Only inn nestled in the reknowned Garden Distric. Well appointed rooms, antiques and today's furnishings. Minutes to main attractions.*

**Sun & Moon B&B**
1037 N. Rampart St.,  70116
504-529-4652
Kathleen Barrow
All year

$$-B&B
2 rooms, 2 pb
C-ltd/S-no/P-no/H-no

Continental breakfast
Refrigerators in rooms
Walking distance to all
French Quarter locations

*French Quarter historic Creole cottage with suites located across courtyard. Includes classic fountain and lush foliage. Queen beds, wet bar, TV, A/C.*

## PRAIRIEVILLE

**Tree House in the Park**
16520 Airport Rd., Port
Vincent,  70769
504-622-2850  800-LE-CABIN
All year

$$$-MAP
4 rooms, 3 pb
MC, Visa, •
S-no/P-no/H-no

Full breakfast
Dinner included
Hot tub on deck, gazebo
heated swimming pool
kyak & pirogues

*Cajun cabin in the swamp. Rooms have private entrance, queen waterbed, TV/VCR, hot tub on deck under stars. Comp. first supper. Cypress trees, moss, ponds.* **10% off stay, ask.**

SHREVEPORT ───────────────────────────────

| **Columns on Jordan, The** | $$$-B&B | Continental plus bkfst. |
|---|---|---|
| 615 Jordan,  71101 | 5 rooms, 4 pb | Comp. wine, snacks |
| 318-222-5912  Fax: 318-227-2424 | AmEx, MC, Visa, • | Sitting room |
| 800-801-4950 | S-yes/P-ltd/H-no | library, bicycles |
| Judith & Edwin Simonton | Spanish | spa, pool |
| All year | | |

*Sleep in the splendor and comfort of an antique bed and have a leisurely breakfast in the morning room. Enjoy the elegance of Southern living.*

───────────────────────────────

| **Fairfield Place B&B Inn** | $$$-B&B | Full breakfast |
|---|---|---|
| 2221 Fairfield Ave,  71104 | 9 rooms, 9 pb | Dining room |
| 318-222-0048 Fax: 318-226-0631 | AmEx, MC, Visa, | Sitting room, whirlpools |
| Jane Lipscomb | *Rated*, • | suites, library, acre of |
| All year | C-ltd/S-ltd/P-ltd/H-no | gardens, weddings |

*Casually elegant 1900s inn. European and American antiques, gourmet breakfast. Ideal for business travelers and tourists.*

───────────────────────────────

| **Slattery House B&B** | $$$-B&B | Full breakfast |
|---|---|---|
| 2401 Fairfield Ave.,  71104 | 4 rooms, 4 pb | Aftn. tea, comp. wine |
| 318-222-6577  Fax: 318-222-7539 | *Rated*, • | Sitting room, library |
| Bill & Adrienne Scruggs | C-yes/S-ltd/P-no/H-no | pool, close to museums |
| All year | | Riverboat Casinos |

*1903 Victorian home-genuine Southern hospitality. Luxurious antique appointed suites. Private pool, balconies, National Register Historic Places-located in Historic District.*

ST. FRANCISVILLE ───────────────────────────────

| **Barrow House Inn** | $$$-B&B | Continental breakfast |
|---|---|---|
| P.O. Box 700,  70775 | 7 rooms, 5 pb | Full breakfast (fee) |
| 9779 Royal St. | *Rated*, • | Dinner (res), comp. wine |
| 504-635-4791  Fax: 504-635-4769 | C-ltd/S-yes/P-no/H-no | sitting room, bicycles |
| Shirley Dittloff | | cassette walking tours |
| All year | | |

*Circa 1809, located in historic district. Balconies & period antiques. Cassette walking tours. Honeymoon packages. Arnold Palmer golf course nearby.* **3rd night 50% off.**

───────────────────────────────

| **Butler Greenwood** | $$$-B&B | Continental plus bkfst. |
|---|---|---|
| 8345 U.S. Highway 61,  70775 | 5 rooms, 5 pb | Meeting facilities |
| 504-635-6312 Fax: 504-635-6370 | Visa, MC, • | library, balloon trips |
| Anne Butler | C-yes/S-ltd/P-ltd/H-no | nature walk, pool, bikes |
| All year | Some French | |

*6 private cottages w/plenty of historic charm, scattered across peaceful landscaped plantation grounds. On Nat'l Register of Historic Places. Antebellum House tour included.*

───────────────────────────────

| **Myrtles Plantation** | $$-B&B | Full breakfast |
|---|---|---|
| P.O. Box 1100,  70775 | 10 rooms, 10 pb | Bar service |
| 7747 Hwy. 61 | MC, Visa, • | Sitting room, piano |
| 504-635-6277 Fax: 504-635-5837 | C-yes/S-yes/P-yes/H-yes | bicycles, ghost tours |
| John & Teeta Moss | | mystery weekends |
| All year | | |

*Romantic 18th-century French-style plantation. Elaborate plaster frieze work & faux bois; period furnishings; unique history includes ghosts; mint juleps.* **Free Historical Tour.**

## WHITE CASTLE

| **Nottoway Plantation Inn** | $$$-B&B | Continental plus bkfst. |
| P.O. Box 160,  70788 | 13 rooms, 13 pb | Restaurant, comp. wine |
| Mississippi River Rd. | MC, Visa, *Rated*,  • | Swimming pool, meeting |
| 504-545-2730 Fax: 504-545-8632 | C-yes/S-yes/P-no/H-ltd | space, sitting room |
| Cindy Hidalgo | French | piano, tennis nearby |
| All year exc. Christmas | | |

*Fresh flowers in your room, chilled champagne, a wake-up call consisting of hot sweet potato biscuits, coffee and juice delivered to your room. Also a guided tour of mansion.*

## More Inns ...

| | |
|---|---|
| Abita Springs | Trail's End B&B, 71648 Maple St., 70808 |
| Bunkie | Homeplace, Rt 2, Box 76A, 71322,  318-826-7558 |
| Carencro | Country House, The,  825 Kidder Rd., 70520,  318-896-6529 |
| Carencro | La Maison de Campagne,  825 Kidder Rd., 70520,  318-896-6529 |
| Darrow | Tezcuco Plantation Village,  3138 Hwy. 44, 70725,  504-562-3929 |
| Jackson | Asphodel Village,  Rt. 2, Box 89 Hwy 68., 70748,  504-654-6868 |
| Jackson | Milbank - Historic House,  102 Bank St., Box 1000, 70748,  504-634-5901 |
| Kenner | Seven Oaks Plantation,  2600 Gay Lynn Dr., 70065,  504-888-8649 |
| Lafayette | Bois de Chenes Inn,  338 N. Sterling St., 70501,  318-233-7816 |
| Lafayette | Mouton Manor Inn,  310 Sidney Martin Rd, 70507,  318-237-6996 |
| Madisonville | Magnolia House B&B, The,  904 Main St., 70447 |
| Monroe | Boscobel Cottage B&B,  185 Cordell Ln., 71418,  318-325-1550 |
| Montegut | Amanda-Magenta Plantation,  P.O. Box 529, 70377,  504-594-8298 |
| Natchitoches | Jefferson House B&B,  229 Jefferson St., 71458,  318-352-3957 |
| New Iberia | Estorge-Norton House,  446 E. Main St., 70560,  318-365-7603 |
| New Iberia | Inn at le Rosier, The,  314 E. Main St., 70560,  318-367-5306 |
| New Iberia | Pourtos House,  4018 Old Jeanerett Rd., 70560,  318-367-7045 |
| New Orleans | 623 Ursulines,  623 Ursulines St., 70116,  504-529-5489 |
| New Orleans | A Hotel...The Frenchmen,  417 Frenchmen, 70116,  504-948-2166 |
| New Orleans | Beau Sejour,  1930 Napoleon Ave., 70115,  504-897-3746 |
| New Orleans | Bougainvillea House,  841 Bourbon St., 70116,  504-525-3983 |
| New Orleans | Chimes Cottages,  1360 Moss St., 70152,  504-525-4640 |
| New Orleans | Claiborne Mansion, The,  2111 Dauphine St., 70116 |
| New Orleans | Columns Hotel,  3811 St. Charles Ave., 70115,  504-899-9308 |
| New Orleans | Creole B&B,  3650 Gentilly Blvd., 70122 |
| New Orleans | Delta Queen Steamboat Co.,  Robin St. Wharf, 70130,  800-543-1949 |
| New Orleans | Dufour-Baldwin House,  1707 Esplanade Ave., 70116,  504-945-1503 |
| New Orleans | Duvigneaud House, The,  2857 Grand Route, 70119 |
| New Orleans | French Qrtr. Lanaux Hse.,  Esplanade, Box 52257, 70152,  800-729-4640 |
| New Orleans | Garden District B&B,  2418 Magazine St., 70130 |
| New Orleans | Glimmer Inn, The,  1631 Seventh St., 70115,  504-897-1895 |
| New Orleans | Grenoble House Inn,  329 Dauphine St., 70112,  504-522-1331 |
| New Orleans | Hedgewood Hotel,  2427 St. Charles Ave., 70130,  504-895-9708 |
| New Orleans | Historic B&B Home,  P.O. Box 52257, 70152,  800-749-4640 |
| New Orleans | Historic Inns/New Orleans,  911 Burgundy St., 70116,  504-524-4401 |
| New Orleans | Hotel Maison de Ville,  727 Toulouse St., 70130,  504-561-5858 |
| New Orleans | Hotel St. Pierre,  911 Burgundy St., 70116,  504-524-4401 |
| New Orleans | Hotel Ste. Helene,  508 Rue Chartres, 70130,  504-522-5014 |
| New Orleans | Hotel Villa Convento,  616 Ursulines St., 70116,  504-522-1793 |
| New Orleans | House on Bayou Road, The,  2275 Bayou Rd., 70119 |
| New Orleans | Jensen's B&B,  1631 Seventh St., 70115 |
| New Orleans | Josephine Guest House,  1450 Josephine St., 70130,  504-524-6361 |
| New Orleans | Levee View, The,  39 Hennesey Ct., 70123,  504-737-5471 |
| New Orleans | Longpre Garden's Gsthouse,  1726 Prytania, 70130,  504-561-0654 |
| New Orleans | MacArthy Park Guest House,  3820 Burgundy St., 70117,  505-943-4994 |
| New Orleans | Maison Orleans,  608 Kerlerac St., 70116 |
| New Orleans | Marigny Guest House,  617 Kerlerec, 70116,  504-944-9700 |
| New Orleans | Mazant Guest House,  906 Mazant St., 70117 |
| New Orleans | McKendrick-Breaux House,  1474 Magazine St., 70130 |
| New Orleans | Mechling's Guest House,  2023 Esplande Ave., 70116,  504-943-4131 |
| New Orleans | Melrose B&B,  937 Esplanade Ave., 70116,  504-944-2255 |
| New Orleans | Nicholas M. Benachi House,  2257 Bayou Rd., 70119 |
| New Orleans | Olivier Estate, a B&B,  1425 No. Prieur St., 70116,  504-949-9600 |
| New Orleans | Parkview Guest House,  7004 St. Charles, 70118,  504-861-7564 |
| New Orleans | Rathbone Inn,  1227 Esplanade Ave., 70116 |
| New Orleans | Robert Gordy House, The,  2630 Bell St., 70119,  504-486-9424 |
| New Orleans | Rue Royal Inn,  1006 Rue Royal, 70116,  800-776-3901 |
| New Orleans | Terrell House Mansion,  1441 Magazine St., 70130,  504-524-9859 |
| New Roads | River Blossom Inn,  300 N. Carolina Ave., 70760,  504-638-8650 |
| Plaquemine | Old Turnerville B&B,  23230 Nadler St., 70764,  504-687-5337 |
| Shreveport | 2439 Fairfield, A B&B,  2439 Fairfield Ave., 71104,  318-424-2424 |

| | |
|---|---|
| Slidell | Salmen-Fritchie House 1895, 127 Cleveland Ave., 70458, 504-643-1405 |
| St. Francisville | Green Springs Plantation, 7463 Tunica Trace, 70775 |
| St. Francisville | Lake Rosemound Inn, 10473 Lindsey Ln., 70775, 504-635-3176 |
| St. Francisville | Rosedown Plantation B&B, 12501 Hwy. 10, 70775, 504-635-3332 |
| St. Francisville | St. Francisville Inn, P.O. Box 1369, 70775, 504-635-6502 |
| St. Martinville | Old Castillo Hotel, The, 220 Evangeline Blvd, 70582, 318-394-4010 |
| Vacherie | Oak Alley Plantation, 3645 Highway 18, 70090, 800-442-5539 |
| Washington | Camellia Cove, 205 West Hill St, 70589, 318-826-7362 |
| Washington | De La Morandiere, P.O. Box 327, 70589, 318-826-3510 |
| Washington | La Chaumiere, 202 S Main St, 70589, 318-826-3967 |
| White Castle | White Castle Inn, 55035 Cambre St., 70788 |
| Wilson | Glencoe Plantation, P.O. Box 178, 70789, 504-629-5387 |

*Lafitte Guest House, New Orleans, LA*

# Maine

## BAR HARBOR

### Balance Rock Inn
| | | |
|---|---|---|
| 21 Albert Meadow,  04609 | $$$$-B&B | Continental breakfast |
| 207-286-2610  800-753-0494 | 14 rooms, 14 pb | Full breakfast (fee) |
| Nancy Cloud | Most CC, *Rated*,  • | Aftn. tea, sitting room |
| May–October 27 | C-ltd/S-ltd/P-no/H-no | hot tubs, fireplaces |
| | French | oceanside heated pool |

*Turn-of-the-century oceanfront mansion w/lovely rooms & spectacular views. Ideal spot for romantic vacations. Walk to downtown. **Disc't. on whale watch or sunset cruise.***

### Black Friar Inn
| | | |
|---|---|---|
| 10 Summer St.,  04609 | $$$-B&B | Full gourmet breakfast |
| 207-288-5091  Fax: 207-288-4197 | 7 rooms, 7 pb | Aftn. tea & refreshments |
| P.& S. Risley, Falke | MC, Visa, Disc. *Rated*, | Sitting room |
| All year | C-ltd/S-no/P-no/H-no | fly fishing trips |
| | | Sea Kayak School-May |

*Rebuilt in 1981 w/antiques & architectural finds from Mt. Desert Island. Victorian & country flavor. Near Acadia National Park, shops, restaurants. 2 day min. stay July-Oct.*

### Castlemaine Inn
| | | |
|---|---|---|
| 39 Holland Ave.,  04609 | $$-B&B | Continental plus bkfst. |
| 207-288-4563 Fax: 207-288-4525 | 12 rooms, 12 pb | All A/C, all cable TV |
| 800-338-4563 | MC, Visa, *Rated*, | Main street 3 blocks |
| T. O'Connell & N. O'Brien | C-ltd/S-ltd/P-no | water 2 blocks, Fax, VCR |
| All year | | |

*The inn is nestled on a quiet side street in Bar Harbor village, surrounded by the magnificent Acadia National Park. Rooms are well-appointed. AAA 3-Diamond rating*

### Graycote Inn
| | | |
|---|---|---|
| 40 Holland Ave.,  04609 | $$$-B&B | Full breakfast |
| 207-288-3044  Fax: 207-288-2719 | 12 rooms, 12 pb | Afternoon refreshments |
| Pat & Roger Samuel  All year | Most CC, *Rated*, | Sitting room, fireplaces |
| | C-ltd/S-ltd/P-no/H-no | king or queen-size beds |
| | | fireplaces, balconies |

*Restored Country Victorian inn located on quiet in-town street. Near Acadia National Park. Short walk to waterfront and fine restaurants, shops & galleries. **Reduced rates off-season**.*

*Castlemaine Inn, Bar Harbor, ME*

BAR HARBOR
**Hatfield B&B**
20 Roberts Ave.,   04609
207-288-9655
Jeffrey & Sandra Miller
All year

$$-B&B
6 rooms, 4 pb
Visa, MC,
C-yes/S-ltd/P-no/H-no

Full breakfast
Afternoon tea
Sitting room

*"Country Comfort" in downtown Bar Harbor. Fantastic breakfast, short walk to the waterfront, 5 minutes to Acadia National Park.*

---

**Hearthside B&B**
7 High St.,   04609
207-288-4533
Susan & Barry Schwartz
All year

$$$-B&B
9 rooms, 9 pb
MC, Visa, *Rated*,
C-ltd/S-no/P-no/H-no

Full breakfast
Comp. wine, cookies
Evening refreshments
3 rooms w/fireplaces, AC
2 bath w/whirlpool jets

*Small, gracious hostelry in quiet in-town location; elegant & comfortable; blend of antiques & traditional furniture. Visit Acadia Nat'l Park.* **Spring packages available.**

---

**Holbrook House Inn, The**
74 Mt. Desert St.,   04609
207-288-4970
Bill & Carol Deike
May-October

$$$-B&B
12 rooms, 12 pb
Visa, MC, *Rated*,
C-ltd/S-no/P-no/H-no

Full breakfast
Afternoon refreshments
Old fashion porch-parlor
library, inn rooms
beautiful furnishings

*A bright and airy restored Victorian summer home on Bar Harbor's Historic Corridor. Close to shops, restaurants, ocean and park. Off-street parking.*

---

**Inn at Bay Ledge, The**
1385 Sand Point Rd.,   04609
207-288-4204 Fax: 207-288-5573
Jack & Jeani Ochtera
All year

$$-B&B
,
*Rated*,
S-no/P-no

Full breakfast
Heated pool, fireplaces
sauna, steam rooms
Jacuzzi in 3 rooms

*Amidst towering pines, the inn literally clings to the cliffs of Mt. Desert Island. Many tiered decks over-look spectacular coastline. Private beach.*

## BAR HARBOR

**Ledgelawn Inn, The**
66 Mount Desert St., 04609
207-288-4596  800-274-5334
Nancy Cloud
April–November

$$-B&B
33 rooms, 33 pb
AmEx, MC, Visa,
*Rated*, •
C-yes/S-yes/P-no/H-no

Continental plus bkfst.
Bar service, comp. tea
Sitting room, library
piano, pool, sauna
modern exercise room

*A graceful turn-of-the-century mansion with antiques, sitting areas, fireplaces, hot tub; in a quiet location, 5-min. walk to downtown. **Disc't on whale watch or sunset sail.***

---

**Manor House Inn**
106 West St., 04609
207-288-3759  Fax: 207-288-2974
800-437-0088
Mac Noyes
May–mid-October

$$$-B&B
14 rooms, 14 pb
AmEx, MC, Visa,
*Rated*,
C-ltd/S-no/P-no/H-no

Full breakfast
Afternoon tea
Sitting room, fireplaces
swimming pool, piano
gardens, tennis courts

*Many special touches. Restored Victorian, National Register, antique furniture. Bedrooms include parlor, bath. Near Acadia National Park. **4th night free off-season weekdays.***

---

**Mira Monte Inn & Suites**
69 Mt. Desert St., 04609
207-288-4263  Fax: 207-288-3115
800-553-5109
Marian Burns
Early May–late October

$$$-B&B
16 rooms, 16 pb
AmEx, MC, Visa,
*Rated*, •
C-ltd/S-ltd/P-no/H-yes

Full breakfast buffet
Comp. wine & cheese
Juice, snacks, piano
sitting & meeting rooms
all rms: phones, A/C, TV

*Renovated Victorian estate; period furnishings, fireplaces; quiet, in-town location, walk to waterfront. Honeymoon packages. Weekly rental.*

---

**Primrose Inn**
73 Mt. Desert St., 04609
207-288-4031  Fax: 207-288-4031
800-543-7842
Bronwen Kaldro
May-October

$$-B&B
15 rooms, 15 pb
Most CC, *Rated*, •
C-yes/S-ltd/P-no/H-ltd

Continental plus bkfst.
Afternoon refreshments
Sitting room
large front porch
sugar free baking

*1878 Victorian guest house on "Historic Corridor." Antique furnishings, some rooms with whirlpool, porch, fireplace. Near Acadia and downtown.*

---

**Ridgeway Inn, The**
11 High St., 04609
207-288-9682
Lucie Rioux Hollfelder
May 1-Mid. November

$$-B&B
5 rooms, 5 pb
*Rated*,
C-ltd/S-no/P-no/H-no
German, Hebrew,
Yiddish

Full 3 course breakfast
Afternoon tea
Complimentary wine
walk to the sea
honeymoon packages

*The Ridgeway is a Victorian home on a tree-lined street in a quiet residential section of Bar Harbor. Guests can park at the inn and walk to nearby restaurants and shops.*

---

**Stratford House Inn**
45 Mt. Desert St., 04609
207-288-5189
Barbara & Norman Moulton
May 15–October

$$-B&B
10 rooms, 8 pb
AmEx, MC, Visa,
C-yes/S-ltd/P-ltd

Continental breakfast
Sitting room
library

*Tudor mansion built by publisher of "Little Women." Close to boating, swimming, tennis, golf, climbing, hiking, stores and restaurants. Quiet area. **3 nights for price of 2, ltd.***

BAR HARBOR ——————————————————————————————

| **Tides, The** | $$$$-B&B | Full breakfast |
| 119 West St.,   04609 | 3 rooms, 3 pb | Sitting room |
| 207-288-4968 | Visa, MC, Disc. *Rated*, | 2nd floor guest living |
| Joe & Judy Losquadro | C-ltd/S-no/P-no/H-no | room w/gas fireplace |
| All year | | |

*Magnificent water views from every bed chamber; private but walk to town; sumptuous full breakfast on the veranda with sweeping views of Frenchman's Bay.*

—————————————————————————————————————————

| **Town Guest House** | $$-B&B/AP | Continental plus bkfst. |
| 12 Atlantic Ave.,   04609 | 9 rooms, 9 pb | Sitting room |
| 207-288-5548 Fax: 207-288-9406 | AmEx, MC, Visa, | 3 rms w/queen sized beds |
| 800-458-8644 | *Rated*, • | no chg. for age 12/under |
| Joe & Paulette Paluga | C-yes/S-no/P-no/H-no | |
| May–October | | |

*Victorian inn offers old-fashioned comfort with modern conveniences. Enjoy period furniture, marble sinks, porches, working fireplaces, private baths in our gracious rooms.*

BASS HARBOR ——————————————————————————————

| **Bass Harbor Cottages &** | $-EP | Kitchen, refrigerators |
| **Inn** | 3 rooms, 3 pb | TVs in cottages |
| P.O. Box 40,   04653 | MC, Visa, *Rated*, | porch overlooks harbor |
| Rt. 102 A | C-yes/S-no/P-no/H-no | by Acadia National Park |
| 207-244-3460 Fax: 207-244-3023 | | |
| Constance L. Howe | | |
| All year | | |

*Our small, intimate inn offers privacy, tranquility & views of the harbor. A staircase leads to the water's edge. Bass Harbor Cottages & Country Inn*

—————————————————————————————————————————

| **Pointy Head Inn** | $$-B&B | Full breakfast |
| HCR 33, Box 2A, Route 102A, | 6 rooms, 3 pb | Sitting room with TV |
|    04653 | C-ltd/S-no/P-no/H-no | porch & deck |
| 207-244-7261 | | overlook harbor |
| Doris & Warren Townsend | | |
| Mid-May–October | | |

*Old sea captain's home on the ocean in Bass Harbor. 1 mile from Bass Harbor Headlight in Acadia National Park. A haven for artists and photographers. Gift shop.*

BATH ———————————————————————————————————————

| **Fairhaven Inn** | $$-B&B | Full breakfast |
| RR 2, Box 85,   04530 | 6 rooms, 6 pb | Tea, soda |
| N. Bath Rd. | *Rated*, • | Piano, library, bicycles |
| 207-443-4391 | C-ltd/S-yes/P-no/H-no | hiking trail, cross-country |
| Susie & Dave Reed | | skiing |
| All year | | winter snowshoeing |

*Quiet country inn on 16 acres of woods, meadows, lawns. Antique & country furnishings. Occasional baking lessons from pastry chef/owner.* **Winter discounts.**

BELFAST ——————————————————————————————————

| **Belfast Bay Meadows Inn** | $$-B&B | Full gourmet breakfast |
| 90 Northport Ave., Route 1, | 12 rooms, 12 pb | Lunch, dinner available |
|    04915 | Most CC, *Rated*, • | Dedicated conference rm. |
| 207-338-5715  800-335-2370 | C-yes/S-no/P-yes/H-ltd | boat & train tour rides |
| John & Patty Lebowitz | | antique shops/auctions |
| All year | | |

*Penobscot Bay view. Antique decor; A/C, phone, TV. Bay view dining deck, enclosed porch, 8 acres of gardens, fields, forest. 17 acres. Summer restaurant. Near golf, art galleries.* **1/3 off 3rd night.**

*The Jeweled Turret Inn, Belfast, ME*

BELFAST ——————————————————————————————

| | | |
|---|---|---|
| **Jeweled Turret Inn, The** | $$-B&B | Full breakfast |
| 40 Pearl St., 04915 | 7 rooms, 7 pb | Aftn. tea by res., ltd |
| 207-338-2304  800-696-2304 | *Rated*, • | Sitting rooms, parlors |
| Carl & Cathy Heffentrager | C-ltd/S-ltd/P-no/H-no | antiques |
| All year | | tennis & pool nearby |

*Intimate & charming. Unique architectural features; turrets, verandahs, beautiful wood-work. Walk to town, shops & harbor. On National Register.* **10% off 2+ nights, ltd.**

BOOTHBAY HARBOR ——————————————————————————

| | | |
|---|---|---|
| **Albonegon Inn** | $$-B&B | Continental breakfast |
| Capitol Island, 04538 | 15 rooms, 3 pb | Afternoon tea |
| 207-633-2521 | MC, Visa, | Sitting room, piano |
| Kim & Bob Peckham | C-ltd | tennis court, beaches |
| July—mid October | Spanish | "grill" your own dinner |

*A very special place to relax. On a private island, perched on the edge of the ocean. Spectacular views! Hike, bird-watch, swim, beachcomb, tennis, sail. Golf nearby.*

| | | |
|---|---|---|
| **Anchor Watch B&B** | $$$-B&B | Full breakfast |
| 3 Eames Rd., 04538 | 4 rooms, 4 pb | Home-grown strawberries |
| 207-633-7565 | *Rated*, • | 3 rooms w/ocean views |
| Diane Campbell | C-ltd/S-no/P-no/H-no | pier on property for |
| All year | | fishing and boating |

*Scenic shore; winter ducks feed near the rocks; flashing lighthouses; lobstermen hauling traps, walk to restaurants, shops, boats.* **Discount on boat trip, "Balmy Day Cruises."**

| | | |
|---|---|---|
| **Atlantic Ark Inn, The** | $$-B&B | Full gourmet breakfast |
| 64 Atlantic Ave., 04538 | 6 rooms, 6 pb | Comp. afternoon beverage |
| 207-633-5690 | *Rated*, • | Sitting room, wrap |
| Donna Piggott | C-ltd/S-ltd/P-no/H-no | around veranda with |
| May—October | | arbor, near town |

*Quaint & intimate, this small inn offers lovely harbor views, antiques, oriental rugs, mahogany beds, flowers. Suite luxurious: 16 windows, private balcony, panoramic view.*

## BOOTHBAY HARBOR

| **Five Gables Inn** | $$$-B&B | Full breakfast |
|---|---|---|
| P.O. Box 335,   04544 | 15 rooms, 15 pb | Fireplaces, games |
| Murray Hill Rd. | *Rated*, • | wraparound veranda |
| 207-633-4551  800-451-5048 | C-ltd/S-no/P-no | pool & boating nearby |
| Mike & De Kennedy | | |

*Charm & elegance of old Victorian decor, the convenience of spotless facilities. All rooms have views of the bay, unique furnishings & private bath. **Cookbook for repeat guests.***

| **Greenleaf Inn** | $$-B&B | Continental plus bkfst. |
|---|---|---|
| 91 Commercial St.,  04538 | 5 rooms, | Fantastic views |
| 207-633-7346 Fax: 207-633-7346 | Visa, MC, | |
| Sara & Wayne Thompson | C-ltd/S-ltd/P-no/H-ltd | |
| May 15–Oct. 15 | | |

*Inn overlooks harbor in 2 directions, east is the yacht filled inner harbor, gift shop, restaurant, tour boats. South is the island studded harbor to the open sea. Beautiful rooms, private baths.*

| **Kenniston Hill Inn** | $$-B&B | Full breakfast |
|---|---|---|
| P.O. Box 125,   04537 | 10 rooms, 10 pb | Sitting room, fireplaces |
| Route 27 | MC, Visa, Disc. *Rated*, | fishing, boating, skiing |
| 207-633-2159  Fax: 207-633-2159 | • | tennis, golf, swimming |
| 800-992-2915 | C-ltd/S-no/P-no/H-ltd | |
| The Straights   All year | | |

*Oldest inn in Boothbay (c. 1786) on 4 peaceful acres offering country antiques, fireplaces & sitting rooms, full country breakfast. Diet restrictions accommodated.*

## BRIDGTON

| **Noble House B&B, The** | $$$-B&B | Full breakfast |
|---|---|---|
| P.O. Box 180,   04009 | 9 rooms, 6 pb | Sitting room, library |
| 37 Highland Ridge Rd. | • | baby grand piano, organ |
| 207-647-3733 Fax: 207-647-3733 | C-ltd/S-ltd/P-no/H-no | canoe, lake, lawn games |
| Jane & Dick Starets | | |
| All year | | |

*Majestic turn-of-the-century home on beautiful Highland Lake. Four-season activities: summer theater, skiing. Family suites, personal attention. Near crafts & antique shops.*

## BROOKSVILLE

| **Breezemere Farm Inn** | $$$-B&B | Full breakfast |
|---|---|---|
| RR1, Box 290,   04617 | 14 rooms, 12 pb | Aftn. tea, group dinners |
| Breezemere Rd. | MC, Visa, • | Sitting room, gameroom |
| 207-326-8628 Fax: 207-326-8912 | C-yes/S-ltd/P-ltd/H-no | hiking trails, bikes |
| 888-223-FARM | | boating, cross-country skiing |
| Laura Johns & Carolyn | | |
| Heller     All year | | |

*Unrivaled scenic beauty—coves, islands, ledges, trees, unparalleled nature—bald eagles, seals, tidal life. Fine eating, sparkling accommodations. 7 cottages available. **10% off week stay.***

| **Oakland House-Shore Oaks** | $$-B&B/MAP | Continental breakfast |
|---|---|---|
| RR 1, Box 400,   04617 | 25 rooms, 22 pb | Full breakfast (MAP) |
| Herrick Rd. | Cash or checks only, • | Snacks, beaches, byokyak |
| 207-359-8521  800-359-7352 | C-ltd/S-ltd/P-ltd/H-no | sitting room, gazebo |
| Jim & Sally Littlefield | | library, boating, hikes |
| Early May-January | | |

*On a half mile of rural ocean front, woodland dirt roads, loons, seals, dock, rowboats, hiking trails, beach lobster picnic & photo perfect views. **7th night free, ltd.***

## CAMDEN

**A Little Dream**
66 High St., 04843
207-236-8742
Joanna Ball, Bill Fontana
All year

$$$-B&B
7 rooms, 7 pb
Visa, MC, AmEx,
S-no/P-no/H-no
Italian, some Fr. & Ger.

Full gourmet breakfast
Comp. sherry
Sitting room
antique books

*Lovely luxury B&B in a turn-of-the-century turreted Victorian. Rooms with view of water, decks, or fireplace. Featured in Country Inns and Glamour magazine.*

---

**Camden Harbour Inn**
83 Bayview St., 04843
207-236-4200 Fax: 207-236-7063
800-236-4266
Sal Vella & Patti Babij
All year

$$$-B&B
22 rooms, 22 pb
Most CC, *Rated*, •
C-ltd/S-yes/P-no/H-yes

Full breakfast from menu
Dinner, bar service
Parlour, porch, patio
lounge with fireplace
meeting facilities

*Historic 1874 Victorian inn with spectacular panorama of harbor, bay and mountains. Fine dining; cocktails in the Thirsty Whale. Meeting facilities.* **Dessert & coffee w/ dinner.**

---

**Edgecombe-Coles House**
RR1, Box 3010, 04843
64 High St.
207-236-2336 Fax: 207-236-6227
800-528-2336
Terry & Louise Price
All year

$$$-B&B
6 rooms, 6 pb
Most CC,
C-ltd/S-yes/P-no/H-no

Full breakfast
Comp. port, aftn. tea
Sitting room, piano
library, bikes, tennis
phones & TVs in rooms

*Distinctive country inn with breathtaking views of Penobscot Bay. Antique furnishings, private baths, hearty breakfasts. Some rooms have VCRs. Maine's most beautiful seaport.* **2nd night 50%, Nov.–Apr.**

---

**Elms B&B, The**
84 Elm St., 04843
207-236-6250 Fax: 207-236-7330
800-755-ELMS
Ted & Jo Panayotoff
All year

$$$-B&B
6 rooms, 6 pb
MC, Visa,
C-ltd/S-no/P-no/H-ltd

Full breakfast
Breakfast, Afternoon tea
Cottage gardens, library
period furniture
fireplaces, restaurants

*Experience the casual warmth of this restored 1806 Colonial. Enjoy collection of lighthouse artwork, books & collectibles. Walk to harbor and shops.* **2nd night free, ltd.**

---

**Hartstone Inn**
41 Elm St., 04843
207-236-4259
Sunny & Peter Simmons
All year

$$-B&B/EP
10 rooms, 10 pb
Most CC, *Rated*, •
C-ltd/S-no/P-no/H-no

Full breakfast
Dinner, picnic sails
Comp. tea, cookies
sitting room, fireplaces
library, TV room, phones

*Stately Victorian inn, centrally located in picturesque village, steps away from harbor. Hearty bkfst., romantic dinners, friendly, relaxed atmosphere.* **Special dinner packages.**

---

**Hawthorn Inn**
9 High St., 04843
207-236-8842 Fax: 207-236-6181
Nick & Patty Wharton
All year

$$$-B&B
10 rooms, 10 pb
MC, Visa, *Rated*, •
C-ltd/S-no/P-no/H-no

Full breakfast
2 sitting rooms
double jacuzzi tubs
fireplaces, decks

*Stately Victorian mansion with light, airy rooms. Views of Camden Harbor and mountains. Minutes to shops, restaurants & harbor activities.* **3 nights for price of 2, ltd.**

## CAMDEN

**Maine Stay Inn**
22 High St., 04843
207-236-9636 Fax: 207-236-0621
Peter Smith, Donny, Diana
All year

$$-B&B
8 rooms, 6 pb
MC, Visa, *Rated*, •
C-ltd/S-yes/P-no/H-no

Full breakfast
2 parlors w/fireplaces
piano, TV room
deck

*Built in 1802, the inn is situated in the high street historic district on two acres of lovely grounds only two blocks from the harbor and village center.*

---

**Swan House**
49 Mountain St. (Rt 52),
04843
207-236-8275 Fax: 207-236-0906
800-207-8275
Lyn & Ken Kohl
All year

$$$-B&B
6 rooms, 6 pb
MC, Visa,
C-ltd/S-no/P-no/H-ltd

Full country breakfast
Sitting rooms, gazebo
enclosed sunporch
mountain hiking trail

*Located in a quiet neighborhood, away from busy Route 1. Short walk to Camden's beautiful harbor, or hike backyard trail to Mt. Battie summit for spectacular views. Antiques.*

---

**Victorian B&B, The**
P.O. Box 1385, 04849
207-236-3785 Fax: 207-236-0017
800-382-9817
Ray & Marie Donner
All year

$$$$-B&B
6 rooms, 6 pb
Visa, MC, *Rated*, •
C-ltd/S-ltd/P-no/H-no

Full breakfast
Afternoon tea
Sitting room
library
elegant hideaway

*Quiet 1881 Victorian. Water views, gardens, fireplaces & relaxation. Queen beds. Full breakfast in sunlit turret room. Five minutes to downtown Camden.*

---

**Windward House B&B**
6 High St., 04843
207-236-9656 Fax: 207-230-0433
Tim & Sandy La Plante
All year

$$$-B&B
8 rooms, 8 pb
MC, Visa,
C-ltd/S-no/P-no/H-no

Full gourmet breakfast
Comp. port and sherry
Sitting rooms, library
garden room
walk to village & harbor

*In Harbor Village; spacious historic 1854 colonial fully restored, beautifully decorated. All rooms have queen beds, some w/canopy beds & gas fireplaces. Gracious hospitality.*

## CAPE ELIZABETH

**Inn by the Sea**
40 Bowery Beach Rd., Route
77, 04107
207-799-3134 Fax: 207-799-4779
800-888-4287
Maureen McQuade
All year

$$$-EP
43 rooms, 43 pb
MC, Visa, AmEx,
*Rated*, •
C-yes/S-no/P-yes/H-yes
French, German

Restaurant (fee)
Snacks, bar service
Library, bicycles
tennis court, pool
croquet, volleyball

*Luxury suites in chippendale cherry or white pine & natural wicker. Overlooking Atlantic, full kitchen, living/dining area. Natural estuaries. **3rd night free, Nov.–Apr.***

## CAPE NEDDICK

**Cape Neddick House, The**
P.O. Box 70, 03902
1300 Rt.1
207-363-2500 Fax: 207-363-4499
Dianne & John Goodwin
All year

$$-B&B
6 rooms, 6 pb
*Rated*,
C-ltd/S-ltd/P-no/H-no

Full breakfast
Comp. wine, tea, coffee
Parlor & living room
bicycles, guitar, trails
horseshoes, picnic area

*Coastal country 4th-gen. Victorian home. Close to beach, antiques, outlets, boutiques. Cultural, historic attractions. Award-winning Apple Butter Nut Cake. **3rd night 50%.***

## CASTINE

**Manor, The**
Box 276,   04421
Battle Ave.
207-326-4861  Fax: 207-326-4066
Sara & Paul Brouillard
All year exc. Christmas

$$-B&B
12 rooms, 10 pb
MC, Visa,  •
C-yes/S-yes/P-ltd/H-no
French, Spanish

Continental plus bkfst.
La Conque Restaurant/bar
Sitting room, library
lounge, billiard room
piano, bicycles, cottage

*Elegant turn-of-the-century mansion. Very quiet, yet close to restaurants & shops. Gourmet dining on-site, Wine Spectator award-winning wine list. 5 acres of lawns. Nat'l Register.*

## COREA

**Black Duck on Corea Harbor**
P.O. Box 39,   04624
Crowley Island Rd.
207-963-2689  Fax: 207-963-7495
Barry & Bob    All year

$$-B&B
5 rooms, 3 pb
Visa, MC,  •
C-ltd/S-no/P-no/H-no
Danish, ltd. French

Full breakfast
Special diets catered
Sitting room, library
bicycles
hiking trails

*Casual elegance, antiques and art. Overlooking working lobster harbor. Village charm with rural atmosphere. Near national park and bird sanctuary.* **10% off for 7+ nights.**

## DEER ISLE

**Pilgrim's Inn**
Box 69,   04627
Main St.
207-348-6615
Jean & Dud Hendrick
Mid-May–mid-October

$$$$-B&B/MAP
13 rooms, 8 pb
*Rated*,  •
C-ltd/S-no/P-yes/H-no

Full breakfast
Supper, tea, coffee, bar
Sitting room, piano
bicycles, library, deck
patio grill area, garden

*Idyllic location on Deer Isle. Elegant yet informal colonial inn, creative cuisine, rustic antique-furnished barn. Commons rooms with 8' fireplaces. Gift shop.* **Special mug.**

## DENNYSVILLE

**Lincoln House Country Inn**
RR1, Box 136A, Rts. 1 and 86,
   04628
207-726-3953  Fax: 207-726-0654
888-726-3953
Mary Carol & Jerry Haggerty
Open mid-May–mid-Oct.

$$-B&B
11 rooms, 4 pb
AmEx, MC, Visa,
*Rated*,  •
C-yes/S-yes/P-no/H-yes

Full breakfast
Sitting room
grand piano, library
fireplaces

*Lovingly restored colonial w/95 acres of hiking, birding, fishing. Centerpiece of N.E. corner of coastal Maine. Internationally acclaimed. Nat'l Register.* **3rd night free.**

## EASTPORT

**Todd House**
1 Capen Ave., Todd's Head,
   04631
207-853-2328
Ruth M. McInnis
All year

$-B&B
7 rooms, 3 pb
C-yes/S-ltd/P-yes/H-yes

Continental plus bkfst.
Babeque deck with a view
Library, fireplace
yard with barbecue
picnic facilities

*Step into the past in our revolutionary-era Cape with wide panorama of Passamaquoddy Bay. Breakfast in common room before huge fireplace.*

**Weston House B&B**
26 Boynton St.,   04631
207-853-2907  800-853-2907
Jett Peterson
All year

$$-B&B
5 rooms,
*Rated*,
C-ltd/S-ltd/P-no/H-no

Full gourmet breakfast
Comp. wine, tea, snacks
Picnic lunch & dinner
sitting room, library
croquet, "secret garden"

*1810 Federal on a hill overlooking Passamaquoddy Bay. On National Register of Historic Places. Furnished with antiques, clocks and family treasures.* **3rd night 50% off.**

*High Meadows B&B, Eliot, ME*

## ELIOT

| | | |
|---|---|---|
| **High Meadows B&B** | $$-B&B | Full breakfast |
| 2 Brixham Rd., Rt. 101, | 5 rooms, 5 pb | Afternoon wine, tea |
| 03903 | S-ltd/P-no/H-no | Sitting room |
| 207-439-0590 | | Barn available for |
| Elaine Raymond | | parties and weddings |
| April–November | | |

*1736 colonial house in the country. Walking & cross-country ski trails. 6.5 miles to historic Portsmouth, New Hampshire; shopping, theater & fine dining.*

## FREEPORT

| | | |
|---|---|---|
| **181 Main Street B&B** | $$$-B&B | Full breakfast |
| 181 Main St.,  04032 | 7 rooms, 7 pb | Comp. coffee, tea, etc. |
| 207-865-1226 | MC, Visa, *Rated*, | Sitting room |
| Ed Hassett & David Cates | S-ltd/P-no/H-no | library |
| All year | French | in-ground pool |

*Cozy, antique-filled 1840 cape, in town, with ample parking, hearty breakfasts. Walk to L.L. Bean and luxury outlets.*

| | | |
|---|---|---|
| **Bayberry Inn** | $-B&B | Continental plus |
| 8 Maple Ave.,  04032 | 5 rooms, 5 pb | Full breakfast, optional |
| 207-865-1868 | Visa, MC, *Rated*, | Sitting room w/cable tv, |
| The Frank Family | C-yes/S-no/P-no/H-no | VCR, books, games or |
| All year | German | conversation |

*Quaint village on the sea coast of Maine. 1853 Federal house with cozy and cheerful guestrooms. Private baths. Walk to village and L.L. Bean.* **disc't on 4 or more nights.**

| | | |
|---|---|---|
| **Country at Heart B&B** | $$-B&B | Full breakfast |
| 37 Bow St.,  04032 | 3 rooms, 3 pb | Afternoon tea, snacks |
| 207-865-0512 | *Rated*, • | Sitting room, fireplace |
| Roger & Kim Dubay | C-yes/P-no/H-no | walk to many restaurants |
| Exc. Thanksgiving, Xmas | | reproduction furnishings |

*Enjoy a stay in 1870 home w/country decorated rooms. Handsome crafts & antiques. Close to L.L. Bean & outlet stores.* **7th night free.**

## FREEPORT

**Harraseeket Inn**
162 Main St.,   04032
207-865-9377  Fax: 207-865-1684
800-342-6423
The Gray Family
All year

$$$-B&B
6 rooms, 6 pb
Visa, MC, AmEx,
*Rated*, •
C-yes/S-ltd/P-no/H-no

Full breakfast buffet
Restaurant, tavern
Afteroon tea, library
sitting rooms, fireplace
ballroom, dining rooms

*Luxury B&B. Private baths (jacuzzi or steam), cable TV, elegant Maine buffet country breakfast. Two blocks north of L.L. Bean. Walk to famous factory outlet shops.*

---

**Isaac Randall House, The**
5 Independence Dr.,   04032
207-865-9295  Fax: 207-865-9003
800-865-9295
J.&G. Friedlander, C. Wellito
All year

$$-B&B
8 rooms, 6 pb
•
C-ltd/S-ltd/P-ltd/H-ltd
Spanish, French

Full breakfast
Comp. beverages/snacks
Sitting room, library
dining porch, playground
caboose, seminar rooms

*Gracious 1823 country inn, elegantly & comfortably furnished with antiques. Pond, woods, picnic areas, playground.* **3rd night 50% off; honeymoon/anniversary champagne.**

---

**Kendall Tavern B&B**
213 Main St.,   04032
207-865-1338  800-341-9572
Jim Whitley
All year

$$-B&B
7 rooms, 7 pb
Most CC, *Rated*, •
C-ltd/S-no/P-no/H-no

Full country breakfast
Sitting room & fireplace
parlor, Steinway piano
hot tub

*Lovingly restored early 1800s farm house on 3.5 acres. Easy 10 minute walk to shopping and dining.* **Off season specials; Local restaurant discounts.**

---

**White Cedar Inn**
178 Main St.,   04032
207-865-9099  800-853-1269
Carla & Phil Kerber
All year

$$$-B&B
6 rooms, 6 pb
Most CC, *Rated*,
C-ltd/S-no/P-no/H-no

Full breakfast
Outdoor grill
Sitting room, Air Cond.
picnic table, patio
all rooms have A/C

*Recently restored 100-year-old home with large uncluttered antique-furnished rooms. Located just 2 blocks from L.L. Bean. Breakfast served on sun porch overlooking landscape.*

## FREEPORT/DURHAN

**Bagley House, The**
1290 Royalsborough Rd.,
  04222
207-865-6566  Fax: 207-353-5878
800-765-1772
S. O'Connor & S. Backhouse
All year

$$-B&B
5 rooms, 5 pb
Most CC, *Rated*, •
C-yes/S-no/P-no/H-no

Full breakfast
Comp. beverages, cookies
Sitting room, library
cross-country skiing
(winter)
6-acre yard, barbecue

*Peace, tranquillity & history abound in this magnificent 1772 country home. A warm welcome awaits you from us & resident dog & cat. 6 miles from downtown Freeport.* **10% off 11/1-6/30, holidays excluded.**

## FRYEBURG

**Admiral Peary House B&B**
9 Elm St.,   04037
207-935-3365  Fax: 207-935-3365
800-237-8080
Nancy & Ed Greenberg
May—Oct. & Dec.—Mar.

$$-B&B
5 rooms, 5 pb
AmEx, MC, Visa,
*Rated*, •
C-ltd/S-no/P-no/H-no
French

Full breakfast
Complimentary beverage
Sitting room, library
bicycles, tennis court
hot tub, billiards, A/C

*Charming historical home in a picturesque White Mountain village. Clay tennis court, skiing, canoeing, hiking, spacious grounds, perennial gardens.* **10% off 5+ nights, ltd.**

*Greenville Inn, Greenville, ME*

## GOULDSBORO

| | | |
|---|---|---|
| **Bluff House Inn, The** | $$-B&B | Continental breakfast |
| P.O. Box 249,   04607 | 8 rooms, 8 pb | Restaurant features BYOB |
| Route 186 | Most CC, *Rated*, | Sitting room, canoes |
| 207-963-7805 | C-yes/S-ltd/P-no/H-no | conference facilities up |
| Joyce & Don Freeborn | | to 30 persons, kayak |
| All year | | |

*A quiet, serene, beautiful setting nestled among whispering pines atop a 200-foot bluff. Overlooking Frenchman Bay and its islands. Large decks with million dollar view.*

## GREENVILLE

| | | |
|---|---|---|
| **Greenville Inn** | $$$-B&B | Continental plus bkfst. |
| P.O. Box 1194,   04441 | 9 rooms, 7 pb | Dinner, restaurant, bar |
| Norris St. | Visa, MC, Disc. *Rated*, | Sitting room, queen beds |
| 207-695-2206 Fax: 207-695-2206 | C-ltd/S-yes/P-ltd/H-ltd | 4 new cottages, suite |
| 888-695-6000 | German | common rooms redecorated |
| The Schnetzers | | |
| May-Oct, Dec 15-Mar 15 | | |

*Restored lumber baron's mansion w/many unique features on a hill in town overlooking Moosehead Lake and Squaw Mountain. 8 miles to Squaw Mountain skiing. Moosewatching tours.* **Complimentary maple syrup.**

## HANCOCK POINT

| | | |
|---|---|---|
| **Crocker House Country Inn** | $$-B&B | Full breakfast |
| | 11 rooms, 11 pb | Restaurant, bar, dinner |
| P.O. Box 171,   04640 | Most CC, *Rated*, | Sitt. rm. liqour lic. |
| HC 77 | C-ltd/S-yes/P-ltd/H-no | spa, vegetarian dining |
| 207-422-6806 Fax: 207-422-3105 | | conference facilities |
| Elizabeth & Richard Malaby | | |
| May—Thanksgiving | | |

*Quiet traditional coastal inn offering simple elegant dining. A little out of the way, but way out of the ordinary. Recently renovated.*

## ISLE AU HAUT

**Keeper's House, The**
P.O. Box 26, 04645
Lighthouse Point
207-367-2261
Jeffrey & Judith Burke
May–October

$$$$-AP
4 rooms,
C-yes/S-no/P-no/H-no
Spanish

Full breakfast
Lunch, dinner included
Snacks
hiking, bicycles
ocean swimming

*Operating lighthouse station on island in Acadia National Park. Tiny fishing village, spectacular natural surroundings. Arrive on mailboat.* **50% off second night, ltd.**

## KENNEBUNK

**Arundel Meadows Inn**
P.O. Box 1129, 04043
Route 1, Arundel ME 04046
207-985-3770 Fax: 207-967-4704
Mark Bachelder, Murray
Yaeger   All year

$$-B&B
7 rooms, 7 pb
MC, Visa *Rated*, •
C-ltd/S-no/P-no/H-ltd

Full gourmet breakfast
Afternoon tea
Set-ups, library
sitting room

*Rooms individually decorated with art, antiques. Some with fireplaces; all with private baths. Gourmet breakfasts and teas. Near shops and beaches.* **10% off 5 nites or more.**

**Sundial Inn, The**
P.O. Box 1147, 04043
48 Beach Ave.
207-967-3850 Fax: 207-967-4719
Pat & Larry Kenny
All year

$$-B&B
34 rooms, 34 pb
AmEx, MC, Visa,
*Rated*,
C-ltd/S-no/P-no/H-yes
French

Continental plus bkfst.
Afternoon tea (winter)
Sitting room
whirlpool tubs
beach & ocean views

*On Kennebunkport beach. Country Victorian antiques, beautiful ocean views. An elevator for your convenience. Near hiking, beach, swimming, shopping, dining, fishing.* **Off-season packages.**

## KENNEBUNK BEACH

**Ocean View, The**
72 Beach Ave., 04043
207-967-2750 Fax: 207-967-5418
Carole & Bob Arena
April-mid December

$$$-B&B
9 rooms, 9 pb
Visa, MC, Disc.,
S-no/P-no/H-no
French

Full breakfast
Late aftn. refreshments
Sitting room, library
exclusive boutique
"Painted Lady" on beach

*"The closest you'll find to a bed on the beach." An intimate oceanfront Inn. Whimsical and colorful. Immaculate and sparkling. A jewel of distinct quality.*

## KENNEBUNKPORT

**1802 House B&B Inn**
P.O. Box 646-A, 15 Locke St.,
  04046
207-967-5632 Fax: 207-967-0780
800-932-5632
Ron & Carol Perry   All year

$$$-B&B
6 rooms, 6 pb
AmEx, MC, Visa,
*Rated*, •
C-ltd/S-no/P-no/H-no

Full breakfast
Guest parlors
gardens, dbl. whirlpool
bathtubs & fireplaces

*Beautifully restored historic inn furnished with antiques. Quiet, secluded location on golf course. Walk to town. Elegant three room suite.* **10% off Nov.–May, off-season rates.**

**Captain Fairfield Inn**
P.O. Box 1308, 04046
Pleasant & Green Sts.
207-967-4454 Fax: 207-967-8537
800-322-1928
Dennis & Bonnie Tallagnon

$$$-B&B
9 rooms, 9 pb
MC, Visa, *Rated*, •
C-yes/S-no/P-no/H-no
some French

Full gourmet breakfast
Afternoon tea
Sitting room,library
lovely park-like gardens
& grounds, beach, boats

*Gracious 1813 Federal Sea Captain's mansion beautifully appointed. Romantic, spacious bedrooms. Some with fireplaces. Chef owner prepares wonderful breakfasts.* **3-day midweek discount Nov.–Apr.**

KENNEBUNKPORT ──────────────────────

| | | |
|---|---|---|
| **Captain Lord Mansion, The** | $$$$-B&B | Full breakfast |
| P.O. Box 800,  04046 | 16 rooms, 16 pb | Afternoon tea, sweets |
| Pleasant & Green Sts. | Most CC, *Rated*, • | Accecories in bathrooms |
| 207-967-3141  Fax: 207-967-3141 | C-ltd/S-ltd/P-no/H-no | sitting room, piano, A/C |
| Bev Davis & Rick Litchfield | | beach towels, umbrellas |
| All year | | |

*An intimate Maine coast inn. Furnished with genuine antiques. AAA 4-Diamond. Mobil 3-Star. Conference room for large meetings. TV, gift shop.*

────────────────────────────────────

| | | |
|---|---|---|
| **Chetwynd House Inn, The** | $$$-B&B | Full multi-course bkfst. |
| P.O. Box 130,  04046 | 4 rooms, 4 pb | Complimentary tea |
| 4 Chestnut St. | • | Sitting room, library |
| 207-967-2235  Fax: 207-967-5406 | C-ltd/S-ltd/P-no/H-no | 2 room suite, all rooms |
| 800-833-3351 | French, Italian | have cable TV & A/C |
| Susan Knowles Chetwynd | | |
| All year | | |

*Pristine rooms. Handsome, lovely furnishings. Rich mahogany & cherry wood antique pieces. Poster beds; tea tables. Room renovations & painting.* **Seasonal & midweek specials.**

────────────────────────────────────

| | | |
|---|---|---|
| **English Meadows Inn** | $$$-B&B | Full breakfast |
| 141 Port Rd.,  04043 | 15 rooms, 15 pb | Afternoon tea, lemonade |
| 207-967-5766  Fax: 207-967-5766 | *Rated*, | Room service for bkfast. |
| 800-272-0698 | C-ltd/S-no/P-yes/H-no | sitting room, piano |
| Charlie Doane | French | studio apt/cottage avail |
| April–October | | |

*1860 Victorian farmhouse. Stroll to beaches, town, restaurants. Inn furnished throughout with antiques and local artworks. Extra-special breakfasts.* **Off-season rates.**

────────────────────────────────────

| | | |
|---|---|---|
| **Harbor Inn** | $$$-B&B | Full buffet breakfast |
| PO Box 538A, 90 Ocean Ave., | 9 rooms, 9 pb | Comp. wine, coffee |
|  04046 | C-ltd/S-yes/P-no/H-no | Sitting room |
| 207-967-2074 | | front porch with wicker |
| Charlotte & Bill Massmann | | large lawn, cottage |
| May 15–October | | |

*Comfortably & elegantly furnished throughout with antiques, canopy & poster beds. "More than just a night's lodging, a delightful experience." Featured in travel magazines.*

────────────────────────────────────

| | | |
|---|---|---|
| **Kennebunkport Inn, The** | $$-B&B | Cont. bkst. (Nov-April) |
| One Dock Square,  04046 | 34 rooms, 34 pb | Full bkfst May-Oct (fee) |
| 207-967-2621  Fax: 207-967-3705 | AmEx, MC, Visa, | Pub, restaurant |
| 800-248-2621 | *Rated*, • | pool, color TV |
| Rick & Martha Griffin | C-yes/P-no/H-no | golf & tennis nearby |
| All year | French | |

*Country inn in old sea captain's home. All rooms w/private baths. Gourmet patio dining, turn-of-the-century bar, piano bar. Historic district.* **3rd night free Nov.–April.**

────────────────────────────────────

| | | |
|---|---|---|
| **King's Port Inn** | $-B&B | Pantry sideboard buffet |
| P.O. Box 1172,  04046 | 32 rooms, 32 pb | Comp. hot beverages |
| 207-967-4340  Fax: 207-967-4810 | Visa, MC, AmEx, • | Fireside parlor |
| 800-286-5767 | C-yes/S-ltd/P-no/H-yes | 5 in room hot tubs |
| Bill Greer | French | wide array of amenities |
| All year | | |

*This New England coastal inn, nestled near the quaint, historical seacoast village of Kennebunkport, offers affordable, comfortable, gracious hospitality.* **7th night free, ltd.**

KENNEBUNKPORT ───────────────────────────────

| Kylemere House 1818 | $$$-B&B | Full gourmet breakfast |
| P.O. Box 1333,  04046 | 4 rooms, 4 pb | Comp. wine, beverages |
| 6 South St. | Visa, MC, *Rated*, • | Sitting rm., porch, lawn |
| 207-967-2780 | C-ltd/S-no/P-no/H-no | featured in Glamour 4/90 |
| Ruth & Helen Toohey | | Regis & Kathie Lee Show |
| May 1–mid December | | |

*Charming federal inn in historic area located within a short walk to shops and beach. Warm, inviting rooms, traditional hospitality & "down east" breakfast. **3rd night 50%, off season only.***

| Lake Brook B&B | $$$-B&B | Full breakfast |
| P.O. Box 762,  04046 | 4 rooms, 4 pb | Golf, tennis nearby |
| 57 Western Ave., 04043 | Visa, MC, • | just ½ mile from |
| 207-967-4069 | C-ltd/S-no/P-no/H-no | downtown Kennebunkport |
| Carolyn A. McAdams | Spanish | |
| Late April thru Feb. | | |

*Nestled at the edge of a salt marsh & tidal brook, Lake Brook offers charming rooms w/ antiques & paddle fans, great breakfasts, extensive gardens & rockers on the porch.*

| Maine Stay Inn & Cottages | $$$-B&B | Full breakfast |
| P.O. Box 500-A-PL, 34 Maine | 17 rooms, 17 pb | Afternoon tea, snacks |
| St.,  04046 | Most CC, *Rated*, • | Sitting room |
| 207-967-2117  Fax: 207-967-8757 | C-yes/S-no/P-no/H-no | swing set, garden, porch |
| 800-950-2117 | | 7 rooms with fireplaces |
| The Copelands   All year | | |

*Victorian inn known for exceptional warmth, hospitality & great breakfasts. Elegant rooms, charming cottages, spacious lawn, A/C, cable TV. **2 night pkg. Nov.–May.***

| Old Fort Inn | $$$$-B&B | Full breakfast |
| P.O. Box M, 8 Old Fort Ave., | 16 rooms, 16 pb | Cable TV, phone in room |
| 04046 | AmEx, MC, Visa, | tennis, swimming pool |
| 207-967-5353  Fax: 201-967-4545 | *Rated*, • | jacuzzis, A/C, bicycles |
| 800-828-3678 | C-ltd/S-no/P-no/H-no | |
| David & Sheila Aldrich | | |

*A luxurious resort in a secluded charming setting. The inn has yesterday's charm with today's conveniences. Within walking distance to the ocean.*

| Tides Inn By-The-Sea, The | $$$-EP | Full breakfast (fee) |
| RR 2, 252 Goose Rocks | 22 rooms, 20 pb | Restaurant |
| Beach,  04046 | Visa, MC, Disc. *Rated*, | Bar service, cozy Pub |
| 207-967-3757 | C-yes/S-ltd/P-no/H-no | sitting room, antiques |
| M. Henriksen & K. Blomberg | | 3 miles of sandy beach |
| May - Mid-October | | |

*Magnificent ocean/island views. Whimsical, charming Victorian inn. Fine dining. Escape from in-room TV & phone on Sandy Goose Rocks beach. Adjacent oceanfront suites w/ TV.*

| Welby Inn | $$$-B&B | Full breakfast |
| P.O. Box 774,  04046 | 7 rooms, 7 pb | Eve. homemade Amaretto |
| 92 Ocean Ave. | AmEx, *Rated*, | Guest pantry, bicycles |
| 207-967-4655 | C-ltd/S-no/P-no/H-no | sitting room, piano |
| David Knox, Betsy Rogers- | | 5 queen, 2 full beds |
| Knox | | |
| All year | | |

*Gracious turn-of-the-century home in historic Kennebunkport. Walk to beach, marina and shops. Deep-sea fishing and harbor cruises available. **Champagne for special occasions.***

## KENNEBUNKPORT

| **White Barn Inn, The** | $$$$-B&B | Continental breakfast |
| P.O. Box 560 C, 37 Beach St., | 24 rooms, 24 pb | Dinner, bar, aftn. tea |
| 04046 | AmEx, MC, Visa, | Swimming pool, landscape |
| 207-967-2321  Fax: 207-967-1100 | *Rated*, • | steam shower, jacuzzy |
| L. Cameron & L. Bongiorno | C-ltd/S-yes/P-no/H-ltd | renovated cottage, VCR |
| All year | | |

*Elegant farmhouse Inn-5-diamond restaurant. Set in the orig., architecturally preserved barn. Mbr. of Relais & Chateaux. Named among best inns in U.S.* **30% disc't. off season.**

## KITTERY

| **Melfair Farm B&B** | $$-B&B | Full breakfast |
| 11 Wilson Rd.,   03904 | 5 rooms, 1 pb | Comp. iced tea, lemonade |
| 207-439-0320 | *Rated*, • | Large sitting room |
| Claire Cane | C-yes/S-yes/P-no/H-no | piano, TV |
| March–December | French | near shopping, beaches |

*1871 New England farmhouse, 9 acres of pastoral setting. Theater, gourmet dining in nearby historical Portsmouth, NH.* **10% off after 3 days.**

## MILFORD

| **A Little Bit Country B&B** | $-B&B | Full breakfast |
| 294 Main Rd.,   04461 | 3 rooms, 1 pb | Afternoon tea |
| 207-827-3036  800-895-3036 | Visa, • | 10%, 3 or more nights |
| Annette Brown | C-ltd/S-no/P-no/H-no | |
| All year | | |

*Home away from home, as our name implies, near major transportation, interstate, coast & mountains. An "old fashioned" from scratch breakfast served daily w/comp. muffin bag to go.*

## MONHEGAN ISLAND

| **Island Inn, The** | $$$-B&B | Full breakfast |
| , 04852 | 36 rooms, 7 pb | Aftn. tea, restaurant |
| 207-596-0371  Fax: 207-594-5517 | Visa, MC, • | Lunch, dinner (fee) |
| P. Truelove & H. Wilbacker | C-yes/S-no/P-yes/H-no | sitting room, library |
| May 25-Oct 14 | | |

*A rustic retreat from the mainland with glorius views of the ocean and setting sun.*

## NAPLES

| **Augustus Bove House, The** | $$-B&B | Full breakfast |
| RR 1, Box 501,   04055 | 12 rooms, 5 pb | Honeymoon/Anniv. tray |
| Corner of Rts. 302 & 114 | AmEx, MC, Visa, | Comp. coffee, tea |
| 207-693-6365 | *Rated*, • | sitting room |
| David & Arlene Stetson | C-yes/S-ltd/P-yes/H-ltd | veranda, lawn |
| All year | | |

*Recently restored, offers authentic colonial accommodations in a relaxing atmosphere. Between 2 lakes, 20 min. from mountain skiing.* **Off season—2nd night 50%; 3rd free.**

| **Inn at Long Lake** | $$-B&B | Continental plus bkfst. |
| P.O. Box 806,   04055 | 16 rooms, 16 pb | Comp. coffee & tea |
| 207-693-6226  800-437-0328 | Most CC, *Rated*, • | Comp. hot chocolate |
| Maynard and Irene Hincks | C-yes/S-no/P-no/H-no | sitting room, library |
| All year | Some French, Spanish | Great Room w/fireplace |

*Restored 16-room inn nestled by Sebago Lake, year-round activities, shopping, fine dining. Romantic elegance, Maine hospitality.* **Midweek discounts, ask.**

NAPLES ────────────────────────

**Lamb's Mill Inn**
RR1, Box 676/PO Box 547,
  04055
Lamb's Mill Rd.
207-693-6253
Laurel Tinkham, Sandy Long
All year

$$-B&B
6 rooms, 6 pb
*Rated*, •
C-yes/S-no/P-no/H-no

Full breakfast
Afternoon tea, snacks
Sitting room, library
hot tubs, outside stone
fire pit & gas grills

*Charming country inn, 1/2 mile from Naples Village, in heart of western Maine's lakes/ mountains region. Ewe hike, ewe bike, ewe ski, ewe zzzz . . . **Stay 5 nights, get 6th free.***

NEW HARBOR ────────────────────

**Gosnold Arms**
HC 61, Box 161,  04554
Route 32, Northside Rd.
207-677-3727  Fax: 207-677-2662
The Phinney Family
Mid-May—October

$$-B&B
26 rooms, 19 pb
MC, Visa, *Rated*,
C-yes/S-ltd/P-no/H-ltd

Full breakfast
Dinner, cocktails
Sitting rm., small wharf
cable TV available in
some rooms & cottages

*Charming country inn and cottages. All-weather dining porch overlooking harbor. Beaches, lobster ponds, parks nearby.*

NEWCASTLE ─────────────────────

**Captain's House B&B, The**
P.O. Box 242,  04553
River Rd.
207-563-1482
Susan Rizzo, Joe Sullivan
All year

$$-B&B
5 rooms, 5 pb
C-yes/S-yes/P-no/H-no

Full breakfast from menu
Complimentary tea
Dinner (winter)
sitting room

*Spacious colonial home overlooking the Damariscotta River offers sunny rooms furnished with antiques. Delicious full Maine breakfast. Omelets a specialty.*

**Newcastle Inn, The**
River Rd.,  04553
207-563-5685  Fax: 207-563-6877
800-832-8669
Howard & Rebecca Levitan
All year

$$-B&B/MAP
15 rooms, 15 pb
MC, Visa, *Rated*, •
C-ltd/S-no/P-no/H-ltd

Full breakfast
Evening reception bar
Dinner, aftn. beverages
sitting room w/fireplace
screened-in porch, deck

*Fine dining and a pampering environment in an intimate, full-service, country inn on the Damariscotta River. Briar Patch Pub; fireside dining. Fireplaces in rooms.*

NOBLEBORO ─────────────────────

**Mill Pond Inn**
50 Main St., Route 215,  04553
207-563-8014
Bobby & Sherry Whear
All year

$$-B&B
5 rooms, 5 pb
MC, Visa,
C-yes/S-yes/P-no/H-ltd

Full breakfast
Comp. wine
Swimming/boating in lake
canoe & mountain bikes
hammock, horseshoes

*Small, private inn with a water view from four rooms, across the road from Damariscotta Lake. Guided fishing trips available with "registered Maine fishing guide."*

OGUNQUIT ──────────────────────

**Beauport Inn**
P.O. Box 1793,  03907
102 Shore Rd.
207-646-8680  800-646-8681
Dan Pender    All year

$$-B&B
4 rooms, 4 pb
MC, Visa,
C-ltd/S-no

Continental plus bkfst.
Sitting room
piano, TV room
antique shop

*Restored cape furnished with antiques. Pine-paneled sitting room with fireplace. Queen-size beds. Walk to beach, Marginal Way and Perkins Cove. **$2 off full New England breakfast.***

## OGUNQUIT

**Blue Shutters Guest House**
P.O. Box 655,  03907
6 Beachmere Place
207-646-2163 Fax: 207-646-7225
800-633-9550
Phyllis & Dick Norton
All year

$$-B&B
11 rooms, 11 pb
C-ltd/S-no/P-no/H-no
Italian

Full bkfst. (guesthouse)
Bkfst. fee-Efficiencies
Sitt. rm. in guesthouse
breakfast room

*Share the peacefulness and ocean view of this special guest house with color coordinated rooms. A short amble to everything, including exquisite little beaches.* **Off season packages available.**

---

**Gazebo, The**
P.O. Box 668,  03907
Rt. 1 N.
207-646-3733  800-486-3294
Tony Fontes
All year exc. January

$$-B&B
9 rooms, 7 pb
MC, Visa,
C-ltd/S-yes/P-no/H-no

Full gourmet breakfast
Sitting room
dining room
heated swimming pool

*150-year-old restored farmhouse serving full gourmet breakfast. Short walk to Ogunquit Beach. Afternoon tea and pate. 5 rooms with queen beds, 1 king, 1 twin.*

---

**Gorges Grant Hotel**
P.O. Box 2240,  03907
239 Main St.
207-646-7003 Fax: 207-646-0660
800-646-5001
Karen J. Hanson

$$-B&B/MAP
56 rooms, 56 pb
Most CC, *Rated*,
C-yes/S-yes/P-no/H-yes

Full breakfast (fee)
Restaurant, bar
Hot tubs, fitness room
indoor & outdoor pool
large saltwater aquarium

*Elegant, small, modern hotel operated w/an inn flavor. Located in Ogunquit near (within short trolley ride) one of the world's best beaches.* **10% off restaurant upon arrival.**

---

**Rockmere Lodge**
PO Box 278, 40 Stearns Rd.,
03907
207-646-2985 Fax: 207-646-6947
Andy Antoniuk & Bob Brown
All year

$$$-B&B
8 rooms, 8 pb
MC, Visa,
C-ltd/S-no/P-no/H-no

Continental plus bkfst.
Aft. tea, comp. wine
Sitting room, library
beach chairs
cool drinks for beach

*Seaside, shingled cottage in out-of-the-way location. Very quiet. Listen to the ocean and relax. Walking distance to everything. Cable TV in all rooms.*

## PORTLAND

**Andrews Lodging B&B**
417 Auburn St.,  04103
207-797-9157  Fax: 207-797-9040
Elizabeth Andrews
All year

$$-B&B
6 rooms, 1 pb
Visa, MC, AmEx,
*Rated*, •
C-ltd/S-no/P-yes/H-no

Full breakfast
Snacks, guest kitchen
Sitting room, library
whirlpool in suite
deck, solarium

*200+-year-old colonial with wonderful gardens on outskirts of Portland. Antiques, quilts, fresh fruit from our garden, great hospitality.*

---

**Inn On Carleton**
46 Carleton St,  04102
207-775-1910  Fax: 207-761-2160
800-639-1779
Sue & Phil Cox
All year

$$-B&B
7 rooms, 3 pb
Visa, MC, Disc. *Rated*,
C-ltd/S-no/P-no/H-no

Full breakfast
Afternoon tea
Sitting room

*Old world charm & elegance in Portland's historic West End District. Walk to Old Port, art museum & many museum houses, antiques shops.*

## PORTLAND

**West End Inn**
146 Pine St., 04112
207-772-1377 800-338-1377
John J. Leonard
All year

$$$-B&B
6 rooms, 6 pb
Most CC, *Rated*, •
C-yes/S-no/P-no/H-no

Full breakfast
Afternoon tea, snacks
Comp. wine, library
sitting room, cable TV
remodeled & redecorated

*Very comfortable, relaxing home atmosphere in the heart of the city in historical district.
Art Museum, theaters and Old Port within walking distance.* **10% off mentioning book.**

## RANGELEY

**Northwoods B&B**
P.O. Box 79, 04970
Main St.
207-864-2440 800-295-4968
Carol & Robert Scofield
1/1-4/1; 5/30-10/15

$$-B&B
4 rooms, 3 pb
MC, Visa, *Rated*, •
C-ltd/S-no/P-no/H-no

Full breakfast
Sitting rooms, library
Antique doll collection
includes 1910 Doll House

*Elegant historic home overlooking lake in Rangeley Village. Spacious rooms, porches &
grounds. Private boat dock. Gourmet breakfasts. Beach swimming, tennis, shops next
door.*

## ROCKLAND

**Lakeshore Inn**
184 Lakeview Dr., 04841
207-594-4209
Joseph McCluskey/
Paula Nicols   All year

$$$-B&B
4 rooms, 4 pb
Visa, MC, *Rated*,
C-yes/S-no/P-no/H-no
Greek

Gourmet full breakfast
Afternoon tea, snacks
Sitting room, library
boat rentals, fishing
para-sailing, swimming

*Hair dryers, special soaps, gels, fluffy robes, 2 miles to Rockland, Schooner - lobster
capital, home of Wyeth Art - shop Camden.* **7th day free, special rates for events, ltd.**

## SEARSPORT

**Brass Lantern Inn**
P.O. Box 407, 04974
81 W. Main St.
207-548-0150 800-691-0150
Pat Gatto & Lee Anne Lee
All year

$$-B&B
4 rooms, 4 pb
Visa, MC, *Rated*,
C-ltd/S-ltd/P-no/H-no

Full breakfast
Sitting room
Family friendly facility

*1850 Victorian built by sea captian. All private baths, hearty breakfasts. Ornate ceilings,
extensive doll collection. Lionel train shop.*

**Homeport Inn**
P.O. Box 647, 04974
121 East Main St.
207-548-2259 Fax: 508-443-6682
800-742-5814
George & Edith Johnson
All year

$$-B&B
11 rooms, 7 pb
Most CC, *Rated*, •
C-ltd/S-ltd/P-no/H-yes

Full breakfast
Mermaid lounge & bar
Soda fountain, garden
antique shop, ocean view
bicycles, golf, tennis

*On Historic Register. Ideal mid-coast location for an extended stay on coast of Maine.
Victorian cottage available by the week.* **3rd night 50% off, ltd, 10% off extended stay.**

**Thurston House B&B Inn**
P.O. Box 686, 04974
8 Elm St.
207-548-2213 Fax: 207-548-2213
800-240-2213
Carl & Beverly Eppig
All year

$$-B&B
4 rooms, 2 pb
MC, Visa, AmEx, •
C-ltd/S-no/P-no/H-ltd

Full breakfast
Snacks (sometimes)
Sitting room
library, shade garden
tennis courts nearby

*Circa 1830 Colonial family inn in quiet village setting. Easy stroll to everything, including
Maritime Museum, tavern, beach park on Penobscot Bay.* **6th night free.**

## SEBASCO ESTATES

| **Edgewater Farm B&B** | $$-B&B | Full gourmet breakfast |
|---|---|---|
| HC 32 Box 464,   04565 | 5 rooms, 3 pb | Dinner, snacks |
| Rte. 216, Smallpoint | Visa, MC, AmEx, | Sitting room, parlor |
| 207-389-1322 | C-yes/S-no/P-no/H-ltd | lawn games, gardens |
| Bill & Carol Emerson | Spanish | shaded deck, near golf |
| May through October | | |

*Charming, comfortable 200-year old farm house; generous memorable gourmet breakfasts; organic gardens; glorious beaches nearby; quiet . . . relaxing . . . the essential Maine.*

## SORRENTO

| **Bass Cove Farm B&B** | $$-B&B | Continental plus bkfst. |
|---|---|---|
| Rte. 185 Box 132,   04677 | 3 rooms, 1 pb | Exercise room, library |
| 207-422-3564 Fax: 207-422-3564 | MC, Visa, | porch, gardens |
| Mary Solet & Michael Tansey | C-ltd/S-no/P-no | sitting room |
| All year | | |

*Coastal Maine farmhouse in active summer colony. Convenient to Acadia Nat'l. Park. Comfortable beds, delicious breakfast. Explore, shop, relax. **4–7 days stay, discounts.***

## SOUTH BROOKSVILLE

| **Buck's Harbor Inn** | $$-B&B | Full breakfast |
|---|---|---|
| P.O. Box 268,   04617 | 6 rooms, | Restaurant, bar service |
| Steamboat Wharf Rd. | MC, Visa, | Sitting room |
| 207-326-8660 Fax: 207-326-0730 | C-yes/S-yes/P-no/H-no | Penobscot Bay views |
| Peter & Ann Ebeling | Spanish, French | access to harbor |
| May–December | | |

*Quiet country inn on Buck's Harbor, important cruising center for Mid-Coast Maine. Recently refurbished. Excellent dining room, lots of sightseeing.*

## SOUTHWEST HARBOR

| **Inn at Southwest, The** | $$-B&B | Full breakfast |
|---|---|---|
| P.O. Box 593,   04679 | 9 rooms, 9 pb | Afternoon tea, snacks |
| 371 Main St. | Visa, MC, *Rated*, | Large wraparound porch |
| 207-244-3835 | C-ltd/S-no/P-no/H-no | hiking, biking trails |
| Jill Lewis | | sitting room w/fireplace |
| Mid April-End of October | | |

*Victorian Inn overlooking the harbor. Within walking distance of shops and restaurants. Gourmet breakfast served by candlelight. Near Acadia National Park.*

| **Island House, The** | $$-B&B | Full breakfast |
|---|---|---|
| P.O. Box 1006,   04679 | 5 rooms, 2 pb | Breakfast for vegetarian |
| 121 Clark Point Rd. | *Rated*, | Sitting room/fireplace |
| 207-244-5180 | C-ltd/S-no/P-no | library, large garden |
| Ann & Charlie Bradford | | fishing docks, harbor |
| All year | | |

*A gracious, restful, seacoast home on the quiet side of Mt. Desert Island. An efficiency apartment available. Near wharves; 5 min. to Acadia National Park. **Discounts, ask.***

| **Kingsleigh Inn** | $$-B&B | Full breakfast |
|---|---|---|
| P.O. Box 1426,   04679 | 8 rooms, 8 pb | Afternoon tea |
| 373 Main St. | MC, Visa, *Rated*, | Sitting room with |
| 207-244-5302 | C-ltd/S-ltd/P-no/H-no | fireplace, library |
| Ken & Cyd Champagne | | |
| Collins | | |
| All year | | |

*A cozy intimate inn overlooking the harbor. Filled with many antiques. Rooms w/harbor views. In the heart of Acadia National Park, walk to shops, restaurants. AAA 3-Diamond.*

*The Hitchborn Inn, Stockton Springs, ME*

## SOUTHWEST HARBOR

**Lambs Ear Inn, The**
P.O. Box 30,   04679
60 Clark Point Rd.
207-244-9828
Elizabeth, Darrell & Monique
May 1 - October 15

$$-B&B
6 rooms, 6 pb
MC, Visa, *Rated*, •
C-ltd/S-no/P-no/H-ltd

Full breakfast
Peace & quiet
sitting room

*This comfortable and serene inn was built in 1857 in the village overlooking South West Harbor and surrounded by Acadia National Park.*

---

**Penury Hall**
P.O. Box 68,   04679
374 Main St.
207-244-7102
Toby & Gretchen Strong
All year

$$-B&B
3 rooms,
C-ltd/S-yes/P-no/H-no

Full breakfast
Comp. wine, coffee, tea
Sitting room, sauna
picnic day sails
canoeing

*Comfortable rambling Maine home for us and our guests. Decor reflects hosts' interests in art, antiques, books, gardening, sailing. Water sports paradise.*

## STOCKTON SPRINGS

**Hichborn Inn, The**
P.O. Box 115,   04981
Church St.
207-567-4183  800-346-1522
Nancy, Bruce & Morgan
Suppes
Reservations Dec-March

$$-B&B
4 rooms, 2 pb
•
C-ltd/S-no/P-no/H-no

Full breakfast
Afternoon tea
Sitting room
music room

*Romantic, elegant National Register Victorian. Ideal home base for coastal day trips. Quiet location. Period furnishings, fine linens, sumptuous breakfasts. **10% disc't off prevailing rate.***

STONINGTON ——————————————————————————

**Burnt Cove B&B**                $$-B&B                     Continental plus bkfst.
RFD 1, Box 2905,  04681         2 rooms,                   Box lunches
Whitman Rd.                       MC, Visa,                  Walking trails
207-367-2392                      C-ltd/S-no/P-no/H-no       shops, restaurants
Bob Williams, Diane Berlew                                   fishing village
May–October

*Waterfront location on Penobscot Bay island; working lobster wharves; multitude of birds; nature conservancy trails. TV, water view available. **Pay for 6, get 7th night free.***

WALPOLE ——————————————————————————

**Brannon-Bunker Inn**           $$-B&B                     Continental plus bkfst.
349 State Route 129,  04573     9 rooms, 4 pb              Kitchen facilities
207-563-5941                      MC, Visa, *Rated*,  •      Sitting room
Jeanne & Joe Hovance             C-yes/S-no/P-no/H-ltd      porch, antique shop
All year                                                    3 room suite for family

*Country B&B; charming rooms furnished with antiques; close to all mid-coast recreational facilities including ocean, beach, boating, golf, antiquing.*

WATERFORD ——————————————————————————

**Kedarburn Inn**                $$-B&B                     Full breakfast
Route 35, Box 61,  04088        7 rooms, 3 pb              Dinner, Sunday brunch
Valley Rd.                        MC, Visa, *Rated*,  •      Afternoon tea, bar
207-583-6182  Fax: 207-583-6424  C-yes/S-yes/P-yes/H-no     sitting rm., piano, lake
Margaret & Derek Gibson          French                     quilting weekends
All year

*A wonderful old home built in 1858, situated on a beautifully landscaped knoll in the center of historic Waterford Village. A romantic country setting. All rooms have A/C. **3rd night 30% off, Mon.–Thur.***

WELD ——————————————————————————

**Kawanhee Inn Lakeside**        $$-EP                      Breakfast (fee)
Mt. Blue, Box 119,  04285       10 rooms, 5 pb             Full service restaurant
7 High St., Farmington           *Rated*,  •                Tennis courts
207-585-2000  207-778-4306       C-yes/S-ltd/P-no/H-yes     lake beach, bicycles
Martha Strunk, Sturges                                       sitting room, piano
Butler
Open June–October 15

*Rustic lodge and cabins on crystal-clear Webb Lake. Cathedral pines, field stone fireplaces, hiking, tennis, canoe, fishing, golf, dining. **Off-season 15% discounts.***

WEST BOOTHBAY HARBOR ——————————————————————————

**Lawnmeer Inn, The**            $$-EP                      Dinner, comp. coffee
Box 505,  04575                 32 rooms,                  Restaurant, bar
Rt 27, 04576                      MC, Visa, *Rated*,  •      sitting room, library
207-633-2544  800-633-7645       C-ltd/S-yes/P-no/H-no      complimentary coffee
Lee & Jim Metzger                some French
May–October

*"The only thing that we overlook is the water." families completly welcome.*

WEST GOULDSBORO ——————————————————————————

**Sunset House B&B**             $$-B&B                     Full breakfast
HCR 60, Box 62,  04607          7 rooms, 3 pb              3rd-floor kitchen
Route 186                         MC, Visa,  •               Fresh water pond for
207-963-7156  800-233-7156       C-ltd/S-no/P-no/H-no       swimming, fishing
Carl & Kathy Johnson                                         great biking, sunporch
All year

*Late Victorian country farm inn on the coast; water views; beautiful sunsets. Near Acadia Nat'l Park. Observe bald eagle, osprey, loons in natural environment.*

## YORK

| | | |
|---|---|---|
| **Dockside Guest Quarters** | $$$-EP | Continental plus (fee) |
| P.O. Box 205, 03909 | 21 rooms, 19 pb | Lunch, dinner, bar room |
| Harris Island Rd. | MC, Visa, *Rated*, • | Restaurant, sitting room |
| 207-363-2868 Fax: 207-363-1977 | C-yes/S-no/P-ltd/H-ltd | porches, lawn games |
| The Lusty Family | | marina, boat rentals |
| Weekends, Nov-May | | |

*Unsurpassed location along edge of harbor. Tranquil, beautiful scenery abounds. Rooms tastefully decorated for warmth & comfort. AAA 3-diamonds. Weddings. Off season rates.*

## YORK HARBOR

| | | |
|---|---|---|
| **Inn at Harmon Park** | $$$-B&B | Full breakfast |
| P.O. Box 495, 03911 | 5 rooms, 5 pb | Afternoon tea |
| 415 York St. | *Rated*, • | Sitting room |
| 207-363-2031 Fax: 207-351-2948 | C-ltd/S-no/P-no/H-no | bicycles |
| Sue Antal | | suite with fireplace |
| All year | | |

*Charming Victorian home close to harbor, beach & cliffwalk. Creative breakfasts, fresh flowers, fireplaces & a warm, friendly atmosphere.* **3rd night 50% off Nov.–May.**

| | | |
|---|---|---|
| **York Harbor Inn** | $$$-B&B | Continental plus bkfst. |
| P.O. Box 573, 03911 | 32 rooms, 26 pb | Lunch, dinner, bar |
| Route 1A | AmEx, MC, Visa, | Sitting room, piano |
| 207-363-5119 Fax: 207-363-3545 | *Rated*, • | bicycles, ocean swimming |
| 800-343-3869 | C-yes/S-yes/P-no/H-ltd | outdoor hot tub, gazebo |
| Garry Dominguez | | |
| All year | | |

*Quiet, authentic country inn (c.1637) listed in Nat'l Register. Overlooks ocean & York Harbor Beach. Oceanview rooms w/decks. Zoo nearby. A/C & phones. AAA rated 3 diamond.* **10% off standard room, ltd.**

# More Inns ...

| | |
|---|---|
| Addison | Pleasant Bay B&B, Box 222 W Side Rd., 04606, 207-483-4490 |
| Ashville | Green Hill Farm, RR 1, Box 328, 04607, 207-422-3273 |
| Bailey Island | Cloverleaf Cottages, RFD 1, Box 75, 04003 |
| Bar Harbor | Bayview Inn, 111 Eden St. (Route 3), 04609, 207-288-5861 |
| Bar Harbor | Breakwater, 45 Hancock St., 04609, 800-238-6309 |
| Bar Harbor | Cleftstone Manor, 92 Eden St., 04609, 207-288-4951 |
| Bar Harbor | Heathwood Inn, 04609, 800-582-3681 |
| Bar Harbor | Maples Cottage Inn, 16 Roberts Ave., 04609, 207-288-3443 |
| Bar Harbor | Shady Maples, RFD #1, Box 360, 04609, 207-288-3793 |
| Bar Harbor | Thornhedge Inn, 47 Mt. Desert St., 04609, 207-288-5398 |
| Bath | Elizabeth's B&B, 360 Front St., 04530, 207-443-1146 |
| Bath | Glad II, 60 Pearl St., 04530, 207-443-1191 |
| Bath | Inn at Bath, The, 969 Washington St., 04530, 207-443-4294 |
| Bath | Levitt Family B&B, 50 Pearl St., 04530 |
| Belfast | Hiram Alden Inn, 19 Church St., 04915, 207-338-2151 |
| Belfast | Horatio Johnson House, 36 Church St., 04915, 207-338-5153 |
| Bethel | Bethel Inn and Count, P.O. Box 26, 04217, 800-654-0125 |
| Bethel | Douglass Place, Route 2, Box 90, 04217, 207-824-2229 |
| Bethel | Hammons House, The, P.O. Box 16, 04217, 207-824-3170 |
| Bethel | L'Auberge Country Inn, P.O. Box 21, 04217, 207-824-2774 |
| Bethel | Norseman Inn, HCR-61 Box 50, 04217, 207-824-2002 |
| Bethel | Sudbury Inn, Lower Main St., 04217, 207-824-2174 |
| Bethel | Sunday River Inn, Sunday River Rd., 04217, 207-824-2410 |
| Biddefordpool | Lodge, 19 Yates, 04006, 617-284-7148 |
| Bingham | Mrs. G's B&B, P.O. Box 389, 04920, 207-672-4034 |
| Bingham | Mrs. G's B&B, P.O. Box 389, 04920 |
| Blue Hill | Arcady Down East, South St., 04614, 207-374-5576 |
| Blue Hill | Blue Hill Farm Country Inn, Route 15, Box 437, 04614, 207-374-5126 |
| Blue Hill | Blue Hill Inn, The, P.O. Box 403, 04614, 207-374-2844 |
| Blue Hill | John Peters Inn, P.O. Box 916, 04614, 207-374-2116 |
| Boothbay Harbor | Admiral's Quarters Inn, 105 Commercial St., 04538, 207-633-2474 |
| Boothbay Harbor | Boothbay Harbor Inn, 37 Atlantic Ave. Box 4, 04538, 207-633-6302 |
| Boothbay Harbor | Captain Sawyer's Place, 87 Commercial St., 04538, 207-633-2290 |

| | |
|---|---|
| Boothbay Harbor | Green Shutters Inn, P.O. Box 543, 04538, 207-633-2646 |
| Boothbay Harbor | Harbour Towne-Waterfront, P.O. Box 266, 04538, 207-633-4300 |
| Boothbay Harbor | Hilltop Guest House, 44 McKown Hill, 04538, 207-633-2941 |
| Boothbay Harbor | Howard House, The, Townsend Ave., 04538, 207-633-3933 |
| Boothbay Harbor | Seafarer B&B Inn, The, 38 Union St., 04538, 207-633-2116 |
| Boothbay Harbor | Thistle Inn, P.O. Box 176, 04538, 207-633-3541 |
| Boothbay Harbor | Topside, McKown Hill, 04538, 207-633-5404 |
| Boothbay Harbor | Welch House Inn, 36 McKown St., 04538, 207-633-3431 |
| Boothbay Harbor | Westgate B&B, 18 West St., 04538, 207-633-3552 |
| Brewster | Tide Watch Inn, P.O. Box 2135, 02631, 207-832-4987 |
| Bridgton | Tarry-a-While B&B Resort, RR 3, Box 68, 04009, 207-647-2522 |
| Brunswick | Aaron Dunning House, 76 Federal St., 04011, 207-729-4486 |
| Brunswick | Captain Daniel Sto, 10 Water St., 04011 |
| Brunswick | Dove B&B, The, 16 Douglas St., 04011, 207-729-6827 |
| Brunswick | Harborgate B&B, RD 2-2260, 04011, 207-725-5894 |
| Brunswick | Harriet Beecher Stowe Hse, 63 Federal St., 04011, 207-725-5543 |
| Bucksport | L'ermitage, P.O. Box 418, 04416, 207-469-3361 |
| Bucksport | Old Parsonage Inn, P.O. Box 1577, 04416, 207-469-6477 |
| Camden | Abigail's B&B Inn, 8 High St., 04843, 207-236-2501 |
| Camden | Blackberry Inn, 82 Elm St., 04843, 207-236-6060 |
| Camden | Blue Harbor House, 67 Elm St., 04843, 207-236-3196 |
| Camden | Camden Main Stay, 22 High St., 04843, 207-236-9636 |
| Camden | Castleview by the Sea, 59 High St., 04843, 207-236-2344 |
| Camden | Chestnut House, 69 Chestnut St., 04843, 207-236-6137 |
| Camden | Goodspeed's Guest House, 60 Mountain St., 04843, 207-354-8077 |
| Camden | High Tide Inn, 04843, 207-236-3724 |
| Camden | Hosmer House B&B, 4 Pleasant St., 04843, 207-236-4012 |
| Camden | Inn at Sunrise Point, P.O. Box 1344, 04843, 207-236-7716 |
| Camden | Lord Camden Inn, 24 Main St., 04843, 207-236-4325 |
| Camden | Norumbega Inn, 61 High St., Route 1, 04843, 207-236-4646 |
| Camden | Owl & Turtle Harbor View, P.O. Box 1265, 04843, 207-236-9014 |
| Camden | Spouter Inn B&B, The, P.O. Box 270, 04849, 207-789-5171 |
| Canton | Green Acres Inn, RFD #112, 04221, 207-597-2333 |
| Cape Neddick | Sea Chimes B&B, RD 1, Shore Rd., 03902, 207-646-5378 |
| Cape Neddick | Wooden Goose Inn, P.O. Box 195, 03902, 207-363-5673 |
| Cape Newagen | Newagen Seaside Inn, Box H, Southport Island, 04552, 207-633-5242 |
| Carrabassett | Sugarloaf Inn, RR1, Box 5000, 04947, 207-237-2701 |
| Castine | Castine Inn, P.O. Box 41, Main St., 04421, 207-326-4365 |
| Castine | Holiday House, P.O. Box 215, 04421, 207-326-4335 |
| Castine | Pentagoet Inn, The, P.O. Box 4, Main St., 04421, 207-326-8616 |
| Center Lovell | Farrington's, Off Route 5, 04016 |
| Center Lovell | Pleasant Point Inn, P.O. Box 218, 04016, 207-925-3008 |
| Chebeague Island | Chebeague Island Inn, P.O. Box 492, South Rd., 04017, 207-846-5155 |
| Cherryfield | Ricker House, P.O. Box 256, 04622, 207-546-2780 |
| Cornish | Cornish Inn, P.O. Box 266, 04020, 207-625-8501 |
| Damariscotta | Down Easter Inn, Bristol Rd Rt. 130, 04543 |
| Dexter | Atlantic Seal B&B, RFD 2, Box 3160, 04930 |
| Dover, Foxcraft | Foxcroft B&B, 25 W. Main St., 04426, 207-564-7720 |
| East Booth Bay | Linekin Village B&B, Route 65, Box 776, 04544, 207-633-3681 |
| East Booth Bay | Ocean Point Inn, Shore Rd., 04544, 207-633-4200 |
| East Machias | East River B&B, P.O. Box 205 High St., 04630, 207-255-8467 |
| East Machias | Mariner Bed & Breakfast, P.O. Bx 40, 04630 |
| Eastport | Artists Retreat, 29 Washington St., 04631, 207-853-4239 |
| Eliot | Ewenicorn Farm B&B, 116 Goodwin Rd., Rt. 10, 03903, 207-439-1337 |
| Ellsworth | Victoria's B&B, 58 Pine St., 04605, 207-667-5893 |
| Farmington | Blackberry Farm B&B, RR3 Box 7048, 04938, 207-778-2035 |
| Five Islands | Coveside, 04546, 207-371-2807 |
| Five Islands | Grey Havens Inn, Box 82, 04546, 207-371-2616 |
| Fort Kent | Daigle's B&B, 96 E. Main St., 04743 |
| Freeport | Atlantic Seal B&B, 25 Main, 04078, 207-865-6112 |
| Freeport | Holbrook Inn, 7 Holbrook St., 04032, 207-865-6693 |
| Freeport | Old Red Farm, Desert of Maine Rd., 04032, 207-865-4550 |
| Freeport | Porter's Landing B&B, 70 South St., 04032, 207-865-4488 |
| Fryeburg | Oxford House Inn, 105 Main St., 04037, 207-935-3442 |
| Greenville | Chesuncook Lake House, Chesuncook Vil. Rt.76 , 04441 |
| Greenville | Lodge at Moosehead, The, Upon Lily Bay Rd., 04441, 207-695-4400 |
| Guilford | Trebor Inn, The, P.O. Box 299, 04443, 207-876-4070 |
| Hancock | Le Domaine Restaurant/Inn, P.O. Box 496, US Rt. 1, 04640, 207-422-3395 |

*Kenniston Hill Inn,*
*Booth Bay, ME*

| | |
|---|---|
| Harpswell | Harpswell Inn, RR1 Box 141, 04079, 207-833-5509 |
| Harrison | Tolman House Inn, P.O. Box 551, Tolman Rd, 04040, 207-583-4445 |
| Hulls Cove | Inn at Canoe Point, Box 216C, Route 3, 04644, 207-288-9511 |
| Islesboro | Dark Harbor House Inn, Box 185, 04848, 207-734-6669 |
| Jonesport | Tootsie's B&B, Trynor Sq., RFD 1,Box 2, 04649 |
| Kennebunk | Alewife House, 1917 Alewive Rd., Rt 35, 04043, 207-985-2118 |
| Kennebunk | Battlehead Cove, P.O. Box 449, 04046, 207-967-3879 |
| Kennebunk | English Meadows Inn, 141 Port Rd., 04043, 207-967-5766 |
| Kennebunk | Kennebunk Inn, 45 Main St., 04043, 207-985-3351 |
| Kennebunk | Waldo Emerson Inn, 108 Summer St., 04043, 207-985-4250 |
| Kennebunkport | Aiello & Co. B&B, P.O. Box 1143, 04046 |
| Kennebunkport | Breakwater Inn, Ocean Ave., 04046, 207-967-3118 |
| Kennebunkport | Bufflehead Cove, P.O. Box 499, 04046, 207-967-3879 |
| Kennebunkport | Captain Jefferds Inn, The, P.O. Box 691, 04046, 207-967-2311 |
| Kennebunkport | Clarion Nonantum Inn, Ocean Ave., Box 2626, 04046, 207-967-4050 |
| Kennebunkport | Dock Square Inn, The, P.O. Box 1123, 04046, 207-967-5773 |
| Kennebunkport | Farm House, RR 1, Box 656, 04046, 207-967-4169 |
| Kennebunkport | Green Heron Inn, The, P.O. Box 2578, 04046, 201-967-3315 |
| Kennebunkport | Inn at Harbor Head, RR 2, Box 1180, 04046, 207-967-5564 |
| Kennebunkport | Inn on South Street, The, P.O. Box 478A, 04046, 207-967-5151 |
| Kennebunkport | Seaside Inn & Cottages, Gooch's Beach/Beach Sts, 04046, 207-967-4461 |
| Kennebunkport | Village Cove Inn, P.O. Box 650, 04046, 207-967-3993 |
| Kingfield | Herbert Country Inn, The, P.O. Box 67, 04947, 207-265-2000 |
| Kingfield | Three Stanley Avenue, P.O. Box 169, 04947, 207-265-5541 |
| Kingfield | Winter's Inn, RR1, Box 1272, 04947, 207-265-5421 |
| Kittery | Gundalow Inn, 6 Water St., 03904, 207-439-4040 |
| Kittery Point | Harbour Watch B&B, R.F.D. 1 Box 42, 03905, 207-439-3242 |
| Kittery Point | Whaleback Inn B&B, Box 162, Pepperrell Rd., 03905, 207-439-9560 |
| Lamoine | Lamoine House, Rt. 184, Box 180, 04605, 207-667-7711 |
| Lincolnville | Red House, HC 60 Box 540, 04849, 207-236-4621 |
| Lincolnville | Sign of the Owl, Route 1 Box 85, 04849, 207-338-4669 |
| Lincolnville | Youngtown Inn & Restaurant, RR 1, Box 4246, 04849, 207-763-4290 |
| Lubec | Home Port Inn, 45 Main St., 04652, 207-733-2077 |
| Lubec | Overview, The, RD 2, Box 106, 04652, 207-733-2005 |
| Machias | Clark Perry House, 59 Court St., 04654, 207-255-8458 |
| Madison | Colony House Inn B&B, The, P.O. Box 251, 04950, 207-474-6599 |
| Milbridge | Moonraker B&B, Main St., Route 1, 04658, 207-546-2191 |
| Monhegan | Monhegan House, 04852, 207-594-7983 |
| Monhegan Island | Shining Sails Inc., Box 344, 04852, 207-596-0041 |
| Moose River | Sky Lodge, P.O. Box 99, 04945 |
| Mount Vernon | Feather Bed Inn, Box 65, 04352, 207-293-2020 |
| Mt. Desert | B&B Year 'Round-MacDonalds, P.O. Box 52, 04660, 207-244-3316 |
| Mt. Desert | Harbour Woods Lodging, P.O. Box 1214, 04679, 207-244-5388 |
| Naples | Charmwoods, 04055, 207-693-6798 |
| Naples | Songo B&B, Songon Locks Rd., 04055, 207-693-3960 |
| New Harbor | Bradley Inn, The, HC 61, Box 361, 04554, 207-677-2105 |
| Newcastle | Glidden House, RR 1 Box 740, 04553, 207-563-1859 |
| Newcastle | Markert House, P.O. Box 224, Glidden, 04553, 207-563-1309 |
| Newport | Lake Sebasticook B&B, 8 Sebasticook Ave., 04953, 207-368-5507 |
| Norridgewock | Norridgewock Colonial Inn, Upper Main St, Rt 2 &20, 04957, 207-634-3470 |
| North Anson | Olde Carrabassett Inn, The, Union St., 04958, 207-635-2900 |
| North Edgecomb | Channelridge Farm, 358 Cross Point Rd., 04556, 207-882-7539 |
| North Haven Island | Pulpit Harbor Inn, RR 1, 704 Crabtree Pt., 04853, 207-867-2219 |
| North Waterford | Olde Rowley Inn, P.O. Box 87, 04267, 207-583-4143 |
| North Windham | Aimhi Lodge, R.R. #3, 04082 |
| North Windham | Sebago Lake Lodge, White Bridge Rd., 04062, 207-892-2698 |
| Northeast Harbor | Grey Rock Inn, 04662, 217-276-9360 |
| Oakland | Pressey House-1850, 85 Summer St., 04963, 207-465-3500 |
| Ogunquit | Colonial Inn, 71 Shore Rd.,PO Box 895, 03907 |
| Ogunquit | Hartwell House, P.O. Box 393, 03907, 207-646-7210 |
| Ogunquit | Morning Dove B&B, The, P.O. Box 1940, 03907, 207-646-3891 |
| Ogunquit | Ogunquit House, P.O. Box 1883, 03907, 207-646-2967 |
| Ogunquit | Puffin Inn, Box 2232, 03907, 207-646-5496 |
| Ogunquit | Trellis House, P.O. Box 2229, 03907, 207-646-7909 |
| Ogunquit | Yardarm Village Inn, Box 773, 130 Shore Rd., 03907, 207-646-7006 |
| Orono | High Lawn B&B, 193 Main St., 04473, 207-866-2272 |
| Otisfield | Claibern's B&B, P.O. Box B, Oxford, 04270, 207-539-2352 |
| Pemaquid Pt. | Bradley Inn @ Pemaquid Pt., H.C.61, Box 361, 04554, 207-677-2105 |
| Port Clyde | Ocean House, Box 66, 04855, 207-372-6691 |
| Portland | Inn at Parkspring, 135 Spring St., 04101, 207-774-1059 |
| Portland | Pomegranate Inn, 49 Neal St., 04102, 207-772-1066 |

*Buck's Harbor Inn,
South Brookfield, ME*

| | |
|---|---|
| Prospect Harbor | Oceanside Meadows Inn, P.O. Box 90, 04669,  207-963-5557 |
| Rangeley | Country Club Inn,  Country Club Dr., 04970 |
| Rangeley | Farmhouse Inn,  P.O. Box 496, 04970,  207-864-5805 |
| Rangeley | Rangeley Inn,  P.O. Box 160, 04970,  207-864-3341 |
| Raymond | Northern Pines Health Rsrt,  04071,  207-655-7624 |
| Rockland | Old Granite Inn, 546 Main St.,  04841,  207-594-9036 |
| Rockport | Sign of the Unicorn House,  P.O. Box 99, 04856,  207-236-8789 |
| Rockport | Twin Gables,  4 Spear St. @ Beauchamp, 04856,  207-236-4717 |
| Sanford | Allen's Inn,  279 Main St., 04073,  207-324-2160 |
| Scarborough | Higgins Beach Inn,  04074,  207-883-6684 |
| Searsport | Capt. Butman Homestead,The,  P.O. Box 306, 04974 |
| Searsport | Captain A.V. Neckels Inn,  U.S. Route 1, Box 38, 04974 |
| Searsport | Carriage House Inn,  P.O. Box 238, 04974,  207-548-2289 |
| Searsport | Fairwinds, Cpt.Pendleton,  428 E. Main St., 04974 |
| Searsport | Flowering Plum, P.O. Box 259, 04974 |
| Searsport | House of Three Chimneys,  Black Rd., Box 397, 04974,  207-548-6117 |
| Searsport | McGilvery House, P.O. Box 588, 04974,  207-548-6289 |
| Searsport | Old Glory Inn,  P.O. Box 461, 04974 |
| Searsport | Sea Captain's Inn,  P.O. Box 518, 04974 |
| Searsport | Summerwood Inn,  P.O. Box 335, 04974 |
| Searsport | Victorian Inn, The,  P.O. Box 807, 04974,  207-548-0044 |
| Searsport | Watchtide,  190 W. Main St., 04974, 207-548-6575 |
| Searsport | William & Mary Inn,  U.S. Rte. 1, PO Box 813, 04974,  207-548-2190 |
| Sebasco Estates | Rock Gardens Inn,  04565,  207-389-1339 |
| Sebasco Estates | Sebasco Lodge,  04565,  207-389-1161 |
| Skowhegan | Brick Farm B&B,  RFD 1, 04976,  207-474-3949 |
| South Bristol | Coveside Inn,  Cove Rd. Christmas, 04568 |
| South Casco | Migis Lodge,  Route 302, 04077,  207-655-4524 |
| South Harpswell | Alfred M. Senter B&B,  Box 830, 04079,  207-833-2874 |
| South Harpswell | Senter B&B,  Route 123, 04079,  207-833-2874 |
| South Thomaston | Weskeag Inn,  Route 73, P.O. Box 213, 04858,  207-596-6676 |
| Southwest Harbor | Claremont,  04679,  207-244-5036 |
| Southwest Harbor | Harbour Cottage Inn,  P.O. Box 258, 04679,  207-244-5738 |
| Southwest Harbor | Harbour Woods Mt. Desert,  P.O. Box 1214, 04679,  207-244-5388 |
| Southwest Harbor | Island Watch B&B,  P.O. Box 1359, 04679,  207-244-7229 |
| Southwest Harbor | Lindenwood Inn,  P.O. Box 1328, 04679,  207-244-5335 |
| Southwest Harbor | Moorings Inn, The,  Shore Rd., 04679,  207-244-5523 |
| Spruce Head | Craignair Inn,  533 Clark Island Rd., 04859,  207-594-7644 |
| Stockton Springs | Whistlestop B&B,  RFD 1, Box 639, 04981 |
| Stratton | Widow's Walk,  Box 150, 04982,  207-246-6901 |
| Sullivan Harbor | Sullivan Harbor Farm,  Box 96, 04664,  207-422-3735 |
| Sunset | Goose Cove Lodge/Deer Isle,  P.O. Box 40, 04683,  207-348-2508 |
| Surry | Surry Inn,  P.O. Box 25, 04684,  207-667-5091 |
| Tenants Harbor | East Wind Inn,  P.O. Box 149, 04860,  207-372-6366 |
| Tenants Harbor | Mill Pond House,  Box 640, 04860,  207-372-6209 |
| Tenants Harbor | Pointed Fir, The,  HCR 35, Box 625, 04860 |
| The Forks | Crab Apple Acres Inn,  Route 201, 04985,  207-663-2218 |
| The Forks | Northern Outdoors,  Russell Walters, 04985,  207-663-4466 |
| Thomaston | Cap'n Frost's B&B,  241 W. Main St., 04861,  207-354-8217 |
| Topsham | Middaugh B&B,  36 Elm St., 04086,  207-725-2562 |
| Van Buren | Farrell-Michaud House,  231 Main St., 04785 |
| Waldoboro | Blackford Inn, The,  P.O. Box 817, 04572,  207-832-4714 |
| Waldoboro | Broad Bay Inn & Gallery,  P.O. Box 607, Main St., 04572,  207-832-6668 |
| Waldoboro | Le Vatout,  Route 32, Box 375, 04572,  207-832-4552 |
| Waldoboro | Letteney Farm Vacations,  RFD 2, Box 166A, 04572,  207-832-5143 |
| Waldoboro | Roaring Lion B&B, The,  Main St., P.O. Box 756, 04572,  207-832-4038 |
| Washington | Windward Farm,  Young's Hill Rd., 04574,  207-845-2830 |
| Waterford | Artemus Ward House,  04088,  207-583-4106 |
| Waterford | Lake House,  P.O. Box 82, 04088,  800-223-4182 |
| Waterford | Waterford Inne, The,  P.O. Box 149, 04088,  207-583-4037 |
| Weld | Weld Inn, The,  P.O. Box 8, 04285,  207-585-2429 |
| Wells | Grey Gull Inn,  321 Webhannet Dr., 04090,  207-646-7501 |
| Wells | Haven, The,  RR 4 Box 2270, 04090,  207-646-4194 |
| West Bath | New Meadows Inn,  Bath Rd., 04530,  207-443-3921 |
| West Harpswell | Vicarage East Ltd.,  Box 368A, 04079,  207-833-5480 |
| West Levant | Terra Field B&B,  Brann Rd. Box 1950, 04456,  207-884-8805 |
| Winterport | Colonial Winterport Inn,  P.O. Box 525, 04496,  207-223-5307 |
| Wiscasset | Stacked Arms B&B, The,  RR 2, Box 146, 04578,  207-882-5436 |

*Windward House,
Camden, ME*

*Bayberry Inn, Freeport, ME*

# Maryland

## ANNAPOLIS

| | | |
|---|---|---|
| **Barn on Howard's Cove, The** | $$$-B&B | Full breakfast |
| 500 Wilson Rd.,  21401 | 2 rooms, 2 pb | Snacks |
| 410-266-6840  Fax: 410-266-7293 | *Rated*, • | Sitting room |
| Mary Gutsche | C-yes/S-no/P-no/H-no | near pool, tennis, dock |
| All year | | deep water docking avail |

*Minutes from Annapolis. 1850 retored horsebarn on Severn River; antiques, quilts, deep-water docking, guestrooms overlooking water.* **$10.00 reduction after 4+ nites for ea. nite.**

| | | |
|---|---|---|
| **Chesapeake Bay Lighthouse** | $$$-B&B | Continental plus bkfst. |
| 1423 Sharps Point Rd.,  21401 | 5 rooms, 5 pb | Snacks |
| 410-757-0248 | MC, Visa, *Rated*, • | 300-foot pier |
| Bill & Janice Costello | C-ltd/S-no/P-no/H-no | TV and game room |
| All year | | pool table, fishing |

*A full-size replica of the Thomas Point Lighthouse on the Chesapeake Bay. It's a working lighthouse called the Sharps Point Light.*

| | | |
|---|---|---|
| **Chez Amis B&B** | $$-B&B | Full breakfast |
| 85 East St.,  21401 | 4 rooms, 2 pb | Snacks |
| 410-263-6631 | Visa, MC, • | Complimentary wine |
| Don & Mickie Deline | C-ltd/S-no/P-no/H-no | sitting room |
| All year | | "European-country" decor |

*Former circa 1900 grocery store, transformed into a B&B in 1989. Perfect location for enjoying historic area, harbor & Academy.* **Complimentary champagne for special occasions.**

| | | |
|---|---|---|
| **College House Suites** | $$$$-B&B | Continental plus (fee) |
| One College Ave., Historic District,  21401 | 2 rooms, 2 pb | Wet bar in one suite |
| | *Rated*, • | Suites w/sitting room |
| 410-263-6124 | S-no/P-no/H-no | A/C, Cable TV |
| Don & Jo Anne Wolfrey | | courtyard, fireplace |
| All year | | |

*Elegant multi-room suites. One suite w/fireplace & private ivy-covered courtyard; other w/superb orientals & antiques. Each suite one floor w/private baths. 2 night minimum.* **Free bottle of wine.**

## ANNAPOLIS

**Dolls' House B&B, The**  $$-B&B                Parlor, flower garden
161 Green St.,   21401     3 rooms, 1 pb         front porch swing
410-626-2028               C-ltd/S-ltd/P-no      terry robes & chocolate
Barbara & John Dugan

*Decorated in Victorian whimsy w/furniture & decorations true to that nostalgic time. The
tiger oak woodwork, Georgia pine floors, brass & tile fireplaces, large windows reflect
the Victorian period.*

---

**Gibson's Lodgings**       $$-B&B                Continental plus bkfst.
110 Prince George St.,  21401   20 rooms,        Comp. evening wine
410-268-5555               •                     Piano, conference fac.
Claude & Jeanne Schrift    C-ltd/S-no/P-no/H-yes  daily maid service
All year                                         parking

*Located in historic district, near City Docks, adjacent to U.S. Naval Academy. Antique
furnishings throughout. Offstreet parking. Daily maid service. Unique conf. facilities.*

---

**Jonas Green House**       $$-B&B                Continental plus bkfst.
124 Charles St.,   21401    3 rooms, 1 pb         Complimentary wine
410-263-5892  Fax: 410-263-5892  Most CC, •      Sitting room, library
Randy & Dede Brown          C-yes/S-no/P-yes/H-no
All year                    Danish

*Lovingly restored 1690s-1740s home; in innkeeper's family since 1738; genuine antiques;
in center of historic district; off-street parking.*

---

**Mary Rob B&B**            $$$-B&B               Full breakfast
243 Prince George St.,  21401   4 rooms, 3 pb     Snacks, near restaurants
410-268-5438               •                      Sitting room, library
Mary Taylor, Rob Carlson    C-ltd/S-no/P-no/H-no  bicycles, cable TV
All year                                          phone in room, Jacuzzi

*Victorian Italianate Villa in heart of Annapolis historic district. Beautifully decorated with
antiques and reproductions. Breakfast to order. Beautyrest mattresses.*

## BALTIMORE

**Abacrombie Badger B&B**   $$$-B&B               Continental plus
58 W. Biddle St.,  21201    12 rooms, 12 pb       Restaurant
410-244-7227  Fax: 410-244-8415  Most CC, *Rated*, •  Bar, sitting room
Paul Bragaw                 C-ltd/S-no/P-no/H-no  A/C, private phones
All year                    German, Dutch, French  parlor, cable TV

*1880 house in the heart of Baltimore's Cultural Center. Walk to symphony, opera, muse-
ums, Antique Row. Near Juner Harbor. Streetcar line one block away.*

---

**Betsy's B&B**             $$$-B&B               Full breakfast
1428 Park Ave.,  21217      3 rooms, 3 pb         Special diet requests
410-383-1274  Fax: 410-728-8957  AmEx, MC, Visa,  Hot tub (by reservation)
800-899-7533                *Rated*, •            piano, TV, bicycles
Betsy Grater                C-ltd/S-ltd/P-no/H-no  swim club privileges
All year

*Charming, 100-yr-old townhouse w/hardwood floors, handsome brass rubbings. 3 blocks
to light rail, Inner Harbor, Oriole Park. Outdoor hot tub.* **10% off Sun.–Thurs, 2 night
minimum.**

## BALTIMORE

**Biltmore Suites Hotel, The**
205 W. Madison St., 21201
410-728-6550  800-868-5064
Robert Dionne
All year

$$$-B&B
27 rooms, 27 pb
Most CC, *Rated*, •
C-yes/S-yes/P-no/H-no

Continental breakfast
Free evening reception
library
courtyard/backyard

*Historic inn, rooms & suites appointed with period antiques and private baths. Short walk to Inner Harbor and Orioles Park.* **Comp. stretch limo within 4 miles.**

---

**Celie's Waterfront B&B**
1714 Thames St., 21231
410-522-2323  Fax: 410-522-2324
800-432-0184
Celie Ives
All year

$$$-B&B
7 rooms, 7 pb
Most CC, *Rated*, •
C-ltd/S-no/P-no/H-yes

Continental plus bkfst.
Refrigerators
Pvt. phones, TV, A/C
bedroom fireplaces
whirlpools, parking

*Urban inn in Fell's Point historic maritime community. Near Harbor Place, business dist. & Orioles Park by water taxi. Harbor front, roofdeck & gardens. Near excellent dining.*

---

**Mr. Mole B&B**
1601 Bolton St., 21217
410-728-1179  Fax: 410-728-3379
Collin Clarke
All year

$$$-B&B
5 rooms, 5 pb
Most CC, *Rated*, •
C-ltd/S-no/P-no/H-no

Continental plus bkfst.
Sitting room, A/C,
garage parking, parlor,
private phones

*Elegant and spacious 1870 Baltimore row house on historic Bolton Hill . . . decorated like a designer's showcase home . . ." (The Discerning Traveler).*

---

**Paulus Gasthaus, The**
2406 Kentucky Ave., 21213
410-467-1688  Fax: 410-467-1688
Lucie & Ed Paulus
All year

$$$-B&B
2 rooms, 1 pb
*Rated*, •
C-ltd/S-no/P-no/H-no
German, some French

Full gourmet breakfast
Comp. sherry in room
Sitting rm, outsd. patio
near golf, fitness trail
free parking, amenities

*Tudor-style home, lovely neighborhood, Gemuetlichkeit. Near Inner Harbor & Johns Hopkins. Guests choose Ger. or Amer. breakfast.* **Weekly discounts, tickets to major museums.**

---

**Union Square House B&B**
23 S. Stricker St., 21223
410-233-9064  Fax: 410-233-4046
Patrice & Joe Debes
Dec. 23—Jan 1 closed

$$$-B&B
4 rooms, 4 pb
Most CC, *Rated*, •
C-ltd/S-ltd/P-ltd/H-ltd

Continental plus bkfst.
Afternoon tea, snacks
Sitt. room, some frplcs.
Murder Mystery Weekend
A/C, color TV in room

*Genteel Victorian townhouse in historic Union Square. 15 blocks west of Inner Harbor/ Stadium area. Period furnishings. Honeymoon/anniv. specials.* **1 week stay, 7th night free.**

## BETTERTON

**Lantern Inn B&B**
P.O. Box 29, 21610
115 Ericsson Ave.
410-348-5809  800-499-7265
Ken & Ann Washburn
All year

$$-B&B
13 rooms, 4 pb
Visa, MC,
C-ltd/S-ltd/P-no/H-no

Full breakfast
Complimentary wine
Beach & tennis, 2 blocks
sitting room
library

*Small quiet town on Chesapeake Bay, One and one half hours from Philadelphia, Baltimore, D.C. Sandy beaches, great cycling, seafood, wildlife preserves, antiquing.*

## BUCKEYSTOWN

| **Catoctin Inn** | $$$-B&B | Full breakfast |
|---|---|---|
| P.O. Box 243,  21717 | 17 rooms, 12 pb | Afternoon tea, snacks |
| 3613 Buckeystown Pike | *Rated*,  • | Sitting room, library |
| 301-874-5555  Fax:301-831-8102 | C-yes/S-no/P-yes/H-no | bicycles, Jacuzzi tub |
| 800-730-5550 | | fireplace, TV's, hot tub |
| Terry & Sarah MacGillivray | | |
| All year | | |

*200 year old mansion furnished w/antiques on 4 acres. King & queen-size beds & private baths. A/C, working frplcs., whirlpools, private cottage w/king bed. Business rates.*

## CAMBRIDGE

| **Sarke Plantation Inn** | $$-B&B | Continental breakfast |
|---|---|---|
| 6033 Todd Point Rd.,  21613 | 5 rooms, 3 pb | Swimming pool, stereo |
| 410-228-7020  800-814-7020 | AmEx, | sitting room, piano |
| Genevieve Finley | C-ltd/S-yes/P-ltd/H-no | pool table, fireplaces |
| All year | | |

*Spacious & scenic country, abundant waterfowl. Breakfast in "sidewalk cafe" with paintings by local artists. Summer house for cards and games. Reduced rate for 2+ nights, ask.*

## CHESTERTOWN

| **Brampton B&B Inn** | $$$-B&B | Full breakfast |
|---|---|---|
| 25227 Chestertown Rd., | 10 rooms, 10 pb | Comp. wine, aftn. tea |
|   21620 | MC, Visa, *Rated*,  • | Sitting room, library |
| 410-778-1860  Fax: 410-778-1805 | C-ltd/S-no/P-no/H-ltd | bicycles, one suite |
| Michael & Danielle Hanscom | French, German | one room sleeps 4 |
| All year | | |

*1860 National Register manor house. 35-acre estate one mile south of historic Chestertown. Luxurious rooms, furnished in antiques and with woodburning fireplaces.*

| **Lauretum Inn B&B** | $$-B&B | Continental plus bkfst. |
|---|---|---|
| 954 High St.,  21620 | 5 rooms, 3 pb | Afternoon tea, snacks |
| 410-778-3236  Fax: 410-778-1922 | Visa, MC, Disc. *Rated*, | Sitting room |
| 800-742-3236 | • | library |
| Peg & Bill Sites | C-ltd/S-no/P-no/H-no | family friendly facility |
| All year | | |

*Quiet, relaxing, restful, historic 1870 Victorian manor on six acres. Charming rooms, screened-in porch, close to everything. 20% midweek disc't (Sun.–Thur.).*

| **White Swan Tavern, The** | $$$-B&B | Continental breakfast |
|---|---|---|
| 231 High St.,  21620 | 5 rooms, 5 pb | Comp. wine, eve. sherry |
| 410-778-2300  Fax: 410-778-4543 | *Rated*,  • | Comp. fruit basket |
| Mary Susan Maisel | C-yes/S-yes/P-no/H-ltd | sitting room, bicycles |
| All year | | terrace, garden, tea rm. |

*18th-century inn nestled in Maryland's historic eastern shore. Genuine antiques, homemade continental breakfast, tea, complimentary wine & fruit. 3rd night 50% off.*

## CUMBERLAND

| **Inn at Walnut Bottom, The** | $$-B&B | Full breakfast |
|---|---|---|
| 120 Greene St.,  21502 | 12 rooms, 10 pb | Restaurant-full service |
| 301-777-0003 Fax:301-777-8288 | Most CC, *Rated*,  • | Afternoon refreshments |
| 800-286-9718 | C-yes/S-no/P-no/H-ltd | sitting room, in-room TV |
| K. Hansen & G. Irving | | telephones, bicycles |
| All year | | |

*Charming traditional country inn. Beautiful mountain town with scenic railroad, historic district, extraordinary hiking, biking, sight-seeing. Fine restaurant.*

EASTON

| | | |
|---|---|---|
| **Bishop's House B&B, The** | $$-B&B | Full breakfast |
| P.O. Box 2217,  21601 | 6 rooms, 5 pb | Comp. wine & beverages |
| 214 Goldsborough St. | • | Sitting rooms, bikes |
| 410-820-7290  Fax: 410-820-7290 | C-ltd/S-no/P-no/H-no | A/C, whirlpool tubs |
| 800-223-7290 | | fireplaces, parking |
| Diane Laird & John Ippolito | | |
| All year | | |

*Historic District c1880 in town Victorian. Romantically furnished in period style. Centraly loated, Easton provides an excellent location for visiting all points of interest.*

ELLICOTT CITY

| | | |
|---|---|---|
| **Wayside Inn, The** | $$-B&B | Continental plus bkfst. |
| 4344 Columbia Rd.,  21042 | 4 rooms, 2 pb | Spring water/soft drinks |
| 410-461-4636  Fax: 410-750-2070 | Most CC, *Rated*, • | Sitting room, music room |
| Margo & John Osantowski | C-ltd/S-no/P-no/H-no | tavern, in room phones |
| All year | | 10% business disc't, ltd |

*Historic Maryland Home pond, antique and reproduction furnishings, convenient to Ellicott City, Columbia, Baltimore, Annapolis and Washington D.C.* **1 night free after 5th visit.**

FREDERICK

| | | |
|---|---|---|
| **Middle Plantation Inn** | $$$-B&B | Continental plus bkfst. |
| 9549 Liberty Rd.,  21701 | 3 rooms, 3 pb | Sitting room, garden |
| 301-898-7128 | *Rated*, • | hen house, brook |
| Shirley & Dwight Mullican | C-ltd/S-no/P-no/H-no | four golf courses nearby |
| All year | | |

*A rustic stone and log B&B, furnished with antiques, television and A/C. Near Gettysburg, Antietam, Harper's Ferry, Washington D.C., and Baltimore.* **$15 disc't w/out breakfast.**

| | | |
|---|---|---|
| **Spring Bank—A B&B Inn** | $$$-B&B | Continental plus bkfst. |
| 7945 Worman's Mill Rd., | 5 rooms, 1 pb | Double parlors, library |
| 21701 | Most CC, *Rated*, • | view from observatory |
| 301-694-0440  800-400-4667 | C-ltd/S-no/P-no/H-no | 10 acres for roaming |
| Beverly & Ray Compton | | |
| All year | | |

*On National Register of Historic Places. Antiques. Near Baltimore, Washington, D.C., and Civil War battlefields. Exceptional dining in Frederick Historic District 2 mi. away.*

HAGERSTOWN

| | | |
|---|---|---|
| **Beaver Creek House B&B** | $$-B&B | Full breakfast |
| 20432 Beaver Creek Rd., | 5 rooms, 5 pb | Afternoon tea, snacks |
| 21740 | Visa, MC, AmEx, | Hiking, antiquing |
| 301-797-4764 | *Rated*, • | sitting room, library |
| Donald & Shirley Day | C-ltd/S-no/P-no/H-no | restaurants nearby |
| All year | | |

*Country Victorian home filled w/family antiques & memorabilia. Full country breakfast served on screened porched. Hiking, civil war battlefields nearby.* **3rd night 50% off.**

| | | |
|---|---|---|
| **Lewrene Farm B&B** | $$-B&B | Full breakfast |
| 9738 Downsville Pike,  21740 | 5 rooms, 3 pb | Bedside snack |
| 301-582-1735 | Visa, MC, | Sitting room, whirlpool |
| Irene & Lewis Lehman | C-ltd/S-no/P-no/H-no | gazebo, large farm |
| All year | Spanish, some German | quilts for sale, piano |

*Quiet farm, cozy colonial home w/fireplace, antiques, candlelight breakfasts, Historic Antietam Battlefield, Harper's Ferry, outlets, restaurants.* **3rd night or more—10% off.**

## HAGERSTOWN

| **Sunday's B&B** | $$-B&B | Full breakfast |
| 39 Broadway,   21740 | 3 rooms, 3 pb | Aftn. tea, snacks, wine |
| 301-797-4331  800-221-4828 | Visa, MC, Dinners,  • | Sitting room, porch |
| Bob Ferrino | C-ltd/S-ltd/P-ltd/H-no | fishing, golf, museums |
| All year | | theatres, skiing nearby |

*Elegant Queen Anne Victorian home. Antiques throughout; personalized service. Gourmet breakfast, afternoon tea, evening wine & cheese. Battlefields nearby.* **3rd night 50%**

## HAVRE DE GRACE

| **Spencer Silver Mansion** | $$-B&B | Full breakfast |
| 200 S. Union Ave.,   21078 | 4 rooms, 1 pb | 2 parlors, fireplace, TV |
| 410-939-1097  800-780-1485 | *Rated*,  • | porch, reading nook |
| Carol & Jim Nemeth | C-yes/S-ltd/P-no/H-no | suite with whirlpool |
| All year | German | |

*In the heart of the historic district, our 1896 mansion takes you to the turn of the century. Antique-filled Victorian-style rooms, informative hosts. Boat rental, jetskis.*

| **Vandiver Inn** | $$-B&B | Full breakfast |
| 301 S. Union Ave,   21078 | 8 rooms, 8 pb | Chef with degree on-site |
| 410-939-5200  Fax: 410-939-1901 | Most CC, *Rated*,  • | 2 rooms private porch & |
| 800-245-1655 | C-ltd/S-ltd/P-no/H-yes | entrance, gazebo |
| Mary McKee | | large front porch |
| All year | | |

*1886 Victorian mansion. Surrounded by historic sites, antiquing, museums, marinas. Dinner served on Friday & Saturday evenings. 2 blocks from Chesapeake Bay. 5$ off if paying cash/check.*

## KEEDYSVILLE

| **Antietam Overlook Farm** | $$$-B&B | Full breakfast |
| P.O. Box 30,   21756 | 5 rooms, 5 pb | Comp. wine, chocolates |
| 301-432-4200  800-878-4241 | Most CC,  • | After dinner drinks |
| John & Barbara Dreisch | C-ltd/S-no/P-no/H-no | sitting room, library |
| All year | | |

*Extraordinary 95-acre mountaintop farm with four-state view at Antietam National Battlefield. Yesterday's architecture—today's comfort. Sumptuous breakfast.*

## LUTHERVILLE

| **Twin Gates B&B Inn** | $$$-B&B | Full gourmet breakfast |
| 308 Morris Ave., Suburb of | 6 rooms, 6 pb | Comp. wine, tea |
| Baltimore,   21093 | *Rated*,  • | Free winery tours |
| 410-252-3131  800-635-0370 | C-ltd/S-no/P-no/H-no | library |
| Gwen & Bob Vaughan | | low fat breakfast avail. |
| All year | | |

*Peaceful Victorian mansions & gardens, close to National Aquarium, Harborplace, and Oriole Park in Baltimore. Excellent seafood restaurants nearby.*

## MIDDLETOWN

| **Stone Manor** | $$$-B&B | Continental plus bkfst. |
| 5820 Carroll Boyer Rd., | 5 rooms, 5 pb | Lunch, dinner (fee) |
| 21769 | Visa, MC, AmEx, | Snacks, restaurant |
| 301-473-5454  Fax: 301-371-5622 | *Rated*, | sitting room, library |
| Judith V. Harne | C-ltd/S-no/P-no/H-yes | fireplaces, whirlpools |
| All year | | |

*Savor the magic of exceptional cuisine, luxurious suites, and 18th-century charm in this 114-acre country estate.* **Comp. fruit & cheese upon arrival; 10% discount, ask.**

NEW MARKET ────────────────────────────────

| | | |
|---|---|---|
| **National Pike Inn** | $$-B&B | Full breakfast |
| P.O. Box 299,  21774 | 5 rooms, 4 pb | Dining in town, snacks |
| 9 W. Main St. | MC, Visa, | Sitting room, tennis |
| 301-865-5055 | C-ltd/S-no/P-no/H-no | Convenient to historic |
| Tom & Terry Rimel | | Frederick |
| All year, by reservation | | |

*Beautiful Federal Home, inviting colonial atmosphere situated in historic village. Antique shopping and excellent restaurant-easy walking.* **3rd night 50% off.**

OAKLAND ────────────────────────────────

| | | |
|---|---|---|
| **Oak & Apple B&B, The** | $$-B&B | Continental plus bkfst. |
| 208 N. Second St.,  21550 | 5 rooms, 3 pb | Afternoon tea, snacks |
| 301-334-9265 | MC, Visa, • | Sitting room, bicycles |
| Jana Brown | C-ltd/S-no/P-no/H-no | sunporch w/swing |
| All year | | fireplaces |

*Colonial revival mansion circa 1915 in historic district of quaint mountain village. Elegant yet relaxed, surrounded by scenic and recreational paradise.*

OLNEY ────────────────────────────────

| | | |
|---|---|---|
| **Thoroughbred B&B** | $$-B&B | Continental breakfast |
| 16410 Batchellor Forest, | 15 rooms, 7 pb | Hot tubs, pool table |
| 20832 | MC, Visa, *Rated*, • | swimming pool, library |
| 301-774-7649  Fax: 301-924-2381 | C-yes/S-no/P-no/H-ltd | golf nearby, sitting rm. |
| Helen M. Polinger    All year | | |

*Beautiful country estate on 18-hole, 72 par golf course. 12 mi. to DC, 6 mi. to Metro. Tennis, some rooms w/fireplaces & whirlpool tubs. Golf Packages available.* **$5 discount if pay by cash or check.**

OXFORD ────────────────────────────────

| | | |
|---|---|---|
| **Robert Morris Inn** | $$$-EP | Full breakfast (fee) |
| P.O. Box 70,  21654 | 33 rooms, 33 pb | Continental (Tues) (fee) |
| 314 N. Morris St. | MC, Visa, *Rated*, • | Restaurant (excl. Tues.) |
| 410-226-5111  Fax: 410-226-5744 | C-ltd/S-no/P-no/H-ltd | bar service |
| Jay Gibson    All year | | non-smoking inn |

*Historic Chesapeake Bay romantic inn. Featuring the best crab cakes on the eastern shore. Tennis, fishing, boating, golfing nearby.* **10% discount Wed. & Thur. except holidays.**

ROCK HALL ────────────────────────────────

| | | |
|---|---|---|
| **Huntingfield Manor B&B** | $$$-B&B | Continental plus bkfst. |
| 4928 Eastern Neck Rd., | 6 rooms, 6 pb | Snacks, comp. wine |
| 21661 | Visa, MC, • | Sitting room, library |
| 410-639-7779  Fax: 410-639-2924 | C-ltd/S-no/P-yes/H-yes | bikes |
| George & Bernie Starken | | |
| All year | | |

*Your hosts welcome you to the shores of Chesapeake Bay, near the village of Rock Hall. Ideal for the single person who is looking for a safe haven, couples who want privacy, groups & business persons.*

SNOW HILL ────────────────────────────────

| | | |
|---|---|---|
| **River House Inn** | $$$-B&B | Full breakfast |
| 201 E. Market St.,  21863 | 8 rooms, 8 pb | Lunch, dinner, snacks |
| 410-632-2722 Fax: 410-632-2866 | MC, Visa, *Rated*, • | Comp. wine/tea, porches |
| Larry & Susanne Knudsen | C-yes/S-no/P-ltd/H-yes | A/C, fishing, boating |
| All year | | country club golf, bikes |

*Come relax at our elegant 1860s riverfront country home in historic Snow Hill. Canoe or bike inn-to-inn. Enjoy Maryland's eastern shore, beaches, bay.* **AAA, AARP 5% discounts.**

*Solomons Victorian Inn, Solomons Island, MD*

## SOLOMONS ISLAND

**Solomons Victorian Inn**
P.O. Box 759,  20688
125 Charles St.
410-326-4811  Fax: 410-326-0133
Helen & Richard Bauer
All year

$$$-B&B
6 rooms, 6 pb
*Rated*,
C-ltd/S-no/P-no/H-no
Spanish, Swedish,
French

Full breakfast
Boating, shops
hiking
restaurants nearby

*Let the Chesapeake romance you from the porch of this charming Queen Anne Victorian. Convenient to Washington, Baltimore and Richmond.*

## ST. MICHAELS

**Kemp House Inn**
P.O. Box 638,  21663
412 Talbot St.
410-745-2243
Steve & Diane Cooper
All year

$$-B&B
8 rooms, 6 pb
MC, Visa, *Rated*, •
C-yes/S-yes/P-yes/H-no

Continental plus bkfst.
Bicycles
queen-sized beds
private cottage avail.

*1805 Georgian house with four-poster beds and working fireplaces in historic eastern shore village; close to restaurants, museums, harbor.*

**Parsonage Inn**
210 N. Talbot (Rt. 33),  21663
401-745-5519  800-394-5519
Anthony Detesu
All year

$$$-B&B
8 rooms, 7 pb
MC, Visa, *Rated*, •
C-ltd/S-no/H-yes

Full gourmet breakfast
Comp. ice tea, tea
Parlor, library, suite
bicycles, shops, museums
fireplaces, restaurants

*Unique brick Victorian, part of historic district. Walking distance to maritime museums. Laura Ashley linens.* **10% off mid week (except July–Oct.).**

TANEYTOWN ─────────────────────────────────

| **Glenburn B&B** | $$-B&B | Full breakfast |
| 3515 Runnymede Rd., 21787 | 3 rooms, 2 pb | Refrigerator, kitchen |
| 410-751-1187 | • | 2 bdr. cottage w/kitchen |
| Robert & Elizabeth Neal | C-yes/S-ltd/P-no/H-no | swimming pool, porches |
| All year | | golf, A/C |

*Georgian house with Victorian addition, antique furnishings, featured in Maryland House & Garden Pilgrimage. Historic rural area close to Gettysburg.* **10% off midweek.**

TILGHMAN ISLAND ─────────────────────────────

| **Black Walnut Point Inn** | $$$-B&B | Continental breakfast |
| P.O. Box 308, 21671 | 7 rooms, 7 pb | Complimenatry wine |
| Black Walnut Rd. | *Rated*, | Sitting room, bicycles |
| 410-886-2452  Fax: 410-886-2053 | S-ltd/P-no/H-yes | tennis, pool, shoreline |
| Tom Ward & Brenda Ward | | 57-acre wildlife reserve |
| All year | | |

*The inn at the end of the road. Key West sunsets. Hammocks by the bay. Quiet and peaceful. Fishing*

| **Chesapeake Wood Duck** | $$$-B&B | Full gourmet breakfast |
| **Inn** | 7 rooms, 7 pb | Aft. tea, snacks |
| P.O. Box 202, 21671 | MC, Visa, *Rated*, • | Comp. wine, sitting room |
| Gibsontown Rd. | C-ltd/S-no/P-no/H-no | sun rm., bikes, kayaking |
| 410-886-2070  Fax: 410-886-2263 | | access to country club |
| 800-956-2070 | | |
| Stephanie & Dave Feith | | |
| All year | | |

*Award winning Southern hospitality on Chesapeake Bay. 1890 Victorian overlooking Dogwood Harbor in Waterman's Village. Porches/decks/sunset sails/frplcs./antiques.* **25% off ltd.**

VIENNA ───────────────────────────────────

| **Tavern House, The** | $$-B&B | Full breakfast |
| P.O. Box 98, 21869 | 3 rooms, | Aftn. tea, comp. wine |
| 111 Water St. | MC, Visa, • | Sitting room |
| 410-376-3347 | C-ltd/S-yes | tennis courts nearby |
| Harvey & Elise Altergott | Spanish, German | |
| All year | | |

*Restored Colonial tavern on Nanticoke River. Simple elegance; stark whites, detailed woodwork. Looking out over river and marshes. Great for bicycling and bird-watching.*

## More Inns ...

| Annapolis | American Heritage B&B, 108 Charles, 21404, 410-280-1620 |
| Annapolis | Annapolis B&B, 235 Prince George Sr., 21401, 301-269-0669 |
| Annapolis | Ark & Dove B&B, 149 Prince George St., 21401, 410-268-6277 |
| Annapolis | Casa Bahia, 262 King George St., 21404 |
| Annapolis | Charles Inn, 74 Charles St., 21401, 301-268-1451 |
| Annapolis | Coggeshall House, 198 King George St., 21404, 410-263-5068 |
| Annapolis | Corner Cupboard Inn, 30 Randall St., 21404, 410-263-4970 |
| Annapolis | Flag House Inn, 26 Randall St., 21404, 410-280-2721 |
| Annapolis | Georgian House B&B, 170 Duke of Gloucester, 21401, 410-263-5618 |
| Annapolis | Heart of Annapolis B&B, 185 Duke of Gloucester , 21404, 301-267-2309 |
| Annapolis | Hunter House B&B, 154 Prince George St., 21401, 410-626-1268 |
| Annapolis | Magnolia House, 220 King George St., 21404, 410-268-3477 |
| Annapolis | Maryland Inn, 58 State Circle, 21401, 800-638-8902 |
| Annapolis | Prince George Inn, 232 Prince George St., 21401, 410-263-6418 |
| Annapolis | Riverwatch, 145 Edgewater Dr., 21037, 410-974-8152 |
| Annapolis | Robert Johnson House, 58 State Circle, 21401, 800-638-8902 |
| Annapolis | William Page B&B Inn, 8 Martin St., 21401, 410-626-1506 |
| Baltimore | Admiral Fell Inn, 888 S. Broadway, 21231, 410-522-7377 |
| Baltimore | Agora, 824 E. Baltimore St., 21202, 301-234-0515 |
| Baltimore | Bolton Hill B&B, 1534 Bolton St., 21217, 301-669-5356 |

| | |
|---|---|
| Baltimore | Eagles Mere B&B, 102 E. Montgomery, 21230, 301-332-1618 |
| Baltimore | Inn at Government House, 1125 North Calvert St., 21202, 301-752-7722 |
| Baltimore | Society Hill–Hopkins, 3404 St. Paul St., 21218, 410-235-8600 |
| Berlin | Atlantic Hotel, The, 2 N. Main St., 21811, 410-641-0189 |
| Bryantown | Shady Oaks of Serenity, P.O. Box 842, 20617, 800-597-0924 |
| Burtonsville | Taylors' B&B, The, P.O. Box 238, 20866, 301-236-4318 |
| Burtonsville | Upsteam Guest House, 3600 Dustin Rd., 20866, 301-421-9163 |
| Cabin John | Winslow House, 8217 Caraway St., 20818, 301-229-4654 |
| Cambridge | Commodore's Cottage B&B, 215 Glenburn Ave., 21613, 800-228-6938 |
| Cambridge | Glasgow B&B Inn, 1500 Hambrooks Blvd., 21613, 410-228-0575 |
| Cambridge | Lodgecliffe on Choptank, 103 Choptank Ter., 21613 |
| Cascade | Bluebird on the Mountain, 14700 Eyler Ave., 21719 |
| Cascade | Inwood Guest House, Box 378, Route 1, 21719, 301-241-3467 |
| Centreville | Academy B&B, The, 100 Academy Lane, 21617, 410-758-2791 |
| Chesapeake City | Bohemia House, 1236 Town Point Rd., 21915, 410-885-3024 |
| Chesapeake City | Inn at the Canal, P.O. Box 187, 21915, 410-885-5995 |
| Chestertown | Hill's Inn, 114 Washington Ave., 21620, 301-778-INNS |
| Chestertown | Imperial House, 208 High St., 21620, 410-778-5000 |
| Chestertown | Widow's Walk Inn, 402 High St., 21620, 410-778-6455 |
| Chevy Chase | Chevy Chase B&B, 6815 Connecticut Ave., 20815, 301-656-5867 |
| Church Creek | Loblolly Landings & Lodge, 2142 Liners Rd., 21622, 410-397-3033 |
| Church Creek | Sportman's Retreat, The, 2142 Liners Rd., 21622, 410-397-3033 |
| Clear Spring | Harbine House B&B, P.O. Box 27, 21722, 301-842-2553 |
| Clear Spring | Wilson House B&B, 14923 Rufus Wilson Rd., 21722, 301-582-4320 |
| Cumberland | Red Lamp Post B&B, 849 Braddock Rd., 21502, 301-777-3262 |
| Easton | Tidewater Inn, Dover & Harrison St., 21601, 301-822-1300 |
| Elkton | Garden Cottage Sinking Spr, 234 Blair Shore Rd., 21921, 410-398-5566 |
| Ellicott City | Hayland Farm, 5000 Sheppard Ln., 21043, 301-531-5593 |
| Ellicott City | White Duck B&B, The, 3920 College Ave., 21043, 410-992-8994 |
| Fairplay | Candlelight Inn, 8620 Sharpsburg Pike, 21733, 301-582-4852 |
| Flintstone | Trailside Country Inn, US 40, 21530, 301-478-2032 |
| Frederick | Townhouse, The, 18-A E. 2nd St., 21701, 301-695-5374 |
| Frederick | Turning Point Inn, 3406 Urbana Pike, 21701, 301-874-2421 |
| Frederick | Tyler Spite House, The, 112 W. Church St., 21701, 301-831-4455 |
| Freeland | Freeland Farm, 21616 Middletown Rd., 21053, 301-357-5364 |
| Gaithersburg | Gaithersbury Hospitality, 18908 Chimney Place, 20879, 301-977-7377 |
| Georgetown | Kitty Knight House, Route 213, 21930, 301-648-5777 |
| Hagerstown | Sword Fireplace Country, 12238 Walnut Pt. Rd., 21740, 301-582-4702 |
| Hagerstown | Wingrove Manor, The, 635 Oak Hill Ave., 21740, 301-733-6328 |
| Huntington | Ches' Bayvu, 4720 Paul Hance Rd., 20639 |
| McHenry | Country Inn, P.O. Box 397, 21541, 301-387-6694 |
| Middletown | Marameade, The, 2439 Old National Pike, 21769, 301-371-4214 |
| Mount Savage | Castle, P.O. Box 578, Route 36, 21545, 301-759-5946 |
| New Market | Inns of the Blue Ridge, P.O. Box 299 FC, 21774, 301-865-5055 |
| New Market | Strawberry Inn, The, P.O. Box 237, 21774, 301-865-3318 |
| North Beach | Angels in the Attic, P.O. Box 70, 20714, 410-257-1069 |
| North Beach | Westlawn Inn, 7th St. & Chesapeake, 20714, 301-855-8410 |
| North East | Mill House, The, 102 Mill Ln., 21901, 301-287-3532 |
| Oakland | Carmel Cove, P.O. Box 644, 21550, 301-387-0067 |
| Oakland | Red Run Inn, Route 5, Box 268, 21550, 301-387-6606 |
| Oxford | 1876 House, P.O. Box 658, 21654, 301-226-5496 |
| Poolesville | Rocker Inn, 17924 Elgin Rd., 20837, 301-972-8543 |
| Princess Anne | Elmwood c. 1770 B&B, P.O. Box 220, 21853, 301-651-1066 |
| Princess Anne | Washington Hotel & Inn, Somerset Ave., 21853, 301-651-2525 |
| Rock Hall | Inn at Osprey, The, 20786 Rock Hall Ave., 21661, 410-639-2194 |
| Royal Oak | Part of Retreat Farm, A, P.O. Box 305, 21662 |
| Scotland | St. Michael's Manor B&B, 50200 St Michaels Manor, 20687, 301-872-4025 |
| Sharpsburg | Ground Squirrel Haller, 6736 Sharpsburg Pike, 21782, 301-432-8288 |
| Sharpsburg | Inn at Antietam, P.O. Box 119, 21782, 301-432-6601 |
| Sharpsburg | Jacob Rohrback Inn, P.O. Box 607, 21782, 301-432-5079 |
| Sharpsburg | Piper House B&B Inn, Antietam Battlefield, 21782, 301-797-1862 |
| Silver Spring | Northwood Inn, 10304 Eastwood Ave., 20901 |
| Silver Spring | Quality International, 10750 Columbia Pike, 20901, 301-236-5032 |
| Smithsburg | Blue Bear B&B, 13810 Frank's Run Rd., 21783, 800-381-2292 |
| Snow Hill | Snow Hill Inn, 104 E. Market St., 21863, 301-632-2102 |
| Solomons | Back Creek Inn B&B, P.O. Box 520, 20688 |
| Solomons | By-The-Bay B&B, P.O. Box 504 Calvert St, 20688 |
| St. Michaels | Inn at Perry Cabin, 308 Watkins Lane, 21663, 410-745-2200 |
| St. Michaels | Two Swan Inn, P.O. Box 727, 21663, 410-745-2929 |
| St. Michaels | Victoriana Inn, 205 Cherry St., Box 449, 21663, 410-745-3368 |
| St. Michaels | Wades Point Inn On The Bay, P.O. Box 7, 21663, 410-745-2500 |
| Stevenson | Gramercy Mansion, 1400 Greenspring Valley, 21153, 410-486-2405 |
| Stevensville | Kent Manor Inn, 500 Kent Manor Dr., 21666, 301-643-5757 |
| Taneytown | Antrim 1844, 30 Trevanion Rd., 21787, 410-756-2744 |
| Thurmont | Cozy Country Inn, 103 Frederick Rd., 21788, 301-271-4301 |
| Tilghman | Harrison's Country Inn, P.O. Box 310, 21671, 301-886-2123 |
| Tilghman Island | Sinclair House B&B, Box 145, 21671, 410-886-2147 |
| Vienna | Governor's Ordinary, P.O. Box 156, 21869, 301-376-3530 |

| | |
|---|---|
| Vienna | Nanticoke Manor House, P.O. Box 248, 21869,  301-376-3530 |
| Westminster | Avondale,  501 Stone Chapel Rd., 21157 |
| Westminster | Judge Thomas House 1893,  195 Willis St., 21157, 301-876-6686 |
| Westminster | Westminster Inn,  5 South Center St., 21157,  301-876-2893 |
| Westminster | Winchester Country Inn,  430 S. Bishop St., 21157, 301-876-7373 |
| Wittman | Christmas Farm, Rte. 33, 21676,  301-822-4470 |
| Woodsboro | Rosebud Inn, 4 N. Main St., 21798,  301-845-2221 |

*Gibson's Lodgings, Annapolis, MD*

# Massachusetts

## AMHERST

**Allen House Victorian Inn**
599 Main St.,   01002
413-253-5000  Fax: 413-253-0846
Alan & Ann Zieminski
All year

$$-B&B
7 rooms, 7 pb
*Rated*,
C-ltd/S-no/P-no/H-no

Full breakfast
Afternoon tea
Evening refreshments
sitting room, library
veranda, gardens, A/C

*Authentic antique-filled 1886 Victorian on 3 acres. Spacious bed chambers, private baths, ceiling fans. Historic Preservation Award winner. Opposite Emily Dickinson Homestead.*

## ATTLEBORO

**Col. Blackinton Inn, The**
203 N. Main St.,   02703
508-222-6022
Allana Schaefer
All year

$$$-B&B
16 rooms, 11 pb
Most CC, *Rated*,  •
C-yes/S-ltd/P-no/H-yes
German

Full breakfast
Afternoon tea, snacks
Bar service, library
2 sitting rooms
walking

*Featuring secluded garden terrace, viewing park-like cemetery & Bungay River. Ideal for touring & business travel in southeastern Massachusetts.*

## AUBURN

**Captain Samuel Eddy House**
609 Oxford St. S.,   01501
508-832-7282
Diedre & Mike Meddaugh
All year

$$-B&B
5 rooms, 4 pb
•
C-ltd/S-no/P-no/H-no

Full breakfast
Afternoon tea
Sitting room, library
bikes

*C.1765 Colonial home, tastefully decorated, common rooms with fireplaces, flower & herb gardens, New England history & antiques, near Worcester & Sturbridge.*

## BARNSTABLE, CAPE COD

**Ashley Manor**
P.O. Box 856,   02630
3660 Old Kings Hwy(Rt 6A)
508-362-8044
Fay & Donald Bain
All year

$$$-B&B
6 rooms, 6 pb
AmEx, MC, Visa,
*Rated*,  •
C-ltd/S-ltd/P-no/H-no

Full gourmet breakfast
Comp. wine/sherry/port
Flowers, fruit, snacks
sitting rm, croquet, A/C
bikes, tennis, garden

*1699 mansion in the historic district; rooms & suites have antiques, fireplaces, & private baths; walk to beach, village & harbor. Canopy beds.* **10% off for stays of 7+ nights.**

## BASS RIVER, CAPE COD

**Captain Isaiah's House**
33 Pleasant St., 02664
508-394-1739
Marge & Alden Fallows
Late June—early Sept

$$-B&B
3 rooms, 3 pb
C-ltd/S-yes/P-no/H-no

Continental breakfast
With home-baked goodies
Sitting room, fireplaces
2 studio apartments
whale watching nearby

*Charming, restored old sea captain's house in historic Bass River area. Most rooms have fireplaces. Studios have kitchens, TV and A/C.* **Free potted plants.**

## BOSTON

**Beacon Hill B&B**
27 Brimmer St., 02108
617-523-7376
Susan Butterworth
All year

$$$-B&B
3 rooms, 3 pb
•
C-ltd/S-no/P-no/H-no
French

Full breakfast
Restaurants nearby
Sitting room
garage nearby

*1869 Victorian townhouse. Fireplaces, riverview. Gas-lit, historically preserved downtown neighborhood. Boston Common, "Cheers" bar, Freedom Trail, Convention Center easy walk*

## BOSTON, BROOKLINE

**Anthony's Town House**
1085 Beacon St., 02146
617-566-3972
Barbara A. Anthony
All year

$-EP
14 rooms,
*Rated*, •
C-yes/S-yes/P-no/H-no

Restaurant/stores nearby
Near major league sports
all hospitals, sitt. rm.
historical sites, TV

*Turn-of-the-century brownstone townhouse; spacious rooms in Victorian atmosphere; family-operated for over 50 years; on trolley line, 10 min. to Boston.* **Special winter rates.**

## BREWSTER

**Bramble Inn & Restaurant**
P.O. Box 807, 02631
2019 Main St.
508-896-7644 Fax: 508-896-9332
Ruth & Clifford Manchester
April—December

$$$-B&B
8 rooms, 8 pb
*Rated*, •
C-ltd/S-yes/P-no/H-ltd

Full breakfast buffet
Lunch, dinner
Sitting room, suite
near beach, tennis
A/C, 3 rooms w/TV

*Romantic country inn in historic district of Cape Cod. Beach, tennis courts, and close to golf, fishing, and museums.* **7th night free.**

**Captain Freeman Inn**
15 Breakwater Rd., 02631
508-896-7481 Fax: 508-896-5618
800-843-4664
Carol & Tom Edmondson
All year

$$$-B&B
12 rooms, 9 pb
Most CC, *Rated*, •
C-ltd/S-no/P-no/H-no

Full breakfast
Menu gardens
Sitting room, jacuzzi
bicycles, badminton, A/C
swimming pool, croquet

*Charming, quiet inn in a sea captain's mansion. Canopy beds, romantic porch. 3 luxury suites w/fireplace. Weekend cooking school, Innkeeping seminars.* **50% off 3rd night, ltd.**

**Old Sea Pines Inn**
P.O. Box 1026, 02631
2553 Main St
508-896-6114 Fax: 508-896-8322
Stephen & Michele Rowan
April—December 22

$$-B&B
14 rooms, 14 pb
Most CC, *Rated*, •
C-ltd/S-ltd/P-no/H-no
Italian, German

Full breakfast
Beverage on arrival
Restaurant, parlor with
fireplace, deck, Sunday
dinner theatre summers

*Turn-of-the-century mansion furnished with antiques. Near beaches, bicycle trails, quality restaurants & shops. Nightly dinner, July & August.* **50% off 3rd night weekdays only.**

## CAMBRIDGE

| **Cambridge House B&B, A** | $$$-B&B | Full breakfast |
| 2218 Massachusetts Ave., | 13 rooms, 11 pb | Comp. wine & cheese |
| 02140 | AmEx, MC, Visa, | Lemonade, coffee, tea |
| 617-491-6300 Fax: 617-868-2848 | *Rated*, • | cookies |
| 800-232-9989 | C-ltd/S-no/P-no/H-no | sitting room |
| Ellen Riley & Tony Femmino | Italian | |
| All year | | |

*"Boston's finest gem"—Country Inns Magazine; "Boston's premier B&B"—BBC; "Our vote goes to Cambridge House"—L.A. Times.* **Winter specials.**

| **Irving House @ Harvard** | $$$-B&B | Continental plus bkfst. |
| 24 Irving St., 02138 | 44 rooms, 27 pb | Sitting room |
| 617-547-4600 Fax: 617-576-2814 | AmEx, MC, Visa, • | library, bicycles |
| 800-854-8249 | C-yes/S-no/P-ltd/H-yes | central A/C, cribs avail |
| Rachael Solem, Stephen | Spanish, some French | |
| Logue All year | | |

*Friendly accommodations in the heart of Cambridge. Off-street parking included. 10 min. walk to Harvard Square. Children under 7 free. Rentals w/kitchens avail.* **10% discount.**

| **Missing Bell B&B, The** | $$-B&B | Continental plus bkfst. |
| 16 Sacramento St., 02138 | 3 rooms, 2 pb | Sitting room |
| 617-876-0987 | C-ltd/S-no/P-no/H-no | |
| JP Massar, Kristin Quinlan | | |
| All year | | |

*Incredible 1883 Victorian in the heart of Cambridge. Wonderful breakfasts; fireplaces, deck, easy access to Boston. Quiet neighborhood.*

## CAPE COD, W. BARNSTABLE

| **Honeysuckle Hill** | $$$-B&B | Full gourmet breakfast |
| 591 Old Kings Hwy., Route | 3 rooms, 3 pb | Choc. chips at bedside |
| 6A, 02668 | Most CC, *Rated*, • | Air conditioning |
| 508-362-8418 Fax: 508-362-4854 | C-ltd/S-no/P-no/H-ltd | screened porch |
| 800-441-8418 | | near beaches |
| Richard & Judith Field | | |
| Memorial Day-September | | |

*Charming, shingled, historic 1810 inn. All rooms/suites have feather beds, air conditioning and private baths. Tranquil country setting with colorful gardens.*

## CHATHAM

| **Captain's House Inn** | $$$$-B&B | Full gourmet breakfast |
| P.O. Box 146, 02650 | 16 rooms, 16 pb | Comp. afternoon tea |
| 369-377 Old Harbor Rd. | AmEx, MC, Visa, | Sitting room |
| 508-945-0127 Fax: 508-945-0866 | *Rated*, • | bikes, lawn croquet |
| 800-315-0728 | C-ltd/S-ltd/P-no/H-no | 3 new suites w/frplcs. |
| David & Janet McMaster | | |
| All year | | |

*Antiques & Williamsburg wallpapers. Charming guest rooms have 4-poster beds, fireplaces. Private 2-acre estate of lawns & gardens. Quiet & elegant. AAA 4-Diamond (1987).*

| **Carriage House Inn** | $$$-B&B | Continental plus bkfst. |
| 407 Old Harbor Rd., 02633 | 3 rooms, 3 pb | Afternoon refreshments |
| 508-945-4688 Fax: 508-945-4688 | Visa, MC, AmEx, | Guest refrigerator |
| 800-355-8868 | *Rated*, • | sitting room w/piano, TV |
| Pam & Tom Patton | C-ltd/S-no/P-no/H-no | Air-conditioning |
| All year | | |

*Charming antique home, spacious grounds, fireplaced rooms, canopy beds, two friendly golden retrievers, warm and welcoming hosts.* **10% discount, ltd.**

## CHATHAM

**Cranberry Inn at Chatham**
359 Main St., 02633
508-945-9232 Fax:508-945-3769
800-332-4667
Ray & Brenda Raffurty
All year

$$$-B&B
18 rooms, 18 pb
Most CC, *Rated*, •
C-ltd/S-ltd/P-no/H-no

Full buffet breakfast
Tap Room, liquor license
Rooms w/phone, TV, A/C
patio, front porch
poster beds, suites

*In heart of Chatham's picturesque seaside village & Historic District. Relaxed & intimate atmosphere, fireplaces, antiques.* **3rd night 50% off, ltd.**

---

**Cyrus Kent House Inn**
63 Cross St., 02633
508-945-9104 Fax:508-945-9104
800-338-5368
Sharon Mitchell Swan
All year

$$$-B&B
11 rooms, 10 pb
AmEx, MC, Visa,
*Rated*,
C-ltd/S-yes/P-no/H-no

Continental plus bkfst.
Porch, deck, gardens
ample parking, phones
art & antique gallery

*Sea captain's house reborn in heart of the quaint seaside village of Chatham. Picturesque stroll to Main St. shops, beaches, restaurants. Re-decorated.* **Free bottle of wine.**

## CHATHAM, CAPE COD

**Moses Nickerson House Inn**
364 Old Harbor Rd., 02633
508-945-5859 Fax:508-945-7087
800-628-6972
Linda & George Watts
All year

$$$$-B&B
7 rooms, 7 pb
AmEx, MC, Visa,
*Rated*,
C-ltd/S-yes/P-no/H-no

Full breakfast
Comp. wine, cheese/fruit
Sitting room near beach
fresh flowers, antiques
turndown service, TV A/C

*Elegant sea captain's home built 1839. Canopy beds, fireplaces, romantic, quiet. Walk to village & beaches. Glass-enclosed breakfast room overlooking garden.* **Off-seas. disc't.**

## CONCORD

**Col. Roger Brown House**
1694 Main St., 01742
508-369-9119 Fax:508-369-1305
800-292-1369
Mrs. Lauri Berlied
All year

$$-B&B
5 rooms, 5 pb
Most CC, •
C-ltd/S-no/P-no/H-no

Continental plus bkfst.
Snacks
Sitting room, library
sauna & swimming pool
next door at Health Club

*National historic register 1775 Colonial; private baths; hearty breakfast; cozy, relaxed atmosphere; near historic areas. Meeting room for 12-18 (fee basis)*

---

**Hawthorne Inn**
462 Lexington Rd., 01742
508-369-5610 Fax:508-287-4949
Gregory Burch, Marilyn
Mudry
All year

$$$-B&B
7 rooms, 7 pb
Most CC, *Rated*, •
C-yes/S-ltd/P-no/H-no

Continental plus bkfst.
Tea & coffee at check-in
Sitting room, garden
yard, small pond, swings
bicycles, tree house

*On the "Battle Road" of 1775, furnished with antiques, quilts and artwork with the accent on New England comfort and charm. Extensive gardens, canopy queen bed.*

## CUMMAQUID

**Acworth Inn, The**
P.O. Box 256, 02637
4352 Old King's Hwy.
508-362-3330 800-362-6363
Cheryl & Jack Ferrell
All year

$$-B&B
6 rooms, 6 pb
Visa, MC, AmEx,
*Rated*, •
C-ltd/S-no/P-no/H-no
German

Continental plus bkfst.
Afternoon tea, snacks
Sitting room
bicycles

*Cape Cod charm in the center of the historic district; especially noted for the hand painted furnishings; easy access to islands.*

*Deerfield Inn, Deerfield, MA*

CUMMINGTON ───────────────────────────────

| **Cumworth Farm** | $$-B&B | Full breakfast |
| 472 W. Cummington Rd., | 6 rooms, | Afternoon tea |
| Route 112,  01026 | *Rated*, | Comp. wine, snacks |
| 413-634-5529 | C-yes/S-ltd | sitting room, hot tub |
| Ed & Mary McColgan | | piano, bicycles |
| All year | | |

*Big, 200-year-old farmhouse; sugarhouse on premises; sheep; berries—pick your own in season. Close to cross-country skiing, hiking trails. Quiet getaway, sweeping views.*

───────────────────────────────────────────

| **Swift River Inn** | $$$-B&B | Continental breakfast |
| 151 South St.,  01026 | 22 rooms, 22 pb | Restaurant, all meals |
| 413-634-5751  Fax: 413-634-5300 | Most CC, *Rated*, • | Snacks, bar service |
| 800-532-8022 | C-yes/S-no/P-no/H-yes | library, bicycles |
| Michael H. Trudeau, CHA | | swimming pool, cross- |
| All year | | country ski |

*Former turn-of-the-century gentleman's daily farm restored for lodging, dining & recreation. Family fun for all seasons: hiking, biking, fishing, hayrides. **3rd night 50%.***

DEERFIELD ───────────────────────────────

| **Deerfield Inn** | $$$-B&B | Full breakfast |
| 81 Old Main St.,  01342 | 23 rooms, | Afternoon tea |
| 413-774-5587  Fax: 413-773-8712 | Most CC, *Rated*, • | Restaurant, bar service |
| 800-926-3865 | C-yes/S-no/P-no/H-yes | lunch, dinner (fee) |
| Karl & Jane Sabo | | sitting room |
| Closed Xmas | | |

*Located in an historic village surrounded by museum houses, our 1884 inn and award-winning restaurant invite you into a gracious past.*

DENNIS ───────────────────────────────────

| **Four Chimneys Inn, The** | $$$-B&B | Continental plus bkfst. |
| 946 Main. St., Rte. 6A,  02638 | 8 rooms, 8 pb | Snacks, dining room |
| 508-385-6317  Fax: 508-385-6285 | Most CC *Rated*, • | Library, swimming |
| 800-874-5502 | C-ltd/S-ltd/P-no/H-no | fishing |
| Russell & Kathy Tomasetti | | porch, perennial gardens |
| April—October | | |

*1881 restored Victorian—stunning decor, spacious rms. all w/pb. Near Cape Cod beaches, Scargo Lake, tennis court, bike trails, Playhouse, Village, auctions.*

## DENNIS

**Isiah Hall B&B Inn**
P.O. Box 1007,  02638
152 Whig St.
508-385-9928  Fax: 508-385-5879
800-736-0160
Marie Brophy
April–mid-October

$$$-B&B
11 rooms, 10 pb
AmEx, MC, Visa,
*Rated*,  •
C-ltd/S-yes/P-no/H-ltd

Continental plus bkfst.
Complimentary tea/coffee
Library, gift shop
2 sitting rooms, gardens
rooms w/priv. bath, A/C

*Enjoy our relaxing quiet country ambience and hospitality in the heart of Cape Cod. Walk to beach, village, Playhouse and restaurants. **Spring Value Packages available.***

## DENNISPORT

**Rose Petal B&B, The**
P.O. Box 974,  02639
152 Sea St.
508-398-8470
Gayle & Dan Kelly
All year

$$-B&B
3 rooms, 2 pb
MC, Visa, *Rated*,  •
C-yes/S-ltd/P-no/H-no
some French

Full breakfast
Complimentary beverages
Sitting rm., TV, gardens
brass beds, piano, A/C
handstitched quilts

*Excellence & sophistication. 1872 home in a delightful seaside resort neighborhood. Pretty gardens, superb full breakfast features home-baked pastries. **10% off 7+ nights.***

## DUXBURY

**Winsor House Inn**
390 Washington St,  02332
617-934-0991  Fax: 617-934-5955
David M. O'Connell
All year

$$$-B&B
3 rooms, 3 pb
Most CC,
C-yes/S-yes/P-no/H-no

Full breakfast
Lunch seasonal (fee)
Sitting room

*Charming 19th-Century sea captain's home located in quaint seaside village of Duxbury, 35 miles S. of Boston, 10 miles from historic Plymouth. Walk to beach and shopping.*

## EAST ORLEANS

**Nauset House Inn**
P.O. Box 774,  02643
143 Beach Rd.
508-255-2195
D & L Johnson, C & J
Vessella    April–October

$$-EP
14 rooms, 8 pb
MC, Visa,
C-ltd/S-ltd/P-no/H-no

Full breakfast (fee)
Wine & hors d'oeuvres
Commons room
conservatory
dining room

*Intimate 1810 inn, unique turn-of-the-century conservatory, warm ambience, a short walk to the sea.*

**Parsonage Inn, The**
P.O. Box 1501,  02643
202 Main St.
508-255-8217  Fax: 508-255-8216
Ian & Elizabeth Browne
All year

$$$-B&B
8 rooms, 8 pb
MC, Visa, *Rated*,  •
C-ltd/S-no/P-no/H-no

Full breakfast
Guest refrigerator
Appetizers, parlor
piano, dining room
suite w/TV, AC, fridge

*A 1770 antique-furnished Cape home. All rooms have queen beds & A/C. Savor breakfast on the patio, walk to restaurants. Biking, golfing, tennis, fishing, Nauset beach nearby. Warm, friendly hosts.*

**Ship's Knees Inn**
P.O. Box 756,  02643
186 Beach Road
508-255-1312  Fax: 508-240-1351
Jean & Ken Pitchford
All year

$$-B&B
25 rooms, 11 pb
*Rated*,  •
C-ltd/S-yes/P-no/H-no

Continental breakfast
Sitting room
swimming pool
tennis courts

*A restored sea captain's house; surrounded by the charm of yesterday while offering the convenience of today. **50% off 3rd night except July, August, holidays.***

## EASTHAM

| **Over Look Inn, The** | $$$-B&B | Full breakfast |
|---|---|---|
| P.O. Box 771,  02642 | 14 rooms, 14 pb | Dinner occ., Aftn. tea |
| 3085 County Rd., Route 6 | *Rated*, • | Sitting room, library |
| 508-255-1886 Fax: 508-260-0345 | C-ltd/S-ltd/P-no/H-ltd | bikes, tours, packages |
| The Aitchison Family | Fr., Sp., It., Port. | 3 suites for families |
| All year | | |

*Victorian country inn & cottage within walking distance of Cape Cod National Seashore. Bike paths & nature trails. Tranquil wooded setting. Children welcome in suite.*

| **Penny House Inn** | $$$-B&B | Full breakfast |
|---|---|---|
| P.O. Box 238,  02651 | 12 rooms, 12 pb | Comp. wine, aftn. tea |
| 4885 County Rd. | MC, Visa, *Rated*, • | Sitting room, gazebo |
| 508-255-6632 Fax: 508-255-4893 | C-ltd/S-yes/P-no/H-no | brick patio, gardens |
| 800-554-1751 | French | great room w/fireplace |
| Margaret Keith | | |
| All year | | |

*Experience original Cape Cod charm & serenity in this 1751 bow-roof rambling Cape conveniently near all Nat'l Seashore Park activities.* **3rd night 50% off.**

| **Whalewalk Inn, The** | $$$-B&B | Full gourmet breakfast |
|---|---|---|
| 220 Bridge Rd.,  02642 | 12 rooms, 12 pb | Comp. hors d'ouevres |
| 508-255-0617 Fax: 508-240-0017 | *Rated*, • | Bar, sitting room, patio |
| Richard & Carolyn Smith | C-ltd/S-ltd/P-no/H-no | all rooms are A/C |
| April–November | | all suites w/fireplaces |

*Restored 1830s whaling master's home. Elegance, hospitality. Uniquely decorated. On quiet road by bay, ocean. Near beach. OUR 1993 INN OF THE YEAR!* **3rd night 50% - ltd.**

## EDGARTOWN

| **Arbor, The** | $$$-B&B | Continental breakfast |
|---|---|---|
| P.O. Box 1228,  02539 | 10 rooms, 8 pb | Comp. wine, beverages |
| 222 Upper Main St. | MC, Visa, *Rated*, • | Parlor, fresh flowers |
| 508-627-8137 | C-ltd/S-ltd/P-no/H-no | garden, courtyard, A/C |
| Peggy Hall | | antique shop in yard |
| May–October | | |

*Turn-of-the-century home in historic Edgartown. Walk to town & harbor. Rooms are delightfully and typically New England. Enchanting one-bedroom cottage available by the week.*

| **Captain Dexter House** | $$-B&B | Continental plus bkfst. |
|---|---|---|
| P.O. Box 2798,  02539 | 11 rooms, 11 pb | Complimentary wine |
| 35 Pease's Point Way | AmEx, MC, Visa, | Hot cider, lemonade |
| 508-627-7289 Fax: 508-627-3328 | *Rated*, • | landscaped garden |
| Rick & Birdie | C-yes/S-yes/P-no/H-no | sitt. rm., beach towels |
| April 15 - Nov. 15 | | |

*Lovely 1840s home; romantic antique-filled guest rooms with canopied beds and working fireplaces. Landscaped gardens. Near harbor, shops and restaurants.*

| **Colonial Inn Martha's Vyd.** | $$$-B&B | Continental plus bkfst. |
|---|---|---|
| P.O. Box 68,  02539 | , | Restaurant, bar |
| 38 N. Water St. | AmEx, MC, Visa, | Sitting room, library |
| 508-627-4711 Fax: 508-627-5904 | *Rated*, • | by tennis, riding, golf |
| 800-627-4701 | C-yes/S-yes/P-no/H-yes | sailing, fishing, beach |
| L. Malcouronne | Portuguese | |
| April-Dec | | |

*Charming, lovingly refurbished inn w/brass beds offers affordable luxury. Some rooms w/refrigerators. 2 suites w/kitchens. Near museums, galleries, shops.* **4th night 50% off.**

## EDGARTOWN

**Edgartown Inn, The**
P.O. Box 1211,  02539
56 North Water St.
508-627-4794
Susanne Hakala
April—October

$$$-EP
22 rooms, 13 pb
*Rated*,
C-ltd/S-yes
French

Full breakfast (fee)
Garden house renovation
many antiques
good fishing 5 minutes

*192-year-old historic inn where Nathaniel Hawthorne, Daniel Webster & John Kennedy stayed. Serving homemade cakes and breads for breakfast in the garden.*

---

**Point Way Inn**
P.O. Box 5255,  02539
104 Main St.
508-627-8633 Fax: 508-627-8579
Linda & Ben Smith
All year

$$-B&B
15 rooms, 15 pb
AmEx, MC, Visa,
*Rated*,  •
C-ltd/S-yes/H-ltd

Continental plus bkfst.
Comp. wine/lemonade/tea
Honor bar, snacks
sitting room, library
croquet, gardens, gazebo

*Located near center of town; 11 rooms w/working fireplaces. Inn is a former whaling captain's mansion. A comp. courtesy car is available to guests. **3rd. night 50%, ltd.***

## EDGARTOWN,MARTHA'S VINYD

**Shiverick Inn, The**
P.O. Box 640,  02539
Peases Point Wy–Pent Ln.
508-627-3797
Denny and Marty Turmelle
All year

$$$$-B&B
10 rooms, 10 pb
AmEx, MC, Visa,  •
C-ltd/S-ltd

Continental plus bkfst.
Comp. tea or coffee
Sitting room, library
dining room, parlor
formal garden, bicycles

*Exquisitely restored 19th-century mansion offering one-of-a-kind suites and guest rooms with fireplaces, library, formal parlor and garden.*

## ESSEX

**George Fuller House**
148 Main St. (Rt. 133),  01929
508-768-7766  Fax: 508-768-6178
800-477-0148
Cindy & Bob Cameron
All year

$$$-B&B
6 rooms, 5 pb
AmEx, MC, Visa,
*Rated*,  •
C-yes/S-ltd/P-no/H-no

Full breakfast
Comp. coffee, tea
Sitting room, fireplaces
learn to sail/charter in
30-foot yacht (midweek)

*Federalist-style with antique furnishings, 4 fireplaces, TV, marsh view. Near antique shops, seafood restaurants. 30-ft yacht for sailing/charters. **3rd night 50%.***

## FALMOUTH

**Capt. Tom Lawrence House**
75 Locust St.,  02540
508-540-1445  Fax: 508-457-1790
800-266-8139
Barbara Sabo-Feller
All year

$$$-B&B
6 rooms, 6 pb
MC, Visa, *Rated*,  •
C-ltd/S-yes/P-no/H-no
German

Full gourmet breakfast
Complimentary tea
Sitting room, library
piano, TV, A/C, porch
apt. avail/sleeps four

*Redecorated Victorian captain's home close to village ctr, beaches, golf, island ferries. Brkfst with homemade, organic bread. Fully furnished apartment with A/C, sleeps 4*

---

**Hewins House B&B**
20 Hewins St., Village Green,
  02540
508-457-4363  800-555-4366
Virginia Price
All year

$$$-B&B
3 rooms, 3 pb
Disc., *Rated*,  •
C-yes/S-no/P-no/H-no

Full breakfast
Sitting room, porch
kitchen facility

*Your home on Olde Cape Cod-National Register Historic District. Gardens, porch, breakfast in dining room. Convenient location for all Cape attractions. **10% disc't 4+ nights.***

*Capt. Tom Lawrence House, Falmouth, MA*

## FALMOUTH

| **Inn at One Main St., The** | $$$-B&B | Full breakfast |
| One Main St.,   02540 | 6 rooms, 6 pb | Snacks |
| 508-540-7469  888-AT-1MAIN | Visa, MC, AmEx, • | Sitting room |
| Karen Hart & Mari Zylinski | C-ltd/S-no/P-no/H-ltd | weddings |
| All year | | |

*This light and airy 1892 Victorian welcomes guests year-round. Walk to shops, beaches, everything. Full breakfast, private baths, A/C.*

| **Inn on the Sound** | $$$-B&B | Full breakfast |
| 313 Grand Ave.,   02540 | 10 rooms, 10 pb | Upscale casual beach |
| 508-457-9666  Fax: 508-457-9631 | MC, Visa, *Rated*, • | house, walk to MA V. |
| 800-564-9668 | C-ltd/S-no/P-no/H-no | ferry, golf, tennis |
| Renee Ross & David Ross | | |
| All year | | |

*Spacious rooms with spectacular ocean view, fireplaces, providing rest, relaxation or endless activities. 40ft deck overlooking Sound. Steps from beach*

| **Village Green Inn** | $$$-B&B | Full gourmet breakfast |
| 40 Main St.,   02540 | 5 rooms, 5 pb | Seasonal beverages |
| 508-548-5621  Fax: 508-457-5051 | *Rated*, • | Parlor, piano |
| 800-237-1119 | C-ltd/S-no/P-no/H-no | fireplaces, open porches |
| Don & Diane Crosby | | bikes, colored cable TV |
| All year | | |

*Old Victorian ideally located on Falmouth's historic green. 19th-c. charm & warm hospitality in lovely spacious rooms. Air conditioned rooms.* **Stay of 2 nights—zip code disc't, Feb-Apr., Sun.–Thurs.**

*Grafton Inn, Falmouth, Cape Cod, MA*

## FALMOUTH, CAPE COD

| | | |
|---|---|---|
| **Grafton Inn** | $$$-B&B | Full gourmet breakfast |
| 261 Grand Ave. S., 02540 | 11 rooms, 11 pb | Comp. wine/cheese |
| 508-540-8688 Fax: 508-540-1861 | MC, Visa, *Rated*, • | Sitting room, porch |
| 800-642-4069 | C-ltd/S-no/P-no/H-yes | bicycles, phone in rooms |
| Liz & Rudy Cvitan | Croatian | all rooms have A/C |
| Feb.–Dec | | |

*Oceanfront-on the beach; panoramic view; delectable croissants from France. Convenient to ferry, shops, restaurants. Gallery throughout. English gardens, beach towels & chairs*

| | | |
|---|---|---|
| **Mostly Hall B&B Inn** | $$$-B&B | Full gourmet breakfast |
| 27 Main St., 02540 | 6 rooms, 6 pb | Coffee, tea, sherry |
| 508-548-3786  800-682-0565 | Most CC, *Rated*, | Sitting room, piano |
| Caroline & Jim Lloyd | S-no/P-no/H-no | gazebo, veranda, porch |
| Feb. –Dec. | German | bicycles, gardens |

*Romantically secluded plantation home built in 1849 for New Orleans bride. Spacious corner rooms. Queen-sized four-poster canopy beds. A/C. Near beaches, shops, ferries.*

| | | |
|---|---|---|
| **Wildflower Inn, The** | $$-B&B | Full gourmet breakfast |
| 167 Palmer Ave., 02540 | 6 rooms, 6 pb | Tea, snacks, comp. wine |
| 508-548-9524  800-294-5459 | Visa, MC, *Rated*, • | Sitting room, library |
| Phil & Donna Stone | C-ltd/S-no/P-no/H-no | bicycles, hot tubs, A/C |
| All year | | fish, golf, tennis near |

*Restored Victorian in historic district close to shops, restaurants, & Island Ferry. Dine in fireplaced gathering room or wraparound porch. **Free champagne on special occasions.***

FALMOUTH, EAST ─────────────────────────────

| | | |
|---|---|---|
| **Bayberry Inn** | $$-B&B | Full breakfast |
| 226 Trotting Park Rd., 02536 | 2 rooms, 2 pb | Afternoon tea, snacks |
| 508-540-2962 | • | Sitting room, library |
| Anna Marie Peterson | C-yes/S-no/P-yes/H-no | enclosed yard for |
| All year | | children & pets |

*Traditional Cape Cod cottage—sunshine & rambler roses. Relax & be pampered. Quiet woodland setting close to beaches, shopping & island ferries. **Free ferry ticket w/2-nights.***

FALMOUTH, WEST ─────────────────────────────

| | | |
|---|---|---|
| **Elms, The** | $$-B&B | Full continental bkfst. |
| P.O. Box 895, 02574 | 9 rooms, 7 pb | Comp. sherry |
| 495 W.Falmouth Hwy Rt 28A | C-ltd/S-ltd/P-no/H-no | Living room, study |
| 508-540-7232 | | gardens, gazebo |
| Betty & Joe Mazzucchelli | | bicycles |
| All year | | |

*Refurbished Victorian home built in the 1800s, filled w/antiques, plants. Boasting cool breezes from Buzzard's Bay. Half mile to beach. **Free bottle of wine for honeymooners.***

GREAT BARRINGTON ─────────────────────────────

| | | |
|---|---|---|
| **Turning Point Inn, The** | $$-B&B | Full breakfast |
| 3 Lake Buel Rd., 01230 | 8 rooms, 6 pb | Comp. tea, coffee, juice |
| 413-528-4777 | AmEx, MC, Visa, | 4-room cottage with bath |
| Irving & Jamie Yost | C-yes/S-no/P-no/H-no | piano, fireplaces |
| All year | | bicycles, cottage |

*We offer a natural environment: whole grain vegetarian breakfast; no smoking. Hiking, skiing, comfort in 18th-century inn near Tanglewood, next to ski slopes.*

| | | |
|---|---|---|
| **Windflower Inn** | $$$-B&B/MAP | Full breakfast |
| 684 S. Egremont Rd., 01230 | 13 rooms, 13 pb | Dinner incl., aftn. tea |
| 413-528-2720 800-992-1993 | *Rated*, • | Snacks, bar service |
| C. & J. Ryan, B. & G. Liebert | C-yes/S-ltd/P-no/H-ltd | sitting room, library |
| All year | | swimming pool, remodeled |

*Elegant small country Inn. Beautiful rooms, some with fireplaces. Summer dining on our screened porch. Produce from our organic garden. **Room upgrade on 2 night stay, ltd.***

GT. BARRINGTON/EGREMONT ─────────────────────────────

| | | |
|---|---|---|
| **Baldwin Hill Farm B&B** | $$-B&B | Full country breakfast |
| 121 Baldwin Hill Rd.N/S, | 4 rooms, 3 pb | Afternoon tea, snacks |
| 01230 | MC, Visa, *Rated*, • | 2 sitting rooms, library |
| 413-528-4092 | C-ltd/S-no/P-no/H-no | screened porch, pool |
| Richard & Priscilla Burdsall | | fireplace, cross-country |
| All year | | skiing |

*Spacious Victorian farmhouse. Mountain views; nature hikes. Restaurants nearby. Hiking, tennis, golf, boating, fishing. Friendly and elegant. **10% discount for 4+ nights.***

HAMILTON ─────────────────────────────

| | | |
|---|---|---|
| **Miles River Country Inn** | $$$-B&B | Full breakfast |
| P.O. Box 149, 01936 | 8 rooms, 5 pb | Afternoon tea |
| 823 Bay Rd. | *Rated*, | Library, gardens |
| 508-468-7206 Fax: 508-468-3999 | C-yes/S-no/P-no/H-no | paths in woods, field |
| Gretel & Peter Clark | Spanish, French, | wildlife, beaches |
| All year | German | |

*200-year-old country Colonial on large estate. Summer breakfast on shaded garden terraces. Winter evenings by your bedroom's fireplace. **20% discount for weekday stays.***

## HARWICH PORT

| **Augustus Snow House** | $$$$-B&B | Full breakfast |
|---|---|---|
| 528 Main St., 02646 | 5 rooms, 5 pb | Afternoon tea |
| 508-430-0528 Fax: 508-432-7995 | Most CC, • | Gazebo and verandah |
| 800-320-0528 | C-ltd/S-no/P-no/H-no | close to quaint shops of |
| Joyce & Steve Roth | | Chatham |
| All year | | |

*Romantic Victorian mansion. Exquisite bedrooms, private baths (some w/jacuzzis), fire-places, TVs, gourmet breakfast, afternoon tea, walk to private beach.* **3rd night free, ltd.**

| **Country Inn** | $$-B&B | Continental plus bkfst. |
|---|---|---|
| 86 Sisson Rd. (Rte. 39), | 6 rooms, 6 pb | Dinner, bar service |
| 02646 | AmEx, MC, Visa, • | Sitting room, piano |
| 508-432-2769 800-231-1722 | C-ltd/S-yes/P-no/H-ltd | A/C, fireplace |
| The Dings Family | | swimming pool, cable TV |
| All year | | |

*Country Inn is a lovely old Cape Cod home on 6 acres w/the essence of yesteryear. Romantic ambience. An Inn of New England tradition.* **$40 restaurant credit w/3 night stay, off-season.**

| **Harbor Walk** | $-B&B | Full breakfast |
|---|---|---|
| 6 Freeman St., 02646 | 6 rooms, 4 pb | Canopy beds |
| 508-432-1675 | • | library, sitting room |
| Marilyn Barry | C-yes/S-no/P-ltd/H-no | tennis & ocean nearby |
| May—October | some French | |

*Victorian charmer, featuring antiques, homemade quilts and queen canopy beds. Walk to beach and most photographed harbor on Cape Cod. Summer sports paradise.*

## HARWICH PORT, CAPE COD

| **Dunscroft By-the-Sea Inn** | $$$-B&B | Full breakfast |
|---|---|---|
| 24 Pilgrim Rd., 02646 | 10 rooms, 10 pb | Comp. wine, juices |
| 508-432-0810 800-432-4345 | *Rated*, • | Library, piano, terrace |
| Alyce & Wally Cunningham | C-ltd/S-ltd/P-no/H-no | 2 person Jacuzzi, A/C |
| All year | | fireplace suite, sleigh |

*Located 300 feet from a beautiful private beach on Nantucket Sound; walk to restaurant, shops. Exclusive residential area. Honeymoon cottage, romance package available.*

## HARWICH WEST

| **Cape Cod Claddagh Inn** | $$$-B&B | Full Irish breakfast |
|---|---|---|
| P.O. Box 667, 02671 | 8 rooms, 8 pb | Restaurant - all meals |
| 77 Main St., Rt. 28 | Most CC, *Rated*, • | Aft. tea, snacks, pub |
| 508-432-9628 Fax: 508-432-6039 | C-yes/S-yes/P-no/H-no | sitting room, art, pool |
| 800-356-9628 | | library, trolly service |
| Eileen & Jack Connell | | |
| All year | | |

*Irish hospitality in Victorian ambiance. A full-service inn yet friendly and intimate. 2 king-size cottage stes. Authentic Irish Pub.* **Complimentary drink with lunch or dinner.**

## HYANNIS

| **Inn on Sea Street, The** | $$$-B&B | Full gourmet breakfast |
|---|---|---|
| 358 Sea St., 02601 | 9 rooms, 7 pb | Fruit & cheese |
| 508-775-8030 Fax: 508-771-0878 | AmEx, MC, Visa, | Library, sitting room |
| Lois Nelson, J.B. Whitehead | *Rated*, | goose down pillows |
| May-November | C-ltd/S-yes/P-no/H-no | 4-room cottage for two |

*Elegant Victorian inn, steps from the beach & Kennedy Compound. Antiques, canopy beds, goose down pillows, radios, fireplace, home-baked delights. A favorite w/travel writers.*

## HYANNIS

| **Sea Breeze Inn** | $$-B&B | Continental plus bkfst. |
|---|---|---|
| 397 Sea St.,   02601 | 15 rooms, 13 pb | Kitchen privileges |
| 508-771-7213 | Disc., *Rated*, • | Sitting room, cable TV |
| Patricia & Martin Battle | C-yes/S-yes/P-no/H-no | bicycles, canopy beds |
| All year | | 3 cottages, A/C |

*Quaint, nautical atmosphere, private setting, beach & Hyannisport Harbor 900 ft., near center of Hyannis. All Cape Cod towns & points of interest within 1 hour.*

## HYANNIS PORT

| **Simmons Homestead Inn** | $$$-B&B | Full breakfast |
|---|---|---|
| 288 Scudder Ave.,   02647 | 10 rooms, 10 pb | Comp. wine and cheese |
| 508-778-4999 Fax: 508-790-1342 | AmEx, MC, Visa, | Sitting room, library |
| 800-637-1649 | *Rated*, • | wrap-around porch |
| Bill Putman   All year | C-yes/S-ltd/P-ltd/H-no | huge yard, beaches |

*Beautifully restored 1820 sea captain's home abounds in art, priceless antiques, canopy beds. Lovely grounds.*

## LEE

| **Devonfield** | $$-B&B | Continental plus bkfst. |
|---|---|---|
| RR1, Box 435,   01238 | 10 rooms, 10 pb | Guest pantry |
| 85 Stockbridge Rd. | MC, Visa, AmEx, | Heated pool, tennis |
| 413-243-3298  Fax: 413-243-1360 | *Rated*, • | bicycles, lawn sports |
| 800-664-0880 | C-ltd/S-ltd/P-no/H-no | sitting room, ski area |
| The Schencks   All year | French, German | |

*Historic revolutionary setting, heated pool, golf, tennis, luxury, comfort, local fine restaurants. Comp. breakfast. Relax in Old World charm.* **3rd night 50%, ltd.**

## LENOX

| **Amadeus House** | $$-B&B | Full breakfast |
|---|---|---|
| 15 Cliffwood St.,   01240 | 8 rooms, 6 pb | Afternoon tea, snacks |
| 413-637-4770  Fax: 413-637-4484 | Most CC, *Rated*, • | Sitting room, library |
| 800-205-4770 | C-ltd/S-no/P-no/H-no | lawn games, porch |
| John Felton & Martha | | classical music, fans |
| Gottron   All year | | |

*Guest comfort comes first at this Victorian B&B on a quiet street. Featuring lovely rooms, delicious breakfast, friendly service. Near Tanglewood.* **10% off Nov. 1–April 30, ltd.**

| **Birchwood Inn** | $$-B&B | Full breakfast |
|---|---|---|
| P.O. Box 2020,   01240 | 12 rooms, 10 pb | Comp. tea, wine & cheese |
| 7 Hubbard St. | Most CC, *Rated*, | Sitting room, library |
| 413-637-2600  Fax: 413-637-2600 | C-ltd/S-ltd/P-no/H-ltd | in-room phones, fax |
| 800-524-1646 | | A/C in assorted rooms |
| Joan, Dick, Dan & Anne | | |
| Toner   All year | | |

*This hilltop inn is the only Lenox Inn on the National Historic Register. Beautifully appointed with fireplaces, grand porch & lovely gardens.* **Mid-week discount.**

| **Blantyre** | $$$$-B&B | Continental breakfast |
|---|---|---|
| P.O. Box 995,   01240 | 23 rooms, 23 pb | Restaurant, bar |
| 16 Blantyre Rd. | Most CC, *Rated*, • | Comp. wine, snacks |
| 413-637-3556  Fax: 413-637-4282 | S-yes/P-no/H-yes | tennis, pool, hot tubs |
| 413-298-3806 | French, German | croquet, bikes, hiking |
| Roderick Anderson | | |
| Open mid May—early Nov. | | |

*A gracious country house hotel surrounded by 85 acres of grounds. The hotel has a European atmosphere and exceptional cuisine. Carriage house.* **Complimentary cheese & Evian.**

LENOX ────────────────────────────────────

**Brook Farm Inn**
15 Hawthorne St., 01240
413-637-3013  Fax: 413-637-4751
800-285-POET
Joe & Anne Miller
All year

$$$-B&B
12 rooms, 12 pb
MC, Visa, *Rated*,
C-ltd/S-no/P-no/H-no

Full breakfast
Comp. tea with scones
Library, sitting room
swimming pool, gardens
poetry library, pantry

*100-year-old inn w/the grace of its Victorian past & comfort of the present. There is poetry here: 650 volumes & 60 poets on tape w/players available.*

---

**Cornell Inn**
203 Main St,  01267
413-637-0562  Fax: 413-637-0927
800-637-0562
Jack D'Elia
All year

$$-B&B
18 rooms, 18 pb
MC, Visa,  •
C-ltd/S-yes/P-no/H-yes

Continental plus bkfst.
Lunch, dinner, tavern
Sitting rooms, sundeck
restaurant bar & lounge
health spa

*Large Victorian home with country charm & modern conveniences. Close to all Berkshire sites. Full-service inn. Condo-style Carriage House wiht all comforts of home. **Packages available**.*

---

**Gables Inn, The**
81 Walker St.,  01240
413-637-3416  Fax: 413-637-3416
800-382-9401
Mary & Frank Newton
All year

$$$-B&B
17 rooms, 17 pb
Most CC, *Rated*,
C-ltd/S-yes/P-no/H-no
Spanish

Full breakfast
Comp. wine, dinner pkgs.
Sitting room, library
tennis courts
swimming pool

*Built in 1885, this gracious "cottage" was the home of Edith Wharton at the turn of the century. Lovingly furnished in period style. 2 new suites: Teddy & Edith Wharton suites*

**Garden Gables Inn**
P.O. Box 52,  01240
141 Main St.
413-637-0193  Fax: 413-637-4554
Mario & Lynn Mekinda
All year

$$-B&B
18 rooms, 18 pb
MC, Visa, *Rated*,
C-ltd/S-ltd/P-no/H-no
German, French

Full breakfast
Comp. port and sherry
Library, fireplace
whirlpools, porches
largest pool in the USA

*220-year-old gabled inn located in center of Lenox on four wooded acres. Furnished with antiques. One mile to Tanglewood and many other attractions. Phones in all rooms.*

---

**Gateways Inn**
51 Walker St.,  01240
413-637-2532  Fax: 413-637-2532
Fabrizio/Rosemary
Chiariello
All year

$$$-B&B
12 rooms, 8 pb
Most CC, *Rated*,
C-ltd/S-no/P-no/H-no
French, German, Italian

Continental breakfast
Dinner, Restaurant, bar
Sitting room w/TV
telephones in room
A/C, fireplaces, tennis

*Gateways Inn is Berkshire's only four-star restaurant. Elegant, luxurious townhouse in heart of Lenox.*

---

**Kemble Inn, The**
2 Kemble St.,  01240
413-637-4113  800-353-4113
John & Linda Reardon
All year

$$-B&B
15 rooms, 15 pb
Visa, MC, AmEx,  •
S-no/P-no/H-yes

Continental breakfast

*Elegant 1881 Georgian mansion, magnificent mountain views, spacious rooms w/private baths, fireplaces, A/C, TV, and 1½ miles to Tanglewood. Ski areas nearby.*

LENOX ─────────────────────────────────────────────

**Seven Hills Country Inn**
40 Plunkett St., 01240
413-637-0060
Fax: 413-637-3651
800-869-6518
All year

$$$-B&B
52 rooms, 52 pb
Most CC, *Rated*, •
C-yes/S-no/P-yes/H-yes
Spanish

Full bkfst. in season
Continental breakfast
Restaurant, bar service
sitting room
tennis courts, pool

*Country Inn on 27 acres of terraced lawns & gardens. Antique filled. Acclaimed restaurant. Swimming, tennis, skiing. Weddings and conferences. 3rd night 50%, off season.*

───────────────────────────────────────────────────

**Summer Hill Farm**
950 East St., 01240
413-442-2057
800-442-2059
Michael & Sonya Wessel
All year

$$-B&B
7 rooms, 7 pb
Visa, MC, AmEx,
*Rated*, •
C-ltd/S-no/P-no/H-yes

Full breakfast
Sitting room
fireplaces
2-room guest cottage

*200 year old Colonial with small horse farm. Elegantly & comfortably furnished with English antiques and oriental rugs. Rural setting, close to all local amenities. Off season & mid-week discounts.*

───────────────────────────────────────────────────

**Village Inn, The**
P.O. Box 1810,   01240
16 Church St.
413-637-0020  Fax: 413-637-9756
800-253-0917
Clifford Rudisill, Ray Wilson
All year

$$-EP
32 rooms, 32 pb
Most CC, *Rated*, •
C-ltd/S-yes/P-no/H-yes
Spanish, French,
German

Full menu avail. (fee)
Restaurant, bar
Sitting room, library
lakes, mountain trails
parks & museums nearby

*Historic 1771 inn reflecting charm & warmth of colonial New England. Rooms furnished in country antiques. Afternoon tea with homemade scones, dinner served July-October. 3rd night 50% off Nov.–May.*

───────────────────────────────────────────────────

**Walker House**
64 Walker St., 01240
413-637-1271
Fax: 413-637-2387
800-235-3098
Peggy & Richard Houdek
All year

$$$-B&B
8 rooms, 8 pb
*Rated*,
C-ltd/S-no/P-ltd/H-ltd
Spanish, French

Continental plus bkfst.
Comp. wine, aftn. tea
Sitting room, piano
library video theatre
opera/film weekends

*Our guests feel like special pampered friends. Lovely country atmosphere on 3 acres. Walk to shops, restaurants. 100-in. video screen shows films, plays. 3rd night 50% off 11/1-4/30, ltd.*

───────────────────────────────────────────────────

**Whistler's Inn**
5 Greenwood St., 01240
413-637-0975
Joan & Lisa Mears
All year

$$$-B&B
14 rooms, 14 pb
AmEx, MC, Visa,
*Rated*, •
C-ltd/S-no/P-no/H-no
Spanish, Polish, French

Full breakfast
Comp. sherry, tea/coffee
Sitting room, piano
library, bicycles
air conditioned, phones

*Elegant, antique-filled Tudor mansion; cozy library & French salon with Steinway piano. Home-baked breads & muffins. Old World charm. Lake nearby. Off-season discounts, ask.*

LEVERETT ─────────────────────────────────────────────

| | | |
|---|---|---|
| **Hannah Dudley House, The** | $$$-B&B | Full breakfast |
| 114 Dudleyville Rd.,   01054 | 4 rooms, 4 pb | Snacks, comp. wine |
| 413-367-2323 | Visa, MC, *Rated*, | Lunch, dinner (fee) |
| Erni & Daryl Johnson | C-ltd/S-no/P-no/H-no | Sitting room, library |
| All year | | pool, romantic getaways |

*Restored 200 yr. old colonial on 110 tranquil acres. Rooms individually decorated. Cozy fireplaces. Hiking trails/meadows/ woods/special places.* **Ask about comp. lobster dinner.**

LEXINGTON ────────────────────────────────────────────

| | | |
|---|---|---|
| **Halewood House** | $$-B&B | Continental plus |
| 2 Larchmont Ln.,   02173 | 2 rooms, | Modern baths, sitt. rm. |
| 617-862-5404 | ● | near tennis, swimming, |
| Carol Halewood | C-ltd/S-no/P-no/H-no | restaurants, shopping |
| All year | | |

*Well-decorated rooms, modern bath. Excellent food. New England charm and architecture. Walking distance to historic sights. Near route 95. .* **5+ nights 20% off.**

LYNN ─────────────────────────────────────────────────

| | | |
|---|---|---|
| **Diamond District Breakfast** | $$-B&B | Full breakfast |
| 142 Ocean St.,   01902 | 9 rooms, 5 pb | Afternoon tea, snacks |
| 617-599-4470   Fax: 617-595-2200 | Most CC, *Rated*, ● | Overlooks garden & ocean |
| 800-666-3076 | C-ltd/S-no/P-ltd | library, home-cooked low |
| Sandra Caron    All year | | fat, vegetarian food |

*1911 clapboard mansion. Gracious foyer, grand staircase winding up three floors. Fireplace liv. room, Mexican mahogany. French doors to large veranda.* **Discounted winter rates.**

MARBLEHEAD ───────────────────────────────────────────

| | | |
|---|---|---|
| **Harbor Light Inn** | $$$-B&B | Continental plus bkfst. |
| 58 Washington St.,   01945 | 20 rooms, 20 pb | Aftn. tea, comp. wine |
| 617-631-2186   Fax: 617-631-2216 | AmEx, MC, Visa, | Sitting rm., conf. room |
| Peter & Suzanne Conway | *Rated*, ● | hot tubs, courtyard |
| All year | C-ltd/S-yes/P-no/H-no | heated swimming pool |

*The north shore's premier inn. Elegant 18th-century Federalist mansion. Jacuzzis, sundecks, in heart of historic Harbor District. Conference facilities.* **Dinner pkgs. in winter months.**

| | | |
|---|---|---|
| **Harborside House** | $$-B&B | Continental plus bkfst. |
| 23 Gregory St.,   01945 | 2 rooms, | Harbor Sweets candy |
| 617-631-1032 | ● | Living room w/fireplace |
| Susan Livingston | C-ltd/S-no/P-no/H-no | deck, period dining room |
| All year | | bicycles available |

*C. 1850 colonial home offers antiques/modern amenities. Homemade baked goods. Sunny porch, flower gardens. Walk to historic sites, shops, beach, restaurants.* **10% off 3+ nights.**

| | | |
|---|---|---|
| **Pheasant Hill Inn** | $$$-B&B | Continental plus bkfst. |
| 71 Bubier Rd,   01945 | 3 rooms, 3 pb | Snacks |
| 617-639-4799 | Visa, MC, AmEx, ● | Sitting room, library |
| Bill & Nancy Coolidge | C-ltd/S-ltd/P-no/H-no | phones, TV, A/C |
| All year | | suite with fireplace |

*Charming 1920 summer estate. Private all-suites, getaway. Country-like setting and views to water. Memorable! Walk to restaurants, shops and beach*

MARTHA'S VINEYARD ISLAND ─────────────────────────────

| **Thorncroft Inn** | $$$$-B&B | Full breakfast |
| P.O. Box 1022,   02568 | 14 rooms, 14 pb | Cont. breakfast in bed |
| 278 Main St. | *Rated*, • | Afternoon tea, TV |
| 508-693-3333 Fax: 508-693-5419 | C-ltd/S-ltd/P-no/H-no | evening turndown service |
| 800-332-1236 | | 3.5 acres, morning paper |
| Karl & Lynn Buder | | |
| All year | | |

*Romantic country inn. AAA 4 diamond; Mobil 4 stars. Fireplaces; central A/C; luxury suites with jacuzzi or private hot tub, balconies; canopied 4-poster beds.*

MARTHAS VYARDS/EDGARTOWN ─────────────────────────

| **Ashley Inn** | $$$-B&B | Continental breakfast |
| P.O. Box 650,   02539 | 10 rooms, 8 pb | Sitting room |
| 129 Main St. | AmEx, MC, Visa, | tea room, grounds |
| 508-627-9655  800-477-9655 | *Rated*, • | badminton, hammock |
| Fred & Janet Hurley | C-ltd/S-yes/P-no/H-no | |
| All year | | |

*1800s sea captain's home with country charm, decorated with period antiques, brass & wicker. A leisurely stroll to shops, beaches, fine foods. Off-season: 3rd night 50%.*

NANTUCKET ─────────────────────────────────────────

| **Carriage House, The** | $$-B&B | Continental plus bkfst. |
| 5 Ray's Court,   02554 | 7 rooms, 7 pb | Guest refrigerator |
| 508-228-0326 | *Rated*, • | Sitting room, library |
| Jeanne McHugh & son, | C-yes/S-no/P-no/H-no | patio, beach towels |
| Haziel | Fr., Ger., Sp., Jap. | discount rates, ask |
| All year | | |

*Converted carriage house on the prettiest country lane; beautifully quiet, yet right in town. B&B and more, since 1974. Tennis, boating and unspoiled beaches nearby.*

| **Centerboard Guest House** | $$$-B&B | Continental plus bkfst. |
| P.O. Box 456,   02554 | 6 rooms, 6 pb | Comp. refreshments |
| 8 Chester St. | AmEx, MC, Visa, | Beach towels |
| 508-228-9696 Fax: 508-228-1963 | *Rated*, • | library, sitting room |
| Marcia Wasserman | C-ltd/S-no/P-no/H-no | suite, jacuzzi |
| All year | Spanish | |

*A Victorian guest house of quiet country elegance; lovingly renovated & restored in 1986-87; located in historic district, Nantucket Center; beaches nearby.*

| **Centre Street Inn** | $$$-B&B | Continental plus |
| 78 Centre Street,   02554 | 13 rooms, 7 pb | Afternoon tea |
| 508-228-0199  800-298-0199 | Visa, MC, AmEx, • | Sitting room, bike rack |
| Sheila & Fred Heap | C-ltd/S-no/P-no | beach towels, yard |
| | | One suite available |

*Delightfully restored 18th century inn minutes from ferry, beaches, and town. Spacious dining/sitting rooms overlooking flower gardens. Some rooms with fireplace.*

| **Corner House** | $$-B&B | Continental plus bkfst. |
| P.O. Box 1828,   02554 | 14 rooms, 14 pb | Afternoon tea |
| 49 Centre St. | Visa, MC, Disc. *Rated*, | Sitt. rm., A/C in summer |
| 508-228-1530 | C-ltd/S-ltd/P-no/H-ltd | screen porch w/wicker |
| John & Sandy Knox- | French, German | secluded garden terrace |
| Johnston | | |
| February 15—December | | |

*Especially comfortable & attractive 18th-century village inn, brought gently into the 20th century. Antiques, canopy beds, cozy fires. Special packages late Oct.–mid-May.*

## NANTUCKET

**Jared Coffin House**
29 Broad St., 02554
508-228-2400 Fax: 508-228-8549
800-248-2405
Philip & Margaret Read
All year

$$-B&B
,
Most CC, *Rated*, •
C-ltd/S-yes/P-ltd/H-no

Full breakfast
Full menu, bar service
Sitting room
piano, meeting rooms
entertainment

*Historically interesting collection of six buildings make up the inn. Convenient location in town near everything. Two excellent restaurants. Mobil 3-star rating.*

---

**La Petite Maison**
132 Main St., 02554
508-228-9242
Holli Martin
April 15–January 15

$$$-B&B
4 rooms, 1 pb
MC, Visa, *Rated*,
C-ltd/S-yes/H-ltd
French

Continental plus bkfst.
Afternoon tea
Sitting room
dining room w/fireplace
Cottage/apt./studio

*Located on upper Main St., a 6 minute walk to town center is our owner managed European guesthouse. Breakfast on the sunporch amid international clientele as you enjoy the ambiance & friendliness.*

---

**Martin House Inn**
P.O. Box 743, 02554
61 Centre St.
508-228-0678
Ceci and Channing Moore
All year

$$-B&B
13 rooms, 9 pb
AmEx, MC, Visa,
*Rated*, •
C-ltd/S-no/P-no/H-no

Continental plus bkfst.
Complimentary sherry
Sitt./Dining rm., frplc.
veranda, beach towels
piano/3 rms. w/fireplace

*Stately 1803 Mariner's home in Nantucket's historic district. Four-poster canopy beds, 13 airy rooms. Spacious living room, dining room, verandah.*

---

**Seven Sea Street Inn**
7 Sea St., 02554
508-228-3577 Fax: 508-228-3578
Matthew & Mary Parker—
Owners
All year

$$$-B&B
11 rooms, 11 pb
AmEx, MC, Visa,
*Rated*, •
C-ltd/S-no/P-no/H-no

Continental plus bkfst.
Sitting rooms
Jacuzzi, A/C-all rooms
guest house next to main

*Red oak post and beam guest house with authentic Nantucket ambiance. Romance, comfort and warmth best describe our colonial inn. **Split of champagne for honeymooners.***

---

**Stumble Inne**
109 Orange St, 02554
508-228-4482 Fax: 508-228-4752
800-649-4482
Mary Kay & Mal Condon
All year

$$$-B&B
13 rooms, 10 pb
AmEx, MC, Visa,
*Rated*, •
C-ltd/S-no/P-no/H-no

Continental plus bkfst
Aftn. tea, comp. wine
Sitting room, parking
spacious grounds
Voted #1-Cape Cod Life

*Nantucket's friendliest bed & breakfast. Delightful Laura Ashley decor. Hearty breakfast in a gracious dining room. Near activities & sites. **Wine, 3rd night 50% Oct.–June** .*

---

**Tuckernuck Inn**
60 Union St., 02554
508-228-4886 Fax: 508-228-4890
800-228-4886
Ken & Phyllis Parker
All year

$$$-B&B
18 rooms, 17 pb
AmEx, MC, Visa,
*Rated*, •
C-ltd/S-no/P-no/H-yes

Continental breakfast
Full breakfast (fee)
Complimentary wine/snack
sitting room, library
full service dining, ltd

*Wonderful in-town location; panoramic harbor view from our widow's walk; spacious lawn with recreational facilities; Colonial ambiance. **50% off Nov.–April.***

*Tuckernuck Inn, Nantucket, MA*

## NANTUCKET

| **Woodbox Inn, The** | $$$-EP | Full breakfast (fee) |
| 29 Fair St.,  02554 | 9 rooms, 9 pb | Dinner (7 and 9pm) |
| 508-228-0587 | *Rated*, | Sitting room, frplc. |
| Dexter Tutein | C-yes/S-yes/P-ltd/H-yes | "Nantucket's most |
| June–mid-October | French, German | romantic dining room" |

*"Probably the best place to stay on Nantucket." Oldest inn (1709) in Nantucket, furnished with period antiques. Breakfast 8:30-10:30.* **Complimentary bottle of wine ltd.**

## NANTUCKET ISLAND

| **Century House, The** | $$$-B&B | Gerry's buffet breakfast |
| 10 Cliff Rd.,  02554 | 9 rooms, 9 pb | Happy hour setups |
| 508-228-0530 | *Rated*, • | Afternoon tea, munchies |
| All year | C-ltd/S-ltd/P-no/H-no | sitting room, veranda |
|  | Fr., Rus., Ger., Jap., | H. Miller player piano |

*Historic sea captain's B&B inn in operation since the mid-1800s. Minutes to beaches, restaurants, galleries, shops. Antiques, Laura Ashley decor. Featured on TV's "Wings."*

| **Ivy Lodge, The** | $$$-B&B | Continental plus bkfst. |
| 2 Chester St,  02554 | 6 rooms, 6 pb | Complimentary sherry |
| 508-228-775 | MC, Visa, *Rated*, | Sitting room |
| Fax: 508-228-0305 | C-ltd/S-no/P-no/H-no | courteous European hosp. |
| Tuge Koseatac | Turkisk, Spanish |  |
| Mid April–Mid October |  |  |

*Corner of Europe tucked away at downtown Nantucket. Close to everything. Rooms furnished with antiques, home baked breakfast at the formal dinning room.* **3rd night 50%, ltd.**

| **Quaker House Inn & Rest.** | $$$-B&B | Full breakfast |
| 5 Chestnut St.,  02554 | 9 rooms, 9 pb | Restaurant-15%off dinner |
| 508-228-0400 | MC, Visa, *Rated*, • | Dinner, beer, wine |
| Fax: 508-228-9156 | C-ltd/S-ltd/P-no/H-no | sitting room, A/C |
| Caroline & Bob Taylor |  |  |
| Memorial Day–September |  |  |

*Located in the heart of Nantucket's historic district. Guest rooms have private baths, queen-size beds, and decorated in 19th-century antiques. Charming candlelit dinners.*

## NEW MARLBOROUGH

**Old Inn on the Green, The**
Star Route 70, Route 57,
  01230
413-229-3131  Fax: 413-229-2053
800-286-3139
B. Wagstaff & L. Miller
All year

$$$-B&B
16 rooms, 12 pb
MC, Visa, •
C-yes/S-yes/P-no/H-yes
French, Ger., Sp.-ltd

Continental plus bkfst.
Restaurant, bar
Dinner (Fri-Sun)
five public rooms
nearby whirlpools

*1760 colonial inn on historic landmark register. 3 public rooms downstairs. Parlor, dining room, old tavern. Inn furnished with antiques. **3rd night, 25% discount.***

## NEWBURYPORT

**Windsor House, The**
38 Federal St.,  01950
508-462-3778 Fax: 508-465-3443
Judith & John Harris
All year

$$$-B&B/MAP
6 rooms, 3 pb
MC, Visa, *Rated*, •
C-ltd/S-no/P-yes/H-no

Full breakfast
Aftn. tea, evening meal
Common rooms, organ
shops, museums

*Federalist mansion/ship's chandlery in restored historic seaport furnished in period antiques; explore our beaches & wildlife refuge. **3rd night 50% off, ltd.***

## NEWTONVILLE

**Sage and Thyme B&B**
65 Kirkstall Rd., 02160
617-332-0695
Ed & Hertha Klugman
All year

$$-B&B
2 rooms,
C-yes/S-no/P-no/H-no
Ger., It., Sp., Fr.

Full breakfast
Comp. coffee, juice
A/C in rooms
Crib, toys, books

*Classic colonial in quiet neighborhood. Downtown Boston only 5 miles away. Outstanding breakfast & congenial hosts & cat. Cozy quilts in winter. 3rd person in room is $20/ night. **8th night free, ltd.***

## NORTHAMPTON

**Knoll, The**
230 N. Main St., (Florence),
  01060
413-584-8164
Leona (Lee) Lesko   All year

$$-B&B
3 rooms,
*Rated*,
C-ltd/S-no/P-no/H-no

Full breakfast

*Large Tudor house in quiet rural setting on 16 acres. Near 5 colleges: Smith, Amherst, Mt. Holyoke, University of Massachusetts, Hampshire.*

## NORTHFIELD

**Northfield Country House**
P.O. Box 617,  01360
RR1, 181 School St.
413-498-2692  800-498-2692
Andrea Dale   All year

$$-B&B
7 rooms,
*Rated*,
C-ltd/S-yes/P-no/H-no

Full gourmet breakfast
Dinner (by reservation)
Sitting room, piano
cross-country skiing, tennis
court; swimming pool

*English manor house softened by firelight & flowers. Personally decorated bedrooms w/ antiques. 3 rooms w/romantic fireplaces. Close to New England activities. **3rd night 50% exc. 9/15-10/31.***

## OAK BLUFFS

**Oak Bluffs Inn, The**
P.O. Box 2477,  02557
Circuit & Pequot Ave.
508-693-7171  800-955-6235
Maryann Mattera   All year

$$$-B&B
10 rooms, 10 pb
AmEx, MC, Visa, •
C-yes/S-yes/P-no/H-no

Continental plus bkfst.
Afternoon tea
Sitt. room, A/C in rooms
60-ft. observation tower
large wraparound porch

*A Victorian masterpiece. Reflects the romance and elegance of the past yet fresh and colorful. Near beaches, nightlife and gingerbread cottages. **Free bottle of wine.***

OAK BLUFFS, M. VINEYARD ────────────

| **Dockside Inn, The** | $$-B&B | Continental plus bkfst. |
| P.O. Box 1206,  02557 | 20 rooms, 20 pb | Bicycles, A/C, sitting |
| Circuit Ave. Extension | Visa, MC, Disc., *Rated, | room, TV, Kitchen suites |
| 508-693-2966 Fax: 508-696-7293 | • | Garden area w/BBQ grill |
| 800-245-5979 | C-ltd/S-yes/P-no/H-yes | |
| Patrick Mullin, Siobhan | | |
| Casey   Mid May - Mid Oct. | | |

*A romantic Victorian Inn on the harbor. Built in 1989 with all the charm of the 1800s and all the amenities of today. Hairdryers have been added to all bathrooms.*

ONSET ─────────────────────────

| **Onset Pointe Inn** | $$-B&B | Continental plus bkfst. |
| P.O. Box 1450,  02558 | 15 rooms, 15 pb | Sitting room, library |
| 9 Eagle Way | Most CC, • | tennis, swimming pool |
| 508-295-8442 Fax: 508-295-5241 | C-ltd/S-no/P-no/H-ltd | massage with notice |
| 800-35-ONSET | | |
| Joe & Debbie Lopes   All yr | | |

*1880 Victorian mansion at the water's edge—uniquely decorated—private baths & balconies—quaint, quiet village—one of a kind views and sunsets.* **3rd night free w/2 night stay, ltd.**

ORLEANS ───────────────────────

| **Academy Place B&B** | $$-B&B | Continental plus bkfst. |
| P.O. Box 1407,  02653 | 5 rooms, 3 pb | Afternoon tea |
| 8 Academy Place | Visa, MC, | Sitting room |
| 508-255-3181 | C-ltd/S-no/P-no/H-no | swimming & fishing close |
| Sandy & Charles Terrell | | |
| Memorial-Columbus Day | | |

*Antique Cape Cod sea captain's home on Village Green. Walk to restaurants & shops. Nat'l seashore 10 minutes away; bike path 1/4 mile.* **5th night 50% off Memorial-Labor Day.**

| **Morgan's Way B&B** | $$$-B&B | Full gourmet breakfast |
| Nine Morgan's Way,  02653 | 3 rooms, 3 pb | Guest refrigerators |
| 508-255-0831 Fax: 508-255-0831 | • | Sitting room, library |
| Page McMahan & Will Joy | C-ltd/S-no/P-no/H-no | fresh flowers, chocolate |
| All year | | firm beds, heated pool |

*Romantic and elegant contemporary hideaway. Five acres of gardens and woodlands, heated pool; a birdwatcher's paradise. Close to beaches. Bedrooms have central A/C*

PEABODY ───────────────────────

| **Joan's B&B** | $$-B&B | Continental plus bkfst. |
| 210R Lynn St.,  01960 | 3 rooms, 1 pb | Afternoon tea, snacks |
| 508-532-0191 | C-ltd/S-no/P-no/H-no | Sitting room, patio |
| Joan Hetherington | | swimming pool, laundry |
| All year | | use of whole house |

*Located 10 min. from historic Salem, 25 min. from Boston, and 25 min. from picturesque Gloucester and Rockport. 2 rooms have A/C.* **Discount on 2nd & 3rd weeks.**

PETERSHAM ──────────────────────

| **Winterwood at Petersham** | $$$-B&B | Continental plus bkfst. |
| P.O. Box 176,  01366 | 6 rooms, 6 pb | Restaurant |
| 19 North Main St. | AmEx, MC, Visa, • | Bar service |
| 508-724-8885 | C-yes/S-ltd/P-no/H-no | sitting room, library |
| Jean & Robert Day | | working fireplaces |
| All year | | |

*Sixteen-room Greek revival mansion—built as private summer home—on National Register of Historic Homes. Beautifully appointed and professionally decorated.*

## PLYMOUTH

| **Foxglove Cottage B&B** | $$$-B&B | Full breakfast |
|---|---|---|
| 101 Sandwich Road, 02360 | 3 rooms, 3 pb | Picnic lunch baskets |
| 508-747-6576 Fax: 508-747-7622 | AmEx, MC, Visa, | Dinner, sitting room |
| 800-479-4746 | *Rated*, • | video library, bicycles |
| Charles & Michael Mary | C-ltd/S-no/P-no/H-no | breakfast on deck |
| Cowan | | |
| All year | | |

*Pastoral setting, minutes to Plymouth Plantation & Mayflower. Day trips to Cape Cod & Islands. Sitting area & fireplace in each room. A touch of tranquility.* **10% off 4+ nights.**

## PROVINCETOWN

| **Cape Codder Guest House** | $-B&B/EP | Continental breakfast |
|---|---|---|
| 570 Commercial St., 02657 | 14 rooms, 1 pb | Private sandy beach |
| 508-487-0131 | MC, Visa, | sun deck, seaside garden |
| Deborah Dionne | C-yes/S-ltd/P-ltd/H-ltd | 1 apt. with private bath |
| Mid-April–October | | |

*Old-fashioned comfort in quiet area; private beach, sun deck; whale-watching and bicycling nearby; informal friendly atmosphere; resident marine biologists! Daily maid*

| **Land's End Inn** | $$$-B&B | Continental breakfast |
|---|---|---|
| 22 Commercial St., 02657 | 14 rooms, 14 pb | Restaurants |
| 508-487-0706 800-276-7088 | C-ltd/S-no/P-no/H-no | Sitting room, near shops |
| Anthony Arakelian | | panoramic views |
| All year | | some queen-size beds |

*Victorian summer house set high on a hill overlooking Provincetown with panoramic views of Cape Cod. With a homelike and friendly atmosphere. Oriental wood carvings, antiques.*

| **Rose and Crown Guest House** | $$-B&B | Continental breakfast |
|---|---|---|
| 158 Commercial St., 02657 | 8 rooms, 5 pb | Comp. wine in room |
| 508-487-3332 | • | Sitting room |
| Sam Hardee | C-yes/S-yes/P-no/H-ltd | |
| All year | | |

*A relaxed, elegant 1780s captain's house. Rooms feature antiques in a homey atmosphere. An unusual eclectic living room is featured.* **Stay 3 nights, get 4 free, off season.**

| **Somerset House** | $$$-B&B | Continental breakfast |
|---|---|---|
| 378 Commercial St., 02657 | 13 rooms, 10 pb | Library, antiques |
| 508-487-0383 Fax: 508-487-4746 | MC, Visa, *Rated*, | original paintings |
| 800-575-1850 | C-yes/S-ltd/P-no/H-no | lithographs |
| Ken Conrad | | |
| All year | | |

*An historic 3 story Victorian house built in 1850. Located in center of town, across the street from beach. Many plants & flowers enhance the decor. AAA 3 diamonds.*

| **White Wind Inn Inc.** | $$-B&B | Continental plus bkfst. |
|---|---|---|
| 174 Commercial St., P.O. Box 1307, 02657 | 11 rooms, 11 pb | Packages in the off season |
| 508-487-1526 Fax: 508-487-3985 | Visa, MC, AmEx, | |
| Sandra Rielt, Russ Dusablon | C-yes/S-yes/P-ltd/H-no | |
| All year | | |

*Lovely white Victorian mansion. Carpeted throughout. Five-minutes walking from everything. Parking.* **3rd night free January through March, except holidays.**

## PROVINCETOWN

| **Windamar House** | $$-B&B | Continental breakfast |
|---|---|---|
| 568 Commercial St.,   02657 | 8 rooms, 6 pb | Guest refrig., microwave |
| 508-487-0599 Fax: 508-487-7505 | • | Sitting room, TV/VCR |
| Bette Adams | S-no/P-no/H-no | film library, tennis |
| Open April–January | French | 2 apartments avail. |

*Stately, seaside captain's home circa 1840, filled with antiques and original artwork, surrounded by manicured lawns and English flower gardens.*

## REHOBOTH

| **Five Bridge Farm B&B** | $$-B&B | Full breakfast |
|---|---|---|
| P.O. Box 462,   02769 | 6 rooms, 3 pb | Lunch, picnic box, bar |
| 154 Pine St. | Most CC, *Rated*, • | Tennis, hot tub, library |
| 508-252-3190  Fax: 508-252-3190 | S-ltd/P-yes/H-yes | sitting room, golf |
| Ann & Harold Messenger | | swimming pool, bicycles |
| All year | | |

*Secluded Georgian Mansion with tennis, swimming, hiking, good food. Friendly innkeepers & 9 Golf Courses within 5 miles.* **Free wine in room; 10% senior discount.**

| **Perryville Inn B&B** | $$-B&B | Continental plus bkfst. |
|---|---|---|
| 157 Perryville Rd.,   02769 | 5 rooms, 4 pb | Comp. wine, tea, coffee |
| 508-252-9239 | AmEx, MC, Visa, | 2 sitting rooms |
| Tom & Betsy Charnecki | *Rated*, • | piano, balloon rides |
| All year | C-yes/S-ltd/P-no/H-no | bicycles |

*Newly renovated 19th-century spacious farmhouse in quiet country setting. Located between Boston, Newport, Providence. On National Register of Historic Homes.* **Family rates.**

## ROCKPORT

| **Addison Choate Inn, B&B** | $$$-B&B | Continental plus bkfst. |
|---|---|---|
| 49 Broadway,   01966 | 9 rooms, 9 pb | Summer bkfst. on porch |
| 508-546-7543 Fax: 508-546-7638 | Most CC, *Rated*, | Living room, TV w/suites |
| 800-245-7543 | C-ltd/S-no/P-no/H-no | King, etc. beds, pool |
| Knox & Shirley Johnson | | comp. aftn. tea/coffee |
| All year | | |

*A village Bed & Breakfast. Relax in a charming nineteenth-century home, and come experiece the joys of coastal New England.* **Off season, winter,& midweek rates, ask.**

| **Inn on Cove Hill, The** | $-B&B | Continental breakfast |
|---|---|---|
| 37 Mt. Pleasant St.,   01966 | 11 rooms, 9 pb | Canopy beds, antiques |
| 508-546-2701 | Visa, MC, *Rated*, | garden, panoramic view |
| John & Marjorie Pratt | C-ltd/S-no/P-no/H-no | porch, all rooms A/C |
| April–October | | |

*This 18th-century inn overlooks a historic harbor. Breakfast is served on fine china in the garden or in your room. Short walk to shops, Art Association, rocky seafront.*

| **Linden Tree Inn** | $$$-B&B | Continental breakfast |
|---|---|---|
| 26 King St,   01966 | 18 rooms, 18 pb | Afternoon tea, cookies |
| 508-546-2494  800-865-2122 | Visa, MC, AmEx, • | Lemonade |
| Jon & Dawn Cunningham | C-yes/S-yes/P-no/H-no | sitting room |
| Open mid-April–end Oct. | | guest livingroom |

*Short walk to beach, shops, restaurants, galleries. Widow's walk views of ocean & mill pond. Local art collection & flower gardens.* **Off-season discounts**.

*Seacrest Manor, Rockport, MA*

## ROCKPORT

**Old Farm Inn**
291 Granite St., Rt 127, 01966
508-546-3237 Fax: 508-546-9308
800-233-6828
Susan & Bill Balzarini
April–December

$$$-B&B
13 rooms, 13 pb
MC, Visa, *Rated*,
C-ltd/S-yes/P-no/H-ltd

Continental plus bkfst.
Comp. sherry, port
Sitting room, bicycles
A/C, telephones in rooms
queen or king beds

*Relax by the fire, nap under a tree, wander on the rocky coastline. Unwind at our friendly, cozy, country farmhouse. Cottage with 2 bedrooms also available.*

---

**Rocky Shores Inn/Cottages**
65 Eden Rd., 01966
508-546-2823 800-348-4003
Renate & Gunter Kostka
April–October

$$$-B&B
22 rooms, 22 pb
*Rated*, •
C-ltd/S-ltd/P-no/H-no
German

Continental plus (inn)
Sitting room
rooms with ocean views
walk to beaches

*Inn & cottages w/unforgettable view of Thatcher Island lights & open sea. Inn has 7 frplcs. & beautiful woodwork. Comp. brkfst. incl. for inn guests. **10% off for "Complete Guide" readers.***

---

**Sally Webster Inn, The**
34 Mt. Pleasant St, 01966
508-546-9251
T. Traynor, D. Muhlenburg
All year

$$-B&B
8 rooms, 8 pb
MC, Visa, *Rated*,
C-ltd/S-yes/P-no/H-no

Full breakfast
Comp. wine/special occ.
sitting room, piano
suite which sleeps 5

*Historic, colonial home built in 1832. Antique decor. Walk to village and sea. Welcome to the charm of yesteryear. **3rd night free in Feb. and March.***

---

**Seacrest Manor**
131 Marmion Way, 01966
508-546-2211
L. Saville, D. MacCormack, Jr
Exc. December–February

$$$-B&B
8 rooms, 6 pb
*Rated*,
C-ltd/S-no/P-no/H-no
some French

Full breakfast
Afternoon tea
Library, sitting room
gardens, sun deck
bicycles, cable TV

*Decidedly small, intentionally quiet inn. Prizewinning gardens overlook woods & sea. Scenic trolley stop, Apr.-Nov. OUR 1988 INN OF THE YEAR! **10% off 2nd consec. week***

ROCKPORT —

| **Tuck Inn B&B, The** | $-B&B | Continental plus bkfst. |
|---|---|---|
| 17 High St., 01966 | 9 rooms, 9 pb | Snacks |
| 508-546-7260 800-789-7260 | Visa, MC, *Rated*, • | Sitting room, A/C |
| Liz & Scott Wood | C-yes/S-no/P-no/H-no | swimming pool, bicycles |
| All year | | scenic walks, beach |

*Lovely 1790 Colonial with a quiet & homey atmosphere. A few minutes' walk to everything. Antiques, gardens, special home-baked breakfast buffet.*

| **Yankee Clipper Inn** | $$$$-B&B | Full breakfast hi-season |
|---|---|---|
| P.O. Box 2399, 01966 | 26 rooms, 26 pb | Continental bkfst winter |
| 96 Granite St. | *Rated*, • | Gourmet dinner, sitt. rm |
| 508-546-3407 Fax: 508-546-9730 | C-yes/S-no/P-no/H-no | concierge service, some |
| 800-545-3699 | | rooms with TV, Jet tubs |
| Bob & Barbara Ellis | | |
| All year exc. Dec 24–27 | | |

*Oceanfront grounds in picturesque Rockport. 3 converted estate buildings. Rooms furnished in antiques, named after clipper ships. Wedding facilities, outdoor heated pool.*

S. LEE, STOCKBRIDGE —

| **Merrell Tavern Inn** | $$-B&B | Full breakfast |
|---|---|---|
| 1565 Pleasant St., Main Street, | 9 rooms, 9 pb | Afternoon refreshments |
| 01260 | Visa, MC, *Rated*, | Fireplace rooms |
| 413-243-1794 Fax: 413-243-2669 | C-ltd/S-no/P-no/H-no | antiques |
| 800-243-1794 | | telephones, A/C |
| Pam Hurst | | |
| All year | | |

*One of New England's most historic stage coach inns, a few miles from Norman Rockwell Museum, Stockbridge. Full country breakfast of your choice.*

SAGAMORE BEACH —

| **Widow's Walk B&B** | $$$-B&B | Continental plus bkfst. |
|---|---|---|
| Box 605, 02562 | 3 rooms, 2 pb | Dinner, snacks |
| 152 Clark Rd. | C-yes/S-no/P-ltd/H-yes | Comp. wine, sitting room |
| 508-888-0762 | | bicycles, tennis |
| Meredith & Bill Chase | | beach equipment |
| May–December | | |

*Our country cape-style home offers wide plank floors, fireplace, sitting room, full gourmet breakfast, backyard tennis courts. 100 yards to sandy beach.*

SALEM —

| **Amelia Payson House** | $$-B&B | Continental plus bkfst. |
|---|---|---|
| 16 Winter St., 01970 | 4 rooms, 4 pb | Restaurant nearby |
| 508-744-8304 | AmEx, MC, Visa, | |
| Ada May & Donald Roberts | C-ltd/S-no | |
| All year | | |

*Celebrating 10 yrs. as a B&B. Elegantly restored 1845 Greek Revival-style home; 5-min. stroll finds restaurants, museums, shopping & train station. Call for color brochure.*

| **Coach House Inn, The** | $$-B&B | Continental breakfast |
|---|---|---|
| 284 Lafayette St., 01970 | 11 rooms, 10 pb | Non-smoking Inn |
| 508-744-4092 800-688-8689 | AmEx, MC, Visa, | completely restored and |
| Patricia Kessler | *Rated*, • | redecorated rooms |
| All year | C-yes/S-no/P-no/H-no | |

*Return to elegance. Enjoy the intimacy of a small European-type inn. Victorian fireplaces highlight the charming decor of each room.*

SALEM ────────────────────────────────

**Inn at Seven Winter St.**
7 Winter St., 01970
508-745-9520 Fax: 508-745-5052
D.L. & Jill Cote, Sally Flint
All year

$$$-B&B
10 rooms, 10 pb
Visa, MC, AmEx, •
C-yes/S-no/P-no/H-no

Continental plus bkfst.
Aftn. tea, comp. sherry
Sitting room

*Come be our guest! Beautiful 1870 French Victorian. Elegant, romantic, relaxing. Situated at the heart of Historic Salem. Enjoy!*

──────────────────────────────────────

**Salem Inn, The**
7 Summer St., 01970
508-741-0680 Fax: 508-744-8924
800-446-2995
Richard & Diane Pabich
All year

$$$-B&B
32 rooms, 32 pb
Most CC, *Rated*, •
C-yes/S-ltd/P-no/H-no

Continental breakfast
Comp. sherry, restaurant
Private garden, phones
TV, A/C, canopy beds
fireplaces, jacuzzi bath

*Spacious, luxuriously appointed rooms in elegantly restored Federal mansion. Some, Jacuzzis, fireplaces & family suites. In the heart of historic district. **Special Getaway Packages!***

──────────────────────────────────────

**Stephen Daniels House**
One Daniels St., at 55 Essex
St., 01970
508-744-5709
Catherine Gill
All year

$$-B&B
5 rooms, 3 pb
*Rated*, •
C-yes/S-yes/P-yes/H-no

Continental plus bkfst.
Compimentary tea
Sitting rooms
walk-in fireplaces
private garden, bicycles

*300-year-old house furnished with canopy beds, antiques throughout, fireplaces in every room. Lovely flower-filled English garden, private for guests. **Discount after 4+ days.***

──────────────────────────────────────

**Stepping Stone Inn, The**
19 Washington Square N.,
01970
508-741-8900  800-338-3022
John W. Brick
All year

$$-B&B
8 rooms, 8 pb
AmEx, MC, Visa,
C-ltd/S-no/P-no

Continental plus bkfst.
Sitting room
available for private
functions

*Step into the past at our elegant inn located in Heritage Trail; continental breakfast in a candlelit dining room; 8 unique guest rooms; rated "best" by The Washington Post.*

──────────────────────────────────────

**Suzannah Flint House**
98 Essex St., 01970
508-744-5281  800-752-5281
Scott Eklind
All year

$$$-B&B
4 rooms, 4 pb
Most CC,
C-yes/S-yes/P-no/H-no

Continental plus bkfst.
Flower garden area

*1806 Federalist Architecture, in historic Salem, walk to attractions, waterfront, shops and restaurants. Spacious rooms, antiques, decorative fireplaces. **Discount 2+ nights.***

SANDWICH ──────────────────────────────

**Bay Beach B&B**
P.O. Box 151, 02563
1-3 Bay Beach Ln.
508-888-8813  800-475-6398
Emily & Reale Lemieux
May 1-November 15

$$$$-B&B
6 rooms, 6 pb
MC, Visa, *Rated*, •
C-ltd/S-no/P-no/H-ltd
French

Continental plus bkfst.
Aftn. tea, comp. wine
Sitting room, CD player
bicycles, phones, A/C
exercise room, jacuzzis

*Located on secluded & private Bay Beach, offering relaxation & privacy. Complimentary wine & cheese/crackers welcomes your arrival. Jacuzzis in rooms.*

SANDWICH ———————————————————————————————————————

| Captain Ezra Nye House | $$$-B&B | Full breakfast |
|---|---|---|
| 152 Main St., 02563 | 6 rooms, 6 pb | Complimentary wine |
| 508-888-6142 Fax: 508-833-2897 | Most CC, *Rated*, • | Sitting room, library |
| 800-388-CAPT | C-ltd/S-no/P-no/H-no | 3 canopy beds, working |
| Elaine & Harry Dickson | Spanish | fireplaces, TV in suite |
| All year | | |

*1829 Federal home; near museums, antique shops, ocean and Heritage Plantation. Voted Best B&B-Upper Cape '93, '94 & '96 , Cape Cod Life Magazine.* **Champ. for special occasions.**

| Isaiah Jones Homestead | $$-B&B | Full breakfast |
|---|---|---|
| 165 Main St., 02563 | 4 rooms, 4 pb | Aftn. tea, lemonade |
| 508-888-9115 800-526-1625 | Visa, MC, AmEx, | Gift shop, phone avail. |
| Shirley & Bud Lamson | *Rated*, • | 2 rooms w/fireplaces & |
| All year | C-ltd/S-no/P-no/H-no | whirlpool tubs |

*Victorian B&B, 4 rooms all with private baths & queen-sized beds, furnished with museum-quality antiques. Breakfast & afternoon tea or bedside goodies, low cholesterol cooking.*

| Seth Pope House 1699 B&B | $$-B&B | Full breakfast (no meat) |
|---|---|---|
| 110 Tupper Rd., 02563 | 3 rooms, 3 pb | Aftn. tea - upon request |
| 508-888-5916 800-699-SETH | Checks accepted, • | Sitting room, A/C, TV |
| John & Beverly Dobel | C-ltd/S-no/P-no/H-no | bicycles rental nearby |
| Open April–October | | tennis court nearby |

*Historic village colonial overlooking salt marsh, spacious rooms, antiques, fireplaces, candlelight breakfast. Walk to historic sites & restaurants.*

| Summer House, The | $$-B&B | Full breakfast |
|---|---|---|
| 158 Main St., 02563 | 5 rooms, 5 pb | Afternoon tea |
| 508-888-4991 | Most CC, | Sitting room, library |
| Marjorie & Keven Huelsman | C-ltd/S-no/P-no/H-no | common room w/color TV, |
| All year | | books & board games |

*Exquisite 1835 Greek Revival in historic Sandwich Village. Large, airy rooms with fireplaces, antiques, hand-stitched quilts, and beautiful English gardens.*

SCITUATE ———————————————————————————————————————

| Allen House, The | $$-B&B | Full gourmet breakfast |
|---|---|---|
| 18 Allen Place, 02066 | 6 rooms, 6 pb | Comp. afternoon tea |
| 617-545-8221 Fax: 617-545-8221 | AmEx, MC, Visa, Disc., | Sitting room |
| Christine & Iain Gilmour | • | library/music center |
| April–Feb. | C-ltd/S-no/P-no/H-yes | whirlpool bath |
| | French, German, | |
| | Spanish | |

*Gourmet cook-owner serves "Fantasy Breakfast" on Victorian porch overlooking harbor in unpretentious fishing town 25 miles south of Boston.*

SHEFFIELD ———————————————————————————————————————

| Race Brook Lodge | $$$-B&B | Continental plus bkfst. |
|---|---|---|
| 864 S. Undermountain Rd, | 20 rooms, 20 pb | Restaurant, wine bar |
| Route 41, 01257 | Visa, MC, AmEx, • | Group retreats, meetings |
| 413-229-2916 Fax: 413-229-6629 | C-yes/S-no/P-no/H-ltd | library, common room |
| Ernie Couse | Spanish | family friendly facility |
| All year | | |

*1790s restored timber-peg barn, handhewn beams, plank floors, stenciling, quilts, eclectic artwork. Hikers heaven. Close to concerts, museums, antiquing.* **$25 discount, 2nd night, midweek.**

## SOUTH EGREMONT

| **Egremont Inn, The** | $$$-B&B/MAP | Continental breakfast |
| P.O. Box 418,  01258 | 20 rooms, 20 pb | Restaurant, snacks, bar |
| 10 Old Sheffield Rd. | Visa, MC, AmEx, Disc., | Sitting room, fireplaces |
| 413-528-2111  Fax: 413-528-3284 | • | tennis courts, pool |
| Steve & Karen Waller | C-yes/S-ltd/P-no/H-no | wraparound porch |
| All year | | |

*Wonderful Colonial inn offering charm & comfort; tavern; restaurant; close to antiquing, cycling, hiking, skiing & Tanglewood—Come join us. Entertainment Thurs. & Sat. **3rd night 50%, restrictions.***

| **Weathervane Inn** | $$$-B&B/MAP | Full breakfast |
| P.O. Box 388,  01258 | 10 rooms, 10 pb | Dinner included Fri/Sat |
| Rt. 23, Main St. | MC, Visa, *Rated*, • | Bar, Cordial in room |
| 413-528-9580  Fax: 413-528-1713 | C-ltd/S-yes/P-no/H-yes | sitting room, library |
| 800-528-9580 | | swimming pool |
| Anne & Vincent Murphy | | |
| All year | | |

*200-year-old hostelry with modern amenities. Hearty breakfasts and superb dining will make your stay memorable. Conference facilities for up to 25 persons, great fly fishing.*

## STERLING

| **Sterling Inn** | $$-B&B | Continental breakfast |
| P.O. Box 609,  01564 | 8 rooms, 6 pb | Lunch, dinner, bar |
| 240 Worcester Rd.(Rt. 12) | AmEx, MC, Visa, | Afternoon cheese & fruit |
| 508-422-6592  Fax: 508-422-3127 | *Rated*, | sitting room |
| 508-422-6333 | C-ltd/S-ltd/P-no/H-ltd | Fireplaced dining rooms |
| The Roy Family | | |
| All year | | |

*Turn-of-the-century setting, unique to the area. Near skiing. Dine outside by our landscaped rock garden. Private dining rooms. One hour to Boston. **3rd night 30% off.***

## STOCKBRIDGE

| **Inn at Stockbridge** | $$$-B&B | Full breakfast |
| P.O. Box 618,  01262 | 8 rooms, 8 pb | Complimentary wine |
| Rt. 7 | Visa, MC, AmEx, | Sitting room, library |
| 413-298-3337  Fax: 413-298-3406 | *Rated*, • | antiques, phones, A/C |
| Alice & Len Schiller | C-ltd/S-no/H-no | swimming pool |
| All year | | |

*Consummate hospitality distinguishes this Georgian estate. In the heart of the Berkshires, close to Norman Rockwell museum, Tanglewood, summer theaters, winter skiing. **3rd weeknight 50% off, ltd.***

## STURBRIDGE

| **Col. Ebenezer Crafts Inn** | $$-B&B | Continental breakfast |
| P.O. Box 187,  01566 | 8 rooms, 8 pb | Comp. tea, breads |
| 66 Fiske Hill Rd. | Most CC, *Rated*, • | Swimming pool |
| 508-347-3313  800-782-5425 | C-yes/S-yes/P-no/H-no | sitting room, piano |
| Shirley Washburn & David | | 2 suites |
| Lane | | |
| All year | | |

*1786 gracious home, under the management of Publick House, is Sturbridge's most beautiful inn. Sweeping views of gentle Massachusetts hills and gracious accommodations.*

STURBRIDGE ─────────────────────────────────

| **Sturbridge Country Inn** | $$-B&B | Continental breakfast |
|---|---|---|
| P.O. Box 60,  01566 | 9 rooms, 9 pb | Restaurant, bar |
| 530 Main St. | AmEx, MC, Visa, | Lunch & dinner in tavern |
| 508-347-5503  Fax: 508-347-5319 | *Rated*, • | comp. champagne |
| Ms. Affenito | C-ltd/S-yes/P-no/H-yes | hot tubs |
| All year | | |

*Close to Old Sturbridge Village lies our grand Greek Revival structure. Each room has period reproductions, fireplaces, and whirlpool tubs.* **Midweek discounts/packages.**

TRURO ─────────────────────────────────────

| **Parker House** | $$-B&B | Continental breakfast |
|---|---|---|
| P.O. Box 1111,  02666 | 2 rooms, | Ocean and bay beaches |
| 15 Truro Center Rd. | S-no/P-no/H-no | national park |
| 508-349-3358 | | tennis |
| Stephen Williams    All year | | |

*A warmly classic 1850 Cape house with many antiques. Close to beaches and charm of Wellfleet and Provincetown.*

VINEYARD HAVEN ───────────────────────────

| **Captain Dexter House** | $$-B&B | Continental plus bkfst. |
|---|---|---|
| P.O. Box 2457,  02568 | 8 rooms, 8 pb | Comp. sherry, aft. tea |
| 100 Main St. | Most CC, *Rated*, • | Library, fireplaces |
| 508-693-6564 Fax: 508-693-8448 | C-yes/S-yes/P-no/H-no | use of beach towels |
| Rick & Birdie | | fresh flowers, sitt. rm. |
| All year | | |

*Beautifully restored 1843 sea captain's home. Furnished with fine antiques. Some rooms have fireplaces and canopied beds. Walk to beach.*

| **Hanover House, The** | $$$-B&B | Continental plus bkfst. |
|---|---|---|
| P.O. Box 2107,  02568 | 15 rooms, 15 pb | Bike racks |
| 10 Edgartown Rd. | Most CC, *Rated*, • | tennis nearby |
| 508-693-1066 Fax: 508-696-6099 | C-ltd/S-no/P-no/H-ltd | completely non-smoking |
| 800-339-1066 | | |
| Kay & Ron Nelson | | |
| All year | | |

*Located on beautifully landscaped grounds; short walk to town ferry. Offers old Island charm with 20th century comforts. 3 rooms with kitchenettes in separate carriage house.*

| **Lambert's Cove Country Inn** | $$$$-B&B | Full breakfast |
|---|---|---|
| RR 1, Box 422,  02568 | 15 rooms, 15 pb | Restaurant, dinner (fee) |
| Lambert's Cove, W.Tisbury | AmEx, MC, Visa, | Afternoon beverages |
| 508-693-2298 Fax: 508-693-7890 | C-yes/S-no/P-no/H-no | sitting room, library |
| Louis & Katherine Costabel | | Lambert's Cove Beach |
| All year | | |

*Quiet and secluded 1790 inn with spacious lawns, gardens, apple orchard & tennis court. Walk to private beach. Delicious breakfast and fine dining restaurant.*

| **Lothrop Merry House, The** | $$-B&B | Continental breakfast |
|---|---|---|
| P.O. Box 1939,  02568 | 7 rooms, 4 pb | Terrace, beach front |
| Owen Park | MC, Visa, | boat cruises |
| 508-693-1646 | C-ltd/S-no/P-no/H-no | canoe, sailing |
| John & Mary Clarke | | |
| All year | | |

*Charming 18th-century guest house. Harbor, view, beach front. Walk from ferry. Fireplaces, antiques. Home-baked continental breakfast served.* **3rd night 50% during off season.**

## WARE

**Wildwood Inn**
121 Church St., 01082
413-967-7798   800-860-8098
F. Fenster & R. Watson
All year

$$-B&B
9 rooms, 7 pb
Visa, MC, AmEx,
*Rated*, •
C-ltd/S-no/P-no/H-yes

Full breakfast
Lemonade, cider
Sitting room
tennis courts, swimming
canoeing, hiking, games

*Relax! Enjoy American antiques & heirloom quilts. Near Sturbridge, Deerfield, Amherst. Canoe, swim, bike, hike. We'll spoil you. **3rd nite 30% off.***

## WAREHAM

**Mulberry B&B**
257 High St., 02571
508-295-0684 Fax: 508-291-2909
Frances A. Murphy
All year

$$-B&B
3 rooms,
AmEx, Disc., •
C-yes/S-no/P-no/H-no

Full breakfast
Afternoon tea, snacks
Sitting room, library
bicycle routes w/maps
restaurant discounts

*Charming 1840s Cape Cod style home built by blacksmith. Used as a general store by B&B owner's grandfather. Restful location, close to Boston. **3rd night 50% off, ltd.***

## WELLFLEET

**Inn at Duck Creeke, The**
P.O. Box 364, 02667
70 Main St.
508-349-9333 Fax: 508-349-0234
Robert Morrill & Judith Pihl
Mid-May-mid-October

$$$-B&B
25 rooms, 17 pb
AmEx, MC, Visa,
*Rated*,
C-yes/S-yes/P-no/H-ltd

Continental plus bkfst.
Dinner, bar
Entertainment
3 porches & lobby
restaurant discounts

*Cozy Sea Captain's house in coastal fishing village. Close to beaches and Audobon Sanctuary. Overlooks salt marsh and duck pond. **Complimentary house wine with dinner.***

## WEST STOCKBRIDGE

**Williamsville Inn, The**
P.O. Box 138, 01266
Rt. 41
413-274-6118   Fax: 413-274-3539
Gail & Kathleen Ryan
All year

$$$-B&B
16 rooms, 16 pb
Visa, MC, AmEx,
*Rated*, •
C-ltd/S-ltd/P-no/H-no

Full breakfast
Restaurant, bar service
Sitting room, library
tennis court, pool
candlelight dining

*1797 farmhouse on ten beautiful acres on a quiet country road in the heart of the Berkshires. Gourmet candlelit dining.*

## WEST YARMOUTH

**Manor House, The**
57 Maine Ave., 02673
508-771-3433  800-962-6679
Rick & Liz Latshaw
All year

$$-B&B
6 rooms, 6 pb
MC, Visa, AmEx,
*Rated*, •
C-ltd/S-no/P-no/H-no

Full breakfast
Afternoon tea
Sitting room, views of
the Bay, turn-down serv.
beach chairs & towels

*Lovely Dutch colonial a block from the water and minutes to Hyannis, the ferries to the islands, and fine dining. **Off season rates. Champagne for honeymooners.***

## WILLIAMSTOWN

**Steep Acres Farm B&B**
520 White Oaks Rd., 01267
413-458-3774
Mary & Marvin Gangemi
All year

$$$-B&B
4 rooms,
*Rated*,
C-ltd/S-no/P-no/H-no

Full gourmet breakfast
Complimentary wine
Sitting room, swimming
1½ acre pond, fishing
hiking trails, boating

*Country home on a high knoll—spectacular views of Berkshire Hills & Vermont's Green Mts. Furnished in country antiques. Trout & swimming pond, 50 acres of woods & pastures.*

## WOODS HOLE

| | | |
|---|---|---|
| **Woods Hole Passage B&B** | $$$-B&B | Full breakfast |
| 186 Woods Hole Rd., 02540 | 5 rooms, 5 pb | Dinner (off season) |
| 508-548-9575 Fax: 508-540-4771 | Most CC, *Rated*, • | Sitting room, library |
| 800-790-8976 | C-ltd/S-no/P-no/H-no | spacious grounds |
| Todd & Robin Norman | Some Spanish | old shade trees |
| All year | | |

*Traditional Cape Code estate with the contemporary flair of the young, energetic hosts. Bike paths, nature trails, beaches, and ferry minutes away.* **3rd night, 50% Nov.–Mar.**

## YARMOUTH PORT

| | | |
|---|---|---|
| **Colonial House Inn** | $$-MAP | Continental plus bkfst. |
| 277 Main St., Rt. 6A, 02675 | 21 rooms, 21 pb | Dinner included (fee) |
| 508-362-4348 Fax: 508-362-8034 | Most CC, *Rated*, • | Game room, bar, pool |
| 800-999-3416 | C-yes/S-yes/P-yes/H-yes | cribs/high chair, TV/VCR |
| Malcolm J. Perna | | jacuzzi, fitness ctr. |
| All year | | |

*Decorated guest rooms furnished w/antiques, canopy beds. Charming grounds by historic homes. Indoor heated pool, conference center.* **Dinner $10 per couple.**

| | | |
|---|---|---|
| **Inn at Cape Cod, The** | $$$$-B&B | Continental breakfast |
| P.O. Box 96, 02675 | 10 rooms, 10 pb | Afternoon tea |
| 508-375-0590 800-850-7301 | Most CC, • | Fireplaces, canopy beds |
| Diana & Lee Malloy | C-ltd/S-no/P-no/H-yes | A/C, TV & phone |
| Closed winter | | plush terry robes |

*Two hundred year old classic Greek Revival, stylish and comfortable with a touch of old world charm. Furnished with antiques and a European flair.*

| | | |
|---|---|---|
| **Liberty Hill Inn, Cape Cod** | $$$-B&B | Full gourmet breakfast |
| 77 Route 6A, 02675 | 5 rooms, 5 pb | Gourmet lunch |
| 508-362-3976 800-821-3977 | MC, Visa, *Rated*, • | Candlelight dinner |
| Jack & Beth Flanagan | C-yes/S-yes/P-no/H-no | sitting room, cable TV |
| All year | | maid service, telephone |

*Elegant inn in gracious Greek Revival Manor house, c. 1825. Shopper's paradise, a romantic hideaway, antique furnishings. 3 rms. A/C.* **Free roundtrip ferry to Martha's Vineyard.**

| | | |
|---|---|---|
| **Olde Captain's Inn** | $-B&B | Continental plus bkfst. |
| 101 Main St., Rt. 6A, 02675 | 5 rooms, 3 pb | Family friendly facility |
| 508-362-4496 888-407-7161 | C-ltd/S-no/P-no/H-no | |
| Sven Tilly & Betsy O'Connor | | |
| All year | | |

*A charming century and a half old Captain's house located in the historic district. Walk to fine restaurants, craft shops and antique shops. Beaches, golf & tennis nearby.* **3rd night free.**

| | | |
|---|---|---|
| **One Centre Street Inn** | $$-B&B | Full breakfast |
| 1 Centre St., 02675 | 6 rooms, 4 pb | Continental plus (summ.) |
| 508-362-8910 | MC, Visa, *Rated*, • | Piano, bicycles |
| Karen Iannello | C-ltd/S-no/P-no/H-no | flower & herb gardens |
| All year | | whale watching close by |

*Vintage antique-furnished sea captain's home, 1 mile to Cape Cod Bay or village. Fireplace avail. Delicious breakfasts in formal dining room or garden deck.* **Dinner pkg., ask.**

YARMOUTH PORT ─────────────────────────────────

| | | |
|---|---|---|
| **Wedgewood Inn** | $$$-B&B | Full breakfast |
| 83 Main St., 02675 | 6 rooms, 6 pb | Afternoon tea, fruit |
| 508-362-5157  Fax: 508-362-5851 | Most CC, *Rated*, • | Common room, fireplaces |
| 508-362-9178 | C-ltd/S-ltd/P-no/H-ltd | private porches |
| Milt & Gerrie Graham | | gardens/gazebo, A/C |
| All year | | |

*Romantic inn in historic area of Cape Cod. Near beaches & restaurants. Antiques, wood-burning fireplaces, plank floors, canopy beds, private sitting rooms*

# More Inns . . .

| | |
|---|---|
| Andover | Andover Inn, Chapel Avenue, 01002, 508-475-5903 |
| Ashfield | Bull Frog B&B, Box 210, Star Route, 01330, 413-628-4493 |
| Barnstable | Beechwood, 2839 Main St., 02630, 508-362-6618 |
| Barnstable | Charles Hinkley House, P.O. Box 723, 02630, 508-362-9924 |
| Barnstable | Cobb's Cove Inn, P.O. Box 208, 02630, 508-362-9356 |
| Barnstable | Goss House B&B, 61 Pine Ln., 02630, 617-362-8559 |
| Barnstable | Thomas Huckins House, P.O. Box 515, 02630, 508-362-6379 |
| Barre | Jenkins Inn, The, P.O. Box 779, 01005, 508-255-6444 |
| Bass River | Anchorage, 122 South Shore Dr., 02664, 617-398-8265 |
| Bass River | Belvedere B&B Inn, 167 Main St., 02664, 508-398-6674 |
| Bass River | Old Cape House, 108 Old Main St., 02664, 617-398-1068 |
| Becket | Canterbury Farm B&B, Fred Snow Rd., 01223, 413-623-8765 |
| Berlin | Stonehedge B&B, 119 Sawyer Hill Rd., 01503, 617-838-2574 |
| Bernardston | Bernardston Inn, Church St., 01337, 413-648-9282 |
| Billerica | Billerica B&B, 88 Rogers St., 01862, 508-667-7317 |
| Blandford | Baird Tavern B&B, Old Chester Rd., 01008, 413-848-2096 |
| Boston | Beacon Inn, 1087 & 1750 Beacon St., 02146, 617-566-0088 |
| Boston | Boston (Brookline) #36, P.O. Box 1142, 02146, 617-277-5430 |
| Boston | Lenox Hotel, Boyleston St. at Copley, 02124 |
| Boston | Newbury Guest House, 261 Newbury St., 02116, 617-437-7666 |
| Boston | Terrace Townehouse, 60 Chandler St., 02116, 617-350-6520 |
| Bourne | Cape Cop Canalside B&B, 7 Coastal Way, 02532, 508-759-6564 |
| Brewster | Brewster Farmhouse Inn, 716 Main St., 02631, 508-896-3910 |
| Brewster | High Brewster, 964 Satucket Rd., 02631, 508-896-3636 |
| Brewster | Inn of the Golden Ox, 1360 Main, 02631, 617-896-3111 |
| Brewster | Isaiah Clark House, P.O. Box 169, 02631, 508-896-2223 |
| Brewster | Ocean Gold B&B, 74 Locust Ln., 02631, 508-255-7045 |
| Brewster | Old Manse Inn, The, P.O. Box 839, 02631, 508-896-3149 |
| Brewster | Poore House, 2311 Main St., 02631, 800-233-6662 |
| Brewster | Ruddy Turnstone Lodge, The, 463 Route 6A, 02631 |
| Brookline | Brookline Manor Guest Hous, 32 Centre St., 02146, 617-232-0003 |
| Buckland | 1797 House, Charlemont Rd., 01338, 413-625-2697 |
| Buckland | Scott House, Hawley Rd., 01338, 413-625-6624 |
| Cambridge | Mary Prentiss Inn, The, 6 Prentiss St., 02140, 617-661-2929 |
| Centerville | Carver House, 638 Main St., 02632, 617-775-9414 |
| Centerville | Copper Beech Inn, 497 Main St., 02632, 508-771-5488 |
| Centerville | Inn at Fernbrook, 481 Main St., 02632, 508-775-4334 |
| Centerville | Long Dell, 436 South Main St., 02632 |
| Centerville | Old Hundred House, 1211 Craigville Beach R, 02632, 617-775-6166 |
| Centerville | Terrace Gardens Inn, 539 Main St., 02632, 617-775-4707 |
| Charlemont | Forest Way Farm, Route 8A (Heath), 01339, 413-337-8321 |
| Chatham | Bow Roof House, 59 Queen Anne Rd., 02633, 617-945-1346 |
| Chatham | Bradford Inn, P.O. Box 750, 02633, 508-945-1030 |
| Chatham | Chatham Town House Inn, 11 Library Ln., 02633, 508-945-2180 |
| Chatham | Old Harbor Inn, The, 22 Old Harbor Rd., 02633, 508-945-4434 |
| Chatham | Queen Anne Inn, 70 Queen Anne Rd., 02633, 617-945-0394 |
| Chatham | Seafarer Motel, Main St., 02633, 617-432-1739 |
| Chester | Frog Hollow Farm, Holcomb Rd, off Skyline, 01011, 413-354-9678 |
| Chestnut Hill | Pleasant Pheasant B&B, 296 Heath St., 02167, 617-566-4178 |
| Colrain | Maple Shade Farm B&B, 34 Nelson Rd., 01340 |
| Concord | Colonial Inn, The, 48 Monument Square, 01742, 508-369-9200 |
| Conway | Poundsworth B&B, Old Cricket Hill Rd., 01341 |
| Cotuit | Salty Dog Inn, 451 Main St., 02635, 508-428-5228 |
| Cummington | Chalk Stone Ledge, RR 1, Box 186, 01026, 413-634-5034 |
| Cummington | Hidden Brook, RR 1, Box 238C, 01026, 413-634-5653 |
| Cummington | Inn at Cummington Farm VII, RR 1, Box 234, 01026, 413-634-5551 |
| Cummington | Windfields Farm, 154 Windsor Bush Rd., 01026, 413-684-3786 |
| Cuttyhunk | Allen House Inn/Restaurant, P.O. Box 27, Main St., 02713, 508-996-9292 |
| Dalton | Dalton House, 955 Main St., 01226, 413-684-3854 |
| Dedham | Iris Bed & Breakfast, P.O. Box 4188, 02026, 617-329-3514 |
| Deerfield S. | Deerfield Yellow Gables, 111 N. Main St., 01373, 413-665-4922 |

| | |
|---|---|
| Dennisport | "By-the-Sea" Guests, 57 Chase Ave., Box 50, 02639, 617-398-8685 |
| East Orleans | Farmhouse at Nauset, The, 163 Beach Rd., 02643, 508-255-6654 |
| East Sandwich | Spring Garden Motel, 578 Rte. 6A, Box 867, 02537, 508-888-0710 |
| East Sandwich | Wingscorton Farm Inn, Olde Kings Hwy, Rt. 6A, 02537, 508-888-0534 |
| Eastham | Great Pond House, P.O. Box 351, 02642, 508-255-2867 |
| Edgartown | Chadwick Inn, The, P.O. Box 1035, 02539, 508-627-4435 |
| Edgartown | Charlotte Inn, S. Summer St., 02539, 617-627-4751 |
| Edgartown | Daggett House, P.O. Box 1333, 02539, 508-627-4600 |
| Edgartown | Edgartown Heritage Hotel, 227 Upper Main St., 02539, 617-627-5161 |
| Edgartown | Governor Bradford Inn, The, P.O. Box 239, 02539, 508-627-9510 |
| Edgartown | Katama Guest House, RFD #108,166 Katama Rd., 02539, 617-627-5158 |
| Edgartown | Victorian Inn, The, P.O. Box 947, 02539, 508-627-4784 |
| Fairhaven | Edgewater B&B, 2 Oxford St., 02719, 508-997-5512 |
| Falmouth | Coonamesset Inn, 02540, 508-548-2300 |
| Falmouth | Elm Arch Inn, Elm Arch Way, 02540, 617-548-0133 |
| Falmouth | Gladstone Inn, 219 Grand Ave. S., 02540, 508-548-9851 |
| Falmouth | Palmer House Inn, The, 81 Palmer Ave., 02540, 508-548-1230 |
| Falmouth | Seawinds, The, P.O. Box 393, 02541, 508-548-3459 |
| Falmouth | Wyndemere House, 718 Palmer Ave., 02540, 617-540-7069 |
| Gay Head | Outermost Inn, The, RR 1, Box 171, 02535, 508-645-3511 |
| Gloucester | Blue Shutters Inn, 1 Nautilus Rd., 01930, 617-281-2706 |
| Gloucester | Williams Guest House, 136 Bass Av., 01930, 617-283-4931 |
| Goshen | Whale Inn, Rt. 9, Main St., Box 6, 01032, 413-268-7246 |
| Great Barrington | Bread & Roses, Star Rt 65, Box 50, 01230, 413-528-1099 |
| Great Barrington | Elling's Guest House B&B, R.D. #3, Box 6, 01230 |
| Great Barrington | Littlejohn Manor, Newsboy Monument, Rt 23, 01230, 413-528-2882 |
| Great Barrington | Round Hill Farm Nonsmokers, 17 Round Hill Rd., 01230, 413-528-6969 |
| Great Barrington | Seekonk Pines Inn, 142 Seekonk Cross Rd., 01230, 413-528-4192 |
| Great Barrington | Thornewood Inn, 453 Stockbridge Rd., 01230, 413-528-3828 |
| Great Barrington | Uttermost Barn, The, 17 Round Hill Rd., 01230, 413-528-3366 |
| Greenfield | Brandt House, The, 29 Highland Ave., 01301, 413-774-3329 |
| Greenfield | Hitchcock House, The, 15 Congress St., 01301, 413-774-7452 |
| Hancock | Mill House Inn, P.O. Box 1079, 01237 |
| Harwich | Victorian Inn at Harwich, P.O. Box 340, 02645, 508-432-8335 |
| Harwich | Winstead, The, 328 Bank St., 02645, 508-432-4586 |
| Harwich Port | Bayberry Shores, 255 Lower County Rd., 02646, 508-432-0337 |
| Harwich Port | Beach House Inn, The, 4 Braddock Ln., 02646, 508-432-4444 |
| Harwich Port | Captain's Quarters B&B Inn, 85 Bank St., 02646, 508-432-1991 |
| Harwich Port | Coach House, The, 74 Sisson Rd., 02646, 508-432-9452 |
| Harwich Port | Dunscroft by-the-Sea, 24 Pilgrim Rd., 02646, 508-432-0810 |
| Harwich Port | Grey Gull Guest House, 547 Main St., 02646, 508-432-0222 |
| Harwich Port | Harbor Breeze of Cape Cod, 326 Lower County Rd., 02646, 508-432-0337 |
| Harwich Port | Inn on Bank Street, 88 Bank St., 02646, 508-432-3206 |
| Harwich Port | No. 10 Bed & Breakfast, 10 Cross St., 02646, 508-432-9313 |
| Hingham | Ripley House, 347 Main St., 02043 |
| Holland | Alpine Haus, Mashapaung Rd., Box 782, 01550, 413-245-9082 |
| Holyoke | Yankee Pedlar Inn, P.O. Box 6206, 01041, 413-532-9494 |
| Hyannis | Captain Sylvester Baxter, 156 Main St., 02601, 508-775-5611 |
| Lanesboro | AMC - Bascom Lodge, P.O. Box 686, 01237, 413-743-1591 |
| Lee | 1777 Greylock House, 58 Greylock St., 01238, 413-243-1717 |
| Lee | Chambery Inn, Main St., 01238, 413-243-2221 |
| Lee | Tollgate Inn, HC 63, Box 98A, 01238, 413-243-0715 |
| Lenox | Apple Tree Inn, 224 West St., 01240, 413-637-1477 |
| Lenox | Candlelight Inn, 53 Walker St., 01240, 413-637-1555 |
| Lenox | Cliffwood Inn, 25 Cliffwood St., 01240, 413-637-3330 |
| Lenox | Forty-Four St. Ann's Ave., P.O. Box 718, 01240, 413-637-3381 |
| Lenox | Rookwood Inn, P.O. Box 1717, 01240, 413-637-9750 |
| Lenox | Strawberry Hill, P.O. Box 718, 01240, 413-637-3381 |
| Lenox | Wheatleigh Inn, 01240, 413-637-0610 |
| Lexington | Ashley's B&B, 6 Moon Hill Rd., 02173, 617-862-6488 |
| Lowell | Sherman-Berry House B&B, 163 Dartmouth St., 01851, 508-459-4760 |
| Marblehead | Lindsey's Garret, 38 High St., 01945, 800-882-3891 |
| Marblehead | Spray Cliff "On the Ocean", 25 Spray Ave., 01945, 617-631-6789 |
| Marblehead | Stillpoint, 27 Gregory St., 01945, 617-631-1667 |
| Marion | Pineywood Farm B&B, P.O. Box 322, 02738, 508-748-3925 |
| Marstons Mill | Osterville Fairways Inn, 1198 Race Ln., 02648, 617-428-2747 |
| Martha's Vineyard | Farmhouse, State Rd., 02568, 617-693-5354 |
| Martha's Vineyard | Harborview Hotel, Edgartown, 02568, 508-627-4333 |
| Martha's Vineyard | Shiverick Inn, The, 02568, 508-627-3797 |
| Martha's Vineyard | Tisbury Inn, Vineyard Haven, 02568, 508-693-2200 |
| Menemsha | Menemsha Inn & Cottages, Box 38, 02552, 508-645-2521 |
| Middlefield | Strawberry Banke Farm B&B, on Skyline Trail, 01243, 413-623-6481 |
| Middleton | Blue Door, The, 20 East St., 01949, 508-777-4829 |
| Nantucket | Anchor Inn, 66 Centre St., 02554, 508-228-0072 |
| Nantucket | Beachside, N. Beach St., 02554, 617-228-2241 |
| Nantucket | Brass Lantern, 11 N. Water St., 02554, 508-228-4064 |
| Nantucket | Carlisle House Inn, 26 N. Water St., 02554, 508-228-0720 |
| Nantucket | Chestnut House, 3 Chestnut St., 02554, 617-228-0049 |

| | |
|---|---|
| Nantucket | Cliff Lodge B&B, 9 Cliff Rd., 02554, 617-228-9480 |
| Nantucket | Cobblestone Inn, 5 Ash St., 02554, 508-228-1987 |
| Nantucket | Dolphin Guest House, 10 N. Beach St., 02554, 617-228-4028 |
| Nantucket | Easton House, Box 1033, 02554, 617-228-2759 |
| Nantucket | Eighteen Gardner St. Inn, 18 Gardner St., 02554, 508-228-1155 |
| Nantucket | Fair Gardens, 27 Fair St., 02554, 617-228-4258 |
| Nantucket | Four Chimneys Inn, 38 Orange St., 02554, 508-228-1912 |
| Nantucket | Great Harbor Inn, 31 India St., 02554 |
| Nantucket | Hawthorn House, 2 Chestnut St., 02554, 617-228-1468 |
| Nantucket | House of the Seven Gables, 32 Cliff Rd., 02554, 617-228-4706 |
| Nantucket | Ive Lodge B&B, The, 2 Chester St., 02554, 508-228-7755 |
| Nantucket | Le Languedoc Inn, 24 Broad St., 02554, 617-228-2552 |
| Nantucket | Lynda Watts B&B, 30 Vestal St., Box 478, 02554, 508-228-3828 |
| Nantucket | Nantucket Landfall, 4 Harbor View Way, 02554, 617-228-0500 |
| Nantucket | Nesbitt Inn, 21 Broad St., 02554, 617-228-0156 |
| Nantucket | Parker Guest House, The, 4 E. Chestnut St., 02554, 508-228-4625 |
| Nantucket | Paul West House, 5 Liberty St., 02554 |
| Nantucket | Roberts House, India & Centre Sts., 02554, 617-228-9009 |
| Nantucket | Safe Harbor Guest House, 2 Harbor View Way, 02554, 508-228-3222 |
| Nantucket | Ships Inn, The, 13 Fair St., 02554, 508-228-0040 |
| Nantucket | Spring Cottage B&B Suites, 98 Orange St., 02554, 508-325-4644 |
| Nantucket | Union Street Inn, 7 Union St., 02554, 508-228-9222 |
| Nantucket | West Moor Inn, Off Cliff Rd., 02554, 617-228-0877 |
| Nantucket Island | Brant Point Inn, 6 N. Beach St., 02554, 508-228-5442 |
| Nantucket Island | Sherburne Inn, 10 Gay St., 02554, 508-228-4425 |
| Needham | Thistle, 31 Fairfield St., 02192, 617-444-5724 |
| New Bedford | Cynthia & Steven's, 36 Seventh St., 02740, 508-997-6433 |
| New Bedford | Melville House, The, 100 Madison St., 02740, 508-990-1566 |
| New Marlborough | Red Bird Inn, P.O. Box 592, 01230, 413-229-2433 |
| Newburyport | House by the River, The, 566 Merrimac St., 01950, 508-463-9624 |
| Newburyport | Morrill Place Inn, 209 High St., 01950, 508-462-2808 |
| North Billerica | Ted Barbour, 88 Rogers St., 01862, 617-667-7317 |
| North New Salem | Bullard Farm B&B, 89 Elm St., 01364, 508-544-6959 |
| Northampton | Autumn Inn, 259 Elm St., 01060, 413-584-7660 |
| Northfield | Centennial House, 94 Main St., 01360, 413-498-5921 |
| Norwell | 1810 House B&B, 147 Old Oaken Bucket Rd, 02061, 617-659-1810 |
| Oak Bluffs | Attleboro House, 11 Lake Ave., 02557, 617-693-4346 |
| Oak Bluffs | Beach House B&B, The, P.O. Box 417, 02557, 508-693-3955 |
| Oak Bluffs | Capricorn House, P.O. Box 855, 02557 |
| Oak Bluffs | Circuit House, Box 2422, 150 Circuit A, 02557, 617-693-5033 |
| Oak Bluffs | Island Country Club Inn, Beach Rd., 02557 |
| Oak Bluffs | Narragansett House, 62 Narragansett Ave., 02557, 617-693-3627 |
| Oak Bluffs | Nashua House, Kennebec and Park Ave., 02557, 617-693-0043 |
| Oak Bluffs | Oak House, The, P.O. Box 299CG, 02557, 508-693-4187 |
| Oak Bluffs | Pequot House, 19 Pequot Ave, Box 1146, 02557 |
| Oak Bluffs | Ship's Inn, Box 1483, 02557, 617-693-2760 |
| Pepperell | Boggastowe Farm, Shattuck St, 01463 |
| Peru | Chalet d'Alicia B&B, E. Windsor Rd., 01235, 413-655-8292 |
| Peru | Stall, The, East Windsor Rd., 01235, 413-655-8008 |
| Pittsfield | Country Hearts B&B, 52 Broad St., 01201 |
| Pittsfield | White Horse Inn B&B, 378 South St, Rts 7 & 2, 01201, 413-443-0961 |
| Plainfield | Rolling Meadow Farm, H.C. 15A Pleasant St., 01070, 415-634-2166 |
| Plymouth | Another Place Inn, 240 Sandwich St., 02360, 548-746-0126 |
| Plymouth | Colonial House Inn, 207 Sandwich St., 02360, 617-746-2087 |
| Plymouth | Hawthorne Hill B&B, 3 Wood St., 02360, 508-746-5244 |
| Plymouth | Morton Park Place, 1 Morton Park Rd., 02360, 508-747-1730 |
| Princeton | Harrington Farm, The, 178 Westminster Rd., 01541, 508-464-5600 |
| Provincetown | Admiral's Landing, 158 Bradford St., 02657 |
| Provincetown | Asheton House, 3 Cook St., 02657, 508-487-9966 |
| Provincetown | Bed 'n B'fast, 44 Commercial St., 02657, 508-487-9555 |
| Provincetown | Bradford Gardens Inn, 178 Bradford St., 02657, 508-487-1616 |
| Provincetown | Captain Lysander Inn, 96 Commercial St., 02657, 508-487-2253 |
| Provincetown | Crosswinds Inn, 140 Bradford St., 02657, 508-487-3533 |
| Provincetown | Fairbanks Inn, The, 90 Bradford St., 02657, 508-487-0386 |
| Provincetown | Lamplighter Inn, 26 Bradford St., 02657, 508-487-2529 |
| Provincetown | Red Inn, 15 Commercial St., 02657, 617-487-0050 |
| Provincetown | Victoria House, 5 Standish St., 02657, 617-487-1319 |
| Richmond | Middlerise B&B, Route 41, Box 17, 01254 |
| Rockport | Beach Knoll Inn, 30 Beach St., 01966, 508-546-6939 |
| Rockport | Cable House, 3 Narwood Ave., 01966, 508-546-3895 |
| Rockport | Lantana House, 22 Broadway, 01966, 508-546-3535 |
| Rockport | Peg Leg Inn & Restaurant, 2 King Street, 01966, 800-346-2352 |
| Rockport | Pleasant Street Inn, 17 Pleasant St., 01966, 508-546-3915 |
| Rockport | Sally Webster Inn, The, 34 Mt. Pleasant St., 01966, 508-546-9251 |
| Rockport | Seaward Inn & Cottages, 62 Marmion Way, 01966, 800-648-7733 |
| Rockport | Seven South St.—The Inn, 7 South St., 01966, 508-546-6708 |
| Rutland | General Rufus Putnam House, 344 Main St., Rt. 122-A, 01543, 508-886-4256 |
| S. Yarmouth | Captain Farris House B&B, 308 Old Main St., 02664, 800-350-9477 |

| | |
|---|---|
| Sagamore | Bed & Breakfast, One Hawes Rd., Box 205, 02562, 508-888-1559 |
| Salem | Nathaniel Bowditch House, 2 Kimball Court, 01970, 508-745-7755 |
| Sandisfield | New Boston Inn, Routes 57 & 8, 01255, 413-258-4477 |
| Sandwich | Barclay Inn, 40 Grove St., 02563, 508-888-5738 |
| Sandwich | Dillingham House, 71 Main St., 02563, 508-833-0065 |
| Sandwich | Hawthorn Hill, P.O. Box 777, 02563, 508-888-3333 |
| Sandwich | Inn at Sandwich Center, 118 Tupper Road, 02563, 508-888-6958 |
| Sandwich | Six Water Street, P.O. Box 1295, 02563, 508-888-6808 |
| Sandwich | Village Inn at Sandwich, P.O. Box 951, 02563, 508-833-0363 |
| Sheffield | Centuryhurst Antiques B&B, P.O. Box 486, 01257, 413-229-8131 |
| Sheffield | Stagecoach Hill Inn, Route 41, 01257, 413-229-8585 |
| Sheffield | Staveleigh House, P.O. Box 608, 01257, 413-229-2129 |
| Shelburne Falls | Country Comfort, 15 Masonic Ave., 01370, 413-625-9877 |
| Shelburne Falls | Parson Hubbard House, Old Village Rd., 01370, 413-625-9730 |
| Siasconset | Summer House, The, P.O. Box 880, S. Bluff, 02564, 508-257-4577 |
| South Chatham | Ye Olde Nantucket House, P.O. Box 468, 02659, 508-432-5641 |
| South Dartmouth | Little Red House, The, 631 Elm St., 02748, 508-996-4554 |
| South Dartmouth | Salt Marsh Farm, 322 Smith Neck Rd., 02748, 508-992-0980 |
| South Deerfield | Orchard Terrace, 330 No. Main St., 01373, 413-665-3829 |
| South Harwich | House on the Hill, P.O. Box 51, 968 Main, 02661, 617-432-4321 |
| South Lee | Federal House, Route 102, 01260, 413-243-1824 |
| South Orleans | Hillbourne House B&B, Route 28, Box 190, 02662, 617-255-0780 |
| South Sudbury | Wayside Inn, 01776, 617-443-8846 |
| South Yarmouth | Four Winds, 345 High Bank Rd., 02664, 508-394-4182 |
| Southfield | Langhaar House, P.O. Box 191, 01259, 413-229-2007 |
| Stow | Amerscot House B&B, P.O. Box 351, 01775, 508-897-0666 |
| Sturbridge | Chamberlain, P.O. Box 187, 01566, 617-347-3313 |
| Sturbridge | Commonwealth Inn, P.O.Box 251, Fiskdale, 01566, 508-347-5503 |
| Sturbridge | Country Motor Lodge, P.O. Box 187, 01566, 617-347-3313 |
| Sudbury | Checkerberry Corner B&B, 5 Checkerberry Circle, 01776, 508-443-8660 |
| Sudbury | Sudbury B&B, 3 Drum Ln., 01776, 617-443-2860 |
| Swampscott | Marshall House, 11 Eastern Ave., 01907, 617-595-6544 |
| Swampscott | Oak Shores, 64 Fuller Ave., 01907, 617-599-7677 |
| Townsend | Wood Farm, 40 Worcester Rd., 01469, 508-597-5019 |
| Tyringham | Golden Goose, P.O. Box 336, 01264, 413-243-3008 |
| Uxbridge | Capron House, 2 Capron St., 01569 |
| Vineyard Haven | Gazebo B&B, Edgartown Rd., 02568, 617-693-6955 |
| Vineyard Haven | High Haven House, Box 289, Summer St., 02568, 617-693-9204 |
| Vineyard Haven | Nancy's Auberge, 102 Main St., Box 4433, 02568, 508-693-4434 |
| Vineyard Haven | Post House, The, P.O. Box 717, 02568, 508-693-5337 |
| Vineyard Haven | Sea Horse Guests, RFD Box 373, 02568, 617-693-0594 |
| Vineyard Haven | Tuckerman House, 45 William St, Box 194, 02568, 617-693-0417 |
| Vineyard Haven | Twin Oaks Inn, P.O. Box 1767, 02568, 508-693-8633 |
| Ware | 1880 Inn B&B, The, 14 Pleasant St., 01082, 413-967-7847 |
| West Boylston | Rose Cottage, 24 Worcester,Rts 12 & 1, 01583, 617-835-4034 |
| West Dennis | Lighthouse Inn, 02670, 508-398-2244 |
| West Falmouth | Old Silver Beach B&B, 3 Cliffwood Lane, Box 6, 02574, 617-540-5446 |
| West Falmouth | Sjoholm Inn B&B, P.O. Box 430, 02574, 508-540-5706 |
| West Harwich | Lion's Head Inn, P.O. Box 444, 02671, 508-432-7766 |
| West Harwich | Tern Inn, The, 91 Chase St., 02671, 508-432-3714 |
| West Hawley | Stump Sprouts Guest Lodge, West Hill Rd., 01339, 413-339-4265 |
| West Tisbury | Bayberry Inn, The, Old Courthouse Rd., 02575, 508-693-1984 |
| West Tisbury | Cove House/Studio House, Box 25, 02575 |
| Weston | Webb-Bigelow House, 863 Boston Post Rd., 02193, 617-899-2444 |
| Whately | Sunnyside Farm, 11 River Rd., 01093, 413-665-3113 |
| Williamsburg | Carl & Lottie Sylvester, 9 South St., 01096, 413-268-7283 |
| Williamsburg | Twin Maples, 106 South St., 01098, 413-268-7925 |
| Williamstown | Field Farm Guest House, 554 Sloan Rd., 01267, 413-458-3135 |
| Williamstown | House On Main Street, 1120 Main St., 01267, 413-458-3031 |
| Williamstown | Le Jardin, 777 Coldspring Rd., 01267, 413-458-8032 |
| Williamstown | Orchards, The, 01267, 800-225-1517 |
| Williamstown | Upland Meadow House, 1249 Northwest Hill Rd., 01267 |
| Woods Hole | Marlborough, The, Box 238, 02543, 508-548-6218 |
| Worthington | Franklin Burr Homestead, HC63 B196, Kinne Brook, 01098, 413-238-5826 |
| Worthington | Heritage, The, Box 444, 01098, 413-238-4230 |
| Worthington | Inn Yesterday, Huntington Rd.-Rt. 11, 01098, 413-238-5529 |
| Worthington | Worthington Inn, Route 143, Old North Rd., 01098, 413-238-4441 |
| Yarmouth Port | Old Yarmouth Inn, 223 Main St., 02675 |

# Michigan

ANN ARBOR ———————————————————

| | | |
|---|---|---|
| **Urban Retreat B&B, The** | $$-B&B | Full breakfast |
| 2759 Canterbury Rd., 48104 | 2 rooms, 1 pb | Sitting room |
| 313-971-8110 | Visa, MC, *Rated*, • | patio, gardens |
| Andre Rosalik & Gloria Krys | C-ltd/S-ltd/P-no/H-no | air-conditioned |
| All year | | |

*Comfortable 1950s ranch home on quiet tree-lined street; furnished with antiques; adjacent to 127-acre meadowland park; minutes from major universities. Resident house cats.*

AU TRAIN ———————————————————

| | | |
|---|---|---|
| **Pinewood Lodge** | $$-B&B | Full breakfast |
| Box 176, 49806 | 8 rooms, 4 pb | Snacks |
| M28W | Disc., Visa, MC, | Library, sitting room |
| 906-892-8300 Fax: 906-892-8510 | C-ltd/S-no/P-no/H-ltd | Hot tub, sauna |
| Jerry & Jenny Krieg | | beach on Lake Superior |
| All year | | |

*Enjoy our Log Home & brkfst. overlooking our sand beach, Lake Superior & AuTrain Island. Hike, swim or relax in our sauna, hot tub, or warm up @ fireside in 2 great rooms.*

BOYNE CITY ———————————————————

| | | |
|---|---|---|
| **Deer Lake B&B** | $$$-B&B | Full breakfast |
| 00631 E. Deer Lake Rd., 49712 | 5 rooms, 5 pb | Afternoon tea, snacks |
| 616-582-9039 | Most CC, *Rated*, • | Sitting room, bikes |
| Shirley & Glenn Piepenburg | C-ltd/S-no/P-no/H-no | pond/lake, boats |
| All year | | all rooms air condition |

*Modern comfort in quiet country setting on lake and pond in an all season resort area. Jewelry class available. **1st nite full price, each additional nite 10% off.***

CHARLEVOIX ———————————————————

| | | |
|---|---|---|
| **Bridge Street Inn, The** | $$-B&B | Continental plus bkfst. |
| 113 Michigan Ave., 49720 | 9 rooms, 3 pb | Close to beaches, |
| 616-547-6606 Fax: 616-547-1812 | *Rated*, • | restaurants, shopping |
| Vera & John McKown | C-ltd/S-no/P-no/H-no | & boating |
| All year | | |

*Recapture grace & charm of a gentler era in this 1895 colonial revival home. 3 stories decorated w/unique, interesting antiques. Each room w/different decor. **3rd night 50%.***

COLDWATER ———————————————————

| | | |
|---|---|---|
| **Chicago Pike Inn** | $$$-B&B | Full breakfast |
| 215 E. Chicago St., 49036 | 8 rooms, 8 pb | Dinner (house bookings) |
| 517-279-8744 800-471-0501 | *Rated*, | Afternoon tea, snacks |
| Rebecca Schultz | C-ltd/S-ltd/P-no/H-no | sitting room, jacuzzi |
| All year | | library, bicycles |

*Victorian elegance—eight beautifully restored rooms surrounded by peace & tranquility. Located in historic district. Two carriage house rooms. OUR 1996 INN OF THE YEAR.*

DOUGLAS ———————————————————

| | | |
|---|---|---|
| **Goshorn House B&B** | $$-B&B | Continental Monday-Fri. |
| 89 S. Washington St., 49406 | 4 rooms, 4 pb | Full breakfast Sat.-Sun. |
| 616-857-1326 | Visa, MC, | Complimentary wine |
| Debra Quade, Chuck Klies | C-ltd/S-ltd/P-no/H-no | afternoon tea |
| All year | | bicycles, sitting room |

*Victorian elegance in our lovingly restored home. Original woodwork, staircase & floors. Screened deck/patio, wraparound porch, central air. Near shops. **7th night free.***

---

**FENNVILLE** ————————————————————————

| | | |
|---|---|---|
| **Hidden Pond B&B** | $$-B&B | Full breakfast |
| P.O. Box 461,  49408 | 2 rooms, 2 pb | Snacks, comp. sherry |
| 5975 - 128th Ave. | *Rated*, • | Sitting room, library |
| 616-561-2491 | C-ltd/S-ltd/P-no/H-no | guest use of home |
| Priscilla & Larry Fuerst | | bicycles, fresh flowers |
| All year | | |

*28 acres of wooded, ravined land for your relaxation. Full gourmet breakfast. Beaches, Saugatuck, Holland & Fennville 10 minutes away. Lovely quiet retreat. **15% off 3+ nights.***

---

**FENNVILLE, SAUGATUCK** ————————————————————

| | | |
|---|---|---|
| **Kingsley House, The** | $$-B&B | Full breakfast |
| 626 W. Main St.,  49408 | 9 rooms, 9 pb | Continental plus wkdays. |
| 616-561-6425 | Most CC, *Rated*, | Sitting rooms, frplc. |
| Gary And Kari King | C-ltd/S-no/H-yes | bicycles, porch swing |
| All year | | 3 suites w/whirlpool tub |

*Turreted, elegant, Queen Anne Victorian built 1886. Just minutes from Saugatuck and Holland, and the sandy beaches of Lake Michigan. Top 50 inn by "Inn Times"*

---

**FLINT** ————————————————————————————

| | | |
|---|---|---|
| **Avon House B&B** | $-B&B | Full breakfast |
| 518 Avon St.,  48503 | 3 rooms, | Formal dining room |
| 810-232-6861  Fax: 810-233-7437 | C-yes/P-no/H-no | Sitting room, A/C |
| Arletta E. Minore | | play yard, grand piano |
| All year | | extended stay rates |

*Enchanting Victorian home close to College & Cultural Center w/art & entertainment. Driving distance to Manufacturer's Marketplace. Children's play yard. Phones in every room. **Discounts, ask.***

---

**GLEN ARBOR** ————————————————————————

| | | |
|---|---|---|
| **Sylvan Inn** | $$-B&B | Continental plus bkfst. |
| P.O. Box 648,  49636 | 14 rooms, 7 pb | Sitting room |
| 6680 Western Ave. (M-109) | MC, Visa, *Rated*, • | whirlpool & sauna room |
| 616-334-4333 | C-ltd/S-no/P-no/H-yes | |
| Jenny & Bill Olson | | |
| May—February | | |

*Luxuriously renovated 1885 historic inn situated in the heart of Sleeping Bear National Lakeshore. Easy access to fine dining, shopping, swimming, biking, skiing.*

---

**GRAND HAVEN** ————————————————————————

| | | |
|---|---|---|
| **Harbor House Inn** | $$$-B&B | Continental plus bkfst. |
| 114 S. Harbor Dr.,  49417 | 17 rooms, 17 pb | Snacks |
| 616-846-0610  Fax: 616-846-0530 | MC, Visa, *Rated*, | Sitting room, library |
| 800-841-0610 | C-ltd/S-ltd/P-no/H-yes | whirlpool baths, TV/VCR |
| Emily Ehlert | | fireplaces in rm., phone |
| All year | | |

*Victorian inn along waterfront. Many rooms w/whirlpool tubs & fireplaces. Cottage with frplc., double whirlpool. Walk to restaurants, shops, beach. Homemade breakfast buffet.*

---

**HOLLAND** ————————————————————————————

| | | |
|---|---|---|
| **Dutch Colonial Inn** | $$-B&B | Full breakfast |
| 560 Central Ave.,  49423 | 5 rooms, 5 pb | Afternoon tea, snacks |
| 616-396-3664  Fax: 616-396-0461 | Most CC, *Rated*, | Sitting room, bicycles |
| B./P. Elenbaas, L. Lutke | C-ltd/S-no/P-no/H-no | Conference facilities |
| All year | | whirlpool tubs, AC |

*Lovely 1928 Dutch Colonial home. Touches of elegance and antiques. Lovely common room w/fireplace. Whirlpool tubs for 2 in private baths; honeymoon suite. **10% off 4+ nights.***

## HOLLAND

**North Shore Inn of Holland**
686 N. Shore Dr.,   49424
616-394-9050  Fax: 616-392-1389
Beverly & Kurt Van
Genderen
All year

$$$-B&B
3 rooms, 2 pb
C-ltd/S-no/P-no/H-no

Full breakfast
Comp. soft drinks
Sitting room
bicycles

*Quiet lakeside location with gardens and woods, yet close to public beaches and historic downtown Holland. Gourmet breakfasts are a specialty.*

**Parsonage 1908 B&B, The**
6 E. 24th St.,   49423
616-396-1316
Bonnie McVoy-Verwys
May—October

$$$-B&B
4 rooms,
*Rated*, •
C-ltd/S-no/P-no/H-no

Full breakfast
Sitting room
TV, games
golf, tennis nearby

*European-style B&B in town famous for May tulip festival. Marvelous alternative to motels for traveling businesswomen. Convenient to several major cities. **Special occasion gift.***

## INTERLOCHEN

**Between the Lakes**
PO Box 280, 4570 Case Blvd.,
  49643
616-276-7751
Barbara & Gordon Evans
All year

$$-B&B
6 rooms, 6 pb
MC, Visa,
C-yes/S-no/P-no/H-yes

Continental deluxe bkfst
Afternoon tea
Sitting room, library
piano, off-season rates
indoor heated lap pool

*This home reflects our Foreign Service in Asia and Africa. Walk to Interlochen Center for the Arts. **10% summer discount for students (and their parents) and seniors***

## JONESVILLE

**Horse & Carriage B&B**
7020 Brown Rd.,   49250
517-849-2732  Fax: 517-849-2732
Keith Brown & Family
All year

$$-B&B
3 rooms, 2 pb
*Rated*,
C-yes/S-no/P-no/H-no
Limited Portuguese

Full breakfast
Picnic lunch, snacks
Sitting room, library
Family friendly facility

*Horse drawn carriage ride awaits you at our quaint 1898 schoolhouse nestled on our peaceful sesquicentennial dairy farm. Hearty breakfast served.*

**Munro House B&B, The**
202 Maumee,   49250
517-849-9292  800-320-3792
Joyce A. Yarde
All year

$$-B&B
7 rooms, 7 pb
Visa, MC, •
C-yes/S-ltd/P-no/H-ltd

Full breakfast
Evening dessert
Sitting room, library
2 rooms with Jacuzzis
5 rooms with fireplaces

*This 1840 Greek Revival home (once a station on the underground railroad) is filled with history and the charm of a bygone era. **3rd night, 50%.***

## KALAMAZOO

**Hall House B&B**
106 Thompson St.,   49006
616-343-2500
Jerry & Joanne Hofferth
All year

$$$-B&B
5 rooms, 5 pb
Visa, MC, *Rated*,
C-ltd/S-no/P-no/H-no

Full breakfast—weekend
Continental plus—wkdays
Afternoon tea & cookies
sitting rooms, sun porch
library, TV & phones

*Stately 1920s Georgian Colonial home, minutes from downtown, on the edge of the Kalamazoo College campus. Common areas for small weedings & receptions.*

LAKESIDE ─────────────────────────────────────────

**Pebble House, The**
15093 Lakeshore Rd.,   49116
616-469-1416
Jean & Ed Lawrence
All year

$$$-B&B
8 rooms, 6 pb
*Rated*,
C-ltd/S-yes/P-no/H-ltd

Full breakfast
Screen house, hammocks
fireplace, bicycles
tennis courts, walkways

*Circa 1910 decorative block & beach pebble house. Arts & Crafts furniture, decorative items. Frplc., woodstove, rocking chairs & lake view. Like going home to Grandma's.* **3rd nite 50%, exc. July & August.**

LUDINGTON ────────────────────────────────────────

**Inn at Ludington, The**
701 E. Ludington Ave.,   49431
616-845-7055  800-845-9170
Diane Shields, David Nemitz
All year

$$-B&B
6 rooms, 6 pb
Most CC,  •
C-ltd/S-no/P-no/H-no

Full buffet breakfast
Picnic lunches (fee)
Sitting room, library
murder mystery weekends
family country suite

*This 1890 Queen Anne painted lady combines the charm of the past w/the comforts of today. Conveniently located on the avenue, walk to shops, restaurants, marina & carferry.*

**Lamplighter B&B, The**
602 E. Ludington Ave.,   49431
616-843-9792  Fax: 616-845-6070
800-301-9792
Judy & Heinz Bertram
All year

$$$-B&B
4 rooms, 4 pb
Most CC,  •
C-ltd/S-no/P-no/H-no
German

Full breakfast
Afternoon tea
Complimentary wine
Sitting room, bicycles
Resident cocker spaniel

*Elegant surroundings in a centennial home. European antiques and original art. Gourmet breakfasts in our gazebo or on the terrace.*

**Snyder's Shoreline Inn**
P.O. Box 667,   49431
903 W. Ludington Ave.
616-845-1261  Fax: 616-843-4441
Angela Snyder & Kate
Whitaker
Open May—Oct.

$$-B&B
44 rooms, 44 pb
Most CC, *Rated*,
C-ltd/S-ltd/P-no/H-yes

Continental breakfast
Box lunches available
Library
hot tub, swimming pool
in room spas

*Country inn with private balconies facing Lake Michigan. In-room spas. Near shopping, restaurants, golf & bike paths. On the beach.* **50% off 3rd night, off season only.**

MACKINAC ISLAND ──────────────────────────────────

**Haan's 1830 Inn**
P.O. Box 123,   49757
3418 Oakwood-Is. Lake, IL
906-847-6244  414-248-9244
Nick & Nancy Haan, Judy
Mark
Mid-May—mid-October

$$$-B&B
7 rooms, 5 pb
*Rated*,
C-yes/S-ltd/P-no/H-no

Continental plus bkfst.
Parlor, porches
antique furnishings
kids 5 and under free

*Restored Greek Revival home on Historic Register. Across street from Haldimand Bay. 3 blocks from Fort Mackinac and downtown. Featured in Summer 1990 Innsider Magazine.*

MANISTEE ──────────────────────────────────────────

**Inn Wick-A-Te-Wah**
3813 Lakeshore Dr., Portage
Lake,   49660
616-889-4396  Fax: 616-889-4396
Len & Marge Carlson
All year

$$-B&B
4 rooms, 1 pb
MC, Visa, *Rated*,  •
C-ltd/S-ltd/P-no/H-no

Full breakfast
Comp. wine, fruit
Snacks, sitting rooms
swimming, games
sunfish (sailing)

*Enjoy tranquility & gracious hospitality in relaxed lakeside setting. Nostalgic atmosphere & cozy comforts bring back memories of simpler times.* **3 nites +: 10% discount.**

*Sans Souci Euro Inn, New Buffalo, MI*

## MENDON

**Mendon Country Inn B&B**
440 W. Main St., 49072
616-496-8132
Fax: 616-496-8403
800-304-3366
Dick & Dolly Buerkle
All year

$$-B&B
18 rooms, 18 pb
Most CC, *Rated*, •
C-ltd/S-ltd/P-no/H-yes
A little Spanish

Continental plus bkfst.
Evening dessert
Hot tubs, sauna
canoe livery trips
bikes for two, tennis

*1843 Stagecoach Inn. 9 antique-filled rooms, 9 jacuzzi suites w/fireplaces. Close to Amish, golfing, canoes, wineries. Rural setting.* **Stay 2 nights 3rd is free, stay 2 nights, 2nd is 50%, Sun.–Thurs.**

## NEW BUFFALO

**Sans Souci Euro Inn**
19265 S. Lakeside Rd., 49117
616-756-3141
Fax: 616-756-5511
Don Kerr
All year

$$$-B&B
9 rooms, 9 pb
Most CC, *Rated*, •
C-ltd/S-ltd/P-no/H-yes
German, Spanish

Full breakfast
Fully equipped kitchens
TV, VCR, phones, golf
private lakes, swim/fish
birdwatching

*Choose your destination to be "without a care."Our Euro vacation home, honeymoon suite, or family cottage come with luxury amenities. Near Lake Michigan.* **Weekly specials & family packages.**

## NORTHPORT

**Old Mill Pond Inn, The**
202 West Third St., 49670
616-386-7341
David Chrobak
June–October

$$-B&B
4 rooms, 2 pb
•
C-ltd/S-yes/P-no/H-no

Full breakfast
Sitting room

*Restored ninety-year-old house decorated with period furniture and an extensive collection of art objects from around the world. Gay friendly.*

### PENTWATER

| **Pentwater Inn** | $$-B&B | Full breakfast |
|---|---|---|
| P.O. Box 98,  49449 | 5 rooms, 5 pb | Evening beverage & snack |
| 180 E. Lowell St. | Visa, MC, *Rated*, | Sitting room, antiques |
| 616-869-5909  Fax: 616-869-7002 | C-yes/S-no/P-no/H-no | hot tub, bicycles - near |
| Donna & Quintus Renshaw | German, French | cross-country ski, |
| All year | | snowmobile |

*1869 Victorian Inn in quiet residential area. Within walking distance of Lake Michigan Beach, village shops & fine dining. Golf, fishing charter. **7th night free.***

### PORT SANILAC

| **Raymond House Inn, The** | $$-B&B | Full breakfast |
|---|---|---|
| P.O. Box 438,  48469 | 7 rooms, 7 pb | Comp. sherry, snacks |
| 111 S. Ridge St. | Visa, MC, Disc., ● | A/C in most rooms |
| 810-622-8800  800-622-7229 | C-ltd/S-no/P-no/H-no | sitting room, deck |
| The Denison Family | | Antique Shop |
| April - December | | |

*120-year-old Victorian home on Michigan's Historic Register, furnished in antiques. On Lake Huron—marina, boating, shipwreck, scuba diving, fishing, swimming.*

### ROCHESTER HILLS

| **Paint Creek B&B** | $-B&B | Full breakfast |
|---|---|---|
| 971 Dutton Rd.,  48306 | 3 rooms, | Snacks |
| 810-651-6785 | *Rated*, ● | Library, sitting room |
| Loren & Rea Siffring | C-yes/S-no/P-ltd/H-no | hike, bike |
| All year | | cross-country skiing |

*Unique setting on 3.5 wooded acres above wetlands & trout stream. Adjacent to hiking, biking trail. Close to Palace and Silverdome. Restaurants, shopping & Oakland University.*

### SAGINAW

| **Montague Inn** | $$-B&B | Continental plus bkfst. |
|---|---|---|
| 1581 S. Washington,  48601 | 18 rooms, 16 pb | Restaurant, bar service |
| 517-752-3939  Fax: 517-752-3159 | Visa, MC, AmEx, | Lunch, dinner (fee) |
| Janet Hoffmann | *Rated*, | library |
| All year | C-yes/S-ltd/P-no/H-yes | |

*Georgian mansion restored to its original splendor. Surrounded by spacious lawns w/ flower & herb gardens. The Inn provides a peaceful & elegant oasis in the heart of the city. **All rooms 50%, Sundays.***

### SAUGATUCK

| **Bayside Inn** | $$$-B&B | Continental plus bkfst. |
|---|---|---|
| P.O. Box 1001,  49453 | 10 rooms, 10 pb | Snacks |
| 618 Water St. | Most CC, *Rated*, | Converted boathouse |
| 616-857-4321  Fax: 616-857-1870 | C-yes/S-no/P-no/H-ltd | private bath/deck ea.rm. |
| 800-548-0077 | | cable TV, phones |
| Marie Diebold | | |
| All year | | |

*Bayside is an old boathouse converted to a B&B on the water, near downtown Saugatuck. Inground, outdoor hot tub situated 4 feet from the waters edge. **3rd night 50% off, ltd.***

| **Kemah Guest House** | $$$-B&B | Continental plus bkfst. |
|---|---|---|
| 633 Allegan St.,  49453 | 5 rooms, 2 pb | Non-alcoholic socials |
| 616-857-2919  800-445-3624 | MC, Visa, *Rated*, ● | Sitting room |
| D. Osborn, C. & T. Tatsch | Spanish | library |
| All year | | |

*Turn-of-the-century mansion sports a combination of Old World flavor, art deco and a splash of southwestern airiness. **Call for specials.***

SAUGATUCK ────────────────────────────────

| **Park House, The** | $$$-B&B | Full breakfast |
|---|---|---|
| 888 Holland St., 49453 | 8 rooms, 8 pb | Soft drinks, juice |
| 616-857-4535  Fax: 616-857-1065 | MC, Visa, *Rated*, • | Sitting room, TV |
| 800-321-4535 | C-ltd/S-yes/P-no/H-yes | 3rd floor game loft |
| J. & L. Petty, L. Matzen | | suites w/jet tub, frplc. |
| All year | | |

*Country home w/New England charm; built in 1857. Nat'l Historic Register Home. Near town, beaches, paddleboat rides, dinner cruises, cross-country skiing, golf.* **10% off stay, ask.**

────────────────────────────────

| **Red Dog B&B, The** | $$-B&B | Full breakfast |
|---|---|---|
| P.O. Box 956, 49453 | 7 rooms, 4 pb | Sitting room, garden |
| 132 Mason St. | MC, Visa, *Rated*, • | bicycles, fire place |
| 616-857-8851  Fax: 616-857-5405 | C-ltd/S-no/P-no/H-no | jacuzzi, A/C, porch |
| 800-357-3250 | | |
| D.Indurante/G.Kott/K. Clark | | |
| All year | | |

*A comfortable place to stay in the heart of Saugatuck. Fireplace suite with jacuzzi for two. No minimum stay required.* **November - March 2nd night is 50% off.**

────────────────────────────────

| **Sherwood Forest B&B** | $$-B&B | Continental plus bkfst. |
|---|---|---|
| P.O. Box 315, 49453 | 5 rooms, 5 pb | Afternoon tea, snacks |
| 938 Center St. | MC, Visa, *Rated*, | Sitting room, bicycles |
| 616-857-1246  800-838-1246 | C-ltd/S-no/P-no/H-no | heated pool, skiing |
| Susan & Keith Charak | | jacuzzi, cottage |
| All year | | |

*Victorian home, wraparound porch, mural room, frplcs., beach access, heated swimming pool, A/C. Near charming shops. Gourmet dinner weekends.*

────────────────────────────────

| **Twin Gables Country Inn** | $$-B&B | Continental plus buffet |
|---|---|---|
| P.O. Box 881, 49453 | 10 rooms, 10 pb | Refreshments |
| 900 Lake St. | MC, Visa, *Rated*, • | Whirlpool, hot tub, pool |
| 616-857-4346 | C-ltd/S-ltd/P-no/H-yes | A/C, bicycles, pond |
| Michael & Denise Simcik | Italian, French, Maltese | garden park, ski equip. |
| All year | | |

*Country charm overlooking Kalamazoo Lake. Guestrooms in delightful theme decor. Short walk to downtown. 3 cottages furnished in antiques available.* **50%off on 3rd nite, ltd.**

────────────────────────────────

| **Twin Oaks Inn** | $$-B&B | Full breakfast |
|---|---|---|
| P.O. Box 867, 49453 | 7 rooms, 7 pb | Afternoon tea, snacks |
| 227 Griffith | Visa, MC, Disc., • | Hot tubs, bicycles |
| 616-857-1600  800-788-6188 | C-yes/S-no/P-no | TVs, VCRs with |
| Nancy & Jerry Horney | | movie library |
| All year | | |

*Our inn was constructed in 1860 and has been restored with special attention to the comfort and convenience of our guests. Jacuzzi tub available.*

SOUTH HAVEN ────────────────────────────

| **A Country Place B&B** | $$-B&B | Full breakfast |
|---|---|---|
| 79 N. Shore Dr. North, 49090 | 5 rooms, 5 pb | Afternoon tea, snacks |
| 616-637-5523 | Most CC, • | Complimentary wine |
| Art & Lee Niffenegger | C-ltd/S-no/P-no/H-yes | sitting room, gift soaps |
| All year | | for special occassions |

*Historic Greek revival, American and English antiques. Woodside setting. Lake Michigan beach access nearby. "Sin"sational breakfast. Complimentary all day refreshments.*

SOUTH HAVEN ———————————————————————————————

**Arundel House**
56 North Shore Dr.,    49090
616-637-4790
Patricia & Thomas Zapal
All year

$$-B&B
7 rooms, 7 pb
Visa, MC, Disc. *Rated*,
C-ltd/S-no/P-no/H-no
French

Continental plus bkfst.
Afternoon tea
Library
sitting room

*Historic inn, registered with Michigan Historic Society. Furnished with Victorian antiques. Walk to shops, restaurants and Lake Michigan beaches.*

———————————————————————————————————————————

**Old Harbor Inn**
515 Williams St.,    49090
616-637-8480  Fax: 616-637-8492
800-433-9210
Gwen DeBruyn
All year

$$-EP
37 rooms, 37 pb
Most CC, *Rated*, •
C-yes/S-yes/P-no/H-yes

Restaurant
Comp. paper, hot tubs
fishing, boating, golf
tennis, beaches, sailing

*Nestled on banks of the Black River, Old Harbor Inn offers guests the charm & grace of a quaint coastal village. Luxury suites, fireplaces, kitchenettes, pool.* **50% Sunday nights, Dec-Apr, ltd.**

———————————————————————————————————————————

**Yelton Manor B&B**
140 North Shore Dr.,    49090
616-637-5220  Fax: 616-637-4957
Elaine & Rob
All year

$$$-B&B
17 rooms, 17 pb
AmEx, MC, Visa,
*Rated*,
C-ltd/S-no/P-no/H-no

Full breakfast
Evening hors d'oeuvres
Fireplaces in 8 rooms
library, screened porch
jacuzzis in 11 rooms

*Fabulous lakeside Victorian mansion. Elegant fireplace and jacuzzi rooms and lake views. Porches, parlors, antiques, award winning gardens, great food. Pampering service.*

TRAVERSE CITY ———————————————————————————————

**Linden Lea On Long Lake**
279 S. Long Lake Rd.,    49684
616-943-9182
Jim & Vicky McDonnell
All year

$$$-B&B
2 rooms, 2 pb
*Rated*, •
C-ltd/S-no
Spanish

Full breakfast
Comp. wine, snacks
Sitting room, whirlpool
tub, lake frontage
sandy beach, boating

*Wooded lakeside retreat with private sandy beach, rowboat & raft. Comfortable country furnishings, window seats, antiques & beveled glass throughout. Heavily wooded. Peaceful.*

UNION PIER ————————————————————————————————

**Gordon Beach Inn**
16220 Lakeshore Rd.,    49129
616-469-0800  Fax: 616-469-1914
Connie Williams
All year

$$-B&B
20 rooms, 20 pb
Visa, MC, Disc., •
S-ltd/P-no/H-yes

Continental breakfast
Dinner (fee), restaurant
Sitting room

*Historic inn built in 1920s, rennovated in 1992. Take a step back in time. Casual, rustic atmosphere, close to antique shops, galleries.* **2 nights for price of 1 special, ask.**

———————————————————————————————————————————

**Inn at Union Pier, The**
P.O. Box 222,    49129
9708 Berrien St.
616-469-4700  Fax: 616-469-4720
Mark & Joyce Erickson Pitts
All year

$$$-B&B
16 rooms, 16 pb
Most CC, *Rated*,
C-ltd/S-no/P-no/H-yes

Full breakfast
Snacks & beverages
Great room, library
bikes, outdoor hot tub
Lake Michigan beach

*Elegantly refurbished inn blending barefoot informality with gracious hospitality. In "Harbor Country,"known for Lake Michigan beaches, antiques, galleries, and wineries. Corporate retreats.*

# More Inns ...

| | |
|---|---|
| Adrian | Briaroaks Inn, 2980 N. Adrian Hwy., 49224,  517-263-1659 |
| Allegan | Castle in the Country,  340 M-40 So., 49010 |
| Allegan | Delano Inn,  302 Cutler, 49010,  616-673-2609 |
| Allegan | Winchester Inn, 524 Marshall St., 49010,  616-673-3621 |
| Allen | Olde Bricke House, P.O. Box 211, 49227,  517-869-2349 |
| Alma | Candlelight Cottage B&B,  910 Vassar, 48801,  517-463-3961 |
| Alma | Saravilla B&B,  633 N. State St., 48801,  517-463-4078 |
| Ann Arbor | B&B on Campus, 921 E. Huron, 48104,  313-994-9100 |
| Ann Arbor | Gladstone House,  2865 Gladstone, 48104,  313-769-0404 |
| Ann Arbor | Homestead B&B,  9279 Macon Rd., 48176,  313-429-9625 |
| Ann Arbor | Reynolds House, 5259 W Ellsworth Rd, 48103,  313-995-0301 |
| Ann Arbor | Wood's Inn,  2887 Newport Rd, 48103,  313-665-8394 |
| Atlanta | Briley Inn, Rt. 2, Box 614 McArthur, 49709,  517-785-4784 |
| AuGres | Point Augres Hotel, 3279 S. Point Ln., 48703,  517-876-7217 |
| Battle Creek | Greencrest Manor, 6174 Halbert Rd, 49017,  616-962-8633 |
| Battle Creek | Old Lamp-Lighter, The,  276 Capital Ave., N.E., 49017,  616-963-2603 |
| Bay City | Clements Inn, 1712 Center Ave., 48708,  517-894-4600 |
| Bay City | Stonehedge Inn B&B, 924 Center Ave. (M-25), 48708,  517-894-4342 |
| Bay City | William Clements Inn, 1712 Center (M-25), 48708,  517-894-4600 |
| Bay View | Gingerbread House, The, P.O. Box 1273, 49770,  616-347-3538 |
| Bay View | Terrace Inn,  216 Fairview Ave., 49770,  616-347-2410 |
| Bellaire | Bellaire B&B,  212 Park St, 49615,  616-533-6077 |
| Bellaire | Grand Victorian - B&B Inn, 402 N. Bridge St., 49615,  800-336-3860 |
| Bellaire | Grass River B&B, 5615 Grass River Rd., 49615,  616-533-6041 |
| Beulah | Brookside Inn, US 31, 49617,  616-882-9688 |
| Beulah | Windermere Inn, 747 Crystal Dr., 49617,  616-882-7264 |
| Big Bay | Big Bay Lighthouse B&B,  No. 3 Lighthouse Rd., 49808,  906-345-9957 |
| Black River | Silver Creek Lodge B&B, 4361 U.S. 23 So., 48721 |
| Blaney Park | Celibeth House B&B, Route 1, Box 58A, 49836,  906-283-3409 |
| Blissfield | H. D. Ellis Inn,  415 W. Adrian, US 223, 49228,  517-486-3155 |
| Blissfield | Hathaway House,  49228,  517-486-2141 |
| Blissfield | Hiram D. Ellis Inn,  415 W. Adrian St., 49228,  517-486-3155 |
| Boyne City | Beardsley House, The,  401 Pearl St., 49712 |
| Boyne City | Duley's State Street Inn, 303 State St, 49712,  616-582-7855 |
| Brooklyn | Chicago Street Inn, 219 Chicago St., 49230,  517-592-3888 |
| Brooklyn | Dewey Lake Manor B&B, 11811 Laird Rd., 49230,  517-467-7122 |
| Brooklyn | Karen's House B&B,  Box 69, 49230 |
| Buchanan | Primrose Path B&B, The,  413 E. Front St., 49107 |
| Cadillac | American Inn B&B,  312 E. Cass, 49601,  616-779-9000 |
| Cadillac | Essenmacher's B&B,  204 Locust Ln., 49601,  616-775-3828 |
| Calumet | Bostrom-Johnson House, 1109 Calumet Ave., 49913,  906-337-4651 |
| Calumet | Calumet House B&B, P.O. Box 126, 49913,  906-337-1936 |
| Calumet | Holly Manor, 714 Pine St., 49913 |
| Caro | Garden Gate B&B, 315 Pearl St., 48723,  517-673-2696 |
| Caseville | Country Charm Farm,  5048 Conkey Rd, 48725,  517-856-3110 |
| Cedar | Jarrold Farm,  Box 215A, County Rd 643, 49621,  616-228-6955 |
| Central Lake | Darmon Street B&B, P.O. Box 284, 49622,  616-544-3931 |
| Champion | Michigamme Lake Lodge B&B, P.O. Box 97, 49814,  906-339-4400 |
| Charlevoix | Bay B&B, 11037 Lakeshore Dr., 49720,  616-599-2570 |
| Charlevoix | Belvedere Inn, 306 Belvedere Ave., 49720,  800-280-4667 |
| Charlevoix | Caine Cottage,  219 Antrim, 49720 |
| Charlevoix | Charlevoix Country Inn,  106 W. Dixon Ave., 49720 |
| Charlevoix | MacDougall House B&B, 109 Petoskey Ave., 49720 |
| Charlevoix | Patchwork Parlour B&B, 109 Petoskey Ave US 31 , 49720,  616-547-5788 |
| Charlotte | Schatze Manor B&B,  1281 W. Kinsel, 48813 |
| Chelsea | Whistlestop B&B, The,  237 Railroad St., 48118 |
| Chesaning | Bonnymill Inn, 710 Broad St., 48616 |
| Chesaning | Stone House B&B, The,  405 W. Broad St., 48616 |
| Clinton | Clinton Inn,  104 W. Michigan Ave., 49236,  517-456-4151 |
| Clio | Chandelier Guest House, 1567 Morgan Rd.,  313-687-6061 |
| Coldwater | Batavia Inn, 1824 W Chicago Rd, 49036,  517-278-5146 |
| Commerce Twp. | Victorian Rose B&B, 815 Sleeth Rd., 48382,  810-360-8221 |
| Constantine | Our Olde Home B&B Inn, 285 Mill St., 49042,  616-435-5365 |
| Corktown | Dobson House, 1439 Bagley, 48216 |
| Dearborn | Dearborn Inn, 200301 Oakwood Blvd., 48124,  313-271-2700 |
| Detroit | Blanche House Inn,  506 Parkview, 48214,  313-822-7090 |
| Dimondale | Bannicks B&B,  4608 Michigan Rd., M-9, 48821,  517-646-0224 |
| Douglas | Kirby House, The,  294 W. Center, 49406,  616-857-2904 |
| Douglas | Rosemont Inn, 83 Lake Shore Dr., 49406,  616-857-2637 |
| Dundee | Dundee Guest House, The,  522 Tecumseh (M-50), 48131,  313-529-5706 |
| East Jordan | Easterly Inn, P.O. Box 366, 49727,  616-536-3434 |
| East Lansing | Coleman Corners B&B,  7733 Old M-78, 48823,  517-339-9360 |
| East Tawas | East Tawas Junction B&B, 514 West Bay, 48730,  517-362-8006 |
| Eastport | Sunrise B&B,  Box 52, 49627,  616-599-2706 |
| Eastport | Torch Lake Sunrise B&B, P.O. Box 52, 49627,  616-599-2706 |
| Elk Rapids | Cairn House B&B,  8160 Cairn Hwy., 49629,  616-264-8994 |

| | |
|---|---|
| Elk Rapids | Candlelight Inn, P.O. Box 476, 49629 |
| Elk Rapids | Widows Walk, 603 River St., 49629, 616-264-5767 |
| Ellsworth | Ellsworth House, Dixon, Rt 1 204 Lake St, 49729, 616-588-7001 |
| Ellsworth | House on the Hill, P.O. Box 206, Lake St., 49729, 616-588-6304 |
| Ellsworth | Lake Michigan's Abiding Pl, 9317 Antrim Ln., 49729 |
| Erie | Lotus Inn, 2310 Lotus Dr., 48133, 313-848-5785 |
| Evart | B&B at Lynch's Dream, 22177 80th Ave., 49631, 616-734-5989 |
| Farmington Hills | Botsford Inn, 28000 Grand River Ave., 48824, 313-474-4800 |
| Farmington Hills | Locust Manor B&B, 24105 Locust Dr., 48335 |
| Fennville | Crane House, The, 6051 - 124th Ave., 49408, 616-561-6931 |
| Fennville | Grandma's House B&B, 2135 Blue Star Hwy., 49408 |
| Fennville | Heritage Manor Inn B&B, 2253 Blue Star Hwy., 49408, 616-543-4384 |
| Fennville | J. Paules' Fenn Inn, 2254 S 58th St, 49408, 616-561-2836 |
| Fennville | Porches B&B, The, 2297 Lakeshore Dr, 49408, 616-543-4162 |
| Fenton | Pine Ridge, N-10345 Old US 23, 48430, 313-629-8911 |
| Flint | Courtyard, The, G-3202 W. Court St., 48532, 313-238-5510 |
| Frankenmuth | B&B at The Pines, 327 Ardussi St., 48734, 517-652-9019 |
| Frankenmuth | Bavarian Town B&B, 206 Beyerlein St, 48734, 517-652-8057 |
| Frankenmuth | Bender Haus, 337 Trinklein St., 48734 |
| Frankenmuth | Frankenmuth Bender Haus, 337 Trinklein St, 48734, 517-652-8897 |
| Frankenmuth | Franklin Haus, 216 S. Franklin St., 48734, 517-652-3383 |
| Frankenmuth | Kueffner Haus B&B, 176 Parker St, 48734, 517-652-6839 |
| Frankfort | Birch Haven Inn, The, Box 411, 219 Leelanau, 49635, 616-352-4008 |
| Frankfort | Haugen's Haven B&B, P.O. Box 913, 49635, 616-352-7850 |
| Frankfort | Hotel Frankfort, P.O. Box 1026, 49635, 616-882-7271 |
| Frankfort | Trillium, 611 S. Shore Dr., 49635, 616-352-4976 |
| Fremont | Gerber House B&B, 6130 W. 56th St., 49412, 800-525-0151 |
| Fruitport | Village Park B&B, 60 West Park St., 49415, 616-865-6289 |
| Galesburg | Byrd House, The, 11483 E. G Ave., 49053, 616-665-7052 |
| Garden | Summer House, P.O. Box 107, State St, 49835, 906-644-2457 |
| Gaylord | Heritage House B&B, 521 E. Main St., 49735, 517-732-1199 |
| Gladstone | Cartwrights' Birdseye Inn, 1020 Minnesota Ave., 49837 |
| Glen Arbor | Glen Arbor B&B, P.O. Box 526, 49636 |
| Glen Arbor | Walker's White Gull B&B, 5926 Hwy M-22, 49636, 616-334-4486 |
| Glen Arbor | White Gull Inn, P.O. Box 351, 49636, 616-334-4486 |
| Glenn | Will O'Glenn Irish B&B, P.O. Box 288, 49416 |
| Gobles | Kal-Haven B&B, 23491 Paulson Rd., 49055 |
| Grand Haven | Boyden House Inn B&B, 301 South 5th St., 49417, 616-846-3538 |
| Grand Haven | Highland Park Hotel B&B, 1414 Lake Ave., 49417, 616-842-6483 |
| Grand Haven | Washington Street Inn, 608 Washington St, 49417, 616-842-1075 |
| Grand Ledge | Edwards' Wind Crest, 11880 Oneida Rd., 48837 |
| Grand Marais | Lakeview Inn, P.O. Box 297, 49839, 906-494-2612 |
| Grand Rapids | Fountain Hill B&B, 222 Fountain, NE, 49503, 616-458-6621 |
| Grand Rapids | Heald-Lear House, 455 College Ave, SE, 49503, 616-459-9055 |
| Grass Lake | Coppys Inn, 13424 Phal Rd., 49240 |
| Grayling | Belknap's Hanson House, 604 Peninsular, 49738 |
| Greenville | Gibson House, The, 311 W Washington, 48838, 616-7546691 |
| Greenville | Winter Inn, 100 N. Lafayette, 48838 |
| Harbor Beach | Wellock Inn, 404 S. Huron Ave., 48441, 517-479-3645 |
| Harbor Springs | Four Acres B&B, 684 W. Bluff Dr., 49740, 616-525-6076 |
| Harbor Springs | Kimberly Country Estate, 2287 Bester Rd, 49740, 616-526-7646 |
| Harbor Springs | Main Street B&B, 403 E Main St, 49740, 616-526-7782 |
| Harbor Springs | Mottls Getaway, 1021 Birchcrest Ct., 49740, 616-526-9682 |
| Harbor Springs | Windy Ridge B&B, 6281 S. Lakeshore Dr., 49740, 800-409-4095 |
| Harrison | Carriage House Inn, P.O. Box 757, 48625 |
| Harrisville | Red Geranium Inn, 508 E. Main St. (M-72), 48740, 517-724-6153 |
| Harrisville | Springport Inn B&B, 659 U.S. 23 South, 48740, 517-724-6308 |
| Harrisville | Stratton's Springport Inn, 659 U.S. 23 So., 48740 |
| Harrisville | Widow's Watch B&B, P.O. Box 245, 48740, 517-724-5465 |
| Hart | Rooms At "The Inn", 515 State St., 49420, 616-873-2448 |
| Hartland | Farmstead B&B, 13501 Highland Rd., 48353, 313-887-6086 |
| Hillsdale | Shadowlawn Manor, 84 Union St., 49242, 517-437-2367 |
| Holland | Old Holland Inn, 133 W. 11th St., 49423 |
| Holland | Old Wing Inn, 5298 E. 147th Ave., 49423, 616-392-7362 |
| Holland | Reka's B&B, 300 N. 152nd Ave., 49424 |
| Holly | Holly Crossing B&B, 304 S. Saginaw, 48442 |
| Homer | Grist Guest House, 310 E. Main St., 49245, 517-568-4063 |
| Houghton | Charleston House B&B, 803 W. Lakeshore Dr., 49931, 906-482-7790 |
| Houghton Lake | Stevens White House, P.O. Box 605, 48629, 517-366-4567 |
| Hudson | Sutton's Weed Farm B&B, 18736 Quaker Rd, 49247, 517-547-6302 |
| Interlochen | Betsie Valley B&B, 4440 US-31 South, 49643, 616-275-7624 |
| Interlochen | Interlochen Aire, 4550 State Park Hwy., 49643, 616-276-6941 |
| Interlochen | Sandy Shores B&B, 4487 State Park Hwy, 49643, 616-276-6941 |
| Ionia | Union Hill Inn, 306 Union, 48846, 616-527-0955 |
| Iron River | Pine Willow B&B, 600 Selden Rd, 49935, 906-265-4287 |
| Ithaca | Chaffin's Balmoral Farm, 1245 W. Washington Rd., 48847, 517-875-3410 |
| Jackson | Rose Trellis B&B, 603 W. Michigan Ave., 49201 |
| Jackson | Summit Place B&B, 1682 W. Kimmel Rd., 49201, 517-787-0468 |

| | |
|---|---|
| Kalamazoo | Bartlett-Upjohn House, 229 Stuart Ave, 49007, 616-342-0230 |
| Kalamazoo | Kalamazoo House, 447 W. South St., 49007, 616-343-5426 |
| Kalamazoo | Stuart Avenue Inn B&B, 405 Stuart Ave., 49007, 616-342-0230 |
| Kearsarge | Belknap's Garnet House, 237 Stuart Ave., 49942, 906-337-5607 |
| Laingsburg | Seven Oaks Farm, 7891 Hollister Rd., 48848, 517-651-5598 |
| Lake City | B & B In The Pines, 1940 Schneider Park Rd., 49651, 616-839-4876 |
| Lake Leland | Centennial Inn, 7251 E. Alpers Rd., 49653, 616-271-6460 |
| Lake Orion | Indianwood, The, 80 Cayuga Rd., 48362 |
| Lakeside | White Rabbit Inn, 14634 Red Arrow Hwy, 49116, 616-469-4620 |
| Lamont | Stagecoach Stop B&B, Box 18, 4819 Leonard Rd, 49430, 616-677-3940 |
| Lanse | Bungalow B&B, Route 1, Box 123, 49946, 906-524-7595 |
| Lansing | Ask Me House, 1027 Seymour, 48906 |
| Lansing | Maplewood B&B, 15945 Wood Rd., 48906, 517-485-1426 |
| Lapeer | Hart House, 244 W Park St, 48446, 313-667-9106 |
| Laurium | Laurium Manor & Vict. Hall, 320 Tamarack St., 49913, 906-337-2549 |
| Lawrence | Oak Cove Resort, 58881 46th St., 49064, 616-674-8228 |
| Leland | Manitou Manor, P.O. Box 864, 49654, 616-256-7712 |
| Leland | Riverside Inn, 302 River St., 49654, 616-256-9971 |
| Leland | Snowbird Inn, P.O. Box 1124, 49654, 616-256-9773 |
| Lewiston | Gorton House, Wolf Lake Dr., 49756, 517-786-2764 |
| Lewiston | Lakeview Hills Country Inn, P.O. Box 365, 49756, 517-786-2000 |
| Lexington | Britannia House English, P.O. Box 5, 48450 |
| Lexington | Governor's Inn B&B, P.O. Box 471, 48450, 313-359-5770 |
| Lexington | Powell House B&B, The, 5076 S. Lakeshore Rd., 48450 |
| Lowell | McGee Homestead B&B, 2534 Alden Nash NE, 49331, 616-897-8142 |
| Ludington | Doll House Inn, 709 E. Ludington Ave., 49431, 616-843-2286 |
| Ludington | Hamlin Lake Cottage B&B, 7035 Harvey Rd., 49431 |
| Ludington | Ludington House, 501 E. Ludington Ave., 49431, 616-845-7769 |
| Mackinac Island | Bogan Lane Inn, P.O. Box 482, 49757, 906-847-3439 |
| Mackinac Island | Cloghaun, P.O. Box 203, 49757, 906-847-3885 |
| Mackinac Island | Metivier Inn, Box 285, 49757, 906-847-6234 |
| Mancelona | Cedar Bend Farm, 1021 Doerr Rd., 49659, 616-587-5709 |
| Manistee | 1879 E.E. Douville House, 111 Pine St., 49660 |
| Manistee | E. E. Douville House, 111 Pine St., 49660, 616-723-8654 |
| Manistee | Ivy Inn, The, 552 Harvard Lane, 49660, 616-723-8881 |
| Manistee | Lake Shore B&B, 3440 Lake Shore Rd., 49660 |
| Manistee | Manistee Country House, 1130 Lakeshore Rd., 49660, 616-723-2367 |
| Manistee | Maples, The, 435 Fifth St., 49660, 616-723-2904 |
| Maple City | Country Cottage B&B, 135 E. Harbor Hwy., 49664, 616-228-5328 |
| Maple City | Leelanau Country Inn, 149 E. Harbor Highway, 49664, 616-228-5060 |
| Marine City | Heather House, 409 N. Main St., 48039, 313-765-3175 |
| Marlette | Country View B&B, 3723 S. Van Dyke, 48453 |
| Marquette | Blueberry Ridge B&B, 18 Oak Dr., 49855, 906-249-9246 |
| Marshall | McCarthy's Bear Creek Inn, 15230 "C" Dr. N., 49068, 616-781-8383 |
| Marshall | National House Inn, 102 S. Parkview, 49068, 616-781-7374 |
| Martin | Pine Manor B&B, 1436 Tenth St., 49070, 616-672-9164 |
| McMillan | Helmer House Inn, Route 3, County Rd. 417, 49853, 906-586-3204 |
| Mecosta | Blue Lake Lodge B&B, P.O. Box 1, 49332, 616-972-8391 |
| Michigamme | Cottage On The Bay B&B, HCR-1, Box 960, 49861, 906-323-6191 |
| Midland | Bramble House B&B, The, 4309 Bramble Ridge, 48640, 517-832-5082 |
| Midland | Jay's B&B, 4429 Bay City Rd., 48640, 517-631-0470 |
| Milford | Hibbard Tavern, 115 E Summit, 48042, 313-685-1435 |
| Mount Pleasant | Country Chalet, 723 S. Meridian Rd., 48858, 517-772-9259 |
| Muskegon | Blue Country B&B, 1415 Holton Rd (M-120), 49445, 616-744-2555 |
| Muskegon | Emery House B&B, 446 W. Webster, 49440 |
| Muskegon | Hackley-Holt House B&B, 523 W. Clay Ave., 49440 |
| Muskegon | Port City Victorian Inn, 1259 Lakeshore Dr., 49441 |
| Muskegon | Village B&B, 1135 Fifth St., 49440, 616-726-4523 |
| Newberry | Macleod House, The, Rt 2, Box 943, 49868, 906-2933841 |
| Niles | Yesterday's Inn, 518 N. 4th, 49120, 616-683-6079 |
| Northport | Birch Brook, 310 S. Peterson Park Rd, 49670, 616-386-5188 |
| Northport | Mapletree Inn B&B, Rt. 1, Box 169-F, M-22, 49670, 616-386-5260 |
| Northport | North Shore Inn, 12794 County Rd. 640, 49670 |
| Northport | Plum Lane Inn, P.O. Box 74, 49670, 616-386-5774 |
| Northport | Wood How Lodge, Route 1 Box 44E, 49670, 616-386-7194 |
| Northville | Atchison House, 501 W. Dunlap St., 48167, 313-349-3340 |
| Omena | Omena Shores B&B, P.O. Box 154, 49674, 616-386-7313 |
| Onekama | Lake Breeze House, 5089 Main St., 49675, 616-889-4969 |
| Onekama | Onekama, Lake Breeze House, 49675, 616-889-4969 |
| Ontonagon | Northern Light Inn, 701 Houghton St., 49953 |
| Oscoda | Huron House, 312A North US-23, 48750, 517-739-9255 |
| Owosso | Mulberry House, 1251 Shiawassee St., 48867, 517-723-4890 |
| Owosso | Sylverlynd, 3452 McBride Rd., 48667, 517-723-1267 |
| Owosso | Victorian Splendor, 426 N. Washington St., 48867, 517-725-5168 |
| Paw Paw | Carrington's Country House, 43799 60th Ave., 49079, 616-657-5321 |
| Pentwater | Candlewyck House B&B, The, 438 E. Lowell St., 49449, 800-348-5827 |
| Pentwater | Historic Nickerson Inn, P.O. Box 109, 49449, 616-869-6731 |
| Pentwater | Pentwater Abbey, P.O. Box 735, 49449, 616-869-4049 |

| | |
|---|---|
| Petoskey | Bear & The Bay, 421 Charlevoix Ave., 49770, 616-347-6077 |
| Petoskey | Bear River Valley, 03636 Bear River Rd., 49770, 616-348-2046 |
| Petoskey | Benson House, 618 E. Lake St., 49770, 616-347-1338 |
| Petoskey | Cozy Spot, 1145 Kalamazoo, 49770, 616-347-3869 |
| Petoskey | Gull's Way, 118 Boulder Lane, 49770, 616-347-9891 |
| Petoskey | Stafford's Bay View Inn, P.O. Box 3 G, 49770, 616-347-2771 |
| Pinckney | Bunn-Pher Hill, 11745 Spencer Lane, 48169, 313-8789236 |
| Plainwell | 1882 John Crispe House B&B, 404 E. Bridge St., 49080, 616-685-1293 |
| Plymouth | Mayflower B&B Hotel, 827 W. Ann Arbor Trail, 48170, 313-453-1620 |
| Port Austin | Garfield Inn, 8544 Lake St., 48467 |
| Port Austin | Questover Inn, 8510 Lake St., 48467, 517-738-5253 |
| Port Huron | Victorian Inn, The, 1229 7th St., 48060, 313-984-1437 |
| Prescott | Duncan's County B&B, 4738 Clark Rd., 48756, 517-873-4237 |
| Prudenville | Spring Brook Inn, P.O. Box 390, 48651, 517-366-6347 |
| Rapid River | Buck Stop B&B, The, P.O. Box 156, 49878, 906-446-3360 |
| Rockford | Village Rose B&B, 161 N. Monroe, 49341, 616-866-7041 |
| Romeo | Country Heritage B&B, 64707 Mound Rd., 48065, 313-752-2879 |
| Romulus | Country Lane B&B, 32285 Sibley Rd., 48174, 313-753-4586 |
| Roscommon | Tall Trees, Route 2, 323 Birch Rd., 48653, 517-821-5592 |
| Rothbury | Double J Resort Ranch, P.O. Box 94, 49452, 616-894-4444 |
| Saginaw | Brockway House B&B, 1631 Brockway St., 48602, 517-792-0746 |
| Saginaw | Heart House, 419 N. Michigan, 48602, 517-753-3145 |
| Saugatuck | Beechwood Manor, 736 Pleasant St., 49453, 616-857-1587 |
| Saugatuck | Fairchild House, P.O. Box 416, 49453, 616-857-5985 |
| Saugatuck | Kirby House, The, Box 1174, 294 W.Center , 49453, 616-857-2904 |
| Saugatuck | Maplewood Hotel, The, P.O. Box 1059, 49453, 616-857-1771 |
| Saugatuck | Newnham Inn, Box 1106, 131 Giffith S, 49453, 616-857-4249 |
| Saugatuck | Wickwood Country Inn, The, P.O. Box 1019, 49453, 616-857-1097 |
| Sault Ste. Marie | Water Street Inn, The, 140 E. Water St., 49783, 906-632-1900 |
| Scottville | Eden Hill B&B, 1483 E. Chauvez Rd., 49454, 616-757-2023 |
| Sebewaing | Rummel's Tree Haven, 41 N. Beck St., 48759, 517-883-2450 |
| South Haven | Country Place B&B, Rt. 5, Box 43, 49090, 616-637-5523 |
| South Haven | Elmhurst Farm Inn, Rt. 4, Box 261, 49090, 616-637-4633 |
| South Haven | Last Resort B&B Inn, 86 N. Shore Dr, 49090, 616-637-8943 |
| South Haven | N. Beach Inn & Restaurant, 51 North Shore Dr., 49090, 616-637-6738 |
| South Haven | Ross B&B House, 229 Michigan Ave., 49090, 616-637-2256 |
| South Haven | Seymour House, The, 1248 Adams Rd., 49090, 616-227-3918 |
| South Haven | Victoria Resort B&B, 241 Oak St., 49090, 616-637-6414 |
| Spring Lake | Seascape B&B, 20009 Breton, 49456, 616-842-8409 |
| St. Clair | Murphy Inn, 505 Clinton Ave., 48079, 313-329-7118 |
| St. Ignace | Colonial House Inn, 90 N. State St., 49781, 906-643-6900 |
| St. Johns | Classic B&B, The, 505 E. Walker St., 48879, 800-528-6486 |
| St. Joseph | South Cliff Inn B&B, 1900 Lakeshore Dr., 49085, 616-983-4881 |
| Stanton | Clifford Lake Hotel, 561 W. Clifford Lake, 48888, 517-831-5151 |
| Stephenson | Csatlos' Csarda, P.O. Box 523, 49887, 906-753-4638 |
| Sturgis | Christmere House Inn, 110 Pleasant St., 49091, 616-651-8303 |
| Suttons Bay | Cottage B&B, The, P.O. Box 653, 49682, 616-271-6348 |
| Suttons Bay | Lee Point Inn on W. Grand, Rt. 2, Box 374B, 49682, 616-271-6770 |
| Suttons Bay | Open Windows B&B, P.O. Box 698, 49682, 616-271-4300 |
| Swartz Creek | Pink Palace Farms, 6095 Baldwin Rd., 48473, 313-655-4076 |
| Tawas City | Sarah's Countryside B&B, 1461 S. Lorenz, 48763, 517-362-7123 |
| Tecumseh | Boulevard Inn, 904 W. Chicago Blvd., 49286, 517-423-5169 |
| Traverse City | Bowers Harbor B&B, 13972 Peninsula Dr., 49684, 616-223-7869 |
| Traverse City | Cider House B&B, 5515 Barney Rd., 49684, 616-947-2833 |
| Traverse City | L'DA RU B&B, 4370 N. Spider Lake Rd., 49684, 616-946-8999 |
| Traverse City | Mission Pt. B&B, 20202 Center Rd., 49684, 616-223-7526 |
| Traverse City | Neahtawanta Inn, 1308 Neahtawanta Rd., 49684, 616-223-7315 |
| Traverse City | Peninsula Manor, 8880 Peninsula Dr., 49686, 616-929-1321 |
| Traverse City | Queen Anne's Castle, 500 Webster, 49684, 616-946-1459 |
| Traverse City | Stonewall Inn, The, 17898 Smokey Hollow Rd., 49684, 616-223-7800 |
| Traverse City | Tall Ship Malabar, 13390-D W. Bayshore Dr., 49684, 616-941-2000 |
| Traverse City | Victoriana 1898, The, 622 Washington St., 49684, 616-929-1009 |
| Traverse City | Warwickshire Inn, 5037 Barney Rd., 49684, 616-946-7176 |
| Traverse City | Wooden Spoon B&B, 316 W. 7th St., 49684, 616-947-0357 |
| Trenton | Bear Haven, 2947 - 4th St., 48183, 313-675-4844 |
| Union City | Victorian Villa Inn, The, 601 N. Broadway St., 49094, 517-741-7383 |
| Union Pier | Pine Garth Inn, P.O. Box 347, 49129, 616-469-1642 |
| Walloon Lake | Walloon Lake Inn, P.O. Box 85, 49796, 616-535-2999 |
| Webberville | Basic Brewer B&B, 5174 Royce, 48892, 517-468-3970 |
| West Branch | Green Inn, 4045 West M-76, 48661, 517-345-0334 |
| White Cloud | Crow's Nest, The, 1440 N. Luce, 49349, 616-689-0088 |
| White Cloud | Shack Country Inn, The, 2263 W. 14th St., 49349, 616-924-6683 |
| White Pigeon | River Haven, 9222 St. Joe River Rd., 49099, 616-483-9104 |
| Ypsilanti | Crickett House, The, 1200 Washtenaw, 48197, 313-484-1387 |

# Minnesota

## ALEXANDRIA

**Cedar Rose Inn B&B**
422 7th Ave. West,  56308
320-762-8430
Aggie & Florian Ledermann
All year

$$-B&B
5 rooms, 4 pb
Visa, MC,
C-ltd/S-no/P-no/H-no

Full breakfast
Snacks, comp. wine
Sitting room, library
bicycles, hot tubs

*Cozy 1903 Tudor-Revival style home, walking distance to downtown, many beautiful roses, located in heart of Minnesota lake country. $25 off 2nd night.*

## ANNANDALE

**Thayer Inn**
P.O. Box 246,  55302
60 W. Elm St.
320-274-8222  Fax: 320-274-8222
800-944-6595
Sharon Gammell
All year

$$$-B&B
13 rooms, 13 pb
Visa, MC, Disc.,  •
C-ltd/S-yes/P-ltd/H-no

Full breakfast
Restaurant - all meals
Aftn. tea, snacks
comp. wine, bar service
sitting room, sauna

*Enjoy Victorian ambiance amidst gracious antique furnishings in restored 1895 inn. Surrounded by lakes, near Mall of America & Twin Cities. Inn is said to be haunted. **Gift bag & 25% off 1st night stay.***

## CANNON FALLS

**Quill & Quilt**
615 W. Hoffman St.,  55009
507-263-5507  800-488-3849
Jim & Staci Smith
All year

$$-B&B
4 rooms, 4 pb
MC, Visa, *Rated*,  •
C-ltd/S-ltd

Full breakfast
Evening dessert
Sitting room w/frplc.
library, antiques

*1897 colonial revival home. Ste. w/whirlpool. In scenic Cannon River Valley; near biking, hiking, skiing, canoeing. 35 min. to Mall of America. **Midweek specials, cider in room.***

## FERGUS FALLS

**Bakketopp Hus B&B**
RR 2, Box 187A,  56537
218-739-2915  800-739-2915
Dennis & Judy Nims
All year

$$-B&B
3 rooms, 3 pb
MC, Visa, Disc. *Rated*,
C-ltd/S-no/P-no/H-no

Full special breakfast
Aft. tea, snacks
Sitting room, antiques
fishing, golf, hot tubs
decks on the lakeside

*Wooded hillside lake view. Listen to loons at dusk, enjoy flowers in tiered gardens or relax in spa. Golf, antiques & restaurants nearby. Group meetings, fishing.*

## GRAND MARAIS

**Dream Catcher B&B**
HC 86, Box 122,  55604
218-387-2876  800-682-3119
Jack & Sue McDonnell
All year

$$$-B&B
3 rooms, 3 pb
Visa, MC, Disc.,  •
C-ltd/S-no/P-no/H-no

Full breakfast
Afternoon tea, snacks
Trail lunch available
sitting room, library
sauna

*Quiet, comfortable seclusion, nestled in the northwoods overlooking Lake Superior. Numerous hiking, mountain biking, skiing trails nearby; canoeing. **10% off midweek, ltd.***

## HASTINGS

**Thorwood Historic Inns** | $$-B&B | Full breakfast
315 Pine, 55033 | 8 rooms, 8 pb | Comp. evening snack
612-437-3297 Fax: 612-437-7962 | AmEx, MC, Visa | Sitting room, library
888-THORWOOD | *Rated*, • | victrolas, fireplaces
Dick & Pam Thorsen | C-yes/S-ltd/P-no/H-no | whirlpools, limousine
All year

*1880 French Second Empire home, listed on National Register. Suite-size rooms, feather comforters, fine local wine with evening snack.* **Third night free April–August.**

## LAKE CITY

**Red Gables B&B Inn** | $$$-B&B | Full breakfast
403 N. High St., 55041 | 4 rooms, 4 pb | Comp. wine, snacks
612-345-2605 | MC, Visa, *Rated*, • | Sitting room, library
Mary & Douglas DeRoos | C-ltd/S-ltd/P-no/H-no | bicycles, tennis nearby
All year | | 3 rooms with A/C

*Graciously restored 1865 Victorian on the shores of the Mississippi River. Enjoy antique decor, quiet elegance and Victorian breakfast. Sailing, swimming, skiing.*

## LANESBORO

**Mrs. B's Historic Inn** | $$ | Full breakfast
P.O. Box 411, 55949 | 10 rooms, 10 pb | 5 course gourmet dining
101 Parkway | *Rated*, • | Comp. sherry, chocolate
507-467-2154 800-657-4710 | C-ltd/S-ltd | great trout fishing
Bill Sermeus & Mimi Abell | | tennis & golf nearby
All year

*Nestled deep in Root River Valley; 1872 limestone bldg. in village on National Register. Serene; rural; famous regional cuisine. Restaurant operates Wed-Sun, 5 course dinners.*

## LUTSEN

**Lindgren's B&B** | $$$-B&B | Full breakfast
P.O. Box 56, 55612 | 4 rooms, 4 pb | Snacks, rest. nearby
County Road 35 | MC, Visa, *Rated*, • | Sauna, horeshoes
218-663-7450 | C-ltd/S-no/P-no/H-no | volleyball court
Shirley Lindgren | | kayaking, fall colors
All year

*Gracious and very charming 1920s log home on walkable shores of Lake Superior. Gourmet breakfast served fireside with full lake view. Golf, hike, ski, bike, fish, skyride.*

## MINNEAPOLIS

**Evelo's B&B** | $$-B&B | Continental plus bkfst.
2301 Bryant Ave. S., 55405 | 3 rooms, | TV, refrigerator
612-374-9656 | AmEx, | coffee maker
David & Sheryl Evelo | C-yes/S-no/P-no/H-no | air conditioning
All year

*1897 Victorian, period furnishings. Located on bus line, walk to Guthrie Theater, Minneapolis Art Institute, children's theater. Near historic Lake District.*

**Nan's B&B** | $-B&B | Full breakfast
2304 Fremont Ave. South, | 3 rooms, | Beautiful porch
55405 | MC, Visa, AmEx, • | antique furnishings
612-377-5118 800-214-5118 | C-yes/S-yes/P-ltd/H-no | near many restaurants
Nan & Jim Zosel
All year

*Comfortable urban 1890s Victorian family home; near best theatres, galleries, restaurants, Minneapolis. Friendly, informative hosts.* **Weekly rate: 1 night free.**

## ONAMIA

| **Cour du Lac B&B** | $$$-B&B | Full breakfast |
| 10654-390th St.,  56359 | 3 rooms, 3 pb | Sitting room, library |
| 320-532-4627 | Visa, MC, | golf & jet skis nearby |
| Frank & Susan Courteau | C-ltd/S-no/P-no/H-no | ice skating, cross-country |
| All year | | skiing |

*A country French home on Mille Lacs Lake. The largest guestroom has a fireplace. Near state parks, casino, golf courses & a bike trail.* **10% off 3 or more nights, ask.**

## SAUK CENTRE

| **Palmer House Hotel/Inn** | $$-EP | Full service restaurant |
| 228 Original Main St.,  56378 | 37 rooms, 4 pb | Tennis courts |
| 612-352-3431  888-222-3431 | C-yes/S-yes/P-yes/H-no | sitting room, piano |
| Al Tingley | German | dinner theatre |
| All year | | |

*Historic site—the "original Main Street" home of Sinclair Lewis, the first American author to win the Nobel Prize for Literature.* **10% off restaurant.**

## SHERBURN

| **Four Columns B&B** | $$-B&B | Full hearty breakfast |
| Rt. 2, Box 75,  56171 | 4 rooms, 4 pb | Snacks |
| I-90 | • | Sitting room, library |
| 507-764-8861 | C-ltd/S-no/P-no/H-ltd | hot tub, bicycles |
| Norman & Pennie Kittleson | | located on a farm |
| All year | | |

*Scandinavian hospitality in antique-filled, lovingly remodeled, 1884 former country inn. Player piano, gazebo, '50s jukebox. Formal dining room for breakfast.*

## SPRING VALLEY

| **Chase's** | $$$-B&B | Full farm breakfast |
| 508 N. Huron Ave.,  55975 | 5 rooms, 5 pb | Complimentary tea |
| 507-346-2850 | MC, Visa, *Rated*, • | Library, sitting room |
| Bob & Jeannine Chase | C-yes/S-no/P-no/H-no | fishing, quiet, solitude |
| May—October | | golf, bike, hike |

*Antiques throughout Chase's 19th-century mansion. Sleep in solitude, breakfast in quietness. Scenic southeastern Minnesota bluff country. Amish area.*

## STILLWATER

| **Elephant Walk Inn, The** | $$$$-B&B | Full 4 course breakfast |
| 801 W. Pine St.,  55082 | 4 rooms, 4 pb | Comp. wine, snacks |
| 612-430-0359  Fax: 612-351-9080 | Visa, MC, *Rated*, | Sitting room |
| Rita Graybil | C-ltd/S-no/P-no/H-no | hot tubs |
| All year | Thai | international flavor |

*Walk to historic Stillwater. Flower gardens. Tour the world, one room at a time. A bit of the tropics in Minnesota! Exotic settings-gourmet breakfasts. Whirlpools, fireplaces.*

| **Rivertown Inn, The** | $$$-B&B | Full breakfast |
| 306 W. Olive St.,  55082 | 8 rooms, 8 pb | Comp. wine on weekends |
| 612-430-2955  Fax: 612-430-9292 | MC, Visa, *Rated*, • | Sitting areas, A/C |
| 800-562-3632 | C-yes/S-ltd/P-no/H-no | screen porch, gazebo |
| Judy & Chuck Dougherty | | whirlpool bath, bicycles |
| All year | | |

*Beautifully restored 1882 3-story lumberman's mansion. Individually decorated rooms with Victorian antiques. 4 blocks from Historic Main St. Stillwater's oldest B&B.* **Midweek discounts.**

## VERGAS ─────────────────────────────────

| | | |
|---|---|---|
| **Log House & Homestead** | $$$-B&B | Full breakfast |
| P.O. Box 130,　56587 | 5 rooms, 4 pb | Welcome tray |
| East Sprit Lake | MC, Visa, *Rated*, | Sitting room, hike, bike |
| 218-342-2318　800-342-2318 | S-ltd/P-no/H-no | whirlpool, cross-country ski |
| Yvonne & Lyle Tweten | French | large suite w/balconies |
| All year | | |

*Romantic, elegant retreat in restored 1889 loghouse & turn-of-the-century homestead. Tranquility & pampered comfort w/charm of a bygone era. **10$ off 2nd and succeeding night.***

## More Inns ...

| | |
|---|---|
| Afton | Afton House Inn, Hwy 95, 55001, 612-436-8883 |
| Albert Lea | Fountain View Inn, 310 N. Washington Ave., 56007, 507-377-9425 |
| Alexandria | Carrington House B&B, Route 5, Box 88, 56308, 612-846-7400 |
| Alexandria | Robards House, The, 518 Lincoln Ave., 56308, 612-763-4073 |
| Blooming Prairie | Pine Springs Inn, 448 Center Ave. N., 55917, 507-583-4411 |
| Breezy Point | Breezy Point Resort, HC 2, Box 70, 56472, 218-562-7811 |
| Brooklyn Center | Inn on the Farm, 6150 Summit Dr., N., 55430, 612-569-6330 |
| Caledonia | Inn on the Green, The, Route #1, Box 205, 55921, 507-724-2818 |
| Carver | Carousel Rose Inn, 217 W. Third St., 55315, 612-448-5847 |
| Chaska | Bluff Creek Inn, 1161 Bluff Creek Dr., 55318, 612-445-2735 |
| Cold Spring | Pillow, Pillar & Pine, 419 Main St., 56320, 612-332-6774 |
| Crookston | Elm Street Inn B&B, 422 Elm St., 56716, 218-281-2343 |
| Crosby | Hallet House, P.O. 247, 56441, 218-546-5433 |
| Deerwood | Walden Woods B&B, Route 1, Box 193, 56444, 612-692-4379 |
| Dodge Center | Eden Bed & Breakfast, RR 1, Box 215, 55927, 507-527-2311 |
| Duluth | Ellery House, 28 S. 21st Ave. E., 55812, 218-724-7639 |
| Duluth | Fitzger's Inn, 600 E. Superior St., 55802, 218-722-8826 |
| Duluth | Mansion, 3600 London Rd., 55804, 218-724-0739 |
| Duluth | Mathew S. Burrows 1890 Inn, 1632 E. 1st St., 55812, 218-724-4991 |
| Duluth | Stanford Inn, 1415 Superior St., 55805, 218-724-3044 |
| Dundas | Martin Oaks B&B, P.O. Box 207, 55019, 507-645-4644 |
| Ely | Three Deer Haven, Hwy 169, 55731, 218-365-6464 |
| Excelsior | Christopher Inn, 201 Mill St., 55331, 612-474-6816 |
| Excelsior | Murray Street Gardens B&B, 22520 Murray St., 55331, 612-474-8089 |
| Faribault | Cherub Hill, 101 NW 1st. Ave., 55021, 507-332-2024 |
| Graceville | Lakeside B&B, 113 W. 2nd St., 56240, 612-748-7657 |
| Grand Marais | Gunflint Lodge, 750 Gunflint Trail, 55604, 800-328-3325 |
| Grand Marais | Pincushion Mountain B&B, 220 Gunflint Trail, 55604, 218-387-1276 |
| Grand Marais | Superior Overlook B&B, The, P.O. Box 963, 55604, 218-387-1571 |
| Hastings | Thornwood Historic Inns, 315 Pine, 55033, 612-437-3297 |
| Hendricks | Triple L Farm, Rt. 1, Box 141, 56136, 507-275-3740 |
| Herman | Lawndale Farm, Rt. 2, Box 50, 56248, 612-677-2687 |
| Hinckley | B&B Lodge, Rt. 3, Box 178, 55037, 612-384-6052 |
| Houston | Bunk House, The, 501 S. Jefferson, 55943, 507-896-2080 |
| Hoveland | Trovall's Inn, Box 98, Hwy. 61, 55606, 218-475-2344 |
| Lake City | Evergreen Knoll Acres, Rt. 1, Box 145, 55041, 612-345-2257 |
| Lake City | Pepin House, 120 S. Prairie St., 55041, 612-345-4454 |
| Lake City | Victorian Bed & Breakfast, 620 South High St., 55041, 612-345-2167 |
| Lanesboro | Carrolton Country Inn, RR 2, Box 139, 55949, 507-467-2257 |
| Lanesboro | Historic Scanlan House B&B, 708 Parkway Ave. S., 55949, 507-467-2158 |
| Little Falls | Pine Edge Inn, 308 First St. SE, 56345, 612-632-6681 |
| Little Marais | Stone Hearth Inn, 1118 Highway 61 E., 55614, 218-226-3020 |
| Lutsen | Woods B&B, The, P.O. Box 158, 55612, 218-663-7144 |
| Mabel | Mabel House B&B, 117 S. Main, 55954, 507-493-5768 |
| Mantorville | Grand Old Mansion, 501 Clay St., 55955, 507-635-3231 |
| Marine | Asa Parker House B&B, 17500 St. Croix Trail N, 55047, 612-433-5248 |
| McGregor | Savanna Portage Inn, HCR 4, Box 96, 55760, 218-426-3500 |
| Minneapolis | 1900 Dupont, 1900 Dupont Ave. S., 55403, 612-374-1973 |
| Minneapolis | Elmwood House, 1 East Elmwood Pl., 55423, 612-822-4558 |
| Minneapolis | Le Blanc House, 302 University Ave. NE, 55413, 612-379-2570 |
| Minneapolis | Nicollet Island Inn, 95 Merriam, Nicollet Is, 55401 |
| Morris | American House, The, 410 E. Third St., 56267, 612-589-4054 |
| Nevis | Park Street Inn, The, Rt. 1, Box 254, 56467, 612-599-4763 |
| New Prague | Schumacher's New Prague, 212 W. Main St., 56071, 612-758-2133 |
| North Branch | Red Pine B&B, 15140 400th St., 55056, 612-583-3326 |
| Northfield | Archer House, P.O. Box 676, 55057, 507-645-5661 |
| Owatonna | Northrop House, 358 East Main St., 55060 |
| Park Rapids | Dickson Viking Huss B&B, 202 E. 4th St., 56470, 218-732-8089 |
| Park Rapids | Dorset Schoolhouse, P.O. Box 201, 56470, 218-732-1377 |
| Pequot Lakes | Stonehouse B&B, HCR 2, Box 9, 56472, 218-568-4255 |

| | |
|---|---|
| Pipestone | Calumet Inn, 104 W. Main, 56164, 507-825-5871 |
| Preston | Inn Town Lodge, 205 Franklin St., 55965, 507-765-4412 |
| Preston | Sunnyside at Forestville, RR 2, Box 119, 55965, 507-765-3357 |
| Ray | Bunt's B&B Inns, Lake Kabetogama, 56669, 218-875-2691 |
| Red Wing | Candlelight Inn, The, 818 W. 3rd St., 55066, 612-388-8034 |
| Red Wing | Pratt Taber Inn, 706 W. 4th, 55066, 612-388-5945 |
| Red Wing | St. James Hotel, 406 Main St., 55066, 612-388-2846 |
| Rochester | Canterbury Inn B&B, 723 2nd St. SW, 55902, 507-289-5553 |
| Round Lake | Prairie House Round Lake, RR 1, Box 105, 56167, 507-945-8934 |
| Rush City | Grant House, Box 87, 55069, 612-358-4717 |
| Shafer | Country B&B, 32030 Ranch Tr., 55074, 612-257-4773 |
| Silver Bay | Guest House B&B, 299 Outer Dr., 55614, 218-226-4201 |
| Silver Bay | Inn At Palisade, The, 384 Hwy. 61 E., 55614, 218-226-3505 |
| Silver Bay | Norsk Kubbe Hus, Box 131 B Highway 61 E., 55614, 218-226-4566 |
| Sleepy Eye | Woodland Inn, The, Rt. 4, Box 68, 56085, 507-794-5981 |
| Spicer | Spicer Castle, P.O. Box 307, 56288, 612-796-5870 |
| Spring Grove | Touch Of The Past, 102 3rd Ave. SE, 55974, 507-498-5146 |
| Spring Lake | Anchor Inn, Hwy. 4, RR, 56680, 218-798-2718 |
| St. Charles | Victorian Lace Inn, 1512 Whitewater Ave., 55972, 507-932-3054 |
| St. Joseph | Lamb's B&B, 29738 Island Lake Rd., 56374, 612-363-7924 |
| St. Paul | Chatsworth B&B, 984 Ashland Ave., 55104, 612-227-4288 |
| St. Paul | Como Villa, 1371 W. Nebraska Ave., 55108, 612-647-0471 |
| St. Paul | Desoto at Prior's B&B, 1522 Desoto St., 55101, 612-774-2695 |
| St. Paul | Garden Gate, The, 925 Goodrich Ave., 55105, 612-227-8430 |
| St. Paul | Miller B&B, 887 James Ave., 55102, 612-227-1292 |
| St. Paul | Sunwood Inn, Bandana Sq. 1010 Banda, 55108 |
| St. Paul | University Club, The, 420 Summit Ave., 55102, 612-222-1751 |
| St. Peter | Park Row B&B, 525 W. Park Row, 56082, 507-931-2495 |
| Stacy | Kings Oakdale Park G.H., 6933 232nd Ave NE, 55029, 612-462-5598 |
| Stillwater | Ann Bean House, The, 319 West Pine St., 55082, 612-430-0355 |
| Stillwater | CoverPark Manor, 306 West Olive Street, 55082, 800-562-3632 |
| Stillwater | Heirloom Inn B&B, The, 1103 S. Third St, 55082, 612-430-2289 |
| Stillwater | James A. Mulvey Inn, 622 W. Churchill St., 55082, 612-430-8008 |
| Stillwater | Laurel Street Inn, 210 E. Laurel St., 55082, 612-351-0031 |
| Stillwater | Lowell Inn, 102 N. Second St., 55082, 612-439-1100 |
| Stillwater | Outing Lodge at Pine Pt., 11661 Myeron Rd., 55082, 612-439-9747 |
| Stillwater | Wm. Sauntry Mansion, 626 N. Fourth St, 55082, 612-430-2653 |
| Taylors Falls | Hudspeth House B&B, 21225 Victory Ln., 55084, 612-465-5811 |
| Taylors Falls | Old Jail Company B&B, The, 100 Government Rd, 55084, 612-465-3112 |
| Taylors Falls | Old Taylors Falls Jail, 102 Government Rd., 55084, 612-465-3112 |
| Tyler | Babette's Inn, 308 S. Tyler St., 56178, 507-247-3962 |
| Wabasha | Anderson House, The, 33 W. Main St., 55981, 612-565-4524 |
| Walker | Chase On The Lake Lodge, P.O. Box 206, 56484, 218-547-1531 |
| Walker | Peacecliff, HCR 73, Box 998D, 56484, 218-547-2832 |
| Winona | Carriage House B&B, 420 Main, 55987, 507-452-8256 |

*Mrs. B's*
*Lanesboro Inn,*
*Lanesboro, MN*

# Mississippi

## JACKSON

**Fairview Inn**
734 Fairview St.,   39202
601-948-3429  Fax: 601-948-1203
888-948-1908
Carol & Bill Simmons
All year

$$$
8 rooms, 8 pb
Most CC, *Rated*, •
C-ltd/S-no/P-no/H-yes
French

Full breakfast
Snacks, comp. wine
Dinner (fee)
sitting room, library
special occasion fac.

*Colonial Revival mansion on National Register of Historic Places. Luxury accommodations. Fine dining by reservation. AAA Four Diamond Award.*

## LONG BEACH

| | | |
|---|---|---|
| **Red Creek Vineyard/Stable** | $-B&B | Continental plus bkfst. |
| 7416 Red Creek Rd., Vineyard | 3 rooms, 3 pb | Full bkfast upon request |
| & Racing Stable,  39560 | *Rated*, • | Coffee, afternoon tea |
| 601-452-3080 Fax: 601-452-4450 | C-yes/S-ltd/P-ltd | hot tub, Racing Stable |
| 800-729-9670 | Spanish | golf packages available |
| Karl & Toni Mertz   All year | | |

*Three-story "raised French cottage" w/6 fireplaces, 64-foot porch, and antiques. Amid 11 acres of live oaks & magnolias near beaches. **Seven nights for price of six.***

## LORMAN

| | | |
|---|---|---|
| **Rosswood Plantation** | $$$-B&B | Full breakfast |
| Rt. 2, Box 6,  39096 | 4 rooms, 4 pb | Sitting room, library |
| Hwy. 552 E. | Most CC, *Rated*, • | hot tubs |
| 601-437-4215  Fax: 601-437-6888 | C-yes/S-ltd/P-no/H-ltd | swimming pool |
| 800-533-5889 | German | |
| Jean & Walt Hylander | | |
| March-December | | |

*Authentic columned mansion on working plantation near Natchez, Vicksburg. Heirloom antiques, canopied beds, Civil War history, slave quarters, all conveniences.*

## NATCHEZ

| | | |
|---|---|---|
| **Briars Inn, The** | $$$$-B&B | Full 5-course breakfast |
| P.O. Box 1245,  39120 | 13 rooms, 13 pb | Bar service, snacks |
| 31 Irving Ln. | AmEx, MC, Visa, | Sitting room, library |
| 601-446-9654 Fax: 601-445-6037 | *Rated*, • | swimming pool, porch |
| 800-634-1818 | C-ltd/S-yes/P-no/H-yes | gardens |
| Newton Wilds & R.E. Canon | | |
| All year | | |

*Circa 1812, unique retreat into 19th century splendor with modern amenities. National Register. 19 acres of gardens overlooking Mississippi River. Entirely antique-furnished.*

| | | |
|---|---|---|
| **Linden** | $$$-B&B | Full Southern breakfast |
| 1 Linden Place,  39120 | 7 rooms, 7 pb | Early morning coffee |
| 601-445-5472 Fax: 601-445-5472 | *Rated*, • | Sitting room |
| 800-2-LINDEN | C-ltd/S-yes/P-no/H-yes | piano |
| Jeanette Feltus | | |
| All year | | |

*Antebellum home furnished with family heirlooms. Park-like setting of mossy live oaks. Occupied by same family since 1849. **Free bottle of wine.***

| | | |
|---|---|---|
| **Pleasant Hill** | $$-B&B | Full breakfast |
| 310 S. Pearl St.,  39120 | 5 rooms, 5 pb | Sitting room |
| 601-442-7674 | MC, Visa, • | |
| Brad & Eliza Simonton | C-yes/S-yes/P-no | |
| All year | | |

*Pleasant Hill is a true family antebellum home with antique-filled rooms plus a lovely garden room where breakfast is served.*

## OLIVE BRANCH

| | | |
|---|---|---|
| **Country Goose Inn, The** | $$$-AP | Full breakfast |
| 350 Hwy. 305,  38654 | 15 rooms, 5 pb | Lunch, dinner, aftn. tea |
| 601-895-3098 Fax: 601-893-0700 | Most CC, • | Snacks, comp. wine |
| 800-895-3098 | C-yes/S-yes/P-no/H-no | sitting room, hot tubs |
| Jeanette Martin | French | swimming pool |
| All year | | |

*Small convention facility, lakeside cottages w/picturesque surroundings. Fishing & pedal boating, horseback riding, playground, suitable for leisure or business travel.*

## PASS CHRISTIAN

| | | |
|---|---|---|
| **Inn at the Pass** | $$-B&B | Full gourmet breakfast |
| 125 E. Scenic Dr., 39571 | 5 rooms, 5 pb | Afternoon tea, snacks |
| 601-452-0333 Fax: 601-452-0449 | Visa, MC, *Rated*, • | Sitting rm., guest phone |
| 800-217-2588 | C-ltd/S-ltd/P-yes/H-no | separate cottage, beach |
| Brenda & Vernon Harrison | | cable TV in each room |
| All year | | |

*Victorian Inn on National Historic Register on beach on Mississippi Gulf Coast. Casinos, restaurants, fishing & golf are available. Gourmet breakfast.* **Free bottle of wine.**

## PORT GIBSON

| | | |
|---|---|---|
| **Oak Square** | $$$-B&B | Full breakfast |
| 1207 Church St., 39150 | 11 rooms, 11 pb | Comp. wine & tea |
| 601-437-4350 Fax: 601-437-5768 | Most CC, *Rated*, • | Victorian parlor |
| 800-729-0240 | C-ltd/S-ltd/P-no/H-ltd | piano, TV, courtyard |
| Mr. & Mrs. William D. Lum | | fountain, gazebo |
| All year | | |

*Antebellum mansion in the town General Ulysses S. Grant said was "too beautiful to burn." Heirloom antiques. Canopied beds. Nat'l Register. AAA 4-diamond rated.*

## TUPELO

| | | |
|---|---|---|
| **Mockingbird Inn B&B, The** | $$-B&B | Full breakfast |
| 305 N. Gloster, 38801 | 7 rooms, 7 pb | Snacks |
| 601-841-0286 Fax: 601-840-4158 | Visa, MC, AmEx, Disc., | L-shaped double jacuzzi |
| Jim & Sandy Gilmer | • | sitting room, library |
| All year | C-ltd/S-no/P-yes/H-yes | romance packages |
| | Spanish | |

*Experience the romance of a different place and time with each room representing a different area of the world and a different era in history.*

## VICKSBURG

| | | |
|---|---|---|
| **Cedar Grove Mansion Inn** | $$$-B&B | Full breakfast |
| 2200 Oak St., 2300 | 29 rooms, 20 pb | Restaurant 6pm-9pm |
| Washington St., 39180 | MC, Visa, *Rated*, • | Cocktails, mint juleps |
| 601-636-1000 Fax: 601-634-6126 | C-ltd/S-ltd/H-yes | hot tubs, roof garden |
| 800-862-1300 | Spanish | pool, tennis, croquet |
| Ted Mackey | | |
| All year | | |

*Antebellum mansion, ca. 1840. Exquisitely furnished w/many original antiques, gaslit chandeliers. Tennis court, croquet, river view roof garden. Relive "Gone With the Wind."*

# More Inns . . .

| | |
|---|---|
| Bay St. Louis | Palm House, 217 Union St., 39520, 601-467-1665 |
| Biloxi | Lofty Oaks Inn, 17288 Highway 67, 39532, 601-392-6722 |
| Chatham | Mount Holly, 140 Lake Washington Rd., 38731, 601-827-2652 |
| Church Hill | Cedars, The, Route 2, Box 298, 39120, 601-445-2203 |
| Columbus | Amzi Love B&B, 305 S. 7th St., 39701, 601-328-5413 |
| Columbus | Cartney-Hunt House, 408 S. 7th St., 39701, 601-327-4259 |
| Corinth | Madison Inn, 822 Main St., 38834, 601-287-7157 |
| Fayette | Springfield Plantation, Rt. 1 Box 201, Hwy 553, 39069, 601-786-3802 |
| Hernando | Sassafras Inn B&B, P.O. Box 612, 38632, 800-882-1897 |
| Iuka | Eastport Inn B&B, 100 S. Pearl Street, 38852, 601-423-2511 |
| Jackson | Millsaps Buie House, 628 N. State St., 39202, 601-352-0221 |
| Natchez | Aunt Clara's Cottage, 718 N. Union, 39120, 601-442-9455 |
| Natchez | Aunt Pitty Pat's, 306 S. Rankin, 39120, 601-446-6111 |
| Natchez | Burn, The, 712 N. Union St., 39120, 601-442-1344 |
| Natchez | Camellia Gardens, 506 S. Union St., 39120, 601-446-7944 |
| Natchez | Clifton Heights, 212 Linton Ave., 39120, 601-446-8047 |
| Natchez | Coyle House, 307 S. Wall St., 39120, 601-445-8679 |
| Natchez | Dorsey House, 305 N. Pearl St., 39120, 601-445-4649 |
| Natchez | Dunleith, 84 Homochitto, 39120, 601-446-8500 |
| Natchez | Elgin Plantation, Elgin Rd., Hwy. 61 S., 39120, 601-446-6100 |

| | |
|---|---|
| Natchez | Glen Auburn, 300 S. Commerce St., 39120 |
| Natchez | Glenfield, 6 Providence Rd., 39120,  601-442-1002 |
| Natchez | Governor Holmes House, 207 S. Wall St., 39120,  601-442-2366 |
| Natchez | Guest House Historic Hotel, 201 N. Pearl St., 39120,  601-442-1054 |
| Natchez | Harper House, 201 Arlington, 39120,  601-445-5557 |
| Natchez | Highpoint, 215 Linton Ave., 39120,  601-442-6963 |
| Natchez | Hope Farm, 147 Homochitto St., 39120,  601-445-4848 |
| Natchez | Lenoir Plantation, P.O. Box 1341, 39121 |
| Natchez | Mark Twain On Main, 320 Main, 39120,  601-442-3544 |
| Natchez | Melrose, 136 Melrose Ave., 39120,  601-446-9408 |
| Natchez | Monmouth Plantation, 36 Melrose Ave., 39120,  800-828-4531 |
| Natchez | Mount Repose, P.O. Box 347, 39121 |
| Natchez | Oakland Plantation, 1124 Lower Woodville Rd, 39120,  601-445-5101 |
| Natchez | Oakwood, Upper Kingston Rd., 39120,  601-445-4738 |
| Natchez | Ravenna, S. Union at Ravenna Ln., 39120,  601-446-9973 |
| Natchez | Ravennaside, 601 S. Union St., 39121,  601-442-8015 |
| Natchez | Riverside, 211 Clifton Ave., 39120,  601-446-5730 |
| Natchez | Riverview, 47 New St., 39120,  601-446-6526 |
| Natchez | Shields Town House, P.O. Box 347, 39121 |
| Natchez | Stanton Hall, 401 High St., 39120 |
| Natchez | Sweet Olive Tree Manor, 700 Orleans St., 39120,  601-442-1401 |
| Natchez | T.A.S.S. House, 404 S. Commerce St., 39120,  601-445-4663 |
| Natchez | Texada, P.O. Box 347, 39121 |
| Natchez | The Russell House, 404 N. Union St., 39120,  601-445-7499 |
| Natchez | The William Harris House, 311 Jefferson St., 39120,  601-445-2003 |
| Natchez | Twin Oaks, P.O. Box 347, 39121 |
| Natchez | Wensel House, 206 Washington St., 39120,  601-445-8577 |
| Natchez | Weymouth Hall, P.O. Box 1091, 39121,  601-445-2304 |
| Natchez | White Wings, 311 N. Wall Street, 39120,  601-442-2757 |
| Oxford | ISOM Place, 1003 Jefferson Ave., 39655 |
| Oxford | Oliver-Britt House, 512 Van Buren Av., 38655,  601-234-8043 |
| Port Gibson | Gibson's Landing, P.O. Box 195, 39150,  601-437-3432 |
| Satartia | No-Mistake Plantation B&B, 5602 Hwy 3, 39155 |
| Vicksburg | Anchuca Mansion & Inn, 1010 First East St., 39180,  601-631-6800 |
| Vicksburg | Balfour House, P.O. Box 781, 39181 |
| Vicksburg | Belle of the Bends, The, 508 Klein St., 39181 |
| Vicksburg | Cherry Street Cottage, 2212 Cherry St., 39180 |
| Vicksburg | Corners, The, 601 Klein St., 39180,  601-636-7421 |
| Vicksburg | Duff Green Mansion, The, P.O. Box 75, 39180,  601-636-6968 |
| Vicksburg | Gray Oaks, 4142 Rifle Range Rd., 39180,  601-638-4424 |
| Vicksburg | Tomil Manor, 2430 Drummond St., 39180,  601-638-8893 |
| West | Alexander House, The, P.O. Box 187, 39192,  800-350-8034 |

# Missouri

## BRANSON

| **Branson Hotel B&B Inn** | $$$-B&B | Full gourmet breakfast |
|---|---|---|
| 214 W. Main,  65616 | 9 rooms, 9 pb | Comp. wine, aftern. tea |
| 417-335-6104 | Visa, MC, *Rated*,  • | Sitting room |
| Teri Murguia | C-ltd/S-no/P-no/H-no | two large verandas |
| All year | | guest refrigerator |

*Elegant little hotel where history and romance await you. Antique decor, king and queen beds, cable TV in 5 rooms, guest phones.* **3rd night, 50%.**

| **Brass Swan B&B, The** | $$-B&B | Full breakfast |
|---|---|---|
| 202 River Bend Rd.,  65616 | 4 rooms, 4 pb | Snacks |
| 417-336-3669  Fax: 417-334-6873 | Visa, MC, Disc, *Rated*, | Sitting room |
| 800-280-6873 | • | hot tubs |
| Dick & Gigi House | C-ltd/S-no/P-no/H-no | |
| All year | | |

*Prepare to be pampered in an elegant, contemporary with quiet surroundings yet only minutes away from shows, attractions and shopping.*

BRANSON ───────────────────────────────────────

**Free Man House**            B&B                        Continental plus bkfst.
1773 Lakeshore Dr.,   65616   3 rooms, 3 pb              Hot tubs, swimming pool
417-334-6262                  Most CC, *Rated*,  •       large meeting/conference
Jim & Jennifer Freeman        C-ltd/S-yes/P-no/H-ltd     rooms, family reunions
All year

*Wooded, natural setting on lakefront, yet close to all Branson attractions. Spas, decks, private baths, gardens, swimming pool, sweetheart packages available.*

──────────────────────────────────────────────────

**Josie's Peaceful Getaway**  $$-B&B                     Full breakfast
HCR 1, Box 1104,   65616      3 rooms, 3 pb              Sitting room, hot tubs
Indian Point                  Most CC, *Rated*,  •       lavish spas, fireplaces
417-338-2978  800-289-4125    C-ltd/S-no/P-no/H-no
Bill & JoAnne Coats
All year

*A pristine, expansive lakefront view! Contemporary design w/Victorian decor. Romance & moonlit nights. Celebrate your anniversary, honeymoon.* **5 night stay, 10% discount.**

CAPE GIRARDEAU ────────────────────────────────────

**Bellevue B&B**              $$-B&B                     Full breakfast
312 Bellevue,   63701         4 rooms, 4 pb              Sitting room
314-335-3302  800-768-6822    Visa, MC, AmEx,  •         bicycles
Jackie & Fred Hoelscher       C-yes/S-no/P-no/H-no       family friendly facility
All year

*1891 Queen Anne Victorian faithfully restored, furnished with period antiques.*

DEFIANCE ──────────────────────────────────────────

**Das Gast Haus Nadler**      $$$-B&B                    Full breakfast
125 Defiance Rd,   63341      4 rooms,                   Complimentary wine
314-987-2200                  Most CC,  •                Sitting room, byke trail
Dave & Jacquie Nadler         C-yes/S-ltd/P-yes/H-no     hot tubs, game room
All year                                                 family friendly facility

*Country luxury and relaxation, less than one hour from St. Louis. Located at the gateway of the Missouri River wine country.*

FULTON ────────────────────────────────────────────

**Loganberry Inn**            $$-B&B                     Full gourmet breakfast
310 W. 7th St.,   65251       4 rooms, 4 pb              Comp. wine,
573-642-9229  888-866-6661    MC, Visa, AmEx             Snacks, beverages
Carl & Cathy McGeorge         *Rated*,  •                sitting room
All year                      C-yes/S-no/P-ltd/H-no

*Historic century-old English-style inn within walking distance of Churchill Memorial and quaint shops. Hosted Margaret Thacher in March of 1996. Special event weekends.*

GERALD ────────────────────────────────────────────

**Bluebird B&B**              $$-B&B                     Full/continental bkfsts.
5734 Mill Rock Rd.,   63037   4 rooms, 2 pb              Other meals avail. ask!
573-627-2515                  Visa, MC,  •               Weekend bridge groups
Mary Jane & Don Boettcher     C-ltd/S-no/P-no/H-no       pond fishing, birding
All year                                                 wine country, antiques

*An English country atmosphere in a secluded woodland setting offering wild birds, rivers, caves, antiques, and wine country attractions for the guests.* **Specials, ask; ltd.**

## HANNIBAL

**Fifth Street Mansion B&B**
213 S. Fifth St., 63401
573-221-0445 Fax: 573-221-3335
800-874-5661
Mike Andreotti
All year

$$-B&B
7 rooms, 7 pb
*Rated*, •
C-ltd/S-yes/P-no/H-no

Full breakfast
Complimentary tea
Sitting room
special event weekends
beer & wine licensed

*Italianate Victorian brick mansion; National Historic Register home near historic district. Special events like mystery weekends, craft workshops, and art shows.*

---

**Garth Woodside Mansion**
RR 3, Box 578, 63401
Off Route 61
573-221-2789
Diane & Irv Feinberg
All year

$$-B&B
8 rooms, 8 pb
MC, Visa, *Rated*,
C-ltd/S-ltd

Full breakfast
Comp. tea or hot cider
Library, tour planning
turndown service
guest nightshirts

*Mark Twain was a guest at this 39-acre country estate. Original Victorian furnishings, double jacuzzi. Elegance, privacy, hospitality. **Nov.–April 2nd night free, ltd.***

---

**LulaBelle's Restaurant/ B&B**
111 Bird St., 63401
573-221-6662 800-882-4890
Mike & Pam Ginsberg
All year

$$$-B&B
7 rooms, 5 pb
Most CC,
C-yes/S-yes/P-no/H-no

Full breakfast
Lunch & dinner (fee)
Snacks, restaurant
sitting room, hot tubs
family friendly facility

*Originally built as a bordello in 1917. Newly renovated fine dining restaurant with 7 charming rooms overlooking the Mississippi River.*

## INDEPENDENCE

**Woodstock Inn B&B**
1212 W. Lexington, 64050
816-833-2233
Jan & Dave Quick
All year

$-B&B
11 rooms, 11 pb
MC, Visa, *Rated*, •
C-yes/S-no/P-no/H-yes
German

Full breakfast
Comp. coffee, tea, etc.
Sitting room
National Frontier Trails
Center 6 blocks away

*Enjoy comfort, privacy and tastefully appointed rooms in this century-old renovated bed and breakfast. Individualized breakfasts. Truman, Missouri history sites nearby.*

## KANSAS CITY

**Behm's Plaza Carriage Hse**
4320 Oak, 64111
816-753-4434 888-832-6000
Shirley & Del Behm
All year

$$$-B&B
5 rooms, 5 pb
MC, Visa, •
C-yes/S-ltd/P-no/H-no

Full breakfast
Comp. wine & cheese
Living room, frplc, TV
jacuzzi, side porch, spa
yard, airport shuttle

*1910 Georgian colonial, fully restored w/elegantly appointed suites. Walk to Country Club Plaza & Nelson-Atkins Art Museum. Room w/private hot tub. **Wine & cheese on arrival.***

---

**Brookside House**
6315 Walnut, 64114
913-491-8950 Fax: 913-381-6256
Vern & Brenda Otte
All year

$$$-B&B
3 rooms, 2 pb
C-ltd/S-no/P-no/H-no

Continental plus bkfst.
Complimentary wine
Sitting room

*Unique B&B experience. Entire 3 bedroom, charming Dutch colonial is yours to enjoy alone or w/family and friends. Close to Plaza. **Free bottle of wine, 10% discount after 1 week.***

## KANSAS CITY

| **Doanleigh Wallagh Inn** | $$$-B&B | Full gourmet breakfast |
|---|---|---|
| 217 E. 37th St.,   64111 | 5 rooms, 5 pb | Snacks in pantry |
| 816-753-2667  Fax: 816-531-5185 | Most CC, *Rated*,  • | Facilities for meetings, |
| T. Maturo & C. Brogdon | C-ltd/S-no/P-no/H-no | weddings, TV, Jacuzzis |
| All year | | phone & dataports in rms |

*Located between the Plaza and Crown Center. Georgian mansion with European and American antiques. Comfortable elegance in the heart of the city.*

| **Kelley's B'nB** | $$-B&B | Full family-style bkfst. |
|---|---|---|
| P.O. Box 17602,  64123 | 3 rooms, | Cont. bkfst. if pref. |
| 321 N. Van Brunt Blvd. | C-yes/S-no/P-no/H-no | Highchair, crib |
| 816-483-8126 | | babysitting arranged |
| Jim & Mary Jo Kelley | | phone, cable TV |
| All year | | |

*Large home located minutes from sports, culture, parks, convention centers, riverboat casinos. Comfortable rooms with decor handcrafted like Grandma's place. Refrig/cable TV.*

| **Southmoreland on the Plaza** | $$$-B&B | Full breakfast |
|---|---|---|
| 116 E. 46th St.,   64112 | 12 rooms, 12 pb | Comp. wine, snacks |
| 816-531-7979  Fax: 816-531-2407 | AmEx, MC, Visa, | Courtyard w/lily pond |
| Susan Moehl & Penni | *Rated*,  • | glass enclosed veranda |
| Johnson | C-ltd/S-ltd/P-no/H-yes | dining room w/fireplace |
| All year | | |

*Only B&B on Country Club Plaza, Kansas City's cultural, shopping, entertainment area. Elegantly restored Colonial revival; special services for business & vacation traveler.*

## KANSAS CITY–PLATTE CITY

| **Basswood Country Inn** | $$-B&B | Deluxe Continental bkfst |
|---|---|---|
| 15880 Interurban Rd.,   64079 | 10 rooms, 10 pb | Fishing lakes, trails |
| 816-858-5556  800-242-2775 | MC, Visa, Disc. *Rated*, | gifts, store, pool |
| Don & Betty Soper | • | shuffleboard, horseshoes |
| All year | C-yes/S-yes/P-no/H-ltd | |

*Historic Basswood Lakes; former millionaire's estate. 8 suites plus mother-in-law cottage & tri-plex. Elegant country French; prvt. baths, patios, kitchens, TV/VCR, phones.*

## LABADIE

| **Hunter's Hollow Inn** | $$$-B&B | Continental breakfast |
|---|---|---|
| P.O. Box 127,  63055 | 3 rooms, 3 pb | Full breakfast available |
| Front Street | Visa, MC, AmEx, | Rest., lunch, dinner |
| 314-458-3326  Fax: 314-742-4820 | S-no/P-no/H-yes | Afternoon tea, snacks |
| D. L Wolfsberger | | sitting room |
| All year | | |

*A "special place in the country" combining fine dining with beautiful B&B cottages, located in the wine country. Special attractions nearby.* **Complimentary wine.**

## PARKVILLE

| **Down to Earth Lifestyles** | $$-B&B | Full breakfast |
|---|---|---|
| 12500 N. Crooked Rd., Route | 4 rooms, 4 pb | Drink on arrival, wine |
| 22,  64152 | • | Sitting room, piano |
| 816-891-1018 | C-yes/S-yes/H-yes | organ, entertainment |
| Lola & Bill Coons | | indoor heated pool |
| All year | | |

*Unique new earth-contact home designed for guests. Private baths, telephones, indoor pool. Closed-in country setting between Kansas City and airport.* **Complimentary drinks and popcorn.**

POINT LOOKOUT ─────────────────────────────────

| **Cameron's Crag** | $$-B&B | Full hearty breakfast |
|---|---|---|
| P.O. Box 526, 65726 | 3 rooms, 3 pb | One suite with kitchen |
| 738 Acacia Club Rd. | Visa, • | Video lib., area sites |
| 417-335-8134  Fax: 417-335-8134 | C-ltd/S-no/P-no/H-no | private entrance & tubs |
| 800-933-8529 | | hot tubs, cable TV/VCR |
| Kay & Elen Cameron | | |
| All year | | |

*Contemporary hideaway on bluff overlooking Lake Taneycomo. Fantastic views! Three separate guest areas, delightful accommodations.* **Stay 3 nights, $10 off each night.**

ROCHEPORT, COLUMBIA ──────────────────────────

| **School House B&B** | $$$-B&B | Full breakfast |
|---|---|---|
| P.O. Box 88, 65279 | 10 rooms, 10 pb | Bicycles, swing, library |
| 504 Third St. | MC, Visa, *Rated*, • | Two rooms have Jacuzzis |
| 573-698-2022 | C-ltd/S-no/P-no/H-no | nature/bike trails |
| John & Vicki Ott, P. Province | French, Spanish | |
| All year | | |

*Historic 3-story brick school building magnificently restored into a 10-room inn. Furnished w/antiques & school memory charm. Local winery, shops, cafes.* **3rd night 50% off.**

SPRINGFIELD ──────────────────────────────────

| **Walnut Street Inn** | $$$-B&B | Full breakfast |
|---|---|---|
| 900 E. Walnut St., 65806 | 12 rooms, 12 pb | Bear & wine available |
| 417-864-6346  Fax: 417-864-6184 | Most CC, *Rated*, • | Sitting room |
| 800-593-6346 | C-yes/S-no/P-ltd/H-yes | hot tubs |
| Gary & Paula Blankenship | | tennis nearby |
| All year | | |

*1894 Victorian showcase inn in Historic District. Gourmet breakfast; walking distance to shops, theatre, live music.* **Corp. acct. discount, ltd.**

ST. LOUIS ─────────────────────────────────────

| **Doelling Haus** | $$-B&B | Full breakfast |
|---|---|---|
| 4817 Towne South, 63128 | 3 rooms, 1 pb | Afternoon tea, snacks |
| 314-894-6796 | MC, Visa, *Rated*, • | Sitting room |
| Carol & David Doelling | C-yes/S-ltd/P-ltd/H-no | color TV & A/C in rooms |
| All year | German | large suite avail. |

*European country flavor. A private home furnished w/antiques, quilts and linens. Homemade truffles and a comfortable atmosphere await your arrival. Very accessible.* **3+nights discount; Corporate discount.**

| **Eastlake Inn B&B** | $$-B&B | Full gourmet breakfast |
|---|---|---|
| 703 N. Kirkwood Rd., 63122 | 3 rooms, 3 pb | Outdoor patios, porch |
| 314-965-0066  Fax: 314-965-0066 | MC, Visa, • | perennial gardens |
| Lori Murray | C-yes/S-no/P-no/H-no | |
| All year | | |

*1920 colonial decorated with Eastlake Victorian furniture. 20 minutes from St. Louis. Walk to antique shops!* **Local restaurant discounts.**

| **Lafayette House B&B** | $$-B&B | Full gourmet breakfast |
|---|---|---|
| 2156 Lafayette Ave., 63104 | 5 rooms, 2 pb | Afternoon tea, snacks |
| 314-772-4429  Fax: 314-664-2156 | Most CC, *Rated*, • | Sitting room |
| 800-641-8965 | C-ltd/S-ltd/P-ltd/H-no | library, cable TV, VCR |
| Bill, Nancy & Anna | | crib available, A/C |
| All year | | |

*Old world charm overlooking historic Lafayette Park. In the center of things to do! Delightful gourmet breakfast.*

ST. LOUIS ─────────────────────────────────────────

| | | |
|---|---|---|
| **Preston Place** | $$-B&B | Full & Cont. breakfast |
| 1835 Lafayette Ave., 63104 | 2 rooms, 2 pb | Snacks |
| 314-664-3429 Fax: 314-664-6929 | Most CC, • | Sitting room |
| Jenny Preston | S-no/P-no/H-no | |
| All year | French | |

*Richly hued, uncluttered Victorian rooms, large private baths, clawfoot tub. Downtown location, phone and Fax. Especially comfortable for businesswomen.*

| | | |
|---|---|---|
| **Soulard Inn, The** | $$-B&B | Full breakfast |
| 1014 Lami, 63104 | 4 rooms, | Aft. tea, snacks |
| 314-773-3002 | *Rated*, • | Sitting room |
| Raymond Ellerbeck | S-yes/H-no | bicycles, transportation |
| All year | | from bus, airport, train |

*The Soulard Inn is one of the oldest buildings in St. Louis. Only moments away from blues & jazz music & restaurants. **3rd night 50% off.***

| | | |
|---|---|---|
| **Winter House, The** | $$-B&B | Full breakfast |
| 3522 Arsenal St., 63118 | 3 rooms, 3 pb | Comp. refreshments |
| 314-664-4399 | Most CC, *Rated*, • | Sitting room, AC |
| Kendall | C-yes/S-ltd/P-no/H-no | suite w/balcony, piano |
| All year except Xmas | | near shops & restaurants |

*1897 Victorian 10-room house with turret. Hand-squeezed O.J. and live piano at breakfast by reservation. Near Missouri Botanical Gardens and fine restaurants. **After 2nd night 10%.***

STE. GENEVIEVE ──────────────────────────────────────

| | | |
|---|---|---|
| **Inn St. Gemme Beauvais** | $$-B&B | Full breakfast |
| 78 N. Main, Box 231, 63670 | 8 rooms, 8 pb | Tea, hors d' oeuvres |
| 573-883-5744 Fax: 573-883-3899 | MC, *Rated*, • | Beer and wine garden |
| 800-818-5744 | C-yes/S-yes/P-no/H-no | special packages avail. |
| Janet Joggerst | | free bicycles, jacuzzis |
| All year | | |

*Charming little Victorian inn located just one hour from St. Louis in small historic French town. Within walking distance of all restored French homes. **3rd night free, ltd.***

| | | |
|---|---|---|
| **Main Street Inn B&B** | $$-B&B | Full breakfast |
| P.O. Box 307, 63670 | 7 rooms, 7 pb | Snacks, comp. wine |
| 221 N. Main St | Most CC, • | Sitting room |
| 573-883-9199 800-918-9199 | C-ltd/S-no/P-no/H-no | |
| Ken & Karen Kulberg | Some French | |
| All year | | |

*1880s inn even husbands enjoy. Antique furniture but free of clutter and country cute. Substantial gourmet breakfasts. Herb & flower garden. **3rd night 50% off.***

TRENTON ─────────────────────────────────────────

| | | |
|---|---|---|
| **Hyde Mansion B&B** | $$-B&B | Full breakfast |
| 418 E. 7th St., 64683 | 5 rooms, 5 pb | Comp. beverages, snacks |
| 816-359-5631 Fax: 816-359-5632 | AmEx, MC, Visa, | Sitting room, library |
| Robert & Carolyn Brown | C-ltd/S-ltd/P-no/H-no | Baby grand piano, patio |
| All year | | screened porch, bicycles |

*Inviting hideaway in rural America, 1949 mansion refurbished for your convenience. Close to Amish country, serves full breakfast*

WARRENSBURG ────────────────────────────────

**Cedarcroft Farm B&B**
431 S.E. "Y" Hwy., 64093
816-747-5728  800-368-4944
Sandra & Bill Wayne
All year

$$-B&B
2 rooms, 2 pb
Most CC, *Rated*, •
C-yes/S-ltd/P-no/H-no

Full breakfast
Lunch, dinner by arrang.
Comp. tea, evening snack
sitting room, parlor
hiking, horseback riding

*Country hospitality, country quiet, more-than-you-can-eat at National Register 1867 farm, 80 acres to roam. Can demo Civil War items. 2-bedroom suites sleeps up to 8.* **20% off 3rd night.**

WASHINGTON ────────────────────────────────

**Schwegmann House B&B**
**Inn**
438 W. Front St., 63069
314-239-5025  Fax: 314-239-3920
800-949-2262
Cathy & Bill Nagel
All year

$$-B&B
9 rooms, 9 pb
MC, Visa, AmEx,
*Rated*, •
C-ltd/S-no/P-no/H-yes

Full breakfast delivered
Thermo massage tub for 2
sitting room, river view
handmade quilts, bicycle

*Missouri Wine Country w/11 wineries & historic communities. Rekindles local flour miller's hospitality of more than 100 years ago. Business meetings.* **Comp. bottle of wine, weekday getaway packages.**

**Washington House B&B**
100 W. Front St., 3 Lafayette
St., 63090
314-742-4360
Mary Imergoot & Sue Black
All year

$$-B&B
2 rooms, 2 pb
Most CC,
C-yes/H-yes

Full breakfast
Cheese, teas, coffees
Sitting room

*Our historic 1837 inn on the Missouri River features antique furnishings and decor, queen-size canopy beds, river views, country breakfasts. Balcony and terrace on riverside.*

## More Inns ...

| | |
|---|---|
| Arrow Rock | Borgman's B&B,  706 Van Buren, 65320,  816-837-3350 |
| Arrow Rock | Cedar Grove B&B/Antiques, Cedar Grove, 65320,  816-837-3441 |
| Arrow Rock | DownOver Inn,  602 Main St., 65320,  816-837-3268 |
| Bonne Terre | 1909 Depot,  Oak St. at Allen St., 63628,  314-731-5003 |
| Boonville | Morgan Street Repose,  611 E. Morgan St., 65233,  816-882-7195 |
| Bourbon | Wildflower Inn, The,  Route 2, Box 101, 65441,  314-468-7975 |
| Branson | Aunt Sadie's Garden Glade,  163 Fountain St., 65616,  417-335-4063 |
| Branson | Barger House B&B,  621 Lakeshore Dr., 65616,  800-266-2134 |
| Branson | Branson House B&B Inn, The,  120 Fourth St., 65616,  417-334-0959 |
| Branson | Emory Creek B&B,  143 Arizona Dr., 65616,  417-334-3805 |
| Branson | Fall Creek B&B,  4988 Fall Creek Rd., 65616,  417-334-3939 |
| Branson | Gaines Landing B&B,  P.O. Box 1369, 65616,  800-825-3145 |
| Branson | Inn at Fall Creek B&B,  391 Concord Ave., 65616,  417-336-3422 |
| Branson | Peaceful Getaway, The,  HCR1, Box 1104, 65616,  417-338-2978 |
| Branson | Rhapsody Inn B&B,  296 Blue Meadows Rd., 65616,  417-335-2442 |
| Branson | Schroll's Lakefront B&B,  418 N. Sycamore St., 65616,  417-335-6759 |
| Branson | Show Me Hospitality,  163 Fountain St., 65616,  417-335-4063 |
| Branson | The Brass Swan B&B,  202 River Bend, 65616,  417-334-6873 |
| Branson | Thurman House B&B,  888 State Hwy. F, 65616,  417-334-6000 |
| Branson | We Lamb Farm,  P.O. Box 338, 65615,  417-334-1485 |
| Camdenton | Ramblewood B&B,  402 Panoramic Dr., 65020,  314-346-3410 |
| Cape Fair | Fantasea Inn,  P.O. Box 123, 65624,  417-538-2742 |
| Carthage | Brewer's Maple Lane Farms,  RR #1, 64836,  417-358-6312 |
| Carthage | Grand Avenue Inn,  1615 Grand Ave., 64836,  417-358-7265 |
| Carthage | Maple Lane Farms,  RR 1, 64836 |
| Columbia | Parkview Farm,  13 Garrison Dr., 65201,  816-664-2744 |
| Eminence | Eminence Cottage & Brkfst,  P.O. Box 276, 65466,  314-226-3642 |
| Eminence | River's Edge B&B Resort,  HCR 1, Box 11, 65466,  314-226-3233 |
| Ethel | Recess Inn,  203 E. Main, 63539,  816-486-3328 |
| Excelsior Springs | Crescent Lake Manor B&B,  1261 St. Louis St., 64024,  816-637-2958 |
| Hannibal | Victorian Guest House,  #3 Stillwell, 63401,  314-221-3093 |
| Hermann | Aunt Flora's B&B,  127 E. 5th St., 65041,  314-486-3591 |

| | |
|---|---|
| Hermann | Birk's Goethe St. Gasthaus, P.O. Box 255, 65041, 314-486-2911 |
| Hermann | Das Brownhaus, RR 3 Box 20C, 65041, 314-486-3372 |
| Hermann | Das Rheinhaus B&B, 126 W. 2nd St., 65041, 314-486-3976 |
| Hermann | Die Hillig Heimat, HCR62 Box 30, 65041, 314-943-6942 |
| Hermann | Esther's Ausblick, 236 W. 2nd St., 65041, 314-486-2170 |
| Hermann | Lark's Nest B&B, HCR 62, Box 102B, 65041, 314-943-6305 |
| Hermann | Market Street B&B, 210 Market St., 65041, 314-486-5597 |
| Hermann | Meyer's Hilltop Farm B&B, RR3, Box 16, 65041, 314-486-5778 |
| Hermann | Mumbrauer Gasthaus, 223 E. 2nd St., 65041, 314-486-5246 |
| Hermann | Schmidt Guesthouse, 300 Market, 65041, 314-486-2146 |
| Hermann | Strassner Suites, 132 E. 4th St., 65041, 314-486-2682 |
| Hermann | White House Hotel-1868-, 232 Wharf St., 65041, 314-468-3200 |
| Hermann | William Klinger Inn, P.O. Box 116, 65041, 314-486-5930 |
| Hollister | Red Bud Cove B&B, 162 Lakewood Dr., 65672, 417-334-7144 |
| Hollister | Ye English Inn, 24 Downing St., 65672, 417-334-4142 |
| Jackson | Trisha's B&B & Tea Room, 203 Bellevue, 63755, 314-243-7427 |
| Jamesport | Richardson House B&B, North Street, 64648, 816-842-4211 |
| Joplin | Visages B&B, 327 N. Jackson, 64801, 417-624-1397 |
| Kansas City | Dome Ridge B&B, 14360 N.W. Walker Rd., 64164, 816-532-4074 |
| Kansas City | Milford House B&B, 3605 Gillham Rd., 64111, 816-753-1269 |
| Kansas City | Pridewell, 600 W. 59th St., 64112, 816-931-1642 |
| Kimberling City | Cinnamon Hill B&B, 24 Wildwood Lane, 65686, 417-739-5727 |
| Kimmswick | Wenom-Drake House, The, P.O. Box 125, 63053, 314-464-1983 |
| Lake Ozark | Shawnee Bluff, Route 72, Box 14-2, 65049, 314-365-2442 |
| Lampe | Grandpa's Farm, Box 476, HCR 1, 65681, 417-779-5106 |
| Lexington | Linwood Lawn B&B Inn, Route 2, Box 192, 64067 |
| Liberty | James Inn, 342 N. Water, 64068, 800-781-3677 |
| Libery | WynBrick Inn, 1701 WynBrick Dr., 64068, 816-781-4900 |
| Lonedell | Peppermint Spings Farm, P.O. Box 240, Hwy FF, 64067, 314-629-7018 |
| Louisiana | Meadowcrest B&B, Route 1, Box 193-A, 63353 |
| Marshfield | Dickey House B&B, The, 331 S. Clay St., 65706, 417-468-3000 |
| Marthasville | Gramma's House, 1105 Highway D, 63357, 314-433-2675 |
| Mexico | Hylas House B&B Inn, 811 S. Jefferson, 65265, 314-581-2011 |
| Mountain View | Jack's Fork Country Inn, Route 1 Box 347, 65548, 805-934-1000 |
| Mountain View | Merrywood Guest House, P.O. Box 42, 65548, 417-934-2210 |
| Nevada | Red Horse Inn, 217 S. Main St., 64772, 417-667-7796 |
| Nixa | Country View B&B, Route 3, Box 593, 65714, 417-725-1927 |
| Paris | Jackson House, 409 W. Caldwell, 65275, 816-327-4283 |
| Perryville | Pecan Corner B&B, 919 Sunset Dr., 63775, 314-883-7171 |
| Reeds Spring | Journey's End B&B, HCR 6, Box 4632, 65737, 417-338-2685 |
| Reeds Spring | Martindale B&B, HCR 4, Box 3570, 65737, 417-338-2588 |
| Rocheport | Roby River Run, 201 N. Roby Farm Rd., 65279, 314-698-2173 |
| Sedalia | Sedalia House Country B&B, Rt 4, Box 25, 65301, 816-826-6615 |
| St. Charles | Boone's Lick Trail Inn, 1000 So. Main St., 63301, 314-947-7000 |
| St. Charles | Saint Charles House B&B, 338 S. Main St., 63301, 314-946-6221 |
| St. Joseph | Harding House B&B, 219 N. 20th St., 64501, 816-232-7020 |
| St. Joseph | Schuster-Rader Mansion, 703 Hall St., 64501, 816-279-9464 |
| St. Louis | Geandaugh House B&B, 3835-37 S. Broadway, 63118, 314-771-5447 |
| St. Louis | Lehmann House B&B, #10 Benton Place, 63104, 314-231-6724 |
| St. Louis | Lemp Mansion Inn, 3322 DeMenil Pl., 63141, 314-664-8024 |
| St. Louis | Mansion Hill Country Inn, 11215 Natural Bridge, 63044, 314-731-5003 |
| St. Louis | Seven Gables Inn, 26 N. Meramec, 63105, 314-863-8400 |
| Ste. Genevieve | Creole House B&B, 339 St. Mary's Rd., 63670, 800-275-6041 |
| Ste. Genevieve | Hotel Sainte Genevieve, Main & Merchant Sts., 63670, 314-883-2737 |
| Ste. Genevieve | Mansion At Elfindale, The, 1701 S. Fort, 65807, 417-831-5400 |
| Ste. Genevieve | Southern Hotel, 146 S. Third St., 63670, 800-275-1412 |
| Ste. Genevieve | Steiger Haus, 1021 Market St., 63670, 314-883-5881 |
| Sullivan | Whip Haven Farm, R.R. 1, Box 395, 63080, 314-627-3717 |
| Versailles | The Hilty Inn, 206 E. Jasper, 65084, 314-378-2020 |
| Walnut Shade | Light in the Window B&B, 8007 Hwy. 160, 65771, 417-561-2415 |
| Weston | Benner House B&B, 645 Main St., 64098, 816-386-2616 |
| Weston | Hatchery, The, 618 Short St., 64098, 816-386-5700 |
| Zanoni | Zanoni MIll Inn, P.O. Box 2, 65784, 417-679-4050 |

# Montana

BIG SKY ───────────────────────────────────────

| | | |
|---|---|---|
| **Lone Mountain Ranch** | $$$-AP | All meals included |
| P.O. Box 160069, 59716 | 23 rooms, 23 pb | Winter sleighride dinner |
| 406-995-4644 Fax: 406-995-4670 | MC, Visa, *Rated*, | Bar, sitting room |
| 800-514-4644 | C-yes/S-no/P-no/H-ltd | hot tub, horses |
| Bob & Vivian Schaap   All yr | | weekly rates |

*Historic guest ranch offering family vacations and Nordic ski vacations near Yellowstone National Park. Beautiful log cabins with fireplaces, conveniences. Yellowstone Park tours.*

BIGFORK ───────────────────────────────────────

| | | |
|---|---|---|
| **Burggraf's Countrylane B&B** | $$$-B&B | Full breakfast |
| | 5 rooms, 5 pb | Comp. wine/cheese/fruit |
| Rainbow Dr., Swan Lk, 59911 | MC, Visa *Rated*, • | Picnic baskets avail. |
| 406-837-4608 Fax: 406-837-2468 | C-ltd/S-ltd/P-no/H-yes | lake, snowmobile rental |
| 800-525-3344 | | boating, canoe, jacuzzi |
| Natalie J. Burggraf  May-Sept | | |

*True log home nestled in heart of Rocky Mt; 7 acres on the shores of Swan Lake; panoramic view; country breakfast. Lawn croquet & putting green.* **10% off stay, 4+ nites**

BOZEMAN ───────────────────────────────────────

| | | |
|---|---|---|
| **Fox Hollow B&B** | $$-B&B | Full breakfast |
| 545 Mary Rd., 59715 | 5 rooms, 5 pb | Dinner (fee), snacks |
| 406-582-8440 Fax: 406-582-8440 | Most CC, • | Sitting room |
| 800-431-5010 | C-ltd/S-no/P-no/H-no | hot tubs |
| Nancy & Michael Dawson | | art gallery |
| All year | | |

*"Without equal-by far the best B&B we have ever stayed in." Jay & Sue, Boca Raton, FL.*

| | | |
|---|---|---|
| **Hyalite Creek Guesthouse** | $$$-EP | Near Yellowstone Park |
| P.O. Box 4308, 59715 | 2 rooms, 2 pb | |
| 406-585-0557 Fax: 406-585-2869 | Visa, MC, • | |
| 800-522-7097 | C-yes/S-no/P-no/H-no | |
| Paula Diegert   All year | | |

*Handsome cedar guesthouse located on wooded creek only minutes from Bozeman, golf, mountain hiking. One and a half hours from Yellowstone National Park.*

| | | |
|---|---|---|
| **Torch & Toes B&B** | $$$-B&B | Full breakfast |
| 309 S. 3rd Ave., 59715 | 4 rooms, 4 pb | Comp.limentary sherry |
| 406-586-7285  800-446-2138 | MC, Visa, *Rated*, • | Sitting room, library |
| Ron & Judy Hess | C-yes/S-no/P-no/H-no | bicycles, porch swing |
| All year | | 6 person carriage house |

*A friendly cat, a gourmet breakfast and unique collections of dolls, mouse traps, and brass rubbings make for a pleasant stay. Nearby skating, band concerts, and market.*

| | | |
|---|---|---|
| **Voss Inn** | $$$-B&B | Full breakfast in parlor |
| 319 S. Willson, 59715 | 6 rooms, 6 pb | Or guest room, aftn. tea |
| 406-587-0982 Fax: 406-585-2964 | Most CC, *Rated*, • | Sitt. rm, parlour, piano |
| Bruce & Frankee Muller | C-ltd/S-ltd/P-no/H-no | trips to Yellowstone Prk |
| All year | | fax/copy machines avail. |

*Warm, elegant historic Victorian mansion beautifully decorated w/period wallpaper & furniture. Walk to university, museums, restaurants, shopping.* **Champagne for honeymooners.**

*The Hostetler House B&B, Glendive, MT*

## CHOTEAU

**Country Lane B&B**
Route 2, Box 232, 59422
406-466-2816 505-865-4412
Ann Arensmeyer
May 15-October 1

$$-B&B
5 rooms, 1 pb
Visa, MC, *Rated*, •
C-ltd/S-no/P-no/H-no

Full breakfast
Snacks
Sitting room
indoor pool, gift shop
hiking nearby, TV, VCR

*Contemporary split level 5,000 square foot country home; cedar/shake construction, private entrance, indoor solar-heated pool, gift shop.*

## COLUMBIA FALLS

**Bad Rock Country B&B**
480 Bad Rock Dr., 59912
406-892-2829 Fax: 406-892-2930
800-422-3666
Jon & Sue Alper
All year

$$$-B&B
7 rooms, 7 pb
Most CC, *Rated*, •
C-ltd/S-no/P-ltd/H-yes

Full breakfast
Complimentary wine/snack
Afternoon tea, hot tubs
sitting room, library
small groups facility

*Four stunning rooms made of hand-hewn square logs, with fireplaces, three beautiful rooms in the home, Old West antiques. Twenty minutes to Glacier National Park.*

## GLENDIVE

**Hostetler House B&B, The**
113 N. Douglas St., 59330
406-365-4505 Fax: 406-365-8456
Craig & Dea Hostetler
All year

$$-B&B
2 rooms,
Visa, MC, Disc., •
C-ltd/S-no/P-no/H-no
Basic German

Full breakfast
Snacks
Sitting room
bikes, tennis court
hot tub

*Charming 1912 historic home with two comfortable guest rooms in casual country. Hot tub, sitting room, sun porch, full breakfast.* **3rd night, 50%.**

## HAMILTON

**Deer Crossing B&B**
396 Hayes Creek Rd., 59840
406-363-2232 800-763-2232
Mary Lynch
All year

$$-B&B
5 rooms, 3 pb
Visa, MC, •
C-yes/S-ltd/P-ltd/H-no

Full country breakfast
Afternoon tea, snacks
Lunch & dinner available
fishing guide, shuttle
horseback riding

*Experience Old West charm & hospitality. 24 acres of pines/pasture. Incredible views. Hearty ranch breakfast. Luxury suites w/double jacuzzi tub.* **10% discount- week long stay.**

## RED LODGE

**Willows Inn**
P.O. Box 886,  59068
224 S. Platt Ave.
406-446-3913
Kerry & Carolyn Boggio
All year

$$-B&B
6 rooms, 4 pb
MC, Visa,  •
C-yes/S-no/P-no/H-no
Finnish, Spanish

Continental plus
Gourmet picnics avail.
TV/VCR parlor w/movies
games/books, local menus
ski racks, sun decks

*Charming Victorian. Delicious homebaked pastries. Spectacular mountain scenery. Yellowstone Park; ski, fish, hike, golf, bike. 2 cottages. **Free wine for honeymoon/anniversary.***

## RONAN

**Timbers B&B, The**
1184 Timberlane Rd.,  59864
406-676-4373  Fax: 406-676-4370
800-775-4373
Doris & Leonard McCravey
Jan.3-Dec.18

$$-B&B
2 rooms, 1 pb
Visa, MC, *Rated*,  •
C-ltd/S-no/P-no/H-no

Full breakfast
Complimentary wine/snack
Hiking, whitewater raft.
sitting room, BBQ garden
library

*Stunning contemporary inn; spectacular mountain views; borders wilderness area, whitewater rafting, horses, Flathead Lake, Nat'l. Bison Range. **One week stay, 10% off.***

## WEST YELLOWSTONE

**Sportsman's High B&B**
750 Deer St.,  59758
406-646-7865 Fax: 406-646-9434
Diana & Gary Baxter
All year

$$$-B&B
5 rooms, 5 pb
MC, Visa, AmEx
*Rated*,
C-ltd/S-no/P-no/H-no

Full gourmet breakfast
Sitting room, FAX
library, wildlife
hot tub, mountains

*Eight miles from Yellowstone Park you'll find country charm at its best amidst aspen and pines, with close and personal views of mountains. Family guest houses available.*

## WHITEFISH

**Good Medicine Lodge**
537 Wisconsin Ave.,  59937
406-862-5488 Fax: 406-862-5489
800-860-5488
Christopher & Susan Ridder
All year

$$-B&B
9 rooms, 9 pb
Visa, MC, *Rated*,  •
C-yes/S-no/P-no/H-yes
German, French

Continental plus bkfst.
Guest bar, no alcohol
Ski boot & glove dryers
hot tubs, library, A/C
sitt. rm., guest laundry

*A classic Montana getaway. Built of solid cedar; has balconies with stunning views, crackling fireplaces, outdoor spa and loads of western hospitality. **Senior discount.***

# More Inns . . .

| | |
|---|---|
| Alberton | Montana Hotel B&B,  Box 423, 59820 |
| Big Sandy | Sky View,  Box 408, 59520,  406-378-2549 |
| Big Timber | Grand Hotel, The,  P.O. Box 1242, 59011,  406-932-4459 |
| Big Timber | Lazy K Bar Ranch,  Box 550, 59011,  406-537-4404 |
| Bigfork | Deck House, The,  Box 865, 59911 |
| Bigfork | Gustin Orchard,  East Lake Shore, 59911,  406-982-3329 |
| Bigfork | Gustin Orchard B&B,  E. Lake Shore, 59911,  406-982-3329 |
| Bigfork | Jubilee Orchards Lake Reso,  836 Sylvan Dr., 59911,  406-837-4256 |
| Bigfork | O'Duachain Country Inn,  675 Ferndale Rd., 59911,  406-837-6851 |
| Bigfork | Schwartz's B&B,  890 McCaffery Rd., 59911,  406-837-5463 |
| Billings | Josephine, The,  514 N. 29th St., 59101 |
| Billings | PJ's B&B,  722 N. 29th St., 59101,  406-259-3300 |
| Bozeman | B&B Western Adventure,  P.O. Box 4308, 59772,  406-259-7993 |
| Bozeman | Kirk Hill B&B,  7960 S. 19th Rd., 59715,  406-586-3929 |
| Bozeman | Lehrkind Mansion,  719 N. Wallace, 59715,  406-586-1214 |
| Bozeman | Lindley House,  202 Lindley Pl., 59715,  406-587-8403 |
| Bozeman | Millers of Montana B&B,  1002 Zacharia Lane, 59715,  406-763-4102 |
| Bozeman | Silver Forest Inn,  15325 Bridger Canyon Rd., 59715,  406-586-1882 |
| Bozeman | Sun House B&B,  9986 Happy Acres West, 59715,  406-587-3651 |
| Broadus | Oakwood Lodge,  S. Pumpkin Creek Rd., 59317 |

| | |
|---|---|
| Butte | Copper King Mansion, 219 W. Granite St., 59701 |
| Butte | Scott B&B, 15 W. Copper, 59701, 800-844-2952 |
| Cameron | Cliff Lake Lodge, P.O. Box 573, 59720, 406-682-4982 |
| Columbia Falls | La Villa Montana, 3800 Hwy. 40, 59912, 800-652-8455 |
| Columbia Falls | Plum Creek House, 985 Vans Ave., 59912 |
| Columbia Falls | Turn in the River Inn, 51 Penny Ln., 59912 |
| Condon | Holland Lake Lodge, S.R. Box 2083, 59826, 800-648-8859 |
| Conner | Bunky Ranch Outfitters, P.O. Box 215, 59827, 406-821-3312 |
| Darby | Triple Creek Ranch, 5551 W. Fork Route, 59829, 406-821-4664 |
| De Borgia | Hotel Albert, P.O. Box 300186, 59830, 406-678-4303 |
| East Glacier | Bison Creek Ranch, Box 144, 59434 |
| Emigrant | Paradise Gateway B&B, P.O. Box 84, 59027, 800-541-4113 |
| Eureka | Trail's End B&B, 57 Trail's End Rd., 59917, 406-889-3486 |
| Gallatin | Gallatin Gateway Inn, P.O. Box 376, 59730 |
| Gardiner | Yellowstone Suites B&B, 506 4th St. (Box 277), 59030, 800-948-7937 |
| Great Falls | Chalet, The, 1204 — 4th Ave. N., 59401, 406-452-9001 |
| Great Falls | Murphy's House B&B, 2020 Fifth Ave. North, 59401 |
| Great Falls | Sovekammer B&B, The, 1109 Third Ave. N., 59401, 406-453-6620 |
| Hamilton | Bavarian Farmhouse B&B, 163 Bowman Rd., 59840, 406-363-4063 |
| Helena | Barrister B&B, 416 N. Ewing, 59601 |
| Helena | Sanders-Helena B&B, The, 328 N. Ewing, 59601, 406-442-3309 |
| Helena | St. James B&B, The, 114 N. Hoback, 59601, 406-449-2623 |
| Helena | Upcountry Inn, 2245 Head Ln., 59601, 406-442-1909 |
| Huson | Schoolhouse and Teacherage, 9 Mile, 59846, 406-626-5879 |
| Huson | Whispering Pines, Box 36, 59846, 406-626-5664 |
| Kalispell | Blaine Creek B&B, 727 Van Sant Rd., 59901 |
| Kalispell | Bonnie's B&B, 265 Lake Blaine Rd., 59901 |
| Kalispell | Creston Inn, 70 Creston Rd., 59901, 800-257-7517 |
| Kalispell | Logan House B&B, 528 Woodland Ave., 59901 |
| Kalispell | River Rock B&B, 179 Schrade Rd., 59901 |
| Kalispell | Stillwater Inn B&B, 206 Fourth Ave. East, 59901, 800-398-7024 |
| Kalispell | Switzer House Inn, 205 Fifth Ave. East, 59901, 406-257-5837 |
| Kalispell | Whitney Mansion, The, 538 Fifth Ave., 59901, 800-426-3214 |
| Lakeside | Angel Point Guest Suites, Box 768, 59922 |
| Lakeside | Shoreline Inn, P.O. Box 568, 59922, 800-645-0255 |
| Libby | Bobtail B&B, 4909 Bobtail Rd., 59923, 406-293-3926 |
| Libby | Kootenai Country Inn, The, 264 Mack Rd., 59923, 406-293-7878 |
| Livingston | Davis Creek, Rt. 38, Box 2179, 59047, 406-333-4353 |
| Livingston | Remember When B&B, 320 S. Yellowstone, 59047, 406-222-8367 |
| Loma | Virgelle Merc., Rural Route 1, 59460, 800-426-2926 |
| Marion | Hargrave Cattle House, Thompson River Valley, 59925, 406-858-2284 |
| Marion | Rocky Meadow Ranch, 400 Lower Lost Prairie, 59925 |
| Missoula | Colonial House, 13655 Turah Rd., 59825 |
| Missoula | Goldsmith Inn, 809 E. Front, 59802, 406-721-6732 |
| Missoula | Gracenote Garden, 1558 S. 6th St., 59801 |
| Missoula | Greenough B&B, 631 Stephens, 59801 |
| Nevada City | Nevada City Hotel, 59755, 406-843-5377 |
| Noxon | Bighorn Lodge, 710 Bull River Rd., 59853, 406-847-5597 |
| Polson | Hammond's B&B, 10141 East Shore, 59860, 406-887-2766 |
| Polson | Hawthorne House B&B, 304 Third Ave. East, 59860, 406-883-2723 |
| Polson | Hidden Pines, 792 Lost Quartz Rd., 59860 |
| Polson | Ruth's B&B, 802 7th. Ave, 59860, 406-883-2460 |
| Polson | Swan Hill B&B, 460 Kings Pt. Rd., 59860, 406-883-5292 |
| Pony | Lodge at Potosi Hot Spring, P.O. Box 651, 59747, 406-685-3594 |
| Red Lodge | Maxwell's Mountain Home, 606 S. Broadway, 59068, 406-446-3052 |
| Red Lodge | Pitcher Guest House, P.O. Box 3450, 59068, 406-446-2859 |
| Roberts | Wolves Den B&B, The, Rt. 1, Box 2123, 59070, 406-446-1273 |
| Seeley Lake | Emily A. The, P.O. Box 350, 59868, 406-677-3474 |
| Sheridan | King's Rest B&B, 55 Tuke Ln., 59749, 406-842-5185 |
| Somers | Osprey Inn, 5557 Hwy 93 So., 59932, 800-258-2042 |
| St. Ignatius | Mandorla Ranch B&B, 6873 Allard Rd., 59865, 406-745-4500 |
| Stevensville | Big Creek Pines B&B, 2986 Hwy. 93, 59870 |
| Stevensville | Country Caboose B&B, 852 Willoughby Rd., 59870, 406-777-3145 |
| Sula | Camp Creek Inn, 7674 Hwy 93 South, 59871, 406-821-3771 |
| Thompson Falls | Lost Ranch Lodge, 606 Blue Slide Rd., 59873 |
| Three Forks | Sacajawea Inn, P.O. Box 648, 59752, 406-285-6515 |
| Townsend | Hidden Hollow Hideaway, Box 233, 59644, 406-266-3322 |
| Troy | Bull Lake Guest Ranch, 15303 Bull Lake Rd., 59935, 406-295-4228 |
| Virginia City | Just an Experience, Highway 287 West, 59755 |
| West Glacier | Mountain Timbers Lodge, Box 94, 59936, 800-841-3835 |
| White Sulpher | Montana Mountain Lodge, 1780 Hwy 89, 59645, 406-547-3773 |
| White Sulphur | Foxwood Inn, Box 404, 59645, 406-547-3918 |
| Whitefish | Angel Connection B&B, 233 E. 2nd St., 59937, 800-557-5800 |
| Whitefish | Castle B&B, 900 S. Baker Ave., 59937, 406-862-1257 |
| Whitefish | Cresnshaw House, 5465 Hwy. 93 S., 59937 |
| Whitefish | Duck Inn, 1305 Columbia Ave., 59937, 406-862-DUCK |
| Whitefish | Eagle's Roost B&B, 400 Wisconsin Ave., 59937 |
| Whitefish | Edgewood, The, 12 Dakota Ave., 59937, 406-862-WOOD |

| | |
|---|---|
| Whitefish | Garden Wall, 504 Spokane Ave., 59937, 406-862-3440 |
| Whitefish | Hibernation House, P.O. Box 1400, 59937, 406-862-3511 |
| Whitefish | Kandahar Lodge, P.O. Box 1659, 59937, 406-862-6098 |
| Whitefish | Maples B&B, 233 2nd St., 59937 |
| Wolf Creek | Bundalow B&B, Box 202, 59648 |

# Nebraska

## ELGIN

| | | |
|---|---|---|
| **Plantation House B&B** | $-B&B | Full breakfast |
| RR 2, Box 17,  68636 | 6 rooms, 3 pb | Sitting room, library |
| 401 Plantation St. | *Rated*, • | family room w/fireplace |
| 402-843-2287 Fax: 402-843-2287 | C-yes/S-no/P-no/H-no | and DSS TV, 1 cottage |
| Merland & Barbara Clark | | |
| All year | | |

*Experience a quieter, gentler era in our historic Greek revival mansion on 4 acres at the edge of a tiny town.* **3rd night, 50%.**

## FUNK

| | | |
|---|---|---|
| **Uncle Sam's Hilltop Lodge** | $-B&B | Full breakfast |
| Box 110,  68940 | 2 rooms, 1 pb | Aftn. tea, snacks |
| R.R. 1 | *Rated*, | Sitting room |
| 308-995-5568 | C-ltd/S-ltd/P-yes/H-no | bikes, racquetball court |
| Sam & Sharon Schrock | | sunken tub for 2 |
| All year | | |

*A modern 4 level country home with a view. Bathtub for two. 3 miles from I-80. Near Kearney.*

## NORTH BEND

| | | |
|---|---|---|
| **Platte Valley Guernsey B&B** | $-B&B | Full breakfast |
| | 3 rooms, | Snacks |
| RR2, Box 28,  68649 | C-ltd/S-no/P-no/H-no | Living room, deck |
| 402-652-3492 | | area attractions |
| Judy Chapman | | |
| All year | | |

*A former dairy farm converted to a B&B. Has all the features of country living except chores! We offer greens fees at local golf course.*

## OMAHA

| | | |
|---|---|---|
| **Offutt House, The** | $$-B&B | Full breakfast |
| 140 North 39th St.,  68131 | 7 rooms, 7 pb | Complimentary wine |
| 402-553-0951 | AmEx, MC, Visa, | Dinner, lunch/groups |
| Janet & Paul Koenig | *Rated*, • | Sitting room, library |
| All year | C-ltd/S-yes/P-ltd/H-no | deep claw-foot tubs |
| | A little Italian | |

*Mansion built in 1894 furnished with antiques. Centrally located near historic "Old Market" area of shops, restaurants. Sun porch, bar on 1st floor.* **Light refreshments at check-in.**

## VERDIGRE

**Commercial Hotel, The**
217 Main St., 68783
402-668-2386 Fax: 402-668-2328
Mike, Jenete & Sarah
Maslonka
All year

$-B&B
7 rooms, 7 pb
Visa, MC, AmEx,
C-yes/S-ltd/P-no/H-yes

Continental plus bkfst.
Snacks
Sitting room, phones in
room, cribs available
family friendly facility

*Historic charm and original furnishing blend with modern luxury at this recently renovated 1900 hotel, listed on the National Register.*

# More Inns ...

| | |
|---|---|
| Ainsworth | Ainsworth Inn, RR1 Box 126, 69210, 402-387-0408 |
| Bartley | Pheasant Hill Farm, HCR 68, Box 12, 69020 |
| Beatrice | Carriage House, The, RR, 68310, 402-228-0356 |
| Beemer | Behrens Inn, P.O. Box 273, 68716, 402-528-3212 |
| Berwyn | 1909 Heritage House, P.O. Box 196, 68819, 308-935-1136 |
| Big Springs | Phelps Hotel, P.O. Box 473, 69122, 308-889-3447 |
| Blair | Nostalgia Inn, 207 S. 16th St., 68008, 402-426-3280 |
| Brewster | Eliza's Cottage, HC 63, Box 34, 68821, 308-547-2432 |
| Brewster | Sandhills Country Cabin, HC 63, Box 13, 68821, 308-547-2460 |
| Broken Bow | Pine Cone Lodge, RR 2, Box 156C, 68822, 308-872-6407 |
| Brownville | Thompson House, Route 1, 68321, 402-825-6551 |
| Cambridge | Cambridge Inn, The, P.O. Box 239, 69022, 308-697-3220 |
| Cedar Rapids | River Road Inn, RR2 Box 112, 68627, 308-358-0827 |
| Chadron | Olde Main Street Inn, P.O. Box 406, 69337, 308-432-3380 |
| Chappell | Cottonwood Inn B&B, The, P.O. Box 446, 69129, 308-874-3250 |
| Columbus | Valley View B&B, 4605 Valley View Dr., 68641, 402-563-2454 |
| Crawford | Fort Robinson Inn, Box 392, 69339, 308-665-2660 |
| Crete | Parson's House, The, 638 Forest Ave., 68333, 402-826-2634 |
| Dannebrog | Heart of Dannebrog, The, 121 E. Elm St., 68831, 308-226-2303 |
| Dannebrog | Nestle Inn, 209 E. Roger Welsch Ave, 68831, 308-226-8252 |
| Dixon | George's, The, Rt. 1, Box 50, 68732, 402-548-2625 |
| Fairbury | Parker House B&B, 515 4th St., 68352, 402-729-5516 |
| Fairbury | Personett House, 615 6th St., 68352, 402-729-2902 |
| Fremont | B&B of Fremont, 1624 E. 25th St., 68025, 402-727-9534 |
| Gering | Monument Heights B&B, 2665 Grandview Rd., 69341, 308-635-0109 |
| Gordon | Bed & Breakfast Bunkhouse, HC 91 Box 29, 69343, 308-282-0679 |
| Gordon | Meadow View Ranch, HC 91 Box 29, 69343 |
| Gordon | Spring Lake Ranch, H.C. 84, Box 103, 69343, 308-282-0835 |
| Grand Island | Bed & Breakfast, 2617 Brahma St., 68801, 308-384-0830 |
| Grand Island | Kirschke House B&B, The, 1124 W. 3rd, 68801, 308-381-6851 |
| Grant | Prairie Jean's B&B, RR 1 Box 167, 69140, 308-352-2355 |
| Gretna | Bundy's B&B, 16906 S. 155th St., 68028, 402-332-3616 |
| Harrison | Sowbelly B&B Hide-a-way, Box 292, 69346, 308-668-2537 |
| Hastings | Grandma's Victorian B&B, 1826 W. 3rd St., 68901, 402-462-2013 |
| Holdrege | Crow's Nest, The, 503 Grant St., 68949, 308-995-5440 |
| Hooper | Empty Nest B&B, RR, 68031, 402-664-2715 |
| Howells | Beran B&B, RR 2 Box 142, 68641, 402-986-1358 |
| Howells | Prairie Garden, RR 1, Box 134, 68641, 402-986-1251 |
| Kearney | George W. Frank Jr. House, 621 W. 27th, 68847, 308-237-7545 |
| Kearney | Walden West, RR #4, Fawn Woods Lake, 68847, 308-237-7296 |
| Lexington | Memories, 900 N. Washington, 68850, 308-324-3290 |
| Lincoln | Atwood House B&B, The, 740 S. 17th St., 68503, 402-438-1416 |
| Lincoln | Capitol Guesthouse B&B, 720 S. 16th St., 68508, 402-476-6669 |
| Lincoln | Rogers House, 2145 "B" St., 68502, 402-476-6961 |
| Lincoln | Sweet Dream, 2721 P St., 68503, 402-438-1416 |
| Lincoln | Yellow House on the Corner, 1603 N. Cotner, 68505, 402-466-8626 |
| Madrid | Clown 'N Country, RR Box 115, 69150, 308-326-4378 |
| McCook | Park Place Guest House, 707 East First St., 69001, 308-345-6057 |
| Merna | Country Nest, The, RR1 Box 62, 68856, 308-643-2486 |
| Merriman | Twisted Pine Ranch B&B, Box 84, 69218, 308-684-3482 |
| Minden | Home Comfort B&B, 1523 N. Brown, 68959, 308-832-0533 |
| Minden | Prairie View, Rt. 2, Box 137, 68959, 308-832-0123 |
| Nebraska City | Peppercricket Farm B&B, RR1, Box 304, 68410 |
| Nebraska City | Whispering Pines B&B, 21st St. & 6th Ave., 68410, 402-873-5850 |
| North Platte | Knoll's Country Inn, 6132 S. Range Rd., 69101, 308-368-5634 |
| Oakland | Benson B&B, 402 N. Oakland Ave., 68045, 402-685-6051 |
| Ogallala | Denim to Lace B&B, 500 N. Spruce, 69153, 308-284-6200 |
| Omaha | Mary Mahoney's Thissen B&B, 6103 Burt St., 68132, 402-553-8366 |
| Osceola | Victorian Times, 160 N. Main, 68651, 402-747-2006 |
| Osmond | Willow Way B&B, Rt. 2, Box A20, 68765, 402-748-3593 |
| Pawnee City | My Blue Heaven, 1041 5th St., 68420, 402-852-3131 |

| | |
|---|---|
| Paxton | Gingerbread Inn, P.O. Box 247, 69155,  308-239-4265 |
| Plainview | Rose Garden Inn, The, P.O. Box 148, 68769,  402-582-4708 |
| Ravenna | Aunt Betty's B&B, 804 Grand Ave., 68869,  308-452-3739 |
| Sidney | Snuggle Inn, 1516 Jackson, 69162,  308-254-0500 |
| Spalding | Esch Haus, Rt. 1, 68665,  308-497-2628 |
| Springview | Big Canyon Inn, HC 82 Box 17, 68778,  402-497-3170 |
| Springview | Larrington's Guest Cottage, HC 82 Box 2, 68778,  402-497-2261 |
| St. Paul | Miss Lizzie's Boardin' Hse, 1023 Kendall St., 68873,  308-754-4137 |
| Steinauer | Convent House, 311 Hickory, 68441,  402-869-2276 |
| Sutton | Maltby House, 409 S. Maltby, 68979,  402-773-4556 |
| Table Rock | Hill Haven Lodge, RR 1, Box 5AA, 68447,  402-839-2023 |
| Tekamah | Deer Run B&B, RR1, Box 142, 68061,  402-374-2423 |
| Trenton | Blue Colonial Inn, The, HC2 Box 120, 69044,  308-276-2533 |
| Trenton | Flying A Ranch B&B, P.O. Box 142, 69044,  308-334-5574 |
| Valentine | Stone House Inn, 559 N. Main, 69201,  402-376-1942 |
| Valentine | Town & Country B&B, P.O. Box 624, 69201,  402-376-2193 |
| Waterloo | J.C. Robinson House B&B, 102 Lincoln Ave., 68069,  402-779-2704 |
| Waterloo | Journey's End B&B, P.O. Box 190, 68069,  402-779-2704 |
| Wayne | Swanson's B&B, Rt.2, 68787,  402-584-2277 |
| Wilber | Hotel Wilber, 203 S. Wilson, 68465,  402-821-2020 |

# Nevada

## CARSON CITY

**Deer Run Ranch B&B**
5440 Eastlake Blvd., Washoe
Valley,  89704
702-882-3643
David & Muffy Vhay
Exc. Thanksgiving & Xmas

$$$-B&B
2 rooms, 2 pb
MC, Visa, AmEx,
C-ltd/S-no/P-ltd/H-no

Full breakfast
Comp. wine, beverages
Snacks, refrigerator
sitting room, library
TV, VCR, private entry

*Western ambiance in a unique architect-designed & built ranch house between Reno & Carson City overlooking Washoe Lake. Pottery, pond, swimming pool, privacy, great bkfst.*

## ELY

**Steptoe Valley Inn**
P.O. Box 151110,  89315
702-289-8687  702-435-1196
Jane & Norman Lindley
June–September

$$$-B&B
5 rooms, 5 pb
AmEx, MC, Visa,
*Rated*, •
C-ltd/S-no/P-no/H-no
Spanish

Full breakfast
Juice and cheese
Sitting room, library
rose garden, back porch
private balconies, TVs

*Romantic, historic structure near railroad museum, reconstructed in 1990. Elegant dining room/library. Rooms have country-cottage decor. Jeep rental.*

## INCLINE VILLAGE

**Haus Bavaria**
P.O. Box 3308,  89450
593 N. Dyer Circle
702-831-6122 Fax: 702-831-1238
800-731-6222
Bick Hewitt
All year

$$$-B&B
5 rooms, 5 pb
AmEx, MC, Visa,
*Rated*, •
C-ltd/S-no/P-no/H-no

Full breakfast
Complimentary wine
Large family room
TV, frplc., ski packages
outdoor jacuzzi

*There's much to do and see in this area, from gambling casinos to all water sports and golf, hiking, tennis and skiing at 12 nearby sites. Conf. facilities. **7th night is free.***

# More Inns ...

| | |
|---|---|
| Fallon | Oasis B&B, 540 W. Williams, 89406 |
| Gardenerville | Nenzel Mansion, 1431 Ezell St., 89410,  702-782-7644 |
| Gardnerville | Sierra Spirit Ranch, 3000 Pinenut Rd., 89410,  702-782-7011 |
| Genoa | Genoa House Inn, P.O. Box 141, 89411,  702-782-7075 |
| Genoa | Wild Rose Inn, 2332 Main St., 89411 |
| Gold Hill | Gold Hill Hotel, P.O. Box 710, 89440,  702-847-0111 |
| Imlay | Old Pioneer Garden B&B, 2805 Unionville Rd., 89418,  702-538-7585 |
| Lamoille | Breitenstein House, 89828,  702-753-6356 |
| Las Vegas | Brittany Acre,  121 E. Robindale Rd., 89123 |
| Reno | B&B South Reno, 136 Andrew Ln., 89511,  702-849-0772 |
| Silver City | Hardwicke House, P.O. Box 96, 89429,  702-847-0215 |
| Smith | Windybrush Ranch, Box 85, 89430,  702-465-2481 |
| Virginia City | Chollar Mansion, 565 S. D St., Box 889, 89440 |
| Virginia City | Edith Palmer's Country Inn, Box 756, South B St., 89440,  702-847-0707 |
| Winnemucca | Robin's Nest Inn, 130 E. Winnemucca, 89445,  702-623-2410 |
| Yerington | Harbor House, 39 N. Center St., 89447 |
| Yerington | Robric Ranch, P.O. Box 2, 89447,  702-463-3515 |

# New Hampshire

## ANTRIM

| | | |
|---|---|---|
| **Steele Homestead Inn, The** | $$-B&B | Full breakfast |
| 125 Keene Rd.,   03440 | 3 rooms, 3 pb | Snacks |
| 603-588-2215 | • | Sitting room, library |
| Barbara & Carl Beehner | C-yes/S-no/P-no/H-no | we accomodate guest with |
| All year | | health or allergy prob. |

*Warm personal attention given to guests in beautifully restored 1810 home. Four seasons activities and relaxation. Health- conscious breakfasts.* **4th. night 30% off.**

## ASHLAND

| | | |
|---|---|---|
| **Glynn House Victorian Inn** | $$$-B&B | Full breakfast |
| P.O. Box 719,   03217 | 9 rooms, 9 pb | Comp. wine, snacks |
| 43 Highland St. | *Rated*, • | Sitting room, bicycles |
| 603-968-3775 Fax: 603-968-3129 | C-ltd/S-yes/P-no/H-no | tennis, lake, golf |
| 800-637-9599 | Polish, Russian | canopy beds, cable TV |
| Betsy & Karol Paterman | | |
| All year | | |

*Fine example of Victorian Queen Anne architecture, among lakes mountains. Antiques, gourmet breakfast, 2 bridal suite with whirlpool, fireplace, TV.* **30% off-season rates ltd.**

## ASHUELOT

| | | |
|---|---|---|
| **Crestwood Pavilion, The** | $$$$-B&B | Full, cont. cont. plus |
| 400 Scofield Mtn. Rd.,   03441 | 4 rooms, 4 pb | Lunch, dinner, snacks |
| 603-239-6393 Fax: 603-239-8861 | AmEx, *Rated*, | Horse & carriage avail. |
| Gary O'Neal | C-yes/S-yes/P-no/H-no | bicycles, sauna, library |
| All year | French | bar service, sitting rm. |

*Private mountain top retreat, century-old chapel, 100-mile views. Marble floors and fireplaces, spacious rooms. Massage on call. Spa cuisine available.* **33% third night, $1000 weekly. Nov-June**

## BARTLETT

**Country Inn at Bartlett**
P.O. Box 327,   03812
Route 302
603-374-2353
Fax: 603-374-2547
800-292-2353
Mark Dindorf
All year

$$-B&B
17 rooms, 17 pb
AmEx, MC, Visa,
*Rated*, •
C-yes/S-ltd/P-ltd

Full breakfast
Comp. tea/coffee, snacks
Sitting room
outdoor hot tub
cross-country ski trails

*A B&B inn for hikers, skiers & outdoors enthusiasts in the White Mountains. New addition of 2-rm. cottage. Expert hiking & trail advice. 3rd night free midwk, ltd.*

## BETHLEHEM

**Mulburn Inn, The**
RR #1, Box 270,   03574
Main St., Route 302
603-869-3389
Fax: 603-869-5633
800-457-9440
The Skeels Family
All year

$$-B&B
7 rooms, 7 pb
Most CC, *Rated*, •
C-yes/S-no/P-no/H-no

Full breakfast
Afternoon tea, snacks
Sitting room, library
ski & golf packages
wraparound porches

*Sprawling summer cottage built 1913 as family retreat known as the Ivie House on the Woolworth Estate. Warm, fireside dining, hot country breakfast. Restaurant discount 10%.*

## BRADFORD

**Mountain Lake Inn**
P.O. Box 443,   03221
Route 114
603-938-2136
800-662-6005
Pat Hendry Lubrano
All year

$$$-B&B
9 rooms, 9 pb
*Rated*,
C-yes/S-yes/P-no/H-no

Full country breakfast
Dinner, tea/coffee/snack
Sitting room, library
full screened porch
piano, bicycles, beach

*165 acres of beautiful vacationland for any season. Built before the Revolution. Near all ski areas. Private sandy beach. 3rd night 50%.*

## BRETTON WOODS

**Bretton Arms Country Inn**
Route 302,   03575
603-278-1000
Fax: 603-278-3603
800-258-0330
Robert M. Clement
All year

$$$-EP
34 rooms, 34 pb
Most CC, *Rated*, •
C-yes/S-yes/P-no/H-yes

Full bkfst. a-la-carte
Dinner, restaurant
Bar service, sitt. room
library, bikes, hot tubs
tennis court, sauna/pool

*Lovingly restored 1896 Inn nestled on picturesque grounds of the historic Mt. Washington Hotel. Cozy country atmosphere, carriage rides, golf. Supervised kids camp May-Oct.*

## BRIDGEWATER

**Inn on Newfound Lake, The**
Rt. 3A,   03222
603-744-9111   Fax: 603-744-3894
800-745-7990
Larry Delangis & Phelps
Boyce
All year

$$-EP
31 rooms, 23 pb
Visa, MC, AmEx, Disc.,
•
C-ltd/S-no/P-no/H-yes

Continental breakfast
Restaurant, bar service
Snacks
sitting room, library
private beach & dock

*One of the few remaining true country inns. We have a 260-ft. private beach and private dock on one of the cleanest lakes in the country. 3rd night is free.*

CAMPTON ─────────────────────────────────────────────

| **Mountain Fare Inn** | $$-B&B | Full breakfast |
|---|---|---|
| P.O. Box 553, 03223 | 8 rooms, 5 pb | Dinner (groups, winter) |
| Mad River Rd. | *Rated*, • | Snacks, sitting room |
| 603-726-4283 | C-yes/S-no/P-ltd/H-no | hiking, biking, golf |
| Susan & Nick Preston | | cross-country & downhill |
| All year | | skiing |

*1840s white clapboard mtn. village home; 3 rm. carriage house w/honeymoon suite. Truly New Hampshire. Skiers, hikers, travelers: come share fun & beauty.* **5th night midweek free.**

CENTER OSSIPEE ─────────────────────────────────────

| **Hitching Post Village Inn** | $$-B&B | Full breakfast |
|---|---|---|
| Old Rt. 16 & Grant Hill, | 9 rooms, 3 pb | Afternoon tea |
| 03814 | C-yes/S-ltd/P-ltd | Sitting & living rooms |
| 603-539-3360 | | library |
| Michael & Jessica Drakely | | screened porch |
| All year | | |

*A 150+-year-old colonial-style inn featuring wide plank wood floors and original Franklin stove. Located next to a steepled church. Must make arrangements for pets.* **Group rates, winter discount.**

CHARLESTOWN ───────────────────────────────────────

| **Maple Hedge B&B Inn** | $$$-B&B | Full 3-course breakfast |
|---|---|---|
| P.O. Box 638, 03603 | 5 rooms, 5 pb | Aftn. tea, comp. wine |
| Main St. | MC, Visa, *Rated*, • | Sitting room, library |
| 603-826-5237 Fax: 603-826-5237 | C-ltd/S-ltd/P-no/H-no | with fireplace |
| 800-9-MAPLE9 | | horseshoes, croquet |
| Joan & Dick De Brine | | |
| April-December | | |

*Luxurious accomodations in elegant home set among lovely gardens & 200 year old maples. Part of longest National District in New Hampshire. Memorable 3 course breakfast.*

CLAREMONT ──────────────────────────────────────────

| **Goddard Mansion B&B** | $$-B&B | Full breakfast |
|---|---|---|
| 25 Hillstead Rd., 03743 | 10 rooms, 3 pb | Snacks |
| 603-543-0603 Fax: 603-543-0001 | Visa, MC, AmEx, | Sitting room, library |
| 800-736-0603 | C-yes/S-no/P-no/H-ltd | bicycles |
| Debbie Albee | Some French | golf & tennis nearby |
| All year | | |

*Delightful, c.1902, 18 room English Manor style mansion, acres of lawns, gardens, easy elegance yet comfortable/homey atmosphere. A romantic Victorian getaway.* **Stay 3 nights, 10% off all nights.**

CONWAY ─────────────────────────────────────────────

| **Darby Field Inn, The** | $$$-B&B | Full breakfast |
|---|---|---|
| P.O. Box D, Bald Hill Rd., | 16 rooms, 14 pb | Dinner, bar, MAP avail. |
| 03818 | AmEx, MC, Visa, | Sitting room, piano |
| 603-447-2181 Fax: 603-447-5726 | *Rated*, • | outdoor pool |
| 800-426-4147 | C-ltd/S-yes/P-no/H-no | entertainment |
| Marc & Maria Donaldson | Spanish | |
| All year | | |

*Cozy country inn overlooking Mt. Washington Valley & Presidential Mountains, rivers. Candlelight dinners, 15 miles of cross-country skiing.* **3rd night 50% Jan.–July.**

## CONWAY

**Mountain Valley Mannor B&B**
P.O. Box 1649,   03818
148 Wash. St./Westside Rd
603-447-3988  Fax: 603-447-1010
Bob & Lynn    All year

$$-B&B
4 rooms, 2 pb
Visa, MC, Disc. *Rated*,
•
C-yes/S-no/P-no/H-no

Full breakfast
Afternoon tea, snacks
Complimentary beverages
sitting room, library
pool, cable TV, A/C

*Friendly restored Victorian at the Kankamaugus Hwy.-200 yds. from two historic Kissing Bridges! Walk to restaurants & outlets. Environmentally clean. **3rd night free, excl. foliage season.***

## EATON CENTER

**Inn at Crystal Lake, The**
Route 153, P.O. Box 12,
   03832
603-447-2120  Fax: 603-447-3599
800-343-7336
Richard & Janice Octeau
All year

$$-B&B/MAP
11 rooms, 11 pb
Most CC, •
C-ltd/S-ltd/P-no/H-no

Full country breakfast
Parlor, TV
Fireplace,lounge, pianos
lake swimming & canoes
hiking & cross-country ski
nearby

*Newly restored country inn—Greek revival with Victorian influence. Relaxing ambience, extraordinary international cuisine presented with elegant appeal. **3rd night 50% off.***

## EXETER

**Inn by the Bandstand, The**
4 Front St.,   03833
603-772-6352  Fax: 603-778-0212
Chuck & Merry Robinson
All year

$$$-B&B
8 rooms, 8 pb
Visa, MC, *Rated*, •
C-yes/S-no/P-no/H-yes

Continental plus bkfst.
Aftn. tea, snacks
Complimentary wine
sitting room, library
antique firechambers

*Premier B&B in Historic District. Crackling fireplaces, complimentary sherry, canopied beds, fine linens. Meetings, conferences are welcome. **3rd night, 50% off.***

**Inn of Exeter, The**
90 Front St.,   03833
603-772-5901  Fax: 603-778-8757
800-782-8444
Carl G. Jensen    All year

$$$-EP
50 rooms, 50 pb
Most CC, *Rated*, •
C-yes/S-yes/P-yes/H-no
French, Spanish

Breakfast available
Restaurant, bar service
Lunch, dinner, snacks
afternoon tea, library
sitting room, sauna

*Three story brick Georgian-style building; on the campus of Phillips Exeter academy; in the Revolutionary capitol of New Hampshire. **3rd night 50%; 7th consecutive day is free.***

## FRANCONIA

**Bungay Jar B&B**
P.O. Box 15,   03580
Easton Valley Rd.
603-823-7775  Fax: 603-444-0100
Kate, Lee, Janet & Julie
All year

$$-B&B
6 rooms, 4 pb
MC, Visa, *Rated*,
C-ltd

Full breakfast
Dinner for groups RSVP
Afternoon tea, snacks
library, antiques, sauna
swimming hole, balconies

*Mountain views on 8 quiet wooded acres w/garden walks to river, waterlily pond, cottage. Frplcs. **10% off on 3rd night, ltd; Comp. bottle of wine to honeymooners & anniversary.***

**Franconia Inn**
1300 Easton Valley Rd., 03580
603-823-5542  Fax: 603-823-8078
The Morris Family
Mem. Day—Oct; 12/15-4/1

$$$-EP
35 rooms, 34 pb
Most CC, *Rated*, •
C-yes/S-yes/P-no/H-no

Full breakfast
Restaurant, full bar
Lounge w/movies, library
bicycles, heated pool
piano, sitt. rm., tennis

*Located in the Easton Valley—Mt. Lafayette & Sugar Hill. Riding stable, ski center. Rooms beautifully decorated. Sleigh rides, horseback riding, soaring, ice-skating rink.*

FRANCONIA ——————————————————————————————————

**Inn at Forest Hills, The**            $$-B&B                   Full breakfast
P.O. Box 783,  03580                    8 rooms, 5 pb            Two large living rooms
Rt. 142                                 MC, Visa, *Rated*, •     Innkpr. is Justice of
603-823-9550 Fax: 603-823-8701          C-ltd/S-no/P-no/H-no     Peace & will marry
800-280-9550
Gordon & Joanne Haym
All year

*Charming, historic 18 rm. Tudor Manor among majestic scenery of the White Mountains.*
*Enjoy tennis, golf, hiking trails, cross-country/downhill skiing.* **3rd night 50% off, ltd.**

GILFORD ——————————————————————————————————

**Cartway House Inn**                   $$-B&B                   Full breakfast
83 Old Lakeshore Rd.,  03246            9 rooms,                 Comp. tea, wine
603-528-1172                            MC, •                    Sitting room
Gretchen & Tony Shortway                C-yes/S-yes/P-yes/H-no
All year                                Italian, French, Spanish

*1791 renovated farmhouse, French country dining room overlooking mountains and*
*lake. Near all attractions, ski area, lake. Casual comfort.* **3rd night, 50%.**

**Inn at Smith Cove, The**              $$$-B&B                  Full breakfast
19 Roberts Rd., Lake                    11 rooms, 11 pb          Sitting room, jacuzzis
Winnepesauki,  03246                    Most CC,                 private beach, gazebo
603-293-1111                            C-ltd/S-no/P-no/H-no     boat slips, antiques
Bob & Maria Ruggiero  All yr

*Circa 1898 Victorian on Lake Winnepesauki. Close to Gunstock ski area, outlet shopping,*
*golf courses, health club. Breakfast in dining room or outside patio.* **Discounts, ask.**

GLEN ——————————————————————————————————————

**Bernerhof Inn**                       $$-B&B                   Full breakfast
P.O. Box 240,  03838                    9 rooms, 9 pb            Lunch ltd, dinner, tea
Rte 302                                 AmEx, MC, Visa,          Snacks, restaurant, pub
603-383-4414 Fax: 603-383-0809          *Rated*,                 bar, sitting room, sauna
800-548-8007                            C-ltd/S-no/P-no/H-no     cooking school
Hollie Smith    All year

*An elegant small hotel featuring antique rooms, many with private spa tubs. Host of the*
*renowned "A Taste of the Mountains" Cooking School.* **3rd night 50% off, ltd.**

GREENFIELD ————————————————————————————————

**Greenfield B&B Inn**                  $-B&B                    Full breakfast
P.O. Box 400,  03047                    13 rooms, 10 pb          Lunch (for groups to 12)
Jct Rts 136 & 31 N.                     MC, Visa, *Rated*, •     Comp. wine, tea, coffee
603-547-6327 Fax: 603-547-2418          C-yes/S-ltd              jacuzzis, hayloft suite
800-678-4144                                                     conference room, cottage
Barbara & Vic Mangini
All year

*Mountain valley Victorian mansion. Antiques. Winter/summer recreation. Carriage*
*house(6). Romantic comfort for 1st & 2nd honeymooners.* **Last min. discount; Dinner,**
**B&B $119/pcoup.**

HAMPSTEAD —————————————————————————————————

**Stillmeadow B&B**                     $$-B&B                   Continental plus bkfst.
P.O. Box 565,  03841                    4 rooms, 4 pb            Comp. wine and cookies
545 Main St.                            MC, Visa, *Rated*,       Croquet, gardens, bikes
603-329-8381 Fax: 603-329-4075          C-ltd/S-no/P-no/H-no     near lake & cross-country
Lori Offord    All year                 Some French, Ger., Sp.   skiing
                                                                 play yard for children

*Discover Southern New Hampshire's best kept secret. Memorable, charming getaway.*
*Inviting Greek Revival Colonial with 5 chimneys and 3 staircases.*

## HAMPTON

**Curtis Field House, The**
735 Exeter Rd.,   03842
603-929-0082
Mary F. Houston
Open May–October

$$-B&B
3 rooms, 2 pb
MC, Visa, *Rated*,
C-ltd/S-ltd/P-no

Full breakfast
Dinner (on request)
Afternoon tea, sundeck
sitting room, library
tennis courts, pool, A/C

*Royal Bairy Wills Cape-country setting. Near Phillips Exeter, antiques, historical area, ocean. Breakfast served on terrace. Lobster dinners on request. 3rd night 20% off.*

## HAMPTON BEACH

**Oceanside, The**
365 Ocean Blvd.,   03842
603-926-3542 Fax: 603-926-3549
Skip & Debbie Windemiller
Mid-May–mid-October

$$$-B&B
10 rooms, 10 pb
Most CC, *Rated*, •
C-ltd

Continental plus bkfst.
Bar service
sitting room, library
beach chair & towels

*Directly across from sandy beach; beautiful ocean views. Active, resort-type atmosphere during mid-summer. Recently renovations, many antiques. 20-30% discounts, ask.*

## HART'S LOCATION

**Notchland Inn, The**
Rt. 302,   03812
603-374-6131  Fax: 603-374-6168
800-866-6131
Les Schoof & Ed Butler
All year

$$$$-MAP
11 rooms, 11 pb
Most CC, *Rated*, •
C-ltd/S-no/P-no/H-ltd

Full breakfast
Dinner
Sitting room, library
hot tubs, sauna
cross-country skiing

*A traditional country inn where hospitality hasn't been forgotten. Working fireplaces in every room, gourmet meals and spectacular mountain views. Hiking & swimming nearby.*

## HENNIKER

**Colby Hill Inn**
P.O. Box 779,   03242
3 The Oaks
603-428-3281 Fax: 603-428-9218
800-531-0330
Ellie, John & Laurel Day
All year

$$$-B&B
16 rooms, 16 pb
AmEx, MC, Visa,
*Rated*, •
C-ltd/S-ltd/P-no/H-ltd

Full breakfast
Dinner, bar
Comp. beverages. cookies
sitt. room, library, A/C
croquet, badminton, pool

*1800 country inn on 5 acres in a quiet village. Antique-filled rooms, smiling hosts, fine dining. Swimming, hiking, skiing, canoeing, kayaking, fishing and cycling all nearby.*

**Meeting House Inn**
35 Flanders Rd.,   03242
603-428-3228 Fax: 603-428-6334
J. & B. Davis, P. & C. Bakke
All year

$$-B&B
6 rooms, 6 pb
AmEx, MC, Visa
*Rated*, •
C-ltd/S-no/P-no/H-no

Full breakfast
Lunch, dinner
Hot tub, sauna, lounge
bicycles
sitting room

*A country retreat with cozy rooms and attention to detail. "Your place to return to again and again." 25% off after three nights.*

## HILLSBOROUGH

**Inn at Maplewood Farm, The**
447 Center Rd.,   03244
603-464-4242  800-644-6695
Laura & Jayme Simoes
Closed April

$$$-B&B
4 rooms, 4 pb
Most CC, *Rated*, •
C-ltd/S-no/P-no/H-no
Portuguese

Full vegetarian bkfst.
Afternoon tea, library
Sitting room, radio with
vintage radio shows
Fax: 464-5401

*For more than 200 years Maplewood Farm has welcomed travelers. Surrounded by open fields & forests, appointed with period antiques the all-suites inn offers a timeless escape.*

## HOLDERNESS

**Inn on Golden Pond, The**
P.O. Box 680,   03245
Route 3
603-968-7269 Fax: 603-968-9226
Bill & Bonnie Webb
All year

$$$-B&B
9 rooms, 9 pb
MC, Visa, *Rated*, •
C-ltd/S-no/P-no/H-no

Full breakfast
Piano

*Located on 55 wooded acres across the street from Squam Lake, setting for "On Golden Pond." Close to major attractions, skiing.*

## INTERVALE

**Forest—A Country Inn, The**
P.O. Box 37,   03845
Route 16A
603-356-9772 Fax: 603-356-5652
800-448-3534
Bill & Lisa Guppy
All year

B&B
12 rooms, 10 pb
Most CC, *Rated*, •
C-ltd/S-no/P-no/H-no

Full breakfast
Snacks
Sitting room
tennis court, pool

*Enjoy our peaceful setting with beautifully served breakfasts, fireplaced rooms, a quaint stone cottage with fireplace, pool and lovely gardens. cross-country skiing from our back door.*

## JACKSON

**Dana Place Inn**
P.O. Box L, Route 16,
Pinkham Notch,   03846
603-383-6822 Fax: 603-383-6022
800-537-9276
The Levine Family
All year

$$$-B&B/MAP
35 rooms, 31 pb
AmEx, MC, Visa,
*Rated*, •
C-yes/S-yes/P-yes/H-no
French

Full breakfast in season
Dinner, pub
Piano, river swimming
indoor pool, cross-country
skiing
tennis courts, Jacuzzi

*Historic country inn at base of Mt. Washington. Cozy rooms, fine dining, afternoon tea. Three 2-room family suites.* **Stay 2nd night Seasonal Escape Pkg. & get 3rd night for $99/couple.**

**Ellis River House**
P.O. Box 656,   03846
Route 16
603-383-9339 Fax: 603-383-4142
800-233-8309
Barry & Barbara Lubao
All year

$$$-B&B
18 rooms, 18 pb
Most CC, *Rated*, •
C-ltd/S-no/P-ltd/H-ltd
Polish

Full country breakfast
Tea, coffee, cookies
Tavern with billiards
darts, Cable, fishing
Atrium w/jacuzzi, sauna

*Romantic fireplaced rooms & 2 person jacuzzi, balconies overlooking the Ellis River, a Honeymoon cottage w/spectacular views. Homemade breads, cross-country skiing.* **Champagne for honeymoon, anniv; 7th nite free.**

**Inn at Jackson**
P.O. Box 807,   03846
Main St. & Thornhill Rd.
603-383-4321 Fax: 603-383-4085
800-289-8600
Lori Tradewell
All year

$$-B&B
14 rooms, 14 pb
Most CC, *Rated*, •
C-ltd/S-ltd/P-no/H-no

Full breakfast
Library, sitting room
fireplaces, A/C, T.V.'s
outdoor hot tub Jacuzzi

*Stanford White mansion in the heart of the White Mountains. Adjacent to Jackson ski touring trails. Spacious rooms, common rooms, porch dining room.* **3rd night 50%, ltd.**

*Inn at Jackson, Jackson, NH*

## JACKSON

**Inn at Thorn Hill**
P.O. Box A, Thorn Hill Rd.,
03846
603-383-4242 Fax: 603-383-8062
800-289-8990
Jim & Ibby Cooper
All year (Apr. wknds)

$$$$-B&B/MAP
19 rooms, 19 pb
Most CC, *Rated*, •
C-ltd/S-no/P-no/H-no

Full country breakfast
4-course dinner w/MAP
Sitt. room, pub, croquet
horseshoes, tobogganing
cross-country ski, hot tub,
A/C

*Stanford-White-designed Victorian-era inn; breathtaking views of the White Mountains. Candlelight dinners. Perfect getaway for lovers, skiers, and nature enthusiasts.* **Extended stay disc't, ask.**

---

**Village House, The**
P.O. Box 359, 03846
Route 16A
603-383-6666 Fax: 603-383-6464
800-972-8343
Robin Crocker    All year

$$-B&B
15 rooms, 13 pb
Most CC, •
C-yes/S-yes/P-no/H-no

Full bkfst.(fall-winter)
Cont. plus (sum.-spring)
Aftn. snack, TV, balcony
pool, tennis courts
living room w/fireplace

*The Village House has been hosting guests for over 100 years. We offer the charms of a small B&B w/the amenities of large inns. Affordable rates w/B&B & kitchenettes avail., outdoor hot tub.*

---

**Whitneys' Inn**
P.O. Box 822, 03846
Rt 16 B
603-383-8916 Fax: 603-383-6886
800-677-5737
Bob & Barb Bowman
All year

$$$-B&B
29 rooms, 29 pb
Most CC, *Rated*, •
C-yes/S-yes/P-ltd/H-no

Full breakfast
Restaurant, dinner (fee)
Aftn. tea, bar service
sitting room, library
tennis, hot tubs, pond

*Classic country inn with a variety of accommodations. Families are welcome. Close to recreational activities in any season. 3 meeting rooms for up to 40 persons.*

## JAFFREY

**Benjamin Prescott Inn**
433 Turnpike Rd. Rt 124,
03452
603-532-6637 Fax: 603-532-6637
Jan & Barry Miller    All year

$$-B&B
11 rooms, 9 pb
MC, Visa, *Rated*, •
C-ltd/S-ltd/P-no/H-no

Full breakfast
Complimentary tea/coffee
Sitting room
bicycles
Air conditioned suites

*Relax ... Indulge ... Less than two hours from Boston, the inn offers the opportunity to reset your pace and explore the Monadnock region.* **3rd night 50% off.**

*Benjamin Prescott Inn, Jaffrey, NH*

## JAFFREY

**Lilac Hill Acres B&B**
5 Ingalls Rd., 03452
603-532-7278
Frank & Ellen McNeill
All year

$$-B&B
6 rooms, 1 pb
C-ltd/S-ltd/P-no/H-no

Full breakfast
Complimentary tea
Sitting room
piano, pond
fishing

*Five-star service in a beautiful setting. Enjoy a bit of life on the farm with a warm personal touch. Join us year-round.*

## JEFFERSON

**Applebrook B&B**
Route 115A, 03583
603-586-7713  800-545-6504
Sandra Conley & Martin Kelly
All year

$$-B&B
12 rooms, 4 pb
Visa, MC. Disc. *Rated*,
•
C-yes/S-no/P-yes/H-no

Full breakfast
Dinner by reservation
Sitting room, library
hot tub under the stars
family suite

*Hike, golf, ski from comfortable Victorian farmhouse. Taste mid-summer raspberries & enjoy mountain views. Stained glass & goldfish pool. **3rd night free, Sun.–Thurs.***

## LACONIA

**Rest Assured**
47 Laighton Ave. S., 03246
603-524-9021 Fax: 603-528-9004
•
Maurice & Helene Gouin
All year

$$-B&B
3 rooms, 1 pb
•
S-no/P-no/H-no
French

Full breakfast
Comp. wine & cheese
2 TV rooms, solarium
seasonal activities
golf, make maple syrup

*Come and share with us a piece of heaven. The serenity of the lake, mountains & woodlands lift one's spirit.*

## LITTLETON

**Beal House Inn**
2 W. Main St., 03561
603-444-2661 Fax: 603-444-6224
Ted & Barbara Snell
All year

$$-B&B
13 rooms, 7 pb
Visa, MC, Amex,
*Rated*,
C-ltd/S-no/P-no/H-no

Full breakfast
Afternoon snacks
Parlor, porch, deck
game room

*Within walking distance of downtown Littleton, quaint shops and tasteful dining, the Beal House offers a genteel setting for the perfect blend of relaxation & a taste of the past.*

## MADISON

**Maple Grove House**
P.O. Box 340,  03849
Maple Grove Rd.
603-367-8208
Celia Pray
All year

$$-B&B
6 rooms, 6 pb
Most CC,
C-ltd/S-no/P-no/H-no

Full breakfast
Afternoon tea, snacks
Sitting room, library
200 acres of hiking
trails, cross-country skiing

*Victorian farmhouse in the country only minutes away from fine restaurants and outlet shopping. Near lakes overlooking the White Mountains.* **4 nights for price of 3.**

## MARLBOROUGH

**Peep-Willow Farm B&B**
51 Bixby St.,  03455
603-876-3807
Fax: 603-876-3320
Noel Aderer
All year

$$-B&B
3 rooms, 1 pb
•
C-yes/S-no/P-yes/H-no

Full breakfast
Complimentary wine
Snacks
sitting room

*I raise thoroughbred horses—you can help with chores (no riding), watch the colts play and enjoy the view all the way to Vermont's Green Mountains.*

## MOULTONBORO

**Olde Orchard Inn**
RR Box 256,  03254
Lee Rd. & Lees Mill Rd.
603-476-5004
Fax: 603-476-5419
800-598-5845
Jim & Mary Senner
All year

$$-B&B
9 rooms, 6 pb
Visa, *Rated*, •
C-yes/S-no/P-ltd/H-ltd
French, Finnish

Full breakfast
Sitting room
library, bicycles

*C.1790 Federal nestled in twelve acre apple orchard. Furnished w/antiques collected by former diplomat owners. Near large lake. 2 rooms w/queen bed, fireplace, Jacuzzi.* **1 Nov.–1 May-3rd night free.**

## MOUNT SUNAPEE

**Blue Goose Inn B&B, The**
24 Route 103B, Box 2117,
   03255
603-763-5519
Fax: 603-763-8720
Meryl & Ronald Caldwell
All year

$$-B&B
5 rooms, 3 pb
MC, Visa, *Rated*, •
C-yes/S-yes/P-no/H-yes

Full breakfast
Dinner on request
Sitting room, bicycles
lake, downhill skiing
picnicking, lawn games

*Adjacent to Mt. Sunapee State Park; 19th-century farmhouse on 3.5 acres. Picnicking, grill, bikes available. Mystery weekends. Non-smoking policy.* **Area events discounts.**

## NEW IPSWICH

**Inn at New Ipswich, The**
P.O. Box 208,  03071
11 Porter Hill Rd.
603-878-3711
Ginny & Steve Bankuti
All year

$$-B&B
7 rooms, 5 pb
MC, Visa, •
C-ltd/S-no/P-no/H-no
Hungarian

Full breakfast
Tea, coffee, snacks
Sitting room, library
game chest, 6 fireplaces
porch, stone walls

*Graceful, lovingly maintained 1790 farmhouse w/fruit trees. Hearty hospitality. Near cross-country & downhill skiing, antiquing, concerts, arts & crafts, hiking.* **10% senior (65+) discount.**

*The Blue Goose Inn, Mt. Sunapee, NH*

## NEW LONDON

**Maple Hill Farm**
200 Newport Rd.,   03257
603-526-2248  Fax: 603-526-4170
800-231-8637
Dennis & Roberta Aufranc
All year

$$-B&B
10 rooms, 2 pb
•
C-yes/S-yes/P-yes/H-ltd

Full breakfast
Dinner by reservation
Sitting room, croquettte
bikes, swimming, canoe
basketball, horseshoes

*160-yr-old farmhouse, newly restored, serving country breakfast. Near golf, cross-country & alpine skiing, all other recreation. Country gourmet dinner: $15-25 pp.* **10% off 3+ nights.**

**New London Inn**
P.O. Box 8,   03257
140 Main St.
603-526-2791  Fax: 603-526-2749
800-526-2791
Kimberley & Terance
O'Mahoney
All year

$$$-B&B
29 rooms, 29 pb
MC, Visa, AmEx,
*Rated*, •
C-yes/S-no/P-no/H-no

Continental plus bkfst.
Restaurant, dinner (fee)
Bar service
sitting room, library
bicycles

*On the town green in this lovely New England college town, this 1792 inn offers exquisite fireside dining and charming rooms. Lakes, golf & skiing nearby.*

## NORTH CONWAY

**1785 Inn & Restaurant, The**
P.O. Box 1785,   03860
3582 White Mountain Hwy
603-356-9025  Fax: 603-356-6081
800-421-1785
Becky & Charlie Mallar
All year

$$-B&B
13 rooms, 8 pb
AmEx, MC, Visa,
*Rated*, •
C-yes/S-ltd/P-ltd/H-ltd
French

Full country breakfast
Restaurant, lounge
2 sitting rooms, piano
classical guitar Sat-Sun
ski/honeymoon pkgs, pool

*Newly redecorated historic inn at The Scenic Vista overlooking the Saco River Valley. Award winning cross-country skiing trails. Won several food & wine accolades.* **4th night free, ltd.**

NORTH CONWAY ─────────────────────────────────────────

**Buttonwood Inn, The**
P.O. Box 1817,  03860
Mt. Surprise Rd.
603-356-2625  Fax: 603-356-3140
800-258-2625
Peter & Claudia Needham
All year

$$-B&B
9 rooms, 5 pb
Most CC, *Rated*, •
C-ltd/S-ltd/P-no/H-no

Full breakfast
Sitting room, library
40-foot swimming pool
TV, lawn sports, skiing

*Tucked away on Mt. Surprise. Quiet, secluded yet only 2 mi. to town-excellent dining, shopping. Near all outdoor activities. Apres-ski gameroom w/frplc. 1 room w/gas frplc.* **Midweek upgrade as available.**

---

**Cabernet Inn**
P.O. Box 489,  03860
3552 White Mtn. Hwy.
603-356-4704  Fax: 603-356-5399
800-866-4704
Chris & Bob Wyner
All year

$$-B&B
10 rooms, 10 pb
Most CC, *Rated*, •
C-ltd/S-ltd/P-no/H-ltd

Full breakfast
Afternoon tea
Sitting room
2 common rms. w/firplcs.
upper deck for breakfast

*Nestled in the heart of the spectacular White Mountains, the Cabernet is the perfect romantic getaway. Guest rooms with Jacuzzi tubs or gas fireplaces, gorgeous views.* **Restaurant/Seasonal discounts.**

---

**Cranmore Mountain Lodge**
P.O. Box 1194,  03860
859 Kearsarge Rd.
603-356-2044  Fax: 603-356-8963
800-356-3596
Dennis & Judy Helfand
All year

$$-B&B
18 rooms, 18 pb
Most CC, *Rated*, •
C-yes/S-yes/P-no/H-no
Danish

Full breakfast
Dinner/BBQ (fee)
Fireplace room
piano, hot tub
swimming, tennis

*Authentic country inn in heart of White Mts. Hearty country breakfast. Tennis court, pool, jacuzzi, tobogganing, skating, cross-country skiing. 2-bdrm townhouse also avail.*

---

**Eastman Inn**
P.O. Box 882,  03860
Main St.
603-356-6707  800-626-5855
Peter & Carol Watson
All year

$$-B&B
14 rooms, 14 pb
Visa, MC, Disc. *Rated*,
•
C-ltd/S-no/P-no/H-no
French

Full country breakfast
Aftn. tea, comp. wine
Sitting room, library
spacious rooms, minutes
from major attractions

*Upscale romantic & elegant 1797 Colonial inn located in the heart of N. Conway. Walking distance to village & outlet shopping. Frplc., living room, all queen/king beds.* **4th night, 50%; Rest. discount.**

---

**Farm by the River, The**
2555 W. Side Rd.,  03860
603-356-2694  Fax: 603-356-2694
888-414-8353
Charlene & Rick Davis
All year

$$-B&B
10 rooms,
Visa, MC, •
S-no/P-no/H-no
Spanish

Full breakfast
Snacks
Sitting room, swim, fly
fish, slieghrides, golf
lake, hiking, shopping

*Award winning New England inn on 65 acres of river, forest & pasture land & has been in 1 family for over 200 yrs. Surrounded by mountains. Dinners for entire inn bookings.* **Ski pkgs., dinner discount.**

NORTH CONWAY

**Merrill Farm Resort**
428 White Mountain Hwy.,
  03860
603-447-3866 Fax: 603-447-3867
800-445-1017
Lynn T. McArdle    All year

$$-B&B
,
Most CC, *Rated*, •
C-yes/S-yes/P-no/H-yes
German

Continental plus bkfst.
Beverages & cookies
Hot tub, sauna, bicycles
sitting room, library
pool, fully A/C

*Let us introduce you to real old-fashioned New England hospitality. A casual country setting with a touch of class.* **10% discount when you mention the Guide.**

---

**Nereledge Inn**
P.O. Box 547,  03860
River Road
603-356-2831 Fax: 603-356-7085
Valerie & Dave Halpin
All year

$$-B&B
11 rooms, 5 pb
AmEx, MC, Visa,
C-yes/S-no/P-no/H-no

Full breakfast
Dinner for groups
Fireplace room with
darts & games, 2 sittup
rooms, 1 w/woodstove

*Cozy 1787 inn, 5 minute walk to village, close to skiing areas, fishing, golf, climbing, canoeing. Home-cooked meals including country-style breakfast.* **Restaurant discount available.**

---

**Old Red Inn & Cottages**
PO Box 467, 2406 White Mt.
Hwy. Rt 16,  03860
603-356-2642 Fax: 603-356-6626
800-338-1356
Don & Winnie White    All yr

$$-B&B
17 rooms, 15 pb
Most CC,
C-yes/S-yes/P-no/H-no
French

Full breakfast
Kitchenettes
Living room w/woodstove
piano, herb garden
gardens, near park

*Four-season 1810 country inn w/10 cottages & award-winning flower gardens. Walking distance to village. Spectacular mountain views of Mt. Washington.* **3rd night 50%.**

---

**Stonehurst Manor**
P.O. Box 1937,  03860
Route 16
603-356-3113 Fax: 603-356-3217
800-525-9100
Peter Rattay    All year

$$$-MAP
25 rooms, 23 pb
AmEx, MC, Visa,
*Rated*,
C-yes/S-yes/P-no/H-yes
German

Full breakfast
Dinner incl., tea/coffee
Library, piano, bar
swimming pool, hot tub
tennis, fireplaces

*Turn-of-the-century mansion with old oak and stained glass. Relax by our fireplace in the library. Mount Washington Valley.* **Call for "Best Buys" packages.**

---

**Wyatt House Country Inn**
P.O. Box 777,  03860
Main St.
603-356-7977  800-527-7978
Bill & Arlene Strickland
All year

$$-B&B
6 rooms, 4 pb
Most CC, *Rated*, •
C-ltd/S-ltd/P-no/H-no

Gourmet candlelit bkfst.
Aftn. tea, cakes, sherry
Parlor, study, veranda
A/C, CCTV, frplc., bikes
swim/fish/hike/cross-
country ski

*Be pampered and enjoy antiqued rooms with panoramic mountain & river views, c.1880. Suites, decks. Walk to village. Restaurant discounts.* **3rd night free, ltd.**

NORTH WOODSTOCK

**Three Rivers House**
RR#1 Box 62,  03262
S. Main St., Rt. 3
603-745-2711 Fax: 603-745-2773
800-241-2711
Brian A. Crete, Diane Brisson
All year

$$-B&B
15 rooms, 15 pb
MC, Visa, *Rated*,
C-ltd/S-yes/P-no/H-no

Full breakfast
Dinner, lounge
Porches with rockers
fireplace sitting room
hot tub in winter

*Warm hospitality since 1875, full country bkfst, in-rm TVs. Located on edge of village near trails, skiing, & attractions. Some rooms w/2 person Jacuzzi, gas fireplace.* **2nd, 3rd night discount, ask.**

## NORTH WOODSTOCK

| | | |
|---|---|---|
| **Wilderness Inn B&B** | $-B&B | Full gourmet breakfast |
| RFD 1, Box 69,　03262 | 8 rooms, 6 pb | Dinner with reservation |
| Route 3 & Hwy 112 | AmEx, MC, Visa, | Aftn. tea, cider, cocoa |
| 603-745-3890　800-200-WILD | *Rated*, ● | swimming hole, 3 porches |
| Michael & Rosanna Yarnell | C-yes/S-yes/P-no/H-no | fireplace in cottage |
| All year | Fr., It., Hindi, Amharic | |

*"The quintessential country inn." Circa 1912, located in quaint New England town. Inn & rooms furnished w/antiques & oriental carpets. 3 mi. to Loon Mtn. skiing. **Discounts,ask.***

## NORTHWOOD

| | | |
|---|---|---|
| **Meadow Farm B&B** | $$-B&B | Full breakfast |
| Jenness Pond Rd.,　03261 | 3 rooms, | Private beach, canoeing |
| 603-942-8619　Fax: 603-942-5731 | C-ltd/S-ltd/P-ltd/H-no | sitting room, antiquing |
| Janet & Douglas Briggs | | cottage on lake for rent |
| All year | | |

*Restored charming 1770 colonial home—50 acres of fields, woods. Private beach on lake. Enjoy walks, canoeing, cross-country skiing. Memorable breakfasts, fishing.*

## RYE

| | | |
|---|---|---|
| **Cable House, The** | $-B&B | Continental plus bkfst. |
| 20 Old Beach Rd.,　03870 | 7 rooms, 2 pb | Sitting room, beach |
| 603-964-5000 | S-yes/P-no/H-no | fishing boat excursions |
| Katherine Kazakis | Greek | whale watching |
| May 15–September 30 | | |

*Named historical site, walk to beach. Landfall of first direct cable between Europe and the USA. **$200 per week: 6th & 7th nights free.***

| | | |
|---|---|---|
| **Rock Ledge Manor B&B** | $$-B&B | Full breakfast |
| 1413 Ocean Blvd., Route 1A,　03870 | 4 rooms, 2 pb | Sitting room |
| | *Rated*, | Period furnishings |
| 603-431-1413 | C-ltd/S-no/P-no/H-no | Ocean view, veranda |
| Norman & Janice Marineau | Some French | |
| May 1-Oct 31 or call | | |

*Seacoast getaway on the ocean, full memorable breakfast served in mahogany-ceilinged breakfast room. Near all NH & ME activities, University of NH.*

## SUGAR HILL

| | | |
|---|---|---|
| **Hilltop Inn, The** | $$-B&B/MAP | Very full breakfast |
| Rt. 117,　03585 | 7 rooms, 7 pb | Dinner w/MAP in Fall |
| 603-823-5695　Fax: 603-823-5518 | Visa, MC, Disc. *Rated*, | Box lunches on request |
| 800-770-5695 | C-ltd/S-ltd/P-yes/H-no | aft. tea, snacks, bar |
| Meri & Mike Hern | | sitting room, library |
| All year | | |

*Rooms redone w/unusual wallpaper borders & stencils, handmade quilts, original local artwork & stained glass, large decks & porches, flower beds. **10% off after 2 days, ltd.***

| | | |
|---|---|---|
| **Homestead Inn, The** | $$-B&B | Full country breakfast |
| Route 117,　03585 | 18 rooms, 9 pb | Afternoon tea |
| 603-823-5564　800-823-5564 | Most CC, *Rated*, ● | Sitting room, library |
| Paul & Melody Hayward | C-yes/S-ltd/P-yes/H-no | gift shop, museum |
| All year | | pets ltd. to certain rms |

*Family inn built in 1802; antiques passed down seven generations. Breathtaking views of three mountain ranges. **3rd night, 50%.***

## SUNAPEE

**Dexter's Inn & Tennis Club**
P.O. Box 703 B, 258
Stagecoach Rd., 03782
603-763-5571 800-232-5571
Frank & Shirley Simpson
May—October

$$$$-MAP
19 rooms, 19 pb
MC, Visa, •
C-yes/S-yes/P-yes/H-no

Full breakfast
Lunch (July-August)
Dinner (exc. Tuesday)
snacks, bar, lawn games
recreation room, tennis

*Inspiring view of the countryside with mountains, meadows, lawns and gardens. Minutes from Lake Sunapee, golf, and summer theater.* **Free court time for 3 day stay.**

**Seven Hearths Inn**
26 Seven Hearths Ln., 03782
603-763-5657 Fax: 603-763-9495
800-237-2464
David & Georgia Petrasko
All year

$$$-B&B
10 rooms, 10 pb
MC, Visa, *Rated*, •
C-yes/S-yes/P-no/H-yes

Full 4 course bkfst.
Restaurant, bar
Afternoon tea, snacks
canopied beds & frplcs.
massage & salon services

*Beautiful country inn on 5 priv. acres. Year round resort area, minutes to beach & ski areas. Guests welcomed to their rooms w/fresh flowers & bowls of fruit.* **5th nite free.**

## WHITEFIELD

**The Spalding Inn**
Mountain View Rd., RR 1,
Box 57, 03598
603-837-2572 Fax: 603-837-3062
800-368-8439
Diane Edwards Cockrell
June-October

$$$-B&B/AP
42 rooms, 42 pb
MC, Visa, *Rated*, •
C-yes/S-yes/P-yes/H-no

Full breakfast
Dinner w/AP, aft. tea
Bar service, sitt. room
library, tennis, pool
family packages avail.

*A premier country inn in the heart of the White Mtns.—200 acres, manicured lawns, perennial gardens, glorious views, magnificent food & a relaxed way of life.* **3rd night free.**

## WILTON CENTER

**Stepping Stones B&B**
6 Bennington Battle Tr.,
Bennington Battle Trail,
03086
603-654-9048
D. Ann Carlsmith
All year

$$-B&B
3 rooms, 1 pb
*Rated*,
C-yes/S-ltd/P-ltd/H-no

Full breakfast
Complimentary tea, wine
Stereo, color TV
library, sitting room
breakfast room

*Quiet country setting in Monadnock hills, near picture-book village. Summer theater & music. Antiquing, hiking, civilized atmosphere.* **3rd night 50% off; 7th night free.**

## WOLFEBORO

**Tuc'Me Inn B&B**
P.O. Box 657, 03894
118 N. Main St, 109 North
603-569-5702
E., T. & T. Foutz, I. Evans
All year

$$-B&B
6 rooms, 2 pb
MC, Visa, *Rated*, •
C-ltd/S-no/P-no/H-no

Continental plus bkfst.
Sitting room
library, no cribs
2 screened porches

*Early 1800s Colonial inn. Homey atmosphere, tastefully furnished. "Cook's whims" breakfast. 2-block walk to downtown & beautiful Lake Winnipesaukee.* **Champagne for special occasions.**

# More Inns ...

| | |
|---|---|
| Alexandria | Mt. Cardigan B&B, Knowles Hill Rd., 03222, 603-744-5803 |
| Alexandria | Stone Rest B&B, 652 Fowler River Rd., 03222, 603-744-6066 |
| Alstead | Darby Brook Farm, Hill Rd., 03602, 603-835-6624 |
| Andover | English House, The, P.O. Box 162, 03216, 603-735-5987 |

| | |
|---|---|
| Antrim Center | Uplands Inn, Miltimore Rd., 03440, 603-588-6349 |
| Ashland | Country Options, P.O. Box 736, 03217, 603-968-7958 |
| Ashland | Rose & The Bear B&B, Sanborn Rd., 03217 |
| Bethlehem | Adair Country Inn, Old Littleton Rd., 03574, 603-444-2600 |
| Bethlehem | Gables of Park and Main, Box 190 Main St., 03574, 603-869-3111 |
| Bethlehem | Highlands Inn, P.O. Box 118C, 03574, 603-869-3978 |
| Bethlehem | Wayside Inn, Rt. 302, 03574 |
| Bradford | Bradford Inn, The, RR 1, Box 40, 03221, 603-938-5309 |
| Bradford | Candlelite Inn B&B, RR 1, Box 408, 03221, 603-938-5571 |
| Bristol | Victorian B&B, 16 Summer St., Rt. 104, 03222, 603-744-6157 |
| Campton | Campton Inn, The, RR 2, Box 12, 03223, 603-726-4449 |
| Campton | Osgood Inn B&B, P.O. Box 419, 03223, 603-726-3543 |
| Canaan | Inn on Canaan St., The, P.O. Box 92, 03741, 603-523-7310 |
| Canaan | Towerhouse Inn, One Parker St., 03741 |
| Center Conway | Lavender Flower Inn, P.O. Box 328, Main St., 03813, 603-447-3794 |
| Center Harbor | Kona Mansion Inn, P O. Box 458, 03226, 603-253-4900 |
| Center Sandwich | Corner House Inn, P.O. Box 204, 03227, 603-284-6219 |
| Centre Harbor | Dearborn Place, Box 997, Route 25, 03226, 603-253-6711 |
| Centre Harbor | Red Hill Inn, RFD 1, Box 99M, 03226, 603-279-7001 |
| Chocorua | Riverbend Inn, Box 347, 03817, 603-323-7440 |
| Chocorua | Staffords in the Field, Box 270, 03817, 603-323-7766 |
| Claremont | Poplars, 13 Grandview St., 03743, 603-543-0858 |
| Colebrook | Monadnock B&B, 1 Monadnock St., 03576, 603-237-8216 |
| Conway | Foothills Farm, The, P.O. Box 1368, 03818, 207-935-3799 |
| Cornish | Home Hill Country Inn, RR 3, Box 235, 03745, 603-675-6165 |
| Danbury | Inn at Danbury, Route 104, 03230, 603-768-3318 |
| Durham | University Guest House, 47 Mill Rd., 03824 |
| East Andover | Highland Lake Inn, P.O. Box 164, Maple St., 03231, 603-735-6426 |
| Epping | Haley House Farm, RFD #1, N. River Rd., 03857, 603-679-8713 |
| Etna | Moose Mountain Lodge, Moose Mountain, 03750, 603-643-3529 |
| Fitzwilliam | Fitzwilliam Inn, 03447, 603-585-9000 |
| Francestown | Francestown B&B, Main St., 03043, 603-547-6333 |
| Francestown | Inn at Crotched Mountain, Mountain Rd., 03043, 603-588-6840 |
| Franconia | Blanche's B&B, 351 Easton Valley Rd., 03580, 603-823-7061 |
| Franconia | Horse and Hound Inn, 205 Wells Rd., 03580, 603-823-5501 |
| Franconia | Lovetts' Inn, Route 18, 03580, 603-823-7761 |
| Franconia | Main St. B&B of Franconia, Main St., 03580, 603-823-8513 |
| Franconia | Pinestead Farm Lodge, Route 116, RFD 1, 03580, 603-823-5601 |
| Franconia | Sugar Hill Inn, Route 117 (Sugar Hill), 03580, 603-823-5621 |
| Franklin | Atwood Inn, The, 71 Hill Rd., Route 3A, 03235, 603-934-3666 |
| Freedom | Freedom House B&B, Box 338, 1 Maple St., 03836, 603-539-4815 |
| Gilford | Gunstock Country Inn, 580 Cherry Valley Rd., 03246, 603-293-2021 |
| Gilmanton | Historic Tavern Inn, P.O. Box 369, 03237, 603-267-7349 |
| Gorham | Gorham House Inn B&B, P.O. Box 267, 03581, 603-466-2271 |
| Greenland | Ayres Homestead B&B, 47 Park Ave., 03840, 603-436-5992 |
| Hampton | Blue Heron Inn, 124 Landing Rd., 03842, 603-926-9666 |
| Hampton | Inn at Elmwood Corners, 252 Winnacunnet Rd., 03842, 603-929-0443 |
| Hancock | John Hancock Inn, Main St., 03449, 603-525-3318 |
| Harrisville | Harrisville Squires' Inn, Box 19, Keene Rd., 03450, 603-827-3925 |
| Henniker | Hanscom House, Box 191, 03242 |
| Henniker | Henniker House, Box 191, 1 Ramsdell Rd., 03242, 603-428-3198 |
| Hillsborough | Stonebridge Inn, 365 W. Main St., 03244, 603-464-3155 |
| Holderness | Manor on Golden Pond, The, P.O. Box T, 03245, 603-968-3348 |
| Hopkinton | Windyledge B&B, 1264 Hatfield Rd., 03229, 603-746-4054 |
| Intervale | New England Inn, The, PO Box 100, Route 16A, 03845, 603-356-5541 |
| Intervale | Old Field House, The, P.O. Box 1, 03845, 603-356-5478 |
| Intervale | Wildflowers Inn, P.O. Box 802, 03845, 603-356-2224 |
| Jackson | Christmas Farm Inn, Route 16B, P.O. Box 176, 03846, 603-383-4313 |
| Jackson | Covered Bridge Motor Lodge, Box 277B, White Mt. Hwy, 03846, 603-383-9151 |
| Jackson | Jackson House B&B, P.O. Box 378, 03846 |
| Jackson | Paisley and Parsley B&B, Box 572, 03846, 603-383-0859 |
| Jackson Village | Nestlenook Farm & Resort, Dinsmore Rd., Box Q, 03846, 603-383-9443 |
| Jackson Village | Wildcat Inn & Tavern, Box T, Main St., 03846, 603-383-4245 |
| Jaffrey | Jaffrey Manor Inn, 13 Stratton Rd., 03452, 603-532-8069 |
| Jaffrey | Mill Pond Inn, 50 Prescott Rd., 03452, 603-532-7687 |
| Jaffrey | Woodbound Inn, 62 Woodbound Rd., 03461, 603-532-8341 |
| Jefferson | Jefferson Inn, The, RFD 1, Box 68A, Route 2, 03583, 603-586-7998 |
| Jefferson | Stag Hollow Inn, Route 115, 03583, 603-586-4598 |

*Colby Hill Inn,
Henniker, NH*

| | |
|---|---|
| Lincoln | Red Sleigh Inn B&B, The,  P.O. Box 562, 03251, 603-745-8517 |
| Lisbon | Ammonoosuc Inn,  Bishop Rd., 03585,  603-838-6118 |
| Littleton | 1895 House,  74 Pleasant St., 03561,  603-444-5200 |
| Loudon | Inn at Loudon Ridge,  Box 195, 03301,  603-267-8952 |
| Lyme | Dowds Country Inn,  P.O. Box 58, 03768,  603-795-4712 |
| Lyme | Loch Lyme Lodge,  RFD 278, 03768,  603-795-2141 |
| Meredith | Nutmeg Inn, The,  80 Pease Road, RFD 2, 03253, 603-279-8811 |
| Meredith | Tuckernuck Inn, The,  RFD 4, Box 88, 03253, 603-279-5521 |
| Milford | Ram in the Thicket,  Maple St., 03055,  603-654-6440 |
| Mt. Sunapee | 1806 House, The,  P.O. Box 54, 03255,  603-763-4969 |
| N. Charlestown | Indian Shutters Inn,  Route 12, 03603,  603-826-4445 |
| New London | Pleasant Lake Inn,  N. Pleasant St., 03257 |
| Newport | Eagle Inn at Coit Mountain,  HCR 63, Box 3, Route 10, 03773,  603-863-3583 |
| North Conway | Center Chimney—1787, The,  P.O. Box 1220, 03860, 603-356-6788 |
| North Conway | Isaac Merrill House Inn,  P.O. Box 8, 03847 |
| North Conway | New England Inn,  P.O. Box 428, Route 16A, 03860, 603-356-5541 |
| North Conway | Schoolhouse Motel,  P.O. Box 302, 03860,  800-638-6050 |
| North Conway | Scottish Lion Inn & Restr.,  P.O. Box 1527, 03860,  603-356-6381 |
| North Conway | Sunny Side Inn,  P.O. Box 557, 03860,  603-356-6239 |
| North Conway | Victorian Harvest Inn, The,  28 Locust Ln., Box 1763, 03860,  603-356-3548 |
| North Salem | George P. Johns, III,  P.O. Box 49, 03073 |
| North Woodstock | Birches B&B, The,  Rt. 175, 03262 |
| North Woodstock | Cascade Lodge/B&B,  Main St., P.O. Box 95, 03262,  603-745-2722 |
| North Woodstock | River's Edge B&B, The,  Rt. 3, 03262 |
| North Woodstock | Woodstock Inn,  80 Main St., 03262,  603-745-3951 |
| Northwood | Aviary,  Bow Lake, Box 268, 03261,  603-942-7755 |
| Northwood | Nostalgia B&B,  Box 520, Route 1, 03261,  603-942-7748 |
| Orford | White Goose Inn,  P.O. Box 17, Route 10, 03777,  603-353-4812 |
| Plymouth | Northway House,  R.F.D. 1, Box 71, 03264,  603-536-2838 |
| Portsmouth | Governor's House B&B,  32 Miller Ave., 03801,  603-431-6546 |
| Portsmouth | Inn at Strawbery Banke,  314 Court St., 03801,  603-436-7242 |
| Portsmouth | Leighton Inn,  69 Richards Ave., 03801,  603-433-2188 |
| Portsmouth | Martin Hill Inn,  404 Islington St., 03801,  603-436-2287 |
| Portsmouth | Sheafe Street Inn,  3 Sheafe St., 03801,  603-436-9104 |
| Portsmouth | Sise Inn,  40 Court St., 03801,  603-433-1200 |
| Portsmouth | Theatre Inn,  121 Bow St., 03801,  603-431-5846 |
| Rindge | Grassy Pond House,  03461,  603-899-5166 |
| Rindge | Tokfarm Inn,  Box 1124, RR 2, 03461,  603-899-6646 |
| Sanbornton | Ferry Point House,  Lower Bay Rd., 03269 |
| Sandbornton | Ferry Point House,  100 Lower Bay Rd., 03269,  603-524-0087 |
| Snowville | Snowvillage Inn,  Box 196, 03849,  603-447-2818 |
| Springfield | Hide-Away Lodge,  P.O. Box 6, New London, 03257,  603-526-4861 |
| Strafford | Province Inn,  P.O. Box 309, 03884,  603-664-2457 |
| Sugar Hill | Foxglove, A Country Inn,  Route 117, 03585,  603-823-5755 |
| Sugar Hill | Ledgeland,  RR1, Box 94, 03585,  603-823-5341 |
| Sugar Hill | Sunset Hill House,  Sunset Rd., 03585,  603-823-5522 |
| Sunapee | Inn at Sunapee, The,  P.O. Box 336, 03782,  603-763-4444 |
| Sunapee | Loma Lodge,  RFD #1 Box 592, 03782,  603-763-4849 |
| Sunapee | Old Governor's House,  P.O. Box 524, 03782,  603-763-9918 |
| Sunapee | Times Ten Inn,  Route 103B, Box 572, 03782,  603-763-5120 |
| Suncook | Suncook House,  62 Main St., 03275,  603-485-8141 |
| Sutton Mills | Village House, The,  Box 151 Grist Mill Rd., 03221,  603-927-4765 |
| Tamworth | Tamworth Inn,  P.O. Box 189, Main St., 03886,  603-323-7721 |
| Temple | Birchwood Inn,  Route 45, 03084,  603-878-3285 |
| Tilton | Black Swan Inn,  308 W. Main St., 03276,  603-286-4524 |
| Tilton | Tilton Manor,  28 Chestnut St., 03276,  603-286-3457 |
| Warren | Black Iris B&B,  P.O. Box 83, 03279,  603-764-9366 |
| Waterville Valley | Silver Squirrel Inn,  Snow's Brook Rd., 03223 |
| Waterville Valley | Snowy Owl Inn,  P.O. Box 407, 03215,  603-236-8383 |
| Wentworth | Hilltop Acres B&B,  P.O. Box 32, 03282,  603-764-5896 |
| Wentworth | Hobson House,  Town Common, 03282,  603-764-9460 |
| West Chesterfield | Chesterfield Inn,  P.O. Box 155, 03443,  603-256-3211 |
| West Franklin | Strolling Woods on Webster,  SW on Lake Shore Dr., 03235 |
| Whitefield | Inn at Whitefield, The,  Rt. 3 N, 03598 |
| Whitefield | Kimball Hill Inn,  P.O. Box 74, 03598,  603-837-2284 |
| Winnisquam | Tall Pines Inn,  P.O. Box 327, 03289,  603-528-3632 |
| Wolfeboro | Wolfeboro Inn,  P.O. Box 1270, 03894,  603-569-3016 |

*Nereledge Inn,*
*Conway, NH*

# New Jersey

## ANDOVER

**Crossed Keys B&B**
289 Pequest Rd.,   07821
201-786-6661
Pat Toye & Peter Belder
All year

$$$-B&B
5 rooms, 3 pb
Visa, MC, AmEx,
*Rated*, •
C-ltd/S-no/P-no/H-no

Full breakfast
Snacks, comp. wine
Sitting room, library
bicycles, shuffleboard
pool table

*Located on 12 acres of beautiful gardens, water ponds and trees. Tastefully furnished with antiques. Stone honeymoon cottage with jacuzzi for two. Homemade country breakfast.*

## AVON-BY-THE-SEA

**Cashelmara Inn**
22 Lakeside Ave.,   07717
908-776-8727  Fax: 908-988-5819
800-821-2976
Mary Wiernasz
All year

$$-B&B
14 rooms, 14 pb
AmEx, MC, Visa
*Rated*,
C-ltd/S-no/P-no/H-no

Full breakfast
Wine available
Sitting room, A/C
resident dog named Cody
some fireplaces, jacuzzi

*Period antiques and water views complemented by designer fabrics and window treatments. In-season complimentary beach badges. In-home "theater." Hearty breakfast served on oceanside verandah.*

## BAY HEAD

**Bay Head Gables**
200 Main Ave.,   08742
908-892-9844  Fax: 908-295-2196
800-984-9536
Don Haurie & Ed Laubusch
Wkends only in Winter

$$$-B&B
11 rooms, 11 pb
Most CC, *Rated*, •
C-ltd/S-no/P-no/H-no

Full breakfast
Snacks, comp. wine
Sitting room
75 yds. to ocean
in room phones & A/C

*A 3-story Georgian Colonial overlooking ocean. Elegant Victorian to ultra contemporary—to please the most discriminating guest. Memorable breakfasts. AAA rates 3 diamonds.*

---

**Bay Head Sands B&B**
2 Twilight Rd.,   08742
908-899-7016
Mary Stockton Glass/Ken
Glass
All year

$$$-B&B
8 rooms, 5 pb
AmEx, MC, Visa,
C-ltd/S-yes/P-no/H-no

Full breakfast
Comp. tea - off season
After beach snacks, TV
sitting room, free
bottle of wine

*Friendly, romantic seaside getaway, Laura Ashley prints, antiques, iron beds, delicious home-baked treats. One block from beach. A special place.*

---

**Conover's Bay Head Inn**
646 Main Ave,   08742
908-892-4664  Fax: 908-892-8748
800-956-9099
Beverly, Carl, & Tim Conover
Exc. wkdys/Dec 15-Feb 15

$$$-B&B
12 rooms, 12 pb
AmEx, MC, Visa,
*Rated*, •
S-no/P-no/H-no

Full breakfast
Comp. tea Oct-April
Sitting rm., dining rm.
library, parlor, porch
sm. conf. room, gardens

*Romantic hideaway furnished w/antiques, handmade pillows, bedcovers, fam. pictures; on ocean. Frplc. in bedrooms. 1995 Waverly Hon. Mention. Dinind tables for 2. **$20.00 off, ltd.***

## BEACH HAVEN

**Amber Street Inn**
118 Amber St., 08008
609-492-1611
Joan & Michael Fitzsimmons
Mid February - November

$$$-B&B
6 rooms, 6 pb
*Rated*,
C-ltd/S-no/P-no/H-no
Spanish

Continental plus bkfst.
Afternoon tea/lemonade
Sitting room, parlor
porch with wicker
English garden

*Victorian seaside B&B; 1/2 block away from the beach. Antiques; great breakfasts; fireplace; English garden; close to everything.* **10% off 4 night midweek stay, Mon-Thurs**

## BELMAR

**Inn at the Shore, The**
301 Fourth Ave., 07719
908-681-3762 Fax: 201-945-2822
Rosemary & Tom Volker
All year

$$$-B&B
12 rooms, 3 pb
Visa, MC, AmEx,
*Rated*, •
C-yes/S-no/P-no/H-no

Continental plus bkfst.
Sitting room, library
bicycles, aquarium
patio & gas grill

*Let us pamper you at our Victorian country inn while rocking away and enjoying the sea and lake breezes on our wraparound porch.* **10% discount, Sun.–Thurs, 9/9–4/30.**

## CAPE MAY

**7th Sister Guesthouse, The**
10 Jackson St., 08204
609-884-2280 Fax: 609-898-9899
Bob & JoAnne Echevarria-
Myers
All year

$$-EP
6 rooms, 1 pb
C-ltd/S-ltd/P-no/H-no
Spanish, French,
German

Guest refrigerator
Piano, library, sunporch
rooms 100 ft. from beach
restaurants, sitt. room

*Ocean view, wicker-filled rooms with a hint of eccentricity. Paintings by the owner/innkeeper, JoAnne Echevarria Myers, hang throughout.* **10% off 1 week stay.**

---

**Abbey B&B, The**
34 Gurney St., At Columbia
Ave., 08204
609-884-4506
Jay & Marianne Schatz
Easter–December

$$$-B&B
14 rooms, 14 pb
MC, Visa, *Rated*,
C-ltd/S-ltd/P-no/H-no

Full breakfast
Bkfast buffet on veranda
Comp. wine, snacks
2 parlors, piano, harp
off-street parking

*Elegantly restored villa, w/period antiques. Genuine merriment in a warm atmosphere. A/C avail. One block from Atlantic Ocean.* **One nite comp. on 2+ nite stay, Mon.-Thurs., ltd.**

---

**Abigail Adams B&B by Sea**
12 Jackson St., 08204
609-884-1371
Kate Emerson
All year

$$$-B&B
5 rooms, 3 pb
MC, Visa, •
C-ltd/S-no/P-no/H-no

Full gourmet breakfast
Continental plus (summ.)
Comp. tea, gardens
sitting room, porch
TV, ocean views, beach

*Intimate, elegant country charm, ocean views, all located in historic Cape May within 100' of beach. Walk to Victorian shopping mall & restaurants.* **3rd night 50% off-season.**

---

**Angel of the Sea**
5 Trenton Ave., 08204
609-884-3369  800-848-3369
Lorie & Greg Whissill
All year

$$$-B&B
27 rooms, 27 pb
AmEx, MC, Visa,
*Rated*, •
C-ltd/S-no/P-no/H-no

Full breakfast
Lunch, comp. fruit bskt.
Wine, tea, sitting rm.
oceanfront porch
fireplaces, bicycles

*Cape May's most luxurious B&B mansion; fabulous ocean views. Rooms have private baths, ceiling fans, ocean views, clawfoot tubs. Free use of bicycles and all beach equipment.*

*Captain Mey's Inn, Cape May, NJ*

## CAPE MAY

**Barnard-Good House**
238 Perry St., 08204
609-884-5381
Nan & Tom Hawkins
April–November 15

$$$-B&B
5 rooms, 5 pb
MC, Visa, *Rated*,
C-ltd/S-ltd/P-no/H-no

Full 4-course breakfast
Wine, snacks (sometimes)
Sitting room, antique
organ, private baths
A/C in rooms

*Victorian splendor in landmark-dotted town. Breakfast is a taste thrill ... sumptuous and lovingly created for you. Awarded best breakfast in N.J.* **10% off discounts, ask.**

---

**Bedford Inn**
805 Stockton Ave., 08204
609-884-4158
Fax: 609-884-0533
Alan & Cindy Schmucker
March–December

$$$-B&B
11 rooms, 11 pb
MC, Visa, *Rated*, •
C-ltd/S-no/P-no/H-no

Full breakfast
Comp. sherry, beverages
Sitting room, parlor
set-up service, A/C,
sun porch, color TVs

*Elegant 1880 Italianate seaside inn w/unusual double staircase; lovely, antique-filled rooms, suites. Near beach & historic shopping district.* **Midweek discount Sept.–June.**

---

**Captain Mey's Inn**
202 Ocean St., 08204
609-884-7793
George & Kathleen Blinn
All year

$$-B&B
8 rooms, 8 pb
MC, Visa, *Rated*, •
C-ltd/S-no/P-no/H-no

Full country breakfast
Comp. wine, refreshments
A/C, on-site parking
beach towel/badge/chair
veranda, queen beds

*Victorian 1890 inn with wrap-around veranda. Period antiques. One block to beach, shops, restaurants. Fireplace in dining room. Victorian parlor.* **10% off midweek off-season.**

CAPE MAY ─────────────────────────────────────────

**Carroll Villa B&B Hotel**
19 Jackson St.,  08204
609-884-9619 Fax: 609-884-0264
Mark Kulkowitz & Pamela
Huber
February 14–December 31

$$-B&B
21 rooms, 21 pb
MC, Visa, *Rated*,  •
C-ltd/S-yes/P-no/H-no
German

Full breakfast
Continental (off season)
Restaurant w/fireplace
sitting room, conf. fac.
garden terrace, AC/heat

*Restored 1881 Victorian hotel. Mid-block between ocean and Victorian Mall. Porch and garden dining. European ambience. Moderate rates. Annual renovations.*

───────────────────────────────────────────────

**Cliveden Inn & Cottage**
709 Columbia Ave.,  08204
609-884-4516  800-884-2420
Sue & Alex De Rosa
All year

$$$-B&B
10 rooms, 10 pb
Visa, MC, AmEx,
C-ltd/S-ltd/P-no/H-no

Full breakfast buffet
Afternoon tea, snacks
Library, veranda
rocking chairs
Victorian cottage avail.

*Fine accommodations, delicious breakfasts and gracious hospitality have made the Cliveden one of the popular inns of Cape May.*

───────────────────────────────────────────────

**Dormer House**
800 Columbia Ave.,  08204
609-884-7446  800-884-5052
Lucille & Dennis Doherty
All year

B&B
10 rooms, 10 pb
Visa, MC, AmEx,
C-ltd/S-no/P-no/H-no

Full breakfast
Afternoon tea
Sitting room
bikes

*One of the great summer houses of the 1890s. Long porches, enjoy full breakfast/tea. An inn for all seasons. "Come for the tea, stay for the night." **Free bottle of wine.***

───────────────────────────────────────────────

**Duke of Windsor B&B Inn**
817 Washington St.,  08204
609-884-1355  800-826-8973
Bruce & Fran Prichard
All year

$$-B&B
9 rooms, 7 pb
MC, Visa, *Rated*,
C-ltd/S-no/P-no/H-no

Full breakfast
Sitting rooms, veranda
organ, bicycles
Christmas grand tour

*Grand in scale and bold in Victorian character. Warm & friendly atmosphere, antiques. Near beaches, restaurants, shopping area, historical area. **Sun–Th nights discounts, ltd.***

───────────────────────────────────────────────

**Fairthorne B&B**
P.O. Box 2381,  08204
111 Ocean St.
609-884-8791 Fax: 609-884-1902
800-438-8742
Ed & Diana Hutchinson
All year

$$$$-B&B
7 rooms, 5 pb
Visa, MC, *Rated*,  •
C-ltd/S-no/P-no/H-no

Full breakfast
Afternoon tea
Public library across
street, bicycles
sitting room, near ocean

*Light and airy, pastel pinks, lace curtains and antique furnishings. Sumptuous breakfasts are served outside on our verandah during warm weather. **3rd night free, ltd.***

───────────────────────────────────────────────

**Gingerbread House**
28 Gurney St.,  08204
609-884-0211
Fred & Joan Echevarria
All year

$$$-B&B
6 rooms, 3 pb
*Rated*,
C-ltd/S-yes/P-no/H-no

Full breakfast
Aftn. tea w/baked goods
Wicker-filled porch
parlor with fireplace
Victorian antiques, A/C

*The G.B.H. offers period furnished rooms—comfortable accommodations within walking distance to major sights. Half block from the beach. **50% discount, ltd.***

CAPE MAY ──────────────────────────────

| | | |
|---|---|---|
| **Humphrey Hughes House, The** | $$$-B&B | Full buffet breakfast |
| 29 Ocean St., 08204 | 10 rooms, 10 pb | Afternoon tea & treats |
| 609-884-4428 | MC, Visa, AmEx, | Library, veranda, beach |
| Lorraine & Terry Schmidt | S-ltd/P-no/H-no | tags, rocking chairs |
| Mid-April — Ocotber | | Victorian cottage |

*Enjoy buffet breakfast & afternoon tea & treats on our large, wraparound veranda. Cozy Victorian cottage. Center of Historic District.*

───────────────────────────────────────

| | | |
|---|---|---|
| **Inn On Ocean, The** | $$$-B&B | Full breakfast |
| 25 Ocean St, 08204 | 5 rooms, 5 pb | Golf, tennis, antiques |
| 609-884-7070 Fax: 609-884-1384 | Most CC, *Rated*, • | birdwatching, fishing |
| 800-304-4477 | C-ltd/S-no/P-no/H-no | near beach/ocean's edge |
| Jack & Katha Davis | | |
| All year | | |

*Fanciful Second Empire style with an exhuberant personality in the heart of Victorian Cape May, horse drawn carriages, gas lit streets, renowned dining, billiard table.*

───────────────────────────────────────

| | | |
|---|---|---|
| **John Wesley Inn** | $$$-B&B | Continental plus bkfst. |
| 30 Gurney St., 08204 | 6 rooms, 4 pb | Sitting room, library |
| 609-884-1012 | • | beach tags, beach chairs |
| Rita Tice | C-ltd/S-no/P-no/H-no | parking |
| All year | | |

*Elegant Victorian interior designed for relaxation & romance. Centrally located in Historic District, 1/2 block from beach. On-site parking.*

───────────────────────────────────────

| | | |
|---|---|---|
| **Mainstay Inn, The** | $$$-B&B | Full breakfst (spr/fall) |
| 635 Columbia Ave., 08204 | 16 rooms, 9 pb | Cont. breakfast (summer) |
| 609-884-8690 | *Rated*, | Aft. tea, 10 A/C rooms |
| Tom & Sue Carroll | C-ltd/S-no/P-no/H-no | piano, 3 sitting rooms |
| April—November | | suites w/whirpools avail |

*Two wealthy 19th-century gamblers spared no expense to build this luxurious villa. Sumptuous Victorian furnishings, garden. New "Officers' Quarters" building.* **Ask about discount.**

───────────────────────────────────────

| | | |
|---|---|---|
| **Manor House** | $$$-B&B | Full gourmet breakfast |
| 612 Hughes St., 08204 | 9 rooms, 7 pb | Refreshments |
| 609-884-4710 Fax: 609-898-0471 | *Rated*, • | Unlimited cookie jar |
| Nancy & Tom McDonald | C-ltd/S-no/P-no/H-no | sitting rooms |
| Closed January | | refreshments |

*Relaxing, comfortable setting, centrally located. Sparkling clean and tastefully decorated rooms. 4-course "made from scratch" breakfast, great buns!*

───────────────────────────────────────

| | | |
|---|---|---|
| **Mason Cottage, The** | $$$-B&B | Full gourmet breakfast |
| 625 Columbia Ave, 08204 | 9 rooms, 9 pb | Afternoon tea |
| 609-884-3358 800-716-2766 | MC, Visa, AmEx, | Sitting room, veranda |
| Dave & Joan Mason | *Rated*, • | parlor, fireplaces, A/C |
| Open Feb.—Dec. | C-ltd/S-no/P-no/H-no | whirlpoool, beach towels |

*An elegant seaside inn located on a quiet, tree-lined street in the center of historic district, 1 block to beach & close to other attractions.* **5% off stay with mention of Guide.**

CAPE MAY ─────────────────────────────────────────

**Mission Inn, The**
1117 New Jersey Ave., 08204
609-884-8380 Fax: 609-884-4191
800-800-8380
Judith DeOrio & Diane
Fischer
Open April–November

$$$-B&B
6 rooms, 6 pb
Visa, MC, AmEx, •
S-no/P-no/H-no

Full breakfast alfresco
Comp. wine, snacks
Sitting room, king &
queen beds, hairdryers
50 yds. to beach

*California casual. Large, bright A/C rooms, breakfast al fresco. A relaxing, fun place to stay. Garden w/fountain. Hospitality begins with your call. Parking on-site.* **Midweek specials, ltd.**

───────────────────────────────────────────────────────

**Mooring, The**
801 Stockton Ave., 08204
609-884-5425 Fax: 609-884-1357
Leslie Valenza
April 3–December 30

$$-B&B
12 rooms, 12 pb
MC, Visa, •
C-ltd/S-no/P-no/H-no

Full breakfast
Afternoon tea
Sitting room
mid–week discounts
Sept-Jan, March–June

*Victorian mansard structure furnished in original period antiques. One block to ocean and easy walking distance to five different restaurants.*

───────────────────────────────────────────────────────

**Perry Street Inn**
29 Perry St., 08204
609-884-4590      Fax: 609-884-
8444 800-29-PERRY
John & Cynthia Curtis
April–November

$$-B&B
20 rooms, 13 pb
MC, Visa, *Rated*, •
C-ltd/S-yes/H-yes

Full breakfast
Afternoon tea, snacks
Sitting room, bicycles
in-room phones, Mystery!
oceanfront porch, phones

*National historic landmark city. Victorian guest house & modern efficiency suites. Beach block; close to unique shopping, fine restaurants.* **$10 off special mystery packages.**

───────────────────────────────────────────────────────

**Poor Richard's Inn**
17 Jackson St., 08204
609-884-3536 Fax: 609-884-2329
Richard Samuelson
Valentines–New Years

$$-B&B
9 rooms, 4 pb
•
C-ltd/S-yes/P-no/H-no

Continental breakfast
Sitting room
oriental rock garden
near beach

*Classic gingerbread guest house offers accommodations w/eclectic Victorian & country decor; friendly, unpretentious atmosphere.* **2nd. night 50%, limited please ask.**

───────────────────────────────────────────────────────

**Queen Victoria, The**
102 Ocean St., 08204
609-884-8702
Dane & Joan Wells
All year

$$$-B&B
19 rooms, 19 pb
AmEx, MC, Visa,
*Rated*,
C-yes/S-ltd/P-no/H-ltd
French

Full buffet breakfast
Afternoon tea
Sitting room, bicycles
kitchen & whirlpool
2 luxury suites, bikes

*A country inn located in the center of the nation's oldest seaside resort; specialty is comfort & service. Morning and evening room cleanings. Large breakfast. A/C in rooms.*

───────────────────────────────────────────────────────

**Sea Holly B&B Inn**
815 Stockton Ave., 08204
609-884-6294 Fax: 609-884-5157
Christy Lacey Igoe
Mid-Feb.–Dec. 31

$$$-B&B
8 rooms, 8 pb
Visa, MC, AmEx,
*Rated*,
S-ltd/P-no/H-no

Full breakfast
Comp. sherry, tea, etc.
Sitting room, books, A/C
beach equipment & tags
rockers, veranda

*Elegant 3-story 1875 Victorian Gothic; some ocean view rooms; period antiques; known for Christy's breakfast treats—have written cookbook!* **Champagne/balloons for special occasions.**

## CAPE MAY

| | | |
|---|---|---|
| **Springside** | $$-B&B | Continental breakfast |
| 18 Jackson St., 08204 | 4 rooms, | King-sized beds, library |
| 609-884-2654 | MC, Visa, • | 1/2 block from beach |
| Meryl & Bill Nelson | C-ltd/S-no/P-no/H-no | 1/2 block from mall |
| All year | | |

*1890 Victorian beach house with bright, airy guest rooms with ocean views. Many creature comforts—big beds, ceiling fans, rockers on veranda, books and good music.*

| | | |
|---|---|---|
| **Summer Cottage Inn, The** | $$$-B&B | Full breakfast |
| 613 Columbia Ave., 08204 | 8 rooms, 8 pb | Snacks, afternoon tea |
| 609-884-4948 | Visa, MC, *Rated*, | Sitting room |
| Skip & Linda Loughlin | C-yes/S-no/P-no/H-no | bicycles, garden |
| All year | French (a little) | queen size beds |

*Enjoy beautiful Cape May, the nation's oldest seashore resort while vacationing in an authentic Victorian summer cottage with gracious hospitality.*

| | | |
|---|---|---|
| **White Dove Cottage** | $$$-B&B | Full breakfast |
| 619 Hughes St., 08204 | 6 rooms, 6 pb | Afternoon tea |
| 609-884-0613 800-321-3683 | *Rated*, • | Complimentary wine |
| Frank and Sue Smith | C-ltd/S-no/P-no/H-no | sitting room |
| All year | | two blocks from ocean |

*Elegant 1866 B&B located in center of Historic District on tree-lined, gas-lit street. A memorable occasion - a delightful retreat. AAA 3 star rating.* **10% off, ltd.**

| | | |
|---|---|---|
| **Windward House** | $$$-B&B | Full breakfast |
| 24 Jackson St., 08204 | 8 rooms, 8 pb | Afternoon tea, sherry |
| 609-884-3368 Fax: 609-884-0533 | MC, Visa, *Rated*, • | Sitting rm, library, A/C |
| Sandy & Son O. Miller | C-ltd/S-ltd/P-no/H-no | ocean view sundeck, TV |
| All year | | bicycles, beach passes |

*Edwardian shingle cottage; sun/shade porches; spacious antique-filled guest rooms; massive oak doors w/stained/leaded glass. Parking. 1/2 blk to beach.* **Midweek discount all year.**

| | | |
|---|---|---|
| **Wooden Rabbit, The** | $$$-B&B | Spring/Summer Cont. Plus |
| 609 Hughes St., 08204 | 4 rooms, 4 pb | Fall/Winter Full Bkfst. |
| 609-884-7293 Fax: 609-898-0842 | MC, Visa, | Sitting room, A/C rooms |
| Greg & Debby Burow | C-yes/S-no/P-no/H-no | sun room, guest phone |
| All year | | suite w/1 king, 2 twins |

*Horse-drawn carriages roll through our quiet, shaded neighborhood. Victorian homes; fine restaurants; antiques. 2 rooms and 2 - 2 bedroom suites. All with private baths.*

| | | |
|---|---|---|
| **Woodleigh House** | $$$-B&B | Full breakfast |
| 808 Washington St., 08204 | 4 rooms, 4 pb | Afternoon refreshments |
| 609-884-7123 Fax: 609-884-5174 | Visa, MC, • | Sitting room, queen beds |
| 800-399-7123 | C-ltd | courtyards, bicycles |
| Buddy & Jan Wood | | romantic packages, suite |
| All year | | |

*Nestled in Cape May's historic district, surrounded by porches and courtyards. This attractive example of "Country Victorian" is charmingly hosted.* **4th night free, M–Th.**

## CHATHAM

**Parrot Mill Inn at Chatham**
47 Main St.,  07928
201-635-7722  Fax: 201-701-0620
Betsy A. Kennedy
All year

$$$-B&B
11 rooms, 10 pb
AmEx, MC, Visa,
*Rated*, •
C-yes/S-no/P-no/H-no

Continental plus bkfst.
Afternoon tea
Sitting room
wedding facilities

*English country elegance. Tastefully decorated bedrooms with private baths, situated ideally near major corporate offices and universities.* **Free bottle of wine, cheese.**

## CLINTON

**Amber House Victorian Inn**
66 Leigh St.,  08809
908-735-7881
Terry Schlegal
April–December

$$-B&B
5 rooms, 4 pb
AmEx, MC, Visa, •
C-ltd/S-no/P-no/H-no
French

Continental plus bkfst.
Restaurant nearby
Sitting room, fireplace
fishing, sailing
tennis nearby

*Lovingly restored inn with cozy fireplace, porch swing and ferns. Authentic Victorian (c.1862) located in picture-book Clinton, where small town America is alive and well.*

## FLEMINGTON

**Cabbage Rose Inn, The**
162 Main St.,  08822
908-788-0247
Pam Venosa & Al Scott
All year

$$$-B&B
5 rooms, 5 pb
AmEx, MC, Visa,
*Rated*,
C-ltd/S-no/P-no/H-no

Continental plus/full
Afternoon refreshments
Complimentary sherry
sitting room, gazebo
sunporch, piano, firepl.

*Victorian romance & roses galore! Fabulous shopping, restaurants, galleries, wineries, theater, Delaware River. Warmest hospitality. "Romance & Roses" pckg.* **3rd night 50% off.**

**Jerica Hill Inn**
96 Broad St.,  08822
908-782-8234 Fax: 908-782-8234
Judith Studer-Hamilton
All year

$$$-B&B
5 rooms, 5 pb
AmEx, MC, Visa,
*Rated*, •
C-ltd/S-no/P-no/H-no

Continental plus bkfst.
Sherry, refreshments
Picnic & wine tours
guest pantry, refrig.
fax on premises

*Gracious Victorian in heart of historic Flemington. Spacious, sunny guest rooms with A/ C. Phones/TV by request. Antiques, liv. rm. w/fireplace, wicker-filled screened porch.* **3rd night, 50%.**

## FRENCHTOWN

**Hunterdon House, The**
12 Bridge St.,  08825
908-996-3632 Fax: 908-996-0942
800-382-0375
Gene Refalvy
All year

$$$-B&B
7 rooms, 7 pb
AmEx, Visa, *Rated*, •
C-ltd/S-no/P-no/H-no

Full breakfast
Comp. fruit & cheese
Comp. cordials, desserts
housekeeping service
sitting room

*Small-town Civil War era mansion furnished in Victoriana. Distinctive guest rooms with emphasis on special touches for comfort and elegance.*

## GLENWOOD

**Apple Valley Inn**
P.O. Box 302,  07418
Corner Rt. 517 & 565
201-764-3735
Mitzi Durham
All year

$$-B&B
6 rooms, 1 pb
*Rated*,
C-ltd/S-ltd/P-no/H-no

Full breakfast
Picnic lunch available
Aftn. tea, comp. wine
sitt. rm., library, pool
tennis court, porches

*Historic 1831 mansion located in Skylands Region, adjacent to Appalachian Trail. Close to ski area, trout stream, water park. Genuine rural refreshment.*

*Jerica Hill Inn, Flemington, NJ*

HIGHLANDS ─────────────────────────────────

**SeaScape Manor B&B**
3 Grand Tour,  07732
908-291-8467 Fax: 908-872-7932
Sherry Ruby, Gloria Miller
All year

$$$-B&B
4 rooms, 4 pb
AmEx,
C-ltd/S-no/P-no/H-no

Full breakfast
Complimentary wine
Sitting room, library
bikes

*Secluded manor nestled in the true covered hills overlooking the blue Atlantic and Sandy Hook Nat'l Recreation area; 45 minutes from NYC; spacious antique filled rooms, private decks.*

LAMBERTVILLE ─────────────────────────────

**Chimney Hill B&B**
207 Goat Hill Rd.,  08530
609-397-1516
Terry & Rich Anderson
All year

$$-B&B
8 rooms, 8 pb
Visa, MC, AmEx,
*Rated*, •
C-ltd/S-no/P-no/H-ltd

Continental plus
Afternoon tea, snacks
Complimentary sherry
sitting room, library
pool, nature trails

*A unique country estate—the perfect setting for a rejuvenating getaway. Romantic with a touch of elegance.* **10% off stay.**

**Inn @ Lambertville Station**
11 Bridge St.,  08530
609-397-4400 Fax: 609-397-9744
800-524-1091
Charles Kroekel
All year

$$$-B&B
45 rooms, 45 pb
Visa, MC, AmEx,
*Rated*,
S-yes/P-no/H-yes
Spanish, German

Continental breakfast
Snacks
Restaurant, bar service
fireplaces, whirlpool
baths

*45 guest rooms, riverviews, Victorian antiques, continental breakfast included. Station rest. serving lunch, dinner, Sunday brunch, creative American cuisine. Conference, banquet facilities available.*

NORTH WILDWOOD ————————————————————————————

| **Candlelight Inn** | $$$-B&B | Full breakfast |
|---|---|---|
| 2310 Central Ave., 08260 | 10 rooms, 10 pb | Refreshments |
| 609-522-6200 Fax: 609-522-6125 | Most CC, *Rated*, • | Sitting room, piano |
| Paul & Diane DiFilippo | S-no/P-no/H-no | hot tub, sun deck, TV, |
| All year exc. January | French | 3 suites, jacuzzi, A/C |

*Seashore B&B with genuine antiques, fireplace, wide veranda. Getaway specials and murder mystery parties available. Close to beach and boardwalk. Carriage house w/ frplcs., Jacuzzi tubs. 7th night 50%.*

OCEAN CITY ————————————————————————————————

| **New Brighton Inn B&B** | $$$-B&B | Full breakfast |
|---|---|---|
| 519 Fifth St., 08226 | 6 rooms, 6 pb | Afternoon tea |
| 609-399-2829 | Most CC, *Rated*, | Sitting room, library |
| Daniel B. & Donna Hand | C-ltd/S-ltd/P-no/H-no | slate patio, bicycles |
| All year | | 2 bedroom cottage |

*Magnificently restored seaside Victorian filled w/antiques. Close to beach, boardwalk, shopping district, restaurants. A charming, romantic inn.*

| **Northwood Inn B&B** | $$$-B&B | Full breakfast |
|---|---|---|
| 401 Wesley Ave., 08226 | 8 rooms, 8 pb | Afternoon tea, snacks |
| 609-399-6071 Fax: 609-398-5553 | MC, Visa, *Rated*, | Porches, roof-top deck |
| Marj & John Loeper | C-ltd/S-no/P-no/H-no | beach passes, game room |
| All year | | regulation pool table |

*Elegantly restored 1894 Victorian with 20th-century comforts. Three blocks to beach and boardwalk. Between Atlantic City and Cape May. Deduct $10/night with 3 night stay midweek.*

| **Scarborough Inn** | $$$-B&B | Continental plus bkfst. |
|---|---|---|
| 720 Ocean Ave., 08226 | 29 rooms, 29 pb | Afternoon refreshments |
| 609-399-1558 Fax: 609-399-4472 | Visa, MC, Disc., • | Sitting room, library |
| 800-258-1558 | C-yes/S-ltd/P-no/H-no | 100-ft. wraparound porch |
| Gus & Carol Bruno | Italian | pocket garden w/fountain |
| May–Oct | | |

*Lovely island inn featuring individually decorated rooms accented with antiques, spacious parlor with upright piano, and thoughtful hospitality. 20% off 5 night mid-week stay.*

OCEAN GROVE ———————————————————————————————

| **Cordova, The** | $-B&B | Continental plus bkfst. |
|---|---|---|
| 26 Webb Ave., 07756 | 21 rooms, 5 pb | Guest kitchen |
| 212-751-9577 Fax: 212-207-4720 | • | Sat. night wine & cheese |
| Doris Chernik | C-yes/S-ltd/P-no/H-no | sitting room, bikes, BBQ |
| Mem. Day–Labor Day | French, Russian | garden, picnic tables |

*Century-old Victorian inn w/antiques, located in lovely historic beach community. You feel like one of the family–experience Old World charm, many amenities. 3rd night free (weekday).*

| **House by the Sea** | $$-B&B | Continental breakfast |
|---|---|---|
| 14 Ocean Ave., 07756 | 20 rooms, 6 pb | Restaurants nearby |
| 908-775-2847 Fax: 908-502-0403 | C-ltd/S-no/P-no/H-no | Library, porches |
| Sally & Alyn Heim | | close to beach |
| Open Memorial–Labor Day | | public tennis court |

*Ocean-front resort on the NJ Coastal Heritage Trail, nestled in a Victorian community. On the Nat'l Historic Register. 60 miles from New York City/Philadelphia areas. 3rd night, 50% discount.*

## PRINCETON

| **Red Maple Farm** | $-B&B | Full country breakfast |
|---|---|---|
| Raymond Rd.,  08540 | 3 rooms, | Sitting room, library |
| 908-329-3821 | *Rated*, | tennis, lawn games |
| Ms. Roberta Churchill | C-ltd/S-no/P-no/H-no | swimming pool, bicycles |
| All year | Some French | |

*Charming, gracious 1740 Historic Register Colonial farm. A 2-acre country retreat minutes from Princeton University and Route 1 business.*

## SPRING LAKE

| **Ashling Cottage** | $$-B&B | Continental plus bkfst. |
|---|---|---|
| 106 Sussex Ave.,  07762 | 10 rooms, 8 pb | Complimentary wine |
| 908-449-3553 Fax: 908-974-0831 | *Rated*,  • | AAA rated 3 diamonds |
| 888-ASHLING | C-ltd/S-ltd/P-no/H-no | TV, VCR, sitting room |
| Goodi & Jack Stewart | German | library, games, bicycles |
| March–December | | |

*Victorian gem furnished w/oak antiques & solarium breakfast room, a block from ocean, in storybook setting. Rowboating on Spring Lake. **50% off 3rd night in May, June, Oct.***

---

| **Hamilton House Inn** | $$$-B&B | Full breakfast |
|---|---|---|
| 15 Mercer Ave.,  07762 | 8 rooms, 8 pb | Snacks, comp. wine |
| 908-449-8282 Fax: 908-449-0206 | MC, Visa, AmEx, | Sitting room |
| Bud & Anne Benz | *Rated*, | pool, tennis courts |
| All year | C-ltd/S-no/P-no/H-no | |

*Warm hospitality in our Victorian home; exquisitely decorated. Pool, steps to the Atlantic Ocean, gourmet breakfasts. Unique seaside experience.*

---

| **Normandy Inn, The** | $$$-B&B | Full breakfast |
|---|---|---|
| 21 Tuttle Ave.,  07762 | 17 rooms, 17 pb | Complimentary wine |
| 908-449-7172 Fax: 908-449-1070 | *Rated*,  • | Sitting/meeting room |
| Michael & Susan Ingino | C-yes/S-ltd/P-no/H-no | bicycles, front porch |
| All year | | newly built suite |

*A country inn at the shore, decorated with lovely Victorian antiques, painted with 5 different Victorian colors. Conference facilities.*

---

| **Sea Crest by The Sea** | $$$-B&B | Full breakfast |
|---|---|---|
| 19 Tuttle Ave.,  07762 | 11 rooms, 11 pb | Afternoon tea |
| 908-449-9031 Fax: 908-974-0403 | Visa, MC, AmEx, | Sitting room, library |
| 800-803-9031 | *Rated*, | bicycles, tennis court |
| John & Carol Kirby | S-no/P-no/H-no | croquet, beach towels |
| All year | | |

*A Spring Lake B&B just for the two of you. A lovingly restored 1885 Queen Anne Victorian with beautiful antiques, ocean views, fireplaces, Carol's famous buttermilk scones.*

---

| **Victoria House** | $$$-B&B | Full breakfast |
|---|---|---|
| 214 Monmouth Ave.,  07762 | 9 rooms, 7 pb | Snacks, comp. wine |
| 908-974-1882 Fax: 908-974-9702 | Visa, MC, AmEx, Disc., | Sitting room, TV, VCR |
| Louise & Robert Goodall | S-no/P-no/H-no | bicycles, tennis pass |
| All year | | local trolley |

*An 1882 quiet seashore Victorian which will charm you with stained glass, antiques, wraparound porch, and old-world hospitality. Bed and breakfast for all seasons.*

STOCKTON ──────────────────────────────

| | | |
|---|---|---|
| **Stockton Inn, The** | $$-B&B | Continental plus bkfst. |
| PO Box C, One Main St., | 11 rooms, 11 pb | Restaurant, bar |
| 08559 | AmEx, MC, Visa, | Sunday brunch, glass rm. |
| 609-397-1250 | *Rated*, | Alfresco dining |
| Andy McDermott, Scott | C-ltd/S-yes/P-no/H-no | 8 suites, gardens |
| Serafin | | |
| All year exc. Christmas | | |

*Unique country inn in riverside town. Distinctive lodging; garden & fireside dining. 3 mi. to Lambertville-New Hope galleries, theaters, antiquing. Suite Retreat discount, ask*

──────────────────────────────

| | | |
|---|---|---|
| **Woolverton Inn** | $$$-B&B | Full country breakfast |
| 6 Woolverton Rd., 08559 | 10 rooms, 10 pb | Weddings, corp. retreats |
| 609-397-0802 Fax: 609-397-4936 | MC, Visa, AmEx, | private parties, bikes |
| 888-AN INN4U | S-no/P-no/H-ltd | fireplaces, Jacuzzis |
| Elizabeth & Michael Palmer | | |
| All year exc. Dec 20-26 | | |

*Newly redecorated/landscaped stately manor country inn, pastoral setting in riverside town. Lambertville 3 miles, New Hope galleries, theaters, antiques.* **Mid-week suite & gourmet dinner special.**

WOODBINE ──────────────────────────────

| | | |
|---|---|---|
| **Henry Ludlam Inn, The** | $$$-B&B | Full 4-course breakfast |
| 1336 Rt. 47, 08220 | 6 rooms, 2 pb | Picnic baskets, wine |
| 609-861-5847 | Most CC, *Rated*, • | Dinner winter (Sat) |
| Chuck & Pat DeArros | C-ltd/S-no/P-no/H-no | sitting room, fireplaces |
| All year | | piano, gazebo, lake |

*Historic B&B situated on 56-acre lake. Creative heart-healthy breakfast. Wood-burning fireplace rooms. Mecca for birders. "We know the hot spots."* **7 nights for price of 5.**

# More Inns ...

| | |
|---|---|
| Andover | Hudson Guide Farm, 07821, 201-398-2679 |
| Asbury Park | Hermitage Guest House, 309 First Ave, 07712, 908-776-6665 |
| Avon-by-the-Sea | Atlantic View Inn, 20 Woodland Ave., 07717, 908-774-8505 |
| Avon-by-the-Sea | Avon Manor Inn, The, 109 Sylvania Ave., 07717, 908-774-0110 |
| Avon-by-the-Sea | Ocean Mist Inn, 28 Woodland Ave., 07717, 908-775-9625 |
| Avon-by-the-Sea | Sands B&B Inn, 42 Sylvania Ave., 07717, 908-776-8386 |
| Avon-by-the-Sea | Summer House, The, 101 Sylvania Ave., 07717, 908-775-3992 |
| Bay Head | Bay Head Harbor Inn, 676 Main Ave., 08742, 908-899-0767 |
| Bay Head | Bentley Inn, The, 694 Main Ave, 08742, 201-892-9589 |
| Beach Haven | Bayberry Barque B&B Inn, 117 Centre St., 08008, 609-492-5216 |
| Beach Haven | Green Gables Inn & Rest., 212 Center St., 08008, 609-492-3553 |
| Beach Haven | Magnolia House, The, 215 Centre St., 08008, 609-492-0398 |
| Beach Haven | Pierrot-by-the-Sea B&B, 101 Centre St., 08008, 609-492-4424 |
| Beach Haven | St. Rita Hotel, 127 Engleside Ave., 08008, 609-492-9192 |
| Beach Haven | Victoria Guest House, 126 Amber St., 08008, 609-492-4154 |
| Belmar | Down the Shore B&B, 201 Seventh Ave., 07719 |
| Belmar | Seaflower, The, 110 Ninth Ave., 07719, 908-681-6006 |
| Bernardsville | Bernards Inn, The, 27 Mine Brook Rd., 07924, 908-766-0002 |
| Cape May | Albert Stevens Inn, The, 127 Myrtle Ave., 08204, 609-884-4717 |
| Cape May | Alexander's Inn, 653 Washington St., 08204, 609-884-2555 |
| Cape May | Brass Bed Inn, The, 719 Columbia Ave., 08204, 609-884-8075 |
| Cape May | Buttonwood Manor, 115 N. Broadway, 08204 |
| Cape May | Colvmns by the Sea, 1513 Beach Dr., 08204, 609-884-2228 |
| Cape May | Delsea, 621 Columbia Ave., 08204, 609-884-8540 |
| Cape May | Doctors Inn at Kings Grant, 2n N. Main St., 08210, 609-463-9330 |
| Cape May | Hanson House, 111 Ocean St., 08204, 609-884-8791 |
| Cape May | Heirloom B&B Inn, 601 Columbia Ave., 08204, 609-884-1666 |
| Cape May | Holly House, 20 Jackson St., 08204, 609-884-7365 |
| Cape May | Inn at 22 Jackson, 22 Jackson St., 08204, 800-452-8177 |
| Cape May | Inn of Cape May, The, P.O. Box 31, 08204, 800-257-0432 |
| Cape May | John F. Craig House, The, 609 Columbia Ave., 08204, 609-884-0100 |
| Cape May | Kelly's Celtic Inn, 24 Ocean St., 08204, 609-898-1999 |
| Cape May | King's Cottage, The, 9 Perry St., 08204, 609-884-0415 |
| Cape May | Leith Hall, 22 Ocean St., 08204 |

| | |
|---|---|
| Cape May | Leith Hall Seashore Inn, 22 Ocean St., 08204, 609-884-1934 |
| Cape May | Linda Lee, 725 Columbia Ave., 08204, 609-884-1240 |
| Cape May | Manse Inn, 510 Hughes St., 08204, 609-884-0116 |
| Cape May | Primrose Inn, 1102 Lafayette St., 08204, 609-884-8288 |
| Cape May | Prince Edward, The, 38 Jackson St., 08204, 609-884-2131 |
| Cape May | Sand Castle, The, 829 Stockton Ave., 08204, 609-884-5451 |
| Cape May | Sevilla, The, 5 Perry St., 08204 |
| Cape May | Stetson B&B Inn, The, 725 Kearney Ave., 08204, 609-884-1724 |
| Cape May | Twin Gables, 731 Columbia Ave., 08204, 609-884-7332 |
| Cape May | Victorian Lace Inn, 901 Stockton Ave., 08204, 609-884-1772 |
| Cape May | Victorian Rose, 719 Columbia Ave., 08204, 609-884-2497 |
| Cape May | Washington Inn, 801 Washington St., 08204 |
| Cape May | Wilbraham Mansion, 133 Myrtle Ave., 08204, 609-884-2046 |
| Chester | Publick House Inn, 111 Main St., Box 85, 07930, 201-879-6878 |
| Cream Ridge | Country Meadows B&B, 38 Jonathan Holmes Rd., 08514, 609-758-9437 |
| Frenchtown | National Hotel, 31 Race St., 08825, 201-996-4871 |
| Hope | Inn at Millrace Pond, The, P.O. Box 359, 07844, 908-459-4884 |
| Island Heights | Studio of John F. Peto, 102 Cedar Ave., 08732, 201-270-6058 |
| Jobstown | Belle Springs Farm, RD 1, Box 420, 08041, 609-723-5364 |
| Lambertville | York Street House, 42 York St., 08530, 609-397-3007 |
| Longport | Winchester Hotel, One S. 24 St., 08403, 609-822-0623 |
| Lyndhurst | Jeremiah J. Yercance House, 410 Riverside Ave., 07071, 201-438-9457 |
| Madison | Garden Suite, 42 Ridgedale, 07940, 201-765-0233 |
| Manahawkin | Goose N. Berry Inn, 190 N. Main St, 08050, 609-597-6350 |
| Milford | Chestnut Hill on Delaware, P.O. Box N, 08848, 201-995-9761 |
| Montclair | Marlboro Inn, The, 334 Grove St., 07042, 201-783-5300 |
| Ocean City | Adelmann's, The, 1228 Ocean Ave., 08226, 609-399-2786 |
| Ocean City | Barnagate B&B, 637 Wesley Ave., 08226, 609-391-9366 |
| Ocean City | Beach End Inn, 815 Plymouth Pl., 08226, 609-398-1016 |
| Ocean City | Enterprise B&B Inn, The, 1020 Central Ave., 08226, 609-398-1698 |
| Ocean City | Top o'the Waves, 5447 Central Ave., 08226, 609-399-0477 |
| Ocean Grove | Amherst Inn, The, 14 Pitman Ave., 07756, 201-988-5297 |
| Ocean Grove | Keswick Inn, 32 Embury Ave., 07756, 201-775-7506 |
| Ocean Grove | Pine Tree Inn, 10 Main Ave., 07756, 908-775-3264 |
| Pemberton | Isaac Hilliard House B&B, 31 Hanover St., 08068, 609-894-0756 |
| Pittstown | Seven Springs Farm B&B, 12 Perryville Rd., 08867 |
| Princeton | B&B of Princeton, P.O. Box 571, 08542, 609-924-3189 |
| Princeton | Candy Lindsay, 19 Corson Rd., 08540 |
| Princeton | Peacock Inn, 20 Bayard Ln., 08540, 609-924-1707 |
| Salem | Ma Bowman's B&B, 156 Harmersville Peck-, 08079, 609-935-4913 |
| Sea Girt | Beacon House B&B, The, 100 & 104 Beacon Blvd., 08750, 908-449-5835 |
| Sea Girt | Holly Harbor Guest House, 112 Baltimore Blvd., 08750, 908-449-9731 |
| Spring Lake | Carriage House, 208 Jersey Ave., 07762, 908-449-1332 |
| Spring Lake | Chateau Inn, 500 Warren Ave., 07762, 908-974-2000 |
| Spring Lake | Colonial Ocean House, 102 Sussex Ave., 07762 |
| Spring Lake | Grand Victorian Hotel, The, 1505 Ocean Ave., 07762, 908-449-5327 |
| Spring Lake | Hewitt Wellington Hotel, 200 Monmouth Ave., 07762, 908-974-1212 |
| Spring Lake | Hollycroft Inn, P.O. Box 448, 07762, 908-681-2254 |
| Spring Lake | Johnson House Inn, 25 Tuttle Ave., 07762, 908-449-1860 |
| Spring Lake | Kenilworth, The, 1505 Ocean Ave., 07762, 908-449-5327 |
| Spring Lake | La Maison, 404 Jersey Ave., 07762, 908-449-0969 |
| Spring Lake | Moulton House, 120 Ludlow Ave., 07762 |
| Spring Lake | Villa Park House, 417 Ocean Rd., 07762, 908-449-3642 |
| Spring Lake | Walden on the Pond, 412 Ocean Rd., 07762, 908-449-7764 |
| Spring Lake | Warren Hotel, P.O. Box 286, 07762, 908-449-8800 |
| Stanhope | Whistling Swan Inn, P.O. Box 791, 07874, 201-347-6369 |
| Whitehouse | Holly Thorn House, 143 Readington Rd., 08889, 908-534-1616 |

*A Sea Crest by the Sea, Spring Lake, NJ*

# New Mexico

## ALBUQUERQUE

**Canyon Crest**
5804 Canyon Crest NE, 87111
505-821-4898
Jan Mansure
All year

$$-B&B
2 rooms, 1 pb
Most CC, •
S-no/P-no/H-no

Continental plus
Afternoon tea
Antiques & collectibles
museums, Batik pictures

*Contemporary cozy hideaway furnished with southwest and country decor sprinkled with flowers and antiques. Convenient to golfing, galleries, balooning and hiking.*

---

**Casas de Suenos, B&B Inn**
310 Rio Grande Blvd. SW,
87104
505-247-4560 Fax: 505-842-8493
800-242-8987
Mari Penshurst-Gersten
All year

$$$-B&B
12 rooms, 12 pb
Most CC, •
C-ltd/S-no/P-no/H-yes
Spanish

Full gourmet breakfast
Afternoon tea
Comp. wine, snacks
sitting room, library
bicycles

*Fresh flower arrangements, blooming gardens, and hospitality. Adjoining Albuquerque's famous old town, with museums, theater, fine dining, galleries, shops, nature trails. **10% discount.***

---

**Sarabande**
5637 Rio Grande Blvd NW,
87107
505-345-4923 Fax: 505-345-9130
800-506-4923
M. Magnussen & B. Vickers
All year

$$$-B&B
3 rooms, 3 pb
MC, Visa, *Rated*, •
S-no/P-no/H-yes

Full breakfast
Aftn. tea, comp. wine
Tennis courts, bicycles
fireplace, jogging path
riding, spa, 50'lap pool

*Nestled in Los Ranchos, a pastoral village: the best of old New Mexico charm. Linger & reminisce by the courtyard fountain or country kitchen. **10% off week long stay.***

## ALGODONES, SANTA FE

**Hacienda Vargas B&B Inn**
P.O. Box 307, 87001
1431 El Camino Real
505-867-9115 Fax: 505-867-1902
800-261-0006
Pablo & Jule De Vargas
All year

$$$-B&B
7 rooms, 7 pb
MC, Visa, *Rated*, •
C-ltd/S-no/P-no/H-ltd
Spanish, German

Full country breakfast
Complimentary wine
Hot tubs, sitting room
library, golf courses
nearby, private jacuzzis

*Hacienda Vargas has 2 bdrms. & 5 suites w/priv. entrances, bathrooms & frplcs. 4 suites have jacuzzi tubs. Large BBQ area also available. Romance packages avail. **10% off ltd.***

## BERNALILLO

**La Hacienda Grande**
21 Baros Ln., 87004
505-867-1887 Fax: 505-867-4621
800-353-1887
Shosh. Zimmerman & Dan'l
Buop
All year

$$$-B&B
6 rooms, 6 pb
Visa, MC, Disc., •
C-ltd/S-ltd/P-no/H-no

Full breakfast
Lunch/dinner/arrangement
Weddings, retreats
jacuzzi for 2, hot tubs
business mtngs., library

*250 year old authentic hacienda. 2 ft. thick walls, wood ceilings, frplcs., priv. baths, A/C. Near Santa Fe, Albuquerque & minutes to most N.M. sites. **50% off 3rd night.***

*Casa del Gavilan, Cimarron, NM*

## CHIMAYO

**La Posada de Chimayo**
P.O. Box 463, 87522
279 Rio Arriba County Rd.
505-351-4605 Fax: 505-351-4605
Sue Farrington
All year

$$$-B&B
6 rooms, 4 pb
*Rated*,
C-ltd/S-yes/P-ltd/H-no
Spanish

Full breakfast
Complimentary wine
Private sitting rooms
fireplace
hiking

*A traditional adobe guest house in beautiful northern New Mexico; brick floors, viga ceilings, corner fireplaces, Mexican rugs. 30 miles to Santa Fe & Taos.*

## CIMARRON

**Casa del Gavilan**
P.O. Box 518, 87714
Hwy 21 South
505-376-2246 Fax: 505-376-2247
800-GAV-ILAN
Mrs. Bettye Knox
All year

$$-B&B
7 rooms, 6 pb
AmEx, MC, Visa, •
C-yes/S-no/P-no/H-yes
Spanish

Full breakfast
Lunch, dinner by arrang.
Aftn. tea, comp. wine
sitting room, library
hiking, skiing, fishing

*Casa del Gavilan, the perfect retreat, overlooking the Santa Fe trail. Service, view, gardens and quiet will delight you.*

## CORRALES

**Casa La Resolana**
7887 Corrales Rd., 87048
505-898-0203 Fax: 505-898-3390
800-884-0203
Jerry and Nancy Thomas
All year

$$$-B&B
3 rooms, 3 pb
Visa, MC, AmEx,
*Rated*, •
C-ltd/S-ltd/P-no/H-no

Full breakfast
Breakfast by waterfall
Sitting room, snacks
hot tubs, aft. tea
golf package, comp. wine

*Southwest Abode, magnificent mountain & bosque views, pastoral setting with spacious suites, winter skiing, golfers paradise.* **Free champagne for newlyweds.**

**Chocolate Turtle, The**
1098 W. Meadowlark Lane,
87048
505-898-1800 Fax: 505-898-5328
800-898-1842
Carole Morgan
All year

$$-B&B
4 rooms, 4 pb
Visa, MC, Amex,
C-ltd/S-no/P-no

Gourmet breakfast
Handmade chocolates
TV/videos, dining room

*Relax in historic Corrales. Located on the northern boundary of Albuquerque, yet in a country-like setting with incredible mountain views, horses, and great golfing.*

## CORRALES

| **Cottonwoods B&B, The** | $$-B&B | Continental plus bkfst. |
|---|---|---|
| P.O. Box 3028,  87048 | 2 rooms, 2 pb | Sitting room, bicycles |
| 415 E. La Entrada | Visa, MC, *Rated*, | swimming pool |
| 505-897-5086 Fax:505-898-9725 | S-no/P-no/H-no | jacuzzi available |
| 888-897-5086 | | |
| Jan McConnell | | |
| All year | | |

*Nestled among cottonwoods near the Rio Grande, rooms have antique furnishings & exposed adobe walls. Walk to restaurants, galleries and nature preserve.*

| **Sagebrush Circle B&B** | B&B | Continental plus bkfst. |
|---|---|---|
| 23 Sagebrush Circle,  87048 | 2 rooms, 2 pb | Afternoon tea, snacks |
| 505-898-5393 Fax:505-898-5393 | C-ltd/S-no/P-no/H-no | Lunch (fee) |
| Barbara & Victor Ferkiss | Some Spanish | library, hot tubs |
| All year | | |

*Magnificent mountain views, antiques/collectibles from abroad. Delicious breakfasts and caring, articulate hosts create a stimulating, yet relaxing haven. 3rd night, 50%.*

| **Sandhill Crane B&B, The** | $$$-B&B | Full breakfast |
|---|---|---|
| 389 Camino Hermosa,  87048 | 4 rooms, 4 pb | Dinner, snacks |
| 505-898-2445 Fax:505-898-2445 | Visa, MC, AmEx, | Hot tubs |
| 800-375-2445 | *Rated*, • | library |
| Carol Hogan & Phil Thorpe | C-ltd/S-no/P-no/H-yes | sitting room |
| All year | | |

*Enjoy memorable sunrises & breakfasts in warm, friendly, casual, southwestern adobe hacienda. Tours, massages, hot tub, central location. 10% off 3 nights or more.*

## ESPANOLA

| **Inn at the Delta** | $$$-B&B | Full breakfast |
|---|---|---|
| 304 Paseo de Onate,  87532 | 10 rooms, 10 pb | Restaurant |
| 505-753-9466 800-995-8599 | Most CC, *Rated*, • | Sitting room, patio |
| The Garcia Family | C-yes/S-ltd/P-ltd/H-ltd | private collection of |
| All year | Spanish, French | Indian & Spanish artwork |

*Beautiful adobe suites with vistas, handcarved furniture, whirlpool tubs, kiva fireplaces and lovely gardens. Centrally located for touring.*

## FARMINGTON

| **Silver River Adobe Inn** | $$$-B&B | Continental plus bkfst. |
|---|---|---|
| **B&B** | 3 rooms, 3 pb | Dinner, ask |
| P.O. Box 3411,  87499 | MC, Visa, • | River walk |
| 3151 West Main 87401 | C-ltd/S-no/P-no/H-yes | wildlife, 5 star golfing |
| 505-325-8219  800-382-9251 | | Weddings, workshops |
| Diana Ohlson & David Beers | | |
| All year | | |

*New Mexico adobe with large timbers. Day trips to Chaco Canyon, Mesa Verde, Aztec ruins, Salmon ruins, Canyon de Chelly. Conferences for up to 12 people. 3rd night 50% off.*

## GALISTEO

| **Galisteo Inn, The** | $$$-B&B | Full breakfast |
|---|---|---|
| HC 75-Box 4,  87540 | 12 rooms, 8 pb | Lunch, dinner, tea |
| 9 La Vega | Visa, MC, Disc.,*Rated*, | Rest., bar, library |
| 505-466-4000 Fax:505-466-4008 | • | hot tubs, sauna, bicycle |
| W. Aarniokoski & J. Kaufman | C-ltd/S-ltd/P-ltd/H-yes | lap pool, horseback |
| Feb-Dec | Spanish | |

*Magical 250 year old Spanish hacienda on eight country acres, half hour from Santa Fe. Exquisite "Fresh Southwest" dinners & breakfasts.*

LAS CRUCES ───────────────────────────────────

**T.R.H. Smith Mansion B&B**
909 N. Alameda Blvd., 88005
505-525-2525 Fax: 505-524-8227
800-526-1914
Marlene K. & Jay Tebo
All year

$$-B&B
4 rooms, 2 pb
Visa, MC, AmEx, •
C-ltd/S-ltd/P-ltd/H-no
German

Full breakfast
Sitting room, library
pool table, game/TV room
music, artist lectures

*Elegant, centrally located historic mansion offers peaceful respite in heart of fertile Mesilla Valley. Full European style breakfast features fruits.* **7th night free.**

LINCOLN ───────────────────────────────────

**Casa de Patron B&B Inn**
P.O. Box 27, 88338
Hwy. #380 East
505-653-4676 Fax: 505-653-4671
Jeremy & Cleis Jordan
All year

$$$-B&B
7 rooms, 7 pb
Visa, MC, *Rated*, •
C-ltd/S-no/P-no/H-ltd

Full breakfast
Continental plus bkfst.
Sitting room
hiking trail
2 casitas for families

*On the scenic way to Carlsbad Caverns. A charmed Adobe hacienda awaits you as it did Billy the Kid! Conference room.*

LOS ALAMOS ───────────────────────────────────

**Canyon Inn**
12 Timber Ridge, 80 Canyon
Rd., 87544
505-662-9595 800-662-2565
Rich Kraemer
All year

$$-B&B
4 rooms, 4 pb
Visa, MC, AmEx,
C-ltd/S-no/P-no/H-no

Continental plus bkfst.
Laundry and kitchen
facilities available
close to downtown

*Convenient to town and national lab. Guests have use of entire house including kitchen and laundry facilities. Ideal for long stays.*

**Casa del Rey**
305 Rover Blvd., 87544
505-672-9401
Virginia King
All year

$-B&B
2 rooms, 1 pb
C-ltd/S-no/P-no/H-no

Continental plus bkfst.
Homemade breads, granola
Sitting room
patio, sun porch, garden
tennis courts nearby

*Quiet residential area, friendly atmosphere, beautiful mountain views from patios. Excellent library, restaurants and recreational facilities nearby.* **Weekly & monthly rates.**

SANTA FE ───────────────────────────────────

**Adobe Abode B&B Inn**
202 Chapelle Street, 87501
505-983-3133 Fax: 505-986-0972
Pat Harbour
All year

$$$-B&B
6 rooms, 6 pb
Visa, MC, Disc, *Rated*,
•
C-ltd/S-ltd/P-no/H-yes
Spanish

Full gourmet breakfast
Comp. cookies & sherry
Sitting rm. w/fireplace
private phones, TV's
off-street parking

*Restored, historic adobe 3 blocks from the Plaza, with a sophisticated mix of Southwest decor and European touches.* **Free champagne for honeymooners & anniversaries.**

**Alexander's Inn**
529 E. Palace Ave., 87501
505-986-1431 Fax: 505-982-8572
Carolyn Lee
All year

$$-B&B
5 rooms, 3 pb
MC, Visa, *Rated*, •
C-ltd/S-no/P-no/H-no
French

Continental plus bkfst.
Afternoon tea, beverages
Sitting room w/fireplace
hot tub in back garden
dbl. jacuzzi in cottage

*Cozy, quiet & romantic, yet just minutes from the Plaza. Full continental breakfast served by fireside or on terrace. Private casita available.* **50% off, ltd.**

*Adobe Abode, Santa Fe, NM*

## SANTA FE

**Arius Compound**
P.O. Box 1111,  87504
1018-1/2 Canyon Rd.
505-982-2621 Fax: 505-989-8280
800-735-8453
Len & Roberta Goodman
All year

$$$-EP
3 rooms, 3 pb
AmEx, MC, Visa,
*Rated*,
C-yes/S-yes/P-ltd/H-no

Full kitchens
Hot tub
near shops & restaurants
1- or 2-bedroom suites

*1- & 2-bedroom guest houses on historic adobe compound. Classic Santa Fe charm; corner fireplaces, complete kitchens, garden patios & fountains, fruit trees. Outdoor hot tub.*

---

**Camas de Santa Fe**
323 E. Palace Ave.,  87501
505-984-1337 Fax: 505-984-8449
800-756-5873
John D. Gundzik
All year

$$-B&B
15 rooms, 14 pb
Most CC,
C-yes/S-no/P-no/H-yes
Spanish, Danish

Continental plus bkfst.
Afternoon tea, snacks
Outside courtyard
sitting room
easy walk to plaza

*Charming, affordable downtown B&B Inn, territorial style; hardwood floors & viga ceilings w/Mexican furniture & private baths. Close to Canyon Road, The Plaza and Ski Basin.*

---

**Casa De La Cuma B&B**
P.O. Box 9925,  87504
105 Paseo de la Cuma
505-983-1717  888-336-1717
Art & Donna Bailey
All year

$$-B&B
7 rooms, 5 pb
*Rated*, •
C-ltd/S-ltd/P-no/H-no
Spanish

Continental plus bkfst.
Complimentary beverages
TV, solarium, garden
patio w/barbecue, A/C
avail. as rental house

*Mountain views! Walking distance to downtown Plaza, shopping, restaurants, galleries, library, museums, banks. City sports facilities across street. **3rd night free, ltd.***

SANTA FE ─────────────────────────────────

**Chapelle St. Casitas**
P.O. Box 9925, 87504
209-211 Chapelle St.
505-988-2883  888-366-1717
Art & Donna Bailey
All year

$$$-EP
4 rooms, 4 pb
Visa, MC, •
C-ltd/S-no/P-no/H-no
Spanish

Continental plus bkfst.
Kitchens
Patio, quite location
some rooms A/C, owners
are long time residents.

*3-room suites (1-4 persons) with private baths & kitchens. Beautiful, quiet downtown location in core historic district. **3rd night free, ltd. Monthly rates.***

---

**Don Gaspar Compound Inn**
623 Don Gaspar Ave., 87501
505-986-8664 Fax: 505-986-0696
Shirley & David Alford
All year

$$$-B&B
12 rooms, 12 pb
•
C-yes/S-no/P-no/H-no

Continental plus bkfst.
Garden courtyard with
fountain, walk to Plaza,
galleries, restaurants

*Located in historic residential neighborhood three blocks from Plaza & The Compounds. Three private suites enjoy secluded flower filled courtyards. **10% disc't 5 days or more.***

---

**Dunshee's B&B**
986 Acequia Madre, 87501
505-982-0988
Susan Dunshee
All year

$$$-B&B
2 rooms, 2 pb
MC, Visa,
C-yes/S-no/P-no/H-no

Full breakfast in suite
Continental in casita
Sitting room
refrig., microwave, TV
patio, porch

*Romantic hideaway in adobe compound in historic zone. Choice of 2-room suite or 2-bedroom guesthouse furnished with antiques, folk art, fresh flowers, fireplaces.*

---

**El Paradero**
220 W. Manhattan, 87501
505-988-1177
Ouida MacGregor & Thom
Allen
All year

$$-B&B
14 rooms, 8 pb
MC, Visa, *Rated*, •
C-ltd/S-ltd/P-ltd/H-ltd
Spanish

Full gourmet breakfast
Gourmet picnic lunches
TV rm, living rm, piano
central cooling in rooms
2 suites available

*180-year-old adobe in quiet downtown location. Gourmet breakfasts, warm atmosphere, detailed visitor information. True southwestern hospitality. **Bottle of wine with reservation.***

---

**Four Kachinas Inn B&B**
512 Webber St., 87501
505-982-2550  800-397-2564
John Daw
All year

$$$-B&B
4 rooms, 4 pb
MC, Visa, Disc, *Rated*,
•
C-ltd/S-no/P-no/H-yes
Spanish, French

Continental plus bkfst.
Afternoon tea
Sitting room
breakfast are vegetarian

*Only 4 blocks from historic Plaza; furnished w/handcrafted furniture, Navajo rugs & Indian art; breakfast, award-winning baked goods served in your room. **Free bottle of wine.***

---

**Grant Corner Inn**
122 Grant Ave., 87501
505-983-6678 Fax: 505-983-1526
Louise Stewart
All year

$$$-B&B
14 rooms, 8 pb
MC, Visa, *Rated*, •
C-ltd/S-yes/P-no/H-yes
Spanish

Full breakfast
Comp. wine & cheese
Gourmet picnic lunches
private club access
(pool, sauna, tennis)

*Elegant colonial home located in the heart of downtown Santa Fe, nine charming rooms furnished with antiques; friendly, warm atmosphere.*

SANTA FE —————————————————————————————————————

**Heart Seed B&B & Spa**
P.O. Box 6019,  87502
516 B County Rd. SS
505-471-7026
Judith Polich
All year

$$$-B&B
4 rooms, 4 pb
Visa, MC, •
C-ltd/S-ltd/P-no/H-no

Full gourmet breakfast
Afternoon tea, snacks
Day spa on premises
50's cowboy - cowgirl
motiff, and camp kitchen

*Spectacular mountain setting on historic Turquoise Trail, day spa, massage, hot tub, 100 acres, full gourmet breakfast, rooms with kitchenettes. **3+ nights 10% off.***

---

**La Tienda Inn**
445-447 W San Francisco,
  87501
505-989-8259 Fax: 505-820-6931
800-889-7611
Leighton & Barbara Watson
All year

$$$-B&B
7 rooms, 7 pb
Visa, MC, •
C-ltd/S-ltd/P-no/H-yes

Continental plus
Afternoon tea
Sitting room, library
bottled water and fresh
flowers in room

*A romantic abode compound just 4 blocks from the Plaza. Private entrances; private baths; fireplaces. Breakfast in your room or in the garden in summer.*

---

**Polly's Adobe Guest House**
410 Camino Don Miguel,
  87501
505-983-9481
Ted & Polly Rose
All year

$$-EP
1 rooms, 1 pb
MC, Visa,
C-ltd/S-ltd/P-ltd

Casita has kitchen
Coffee, tea, staples
Private garden patio
separate telephone
as private as you want

*Adobe casita, comfortably furnished; Southwestern books, nice kitchen, cozy garden patio; Canyon Road neighborhood. Walk to Plaza, museums, restaurants, shopping, foothills.*

---

**Preston House, The**
106 Faithway St.,  87501
505-982-3465 Fax: 505-982-3465
Signe Bergman
All year

$-B&B
14 rooms, 14 pb
MC, Visa, *Rated*,
C-ltd/S-ltd/P-no/H-no

Continental plus bkfst.
Afternoon tea & dessert
Sitting room
lawn

*Historic 100-year-old Queen Anne house on National Register with fireplaces and antiques; quiet location 3 blocks from Plaza.*

---

**Pueblo Bonito B&B Inn**
138 W. Manhattan,  87501
505-984-8001 Fax: 505-984-3155
800-461-4599
Herb & Amy Behm
All year

$$-B&B
14 rooms, 14 pb
Most CC, *Rated*, •
C-yes/S-ltd/P-no/H-ltd

Continental plus to room
Aft. tea, snacks
Laundry, cable TV
tours, sightseeing arr.
airport pickup, hot tub

*Secluded historic adobe; 5-minute walk from Santa Fe Plaza. Traditional New Mexico living and decor. 15 guest rooms with private bath and fireplace. Landscaped grounds.*

---

**Territorial Inn**
215 Washington Ave.,  87501
505-989-7737  Fax: 505-986-9212
Lela McFerrin
All year

$$-B&B
10 rooms, 8 pb
MC, Visa, *Rated*, •
C-ltd/S-ltd/P-no/H-yes

Continental plus bkfst.
Comp. brandy, cookies
Sitting room
hot tubs

*Elegantly furnished 100-year old home. One block from Historic Plaza. Seasonal rates "Peak" (Thanksgiving, Christmas & May1-Oct 30th) $90-160. All rest of year $70-120.*

## SILVER CITY

**Carter House, The**
101 N. Cooper St., 88061
505-388-5485
Lucy Dilworth
All year

$$-B&B
5 rooms, 5 pb
Visa, MC *Rated*,
C-yes/S-ltd/P-no/H-yes
Italian, Spanish

Full breakfast
Afternoon tea
Sitting room, library
22 bed Hostelling
International facility

*Stately historic district home with ornate interior oak trim. Panoramic view of mountains from large front porch. Close to galleries and museums.*

## TAOS

**Adobe & Stars B&B Inn**
P.O. Box 2285, 87571
584 State Hwy. 150
505-776-2776 Fax: 505-776-2872
800-211-7076
Judy Salathiel
All year

$$-B&B
7 rooms, 7 pb
Most CC, *Rated*, •
C-yes/S-no/P-ltd/H-yes
Spanish

Full breakfast
Afternoon tea, snacks
Comp. wine, sitting room
library, jacuzzi tubs
starry skies

*Brand new southwestern style inn with beamed ceilings, kiva fireplaces, jacuzzi tubs, sweeping mountain views. Mountain biking/hiking trails accessible.* **3rd night 50%, ltd.**

**Amer.Artists Gallery B&B**
P.O. Box 584, 87571
132 Frontier Ln.
505-758-4446 Fax: 505-758-0497
800-532-2041
LeAn & Charles Clamurro
All year

$$-B&B
10 rooms, 10 pb
Visa, MC, AmEx,
*Rated*, •
C-ltd/S-no/P-no/H-ltd
Spanish

Full breakfast
Afternoon snacks/goodies
Hot tub, sitting room
skiing, hiking, kayaking
art gallery, kiva frplc.

*Charming southwestern hacienda filled with artwork. Fireplaces, hot tub, gardens. Magnificent view of mountains. Minutes from plaza, galleries, skiing, historic attractions. Jacuzzi suites.*

**Brooks Street Inn, The**
P.O. Box 4954, 87571
119 Brooks St.
505-758-1489 800-758-1489
Carol Frank
All year

$$-B&B
7 rooms, 5 pb
MC, Visa, *Rated*,
C-ltd/H-yes
Spanish

Full breakfast
Comp. espresso bar
Snacks
sitting room, library
shaded patio, hammock

*Rambling adobe with charming guest house. Fireplaces and cozy alcoves. Quiet, tree-shaded garden. Short walk to historic plaza and galleries. Vegetarian breakfasts available.*

**Casa Europa Inn & Gallery**
HC 68, Box 3F, 840 Upper
Ranchitos Rd., 87571
505-758-9798 888-758-9798
Rudi & Marcia Zwicker
All year

$$$-B&B
6 rooms, 6 pb
MC, Visa, *Rated*, •
C-yes/S-no/P-no/H-no
German

Full breakfast
Afternoon tea
Comp. wine, snacks
hot tub in one room
art gallery

*Luxury country inn-historical Southwest estate; horses, views, ambiance. Romantic rooms/suites; marble baths (hot tubs), fireplaces. Pamper yourself with the best!*

**Casa Zia**
P.O. Box 5107, 87571
513 Zia
505-751-1861

$$$-B&B

Continental plus bkfst.

*Our suite has a cathedral ceiling, king bed & sleeper, private entrance & bath, hot tub. Walk to Plaza, short drive to ski valley & river rafting.*

TAOS —————————————————————————————————

**Cottonwood Inn**
HCR 74 Box 24609, 87529
#2 State Rt. 230, 87514
505-776-5826 Fax: 505-776-5826
800-324-7120
Bill & Kit Owen
All year

$$$-B&B
7 rooms, 7 pb
Visa, MC, •
C-yes/S-ltd/P-no/H-yes
Spanish, German

Full breakfast
Afternoon tea, snacks
Complimentary wine
sitting room, library
hot tubs, sauna

*Exceptional views. Distinctive rooms w/frplcs., whirlpools & southwestern art. Full breakfasts, aftn. refreshments. Convenient to town & ski slopes. **10% discount on 5 night stay, ltd.***

---

**Hacienda Del Sol B&B**
P.O. Box 177, 87571
109 Mabel Dodge Ln.
505-758-0287
John & Marcine Landon
All year

$$-B&B
9 rooms, 9 pb
MC, Visa, *Rated*, •
C-yes/S-no/P-no/H-ltd

Full breakfast
Complimentary snacks
Lib., frplcs., gallery
outdoor hot tub, robes
golf nearby, gardens

*180-yr-old large adobe hideaway purchased by Mabel Dodge for Indian husband, Tony. Adjoins vast Indian lands yet close to Plaza. Tranquillity, mountain views. Comp. newspaper.*

---

**Historic Taos Inn, The**
125 Paseo del Pueblo N.,
87571
505-758-2233 Fax: 505-758-5776
800-TAOS-INN
Carolyn Haddock/Doug
Smith
All year

$$$-EP
36 rooms, 36 pb
Visa, MC, DC, *Rated*,
•
C-yes/S-yes/P-no/H-ltd
Spanish, French

Breakfast coupon avail.
Full service restaurant
Bar, library, hot tubs
musical entertainment
ski (wint.), swim (sum.)

*Historic adobe property, a block north of Plaza. Guest rooms feature antiques, hand-loomed Indian bedspreads, pueblo-style fireplaces, and handcrafted furniture.*

---

**La Posada de Taos**
P.O. Box 1118, 87571
309 Juanita Ln.
505-758-8164 Fax: 505-751-3294
800-645-4803
Bill Swan & Nancy Brooks-
Swan
All year

$$$-B&B
6 rooms, 6 pb
*Rated*, •
S-yes/P-yes/H-yes

Full breakfast
Large dining room
Sitting room, patios
sun room, portals
fireplaces, courtyards

*We have a new large dining room with 13' high beamed ceiling overlooking the garden & Taos Mountain. Also added private patios for 2 rooms. Host meetings & classes.*

---

**Laughing Horse Inn**
P.O. Box 4889, 87571
729 Paseo del Pueblo No.
505-758-8350 Fax: 505-751-1123
800-776-0161
P. Loumena & A. Lorraine
All year

$-EP
14 rooms, 4 pb
Visa, MC, AmEx, •
C-yes/S-no/P-yes/H-no

Guest kitchen, food, bev
Bar service, library
bicycles, hot tubs
sauna, sitting room

*An 1887 southwestern adobe that was once home to the publisher of The Laughing Horse magazine and his guests, D.H. Lawrence and Georgia O'Keefe. **3rd night 20% off, ltd.***

TAOS

**Orinda B&B**
P.O. Box 4451,　87571
461 Valverde
505-758-8581　Fax: 505-751-4895
800-847-1837
Cary & George
All year

$$-B&B
4 rooms, 4 pb
Visa, MC, Disc., •
C-ltd/S-no/P-no/H-no

Full breakfast
Snacks
Sitting room, library
tennis court, hot tubs
sauna, swimming pool

*Quiet, pastoral setting on 2 acres, southwest adobe home close to town, shops, galleries and skiing (16 miles). Free pass to health spa and tennis.* **Discounts offered for certain periods.**

---

**Salsa del Salto B&B Inn**
P.O. Box 1468,　87529
543 Taos Ski Valley Rd.
505-776-2422　Fax: 505-776-2422
800-530-3097
Mary Hockett, Dadou Mayer
All year

$$$-B&B
10 rooms, 10 pb
MC, Visa, *Rated*, •
C-ltd/S-no/P-no/H-no
French, Spanish

Full gourmet breakfast
Afternoon tea, snacks
Sitting room, library
private tennis & pool
hot tubs, ski packages

*Beautiful blend of southwestern style and ambiance. Mountain views, sunsets, a million stars, and a hot tub. French chef. 10 miles from Taos ski valley & Taos Pueblo.*

---

**San Geronimo Lodge**
216M Paseo del Pueblo, N167,　87571
505-751-3776　Fax: 505-751-1493
800-894-4119
Allison & Shaunessy Everett
All year

$$$-B&B
18 rooms, 18 pb
Visa, MC, AmEx,
*Rated*, •
C-yes/S-no/P-no/H-yes
Spanish

Full breakfast
Afternoon tea
Library
hot tubs, swimming pool
phones & TVs in rooms

*San Geronimo Lodge is Taos' finest mountain inn. Comfortable rooms, spacious common areas, delicious breakfasts, spectacular views on 2.5 acres.* **3rd night, 50%.**

---

**Stewart House B&B**
P.O. Box 3020,　87571
Hwy. 150, Ski Valley Rd.
505-776-2557
Carl Fritz & Sharon Flagler
All year

$$-B&B
4 rooms, 4 pb
Visa, MC, •
C-yes/S-no/P-no/H-yes
German, Spanish

Full breakfast
Afternoon tea
Sitting room, library
hot tubs

*Unique country inn; magical view of spectacular Taos Mountain; warm, friendly old west ambiance; hot tub; fireplaces; gourmet breakfast.*

---

**Touchstone B&B**
P.O. Box 2896,　87571
110 Mable Dodge Lane
505-758-0192　Fax: 505-758-3498
800-758-0192
Bren Price
All year

$$$-B&B
8 rooms, 8 pb
Visa, MC, AmEx,
*Rated*, •
C-ltd/S-no/P-no/H-no
Spanish

Full gourmet breakfast
Sitting room, library
hot tubs
video & casette library

*Luxurious historic adobe; secluded acres, trees, river, wildflowers; Taos Plaza nearby; classic Southwestern, private baths, Jacuzzi tubs, fireplaces. Gourmet breakfasts.* **Ask about seasonal rates.**

---

## More Inns ...

| | | |
|---|---|---|
| Abiquiu | Casa Del Rio, P.O. Box 702, 87510,　505-753-2035 | |
| Albuquerque | Adobe and Roses B&B, 1011 Ortega NW, 87114,　505-898-0654 | |
| Albuquerque | Anderson's Victorian House, 11600 Modesto Ave. NE, 87122,　505-856-6211 | |
| Albuquerque | Bottger Mansion, The, 110 San Felipe NW, 87104,　505-243-3639 | |

| | |
|---|---|
| Albuquerque | Casa Del Granjero, 414 C de Baca Lane N.W., 87114, 505-897-4144 |
| Albuquerque | Casita Chamisa B&B, 850 Chamisal Rd. NW, 87107, 505-897-4644 |
| Albuquerque | Corner House, The, 9121 James Place NE, 87111 |
| Albuquerque | Hacienda Antigua, 6708 Tierra Dr. NW, 87107, 505-345-5399 |
| Albuquerque | Inn at Paradise, The, 10035 Country Club Ln., 87114, 505-898-6161 |
| Albuquerque | Las Palomas Inn, 2303 Candelaria Rd. NW, 87107, 505-345-7228 |
| Albuquerque | Rio Grande House, 3100 Rio Grande Blvd NW, 87107, 505-345-0120 |
| Albuquerque | W.E. Mauger Estate, The, 701 Roma Ave., 87102, 505-242-8755 |
| Alto | Sierra Mesa Lodge, P.O. Box 463, 88312, 505-336-4515 |
| Angel Fire | Monte Verde Ranch B&B, Box 173, 87710, 505-377-6928 |
| Arroyo Hondo | New Buffalo B&B, Box 257, 87513, 505-776-2015 |
| Arroyo Hondo | Taos Trace, P.O. Box 436, 87513, 505-776-2538 |
| Caliente | Inn at Ojo, The, P.O. Box 215, 87549 |
| Chimayo | Casa Escondida B&B, P.O. Box 142, 87522, 505-351-4805 |
| Chimayo | Rancho do Chimaya, P.O. Box 11, 87522 |
| Cloudcroft | Lodge at Cloudcroft, P.O. Box 497, 88317, 505-682-2566 |
| Corrales | Casa Entrada B&B, P.O. Box 2320, 87048, 505-897-0083 |
| Corrales | Corrales Inn B&B, P.O. Box 1361, 87048, 505-897-4422 |
| Corrales | Yours Truly, P.O. Box 2263, 87048, 505-898-7027 |
| Costilla | Costilla B&B, P.O. Box 186, 87524, 505-586-1683 |
| Dixon | La Casita Guesthouse, P.O. Box 103, 87527, 505-579-4297 |
| El Prado | Little Tree, P.O. Box 960, 87529, 505-776-8467 |
| Espanola | La Puebla House B&B, Route 3, Box 172-A, 87532 |
| Espanola | O'Keefe Country, P.O. Box 92, 87532 |
| Farmington | Casa Blanca B&B, 505 E. La Plata St., 87401, 505-327-6503 |
| Jemez Springs | Dancing Bear B&B, The, P.O. Box 128, 87025, 505-829-3336 |
| Jemez Springs | Jemez River B&B Inn, 16445 Scenic Hwy. 4, 87025, 505-829-3262 |
| Las Cruces | Hilltop Hacienda B&B, 2600 Westmoreland Rd., 88012, 505-382-3556 |
| Las Cruces | Lundeen Inn of the Arts, 618 S. Alameda Blvd., 88005, 505-526-3327 |
| Las Vegas | Carriage House B&B, 925 Sixth St., 87701, 505-454-1784 |
| Las Vegas | Plaza Hotel, 230 Old Town Plaza, 87701, 505-425-3591 |
| Lincoln | Wortley Hotel, Box 96, 88338, 505-653-4500 |
| Los Alamos | Bud's B&B, 1981 B North Rd., 87544, 505-662-4239 |
| Los Alamos | Lost Viking Inn Slp.Hollow, 135 La Senda-White Rock, 87544, 505-672-9494 |
| Los Alamos | North Road B&B, 2127 North Rd., 87544, 505-662-3678 |
| Los Alamos | Orange Street B&B, 3496 Orange St., 87544, 505-662-2651 |
| Los Ojos | Casa De Martinez B&B Inn, P.O. Box 96, 87551, 505-588-7858 |
| Mesilla | Meson de Mesilla, P.O. Box 1212, 88046, 505-525-9212 |
| Mesilla Park | Elms, P.O. Box 1176, 88001, 505-524-1513 |
| Nogal | Monjeau Shadows Inn, Bonito Route, 88341, 505-336-4191 |
| Pilar | Plum Tree B&B, The, Box A-1, State Rd. 68, 87531, 505-758-0090 |
| Placitas | Hacienda de Placitas B&B, 491 Hwy 165, 87043, 505-867-3775 |
| Ramah | Vogt Ranch B&B, The, Box 716, 87321, 505-783-4362 |
| Rancho de Taos | Don Pasqual Martinez B&B, P.O. Box 1205, 87557 |
| Ranchos De Taos | Adobe & Pines Inn, P.O. Box 837, 87557, 800-723-8267 |
| Ranchos de Taos | Ranchos Ritz B&B, P.O. Box 669, 87557, 505-758-2640 |
| Raton | Red Violet Inn, 344 N. Second St., 87740, 505-445-9778 |
| Red River | El Western Lodge, Box 301, Gilt Edge, 87558, 505-754-2272 |
| Rinconada | Casa Rinconada del Rio, Box 10A, Taos Hwy 68, 87531, 505-579-4466 |
| San Juan Pueblo | Chinguague Compound, P.O. Box 1118, 87566, 505-852-2194 |
| Sandia Park | Pine Cone Inn B&B, Box 94, 13 Tejano Canyo, 87047, 505-281-1384 |
| Santa Fe | Canyon Road Casitas, 652 Canyon Rd., 87501, 505-988-5888 |
| Santa Fe | Dancing Ground of the Sun, 711 Paseo de Peralta, 87501, 505-986-9797 |
| Santa Fe | El Farolito B&B, 514 Galisteo St., 87501 |
| Santa Fe | Guadalupe Inn, The, 604 Agua Fria, 87501, 505-989-7422 |
| Santa Fe | Inn of the Animal Tracks, 707 Paseo de Peralta, 87501, 505-988-1546 |
| Santa Fe | Inn of the Victorian Bird, P.O. Box 3235, 87501, 505-455-3375 |
| Santa Fe | Inn on the Alameda, 303 E. Alameda, 87501, 505-984-2121 |
| Santa Fe | La Posada de Santa Fe, 330 E. Palace Ave., 87501, 800-727-5276 |
| Santa Fe | Manzano House, 661 Garcia St., 87501, 505-983-2054 |
| Santa Fe | Open Sky, 134 Turquoise Trail, 87505, 800-244-3475 |
| Santa Fe | Rancho Jacona, Route 5, Box 250, 87501, 505-455-7948 |
| Santa Fe | Spencer House, 222 McKenzie, 87501, 505-988-3024 |
| Santa Fe | Triangle Inn, P.O. Box 3235, 87501 |
| Santa Fe | Water Street Inn, 427 W. Water St., 87501 |
| Sante Fe | Hotel St. Francis, 210 Don Gaspar Ave., 87501, 505-983-5700 |
| Socorro | Eaton House B&B Inn, 403 Eaton Ave., 87801, 505-835-1067 |
| Taos | Blue Door, The, P.O. Box 1916, 87571, 505-758-8360 |
| Taos | Casa Benarides B&B, 137 Kit Carson Rd., 87571, 505-758-1772 |
| Taos | Casa Encantada, P.O. Box 6460, 87571, 505-758-7477 |
| Taos | Casa Feliz B&B, 137 Bent St., 87571, 505-758-9790 |
| Taos | Casa de Las Chimeneas, 405 Cordoba, Box 5303, 87571, 505-758-4777 |
| Taos | Casa de Milagros B&B, P.O. Box 2983, 87571, 505-758-8001 |
| Taos | Dasburg House & Studio, Box 2764, 87571, 505-758-9513 |
| Taos | El Rincn B&B, 114 Kit Carson, 87571, 505-758-4874 |
| Taos | Harrison's B&B, P.O. Box 242, 87571, 505-758-2630 |
| Taos | Mabel Dodge Lujan House, P.O. Box 3400, 87571, 505-758-9456 |
| Taos | Old Taos Guesthouse, Box 6552, 87571, 505-758-5448 |

| | |
|---|---|
| Taos | Rancho Rio Pueblo Inn,  Box 2331, 87571,   505-758-4900 |
| Taos | Ruby Slipper, The,  Box 2069, 87571,   505-758-0613 |
| Taos | Suite Retreat, The,  Box 85, 87571,   505-758-3960 |
| Taos | Taos Hacienda Inn,  Box 4159, 87571,   800-530-3040 |
| Taos | Zia House,  Box 5017, 87571,   505-751-0697 |
| Taos Ski Valley | Amizette Inn & Restaurant,  P.O. Box 756, 87525,   505-776-2451 |
| Taos Ski Valley | Hotel Edelweiss,  P.O. Box 83, 87525,   505-776-8687 |
| Truchas | Rancho Arriba B&B,  P.O. Box 338, 87578,   505-689-2374 |
| Vallecitos | Vallecitos Retreat,  P.O. Box 226, 87581,   505-582-4226 |

# New York

ADDISON ─────────────────────────────────────

| **Addison Rose B&B** | $$-B&B | Full breakfast |
|---|---|---|
| 37 Maple St.,   14801 | 3 rooms, 3 pb | Afternoon tea |
| 607-359-4650 | *Rated*, | Antiques |
| Bill & Mary Ann Peters | S-no/P-no/H-no | near golf, hiking |
| All year | | skiing, lakes & streams |

*Discover "Victorian elegance in the heart of the country" in this restored, period-furnished "painted lady."Minutes from Corning and Finger Lakes Wineries.*

ALBANY ─────────────────────────────────────

| **Pine Haven B&B** | $-B&B | Continental plus bkfst. |
|---|---|---|
| 531 Western Ave.,   12203 | 5 rooms, 2 pb | Dining room w/fireplace |
| 518-482-1574 | • | Living room, TV, books |
| Janice Tricarico | C-ltd/S-no/P-no/H-no | board games, antiques |
| All year | | original oak woodwork |

*Victorian ambiance in the heart of the city. Century old Victorian in a beautiful residential area of the state's capital. Features iron & brass beds, feather mattresses. 10% off, ask.*

ALBION ─────────────────────────────────────

| **Friendship Manor B&B** | $$-B&B | Continental plus bkfst. |
|---|---|---|
| 349 S. Main St.,   14411 | 4 rooms, 4 pb | Aftn. tea, snacks |
| 716-589-7973 | *Rated*, • | Sitting room, library |
| John Baker | C-yes/S-no/P-no/H-no | bicycles, tennis court |
| All year | | pool, grill & tables |

*Historical rural town. Ride on Erie Canal, fish in Lake Ontario. Homemade fudge, pastries, ice cream waffle cone. Pick your own fresh fruit. Putting green. 3rd night 50%.*

AMENIA ─────────────────────────────────────

| **Troutbeck Country Inn** | $$$$-AP | Full breakfast excl. Sun |
|---|---|---|
| Leedsville Rd.,   12501 | 42 rooms, 37 pb | Six meals & open bar |
| 914-373-9681 Fax: 914-373-7080 | AmEx, *Rated*, • | Pub. rooms, piano, lib. |
| James Flaherty | C-ltd/S-yes/P-no/H-no | tennis courts, ballroom |
| All year | Sp., Port., It., Fr. | year-round swimming pool |

*Historic English country estate on 422 acres, with indoor and outdoor pools, fine chefs, 12,000 books, lovely grounds. A quiet retreat. 10% off a full weekend.*

## AVERILL PARK

**Gregory House Country Inn**
P.O. Box 401,   12018
518-674-3774   Fax: 518-674-8916
800-497-2977
Bob & Bette Jewell    All year

$$$-B&B
12 rooms, 12 pb
Most CC, *Rated*, •
C-ltd/S-no/P-no/H-no

Continental breakfast
Restaurant (Tues-Sun)
Bar, comp. sherry, pool
common room w/fireplace
direct dial phones in rm

*Country charm centrally located—near Albany, Troy, Saratoga, Tanglewood, mountains, lakes & skiing. Vermont & Berkshires 45 min. away.* **3rd night 50% off.**

## BAINBRIDGE

**Berry Hill Gardens B&B**
RD1, Box 128,   13733
Ward-Loomis Rd.
607-967-8745   Fax: 607-967-2227
800-497-8745
Jean Fowler & Cecilio Rios
All year

$$-B&B
4 rooms, 1 pb
Visa, MC, *Rated*, •
C-yes/S-ltd/P-no/H-no
Sp., Fr., Ger., It.

Full country breakfast
Herb/flower garden, shop
nature trails, cross-country
ski
swimming & beaver ponds

*Comfortably restored 1820s farmhouse on hilltop surrounded by acres of woods, meadows, extensive perennial flower gardens. Antiques. Near tennis, golf.* **7th night free.**

## BALDWINSVILLE

**Pandora's Getaway**
83 Oswego St.,   13027
315-635-9571   888-638-8668
Sandra Wheeler    All year

$$-B&B
4 rooms, 3 pb
Visa, MC, Disc., •
S-ltd/P-no

Full breakfast
Sitting room
family friendly facility

*Historic Greek Revival, minutes from all locations in Syracuse. Decorated with antiques, collectables with country charm. Fireplace in one bedroom.*

## BERLIN

**Sedgwick Inn, The**
P.O. Box 250,   12022
Route 22
518-658-2334
Edith Evans    All year

$$-B&B
11 rooms, 11 pb
Most CC, *Rated*, •
C-ltd/S-ltd/P-ltd/H-no
German, French

Full breakfast
Lunch/Dinner, restaurant
Bar service, sitt. room
library, tennis nearby
swimming lakes, hiking

*1791 "quintessential Country Inn" - old-world charm, casual elegance, fine food. In tristate corner near excellent theatre, music, hiking, skiing.*

## BURDETT

**Red House Country Inn**
4586 Picnic Area Rd., Finger
Lakes Nat'l Forest,   14818
607-546-8566
Sandy Schmanke & Joan
Martin
All year

$$-B&B
5 rooms,
Most CC, *Rated*, •
C-ltd/S-no/P-no

Full breakfast
Comp. tea, coffee
Large in-ground pool
sitting room, piano
nature trails

*Within national forest; 28 miles of trails. Beautiful rooms in gorgeous setting. Near famous Watkins Glen, eastside Seneca Lake. Small conf. fac.- all meals. Call for details.*

## BURLINGTON FLATS

**Chalet Waldheim**
RD 1, Box 51-G-2,   13315
607-965-8803   800-654-8571
Franzi & Heinz Kuhne
All year

$$-B&B
2 rooms, 2 pb
*Rated*,
C-ltd/S-no/P-no/H-no
German

Continental plus bkfst.
Afternoon tea, snacks
Complimentary wine
sitting room, antiques
patio, deck, pond

*15 min. to town center, unique, quiet chalet; authentic antiques; private entrance; 75 acres of trails; gourmet breakfast; golf, Lake Otsego, Opera.* **15% senior disc't 3+ nite.**

### CANANDAIGUA

**Acorn Inn**
P.O. Box 334,  14424
4508 Rte. 64 South
716-229-2834 Fax: 716-229-5046
Louis & Joan Clark
All year

$$$-B&B
4 rooms, 4 pb
Most CC, *Rated*,  •
C-ltd/S-no/P-ltd/H-no

Full gourmet breakfast
Dinner in ski season
Snacks, comp. beverages
sitting room, library
tennis nearby, hot tubs

*Charming 1795 inn furnished with period antiques, canopy beds, luxury baths, colonial fireplace in book lined common room. Beautiful gardens in heart of finger lakes. **2nd night 50%, Nov.–Apr.***

**Habersham Country Inn**
6124 Routes 5 & 20,  14425
716-394-1510
Cindy McAvoy
All year

$$$-B&B
5 rooms, 5 pb
Most CC,  •
C-yes/S-no/P-no/H-no

Full gourmet breakfast
Aftn. tea, comp. wine
Sitting room
fishing, ice skating
skiing nearby

*Charming 18th-century Federal-style inn; comfortable period decor; romantic country suite; gourmet breakfast; gift shop. Close to lake, skiing and wineries.*

### CATSKILL MTS./PALENVILLE

**Palenville House B&B**
P.O. Box 465,  12463
Junction Rts. 23A & 32A
518-678-5649
James Poretta/James Forster
All year

$$-B&B
4 rooms, 3 pb
 •
C-ltd/S-no/P-no

Full breakfast
Comp. snacks, tea, cider
10 person hot tub
one deluxe suite with
fireplace & whirlpool

*1901 charming Queen Anne home. Close to skiing, hiking, swimming and golfing. 2 hours from New York City. Full breakfast & lots of peace & comfort. **10% disc't 2 or more nights.***

### CAZENOVIA

**Brae Loch Inn**
5 Albany St.,  13035
315-655-3431 Fax: 315-655-4844
Jim & Valerie Barr
All year

$$-B&B
12 rooms, 12 pb
Most CC, *Rated*,  •
C-yes/S-yes/P-no/H-yes

Continental plus bkfst.
Restaurant, bar
Banquet fac., catering
meeting rooms, lounge
phones in all rooms

*Victorian inn built in 1805, decorated in Scottish motifs w/antiques, tartan plaids. Unique Scottish gifts. 1 room w/king bed & jacuzzi. **Winter Special, call for details.***

**Brewster Inn, The**
P.O. Box 507,  13035
6 Ledyard Ave., Route 20
315-655-9232 Fax: 315-655-2130
Richard A. Hubbard
All year

$$-B&B
17 rooms, 17 pb
Most CC, *Rated*
C-yes/S-ltd/P-no/H-ltd

Continental breakfast
Restaurant - dinner
Bar service, fishing in
lake, sitting room
4 rooms w/jacuzzi

*Excellent food/wine list. Unspoiled, "non-touristy" town w/quaint shops & outdoor activities: swimming, cross-country skiing, Chittenango Falls Park. Quiet & relaxing.*

### CHAZY

**Grand-Vue B&B**
2423 Lake Shore Rd.,  12921
518-846-7857  518-297-5700
Rita-Rae Laurin
All year

$$-B&B
5 rooms, 1 pb
*Rated*
C-yes/S-ltd/P-yes/H-no
French

Full breakfast
Afternoon tea, snacks
Sitting room

*Farm house built in 1867 was bootleggers gathering. Pet animals walk countryside. Boat launch 1/4 mile north. Montreal and Vermont 1 hour away. **10% discount, ltd.***

## CHEMUNG/ELMIRA

**Halcyon Place B&B** | $$-B&B | Full gourmet breakfast
P.O. Box 244,  14825 | 3 rooms, 1 pb | Homemade herb cheese
197 Washington St. | Most CC, *Rated* | Lemon herb tea bread
607-529-3544 | C-ltd/S-no/P-no | bicycles, wineries
Yvonne & Douglas Sloan | Some German | jazz & classical music
All year

*1825 Greek Revival home offers peace, tranquillity and gracious hospitality for the discerning traveler. Period antiques. Herb Series. **3rd night 50% off; Special packages.***

## CHESTERTOWN

**Friends Lake Inn** | $$$$-MAP | Full country breakfast
Friends Lake Rd.,  12817 | 14 rooms, 14 pb | Restaurant, bar service
518-494-4751  Fax:518-494-4616 | MC, Visa, *Rated*, • | Sitting room, library
Greg & Sharon Taylor | C-ltd/S-ltd/P-no/H-no | bikes, swimming, cross-
All year | | country ski
 | | Adirondack suites w/view

*Fully restored 19th century inn with lake view. Award-winning restaurant and wine list. 14 romantic guest rooms, cross country skiing & mountain biking. **Jacuzzis in some rooms.***

## CLARENCE

**Asa Ransom House** | $$$-B&B | Full breakfast
10529 Main St., Rt. 5,  14031 | 9 rooms, 9 pb | Dinner, bar, snacks
716-759-2315  Fax: 716-759-2791 | Visa, MC, Disc. *Rated*, | Sitting room, library
Robert Lenz, Judy Lenz | • | most rooms w/fireplace
All year exc. January | C-ltd/S-ltd/P-no/H-ltd | herb garden, bicycles

*Village inn furnished with antiques, period reproductions; gift shop, herb garden, regional dishes, homemade breads & desserts. **3rd night 50% off Mon.–Thur.***

## CLAYTON

**Thousand Islands Inn** | $-EP | Full breakfast (fee)
P.O. Box 69,  13624 | 13 rooms, 13 pb | All meals served
335 Riverside Dr. | Most CC, *Rated*, | Piano
315-686-3030  800-544-4241 | C-yes/S-yes/P-no/H-no | near public tennis
Susan & Allen Benas | | courts and pool
Memorial Day-late Sept

*The last full-service inn in the Islands. 1000 Islands salad dressing originated here in the early 1900s. Original recipe still used. 1993 was our 96th year! **$15 3rd night discount.***

## COLD SPRING

**Hudson House, Country** | $$$-B&B | Continental breakfast
**Inn** | 15 rooms, 13 pb | All meals available
2 Main St.,  10516 | Most CC, *Rated*, | Bar service
914-265-9355  Fax: 914-265-4532 | C-yes/S-no/P-no/H-no | sitting room, A/C
Joe & Kathleen Klingelsmith | | private balconies
All year

*Historic landmark completely restored and furnished with pine antiques. Outdoor dining overlooking the Hudson River. All rooms are non-smoking. **Free bottle of wine, ltd.***

## COLDEN

**Back of the Beyond** | $$-B&B | Full country breakfast
7233 Lower E. Hill Rd.,  14033 | 3 rooms, | Comp. beverages & snacks
716-652-0427 | C-yes/S-no/P-no/H-no | Kitchen, fireplace
Shash Georgi    All year | | pool table, gift shop
 | | swimming pond, cross-
 | | country ski

*Charming mini-estate 50 mi. from Niagara Falls. Organic herb, flower & vegetable gardens. Breakfast served on deck/living room. Hiking. **Kids under 10 free.***

COOPERSTOWN ───────────────────────────────────

| **Angelholm B&B** | $$$-B&B | Full breakfast |
| P.O. Box 705, 13326 | 5 rooms, 5 pb | Deluxe & aftn. tea |
| 14 Elm St. | MC, Visa, *Rated*, • | Sitting room, library |
| 607-547-2483 Fax: 607-547-2309 | C-ltd/S-no/P-no/H-no | porch, piano, TV room |
| Jan & Fred Reynolds | | specialty diets |
| All year | | |

*Historic 1805 Federal Colonial with off-street parking. Walking distance to shops, restaurants and Hall of Fame Museum. Comfortably elegant. 25% off Nov. 1–May 15.*

| **Briar Hill Farm B&B** | $$-B&B | Full breakfast |
| RR2, Box 634, 13326 | 1 rooms, 1 pb | Afternoon tea |
| 607-264-8100 | *Rated*, | Sitting room |
| Nancy & Webster Tilton | C-ltd/S-no/P-no/H-no | swimming pool |
| All year | | |

*Surrounded by 135 acres of fabulous farmlands in forestry which date back to Indian days of 1746. Briar Hill exudes the charm of Early American embellished w/the luxury of modern day fastidiousness.*

| **Brown-Williams House** | $$$ | Full breakfast buffet |
| R.R. #1 Box 337 Rt. 28N, | 5 rooms, 4 pb | Aftn. refreshment/snacks |
| 13326 | S-ltd/P-no/H-no | Sitting room, library |
| 607-547-5569 | | outdoor spa |
| Deborah Bathen | | outdoor playground |
| All year | | |

*C. 1825 Federal Inn; 4.5 acres of lawns & gardens. Privacy, breath-taking views, hand-painted wall finishes, stenciling, Shaker–Federal furnishings. **Complimentary wine on special occasions.***

| **Chestnut Street** | $$$-B&B | Continental plus bkfst. |
| **GuestHouse** | 4 rooms, 4 pb | Restaurants nearby |
| 79 Chestnut St., 13326 | AmEx, | Sitting room |
| 607-547-5624 | C-ltd/S-no/P-no/H-no | walk to 3 museums |
| John & Pam Miller | | tennis nearby |
| All year | | |

*Park your car and enjoy the beauty of our delightful village. Warm hospitality and a lovely home await you. Please come share it with us.*

| **Inn at Cooperstown, The** | $$$-B&B | Continental breakfast |
| 16 Chestnut St., 13326 | 18 rooms, 18 pb | 1986 NY State Historic |
| 607-547-5756 800-437-6303 | Most CC, *Rated*, • | Preservation award |
| Michael Jerome | C-ltd/S-yes/P-no/H-yes | winner, conf. facilities |
| All year | | |

*Restored Victorian inn providing genuine hospitality; close to Baseball Hall of Fame, Fenimore House and Farmer's Museum; open all year. Holiday shopping packages.*

| **Litco Farms B&B** | $$-B&B | Full breakfast |
| P.O. Box 1048, 13326 | 4 rooms, 2 pb | Sitting room, swimming |
| Route 28, Fly Creek | *Rated*, • | library, pool, hikes |
| 607-547-2501 Fax: 607-547-2067 | C-yes/S-yes/P-no/H-no | cross-country ski |
| Jim & Margaret Wolff | | trails,ponds |
| All year | | |

*Families & couples enjoy 20'x40' pool, 70 acres & nature trails. Handmade quilts by resident quilter. Warm hospitality; marvelous breakfasts. **35% off 3rd night.***

## COOPERSTOWN

| **Thistlebrook B&B Inn** | $$$-B&B | Full breakfast |
| RDI Box 26,   13326 | 5 rooms, 5 pb | Comp. port & sherry |
| 607-547-6093  800-596-9305 | • | Sitting room, library |
| Paula & Jim Bugonian | C-ltd/S-no/P-no/H-yes | oversized guest rooms |
| Open May–November | | |

*Voted as a "Top Twelve Inn" in 1992 by Country Inns magazine. Circa 1866 barn with European, American, antique furnishings. Beautiful valley views. Antique & collectible shop.*

## CORINTH

| **Agape Farm B&B** | $$-B&B | Full breakfast |
| 4894 Rt. 9 N,   12822 | 6 rooms, 6 pb | Snacks |
| 518-654-7777 | Visa, MC, Disc., | Gardens, trout stream |
| All year | C-yes/S-no/P-no/H-yes | farm animals, dogs, cats |
| | | family friendly facility |

*Enjoy an old farm atmosphere in our large country home. Six guest rooms, one handicapped equipped. Convenient to area attractions.*

## CORNWALL

| **Cromwell Manor Inn** | $$$-B&B | Full breakfast |
| Angola Rd., West Point area, | 13 rooms, 13 pb | Aftn. tea, picnic basket |
|    12518 | Visa, MC, *Rated*, • | Sitting room, fireplaces |
| 914-534-7136 | C-ltd/S-no/P-no/H-ltd | hot tubs, 7 acres garden |
| Dale & Barbara Ohara | | hiking, biking, wineries |
| All year | | |

*Historic 1820 Greek revival mansion on a seven-acre estate. Formal mountain setting, fully restored inn. 5 miles to West Point, 1 hour north of New York City.*

## CROTON-ON-HUDSON

| **Alexander Hamilton** | $$$-B&B | Full gourmet breakfast |
| **House** | 9 rooms, 9 pb | Fireplaces, bicycles |
| 49 Van Wyck St.,   10520 | AmEx, MC, Visa, | gardens, swimming pool |
| 914-271-6737  Fax: 914-271-3927 | *Rated*, • | bridal chamber w/jacuzzi |
| Barbara & Brenda | C-yes/S-no/P-no/H-no | |
| All year | French | |

*1889 Victorian, many fireplaces & Jacuzzis. TV in all rooms, telephone, answering machine, antiques. 1 hour to NYC. Close to West Pt., Lyndhurst, Sunnyside. Massage available ($50/hr.). **7th nite free.***

## CROWN POINT

| **Crown Point B&B** | $$-B&B | Continental plus bkfst. |
| P.O. Box 490,   12928 | 6 rooms, 5 pb | Aft. tea, wine, snacks |
| Main St., Route 9N | Visa, MC, *Rated*, • | Sitting room, gift shop |
| 518-597-3651  Fax: 518-597-4451 | C-ltd/S-no/P-no/H-yes | bicycles, jacuzzi |
| Al & Jan Hallock | Spanish | robes/slippers, croquet |
| All year | | |

*Victorian manor house rich in raised paneled woodwork, decorated w/antiques & customized linens. Home baking done daily. **Comp. wine at restaurant; free bottle of wine at inn.***

## DE BRUCE

| **De Bruce Country Inn** | $$$$-MAP | Full breakfast |
| De Bruce Rd. #286-A,   12758 | 15 rooms, 15 pb | Dinner included, bar |
| 914-439-3900 | • | Library, sauna, pool |
| All year | C-yes/S-yes/P-yes/H-no | private preserve |
| | French | trout pond, art gallery |

*Within the Catskill Forest Preserve with its trails, wildlife, famous trout stream, our turn-of-the-century inn offers superb dining overlooking the valley.*

DEPOSIT ————————————————————————————————————

**Alexander's Inn**
770 Oquaga Lake Rd.,   13754
607-467-6023  Fax: 607-467-6098
Alexander Meyer
All year

$$-B&B
5 rooms, 3 pb
Most CC, *Rated*,  •
C-yes/S-ltd/P-yes/H-ltd
German, French

Full breakfast
Dinner by appointment
Boats, waterskiing
bicycles, hiking
sauna, hot tub, pool

*Beautiful lake, elegant & relaxing meeting place for world travellers. Golf, fishing. Day trips to Catskills, Finger Lakes, Niagara Falls. **3rd night 50% off.***

---

**Chestnut Inn @ Oquaga
Lake**
498 Oquaga Lake Rd.,   13754
607-467-2500  Fax: 607-467-5911
800-467-7676
Tom Spaulding    Apr.–Dec.

$$-EP
31 rooms, 7 pb
Most CC, *Rated*,  •
C-yes/S-ltd/P-no/H-yes

Lunch, dinner avail.
Restaurant, bar service
sitting room, library
bicycles, tennis court

*Built in 1928, the Chestnut Inn is a classic example of architecture and building construction at its best. A luxury country inn with amenities of a lakeside resort.*

---

**Scott's Oquaga Lake House**
P.O. Box 47,   13754
607-467-3094  Fax: 607-467-2370
R.J. Scott
May 24 - October 14

$$$-AP
148 rooms, 138 pb
Visa, MC, Disc.,  •
C-yes/P-ltd/H-yes

Full breakfast
Lunch & dinner included
Sitting room, library
bikes, tennis courts
recreation

*1100 acre mountain-lake setting, 3 meals, free golf, multiple recreational facilities, daily live music, dancing, entertainment, all included. "I Love NY" award for Best Family Value.*

DOLGEVILLE ————————————————————————————————

**Adrianna B&B**
44 Stewart,   13329
315-429-3249  800-335-4233
Adrianna Naizby
All year

$$-B&B
3 rooms, 1 pb
Visa, MC, *Rated*,  •
C-ltd/S-ltd/P-no/H-no

Full breakfast
Snacks
Swimming pool
historic sites
hiking trials, skiing.

*Rural setting in Adirondack Foothills near I-90. Cozy residence in charming village features eclectic blend of antique & contemporary furnishings. Convenient to Saratoga.*

---

**Gatehouse Herbs B&B**
98 Van Buren St.,   13329
315-429-8366  Fax: 315-429-8366
Carol & Kermit Gates
June-Sept.

$$-B&B
3 rooms, 3 pb
C-ltd/S-no/P-no/H-no

Full breakfast
Aftn. tea, Comp. wine
Sitting room, library
bicycles, swimming pool
historic, scenic

*Queen Anne Victorian furnished with family antiques. Perennial gardens, wooded walks, brook, lily pond, Adirondack hiking, biking and canoeing.*

EAST HAMPTON ——————————————————————————————

**Maidstone Arms Inn/Rest.**
207 Main St,   11937
516-324-5006
Rita & Gary Reiswig
All year exc. February

$$$-B&B
19 rooms, 19 pb
AmEx, MC, Visa,  •
C-yes/S-yes/P-no/H-no

Continental breakfast
Dinner, bar service
Library
sitting room
entertainment

*Country charm, elegant restaurant. Choose one of sixteen rooms and three cottages. Breakfast served on the wicker sun porch.*

## EAST HAMPTON

| **Mill House Inn** | $$$$-B&B | Buffet breakfast |
|---|---|---|
| 33 N. Main St.,   11937 | 8 rooms, 8 pb | Cooking workshops |
| 516-324-9766  Fax: 516-324-9793 | Visa, MC, AmEx, | Air conditioning, spa |
| Katherine & Don Hartnett | *Rated*, | in-room fireplaces |
| All year | C-yes/S-no/P-no/H-yes | whirlpool tubs |
| | Spanish | |

*Magnificently restored 1790 B&B located across from historic Windmill. Delicious buffet breakfasts. Experience the charm, luxury, hospitality. Families/children welcome.*

| **Pink House, The** | $$$$-B&B | Full breakfast |
|---|---|---|
| 26 James Ln.,   11937 | 5 rooms, 5 pb | Sitting room |
| 516-324-3400  Fax: 516-324-5254 | Most CC, | porch |
| Sue Calden, Ron Steinhilber | C-ltd/S-no/P-no/H-no | swimming pool |
| All year | Spanish | |

*A distinctive B&B located in the historic district of East Hampton. Newly renovated with marble bathrooms, lush bathrobes & special emphasis on personal service.*

## ELBRIDGE

| **Fox Ridge Farm B&B** | $$-B&B | Full breakfast |
|---|---|---|
| 4786 Foster Rd.,   13060 | 3 rooms, 1 pb | Aftn. tea, snacks |
| 315-673-4881 | Most CC, | Sitting room, library |
| Marge & Bob Sykes | C-yes/S-no/P-no/H-no | hiking/nature trails |
| All year | | cross-country skiing |

*Country B&B secluded and quiet with miles of hiking and cross-country country ski trails through woods, meadows and along streams. **Dec-Mar, 50% off 2nd night.***

## ELIZABETHTOWN

| **Stony Water B&B** | $$-B&B | Full breakfast |
|---|---|---|
| RR 1, P.O. Box 69,   12932 | 4 rooms, 4 pb | Lunch, dinner (seasonal) |
| 518-873-9125  800-995-7295 | MC, Visa, AmEx, | Afternoon tea, snacks |
| Winifred Thomas/Sandra | *Rated*, | sitt. rm, lib., screened |
| Murphy | C-yes/S-no/P-no/H-yes | gazebo, in-ground pool |
| All year | | |

*Stony Water's tranquil setting on 87 wooded acres provides a perfect refuge from the complexities of today's world. 2 bedroom cottage also available. Small retreats, family reunions. **7th night free.***

## FLEISCHMANNS

| **River Run B&B Inn** | $$-B&B | Continental plus bkfst. |
|---|---|---|
| Main St., Box D-4,   12430 | 9 rooms, 6 pb | Fireplace, stained glass |
| 914-254-4884 | MC, Visa, *Rated*, • | beautiful grounds, piano |
| Larry Miller | C-yes/S-ltd/P-yes/H-no | front porch/trout stream |
| All year | | |

*Exquisite country village Victorian, at the edge of the Catskill Forest. Enjoy hiking trails, superb skiing, antiquing, auction, fishing, golf & tennis. **3rd night 25% off, ltd.***

## GARRISON

| **Bird & Bottle Inn, The** | $$$$-B&B/MAP | Full breakfast |
|---|---|---|
| Route 9, Old Albany Post Rd., | 4 rooms, 4 pb | Dinner included, bar |
| 10524 | AmEx, MC, Visa, | Gazebo near brook |
| 914-424-3000  Fax: 914-424-3283 | *Rated*, • | cedar shake roof |
| Ira Boyar | C-ltd/S-ltd/P-no/H-no | special diets available |
| All year | | |

*Established in 1761, the inn's history predates the Revolutionary War. Each room has period furniture, a working fireplace & four-poster or canopy bed. **3rd night 50% off; Free bottle of wine.***

GENEVA ───────────────────────────────────

| | | |
|---|---|---|
| **Geneva on the Lake** | $$$-B&B | Continental breakfast |
| 1001 Lochland Rd., Rt. 14 | 29 rooms, 29 pb | Full breakfast (fee) |
| South,  14456 | AmEx, MC, Visa, | Dinner wkend eves, music |
| 315-789-7190 | *Rated*,  • | swimming pool, gardens |
| Fax: 315-789-0322 | C-yes/S-yes/P-no/H-yes | sailing, bicycles, piano |
| 800-3-GENEVA | | |
| William J. Schickel | | |
| All year | | |

*Italian Renaissance villa w/terrace, formal gardens & pool overlooking Seneca Lake. Enchanting ten acres include, column-ringed swimming pool, secluded nooks, naturally landscaped.*

GREENPORT ───────────────────────────────────

| | | |
|---|---|---|
| **Bartlett House Inn** | $$-B&B | Continental plus buffet |
| 503 Front St.,  11944 | 10 rooms, 10 pb | Sitting room |
| 516-477-0371 | Visa, MC, AmEx, | fireplace |
| Diane & Bill May | *Rated*, | |
| All year | C-ltd/S-ltd/P-no/H-no | |

*Stately Victorian home furnished with brass beds & period antiques. Conveniently located near North Fork Wineries, beaches, Greenport village and Shelter Island. **Discount available, ask.***

GREENVILLE ───────────────────────────────────

| | | |
|---|---|---|
| **Greenville Arms 1889 Inn** | $$$-B&B | Full breakfast from menu |
| P.O. Box 659,  12083 | 14 rooms, 14 pb | Elegant country dining |
| Rt. 32 South St. | Visa, MC, Disc.,*Rated*, | Library, pool |
| 518-966-5219 | • | living/sitting rooms |
| Fax: 518-966-8754 | C-ltd/S-no/P-no/H-no | art workshops, croquet |
| Eliot & Letitia Dalton | | |
| Closed December | | |

*Historic Victorian country inn on 6 acres, with established shade trees, gardens, outdoor pool. Hudson Valley mansions, hiking, biking, and relaxing. **Winter discounts.***

HADLEY ───────────────────────────────────

| | | |
|---|---|---|
| **Saratoga Rose Inn** | $$$-B&B | Full gourmet breakfast |
| 4174 Rockwell St.,  12835 | 4 rooms, 4 pb | Restaurant, bar, dinner |
| 518-696-2861 | AmEx, MC, Visa,  • | Comp. wine, library, in- |
| 800-942-5025 | C-ltd/S-ltd/P-no/H-no | room frpl. & jacuzzi, |
| Chef Anthony & Nancy | | gift shop, garden/gazebo |
| Merlino | | |
| All year | | |

*Romantic Victorian inn/restaurant. Near Saratoga, Lake George, skiing, recreation. Carriage House w/spa & fireplace. Gourmet meals. **Mention guide with res./free champagne.***

HAMMONDSPORT ───────────────────────────────

| | | |
|---|---|---|
| **Another Tyme B&B** | $$-B&B | Full gourmet breakfast |
| P.O. Box 134,  14840 | 3 rooms, 1 pb | Afternoon tea & snacks |
| 7 Church St. | MC, Visa, *Rated*,  • | Sitting room |
| 607-569-2747 | C-ltd/S-no/P-no/H-no | Comp. wine at local |
| Carolyn Clark | | restaurants |
| All year | | |

*3 guest rooms recapture the grace and charm of another tyme. Close to wineries, Watkins Glen racetrack, museums. Lake nearby.*

HAMMONDSPORT ─────────────────────────────

**Blushing Rose B&B, The**          $$$-B&B                     Early continental bkfst.
11 William St.,   14840              4 rooms, 4 pb               Full bkfast after 9 a.m.
607-569-3402 Fax: 607-569-3483       *Rated*,                   Afternoon refreshment
800-982-8818                         C-ltd/S-no/P-no/H-no        bicycles, sitting room
Ellen & Bucky Laufersweiler                                     lake nearby
All year

*An 1843 Victorian Italianate located in heart of a historic village. Enjoy museums, wineries, Corning, swimming, fishing, boating or just strolling.* **Corporate discounts.**

HAMPTON BAYS ─────────────────────────────

**House on the Water**               $$-B&B                     Full breakfast
P.O. Box 106,   11946                2 rooms, 2 pb              Complimentary coffee/tea
33 Rainpasture Rd.                   *Rated*,  •                Full kitchen privileges
516-728-3560                         C-ltd/S-ltd/P-no/H-no      barbecue, windsurfer
Hostess: Mrs. Ute                    German, Spanish,           sail/pedal boats, bikes
May—November                         French

*Seven miles to Southampton Village. Museum, art gallery, stores. Short drive to beaches. Breakfast on terrace, relax in garden, kitchen privileges (snacks).* **Discounts, ask.**

HARTSDALE ─────────────────────────────

**Krogh's Nest B&B**                 $$-B&B                     Full breakfast
4 Hillcrest Rd.,   10530             3 rooms, 2 pb              Sitting room
914-946-3479                         AmEx,                      hammock, lawn swing
Claudia & Paul Krogh                 C-yes/S-ltd/P-no/H-ltd     picnic table
All year

*100 year old home on hillside acre with country atmosphere. Walk to 10 restaurants and train. 21 rail miles to NY City.* **Student discounts, ltd.**

HEMPSTEAD BY GARDEN CITY ─────────────────────────────

**Country Life B&B**                 $$-B&B                     Full breakfast weekend
237 Cathedral Ave., Garden           5 rooms, 3 pb              Continental plus weekday
City Border,   11550                 *Rated*,  •                Comp. wine and snacks
516-292-9219  Fax: 516-292-2393      C-yes/S-no/P-no/H-ltd      stereo, patio, backyard
Richard & Wendy Duvall               Spanish, German,           color TV & A/C in rooms
All year                             French

*Charming old Dutch colonial; close to New York City, beaches, airports and public transportation, Fifth Avenue of Long Island, tourist sights. Swing set.* **10% off midweek, ltd.**

HILLSDALE ─────────────────────────────

**Swiss Hutte Country Inn**          $$-MAP/EP                  Full breakfast
Route 23,   12529                    16 rooms, 16 pb            Restaurant, bar service
518-325-3333  Fax: 413-528-6201      MC, Visa, *Rated*,         Vegetarian dishes, in-
413-528-6200                         C-yes/S-yes/P-yes/H-yes     room phones, parlor room
Mr.& Mrs. Gert, Cindy Alper          German                     tennis, pool, skiing
April 15—March

*Swiss chef & owner. Nestled in a hidden wooded valley. French continental decor. Indoor/outdoor garden dining. Business groups welcome.* **Daily bar menu, bistro style.**

HYDE PARK ─────────────────────────────

**Saltbox B&B, The**                 $$-B&B                     Full breakfast
255 Ruskey Ln.,   12538              2 rooms, 1 pb              Snacks
914-266-3196                         C-ltd/S-no/P-no/H-no       Swimming pool
Sue De Lorenzo                                                  sitting room
April thru December                                            colleges/wineries nearby

*Featuring hospitality & quaint country charm in an 1840 "Saltbox"; low beamed ceilings, fireplaces, high post beds, period antiques. Convenient to historic mansions, antique shops.* **3rd night 50%.**

ITHACA ──────────────────────────────────

| | | |
|---|---|---|
| **Federal House B&B, The** | $$-B&B | Full breakfast |
| P.O. Box 4914,   14852 | 4 rooms, 4 pb | Snacks |
| 175 Ludlowville, Lansing | Most CC, *Rated*,  • | Sitting room |
| 607-533-7362 Fax: 607-533-7899 | C-ltd/S-no/P-no/H-no | bicycles, A/C |
| 800-533-7362 | | |
| Diane Carroll | | |
| All year | | |

*Gracious, antique-filled 1815 inn. Quiet location near colleges, state parks, wineries, lake. Great fishing, biking, hiking, swimming. Suite w/fireplace.* **Midweek discount, ltd.**

| | | |
|---|---|---|
| **Hanshaw House B&B Inn** | $$-B&B | Full gourmet breakfast |
| 15 Sapsucker Woods Rd., | 4 rooms, 4 pb | Afternoon tea |
| 14850 | AmEx, MC, Visa, | Snacks, sitting room |
| 607-257-1437  800-257-1437 | *Rated*, | patio, pond, gardens |
| Helen Scoones | C-yes/S-no/P-no/H-no | formal dining room |
| All year | | |

*Elegantly remodeled 1830s farmhouse overlooking pond & woods. Furnished with antiques, colorful chintzes, down comforters. Gardens, A/C.* **Free bottle of wine.**

| | | |
|---|---|---|
| **Hound & Hare B&B, The** | $$$-B&B | Full breakfast |
| 1031 Hanshaw Rd.,   14850 | 4 rooms, 4 pb | Afternoon tea, snacks |
| 607-257-2821 Fax: 607-257-3121 | Visa, MC, *Rated*, | Sitting room, library |
| 800-652-2821 | C-ltd/S-no/P-no/H-no | bicycles |
| Zetta Sprole    All year | Spanish | |

*White brick Colonial built on land given to my forbearers by General George Washington for service in Revolutionary War. Gourmet candlelight breakfast. A Victorian Fantasy.*

| | | |
|---|---|---|
| **Rose Inn** | $$$-B&B | Full breakfast |
| P.O. Box 6576,   14851 | 16 rooms, 16 pb | Gourmet dinner by resv. |
| Rt. 34 N. | AmEx, *Rated*,  • | Antique shop, parlor |
| 607-533-7905 Fax: 607-533-7908 | C-ltd/S-no/P-no/H-no | 2nd nite free, ask, ltd |
| Charles & Sherry Rosemann | German, Spanish | piano, bikes, jacuzzis |
| All year | | |

*The inn has a non-smoking Jazz Club with a-la-carte dinner on Fri. & Sat. night April-Dec. Conference facility in restored 1850s Carriage House for 60 people.*

JAY ──────────────────────────────────

| | | |
|---|---|---|
| **Book & Blanket B&B, The** | $$-B&B | Full breakfast |
| P.O. Box 164,   12941 | 3 rooms, 1 pb | Afternoon tea - request |
| Rte 9N | C-yes/S-no/P-no/H-no | Sitting room, library |
| 518-946-8323 Fax: 518-946-8323 | | fireplace, porch swing |
| Kathy/Fred/Sam & | | piano, covered bridge |
| Daisy(Hound)   All year | | |

*1850s Greek Revival near Lake Placid. Picturesque Adirondack hamlet w/covered bridge & swimming hole. Bedrooms honor famous authors. Resident Basset Hound.* **25% off 3rd night.**

LAKE GEORGE, BOLTON LDG. ──────────────────────

| | | |
|---|---|---|
| **Hilltop Cottage B&B** | $$-B&B | Full breakfast |
| P.O. Box 186,   12814 | 4 rooms, 2 pb | |
| 6883 Lakeshore Dr. | MC, Visa, *Rated*,  • | |
| 518-644-2492 | C-yes/S-ltd/P-no/H-no | |
| Anita & Charles Richards | German | |
| All year | | |

*Beautiful Lake George—Eastern Adirondack region. Clean, comfortable. Renovated farmhouse. Walk to beach, restaurants, marinas. Friendly hosts familiar w/area.* **7th night free.**

## LAKE LUZERNE

**Lamplight Inn B&B, The**
P.O. Box 70, 12846
231 Lake Ave.
518-696-5294 Fax: 518-696-5256
800-262-4668
Gene & Linda Merlino
All year

$$$-B&B
10 rooms, 10 pb
AmEx, MC, Visa,
*Rated*, •
C-ltd/S-ltd/P-no/H-ltd

Full breakfast
Comp. tea & coffee
Sitting rm. w/fireplaces
porch w/swing, gardens
lake swimming, jacizzi

*Romantic 1890 Victorian, 5 fireplaced bedrooms, antiques, comfortable atmosphere. Spacious sun porch breakfast room. OUR 1992 INN OF THE YEAR!* **Honeymoon packages.**

## LAKE PLACID

**South Meadow Farm Lodge**
HCR 1, Box 44, 12946
Cascade Rd.
518-523-9369 800-523-9369
Tony & Nancy Corwin
All year

$$-B&B
5 rooms,
MC, Visa, •
C-yes/S-yes/P-no/H-no

Full breakfast
Trail lunch, farm dinner
Comp. hot cider (winter)
sitting room, piano
swimming pond

*Enjoy the Olympic cross-country ski trails that cross our small farm, the view, our fireplace, and home-grown meals.*

**Stagecoach Inn**
370 Old Military Rd., 12946
518-523-9474
H. Peter Moreau
All year

$$-B&B
9 rooms, 5 pb
Visa, MC, •
C-ltd/S-yes/P-ltd/H-ltd

Full breakfast
Front porch with swing
rocking chairs
sitting room

*An Adirondack experience since 1833. Quiet, convenient location. Rooms decorated with quilts, wicker and antiques. Outstanding "great room."* **3rd night 50% off.**

## LEW BEACH

**Beaverkill Valley Inn**
Box 136 Beaverkill Rd.,
12753
914-439-4844 Fax: 914-439-3884
Graham Watson
All year

$$$$-B&B
21 rooms, 13 pb
Visa, MC, AmEx,
*Rated*, •
S-no/P-no/H-yes

Full breakfast
Lunch, dinner, bar serv.
Tennis, swimming pool
fly fishing, kids playrm
self-serv.ice.crm.parlor

*Understated elegance amidst the beauty of the Catskills. Outstanding cuisine, antique furnishings, distinctive artwork, period rooms, expansive grounds, cross-country skiing.*

## LOCKPORT

**Hambleton House B&B**
130 Pine St., 14094
716-439-9507 716-634-3650
Ted Hambleton
All year

$$-B&B
3 rooms, 3 pb
MC, Visa, *Rated*, •
C-ltd/S-ltd/P-no/H-no

Continental plus bkfst.
Snacks
Sitting room
Private baths all rooms
Air conditioning

*Gracious, historic city home where Lockport carriage maker resided in the 1850s. Each room a delicate blending of the past and present. Walk to city's main street.*

## MUMFORD, ROCHESTER

**Genesee Country Inn, The**
948 George St., 14511
716-538-2500 Fax: 716-538-4565
800-NY-STAYS
Glenda Barcklow
All year

$$$-B&B
12 rooms, 12 pb
Most CC, *Rated*, •
C-ltd/S-no/P-no/H-ltd

Full breakfast
Afternoon tea, snacks
Common rooms, fireplaces
canopy beds, gift shop
A/C, fly fishing, TVs

*17-room 1833 stone mill specializing in hospitality and quiet, comfortable retreats. Unique natural setting—woods, gardens, waterfalls. Near Village-Museum.*

## NEW ROCHELLE

**Rose Hill Guest House**
44 Rose Hill Ave., 10804
914-632-6464
Marilou Mayetta
All year

$$-B&B
2 rooms,
•
C-yes/S-yes/P-ltd/H-no

Continental plus bkfst.
Comp. wine, tea
Sitting room, library
VCR, cable TV
bicycles

*Beautiful Norman Rockwell home 20 min. from Manhattan or Greenwich. Enjoy "Big Apple" & country living in one. Horseback riding, golfing, sailing, etc.* **10% off after 1 week.**

## NEW YORK

**Broadway B&B Inn**
264 W. 46th St., 10036
212-997-9200 Fax: 212-768-2807
800-826-6300
Al & Gloria Milner
All year

$$$-B&B
40 rooms,
Most CC, •
C-yes/S-yes/P-no/H-no
French, German,
Spanish

Continental breakfast
Afternoon tea, snacks
Lunch, dinner (fee)
sitting room, library
hot tubs

*A small inn located in the heart of Times Square. We operate as a European style B&B— quaint, personal and charming. Built in 1918 & completely renovated this past July.*

---

**Hospitality Company, A**
580 Broadway, #1009, 10009
212-965-1102
Howard Pitter
All year

$$$-B&B
,
Visa, MC, Disc., •
C-yes/S-ltd/P-no/H-yes

Continental breakfast
Family friendly

*Lovely treelined street; centrally located; convenient to all locations; antique furnishings. Warm friendly atmosphere.* **Free bottle of wine.**

## NIAGARA FALLS

**Cameo Inn & Cameo Manor**
3881 Lower River Rd., Route 18F, 14174
716-745-3034 716-754-2075
Greg & Carolyn Fisher
All year

$$-B&B
8 rooms, 4 pb
Visa, MC, Disc., •
C-ltd/S-no/P-no/H-no

Full breakfast
Antiquing, fishing
bicycling, cross-country ski
relax by river, library

*Choose Victorian elegance in a romantic river setting or a secluded English manor, both just minutes from Niagara Falls.* **Off-season specials.**

---

**Manchester House**
653 Main St., 14301
716-285-5717 Fax: 716-282-2144
800-489-3009
Lis & Carl Slenk
All year

$$-B&B
3 rooms, 3 pb
Visa, MC, *Rated*, •
C-yes/S-no/P-no/H-no
German

Full breakfast
Sitting room
Health club membership
during stay available

*Award-winning renovated former doctor's office and residence provides a comfortable, convenient home for your visit. Ample off-street parking.* **Off season rates available.**

---

**Red Coach Inn, The**
2 Buffalo Ave., 14303
716-282-1459 Fax: 716-282-2650
800-282-1459
Thomas Reese
All year

$$$-B&B
8 rooms, 8 pb
Visa, MC, *Rated*, •
C-yes/S-no/P-no/H-no

Continental plus bkfst.
Snacks, comp. wine
Lunch, dinner (fee)
restaurant, bar service
sitting room

*English country inn 1500 feet from Niagara Falls. Walk to all Falls attractions. Luxury suites with period reproductions and antiques.*

## NORTH RIVER

**Garnet Hill Lodge**
13th Lake Rd.,    12856
518-251-2444  Fax: 518-251-3089
800-497-4207
George & Mary Heim
Exc. June & November

$$-MAP
19 rooms, 19 pb
*Rated*,  •
C-yes/S-ltd/P-no/H-ltd

Full breakfast
Dinner incl., bar
Sitting room, piano
wide variety of features
beach, lake swimming

*Mountain retreat with freshly baked breads, cross-country skiing, hiking trails on premises. Alpine skiing and Adirondack Museum nearby. **Discount on 4+ nights.***

## OGDENSBURG

**Way Back In B&B**
247 Proctor Ave.,    13669
315-393-3844
Rena S. Goldberg
All year

$$-B&B
2 rooms,
C-yes/S-no/P-no/H-no

Full breakfast
Afternoon tea, snacks

*Enjoy a deluxe breakfast viewing the St. Lawrence River, in our bright "Florida Room." Only minutes from the Frederic Remington Art Museum.*

## OLD CHATHAM

**Old Sheepherding Co. Inn**
99 Shaker Museum Rd.,
12136
518-794-9774  Fax: 518-794-9779
George Shattuck
All year

$$$$-B&B
10 rooms, 10 pb
Visa, MC, AmEx,
C-yes/S-no/P-no/H-no

Full breakfast
Afternoon tea
Lunch, dinner (fee)
sitting room, bikes
tennis courts

*Antiqued filled 1790 manor house on 500 acres dotted with sheep. Luxurious lodging and exquisite dining. Two and a half hours from NYC and Boston.*

## OLIVEREA

**Slide Mtn. Forest House**
805 Oliverea Rd.,    12410
914-254-5365  914-254-4269
Ralph & Ursula Combe
All year

$$-B&B
21 rooms, 17 pb
MC, Visa, Disc.,
C-yes/S-yes/P-no/H-no
German

Full breakfast
Lunch & dinner (fee)
Restaurant, bar, pool
sitting room, hiking
tennis courts, fishing

*Fresh air, nature & a touch of Old World charm await you at our German/American Catskill Mountains Inn. Congenial family atmosphere. **3rd nite 50% off midweek only.***

## OVID

**Driftwood Inn B&B, The**
7401 Wyers Point Rd.,    14521
607-532-4324
James & Tammy Steuer
All year

$$-B&B
5 rooms, 3 pb
Most CC,
C-ltd/S-no/P-no/H-no

Full breakfast
Sitting room, library
bikes, lake front
property

*The Driftwood is located directly on Cayuga Lake in the Finger Lakes region of New York. We are centrally located for wine touring and many tourist attractions. **Free bottle of wine with your stay.***

## PHOENICIA

**Ramble Brook House**
P.O. Box 606,    12464
Rte. 42, Shandaken
914-688-5784  Fax: 914-688-5784
Margie
All year

$$-B&B
2 rooms, 1 pb
•
C-yes/S-no/P-no/H-no
Spanish, Portugese

Full breakfast
Afternoon tea, snacks
Sitting room, private
decks, trout stream
oversized video screen

*Warm hospitality in gracious country setting. Tasteful decor & cheerful ambience. 4 season sportsman's paradise. Close to cultural/recreational activities. **3rd nite 30% off.***

PITTSFORD ──────────────────────────────

| **Oliver Loud's Inn** | $$$$-B&B | Continental plus bkfst. |
|---|---|---|
| 1474 Marsh Rd., 14534 | 8 rooms, 8 pb | Restaurant, welcome tray |
| 716-248-5200 Fax: 716-248-9970 | Most CC, *Rated*, ● | Comp. cocktails/dessert |
| Vivienne Tellier | C-ltd/S-ltd/P-no/H-yes | snacks, sitting room |
| All year | French, Spanish | jogging, cross-country skiing |

*English country-house charm & service in restored c. 1810 stagecoach inn on banks of Erie Canal. 12 minutes from downtown Rochester.* **Corporate rates; Comp. cocktail & dessert.**

POUGHKEEPSIE ──────────────────────────

| **Inn at the Falls** | $$$-B&B | Continental plus bkfst. |
|---|---|---|
| 50 Red Oaks Mill Rd., 12603 | 36 rooms, 36 pb | Comp. eve. snack/port |
| 914-462-5770 Fax: 914-462-5943 | *Rated*, ● | Hike on country roads |
| Barbara and Arnold Sheer | C-yes/S-yes/P-no/H-yes | landscaped grounds |
| All year | | |

*Quiet country inn, well off the main highway. Glass-enclosed common area w/fireplace. Near Vassar College, historic sights. Borders Wappingers Creek.* **Comp. bottle of wine.**

QUEENSBURY ────────────────────────────

| **Crislip's B&B** | $$-B&B | Full breakfast |
|---|---|---|
| 693 Ridge Road, 12804 | 3 rooms, 3 pb | Sitting room |
| 518-793-6869 | AmEx, MC, Visa, | Just minutes from Lake |
| Ned & Joyce Crislip | *Rated*, | George/Saratoga Springs |
| All year | C-yes/S-no/P-ltd/H-no | |

*This Quaker-built Federal home provides spacious accommodations complete w/period antiques, 4 poster beds & down comforters. Enjoy lawns & gardens.* **Disc't for longer stays.**

RHINEBECK ─────────────────────────────

| **Veranda House B&B** | $$$-B&B | Full gourmet breakfast |
|---|---|---|
| 82 Montgomery St., 12572 | 4 rooms, 4 pb | Complimentary wine |
| 914-876-4133 Fax: 914-876-6218 | C-yes/S-no/P-no/H-no | Sitting room, library |
| Linda & Ward Stanley | | A/C, concierge service |
| All year | | veranda with wicker |

*Charming 1845 Federal house located in historic Hudson Valley. Restaurants, fairs, antiques. Gourmet breakfasts, complimentary wine & cheese Saturday evenings.*

ROCHESTER ─────────────────────────────

| **Dartmouth House B&B** | $$$-B&B | Full gourmet breakfast |
|---|---|---|
| 215 Dartmouth St., 14607 | 4 rooms, 4 pb | Complimentary beverages |
| 716-271-7872 Fax: 716-473-0778 | AmEx, Visa, MC, | Sitting room, porches |
| Ellie & Bill Klein | *Rated*, ● | grand piano, organ |
| All year | C-ltd/S-no/P-no/H-no | bicycles, A/C, TV |

*Spacious 1905 Tudor home near everything. Architecturally fascinating, residential neighborhood. Hosts are well traveled & love people! Great breakfasts! Walk to museums*

| **Strawberry Castle B&B** | $$-B&B | Full country breakfast |
|---|---|---|
| 1883 Penfield Rd, Penfield, 14526 | 3 rooms, 3 pb | Sitting room, piano |
| 716-385-3266 Fax: 716-385-3266 | AmEx, MC, Visa, | swimming pool, patio |
| | *Rated*, ● | bicycles |
| Anne Felker & Robert Houle | C-ltd/S-yes/P-no/H-no | |
| All year | | |

*Landmark Victorian mansion on 3 acres. Large rooms & suites with antique furnishings. Small-town advantages, convenient to Finger Lakes.* **3rd night 50% off if mention book.**

## ROCHESTER, FAIRPORT

| | | |
|---|---|---|
| **Woods Edge B&B** | $$-B&B | Full breakfast |
| P.O. Box 444,  14450 | 3 rooms, 3 pb | Afternoon tea, snacks |
| 151 Bluhm Rd. | *Rated*, • | Sitting room, library |
| 716-223-8877  Fax: 716-223-5508 | C-yes/S-no/P-no/H-no | bicycles, hiking |
| Betty Kinsman | | tennis court 1 mile away |
| Closed Feb, July, August | | |

*Quiet country hideaway nestled in fragrant pines. Romantic guest house plus two rooms in main house. All rooms have private baths. Near exit 45 on NY State I-90.*

## ROME

| | | |
|---|---|---|
| **Maplecrest B&B** | $$-B&B | Full breakfast |
| 6480 Williams Rd.,  13440 | 3 rooms, 1 pb | Beverage on arrival |
| 315-337-0070 | • | Frig use, central A/C |
| Diane Saladino | C-ltd/S-no/P-no/H-no | sitting room, bicycles |
| All year | Italian | grill, picnic facilities |

*Modern split-level home. Formal country breakfast. Close to historic locations. Adirondack foliage, lakes, & skiing. Near Griffiss Air Force Base.* **Special disc't on term rates; Comp. beverage at restaurant.**

## SARATOGA SPR., BALLSTONE

| | | |
|---|---|---|
| **Apple Tree B&B** | $$-B&B | Full breakfast |
| 49 West High St.,  12020 | 4 rooms, 4 pb | Sitting room, TV/VCR |
| 518-885-1113 | Visa, MC, AmEx, | tennis court |
| Dolores & James Taisey | *Rated*, • | whirlpool tub |
| All year | C-ltd/S-no/P-no/H-no | |

*Second Empire Victorian w/romantic ambiance. Close to SPAC, spa Park & Saratoga attractions. Delightful breakfast, private baths w/whirlpool.* **3rd night 50%, ltd.**

## SARATOGA SPRINGS

| | | |
|---|---|---|
| **Adelphi Hotel, The** | $$$-B&B | Continental plus bkfst. |
| 365 Broadway,  12866 | 20 rooms, 20 pb | Summer dinners, bar |
| 518-587-4688  Fax: 518-587-0857 | AmEx, MC, Visa, | Entertainment |
| Gregg Siefker, Sheila Parkert | *Rated*, • | sitting room, library |
| May–November | C-yes/S-yes/P-no/H-no | piano, swimming pool |

*Charming accommodations. Opulently restored high Victorian hotel located in the historic district of the renowned resort and spa of Saratoga Springs. Landscaped outdoor pool.*

| | | |
|---|---|---|
| **Batcheller Mansion Inn** | $$$-B&B | Continental plus bkfst. |
| 20 Circular St.,  12866 | 9 rooms, 9 pb | Afternoon tea, snacks |
| 518-584-7012  Fax: 518-581-7746 | Visa, MC, AmEx, • | Sitting room, library |
| 800-616-7012 | C-ltd/S-ltd/P-no/H-no | baby grand piano, big |
| Lorena L. Lund | | screen TV, jacuzzis |
| All year | | |

*Saratoga's most spectacular Victorian residence is now an Inn with 9 guest rooms, all with private baths, telephones, televisions, and large, elegant common areas.*

| | | |
|---|---|---|
| **Chestnut Tree Inn** | $$-B&B | Continental breakfast |
| 9 Whitney Place,  12866 | 10 rooms, 7 pb | Afternoon tea, lemonade |
| 518-587-8681  800-CHES-NUT | MC, Visa, • | Comp. wine, snacks |
| Cathleen & Bruce DeLuke | C-ltd/S-no/P-no/H-no | sitting room, antiques |
| Mid-April–November | | porch, spas |

*Restored turn-of-the-century guest house. Walk to racetrack & downtown. Furnished with antiques; large wicker porch. Soft drinks, coffee, fruit always available.* **3rd nite 50%, ltd.**

*Saratoga B&B, Saratoga Springs, NY*

## SARATOGA SPRINGS

| **Inn on Bacon Hill, The** | $$-B&B | Full breakfast |
| P.O. Box 1462,  12866 | 4 rooms, 2 pb | Comp. bev. & snacks |
| 518-695-3693 | MC, Visa, *Rated*, • | Sitting room, piano |
| Andrea Collins-Breslin | C-ltd/S-no/P-no/H-no | library, screened gazebo |
| All year | | close to ski areas |

*10 min. to Saratoga Springs — elegant 1862 restored Victorian. Rural setting, warm hospitality, sumptuous bkfsts, central A/C. Innkeeping course offered.* **3rd nite 50%, ltd.**

| **Lombardi Farm B&B, The** | $$$-B&B | 4-course breakfast |
| 41 Locust Grove Rd.,  12866 | 4 rooms, 4 pb | Afternoon tea, snacks |
| 518-587-2074  Fax: 518-587-2074 | *Rated*, • | Sitting room, hot tubs |
| Dr. V & Kathleen Lombardi | C-yes/S-yes/P-no/H-yes | exercise machine |
| All year | | National museums |

*Informal friendly Gentleman's farm w/beauty, warmth, privacy, peace. Four-course heart-smart gourmet breakfast. Hot tub/jacuzzi in Florida Room.* **3rd night 50%, ltd.**

| **Saratoga B&B** | $$-B&B | Full Irish breakfast |
| 434 Church St.,  12866 | 8 rooms, 8 pb | Sitting rooms, A/C |
| 518-584-0920  Fax: 518-584-4500 | Most CC, *Rated*, • | water garden, bikes |
| 800-584-0920 | C-ltd/S-no/P-ltd/H-no | phones, TVs, parking |
| Kathleen & Noel Smith | French | |
| All year | | |

*C.1850. Romantic rooms with fireplaces, king beds. Historic Victorian city with excellent restaurants, soothing spas and intriguing museums. AAA 3 diamonds.* **Midweek discounts.**

| **Six Sisters B&B** | $$-B&B | Full gourmet breakfast |
| 149 Union Ave.,  12866 | 4 rooms, 4 pb | Complimentary beverages |
| 518-583-1173  Fax: 518-587-2470 | Visa, MC, AmEx, | Sitting room, porch, A/C |
| Kate Benton & Steve Ramirez | *Rated*, • | rooms have TV & fridge |
| All year | C-ltd/S-no/P-no | mineral bath/massage |

*Beautifully appointed 1880 Victorian, recommended by Gourmet, NY Times, & McCall's. 3 rooms w/private balconies. Near numerous attractions. Whirlpool tub.* **3rd nite 50%, ltd.**

SARATOGA SPRINGS ───────────────────────────────

| **Union Gables B&B** | $$$-B&B | Continental plus bkfst. |
|---|---|---|
| 55 Union Ave.,  12866 | 12 rooms, 12 pb | Hot tub outdoors, tennis |
| 518-584-1558  Fax: 518-583-0649 | AmEx, MC, Visa, | telephones, TVs, A/C |
| 800-398-1558 | *Rated*,  • | sitting room, bicycles |
| Tom & Jody Roohan  All year | C-yes/S-ltd/P-yes/H-no | |

*Restored turn of the century Queen Ann Victorian. Gigantic front porch. Great downtown location; walk to everything. Small meetings welcome.*

| **Westchester House B&B, The** | $$-B&B | Continental plus bkfst. |
|---|---|---|
| P.O. Box 944,  12866 | 7 rooms, 7 pb | Complimentary beverages |
| 102 Lincoln Ave. | AmEx, MC, Visa, | Sitting room, library |
| 518-587-7613  800-581-7613 | *Rated*,  • | wraparound porch, piano |
| Bob & Stephanie Melvin | C-ltd/S-ltd/P-no/H-no | A/C, games, cross-country |
| All year | French, German | skiing |

*Gracious Queen Anne Victorian. Old-World ambiance w/up-to-date comforts. Old-fashioned gardens. Walk to attractions. AAA 3 Diamonds. King & queen beds. **Off season discounts.***

SHANDAKEN ───────────────────────────────

| **Copperhood Inn & Spa, The** | $$$$-MAP | Full breakfast |
|---|---|---|
| Route 28,  12480 | 19 rooms, 19 pb | Dinner, aftn. tea |
| Elizabeth Winograd | Visa, MC, AmEx, | Bar service, sitting rm. |
| All year | *Rated*,  • | library, bicycles,tennis |
| | C-ltd/S-ltd/P-ltd/H-no | hot tubs, sauna, pool |
| | Polish, French | |

*Intimate spa and resort with impressive facilities & incredible line of services, helping you to pamper and restore your body, mind and spirit. **Late check out on 2+ nights.***

SHARON SPRINGS ───────────────────────────────

| **Edgefield** | $$$-B&B | Full breakfast |
|---|---|---|
| P.O. Box 152,  13459 | 5 rooms, 5 pb | Aftn. tea, comp. wine |
| Washington St. | C-ltd/S-no/P-no/H-no | Living room |
| 518-284-3339 | | queen & twin beds |
| Daniel M. Wood   All year | | friendly host & cat |

*A well-appointed Edwardian home in quaint village. Comfortable, elegant English country-house decoration, antiques, fireplace. Close to Glimmerglass Opera, Cooperstown museums. **Special rates M–Th, ltd.***

SODUS BAY, WOLCOTT ───────────────────────────────

| **Bonnie Castle Farm B&B** | $$-B&B | Full breakfast |
|---|---|---|
| P.O. Box 188,  14590 | 8 rooms, 8 pb | Hot tubs, sitting room |
| 6603 Bonnie Castle Rd. | Most CC, *Rated*,  • | library, onsite swimming |
| 315-587-2273  Fax: 315-587-4008 | C-yes/S-no/P-no/H-no | all rooms have A/C |
| 800-887-4006 | | |
| Eric & Georgia Pendleton | | |
| All year | | |

*"Turn of the Century" waterfront home on Sodus Bay, Northern Finger Lakes, between Rochester & Syracuse. Waterfront location. Near Renaissance Festival. **Call for update.***

SOUTHAMPTON ───────────────────────────────

| **Old Post House Inn** | $$$-B&B | Continental breakfast |
|---|---|---|
| 136 Main St.,  11968 | 7 rooms, 7 pb | Sitting room, library |
| 516-283-1717 | Visa, MC, Disc., | tennis nearby |
| Cecile & Edward Courville | C-ltd/S-yes/P-no/H-no | ocean nearby |
| All year | | |

*Clean country charm less than two hours from Manhattan. National Register. Pristine Atlantic beaches one mile away. Complimentary van transport.*

*Lakehouse on Golden Pond, Stanfordville, NY*

## SOUTHHAMPTON

| | | |
|---|---|---|
| **Mainstay Bed & Breakfast** | $$$-B&B | Continental plus bkfst. |
| 579 Hill St.,   11968 | 8 rooms, 5 pb | Restaurant nearby |
| 516-283-4375 | Most CC, *Rated*, | Sitting room |
| Fax: 516-287-6240 | C-ltd/S-no/P-no/H-no | bikes, tennis court |
| Elizabeth Main | | swimming pool |
| All year | | |

*1870s Colonial guest house, all antique iron beds & country pine furniture. Minutes to ocean beaches, town and shopping.* **20% discount, midweek. Off season rates.**

## SOUTHOLD

| | | |
|---|---|---|
| **Goose Creek Guesthouse** | $$-B&B | Full country breakfast |
| P.O. Box 377,   11971 | 3 rooms, 1 pb | Tea, snacks |
| 1475 Waterview Dr. | ● | Homegrown vegetables & |
| 516-765-3356 | C-yes/S-no/P-ltd/H-no | fruit |
| Mary Mooney-Getoff | Spanish | sitting room, library |
| All year | | |

*Pre-Civil War farmhouse, secluded in 7 acres of woods, near golf, beaches and ferries. Gourmet country breakfasts, garden-fresh food.* **$5.00 off after 2+ nights.**

## STANFORDVILLE

| | | |
|---|---|---|
| **Lakehouse Inn Golden Pond** | $$$-B&B | Full gourmet breakfast |
| Shelley Hill Rd.,   12581 | 8 rooms, 8 pb | Afternoon appetizers |
| 914-266-8093 | AmEx, MC, Visa, | 7-acre private lake |
| Fax: 914-266-4051 | *Rated*, ● | swimming, boating |
| 800-726-3323 | C-ltd/S-no/P-no/H-no | bass fishing |
| Judy & Rich Kohler | | |
| All year | | |

*Priv. country estate overlooking the lake. Rooms with jacuzzis and fireplaces. Scrumptious breakfast served in room.* **3rd night free in a jacuzzi room/excludes holidays.**

## STONE RIDGE

| **Inn at Stone Ridge, The** | $$-B&B | Full breakfast |
| P.O. Box 76, 12484 | 11 rooms, 2 pb | Restaurant, bar service |
| Rt. 209 | Visa, MC, Disc, *Rated*, | Dinner available |
| 914-687-0736 Fax: 914-687-0112 | C-ltd/P-yes/H-ltd | sitting room, library |
| Suzanne & Dan Hausping | | billiard room, pool |
| All year | | |

*18th-century Dutch Colonial mansion with beautiful gardens & grounds at the foot of the Shawangunk Ridge in the heart of the Catskill Mountains. Perfect for every season.*

## TANNERSVILLE

| **Eggery Inn, The** | $$$-B&B | Full breakfast from menu |
| County Rd. 16, Box 4, 12485 | 15 rooms, 15 pb | Wine list |
| 518-589-5363 Fax: 518-589-5774 | AmEx, MC, Visa, | Dinner for groups |
| Julie & Abe Abramczyk | *Rated*, | cable TV in rooms |
| All year | C-yes/S-ltd/P-no/H-ltd | Newly renovated 3rd flr. |

*Majestic setting, panoramic views, dining in a garden setting, fireplaces atmosphere and individualized attention. Near Hunter Mountain ski slopes.* **Ask about seasonal rates.**

## UTICA

| **Iris Stonehouse B&B** | $-B&B | Full breakfast |
| 16 Derbyshire Place, 13501 | 4 rooms, 2 pb | Snacks |
| 315-732-6720 800-446-1456 | Most CC, *Rated*, • | Sitting room |
| Shirley & Roy Kilgore | C-ltd/S-no/P-no/H-no | central A/C |
| All year | | |

*City charm, close to everything. Full breakfast served from menu. Central A/C for hot days; blazing fireplace for cold days. Easy access to I-90, exit 31 and route 5, 8 & 12.*

## VICTOR

| **Golden Rule B&B** | $$-B&B | Full breakfast |
| 6934 Rice Rd., 14564 | 2 rooms, | Aft. tea, picnic area |
| 716-924-0610 Fax: 716-924-0610 | *Rated*, | Sitting room, hammock |
| Karen L. deMauriac | C-ltd/S-no/P-no/H-no | inground swimming pool |
| All year | | lawn games, gazebo |

*A uniquely renovated and enlarged 1865 country schoolhouse furnished with many antiques. Sumptuous gourmet candlelight breakfast. Many area attractions.* **25% disc't Nov-Apr; 10% disc't weekday May–Oct.**

## WARRENSBURG

| **Country Road Lodge** | $$-B&B | Full breakfast |
| HCR 1 Box #227, Hickory Hill | 4 rooms, 2 pb | Sitting room |
| Rd., 12885 | • | library |
| 518-623-2207 Fax: 518-623-4363 | S-no/P-no/H-no | birdwatching, hiking |
| Steve & Sandi Parisi | | |
| All year | | |

*Quiet, idyllic setting along Hudson River at the end of a country road. Discreetly sociable host. No traffic or TV. Southern Adirondack Mountains, near Lake George. Since 1974.*

| **House on the Hill B&B** | $$$-B&B | Full bkfst. in sunroom |
| Rt. 28, Box 248, 12885 | 5 rooms, 1 pb | Snacks |
| 518-623-9390 Fax: 518-623-9396 | Most CC, *Rated*, • | Sitting room |
| 800-221-9390 | C-ltd/S-no/P-no | hiking, cross-county ski |
| Joe & Lynn Rubino | Italian, French | mountain biking |
| All year | | |

*18th-century Federal home in southern Adirondacks; thoughtfully decorated w/art & antiques. 7 miles to Lake George, 16 miles to Gore Mtn.* **3rd nite free, ltd. Special packages.**

*House on the Hill, Warrensburg, NY*

WARRENSBURG ─────────────────────────────────

**Merrill Magee House, The**
Box 391,   12885
2 Hudson St.
518-623-2449
Ken & Florence Carrington
All year

$$-B&B
13 rooms, 10 pb
Most CC, *Rated*, •
C-ltd/S-yes/P-no/H-yes

Full breakfast
Restaurant, bar, dinner
Comp. coffee, tea, cocoa
sitting room, library
swimming pool, hot tubs

*Elegant Victorian setting w/decidedly 20th-C. comforts in the center of a charming Adirondack Mountain village. Family suite avail. w/TV, frig, pvt. bath.* **3rd night free, ltd.**

───────────────────────────────────────────

**North Country Lodge B&B**
Rt. 9,   12885
518-623-3220  Fax: 518-623-3922
Anthony Sapienza
All year

$$-B&B
11 rooms, 11 pb
Visa, MC, •
C-ltd/S-no/P-no/H-yes
Italian

Full breakfast
Restaurant, bar service
Sitting room, library
pool, cross-country ski
snowmobile, snowshoeing

*All the amenities of a first class B&B with your privacy in mind. Gourmet breakfast served by candlelight (in our art gallery).* **3rd night 50%.**

───────────────────────────────────────────

**White House Lodge**
53 Main St.,   12885
518-623-3640
Ruth & Jim Gibson
All year

$$$-B&B
3 rooms,
MC, Visa,
C-ltd/S-ltd/P-no/H-no

Continental breakfast
Comp. wine, cookies
Homemade cakes, pies
sitting room, television
front porch

*Pre-Civil War mansion, four miles from beautiful Lake George. Eight miles from Gore Mountain. Queen village of the Adirondacks.*

WESTFIELD ───────────────────────────────────

**Westfield House**
P.O. Box 505,   14787
E. Main Rd., Route 20
716-326-6262
Betty & Jud Wilson
All year

$$-B&B
7 rooms, 7 pb
MC, Visa, *Rated*, •
C-yes/S-no/P-no/H-yes

Full breakfast
Comp. wine, snacks
Sitting room, bicycles
needlework shop
small meeting facilites

*Elegant red brick Gothic Revival inn amid maples overlooking vineyards. Near antique shops, recreational & cultural activities.* **Midweek discounts.**

WESTFIELD

**William Seward Inn, The**
6645 S. Portage Rd., Route
394, 14787
716-326-4151   Fax: 716-326-4163
800-338-4151
Jim & Debbie Dahlberg
All year

$$$-B&B
14 rooms, 14 pb
Visa, MC, Disc. *Rated*,
•
C-ltd/S-no/P-no/H-yes

Full gourmet breakfast
Dinner & wine avail.
Sitting room, library
king/queen beds
4 rms. double jacuzzi

*Country mansion w/period antiques; close to major antique center, wineries, ski slopes & cross-country, & charming Lake Chatauqua. **3rd night 40% off.***

WESTHAMPTON BEACH

**1880 House**
2 Seafield Ln.,   11978
516-288-1559
Fax: 516-288-0721
800-346-3290
Elsie P. Collins
All year

$$$-B&B
3 rooms, 3 pb
*Rated*, •
C-yes/S-no/P-no/H-no

Full breakfast
Comp. sherry & muffins
Sitting room, piano
tennis court, library
pool, tennis court

*Country hideaway w/3 suites furnished in antiques. Gourmet breakfast served in lovely decorated dining room or enclosed porch overlooking pool. **3rd night 50%.***

WESTPORT

**All Tucked Inn**
P.O. Box 324,   12993
53 So. Main St.
518-962-4400
888-ALL-TUCK
Claudia Ryan & Tom Haley
All year

$$-B&B
9 rooms, 9 pb
*Rated*,
C-ltd/S-no/P-no/H-no

Full breakfast
Dinner, snacks, wine
Championship golf
beach, marina close by
sitting room

*Four season inn overlooking Lake Champlain. Cozy rooms, fireplaces. Enjoy championship golf and the year round activities of the Adirondacks. **3rd night 50%.***

**Inn on the Library Lawn**
P.O. Box 390,   12993
One Washington St.
518-962-8666
Donald & Susann Thompson
All year

$$-B&B
10 rooms, 10 pb
Visa, MC, AmEx, •
C-ltd/S-no/P-no/H-no

Full breakfast
Snacks, comp. wine
Lunch served on weekends
May-Oct. conference fac.
library, sitting room

*Elegant Victorian inn with period decor & furnishings. Spectacular Lake Champlain views. Walk to restaurants, marina, beach, golf, theatre & shopping. **Golf/inn pkg. discounts.***

WINDHAM

**Albergo Allegria**
P.O. Box 267,   12496
Rt. 296
518-734-5560
Fax: 518-734-5570
800-6ALBERGO
Vito & Lenore Radelich
All year

$$-B&B
21 rooms, 21 pb
Visa, MC, *Rated*,
C-yes/S-yes/P-no/H-yes
Croatian, Italian

Full gourmet breakfast
Lunch, dinner (fee)
Restaurants, bar service
sitting room
bikes & tennis (fee)

*1876 Victorian mansion nestled in the Catskill Mountain Forest Preserve. Activities nearby; P.G.A. golf courses, alpine ski area, hiking, antiquing, Jacuzzi & fireplace suites. **Incredible packages.***

## WOODSTOCK

**Twin Gables of Woodstock** | $$-EP | State parks close by
73 Tinker St., 12498 | 9 rooms, 3 pb | swimming, fishing and
914-679-9479 | Most CC, *Rated*, | skiing nearby
Mr. & Mrs. Albert Hoffman | C-yes/S-no/P-no/H-no
All year

*1930s ambiance revives the easy living of the time. Woodstock "Colony of the Arts," world-wide reputation for art, literature and music.*

## More Inns ...

Acra                Lange's Grove Side, Rt. 23/P.O. Box 79, 12405,  518-622-3393
Albany              Mansion Hill Inn, 115 Philip St., 12202,  518-465-2038
Alder Creek         Alder Creek Bed & Breakfas, Route 12, P.O. Box 5, 13301,  315-733-0040
Alexandria Bay      Bach's Alexandria Bay Inn, 2 Church St., 13607,  315-482-9697
Alexandria Bay      S. S. Suellen B&B, 24 Otter St., 13607
Altamont            Appel Inn, Box 18, RD#3, 12009,  518-861-6557
Amagansett          21 House, Montauk Hwy. Box 149, 11930,  800-888-8888
Amagansett          Mill-Garth-Mews Inn, P.O. Box 700, 11930,  516-267-3757
Amenia              Marshfield B&B, RR 1, Box 432, 12501,  914-868-7833
Ashville            Green Acres, RD 1, Route 474, 14710,  716-782-4254
Auburn              Fay's Point Beachhouse, RD 1, Box 1479, 13021
Auburn              Irish Rose, 102 South St., 13021,  315-255-0196
Auburn              Springside Inn, P.O. Box 327, 13021,  315-252-7247
Aurora              Aurora Inn, Main St., Route 90, 13026,  315-364-8842
Averill Park        Ananas Hus B&B, Route 3, Box# 301, 12018,  518-766-5035
Avoca               Patchwork Peace B&B, 4279 Waterbury Hill Rd., 14809,  607-666-2443
Avon                Mulligan Farm B&B, 5403 Barber Rd., 14414,  716-226-6412
Ballston Spa        House On Saratoga Lake, 143-51 Manning Rd., 12020,  518-584-5976
Barryville          All Breeze Guest Farm, Haring Rd., 12719, 914-557-6485
Bearsville          Bearsville B&B, P.O. Box 11, 12409
Beaver Dams         Vrede Landgoed, Dug Rd., RD #2, 14812,  607-535-4108
Bengall             Beaverbrook House, Duell Rd., 12545,  914-868-7677
Binghamton          Pickle Hill B&B, 795 Chenango St., 13901,  607-723-0259
Blue Mt. Lake       Potter's Resort, Jct Rts 28 & 30, 12812,  518-352-7331
Boicerille          Cold Brook Inn, P.O. Box 251, 12412,  914-657-6619
Bolton Landing      Candlelight Cottages, Route 9N Box 133 N, 12814,  518-644-3321
Bolton Landing      Port Jerry Resort, H.C.R. Box 27, 12814,  518-644-3311
Boonville           Greenmeadow, RD #3, Alder Creek Rd., 13309,  315-733-0040
Branchport          Four Seasons B&B, 470 W. Lake Rd., Rt.54A, 14418,  607-868-4686
Brockport           Portico B&D, The, 3741 Lake Rd., 14420,  716-637-0220
Brockport           Victorian B&B, The, 320 Main St., 14420,  716-637-7519
Brockport           White Farm B&B, The, 854 White Rd., 14420,  716-637-0459
Bronxville          Villa, The, 90 Rockledge Rd., 10708,  914-337-7050
Brookfield          Bivona Hill B&B, Academy Rd., 13314,  315-899-8921
Brooklyn            A.J. Bluestone, 432 Eighth St., 11215,  718-499-1401
Brooklyn            B&B on the Park, 113 Prospect Park West, 11215,  718-499-6115
Brooklyn            Brooklyn B&B, 128 Kent St., 11222,  718-383-3026
Buffalo             Alan Dewart B&B, 701 Seneca St., 14210
Buffalo             Beau Fleuve B&B Inn, 242 Linwood Ave., 14209,  716-882-6116
Buffalo             Betty's B&B, 398 Jersey St., 14213,  716-881-0700
Buffalo             Bryant House, 236 Bryant St., 14222
Burlington Flats    Chalet Waldheim, RD 1, Box 51-G-2, 13315,  607-965-8803
Burlington Flats    Hogs Hollow Farm B&B, RD 1, Box 165, 13315,  607-965-8555
Cairo               Cedar Terrace Resort, R 2, Box 407, 12413,  518-622-9313
Caledonia           Roberts-Cameron House, 68 North St.,, 14423,  716-538-6316
Cambridge           Battenkill B&B Barn, Rt 313, RD 1, Box 143, 12816,  518-677-8868
Cambridge           Cambridge Inn B&B, 16 West Main St, 12816,  518-677-5741
Cambridge           Maple Ridge Inn, Rt. 372, Rt. 1,Box 391C, 12816,  518-677-3674
Camillus            Green Gate Inn, Two Main St., 13031,  315-672-9276
Campbell Hall       Point of View B&B, RR2, Box 766H, 10916

*Dartmouth House, Rochester, NY*

| | |
|---|---|
| Canaan | Inn at Shaker Mill Farm, Cherry Ln., 12029, 518-794-9345 |
| Canaan | Mountain Home B&B, Box 280, 12029, 518-392-5136 |
| Canandaigua | Clawson's B&B, 3615 Lincoln Hill Rd., 14424, 800-724-6379 |
| Canandaigua | Nottingham Lodge Bed & Bre, 5741 Bristol Valley, Rt, 14424, 716-374-5355 |
| Canandaigua | Thendara Inn & Restaurant, 4356 East Lake Rd., 14424, 518-394-4868 |
| Canaseraga | Country House, Box 146, 37 Mill St., 14822, 607-545-6439 |
| Candor | Edge of Thyme, The, P.O. Box 48, 13743, 607-659-5155 |
| Canoga | Locustwood Inn, 3563 Route 89, 13148, 315-549-7132 |
| Cape Vincent | Tymes Remembered, 9494 Point St., Box 406, 13618, 315-654-4354 |
| Castile | Eastwood House, P.O. Box 24, 14427, 716-493-2335 |
| Cazenovia | Edgewater Hollow B&B, 4880 West Lake Rd., 13035, 315-655-8407 |
| Cazenovia | Lincklaen House, 79 Albany St., 13035, 315-655-8171 |
| Central Valley | Gasho Inn, Route 32, Box M, 10917, 914-928-2277 |
| Chappaqua | Crabtree's Kittle House, 11 Kittle Rd., 10514, 914-666-8044 |
| Chautauqua | Longfellow Inn, 11 Roberts Ave., Box Y, 14722, 716-357-2285 |
| Chautauqua | Plumbush—A Victorian B&B, P.O. Box 864, 14722, 716-789-5309 |
| Chautauqua | Rose Cottage, The, 2 Roberts Ave, 14722, 716-357-5375 |
| Chautauqua | Shenango Inn, 20 Ramble, P.O. Box 34, 14722 |
| Chautauqua | St. Elmo Hotel, P.O. Box Y, 14722, 716-357-3566 |
| Chestertown | Balsam House, The, Box 171, 12817, 518-494-2828 |
| Chestertown | Chester Inn, The, Box 163, Main St, 12817, 518-494-4148 |
| Chichester | Maplewood, P.O. Box 40, 12416, 914-688-5433 |
| Cincinnatus | Alice's Dowry B&B, P.O. Box 306, 13040, 607-863-3934 |
| Cleveland | Melody Inn, The, Box 130, East Lake Rd., 13042 |
| Clinton | Clinton House, 21 W. Park Row, 13323, 315-853-5555 |
| Clinton | Victorian Carriage House, 46 William St., 13323, 315-853-8389 |
| Clinton Corners | Bed & Breakfast, Sunset Trail, 12514, 914-266-3922 |
| Clintondale | Orchard House, P.O. Box 413, 12515, 914-883-6136 |
| Cobleskill | Gables Bed & Breakfast, Th, 62 & 66 West Main St., 12043, 518-234-4467 |
| Cold Spring | Olde Post Inn, The, 43 Main St., 10516, 914-265-2510 |
| Cold Spring | One Market Street, One Market St., 10516, 914-265-3912 |
| Cold Spring | Pig Hill Inn B&B, Box 357, 10516, 914-265-9247 |
| Cooperstown | Baseball B&B, 54 Chestnut St., 13326, 607-547-5943 |
| Cooperstown | Bassett House Inn, The, 32 Fair St., 13326, 607-547-7001 |
| Cooperstown | Blacksmith's Guest House, RR4, Box 74, 13326, 607-547-2317 |
| Cooperstown | Burrow's B&B, 23 Leatherstocking St., 13326, 607-547-8137 |
| Cooperstown | Cooper Inn, P.O. Box 311, 13326, 607-547-2567 |
| Cooperstown | Creekside, R.D.1, Box 206, 13326 |
| Cooperstown | Edward's B&B, 83 Chestnut St., 13326, 607-547-8203 |
| Cooperstown | Ellsworth House B&B, 52 Chestnut St., 13326, 607-547-8369 |
| Cooperstown | Evergreen, A B&B, RD 2, Box 74, 13326, 607-547-2251 |
| Cooperstown | Gray Goose B&B, RD 1, Box 21, 13326, 607-547-2763 |
| Cooperstown | Hickory Grove Inn, Rd. 2, Box 898, 13326, 607-547-8100 |
| Cooperstown | Inn at Brook Willow Farm, CR 33, RD 2, Box 5, 13326 |
| Cooperstown | J. P. Sill House B&B, 63 Chestnut St., 13326 |
| Cooperstown | Main Street B&B, 202 Main Street, 13326, 607-547-9755 |
| Cooperstown | Nineteen Church St. B&B, 19 Church St., 13326, 607-547-8384 |
| Cooperstown | Otesaga, The, P.O. Box 311, 13326, 607-547-9931 |
| Cooperstown | Overlook B&B, 8 Pine Blvd., 13326, 607-547-5178 |
| Cooperstown | Plane Old House, The, RR 4, Box 623, 13326, 607-286-3387 |
| Cooperstown | Serendipity, RD 2, Box 1050, 13326, 607-547-2106 |
| Cooperstown | Sunny Slope B&B, RD 3, Box 255, 13326, 607-547-8686 |
| Cooperstown | TJ's Country Inn, 124 Main St., 13326, 315-858-0129 |
| Cooperstown | Tunnicliff Inn, 34-36 Pioneer St., 13326, 607-547-9611 |
| Cooperstown | Whisperin' Pines Chalet, RD 3, Box 248, Rt 11, 13326, 607-547-5640 |
| Cooperstown | Wynterholm, 2 Chestnut St., 13326, 607-547-2308 |
| Corinth | Inn at Edge of the Forest, 11 E. Dayton Dr., 12822, 518-654-6656 |
| Corning | "1865" White Birch B&B, 69 E. 1st. St., 14830, 607-962-6355 |
| Corning | Delevan House, 188 Delevan Ave., 14830, 607-962-2347 |
| Corning | Rosewood Inn, 134 E. First St., 14830, 607-962-3253 |
| Cortland | Country View B&B, 1500 Route 392, 13045, 607-835-6517 |
| Cuba | 33 South, 33 South St., 14727, 716-968-1387 |
| Cuba | Helen's Tourist Home, 7 Maple St., 14727 |
| Dandee | 1819 Red Brick Inn, RD 2, Box 57A, 14837, 607-243-8844 |
| Deposit | White Pillars Inn, The, 82 Second St., 13754, 607-467-4191 |
| Dover Plains | Old Drovers Inn, P.O. Box 675, 12522, 914-832-9311 |
| Downsville | Adams' Farmhouse B&B, P.O. Box 18, 13755, 607-363-2757 |
| Dryden | Sarah's Dream Village Inn, P.O. Box 1087, 13053, 607-844-4321 |
| Dundee | Glenora Guests, 65 N. Glenora Rd., 14837, 607-243-7686 |
| Dundee | Glenora Tree Farm B&B, 546 S. Glenora Rd., 14837, 607-243-7414 |
| Dundee | Willow Cove, 77 S. Glenora Rd., RD 4, 14837, 607-243-8482 |
| Durhamville | Towering Maples B&B, 217 Foster Corners Rd., 13054, 315-363-9007 |
| Eagle Bay | Big Moose Inn, on Big Moose Lake, 13331, 315-357-2042 |
| East Aurora | Roycroft Inn, 40 S. Grove St., 14052, 716-652-9030 |
| East Bloomfield | Holloway House, Routes 5 & 20, 14443, 716-657-7120 |
| East Hampton | 1770 House, 143 Main St., 11937, 516-324-1770 |

| | |
|---|---|
| East Hampton | Bassett House, 128 Montauk Hwy., 11937, 516-324-6127 |
| East Hampton | Centennial House, 13 Woods Ln., 11937, 516-324-9414 |
| East Hampton | Huntting Inn, 94 Main St., 11937, 516-324-0410 |
| East Quogue | Caffrey House, Squires Ave., 11942, 516-728-1327 |
| Eaton | Eaton B&B, P.O. Box 4, Rte. 26, 13334 |
| Eden | Eden Inn B&B, 8362 N. Main St., 14057, 716-992-4814 |
| Edmeston | Pathfinder Village Inn, RR 1, Box 32 A, Rt 80, 13335, 607-965-8377 |
| Elbridge | Cozy Cottage Guest House, 4987 Kingston Rd., 13060, 315-689-2082 |
| Elka Park | Redcoat's Return, The, Dale Ln., 12427, 518-589-6379 |
| Elka Park | Windswept B&B, County Rd. 16, 12427, 518-589-6275 |
| Elmira | Lindenwald Haus, 1526 Grand Central Ave., 14901, 607-733-8753 |
| Elmira | Strathmont—A B&B, 740 Fassett Rd., 14905, 607-733-1046 |
| Essex | Stonehouse, The, Box 43, Church @ Elm, 12936, 518-963-7713 |
| Fair Haven | Brown's Village Inn B&B, Box 378, Stafford St., 13064, 315-947-5817 |
| Fair Haven | Frost Haven Resort B&B, West Bay Rd., 13064, 315-947-5331 |
| Fair Haven | Issac Turner House, 739 Main St., 13064, 315-947-5901 |
| Fairport | Woods Edge, 151 Bluhm Rd., 14450, 716-223-8877 |
| Fayetteville | Beard Morgan House B&B, 126 E. Genesee St., 13066, 315-637-4234 |
| Fayetteville | Collin House, A B&B, 7860 E. Genesee St., 13066, 315-637-4671 |
| Fly Creek | Blueberry Acres Farm, P.O. Box 210, 13337, 607-547-8661 |
| Fly Creek | Toad Hall, the B&B, RD 1, Box 120, 13337, 607-547-5774 |
| Forestburgh | Inn at Lake Joseph, RD 5, Box 85, 12777, 914-791-9506 |
| Fosterdale | Fosterdale Heights House, 205 Mueller Rd., 12726, 914-482-3369 |
| Fredonia | White Inn, 52 E. Main St., 14063, 716-672-2103 |
| Freeville | Tounley House, 304 Peruville Rd., 13068 |
| Friendship | Merry Maid Inn B&B, 53 W. Main St., 14739, 716-973-7740 |
| Fulton | Battle Island Inn, R.R. #1, Box 176, 13069, 315-593-3699 |
| Galway | Salt Hill Farm, 5209 Lake Rd, 12074, 518-882-9466 |
| Geneva | Cobblestones, The, 1160 Routes 5 & 20, 14456, 315-789-1890 |
| Geneva | Inn at Belhurst Castle, P.O. Box 609, 14456, 315-789-0359 |
| Glens Falls | East Lake George House, 492 Glen St., 12801, 378-656-9452 |
| Gowanda | Teepee, The, RD #1, Box 543. Rte 438, 14070, 716-532-2168 |
| Grafton | Grafton Inn, P.O. Box 331, 12082, 518-279-9489 |
| Greenfield | Wayside Inn, 104 Wilton Rd., 12833, 518-893-2884 |
| Greenfield Park | Greenfield Pole Club, Birchall Rd., Box 83, 12435, 916-647-3240 |
| Greenhurst | Spindletop on Chautauqua, Polo Dr off East Ave., 14742, 716-484-2070 |
| Greenville | Homestead, The, Red Mill Rd., 12083, 518-966-4474 |
| Groton | Benn Conger Inn, 206 W. Cortland St., 13073, 607-898-5817 |
| Hague | Ruah B&B, RR 1, Box 34, 12836, 518-543-8816 |
| Hamilton | Colgate Inn, 13346, 315-824-2134 |
| Hamlin | Sandy Creek Manor House, 1960 Redman Rd., 14464, 800-594-0400 |
| Hammondsport | Bowman House, 61 Lake St., 14840, 607-569-2516 |
| Hammondsport | Cedar Beach Bed & Breakfas, 642 West Lake Rd., 14840, 607-868-3228 |
| Hammondsport | Gone With the Wind B&B, 453 W. Lake Rd., 14840, 607-868-4603 |
| Hammondsport | J.S. Hubbs B&B, 17 Sheather St., 14840, 607-569-2440 |
| Hampton Bays | Twin Forks B&B, P.O. Box 657, 11946, 516-728-5285 |
| Hartford | Brown's Tavern B&B, RD #2, Box 2049, 12885, 518-632-5904 |
| Henderson | Dobson House B&B, The, RR 1, Box 671, 13650, 315-938-5901 |
| Henderson Harbor | Gill House Inn, Harbor Rd., 13651, 315-938-5013 |
| Herkimer | Bellinger Woods, 611 W. German St., 13350, 315-866-2770 |
| High Falls | House on the Hill, Box 86 Old Route 213, 12440, 914-687-9627 |
| Hillsdale | Linden Valley, P.O. Box 157, 12529, 518-325-7100 |
| Hobart | Breezy Acres Farm B&B, RD 1, Box 191, 13788, 607-538-9338 |
| Homer | David Harum House, 80 S. Main St., 13077, 607-749-3548 |
| Honeoye | Greenwoods B&B Inn, The, 8136 Quayle Rd., 14471, 716-229-2111 |
| Hoosick | Hoosick B&B, P.O. Box 145, 12089, 518-686-5875 |
| Hopewell Junction | Bykenhulle House, 21 Bykenhulle Rd., 12533, 914-221-4182 |
| Hopewell Junction | Le Chambord Inn, Route 52, Box 3, 12533, 914-221-1941 |
| Hornell | Williams Inn, 27 Main St., 14843, 518-324-7400 |
| Horseheads | Burch Hill Bed & Breakfast, 2196 Burch Hill Rd., 14845, 607-739-2504 |
| Horseheads | Muse, The, 5681 Middle Rd., 14845, 607-739-1070 |
| Hudson | Inn at Blue Stores, Box 99, Star Rt., Rt. 9, 12534, 518-537-4277 |
| Hunter | Washington Irving Lodge, P.O. Box 675, Rt. 23A, 12442, 518-589-5560 |
| Hyde Park | Back of Tranquility, 37 Lawrence Road, 12538, 914-229-7485 |
| Hyde Park | Fala B&B, E. Market St., 12538, 914-229-5937 |
| Ilion | Chesham Place, 317 W. Main St., 13357, 315-894-3552 |
| Inlet | Cinnamon Bear B&B, P.O. box 538, 13360 |
| Ithaca | Austin Manor B&B, 210 Old Peruville Rd., 13073, 607-898-5786 |
| Ithaca | Buttermilk Falls B&B, 110 E. Buttermilk Falls, 14850, 607-272-6767 |

*The Inn on*
*Bacon Hill,*
*Saratoga*
*Springs, NY*

| | |
|---|---|
| Ithaca | Elmshade Guest House, 402 S. Albany St., 14850, 607-273-1707 |
| Ithaca | Hillside Inn, 518 Stewart Ave, 14850, 607-272-9507 |
| Ithaca | Kinship B&B, RD 1, Box 23, Rt. 38N, 13736, 607-657-4455 |
| Ithaca | Log Country Inn B&B, P.O. BOx 581, 14851, 800-274-4771 |
| Ithaca | Peirce House B&B, 218 S. Albany St., 14850, 518-273-8043 |
| Ithaca | Peregrine House Inn, 140 College Ave., 14850, 607-272-0919 |
| Ithaca | Terence Forbes B&B, 168 Pleasant Grove Rd., 14850 |
| Ithaca | Welcome Inn B&B, 529 Warren Rd., 14850, 607-257-0250 |
| Jamestown | Highland View Farms B&B, W. Main St., 14772, 716-358-2992 |
| Jamesville | High Meadow B&B, 3740 Eager Rd, 13078, 315-492-3517 |
| Keene | Bark Eater Inn, The, Alstead Mill Rd Box 139, 12942, 518-576-2221 |
| Keene Valley | High Peaks Inn, P.O. Box 701, 12943, 518-576-2003 |
| Keene Valley | Trail's End, Trail's End Rd., 12943, 518-576-9860 |
| Kent | Ward's Farm House, 14846 Rte 18, 14477, 716-682-3037 |
| Kerhonkson | Maybrook Lodge, #2 P.O. Box 80, 12446, 914-626-9823 |
| Kingston | Rondout B&B, 88 W. Chester St., 12401, 914-331-2369 |
| Lake George | Corner Birches B&B Guests, 86 Montcalm St., 12845, 518-668-2837 |
| Lake George | McEnaney's Lincoln Log, Route 9, 12845, 518-668-5326 |
| Lake Placid | Blackberry Inn B&B, 59 Sentinel Rd., 12946, 518-523-3419 |
| Lake Placid | Brook's Sunshine Cottage, 6 Maple St., 12946, 518-523-3661 |
| Lake Placid | Highland House Inn, 3 Highland Pl., 12946, 518-523-2377 |
| Lake Placid | Interlaken Inn/Restaurant, 15 Interlaken Ave., 12946, 518-523-3180 |
| Lake Placid | Spruce Lodge, 31 Sentinel Rd., 12946, 518-523-9350 |
| Lake Pleasant | Hummingbird Hill, Route 8, 12108 |
| Lansing | Bay Horse Bed & Breakfast, 813 Ridge Rd., 14882, 607-533-4612 |
| Leonardsville | Horned Dorset Inn, 13364, 315-855-7898 |
| Lewiston | Cameo Inn, The, 4710 Lower River Rd., 14092, 716-754-2075 |
| Lewiston | Little Blue House B&B, 115 Center St., 14092, 716-754-9425 |
| Little Falls | Buttermilk Bear, 37 Milligan St., 13365, 315-823-3378 |
| Livingston Manor | Lanza's Country Inn, RD 2, Box 446, 12758, 914-439-5070 |
| Livingston Manor | R.M. Farm, P.O. Box 391, 12758, 914-439-5511 |
| Lowville | Hinchings Pond B&B Inn, P.O. Box 426, 13367, 315-376-8296 |
| Lowville | Parkside Manor B&B, 7701 N. State St., 13367, 316-376-4453 |
| Macedon | Iris Farm, 162 Hook Rd., 14502, 315-986-4536 |
| Maine | Killarney B&B, P.O. Box 337, 13802 |
| Marathon | Three Bear Inn, 3 Broom St., Box 507, 13803, 607-849-3258 |
| Margaretville | Margaretville Mountain Inn, Margaretville Mountain, 12455, 914-586-3933 |
| Mayville | Village Inn B&B, 111 S. Erie St., 14757, 716-753-3583 |
| Milford | 1860 Spencer House B&B, RD 1, Box 65, 13807, 607-286-9402 |
| Milford | Cat's Pajamas B&B, The, RD 1, Box 98, 13807, 607-286-9431 |
| Milford | Country Meadow Inn, The, P.O. Box 355, 13807, 607-286-9496 |
| Milford | Main Street B&B, RD 1, Box 105A, 13807, 607-547-9530 |
| Milford | Maple Shade B&B, RD 1, 13807 |
| Millbrook | Cottonwood Inn & Motel, Route 44, 13807, 914-677-3919 |
| Millerton | Simmons Way Village Inn, Main St., Route 44, 12546, 518-789-6235 |
| Millsboro | Champlain Vistas, 183 Lake Shore Rd., 12996, 518-963-8029 |
| Montauk | Shepherds Neck Inn, P.O. Box 639, 11954, 516-668-2105 |
| Mount Tremper | Mount Tremper Inn, P.O. Box 51, 12457, 914-688-5329 |
| Mt. Morris | Allan's Hill B&B, 2446 Sand Hill Rd., 14510, 716-658-4591 |
| Mt. Morris | Allegiance B&B Inn, 145 Main St., 14510, 716-658-2769 |
| Mt. Vision | B&B at Twin Fawns, 166 Otto Stahl Rd. RD 1, 13810, 607-293-8009 |
| Naples | Landmark Retreat, 6006 Route 21, 14512, 716-396-2383 |
| Nelliston | Historian, The, Route 5, Box 224, 13410, 315-733-0040 |
| New Berlin | Preferred Manor, 1 Preferred Way, 13411, 607-847-6161 |
| New Berlin | Sunrise Farm, RD 3, Box 95, 13411, 607-847-9380 |
| New Harford | Globe, The, 45 Pearl St., 13413, 315-733-0040 |
| New Paltz | Mohonk Mountain House, Lake Mohonk, 12561, 914-255-1000 |
| New Paltz | Nana's B&B, 54 Old Ford Rd., 12561, 914-255-5678 |
| New Paltz | Nieuw Country Loft, 41 Allhuson Rd., 12561, 914-ALL-OLD |
| New Paltz | Ujjala's B&B, 2 Forest Glen Rd., 12561 |
| New York | AA Village B&B, 131 E. 15th, #2N, 10003, 212-387-9117 |
| New York | Abode B&B, P.O. Box 20022, 10028, 212-472-2000 |
| New York | Chelsea Pines Inn, 317 W. 14th St., 10014, 212-929-1023 |
| New York | Incentra Village House, 32 8th Ave., 10014, 212-206-0007 |
| New York | James House, The, 131 E. 15th. St, 10003, 212-213-1484 |
| Newark | Chapman's Blue Brick Inn, 201 Scott St., 14513, 315-331-3226 |
| Newburgh | Birch Creek B&B, 31 Fowler Ave., 12550, 914-254-5222 |
| Newport | What Cheer Hall, P.O. Box 417, N. Main, 13416, 315-845-8312 |
| Niagara Falls | Holley Rankine House, The, 525 Riverside Dr., 14303, 716-285-4790 |
| Niagara Falls | Linen'n'Lace B&B Home, 659 Chilton Av., 14301, 518-285-3935 |
| Niagara Falls | Rainbow Guest House, 423 Rainbow Blvd, So., 14092, 716-282-1135 |
| Nicholville | Chateau L'Esperance, Star Rte. - Hwy. 11B, 12965, 315-328-4669 |
| North Creek | Copperhill Inn, 12853, 518-251-5200 |
| North River | Highwinds Inn, Barton Miners Rd, 12856, 518-251-3760 |
| North Rose | Tollhouse B&B, The, 9683 Ridge Rd., 14516, 315-587-4227 |
| Ocean Beach | Jerry's Accommodations, 168 Cottage Walk, 11770, 516-583-8870 |

| | |
|---|---|
| Ocean Beach | Ocean Beach Inn/Restaurant, Bay Walk, 11770, 516-583-5558 |
| Ogdensburg | Maple Hill Country Inn, Route 2, Box 21, 13669, 315-393-3961 |
| Olcott | Bayside Guest House, P.O. Box 34, 14126, 716-778-7767 |
| Olean | Castle Inn, 3220 W. State Rd., 14760, 518-422-7853 |
| Olean | White House, The, 505 W. Henley St., 14760, 716-373-0505 |
| Oliverea | Alpine Inn, Alpine Rd., 12462, 914-254-5026 |
| Oliverea | Catskill Mountain Lane, Route 47, 12462, 914-254-5498 |
| Oneida | Pollyanna, The, 302 Main St., 13421, 315-733-0040 |
| Oneonta | Agnes Hall Tourist Home, 94 Center St., 13820, 607-432-0655 |
| Oneonta | Cathedral Farms Inn, RD 1, Box 560, 13820, 607-432-7483 |
| Oneonta | Walnut Street B&B, 18 Walnut St., 13820 |
| Ontario | Tummonds House, 5392 Walworth/Ontario, 14519, 315-524-5381 |
| Oswego | Chestnut Grove Inn, R.D.7, Box 10, 13069, 315-342-2547 |
| Painted Post | Dannfield, 50 Canada Rd., 14870, 607-962-2740 |
| Palmyra | Canaltown B&B, 119 Canandaigua St., 14522, 315-597-5553 |
| Parish | Springbrook Farms B&B, CR 38, RD 2, 13131 |
| Parksville | Arrowhead Ranch, 607 Colley Rd., 12768, 914-292-6267 |
| Patchogue | Halcyon Manor, 380 Bay Av., 11772, 516-289-9223 |
| Pawling | Sharadu B&B, 4 Smith St., 12564, 914-855-1790 |
| Penn Yan | Finton's Landing, 661 E. Lake Rd., 14527, 315-536-3146 |
| Penn Yan | Fox Inn, The, 158 Main St., 14527 |
| Penn Yan | Fox Run Vineyards B&B, 670 Route 14, RD 1, 14527, 315-536-2507 |
| Penn Yan | Heirlooms B&B, 2756 Coates Rd., 14527, 315-536-7682 |
| Penn Yan | Wagener Estate B & B, 351 Elm St., 14527, 315-536-4591 |
| Phoenix | Merritt House, 1110 Main St., 13135, 315-695-5601 |
| Pine Bush | Milton Bull House, The, 1065 Route 302, 12566, 914-361-4770 |
| Pine Hill | Belleayre Youth Hostel, P.O. Box 665, 12465, 914-254-4200 |
| Pine Hill | Colonial Inn, Main St., 12465, 914-254-5577 |
| Pine Hill | Pine Hills Arms, P.O. 225, 12465, 914-254-4012 |
| Pine Plains | Hammertown Inn, RD 2, Box 25, 12567, 518-398-7539 |
| Plattsburgh | Marshall House, The, 115 Court St., 12901, 518-566-8691 |
| Plattsburgh | Sunny Side Up B&B, RD 1, Box 58, Butler Rd, 12901, 518-563-5677 |
| Port Jefferson | Captain Hawkins Inn, 321 Terryville Rd., 11776, 516-473-8211 |
| Port Jefferson | Danford's Inn, 25 E. Broadway, 11777, 516-928-5200 |
| Portageville | Genesee Falls Hotel, P.O. Box 396, 14536, 716-493-2484 |
| Prattsville | Hideaway Hotel, Huntersfield Rd., 12468, 518-299-3616 |
| Pulaski | Sequoia Inn, 7686 N. Jefferson St., 13142, 315-298-4407 |
| Purdy's | Box Tree Hotel, P.O. Box 477, 10578, 914-277-3677 |
| Purling | Shepherd's Croft, 263 Mountain Ave., 12470, 518-622-9504 |
| Queensbury | Berry Farm B&B, The, 623 Bay Road, 12804, 518-792-0341 |
| Queensbury | Sanford's Ridge B&B, 749 Ridge Rd., 12804, 518-793-4923 |
| Remsen | Stor Felen, RD #2, Box 9, 13438 |
| Rensselaer | Tibbitt's House Inn, 100 Columbia Turnpike, 12144, 518-472-1348 |
| Rexford | Rexford Crossings B&B, 1643 Route 146, 12148, 518-399-1777 |
| Rhinebeck | Beekman Arms, Route 9, 12572, 914-876-7077 |
| Rhinebeck | Delamater House, 44 Montgomery St., 12572, 914-876-7077 |
| Rhinebeck | Mary Sweeney B&B, "Bantry," Asher Rd., 12572, 914-876-6640 |
| Rhinebeck | Whistle Wood Farm, 11 Pells Rd., 12572, 914-876-6838 |
| Rhinecliff | Rhinecliff B&B, Box 167,William & Grinn, 12574, 914-876-3710 |
| Richfield Springs | Country Spread B&B, P.O. Box 1863, 13439, 315-858-1870 |
| Richfield Springs | Jonathan House B&B, 39 E. Main St., 13439, 315-858-2870 |
| Richfield Springs | Summerwood B&B, P.O. Box 388, 13439, 315-858-2024 |
| Rochester | "428 Mt. Vernon"-A B&B Inn, 428 Mt. Vernon Ave., 14620, 716-271-0792 |
| Rochester | Rose Mansion & Gardens, 625 Mt. Hope Ave., 14620, 716-546-5426 |
| Rock City Falls | Mansion, The, Rt29,W of Saratoga, 12863, 518-885-1607 |
| Rock Stream | Reading House, 4610 Rte. 14, 14878, 607-535-9785 |
| Rome | Little Schoolhouse, The, RD #2, 6905 Dix Rd., 13440 |
| Roscoe | Antrim Lodge Hotel, 12776, 607-498-4191 |
| Rosendale | Astoria Hotel, 25 Main St., 12472, 914-658-8201 |
| Round Lake | Olde Stone House Inn, The, P.O. Box 451, 12151, 518-899-5040 |
| Round Top | Pickwick Lodge, 12473, 518-622-3364 |
| Rushford | Klartag Farms B&B, W. Branch Rd., 14777, 716-437-2946 |
| Rushville | Lake View Farm B&B, 4761 Route 364, 14544, 716-554-6973 |
| Sabael | Burke's Cottages, Lake Shore Dr., 12864, 516-281-4983 |
| Salt Point | Mill At Bloomvale Falls, Rt. 82, 12578, 914-266-4234 |
| Sandy Creek | Tug Hill Lodge, 8091 Salisbury St., 13083, 315-387-5326 |
| Saranac Lake | Fogarty's B&B, 37 Riverside Dr., 12983, 518-891-3755 |
| Saratoga Springs | Eddy House, The, 4 Nelson Ave. Ext., 12866, 518-587-2340 |
| Saratoga Springs | Inn at Saratoga, 231 Broadway, 12866, 518-583-1890 |
| Saratoga Springs | Smart Choice, A, 15 Rock St., 12866, 518-584-7835 |
| Saratoga Springs | Springwater Inn, 139 Union Ave., 12866, 518-584-6440 |
| Saratoga Springs | Washington Inn, South Broadway, 12866, 518-584-9807 |
| Saratoga Springs | Willow Walk B&B, 120 High Rock Ave., 12866, 518-584-4549 |
| Saugerties | High Woods Inn, 7472 Glasco Turnpike, 12477, 914-246-8655 |
| Saugerties | House on the Quarry, 7480 Pine Rd., 12477, 914-246-8584 |
| Sauquoit | Hayfield House B&B, 2805 Oneida St., 13456 |
| Schenevus | Julia's Farm House, Elk Creek Rd., 12155 |
| Schroon Lake | Woods Lodge, 12870, 518-532-7529 |

| | |
|---|---|
| Schuylerville | Kings-Ransom Farm, 178 King Road, 12871, 518-695-6876 |
| Scio | Scio House, RD 1, Box 280F, 14880, 716-593-1737 |
| Shandaken | Auberge Des 4 Saisons, Rt. 42, 12480, 914-688-2223 |
| Shandaken | Two Brooks B&B, SR 108, Route 42, 12480, 914-688-7101 |
| Sharon Springs | Clausen Farms B&B Inn, Box 395, 13459, 518-284-2527 |
| Shelter Island | Bayberry B&B, The, P.O. Box 538, 11964, 516-749-3375 |
| Shelter Island | Belle Crest House, The, P.O. Box 891, 11965, 516-749-2041 |
| Shelter Island | Chequit Inn, 23 Grand Ave., 11965, 516-749-0018 |
| Shelter Island | Shelter Island Resort, P.O. Box 3039, 11965, 516-749-2001 |
| Skaneateles | Gray House, The, 47 Jordan St., 13152, 315-685-5224 |
| Sodus | Maxwell Creek Inn, 7563 Lake Rd., 14551, 315-483-2222 |
| Sodus Point | Carriage House Inn, Wickham Blvd & Ontario, 14555, 315-483-2100 |
| Sodus Point | Silver Waters Guesthouse, 8420 Bay St., 14555, 315-483-8098 |
| South Dayton | Town & Country B&B, P.O. Box 208, Pine St., 14138, 716-988-3340 |
| Speculator | Zeiser's Oak Mtn. Lodge, Route 30, 12164, 518-548-7021 |
| Spring Glen | Gold Mountain Chalet, Tice Rd. Box 456, 12483, 914-395-5200 |
| Springfield Center | Country Memories Lodge, P.O. Box 430, 13468, 315-858-2691 |
| Springfield Center | Sweet Dreams B&B, P.O. Box 414, 13468, 315-858-1319 |
| Springville | Leland House, 26 E. Main St., 14141, 518-592-7631 |
| St. Johnsville | Five Acre Farm, RD #3, Box 60, 13452, 315-733-0040 |
| Staatsburg | Scenery Hill, N. Cross Rd., 12580, 914-889-4812 |
| Stamford | Lanigan Farmhouse, Box 399, RD 1, 12167, 607-652-7455 |
| Stephentown | Millhof Inn, Route 43, 12168, 518-733-5606 |
| Stephentown | Mountain Changes Inn, RR 1, Box 124, 12168, 518-733-6923 |
| Stillwater | Lee's Deer Run B&B, 411 Country Rd. #71, 12170, 518-584-7722 |
| Stillwater | River's Edge B&B, 90 Wrights Loop, 12170, 518-664-3276 |
| Stone Ridge | Bakers B&B, RD 2 Box 80, 12484, 914-687-9795 |
| Stony Brook | Three Village Inn, 150 Main St., 11790, 516-751-0555 |
| Syracuse | B&B Wellington, 707 Danforth St., 13208, 315-471-2433 |
| Syracuse | Benedict House B&B, 1402 James St., 13203, 315-476-6541 |
| Syracuse | Giddings Garden B&B, 290 W. Seneca Turnpike, 13207, 315-492-6389 |
| Syracuse | Russell-Farrenkopf B&B, 209 Green St., 13203, 315-472-8001 |
| Tannersville | Washington Irving Lodge, Route 23A, 12485, 518-589-5560 |
| Thendara | Moose River House, P.O. Box 184, 13472, 315-369-3104 |
| Three Mile Bay | Le Muguet, 2553 Church St., 13693, 315-649-5896 |
| Ticonderoga | Ranchouse at Baldwin, Baldwin Rd., 12883, 518-585-6596 |
| Troy | Sharon Fern's B&B, 8 Ethier Dr., 12180, 518-279-1966 |
| Trumansburg | Taughannock Farms Inn, 2030 Gorge Rd. (Rte.89), 14886, 607-387-7711 |
| Trumansburg | Westwind B&B, 1662 Taughannock Blvd., 14886, 607-387-3377 |
| Turin | Towpath Inn, Route 26 and West Rd., 13473, 315-348-8122 |
| Upper Saranac | Land's End, HCR-1, Box 4C, 12983, 800-859-9224 |
| Utica | Adam Bowman Manor, 197 Riverside Dr., 13502, 315-738-0276 |
| Valley Falls | Maggie Towne's B&B, Box 82, RD 2, 12185, 518-663-8369 |
| Vernon | Lavender Inn, 5950 State Rt 5, 13476, 315-829-2440 |
| Vestal | Strawberry Hill B&B Inn, 564 Jones Rd., 13850, 607-785-5058 |
| Wallkill | Audreys Farmhouse B&B Corp, RD 1, Box 268A, 12561, 914-895-3440 |
| Walloomsac | Gypsy Lady, N. Bennington, Rt. 6, 12090, 518-686-4880 |
| Warrensburg | Bent Finial Manor, 194 Main St, 12885, 518-677-5741 |
| Warrensburg | Donegal Manor B&B, 117 Main St, 12885, 518-623-3549 |
| Water Mill | Ocean View Farm, 342 Lopers Path, 11976 |
| Water Mill | Seven Ponds, P.O. Box 98, 11976, 516-726-7618 |
| Waterloo | Historic James R. Webster, 115 E. Main St., 13165, 315-539-3032 |
| Waterloo | James Russell Webster Inn, 115 East Main St, 13165, 315-539-3032 |
| Waterville | B&B of Waterville, 211 White St., 13480, 315-841-8295 |
| Watkins Glen | Chalet Leon, 3835 Rt. 414 Box 388, 14891, 518-546-7171 |
| Watkins Glen | Rose Window B&B, The, 430 S. Franklin St., 14891, 607-535-4687 |
| Webster | Denonville Inn, 1750 Empire Blvd., 14580, 518-671-1550 |
| West Camp | Buena Vista Manor, Route 9W, Box 144, 12490, 914-246-6462 |
| West Shokan | Glen Atty Farm, Box 578, 12494, 914-657-8110 |
| West Shokan | Haus Elissa B&B, P.O. Box 95, 12494, 914-657-6277 |
| West Winfield | Five Gables, 489 E. Main St., 13491, 315-822-5764 |
| West Winfield | Old Stone House, Box 229, 13491 |
| Westfield | Brewer House Inn, 112 E. Main St., 14787, 716-326-2320 |
| Westkill | Sunshine Valley House, Spruceton St., 12492 |
| Wevertown | Mountainaire Adventures, Route 28, 12886, 518-251-2194 |
| Whitehall | Apple Orchard Inn, RD 2, Box 85, 12887 |
| Willet | Woven Waters, HC 73 Box 193E Rt. 41, 13863, 607-656-8672 |
| Wilmington | Whiteface Chalet, Springfield Rd., 12997, 518-946-2207 |
| Windham | Point Lookout Mountain Inn, Mohican Trail, Rt. 23, 12439, 518-734-3381 |
| Woodridge | Fannie Schaffer Vegetarian, P.O. Box 457 M, 12789, 914-434-4455 |
| Worcester | Wild Turkey Farm B&B, W. Hill Rd., RD 1, 121B, 12197, 607-397-1805 |

# North Carolina

ANDREWS ───────────────────────────────────

**Cover House, The**
34 Wilson St.,   28901
704-321-5302 Fax: 704-321-2145
704-321-2145
Gayle Lay
All year

$$-B&B
5 rooms, 3 pb
Visa, MC, •
C-yes/S-no/P-no/H-ltd

Full breakfast
Family cottage available
Whitewater rafting, fish
train rides, hiking,
antique shops

*Charming historic home furnished w/antiques & beautiful artwork where you can "sit a spell" & enjoy mountain views from the valley town. 2 bedroom/2 bath cottage available.*

ASHEVILLE ───────────────────────────────────

**Abbington Green B&B Inn**
46 & 48 Cumberland Cir.,
  28801
704-251-2454 Fax: 704-251-2872
800-251-2454
V., J. & G. Larrea
All year

$$$-B&B
6 rooms, 6 pb
Visa, MC, AmEx,
*Rated*, •
C-ltd/S-no/P-no

Full breakfast
Afternoon tea
Sitting room & library
with piano, chess, etc.
bicycles, A/C

*Elegant, light-filled, historic home—English garden theme with antiques throughout and six working fireplaces. Sumptuous, full breakfast. Carriage house suite.*

---

**Acorn Cottage B&B**
25 St. Dunstan's Circle,
  28803
704-253-0609 Fax: 704-258-2129
800-699-0609
Sharon Tabor

$$$-B&B
4 rooms, 4 pb
Visa, MC, Disc., •
C-ltd/S-no/P-no/H-no

Full breakfast
Afternoon tea
Sitting room
TV in all rooms

*Charming English country cottage, 1/4 mile from Biltmore Estate. Four lovely guest rooms with private bath. Woodland setting in historic neighborhood.* **2 and 3 night packages.**

---

**Albemarle Inn**
86 Edgemont Rd.,   28801
704-255-0027  800-621-7435
Kathy & Dick Hemes
All year

$$$-B&B
11 rooms, 11 pb
MC, Visa, Disc. *Rated*,
•
C-ltd/S-no/P-no/H-no

Full breakfast
Comp. wine, snacks
Sitting rooms, pool
TV & phone in all rooms
golf & tennis nearby

*Unmatched hospitality in a comfortably elegant Greek Revival mansion. Exquisite carved oak staircase, balcony and panelling. Beautiful residential area. Delicious breakfasts.*

---

**Applewood Manor B&B**
62 Cumberland Circle,   28801
704-254-2244 Fax: 704-254-0899
800-442-2197
Johan & Coby Verhey
All year

$$$-B&B
4 rooms, 4 pb
Visa, MC, Disc. *Rated*,
•
C-ltd/S-no/P-no/H-no

Full gourmet breakfast
Complimentary beverages
Sitting room, library
free fitness club, bikes
badminton, croquet

*Balconies, frplcs., priv. baths, delicious breakfasts & aftn. tea-just to mention a few pleasures. Come romance yourselves w/a stay. Cottage for 4 avail.* **7th night free.**

*Albemarle Inn, Asheville, NC*

## ASHEVILLE

**Bridle Path Inn**
30 Lookout Rd., 28804
704-252-0035 Fax: 704-252-0035
Carol & Fred Halton
All year

$$-B&B
8 rooms, 8 pb
Visa, MC, AmEx, •
C-yes/S-ltd/P-no/H-yes

Full breakfast
Dinner by great cooks
Sitting room
verandah, picnic baskets
hiking trails

*Comfortable and secluded on mountain overlooking downtown Asheville. Full breakfast served on verandah. Ten minutes to Biltmore Estate. **3rd night, 50%.***

---

**Cedar Crest Victorian Inn**
674 Biltmore Ave., 28803
704-252-1389 Fax: 704-253-7667
800-252-0310
Jack & Barbara McEwan
All year

$$$-B&B
11 rooms, 11 pb
MC, Visa, *Rated*, •
C-ltd/S-ltd/P-no/H-no

Full breakfast
Afternoon refreshments
Evening beverages/sweets
sitting room, piano
A/C, phones, desks

*The essence of Victoriana—carved woodwork, beveled glass, period antiques, fireplaces. Breakfast & tea on veranda. Winter discounts. **Spring package w/Biltmore Estate tickets.***

---

**Colby House, The**
230 Pearson Dr., 28801
704-253-5644 Fax: 704-259-9479
800-982-2118
Everett & Ann Colby
All year

$$$-B&B
4 rooms, 4 pb
*Rated*,
C-ltd/S-no/P-no/H-no

Full breakfast
Refreshments all day
Library, fireplaces
lovely gardens

*Historic Dutch Tudor home of charm and elegance. Full gourmet breakfast varies daily. Hosts' personal attention to every guest's needs.*

## ASHEVILLE

**Corner Oak Manor**
53 St. Dunstans Rd., 28803
704-253-3525
Karen & Andy Spradley
All year

$$$-B&B
4 rooms, 4 pb
Most CC, *Rated*,
C-yes/S-no/P-no/H-no

Full breakfast
Picnic baskets, snacks
Sitting room, A/C
fireplace, hot tub
cottage has TV, frplc.

*Elegant & comfortable; full gourmet breakfast; queen-size beds; outdoor deck w/Jacuzzi; flowers/chocolates. Minutes from Biltmore Estate & Blue Ridge Parkway.* **10% off 4 or more nights.**

---

**Dogwood Cottage Inn**
40 Canterbury N, 28801
704-258-9725
Joan & Don Tracy
All year

$$$-B&B
4 rooms, 4 pb
Visa, MC, AmEx,
*Rated*, •
C-yes/S-ltd/P-yes/H-yes

Full breakfast
Aft. tea/snacks/wine
Sitting room, library
swimming pool, veranda
Blue Ridge views

*Historical, rustic brown shingled lodge, wood floors, French doors, wood-burning fireplaces, beamed ceilings, 40 foot porch, stunning views, great location, pool.*

---

**Lion & the Rose B&B, The**
276 Montford Ave., Montford
Historic Dist., 28801
704-255-7673 800-546-6988
Rice & Lisa Yordy
All year

$$$-B&B
4 rooms, 4 pb
MC, Visa, *Rated*, •
C-ltd/S-ltd

Full gourmet breakfast
Comp. wine, aftn. tea
TV and card rooms
suite available
lovely verandas

*Classic, elegantly restored & furnished English Queen Anne 1898 townhome. Full gourmet breakfasts, varied daily. Four deluxe suites. Lots of pampering.* **10% off Monday-Thursday.**

---

**Mountain Springs Cabins**
P.O. Box 6922, 28816
Hwy. 151, Candler
704-665-1004 Fax: 704-667-1581
Sara & John Peltier
All year

$$$-EP
9 rooms, 9 pb
*Rated*,
C-yes/P-no/H-no

Grills, picnicing
Fishing, swimming, cabin
horseback riding, hiking
badminton, horseshoes

*The place you dream of but never expect to find. Porches overlooking mountain stream. Cottages furnished with a "Touch of Yesteryear." 15 mi west of Asheville.* **Extra persons $10.**

---

**North Lodge on Oakland**
84 Oakland Rd., 28801
704-252-6433 Fax: 704-252-3034
Herb & Lois Marsh
All year

$$$-B&B
4 rooms, 4 pb
Visa, MC, Disc.,
C-ltd/S-no/P-no/H-no

Full breakfast
Afternoon tea, snacks
Sitting room, library
enclosed porch
front parlor, TV, phones

*Warm, friendly environment. English antiques and contemporary decor. Deluxe breakfasts! Can satisfy special dietary needs. Centrally located; quiet shady street.*

---

**Old Reynolds Mansion, The**
100 Reynolds Heights, 28804
704-254-0496
Fred & Helen Faber
Exc. weekdays Dec–Mar

$$-B&B
10 rooms, 7 pb
*Rated*,
C-ltd/S-yes/P-no/H-no

Continental plus
Complimentary wine
Afternoon beverages
sitting room, verandas
pool, A/C, guest cottage

*A restored 1850 antebellum mansion in a country setting. Wide verandas, mountain views, woodburning fireplaces, huge old swimming pool. On the National Register.*

## ASHEVILLE

**Reed House**
119 Dodge St.,   28803
704-274-1604
Marge Turcot
May–October

$$-B&B
3 rooms, 1 pb
MC, Visa,
C-yes/S-yes/P-no/H-no

Continental plus bkfst.
Sitting room, piano
pool table, play area
family cottage w/crib

*Children welcome in our Victorian home in Biltmore: breakfast on the porch, relaxing rocking chairs everywhere. 2-bedroom cottage w/kitchen. Listed in the National Register.*

---

**Wright Inn Carriage House**
235 Pearson Dr.,   28801
704-251-0789 Fax: 704-251-0929
800-552-5724
Carol & Art Wenczel
All year

$$$-B&B
9 rooms, 9 pb
MC, Visa, *Rated*,
C-ltd/S-no/P-no/H-no

Full breakfast (inn)
Afternoon tea, snacks
TVs, phones, hairdryers
in all rooms - Carriage
House sleeps 8, bikes

*This elegantly restored Queen Anne Victorian allows you to step back to the peaceful and gracious time at the turn of the century.* **50% off 3rd weekday night w/mention of offer.**

## BALSAM

**Angel Haven**
PO Box 7, 331 Westview Dr.,
  28707
704-452-9455
Gail & Bobby Russell
All year

$$$-B&B
4 rooms, 2 pb
Visa, MC,
C-ltd/S-ltd/P-no/H-no

Full breakfast
Picnic baskets, lunch
Afternoon tea, snacks
sitting room, library
steam sauna - not bricks

*Magnificent mountain retreat, rushing streams, walking path, full breakfast. Great room overlooking mountains, jacuzzi, centrally located, warm, gracious host.* **A free gift.**

---

**Balsam Mountain Inn**
P.O. Box 40,   28707
Seven Springs Rd.
704-456-9498 Fax: 704-456-9298
800-224-9498
Merrily Teasley/George
Austin    All year

$$$-B&B
50 rooms, 50 pb
MC, Visa, Disc. *Rated*,
•
C-ltd/S-ltd/P-no/H-yes
French

Full breakfast
Restaurant
Game room, porches
26 acres, springs
rhododendron forest

*Rest, read, ramble, romp and revel in the easy going hospitality of our southern mountains. Magical enchantment awaits at our historic inn.* **3rd night 50% off, ltd.**

---

**Hickory Haven Inn**
P.O. Box 88,   28707
41 Hickory Hill
704-452-1106  800-684-2836
C. Nicholson & J. Eukers
Closed January

$$$-B&B
6 rooms, 6 pb
Visa, MC, •
C-ltd/S-no/P-no/H-yes

Full breakfast
Aftn. tea, snacks, wine
Sitting room, library
hot tubs, adjacent to
Blue Ridge Parkway

*Romantic mountain hideaway. Elegant yet casual. King beds, whirlpools, fireplaces, wrap-around veranda. Peaceful woodland setting.* **7th night free, free bottle of wine.**

## BANNER ELK

**Archers Mountain Inn**
Route 2, Box 56-A,   28604
704-898-9004 Fax: 704-898-9004
Candi McClamma & Tony
Catie
All year

$$-B&B
15 rooms, 14 pb
MC, Visa, *Rated*, •
C-yes/S-yes/P-no/H-ltd

Full breakfast
Dinner available
Library, sitting room
large hot tub for guests
2 rooms with Jacuzzis

*Quaint country inn with long-range view and fireplaces in most rooms. Two miles from the ski slopes. Hiking trail on premises.* **Discount for Sun.–Thur stay. Winter ski packages.**

## BEAUFORT

**Cedars Inn by the sea, The**
305 Front St., 28516
919-728-7036 Fax: 919-728-1685
Linda & Sam Dark
All year

$$$-B&B
12 rooms, 12 pb
MC, Visa, *Rated*, •
C-ltd/S-ltd/P-no/H-no

Full breakfast
Wine bar
Private Cottage, jacuzzi
Cooking classes, TV, A/C
priv sitt rms, bicycles

*Selected as one of North Carolina's 10 best inns. Perfect for romantic and intimate getaways. Waterfront setting, shopping, restaurants, tours, and golfing.*

**Delamar Inn**
217 Turner St., 28516
919-728-4300 Fax: 919-728-1471
800-349-5823
Tom & Mabel Steepy
All year

$$-B&B
4 rooms, 4 pb
MC, Visa, *Rated*, •
C-ltd/S-ltd/P-no/H-no

Continental plus bkfst.
Complimentary wine, ltd.
Snacks, sitting room
library, bicycles
tennis, beach furniture

*Authentically furnished guestrooms in charming Civil War home. Enjoy a lavish breakfast. Historic homes tour, 2nd yr.* **5th night discounted, ltd.**

**Langdon House B&B**
135 Craven St., 28516
919-728-5499
Jimm Prest
All year

$$$-B&B
4 rooms, 4 pb
*Rated*,
C-ltd/S-ltd/P-no/H-no

Full breakfast
Dinner reservations
Refreshments
sitting room, bicycles
fishing & beach supplies

*Friends who help you make the most of your visit. Restored 18th-century home in historic seaside hamlet on the outer banks. Wonderful waffle breakfasts!* **5th night 50%.**

**Pecan Tree Inn**
116 Queen St., 28516
919-728-6733
Susan & Joe Johnson
All year

$$-B&B
7 rooms, 7 pb
MC, Visa, Disc, *Rated*,
•
C-ltd/S-no/P-no/H-no

Continental plus bkfst.
Soda & juices
Jacuzzi in 1 room
sitting room, library
bicycles, beach chairs

*Antique-filled 1866 Victorian home in the heart of Beaufort's Historic District. Half a block from waterfront. Bridal suite with jacuzzi.* **5th night free.**

## BELHAVEN

**River Forest Manor**
600 E. Main St., 27810
919-943-2151 Fax: 919-943-6628
800-346-2151
Melba G. Smith
All year

$$-EP
12 rooms, 12 pb
Most CC, *Rated*,
C-yes/S-yes/P-no/H-yes

Restaurant, full bar
Sitting room, laundry
swimming pool, hot tubs
tennis court, bicycles

*A true country inn located on the Intercoastal Waterway. Opened in 1947 as an Inn, restaurant & marina. Each evening a superb smorgasbord is served with 75 dishes.*

## BLACK MOUNTAIN

**Black Mountain Inn**
718 W. Old Hwy 70, 28711
704-669-6528 800-735-6128
June Bergeron
April–December

$$-B&B
7 rooms, 7 pb
•
C-ltd/S-no/P-no/H-no

Full breakfast buffet
Vegetarian food avail.
Sitting room

*Turn-of-the-century mountain home, nestled on three acres—a restful retreat for body and soul. Full breakfast buffet.*

## BLACK MOUNTAIN

**Friendship Lodge B&B**
P.O. Box 877,   28711
E. Old Hwy. 70
704-669-9294
Bob & Sarah LaBrant
May 23-Mid November

$$-B&B
10 rooms, 8 pb
C-yes/S-no/P-no/H-no

Full breakfast
Antique shops & golf
nearby

*Located close to Black Mountain (known for its antique shops). Cozy and comfortable guest rooms. A delicious full breakfast is served. Our guests feel like they are family.*

## BLOWING ROCK

**Gideon Ridge Inn**
P.O. Box 1929,   28605
202 Gideon Ridge Rd.
704-295-3644 Fax: 704-296-4586
The Milners
All year

$$$-B&B
10 rooms, 9 pb
MC, Visa,  •
C-ltd/S-no/P-no/H-yes

Full breakfast
Dinner, afternoon tea
Sitting rooms, piano
fireplaces, whirlpools
stone terraces

*Elegance, privacy, relaxation with an unbelievable view of the mountains—cool summers, brilliant falls, skiing in winter.*

---

**Inn at Ragged Gardens, The**
P.O. Box 1927,   28605
203 Sunset Dr.
704-295-9703
Lee & Jana Hyett
Exc. January 6—March

$$$-B&B
8 rooms, 8 pb
AmEx, MC, Visa,
*Rated*,
C-ltd/S-no/P-no/H-no

Continental plus bkfst.
Comp. champagne/
newlywed
Completely renovated '96
beautiful walled garden
whirlpool baths

*Near Blue Ridge Parkway and majestic Grandfather Mountain. People come here for the fantastic cool summers and the scenery. Every room has fireplace, 4 rooms with jacuzzi.*

---

**Maple Lodge**
P.O. Box 1236,   28605
152 Sunset Dr.
704-295-3331
Marilyn & David Bateman
January closed

$$-B&B
11 rooms, 11 pb
Most CC, *Rated*,  •
C-ltd/S-no/P-no/H-no

Full breakfast
Complimentary sherry
Parlors, fireplace
canopy beds, quilts
splendor packages

*Perenial gardens. Gracious charm in the heart of village, offering privacy, personal attention & understated elegance. Blue Ridge Pkway one mile. Near golf, fishing & hiking.*

## BOONE

**Grandma Jean's B&B**
254 Meadowview Dr.,   28607
704-262-3670 Fax: 704-262-3670
Dr. Jean Probinsky
All year

$$-B&B
4 rooms, 2 pb
*Rated*,  •
C-yes/S-yes/P-no/H-no
Spanish

Continental plus bkfst.
Comp. wine, snacks
Porch swing, hammock
country garden
mother/daughter weekends

*Hook a trout, sit a spell, ride a horse, climb a mountain, hike a trail, play 18 holes, buy some folk art. Charming 70 year-old country home in the heart of Blue Ridge Mtn.*

## BREVARD

**Inn at Brevard, The**
410 E. Main St.,   28712
704-884-2105
Eileen & Bertrand Bourget
March—December

$$$-B&B
13 rooms, 11 pb
*Rated*,
C-ltd/S-ltd/P-no/H-no

Full breakfast
Lunch, dinner ltd. (fee)
Sunday brunch, weddings
sitting room, color TV
cocktails, aft. tea

*Antique furnishings, gracious hospitality, restful beauty. Main building recently placed on the National Register of Historic Places. Conference facility, dinner parties.*

*Folkestone Inn, Bryson City, NC*

## BREVARD

| | | |
|---|---|---|
| **Red House Inn B&B, The** | $-B&B | Full breakfast |
| 412 W. Probart St.,　28712 | 5 rooms, 3 pb | Comp. wine |
| 704-884-9349 | ● | Sitting room, porches |
| Marilyn Ong | C-ltd/S-ltd/P-no/H-no | air conditioned |
| All year | | off-street parking |

*Lovingly restored antebellum home. Former trading post, courthouse, school and more. Near park, outlets, theater and sights. Completely furnished in antiques.* **7th nite free.**

| | | |
|---|---|---|
| **Womble Inn** | $$-B&B | Continental plus bkfst. |
| 301 W. Main St.,　28712 | 6 rooms, 6 pb | Full breakfast (fee) |
| 704-884-4770 | C-yes/S-yes/P-no/H-yes | Sitting room |
| Steve & Beth Womble　All yr | | piano |

*Gracious atmosphere of antiquity, breakfast served in your room, private baths, near town and Brevard Music Center, wonderful Christmas shop.*

## BRYSON CITY

| | | |
|---|---|---|
| **Folkestone Inn** | $$-B&B | Full gourmet breakfast |
| 101 Folkestone Rd.,　28713 | 10 rooms, 10 pb | Comp. snacks, wine |
| 704-488-2730 Fax: 704-488-0722 | Visa, MC, Disc. *Rated*, | Sitting room, library |
| Ellen & Charles Snodgrass | C-ltd/S-ltd/P-no/H-no | porch, rocking chairs |
| All year | | balconies, antiques |

*Comfortable country farmhouse, beside mountain brook. Walk to 3 waterfalls in the Smokies. Hiking, fishing, birding, scenic railway, whitewater rafting.*

| | | |
|---|---|---|
| **Fryemont Inn** | $$$-MAP | Full breakfast menu |
| P.O. Box 459,　28713 | 44 rooms, 44 pb | Full dinner included |
| 1 Fryemont Dr. | MC, Visa, Disc. *Rated*, | Full service lounge |
| 704-488-2159　800-845-4879 | C-yes/S-no/P-no/H-no | library, sitting room |
| Sue/George/Monica/ | | swimming pool |
| George Jr. | | |
| April–November | | |

*Located on a mountain shelf overlooking the Great Smoky Mountains National Park. A tradition in mountain hospitality since 1923. 2 bedroom family suites avail. Price includes dinner!*

## BRYSON CITY

**Nantahala Village**
9400 Hwy 19 West,   28713
704-488-2826
Fax: 704-488-9634
800-438-1507
John Burton & Jan Letendre
Mid March — December

$$-EP
54 rooms, 54 pb
Most CC, *Rated*, •
C-yes/S-ltd/P-no/H-ltd

Restaurant, meals avail.
Pool, Rec. hall
tennis court, volleyball
rafting, horsebackriding

*Family mountain resort with 14 rooms and 46 cabins; 200 acres in the Nantahala Mountains, Western N.C., great base for a wide variety of sightseeing activities.*

## BRYSON CITY, DILLSBORO

**Chalet Inn, The**
285 Lone Oak Dr., Whittier,
   28789
704-586-0251
Fax: 704-586-0251
George & Hanneke Ware
All year

$$-B&B
6 rooms, 6 pb
Visa, MC, •
C-ltd/S-no/P-no/H-no
German, Dutch, French

Full European breakfast
Snacks, comp. wine, tea
Great room w/library
private balconies/views
brook, hiking trails

*Authentic Alpine Chalet (Gasthaus) nestled in mountain cove of Blue Ridge Mtns. Secluded with spectacular views, convenient to attractions. Picnic area, lawn games. **3rd night 50%, ltd.***

## BURNSVILLE

**Estes Mountain Retreat**
Rt. 1, Box 1316 A, Baker's
Creek Rd.,   28714
704-682-7264
Bruce & Maryallen Estes
All year

$$-B&B
2 rooms, 2 pb
C-ltd/S-no/P-no/H-no
Some French

Full breakfast
Afternoon tea
Sitting room, library
near fishing, ski resort
golf, Country Club

*Log home. Beautiful mountain views. Delicious breakfast served on front porch. Evening dessert. Nature trails-seasonal wildflowers, colorful fall leaves. **10% senior (65+) & 6-night stay 15% discount.***

**NuWray Inn**
PO Box 156, Town Square,
   28714
704-682-2329
800-368-9729
Chris & Pam Strickland
All year

$$-B&B
26 rooms, 26 pb
AmEx, MC, Visa,
*Rated*, •
C-yes/S-no/P-no/H-yes

Full breakfast
Family-style dinners
Afternoon snacks
2 parlors, antiques
library, porch

*Historic Country inn . . . since 1833. Quaint town square setting, nestled in the Blue Ridge Mountains. Near Asheville, Parkway, crafts & golf. **7th night free**.*

## CASHIERS

**Millstone Inn**
P.O. Box 949,   28717
Hwy 64 West
704-743-2737  Fax: 704-743-0208
888-645-5786
Paul & Patricia Collins
March—early January

$$$-B&B
11 rooms, 11 pb
MC, Visa, Disc. *Rated*,
C-ltd/S-ltd/P-no/H-no

Full breakfast
Complimentary sherry
Sitting room, porch
library, games
hiking

*Elegantly furnished in a quiet and romantic setting. Spectacular mountain and forest views, with waterfalls and fishing nearby. **Off-season discount.***

*The Inn at Bingham School, Chapel Hill, NC*

## CHAPEL HILL

| | | |
|---|---|---|
| **Inn at Bingham School, The** | $$-B&B | Full breakfast |
| P.O. Box 267, 27514 | 5 rooms, 5 pb | Snacks, comp. wine |
| NC 54 @ Mebane Oaks Rd. | Visa, Mc, AmEx, | Sitting room, library |
| 919-563-5583 Fax: 919-563-9826 | C-yes/S-no/P-no/H-no | small meetings |
| 800-566-5583 | French, Spanish | wedding facilities |
| Francois & Christina Deprez | | |
| All year | | |

*Step back to a slower time, a slower pace. Rock by the fire with your wine or stroll the surrounding woodlands.* **Extended stay discounts.**

## CHARLOTTE

| | | |
|---|---|---|
| **Still Waters B&B** | $$-B&B | Full breakfast |
| 6221 Amos Smith Rd., 28214 | 4 rooms, 4 pb | Sport court, tennis |
| 704-399-6299 Fax: 704-399-5406 | MC, Visa, *Rated*, ● | basketball, volleyball |
| Janet & Rob Dyer  All year | C-ltd/S-no/P-no/H-no | boat ramp, dock, gazebo |

*Log resort home on two wooded acres overlooking Lake Wylie. Near Charlotte downtown & airport. Full breakfast featuring homemade bread. Guest cottage available*

## CLINTON

| | | |
|---|---|---|
| **Shield House The** | $$-B&B | Continental plus bkfst. |
| 216 Sampson St., 28328 | 24 rooms, 21 pb | Comp. coffee, sodas |
| 910-592-2634 800-462-9817 | Most CC, ● | Sitting room |
| Anita Green & Juanita | C-yes/S-ltd/P-no/H-no | tennis & golf nearby |
| McLamb  All year | | 2-bedroom bungalow avail |

*Reminiscent of Gone With The Wind. Elegant furnishings; outstanding architectural features. Listed in National Register. I-40 10 miles; I-95 29 miles.* **10% off for seniors, ltd.**

## CLYDE

| | | |
|---|---|---|
| **Windsong: A Mountain Inn** | $$$-B&B | Full breakfast |
| 120 Ferguson Ridge, 28721 | 6 rooms, 6 pb | Continental in suite |
| 704-627-6111 Fax: 704-627-8080 | Most CC, *Rated*, ● | Lounge, wet bar, pool |
| Donna & Gale Livengood | C-ltd/S-no/P-no/H-no | pool table, llama treks |
| All year | | tennis, piano |

*Secluded, contemporary rustic log inn set high in the Smoky Mountains. Rooms have fireplaces, tubs and private deck. Breathtaking views.* **10% for 5 nite+, 10% for singles.**

*Still Waters B&B, Charlotte, NC*

## COROLLA, THE OUTER BANKS

| | | |
|---|---|---|
| **Inn at Corolla Light, The** | $$$-B&B | Continental breakfast |
| 1066 Ocean Trail, 27927 | 42 rooms, 42 pb | Library, bikes |
| 919-453-3340 Fax: 919-453-6947 | Visa, MC, • | tennis court, hot tubs |
| 800-215-0772 | C-yes/S-no/P-no/H-yes | sauna, swimming pool |
| Bob White | | |
| All year | | |

*New, quiet, undiscovered, romantic. Luxurious soundfront accommodations in the premier ocean-to-sound resort on the Outer Banks. Oceanfront pool/restaurant. **Ask about seasonal packages.***

## DAVIDSON

| | | |
|---|---|---|
| **Davidson Village Inn** | $$$-B&B | Continental plus bkfst. |
| P.O. Box 1463, 28036 | 18 rooms, 18 pb | Afternoon tea, snacks |
| 117 Depot St. | Most CC, *Rated*, • | Library, sitting room |
| 704-892-8044 Fax: 704-896-2184 | C-yes/S-ltd/P-no/H-yes | lakefront recreation |
| Gordon & Rebecca Clark | | metropolitan amenities |
| All year | | |

*Warm relaxed inn, located in a quaint college town serving a unique blend of historic and contemporary southern pleasures. **Free Ben & Jerry's ice cream coupon.***

## DILLSBORO

| | | |
|---|---|---|
| **Dillsboro Inn, The** | $$$-B&B | Continental plus bkfst. |
| P.O. Box 270, 28725 | 4 rooms, 4 pb | Sitting room, library |
| 225 River Rd. | Visa, MC, | hot tub, yoga |
| 704-586-3898 Fax: 704-586-3898 | C-ltd/S-no/P-no/H-no | excercise/conference rm. |
| All year | | |

*Peaceful riverfront B&B with waterfall. Near hiking, mountain biking, rafting & more. Gourmet coffee, herbal teas, healthy breakfasts. Retreats available & welcome.*

## DUCK

| | | |
|---|---|---|
| **Sanderling Inn Resort** | AP | Full buffet breakfast |
| 1461 Duck Rd., 27949 | 60 rooms, 60 pb | Restaurant, comp. wine |
| 919-261-4111 | *Rated*, • | All meals included |
| Christine J. Berger | C-yes/S-yes/P-no/H-yes | bar service, sitting rm. |
| All year | | library, hot tubs |

*Private porches, bathrobes, kitchenettes or wetbars, whirlpool, tennis, swimming, health club, jogging trail, sauna, oceanfront. **Welcome gift.***

## DURHAM

| **Arrowhead Inn** | $$$-B&B | Full breakfast |
|---|---|---|
| 106 Mason Rd., 27712 | 8 rooms, 8 pb | Complimentary tea |
| 919-477-8430  Fax: 919-477-8430 | Most CC, *Rated*, • | Sitting room, swings |
| 800-528-2207 | C-yes/S-ltd/P-no/H-yes | piano, patio |
| Barb, Jerry & Cathy Ryan | French | A/C, Fax, copier |
| All year | | |

*1775 manor house offers tasteful period rooms with modern conveniences. New log cabin on our 4 acres. Children's museum nearby. Winner of 1st US Micro Business Award!*

| **Blooming Garden Inn, The** | $$$-B&B | Full gourmet breakfast |
|---|---|---|
| 513 Holloway St., 27701 | 5 rooms, 5 pb | Comp. wine, tea, snacks |
| 919-687-0801  Fax: 919-688-1401 | Most CC, *Rated*, • | Sitting rooms, library |
| Frank & Dolly Pokrass | C-yes/S-no/P-no/H-no | 145 foot porch, antiques |
| All year | | 2 rm. suite w/footed tub |

*Vibrant colors transform this restored Victorian into a cozy, memorable retreat in downtown historic Durham. Abundant flower gardens. **Inquire about extended stay discounts.***

## EDENTON

| **Lords Proprietors' Inn** | $$$$-MAP | Full breakfast |
|---|---|---|
| 300 N. Broad St., 27932 | 20 rooms, 20 pb | Dinner included |
| 919-482-3641  Fax: 919-482-2432 | *Rated*, • | Tea, homemade cookies |
| Arch & Jane Edwards | C-ltd/S-yes/P-no/H-no | sitting room, bicycles |
| All year | | private pool privileges |

*Edenton's oldest and most elegant inn offering the finest dining in eastern North Carolina. **3rd night free if noted at time of reservation, excl. Sat. or holiday.***

| **Trestle House Inn** | $$$-B&B | Full breakfast |
|---|---|---|
| 632 Soundside Rd., Rt 4, | 4 rooms, 4 pb | BYOB |
| 27932 | Most CC, *Rated*, • | Sitting room, billiards |
| 919-482-2282 | C-ltd/S-ltd/P-no/H-no | steam, exercise room, TV |
| Peter L. Bogus & Wendy | | shuffleboard, fishing |
| Jewett | | |
| All year | | |

*Immaculate accommodations. Tranquil setting overlooking private 15-acre fishing lake and 60 acres of trees. Five miles from historic Edenton. **3 nights for price of 2.***

## EMERALD ISLE

| **Emerald Isle Inn B&B** | $$-B&B | Full gourmet breakfast |
|---|---|---|
| 502 Ocean Dr., 28594 | 4 rooms, 4 pb | Afternoon tea |
| 919-354-3222  Fax: 919-354-3222 | *Rated*, | Sitting room, library |
| Marilyn Detwiller | C-yes/S-ltd/P-no/H-ltd | direct ocean access |
| All year | | beach chairs, umbrellas |

*Enjoy a warm, relaxing getaway at the beach. Ocean/bay views, gourmet breakfasts. Fishing, windsurfing, www surfing, small weddings, reunions. "Your home away from home."*

## FLAT ROCK

| **Woodfield Inn, The** | $$$-B&B | Continental breakfast |
|---|---|---|
| P.O. Box 98, 28731 | 18 rooms, 10 pb | Lunch, dinner |
| Hwy. 25 S. | Most CC, | Sitting room, piano |
| 704-693-6016  800-533-6016 | C-yes/S-yes/P-yes/H-yes | badminton, croquet |
| Jeane Smith | | entertainment |
| All year | | |

*A wonderful place to unwind and get away from everyday routine. Winner of Dinner Club of America Silver Spoon Award. Nature trail, golf.*

FRANKLIN ――――――――――――――――――――――――――――

| **Buttonwood Inn** | $$-B&B | Full breakfast |
|---|---|---|
| 190 Georgia Rd., 28734 | 4 rooms, 2 pb | Sitting room, TV |
| 704-369-8985 | *Rated*, • | golf nearby |
| Liz Oehser | C-ltd/S-ltd/P-no/H-no | |
| All year | | |

*Completely surrounded by tall pines, small and cozy Buttonwood will appeal to the person who prefers simplicity and natural rustic beauty.* **3rd night 20% off.**

| **Franklin Terrace, The** | $$-B&B | Continental plus bkfst. |
|---|---|---|
| 159 Harrison Ave., 28734 | 9 rooms, 9 pb | Comp. refreshments |
| 704-524-7907 800-633-2431 | MC, Visa, • | 2 beautiful sitting rms. |
| Ed & Helen Henson | C-ltd/S-ltd/P-no/H-no | color/cable TV, A/C |
| May–October | | 2 porches with rockers |

*All rooms furnished with antiques. First floor houses dessert shop with cheesecakes, homemade pies & cakes–also antique shop. In town. Beautiful views.*

HENDERSONVILLE ――――――――――――――――――――――――

| **Claddagh Inn, The** | $$-B&B | Full breakfast |
|---|---|---|
| 755 N. Main St., 28792 | 14 rooms, 14 pb | Aft. tea, Sunday brunch |
| 704-697-7778 Fax: 704-697-8664 | Most CC, *Rated*, • | Sitting room, library |
| 800-225-4700 | C-yes/S-yes/P-no/H-no | TV, phone & A/C in rooms |
| August & Geraldine | | tennis, shuffleboard |
| Emanuele | | |
| All year | | |

*On National Register of Historic Places. Beautiful country inn located in downtown Hendersonville provides a homelike atmosphere where love and lasting friendships prevail.*

| **Waverly Inn, The** | $$$-B&B | Full breakfast |
|---|---|---|
| 783 N. Main St., 28792 | 16 rooms, 16 pb | Comp. wine, beverages |
| 704-693-9193 Fax: 704-692-1010 | Most CC, *Rated*, • | Sitting room, A/C |
| 800-537-8195 | C-yes/S-yes/P-no/H-ltd | telephones in all rms. |
| J & D Sheiry, D. Olmstead | | tennis court, social hr. |
| All year | | |

*A landmark near downtown shopping park, quaint restaurants. On National Register. Beautiful antiques. Spotlessly clean. AAA Approved. Fresh goods baked daily.*

HIGH POINT ――――――――――――――――――――――――――――

| **Bouldin House B&B, The** | $$$-B&B | Full breakfast |
|---|---|---|
| 4332 Archdale Rd., 27263 | 4 rooms, 4 pb | Evening beverage, snacks |
| 910-431-4909 | Most CC, *Rated*, • | Sitting room |
| Larry & Ann Miller | C-ltd/S-ltd/P-no/H-no | large verandah |
| All year | | board games, TV |

*Country atmosphere; relaxed and casual, yet elegant. Better than home away from home. Furniture showrooms minutes away. Come indulge yourself.*

HIGHLANDS ――――――――――――――――――――――――――――

| **Colonial Pines Inn** | $$-B&B | Full breakfast |
|---|---|---|
| Rt 1, Box 22B, 541 Hickory St., | 9 rooms, 9 pb | Afternoon refreshments |
| 28741 | MC, Visa, | Sitting room, kitchen |
| 704-526-2060 | C-ltd/S-ltd/P-no/H-no | grand piano, picnic area |
| Chris & Donna Alley | | 2 new suites |
| All year | | |

*Two acres of lawn and trees. Mountain view from veranda. Antique furnishings and country charm. Guest house with fireplace, sleeps up to six.* **3rd. night free, ltd.**

## HIGHLANDS

| **Long House B&B** | $$-B&B | Full breakfast |
|---|---|---|
| P.O. Box 2078,  28741 | 4 rooms, 4 pb | Snacks |
| Highway 64 East | MC, Visa, | Sitting room |
| 704-526-4394  800-833-0020 | C-yes/S-no/H-no | near golf, hiking paths, |
| The Longs   All year | | fishing |

*Rustic mountain home at the 4000-foot level in the Blue Ridge Mountains. Country comfort, large deck, and wonderful breakfast.*

| **Morning Star Inn** | $$$-B&B | Full gourmet breakfast |
|---|---|---|
| 480 Flat Mt.Estates Rd., | 5 rooms, 5 pb | Aftn. tea, comp. wine |
| 28741 | Visa, MC, *Rated*, • | Sitting room |
| 704-526-1009  Fax: 704-526-4474 | C-ltd/S-ltd/P-no/H-no | beautiful grounds |
| Pat & Pat Allen   All year | | romantic escape |

*Beautiful grounds, mountain view, birds, flowers, hammocks, wicker, elegant rooms, gourmet bkfst., wine & hors d'oeuvres. Mozart, antiques, whirlpool for 2. Romantic escape.*

| **Ye Olde Stone House B&B** | $$-B&B | Full breakfast |
|---|---|---|
| 1337 S. 4th St.,  28741 | 4 rooms, 4 pb | Snacks |
| 704-526-5911 | Visa, MC, | Sitting room |
| Jim & Rene Ramsdell | C-ltd/S-no/P-no/H-no | families welcome in |
| All year | | guest houses |

*Hidden in a vale, enjoy a touch of yesterday. Savor a delicious country breakfast and true Southern hospitality you'll long remember.*

## HILLSBOROUGH

| **Hillsborough House Inn** | $$$-B&B | Continental breakfast |
|---|---|---|
| P.O. Box 880,  27278 | 5 rooms, 5 pb | Snacks |
| 209 E. Tryon St. | MC, Visa, *Rated*, • | Library, swimming pool |
| 919-644-1600  Fax: 919-644-1600 | C-ltd/S-no/P-no/H-no | 7 acres nature paths |
| 800-616-1660 | | separate suite w/kitchen |
| Katherine Webb, Kat Benz | | |
| Closed Xmas - New Years | | |

*Italianate mansion w/dream of a front porch(80 ft.)on 7 acres in the Historic District. Eclectic, gracious & convenient. Extensive gardens. Cater to special diets.* **10% off stay.**

## KILL DEVIL HILLS

| **Cherokee Inn B&B** | $$-B&B | Continental breakfast |
|---|---|---|
| 500 N. Virginia Dare Tr, | 6 rooms, 6 pb | Wraparound porches |
| 27948 | Most CC, *Rated*, • | overhead ceiling fans |
| 919-441-6127  Fax: 919-441-1072 | C-ltd/S-ltd/P-no/H-no | Sr. citizen discount |
| 800-554-2764 | | |
| Bob & Kaye Combs | | |
| March - November | | |

*Beach house with rustic cypress interior. Small, private, quiet. Atlantic Ocean 600 feet away. Near historic sites, shops & restaurants.*

## LAKE LURE

| **Lodge on Lake Lure** | $$$-B&B | Full breakfast |
|---|---|---|
| Box 519,  28746 | 11 rooms, 11 pb | complimentary wine |
| Charlotte Dr. | AmEx, MC, Visa, | Sitt. rm., lib., piano |
| 704-625-2789  Fax: 704-625-2421 | *Rated*, • | lake swimming, 2 docks |
| 800-733-2785 | C-ltd/S-no/P-no/H-no | tennis, golf nearby |
| Jack & Robin Stanier | | |
| April–November | | |

*Adult getaway in the Blue Ridge Mountains. Giant stone frplc., breathtaking view of mtns. and lake. "Cove Room" overlooking cove. Only public facility actually on Lake Lure.*

*Cherokee Inn B&B, Kill Devil Hills, NC*

LAKE TOXAWAY ──────────────────────

| **Earthshine Mountain Lodge**<br>Route 1, Box 216-C, Golden Rd., 28747<br>704-862-4207<br>Marion & Kim Boatwright<br>All year | $$$$-AP<br>10 rooms, 10 pb<br>•<br>C-yes/S-no/P-no/H-yes | Full breakfast<br>Lunch, dinner incl.<br>Comp. set-ups after 5 pm<br>hiking, horseback riding<br>programs for all ages |

*Rustic luxury mountain top lodge. Spectacular views. 70 acres homestead setting. Borders Pisgah National Forest. Perfect for families. Complimentary evening entertainment.*

| **Greystone Inn, The**<br>Greystone Lane, 28747<br>704-966-4700 Fax: 704-862-5689<br>800-824-5766<br>Tim & BooBoo Lovelace<br>All year | $$$$-MAP<br>33 rooms, 33 pb<br>Visa, MC, AmEx,<br>*Rated*, •<br>C-ltd/S-ltd/P-no/H-yes | Full breakfast<br>Dinner included<br>Restaurant, bar service<br>Aft. tea, sitting room<br>jacuzzis in all rooms |

*Romantic elegance. Located on a spectacular mountain lake. Luxurious rooms, gracious service, Southern cuisine & activities. Tennis court, bicycles, pool.*

LITTLE SWITZERLAND ──────────────────

| **Big Lynn Lodge**<br>P.O. Box 459, 28749<br>Highway 226-A<br>704-765-6771 800-654-5232<br>Gale & Carol Armstrong<br>April 15–October | $$$-MAP<br>40 rooms, 40 pb<br>Visa, MC, Disc, *Rated*,<br>•<br>C-ltd/S-yes/P-no/H-ltd<br>German | Full breakfast<br>Dinner included, fruit<br>Sitting room, library<br>player piano lounge, TV<br>billards, shuffleboard |

*Old-fashioned country inn. Dinner and bkfast incl. with room. Cool mountain air; elevation 3200 ft. Breathtaking view. Rocking chairs on porches; some suites with whirlpools.*

MADISON ─────────────────────────────

| **Boxley B&B, The**<br>117 E. Hunter St., 27025<br>910-427-0453 Fax: 910-427-4154<br>800-429-3516<br>JoAnn & Monte McIntosh<br>All year | $$-B&B<br>4 rooms, 4 pb<br>Visa, MC, AmEx,<br>*Rated*,<br>C-yes/S-ltd/P-no/H-yes | Full breakfast<br>Complimentary wine<br>Sitting room<br>gardens<br>yard |

*A gracious home furnished with antiques and filled with southern hospitality. Peacefulness and serenity abound in yard and gardens. Located 22 miles north of Greensboro.*

*Lodge on Lake Lure, Lake Lure, NC*

MOCKSVILLE ───────────────────────────

**Boxwood Lodge**
Hwy 601 at 132 Becktown, 27028
704-284-2031
Martha Hoffner
All year

$$-B&B
8 rooms,
Visa, MC, •
S-no/P-ltd/H-no

Full breakfast
Snacks, afternoon tea
Fishing, pool table
library, guest passes to
YMCA-sauna/pool/weights

*Country mansion hideaway convenient to High Point Furniture Market, Winston-Salem, historic Mocksville and Salisbury, NC.*

MOUNT AIRY ───────────────────────────

**Pine Ridge Inn**
2893 West Pine, Hwy 89, 27030
910-789-5034
Jodi & Tyler Sloan
All year

$$-B&B
6 rooms, 6 pb
Most CC, *Rated*, •
C-yes/S-yes/P-no/H-yes

Full breakfast
All meals available
Comp. tea, wine & cheese
sitting room, piano
hot tub, swimming pool

*Elegant luxury at foot of Blue Ridge Mountains. A country inn with amenities of a grand hotel. All meals available on request. Jacuzzi, sauna.* **Package deals start at $199.00.**

MURPHY ───────────────────────────

**Huntington Hall B&B**
500 Valley River Ave., 28906
704-837-9567 Fax: 704-837-2527
800-824-6189
Bob & Kate Delong
All year

$$-B&B
5 rooms, 5 pb
AmEx, MC, Visa,
*Rated*, •
C-yes/S-yes/P-no/H-ltd

Full breakfast
Complimentary wine
Sitting room, library
public pool & tennis
white water rafting pkg.

*A Bed & Breakfast well done! Circa 1881, former mayor's home, delightful country Victorian. Sumptous breakfast, cool mountain breezes await you! Murder Mystery wkend package.*

## NAGS HEAD

**First Colony Inn, The**
6720 S. Virginia Dare,   27959
919-441-2343  Fax: 919-441-9234
800-368-9390
The Lawrences    All year

$$$-B&B
26 rooms, 26 pb
Visa, MC, Disc, *Rated*,
•
C-yes/S-ltd/P-no/H-yes

Continental plus buffet
Aftn. tea, comp. wine
Sitting room, library
verandas, pool, croquet
ocean beach, fishing

*With verandahs along all four sides; antiques, wonderful big beds. Ocean views on 2nd & 3rd floors. Access to uncrowded private beach. **Stay Sun.–Thur. nights, Thurs. night free.***

## NEW BERN

**Harmony House Inn**
215 Pollock St.,   28560
919-636-3810  Fax: 919-636-3810
800-636-3113
Ed & Sooki Kirkpatrick
All year

$$$-B&B
10 rooms, 10 pb
AmEx, MC, Visa,
*Rated*, •
C-yes/S-no/P-no/H-no

Full breakfast
Comp. drinks/wine/sherry
Victorian pump organ
1 suite, parlor, porch
w/swings, rocking chairs

*Unusually spacious circa 1850 home, rocking chairs on porch, lovely yard. In the historic district, near Tryon Palace; shops, fine restaurants. **4th night 50% off.***

**King's Arms Colonial Inn**
212 Pollock St.,   28560
919-638-4409  Fax: 919-638-2191
800-872-9306
Richard & Pat Gulley
All year

$$$-B&B
11 rooms, 8 pb
AmEx, MC, Visa,
*Rated*, •
C-yes/S-yes/P-no/H-no

Continental plus bkfst.
Breakfast by candlelight
Furnished with antiques
fireplaces, sitting room
suite with view of river

*In heart of historic district. Delicious hot breakfast. Southern hospitality. Information on sightseeing and dining. Three blocks from Tryon Palace. **Special occasion drinks.***

**New Bern's Magnolia House**
315 George St.,   28562
919-633-9488  Fax: 919-633-9488
800-601-9488
Kim & John Trudo    All year

$$$-B&B
3 rooms, 3 pb
Most CC,
C-ltd/S-ltd/P-no/H-no

Full breakfast
Afternoon tea, snacks
Sitting room, library
bicycles, near shops,
museums & historic sites

*Romance yourself in one of our 3 Victorian rooms. Full breakfast in our dining room, front porch or under the magnolia tree. 2 doors from Tryon Palace in Historic District. **3rd night 50% off.***

## OCRACOKE

**Berkley Center Country Inn**
P.O. Box 220,   27960
919-928-5911
Ruth & Wes Egan
March–November

$$-B&B
11 rooms, 9 pb
*Rated*, •
C-yes/S-yes/P-no/H-yes

Continental breakfast
Sitting room
bicycles
fishing

*Beautifully restored estate on harbor of outer banks fishing village located in U.S. National Seashore. 19 miles of uncommercialized beach.*

## OLD FORT

**Inn at Old Fort, The**
P.O. Box 1116,   28762
116 W. Main St.
704-668-9384  800-471-0637
Debbie & Chuck Aldridge
All year

$$-B&B
4 rooms, 4 pb
•
C-yes/S-ltd/P-no/H-no

Continental plus bkfst.
Snacks
Parlor and library
cable TV, large porch
breakfast on garden deck

*1880s Victorian cottage furnished w/antiques, library, large porch for rocking, lawn and many special gardens with sitting areas set on 3.5 acres overlooking Blue Ridge town near Asheville, Lake Lure.*

## ORIENTAL

**Tar Heel Inn, The**
P.O. Box 176,  28571
508 Church St.
919-249-1078
Shawna & Robert Hyde
All year

$$-B&B
8 rooms, 8 pb
*Rated*,
C-yes/S-no/P-no/H-ltd

Full breakfast
Comp. wine w/2+ nights
Library, bicycles
tennis courts, croquet
horseshoes

*Romantic English-style inn. Secluded coastal NC village, known as sailing capital of Carolinas. Within walking distance to shops, galleries & fine restaurants. 3rd night 50%.*

## PISGAH FOREST

**Key Falls Inn**
151 Everett Rd.,  28768
704-884-7559
C. & P. Grosvenor,
J.Fogleman
All year

$$-B&B
5 rooms, 5 pb
AmEx, MC, Visa,  •
C-ltd/S-ltd/P-no/H-no
Spanish

Full breakfast
Afternoon tea, lemonade
Sitting room, cable TV
VCR, trail to waterfall
tennis ct., fishing pond

*Charming, restored Victorian farmhouse furnished w/antiques on 28 acres near Brevard. Porches, mountain view, waterfall, wooded setting & sumptuous breakfasts. 7th nite free.*

**Pines Country Inn, The**
719 Hart Rd.,  28768
704-877-3131
Tom & Mary McEntire
June 1-October 31

$$-B&B/MAP
22 rooms, 19 pb
C-yes/S-yes/P-no/H-ltd

Full breakfast
Dinner Fri-Sat (option.)
Sitting room, piano
children play yard
great biking & hiking

*Quiet, homey country inn. Fantastic view. Accommodations in the Inn or the 4 cabins and cottages. Where guests are treated like family at Grandma's house. 10% off 7+ day stay.*

## PITTSBORO

**Fearrington House Inn**
2000 Fearrington,  27312
919-542-2121  Fax: 919-542-4202
The Fitch Family
All year

$$$$-B&B
28 rooms, 28 pb
MC, Visa, *Rated*,  •
C-ltd/S-ltd/P-no/H-yes

Full breakfast
Lunch, dinner
Afternoon tea
sitting room, pool
meeting facilities

*Classic countryside elegance in suites furnished with English antiques. Charming courtyard and gardens. Delicately prepared regional cuisine. Member of Relais & Chateaux.*

## RALEIGH

**Oakwood Inn**
411 N. Bloodworth St.,  27604
919-832-9712  Fax: 919-836-9263
800-267-9712
Vara & Jim Cox
All year

$$-B&B
6 rooms, 4 pb
MC, Visa, *Rated*,  •
C-ltd/S-no/P-no/H-no

Full breakfast
Comp. wine, aftn. tea
Bedside treat, snacks
sitting room, piano
parlor, porch

*Charming inn in Victorian home built in 1871. On National Register and furnished with period antiques reflecting charm of yesteryear. In room phones, cable & Showtime, fax & copy service.*

## ROBBINSVILLE

**Snowbird Mountain Lodge**
275 Santeetlah Rd.,  28771
704-479-3433  Fax: 704-479-3473
Karen & Robert Rankin
April 15—November 6

$$-AP
21 rooms, 21 pb
Most CC, *Rated*,
C-ltd/S-ltd/P-no/H-ltd

Full breakfast
Lunch & dinner included
Sitting room, piano
vegetarian meals
wildflower hikes

*Located in the heart of the National Forest. Fishing, hiking, mountain stream swimming, canoeing, whitewater rafting, shuffleboard, and horseback riding.*

## SALISBURY

**Rowan Oak House**
208 S. Fulton St., 28144
704-633-2086 800-786-0437
Barbara & Les Coombs
All year

$$$-B&B
4 rooms, 4 pb
Visa, MC, *Rated*, •
C-ltd/S-ltd/P-no

Full breakfast
Complimentary snacks
Library, sitting room
bicycles, antiques
jacuzzi tub in one room

*"Lavish, luxurious and unique" describes our Queen Anne home with antiques, flowers, porches, gardens, and historic Salisbury's small-town atmosphere. AAA approved!*

## SALUDA

**Ivy Terrace B&B Inn**
P.O. Box 639, 28773
Hwy. 176, Main St.
704-749-9542 Fax: 704-749-2017
800-749-9542
D. & H. McGuire, W. Hoover
All year

$$$-B&B
7 rooms, 7 pb
Visa, MC, *Rated*, •
C-ltd/S-ltd/P-no/H-yes

Full breakfast
Snacks
Sitting room, porches
conference building
porches, terraces

*A restful mountain haven in a garden setting. Walk to historic downtown Saluda, tour highway 176 a North Carolina scenic byway. Conference facility.*

**Oaks, The**
Rt. 1, Box 10, 28773
10 Greenville St.
704-749-9613 Fax: 704-749-9613
800-893-6091
Crowley & Terry Murphy
All year

$$$-B&B
5 rooms, 5 pb
MC, Visa, •
C-ltd/S-ltd/P-no/H-no

Full breakfast
Afternoon tea, snacks
Complimentary wine

*Charming Victorian with wrap-around porch furnished with American and Oriental antiques. In small town in western North Carolina mountains.*

## SILER CITY

**B&B at Laurel Ridge**
3188 SC-Snow Camp Rd.,
  27344
919-742-6049 800-742-6049
David Simmons & Lisa
Reynolds
All year

$$-B&B
3 rooms, 3 pb
Visa, MC, AmEx, •
C-yes/S-no/P-no/H-no

Full breakfast
Aft. tea, snacks
Sitting room, large deck
tennis court, screened
porch, 2 person jacuzzi

*Located in heart of North Carolina, post-and-beam country home on 26 acres, overlooks Rocky River. Gourmet breakfast by award-winning chef/owner. 1 cottage with jacuzzi.*

## SOUTHERN PINES

**Knollwood House**
1495 W. Connecticut Ave,
  28387
910-692-9390 Fax: 910-692-0609
Dick & Mimi Beatty All year

$$$-B&B
7 rooms, 7 pb
Visa, MC, *Rated*, •
C-ltd/S-ltd/P-no/H-no

Full breakfast buffet
Comp. hors d'oeuvres
Golf packages includes
breakfast, lodgings
dinner and greens fee.

*A luxurious English manor house with 18th century antiques & contemporary comforts in the heart of golf country*

## SPRUCE PINE

**Fairway Inn B&B, The**
110 Henry Ln., 28777
704-765-4917 704-765-8559
Margaret and John P. Stevens
May—October

$$-B&B
5 rooms, 5 pb
MC, Visa,
C-ltd/S-ltd/P-no/H-no

Full breakfast
Comp. wine & cheese
Sitting room
wake-up service
daily newspaper

*Nestled in the Blue Ridge Mountains & overlooking the golf course, we offer attractive rooms and breakfast in your room. Warmth, good cheer, and personalized service. **Military, AARP, skier discount, ask.***

SPRUCE PINE ─────────────────────────────────────

| **Richmond Inn B&B, The** | $$-B&B | Full breakfast |
|---|---|---|
| 101 Pine Ave., 28777 | 7 rooms, 7 pb | Snacks, comp. wine |
| 704-765-6993 | Visa, MC, *Rated*, • | Sitting room |
| Bill Ansley & Lenore | C-yes/S-no/P-no/H-no | library |
| Boucher | | |
| All year | | |

*Guest awaken each morning to the aromas of brewing coffee, baking muffins and simmering apples, all part of the full country breakfast served daily.*

TARBORO ─────────────────────────────────────

| **Barracks Inn, The** | $$-B&B | Continental plus bkfst. |
|---|---|---|
| 1100 Albemarle Ave., 27886 | 2 rooms, 2 pb | Full bkfst. by request |
| 919-641-1614  Fax: 919-641-1828 | Visa, MC, AmEx, • | Lunch, dinner (fee) |
| Tom & Patty Zelaney | C-yes/S-yes/P-ltd/H-yes | snacks, restaurant |
| All year | French | sitting room, library |

*Historic home furnished in period antiques; gourmet breakfasts served in dining room or in rose garden by fish pond; dine in full gourmet restaurant.* **50% off second dinner for 2.**

| **Little Warren B&B** | $$-B&B | Continental plus or Full |
|---|---|---|
| 304 E. Park Ave., 27886 | 3 rooms, 3 pb | Complimentary beverage |
| 919-823-1314  800-309-1314 | Most CC, *Rated*, • | Sitting room |
| Patsy & Tom Miller | C-ltd/S-yes/P-no/H-no | tennis courts |
| All year | Spanish | Antique shop downtown |

*Gracious, Edwardian home full of antiques & collectibles. In quiet neighborhood, historic district.* **Special attention to newlyweds, anniversary couples, business guests.**

TRYON ─────────────────────────────────────

| **Mill Farm Inn** | $$-B&B | Continental plus bkfst. |
|---|---|---|
| P.O. Box 1251, 28782 | 10 rooms, 8 pb | Sitting porch, TV, fax |
| Harmon Field Rd. | C-yes/S-no/P-no/H-no | large living rm, library |
| 704-859-6992  800-545-6992 | French | confortable, traditional |
| Chip & Penny Kessler | | |
| All year | | |

*Fine guest inn, including complimentary breakfast—homelike atmosphere, bird-watcher's paradise, plus cultural living experience. Mountains, small town.*

| **Pine Crest Inn** | $$$-B&B | Continental |
|---|---|---|
| 200 Pine Crest Ln., 28782 | 32 rooms, 32 pb | Dinner (fee), aft. tea |
| 704-859-9135  800-633-3001 | AmEx, MC, Visa, | Restaurant, bar, snacks |
| Jennifer & Jeremy | *Rated*, • | sitting room, fireplaces |
| Wainwright | C-yes/S-ltd/P-no/H-ltd | library, club privileges |
| All year | French | |

*Elegant country inn located in foothills of North Carolina. Near the Blue Ridge Parkway. Gourmet restaurant, library, bar and wide verandas add to the casual elegance.*

| **Stone Hedge Inn** | $$-B&B | Full breakfast |
|---|---|---|
| P.O. Box 366, 28782 | 5 rooms, 5 pb | Restaurant, dinner |
| 300 Howard Gap Rd. | MC, Visa, *Rated*, • | Swimming pool |
| 704-859-9114  800-859-1974 | C-ltd/S-yes/P-no/H-yes | hiking in wooded meadows |
| T. Dinsmore; G. Shidaker | | receptions & reunions |
| All year | | |

*Restaurant and lodge on peaceful 28-acre estate. Small meetings, conferences, weddings. Contemporary fine dining.* **7th night free, discount, 7 days or more.**

WASHINGTON ――――――――――――――――――――――――――――

| **Acadian House B&B** | B&B | Full breakfast |
|---|---|---|
| 129 Van Norden St.,  27889 | 4 rooms, 4 pb | Afternoon tea |
| 919-975-3967  Fax: 919-975-1148 | C-ltd/S-no/P-no/H-no | Sitting room, library |
| Leonard & Johanna Huber | | bikes |
| February 1 - December 15 | | |

*Located in the historic downtown district. Southern Lousiana's delicacies such as beignets, cafe au lait, and pain perdu often served at breakfast.*

WAYNESVILLE ――――――――――――――――――――――――――――

| **Grandview Lodge** | $$-MAP | Full breakfast |
|---|---|---|
| 809 Valley View Ci.,  28786 | 15 rooms, 15 pb | Dinner incl., lunch |
| 704-456-5212 Fax: 704-452-5432 | *Rated*,  • | Restaurant (resv), Fax |
| 800-255-7826 | C-yes/S-no | library, piano, golf |
| Stan & Linda Arnold | Polish, Russian, German | tennis, shuffleboard |
| All year | | |

*Inn located on rolling land, w/an orchard & arbor. Breakfast features homemade jams & jellies. Dinner includes fresh vegetables, baked breads & desserts. **3rd nite 50%, ltd.***

| **Hallcrest Inn** | $$-MAP | Full breakfast |
|---|---|---|
| 299 Halltop Circle,  28786 | 12 rooms, 12 pb | Dinner included |
| 704-456-6457  800-334-6457 | Visa, MC, Disc.,  • | Tea/coffee/cocoa/juice |
| Martin & Tesa Burson | C-ltd/S-ltd/P-no/H-no | library, living room |
| June—October | | |

*Small country inn in over 100-year-old farmhouse with adjacent modular unit. Family-style dining around lazy-susan tables and beautiful view of the mountain.*

| **Haywood House** | $$-B&B | Full breakfast |
|---|---|---|
| 409 South Haywood St., | 4 rooms, 2 pb | Comp. beverage, snacks |
| 28786 | MC, Visa, AmEx, | Sitting room, library |
| 704-456-9831 Fax: 704-456-4400 | C-ltd/S-no/P-no/H-no | laundry fac., Fax |
| Lynn & Chris Sylvester | | veranda & picnic areas |
| All year | | |

*Rock, relax, view the mountains/enjoy small town charm. Comfortable, beautifully furnished historic home. Warm hospitality & delightful breakfasts. Walk to shops/restaurants.*

| **Old Stone Inn-Heath Lodge** | $$$-EP | Full breakfast |
|---|---|---|
| 900 Dolan Rd.,  28786 | 22 rooms, 22 pb | Fireside dining |
| 704-456-3333  800-432-8499 | *Rated*, | Sitting room, library |
| Robert & Cindy Zinser | C-yes/S-yes/P-no/H-ltd | outdoor deck, gift shop |
| All year | Spanish | color TV in rm, 2 pianos |

*On a wooded hillside—mountain inn w/beamed ceilings & country furnishings. Golf, train ride, whitewater pkgs. Celebrating 50 years. **Comp. bottle of wine.***

| **Yellow House, The** | $$$-B&B | Full breakfast |
|---|---|---|
| 610 Plott Creek Rd.,  28786 | 6 rooms, 6 pb | Snacks, comp. wine |
| 317-452-0991  Fax: 317-452-1140 | Visa, MC,  • | Sitting room, library |
| 800-563-1236 | C-ltd/S-no/P-no/H-no | bikes, tennis court |
| Ron & Sharon Smith | | hot tubs, swimming pool |
| All year | | |

*Western North Carolina's most romantic inn; gourmet breakfast may be served in your room. Every quarter has fireplace, coffee service, robes, & music. 2.5 acres of lawn, lilly pond & gardens.*

*The Old Stone Inn-Heath Lodge, Waynesville, NC*

WEAVERVILLE ─────────────────────────────────

**Dry Ridge Inn**
26 Brown St.,   28787
704-658-3899
800-839-3899
Paul & Mary Lou Gibson
All year

$$-B&B
7 rooms, 7 pb
MC, Visa, *Rated*, •
C-yes/S-ltd

Full breakfast
Complimentary wine
Sitting room, A/C
outdoor spa, gift shop
art gallery, antiques

*Convenient to Asheville and Blue Ridge Parkway with small town charm. Large comfortable guest rooms; antiques and homemade quilts. **Stay 3 nights, get 10% discount.***

WILMINGTON ─────────────────────────────────

**Anderson Guest House**
520 Orange St.,   28401
910-343-8128
Connie Anderson
All year

$$-B&B
2 rooms, 2 pb
C-ltd/S-yes/P-yes/H-no

Full breakfast
Comp. wine, mixed drinks
Afternoon tea, fireplace
restaurant nearby
baby-sitting service

*1851 Italianate townhouse; separate guest quarters overlooking private garden. Furnished with antiques, ceiling fans, fireplaces. Drinks upon arrival. Delightful breakfasts.*

**Catherine's Inn**
410 S. Front St.,   28401
910-251-0863
800-476-0723
Catherine & Walter AcKiss
All year

$$$-B&B
3 rooms, 3 pb
AmEx, MC, Visa,
*Rated*, •
C-yes/S-yes/P-no/H-no

Full breakfast
Comp. wine, snacks, tea
Bar service
sitting room, library
swimming pool

*In heart of the historical district. Experience warm gracious hospitality, tasty breakfasts. Near Wilmington attractions. **Free wine for special occasions, restaurant comp. wine.***

## WILMINGTON

| **Inn at St. Thomas Court** | $$$-B&B | Continental plus bkfst. |
|---|---|---|
| 101 S. Second St, 28401 | 34 rooms, 34 pb | In suites–kitchen inc. |
| 910-343-1800  Fax: 910-251-1149 | AmEx, MC, Visa, | Concierge, conservatory |
| 800-525-0909 | *Rated*, • | billiard room, courtyard |
| T.K. Scott, M.L. Compton | C-ltd/S-yes/H-yes | pub in house |
| All year | | |

*Elegant accommodations for discriminating travelers, located in romantic Historic District. Walk along Cape Fear River paths to fine restaurants, museums and specialty shops.*

| **James Place B&B** | $$-B&B | Full breakfast |
|---|---|---|
| 9 S. Fourth St., 28401 | 3 rooms, 3 pb | Comp. wine, snacks |
| 910-251-0999  Fax: 910-251-1150 | Visa, MC, *Rated*, • | Sitting room |
| 800-303-9444 | C-yes/S-no/P-no/H-no | in-room jacuzzi tubs |
| Tony & Maureen Spataro | | large front porch |
| All year | | |

*In the heart of Wilmington's historic district, our comfortable at-home atmosphere will make you feel welcome throughout your visit.* **3rd night 30% off.**

| **Taylor House Inn** | $$$-B&B | Full breakfast |
|---|---|---|
| 14 N. Seventh St., 28401 | 5 rooms, 5 pb | Comp. wine, snacks, tea |
| 910-763-7581  800-382-9982 | AmEx, MC, Visa, | Sitting room |
| Glenda Moreadith | *Rated*, • | library |
| All year | C-ltd/S-yes/P-no/H-no | piano |

*Authentically restored, spacious guest rooms furnished with antiques. Elegant dining room. Private baths, clawfoot tubs.* **25% off 3rd night. ltd.**

| **Worth House, The** | $$$-B&B | Full breakfast |
|---|---|---|
| 412 S. Third St., 28401 | 7 rooms, 7 pb | Complimentary beverages |
| 910-762-8562  Fax: 910-763-2173 | Most CC, *Rated*, • | Coffee, 3 sitt. rms. fax |
| 800-340-8559 | C-ltd/S-no/P-no/H-no | laundry, modem, porches, |
| Francie & John Miller | | gardens, fireplaces. |
| All year | | |

*1893 Queen Anne in historic district. 7 rms. w/priv. baths, a/c, period art and furnishings. With our 7 guest rms. and 4 common rms., we are ideal for reunions & retreats*

## WILSON

| **Miss Betty's B&B Inn** | $$-B&B | Full breakfast |
|---|---|---|
| 600 W. Nash St., 27893 | 10 rooms, 10 pb | 3 parlors, antique shop |
| 919-243-4447  Fax: 919-243-4447 | Most CC, *Rated*, | A/C, golf, swimming pool |
| 800-258-2058 | S-yes/P-no/H-yes | games, suites |
| Betty & Fred Spitz | | |
| All year | | |

*Selected as one of the "best places to stay in the South." A touch of Victorian elegance and beauty. Close to main North-South Route I-95.*

## WINSTON, SALEM

| **Augustus T. Zevely Inn** | $$$-B&B | Continental plus–wkdays |
|---|---|---|
| 803 S. Main St., 27101 | 12 rooms, 12 pb | Full breakfast–weekends |
| 910-748-9299  Fax: 910-721-2211 | Visa, MC, AmEx, | Aft. tea, snacks, wine |
| 800-928-9299 | *Rated*, • | sitting room, library |
| Linda Anderson | C-yes/S-yes/P-no/H-yes | bikes, sauna, pool |
| All year | | |

*Moravian-style B&B restored to museum quality, overlooking historic Old Salem. Formal dining room & parlor, spacious covered porch. Period garden and orchard. Health facility.*

*The Worth House, Wilmington, NC*

WINSTON, SALEM ───────────
**Colonel Ludlow Inn**
434 Summit at W. 5th,   27101
910-777-1887  Fax: 910-777-1890
800-301-1887
Constance Creasman
All year

$$$$-B&B
12 rooms, 12 pb
AmEx, MC, Visa,
*Rated*, •
C-ltd/S-yes/P-no/H-no

Full breakfast
King bed, some frplcs.
in-room CDs/tapes/VCR
pool table, swim pool

*Two adjacent beautifully restored 1887 & 1890 National Register homes. Exercise room, antiques. Deluxe rooms with private 2-person Jacuzzi in romantic alcove. Near downtown, shops, fine restaurants.*

**Lady Anne's Victorian B&B**
612 Summit St.,   27101
910-724-1074
Shelley Kirley
All year

$$-B&B
4 rooms, 3 pb
AmEx, MC, Visa,
C-ltd/S-no/P-no/H-no

Full breakfast
Afternoon tea, snacks
Sitting room, hot tubs
cable TV, stereo, tapes
room refrig., coff. mak.

*1890 Victorian. Some suites w/antiques, private porch, bath, 2-person whirlpool. Full breakfast & evening dessert. Close to everything.* **Discount rates Sunday–Thursday.**

# More Inns . . .

| | |
|---|---|
| Aberdeen | Inn at the Bryant House, 214 N. Poplar St., 28315,  919-944-3300 |
| Andrews | Walker Inn, 39 Junaluska Rd., 28901,  704-321-5019 |
| Asheboro | Doctor's Inn, 716 S. Park St., 27203,  919-625-4916 |
| Asheville | Aberdeen Inn B&B, 64 Linden Ave., 28801,  704-254-9336 |
| Asheville | Beaufort House, 61 N. Liberty St., 28801,  704-254-8334 |
| Asheville | Black Walnut B&B Inn, The,  288 Montford Ave., 28801,  704-254-3878 |
| Asheville | Blake House Inn & Rest., 150 Royal Pines Dr., 28704,  704-684-1847 |
| Asheville | Cairn Brae, 217 Patton Mountain Rd., 28804,  704-252-9219 |
| Asheville | Carolina B&B, 177 Cumberland Ave., 28801,  704-254-3608 |
| Asheville | Flint Street Inns, 100 & 116 Flint St., 28801,  704-253-6723 |

| | |
|---|---|
| Asheville | Inn on Montford, The, 296 Montford Ave., 28801, 704-254-9569 |
| Asheville | Ray House B&B, The, 83 Hillside St., 28801, 704-252-0106 |
| Asheville | Richmond Hill Inn, 87 Richmond Hill Dr., 28806, 704-252-7313 |
| Bakersville | Bakersville B&B, Route 4, Box 427, 28705, 704-688-3451 |
| Balsam | Balsam Lodge B&B, P.O. Box 279, 28707, 704-456-6528 |
| Banner Elk | Banner Elk Inn B&B, The, P.O. Box 1953, 28604, 704-898-6223 |
| Bat Cave | Old Mill Inn & Antiques, P.O. Box 252, 28710, 704-625-4256 |
| Bat Cave | Orig. Hickory Nut Gap Inn, P.O. Box 246, 28710, 704-625-9108 |
| Bath | Bath Guest House, So. Main St., 27808, 919-923-6811 |
| Beaufort | Beaufort Inn, 101 Ann St., 28516, 919-728-2600 |
| Beaufort | Captains' Quarters, 315 Ann St., 28516, 919-728-7711 |
| Beaufort | Inlet Inn, 601 Front at Queen Sts., 28516, 919-728-3600 |
| Beech Mountain | Beech Mountain Inns, Two Beech Mt. Parkway, 28604, 704-387-2252 |
| Black Mountain | B&B Over Yonder, 433 N. Fork Rd., 28711, 704-669-6762 |
| Black Mountain | Blackberry Inn, P.O. Box 965, 28711, 704-669-8303 |
| Blowing Rock | Farm House, P.O. Box 126, 28605 |
| Blowing Rock | Hound Ears Lodge and Club, P.O. Box 188, 28605, 704-963-4321 |
| Blowing Rock | Meadowbrook Inn, P.O. Box 2005, 28605, 704-295-4300 |
| Blowing Rock | Sunshine Inn, P.O. Box 528, Sunset Dr, 28605, 704-295-3487 |
| Bryson City | Hemlock Inn, 28713, 704-488-2885 |
| Bryson City | Randolph House Country Inn, P.O. Box 816, 28713, 704-488-3472 |
| Bryson City | West Oak Bed & Breakfast, Fryemont Rd., 28713, 704-488-2438 |
| Burnsville | Hamrick Inn B&B, 7787 Hwy 80 South, 28714, 704-675-5251 |
| Buxton | Cape Hatteras B&B, P.O. Box 490, 27920, 919-995-4511 |
| Cashiers | High Hampton Inn, P.O. Box 338, Hwy. 107S, 28717, 704-743-2411 |
| Cashiers | Laurelwood Mountain Inn, P.O. Box 188, 28717, 704-743-9939 |
| Chapel Hill | Hillcrest House, 209 Hillcrest Rd., 27514, 919-942-2369 |
| Chapel Hill | Windy Oaks, Route 7, Box 587, 27514, 919-942-1001 |
| Charlotte | Elizabeth, The, 2145 East 5th St., 28204, 704-358-1368 |
| Charlotte | Homeplace B&B, The, 5901 Sardis Rd., 28270, 704-365-1936 |
| Charlotte | Inn Uptown, The, 129 N. Poplar St., 28202, 704-342-2800 |
| Charlotte | McElhinny House, 10533 Fairway Ridge Rd., 28277, 704-846-0783 |
| Charlotte | Morehead Inn, The, 1122 E. Morehead St., 28204, 704-376-3357 |
| Charlotte | Overcarsh House, 326 West Eighth St., 28202, 704-334-8477 |
| Chimney Rock | Dogwood Inn, P.O. Box 70, Hwy 64 &74, 28720, 704-625-4403 |
| Chimney Rock | Esmeralda Inn, Box 57, 28720, 704-625-9105 |
| Chimney Rock | Gingerbread Inn, P.O. Box 187, Hwy 74, 28720, 704-625-4038 |
| Clemmons | Tanglewood Manor House B&B, P.O. Box 1040, 27012, 919-766-0591 |
| Cullowhee | Cullowhee B&B, 150 Ledbetter Rd., 28723, 704-293-5447 |
| Dillsboro | Jarrett House, The, P.O. Box 219, 28725, 704-586-0265 |
| Dillsboro | Squire Watkins Inn, P.O. Box 430, 28725, 704-586-5244 |
| Durham | Old North Durham Inn, 922 North Mangum St., 27701, 919-683-1885 |
| Edenton | Captain's Quarters Inn, 202 W. Queen St., 27932, 919-482-8945 |
| Edenton | Governor Eden Inn, 304 N. Broad St., 27932, 919-482-2072 |
| Edenton | Granville Queen Inn, 108 S. Granville St., 27932, 919-482-5296 |
| Edenton | Jason House Inn, Granville St., 27932, 919-482-3400 |
| Elizabeth | Culpepper Inn, 609 W. Main St., 27090, 919-335-1993 |
| Elizabeth City | Elizabeth City B&B, 108 E. Fearing St., 27909, 919-338-2177 |
| Elizabeth City | River City B&B, 1004 W. Williams Circle, 27909, 919-338-3337 |
| Fayetteville | Pines Guest Lodge, 1003 Arberdale Dr., 28304, 919-864-7333 |
| Franklin | Country Time B&B, 510 Potts Branch Dr., 28734, 704-369-3648 |
| Franklin | Heritage Inn, 101 Heritage Hollow, 28734, 704-524-4150 |
| Franklin | Lullwater Farmhouse Inn, Route 5, Box 540, 28734, 704-524-6532 |
| Franklin | Olde Mill House, 44 McClure Mill Rd., 28734, 704-524-5226 |
| Franklin | Poor Richard Summitt Inn, E. Rogers St., 28734, 704-524-2006 |
| Germanton | MeadowHaven B&B, P.O. Box 222, 27019, 910-593-3996 |
| Glendale Springs | Mountain View Lodge, P.O. Box 90, 28629, 919-982-2233 |
| Greensboro | Biltmore Greensboro Hotel, 111 W. Washington St., 27401, 910-272-3474 |
| Greensboro | College Hill B&B, 922 Carr St., 27407, 919-274-6829 |
| Greensboro | Greenwich Inn, 111 W. Washington St., 27401, 919-272-3474 |
| Greensboro | Plaza Manor, 511 Martin St., 27406, 919-274-3074 |
| Hartford | 1812 on the Perquimans, Box 10, Route 3, 27983, 919-426-1812 |
| Hazelwood | Belle Meade Inn, P.O. Box 1319, 28738, 704-456-3234 |
| Henderson | La Grange Plantation Inn, Route 3, Box 610, 27536, 919-438-2421 |
| Hendersonville | Echo Mountain Inn, 2849 Laurel Park Hwy., 28739, 704-693-9626 |
| Hendersonville | Havenshire Inn, Route 13, Box 366, 28739, 704-692-4097 |
| Hendersonville | Reverie, 1197 Greenville Hwy, 28739, 704-693-8255 |
| Hickory | Hickory B&B, The, 464 7th St., 28602, 704-324-0548 |
| Hiddenite | Hidden Crystal Inn, School Rd., 28636, 704-632-0063 |
| High Point | Premier B&B, The, 1001 Johnson St., 27262, 919-889-8349 |
| Highlands | Chandler Inn, P.O. Box 2156, 28741, 704-526-5992 |
| Highlands | Guest House, The, Rt 2, Box 65914, 28741, 704-526-4536 |
| Highlands | Highlands Inn, The, P.O. Box 1030, 28741, 704-526-9380 |
| Highlands | Old Edwards Inn, The, P.O. Box 1030, 28741, 704-526-5036 |
| Highlands | Phelp's House, Route 1, Box 55, 28741, 704-526-2590 |
| Hillsborough | Colonial Inn, 153 W. King St., 27278, 919-732-2461 |
| Hillsborough | Inn At Teardrop, 175 W. King St., 27278, 919-732-1120 |
| Lake Junaluska | Brookside Lodge, P.O. Box 925, 28745, 704-456-8897 |
| Lake Junaluska | Providence Lodge, 207 Atkins Loop, 28745, 704-456-6486 |

| | |
|---|---|
| Lake Junaluska | Sunset Inn, 300 N. Lakeshore Dr., 28745,   704-456-6114 |
| Lake Lure | Fairfield Mountains,  Route 1, Buffalo Rd., 28746,   704-625-9111 |
| Lake Lure | Lake Lure Inn,  P.O. Box 6, Hwy 74, 28746,   704-625-2525 |
| Lake Waccamaw | B&B By the Lake,  P.O. Box 218, 28450,  919-646-4744 |
| Laurel Springs | Burgiss Farm B&B,  Rte. 1, Box 300, 28644,  919-359-2995 |
| Lenoir | Summer Hill,  1248 Harrisburg Dr. SW, 28645,   800-757-0204 |
| Lexington | Lawrences,  Route 1, Box 641, 27292,   704-249-1114 |
| Lillington | Waverly's of Lillington,  P.O. Box 25, 27546,   919-893-6760 |
| Little Switzerland | Alpine Inn,  Hwy 226-A, 28749,  704-765-5380 |
| Louisburg | Hearthside Inn, The,  305 N. Main St., 27549,   919-496-6776 |
| Maggie Valley | Cataloochee Ranch,  Rt. 1, Box 500, 28751 |
| Maggie Valley | Smokey Shadows Lodge,  P.O. Box 444, 28751 |
| Maggie Valley | Snuggle Inn,  US Hwy 19, P.O. Box 416, 28751,   704-926-3782 |
| Manteo | Scarborough Inn,  Hwy 64/264, Box 1310, 27954,   919-473-3979 |
| Manteo | Tranquil House Inn,  P.O. Box 2045, 27954,   919-473-1404 |
| Mars Hill | Baird House, Ltd. B&B Inn,  P.O. Box 749, 28754,   704-689-5722 |
| Marshall | Marshall House,  S. Hill St P.O. Box 865, 28753 |
| Montreat | Glen Rock Inn,  421 Kentucky Rd., 28756 |
| Morehead City | Dill House,  1104 Arendell St., 28557,  919-726-4449 |
| Morehead City | Morehead Manor B&B,  107 N. 10th St., 27410,  919-726-9233 |
| Mount Airy | Merritt House B&B,  618 N. Main St., 27030,  800-290-6090 |
| Mount Airy | William E Merritt House,  618 N. Main, 27030 |
| Murphy | Hilltop House B&B,  104 Campbell St., 28906,   704-837-8661 |
| Murphy | Hoover House,  306 Natural Springs Dr., 28906,   704-837-8734 |
| Nashville | Griffin-Pace House,  Rt. 4, Box 300, Hwy 58N, 27856,  919-459-4746 |
| New Bern | Aerie Inn, The,  509 Pollock St., 28560,  919-636-5553 |
| New Bern | Lighthouse, An Irish Inn,  315 George St., 28562,  919-633-9488 |
| New Bern | New Berne House B&B Inn,  709 Broad St., 28560,  919-636-2250 |
| Ocracoke | Boyette House,  Box 39, 27960,  919-928-4261 |
| Ocracoke | Ships Timbers B&B,  Box 10, 27960,  919-928-6141 |
| Ocracoke Island | Island Inn,  Box 7, 27960,  919-928-4351 |
| Ocracoke Island | Oscar's House,  Box 206, 27960,  919-928-1311 |
| Penland | Chinquapin Inn,  P.O. Box 145, 28765,  704-765-0064 |
| Pilot Mountain | Pilot Knob,  P.O. Box 1280, 27041,  919-325-2502 |
| Pinebluff | Pine Cone Manor B&B,  P.O. Box 1208, 28373,  910-281-5307 |
| Pinehurst | Holly Inn,  Box 23, Cherokee Rd., 28374 |
| Pinehurst | Magnolia Inn,  Box 266, 28374,  919-295-6900 |
| Plymouth | Four Gables,  P.O. Box 538, 27962,  919-793-6696 |
| Ridgecrest | Old House B&B,  Old US 70, P.O. Box 384, 28770,   704-669-5196 |
| Robbinsville | Blue Boar Lodge,  200 Santeetlah Rd., 28771,  704-479-8126 |
| Rocky Mount | Sunset Inn,  1210 Sunset Ave., 27804,  919-446-9524 |
| Rosman | Red Lion Inn,  Star Route, Box 200, 28772,  704-884-6868 |
| Rutherfordton | Pinebrae Manor,  RR 5, Box 479-A, 28139,  704-286-1543 |
| Saluda | Bear Creek Lodge,  Route 1, Box 335, 28773,  704-749-2272 |
| Sapphire | Fairfield Sapphire Valley,  4000 Hwy. 64, W., 28774 |
| Shelby | Inn at Webbley,  P.O. Box 1000, 28150,  704-481-1403 |
| Southport | Dosher Plantation House,  Route 5, Box 100, 28461,  919-457-5554 |
| Southport | Indian Oak Inn, The,  120 W. Moore St., 28461,  910-457-0209 |
| Southport | River's End B&B,  120 W. Moore St., 28461,  919-457-9939 |
| Sparta | Bella Columns,  Route 2, Box 228-B, 28675 |
| Sparta | Turby-Villa,  East Whitehead St., 28675,  919-372-8490 |
| Spruce Pine | Pinebridge Inn,  101 Pinebridge Ave., 28777,  704-765-5543 |
| Statesville | Aunt May's B&B,  532 E. Broad St., 28677,  704-873-9525 |
| Statesville | Cedar Hill Farm B&B,  778 Elmwood Rd., 28677,  704-873-4332 |
| Statesville | Madelyn's B&B,  514 Carroll St., 28677,  704-872-3973 |
| Sugar Grove | Bedside Manor,  Route 1, Box 90A, 28679,  704-297-1120 |
| Swansboro | Mt. Pleasant B&B,  310 Journey's End, 28584,  919-326-7076 |
| Swansboro | Scotts Keep B&B,  308 Walnut St., 28584,  919-326-1257 |
| Tabor City | Kate's Four Rooster Inn,  205 Pireway Rd., 28463,  910-653-3878 |
| Tabor City | Todd House,  6 Live Oak St., 28463,  919-653-3778 |
| Tarboro | Main Street Inn, The,  912 Main St., 27886,  919-823-2560 |
| Taylorsville | Phyllis Bardley,  Route 6, Box 12, 28681 |
| Valle Crucis | Bluestone Lodge,  P.O. Box 736, 28691,  704-963-5177 |
| Valle Crucis | Inn at the Taylor House,  Hwy 194, Box 713, 28691,  704-963-5581 |
| Valle Crucis | Mast Farm Inn,  P.O. Box 704, 28691,  704-963-5857 |
| Wanchese | C.W. Pugh's B&B,  P.O. Box 427, 27981,  919-473-5466 |
| Warrenton | Traub's Inn,  116 W. Macon St., 27589,  919-257-2727 |
| Washington | Pamlico House B&B,  400 E. Main St., 27889,  919-946-7184 |
| Waynesville | Belle Meade Inn,  P.O. Box 1319, 28786,  704-456-3234 |
| Waynesville | Palmer House B&B,  108 Pigeon St., 28786,  704-456-7521 |
| Waynesville | Swag Country Inn, The,  Route 2, Box 280-A, 28786,  704-926-0430 |
| Waynesville | Way Inn,  299 S. Main St., 28786,  704-456-3788 |
| Weaverville | Weaverville Feather B&B,  3 Le Perrion Ln., 28787,  704-645-7594 |
| Weldon | Weldon Place Inn,  500 Washington Ave., 27890,  919-536-4582 |
| Wilmington | Graystone Guesthouse,  100 S. Third St., 28401,  919-762-0358 |
| Wilmington | Market Street B&B,  1704 Market St., 28403,  919-763-5442 |
| Wilmington | Murchison House B&B Inn,  305 S. 3rd St., 28401,  919-343-8580 |
| Wilmington | Stemmerman's 1855 Inn,  138 S. Front St., 28401 |

| Winston, Salem | Brookstown Inn B&B, 200 Brookstown Ave., 27101, 919-725-1120 |
| Winston, Salem | Henry F. Shaffner House, 150 S. Marshall St., 27101, 919-777-0052 |
| Winston, Salem | Mickle House B&B, 927 W. Fifth St., 27101, 919-722-9045 |
| Winston, Salem | Wachovia B&B, Inc., 513 Wachovia, 27101, 919-777-0332 |

*The Barracks Inn, Tarboro, NC*

# North Dakota

## JAMESTOWN

**Country Charm B&B**
7717 35th St. S.E.,   58401
701-251-1372
Tom & Ethel Oxtoby
All year

$$-B&B
3 rooms, 2 pb
*Rated*,
C-ltd/S-no

Full breakfast
Lunch, dinner (fee)

*"Country charm at its best."* 1897 farm home on 12 groomed acres lined with tall pines and cottonwood trees.

## More Inns . . .

| Bismark | White Lace, 807 N. 6th St., 58501,  701-258-4142 |
| Bowman | Logging Camp Ranch B&B, P.O. Box 27, 58623,  701-279-5702 |
| Carrington | Kirkland B&B 1886,  RR 2, Box 18, 58421,  701-652-2775 |
| Devils Lake | Dakotah Friend B&B, P.O. Box 280A, 58301,  701-662-6327 |
| Fargo | Bohlig's B&B, 1418 3rd Ave. S., 58103,  701-235-7867 |
| Fessenden | Beiseker Mansion, The,  P.O. Box 187, 58438,  701-547-3411 |
| Grand Forks | 511 Reeves, 511 Reeves Dr., 58201,  701-772-9663 |
| Grand Forks | Lord Byron's B&B, 521 S. 5th St., 58201,  701-775-0194 |
| Grand Forks | Upstairs Inn, The, 1120 University Ave., 58203,  701-772-3853 |
| Kemare | Farm Comfort, 58746,  701-848-2433 |
| Leonard | Lady Bird B&B Inn, P.O. Box 177, 58052,  701-645-2509 |
| Lidgerwood | Kaler's B&B, 9650 Highway 18, 58053,  701-538-4848 |
| Luverne | Grandma's House Farm B&B, P.O. Box 12, 58056,  701-845-4994 |
| Luverne | Volden Farm B&B, RR 2, Box 50, 58056,  701-769-2275 |
| McClusky | Midstate B&B, P.O. Box 28, 58463,  701-363-2520 |
| Minnewaukan | Minnewaukan B&B Inn, 230 2nd St. E., 58351,  701-473-5731 |
| Minot | Broadway Inn B&B, 433 N. Broadway, 58701,  701-838-6075 |
| Minot | D-Over-L B&B, P.O. Box 187, 58701,  701-722-3326 |
| Minot | Dakotah Rose B&B, 510 4th Ave. NW, 58701,  701-838-3548 |
| Minot | Lois & Stan's B&B, 1007 11th Ave. NW, 58701,  701-838-2244 |
| New Salem | Prairie View B&B, Route 2, 58563,  701-843-7236 |
| Northwood | Twin Pine B&B, P.O. Box 30, 58267,  701-587-6075 |
| Reeder | Rocking Chair B&B Inn, P.O. Box 236, 58649,  701-853-2204 |
| Regent | Prairie Vista, 101 Rural Ave., SW, 58650,  701-563-4542 |
| Scranton | Jacobson Mansion, Route 2, Box 27, 58653,  701-275-8291 |
| Stanley | Triple T Ranch, Route 1, Box 93, 58784,  701-628-2418 |
| Tower City | Tower City Inn B&B, 502 Church St., 58071,  701-749-2660 |
| Velva | Hagenhus B&B Inn, 406 W. 2nd St., 58790,  701-338-2714 |
| Wahpeton | Adama Fairview Bonanza B&B, 17170 82nd St. SE, 58075,  701-274-8262 |
| Wing | Eva's B&B, HCR's Box 10, 58494,  701-943-2461 |

# Ohio

## CLEVELAND

**Baricelli Inn**
2203 Cornell Rd., 44106
216-791-6500 Fax: 216-791-9131
Paul A. Minnillo
All year

$$$-B&B
7 rooms, 7 pb
Most CC, *Rated*,
C-ltd/S-ltd/P-no/H-yes
Spanish

Continental plus bkfst.
Restaurant, bar service
Dinner (fee)

*Turn-of-the-century brownstone mansion - European flair. One of the top rated restaurants in town.*

## DANVILLE

**White Oak Inn, The**
29683 Walhonding Rd.,
43014
614-599-6107
Ian & Yvonne Martin
All year

$$-B&B
10 rooms, 10 pb
Most CC, *Rated*, •
C-ltd/S-no/P-no/H-no

Full breakfast
Dinner with notice
Afternoon snacks
common room, porch
screen house, lawn games

*Large country home nestled in wooded area. Outdoor enthusiasts' paradise. Comfortable antique decor; 3 frplc. rooms. Near Amish country/antiques.* **2 nite pkg. w/dinner one nite.**

## DAYTON

**Prices' Steamboat House**
6 Josie St., 45403
513-223-2444
Ruth & Ron Price
All year

$$-B&B
3 rooms, 3 pb
•
C-ltd/S-no/P-no/H-no

Continental plus bkfst.
Comp. beverages
Sitting room
library
tennis courts

*On the National Register, this 1852 Victorian mansion—Steamboat Gothic—is furnished with exquisite antiques and overlooks downtown Dayton.*

## DELLROY

**Whispering Pines B&B**
P.O. Box 340, 44620
1268 Magnolia - SR 542
330-735-2824
Bill & Linda Horn
All year

$$$-B&B
5 rooms, 5 pb
Visa, MC, *Rated*, •
C-ltd/S-no/P-no/H-no

Full breakfast
Dinner, afternoon tea
Sitt. rm., swimming
hot tubs, boat rental
tennis courts, fishing

*Guestrooms feature spectacluar lakeviews of Atwood Lake, woodburning fireplaces, jacuzzi, balconies, fine Victorian antiques, A/C, golf, boating, & private 5-course dinners.*

## DOVER

**Olde World B&B**
2982 State Route 516 NW,
44622
216-343-1333 800-447-1273
Jonna Sigrist
All year

$$-B&B
5 rooms, 5 pb
Visa, MC, Disc, *Rated*,
C-ltd/S-no/P-no/H-no

Full breakfast
Lunch, comp. wine
Hot tubs
sitting room
outdoor veranda w/grill

*Stately 1881 Victorian home; suites include Victorian, Oriental, Parisian, Mediterranean & Alpine. Surrounded by historic sites & old fashioned cultures.* **3rd night 50% off.**

EAST FULTONHAM —————————————————————

| **Hill View Acres B&B** | $-B&B | Full breakfast |
| 7320 Old Town Rd., 43735 | 2 rooms, 1 pb | Snacks, picnic lunch |
| 614-849-2728 | Visa, MC, Amex, • | Sitting room |
| Jim & Dawn Graham | C-yes/P-no/H-yes | hot tubs, large deck |
| All year | | pond, swimming pool |

*Spacious country getaway with old world hospitality. Homemade breads, jams, jellies and country cooking. Area popular for antiques, pottery and outdoor activities.*

LOGAN —————————————————————————

| **Inn at Cedar Falls, The** | B&B | Full breakfast |
| 21190 St. Rt. 374, 43138 | 14 rooms, 14 pb | Lunch, dinner (fee) |
| 614-385-7489 800-653-2557 | Visa, MC, *Rated*, • | Restaurant, bar service |
| Ellen Grinsfelder | | sitting room, library |
| Closed Christmas | | Call for winter rates |

*1840s log cabin houses-open kitchen, dining room. Gourmet meals prepared from inn's organic garden. Antiqued furnished rooms & log cabins surrounded by Hocking State Parks.*

LOUISVILLE ————————————————————————

| **Mainstay B&B** | $-B&B | Full breakfast |
| 1320 E. Main St., 44641 | 3 rooms, 3 pb | Snacks |
| 330-875-1021 | Visa, MC, • | Sitting room, hot tubs |
| Mary & Joe Shurilla | C-yes/S-no/P-no/H-no | 2nd room discount for |
| All year | | child occupancy |

*Century old Victorian filled with antiques. Comp. fruit, cheese, sparkling beverage. Within 15 minutes of Professional Nat'l Football Hall of Fame. Near Amish Country.* **10% off 3+ nights.**

MARBLEHEAD —————————————————————

| **Old Stone House on Lake** | $$$-B&B | Full breakfast |
| 133 Cemons St., 43440 | 13 rooms, 2 pb | Sitting room |
| 419-798-5922 | Visa, MC, Disc., • | swimming in lake |
| Dan & Brenda Anderson | C-yes/S-no/P-no/H-no | family friendly facility |
| All year | | |

*Stately stone mansion located on the Lake Erie shore. On the Historic Register. Tastefully decorated in antiques.* **3rd night, 50%.**

PAINESVILLE —————————————————————

| **Rider's 1812 Inn** | $$-B&B | Full breakfast |
| 792 Mentor Ave., 44077 | 12 rooms, 7 pb | Lunch, dinner (fee) |
| 216-354-8200 800-TENT-NET | AmEx, MC, Visa | Restaurant, bar service |
| Elaine, Courtney, Dick & | *Rated*, • | sitting room, library |
| Gary | C-ltd/S-no/P-ltd/H-no | ask about tour surprise |
| Closed Christmas Day | Spanish | |

*Built as a stagecoach inn in 1812-we offer a tasled history today. Furnished w/antiques, we specialize in one night retreats & getaways, tailored trips to our Amish communities.* **3rd night 50%.**

POLAND ——————————————————————————

| **Inn At The Green** | $$-B&B | Continental breakfast |
| 500 S. Main St., Youngstown, | 5 rooms, 4 pb | Complimentary wine |
| 44514 | MC, Visa, *Rated*, • | Oriental rugs, deck |
| 216-757-4688 | C-ltd/S-no/P-no/H-no | patio, antiques, garden |
| Ginny & Steve Meloy | | Sitting rm., fireplaces |
| All year | | |

*Authentically restored Victorian townhouse in preserved Western Reserve village near Youngstown. Convenient to Turnpike and I-80. Poland is 7 mi. S.E. of Youngstown*

## PUT-IN-BAY

**Fether B&B**
1539 Langram Rd.,   43456
419-285-5511
Eleanor D. Fether
April–October

$$$-B&B
4 rooms, 3.5 pb
MC, Visa,
C-ltd/S-no/P-no/H-no

Full breakfast
All rooms have air
conditioning
weddings, receptions

*Relax while viewing everchanging Lake Erie waters from either a rocking chair or a wrap-around porch swing in the country quiet of South Bass Island.* **Special occasion free wine.**

## SANDUSKY

**Wagner's 1844 Inn**
230 E. Washington St.,   44870
419-626-1726  Fax: 419-626-8465
Walt & Barb Wagner
All year

$$-B&B
3 rooms, 3 pb
MC, Visa, *Rated*,  •
S-ltd/P-no/H-no

Continental plus bkfst.
Comp. wine, chocolates
Billard room with TV
air-conditioning

*Elegantly restored Victorian home. Listed on National Register of Historic Places. Near Lake Erie attractions. Air-conditioned rooms.* **10% discount 5 days or more.**

## WEST UNION

**Murphin Ridge Inn**
750 Murphin Ridge Rd.,
   45693
513-544-2263
Mary & Robert Crosset
Mid February thru Dec.31

$$$-AP
10 rooms, 10 pb
*Rated*,
C-yes/S-no/P-no/H-yes
Ltd. Spanish, Russian

Full breakfast
Lunch, dinner,restaurant
Sitting room, library
tennis court, pool
basketball, horseshoes

*Relax in the comfort of a 1990 Guest House. Enjoy exquisite dining in the 1810 Farm House. Experience unique trails on 717 acres of wooded lands.*

## ZOAR

**Assembly House, The**
P.O. Box 611,   44697
117 E. 3rd St.
330-874-2239  Fax: 330-874-2715
Tim B. Whitemyer
All year

$$-B&B
3 rooms, 1 pb
Visa, MC, AmEx,
C-ltd/S-no/P-no/H-no

Continental plus bkfst.
Sitting room

*Located in the heart of historic Zoar village, close to Cleveland, Columbus and Pittsburgh. Spacious rooms, elegantly appointed with antiques.* **3rd night 50%.**

---

**Cobbler Shop B&B Inn**
P.O. Box 650,   44697
121 East 2nd St.
330-874-2600  800-287-1547
Marian "Sandy" Worley
All year

$$-B&B
5 rooms, 2 pb
AmEx, MC, Visa,  •
C-ltd/S-ltd/P-no/H-no

Full breakfast
Comp. wine, snacks, tea
Sitting room
canopied 4-poster bed
screened porch, garden

*Original structure in historic village; 18th/19th century antiques; close to museum and charming shops. Have breakfast on porch overlooking priv. gardens.* **25% off 3rd night.**

---

**Inn at Cowger House #9**
Box 527,   44697
197 4th St.
330-874-3542  800-874-3542
Ed & Mary Cowger
All year

$$-B&B
10 rooms, 10 pb
*Rated*,  •
C-ltd/S-yes/P-no/H-no

Full country breakfast
Lunch & dinner by RSVP
Entertainment
honeymoon suite with
fireplace & jacuzzi

*A little bit of Williamsburg. 1817 log cabin with 2-acre flower garden maintained by the Ohio Historic Society. 1865 re-enactment dinners.*

# More Inns . . .

| | |
|---|---|
| Akron | Helen's Hospitality House, 1096 Palmetto, 44306,  216-724-7151 |
| Akron | Portage House, 601 Copley Rd, ST 162, 44320,  216-535-1952 |
| Archbold | Sauder Village, P.O. Box 235, 43502 |
| Avon Lake | Williams House, 249 Vinewood, 44012,  216-933-5089 |
| Baltimore | Canal View B&B,  710 Canal Rd., 43105 |
| Bellville | Frederick Fitting House,  72 Fitting Ave., 44813,  419-886-2863 |
| Blue Rock | McNutt Farm II/Outdoorsman,  6120 Cutler Lake Rd., 43720,  614-674-4555 |
| Bryan | Elegant Inn B&B, The,  215 Walnut St., 43506,  419-636-2873 |
| Bucyrus | Hide Away B&B,  1601 St. Rt. 4, 44820,  419-562-3013 |
| Centerville | Yesterday B&B,  39 S. Main St., 45458,  513-433-0785 |
| Charm | Charm Countryview Inn, The,  P.O. Box 100, 44617,  216-893-3003 |
| Chillicothe | Chillicothe B&B,  202 S. Paint St., 45601,  614-772-6848 |
| Chillicothe | Old McDill-Anderson Place,  3656 Polk Hollow Rd., 45601,  614-774-1770 |
| Cincinnati | Parker House B&B, The,  2323 Ohio Ave., 45219,  513-579-8236 |
| Cincinnati | Prospect Hill B&B,  408 Boal St., 45210,  513-421-4408 |
| Cleveland | Glidden House,  1901 Ford Dr., 44106,  216-231-8900 |
| Cleveland | Tudor House,  P.O. Box 18590, 44118,  216-321-3213 |
| Columbus | 50 Lincoln,  50 E. Lincoln St., 43215,  614-291-5056 |
| Columbus | Harrison House,  313 W 5th Ave., 43201,  614-421-2202 |
| Columbus | Victorian B&B,  78 Smith Place, 43201,  614-299-1656 |
| Coshocton | Roscoe Village Inn,  200 N. Whiteman St., 43812 |
| Cuyahoga Falls | Studio 12 B&B,  2850 Bailey Rd., 44221 |
| Dayton | Candlewick B&B,  4991 Bath Rd., 45424,  513-233-9297 |
| Dayton | Prices' Steamboat House,  6 Josie St., 45403,  513-223-2444 |
| Deersville | Mulberry Lane,  224 W Main, P.O. Box 61, 44693,  614-922-0425 |
| Delaware | Camelot at Heater's Run,  676 Taggart Rd., 43015 |
| Dellroy | Candleglow B&B,  4247 Roswell Rd., S.W., 44620,  216-735-2407 |
| Dellroy | Dripping Rock Farm,  4247 Roswell Rd. SW, 44620,  216-735-2987 |
| Dellroy | Pleasant Journey Inn,  4247 Roswell Rd. SW, 44620,  216-735-2987 |
| Dover | Mowrey's Welcome Home,  4489 Dover-Zoar Rd. NE, 44622,  216-343-4690 |
| Fredericktown | Heartland Country Resort,  2994 Township Rd. 190, 43019,  809-230-7030 |
| Gahanna | Shamrock B&B,  5657 Sunbury Rd., 43230,  614-337-9849 |
| Geneva | Otto Court B&B,  5653 Lake Rd., 44041,  216-466-8668 |
| Granville | Buxton Inn,  313 E. Broadway, 43023 |
| Greenfield | Mertz Place, The,  240 Mirabeau St., 45123,  513-981-2613 |
| Grove City | Maxwell House, The,  590 Hibbs Rd., 43137,  614-871-9030 |
| Hillsboro | Victoria House, The,  245 E. Main St., 45133,  513-393-2743 |
| Huron | Beach House,  213 Kiwanis Ave., 44839,  419-433-5839 |
| Huron | Captain Montague's B&B,  229 Center St., 44839,  419-433-4756 |
| Jackson | Maples, The,  14701 State Route 93, 45640,  614-286-6067 |
| Kelley's Island | Beatty House,  S. Shore Dr., 43438,  419-746-2379 |
| Kelley's Island | Cricket Lodge B&B,  Lakeshore Dr., 43438,  419-746-2263 |
| Kinsman | Hidden Hollow B&B,  9340 State Route 5 NE, 44428,  216-876-8686 |
| Lakeside | Poor Richards Inn,  317 Maple, 43440 |
| Lakeville | Quiet Country B&B,  14758 TWP Rd. 453, 44638,  216-378-3882 |
| Lakewood | Idlewyld B&B,  13458 Parkway, 44107,  419-798-4198 |
| Lakewood | Summer House, The,  16934 Edgewater Dr., 44107,  216-226-6934 |
| Lancaster | Shaw's Restaurant & Inn,  123 N. Broad St., 43130,  800-654-2477 |
| Laurelville | Hocking House B&B,  18597 Laurel St., 43135,  614-332-1655 |
| Lebanon | Golden Lamb,  27 S. Broadway, 45036 |
| Lebanon | Hexagon House,  419 Cincinnati Ave., 45036,  513-932-9655 |
| Lebanon | White Tor,  1620 Oregonia Rd., 45036,  513-932-5892 |
| Lexington | White Fence Inn,  8842 Denmanu Rd., 44904,  419-884-2356 |
| Logan | Log Cabin,  7657 TWP Rd. 234, 43138,  614-385-8363 |
| Loudonville | Blackfork Inn,  303 N. Water St., 44842,  419-994-3252 |
| Marblehead | Clemons Manor,  133 Clemons St., 43440,  419-798-5922 |
| Marietta | Clair E,  127 Ohio St., 45750,  614-374-2233 |
| Martins Ferry | Mulberry Inn,  53 N. Fourth St., 43935,  614-633-6058 |
| McConnellsville | Outback Inn, The,  171 E. Union Ave., 43756,  614-962-2158 |
| Medina | Livery Building, The,  254 E. Smith Rd., 44256,  216-722-1332 |
| Miamisburg | English Manon,  505 E. Linden Ave., 45342,  513-866-2288 |
| Milan | Coach House Inn B&B, The,  304 St. Rt. 113 W., 44846,  419-499-2435 |
| Milan | Gastier Farm B&B,  1902 Strecker Rd., 44846,  419-499-2985 |
| Millersburg | Inn at Honey Run, The,  6920 Country Rd. #203, 44654,  216-674-0011 |
| Mount Vernon | Oak Hill B&B,  16720 Park Rd., 43050,  614-393-2912 |
| Mount Vernon | Russell-Cooper House, The,  115 E. Gambier St., 43050,  614-397-8638 |
| New Concord | Bogart's B&B,  1030 Friendship Dr., 43762,  614-826-7439 |
| Newark | Pitzer-Cooper House,  6019 White Chapel Rd., 43056,  614-323-2680 |
| North Ridgeville | St. George House,  33941 Lorain Rd., 44039,  216-327-9354 |
| Old Washington | Zane Trace B&B,  P.O. Box 115, 43768,  614-489-5970 |
| Peebles | Bayberry Inn B&B,  25675 St., Route 41 N., 45660,  513-587-2221 |
| Peninsula | Centennial House,  5995 Center St., Box 67, 44264,  216-657-2506 |
| Peninsula | Peninsula B&B,  5964 Center St., 44264 |
| Pettisville | Tudor Country Inn,  Box 113, 43553,  419-445-2531 |
| Port Clinton | Island House Hotel,  102 Madison St., 43452,  419-734-2166 |
| Powell | Buckeye B&B,  P.O. Box 130, 43065,  614-548-4555 |

| | |
|---|---|
| Put-In-Bay | Arlington House, The, P.O. Box 395, 43456 |
| Put-In-Bay | Vineyard, The, P.O. Box 283, 43456 |
| Ripley | Baird House, The, 201 N. 2nd. St., 45167, 513-392-4918 |
| Sagamore | Inn at Brandywine Falls, 8230 Brandywine Rd., 44067, 216-467-1812 |
| Sandusky | Big Oak, 2501 S. Campbell St., 44870 |
| Sandusky | Bogart's Corner B&B, 1403 E. Bogart Rd., 44870, 419-627-2707 |
| Sandusky | Pipe Creek B&B, 2719 Columbus Ave., 44870, 419-626-2067 |
| Sandusky | Red Gables, The, 421 Wayne St., 44870, 419-625-1189 |
| Sandusky | Sanduskian, The, 232 Jackson St., 44870, 419-626-6688 |
| Sharon Center | Hart & Mather Guest Home, P.O. Box 93, 44274 |
| Somerset | Somer Tea B&B, 200 S Columbus, Box 308, 43783, 614-743-2909 |
| South Amherst | Birch Way Villa, 111 White Birch Way, 44001, 216-986-2090 |
| Spring Valley | 3 B's Bed-n-Breakfast, 103 E. Race St., 45370, 513-862-4278 |
| St. Clairsville | My Father's House B&B, 173 S. Marietta St., 43950, 614-695-5440 |
| Stout | 100 Mile House B&B, U.S. 52, Box 4866D, 45684, 614-858-2984 |
| Tiffin | Zelkova Inn, 2348 S. County Rd. #19, 44882, 419-447-4043 |
| Tipp City | Willowtree Inn, 1900 W. State Route 571, 45371, 513-667-2957 |
| Toledo | Mansion View Inn B&B, 2035 Collingwood Ave., 43620, 419-244-5676 |
| Troy | Allen Villa B&B, 434 S. Market St., 45373, 513-335-1181 |
| Uhrichsville | Someday Valley Health Spa, 4989 Spanson Dr. S.E., 44683, 614-922-3192 |
| Waverly | Governor's Lodge, SR 552, 45690, 614-947-2266 |
| West Milton | Locust Lane Farm B&B, 5590 Kessler Cowlesvlle, 45383, 513-698-4743 |
| Westerville | Priscilla's B&B, 5 South West St., 43081 |
| Wooster | Howey House, 340 N. Bever St., 44691, 216-264-8231 |
| Worthington | Worthington Inn, The, 649 High St., 43085, 614-885-2600 |
| Zoar | Weaving Haus, P.O. Box 431, 44697, 216-874-3318 |
| Zoar | Zoar Tavern & Inn, The, P.O. Box 509, 44697, 216-874-2170 |

# Oklahoma

## EDMOND

| **Arcadian Inn, The** | $$$-B&B | Full breakfast |
|---|---|---|
| 328 East First, 73034 | 5 rooms, 5 pb | Dinner by reservation |
| 405-348-6347 Fax: 405-348-8100 | AmEx, MC, Visa, | Sitting room |
| 800-299-6347 | *Rated*, ● | hot tubs |
| Martha & Gary Hall | C-ltd/S-no/P-no/H-no | |
| All year | | |

*Luxurious, romantic setting, sumptuous homemade breakfast. Intimate getaway for couples, perfect for the business traveler. Specializing in preferential treatment.*

## GUTHRIE

| **Harrison House Inn** | $$-B&B | Continental plus bkfst. |
|---|---|---|
| P.O. Box 977, 73044 | 35 rooms, 35 pb | The Sand Plum restaurant |
| 124 W. Harrison | AmEx, MC, Visa, | Sitting room, gift shops |
| 405-282-1000 Fax: 405-282-7091 | *Rated*, ● | TVs in parlors |
| 800-375-1001 | C-yes/S-yes/P-ltd/H-yes | games, elevators |
| Helen Machtolff | | |
| All year | | |

*35-room historic inn, nestled in the heart of a giant Historic District. Surrounded by live theater, museums, trolley rides and turn-of-the-century homes.*

## NORMAN

| **Holmberg House B&B** | $$-B&B | Full breakfast |
|---|---|---|
| 766 De Barr, 73069 | 4 rooms, 4 pb | Restaurants close by |
| 405-321-6221 Fax: 405-321-6221 | Most CC, *Rated*, ● | Near historic shopping |
| 800-646-6221 | C-ltd/S-no/P-no/H-no | sitting room & library |
| Jo Meacham | | herb & flower gardens |
| All year | | |

*Historic home across the st. from the U of O. Built in 1914, National Register. Entirely furnished with antiques. Shopping nearby. Facilities for weddings & receptions.*

*Montford Inn, Norman, OK*

## NORMAN

**Montford Inn**
322 W. Tonhawa,   73069
405-321-2200  Fax: 405-321-8347
800-321-8969
Ron, Phyllis & William
Murray
All year

$$$-B&B
10 rooms, 10 pb
Most CC, *Rated*, •
C-yes/S-no/P-no/H-yes

Full breakfast
Afternoon tea, wine
Sitting room, library
frplcs. in rms., gym
2 outdoor/priv. hot tubs

*New urban inn w/antiques & gift shop. Restaurants, shops, parks, Oklahoma University nearby. Off-street parking. 2 suite cottage with 2 person jacuzzi.*

## More Inns ...

| | |
|---|---|
| Broken Bow | Sojourners' B&B, Rt. 2, Box 998-1, 74728,  405-584-9324 |
| Checotah | Sharp House B&B, The, 301 NW Second St., 74426,  918-473-2832 |
| Claremore | Country Inn, Route 3, Box 1925, 74017,  918-342-1894 |
| Clayton | Clayton Country Inn,  Rt 1, Box 8, Hwy 271, 74536,  918-569-4165 |
| Coalgate | Memories B&B, 120 West Queen, 74538,  405-927-3590 |
| Coweta | Sandhill B&B, Route 1, 74429,  918-486-1041 |
| Davis | Cedar Green B&B, 909 S. 4th, 73030,  405-369-2396 |
| Grove | Oak Tree B&B, 1007 So. Main, 74344 |
| Guthrie | Guthrie B&B Association, 1016 W. Warner, 73044,  405-282-0012 |
| Guthrie | Stone Lion Inn B&B, 1016 W. Warner, 73044 |
| Guthrie | Victorian Rose B&B, 415 E. Cleveland, 73044,  405-282-3928 |
| Guymon | Prairie View B&B, RR 2, Box 163 A, 73942,  405-338-3760 |
| Keyes | Cattle Country Inn, HCR 1 Box 34, 73947 |
| Lawton | Quinette House, 102 NW Fort Sill Blvd., 73507,  405-355-4012 |
| Mannford | Chateau in the Woods, P.O. Box 449, 74044 |
| Muskogee | Graham-Carroll House, 501 N. 16th St., 74401,  918-683-0100 |
| Norman | Cutting Garden B&B, The, 927 W. Boyd St., 73069,  405-329-4522 |
| Oklahoma City | Country House B&B, 10101 Oakview Rd., 73112,  405-840-3157 |
| Oklahoma City | Flora's B&B, 2312 NW 46th, 73112,  405-840-3157 |
| Oklahoma City | Grandison, The, 1841 NW 15th St., 73106,  405-521-0011 |
| Oklahoma City | Newton & Joann, 23312 W.W. 46, 73112 |
| Oklahoma City | Willow Way, 27 Oakwood Dr., 73112,  405-427-2133 |
| Pawhuska | Inn at Woodyard Farms, The, Rt. 2, Box 190, 74058,  918-287-2699 |
| Ponca City | Davarnathey Inn, 1001 W. Grand, 74601,  405-765-9922 |
| Poteau | Kerr Country Mansion, The, 1507 S. McKenna, 74953,  918-647-8221 |
| Ramona | Jarrett Farm, Route 1, Box 1480, 74061 |
| Stillwater | Friend House B&B, 404 S. Knoblock, 74074,  405-372-1982 |
| Stillwater | Thomasville, 4115 N. Denver, 74075,  405-372-1203 |
| Stroud | Stroud House B&B, 110 E. Second St., 73079,  800-259-2978 |
| Sulphur | Artesian B&B, 1022 W. 12th St., 73086,  405-622-5254 |
| Tulsa | Lantern Inn, The, 1348 E. 35th St., 74105,  918-743-8343 |
| Watonga | Kennedy Kottage, 1017 N. Prouty, 73772,  405-623-4384 |
| Watonga | Redbud Manor B&B, 900 N. Burford, 73772,  405-623-8587 |
| Wilburton | Dome House, The, 315 E. Main, 74578 |
| Woodward | Anna Augusta Inn, 2612 Lakeview Dr., 73801,  405-254-5400 |

# Oregon

ASHLAND ───────────────────────────────

**Country Willows B&B Inn**
1313 Clay St.,  97520
541-488-1590  Fax:541-488-1611
800-WILLOWS-
Dan Durant
All year

$$$-B&B
9 rooms, 9 pb
MC, Visa, *Rated*, •
C-ltd/S-ltd/P-no/H-yes

Full breakfast
Sitting room, hot tubs
library, outdoor jacuzzi
heated swimming pool

*Romantic, peaceful, rural setting. 1896 farmhouse, 5 acres. Rooms in house, cottage & barn with mountain views. Hiking, porches, duck pond, bikes.*

---

**Grapevine Inn**
486 Siskiyou Blvd.,  97520
541-482-7944  800-500-VINE
Shirley Grega
All year

$$$-B&B
3 rooms, 3 pb
Visa, MC,
C-ltd/S-ltd/P-no/H-no

Full breakfast
Snacks, comp. wine
Sitting room
all rooms have A/C
shops, galleries nearby

*Romantic 1909 Dutch Colonial. Down comforters and cozy fireplaces. Gourmet breakfasts served in lush garden gazebo. Walk to town & theatres.* **20% discount (2 night minimum) 11/1-2/15.**

---

**Hersey House & Bungalow**
451 N. Main St.,  97520
503-482-4563  800-482-4563
Gail Orell, Lynn Savage
Late April–October

$$$-B&B
4 rooms, 4 pb
Visa, *Rated*, •
C-ltd/S-ltd/P-no/H-no

Full bkfst. - main house
Cont. bkfst. - bungalow
Comp. tea, wine, snacks
sitting rm, player piano
balcony, near theatres

*Elegantly restored turn-of-the-century Victorian w/family antiques, china, silver, linens, queen beds, thermostats in each room. English garden. Hersey Bungalow sleeps 4-6.*

---

**Morical House Garden Inn**
668 N. Main St.,  97520
541-482-2254  Fax:541-482-1775
800-208-0960
Gary & Sandye Moore
All year

$$$-B&B
7 rooms, 7 pb
Most CC, *Rated*, •
C-ltd/S-ltd/P-no/H-yes

Full breakfast
Afternoon refreshments
Parlor with piano
gardens with ponds

*An 1880s house, set in an acre of lawn and gardens, restored to the simple elegance of its Victorian heritage.*

---

**Mousetrap Inn**
312 Helman St.,  97520
541-482-9228  Fax:541-482-9228
800-460-5453
All year

$$-B&B
6 rooms, 6 pb
Visa, MC, *Rated*, •
C-yes/S-no/P-no/H-no

Full vegetarian bkfst.
Afternoon tea, snacks
Outdoor dining
sitting room, English
garden, hammock

*A colorful eclectic environment combining contemporary art and antiques that compliment this 100 year old home. Full vegetarian breakfast, great coffee.* **3rd night 50%, ltd.**

---

**Mt. Ashland Inn**
550 Mt. Ashland Rd.,  97520
541-482-8707  Fax:541-482-8707
800-830-8707
Chuck & Laurel Biegert
All year

$$$-B&B
5 rooms, 5 pb
MC, Visa, *Rated*, •
C-ltd/S-no/P-no/H-no

Full breakfast
Complimentary beverages
Library, outdoor spa and
sauna, snowshoes, sleds
mountain bikes (no fee)

*Handcrafted luxury log chalet on mountain ridge with spectacular views. Hike and cross-country ski from inn. Downhill ski nearby.* **Off-season midweek discounts, ltd.**

## ASHLAND

**Peerless Hotel, The**
243 Fourth St., 97520
541-488-1082 Fax:541-482-1012
800-460-8758
Crissy Barnett
All year

$$-B&B
6 rooms, 6 pb
Visa, MC, AmEx, •
C-ltd/S-ltd/P-no/H-yes

Continental plus bkfst.
Comp. wine, snacks
Evening cordial, truffle
sitting room, A/C, bikes
in room phones, music

*Restored intimate European style inn in the Historic Railroad District. Art, antiques and character. 3 blocks to town. Ski & romantic getaway packages.* **Free bottle of wine.**

## ASTORIA

**Captain's Inn**
1546 Franklin Ave., 97103
503-325-1387 Fax:503-325-8096
800-1467-1387
Joni R. Sherman
All year

$$-B&B
5 rooms, 5 pb
*Rated*, •
C-yes/S-ltd/P-no/H-yes

Full gourmet breakfast
Afternoon tea, snacks
Sitting room, library
family friendly facility
2 rooms have TV/VCR

*Elegant Victorian Italianate built in 1876. Beautiful European antiques. Iron & brass beds, magnificent art collection. Close to downtown & museums.* **50% off Oct. 15–Apr 15; Long term corporate stays available.**

**Grandview B&B**
1574 Grand Ave., 97103
503-325-5555 800-488-3250
Charleen Maxwell
All year

$-B&B
9 rooms, 7 pb
Most CC, *Rated*, •
C-ltd

Full breakfast
Snacks
Sitt. rm., canopy beds
books, games, binoculars
liquor not permitted

*Light, airy, cheerful Victorian close to superb Maritime Museum, Lightship, churches, golf, clam-digging, fishing, beaches and rivers. Sleeps 21.* **2nd night free Nov. 1–May 20.**

**Martin & Lilli Foard House**
690 17th St., 97103
503-325-1892
Melissa Yowell
Feb.-Oct.

$-B&B
2 rooms,
C-ltd/S-no/P-no/H-no

Continental plus bkfst.
Pastry, fruit, coffee
English garden
overlooks Columbia River

*1892 Queen Anne Victorian, with English garden, located in a neighborhood of Victorian homes on a hill overlooking the Columbia River.*

## BANDON

**Sea Star Guesthouse**
375 2nd St., 370 1st St., 97411
541-347-9632 Fax:541-347-9533
Eileen Sexton
All year

$-EP
4 rooms, 4 pb
Visa, MC, AmEx,
C-yes/S-no/P-no/H-no

Optional breakfast
Comp. tea/wine in room
Comp. wine, restaurant
library, decks, skylight
suites w/full kitchens

*Coastal getaway on harbor in "Oldtown" with bistro. Romantic retreat with European flair. Beachwalks, natural beauty; theater, galleries.* **3rd night 50% off.**

## BEND

**Sather House B&B, The**
7 N.W. Tumalo Ave., 97701
541-388-1065
Robbie Giamboi
All year

$$-B&B
4 rooms, 2 pb
Visa, MC, Disc.,
C-ltd/S-ltd/P-no/H-no

Full breakfast
Comp. wine, aftn. tea
Sitting room
year-round recreation of
every kind and beauty

*Charming and elegant historicai home. Uniquely decorated with period furnishings. Near ski slopes. Walking distance to downtown, park, & river.* **10% discount for 4 or more nights.**

## BROOKINGS

| | | |
|---|---|---|
| **Chetco River Inn** | $$$-B&B | Full breakfast |
| 21202 High Prairie Rd.,  97415 | 3 rooms, 3 pb | Lunch, dinner with resv. |
| 503-469-8128  800-327-2688 | MC, Visa, *Rated*, • | Beverages & cookies |
| Sandra Brugger | C-ltd/S-ltd/P-no/H-no | Sitting room, library |
| Exc. Thanksgiving & Xmas | | games, hiking, river |

*Relax in peaceful seclusion of our private 35-acre forest, bordered on 3 sides by the Chetco River. Enjoy "Old World" hospitality & "New World" comfort. **3rd night 50% off.***

| | | |
|---|---|---|
| **Holmes Sea Cove B&B** | $$$-B&B | Continental plus bkfst. |
| 17350 Holmes Dr.,  97415 | 3 rooms, 3 pb | Tea, coffee, cocoa |
| 541-469-3025 | MC, Visa, • | Trail to private park, |
| Lorene & Jack Holmes | C-ltd/S-no/P-no/H-no | creek and beach |
| All year | | airport pickup |

*Delightful seacoast hideaway. Three cozy rooms with spectacular ocean views, private entrances, baths. Cottage available. Tasty continental plus breakfast served in rooms.*

| | | |
|---|---|---|
| **Oceancrest House B&B** | $$$-B&B | Continental plus |
| 15510 Pedrioli, P.O. Box 2820, | 2 rooms, 2 pb | Library, hot tubs, deck |
| 97415 | Most CC, *Rated*, • | refrig/micro. available |
| Harbor | C-ltd/S-ltd/P-no/H-no | near beach, airport ride |
| 541-469-9200  Fax: 541-469-8864 | French | |
| 800-769-9200 | | |
| Georgine Paulin | | |
| All year | | |

*Oceanfront on rugged Oregon coast; very private and quiet; comfortable elegance; generous continental breakfast served in room; near redwood groves.*

## CLOVERDALE

| | | |
|---|---|---|
| **Hudson House B&B Inn** | $$-B&B | Full breakfast |
| 37700 Hwy. 101 S.,  97112 | 4 rooms, 4 pb | Aftn. tea, snacks |
| 503-392-3533  Fax: 503-392-3533 | Most CC, | Sitting room, library |
| Richard & Judy Shinton | C-ltd/S-no/P-no/H-no | bicycles |
| All year | | |

*Escape to quieter times. Great breakfasts, afternoon snacks; family heirlooms, period antiques; historic 1906 Tillamook country farmhouse near beautiful beaches.*

## CORVALLIS

| | | |
|---|---|---|
| **Abed & Breakfast at Sparks** | $$-B&B | Full breakfast |
| 2515 SW 45th St.,  97333 | 4 rooms, 2 pb | Coffee, tea and soda |
| 541-757-7321  Fax: 541-753-4332 | Most CC, | Sitting rm., dining rm. |
| Neoma & Herb Sparks | C-ltd/S-no/P-no/H-no | hot tubs, TV, VCR |
| All year | | deck with heated spa |

*Peaceful setting on private golf course. Large living & entertainment rooms, huge deck, and outdoor spa dedicated to guests' enjoyment. Plush robes, complimentary wine.*

## ELMIRA

| | | |
|---|---|---|
| **McGillivray's Log Home B&B** | $$-B&B | Full breakfast |
| 88680 Evers Rd.,  97437 | 2 rooms, 2 pb | |
| 541-935-3564 | MC, Visa, | |
| Evelyn R. McGillivray | C-yes/H-yes | |
| All year | | |

*Enjoy hearty breakfasts in this secluded country home. Rooms feature king beds, private baths, and air-conditioning. 14 miles west of Eugene, Oregon.*

## EUGENE

| **Campbell House, a City Inn** | $$-B&B | Full breakfast |
|---|---|---|
| 252 Pearl St.,  97401 | 14 rooms, 14 pb | Lunch & dinner arranged |
| 541-343-1119  Fax: 541-343-2258 | Visa, MC, AmEx, | Aftn. tea, jetted tubs |
| 800-264-2519 | *Rated*, • | beer & wine for sale |
| Myra Plant & Judith | C-ltd/S-no/P-no/H-yes | sitting room, library |
| Whipkey | | |
| All year | | |

*Built in 1892 and restored in the tradition of a small European hotel. "Classic elegance, exquisite decor and impeccable service."* **Free bottle of champagne or sparkling cider.**

| **Kjaer's House in the** | $$-B&B | Full breakfast |
|---|---|---|
| **Woods** | 2 rooms, 2 pb | Afternoon tea, snacks |
| 814 Lorane Hwy,  97405 | *Rated*, • | Sitting room, library |
| 541-343-3234 | C-yes/S-no/P-no/H-no | port-a-crib & games for |
| George & Eunice Kjaer | German | children |
| All year exc. Christmas | | |

*1910 Craftsman home in parklike setting among tall firs. Furnished with antiques and provides urban convenience with suburban tranquillity.* **3rd night, 50%.**

| **Maryellen's Guest House** | $$$-B&B | Full breakfast |
|---|---|---|
| 1583 Fircrest,  97403 | 2 rooms, 2 pb | Snacks |
| 541-342-7375  800-736-1475 | MC, Visa, *Rated*, • | Bicycles, hot tubs |
| Maryellen & Bob Larson | C-yes/S-ltd/P-no/H-no | swimming pool (no kids) |
| All year | | sitting rm., cedar decks |

*Our guests are pampered! The suites are private and spacious, one with double showers and deep soaking tub. Outdoors enjoy swimming pool & hot tub Jacuzzi.*

| **Oval Door B&B Inn, The** | $$-B&B | Full breakfast |
|---|---|---|
| 988 Lawrence St.,  97401 | 4 rooms, 4 pb | Tea, soft drinks, cookie |
| 503-683-3160  Fax: 503-485-5339 | Visa, MC, AmEx, | Sitting room, library |
| 800-882-3160 | *Rated*, • | jacuzzi |
| Judith McLane | C-ltd/S-no/P-no/H-no | |
| All year | | |

*Offering warm hospitality. Private baths, bountiful breakfast, home-baked treats, walk to restaurants.* **3rd night 20% off.**

| **Pookie's B&B College Hill** | $$-B&B | Full breakfast |
|---|---|---|
| 2013 Charnelton St.,  97405 | 3 rooms, 2 pb | Snacks, gas BBQ in back |
| 541-343-0383  Fax: 541-343-0383 | Checks accepted, | Sitting room, library |
| 800-558-0383 | C-ltd/S-ltd/P-no/H-no | shad trees, antiques |
| Pookie & Doug Walling | | Bartolette suite for 3 |
| All year | | |

*Our restored craftsman home built in 1918 is in a quiet, older neighborhood. Sitting room & bedroom are done in a mixture of antiques. Suite available.* **10% off stay, ltd.**

## EUGENE, CRESWELL

| **Country House, The** | $$$-B&B | Full breakfast |
|---|---|---|
| 30930 Camas Swale Rd., | 2 rooms, 2 pb | Dinner (fee), snacks |
| 97426 | *Rated*, • | Comp. beverages, library |
| 541-895-3924  Fax: 541-895-2918 | C-ltd/S-ltd/P-no/H-no | sitt. room, hot tub |
| Michael & Susie Hanner | | rec. room, croquet court |
| All year | | |

*Large, romantic country house on 68 acres of peaceful rolling woodlands. King beds, generous common area. A/C. Tranquility is our specialty.* **Free bottle of wine.**

## FLORENCE

| **Edwin K B&B** | $$$-B&B | Full gourmet breakfast |
|---|---|---|
| P.O. Box 2687,   97439 | 6 rooms, 6 pb | Snacks |
| 1155 Bay St. | Visa, MC, *Rated*, | Sitting room, fireplace |
| 503-997-8360  800-833-9465 | C-yes/S-no/P-no/H-no | rental cottage sleeps 6 |
| Sid & Bob Steen | | children welcome |
| All year | | |

*The romantic show place facing the Siuslaw River and dunes. Walking distance of "Old Town" shops and restaurants. Gourmet breakfast fit for a king. Vacation rentals.*

| **Johnson House B&B, The** | $$$-B&B | Full breakfast |
|---|---|---|
| P.O. Box 1892,   97439 | 6 rooms, 3 pb | Afternoon tea |
| 216 Maple St. | MC, Visa, *Rated*, • | Sitting room, 3 deluxe |
| 541-997-8000 Fax: 541-997-8000 | S-no/P-no/H-no | rooms w/private baths |
| 800-768-9488 | French, Swedish | "Moonset" cabin avail. |
| Jayne & Ronald Fraese | | |
| All year | | |

*Beautifully restored 1892 Victorian; down comforters; genuine antiques throughout; turn-of-the-century charm; in Old Town one block from bayfront.* **3rd night free, Nov. 1– April 30.**

## GARIBALDI

| **Pelican's Perch** | $$$-B&B | Full breakfast |
|---|---|---|
| P.O. Box 543,   97118 | 4 rooms, 4 pb | Picnic lunch, comp. wine |
| 112 E. Cypress Ave. | Visa, MC, • | Hot tubs, snacks, sauna |
| 503-322-3633 | C-ltd/S-ltd/P-no/H-no | deep sea fishing arrang. |
| Dianna & Bill Moore | | sitting room, grill |
| Some winter weeks closed | | |

*Romantic coastal lodge filled w/southern antiques. We delight in helping guests experience the (true) fun of relaxed coastal living.* **Champagne/spec. occ., 4th night disc't.**

## GOLD BEACH

| **Endicott Gardens** | $$-B&B | Extended cont. breakfast |
|---|---|---|
| 95768 Jerry's Flat Rd,   97444 | 4 rooms, 4 pb | Decks, gardens |
| 503-247-6513 | *Rated*, | ocean nearby |
| Mary & Beverly Endicott | C-ltd/S-ltd/P-no/H-no | river nearby |
| All year | | |

*Unique garden setting—restful homemade hospitality. Decks with forest and mountain views.*

| **Inn at Nesika Beach** | $$$-B&B | Full breakfast |
|---|---|---|
| 33026 Nesika Rd.,   97444 | 4 rooms, 4 pb | Snacks |
| 503-247-6434 | *Rated*, | Sitting room |
| Ann G. Arsenault | S-no/P-no/H-no | Jacuzzi tubs |
| All year | | fishing nearby |

*New, large Victorian home bordering Pacific Ocean, with fireplaces, featherbeds, Jacuzzi tubs in rooms. Gourmet breakfast. The theme is relaxation and comfort.*

## GRANTS PASS

| **Flery Manor B&B** | $$-B&B | Full gourmet breakfast |
|---|---|---|
| 2000 Jumpoff Joe Cr. Rd, | 4 rooms, 3 pb | Afternoon tea, snacks |
| 97526 | Visa, MC, *Rated*, • | Complimentary wine |
| 541-476-3591 Fax: 541-471-2303 | C-ltd/S-no/P-no/H-no | sitting room, library |
| Marla & John Vidrinskas | Lithuanian, Russian | ponds, waterfall |
| All year | | |

*Elegant country manor nestled on 7 acres of mountain-side. Healthy gourmet breakfast in formal dining room. Romantic suite w/Jacuzzi, fireplace, private balcony. "Get away from the hurried world."*

## GRANTS PASS

| **Lawnridge House B&B** | $$-B&B | Full breakfast |
|---|---|---|
| 1304 NW Lawnridge,   97526 | 2 rooms, 2 pb | Room refrig w/beverages |
| 541-476-8518 | *Rated*, • | Alfresco dining |
| Barbara Head | C-yes/S-ltd | secluded deck & porch |
| All year | Spanish, some French | filled bookshelves, VCP |

*1909 historic home w/antique furnishings, canopy beds, fireplace, beamed ceilings, dark wood floors, oriental rugs, cable TV, phone, A/C. Family suite available.* **3rd night 30% off.**

## GRANTS PASS, MERLIN

| **Pine Meadow Inn** | $$$-B&B | Healthy full breakfast |
|---|---|---|
| 1000 Crow Rd.,   97532 | 4 rooms, 3 pb | Seasonal fruits/vegys |
| 541-471-6277  Fax: 541-471-6277 | *Rated*, • | Sitting room, library |
| 800-554-0806 | C-ltd/S-no/P-no/H-no | hot tub, deck |
| Maloy & Nancy Murdock | | walking paths |
| All year | | |

*Secluded country retreat on nine acres of meadows & woods near the Rogue River. Wraparound porch, gardens, koi pond. Fruits & vegetables from our gardens.* **3rd night, 50%.**

## HOOD RIVER

| **Columbia Gorge Hotel** | $$$$-B&B | Full farm breakfast |
|---|---|---|
| 4000 Westcliff Dr.,   97031 | 42 rooms, 42 pb | Restaurant, bar |
| 541-386-5566  Fax: 541-387-5566 | Most CC, • | Bicycles, skiing, golf |
| 800-345-1921 | C-yes/S-yes/P-yes/H-yes | Family owned and |
| Boyd & Halla Graves | Spanish, French | operated romantic inn |
| All year | | |

*Famous for its spectacular setting high above the Columbia River, with sweeping vistas of Mount Hood, and 206-foot Wah Gwin Gwin Falls. 4 hours south of Seattle, exit 62 I-84.*

## JACKSONVILLE

| **Jacksonville Inn** | $$$-B&B | Full breakfast |
|---|---|---|
| P.O. Box 359,   97530 | 11 rooms, 11 pb | Restaurant, lounge |
| 175 E. California St. | All major CC, *Rated*, | Lunch & dinner (fee) |
| 541-899-1900  Fax: 541-899-1373 | • | luxurious cottages with |
| 800-321-9344 | C-yes/S-no/P-no/H-no | many amenities avail. |
| Jerry Evans       All year | Greek, Danish, Italian | |

*Built in 1861 and located in center of historic village. 8 rooms and 3 cottages. Private baths & award-winning restaurant w/over 1500 wines. Steam shower & spa tubs available.*

## LANGLOIS

| **Floras Lake House/By Sea** | $$$-B&B | Continental plus |
|---|---|---|
| 92870 Boice Cope Rd.,   97450 | 4 rooms, 4 pb | Complimentary cocoa, tea |
| 541-348-2573  Fax: 541-348-2573 | Visa, MC, Disc., | Windsurfing lessons with |
| Llz & Will Brady | C-yes/S-no/P-no/H-ltd | rentals available, sauna |
| Mid Feb.-Mid Nov. | | hiking, family friendly |

*Our newly built cedar home offers views of the lake and ocean. Windsurfing lessons and rentals available. Incredibly scenic hiking and beachcombing nearby.* **10% off 6+ nights.**

## LINCOLN CITY

| **Brey House Ocean View Inn** | $$-B&B | Full breakfast |
|---|---|---|
| 3725 N.W. Keel,   97367 | 4 rooms, 4 pb | Sitting room, hot tubs |
| 541-994-7123 | Visa, MC, Disc., • | ocean view deck |
| Milt & Shirley (owners) | C-yes/S-ltd/P-no/H-no | landscaped yard |
| All year | | |

*The ocean awaits you just across the street. We are located within the city limits of Lincoln City. Fireplace in Admiral's Room. Casino 2 blocks away.* **Winter stays booked receive Mon., Tues. free.**

## LINCOLN CITY

**Pacific Rest B&B**
1611 Northeast 11th,   97367
541-994-2337  Fax: 541-994-2337
R. & J. Waetjen, B. Beard
All year

$$-B&B
2 rooms, 2 pb
C-yes/S-ltd/P-ltd/H-yes

Full gourmet breakfast
Snacks
Family friendly facility
suites for families

*New home especially designed with the "B&B" guest in mind. Relaxed, restful atmosphere just 4 blocks to beach. Onsite art gallery. 3rd night 50% off.*

## McMINNVILLE

**Steiger Haus B&B**
360 Wilson St.,   97128
503-472-0821
Dale & Susan DeRette
All year

$$-B&B
5 rooms, 5 pb
*Rated*, •
C-ltd/S-no/P-no

Full breakfast
Conference room
decks, terraces
English garden

*In the heart of the Oregon wine country. Unique architecture in parklike town setting. Close to gourmet restaurants. Charm and hospitality plus! Sitting room TV, games.*

## MERLIN

**Morrison's Rogue River**
8500 Galice Rd.,   97532
541-476-3825  800-826-1963
Michelle Hanten
May–Nov. 15

$$$$-AP
13 rooms, 13 pb
MC, Visa, Disc., •
C-yes/S-yes/P-no/H-no

Full gourmet breakfast
Dinner, (Lunch in fall)
Sitting room, pool
tennis, putting green
trails, fishing, rafting

*On the bank of the legendary Rogue River. Gourmet dinners, riverview cottages, peaceful wooded setting, romantic atmosphere, fishing trips & white water raft trips available.*

## MT HOOD AREA, GOV'T CAMP

**Falcon's Crest Inn**
P.O. Box 185,   97028
87287 Gov't Camp Loop Hwy
503-272-3403  Fax: 503-272-3454
800-624-7384
B.J. & Melody Johnson
All year

$$$-B&B
5 rooms, 5 pb
Most CC, *Rated*, •
C-ltd/S-no/P-no/H-no

Full breakfast
Gourmet restaurant
Dinner, VCR, fishing
Alcoholic beverages
hot tubs, golf, hiking

*Elegance in heart of Mt. Hood Nat'l. Forest. Gourmet restaurant. Inn special events, movie collection, outdoor recreation, ski packages, Christmas Holiday Specialists. 3rd night 50% off of rack rate.*

## NEWBERG

**Spring Creek Llama Ranch**
14700 NE Spring Ck. Ln.,
   97132
503-538-5717  Fax: 503-538-5717
Dave & Melinda Van Bossuyt
All year

$$-B&B
2 rooms, 2 pb
*Rated*, •
C-yes/S-no/P-no/H-no
Spanish

Full breakfast
Snacks
Library
Working llama ranch
hiking trails

*"Quiet, peaceful, relaxing, beautiful setting, lovely home, wonderful hospitality." The spacious and immaculate home is nestled in the midst of rolling pasture and forest.*

## NEWPORT

**Oar House B&B**
520 S.W. 2nd st.,   97365
541-265-9571  800-252-2358
Jan LeBrun
All year

$$$-B&B
4 rooms, 4 pb
Visa, MC,
S-no/P-no/H-no
Spanish

Full breakfast
Snacks, tea
Sitting room w/fireplace
libraries, art, music
lighthouse tower

*Lincoln Country historic landmark built 1900. Renovated, expanded 1993. Lighthouse tower with widow's walk-panoramic views. Spacious, elegant guest areas. Reduced winter rates.*

NEWPORT ──────────────────────────

**Ocean House B&B**
4920 NW Woody Way,  97365
541-265-6158  800-56BandB
Bob Garrard
All year

$$$-B&B
5 rooms, 5 pb
MC, Visa, *Rated*,
S-no/P-no/H-no

Full breakfast
Snacks, coffee, tea
Sitting room, library
3 rms. w/spas, 4 w/decks
All rooms w/ocean views

*Near the center of coastal activities & fun. Large comfortable home w/beautiful surroundings, expanded garden w/ocean decks. Near Yaquina Head Lt. House. **10% off stay Oct.–Apr.***

**Tyee Lodge-Oceanfront B&B**
4925 NW Woody Way,  97365
541-265-8953  888-553-TYEE
Mark & Cindy McConnell
All year

$$$-B&B
5 rooms, 5 pb
Visa, MC,
C-ltd/S-ltd/P-no/H-no
Spanish, French,
German

Full breakfast
Convenience bar
Private trail to beach
sitting room, fireplace
accomadate special diets

*Our park-like setting is unequaled on the Oregon Coast. Sit by your window, or by the fire, and watch the waves. **Complimentary wine. Two or more nights reduced rates.***

OREGON CITY ──────────────────────────

**Inn of the Oregon Trail**
416 S. McLoughlin,  97045
503-656-2089  888-650-9322
Mary & Tom DeHaven
All year

$$-B&B
4 rooms, 4 pb
Visa, MC,
C-ltd/S-no/P-no/H-ltd
Some Japanese

Full breakfast
Lunch for public Tue-Fri
Lunch/brunch on Saturday
candlelight dinner by
reservation

*An 1867 Gothic Revival home on the National Historic Register in Oregon City—the "End of the Oregon Trail" and beginning of Oregon history.*

PORT ORFORD ──────────────────────────

**Home by the Sea B&B**
P.O. Box 606,  97465
444 Jackson St.
541-332-2855  Fax: 541-332-7585
Alan & Brenda Mitchell
All year

$$-B&B
2 rooms, 2 pb
MC, Visa,
C-ltd/S-no/P-no/H-no

Full breakfast
Refrigerator, laundry
beach access, ocean view
cable TV, phones, spa

*Enjoy dramatic views of the ocean, direct beach access and miles of unspoiled public beaches in this quiet fishing village.*

PORTLAND ──────────────────────────

**General Hooker's B&B**
125 SW Hooker St.,  97201
503-222-4435  Fax: 503-295-6410
800-745-4135
Lori Hall
All year

$$-B&B
4 rooms, 2 pb
AmEx, MC, Visa,
*Rated*, •
C-ltd/S-no/P-no/H-no

Continental plus - veg.
Comp. wine & beverages
Sitting room, library
A/C, roof deck, cat
TV, VCR, phones in rooms

*Casually elegant Victorian in quiet, historic neighborhood; walking distance of City Center. Classical music throughout. **½ price day pass at nearby, posh YMCA.***

**John Palmer House B&B Inn**
4314 N. Mississippi Ave,
  97217
503-284-5893  Fax: 503-284-1239
800-518-5893
Mary & Richard Sauter
All year

$$-B&B
10 rooms, 5 pb
MC, Visa, *Rated*, •
C-ltd/S-no/P-no/H-no
Sign Language

Full breakfast
Aft. tea by reservation
bathrobes, massages
bicycles, library, piano

*Gourmet summer breakfasts on the veranda. Flowers, wines, beer, chocolates. Two units have kitchens, space for small meetings. **3rd night free, Nov.–March, ltd.***

## PORTLAND

**Lion and the Rose B&B, The**
1517 NE Schuyler, 1810 NE 15th St., 97212
503-287-9245 Fax: 503-287-9247
800-955-1647
Kay Peffer
All year

$$$-B&B
6 rooms, 4 pb
Visa, MC, AmEx,
*Rated*,
C-ltd/S-ltd/P-no/H-no

Full breakfast
Dinner, aft. tea, snacks
Sitting room
bicycles

*Our 1906 10,000 sq. ft. Mansion, boasts comfortable Victorian Elegance. The perfect place for someone who loves all things Victorian.*

**Plum Tree B&B**
2005 NE 22nd Ave., 97212
503-280-0679
Bonne & Peter Posert
All year

$$-B&B
3 rooms, 1 pb
Visa, MC,
C-ltd/S-no/P-no/H-no

Full breakfast
Family friendly facility
library, sitting room
fluffy cat

*The towering Plum Tree, rose covered picket fence, gourmet breakfast, elegant decor and friendly hosts combine for an enchanting stay.*

**Portland Guest House**
1720 N.E. 15th Ave., 97212
503-282-1402
Susan Gisvold
All year

$$-B&B
7 rooms, 5 pb
AmEx, MC, Visa,
*Rated*, •
C-yes/S-no/P-no

Full breakfast
Comp. beverages
Room phones, antiques
jogging routes, crtyard
bus & light rail tickets

*1890 Victorian in historic Irvington neighborhood. All rooms have phones, antiques, heirloom linens, great beds. Luscious breakfasts. Family suite w/3 beds. Walk to restaurants, movies, coffee shops.*

## ROSEBURG

**House of Hunter**
813 S.E. Kane St., 97470
541-672-2335 800-540-7704
Walt & Jean Hunter
All year

$$-B&B
5 rooms, 3 pb
MC, Visa, *Rated*, •
C-ltd/S-no/P-no/H-no

Full breakfast
Comp. bev, refrig.
Phone, patio, VCR, TV
near golf & downtown
laundry facilities, A/C

*Restored 1900 historic home, mixture of antiques & modern, quiet neighborhood, close to restaurants & shopping. Use our raft to float the UMPQUA River.*

**Oak Ridge B&B**
3010 W. Military Ave., 97470
541-672-2168 800-428-2428
Nita & Bob Butcher
All year

$$-B&B
2 rooms, 2 pb
S-no/P-no

Full breakfast

*Scenic hillside home. Enjoy the Indian artifacts, nature photos, custom woodwork. Airy master suite, guest carport. Host is a retired park ranger.*

## SANDLAKE

**Sandlake Country Inn**
8505 Galloway Rd, 97112
503-965-6745
Femke & David Durham
All year

$$$-B&B
4 rooms, 4 pb
MC, Visa, Disc. *Rated*,
•
C-ltd/S-no/P-no/H-yes

Full 3-course breakfast
Sitting room, robes
picnic baskets $34
all rms. w/whirlpool tub

*A private, peaceful place for making memories on the Oregon Coast. Old roses, hummingbirds, breakfast "en suite,"fireplaces and jacuzzis.*

## SALEM

**Marquee House**
333 Wyatt Ct NE,  97301
503-391-0837  800-949-0837
Rickie Hart
All year

$$-B&B
5 rooms, 3 pb
Visa, MC,  •
C-ltd/S-no/P-no/H-no

Full breakfast
Snacks
Sitting room
nightly movies

*Mt. Vernon Colonial; has antiques, fireplace. Nightly film showing with "bottomless" popcorn bowl. Walk to the capitol. Pillow talk room (private bath) now has a queen & a twin bed.*

## SHANITIO

**Historic Shanitio Hotel**
P.O. Box 86,  97057
4th & "E" Sts.
541-489-3441  800-483-3441
Jean F. Farrell
All year

$$$-B&B
18 rooms, 18 pb
MC, Visa,  •
C-yes/S-no/P-no/H-no

Full breakfast
Lunch, dinner

*Historic setting in old wool shipping center and authentic ghost town. Close to fishing. On U.S. Hwy. 97, 40 miles N. of Medras. 56 miles S. of the Columbia River.*

## SISTERS

**Cascade Country Inn**
P.O. Box 834,  97759
15870 Barclay Dr.
541-549-4666  800-316-0089
Judy & Victoria Tolonen
All year

$$$-B&B
7 rooms, 7 pb
MC, Visa, *Rated*,  •
C-yes/S-no/P-no/H-yes

Full breakfast
Sitting room
bicycles
family friendly

*Fly in to Sisters Eagle Air in your private plane. Outdoor activities summer, winter, spring & autumn. Awesome mountain views as well as quite and restfull.* **15% discount, ltd.**

**Conklin's Guest House**
69013 Camp Polk Rd.,  97759
541-549-0123  800-549-4262
Frank & Marie Conklin
All year

$$$-B&B
5 rooms, 5 pb
C-ltd/S-ltd/P-ltd/H-yes
Spanish

Full breakfast
Snacks, comp. wine
Sitting room
heated swimming pool
trout ponds

*A spectacular country paradise of spacious grounds, ponds, & mountain vistas. Tasteful country decor & gourmet breakfasts complete the setting.*

**Squaw Creek B&B Inn**
P.O. Box 1993,  97759
68733 Junipine Ln.
541-549-4312  Fax: 541-549-4312
800-930-0055
Susie and Keith Johnson
All year

$$-B&B
4 rooms, 4 pb
Visa, MC,
C-yes/S-no/P-yes/H-no

Big country breakfast
Lunch, dinner on request
Sitting room, hot tubs
horeshoes, Squaw Creek
8.5 acres to walk

*Just minutes from Sisters, this beautiful country hideaway features a big country breakfast, Jacuzzi, walking trails, deer and mountain fresh air.* **3rd night, 50% off.**

## STEAMBOAT

**Steamboat Inn**
42705 N. Umpqua Hwy.,
  97447
541-498-2411  Fax: 541-498-2411
800-840-8825
Sharon & Jim Van Loan
All year

$$$-EP
12 rooms, 12 pb
MC, Visa,  •
C-yes/S-ltd/P-no/H-ltd

Full breakfast (fee)
Lunch, dinner
Library/conference room

*A fishing lodge/country inn that serves excellent food. At night we close to the public and serve our famous fisherman dinner by reservation only!*

## TILLAMOOK

| **Blue Haven Inn** | $$-B&B | Full breakfast |
|---|---|---|
| 3025 Gienger Rd., 97141 | 3 rooms, 1 pb | Dinner |
| 503-842-2265 | • | Sitting room |
| Joy & Ray Still | C-ltd/S-no/P-no/H-no | library |
| All year | | |

*Peaceful, quiet country setting surrounded by tall evergreens; gourmet breakfast served in formal dining room. Furnished with antiques (also for sale).* **3rd night 50%, 10% disc't weekly stays.**

## WALDPORT

| **Cliff House** | $$$-B&B | Full breakfast |
|---|---|---|
| P.O. Box 436, 97394 | 4 rooms, 4 pb | Aftn. tea, comp. wine |
| 1450 Adohi Rd. | Visa, MC, Disc, *Rated*, | Restaurant |
| 541-563-2506 Fax: 541-563-4393 | S-ltd/P-no/H-ltd | sitting room, library |
| Gabrielle Duvall | Spanish | hot tubs, sauna, ocean |
| All year | | |

*Pampered elegance by the sea. Perched high on a cliff, we offer gourmet breakfasts, spa, sauna, massage (by appointment) and luxury rooms.*

## WINCHESTER BAY

| **Salmon Harbor Belle B&B** | $$$-B&B | Full gourmet breakfast |
|---|---|---|
| PO Box 1208, Salmon Harbor | 6 rooms, 6 pb | Sitting room |
| Marina, 97467 | Visa, MC, AmEx, • | |
| 541-271-1137 Fax: 541-271-7497 | C-ltd/S-no/P-no/H-no | |
| 800-348-1922 | | |
| Sherry Porter | | |
| All year | | |

*Newly constructed sternwheel riverboat, designed as a B&B. A main salon with woodstove, and all the alluring and freshly made gourmet breakfast.* **3rd night 50%.**

## YACHATS

| **Oregon House, The** | $$-EP | Some in room fireplaces, |
|---|---|---|
| 94288 Hwy. 101 S., 97498 | 10 rooms, 10 pb | Jacuzzis, hot tubs |
| 541-547-3329 | Most CC, | kitchens |
| Joyce & Bob | C-ltd/S-no/P-no/H-ltd | |
| All year | | |

*Forest, lawn, creek crossed by arched wooden bridges, lighted trail down the cliff to the beach.*

## YAMHILL

| **Flying M Ranch** | $$-EP | Breakfast (fee) |
|---|---|---|
| 23029 NW Flying M Rd., | 28 rooms, 28 pb | Restaurant, bar |
| 97148 | AmEx, MC, Visa, • | Private airstrip, horses |
| 503-662-3222 Fax: 503-662-3202 | C-yes/S-ltd/P-ltd/H-yes | tennis court, piano |
| Bryce & Barbara Mitchell | | honeymoon cabin, fishing |
| All year exc. Dec 24-25 | | |

*Rustic & warm log lodge offers dining, dancing, mountain trail rides, camping, fishing, swimming pond, airstrip & wineries nearby. Honeymoon cabin with fireplace, jacuzzi tub.*

# More Inns . . .

| Albany | Brier Rose Inn B&B, 206 Seventh Ave. SW, 97321 |
|---|---|
| Albany | Farm "Mini Barn" House, 7070 Springhill Dr. N., 97321, 503-928-9089 |
| Ashland | Albion Inn, 34 Union St., 97520, 503-488-3905 |
| Ashland | Antique Rose Inn, 91 Gresham, 97520 |
| Ashland | Arden Forest Inn, 261 W. Hersey, 97520, 503-488-1496 |
| Ashland | Ashland Colony Inn, 725 Terra, 97520, 503-482-2668 |
| Ashland | Ashland Valley Inn, 1193 Siskiyou Blvd., 97520, 503-482-2641 |

| | |
|---|---|
| Ashland | Ashland's Victory House, 217 Beach St., 97520,  503-488-4828 |
| Ashland | Asland's Knight's Inn, 2359 Hwy. 66, 97520,  503-482-5111 |
| Ashland | Auburn Street Cottage, 549 Auburn St., 97520,  503-482-3004 |
| Ashland | Best Western Bard's Inn, 132 N. Main St., 97520,  503-482-0049 |
| Ashland | Buckhorn Spring's, 2200 Buckhorn Spring's, 97520,  503-488-2200 |
| Ashland | Cedarwood Inn of Ashland, 1801 Siskiyou Blvd., 97520,  503-488-2000 |
| Ashland | Chanticleer Inn, 120 Gresham St., 97520,  503-482-1919 |
| Ashland | Columbia Hotel, 262 1/2 E. Main, 97520,  503-482-3726 |
| Ashland | Coolidge House, 137 N. Main St., 97520,  503-482-4721 |
| Ashland | Country Walrus Inn, 2785 E. Main St., 97520,  503-488-1134 |
| Ashland | Cowslip's Belle B&B, 159 N. Main St., 97520,  503-488-2901 |
| Ashland | Fadden's Inn, 326 Main St., 97520,  503-488-0025 |
| Ashland | Fiddle Family Inn, 111 B St., 97520 |
| Ashland | Fox House Inn, 269 "B" St., 97520,  503-488-1055 |
| Ashland | Hillside Inn, 1520 Siskiyou Blvd., 97520,  503-482-2626 |
| Ashland | Iris Inn, The, 59 Manzanita St., 97520,  503-488-2286 |
| Ashland | Laurel Street Inn, 174 N. Main St., 97520,  503-488-2222 |
| Ashland | Lithia Rose Lodging, 163 Granite St., 97520,  503-482-1882 |
| Ashland | Lithia Springs Inn, 2165 W. Jackson Rd., 97520 |
| Ashland | McCall House, 153 Oak St., 97520,  503-482-9296 |
| Ashland | Neil Creek House, 341 Mowetza Dr., 97520,  503-482-1334 |
| Ashland | Oak Hill Country B&B, 2190 Siskiyou Blvd., 97520,  541-482-1554 |
| Ashland | Oak Street Station B&B, 239 Oak St., 97520,  503-482-1726 |
| Ashland | Parkside, 171 Granite St., 97520,  503-482-2320 |
| Ashland | Pelton House, 228 B St., 97520 |
| Ashland | Queen Anne, 125 N. Main St., 97520,  503-482-0220 |
| Ashland | Redwing B&B, 115 N. Main St., 97520,  503-482-1807 |
| Ashland | Romeo Inn, 295 Idaho St., 97520,  503-488-0884 |
| Ashland | Royal Carter House, 514 Siskiyou Blvd., 97520 |
| Ashland | Shrew's House, 570 Siskiyou Blvd., 97520,  503-482-9214 |
| Ashland | Studio's Inn, The, 550 E. Main, 97520,  503-488-5882 |
| Ashland | Wimer Street Inn, 75 Wimer St., 97520,  503-488-2319 |
| Ashland | Winchester Inn, 35 S. 2nd St., 97520,  503-488-1113 |
| Ashland | Woods House B&B, The, 333 N. Main St., 97520,  503-488-1598 |
| Astoria | Astoria Inn B&B, 3391 Irving Ave., 97103 |
| Astoria | Clementine's B&B, 847 Exchange, 97103,  503-325-2005 |
| Astoria | Columbia River Inn B&B, 1681 Franklin Ave., 97103,  503-325-5044 |
| Astoria | Franklin St. Station, 1140 Franklin, 97103,  503-325-4314 |
| Astoria | Inn-Chanted B&B, 707-8th St., 97103,  503-325-5223 |
| Astoria | Windover House B&B, 550 W. Lexington Ave., 97103 |
| Aumsville | Meadow View Inn B&B, 11221 Steinkamp Rd. SE, 97325 |
| Azalea | Havenshire B&B, 1098 Hogum Creek Rd., 97410,  503-837-3511 |
| Baker | Powder River B&B, HCR 87, Box 500, 97814,  503-523-7143 |
| Bandon | Bailey's Cedar House B&B, 2226 Seven Devils Rd., 97411 |
| Bandon | Lighthouse Inn B&B, P.O. Box 24, 97411,  503-347-9316 |
| Bandon | Na-So-Mah, Rte. 2 Box 2485, 97411,  503-347-1922 |
| Bandon | Riverboat B&B, Rt. 2 Box 2485, 97411,  503-347-1922 |
| Beaverton | Yankee Tinker B&B, The, 5480 SW 183rd Ave., 97007,  503-649-0932 |
| Bend | Farewell Bend B&B, 29 N.W. Greeley, 97701,  541-382-4374 |
| Bend | Gazebo B&B, 21679 Obsidian Ave., 97702,  503-389-7202 |
| Bend | Heidi Haus, 62227 Wallace Rd., 97701,  503-388-0850 |
| Bend | Lara House B&B, 640 N.W. Congress, 97701,  503-388-4064 |
| Bend | Mill Inn, 642 NW Colorado, 97701,  503-389-9198 |
| Bend | Mirror Pond House, 1054 NW Harmon Blvd., 97701,  503-389-1680 |
| Bend | Three Sisters B&B, 20150 Tumalo Rd., 97701 |
| Boring | Lariat Gardens B&B, 29440 SSE Lariat Ln., 97009,  503-663-1967 |
| Bridal Veil | Bridal Veil Lodge, P.O. Box 87, 97010,  503-695-2333 |
| Brookings | Casa Rubie, P.O. Box 397, 97415 |
| Brookings | Chart House Lodge & Outf., P.O. Box 6898, 97415 |
| Brookings | Hemlock Garden Guest Haus, P.O. Box 7994, 97415 |
| Brookings | Lowden's Beachfront B&B, 14626 Wollan Rd., 97415 |
| Brookings | South Coast Inn, 516 Redwood St., Box 86, 97415,  503-469-5557 |
| Brownsville | Atavista Farm B&B, 35580 Hwy. 228, 97327,  503-466-5566 |
| Brownsville | Kirk's Ferry B&B, 203 Washburn, 97327,  503-466-3214 |
| Cannon Beach | Cannon Beach Hotel, P.O. Box 943, 97110,  503-436-1392 |
| Cannon Beach | Tern Inn B&B, 3663 S.Hemlock, Box 952, 97110,  503-436-1528 |
| Cascade Locks | Inn at the Locks, P.O. Box 39, 97104,  702-374-8222 |
| Cascade Locks | Shakala at the Locks, P.O. Box 39, 97104 |
| Cave Junction | Oregon Caves Chateau, P.O. Box 128, 97523,  503-592-3400 |
| Clatskanie | King Salmon Lodge, P.O. Box 1242, 97016 |
| Coburg | Wheeler's B&B, Box 8201, 97401,  503-344-1366 |
| Coos Bay | Blackberry Inn B&B, 843 Central, 97420,  503-267-6951 |
| Coos Bay | Coos Bay Manor, 955 South Fifth St., 97420,  503-269-1224 |
| Coos Bay | Manor B&B, 955 S. 5th St., 97420,  503-269-1224 |
| Coos Bay | Old Tower House B&B, The, 476 Newmark, 97420,  503-888-6058 |
| Coos Bay | Talavar Inn & Retreat, P.O. Box 364, 97420 |
| Coos Bay | Upper Room Chalet, The, 306 N. 8th St., 97420,  503-269-5385 |
| Coquille | Barton House, The, 715 E. First St., 97423 |

| | |
|---|---|
| Corvallis | Hanson Country Inn, The, 795 Hanson St., 97333, 503-752-2919 |
| Corvallis | Harrison House, 2310 NW Harrison Blvd., 97330, 503-752-6248 |
| Corvallis | Wedgwood Inn, 563 SW Jefferson Ave., 97333, 503-758-7377 |
| Cottage Grove | Apple Inn B&B, 30697 Kenady Ln., 97424 |
| Cottage Grove | Deermeadow Inn B&B, 78876 Bryson Sears Rd., 97424, 503-942-4878 |
| Cottage Grove | Inn at Cottage Gove Lake, 32670 Glaisyer HIll Rd., 97424, 503-942-2958 |
| Cottage Grove | Ivanoffs' Inn, 3101 Bennett Creek Rd., 97424 |
| Cottage Grove | Lilly of the Field B&B, P.O.Box 831, 97424, 503-942-2049 |
| Cottage Grove | River Country Inn, 71864 London Rd., 97424 |
| Creswell | Country House, The, 30930 Camas Swale Rd., 97426 |
| Crooked River | Crooked River Ranch B&B, P.O. Box 1334, 97760, 503-548-4804 |
| Dallas | Woodridge Haven B&B, 1830 Woodridge Ct. SW, 97338 |
| Dayton | WineCountry Farm, 6855 Breyman Orchards, 97114, 503-864-3446 |
| Depoe Bay | Channel House B&B, The, P.O. Box 56, 97341, 503-765-2140 |
| Depoe Bay | Gracie's Landing, 235 S.E. Bay View Ave., 97341, 800-228-0448 |
| Depoe Bay | Pirate's Cove B&B, P.O. Box 701, 97341 |
| Detroit | Repose & Repast, P.O. Box 587, 97342 |
| Elkton | Equua Lodge, 221 Main St., 97400 |
| Elmira | Dome B&B, The, 24454 Warten Rd., 97437, 503-935-3138 |
| Enterprise | Lozier's Country Loft, 81922 Fish Hatchery Ln., 97828 |
| Eugene | Atherton Place B&B, 690 W. Broadway, 97402, 503-683-2674 |
| Eugene | Backroads B&B, 85269 Lorane Hwy., 97405, 503-485-0464 |
| Eugene | Campus Cottage B&B Inn, 1136 E. 19th Ave., 97403, 503-342-5346 |
| Eugene | Chambers House B&B Inn, 1006 Taylor St., 97402, 503-686-4242 |
| Eugene | Fort Smith B&B, 2645 Emerald, 97403, 503-687-9079 |
| Eugene | Getty's Emerald Garden B&B, 640 Audel Ave., 97404, 503-688-6344 |
| Eugene | Glendale Resort B&B, 2252 Ridgeway Dr., 97401, 503-726-2064 |
| Eugene | House in the Woods, The, 814 Lorane Highway, 97405, 503-343-3234 |
| Eugene | Lorane Valley B&B, 86621 Lorane Hwy, 97405, 503-686-0241 |
| Florence | Blue Heron Inn, The, P.O. Box 1122, 97439, 541-997-4091 |
| Forest Grove | Main Street B&B, 1803 main St., 97116, 503-357-9812 |
| Garibaldi | Hill Top House B&B, P.O. Box 145, 97118, 503-322-3221 |
| Garibaldi | No-How Inn B&B, 119 E. Driftwood, 97118 |
| Gates | Dragovich House, P.O. Box 261, 97346, 503-897-2157 |
| Glendale | Mt. Reuben Inn, 150 Rattlesnake Rd., 97442 |
| Gold Beach | Heather House B&B, 190 11th St., 97444, 503-247-2074 |
| Gold Beach | Hig Seas Inn, 105 Walker St. Box 3, 97441 |
| Gold Beach | Tu Tu' Tun Lodge, 96550 N. Bank Rogue, 97444, 503-247-6664 |
| Gold Hill | Willowbrook Inn B&B, 628 Foots Creek Rd., 97525, 503-582-0075 |
| Grants Pass | Ahlf House Inn, The, 762 NW Sixth St., 97526, 503-474-1374 |
| Grants Pass | Chriswood Inn, 220 NW "A" St., 97526, 503-474-9733 |
| Grants Pass | Home Farm B&B, 157 Savage Creek Rd., 97527 |
| Grants Pass | Martha's B&B Inn, 764 N.W. 4th St., 97526, 503-476-4330 |
| Grants Pass | Wilson House Inn, The, 746 N.W. Sixth St, 97526, 503-479-4754 |
| Halfway | Birch Leaf Lodge, RR 1, Box 91, 97834, 503-742-2990 |
| Halfway | Clear Creek Farm B&B, P.O. Box 737, 97834, 503-742-2238 |
| Hillsboro | Hawthorne Estate, The, 5611 NE Elam Young Pkwy, 97124 |
| Hillsboro | Leighton Bussard B&B, 13662 SW Whitmore Rd., 97123 |
| Hood River | Beryl House, The, 4079 Barrett Dr., 97212 |
| Hood River | Cascade Avenue B&B, 823 Cascade Ave., 97031 |
| Hood River | Hackett House, 922 State St., 97031, 503-386-1014 |
| Hood River | Lakecliff Estate B&B, P.O. Box 1220, 97031, 503-386-5918 |
| Hood River | State Street Inn, B&B, 1005 State St., 97031, 503-386-1899 |
| Independence | Davidson House, 887 Monmouth St., 97351, 503-838-3280 |
| Independence | Out of the Blue B&B, 386 Monmouth St., 97351, 503-838-3636 |
| Jacksonville | Colonial House B&B, P.O. Box 1298, 97530, 503-770-2783 |
| Jacksonville | McCully House Inn, P.O. Box 13, 97530, 503-899-1942 |
| Jacksonville | Touvelle House, The, P.O. Box 1891, 97530, 503-899-8938 |
| Joseph | Tamarack Pines Inn, 60073 Wallowa Lake Hwy., 97846, 503-432-2920 |
| Junction City | Black Bart B&B, 94125 Love lake Rd., 97448, 503-998-1904 |
| Kerby | Kerbyville Inn, 24304 Redwood Hwy., 97531 |
| Kimberly | Lands Inn B&B, Star Route 1, 97848, 503-934-2333 |
| Klamath Falls | Klamath Manor B&B, 219 Pine St., 97601, 503-883-5459 |
| Klamath Falls | Thompson's B&B By the Lake, 1420 Wild Plum Ct., 97601, 503-882-7938 |
| Klamath Falls | Wasthaven Bed & Breakfast, 2059 Lakeshore Dr., 97601 |
| La Grande | Pitcher Inn B&B, 608 "N" Ave., 97850, 503-963-9152 |
| La Pine | Big Blue House B&B, 53223 Riverview Dr., 97739, 503-536-3879 |
| Lafayette | Kelty Estate B&B, P.O. Box 817, 97127 |
| Leaburg | Marjon B&B Inn, 44975 Leaburg Dam Rd., 97489, 503-896-3145 |
| Leaburg | Marjon Bed & Breakfast Inn, 44975 Leaburg Dam Rd., 97489, 503-896-3145 |
| Lebanon | Historical Booth House, 486 Park St., 97355, 503-258-2954 |
| Lincoln City | Beach Retreat, 1736 N.W. 37th, 97367 |
| Lincoln City | Enchanted Cottage, The, 4507 SW Coast, 97367, 530-996-4101 |
| Lincoln City | Palmer House B&B Inn, 646 NW Inlet, 97367, 503-994-7932 |
| Lincoln City | Rustic Inn, The, 2313 NE Holmes Rd., 97367, 503-994-5111 |
| Lincoln City | Spyglass Inn B&B, 2510 S.W. Dune, 97367, 503-994-2785 |
| Lincoln City | Young's B&B, 3848 NW Lee Ave., 97367, 503-944-6575 |
| Manzanita | Arbors at Manzanita, P.O. Box 68, 97130 |

| | |
|---|---|
| Maupin | C&J Lodge & B&B, P.O. Box 130, 97037, 503-395-2404 |
| McMinnville | Baker Street B&B Inn, 129 S. Baker St., 97128,  503-472-5575 |
| McMinnville | Garden Cottage B&B, 935 Yamhill St., 97128,  503-434-5523 |
| McMinnville | Mattey House B&B, 10221 NE Mattey Ln., 97128 |
| McMinnville | Orchard View Inn, 16540 N.W. Orchard View, 97128,  503-472-0165 |
| McMinnville | Youngberg Hill Farm B&B, 10660 Youngberg Hill Rd, 97128,  503-472-2727 |
| Medford | Cedar Lodge Motor Inn, 518 N. Riverside, 97501,  503-773-7361 |
| Medford | Nendels Inn, 2300 Crater Lake Hwy., 97504,  503-779-3141 |
| Medford | Petera Ahn Reuthlinger, 7770 Griffin Creek Rd., 97501,  503-535-7423 |
| Medford | Under the Greenwood Tree, 3045 Bellinger Ln., 97501, 503-776-0000 |
| Medford | Waverly Cottage, 305 N. Grape, 97501,  503-779-4716 |
| Mill City | Ivy Creek B&B, P.O. Box 757, 97360,  503-897-2001 |
| Milton | Birch Tree Manor B&B, 615 S. Main St., Hwy 11, 97862,  503-938-6455 |
| Milwaukie | Broetiea House, 3101 S.E. Courtney Rd., 97222,  503-659-8860 |
| Monmouth | Howell's B&B, 212 N. Knox, 97361,  503-847-5523 |
| Myrtle Creek | Sonka's Sheep Station Inn, 901 NW Chadwick Ln., 97457,  503-863-5168 |
| Newberg | Belanger's Secluded B&B, 19719 NE Williamson Rd., 97132 |
| Newberg | Owl's View B&B, 29585 NE Owls Ln., 97132,  503-538-6498 |
| Newberg | Secluded B&B, 19719 NE Williamson Rd., 97132,  503-538-2635 |
| Newberg | Smith House B&B, 415 N. College St., 97132 |
| Newberg | Springbrook Hazenut Farm, 30295 Hwy. 99W, 97132,  503-538-4606 |
| Newport | Sea Cliff B&B, 749 NW 3rd, 97365,  503-265-6664 |
| Newport | Sylvia Beach Hotel, 267 N.W. Cliff St., 97365,  503-265-5428 |
| North Bend | 2310 Lombard B&B, 2310 Lombard St., 97459, 503-756-3857 |
| North Bend | Itty Bitty Inn, 1504 Sherman Ave., 97459,  503-756-6398 |
| North Bend | Sherman House B&B, 2380 Sherman Ave., 97459,  503-756-3496 |
| Oakland | Beckley House B&B, P.O. Box 198, 97462, 503-459-9320 |
| Oceanside | Three Capes B&B, 1685 Maxwell Mnt. Rd., 97134,  503-842-6126 |
| Oregon City | Fellows House, 416 S. McLoughlin, 97045,  503-656-2089 |
| Oregon City | Hydrangea B&B, 716 Center St., 97045 |
| Oregon City | Jagger House B&B, 512 Sixth St., 97045,  503-657-7820 |
| Oregon City | Tolle House, 15921 Hunter Ave., 97045,  503-655-4325 |
| Otis | Salmon River B&B, 5622 Salmon River Hwy, 97368,  503-994-2639 |
| Parkdale | Mt. Hood B&B, 8885 Cooper Spur Rd., 97041 |
| Pendelton | Graham's B&B, 704 S. Main St., 97801,  503-278-1743 |
| Pendelton | Swift Station Inn B&B, 602 SE Byers, 97801,  503-276-3739 |
| Portland | A Tudor House, 2321 NE 28th Ave., 97212,  503-287-9476 |
| Portland | Clinkerbrick House, 2311 N.E. Schuyler, 97212,  503-281-2533 |
| Portland | Gedney Gardens, 2651 NW Cornell Rd., 97210 |
| Portland | Georgian House B&B, 1828 NE Siskiyou, 97212,  503-281-2250 |
| Portland | Hampshire House B&B, 10 NE 24th Ave., 97232,  503-370-7081 |
| Portland | Heron Haus, 2545 NW Westover Rd., 97210,  503-274-1846 |
| Portland | MacMaster House B&B Inn, 1041 SW Vista Ave., 97205,  503-223-7362 |
| Portland | Pittock Acres B&B, 103 NW Pittock Ave., 97210,  503-226-1163 |
| Portland | Portland's White House, 1914 NE 22nd, 97212,  503-287-7131 |
| Portland | Sauvie Island B&B, 26504 NW Reeder Rd., 97231 |
| Portland | Sullivan's Gulch B&B, 1744 NE Clackamas St., 97232 |
| Portland | Terwilliger Vista House, 515 SW Westwood Dr., 97201,  503-244-0602 |
| Portland | Westlund's River's Edge, 22502 NW Gillihan Rd., 97213,  503-621-9856 |
| Roseburg | Hokanson's Guest House, 848 SE Jackson, 97470,  503-672-2632 |
| Roseburg | Thee Manor B&B, 927 S.E. Mill St., 97470,  503-672-9545 |
| Roseburg | Umpqua House, The, 7338 Oakhill Rd, 97470,  503-459-4700 |
| Roseburg | Woods B&B, The, 428 Oakview Dr., 97470,  503-672-2927 |
| Salem | Cottonwood Cottage B&B, 960 E. Street NE, 97301 |
| Salem | Eagle Crest B&B, 4401 Eagle Crest NW, 97304 |
| Salem | Harbison House, 1845 Commercial S.E., 97302,  503-581-8118 |
| Salem | State House B&B, 2146 State St., 97301,  503-588-1340 |
| Sandy | Auberge des Fleurs, 39391 SE Lusted Rd., 97055, 503-663-9449 |
| Scio | Wesley House, 38791 Hwy 226, 97374,  503-394-3210 |
| Seal Rock | Blackberry Inn B&B, P.O. Box 188, 97376,  503-563-2259 |
| Seaside | 10th Ave. Inn B&B, 125-10th Ave., 97138,  503-738-0643 |
| Seaside | Anderson's Boarding House, P.O. Box 573, 97138 |
| Seaside | Beachwood, 671 Beach Dr., 97138,  503-738-9585 |
| Seaside | Boarding House, 208 N. Holladay Dr., 97138,  503-738-9055 |
| Seaside | Chocolates for Breakfast, 606 N. Holiday, 97138,  503-738-3622 |
| Seaside | Custer House, 811 First Ave., 97138,  503-738-7825 |
| Seaside | Gilbert House, 341 Beach Dr., 97138, 503-738-9770 |
| Seaside | Rita Mae's B&B, 486 Necanicum Dr., 97138,  503-738-8800 |
| Seaside | Riverside Inn B&B, 430 S. Holladay Dr., 97138,  503-738-8254 |
| Seaside | Sand Dollar Inn, 606 N. Holladay Dr., 97138 |
| Seaside | Summer House, 1221 N. Franklin, 97138 |
| Seaside | Victoriana B&B, 606 12th Ave., 97138,  503-738-8449 |
| Seaside | Walker House, 811 First Ave., 97138,  503-738-5520 |
| Sheridan | Thre'Pence B&B, 27175 SW Frys Lane, 97378,  503-843-4984 |
| Silverton | Abiqua Creek Farms B&B, 11672 Nusom Rd., 97381 |
| Silverton | Egg Cup Inn B&B, The, 11920 Sioux St., 97381 |
| Sisters | Lake Creek Lodge, Star Route, 97759,  503-595-6331 |
| Spray | Pioneer B&B, Star Route, 97874,  503-462-3934 |

| | |
|---|---|
| St Helens | Hopkins House B&B, 105 S. First St., 97051, 503-397-4676 |
| Stayton | Gardner House B&B, 633 N. 3rd Ave., 97383 |
| Stayton | Horncroft, 42156 Kingston-Lyons Dr, 97383, 503-769-6287 |
| Sublimity | Silver Mountain B&B, 4672 Drift Creek Rd. SE, 97447 |
| The Dalles | Bigelow B&B, 308 E. Fourth St., 97058, 503-298-8239 |
| The Dalles | Williams House Inn, 608 W. 6th St., 97058, 503-296-2889 |
| Tualatin | Stafford Road Country Inn, 22262 SW Stafford Rd., 97062 |
| Vida | Eagle Rock Lodge, 49198 McKenzie Hwy., 97488, 503-822-3962 |
| Vida | McKenzie River Inn, 49164 McKenzie Hwy, 97488, 503-822-6260 |
| Waldport | Colleen's Country B&B, 1806 Lucy Lane, 97394, 503-563-3201 |
| Wallowa | McCrae House, 71031 Whiskey Creek Rd., 97885, 503-886-4352 |
| Welches | Mountain Shadows B&B, Box 147, 97067, 503-622-4746 |
| Welches | Old Welches Inn B&B, 26401 E. Welches Rd., 97067 |
| Westfir | Westfir Lodge B&B Inn, 47365 First St., 97492, 503-782-3103 |
| Wolf Creek | Valley Creek Cottage, 4231 Placer Rd/Box 124, 97497 |
| Wolf Creek | Wolf Creek Tavern, P.O. Box 97, 97497, 503-866-2474 |
| Woodburn | Carriage House, The, 515 S. Pacific Hwy., 97071, 503-982-6321 |
| Yachats | Adobe, 97498, 503-547-3141 |
| Yachats | Amaroo Inn B&B, P.O. Box 597, 97498, 503-547-3639 |
| Yachats | Bird's Nest Inn B&B, 97498, 503-547-3683 |
| Yachats | Kittiwake, The, 95368 Highway 101, 97498, 503-547-4470 |
| Yachats | Sanderling B&B, The, 7304 SW Pac. Coast Hwy., 97498 |
| Yachats | Sea Quest B&B, P.O. Box 448, 97498, 541-547-3782 |
| Yachats | Serenity B&B, 5985 Yachats River Rd., 97498, 503-547-3813 |
| Yachts | Ziggurat B&B, P.O. Box 757, 97498, 503-547-3925 |

# Pennsylvania

## ADAMSTOWN

**Adamstown Inn**
P.O. Box 938,   19501
62 W. Main St.
717-484-0800  800-594-4808
Tom & Wanda Berman
All year

$$-B&B
8 rooms, 5 pb
MC, Visa, *Rated*, •
C-ltd/S-ltd/P-no/H-no

Continental plus bkfst.
Afternoon tea, snacks
Sitting room, fireplaces
jacuzzis in 3 rooms
public tennis and pool

*Small charming Victorian inn in the antique district & Pennsylvania Dutch countryside. Minutes from Reading/Lancaster factory outlets. Morning coffee/tea.* **7th night free.**

## AIRVILLE

**Spring House**
1264 Muddy Crk Forks Rd,
17302
717-927-6906
Ray Constance Hearne
All year

$$-B&B
5 rooms, 3 pb
•
C-yes/S-no/P-no/H-yes
Spanish

Full breakfast
Comp. wine, tea, cookies
Sitting room, piano
bicycles, meadows
creek swimming

*18th-century stone house in river valley settlement near Lancaster, York. Feather beds, gourmet country breakfast, vegetarian avail. Hiking, fishing, wineries.* **3rd night 50%, except holiday weekends.**

## AKRON

**Springhouse Inn B&B**
806 New St.,   17501
717-859-4202
Ray & Shirley Smith
All year

$$-B&B
4 rooms, 2 pb
Visa, MC,
C-ltd/S-no/P-no/H-no

Full breakfast
Snacks
Sitting room, library
perennial & herb gardens

*18th-Century farmhouse in historic Lancaster County. Breakfast by the fireplace. Cozy stenciled rooms with queen beds. Spacious grounds with spring house.*

## ALLENTOWN

**Coachaus Inn**
107-111 N. Eighth St.,   18101
610-821-4854  Fax: 610-821-6862
800-762-8680
Barbara Kocher
All year

$$$-B&B
24 rooms, 24 pb
Most CC, *Rated*, •
C-ltd/S-ltd/P-ltd/H-no

Full breakfast
Complimentary wine
Sitting room
TV, room phones
air conditioning, Fax

*Graciously restored & appointed; blessed w/amenities of the finest hotels. Fine dining, shops, theater nearby. 2 & 3 bedroom units with private baths & full kitchens*

**Hamilton House B&B**
22 S. 18th St.,   18104
610-433-3919
Richard & Clare Butcher
All year

$$-B&B
4 rooms, 1 pb
•
C-yes/S-ltd/P-ltd/H-no
French

Full or Continental
 breakfast
Catered lunch & dinner
Afternoon tea, snacks
sitting room, library

*Cozy yet elegant Federal-style house in historic "Mansion Row" near downtown. Beautiful, safe, fully-equipped Dorney Park next door. **Special weekly & monthly rates.***

## AVELLA

**Weatherbury Farm**
1061 Sugar Camp Rd.,   15312
412-587-3763  Fax: 412-587-0125
Dale, Marcy & Nigel Tudor
All year

$$-B&B
4 rooms, 4 pb
Visa, MC,
C-yes/S-ltd/P-no/H-no
German

Full breakfast
Snacks
Sitting room, library
bicycles, swimming pool

*1860s farmhouse on working farm. Meadows and gardens. Spectacular views. Perfect getaway from everyday pressures. Bountiful farm breakfast. Convenient to Pittsburgh.*

## BELLEFONTE

**Reynolds Mansion**
1101 W. Linn St.,   16823
814-353-8407  800-899-3929
Joseph & Charlotte Heidt
All year

$$$-B&B
3 rooms, 3 pb
Visa, MC, •
C-ltd/S-ltd/P-no/H-no

Full breakfast
Complimentary brandy
Sitting room, library
bikes, billiards room
jacuzzi, fireplaces

*Beautiful Victorian mansion - perfect for romantic getaways! Rooms with jacuzzis and fireplaces; billiards room. Near Penn State and I-80. Steam shower in rooms.*

## BIRD-IN-HAND

**Village Inn Bird-in-Hand**
Box 253,   17505
2695 Old Philadel. Pike
717-293-8369  Fax: 717-768-1511
800-914-2473
Richmond & Janice Young
All year

$$-B&B
11 rooms, 11 pb
Most CC, *Rated*, •
C-yes/S-ltd/P-no/H-no

Continental plus bkfst.
Evening snacks
Sitting room
Dutch Country bus tour
hot tubs in 2 suites

*Beautifully restored historic inn located in Pennsylvania Dutch Country. Country setting. Victorian-style architecture and furnishings. Individually decorated deluxe rooms.*

## BLOOMSBURG

**Inn at Turkey Hill, The**
991 Central Rd.,   17815
717-387-1500  Fax: 717-784-3718
Andrew B. Pruden
All year

$$$-B&B
18 rooms, 18 pb
Most CC, *Rated*, •
C-yes/S-yes/P-yes/H-yes

Continental full bkfst.
Sunday brunch, dinner
Bar, vegetarian also
library, fax machine
tennis courts nearby

*Nestled amid Pennsylvania's rolling hills & farmlands, the inn extends warmth, comfort, charm & hospitality. The inn is, as one guest says, "an unexpected find." AAA 4-diamond*

## BOYERTOWN

| | | |
|---|---|---|
| **Twin Turrets Inn, The** | $$$-B&B | Full breakfast |
| 11 E. Philadelphia Ave., | 10 rooms, 10 pb | Aftn. tea, snacks |
| 19512 | Most CC, *Rated*, • | Comp. wine |
| 610-367-4513  Fax: 610-369-7898 | S-no/P-no/H-no | library |
| Marianne Renninger | | |
| All year | | |

*This restored Boyer mansion celebrates you! Internationally recognized as the home-away-from-home to the corporate and pleasure traveler.*

## CANADENSIS

| | | |
|---|---|---|
| **Brookview Manor B&B Inn** | $$$-B&B | Full breakfast |
| Rt. 447, RR 1, Box 365,  18325 | 10 rooms, 10 pb | Afternoon tea, snacks |
| 717-595-2451  Fax: 717-595-2065 | Most CC, *Rated*, • | Sitting room, library |
| 800-585-7974 | C-ltd/S-ltd/P-no/H-no | pool table, ping pong |
| Maryanne Buckley   All year | | lawn games, waterfall |

*On 400 picturesque acres, wrap-around porch, panoramic view of the forest. Hiking trails, golf, skiing, excellent dining nearby. 2 rooms w/jacuzzi tubs and 1 room w/ fireplace.*

| | | |
|---|---|---|
| **Pine Knob Inn** | $$$-B&B/MAP | Full breakfast |
| P.O. Box 295,  18325 / Rt. 447 | 27 rooms, 18 pb | Dinner included, bar |
| 717-595-2532  Fax: 717-595-6429 | MC, Visa, *Rated*, • | Sitting room, tennis |
| 800-426-1460 | C-ltd/S-no/P-no/H-no | Steinway grand piano |
| Cheryl & John Garman | | swimming pool, hiking |
| All year | | |

*The inn is in a lovely country setting in the Pocono Mountains. Antiques and art abound. Nightly turndown service. Best of all, the food is scrumptious.* **3rd night $99, MAP rates, ltd.**

## CHADDS FORD

| | | |
|---|---|---|
| **Hedgerow B&B** | $$$-B&B | Continental plus bkfst. |
| 268 Kennett Pike, Rt. 52, | 3 rooms, 3 pb | Aftn. tea, snacks |
| 19317 | • | Bar service |
| 610-388-6080  Fax: 610-388-6080 | C-ltd/S-no/P-no/H-no | sitting room, library |
| Barbara & John Haedrich | | horseback riding |
| All year | | |

*Between Longwood and Winterthur, beautifully restored separate Carriage House. Three luxurious, quiet, suites. Private baths, central A/C. Best location.* **Pkg. for museums, restaurants, attractions.**

## CHAMBERSBURG

| | | |
|---|---|---|
| **Shultz Victorian Mansion** | $$-B&B | Full breakfast |
| 756 Philadelphia Ave.,  17201 | 9 rooms, 9 pb | Sitting room |
| 717-263-3371  800-804-0826 | Visa, MC, *Rated*, | large lawn |
| Joe & Doris Shultz   All year | C-ltd/S-no/P-no/H-no | Victorian gardens |

*Charming 1880 historic home, elaborate wood carving throughout; furnished with antiques, A/C, beautiful gardens and lawn, near Gettysburg and ski slope.* **Free drinks on arrival.**

## CHURCHTOWN

| | | |
|---|---|---|
| **Churchtown Inn B&B** | $$-B&B | Full 5-course breakfast |
| 2100 Main St.,  17555 | 8 rooms, 6 pb | Dinner with Amish family |
| 717-445-7794 | AmEx, MC, Visa, | Glass garden room, piano |
| H. & S. Smith, J. Kent | *Rated*, • | game rm., carriage house |
| All year | C-ltd/S-ltd/P-no | theme weekends |
| | German | |

*In the heart of Pennsylvania Dutch country. Historic circa 1735 stone federal colonial. Antiquing, farm markets and outlets. On National Historic Register.* **7th night free.**

COLUMBIA ——————————————————————

**Columbian, A B&B Inn, The**
360 Chestnut St., 17512
717-684-5869 800-422-5869
Chris & Becky Will
All year

$$-B&B
6 rooms, 6 pb
MC, Visa,
C-yes/S-no/P-no/H-no

Full breakfast
Complimentary beverages
Sitting room, A/C, TVs
one room w/fireplace
Winter Getaway Package

*1897 brick Colonial Revival mansion in historic river town. Near antiques, restaurants, art galleries, museums and outlets. Ice cream parlor on premises. **Restaurant disc'ts.***

COOKSBURG ——————————————————————

**Gateway Lodge & Restaurant**
Route 36 Box 125, 16217
Cook Forest
814-744-8017  Fax: 814-744-8017
800-843-6862
Jos. & Linda Burney  All year

$$$-B&B/EP/MAP
8 rooms, 3 pb
*Rated*,
C-ltd/S-yes/P-ltd/H-ltd

Full breakfast
Snacks, lunch/din. (fee)
Piano, buggy rides
sitting room, hot tubs
heated pool, sauna

*Log cabin inn w/large stone fireplace. Fine dining by lantern light. Hand-hewn beds w/ quilts. Tea time daily 4-5 p.m. Romantic suites w/king beds, Jacuzzi, fireplace. **Amenity pkgs. available.***

CRESCO ——————————————————————

**La Anna Guesthouse**
RD 2, Box 1051, 18326
717-676-4225  Fax: 717-676-4225
Kay Swingle  All year

$-B&B
3 rooms,
C-ltd/S-yes/P-ltd/H-no

Continental plus bkfst.
Sitting room, piano
cross-country skiing
fishing, swimming, golf

*Private Victorian home nestled in Pocono Mountain village welcomes guests. Furnished with antiques. Skating ponds, waterfalls, woodland walks.*

DANVILLE ——————————————————————

**Pine Barn Inn**
#1 Pine Barn Pl., 17821
717-275-2071  Fax: 717-275-3248
800-627-2276
Martin Walzer
All year

$$-EP
75 rooms, 69 pb
Most CC, *Rated*, •
C-yes/S-yes/P-yes/H-ltd
Spanish

Full breakfast (fee)
Lunch, dinner, bar
Dining patio

*Main inn is 19th-century barn; guest rooms located in new lodge building. Located in residential part of community. Especially popular locally for fine food.*

DOYLESTOWN ——————————————————————

**Sign of The Sorrel Horse**
4424 Old Easton Rd., 18901
215-230-9999  Fax: 215-230-8053
800-282-5289
M. Gaumont-Lanvin, J. Atkin
All year

$$$-B&B/EP
5 rooms, 5 pb
AmEx, MC, Visa,
*Rated*,
C-ltd/S-no/P-yes/H-no
French, German

Continental breakfast
Restaurant, bar, dinner
Comp. sherry & fruits
sitting room, bicycles
meeting room for parties

*Built in 1714 as a gristmill, in the heart of Bucks County—now a gracious historic inn. Fine gourmet dining. Garden weddings a specialty. **Weekday upgrade.***

EAGLES MERE ——————————————————————

**Eagles Mere Inn**
1 Mary Ave., 17731
717-525-3273  800-426-3273
S. & P. Glaubitz, G. Adams
All year

$$$$-MAP
17 rooms, 17 pb
MC, Visa, *Rated*, •
C-yes/S-ltd/P-no/H-ltd

Full breakfast
5-course dinner incl.
Bar, sitting room
tennis, swimming
golf, skiing, hunting

*Charming country inn located in a quiet Victorian town high in the Endless Mountains. Superb food & wine list. Beautiful lake with sandy beach nearby. Undisturbed nature. Conference facilities.*

## EAGLES MERE

| **Shady Lane B&B** | $$-B&B | Full breakfast |
|---|---|---|
| P.O. Box 314,  17731 | 8 rooms, 8 pb | Comp. wine, aftn. tea |
| Allegheny Ave. | *Rated*, • | Two sitting rooms |
| 717-525-3394  800-524-1248 | C-ltd/S-no/P-no/H-yes | tennis court, lake |
| Pat & Dennis Dougherty | | golf, skiing, ice skate |
| All year | | |

*Picturesque mountaintop resort near hiking, swimming, fishing, skiing & tobogganing. Eagles Mere: "the town time forgot." Summer craft & antique shops.* **3rd night 50% off.**

## EAST PETERSBURG

| **George Zahm House B&B** | $$-B&B | Continental plus |
|---|---|---|
| 6070 Main St.,  17520 | 4 rooms, 4 pb | Afternoon tea, snacks |
| 717-569-6026 | Visa, MC, | Sitting room |
| Robyn Kemple-Keeports | C-ltd/S-no/P-no | |
| All year | | |

*Restored federal period home in Lancaster County-richly decorated-furnished with antiques and family heirlooms-breakfast in formal dining room.* **Senior and extended stay discount.**

## EAST STROUDSBURG

| **Inn at Meadowbrook, The** | $$-B&B | Full breakfast |
|---|---|---|
| RD 7, Box 7651,  18301 | 18 rooms, 12 pb | Dinner |
| 717-629-0296  Fax: 717-620-1754 | MC, Visa, *Rated*, • | Sitting room, swimmimg |
| 800-249-6861 | C-ltd/S-yes/P-no/H-no | pool, hoseback riding |
| Bob & Kathy Overman | | tennis,bicycles, fishing |
| All year | | |

*Forty acres of meadows and woods located in the heart of the Poconos. Close to skiing and major attractions.* **Midweek, non-holiday: 3rd night free.**

## ELIZABETHTOWN

| **West Ridge Guest House** | $$-B&B | Full breakfast |
|---|---|---|
| 1285 West Ridge Rd.,  17022 | 9 rooms, 9 pb | Hot tubs |
| 717-367-7783  Fax: 717-367-8468 | AmEx, MC, Visa, | TV, phones |
| Alice Heisey | *Rated*, • | tennis court |
| All year | C-ltd/S-no/P-no | |

*Country setting. Each room decorated in a different decor. Some rooms with decks and fireplaces. Fishing pond.*

## EPHRATA

| **Clearview Farm B&B** | $$$-B&B | Full breakfast |
|---|---|---|
| 355 Clearview Rd.,  17522 | 5 rooms, 5 pb | Tastefully decorated |
| 717-733-6333 | Most CC, *Rated*, | rooms with antiques |
| All year | C-ltd/S-no/P-no/H-no | |

*Located on 200 acres of peaceful farmland-old limestone restored house, manicured lawn, lots of flowers, pond graced with swans. 4 excellent restaurants within 5 minutes.*

| **Inns at Doneckers, The** | $$-B&B | Continental plus buffet |
|---|---|---|
| 251,318-324 N.State St., 409 N. | 31 rooms, 29 pb | Restaurant |
| State St.,  17522 | Most CC, *Rated*, • | Comp. tea, jacuzzis, TV |
| 717-738-9502  Fax: 717-738-9554 | C-yes/S-yes/P-no/H-yes | sitting room, library |
| Linda Bobonich | | porch, Farmer's Market |
| All year | | |

*Unique getaway w/country simplicity & genteel luxury. Elegance w/antiques & folk art; fine dining, splendid shopping. 2 carriage suites, decks. Conference facilities.*

EPHRATA ————————————————————————————————

**Martin House**
265 Ridge Ave., 17522
717-733-6804  888-651-8418
Vera & Moses Martin
All year

$$-B&B
4 rooms, 3 pb
C-yes/S-no/P-no/H-no

Full breakfast
Snacks
Sitting room
hot tubs
efficiency sleeps 6

*Traditional home on wooded hillside near town and major highways. Quiet surroundings. Beautiful area.* **10% discount, 3 or more nights.**

**Smithton Inn, The**
900 W. Main St., 17522
717-733-6094
Dorothy Graybill
All year

$$-B&B
9 rooms, 9 pb
MC, Visa, *Rated*,
C-ltd/S-no/P-ltd/H-ltd

Full breakfast
Comp. tea, snacks
Sitting room, fireplaces
whirlpool baths, gardens
library, canopy beds

*Picturesque 1763 Penn. Dutch Country Inn. Fireplaces in parlor, dining and guest rooms. Chamber music; canopy four-poster beds, refrigerator, quilts and candles in each room.*

ERWINNA ————————————————————————————————

**Evermay on-the-Delaware**
P.O. Box 60, 18920
Headwaters & River Rds.
610-294-9100  Fax: 610-294-8249
William & Danielle Moffly
All year exc. Dec 24

$$$-B&B
16 rooms, 16 pb
MC, Visa, •
C-ltd/S-ltd/P-no/H-yes

Continental plus bkfst.
Comp. sherry in parlor
Cordial in rm., bar, tea
restaurant (weekends)
sitting room, piano

*Romantic Victorian inn on 25 acres of gardens, woodlawn paths and pastures. Elegant dinner served Friday-Sunday & holidays. Rooms face the picturesque Delaware River.*

**Golden Pheasant Inn**
763 River Rd. (Rt. 32), 18920
610-294-9595
Barbara J. Faure
All year

$$$-B&B
5 rooms, 1 pb
MC, Visa, *Rated*,
C-ltd/S-ltd/P-no
French, Spanish, Italian

Continental breakfast
Dinner (Tues.—Sun.)
Restaurant, bar, canoes
Delaware Canal & River
wine in room, solarium

*1857 fieldstone inn situated between river and canal. Five rooms furnished with incredible blend of antiques. Quiet. Plant-filled solarium for romantic candlelight dining.*

FOGELSVILLE ————————————————————————————————

**Glasbern**
Box 250 Rd 1, 2141 Pack
House Rd., 18051
610-285-4723
Beth & Al Granger
All year

$$$-MAP
23 rooms, 23 pb
Visa, MC, *Rated*,
C-ltd/S-yes/P-no/H-yes

Full breakfast
Dinner, restaurant
Bar service
bicycles, hot tubs
swimming pool

*At Glasbern, guests feel completely removed from civilization. Here, one can savor views of trout ponds and a sparkling stream, as horses gambol in the gently rolling fields.*

FRANKLIN ————————————————————————————————

**Quo Vadis B&B**
1501 Liberty St., 16323
814-432-4208  800-360-6598
Cherie & David
All year

$$-B&B
6 rooms, 6 pb
Visa, MC, AmEx,
*Rated*, •
C-yes/S-no/P-no/H-no

Full breakfast
Sitting room, library
near hiking, canoeing,
museums, restaurants

*1867 Queen Anne, elegant Victorian, 6 guestrooms each w/private bath. Heirloom antiques. Discover history, architecture & recreational variety in the Allegheny River Valley.*

GAP ───────────────────────────────────

| | | |
|---|---|---|
| **Fassitt Mansion B&B** | $$$-B&B | Full country breakfast |
| 6051 Philadelphia Pike, | 5 rooms, 5 pb | Coffee, tea, pies, cakes |
| 17527 | Visa, MC, *Rated*, • | Sitting room w/fireplace |
| 717-442-3139 | C-ltd/S-no/P-no/H-no | TV room, bicycle tours |
| Bill & Patricia Collins | | dinner w/Amish Family |
| All year | | |

*Romantic 1845 country mansion with 12 foot ceilings & antiques conveniently located in Lancaster County, easy access to all Amish attractions. **3rd night, 50%.***

GETTYSBURG ───────────────────────────

| | | |
|---|---|---|
| **Brafferton Inn, The** | $$-B&B | Full breakfast |
| 44 York St., 17325 | 10 rooms, 10 pb | Coffee, tea |
| 717-337-3423 | Most CC, *Rated*, • | Library, atrium, piano |
| Jane & Sam Back | C-ltd/S-no/P-no/H-yes | hat collection, old mags |
| All year | | primitive mural |

*Stone and clapboard inn circa 1786 near the center square of Gettysburg. The rooms have stenciled designs, antiques. Walk to battlefield and restaurants.*

---

| | | |
|---|---|---|
| **Doubleday Inn, The** | $$$-B&B | Full breakfast |
| 104 Doubleday Ave., 17325 | 9 rooms, 5 pb | Afternoon tea, snacks |
| 717-334-9119 | Visa, MC, Disc. *Rated*, | Sitting room |
| Charles & Ruth Anne Wilcox | • | battlefield guide |
| All year | C-ltd/S-no/P-no/H-no | presentations |

*The only inn directly on Gettysburg Battlefield. Cozy antiques, Civil War accents and splendid views. Discussion of Battle of Gettysburg with knowledgeable battlefield historians on selected days.*

---

| | | |
|---|---|---|
| **Hickory Bridge Farm** | $$$-B&B | Full breakfast |
| 96 Hickory Bridge Rd., | 7 rooms, 6 pb | Fri, Sat., Sun. dinner |
| Orrtanna, 17353 | MC, Visa, *Rated*, | Sitting room, fireplces |
| 717-642-5261 | C-ltd/S-yes/P-no/H-no | bicycles, fishing |
| Robert & Mary Lynn Martin | | 8 miles from Gettysburg |
| All year | | |

*Relax in the country by enjoying a cozy cottage by the stream, a hearty breakfast at the farmhouse, and dine in restored PA barn during the weekends. Innkeeping for 25 years.*

---

| | | |
|---|---|---|
| **Keystone Inn B&B** | $$-B&B | Full breakfast from menu |
| 231 Hanover St., 17325 | 5 rooms, 5 pb | Lemonade, coffee, tea |
| 717-337-3888 | MC, Visa, | Sitting room, library |
| Doris Martin | C-yes/S-ltd/P-no | suite w/TV, microwave & |
| All year | | refrig. tennis nearby |

*Unique decor, antiques and lots of natural chestnut and oak; comfort our priority. Area rich in history; antique lover's paradise. Country breakfast. **Weekday 4 nights, pay for 3.***

---

| | | |
|---|---|---|
| **Old Appleford Inn, The** | $$$-B&B | Full breakfast |
| 218 Carlisle St., 17325 | 10 rooms, 10 pb | Aftn. tea, snacks, wine |
| 717-337-1711  Fax: 717-334-6228 | Most CC, *Rated*, • | Sitting room, library |
| 800-275-3373 | C-ltd/S-no/P-no/H-ltd | grand piano |
| John & Jane Wiley | | |
| All year | | |

*1867 elegant Victorian mansion/antiques. 2 blocks from town square, 1 block from college; delicious full breakfast; fireplaces, candlelight, canopies. **3rd nite 50% off.***

## GETTYSBURG

| | | |
|---|---|---|
| **Tannery B&B, The** | $$-B&B | Continental plus bkfst. |
| 449 Baltimore St.,   17325 | 9 rooms, 9 pb | Complimentary wine/snack |
| 717-334-2454  Fax: 717-337-2138 | MC, Visa, *Rated*, | Sitting room, library |
| Deb & Charlie Raffensperger | C-ltd/S-no/P-no/H-no | rocking chairs on |
| All year | | front porch, golf nearby |

*Built in 1868 Gothic structure, The Tannery is within walking distance of historical sites, museums, restaurants. 7 rooms with private baths, 2 suites.* **15% winter discount.**

## GORDONVILLE

| | | |
|---|---|---|
| **Osceola Mill House** | $$$-B&B | Full gourmet breakfast |
| 313 Osceola Mill Rd.,   17529 | 4 rooms, 2 pb | Comp. beverages |
| 717-768-3758 | • | Sitting room |
| Robin & Sterling Schoen | C-ltd/S-no/P-no/H-no | bicycles nearby |
| Exc. Christmas & Easter | German | fireplaces, antiques |

*Classic 1766 Georgian limestone mansion in historic setting on quiet country lane, surrounded by Amish farms. Furnished w/canopy beds & antiques. Featured in Country Living.*

## GREENCASTLE

| | | |
|---|---|---|
| **Welsh Run Inn B&B** | $$-B&B | Full breakfast |
| 11299 Welsh Run Rd.,   17225 | 3 rooms, 1 pb | Afternoon tea, snacks |
| 717-328-9506 | Visa, MC, Amex, • | Dinner reservations |
| Bob & Ellie Neff | C-yes/S-ltd/P-no/H-no | at local pub, comp. wine |
| All year | | Sitting room, ski nearby |

*Lovely Victorian home in historic Pennsylvania village. Full breakfast by candlelight in formal, hand stenciled dining room. Relaxed, comfortable atmosphere.*

## GREENSBURG

| | | |
|---|---|---|
| **Huntland Farm B&B** | $$$-B&B | Full breakfast |
| RD 9, Box 21,   15601 | 4 rooms, | Afternoon tea |
| 412-834-8483  Fax: 412-838-8253 | AmEx, • | Sitting room |
| Robert & Elizabeth Weidlein | C-ltd/S-ltd/P-no/H-no | screened porch |
| All year | French | |

*1848 house furnished with antiques and surrounded by gardens. Close to Laurel Highlands area. Good restaurants and antique stores nearby.*

## HANOVER

| | | |
|---|---|---|
| **Beechmont Inn** | $$$-B&B | Full breakfast |
| 315 Broadway,   17331 | 7 rooms, 7 pb | Snacks |
| 717-632-3013  800-553-7009 | Most CC, *Rated*, • | Afternoon tea |
| William & Susan Day | C-ltd/S-no/P-no/H-no | sitting room, library |
| All year | | honeymoon/golf packages |

*Federal period elegance; echoes of Civil War memories; a refuge from the 20th century rush–a bridge across time. Near Gettysburg, antiquing. Whirlpool tub, fireplace avail.*

## HAWLEY

| | | |
|---|---|---|
| **Academy Street B&B** | $$-B&B | Full breakfast buffet |
| 528 Academy St.,   18428 | 7 rooms, 4 pb | Comp. wine, coffee, cake |
| 717-226-3430  Fax: 201-335-5051 | Visa, • | Afternoon tea |
| Judith & Sheldon Lazan | C-ltd/S-yes/P-no/H-no | sitting room, TV |
| May–October | | A/C in rooms |

*Magnificent Victorian in Poconos near Lake Wallenpaupack. European gourmet breakfast, afternoon coffee and cheesecake. Near restaurants, all activities.*

HAWLEY ───────────────────────────────────────────────

**Settlers Inn, The**        $$-B&B              Full breakfast
4 Main Ave., 18428           18 rooms, 18 pb     Lunch, dinner, bar
717-226-2993 Fax: 717-226-1874  Most CC, *Rated*, •  Sitting room, library
800-833-8527                 C-yes/S-yes/P-ltd/H-no  phones in rooms, bikes
Grant & Jeanne Genzlinger                        tennis, piano, gift shop
All year

*Delightful country inn of Tudor architecture, with gift shops and art gallery. Lake Wallen-*
*paupack and shopping are nearby. Air conditioned rooms.* **3rd night 50% off.**

INTERCOURSE ────────────────────────────────────────

**Carriage Corner B&B**      $$-B&B              Full breakfast
P.O. Box 371, 17534          5 rooms, 5 pb       Aft. tea, use of fridge
3705 E. Newport Rd.          MC, Visa, *Rated*,  Sitting room, central AC
717-768-3059 800-209-3059    C-ltd/S-no/P-no/H-no  cable TV in rooms
Gordon & Gwen Schutt                             free attractions coupons
All year

*At the hub of the Amish area, our B&B offers a relaxing country atmosphere. Dinner with*
*an Amish family arranged. Special diets will be accommodated.* **3rd night 15% off.**

JIM THORPE ──────────────────────────────────────────

**Harry Packer Mansion, The**  $$$-B&B           Full breakfast
P.O. Box 458, 18229          13 rooms, 8 pb      Sitting room, library
Packer Hill                  MC, Visa, *Rated*, •  tennis, water sports
717-325-8566                 C-ltd/S-ltd/P-no/H-no  murder mystery weekends
Robert & Patricia Handwerk
All year

*Magnificent Victorian mansion in historic district with period furnishings, original wood-*
*work and stained glass. Gracious and friendly atmosphere with sports activities near.*

KENNETT SQUARE ─────────────────────────────────────

**Meadow Spring Farm B&B**   $$$-B&B             Full country breakfast
201 E. Street Rd., Route 926,  6 rooms, 3 pb     Dinner upon request
   19348                     AmEx, •             Comp. wine, tea, snacks
610-444-3903                 C-yes/S-yes/P-no/H-no  hot tubs, game room
Anne Hicks   All year                            pool, pond for fishing

*1836 farmhouse on working farm with sheep, pigs & cows; filled with antiques, dolls &*
*teddy bears. Full country breakfast served on porch, spacious dining room or by the pool.*

LACKAWAXEN ──────────────────────────────────────────

**Roebling Inn on Delaware**  $$-B&B             Full breakfast
P.O. Box 31, 18435           6 rooms, 6 pb       Afternoon tea
Scenic Drive                 Visa, MC, AmEx,     Sitting room, tennis
717-685-7900 Fax: 717-685-1718  C-yes/S-ltd/P-no/H-no  A/C, TV, queen beds
Don & JoAnn Jahn                                 outdoor recreation, ask
All year

*A jewel of the upper Delaware River, amid scenery to soothe the senses. Enjoy a stroll*
*through our beautiful region.* **Stay 2 nights midweek, 3rd night free.**

LAHASKA ─────────────────────────────────────────────

**Golden Plough Inn**        $$$-B&B             Continental plus bkfst.
P.O. Box 218  18931          60 rooms, 60 pb     Restaurant - all meals
Rte. 202 & Street Rd.        Most CC, *Rated*, •  Snacks, comp. champagne
215-794-4004 Fax: 215-794-4001  C-yes/S-yes/P-no/H-yes  library, some rooms with
Donna Jamison                                    fireplaces, jacuzzi tubs
All year

*Guest rooms located above shops of Peddler's Village, an attraction of 80 shops and*
*restaurants and Carousel World Museum with operating carousel.*

*The Apple Bin Inn B&B, Lancaster, PA*

## LAMPETER

| | | |
|---|---|---|
| **Australian Walkabout Inn** | $$$-B&B | Full Aussie breakfast |
| P.O. Box 294,  17537 | 5 rooms, 5 pb | Afternoon tea |
| 837 Village Rd. | AmEx, MC, Visa, | Library, antique shop |
| 717-464-0707  Fax: 717-464-2501 | *Rated*, ● | in-room whirlpool/hot tub |
| Richard & Margaret Mason | C-ltd/S-no/P-no/H-no | outdoor jacuzzi, gardens |
| All year | | |

*"This is an award winning residence. Thanks so much for a great time. We'll be back." F. Murray Abraham (Oscar for Amadeus).* ***Restaurant coupons, some free dinners.***

## LANCASTER

| | | |
|---|---|---|
| **The Apple Bin Inn B&B** | $$-B&B | Full breakfast |
| 2835 Willow St. Pike, Willow | 4 rooms, 2 pb | Afternoon tea, snacks |
| Street,  17584 | MC, Visa, *Rated*, | Sitting room, patios |
| 717-464-5881  Fax: 717-464-1818 | C-ltd/S-no/P-no/H-no | 2 story Carriage House |
| 800-338-4296 | | w/frplc., living room |
| Debbie & Barry Hershey | | |
| All year | | |

*Warm colonial charm w/country flavor. Antiques, reproductions. Near Amish community, antique & craft shops, excellent restaurants & historical sites. A/C & cable TV in rooms.*

| | | |
|---|---|---|
| **B&B—The Manor** | $$$-B&B | Full breakfast |
| 830 Village Rd,  17537 | 5 rooms, 2 pb | Lunch, dinner |
| 717-464-9564 | MC, Visa, | Snacks, sitting room |
| Jackie Curtis/MaryLou | C-yes/S-no/P-no/H-yes | A/C, swimming pool |
| Paolini | | winter & group discounts |
| All year | | |

*Cozy farmhouse centrally located in scenic Amish country. Deluxe swimming pool, full gourmet breakfast. Children welcome, group discount rates.* ***10% winter discount***.

*Gardens of Eden B&B, Lancaster, PA*

LANCASTER ─────────────────────────────────

| **Gardens of Eden B&B** | $$$-B&B | Full breakfast |
| 1894 Eden Rd., 17601 | 4 rooms, 4 pb | Amish dinners arranged |
| 717-393-5179 | Visa, MC, | Sitting room, rowboats |
| Marilyn & Bill Ebel | C-ltd/S-no/P-no/H-no | canoes, tours, tea/fruit |
| All year | | on arrival, private bath |

*Eden exists along the Conestoga River where wild flowers, herbs, and perennials bloom among the trees and lawns of this circa 1867 Iron Masters mansion.* **10% off 5 days or more.**

| **Hollinger House B&B** | $$$-B&B | Full country breakfast |
| 2336 Hollinger Rd., 17602 | 5 rooms, 5 pb | Picnic baskets |
| 717-464-3050 | Most CC, *Rated*, | Pastry, hor d'oeuvres |
| Gina & Jeff Trost | C-ltd/S-ltd/P-no/H-no | sitting room, library |
| All year | | private party site |

*Your special haven. Friendly, romantic & comfortable. 1870 Adams period brick home. Wraparound porch, lavish breakfast, near attractions.* **Seniors & extended stay discounts.**

| **King's Cottage, A B&B Inn** | $$-B&B | Full breakfast |
| 1049 E. King St., 17602 | 9 rooms, 9 pb | Afternoon tea, cordials |
| 717-397-1017  Fax: 717-397-3447 | MC, Visa, *Rated*, ● | Sitting room, library |
| 800-747-8717 | C-ltd/S-no/P-no/H-yes | water garden, Dinner w/ |
| Karen & Jim Owens | Spanish | Amish family available |
| All year | | |

*Enjoy National Register award-winning architecture & elegance. Near Amish farms, restaurants, antiques, outlets, quilts, historic sites.* **3rd night free, ltd.**

| **Lincoln Haus Inn B&B** | $$-B&B | Full breakfast (rooms) |
| 1687 Lincoln Hwy. E., 17602 | 8 rooms, 8 pb | Amish meals by my cousin |
| 717-392-9412 | *Rated*, ● | No alcohol on premises |
| Mary K. Zook | C-ltd/S-no/P-no/H-ltd | honeymoon suite avail. |
| All year | Dueisch, German | Amish crafts nearby |

*Unique suburban home, built in late 1800s, w/rooms & apts. Natural oaks woodwork, antiques. Owner is a member of the old order Amish church.* **10% discount in winter months.**

## LANCASTER

| **Maison Rouge B&B** | $$$-B&B | Full breakfast |
|---|---|---|
| P.O. Box 6243,  17607 | 4 rooms, 4 pb | Afternoon tea |
| 2236 Marietta Ave. | Visa, MC, AmEx, | Sitting room |
| 717-399-3033  800-309-3033 | C-ltd/S-no/P-no/H-no | library |
| R. Petrocci & W. Stomski | | gardens |
| All year | | |

*Romantic Victorian setting in 1882 mansion. Serving four course gourmet breakfast with antique china & crystal beneath elegant waterford chandelier.* **4th nite 50%.**

| **O'Flaherty's Dingeldein Hs** | $$-B&B | Full breakfast |
|---|---|---|
| 1105 E. King St.,  17602 | 4 rooms, 2 pb | Amish meal if reserved |
| 717-293-1723  Fax: 717-293-1947 | Visa, MC, Disc., • | Sitting room, library |
| 800-779-7765 | C-yes/S-no/P-no/H-no | Amish farmlands nearby |
| Jack & Sue Flatley | | farmers mkt, mall outlet |
| All year | | |

*For the business traveler, why spend another night in impersonal hotel room, greeted by lonely cup of coffee. Instead, join us for all the comforts of home in our home.*

| **Witmer's Tavern—1725 Inn** | $$-B&B | Continental plus bkfst. |
|---|---|---|
| 2014 Old Phila. Pike,  17602 | 4 rooms, 4 pb | Popcorn poppers |
| 717-299-5305 | Personal Checks OK, • | Antique shop, sitting rm |
| Brant E. Hartung | C-ltd/S-ltd/P-no/H-no | air field, honeymoon rm. |
| All year | | National Register |

*Lancaster's only pre-Revolutionary inn & Museum still lodging travelers. Fireplaces, antiques, quilts & fresh flowers in romantic rooms.* **8th night free.**

## LANCASTER, LEOLA

| **Millport Manor** | $$-B&B | Full breakfast |
|---|---|---|
| 924 Log Cabin Rd.,  17540 | 2 rooms, 2 pb | Snacks, comp. wine |
| 717-627-0644 | C-ltd/S-no/P-no/H-no | Sitting room, A/C and TV |
| Joy Sawyer | German | in rooms, large front |
| All year | | porch |

*Country hideaway in Amish country; antiques throughout; generous breakfast; close to historic towns, cities and Adamstown Antique Mall; maps provided.* **3rd night, 50% off.**

## LANCASTER, MANHEIM

| **Penns Valley Farm** | $$-B&B | Full breakfast |
|---|---|---|
| 6182 Metzler Rd.,  17545 | 2 rooms, 1 pb | Farmhouse |
| 717-898-7386 | Visa, MC, AmEx, | open hearth |
| Mel & Gladys Metzler | C-yes/S-no/P-no/H-no | TV, A/C |
| All year | | |

*A cozy, getaway guest house that sleeps up to seven people in beautiful Lancaster County farmland, but close to attractions.*

## LEBANON

| **Zinns Mill Homestead B&B** | $$ | Full breakfast |
|---|---|---|
| 243 N. Zinns Mill Rd.,  17042 | 4 rooms, 1 pb | Afternoon tea, snacks |
| 717-272-1513  Fax: 717-272-1513 | Visa, MC, *Rated*, | Library, bicycles |
| 800-871-1513 | C-ltd/P-no/H-no | hot tubs, swimming pool |
| Judy & Bob Heisey | | gazebo, pond, game room |
| Closed Nov.-April | | |

*Restored limestone farmhouse in the PA Dutch Country. Beautiful country setting. In room TV, swimming pool & hot tub. Handy to Hershey, Reading & Lancaster.*

*Zinn's Mill Homestead, Lebanon, PA*

## LEWISBURG

**Pineapple Inn**
439 Market St,   17837
717-524-6200
Charles & Deborah North
All year

$$-B&B
6 rooms, 2 pb
Most CC, *Rated*,
C-ltd/S-ltd/P-no/H-no
German

Full country breakfast
Comp. tea, snacks
All rooms A/C, tea room
piano, sitting room
tennis, pool nearby

*This c.1857 home of Federalist design is decorated w/period antiques. Just blocks from Bucknell University. Upside-Down Shoppe.* **10% off over 3 nights.**

## LITITZ

**Alden House**
62 E. Main St.,   17543
717-627-3363  800-584-0753
Fletcher & Joy Coleman
All year

$$$-B&B
5 rooms, 5 pb
MC, Visa, •
C-ltd/S-no/P-no/H-no

Full breakfast
Afternoon tea
Sitting room
suites with fireplaces

*1850 brick Victorian home in the heart of Pennsylvania Dutch Country. Walk to all local attractions and fine dining.*

## MANHEIM

**Rose Manor**
124 S. Linden St.,   17545
717-664-4932  Fax: 717-664-1611
800-666-4932
Susan & Anne Jenal
All year

$$-B&B
5 rooms, 4 pb
Visa, MC, •
C-ltd/S-no/P-no

Full breakfast
Aftn. tea, comp. sherry
Picnic baskets
Sitting room, gift shop
conservatory, gardens

*Lancaster County 1905 manor house. Comfortable Victorian decor & cooking reflect "herbal" theme. Near antiquing, PA Dutch attractions, Hershey.* **15% off 3rd night, ltd.**

## MARIETTA

**Noble House, The**
113 West Market St., 17547
717-426-4389 Fax: 717-426-4012
Elissa & Paul Noble
All year

$$-B&B
3 rooms, 3 pb
•
C-ltd/S-no/P-no/H-no

Full breakfast
Aftn. tea, restaurant
Sitting room, library
bicycles, conference rm.
wedding facilities

*Spend an intimate & romantic weekend in a 185-year-old Federal style home located in the historic district of Marietta. Small parties, family reunions.* **3rd night 50% off.**

## MERCER

**Magoffin Inn**
129 S. Pitt St., 16137
412-662-4611 800-841-0824
Jacque McClelland/Gene
Slagle
All year

$$-B&B
7 rooms, 7 pb
AmEx, MC, Visa,
*Rated*,
C-yes/S-no/P-no/H-no

Full breakfast
Dinner available
Cordial, snacks, library
tennis courts, pool
Amish suite w/two baths

*1884 Queen Anne Victorian. Affordable elegance in ideal location. Outdoor activities abound: boating, fishing, golf, cross-country skiing. Near I-79 and I-80.* **10% off dinner.**

## MERCERSBURG

**Mercersburg Inn, The**
405 S. Main St., 17236
717-328-5231 Fax: 717-328-3403
Walt & Sandy Filkowski
All year

$$$-B&B
15 rooms, 15 pb
MC, Visa, *Rated*, •
C-ltd/S-ltd/H-no
Spanish

Full breakfast
6-course dinner (fee)
Bar, TV in game room
golf/ski/tennis nearby
phones in all rooms

*Elegant, restored mansion in south central Pennsylvania. 90 minutes from Washington, D.C. Gourmet dining by candlelight. Handmade canopy beds, antiques & crackling fireplace.*

**Steiger House, The**
33 North Main St., 17236
717-328-5757 Fax: 717-328-5627
Ron & Nancy Snyder
All year

$$-B&B
3 rooms, 3 pb
MC, Visa, Disc.,
C-ltd/S-no/P-no/H-no

Full breakfast
Snacks, comp. wine
Sitting room
7 fireplaces
Fax available

*Circa 1820 home in historic Mercersburg, PA. Boyhood home of President James Buchanan. Nearby restaurants, White Tail ski resort, golf.* **$5.00 off on room, ask.**

## MERTZTOWN

**Longswamp B&B**
1605 State St., 19539
610-682-6197 Fax: 610-682-4854
Elsa Dimick
All year

$$$-B&B
10 rooms, 6 pb
•
C-yes/S-ltd/P-no/H-ltd
French

Full breakfast
Comp. wine, cheese, etc.
Picnics, sitting room
library, piano, bicycles
horseshoes, bocce court

*Historic country farmhouse near Amish country and skiing. Tempting delicacies prepared by area chef. Book and music collection for guests' use.* **3rd night 50% off.**

## MILFORD

**Black Walnut Country Inn**
P.O. Box 1024, 18337
RD2 Box 9285-Firetower Rd
717-296-6322 800-866-9870
Stewart Schneider
All year

$$-B&B
14 rooms, 8 pb
AmEx, MC, Visa,
*Rated*,
C-yes/S-ltd/P-no/H-no

Full breakfast
Restaurant, comp. sherry
Pool table, lawn games
piano, pond, hot tub
riding lessons, trails

*Large secluded estate for an exclusive clientele. Tudor-style stone house w/marble frplc., charming bdrms. w/antiques & brass beds. Overlooks lake. Riding stable.* **3rd nite 50%.**

MILFORD —————————————————————————————————

| **Cliff Park Inn & Golf Crs.** | $$-B&B/MAP/AP | Full breakfast |
| RR 4, Box 7200,  18337 | 18 rooms, 18 pb | Restaurant, bar |
| Cliff Park Rd. | Most CC, *Rated*,  • | Sitting room |
| 717-296-6491  Fax: 717-296-3982 | C-yes/S-yes/P-no/H-ltd | library, 8 rooms with |
| 800-225-6535 | French, Spanish | fireplace & Jacuzzi |
| Harry W. Buchanan | | |
| All year | | |

*Historic country inn surrounded by long-established golf course & school on secluded 600-acre estate. Midweek golf packages. cross-country skiing. Gourmet dining. Mobil 3-Star rating.*

| **Pine Hill Farm B&B** | $$$-B&B | Full breakfast |
| P.O. Box 1001,  18337 | 5 rooms, 5 pb | Restaurants nearby |
| Cummins Hill Rd. | Visa, Disc., *Rated*, | Sitting room, VCR |
| 717-296-7395 | C-ltd/S-ltd/P-no/H-no | color TV, A/C |
| Lynn & Bob Patton | German | trails, two streams |
| All year | | |

*Private 268-acre mountaintop estate above Delaware River. 1870s manor house; carriage house suites. Breakfast on stone terrace, or fireside. Antique shop in barn.*

MOUNT JOY ————————————————————————————————

| **Cedar Hill Farm** | $$-B&B | Continental plus bkfst. |
| 305 Longenecker Rd.,  17552 | 5 rooms, 5 pb | Central A/C, porch |
| 717-653-4655 | Most CC, *Rated*,  • | 1 room w/private balcony |
| Russel & Gladys Swarr | C-ltd/S-no/P-no/H-no | 1 room w/whirlpool tub |
| All year | | |

*Host born in this 1817 Fieldstone farmhouse. Quiet area overlooks stream. Near Lancaster's Amish country & Hershey. Near farmers' markets & quaint villages.* **Last night free w/weeks stay.**

| **Hillside Farm B&B** | $$-B&B | Full breakfast |
| 607 Eby Chiques Rd.,  17552 | 5 rooms, 3 pb | Sitting room, library |
| 717-653-6697  Fax: 717-653-5233 | *Rated*,  • | baby grand piano |
| Deb & Gary Lintner | C-ltd/S-no/P-no/H-no | barn cats, central A/C |
| All year | | |

*1863 farmhouse in Amish Country, furnished w/dairy farm antiques & milk bottles. Secluded, near creek & waterfall. Biking, hiking, outlets, antique shops, wineries.* **Discounts.**

MUNCY ——————————————————————————————————

| **Bodine House, The** | $$-B&B | Full breakfast |
| 307 S. Main St.,  17756 | 5 rooms, 5 pb | Complimentary wine |
| 717-546-8949 | Most CC, *Rated*,  • | Sitting room, library |
| David & Marie Louise Smith | C-ltd/S-no/P-no/H-yes | bicycles |
| All year | | new cottage accom. 4-6 |

*Restored townhouse circa 1805 with period antiques & reproductions. Located in Nat'l Historic District. Full breakfast served by candlelight.* **10% discount for 3+ nights.**

NEW BERLIN ————————————————————————————————

| **Inn at Olde New Berlin** | $$$-B&B | Full breakfast |
| P.O. Box 390,  17855 | 5 rooms, 5 pb | Lunch dinner available |
| 321 Market St. | Visa, MC, *Rated*, | Restaurant & bar service |
| 717-966-0321  Fax: 717-966-9557 | C-ltd/S-no/P-no/H-no | sitting rm, snacks,piano |
| John & Nancy Showers | | tennis nearby, gift shop |

*"A luxurious base for indulging in a clutch of quiet pleasures."—Phila. Inquirer. Fine dining and lodging amidst Victorian ambiance; tranquil setting.*

*Hillside Farm B&B, Mount Joy, PA*

## NEW HOPE

**Aaron Burr House Inn**
80 W. Bridge St., corner of
Chestnut St., 18938
215-862-2520  Fax: 215-862-2570
N. Silnatger & C. Glassman
All year

$$$-B&B
6 rooms, 6 pb
AmEx, *Rated*, •
C-ltd/S-no/P-no/H-yes
French, Spanish

Continental plus bkfst.
Comp. liqueur, snacks
Afternoon tea, library
2 new fireplace suites
white wicker porch, pool

*Discover "safe haven" in vintage village Victorian inn—Aaron Burr did after his famous pistol duel w/Alexander Hamilton in 1804! Innkeeping seminars. 3rd night 50%, ltd.*

**Wedgewood Inn of New Hope**
111 W. Bridge St., 18938
215-862-2570  215-862-2520
Carl & Jessica Glassman
All year

$$$-B&B
18 rooms,
*Rated*, •
C-ltd/S-ltd/P-ltd/H-ltd
Fr., Hebr., Dutch, Ger.

Continental plus bkfst.
Aftn. tea & refreshments
Victorian gazebo, parlor
horsedrawn carriage ride
club w/tennis, swimming

*Victorian mansion. Wedgewood china, fresh flowers & original art. Innkeepers make your stay as pleasant as surroundings. OUR 1989 INN OF THE YEAR! 3rd night 50%(Jan.–Apr.).*

**Whitehall Inn, The**
1370 Pineville Rd., 18938
215-598-7945  888-37-WHITE
Mike & Suella Wass
All year

$$$$-B&B
6 rooms, 4 pb
Most CC, *Rated*, •
C-ltd/S-no/P-no/H-no

Full candlelight bkfst.
High tea, comp. sherry
Pool & rose garden
library, sun room
piano & pump organ

*Experience our four-course candlelit breakfast using European china and crystal and heirloom sterling silver. Formal tea; fireplaces; working dressage horse farm.*

## NEW HOPE, HOLICONG

| **Barley Sheaf Farm** | $$$-B&B | Full farm breakfast |
| P.O. Box 10,  18928 | 12 rooms, 12 pb | Afternoon tea |
| 5281 York Rd., Rt 202 | *Rated*, • | Swimming pool |
| 215-794-5104  Fax: 215-794-5332 | C-ltd/S-no/P-no/H-yes | sitting room |
| Veronica & Peter Suess | French, German | conference center |
| All year | | |

*30-acre working farm—raise sheep. Rooms all furnished in antiques. Good antiquing and historic sights in area.*

## NEW HOPE, PT. PLEASANT

| **Tattersall Inn** | $$-B&B | Continental plus bkfst. |
| P.O. Box 569,  18950 | 6 rooms, 6 pb | Apple cider, snacks |
| Cafferty & River Rds. | Most CC, *Rated*, • | Library, sitting room |
| 215-297-8233  Fax: 215-297-5093 | C-ltd/S-ltd/P-no/H-no | piano, veranda, meetings |
| 800-297-4988 | | walk-in fireplace |
| Gerry & Herb Moss | | |
| All year | | |

*Bucks County historic mansion circa early 1800s. Antique phonograph collection. River canoeing & tubing, antique shops, art galleries.* **2nd night 50% off Sun-Wed, no holidays.**

## NEW HOPE, WRIGHTSTOWN

| **Hollileif B&B** | $$$-B&B | Full gourmet breakfast |
| 677 Durham Rd.,  18940 | 5 rooms, 5 pb | Comp. wine, refreshments |
| 215-598-3100 | MC, Visa, *Rated*, • | Accommodate special diet |
| Ellen & Richard Butkus | C-ltd/S-no/P-no/H-no | volleyball, croquet |
| All year | some Spanish | badminton, horseshoes |

*We pamper you in our romantic 18th-century home on 5.5 beautiful country treed acres, gardens, stream. Charming country furnishings, 2 gas firepelaces.* **3rd night 50%, ltd.**

## NEWFOUNDLAND

| **White Cloud Inn** | $$-B&B | Full breakfast (fee) |
| RD 1, Box 215,  18445 | 20 rooms, 7 pb | Restaurant |
| 717-676-3162  800-820-0370 | Most CC, • | Sitting room, piano |
| Dalle Teel & Pam Leland | C-yes/S-no/P-yes/H-no | chapel, tennis courts |
| All year | French, German in | outdoor swimming pool |
| | summer | |

*Country inn on fifty wooded acres w/emphasis on peace, quiet & good food. Come study, meditate or commune w/nature. Meatless, natural food restaurant.* **50% off 3rd night, ltd.**

## PARADISE

| **Pequea Creekside Inn** | $$-B&B | Full breakfast |
| P.O. Box 435,  17562 | 6 rooms, 5 pb | Afternoon tea, snacks |
| 44 Leacock Rd. | Visa, MC, | Sitting room |
| 717-687-0333  Fax: 717-687-8200 | C-ltd/S-no/P-no/H-no | air conditioning |
| Cathy & Dennis | | 2 guest rms. w/frplcs. |
| Zimmermann | | |
| All year | | |

*Beautifully restored 1781 stone house on Pequea Creek in the heart of Amish country. Antique furnishings, fireplace rooms, gourmet breakfast.*

## PHILADELPHIA

**Penn's View Inn, The**
14 N. Front St., Front &
Market Streets,   19106
215-922-7600  Fax: 215-922-7642
800-331-7634
The Sena Family
All year

$$$-B&B
38 rooms, 38 pb
Most CC, *Rated*, •
C-yes/S-yes/P-no/H-no
Italian, Spanish

Continental plus bkfst.
Lunch & dinner available
Restaurant, bar service
jacuzzis, fireplaces
individual wine tasting

*Charming European-style hotel. Short walk to historic attractions. Award-winning Italian restaurant featuring 120 wines by the glass!*

---

**Queen Anne Inn**
44 West End Ave., Inn located
in NJ,   08033
609-428-2195  Fax: 609-354-1273
Nancy Lynn
All year

$$$-B&B
10 rooms,
AmEx, MC, Visa, •
C-ltd/S-ltd/P-no/H-no

Continental plus bkfst.
Comp. wine, refreshments
Sitting rooms, porch
laundry facilities
bathrobes

*Restored, historic Victorian treasure. Walk to the safe & comfortable Hi-speed line. Be in Philadelphia in 20 min., connections to Atlantic City, NY, etc. Walk to shops, etc.*

---

**Shippen Way Inn**
46-418 Bainbridge St.,   19147
215-627-7266  800-245-4873
Ann Foringer & Raymond
Rhule
All year

$$$-B&B
9 rooms, 9 pb
AmEx, MC, Visa,
*Rated*, •
C-ltd/S-ltd/P-no/H-ltd

Continental plus bkfst.
Afternoon tea
Comp. wine
sitting room

*Friendly family owned and operated Inn with a country feel in the city. Colonial herb and rose garden. Fireplaces.*

---

**Society Hill Hotel**
301 Chestnut St. @ 3rd.,
  19106
215-925-1919
Judith Kleinman
All year

$$$-B&B
12 rooms, 12 pb
Most CC, *Rated*, •
C-yes/S-yes/P-ltd

Continental breakfast
Restaurant
Piano bar
telephones

*An "urban inn" located in the midst of Philadelphia's Historic Park. Fresh flowers, chocolates and brass double beds grace each room.*

---

**Thomas Bond House**
129 S. Second St.,   19106
215-923-8523  Fax: 215-923-8504
800-845-BOND
Joe Killingsworth
All year

$$$-B&B
12 rooms, 12 pb
AmEx, MC, Visa,
*Rated*, •
C-yes/S-yes/P-no/H-no

Continental plus—wkdays
Full breakfast—weekends
Hair dryers, TV, phone
fresh-baked cookies
whirlpool tubs, parlor

*Colonial period (c. 1770), listed in Nat'l Register. Individually decorated rooms. In Independence National Historical Park; next to historic shrines. **10% off, ask.***

## POCONO MOUNTAINS

**Nearbrook B&B**
RD 1, Box 630,   18325
Rt. 447, Canadensis
717-595-3152
Richard & Barb Robinson
All year

$-B&B
3 rooms, 1 pb
*Rated*,
C-yes/P-ltd/H-no

Heart brkfst. on porch
Menus for local rest.
Art instruction; one wk.
seminars, informal
atmosphere for piano

*Meander through rock garden paths and woods to mountain streem. Hiking, skiing, trail rides, swimming, boating, golf, museums, sight seeing, alpine slide, discount stores. Personalized maps.*

---

**POTTSTOWN**

| | | |
|---|---|---|
| **Coventry Forge Inn** | $$-B&B | Continental breakfast |
| 3360 Coventryville Rd., 19465 | 5 rooms, 5 pb | Restaurant, bar |
| 610-469-6222 | Most CC, *Rated*, | Dinner available |
| Wallis and June Callahan | C-yes/S-yes/P-no/H-no | sitting room, library |
| All year | | |

*Superb French restaurant in Chester County horse country. Brandywine Valley & Amish country nearby. Excellent antiquing.*

**QUARRYVILLE**

| | | |
|---|---|---|
| **Runnymede Farm** | $-B&B | Full breakfast (fee) |
| **Guesthouse** | 3 rooms, | Snacks |
| 1030 Robert Fulton Hwy., | *Rated*, | Piano |
| R.222 S., 17566 | C-yes/S-no/P-no/H-no | sitting room |
| 717-786-3625 | | pleasant porch |
| Herb & Sara Hess | | |
| All year | | |

*Enjoy old-fashioned hospitality when you vacation in our clean, comfortable farm home. Full country breakfast. Bicycling, hiking, picnicking.*

**REAMSTOWN**

| | | |
|---|---|---|
| **Hitchcock House** | $$-B&B | Full breakfast |
| P.O. Box 322, 17567 | 4 rooms, 4 pb | Sitting room |
| 31 E. Church St. | Visa, MC, | tennis courts, pool |
| 717-335-3510 | C-ltd/S-no/P-no/H-no | ideal for bicyling |
| Darryl & Annette | | |
| Hitchcock | | |
| All year | | |

*Adjacent to park with walking paths, swimming pool, tennis courts. 1889 brick Victorian town house, 10 foot ceilings, walls draped with botanical stencils, antique chandeliers*

**REBERSBURG**

| | | |
|---|---|---|
| **Centre Mills B&B** | $$$-EP | Full breakfast |
| HCR Box 210, 16872 | 4 rooms, 4 pb | Afternoon tea |
| 814-349-8000 | Visa, MC, | Sitting room, library |
| Fax: 814-422-8368 | C-ltd/S-no/P-ltd/H-no | hiking, biking, fishing |
| Maria Davison | German | antiquing |
| All year | | |

*1813 stone country inn furnished in authentic antiques & mill on 26 acres overlooking limestone trout stream w/mountain backdrop. Secluded country setting in Amish neighborhood. Flyfisher's paradise.*

**RIDGWAY**

| | | |
|---|---|---|
| **Faircroft B&B** | $$-B&B | Full breakfast |
| 17 Montmorenci Rd., 15853 | 3 rooms, 3 pb | Comp. beverages, snacks |
| 814-776-2539 | Most CC, *Rated*, | Sitting room, fireplace |
| Lois & John | C-ltd/S-no/H-no | hiking trails, hunting |
| Shoemaker | | fishing, swimming, golf |
| All year | | |

*2 miles from Rt. 219. Warm, comfortable, 1870 farmhouse on 75 acres; all rooms have A/C. Antiques, Swedish foods. Next to Allegheny Nat'l Forest.* **Comp. wine basket–special occasions.**

## RONKS

**Candlelight Inn B&B**
2574 Lincoln Hwy East, Route
30 East,   17572
717-299-6005  Fax: 717-299-6397
800-77CANDLE
Tim & Heidi Soberick
All year

$$-B&B
6 rooms, 4 pb
MC, Visa, Disc., •
C-ltd/S-no/P-no/H-no
French, Italian

Full breakfast
Afternoon tea & snacks
Sitting room
antiques & oriental rugs
Victorian style

*Large country home, elegantly decorated w/Victorian antiques & oriental rugs. Surrounded by Amish farms in the heart of PA Dutch country. Romantic candlelit bkfst., convenient location.* **10% off, ask.**

## SCHELLSBURG

**Bedford's Covered Bridge**
Rd. 2, Box 196,   15559
814-733-4093
Greg & Martha Lau
All year

$$-B&B
7 rooms, 7 pb
Most CC, *Rated*, •
S-no/P-no/H-no

Full breakfast
Snacks
Sitting room, library
bikes, 2 bedroom cottage
available for families

*Quiet, romantic countryside accommodations beside a covered bridge. On-site hiking, biking, fly fishing, cross-country skiing. Downhill skiing, antiquing, golf, museums nearby.*

## SCOTTDALE

**Pine Wood Acres B&B**
Rt 1, Box 634,   15683
412-887-5404  Fax: 412-887-3111
All year

$$-B&B
3 rooms, 2 pb
•
C-yes/S-no/P-no/H-no

Full breakfast
Afternoon tea & snacks
Herb & perennial gardens
porch
cater to special diets

*An 1880 farm house in a country setting. Antiques, herbs, flowers. Near Wright's Fallingwater, Youghiogheny River Bike Trail, hiking, rafting, ski resorts, historic sites.*

**Zephyr Glen B&B**
205 Dexter Rd.,   15683
412-887-6577
Noreen & Gil McGurl
All year

$$-B&B
3 rooms, 3 pb
Visa, MC, Disc., •
C-ltd/S-no/P-no/H-no
Some German

Full breakfast
Afternoon tea, snacks
Sitting room

*1822 Federal Farmhouse, antique filled, country decor, hearty breakfast, warm hospitality, near antiques, whitewater, skiing, biking, hiking, historical sites.* **10% off, ltd.**

## SMOKETOWN

**Homestead Lodging**
184 E. Brook Rd., Route 896,
17576
717-393-6927  Fax: 717-393-6927
Robert & Lori Kepiro
All year

$-B&B
4 rooms, 4 pb
MC, Visa, *Rated*,
C-yes/S-yes/H-yes

Continental breakfast
Microwave, refrigerator
A/C, sandbox, large yard
color TV w/stereo radio
Amish country tours

*Quiet country lodging in hand-stenciled rooms. Gift shop with local handcrafts. Located beside Amish farm. Walk to restaurants & outlets. Gift shop, tennis court. Queen beds.*

## SOMERSET

**Bayberry Inn B&B**
611 N. Center Ave., Route 601,
15501
814-445-8471
Robert & Marilyn Lohr
All year

$-B&B
11 rooms, 11 pb
Most CC, *Rated*, •
C-ltd/S-no/P-no/H-no

Continental plus bkfst.
Snacks
Sitting room, library
TV room with VCR/stereo

*One and one-half blocks from turnpike exit, near Georgian Place outlet mall. Seven Springs and Hidden Valley ski resorts, whitewater rafting, "Fallingwater."*

## STATE COLLEGE

**Chatelaine (SPF) B&B, The**
P.O. Box 326,  16868
347 W. Pine Grove Rd.
814-238-2028  800-251-2028
Mae McQuade
All year

$$-B&B
4 rooms, 2 pb
Visa, MC, Disc.,*Rated*,
•
C-ltd/S-no/P-no/H-no
Some Spanish &
Portugese

Full breakfast
Complimentary liqueur,
Sodas & hot beverages
sitting room

*Serene setting w/handsome furnishings, exciting decor, & cosmopolitan antiques. Wine for bride & groom/restaurant disc't. Lovingly known as Chatelaine at Split-Pine Farmhouse.*

## STRASBURG

**Decoy B&B, The**
958 Eisenberger Rd.,  17579
717-687-8585  Fax: 717-687-8585
800-726-2287
Debby & Hap Joy  All year

$$-B&B
4 rooms, 4 pb
*Rated*,
C-yes/S-no/P-no/H-no

Full breakfast
Dinner with Amish family
Sitting room, library
A/C, bike tours
quilting seminars

*Spectacular view; quiet rural location in Amish farm country. Former Amish home. We are part of 3+ night inn to inn bicycle tour. Two cats in residence! Family reunions.*

## UPPER BLACK EDDY

**Bridgeton House**
PO Box 167, 1525 River Rd.,
  18972
215-982-5856
Charles & Bea Briggs  All yr

$$-B&B
8 rooms, 8 pb
AmEx, MC, Visa,
C-ltd/S-ltd/P-no/H-no

Full gourmet breakfast
Complimentary sherry
Sitting room
river swimming
restaurant & shops dis't

*Romantic guest rooms in 1836 inn on Delaware River. French doors with river views, screened porches, flowers & fruit. Featured in New York Times & Woman's Day Magazine.*

## WASHINGTON CROSSING

**Inn to the Woods B&B**
150 Glenwood Dr.,  18977
215-493-1974  Fax: 215-493-7592
800-982-7619
Rosemary & Barry Rein
All year

$$$-B&B
6 rooms, 6 pb
MC, Visa, *Rated*, •
C-ltd/S-no/P-no/H-no
Slovak

Continental plus wkdays
Full breakfast weekends
Sitting room, king beds
Sunken tub, garden
use as small conf. ctr.

*Nestled on 10 wooded acres. Enjoy delicious breakfasts in rural, relaxing Bucks County. Close to New York, Philadelphia, Princeton.* **50% off of the 3rd night.**

## WELLSBORO

**Kaltenbach's B&B**
RD #6 Box 106A, Stonyfork
Rd.,  16901
717-724-4954  800-722-4954
Lee Kaltenbach
All year

$$-B&B
10 rooms, 8 pb
Visa, MC, *Rated*,
C-yes/S-no/P-no/H-yes
Spanish

Full breakfast
Aft. tea, snacks, wine
Lunch/dinner by reserv.
sitting room, library
tennis court, hot tubs

*Famous for all-you-can-eat country-style breakfast—homemade jellies, jams, blueberry muffins, farm-raised pork, ham, bacon, sausage. Golf, skiing, hunting, fishing nearby.*

## WEST CHESTER

**Bankhouse B&B**
875 Hillsdale Rd.,  19382
610-344-7388
Diana & Michael Bove
All year

$$$-B&B
2 rooms,
*Rated*,
C-ltd/S-no/P-no/H-no

Full breakfast
Snacks
Sitting room, porch
library, A/C
private entrances

*Charming 18th-century "bankhouse" located across from a 10-acre horse farm. Convenient to Longwood Gardens, Winterthur, etc. Quiet country setting.* **10% off 4+ nights stay.**

WESTCHESTER ───────────────────────────────

| | | |
|---|---|---|
| **Lenape Springs Farm** | $$-B&B | Full breakfast |
| 580 W. Creek Rd., P.O. Box | 5 rooms, 5 pb | Sitting room, library |
| 176, 19382 | Visa, MC, *Rated*, • | game room w/fireplace |
| Pocopson | C-yes/S-ltd/P-no/H-no | pool table, hot tubs |
| 610-793-2266  800-793-2234 | | |
| Bob & Sharon Currie | | |
| Mar- Mid July/Sept-Dec | | |

*Secluded farm convenient to all Brandywine Valley attractions. Hosts friendly and helpfull with local information. All rooms have private baths. **3rd night, 50%.***

WILKES-BARRE ───────────────────────────────

| | | |
|---|---|---|
| **Ponda-Rowland B&B Inn** | $$-B&B | Full candlelight bkfst. |
| RR1, Box 349, 18612 | 5 rooms, 5 pb | Picnics, special diets |
| 717-639-3245  Fax: 717-639-5531 | Most CC, *Rated*, • | Satellite TV, fireplaces |
| 800-854-3286 | C-yes/S-no/P-no | wildlife sanctuary, pond |
| Jeanette & Cliff Rowland | | hiking, all rooms A/C |
| All year | | |

*130-acre farm in the Endless Mtns. Beautiful mountain and forest scenery. Farm includes 30-acre wildlife refuge, canoeing and swimming.*

WILLIAMSPORT ───────────────────────────────

| | | |
|---|---|---|
| **Reighard House, The** | $$-B&B | Full breakfast |
| 1323 E. 3rd St., 17701 | 6 rooms, 6 pb | Afternoon tea |
| 717-326-3593 | Most CC, *Rated*, • | Comp. wine, beer, snacks |
| Susan L. Reighard | C-yes/S-no/P-no/H-no | sitting room, library |
| Exc. Xmas, New Years | | club membership at YMCA |

*1905 stone and brick Victorian house; formal parlor, music room, formal dining room. Six large bedrooms with private baths, color TV, phone, carpeting, air conditioning.*

# More Inns . . .

| | |
|---|---|
| Annville | Swatara Creek Inn B&B, Box 692, RD #1, 17003,  717-865-3259 |
| Bangor | Hurryback Riverhouse B&B, RR 2, Box 2176A, 18013,  215-498-3121 |
| Beach Lake | Beach Lake Hotel, Main & Church, 18405,  717-729-8239 |
| Beach Lake | East Shore House, P.O. Box 12, 18405,  717-729-8523 |
| Beach Lake | Morning Dove Manor, P.O. Box 33, 18405 |
| Bedford | Bedford House, 203 W. Pitt St., 15522,  814-623-7171 |
| Bedford | Golden Eagle Inn, The, 131 East Pitt St., 15522 |
| Bedford | Jean Bonnet Tavern, R.D.2, Box 724, 15522,  814-623-2250 |
| Berlin | Vietersburg Inn B&B, 1001 E. Main St., 15530,  814-267-3696 |
| Bernville | Sunday's Mill Farm B&B, R.D.2, Box 419, 19506,  215-488-7821 |
| Bethlehem | Bethlehem Inn, 476 N. New St., 18018,  215-867-4985 |
| Bethlehem | Wydnor Hall Inn, Rd 3, 18015,  215-867-6851 |
| Bird-In-Hand | Greystone Manor B&B, P.O. Box 270, 17505,  717-393-4233 |
| Bloomsburg | Irondale Inn B&B, 100 Irondale Ave., 17815,  717-784-1977 |
| Boiling Springs | Yellow Breeches House, P.O. Box 221, 17007,  717-258-8344 |
| Boyertown | Little House, The,  RD3, Box 341, 19512,  215-689-4814 |
| Brackney | Indian Mountain Inn B&B, Box 68, Trip Lake Rd., 18812,  717-663-2645 |
| Buck Hill Falls | Buck Hill Inn, 18232,  800-233-8113 |
| Buffalo Mills | Buffalo Lodge, R.D.1, Box 277, 15534,  814-623-2207 |
| Cambridge Springs | Bethany Guest House, 325 So. Main St., 16403,  814-398-2046 |
| Canadensis | Dreamy Acres, Rt. 447 & Seese Hill Rd, 18325,  717-595-7115 |
| Canadensis | Laurel Grove Inn, 18325,  717-595-7262 |
| Canadensis | Overlook Inn, Dutch Hill Rd., Box 680, 18325,  717-595-7519 |
| Canadensis | Pump House Inn, RR1 Box 430, Skytop Rd., 18325,  717-595-7501 |
| Carbondale | Fern Hall,  Box 1095, RD 1, Crystal, 18407,  717-222-3676 |
| Carlisle | Line Limousin Farmhouse, 2070 Ritner Highway, 17013,  717-243-1281 |
| Cashtown | Historic Cashtown Inn, The,  Old Route 30, Box 103, 17310,  717-334-9722 |
| Cedar Run | Cedar Run Inn, 17727,  717-353-6241 |
| Chadds Ford | Brandywine River Hotel, P.O. Box 1058, 19317,  215-388-1200 |
| Chadds Ford | Chadds Ford Inn, Rts. 1 & 100, 19317,  215-388-1473 |
| Chadds Ford | Hill House, Creek Rd., 19317 |
| Chalfont | Butler Mill House B&B, 116 E. Butler Ave., 18914,  215-822-3582 |
| Chalfont | Sevenoaks Farm B&B, 492 New Galena Rd., 18914,  215-822-2164 |
| Clark | Tara—A Country Inn, 3665 Valley View Rd., 16113,  412-962-3535 |
| Clark's Summit | C & L B&B, 1327 Fairview Rd., 18411 |

| | |
|---|---|
| Clearville | Conifer Ridge Farm, RD 2, P.O. Box 202A, 15535,  814-784-3342 |
| Confluence | River's Edge Cafe/B&B, 203 Yough St., 15424,  814-395-5059 |
| Cowansville | Garrott's B&B, RD 1, Box 73, 16218,  412-545-2432 |
| Cranberry TWP | Cranberry B&B, P.O. Box 2005, 16066,  412-776-1198 |
| Danville | Melanie Ann's B&B, 120 Center St., 17821 |
| Downingtown | Duck Hill Farm, R.D. 1, 19335 |
| Doylestown | Inn at Fordhook Farm, The,  105 New Britain Rd., 18901,  215-345-1766 |
| Doylestown | Pine Tree Farm, 2155 Lower State Rd., 18901,  215-348-0632 |
| Dushore | Cherry Mills Lodge, RR 1, Box 1270, 18614,  717-928-8978 |
| Dushore | Heritage Guest House, Rte 87 & 487, 18614 |
| East Berlin | Bechtel Mansion Inn, 400 West King St., 17316,  717-259-7760 |
| Easton | Lafayette Inn, The,  525 W. Monroe St., 18042,  215-253-4500 |
| Ebensburg | Noon-Collins Inn,  114 East High St., 15931,  814-472-4311 |
| Elizabeth | John Butler House B&B, The,  800 Rock Run Rd., 15037,  412-751-6670 |
| Elizabethville | Inn at Elizabethville, 30 W. Main St., 17023 |
| Elm | Elm Country Inn, P.O. Box 37, 17521,  717-664-3623 |
| Emigsville | Emig Mansion, Box 486, 3342 N.George , 17318,  717-764-2226 |
| Ephrata | Gerhart House B&B,  287 Duke St., 17522,  717-733-0263 |
| Erwinna | Issac Stover House, P.O. Box 68, 18920 |
| Exton | Duling-Kurtz House & Inn,  146 S. Whitford Rd., 19341,  610-524-1830 |
| Fairfield | Historic Fairfield Inn,  15 W. Main St., Box 196, 17320,  717-642-5410 |
| Franklin | Franklin B&B, 1501 Liberty St., 16323,  814-432-4208 |
| Gap | Ben-Mar Farm Lodging, R. D. 1, Box 106, 17527 |
| Gardenville | Maplewood Farm B&B,  P.O. Box 239, 18926,  215-766-0477 |
| Gettysburg | Cozy Comfort Inn,  264 Baltimore St., 17325,  717-337-3997 |
| Gettysburg | Dobbin House Tavern Gettys, 89 Steinwehr Ave., 17325,  717-334-2100 |
| Gettysburg | Herr Tavern Publick House,  900 Chambersburg Rd., 17325,  717-334-4332 |
| Gettysburg | Historic Farnsworth House,  401 Baltimore St., 17325,  717-334-8838 |
| Gettysburg | Swinn's Lodging,  31 E. Lincoln Ave., 17325, 717-334-5255 |
| Glen Mills | Crier In The Country, Route 1, 19342, 215-358-2411 |
| Glen Mills | Sweetwater Farm, 50 Sweetwater Rd., 19342,  610-459-4711 |
| Glen Rock | Dogwood @ Spoutwood Farm, RD 3, Box 66, 17327,  717-235-6610 |
| Glen Rock | Spoutwood Farm,  RD 3, Box 66, 17327, 717-235-6610 |
| Greencastle | Phaeton Farm B&B, 9762 Browns Mill Rd., 17225,  717-597-8656 |
| Hallstead | Log Cabin B&B, Box 393, Rt. 11, 18822,  717-879-4167 |
| Hawley | Morning Glories, 204 Bellemonte Ave., 18428 |
| Hershey | Gibson's B&B, 141 W. Caracas Ave., 17033 |
| Hershey | Horetsky's Tourist Home, 217 Cocoa Ave., 17033,  717-533-5783 |
| Hershey | Pinehurst Inn B&B, 50 Northeast Dr., 17033,  717-533-2603 |
| Hesston | Aunt Susie's Country Vac., RD 1, Box 225, 16647,  814-658-3638 |
| Hickory | Shady Elms Farm B&B, Box 188, R.D.1, 15340,  412-356-7755 |
| Huntingdon | Yoder's B&B, RD 1, Box 312, 16652,  814-643-3221 |
| Jamestown | Willowood Inn B&B, 215 W. Lake Rd., 16134,  412-932-3866 |
| Jim Thorpe | Inn at Jim Thorpe, The, 24 Broadway, 18229,  717-325-2599 |
| Johnstown | Meadowbrook School B&B, 160 Engbert Rd., 15902,  814-539-1756 |
| Kane | Kane Manor B&B, 230 Clay St., 16735,  814-837-6522 |
| Kempton | Hawk Mountain Inn, RD 1, Box 186, 19529,  215-756-4224 |
| Kennett Square | Buttonwood Farm, 231 Pemberton Rd., 19348,  215-444-0278 |
| Kennett Square | Scarlett House B&B, 503 W. State St., 19348,  610-444-9592 |
| Kintnersville | Bucksville House, R.D.2, Box 146, 18930,  215-847-8948 |
| Kintnersville | Light Farm, 2042 Berger Rd., 18930,  610-847-3276 |
| Kinzer | Groff Tourist Farm Home, 766 Brackbill Rd., 17535,  717-442-8223 |
| Kutztown | Around the World B&B, 30 S. Whiteoak St., 19530,  610-683-8885 |
| Lahaska | Peddler's Village, P.O. Box 218, 18931 |
| Lancaster | Boxwood Inn, P.O. Box 203, 17501,  717-859-3466 |
| Lancaster | Flowers & Thyme B&B, 238 Strasburg Pike, 17602,  717-393-1460 |
| Lancaster | Inn at Twin Linden, 2092 Main St., Route 23, 17555,  215-445-7619 |
| Lancaster | Landyshade Farms, 1801 Colebrook Rd., 17601,  717-898-7689 |
| Lancaster | Limestone Inn B&B, 33 E. Main St., 17579,  717-687-8392 |
| Lancaster | Little Britain Manor, 20 Brown Rd., 19362,  717-529-2862 |
| Lancaster | Meadowview Guest House, 2169 New Holland Pike, 17601,  717-299-4017 |
| Lancaster | New Life Homestead B&B, 1400 E. King St. Rt.462, 17602,  717-396-8928 |
| Lancaster | Oregon B&B, 1500 Oregon Rd., 17540,  717-656-2644 |
| Lansford | Liberty Hill B&B, 245 East Patterson St., 18232 |
| Laughlintown | Ligonier Country Inn, P.O. Box 46, Rt. 30 E, 15655,  412-238-3651 |
| Leesport | Loom Room, RD 1, Box 1420, 19533,  215-926-3217 |
| Leetsdale | Whistlestop, 195 Broad St., 15056,  412-251-0852 |
| Leola | Turtle Hill Road B&B, 111 Turtle Hill Rd., 17540 |
| Lewisburg | Brookpark Farm B&B, 100 Reitz Blvd., Rt. 45, 17837,  717-524-7733 |

*The Inn at Doneckers,
Ephrata, PA*

| | |
|---|---|
| Lewisburg | Inn on Fiddler's Tract, RD 2, Box 573A, 17837, 717-523-7197 |
| Lincoln | Royalview Dairy Farm, Box 93, 19352 |
| Lititz | Carter Run Inn B&B, 511 E. Main St.,Rte 772, 17543, 717-626-8807 |
| Lititz | General Sutter Inn, 14 E. Main St., 17543, 717-626-2115 |
| Lititz | Historic Gen. Sutter Inn, 14 East Main St., 17543, 717-626-2115 |
| Lititz | Spahr's Century Farm, 192 Green Acre Rd., 17543, 717-627-2185 |
| Lititz | Swiss Woods B&B, 500 Blantz Rd., 17543, 717-627-3358 |
| Lumberville | 1740 House, River Rd., 18933, 215-297-5661 |
| Lumberville | Black Bass Hotel, 3774 River Rd., Rt. 32, 18933, 215-297-5770 |
| Malvern | General Warren Inne, Old Lancaster Hwy., 19355, 610-296-3637 |
| Manheim | Herr Farmhouse Inn, 2256 Huber Dr., 17545, 717-653-9852 |
| Manheim | Inn at Mt. Hope, The, 2232 E. Mt. Hope Rd., 17545, 717-664-4708 |
| Manheim | Jonde Lane Farm, R.D.7, Box 363, 17545 |
| Marietta | Morning Meadows Farm, 103 Fuhrman Rd., 17547, 717-426-1425 |
| Marietta | Railroad House B&B, W. Front & S. Perry, 17547, 717-426-4141 |
| Marietta | River Inn, The, 258 West Front St., 17547, 717-426-2290 |
| Marietta | Vogt Farm, 1225 Colebrook Rd., 17547, 717-653-4810 |
| McKeesport | Guest Home, 1040 Lincoln Way, 15132, 412-751-7143 |
| Mechanicsburg | Moores Mountain Inn, 450 Moores Mountain Rd., 17055, 717-766-3412 |
| Mendenhall | Fairville Inn, P.O. Box 219, 19357, 215-388-5900 |
| Mercer | Stranahan House B&B, The, 117 E. Market St., 16137, 412-662-4516 |
| Mercersburg | Guest Farm, 11335 Punch Bowl Rd., 17236, 800-296-7211 |
| Mercersburg | Maplebrow, 11771 Mercersburg Rd., 17236, 717-328-3172 |
| Mifflinville | Ye Olde Hotel, 124 W. Third St., 18631 |
| Milheim | Milheim Hotel, Main St., 16854, 814-349-5994 |
| Millersburg | Victorian Manor Inn, 312 Market St., 17061, 717-692-3511 |
| Millersville | Walnut Hill B&B, 113 Walnut Hill Rd., 17551, 717-872-2283 |
| Mohnton | Windy Hill Bed & Breakfast, Candy Rd, RD1, Box 1085, 19540, 215-775-2755 |
| Montoursville | Carriage House @ Stonegate, RR 1, Box 11A, 17754, 717-433-4536 |
| Montrose | Montrose House, The, 26 S. Main St., 18801, 717-278-1124 |
| Mount Bethel | Elvern Country Lodge, RR 2, Box 2099A, 18343 |
| Mount Gretna | Mount Gretna Inn, P.O. Box 690, 17064, 717-964-3234 |
| Mount Joy | Brenneman Farm - B&B, RD 1, Box 310, 17552, 717-653-4213 |
| Mount Joy | Cameron Estate Inn, RD 1, Box 305, 17752, 717-653-1773 |
| Mount Joy | Country Stay B&B, The, 2285 Bull Moose Rd., 17552, 717-367-5167 |
| Mount Joy | Donegal Mills Plantation, Box 257, 17552, 717-653-2168 |
| Mount Joy | Nolt Farm Guest Home, S. Jacob St. Farm, 17552, 717-653-4192 |
| Mount Joy | Olde Square Inn, The, 127 E. Main St., 17552, 717-653-4525 |
| Mountville | Mountville Antiques B&B, 407 E. Main St., Rt. 4, 17554, 717-285-5956 |
| Myerstown | Tulpehocken Manor Inn, Route 422, RD 2, 17067 |
| New Albany | Waltman's B&B, RD 1, Box 87, 18833, 717-363-2295 |
| New Bloomfield | Tressler House B&B, The, P.O. Box 38, 17068, 717-582-2914 |
| New Cumberland | Farm Fortune, 204 Lime Kiln Rd., 17070, 717-774-2683 |
| New Hope | Ash Mill Farm B&B, P.O. Box 202, 18928, 215-794-5373 |
| New Hope | Back Street Inn, 144 Old York Rd., 18938, 215-862-9571 |
| New Hope | Central Bridge Inn, River Rd., 18938 |
| New Hope | Centre Bridge Inn, 2998 N. River Rd., 18938, 215-862-9139 |
| New Hope | Hacienda Inn, 36 W. Mechanics St., 18938, 215-862-2078 |
| New Hope | Hotel du Village, N. River Rd., 18938, 215-862-9911 |
| New Hope | Inn at Phillips Mill, North River Rd., 18938, 215-862-9919 |
| New Hope | Logan Inn, 10 W. Ferry St., 18938, 215-862-2300 |
| New Wilmington | Behm's B&B, 166 Waugh Ave., 16142, 412-946-8641 |
| New Wilmington | Tavern, Box 153, On the Square, 16142, 412-946-2020 |
| Newport | Temperance House, The, 5-11 S. State St., 18940, 215-860-0474 |
| Newtown Sq. | Fifer's Folly B&B, 3561 N. Providence Rd., 19073, 215-353-3366 |
| North Wales | Joseph Ambler Inn, 1005 Horsham Rd., 19454, 215-362-7500 |
| Oil City | Flower Cottage B&B, 515 W. 6th St., 16301 |
| Orrtanna | Mt. Carmel Inn, 1391 Mt. Carmel Rd., 17353, 800-642-6255 |
| Ottsville | Frankenfield Farm B&B, P.O. Box 238, 18942, 610-847-2771 |
| Oxford | John Hayes House, 8100 Limestone Rd., 19363, 215-932-5347 |
| Paradise | Maple Lane Farm B&B, 505 Paradise Ln., 17562, 717-687-7479 |
| Paradise | Neffdale Farm, 604 Strasburg Rd., 17562, 717-687-7837 |
| Paradise | Rayba Acres Farm, 183 Black Horse Rd., 17562, 717-687-6729 |
| Paradise | Verdant View Farm, 429 Strasburg Rd., 17562, 717-687-7353 |
| PeachBottom | Pleasant Grove Farm, R. D. 1, Box 132, 17563 |
| Philadelphia | Abigail Adams' B&B, 1208 Walnut St., 19107, 215-546-7336 |
| Philadelphia | Appel's B&B—Society Hill, 414 Spruce St., 19106, 215-922-2626 |
| Philadelphia | Hotel La Reserve, 1804 Pine St., 19103, 215-735-0582 |
| Philadelphia | Independence Park , 235 Chestnut St., 19106 |
| Philadelphia | Steele Away B&B, 7151 Boyer St., 19119, 215-242-0722 |
| Philadelphia | Village Guest House B&B, 808 S. 2nd St., 19147, 215-755-9770 |
| Phoenixville | Valley Forge B&B, 137 Forge Hill Ln., 19460, 215-933-6460 |
| Pine Bank | Cole's Log Cabin B&B, RD 1, Box 98, 15354, 412-627-9151 |
| Pine Grove | Forge, The, RD 1, Box 438, 17963, 717-345-8349 |
| Pittsburgh | Columbus Inn, The, 400 Landmarks Bldg., 15219, 412-471-5420 |
| Pittsburgh | Oakwood, 235 Johnston Rd., 15241, 412-835-9565 |
| Pittsburgh | Priory—A City Inn, The, 614 Pressley St., 15212, 412-231-3338 |
| Pittsburgh | Shadyside B&B, 5516 Maple Heights Rd., 15232, 412-683-6501 |

| | |
|---|---|
| Pottstown | Fairway Farm, Vaughan Rd., 19464, 215-326-1315 |
| Quakertown | Country Country, 243 Old Bethlehem Rd., 18951, 214-536-3630 |
| Reading | Hunter House B&B, 118 S. Fifth St., 19602, 215-374-6608 |
| Reading | Inn at Centre Park, 730 Centre Ave., 19601, 215-374-8557 |
| Regent Sq. | Bianconi's B&B, 727 East End Ave, 15221, 412-731-2252 |
| Riegelsville | Riegelsville Hotel, 10-12 Delaware Rd., 18077, 215-749-2469 |
| Roaring Spring | Spring Garden Farm B&B, RD 1 Box 522, 16673 |
| Rockwood | Brookview B&B, R.D. #3, 15557, 814-926-2241 |
| Rockwood | Carousel Inn, RR #2, Box 280, 15557, 814-926-2666 |
| Rockwood | In Town Inn, 822 E. Broadway, 15557, 814-926-4131 |
| Rockwood | Trenthouse Inn, R.D. #2, Box 140A, 15557, 814-352-8492 |
| Ronks | Wee Three Guest Haus, 233 Hartman Bridge Rd., 17572, 717-687-8146 |
| S. Sterling | French Manor, The, Box 39, 18460, 717-676-3244 |
| S. Sterling | Sterling Inn, The, Rt. 191, 18460, 717-676-3311 |
| Scenery Hill | Century Inn, S, 15360, 412-945-6600 |
| Selinsgrove | Blue Lion Inn, The, 350 S. Market St., 17870, 717-374-2929 |
| Sewickley | Greissinger's Farm, 2397 Springdale Ln., 15143, 412-741-2597 |
| Shartlesville | Haag's Hotel, Main St., 19554, 215-488-6692 |
| Shawnee | Eagle Rock Lodge, River Rd., 18356, 717-421-2139 |
| Shippensburg | Field & Pine B&B, 2155 Ritner Hwy., 17257, 717-776-7179 |
| Sigel | Discoveries B&B, RD #1, Box 42, 15680, 814-752-2632 |
| Slippery Rock | Applebutter Inn, 666 Centreville Pike, 16057, 412-794-1844 |
| Smoketown | Smoketown Village, 2495 Old Phila. Pike, 17576, 717-393-5975 |
| Solebury | Hollyhedge English Estate, Box 213, 18963, 215-862-3136 |
| Somerset | Country Woodland House, R.D. #2, Riggs Rd. Ext., 15501, 814-445-3481 |
| Somerset | Glades Pike Inn, RD 6, Box 250, 15501, 814-443-4978 |
| Somerset | H.B.'s Cottage, 231 W. Church St., 15501, 814-443-1204 |
| Somerset | Highland Farm Guest House, R.D. #2, Box 94A, 15501, 814-445-4015 |
| Somerset | Inn at Georgian Place, The, 800 Georgian Place Dr., 15501, 814-443-1043 |
| St. Marys | Towne House Inn, 138 Center St., 15857, 814-781-1556 |
| Starlight | Inn at Starlight Lake, The, P.O. Box 27, 18461, 717-798-2519 |
| Starrucca | Nethercott Inn B&B, The, P.O. Box 26, 18462, 717-727-2211 |
| Strasburg | Strasburg Village Inn, One W. Main St., 17579, 717-687-0900 |
| Susquehanna | April Valley B&B, RR 1, Box 141, 18847, 717-756-2688 |
| Thompson | Jefferson Inn, RD 2, Box 36, Route 171, 18465, 717-727-2625 |
| Thornton | Pace One Country Inn, P.O. Box 108, 19373, 610-459-3702 |
| Towanda | Victorian Guest House, 118 York Av., 18848, 717-265-6972 |
| Troy | Silver Oak Leaf B&B, The, 196 Canton St., 16947, 717-297-4315 |
| Tyler Hill | Tyler Hill B&B, P.O. Box 62, Route 371, 18469, 717-224-6418 |
| Upper Black Eddy | Tara, 1 Bridgeton Hill, 18972, 215-982-5457 |
| Valley Forge | B&B of Valley Forge, P.O. Box 562, 19481, 800-344-0123 |
| Valley Forge | Valley Forge Mountain B&B, Box 562, 19481 |
| Warfordsburg | Buck Valley Ranch, Rt 2, Box 1170, 17267, 717-294-3759 |
| Warriors Mark | Laurel Ridge B&B, 129 Laurel Court, 16877, 814-632-6813 |
| Waterford | Altheim B&B, 104 Walnut St., 16441 |
| West Chester | Crooked Windsor, 409 S. Church St., 19382, 215-692-4896 |
| West Chester | Dilworthtown Inn, Old Wilmington Pike, 19382, 215-399-1390 |
| West Chester | Faunbrook B&B, 699 W. Rosedale Ave., 19382, 215-436-5788 |
| West Chester | Highland Manor B&B, 855 Hillsdale Rd., 19382, 215-686-6251 |
| Willow Street | Cook's Guest House, 22 West Penn Grant Rd., 17584, 717-464-3273 |
| Willow Street | Green Gables B&B, 2532 Willow St. Pike, 17584, 717-464-5546 |
| Woodbury | Waterside Inn B&B, RD #1, Box 52, 16695, 814-766-3776 |
| Wycombe | Wycombe Inn, P.O. Box 204, 18980, 215-598-7000 |
| York | Briarwold B&B, 5400 Lincoln Hwy., 17406, 717-252-4619 |
| York | Inn at Mundis Mills, RD 22, Box 15, 17402, 717-755-2002 |

# Rhode Island

## BLOCK ISLAND

**1661 Inn & Hotel Manisses**
Spring Street, 02807
401-466-2063 Fax: 401-466-2858
800-MANISSES
J&J Abrams, R&S Draper
May–October

$$$-B&B
25 rooms, 16 pb
AmEx, MC, Visa,
*Rated*, •
C-ltd/S-yes/P-no/H-yes

Full buffet breakfast
Lunch, dinner, full bar
New Gazebo Room added
with glass walls
overlooking the gardens

*Island country inn overlooking Atlantic Ocean—full buffet breakfast, wine & nibble hour, flaming coffees served on ocean view deck. **Mid-week packages, off-season.***

BLOCK ISLAND ──────────────────────────

| **Atlantic Inn, The** | $$$-B&B | Continental plus bkfst. |
| P.O. Box 188,  02807 | 21 rooms, 21 pb | Dinner, afternoon tea |
| High St. | Visa, MC, *Rated*, • | Restaurant, bar service |
| 401-466-5883 Fax: 401-466-5678 | C-yes/S-no/P-no/H-no | beach, garden, tennis |
| Anne & Brad Marthens | | nature trails, buffet |
| April-Nov | | |

*Situated atop a hill on six acres of rolling green lawns, Atlantic Inn offers a commanding view of the village & exquisite beaches but it is set apart from the noise & traffic*

| **Rose Farm Inn, The** | $$$-B&B | Continental plus bkfst. |
| Roslyn Rd.,  02807 | 10 rooms, 8 pb | Whirlpool baths, decks |
| 401-466-2034 Fax: 401-466-2053 | AmEx, MC, Visa, Disc., | bicycle rental shop |
| Judith B. Rose | • | stone porch, gardens |
| Open May–October | C-ltd/S-ltd/P-no/H-no | |

*Sea & country setting. Furnished w/antiques, queen or king size beds, some w/canopy. Bicycle or stroll to waterfront shops & sights. 5% discount on room rate.*

| **Sheffield House B&B, The** | $$-B&B | Continental plus bkfst. |
| P.O. Box C-2, Hight St.,  02807 | 7 rooms, 5 pb | Comp. tea and cookies |
| 401-466-2494 Fax: 401-446-5067 | AmEx, MC, Visa, • | Bicycles & tennis nearby |
| Steve & Claire McQueeny | S-ltd/P-no/H-yes | beaches, hiking trails |
| All year | | bird sanctuaries, nature |

*1886 Victorian home in historic district; walk to beach, shops, restaurants. Quiet, gracious home furnished in family antiques & collections. 3rd night free midweek, Sept.–June.*

BRISTOL ──────────────────────────

| **Reynolds House Inn** | $$-B&B | Full breakfast |
| P.O. Box 5,  02809 | 4 rooms, 2 pb | Comp. tea, sherry, wine |
| 956 Hope St. | Visa, MC, AmEx, | Lunch/dinner/snack avail |
| 401-254-0230 Fax: 401-254-2610 | *Rated*, • | sitting room, library |
| 800-754-0230 | C-ltd/S-no/P-yes/H-no | bikes & tennis nearby |
| Wendy Anderson | Some French & German | |
| All year | | |

*National Historic landmark circa 1680-1695. Lafayette's military headquarters in 1778. Featured in Philadelphia Inquirer. Spectacular food, showcased at Bloomingdales NY 1996.*

| **William's Grant Inn B&B** | $$-B&B | Full breakfast |
| 154 High St.,  02809 | 5 rooms, 3 pb | Aftn. tea, comp. sherry |
| 401-253-4222  800-596-4222 | Most CC, *Rated*, • | Sitting room, library |
| Michael Rose | C-ltd/S-ltd/P-no/H-ltd | bicycles |
| All year | | box lunches for picnics |

*On a quiet tree-lined street. Filled with family antiques and artist's fine work. Featured in NY Times travel section, May 1993. Midweek Miser Pkg.; call for details.*

LITTLE COMPTON ──────────────────────────

| **Stone House Club** | $$$-B&B | Continental plus bkfst. |
| 122 Sakonnet Point Rd, | 13 rooms, 9 pb | Restaurant, bar service |
|   02837 | Visa, MC, | Beach, nature trails, |
| 401-635-2222 Fax: 401-635-2822 | C-yes/S-ltd/P-no/H-ltd | yacht club closeby |
| Margaret & Peter Tirpaeck | | sitting room, library |
| All year | | |

*Private ocean view Victorian Inn, Early American tavern and restaurant, banquet facility and executive retreat. Inquire about our membership and monthly newsletter.*

## MIDDLETOWN

**Inn at Shadow Lawn, The**
120 Miantonomi Ave., 02842
401-849-1298 Fax: 401-849-1306
800-828-0000
Selma & Randy Fabricant
All year

$$-B&B
8 rooms, 8 pb
Visa, MC, *Rated*, •
C-yes/S-no/P-no/H-no

Continental plus bkfst.
Complimentary wine
Sitting room, library
Tiffany lighting
rolling lawns, wicker

*Step back in time and take a leisurely stroll around the beautiful rolling lawns, at our 1853 Victorian mansion. Minutes from Newport.* **Special packages available**

## NARRAGANSETT

**Richards, The**
144 Gibson Ave., 02882
401-789-7746
Steven & Nancy Richards
All year

$$-B&B
2 rooms, 2 pb
C-ltd/S-no/P-no/H-no

Full gourmet breakfast
Comp. sherry in room
Library w/fireplace
tennis courts nearby
fireplaces in bedrooms

*Gracious accommodations in a country setting. Awaken to the smell of gourmet coffee and freshly baked goods. Walk to the beach. 2 bedroom suite w/sitting room & private bath.*

**Sea Gull Guest House**
50 Narragansett Ave., 02882
401-783-4636 Fax: 401-783-4636
Kimber Wheelock
All year

$-EP
5 rooms,
MC, Visa, *Rated*,
C-ltd/S-yes/P-no/H-no

Bar service
Tennis courts nearby
near gambling casino
ocean beach 1 block

*Large rooms cooled by ocean breezes. Close to everything. Swim, sun, sail & fish. Efficiency apartment available. Water sports in the area.* **Stay 5 nights, pay for only 4, ltd**

**White Rose B&B**
22 Cedar St., 02882
401-789-0181  401-465-4149
Pat & Sylvan Vaicaitis
All year

$$-B&B
4 rooms,
*Rated*, •
C-ltd/S-no/P-no/H-no
Some French & Spanish

Full breakfast
Refrigerator, comp. wine
Sitting room with TV
bikes, 1 block to ocean
fishing, tennis nearby

*A classic Victorian where the upbeat atmosphere is simple and elegant. Enjoy the breeze of the front porch or soak up the sun in our large yard.* **Various local discounts**

## NEWPORT

**Admiral Benbow Inn**
8 Fair St., 93 Pelham St.,
02840
401-848-8000 Fax: 401-848-8006
800-343-2863
Cathy Darrigan
February—December

$$$-B&B
15 rooms, 15 pb
AmEx, MC, Visa,
*Rated*, •
C-ltd/S-no/P-yes/H-no

Continental plus bkfst.
Comp. wine—special occ.
Breakfast/conf. room
air conditioning
telephone service, Fax

*Brass beds, antiques and atmosphere, deck and spectacular view of Narragansett Bay. A treasure on our island.* **Ask about Winter Getaway.**

**Admiral Farragut Inn**
8 Fair St., 31 Clarke St., 02840
401-848-8000 Fax: 401-848-8006
800-343-2863
Jack & Janice Oak
All year

$$$-B&B
8 rooms, 8 pb
AmEx, MC, Visa,
*Rated*, •
C-yes/S-ltd/P-no/H-yes

Full breakfast
Afternoon tea
Sitting room
air conditioning
telephones, Fax

*Carefully restored 1702 colonial, furnished w/English antiques. All hand-made pencil four-poster beds, comfortable accommodations. A truly unique inn.* **Ask about Winter Getaway.**

NEWPORT

**Admiral Fitzroy Inn**
8 Fair St., 398 Thames St.,
02840
401-848-8000 Fax: 401-848-8006
800-343-2863
Sheryl Sealey
All year exc. January

$$$-B&B
18 rooms, 18 pb
AmEx, MC, Visa,
*Rated*, •
C-yes/S-yes/P-no/H-yes

Full breakfast
Afternoon tea, snacks
Refrig., cable TV, decks
telephone & coffee maker
in room, hair dryer, A/C

*Small hotel located in town near harbor. Harborviews, gracious, attentive service. Large, comfortable rooms ind. decorated w/hand-painted walls. Ask about Winter Getaways.*

**Bellevue House**
14 Catherine St., 02840
401-847-1828 Fax: 401-847-4946
800-820-1828
Joan & Vic Farmer
Late May–late October

$$-B&B
8 rooms, 6 pb
•
C-ltd/S-no/P-no/H-no

Continental breakfast
Restaurant near, sundeck
laundry, patio, parking
sail package, A/C

*Centrally located on Historic Hill; easy walk to harbor front; mile to beach; combines Victorian charm, colonial history and nautical decor. Guest accommodations since 1828.*

**Brinley Victorian Inn**
23 Brinley St., 02840
401-849-7645 Fax: 401-845-9634
800-999-8523
John & Jennifer Sweetman
All year

$$$-B&B
17 rooms, 12 pb
*Rated*, •
C-ltd/S-yes/P-no/H-no

Continental plus bkfst.
Wine & lobster dinner
Sitting room
landscaped courtyard
A/C, gardens

*Romantic Victorian uniquely decorated w/antiques, period wallpapers. Brick courtyard planted w/Victorian flowers. Park & walk to historic sites/beaches.*

**Castle Hill Inn & Resort**
Ocean Dr., 02840
401-849-3800 Fax: 401-849-3838
Derek Sylvester
All year

$$-B&B
39 rooms, 39 pb
Visa, MC, AmEx,
C-ltd/S-no/P-no/H-no

Full breakfast
Restaurant, bar service
Sitting room, bikes
private beach, trails
all with ocean views

*Experience Victorian splendor-private waterfront retreat on Newport's picturesque Ocean Dr. Tastefully appointed rooms & suites, beach cottages, superb NE regional cuisine. Off season pkgs. available.*

**Cliff View Guest House**
4 Cliff Terrace, 02840
401-846-0885
Pauline Shea
May 1–November 1

$$-B&B
4 rooms, 2 pb
MC, Visa,
C-ltd/S-ltd/P-no/H-no

Continental plus bkfst.
Sitting room
piano
2 rooms with A/C

*Two-story Victorian c.1870. East side has view of Atlantic Ocean. Two porches, open sun deck. Walk to beach or Cliff Walk. July & August french grandson on premises.*

**Cliffside Inn**
2 Seaview Ave., 02840
401-847-1811 Fax: 401-848-5850
800-845-1811
Stephan Nicolas
May-Oct.

$$$$-B&B
15 rooms, 15 pb
AmEx, MC, Visa,
*Rated*, •
C-ltd/S-no/P-no/H-no

Full gourmet breakfast
Victorian tea, comp.
Coffee/tea in rooms
12 rms. with Jacuzzis
12 rms. with fireplaces

*Gracious Victorian home near beach & Cliff Walk. Each room individually & tastefully decorated w/antiques. 2 suite cottage avail. Nov.–May stay 3 nights, get 1 free, mid-week, ltd.*

NEWPORT ————————————————————————————————

| **Flag Quarters** | $$$-B&B | Full breakfast |
|---|---|---|
| 54 Malbone Rd., 02840 | 2 rooms, | Private bath, phone |
| 401-849-4543 | • | private entrance, A/C |
| Rich & Joan Hulse | C-ltd/S-no/P-no/H-no | color/cable TV, antiques |
| April 15-October 1 | | |

*A 15 minute walk of the historic section, waterfront, shops & restaurants. Offers all the amenities of a fine hotel with all the coziness of a B&B. Victorian c.1880.* **3rd night 50%, mid-week.**

| **Harborside Inn** | $$$-B&B | Continental plus bkfst. |
|---|---|---|
| Christie's Landing, 02840 | 14 rooms, 14 pb | Afternoon tea & mixers |
| 401-846-6600 Fax: 401-849-3023 | Most CC, | Harbor Room |
| 800-427-9444 | C-yes/S-yes/P-no/H-no | refrigerators, wet bars |
| Ann McFarland | | TVs, decks |
| All year | | |

*On Newport's historic waterfront, a new inn with each suite featuring a wet bar, refrigerator, color TV, sleeping loft, deck. Homebaked breads each morning.* **Midweek specials.**

| **Hydrangea House Inn** | $$-B&B | Full breakfast buffet |
|---|---|---|
| 16 Bellevue Ave., 02840 | 6 rooms, 6 pb | Sitting room |
| 401-846-4435 Fax: 401-846-4435 | MC, Visa, *Rated*, • | parlor w/fireplace |
| 800-945-4667 | C-yes/S-no/P-no/H-no | A/C, private parking |
| Dennis Blair, Grant | | |
| Edmondson | | |
| All year | | |

*Within Newport's "Walking District." A gratifying hot breakfast buffet served in our contemporary art gallery. AAA rated 2 stars. Fireplace suite w/whirlpool & canopy king bed.*

| **InnTowne Inn** | $$$-EP | Continental plus bkfst. |
|---|---|---|
| 6 Mary St., 02840 | 26 rooms, 26 pb | Afternoon tea |
| 401-846-9200 Fax: 401-846-1534 | Visa, MC, AmEx, • | Sitting room, library |
| 800-457-7803 | C-ltd/S-yes/P-no/H-no | swimming pool, health |
| Carmella L. Gardner | | club facilities, sundeck |
| All year | | |

*Elegant traditional Inn situated in the heart of Newport. Sun deck, four poster beds, use of health club/pool nearby. Close to Mansions, shopping, beaches & fine restaurants.*

| **Ivy Lodge** | $$$-B&B | Full breakfast |
|---|---|---|
| 12 Clay St., 02840 | 8 rooms, 8 pb | Afternoon tea, snacks |
| 401-849-6865 | AmEx, MC, Visa, | Comp. wine, bicycles |
| Maggie & Terry Moy | C-yes/S-ltd/P-no/H-no | sitting room |
| All year | | gardens |

*A romantic Inn in the heart of Newport's famous mansion area. Walking distance to cliff walk, mansions, restaurants, shopping. Rooms are spacious and private.*

| **Marshall Slocum Guest Hse.** | $$-B&B | Full breakfast |
|---|---|---|
| 29 Kay St., 02840 | 5 rooms, 1 pb | Lunch & dinner available |
| 401-841-5120 Fax: 401-846-3787 | Visa, MC. AmEx, • | Aft. tea, comp. wine |
| 800-372-5120 | C-ltd/S-no/P-no/H-no | sitting room, library |
| Joan Wilson | | front porch w/rockers |
| All year | | |

*A charming Victorian private home with rooms for guests. Serving an extraordinary breakfast each morning. Located a scant block from town in a residential neighborhood.*

## NEWPORT

| | | |
|---|---|---|
| **Melville House Inn** | $$$-B&B | Full breakfast in bed |
| 39 Clarke St., 02840 | 7 rooms, 5 pb | Champagne on arrival |
| 401-847-0640 Fax: 401-847-0956 | Most CC, *Rated*, • | Eve. drinks w/turndown |
| Vincent DeRico, David Horan | C-ltd/S-no/P-no/H-no | bicycles, winter frplc. |
| All year | | suite Nov-Apr pkg. deal |

*1750 colonial inn, heart of historic district, close to shops, restaurants, wharfs. Our garden fresh herbs used in cooking. Nat'l Register of Historic Places. **Off-season discount.***

| | | |
|---|---|---|
| **Merritt House Guests** | $$-B&B | Full breakfast |
| **c1850** | 2 rooms, 1 pb | Hot or iced tea |
| 57 Second St., 02840 | *Rated*, • | Sitting room |
| 401-847-4289 | C-ltd | private dining room |
| Angela R. Vars | | patio, A/C in rooms |
| All year | | |

*Historic home (circa 1850) in Point Section, close to bay & center of city, beaches & mansions. Nominated one of 100 Best B&B Homes in North America. **10% off 2nd visit.***

| | | |
|---|---|---|
| **Murray House B&B** | $$$-B&B | Continental plus bkfst. |
| 1 Murray Place, 02840 | 5 rooms, 3 pb | Snacks, comp. wine |
| 401-846-3337 Fax: 401-846-3337 | • | Sitting room |
| Noreen O'Neil | C-ltd/S-ltd/P-yes/H-no | swimming pool, tennis |
| Closed winter | | |

*Charming, attractive, and spotless. Short walk to beach, famous turn of the century mansions. Quiet, Southern tip of the island. **3rd night, 50% off on special days.***

| | | |
|---|---|---|
| **Old Beach Inn, The** | $$$-B&B | Continental plus bkfst. |
| 19 Old Beach Rd., 02840 | 9 rooms, 9 pb | Gazebo, fish pond, patio |
| 401-849-3479 Fax: 401-847-1236 | AmEx, MC, Visa, | Sitting room, fireplaces |
| Cyndi & Luke Murray | C-ltd/S-no/P-no/H-no | garden, some A/C & TVs |
| All year | | |

*An intimate inn built in 1879 with elegant accommodations; close to beaches, fabled mansions, cliff-walk, restaurants and historic harborfront. **10% off 3 or more nights.***

| | | |
|---|---|---|
| **Pilgrim House Inn** | $$-B&B | Continental plus bkfst. |
| 123 Spring St., 02840 | 10 rooms, 8 pb | Comp. sherry, shortbread |
| 401-846-0040 Fax: 401-838-0537 | MC, Visa, *Rated*, | Deck w/view of harbor |
| 800-525-8373 | C-ltd/S-yes/P-no/H-no | living room w/fireplace |
| Pam & Bruce Bayuk | | Close to attractions. |
| Closed January | | |

*Elegant Victorian inn, two blocks from the harbor in Newports historic district. Immaculate rooms & wonderful atmosphere awaits you. Meetings of up to 25 people. **3rd night 50% off, ltd.***

| | | |
|---|---|---|
| **Spring Street Inn** | $$-B&B | Full gourmet breakfast |
| 353 Spring St., 02840 | 5 rooms, 5 pb | Afternoon tea |
| 401-847-4767 | MC, Visa, *Rated*, • | Sitting room |
| Patricia Golder & Jack Lang | C-yes/S-yes/P-no/H-no | parking, bus loop |
| All year | | two blocks from harbour |

*Charming restored Empire Victorian house, c.1858. Harbour-view suite with private deck & living room. Short walk to Newport's historic sights, mansions, shops & restaurants.*

NEWPORT ——————————————————————————————

**Stella Maris Inn**                  $$$-B&B                Continental plus bkfst.
91 Washington St.,  02840    8 rooms, 8 pb           Afternoon tea
401-849-2862                        *Rated*,                   Complimentary wine
Dorothy & Ed Madden          C-ltd/S-no/P-no/H-no  Sitting room, library
All year                                Minimal French         small meetings possible

*1861 Victorian mansion. Newly renovated, water view rooms, fireplaces, spacious porch
and gardens, antique decor, homemade muffins, walk to town. Elegant & romantic.*

**Villa Liberte**                      $$$-B&B                Continental plus bkfst.
22 Liberty St.,  02840          15 rooms, 15 pb        Afternoon tea
401-846-7444 Fax: 401-849-6429  MC, Visa, AmEx,   Sitting room
800-392-3717                        C-ltd/S-ltd/P-no/H-no  4 star rest. nearby
Leigh Anne Mosco
April 1 - November 15

*Elegance w/the intimacy of a guest house. Master suites, queen rooms & apartment suites
in a 1910 "House of the Evening." Located off historic Bellevue Ave. in the heart of
Newport.* **Sunday–Thursday specials.**

**Wayside**                           $$$$-B&B               Continental plus bkfst.
406 Bellevue Ave.,  02840    8 rooms, 8 pb           BBQ facilities
401-847-0302 Fax: 401-848-9374  Personal Checks OK,  Sitting room
800-653-7678                        C-yes/S-yes/P-no/H-no  flower beds
Al, Dorothy & son Don Post                                      outdoor swimming pool
All year

*Large, attractive, comfortable Georgian-style island home. Ideally located within short
walk of mansions, cliff walk, & harborfront activities.* **3rd night 50% ltd.**

**Willows of Newport, The**   $$$-B&B                Continental plus bkfst.
8 Willow St., Historic Point  5 rooms, 5 pb           Black-Tie-Bkfst.-in-Bed
District,  02840                   *Rated*, •                Victorian parlor, wet
401-846-5486 Fax: 401-849-8215  S-ltd/P-no/H-no    bar, Victorian garden
Pattie Murphy                                                     3 ultra wedding rooms
February–January 3

*Elegant breakfast in bed—cut flowers, mints on your pillow. Private parking and private
bath, air conditioning. Featured nationally on PM Magazine.*

NEWPORT, MIDDLETOWN ——————————————————————

**Lindsey's Guest House**      $$-B&B                 Continental plus bkfst.
6 James St.,  02842             4 rooms, 3 pb           Tennis nearby, sitting
401-846-9386                        MC, Visa, *Rated*, •  room, large yard, deck
Anne Lindsey                       C-ltd/H-yes               ceiling fans in all rms
All year

*Quiet, 10 min. walk to beaches and restaurants. One mile Bellevue Avenue mansions.
Two miles downtown Newport harborfront. Off-street parking.* **Weekday discount packages.**

PAWTUCKET, PROVIDENCE ——————————————————————

**Historic Jacob Hill Farm**  $$-B&B                 Full gourmet breakfast
15 Park St., 120 Jacob St.,    5 rooms, 3 pb           Snacks, comp. wine, tea
Seekonk MA,  02860            Visa, MC, Disc. *Rated*,  Sitting rms., fireplaces
508-336-9165 Fax: 508-336-0951  •                       tennis, pool, gazebo
888-336-9165                        C-ltd/S-ltd/P-no/H-no  A/C, whirlpool bath
Bill & Eleonora Rezek          Polish
All year

*1722 newly renovated Colonial, quiet country setting. Located in Massachusetts 3 miles
from Brown University. Central to Newport, Boston or Cape Cod. Romantic Getaway.* **4th
night free.**

## PROVIDENCE

| **Old Court B&B, The** | $$$-B&B | Full breakfast |
|---|---|---|
| 144 Benefit St.,  02903 | 10 rooms, 10 pb | Comp. tea, asst'd. bread |
| 401-751-2002  Fax: 401-272-4830 | Most CC, *Rated*, • | Apt. avail; kitchen, W/D |
| David "Dolby" Dolbashian | C-ltd/S-yes/P-no/H-no | antiques, common TV room |
| All year | French | wet bars in some rooms |

*Built in 1863, Italianate in design and in ornate details; combines tradition with contemporary standards of luxury; filled with antique furniture, chandeliers. Private baths.*

| **State House Inn** | $$$-B&B | Full breakfast |
|---|---|---|
| 43 Jewett St.,  02908 | 10 rooms, 10 pb | Snacks |
| 401-351-6111  Fax: 401-351-4261 | AmEx, MC, Visa, | Sitting room |
| Monica Hopton | *Rated*, • | Shaker art & furniture |
| All year | C-yes/S-no/P-no/H-no | |

*Charming country B&B decorated with Shaker and colonial furnishings with all the privacy and amenities frequent travelers desire.* **3rd night 50% off.**

## WAKEFIELD

| **Larchwood Inn, The** | $-EP | All meals (fee) |
|---|---|---|
| 521 Main St.,  02879 | 19 rooms, | Restaurant, bar |
| 401-783-5454  Fax: 401-783-1800 | Most CC, *Rated*, • | Cocktail lounge |
| 800-275-5450 | C-yes/S-yes/P-yes/H-no | sitting room |
| Francis & Diann Browning | Spanish, French | |
| All year | | |

*Intimate country inn in New England townhouse style. circa 1831. Conveniently located near Newport, Mystic Seaport, Block Island and Univ. of Rhode Island.*

## WESTERLY

| **Villa, The** | $$$-B&B | Continental plus bkfst. |
|---|---|---|
| 190 Shore Rd.,  02891 | 7 rooms, 7 pb | Hot tubs, swimming pool |
| 401-596-1054  Fax: 401-596-6268 | *Rated*, • | fireplace/jacuzzi suites |
| 800-722-9240 | C-ltd/S-yes/P-yes | 1.5 acres of lawn/garden |
| Jerry & Rose Maiorano | Italian | |
| All year | | |

*Escape to our Mediterranean villa. We set the stage for your romantic get-away. You'll fall in love and want to return. Outdoor pool and hot tub. Adjacent to golf course.*

| **Woody Hill B&B** | $$-B&B | Full country breakfast |
|---|---|---|
| 149 S. Woody Hill Rd.,  02891 | 3 rooms, 3 pb | Extensive library |
| 401-322-0452 | • | porch with swing, pool |
| Dr. Ellen L. Madison | C-yes/S-no/P-no/H-ltd | winter hearth cooking |
| All year | | |

*Near beaches and Mystic Seaport, secluded country atmosphere. In-ground pool. Handmade quilts, antiques, wide-board floors, gardens, casual Colonial feeling.* **3rd night 10% off.**

## WYOMING

| **Cookie Jar B&B, The** | $$-B&B | Full breakfast |
|---|---|---|
| 64 Kingstown Rd., Route 138, | 3 rooms, 3 pb | Snacks |
| just off I-95,  02898 | *Rated*, • | Library, 3 acres with |
| 401-539-2680  800-767-4262 | C-yes/S-no/P-no/H-no | fruit trees & gardens |
| Dick & Madelein Sohl | | each room w/TV & A/C |
| All year | | |

*Outside, a simple farmhouse—unusually attractive inside. Living room was a 1732 blacksmith shop. Pool & golf nearby. Private adjoining sitting room in each guestroom.*

# More Inns . . .

| | |
|---|---|
| Block Island | Barrington Inn, P.O. Box 397, 02807, 401-466-5510 |
| Block Island | Blue Dory Inn, The, Box 488, Dodge St., 02807, 401-466-5891 |
| Block Island | Driftwind Guests, High St., 02807, 401-466-5548 |
| Block Island | Gables Inn, P.O. Box 516, 02807, 401-466-2213 |
| Block Island | Holiday Haven Guest House, Center Rd. Box 24, 02807, 401-466-2676 |
| Block Island | Inn at Old Harbour, The, Water St., 02807 |
| Block Island | Island Home, P.O. Box 737 Beach Ave., 02807 |
| Block Island | Island Manor Resort, Chapel St., 02807, 401-466-5567 |
| Block Island | Lewis Farm, Cooneymas Rd., 02807, 401-466-2428 |
| Block Island | Mill Pond Cottages, Old Town Rd., 02807, 401-466-2423 |
| Block Island | New Shoreham House Inn, P.O. Box 160, 02807, 401-466-2651 |
| Block Island | Old Town Inn, Old Town Rd, P.O. Box 3, 02807, 401-466-5958 |
| Block Island | Samuel Peckham Inn, New Harbor, 02807, 401-466-2439 |
| Block Island | Sea Breeze Inn, Spring St., Box 141, 02807, 401-466-2275 |
| Block Island | Seacrest Inn, 207 High St., 02807, 401-466-2882 |
| Block Island | Spring House Hotel, The, P.O. Box 902, 02807, 401-466-5844 |
| Block Island | White House, The, Spring St., 02807, 401-466-2653 |
| Block Island | Willow Grove, P.O. Box 156, 02807, 401-466-2896 |
| Bristol | Rockwell House Inn, 610 Hope St., 02809, 401-253-0040 |
| Carolina | Country Acres B&B, Box 551, 02812, 401-364-9134 |
| Charleston | Ye Ole General Stanton Inn, P.O. Box 1263, 02813, 401-364-0100 |
| Charlestown | "Hathaways", Box 731, 02813, 401-364-6665 |
| Charlestown | Inn the Meadow, 1045 Shannock Rd., 02813, 401-789-1473 |
| Green Hill | Fairfield-by-The-Sea B&B, 527 Green Hill Beach Rd, 02879, 401-789-4717 |
| Jamestown | Mary W. Murphy, 59 Walcott Ave., 02835, 401-423-1338 |
| Kingstown | Farmer Brown House, The, 2492 Kingstown Rd., 02881, 401-783-5477 |
| Little Compton | Ballyvoreen, 75 Stone Church Rd., 02837, 401-635-4396 |
| Middletown | Briar Patch, The, 42 Briarwood Ave., 02842, 401-841-5824 |
| Middletown | Whimsey Cottage, 42 Briarwood Ave, 02840, 401-841-5824 |
| Misquamicut | Andrea Hotel, 89 Atlantic Ave., 02891, 401-348-8788 |
| Misquamicut | Ocean View, Atlantic Ave., 02891, 401-596-7170 |
| N. Kingstown | Meadowland B&B Ltd., 765 Old Baptist Rd., 02852, 401-294-4168 |
| Narragansett | 1900 House, 59 Kingstown Rd., 02882, 401-789-7971 |
| Narragansett | Chestnut House, 11 Chestnut St., 02882, 401-789-5335 |
| Narragansett | Going My Way, 75 Kingstown Rd., 02882, 401-789-3479 |
| Narragansett | Grinnell Inn, 83 Narragansett Ave., 02882 |
| Narragansett | Ilverthorpe Cottage, 41 Robinson St., 02882, 401-789-2392 |
| Narragansett | Kenyon Farms, P.O. Box 648, 02882, 401-783-7123 |
| Narragansett | Mon Reve, 41 Gibson Ave., 02882, 401-783-2846 |
| Narragansett | Murphy's B&B, 43 South Pier Rd., 02882, 401-789-1824 |
| Narragansett | Phoenix House, 29 Gibson Ave., 02882, 401-783-1918 |
| Narragansett | Pier House Inn, 113 Ocean Rd., 02882, 401-783-4704 |
| Narragansett | Stone Lea, 40 Newton Ave., 02882, 401-783-9546 |
| Narragansett | Twenty-Three Perkins, 23 Perkins, 02882, 401-783-9158 |
| Newport | A Viewpoint, 231 Coggeshall Ave., 02840 |
| Newport | Anna's Victorian, 5 Fowler Av., 02840, 401-849-2489 |
| Newport | Blue Stone, 33 Russell Ave., 02840, 401-846-5408 |
| Newport | Castle Keep, 44 Everett, 02840, 401-846-0362 |
| Newport | Clarkeston, The, 28 Clarke St., 02840, 401-524-1386 |
| Newport | Cliff Walk Manor, 117 Memorial Blvd., 02840, 401-847-1300 |
| Newport | Commodore Perry, 8 Fair St., 02840, 401-846-4256 |
| Newport | Country Goose B&B, The, 563 Greenend Ave., 02842, 401-846-6308 |
| Newport | Covell Guest House, 43 Farewell St., 02840, 401-847-8872 |
| Newport | Elm Tree Cottage, 336 Gibbs Av., 02840, 401-849-1610 |
| Newport | Francis Malbone House, The, 392 Thames St, 02840, 401-846-0392 |
| Newport | Hammett House Inn, 505 Thames St., 02840, 800-548-9417 |
| Newport | Jailhouse Inn, 13 Marlborough St., 02840, 401-847-4638 |
| Newport | John Banister House, 56 Pelham St., 02840, 401-846-0050 |
| Newport | La Forge cottage, 96 Pelham St., 02840, 401-847-4400 |
| Newport | Mill Street Inn, 75 Mill St., 02840, 401-849-9500 |
| Newport | Mount Vernon Inn, 24 Mount Vernon St., 02840, 401-846-6314 |
| Newport | Ocean Cliff, Ocean Dr., 02840, 401-849-9000 |
| Newport | Old Dennis House, 59 Washington St., 02840, 401-846-1324 |
| Newport | Rhode Island House, 77 Rhode Island Ave., 02840, 401-849-7765 |
| Newport | Samuel Honey House, 12 Francis St., 02840, 401-847-2669 |
| Newport | Sea Quest, 9 Cliff Terrace, 02840, 401-846-0227 |
| Newport | Thames Street Inn, 400 Thames St., 02840, 401-847-4459 |
| Newport | Victorian Ladies, The, 63 Memorial Blvd., 02840, 401-849-9960 |
| Newport | William Fludder House, 30 Bellevue Ave., 02840, 401-849-4220 |
| Pawt | Constance Delange, 30 South St. #3, 02860 |
| Portsmouth | Twin Spruce Tourist, 515 Turnpike Ave., 02871 |
| Providence | Cady House, 127 Power St., 02906, 401-273-5398 |
| S. Kingstown | Admiral Dewey Inn, 668 Matunuck Beach Rd., 02879, 401-783-2090 |
| Smithfield | Newport Collection, The, 445 Putman Pike, 02828, 800-947-4667 |
| Wakefield | "Almost Heaven" B&B, 49 W. St., 02879, 401-783-9272 |
| Warwick | Open Gate Motel, 840 Quaker Ln., 02886, 401-884-4490 |

| | |
|---|---|
| Watch Hill | Ocean House, 2 Bluff Ave, 02891, 401-348-8161 |
| Watch Hill | Watch Hill Inn, 50 Bay St., 02891, 401-348-8912 |
| Westerly | Grandview B&B, 212 Shore Rd., 02891, 401-596-6384 |
| Westerly | Harbour House, Bay St., 02891 |
| Westerly | J. Livingston's Guesthouse, 39 Weekapang Rd., 02891, 401-322-0249 |
| Westerly | Shelter Harbor Inn, 10 Wagner Rd., 02891, 401-322-8883 |
| Wickford | Moran's B&B, The, 130 W. Main St., 02852, 401-294-3497 |

# South Carolina

## AIKEN

| **Holley Inns** | $$-B&B | Continental breakfast |
|---|---|---|
| 235 Richland Ave., 29801 | 48 rooms, 48 pb | Aftn. tea, comp. wine |
| 803-648-4265 | Most CC, • | Restaurant, bar service |
| Forrest Holley | C-yes/S-ltd/P-ltd/H-yes | tennis nearby, pool |
| All year | | golf at private club |

*B&B Inn also elegant small guesthouse motel. 48 beautiful rooms, center of beautiful, historic city, walking distance of excellent restaurants, shops. We have courtyard dining.* **Comp. drink on arrival.**

| **New Berry Inn B&B** | $$-B&B | Full breakfast weekends |
|---|---|---|
| 240 New Berry St. SW, 29801 | 4 rooms, 4 pb | Complimentary beverages |
| 803-649-2935 | Most CC, • | Sitting room, cable TV |
| Mary Ann & Hal Mackey | C-ltd/S-no/P-no/H-ltd | fine restaurants, phones |
| All year | | weddings, meetings |

*Relaxed atmosphere of the South in a New England-style home. 4 large rooms with private baths and antiques. Historic area. Golf, hiking, horse country.* **Govt. & corp. rates.**

## BEAUFORT

| **Beaufort Inn, The** | $$$-B&B | Full breakfast |
|---|---|---|
| 809 Port Republic St., 29902 | 13 rooms, 13 pb | Restaurant, bar service |
| 803-521-9000 Fax:803-521-9000 | Most CC, *Rated*, • | Bicycles, cooking class |
| Debbie & Russell Fielden | C-ltd/S-ltd/P-no/H-yes | sitting room, library |
| All year | Dutch | low country excursions |

*Local owners have rebuilt Beaufort's largest historic inn. The inn's three-story winding staircase leads you to some of the south's most beautiful guest rooms.*

| **Old Point Inn** | $$-B&B | Full breakfast |
|---|---|---|
| 212 New St., 29902 | 4 rooms, 4 pb | Comp. wine |
| 803-524-3177 Fax:803-525-6544 | AmEx, MC, Visa, | Library, piano, tennis |
| Joan and Joe Carpentiere | C-ltd/S-ltd/P-no/H-no | Garden, Fax, beach |
| All year | | carriage rides, golf |

*1898 Queen Anne, heart of historic district near shops, restaurants, park. Relax on verandas, nap in our hammock; enjoy low-country hospitality.*

| **TwoSuns Inn B&B** | $$$-B&B | Full breakfast |
|---|---|---|
| 1705 Bay St., 29902 | 5 rooms, 5 pb | Aft. tea, comp. wine |
| 803-522-1122 Fax:803-522-1122 | AmEx, MC, Visa, | Sitting room, bicycles |
| 800-532-4244 | *Rated*, • | public tennis courts |
| Carrol and Ron Kay | C-ltd/S-no/P-no/H-yes | computer, Fax, cable TV |
| All year | | |

*1917 Certified Historic Building w/finest bayview. Breakfast fare, modern amenities. Resident owner hospitality in Beufort. Handwoven creations by Carrol.* **10% off, ltd.**

*TwoSuns Inn B&B, Beaufort, SC*

## BLUFFTON

**Fripp House Inn**
PO Box 74,
48 Bridge St.,   29910
803-757-2139
Dana & Grant
Tuttle
All year

$$-B&B
3 rooms, 3 pb
MC, Visa,  •
C-yes/S-ltd/P-no/H-no

Full breakfast
Snacks, set-up bar
Sitting room
bicycles, swimming pool
golf, beaches nearby

*Historic landmark in a quiet village on the May River. Private gardens, fountains, fireplaces, antiques. Minutes from Hilton Head Island. Fine restaurants nearby.*

## CHARLESTON

**27 State Street B&B**
27 State St.,   29401
803-722-4243
Paul & Joye
Craven
All year

$$$-B&B/EP
5 rooms, 5 pb
*Rated*,  •
C-ltd/S-no/P-no/H-no

Continental plus (fee)
Bicycles, sitting room
tennis nearby
morning paper, flowers

*Charming & unique with pronounced old world influence. In French Quarter of the original walled city. 2 suites B&B, 2 suites EP. Some with fireplaces.*

**Ann Harper's B&B**
56 Smith St.,   29401
803-723-3947
Ann D. Harper
All year

$$-B&B
2 rooms, 1 pb
C-ltd/S-ltd/P-no/H-no

Full breakfast
Small garden
off-street parking

*Charming circa 1870 home located in Charleston's historic district. The owner, a retired medical technologist, enjoys serving a full Southern breakfast each morning.*

## CHARLESTON

**Ashley Inn B&B**
201 Ashley Ave.,  29403
803-723-1848
Sally & Bud Allen
All year

$$-B&B
7 rooms, 7 pb
MC, Visa, *Rated*, •
C-ltd/S-ltd/P-no/H-no

Full breakfast
Aft. tea, snacks
Complimentary wine
sitting room
bicycles

*Sleep until the fragrance of southern cooking lures you to garden breakfast. Fireplaces, private baths & bikes assure the best Charleston experience. **Comp. aft. sherry & tea.***

**Barksdale House Inn, The**
27 George St.,  29401
803-577-4800 Fax: 803-853-0482
George & Peggy Sloan
All year exc. Christmas

$$$-B&B
14 rooms, 14 pb
MC, Visa, *Rated*, •
C-ltd/S-yes/P-no/H-no

Continental breakfast
Complimentary tea, wine
Sitting rm., bike rental
whirlpool baths, decks
renovated carriage house

*Circa 1778, elegant inn with whirlpool baths, fireplaces, built-in dry bars, elaborate furnishings and antiques; adjacent to the historic shopping district. **10% off-AARP, AAA, Mobil.***

**Battery Carriage House Inn**
20 S. Battery,  29401
803-727-3100 Fax: 803-727-3130
800-775-5575
Katherine G. Hastie
All year

$$$-B&B
11 rooms, 11 pb
Most CC, *Rated*, •
C-ltd/S-ltd/P-no/H-no

Continental breakfast
Complimentary wine
3 whirlpool baths
4 steam showers

*Very romantic, elegant. Located in garden of historic mansion on the Battery; silver tray breakfast, friendly and professional staff.*

**Belvedere B&B, The**
40 Rutledge Ave.,  29401
803-722-0973
David Spell & Rick Zender
All year

$$$-B&B
3 rooms, 3 pb
*Rated*,
C-ltd/S-yes/P-no/H-no

Continental plus bkfst.
Sherry
Sitting room, newspaper
TV, A/C, porch with view
of lake

*We offer hospitable accommodations in our gracious mansion overlooking beautiful Colonial Lake. Sherry and other extras. **2 nights plus, free color print of Inn.***

**Brasington House B&B**
328 E. Bay St.,  29401
803-722-1274 Fax: 803-722-6785
Dalton & Judy Brasington
All year

$$$-B&B
4 rooms, 4 pb
MC, Visa, *Rated*,
S-no/P-no/H-no

Full breakfast
Complimentary beverages
Coffee/tea making
facilites in room
Sitting room, books

*200-year-old antebellum house elegantly furnished w/antiques. Located in Historic District. Breakfast in formal dining room, wine and liquors included. Gracious hospitality.*

**Cannonboro Inn B&B**
184 Ashley Ave.,  29403
803-723-8572
Sally & Bud Allen
All year

$$-B&B
6 rooms, 6 pb
MC, Visa, *Rated*, •
C-ltd/S-no/P-no/H-no

Full breakfast
Comp. sherry, tea
Sitting room, library
garden, tennis courts
comp. touring bikes

*Antebellum home c.1850 in Charleston's historic district. Breakfast served on a piazza overlooking a country garden. Fireplaces in rooms. 1994 "Fodor's Choice" for SC.*

*Cannonboro Inn B&B, Charleston, SC*

CHARLESTON ────────────────────────────────

**Country Victorian B&B**
105 Tradd St.,  29401
803-577-0682
Diane Deardurff Weed
All year

$$-B&B
2 rooms, 2 pb
C-ltd/S-no/P-no/H-no

Continental plus bkfst.
Afternoon tea, snacks
Parking, bicycles
TV, restaurants nearby
piazzas

*Private entrances, antique iron and brass beds, old quilts, antique oak and wicker furniture. Situated in the historic district. Walk to everything. Many extras.*

────────────────────────────────

**Fulton Lane Inn**
202 King St.,  29401
803-720-2600 Fax: 803-720-2940
800-720-2688
Randall Felkel
All year

$$$-B&B
27 rooms, 27 pb
Most CC, *Rated*, •
C-yes/S-no/P-no/H-yes

Continental plus bkfst.
Bar service
Comp. wine, sitting rm.
Sts. avail., babysitters
hot tubs, conf. facility

*Victorian inn built in 1870 by Confederate blockade runner John Rugheimer, on quiet pedestrian lane. Furnished with antiques & historically accurate reproductions.*

────────────────────────────────

**John Rutledge House Inn**
116 Broad St.,  29401
803-723-7999 Fax: 803-720-2615
800-476-9741
Linda Bishop
All year

$$$$-B&B
19 rooms, 19 pb
AmEx, MC, Visa,
*Rated*, •
C-yes/S-ltd/P-no/H-yes

Continental plus(fee)
Comp. wine/brandy/sherry
Bar, sitting room
concierge, turndown serv
babysitters, hot tubs

*John Rutledge, a signer of US Constitution, built this elegant home in 1763. Visit and re-live history. Downtown location near shopping & historic sites. AAA 4 diamond.*

## CHARLESTON

**King George IV Inn**
32 George St.,   29401
803-723-9339 Fax: 803-727-0065
Debbie, B.J., & Mike
All year

$$-B&B
8 rooms, 8 pb
MC, Visa, •
C-yes/S-no/P-ltd/H-ltd

Continental plus bkfst.
Comp. coffees & teas
Three levels of porches
parking, refrigerators
beaches, boat rides

*Circa 1790s Federal style historic house. All rooms have fireplaces, hardwood floors, high ceilings w/moldings, antiques. Walk to all historic sights, shopping & restaurants. 30%-45% off Nov.–Feb.*

---

**Kings Courtyard Inn**
198 King St.,   29401
803-723-7000 Fax: 803-720-2618
800-845-6119
Laura Fox
All year

$$$-B&B
41 rooms, 41 pb
Most CC, *Rated*, •
C-yes/S-yes/P-no/H-yes

Continental plus bkfst.
Comp. wine/sherry/brandy
Sitting room, parking
hot tub, bicycles
conference/party room

*1853 historic inn, rooms with period furnishings, canopied beds, fireplaces, overlook two inner courtyards. Concierge service, evening turndown with brandy and chocolate.*

---

**Kitchen House (c.1732)**
126 Tradd St.,   29401
803-577-6362
Lois Evans
All year

$$$-B&B
2 rooms, 2 pb
MC, Visa, *Rated*, •
C-ltd/S-yes/P-no/H-no

Full breakfast
Kitchen, afternoon tea
Comp. sherry
sitting room, cable TV
concierge service

*Restored, pre-Revolutionary house in the historic district. Patio, herb garden & fish pond. Featured in Colonial Homes Magazine. Honeymoon packages.* **Free bottle wine with mention of book.**

---

**Maison Du Pre**
317 E. Bay St., at George St.,
29401
803-723-8691  800-662-INNS
Lucille/Bob/Mark
Mulholland
All year

$$$-B&B
15 rooms, 15 pb
Most CC, *Rated*, •
C-yes/S-yes/P-no/H-no

Continental breakfast
Low country tea party
(wine, hors d'oeuvres)
drawing room
porch, patio, bicycles

*Ideally located in Charleston's historic district. 15 guest rms w/private baths. Antiques, carriage rides. Honeymoon suites, kitchen suites, executive suites.* **Golf packages.**

---

**Palmer Home, The**
5 E. Battery,   29401
803-723-2308
Francess P. Hogan
All year

$$$-B&B
3 rooms, 3 pb
C-yes/S-no/P-no/H-no

Continental breakfast
Sitting room, piano
sauna, historic district
swimming pool

*One of the fifty famous homes in the city; furnished in period antiques; piazzas overlook harbor and Fort Sumter where Civil War began.* **3rd night 25% off.**

---

**Planters Inn**
112 N. Market St.,   29401
803-722-2345 Fax: 803-577-2125
800-845-7082
Larry J. Spelts, Jr.
All year

$$$-B&B
,
Most CC, *Rated*, •
C-yes/S-yes/P-no/H-yes

Continental plus bkfst.
Comp. hors d'oeuvres
Wine by Chef Nuetzi
valet parking
full turndown service

*Beautifully restored and furnished 1840s building at the center of Charleston's historic district. High ceilinged rooms all individually decorated. AAA 4 diamond rating.*

**CHARLESTON** ─────────────────────────────────────

| | | |
|---|---|---|
| **Rutledge Victorian Inn** | $$-B&B | Continental plus bkfst. |
| 114 Rutledge Ave., 29401 | 11 rooms, | 24-hour refrshmnt. table |
| 803-722-7551 Fax: 803-727-0065 | MC, Visa, • | Porch with rocking chair |
| Debbie, B.J. & Mike | C-yes/S-ltd | TV, A/C, refrigerator |
| All year | | parking, student rates |

*Elegant, decorative house in historic district. All rms. have 12 foot ceilings w/plaster moldings, frplcs., hardwood floors, antiques. "Step into the past." Porch w/rocking chairs.* **30%-45% off Nov.–Feb.**

| | | |
|---|---|---|
| **Thirty Six Meeting St. B&B** | $$$-B&B | Continental plus bkfst. |
| 36 Meeting St., 29401 | 3 rooms, 3 pb | Bicycles |
| 803-722-1034 Fax: 803-723-0068 | MC, Visa, *Rated*, • | walled garden |
| Anne & Vic Brandt | C-ltd/S-no/P-no/H-no | kitchenettes |
| All year | | |

*1740 Charleston Single House in heart of Historic District. Suites elegantly furnished with mahogony rice beds, kitchenetts.*

| | | |
|---|---|---|
| **Thomas Lamball House B&B** | $$$-B&B | Continental plus bkfst. |
| 19 King St., 29401 | 2 rooms, 2 pb | Swimming, tennis, golf |
| 803-723-3212 Fax: 803-724-6352 | C-yes/S-no/P-no/H-no | nearby, harbor views |
| Marie & Emerson Read | | off street parking |
| All year | | |

*Historic home off Battery. Elegantly furnished bedrooms with piazza and harbor views. Private baths, central air, fireplaces, cable, and telephone.*

| | | |
|---|---|---|
| **Timothy Ford's Kitchen** | $$$-B&B | Continental plus bkfst. |
| 54 Meeting St., 29401 | 2 rooms, 2 pb | Complimentary wine |
| 803-577-4432 | C-ltd/S-no/P-no/H-no | Living room, dining room |
| Mrs. Helen A. Pruitt | | kitchen |
| All year | | |

*"Kitchen House," furnished with antiques, 2 bedrooms, 2 bath. Off-street parking; famous garden; center of Historic District.*

| | | |
|---|---|---|
| **Vendue Inn** | $$$$-B&B | Continental plus bkfst. |
| 19 Vendue Range, 29401 | 34 rooms, 34 pb | Wine, cheese, cordials |
| 803-577-7970 Fax: 803-577-2913 | AmEx, MC, Visa, | Sitting room, piano |
| 800-845-7900 | *Rated*, • | chamber music, library |
| Evelyn & Morton Needle | C-yes/S-yes/P-no/H-yes | bicycles, jacuzzi |
| All year | Spanish, Hebrew, French | |

*Chamber music during wine & cheese hours. A small European hotel with Old South charm & gentility.* **Mention Guide and get 10% disc't in restaurant.**

| | | |
|---|---|---|
| **Victoria House Inn** | $$$-B&B | Continental plus bkfst. |
| 208 King St., 29401 | 18 rooms, 18 pb | Bar service |
| 803-720-2944 Fax: 803-720-2930 | Disc., MC, Visa *Rated*, | Conference facilities |
| 800-933-5464 | • | some hot tubs |
| Mary Kay Smith | C-yes/S-ltd/P-no/H-ltd | babysitter available |
| All year | | |

*Victorian inn built in 1889. Document wallpapers and paint colors. Furnished with antiques and historically accurate reproductions. Located in a historic district.*

## CHARLESTON

**Villa de La Fontaine B&B**
138 Wentworth St.,   29401
803-577-7709
Aubrey Hancock, Bill
Fontaine
All year

$$$-B&B
6 rooms, 6 pb
MC, Visa,
C-ltd

Full breakfast
Garden, terraces, tennis
Canopy beds
off-street parking

*Southern colonial mansion, circa 1838, in historic district; half-acre garden; fountain and terraces. Furnished with 18th-century museum pieces. Walk to places of interest.*

## COLUMBIA

**Claussen's Inn**
2003 Greene St.,   29205
803-765-0440 Fax: 803-799-7924
800-622-3382
Dan O. Vance
All year

$$$-B&B
29 rooms, 29 pb
Most CC, *Rated*, •
C-yes/S-yes/P-no/H-no

Continental plus bkfst.
Comp. wine/sherry/brandy
Morning paper
turn-down service with
chocolate & brandy

*Restored old bakery building close to the university, shops, dining, entertainment. Some rooms have kitchenettes. Conference facilities.*

## GEORGETOWN

**"Shipwright's" B&B**
609 Cypress Ct.,   29440
803-527-4475
Leatrice M. Wright
All year

$$-B&B
2 rooms, 2 pb
*Rated*,
C-yes/S-no/P-no/H-ltd

Full breakfast
Aftn. tea, snacks
Complimentary wine
sitting room, library
bicycles, tennis court

*Quiet, quaint, historic Georgetown, on the intercoastal waterway, is a haven for the weary. Four-rocker front porch overlooks marsh & avenue of live oaks. **3rd night 50%, ltd.***

**1790 House-B&B Inn**
630 Highmarket St.,   29440
803-546-4821  Fax: 803-890-7432
800-890-7432
John & Patricia Wiley
All year

$$$-B&B
6 rooms, 6 pb
Most CC *Rated*, •
C-yes/S-ltd/P-no/H-yes

Full breakfast
Afternoon tea, snacks
Sitting room, gardens
bikes, central air/heat
cottage with jacuzzi

*200-year-old plantation-style inn w/spacious rooms. Walk to shops, restaurants, tours. Near Myrtle Beach & Charleston. **3rd night 25% off.***

**Shaw House, The**
613 Cyprus Ct.,   29440
803-546-9663
Mary & Joe Shaw
All year

$$-B&B
3 rooms, 3 pb
*Rated*, •
C-yes/S-yes/P-no/H-ltd

Full breakfast
Comp. wine, tea, coffee
Sitting room
piano
bicycles

*Spacious rooms furnished with antiques. Bird-watching from glassed-in den overlooking Willowbank Marsh. Walk to Historic District. **7 nights 10% discount, AAA discount.***

## GREENVILLE

**Pettigru Place B&B**
302 Pettigru St.,   29601
864-242-4529 Fax: 864-242-1231
G. Hendershot & Janice
Beatty
All year

$$$-B&B
5 rooms, 5 pb
Visa, MC, AmEx,
*Rated*,
C-ltd/S-no/P-no/H-no

Full breakfast
Aft. tea, comp. wine
Sitting room
private phones in rooms

*Comfortable, casual elegance. Historic register, circa early 1920s. Residential atmosphere in prime downtown location. Perfect for business (meeting rooms) or pleasure.*

*Montgomery's Grove, Marion, SC*

## LANDRUM

**Red Horse Inn, The**
310 N. Campbell Rd.,  29356
864-895-4968 Fax: 864-895-4968
Mary & Roger Wolters
All year

$$$-B&B
5 rooms, 5 pb
•
C-yes/S-ltd/P-ltd/H-no

Continental breakfast
Each cottage has kitchen
Dining area, living room
fireplace, bedroom, bath
sitting area, TV, A/C

*Situated on 190 rolling acres in the midst of horse country with extraordinary mountain views. The Red Horse Inn offers charming Victorian cottages, exquisitely decorated.*

## LITTLE RIVER

**Stella's Guest Home**
P.O. Box 564,  29566
803-249-1871
Stella McLamb    All year

$-EP
3 rooms, 3 pb
S-yes/P-no/H-no

Full breakfast (fee)
Dinner
Sitting room, piano

*Old-fashioned Southern hospitality and elegance. Rooms have private entrance and color TV. Special Southern breakfast.*

## MARION

**Montgomery's Grove**
408 Harlee St.,  29571
803-423-5220
Coreen & Rick Roberts
All year

$$-B&B
5 rooms, 4 pb
•
C-ltd/S-ltd/P-no

Full breakfast
Afternoon tea, snacks
Lunch, dinner (fee)
sitting room, library
bikes, hot tub

*1893 Victorian manor in historic village between I-95 and Myrtle Beach. Dramatic architecture, stunning rooms. Five acres to explore, restful porches.*

## McCLELLANVILLE

**Laurel Hill Plantation**
P.O. Box 190,  29458
8913 N. Hwy 17
803-887-3708
Jackie & Lee Morrison
All year

$$$-B&B
4 rooms, 4 pb
MC, Visa, *Rated*, •
C-ltd/S-ltd/P-no/H-no

Full breakfast
Complimentary wine/snack
Sitting room
fishing boat trip
freshwater fish pond

*Located with a fantastic waterfront view of Cape Romain and the Atlantic Ocean, this 1850s plantation home is furnished with country antiques.*

## MONCKS CORNER

| **Rice Hope Plantation Inn** | $$-B&B | Continental plus bkfst. |
|---|---|---|
| 206 Rice Hope Dr., 29461 | 5 rooms, 3 pb | Lunch, dinner, aftn. tea |
| 803-761-4832  Fax: 803-761-1866 | MC, Visa, *Rated*, • | Snacks, comp. wine |
| 800-569-4038 | C-ltd/S-no/P-no/H-no | restaurant, sitting room |
| Doris Kasprak | | bicycles, tennis court |
| All year | | |

*Less than 1 hour from Charleston. Large mansion set among live oaks overlooking the river. Calm, quiet, friendly atmosphere. Family reunion special, ask.* **3rd night 50%.**

## MT. PLEASANT

| **Guilds Inn** | $$$-B&B | Continental plus bkfst. |
|---|---|---|
| 101 Pitt St., 29464 | 6 rooms, 6 pb | Restaurant |
| 803-881-0510  Fax: 803-881-3907 | AmEx, MC, Visa, | Sitting room |
| 800-331-1510 | *Rated*, | tennis court |
| Guilds & Joyce Hollowell | C-yes/S-yes/P-ltd/H-yes | whirlpool tubs |
| All year | | |

*Circa 1888 six room inn located in historic village, 5 mi. from historic Charleston & 4 mi. from beaches. Furnishings all historic reproductions.* **3rd night 50% off.**

| **Sunny Meadows** | $$-B&B | Full breakfast |
|---|---|---|
| 1459 Venning Rd., 29464 | 2 rooms, 2 pb | Snacks, comp. wine |
| 803-884-7062 | C-ltd/S-no/P-no/H-no | Sitting room |
| Charles & Agnes Houston | | 18th century antiques |
| All year | | and reproductions |

*Convenient to historic Charleston (15 min.) but far enough away to be peaceful. Elegant country setting. Five minute drive to beaches.*

## MYRTLE BEACH

| **Brustman House B&B** | $$-B&B | Full breakfast |
|---|---|---|
| 400 25th Ave. South, 29577 | 5 rooms, 5 pb | Aftn. tea, comp. wine |
| 803-448-7699  Fax: 803-626-2478 | *Rated*, • | Bicycles, basketball |
| 800-448-7699 | C-ltd/S-no/P-no/H-no | veranda, air-conditioned |
| Dr. Wendell Brustman | | golf & tennis nearby |
| All year | | |

*Estate property; 300 yards to beach; rose/herb gardens; honeymoon suites with private whirlpool tubs; family suite w/kitchen. Free airport pickup. Family suite for 3-8 persons.*

| **Serendipity Inn** | $$-B&B | Continental plus bkfst. |
|---|---|---|
| 407 N. 71st Ave., 29572 | 14 rooms, 14 pb | Grill |
| 803-449-5268  800-762-3229 | MC, Visa, *Rated*, • | Heated pool, hot tub |
| Terry & Sheila Johnson | C-ltd/S-ltd/P-no/H-no | color TV & A/C in rooms |
| Closed December | | garden room, sitting rm. |

*Lovely Spanish mission style, surrounded by lush tropical vegetation. Winner of Myrtle Beach "Keep America Beautiful" Award.* **10% off 5+ days, ltd.**

## PAWLEYS ISLAND

| **Litchfield Plantation** | $$$$-B&B | Continental plus |
|---|---|---|
| P.O. Box 290, 29585 | 24 rooms, 22 pb | Dinner (fee), restaurant |
| Kings River Rd. | Most CC, *Rated*, • | Tennis courts, pool |
| 803-237-9121  Fax: 803-237-8558 | C-ltd/S-ltd/P-no/H-ltd | golf, concierge service |
| 800-869-1410 | | oceanfront beachhouse |
| Tracey Weaver & Matt | | |
| Willson | | |
| All year | | |

*Escape down our avenue of live oaks to the Plantation House c.1750 or well appointed cottages. Premier amenities, fine dining. Romance packages.* **7th night free.**

## SALEM

| | | |
|---|---|---|
| **Sunrise Farm B&B** | $$-B&B | Full breakfast - rooms |
| P.O. Box 164,  29676 | 6 rooms, 6 pb | Cont. plus - cottages |
| 325 Sunrise Dr. | *Rated*, • | Sitting room |
| 803-944-0121 | C-ltd/S-no/P-no/H-no | 2 cottages with kitchens |
| Jean Webb | | close to Clemson Univ. |
| All year | | |

*Charming country Victorian farmhouse set on 74 acre cattle farm. Close to Blue Ridge Mts., parks, waterfalls and nature trails. **3rd night 50% off.***

## SUMTER

| | | |
|---|---|---|
| **B&B of Sumter, The** | $$-B&B | Full gourmet breakfast |
| 6 Park Ave.,  29150 | 4 rooms, 2 pb | Comp. beverages |
| 803-773-2903 Fax: 803-775-6943 | Most CC, *Rated*, • | Victorian parlor |
| Jess & Suzanne Begley | C-ltd/S-no/P-no/H-no | TV sitting room |
| All year | | golf nearby, Swanlake |

*Historic Distr.-1896 home; lrg. front porch facing lush, green, quiet park; spacious fire-placed rms., antiques, ancient artifacts. 18 area golf course. **$5 off each day after 1st.***

# More Inns ...

| | |
|---|---|
| Abbeville | Abbewood B&B, 509 N. Main St., 29620,  803-459-5822 |
| Abbeville | Belmont Inn, 106 E. Pickens St., 29620,  803-459-9625 |
| Abbeville | Painted Lady, The, 307 N. Main St., 29620,  803-459-8171 |
| Aiken | Briar Patch, The, 544 Magnolia Ln., 29801,  803-649-2010 |
| Aiken | Brodie Residence, The, 422 York St., 29801,  803-648-1445 |
| Aiken | Chancellor Carroll House, 112 Gregg Ave., 29801,  803-649-5396 |
| Aiken | Hair Residence, 544 Magnolia Lane S.E., 29801 |
| Aiken | Hollie Berries Inn, 1560 Powderhouse Rd. S., 29801,  803-648-9952 |
| Aiken | Pine Knoll Inn, 305 Lancaster St. SW, 29801,  803-649-5939 |
| Aiken | Willcox Inn, The, 100 Colleton Ave., 29801,  803-649-1377 |
| Anderson | Evergreen Inn, 1109 South Main St., 29621,  803-225-1109 |
| Anderson | River Inn, 612 E. River St., 29624,  803-226-1431 |
| Beaufort | Bay Street Inn, 601 Bay St., 29902,  803-522-0050 |
| Beaufort | Rhett House Inn, The, 1009 Craven St., 29902,  803-524-9030 |
| Beaufort | Twelve Oaks Inn, P.O. Box 4126, 29902,  803-525-1371 |
| Belton | Belton Inn, 324 S. Main St., 29627,  803-338-6020 |
| Bennettsville | Breeden Inn-Carriage House, 404 East Main St., 29512,  803-479-3665 |
| Bishopville | Foxfire B&B, The, 416 N. Main St., 29010,  803-484-5643 |
| Blacksburg | White House Inn, 607 West Pine St., 29702,  803-839-3000 |
| Blackville | Floyd Hall Inn B&B, 111 Dexter St., 29817,  803-284-3736 |
| Branchville | Branchville Country Inn, 1 Carroll St., 29432,  803-274-8894 |
| Calhoun Falls | Latimer Inn, P.O. Box 295, 29628,  803-391-2747 |
| Camden | Aberdeen, 1409 Broad St., 29020,  803-432-2524 |
| Camden | Carriage House, The, 1413 Lyttleton St., 29020,  803-432-2430 |
| Camden | Greenleaf Inn, 1308/10 Broad St., 29020,  803-425-1806 |
| Camden | Inn on Broad, 1308/10 Broad St., 29020,  803-425-1806 |
| Charleston | 1837 B&B/Tearoom, 126 Wentworth St., 29401,  803-723-7166 |
| Charleston | Anchorage Inn, The, 26 Vendue Range, 29401,  803-723-8300 |
| Charleston | Ansonborough Inn, 21 Hasell St., 29401,  803-723-1655 |
| Charleston | Capers Motte House, 69 Church St., 29401,  803-722-2263 |
| Charleston | Church St. Inn, 177 Church St., 29401,  803-722-3420 |
| Charleston | Colonial Lake B&B, 32 Rutledge Ave., 29401,  803-722-6476 |
| Charleston | Elliott House Inn, 78 Queen St., 29401,  803-723-1855 |
| Charleston | Hayne House B&B, The, 30 King St., 29401,  803-577-2633 |
| Charleston | Historic Charleston B&B, 57 Broad St., 29401,  803-722-6606 |
| Charleston | Indigo Inn, One Maiden Ln., 29401,  803-577-5900 |
| Charleston | Jasmine House, 8 Cumberland, 29401,  803-577-5900 |
| Charleston | Johnson's Six Orange St BB, 6 Orange St., 29401,  803-722-6122 |
| Charleston | Kings Inn, 136 Tradd St., 29440 |
| Charleston | Lodge Alley Inn, 195 E. Bay St., 29401,  800-722-1611 |
| Charleston | Loundes Grove Inn, 266 St. Margaret St., 29403,  803-723-3530 |
| Charleston | Middleton Inn @ Middleton, Ashley River Rd., 29414,  803-556-0500 |
| Charleston | Sword Gate Inn, 111 Tradd St., 29401,  803-723-8518 |
| Charleston | Two Meeting Street Inn, 2 Meeting St., 29407,  803-723-7322 |
| Cheraw | 501 Kershaw St., 29520,  803-537-7733 |
| Cheraw | 505 Market St., 505 Market St., 29520,  803-537-9649 |
| Cheraw | Spears B&B, 501 Kershaw St., 29520,  803-537-7733 |
| Clemson | Nord-Lac, P.O. Box 1111, 29633,  803-639-2939 |
| Clio | Henry Bennett House B&B, 301 Red Bluff St., 29525,  803-586-2701 |

| | |
|---|---|
| Columbia | Chesnut Cottage B&B, 1718 Hampton St., 29201, 803-256-1718 |
| Columbia | Richland Street B&B, 1425 Richland St., 29201, 803-779-7001 |
| Dale | Coosaw Plantation, P.O. Box 160, 29914, 803-723-6516 |
| Darlington | Croft Magnolia Inn, 306 Cashua Street, 29532, 803-393-1908 |
| Edgefield | Carnoosie Inn, 407 Columbia Rd., 29824, 800-622-7124 |
| Edgefield | Inn On Main, The, 303 Main St., 29824, 803-637-3678 |
| Edgefield | Plantation House, The, Ct. House Square, 29824, 803-637-3789 |
| Edisto Island | Cassina Point Plantation, P.O. Box 535, 29438, 803-869-2535 |
| Ehrhardt | Ehrhardt Hall, 400 South Broadway, 29081, 803-267-2020 |
| Estill | John Lawton House, 159 3rd St. E, 29918, 803-625-3240 |
| Fort Mill | Pleasant Valley, P.O. Box 446, 29715, 803-547-7551 |
| Georgetown | Ashfield Manor, 3030 S. Island Rd., 29440, 803-546-5111 |
| Greenwood | Grace Place B&B, 115 Grace St., 29646, 803-229-0053 |
| Greenwood | Inn on the Square, 104 Court St., 29646, 803-223-4488 |
| Hartsville | Missouri Inn B&B, 314 E. Home Ave., 29550, 803-383-9553 |
| Hilton Head | Ambiance B&B, 8 Wren Dr., 29928, 803-671-4981 |
| Hilton Head | Home Away B&B, 3 Pender Ln., 29928, 803-671-5578 |
| Honea Path | Sugerfoot Castle, 211 S. Main St., 29654, 803-369-6565 |
| James Island | Almost Home B&B, 1236 Oceanview Rd., 29412, 803-795-8705 |
| Johnston | Cox House Inn, P.O. Box 486, 29832, 803-275-4552 |
| Landrum | Lakeshore B&B, 1026 E. Lakeshore Dr., 29356, 803-457-5330 |
| Laurens | Two Sisters Inn, 814 S. Harper, 29360, 803-984-4880 |
| Leesville | Able House Inn, 244 E. Columbia Ave., 29070, 803-532-2763 |
| Lexington | Lake Murray House, 2252 Old Cherokee Rd., 29072, 803-957-3701 |
| Long Creek | Chauga River House, Cobb's Bridge Rd., 29658, 803-647-9587 |
| Marion | Cantey Redidence, 108 Wilcox Ave., 29571, 803-423-5578 |
| Mayesville | Windsong, Rt 1, Box 300, 29104, 800-453-5004 |
| McClellanville | McClellan's B&B, P.O. Box 4, 29458, 803-887-3371 |
| McClellanville | Village B&B, 333 Mercantile Rd., 29458, 803-887-3266 |
| Montmorenci | Annie's Inn, P.O. Box 311, 29839, 803-649-6836 |
| Mt. Pleasant | Charleston East B&B, 1031 Tall Pine Rd., 29464, 803-884-8208 |
| Mt. Pleasant | Tara Oaks B&B, 1199 Long Point Rd., 29464, 803-884-7082 |
| Mullins | Webster's Manor, 115 E. James St., 29574, 803-464-9632 |
| Myrtle Beach | Cain House B&B, 206 29th Ave. S., 29577, 803-448-3063 |
| Newberry | College St. Tourist B&B, 1710 College St., 29108, 803-321-9155 |
| North Augusta | Bloom Hill, 772 Pine Log Rd., 29841, 803-593-2573 |
| Pawley's Island | Sea View Inn, P.O. Box 210, 29858, 803-237-4253 |
| Pendleton | Liberty Hall Inn, 621 S. Mechanic St., 29670, 803-646-7500 |
| Pickens | Schell Haus, The, 4913 SC 11, 29671, 803-878-0078 |
| Ridgeland | Lakewood Plantation, Rt. 2, P.O. Box 3, 29936, 803-726-5141 |
| Rock Hill | Book & The Spindle, The, 626 Oakland Ave., 29730, 803-328-1913 |
| Rock Hill | East Main Guest House, 600 E. Main St., 29730, 803-366-1161 |
| Simpsonville | Hunter House B&B, 201 E. College St., 29681, 803-967-2827 |
| Starr | Gray House, The, 111 Stones Throw Ave., 29684, 803-352-6778 |
| Sullivan's Island | Palmettos, P.O. Box 706, 29482, 803-883-3389 |
| Summerville | B&B Of Summerville, 304 S. Hampton St., 29483, 803-871-5275 |
| Sunset | Laurel Springs Country Inn, 1137 Moorefield Hwy., 29685, 803-878-2252 |
| Union | Inn at Merridun, The, 100 Merrridun Pl., 29379, 864-427-7052 |
| Walhalla | Liberty Lodge, Rt. 1, P.O. Box 77, 29691, 803-638-8639 |
| Walhalla | Walhalla Liberty Lodge B&B, 105 Liberty Lane, 29691, 8646380940 |
| Winnsboro | Brakefield B&B, 214 High St., 29180, 803-635-4242 |

*Sunrise Farm,*
*Salem, SC*

# South Dakota

## CANOVA

**Skoglund Farm**
Route 1, Box 45,  57321
605-247-3445
Alden & Delores Skoglund
All year

$-MAP
6 rooms,
•
C-yes/S-ltd/P-yes/H-no
Swedish

Full breakfast
Dinner included
Sitting room, piano
bicycles

*Enjoy overnight on the South Dakota prairie. Return to your childhood—animals, country walking, home-cooked meals.* **Children 5 & under are free.**

## CUSTER

**Custer Mansion B&B**
35 Centennial Dr., 57730
605-673-3333
Mill & Carole Seaman
All year

$$-B&B
5 rooms, 4 pb
*Rated*, •
C-yes/S-no/P-no/H-no
Spanish

Full breakfast
Restaurant, aft. tea
Sitting room, bicycles
tennis, golf nearby
2 honeymoon suites

*Historic 1891 Victorian on 1 acre in heart of unique Black Hills. Western hospitality & delicious, home-baked food. On National Register of Historic Places. **7th night free.***

## FREEMAN

**Farmers Inn**
28193 US 81, 57029
605-925-7580
Marjean Waltner
All year

$-B&B/AP
4 rooms, 4 pb
C-ltd/S-no/P-no/H-no
German

Full breakfast
Aftn. tea, snacks
Comp. wine, restaurant
sitting room, library
bikes, sauna, game room

*Turn of the century farmhouse on US 81. Tastefully decorated with fine antiques and served with farmer's breakfast. **Champagne for anniversaries, birthdays.***

## HERMOSA

**Bunkhouse B&B**
14630 Lower Spr.Crk.Rd.,
  57744
605-342-5462 Fax: 605-343-1916
Carol Hendrickson
May 1-Dec. 31

$$-B&B
3 rooms, 1 pb
Visa, MC, *Rated*, •
C-yes/S-ltd/P-no/H-ltd

Full breakfast
Snacks
Hiking trails, cattle
sitting room, working
ranch, bring your horse

*Our decor is western/antique. We feature "all you can eat" breakfast, facilities for you to bring your own horse to ride on our working ranch.*

## HILL CITY

**Pine Rest Cabins**
P.O. Box 377, 57745
24063 Hwy. 385
605-574-2416 800-333-5306
Jan & Steve Johnson
All year

$$-EP
9 rooms, 9 pb
Visa, MC, Disc.,
C-yes/S-ltd/P-ltd/H-no

Equipped kitchens
Restaurant nearby
bicycles nearby
tennis court nearby

*Perfect location for day trips anywhere in the Black Hills. Custer State Park, Mt. Rushmore less than 20 minutes. Simple country cabins in the pines. Hot tub coming soon!*

## HOT SPRINGS

**Villa Theresa Guest House**
801 Almond St., 57747
605-745-4633
Susan W. Watt
All year

$$-B&B
7 rooms, 7 pb
Most CC, *Rated*, •
C-ltd/S-no/P-no/H-no

Full breakfast
Each guest room has its
own special theme. On
Nat'l Historic Register

*Victorian hideaway on high bluff overlooking town. Historic walking tours, Angostura Reservoir, Fall River County Museum, Wind Cave National Park and lost more to do.*

## LEAD

**Cheyenne Crossing B&B**
Box 1220, 57754
HC-37
605-584-3510 800-400-7722
Bonnie & Jim LeMar
All year

$$$-B&B
3 rooms, 1 pb
Visa, MC, Disc., •
C-yes/S-ltd/P-no/H-no

Full breakfast
Restaurant, lunch, din.
Liv. rm., TV, VCR, games
library, sitting room
creekside 2-bdrm. cabin

*Voted "Best Small Town Cafe in South Dakota" for the past two years. Mountain Valley location on excellent trout streams. **Group rates available.***

**LEAD**

**Deer Mountain B&B**
HC 37 - Box 1214,   57754
605-584-2473 Fax: 605-584-3045
Vonnie, Bob & Carrie
Ackerman
All year

$$-B&B
4 rooms, 2 pb
MC, Visa, •
C-ltd/S-ltd/P-yes/H-no

Full breakfast
Dinner with adv. notice
Snacks, pool table
box lunch available
sitting room, hot tubs

*Unique log home. Skiing & snowmobiling minutes away. Near historic Deadwood gambling town. Mt. Rushmore, hunting, fishing all close by. **3rd night 25% off.***

**RAPID CITY**

**Abend Haus & Audrie's**
23029 Thunderhead Falls,
  57702
605-342-7788
Hank & Audry Kuhnhauser
All year

$$$-B&B
3 rooms, 3 pb
*Rated*,
S-no/P-no/H-no

Full breakfast
Comp. wine, snacks
Restaurant nearby
trout fishing, hiking
bicycles, hot tubs

*Each quiet room has a private patio, entrance, bath and spa. A full breakfast is served in your room. Fishing, hiking, biking on site.*

**Carriage House B&B**
721 West Blvd.,   57701
605-343-6415
Betty King
All year

$$-B&B
5 rooms, 2 pb
MC, Visa,
S-no/P-no/H-no

Full breakfast
Library, sitting room
piano
video & music libraries

*Located on historic West Boulevard, the inn has English Country interior with antiques, hardwood floors & oil paintings. Relax on veranda or balcony.*

**First Thunder Ranch**
P.O. Box 9008,   57709
23340 First Thunder Rd.
605-341-7080  800-361-7080
Jan Hagen
June 1- Oct. 30

$$$-B&B
4 rooms, 4 pb
Most CC, •
C-ltd/S-no/P-no/H-ltd

Full breakfast
Afternoon tea, snacks
Library
National Forest
Fax: 605-341-7180

*Surrounded by National Forest, an elegant abode lodge, close to Rapid City, but nestled in the hills. Gourmet breakfast.*

**Willow Springs Cabins B&B**
11515 Sheridan Lake Rd.,
  57702
605-342-3665
Joyce Payton
All year

$$$-B&B
2 rooms, 2 pb
Visa, MC, •
C-ltd/S-no/P-no/H-no

Full breakfast
Snacks
Outdoor hot tubs
hiking trails, swimming
mountain stream

*Privacy at its best! Secluded log cabins in the beautiful Black Hills National Forest. Great views, gourmet breakfasts, private hot tubs. Hiking trails directly off of the front porch.*

**SPEARFISH**

**Eighth Street Inn, The**
735 Eighth St.,   57783
605-642-9812  800-642-9812
Brad & Sandy Young
All year

$$-B&B
5 rooms, 2 pb
Visa, MC, •
C-yes/S-ltd/P-ltd/H-no

Full breakfast
Sitting room, library
bikes, hot tubs
family friendly facility

*Experience history, enjoy the deck hot tubs, savor breakfast, all fresh for you. Adventure will find you at your table. **3rd night 50% off.***

## WEBSTER

**Lakeside Farm B&B**  $-B&B                Full breakfast
RR 2, Box 52,  57274      2 rooms,             Other meals possible
605-486-4430              C-yes/S-no/P-no/H-no Comp. coffee, tea, snack
Glenn & Joy Hagen                              sitting room, bicycles
All year                                       Museum, factory outlet

*Sample country life with us. A family-owned/operated dairy farm. Northeastern SD lakes area. Fresh air, open spaces. Fresh milk, homemade cinnamon rolls.* **Comp. snacks.**

## WHITEWOOD

**Rockinghorse B&B**      $$-B&B               Full breakfast
RR1 Box 133,  57793       3 rooms, 3 pb        Aftn. tea, restaurant
605-269-2625              Vica, MC,  •         Horseback riding (fee),
Sharleen & Jerry Bergum   C-yes/S-ltd/P-ltd/H-ltd  nature walks, hiking
All year                                       pet farm

*Early 1900s country getaway; Black Hills meadow. Coyote choirs, star studded skies-panoramic views. Hiking, horses, pet farm. Country breakfast.* **3rd night, 50%.**

# More Inns ...

| | |
|---|---|
| Rapid City | Flying B Ranch B&B, RR 10, Box 2640, 57701,  605-342-5324 |
| Rapid City | H-Bar-D Lodge,  23101 Triangle Trail-Hi, 57702 |
| Rapid City | Hayloft B&B,  9356 Neck Yoke Rd., 57701 |
| Rapid City | Hillside Country Cottages,  HC 33, Box 1901, 57702,  605-342-4121 |
| Rapid City | Madison Ranch B&B,  Rt. 1, Box 1490, 57702,  605-342-6997 |
| Rapid City | Rimrock, The,  13145 Big Bend Rd., 57702 |
| Salem | Jacobson Farm,  RR 2, Box 428, 57058,  605-247-3247 |
| Sioux Falls | Pine Crest Inn,  4501 W. 12th St., 57106,  605-336-3530 |
| Spearfish | Christensen's Country Home,  432 Hillsview, 57783,  605-642-2859 |
| Spearfish | Flying Horse B&B,  630 - 8th St., 57783,  605-642-1633 |
| Spearfish | Kelly Inn,  540 E. Jackson, 57783,  605-642-7795 |
| Sturgis | Old Stone House,  1513 Jackson St., 57785,  605-347-3007 |
| Vale | Dakota Shepherd,  RR3, Box 25C, 57788 |
| Vivian | Rafter L Ranch B&B,  P.O. Box 67, 57576,  605-895-2202 |
| Wall | Western Dakota Ranch,  HCR 1, 57790,  605-279-2198 |
| Wessington Springs | Winegar Farms,  37292 231st St., 57382 |
| Yankton | Mulberry Inn,  512 Mulberry St., 57078,  605-665-7116 |

# Tennessee

## CHATTANOOGA

| **Adams Hilborne** | $$$-B&B/MAP | Continental breakfast |
|---|---|---|
| 801 Vine St.,   37403 | 10 rooms, 10 pb | The Porch Cafe |
| 423-265-5000 Fax: 423-265-5555 | Visa, MC, AmEx, | Hot tubs, library |
| Wendy Adams | *Rated*,  • | sitting room, TV, VCR |
| All year | C-ltd/S-no/P-no/H-yes | 1995 Decorator Showhouse |

*Adams Hilborne, a magnificent stone mansion built by the mayor of Chattanooga in 1889. On the National Register, it boasts innumerable beautiful features. **Disc't at rest., ltd.***

| **Lookout Lake B&B** | $$$-B&B | Full breakfast |
|---|---|---|
| 3408 Elder Mtn. Rd.,   37419 | 10 rooms, 9 pb | Limited bar service |
| 423-821-8088  888-804-0825 | Visa, MC, AmEx, | Sitting room, library |
| All year | C-yes/S-ltd/P-yes/H-ltd | bikes, mini-gym |
| | Limited Spanish | pool, Jacuzzi, fishing |

*Unique 2 story brick home on its own 9 acre lake offers comfort & convenience of a luxury hotel w/warmth & hospitality of a home. 60 acre property w/view of mnts. **3rd night 50%, free bottle of wine.***

## DUCKTOWN

| **White House B&B, The** | $$-B&B | Full breakfast |
|---|---|---|
| P.O. Box 668,   37326 | 3 rooms, 1 pb | Aftn. tea, snacks |
| 104 Main St. | MC, Visa, *Rated*,  • | Evening dessert buffet |
| 423-496-4166  Fax: 423-496-4166 | C-ltd/S-ltd/P-no/H-no | wrap-around porches |
| 800-775-4166 | | rocking chairs, TV |
| Mardee & Dan Kauffman | | |
| All year | | |

*Beautiful mountain area, close to whitewater rafting, 4 TVA lakes 1 hr. away, trout fishing, golf. Lovely porch w/rocking chairs. Country breakfast. **Jan.-March 10% discount.***

## FRANKLIN

| **Namaste Acres Barn B&B** | $$-B&B | Full country breakfast |
|---|---|---|
| 5436 Leipers Creek Rd., | 3 rooms, 3 pb | Lunch avail., snacks |
|   37064 | Most CC, *Rated*,  • | Hot tubs, exercise room |
| 615-791-0333  Fax: 615-591-0665 | C-ltd/S-ltd/P-no/H-no | bicycles, pool, TV/VCR |
| Bill, Lisa & Lindsay Winters | | hiking & riding trails |
| All year | | |

*Peaceful valley setting in terraced hills of TN. Each suite offers; TV, VCR, video library, coffee, sitting area, private entrance. Sun decks. **10% off Sun.–Thur.***

## GATLINBURG

| | | |
|---|---|---|
| **Butcher House-Mountains** | $$$-B&B | Full European breakfast |
| 1520 Garrett Ln., 37738 | , | Afternoon tea, snacks |
| 423-436-9457 Fax: 423-436-9884 | MC, Visa *Rated*, • | Sitting room with TV |
| Hugh & Gloria Butcher | C-ltd/S-no/P-no/H-no | guest kitchen, deck |
| All year | It., some Sp. & Fr. | Dessert offered in eve. |

*Cradled 2800 feet above Gatlinburg. Swiss chalet with many museum-quality antiques. One mile from the slopes. Original gourmet recipes. **Theater & Restaurant discounts.***

| | | |
|---|---|---|
| **Colonel's Lady, The** | $$$-B&B | Full gourmet breakfast |
| 1120 Tanrac Trail, 37738 | 9 rooms, 9 pb | Snacks |
| 423-436-5432 Fax: 423-436-7855 | Visa, MC, Disc. *Rated*, | Sitting room, library |
| 800-515-5432 | • | view the Great Smokies |
| Bill, Anita, Chloe & Wm. Cate | C-ltd/S-no/P-no/H-no | hot tubs, gardens |
| All year | | |

*Elegant country inn furnished in antiques collected from around the world. Unsurpassed views, gourmet food, perfect elegant setting for intimate celebrations.*

| | | |
|---|---|---|
| **Olde English Tudor Inn B&B** | $$$-B&B | Full breakfast |
| 135 W. Holly Ridge Rd., | 7 rooms, 7 pb | Snacks |
| 37738 | Visa, MC, AmEx, • | Sitting room |
| 423-436-7760 Fax: 423-430-7308 | C-yes/S-no/P-no/H-no | family friendly facility |
| 800-541-3798 | | golf, fishing nearby |
| Kathy & Larry Schuh | | |
| All year | | |

*Downtown Gatlinburg one block from major shops, dining. One-half mile to National Park entrance. Award winning garden & waterfall. Community room. Cable TV/HBO. **5th night free.***

| | | |
|---|---|---|
| **Tennessee Ridge Inn** | $$$-B&B | Full gourmet breakfast |
| 507 Campbell Lead, 37738 | 7 rooms, 7 pb | Afternoon tea, snacks |
| 423-436-4068 800-737-7369 | Most CC, *Rated*, • | Sitting room, library |
| Dar Hullander | S-ltd/P-no/H-yes | fireplaces, balconies |
| All year | | jacuzzi, honeymoon stes. |

*View the Smokies by day & the city lights of Gatlinburg by night. Jacuzzis, fireplaces, private balconies, king beds, swimming pool.*

## GREENEVILLE

| | | |
|---|---|---|
| **Big Spring Inn** | $$$-B&B | Full breakfast |
| 315 N. Main St., 37745 | 6 rooms, 6 pb | Dinner (in advance) |
| 423-638-2917 | Visa, MC, AmEx, | Aftn. tea, snacks |
| Marshall & Nancy Ricker | *Rated*, • | 2 rooms with fireplaces |
| All year | C-ltd/S-no/P-no/H-no | sitting room, pool |

*Beautiful Greek Revival home in historic district: large porches, gardens, swimming pool, close to Cherokee Nat'l Forest & Jonesboro. **Chocolate torte—honeymooners/anniversary.***

| | | |
|---|---|---|
| **Hilltop House B&B Inn** | $$-B&B/MAP | Full breakfast |
| 6 Sanford Circle, 37743 | 3 rooms, 3 pb | Afternoon tea |
| 423-639-8202 | Most CC, *Rated*, • | Sitting room, library |
| Denise M. Ashworth | C-ltd/S-no/P-no/H-no | hiking trails, rafting |
| All year | | trout fishing, gardens |

*Comfortable country home with panoramic mountain views and English antiques. Visit historic towns, hike mountain trails with local hiking club. Gourmet meals. **6th night free.***

*Lynchburg Bed & Breakfast, Lynchburg, TN*

## JOHNSON CITY

**Hart House B&B**
207 East Holston Ave.,  37601
423-926-3147
Francis & Vanessa Gingras
All year

$$-B&B
3 rooms, 3 pb
MC, Visa,  •
C-yes/S-no/P-no/H-no

Full breakfast
Afternoon tea, snacks
Sitting room, library
basketball ct, weight rm
tapes/toys for children

*1910 Dutch Colonial home lovingly restored to its original grandeur. Relax on the front porch or spend an evening by the fireplace.*

## KODAK

**Grandma's House B&B**
PO Box 445, 734 Pollard Rd.,
   37764
615-933-3512  800-676-3512
Charlie & Hilda Hickman
All year

$$-B&B
3 rooms, 3 pb
*Rated*,  •
C-ltd/S-no/P-no/H-no

Full country breakfast
Coffee/soft drinks/cake
Sitting room, bicycles
balcony
10% off over 4 days

*On quiet country lane near Great Smoky Mountains. Hosts are both native East Tennesseans, always on premises. Hilda's special treats make up the Southern farm-style breakfast.*

## LYNCHBURG

**Lynchburg B&B**
P.O. Box 34,  37352
Mechanic
615-759-7158
Virginia & Mike Tipps
All year

$$-B&B
3 rooms, 3 pb
MC, Visa,
C-yes/S-no/P-no/H-yes

Continental breakfast
Afternoon tea

*Stay in one of the oldest homes in historic Lynchburg, home of Jack Daniel Distillery. Antique furnished. Private baths.*

## McMINNVILLE

**Historic Falcon Manor B&B**
2645 Faulkner Springs, 37110
615-668-4444 Fax: 615-815-4444
George & Charlien McGlothin
All year

$$-B&B
6 rooms, 2 pb
•
C-ltd/P-no/H-yes
Spanish

Full breakfast
Victorian gift shop
sitting room, library
rocking-chair, verandas

*1890 Victorian mansion—one of the South's finest. Museum-quality antiques, giant trees, intriguing innkeepers. Between Nashville & Chattanooga. Weddings, banquets.*

## MONTEAGLE

**Adams Edgeworth Inn**
Monteagle Assembly, 37356
615-924-4000 Fax: 615-924-3236
Wendy & David Adams
All year

$$-B&B
12 rooms, 12 pb
MC, Visa, AmEx,
*Rated*, •
C-ltd/S-ltd/P-no/H-ltd
French

Full gourmet breakfast
Candle-lit dining
Gift shop, library
Verandas, swim, hike
completely redecorated

*Victorian village on mountain top. Canopy beds, fireplaces, antiques, prize-winning gardens, A/C, 1200-acre wilderness w/trails, Sewanee U. 6 miles. Gourmet dinners available. **10% off midweek stay.***

## MURFREESBORO

**Clardy's Guest House**
435 E. Main St., 37130
615-893-6030
Barbara & Robert Deaton
All year

$-B&B
3 rooms, 2 pb
*Rated*, •
C-yes/S-yes/P-no/H-no

Continental plus bkfst.
Complimentary beverages
Sitting room w/cable TV
porch

*Built in 1898 during opulent & decorative times, the house is completely furnished with beautiful antiques. Murfreesboro is the South's antique center. **7 nights for price of 5.***

## NASHVILLE

**Lyric Springs Country Inn**
P.O. Box 120428, 37212
7306 S. Harpeth, Franklin
615-329-3091 Fax: 615-329-3381
800-621-7824　All year

$$$-B&B
4 rooms, 4 pb
Most CC, *Rated*, •
S-no/P-no/H-yes

Full breakfast
Lunch, dinner on request
Sitting room, library
swimming pool, billiards
massage/manicure/facial

*Elegant antique filled creek-side inn featured in Better Homes and Gardens, Country Inn and USA Today. Haven for romance and retreat. Charm and pampering in the home of a famous songwriter.*

## PIGEON FORGE

**Hilton's Bluff B&B Inn**
2654 Valley Heights Dr.,
　37863
423-428-9765　800-441-4188
Jack & Norma Hilton
All year

$$$-B&B
10 rooms, 10 pb
AmEx, MC, Visa,
*Rated*, •
C-ltd/S-no/P-no/H-no

Full breakfast
Lunch & dinner (groups)
Refreshments, snacks
sitting room, library
golf, swimming nearby

*Elegant country living. View of Smoky Mountains. Romantic mingling of old & new. Enjoy covered decks/rockers. Near crafts/outlet shopping. **10% off Mon.–Thur, ltd.***

## PIKEVILLE

**Fall Creek Falls B&B Inn**
Rt. 3, Box 298B, 37367
423-881-5494 Fax: 423-881-5040
Rita & Doug Pruett
Closed 12/22–2/1

$$-B&B
8 rooms, 8 pb
Visa, MC, *Rated*, •
C-ltd/S-no/P-no/H-no

Full breakfast
Sitting room, AC
room with whirlpool
phones, massage therapy

*Romantic mountain getaway, one mile from nationally acclaimed Fall Creek Falls State Resort Park, featuring golfing, fishing, hiking, swimming, boating. **10% off 3+ nights.***

ROGERSVILLE ─────────────────────────

| | | |
|---|---|---|
| **Hale Springs Inn** | $-B&B | Continental breakfast |
| Town Square,   37857 | 10 rooms, 10 pb | Restaurant |
| 423-272-5171 | AmEx, MC, Visa, | Central A/C and heat |
| Capt. & Mrs. Netherland- | *Rated*, • | fireplaces, guided tours |
| Brown | C-yes/S-yes/P-ltd/H-no | formal gardens & gazebo |
| All year | | |

*Restored 1824 brick. Fronts Village Green with other antebellum buildings. Antiques, poster beds, working fireplaces, plush large rooms—near Gatlinburg.*

SEVIERVILLE ─────────────────────────

| | | |
|---|---|---|
| **Calico Inn** | $$$-B&B | Full delicious breakfast |
| 757 Ranch Way,  37862 | 3 rooms, 3 pb | Afternoon tea, snacks |
| 423-428-3833  800-235-1054 | Visa, MC, | Nature lovers delight |
| Lill & Jim Katzbeck | C-yes/S-ltd/P-no/H-no | near malls/outdoor sport |
| All year | | shopping/entertainment |

*Log inn with magnificent mountain view, antiques and country decor. Minutes from Dollywood, Smoky Mountain National Park.* **10% discount 4 nights, ltd.**

| | | |
|---|---|---|
| **Little Greenbrier Lodge** | $$-B&B | Full breakfast |
| 3685 Lyon Springs Rd., | 11 rooms, 8 pb | Snacks |
| 37862 | Visa, MC, Disc., • | Family friendly facility |
| 615-429-2500  Fax: 615-429-4093 | C-ltd/S-no/P-no/H-no | sitting room |
| 800-277-8100 | | mountain hiking |
| Charles & Susan LeBon | | |
| All year | | |

*Rustic lodge nestled on mountain. Beautiful vista, 150 yards to Great Smoky Mtns. Near Gatlinburg, Dollywood, Pigeon Forge. Shopping, hiking.* **Sun.–Thurs. 10% off per night.**

| | | |
|---|---|---|
| **Von-Bryan Inn** | $$$-B&B | Full breakfast |
| 2402 Hatcher Mtn. Rd., | 6 rooms, 6 pb | Snacks |
| 37862 | Most CC, *Rated*, • | Sitting room, library |
| 423-453-9832  Fax: 423-428-8634 | C-ltd/S-ltd/P-no/H-no | hot tubs |
| 800-633-1459 | | swimming pool |
| The Vaughn Family | | |
| All year | | |

*Mountaintop vistas, cool breeze, brisk walks, inviting nooks, sharing stories with friendly folks. Rockers & relaxation. Near Gatlinburg.* **10% off 2+ nights midweek.**

TALBOTT ─────────────────────────

| | | |
|---|---|---|
| **Arrowhill** | $$-B&B | Full breakfast |
| 6622 W. Andrew Johnson, | 3 rooms, 1 pb | Afternoon tea, snacks |
| 37877 | Visa, MC, AmEx, • | Dinner (fee) |
| 423-585-5777 | C-ltd/S-no/P-no/H-ltd | Sitting room, library |
| Gary & Donna Davis | | hot tubs |
| All year | | |

*Antique filled, Antebellum home with 12 foot ceilings, three story spiral staircase, widow's walk. Historic Civil War site. Near Smoky Mountaints.* **7th night free.**

# More Inns ...

| | |
|---|---|
| Bolivar | Magnolia Manor B&B, 418 N. Main St., 38008, 901-658-6700 |
| Brentwood | English Manor B&B, 6304 Murray Lane, 37027, 615-373-4627 |
| Chattanooga | Bluff View Inn, 412 E. Second St., 37403, 615-265-5033 |
| Chattanooga | Milton House B&B, The, 508 Fort Wood Place, 37403, 615-265-2800 |
| Chuckey | Harmony Hill Inn, Rt. 3 Box 1937, 37641, 615-257-3893 |
| Clarksville | Hachland Hill Inn, 1601 Madison St., 37042, 615-647-4084 |
| Clarksville | South Sycamore B&B, 2700 Seven Miles Ferry, 37040, 615-645-4328 |
| Cleveland | Brown Manor, 215 - 20th St. NE, 37311, 615-476-8029 |
| Cleveland | Chadwick House, 2766 Michigan Ave Rd NE, 37312, 615-339-2407 |
| College Grove | Peacock Hill, 6994 Giles Hill Rd., 37046, 800-327-6663 |
| Covington | Havenhall Farm, 183 Houston Gordon Rd., 38019, 901-476-7226 |
| Culleoka | Sweetwaer Inn, 2346 Campbells Station, 38451, 615-987-3077 |
| Dandridge | Mountain Harbor, 1199 Highway 139, 37725, 615-397-3345 |
| Dandridge | Sugar Fork B&B, 743 Garrett Rd., 37725, 615-397-7327 |
| Dickson | Inn on Main Street, The, 112 S. Main St., 37055, 615-441-6879 |
| Duck River | McEwen Farm Log Cabin B&B, P.O. Box 97, Bratton Ln, 38454, 615-583-2378 |
| Ducktown | Ducktown's Cozy Corner, 301 Hwy 68 North, 37326, 800-933-3499 |
| Elizabethton | Old Main Manor, 708 N. Main St., 37643, 615-543-6945 |
| Fairview | Sweet Annie's B&B Barn, 7201 Crow Cut Rd. S.W., 37062, 615-799-8833 |
| Fayetteville | Old Cowan Plantation, Rt 9, Box 17, 37334, 615-433-0225 |
| Flat Creek | Bottle Hollow Lodge, P.O. Box 92/Shelbyville, 37160, 615-695-5253 |
| Franklin | Blueberry Hill B&B, 4591 Peytonsville Rd., 37064, 615-791-9947 |
| Franklin | Carothers House B&B, 4301 S. Carothers Rd., 37064, 615-794-4437 |
| Franklin | Franklin House, 302 South Third St., 37064, 615-794-0848 |
| Franklin | Inn Town B&B, 1022 West Main St., 37064, 615-794-3708 |
| Franklin | Windsong, 3373 Sweeney Hollow Rd, 37064 |
| Gatlinburg | 7th Heaven Log Inn, 3944 Castle Rd., 37738, 615-430-5000 |
| Gatlinburg | Brevard Inn, The, P.O. Box 326, 37738, 615-436-7233 |
| Gatlinburg | Buckhorn Inn, 2140 Tudor Mtn. Rd., 37738, 615-436-4668 |
| Gatlinburg | Castle on the Green, 3950 Castle Road, 37738, 615-675-2462 |
| Gatlinburg | Eight Gables Inn, 219 N. Mtn. Trail, 37738, 615-430-3344 |
| Gatlinburg | Hippensteal's Mtn. View, P.O. Box 707, 37738, 615-436-5761 |
| Goodlettsville | Drake Farm - Lumsley Creek, P.O. Box 875, 37072, 615-859-2425 |
| Goodlettsville | Woodshire B&B, 600 Woodshire Dr., 37072, 615-859-7369 |
| Gordonsville | Pride Hollow, Route 1, Box 86, 38563, 615-683-6396 |
| Greenbrier | Triple Springs B&B, 2120 Hwy 41 S., 37073, 800-816-3114 |
| Greeneville | Oak Hill Farm B&B, 3035 Lonesome Pine Trai, 37743, 615-639-2331 |
| Hendersonville | Music City Respite, 111 Wonder Valley Rd., 37075 |
| Jonesborough | Aiken-Brow House, 104 3rd Avd. South, 37659, 615-753-9440 |
| Jonesborough | Bugaboo B&B, 211 Semore Dr., 37659, 615-753-9345 |
| Jonesborough | Hawley House B&B, 114 E. Woodrow Ave., 37659, 615-753-8869 |
| Jonesborough | Jonesborough B&B, P.O. Box 722, 37659, 615-753-9223 |
| Jonesborough | Robertson House B&B Inn, 212 E. Main St., 37659, 615-753-3039 |
| Knoxville | Maple Grove Inn, 8800 Westland Dr., 37923, 615-690-9565 |
| Knoxville | Middleton House B&B, P.O. Box 196, 37901, 615-524-8100 |
| Knoxville | Windy Hill B&B, 1031 W Park Dr., 37909, 615-690-1488 |
| LaFollette | Blue Moon B&B, Rt 2, Box 236G3, 37766, 800-340-8832 |
| LaFollette | Dogwood Acres B&B Inn, Rt. 4, Box 628, 37766, 615-566-1207 |
| LaFollette | Mountain-Ayer, P.O. Box 1467, 37766, 615-562-4941 |
| Lawrenceburg | Granville House, 229 Pulaski St., 38464, 615-762-3129 |
| Limestone | Snapp Inn B&B, 1990 Davy Crockett Rd., 37681, 615-257-2482 |
| Loudon | Mason Place B&B, The, 600 Commerce St., 37774, 423-458-3921 |
| Madisonville | Hillside Heaven B&B, 2920 Highway 68, 37354, 615-337-2714 |
| McEven | White Oak Creek B&B, Rt. 2, Box 184, 37101, 615-582-3827 |
| Memphis | Lowenstein-Long House, 217 N. Waldran, 38105, 901-527-7174 |
| Monteagle | North Gate Inn, P.O. Box 858, 37356, 615-924-2799 |
| Morristown | Victoria Rose B&B, 307 E. Second North St., 37814, 615-581-9687 |
| Mountain City | Hidden Acres Farm B&B, Hwy. 67, Rt. 3, Box 39, 37683, 615-727-6564 |
| Murfreesboro | Quilts and Croissants, 2231 Riley Rd., 37130, 615-893-2933 |
| Nashville | Apple Brook B&B, 9127 Hwy 100, 37221, 615-646-5082 |
| Nashville | Hillsboro House, 1933 20th Avenue South, 37212, 615-292-5501 |
| Nashville | Monthaven B&B, 1154 W. Main St., 37075, 615-824-6319 |
| Nashville | Ms. Rickies B&B, 1614 19th Ave. S., 37212, 615-269-3850 |
| Nashville | Rose Garden, 6213 Harding Rd., 37205, 615-356-8003 |
| Newport | Christopher Place Inn, 1500 Pinnacles Way, 37821, 423-623-6555 |
| Normandy | Parish Patch Farm & Inn, 625 Cortner Rd., 37360, 615-857-3017 |
| Orlinda | Aurora B&B, 8253 Hwy. 52, 37141, 615-654-4266 |
| Pigeon Forge | Day Dreams Country Inn, 2720 Colonial Dr., 37863 |
| Red Boiling Spring | Armour's Red Boiling Sprng, 321 E. Main St., 37150, 615-699-2180 |
| Rockford | Wayside Manor B&B, 4009 Old Knoxville Hwy, 37853, 615-970-4823 |
| Rugby | Clear Fork Farm, 328 Shirley Ford Rd., 37852, 615-628-2967 |
| Rugby | Grey Gables B&B, P.O. Box 5252, Hwy. 52, 37733, 615-628-5252 |
| Rugby | Newbury House Inn, P.O. Box 8, Hwy 52, 37733, 615-628-2441 |
| Rugby | Ted & Barbara's B&B, Shirley Ford Rd., 37733, 615-628-2967 |
| Savannah | Ross House, P.O. Box 398, 38372, 901-925-3974 |
| Sevierville | Blue Mountain Mist Country, 1811 Pullen Rd., 37862, 615-428-2335 |
| Sevierville | Gallery House, The, P.O. Box 5274, 37864, 615-428-6937 |
| Sevierville | Huckleberry Inn B&B, 1754 Sandstone Way, 37876, 615-428-2475 |

| | | |
|---|---|---|
| Sevierville | LeConte Lodge, 250 Apple Valley Rd., 37862,  615-436-4473 | |
| Sevierville | Moss Rose Inn & Cafe, The,  1421 Silver Poplar Ln., 37876,  901-423-4777 | |
| Sevierville | Place of the Blue Smoke,  3760 Cove Mountain Rd., 37862,  800-453-4216 | |
| Seymour | Country Inn, The,  701 Chris-Haven Dr., 37865,  615-577-8172 | |
| Shelbyville | Cinnamon Ridge B&B,  799 Whitthorne St., 37160,  615-685-9200 | |
| Signal Mt. | Charlet House, The,  111 River Pt. Rd., 37377,  615-886-4880 | |
| Smithville | Evins Mill Retreat, P.O. box 606, 37166,  615-597-2088 | |
| Sweetwater | Flow Blue Inn, P.O. Box 495, 37874,  615-442-2964 | |
| Townsend | Richmont Inn,  220 Winterberry Ln., 37882,  615-448-6751 | |
| Townsend | Tuckaleechee Inn, 160 Bear Lodge Dr., 37882,  615-448-6442 | |
| Tullahoma | Tullahoma B&B, 308 N. Atlantic St., 37388,  615-455-8876 | |
| Vonore | Turkey Penn Resort, Rt. 1, 37885,  615-295-2400 | |
| Walland | Inn @ Blackberry Farm, The,  West Millers Cove Rd., 37886,  615-984-8166 | |
| Wartrace | Walking Horse Hotel,  P.O. Box 266, 37183 | |
| Watertown | Watertown B&B, 116 Depot St., 37184,  615-237-9999 | |
| Winchester | Antebellum Inn, The,  974 Lynchburg Rd., 37398,  615-967-5550 | |

# Texas

## ALPINE

**Holland Hotel**
P.O. Box 444,   79830
209 W. Holland Ave.
915-837-3844  Fax: 915-837-5129
800-535-8040
Carla McFarland/Juliann
Hafen
All year

$-B&B
12 rooms, 12 pb
Visa, MC,  •
C-yes/S-yes/P-yes/H-yes
Spanish

Continental plus bkfst.
Sitting room
catering/banquet rooms

*Enjoy the breathtaking Big Bend at Alpine's only downtown B&B (across from Amtrak). Concierge style service/catering for your special occasion.*

## AMARILLO

**Parkview House B&B**
1311 S. Jefferson St.,   79101
806-373-9464
Carol & Nabil Dia
All year

$$-B&B
6 rooms, 4 pb
Visa, MC, AmEx,  •
C-ltd/S-no/P-no/H-no
Arabic

Continental plus bkfst.
Complimentary wine
Sitting room, bikes
tennis courts, hot tubs
romantic, friendly

*Historic Victorian home, antiques throughout. Homemade continental breakfast, rose/ herb garden, shaded porch. Friendly Texas hospitality. A bit of the old west in contemporary setting.* **25% off.**

## AUSTIN

**Austin's Wildflower Inn**
1200 W. 22½ St.,   78705
512-477-9639  Fax: 512-474-4188
Kay Jackson
All year

$$$-B&B
4 rooms, 2 pb
AmEx, MC, Visa,
*Rated*,
C-ltd/S-no/P-no/H-no

Full breakfast
Afternoon tea, snacks
Sitting room, deck
nearby public tennis
hiking & biking trails

*Lovely old home furnished w/antiques; located on tree-shaded street; delicious full bkfst. served on deck overlooking garden; near University of Texas and State Capitol. Front verandah w/ceiling fans.*

## AUSTIN

**Brook House B&B, The**
609 W. 33rd St.,   78705
512-459-0534
Barbara Love
All year

$$-B&B
6 rooms, 6 pb
Most CC, •
C-ltd/S-no/P-no/H-no

Full breakfast
Comp. wine, beverages
Sitting room
gazebo, screened porch

*1922 Colonial Revival style home near University of Texas and state capitol. A private cottage and a friendly dog.*

---

**Carrington's Bluff B&B**
1900 David St.,   78705
512-479-0638  Fax: 512-476-4769
800-871-8908
Lisa Mugford
All year

$$-B&B
17 rooms, 15 pb
AmEx, *Rated*, •
C-ltd/S-no/P-no/H-no
French

Full breakfast
Comp. coffee, soda
Afternoon tea
sitting room
babysitting avail. (fee)

*An English country inn located on a tree-covered acre in the heart of the city. Antique-filled rooms and fabulous breakfasts.*

---

**Casa Loma**
5512 Cuesta Verde,   78746
512-327-7189  Fax: 512-327-9150
800-222-0248
Sharon Hillhouse
All year

$$$-B&B
3 rooms, 3 pb
Visa, MC,
C-ltd/S-no/P-no/H-no

Full breakfast
Sitting room, library
hot tubs, sauna, pool
fitness ctr., 2 rm suite

*Newly constructed Mediterranean villa overlooking Lake Austin and bridge, Austin sky-line, University of Texas Tower and Texas Hill Country.*

---

**Chequered Shade B&B, The**
2530 Pearce Rd.,   78730
512-346-8318
Millie Scott
All year

$$-B&B
3 rooms, 2 pb
AmEx, MC, Visa,
C-ltd/S-ltd/P-no/H-no

Full breakfast
Breakfast on the porch
Library, bicycles
antiques, porches, patio
10% off after 3rd. night

*Secluded inn with views of Lake Austin. 15 minutes from restaurants and shopping. Plenty of wildlife in the area. Secluded, ideal get-away with lake vistas, trails, wildlife*

---

**Fairview, A B&B**
1304 Newning Ave.,   78704
512-444-4746  Fax: 512-444-3494
800-310-4746
Duke & Nancy Waggoner
All year

$$$-B&B
6 rooms, 6 pb
Most CC, *Rated*, •
C-ltd/S-ltd/P-no/H-no

Full breakfast
Comp. refreshments
Sitting room, library
tennis close by
cable TV, phones in rms.

*1910 Austin landmark. 1 acre of landscaped grounds in downtown area. Quiet, relaxing, spacious. Antique furnishings.* **Weekly rates & extended stay rates.**

---

**Governor's Inn, The**
611 W. 22nd St.,   78705
512-479-0638  Fax: 512-476-4769
800-871-8908
All year

$$-B&B
10 rooms, 10 pb
Most CC,
C-yes/S-ltd/P-ltd/H-ltd
Spanish, French

Full breakfast
Aftn. tea, snacks
Sitting room
library

*Grand neo-classical Victorian mansion built in 1897. Historical designation, lovely rooms with private baths, cable TV, phones, and beautiful antiques.*

## AUSTIN

**McCallum House, The**
613 W. 32nd,  78705
512-451-6744  Fax: 512-451-6744
Nancy & Roger Danley
All year

$$$-B&B
5 rooms, 5 pb
MC, Visa, *Rated*,  •
C-ltd/S-no/P-no/H-no

Full breakfast
Private kitchens
Sitting area in room
some rooms w/pvt. porch
color TV, phone in rooms

*Explore beautiful Austin from this historic, antique-filled Victorian. Ten blocks from UT-Austin, 20 blocks from Capitol & downtown. $10 off per nite for 2+ consec. weeknites.*

---

**Peaceful Hill B&B**
6401 River Place Bldv.,
  78730
512-338-1817
Mrs. Peninnah Thurmond
All year

$$-B&B
2 rooms, 2 pb
MC, Visa,
C-yes/S-ltd/P-no/H-no

Full breakfast
Porch swing, hammock
grand stone fireplace
25X20 living rm. rockers

*Hill country getaway overlooking panoramic view of city. Swimming, tennis, 18-hole golf-2 miles- at River Place C.C. 15 min. to city; 5 min. to Lake Travis & the Oasis.*

---

**Southard-House**
908 Blanco,  78703
512-474-4731
Jerry & Rejina Southard
All year

$$-B&B
16 rooms, 16 pb
AmEx, MC, Visa,
*Rated*,  •
C-ltd/S-yes/P-no/H-yes

Continental plus wkdays
Full breakfast weekends
Sitting room
porches, pool, laundry
room, garden, gazebo

*Elegant historic home. Clawfoot tub, cutwork linens. Dine by a roaring fire. Caring hosts in the grand Texas style. Downtown. Separate 1920s bungalow w/kitchen suite.*

## BIG SANDY

**Annie's B&B Country Inn**
P.O. Box 928,  75755
105 N. Tyler
903-636-4355  Fax: 903-636-5163
800-BB-ANNIE
Clifton & Kathy Shaw
All year

$$-B&B
12 rooms, 8 pb
MC, Visa, *Rated*,  •
C-ltd/S-no/P-no/H-yes

Full breakfast
Gourmet Restaurant
Sitting room, piano
library, conference
facility for up to 150

*Restored Victorian home with antiques and imported rugs; handmade quilts. Some rooms feature balconies overlooking beautiful flower and water gardens. Low fat dining*

## BOERNE

**Borgman's Sunday House B&B**
911 S. Main,  78006
210-249-9563  800-633-7339
Mike & Mary Jewell
All year

$-B&B
12 rooms, 12 pb
Most CC, *Rated*,  •
C-ltd/S-ltd/P-no/H-ltd

Full breakfast
Restaurant nearby
Refreshments served from
4 to 6 pm, private baths
A/C, cable TV, telephone

*Texas Hill Country. Unique rooms, most furnished with antiques. Craft and antique shops nearby, also nature walk. 25 miles from San Antonio.*

---

**Guadalupe River Ranch**
P.O. Box 877,  78006
605 FM 474
210-537-4837  Fax: 210-537-5249
800-460-2005
Elisa McClure
Closed Christmas week

$$$$-B&B
46 rooms, 46 pb
Most CC,  •
C-yes/S-no/P-no/H-yes
Spanish

Snacks
Lunch, dinner, bar serv.
sitting room, library
bikes, tennis, hot tubs

*Hideaway in this perfect Texas Hill Country Retreat. Dramatic views, attentive staff, gourmet cuisine, horses, canoeing, hiking, nature and more.*

BOERNE ─────────────────────────────────────────────

**Ye Kendall Inn**
128 W. Blanco,  78006
210-249-2138  800-364-2138
Manuel Garcia
All year

$$$-B&B
13 rooms, 13 pb
Visa, MC, AmEx,
*Rated*,  •
C-ltd/S-no/P-no/H-no

Continental plus bkfst.
Restaurant
Bar service, confrence
facilities, sitting room
close to shops in Boerne

*1859 national landmark in the Texas Hill Country. Over the years many famous people found shelter at the inn, including Jefferson Davis, and Dwight D. Eisenhower.*

BURNET ─────────────────────────────────────────────

**Airy Mount Historic Inn**
P.O. Box 351,  78611
Rt. 3, Box 280
512-756-4149
All year

$$$-B&B
3 rooms, 3 pb
Visa, MC,
C-ltd/S-no/P-no/H-yes

Full breakfast
Living room
BBQ, porch
Champagne optional

*This 120 yr. old Texas Limestone Barn is an historic landmark built by General Adam R. Johnson of the Civil War. Gourmet breakfasts served by candlelight & made by owners themselves. 3rd night, 50%.*

CANYON ─────────────────────────────────────────────

**Hudspeth House B&B**
1905 4th Ave.,  79015
806-655-9800  Fax: 806-655-7457
800-655-9809
Mark & Mary Clark
All year

$$-B&B
8 rooms, 8 pb
Most CC, *Rated*,  •
C-yes/S-no/P-no/H-no

Full breakfast
Computerized phone serv.
Fax serv., Conference rm
room fireplaces, hot tub

*Retired historical 1909 university faculty home on main road to Palo Duro Canyon State Park (home of "Texas" outdoor musical drama) and state's largest & oldest museum. Newly restored. 35% disc't, ltd.*

CONROE ─────────────────────────────────────────────

**Heather's Glen. . .A B&B**
200 E. Phillips,  77301
409-441-6611  Fax: 409-441-6603
800-66-JAMIE
Jamie George
All year

$$-B&B
5 rooms, 5 pb
Most CC, *Rated*,  •
C-ltd/S-ltd/P-ltd/H-ltd
Spanish

Full breakfast
Snacks
Sitting room
private Jacuzzis for 2
in some bedrooms

*1900 Victorian 3 story mansion; restored with elegant, modern conveniences. 5 romantic rooms, all with private bathrooms. Area antique shops/auctions, lake sports, golf. 3rd night 50% off.*

CORPUS CHRISTI ─────────────────────────────────────

**Bay Breeze B&B**
201 Louisiana,  78404
512-882-4123  Fax: 512-643-5413
Perry & Frank Tompkins
All year

$$-B&B
4 rooms, 4 pb
•
C-ltd/S-ltd/P-no/H-no

Full breakfast
Sitting room, library
suites w/private baths
endless bayfront venues

*This fine home is within view of the bay waters and radiates the charm and ambiance of days gone by. 7th day free.*

FORT WORTH ─────────────────────────────────────────

**Texas White House, The**
1417 8th Ave.,  76104
817-923-3597  Fax: 817-923-0410
800-279-6491
Jamie & Grover McMains
All year

$$$-B&B
3 rooms, 3 pb
Most CC, *Rated*,  •
C-ltd/S-ltd/P-no/H-no

Full breakfast
Afternoon tea, snacks
Dinner (fee)
sitting room

*Historically designated, award winning, country style home, centrally located; as warm and generous as old family friends; gracious and simply elegant.*

## FREDERICKSBURG

**Delforge Place, The**
710 Ettie St.,  78624
210-997-6212  800-997-0462
Betsy, George & Pete
Delforge
All year

$$$-B&B
4 rooms, 4 pb
Visa, MC, Disc, *Rated*,
•
C-ltd/S-no/P-no
French, Spanish

Full gourmet breakfast
Picnic baskets, snacks
Aft. tea, porch swing
pvt. patio, horseshoes
croquet/archery, library

*1898 Victorian in town. Historical antiques, many authentic Clipper-ship period heirlooms. "World-class breakfast" (Gourmet Mag.) Warm, friendly ambiance. **7th night is free.***

---

**Magnolia House**
101 E. Hackberry,  78624
210-997-0306  Fax: 210-997-0766
800-880-4374
Joyce & Patrick Kennard
All year

$$-B&B
6 rooms, 4 pb
Visa, MC, *Rated*, •
C-ltd/S-no/P-no/H-ltd

Full breakfast
Snacks, comp. wine
Sitting room
swimming, tennis
health facility nearby

*1923 Texas Historical Home. Elegant, southern hospitality. Your home away from home. **10% discount, Mon.–Thurs.***

---

**Rose Cottage &**
**Guesthouse**
231 W. Main,  78624
210-997-5612  Fax: 210-997-8282
Gastehaus Schmidt
All year

$$
3 rooms, 3 pb
Visa, MC, Disc., •
C-yes/S-no/P-yes

Coffee & tea only
TV, VCR, parking
front porch with swing

*Historic district guesthome–Rich, warm decor representative of the 1920's era. Exquisite dining room, exposed wood trims throughout. **Seventh consecutive night no charge!***

---

**Schildknecht-Weidenfeller**
231 W. Main,  78624
210-997-5612  Fax: 210-997-8282
Ellis & Carter Schildknecht
All year

$$$-B&B
8 rooms, 2 pb
Visc, MC, Disc., •
C-ltd/S-no/P-no/H-no

German breakfast
Fireplace, porch
rocking chairs, yard
rent entire house

*1880s German limestone house. Primitive antiques. Handmade quilts. Featured on historic home tours and in "Country Decorating Ideas." Sleeps 10. **7th consecutive night free.***

---

**Schmidt Barn B&B**
231 W. Main St.,  78624
210-997-5612  Fax: 210-997-8282
Donna Mittel
All year

$$-B&B
1 rooms, 1 pb
Visa, MC, Disc., •
C-yes/S-yes/P-ltd
German

Continental plus bkfst.
German breakfast platter
Deer and wildlife

*130-year-old limestone barn. Featured in Country Living Magazine. Modern facilities with old-world charm. Spring flower & herb garden.*

## GALVESTON

**Gilded Thistle, The**
1805 Broadway,  77550
409-763-0194  800-654-9380
Helen & Pat Hanemann
All year

$$$$-B&B
3 rooms,
MC, Visa, *Rated*, •
C-yes

Full breakfast (hearty)
Snack tray in evening
Coffee, juice tray a.m.
porches, gardens, bench
Fax, modem, printer

*Experience the graciousness of times gone by. A family service of excellence since 1981. Aimed at the business traveler & hearing-impaired tourist. **Free teddy bear.***

## GALVESTON

| **Madame Dyer's B&B** | $$$-B&B | Full breakfast |
|---|---|---|
| 1720 Postoffice St., Galveston | 3 rooms, 3 pb | Complimentary wine/snack |
| Island, 77550 | Visa, MC, • | Dinners - arrangements |
| 409-765-5692 | C-yes/S-ltd/P-no/H-no | 15% off 3 night stay |
| Linda & Larry Bonnin | | Champagne & Choc. 2 nite |
| All year | | |

*A unique way to enjoy Galveston's growing popularity & experience a traditional B&B is a stay at Madame Dyer's. Delightful antiques bring back memories of days gone by.*

## GLEN ROSE

| **Hummingbird Lodge** | $$$-B&B | Continental plus |
|---|---|---|
| P.O. Box 128,  76043 | 6 rooms, 6 pb | Sitting room, library |
| F.R. 203 | Visa, MC, *Rated*, • | hot tubs, 20 miles to GC |
| 817-897-2787  Fax: 817-897-3459 | C-yes/S-no/P-no/H-ltd | 5 min. to Wildlife Park |
| Sherry & Richard Fowlkes | | |
| All year | | |

*140 wooded acres - furnished with original art work, antiques and primitive Texas furniture. Grounds have walking trails and a stocked fishing pond. Dining room has frplc.*

| **Ye Ole Maple Inn** | $$-B&B | Full breakfast |
|---|---|---|
| P.O. Box 1141,  76043 | 2 rooms, 2 pb | Snacks |
| 1509 Van Zandt | *Rated*, | River with swimming |
| 817-897-3456 | S-no/P-no/H-yes | tubbing |
| Roberta Maple | | |
| All year | | |

*Quilt country getaway. Inviting porch swing and rockers. Great breakfast and desserts. Unique sightseeing attraction and golf course nearby. $10 off Sun-Thursday.*

## GONZALES

| **St. James Inn** | $$-B&B | Full breakfast |
|---|---|---|
| 723 St. James,  78629 | 7 rooms, 7 pb | Picnic baskets, romantic |
| 210-672-7066 | Visa, MC, AmEx, | Dinners by appointment |
| J.R. & Ann Covert | C-ltd/S-ltd/P-no | browse antique shops |
| All year | | enjoy the scenery |

*The home has exceptionally large rooms, private baths, fireplaces and porches. Decorated with a mixture of period & contemporary furniture w/the guests' relaxation and comfort in mind.*

## GRANBURY

| **Iron Horse Inn, The** | $$-B&B | Full breakfast |
|---|---|---|
| 616 Thorp Spring Rd.,  76048 | 6 rooms, 6 pb | Aftn. tea, snacks |
| 817-579-5535 | Visa, MC, AmEx, | Comp. wine |
| Bob & Judy Atkinson | C-ltd/S-no/P-no/H-no | sitting room, library |
| All year | | |

*Elegant 1905 Craftsman home-large front porch, beveled/leaded glass, warm woodwork create an inviting atmosphere in this historic town.*

| **Pearl Street Inn B&B** | $$-B&B | Full breakfast |
|---|---|---|
| 319 W. Pearl St.,  76048 | 5 rooms, 5 pb | Dinners by reservation |
| 817-279-7465  888-732-7578 | *Rated*, • | Sitting room, snacks |
| Danette D. Hebda | C-ltd/S-ltd/P-no/H-no | king beds, private baths |
| All year | | outdoor hot tub |

*Centrally located historic home features antique clawfoot tubs, period furnishings, porches. Relax & reminisce "where days move gently in all seasons." Free sample Pearl St. Inn coffee.*

HOUSTON ───────────────────────────────

| **Durham House B&B Inn** | $$-B&B | Full breakfast |
| 921 Heights Blvd., 77008 | 9 rooms, 9 pb | Comp. wine, refreshments |
| 713-868-4654 Fax: 713-868-7965 | AmEx, MC, Visa, | Sitting room, gazebo |
| 800-722-8788 | *Rated*, • | tandem bicycles |
| Marguerite Swanson | C-ltd | Murder mystery evenings |
| All year | German | |

*Authentic Victorian on Nat'l Register of Historic Places. Antique furnishings. Romantic getaway/wedding location. Near downtown Houston. Carriage house avail. 3rd night 50%.*

| **Highlander, The** | $$$-B&B | Full breakfast |
| 607 Highland Ave., 77009 | 3 rooms, 3 pb | Snacks |
| 713-861-6110 Fax: 713-861-0056 | • | Sitting room, library |
| 800-807-6110 | C-ltd/S-no/P-no/H-no | hot tubs, gazebo, pond |
| Georgie McIrvin | | Urban Wildlife Garden |
| All year | | |

*A tranquil oasis in the center of dynamic downtown Houston. From hairdryers to modem connections, we try to anticipate your every need. Free "Love, Laughter & Romance" book.*

| **Patrician B&B Inn, The** | $$$-B&B | Full breakfast |
| 1200 Southmore Ave., 77004 | 4 rooms, 4 pb | Comp. wine, snacks |
| 713-523-1114 Fax: 713-523-0790 | Most CC, *Rated*, • | Sitting room, near golf |
| 800-553-5797 | C-ltd/S-no/P-no/H-no | perfect for weddings |
| Pat Thomas | | parties or receptions |
| All year | | |

*1919 mansion minutes to downtown Houston, Texas Medical Center, Museum of Fine Arts and Rice University. Some claw foot tubs. Telephone & TV in all rooms. 4+ nights 10% off.*

JEFFERSON ───────────────────────────────

| **Falling Leaves B&B** | $$$-B&B | Full breakfast |
| 304 Jefferson St., 75657 | 4 rooms, 4 pb | Refreshments |
| 903-665-8803 | Visa, MC, • | Sitting room, library |
| Barbara & Joe Bell | S-no/P-no/H-no | screened porch w/rockers |
| All year | | cable TV in each room |

*Early Greek Revival, CA 1855, in historic district. King-size beds, filled with antiques, private baths, gourmet breakfast, refreshments available. Sun.–Thurs $10 off, ltd.*

MARBLE FALLS ───────────────────────────────

| **La Casita B&B** | $$-B&B | Full breakfast |
| 1908 Redwood Dr., 78654 | 1 rooms, 1 pb | Comp. drink on arrival |
| 210-598-6443 800-798-6443 | • | Refrigerator, garden |
| Joanne & Roger Scarborough | C-yes/S-ltd/P-no/H-ltd | library, queen-sized bed |
| All year | | flowers, swimming, sink |

*A single, priv. Hill Country cottage W. of Marble Falls, among wildlife & wildflowers, near lake LBJ, river cruises & vineyards. Ideal for birthdays, anniv, wkend get-a-aways.*

NACOGDOCHES ───────────────────────────────

| **Llano Grande Plantation** | $$-B&B | Continental plus bkfst. |
| Route 4, Box 9400, 75964 | 3 rooms, 3 pb | Private kitchen |
| 409-569-1249 | *Rated*, | Sitting room |
| Captain Charles & A. Phillips | C-ltd/S-ltd/P-ltd/H-no | historic tours |
| All year | | library |

*Authentically furnished historic house on 600 wooded acres only 2½ miles from the oldest town in Texas. Homemade bread, sausage.*

**Texas**

## NEW BRAUNFELS

**Kuebler Waldrop Haus**
1620 Hueco Springs Loop,
  78132
210-625-8372  Fax: 210-625-8372
800-299-8372
Margaret & son Darrell
All year

$$$-B&B
7 rooms, 7 pb
Most CC, •
C-yes/S-ltd/P-ltd/H-yes
Spanish

Full breakfast
Snacks, comp. wine
Sitting room, library
gift shop
walking trails

*Relax! 43 beautiful hill country acres near rivers, Gruene, New Braunfels, San Antonio, Austin. Delicious candlelight breakfast brunch. Whirlpools, kitchenettes, porches. **13% disc't off season.***

## PLANO

**Inn on the River**
P.O. Box 861900,  76086
205 SW Barnard, Glen Rose
214-424-7119  Fax: 214-424-9766
800-575-2101
Kathi Thompson
All year

$$$-B&B
22 rooms, 22 pb
Most CC, *Rated*, •
C-ltd/S-ltd/P-no/H-ltd
Spanish

Full gourmet breakfast
Dinner on Fri. & Sat.
Library, sitting room
state of the arts 1,000
sq.ft. conference center

*Casual elegance & relaxing atmosphere on the Paluxy River. 300 yr. old oak tree, swimming pool, gourmet meals, featherbeds. State of the art conference center w/view of river.*

## PORT ISABEL

**Yacht Club Hotel**
P.O. Box 4114,  78578
700 Yturria St.
210-943-1301  Fax: 210-943-1301
Ron & Lynn Speier
All year

$-B&B
2 rooms, 1 pb
Most CC, *Rated*, •
C-yes/S-yes/P-no/H-yes
Spanish

Continental breakfast
Restaurant, bar, dinner
Swimming pool
A/C & cable TV in rooms
fishing charters avail.

*Port Isabel's finest accommodation. Spanish architecture with the elegance and ambiance of the 1920s. Gourmet restaurant specializing in seafood. Just 20 minutes to Mexico.*

## ROLSTOWN

**Fortuna Bay B&B**
Rt. 4, Box 115P1, 15405
Fortuna Bay Dr.,  78380
512-387-5666
John & Jackie Fisher
All year

$$$-B&B
2 rooms, 2 pb
C-ltd/S-no/P-no/H-yes
Limited Spanish

Continental plus
Snacks, restaurant
Bar service, tennis
pool

*Hideaway on Texas North Padre Island with white sand beaches. Country Club privileges, fishing off our deck. Condo living Caribbean style. **10% disc't, ltd.***

## SAN ANTONIO

**A Yellow Rose**
229 Madison St.,  78204
210-229-9903  Fax: 210-229-1691
800-950-9903
Dev Field & Kit Walker
All year

$$$-B&B
5 rooms, 5 pb
Most CC, *Rated*, •
C-ltd/S-no/P-no/H-no

Full breakfast
Aft. tea, snacks
Comp. wine
sitting room
2 blocks from river walk

*Located King William Historic District, 2 blocks to Riverwalk, walk to Alamo, Convention Center, antiques, off street parking. Suite has 2 queen-size beds. Fine art hanging in public areas*

## SAN ANTONIO

**Adams House B&B Inn**
231 Adams St., 78210
210-224-4791  Fax: 210-223-5125
800-666-4810
Scott Lancaster
All year

$$-B&B
3 rooms, 3 pb
AmEx, MC, Visa,
*Rated*, •
C-ltd/S-ltd/P-no/H-no
Spanish

Full gourmet breakfast
Aft. tea, snacks
Comp. wine, sitting room
library, computer, fax
carriage house

*Three story brick; King William Historic District, near Riverwalk/downtown; furnished in period antiques; spacious verandas; Gourmet breakfast served in dining room.*

**Beckmann Inn/Carriage Hse**
222 E. Guenther St., 78204
210-229-1449  Fax: 210-229-1061
800-945-1449
Betty Jo & Don Schwartz
All year

$$$-B&B
5 rooms, 5 pb
*Rated*, •
C-ltd/S-ltd/P-no/H-ltd

Full gourmet breakfast
Welcome tea
Sitting room, historic
district, scenic river
walk, trolley, TV's

*Beautiful historic district, scenic riverwalk, Alamo, trolley, gourmet breakfast w/dessert, ornate antique beds featured, warm & gracious hospitality. Featured in Country Inns*

**Brackenridge House**
230 Madison, 78204
210-271-3442  Fax: 210-271-3442
800-221-1412
Bennie & Sue Blansett
All year

$$$-B&B
5 rooms, 5 pb
AmEx, MC, Visa,
*Rated*, •
C-ltd/S-no/P-ltd/H-no

Full breakfast
Comp. drinks on arrival
Veranda, off-street park
king & full beds
6 blocks to downtown

*Lovely blend of comfort and nostalgia. Original pine floors, double-hung windows, high ceilings and antique furniture. Guest house for families with small children & pets.*

**Brookhaven Manor**
128 W. Mistletoe, 78212
210-733-3939  Fax: 210-733-3884
800-851-3666
Nancy E. Forbes
All year

$$-B&B
4 rooms, 4 pb
Visa, MC, *Rated*, •
C-ltd/S-no/P-no/H-no

Full breakfast
Snacks
Sitting room, library
grande piano

*Elegant 3 story home built in 1914. Brookhaven Manor features high ceilings, wood floors & fireplaces. Close to everything.* **Comp. flowers, balloons, champagne for special occasions.**

**Bullis House Inn**
P.O. Box 8059, 78208
621 Pierce St.
210-223-9426  Fax: 210-299-1479
Steve & Alma Cross
All year

$-B&B
7 rooms, 2 pb
Most CC, *Rated*, •
C-yes/S-yes/P-no/H-no
Spanish

Continental plus bkfst.
Guest kitchen, snacks
Library, phones, veranda
movie night w/snacks
poolside BBQs

*Historic 3-story, white mansion, minutes from Alamo, Riverwalk, downtown. Chandeliers, fireplaces, decorative 14-ft. ceilings, geometrically patterned floors of fine woods.* **10% disc't on weekday stay.**

**Columns on Alamo, The**
1037 South Alamo, 78210
210-271-3245  Fax: 210-271-3245
800-233-3364
Ellenor & Art

$$$-B&B
11 rooms, 11 pb
Visa, MC, AmEx, •
C-ltd/S-no/P-no
German

Full breakfast
Queen & king beds
in-room TV & phones
off-street parking

*1892 mansion & guesthouse—historic district, antiques, oriental rugs, spacious common areas, verandas. Walk to restaurants, shopping, downtown, Alamo, riverwalk!*

## SAN ANTONIO

| | | |
|---|---|---|
| **Falling Pines B&B** | $$$-B&B | Full breakfast |
| 300 W. French Pl., 78212 | 4 rooms, 4 pb | Comp. wine/brandy in rm. |
| 210-733-1998 800-880-4580 | *Rated*, | Sitting room, library |
| Grace & Bob Daubert | C-ltd/S-no/P-no/H-no | tennis courts |
| All year | | bicycles |

*Near downtown, riverwalk (5 minutes), three-story mansion in historic district with towering trees in parklike setting. Pristine restoration.*

| | | |
|---|---|---|
| **La Mariposa** | $$$-B&B | Continental breakfast |
| 104 Adams St., 78283 | 1 rooms, 1 pb | Sitting room |
| 210-225-7849 Fax: 210-225-7828 | Visa, MC, | library |
| Bitsy Gorman | S-no/P-no/H-no | automatic gated parking |
| All year | Spanish | |

*1884 home; private, spacious, dramatic; urban conveniences; intriguing folk art; Indonesian Wedding Bed; well-travelled hostess shares San Antonio secrets.*

| | | |
|---|---|---|
| **Noble Inns** | $$$-B&B | Full breakfast |
| 102 Turner St., 107 Madison | 10 rooms, 10 pb | Afternoon tea, snacks |
| St., 78204 | Most CC *Rated*, • | Sitting room, library |
| 210-225-4045 Fax: 210-979-6825 | C-ltd/S-no/P-no/H-yes | hot tub, heated pools |
| 800-221-4045 | Spanish | kitchens, phones, TV |
| Don & Liesl Noble | | |
| All year | | |

*Luxurious, meticulously restored Victorian homes. King William District. Beautiful antiques, fireplaces, marble baths, Jacuzzis. Walk to Riverwalk, Alamo, Convention Center.* **Weekday discounts.**

| | | |
|---|---|---|
| **Oge House on the** | $$$$-B&B | Continental plus bkfst. |
| **Riverwalk** | 10 rooms, 10 pb | Sitting room, library |
| 209 Washington St., | Most CC, *Rated*, • | A/C, cable TV, phone |
| 210-223-2353 Fax: 210-226-5812 | C-ltd/S-ltd/P-no/H-no | set on 1/5 acres |
| 800-242-2770 | | |
| Patrick or Sharrie Magatagan | | |
| All year | | |

*Elegant, romantic Antebellum mansion on 1½ acres on the Riverwalk. European antiques, quiet comfort and luxury. Shopping, dining and Alamo 5 blocks.*

| | | |
|---|---|---|
| **Riverwalk Inn** | $$$-B&B | Full breakfast |
| 329 Old Guilbeau, 78204 | 11 rooms, 11 pb | Bicycles, refrigerators |
| 800-254-4440 | Most CC, *Rated*, • | porch, fireplace, phones |
| Jan & Tracy Hammer | C-ltd/S-ltd/P-no/H-yes | Fax: 210-229-9422 |
| All year | Spanish | |

*The Riverwalk Inn, c1840, has been restored on the San Antonio Riverwalk, and tastefully decorated in period antiques giving a feeling of "country elegance."*

## SAN MARCOS

| | | |
|---|---|---|
| **Crystal River Inn** | $$$-B&B | Full breakfast |
| 326 W. Hopkins, 78666 | 12 rooms, 12 pb | Comp. brandy, chocolates |
| 512-396-3739 Fax: 512-353-3248 | AmEx, MC, Visa, | Fireplaces, courtyard |
| Mike, Cathy & Sarah Dillon | *Rated*, • | piano, fountain, bikes |
| All year | C-ltd/S-ltd/P-no/H-yes | 2-room suites, picnics |

*Romantic, luxurious Victorian captures matchless spirit of Texas Hill Country. Fresh flowers, homemade treats. 4-room garden cottage available: fireplace.* **3rd. nite 50%, ltd.**

SMITHVILLE —————————————————————————————————

**Katy House, The**        $$-B&B                    Full country breakfast
P.O. Box 803,   78957       4 rooms, 4 pb             One suite w/kitchen
201 Ramona                  Visa, MC *Rated*,  •      Sitting room
512-237-4262  Fax: 512-237-2239   C-ltd/S-no/P-ltd/H-no   bicycles
800-843-5289                                         queen-size beds
Sallie Blalock
All year

*Historic pecan-shaded home in beautiful central Texas. Railroad memorabilia & antique*
*furnishings. A gracious, comfortable, charming home.*

STEPHENVILLE ————————————————————————————————

**Oxford House, The**       $$-B&B                    Full breakfast
563 N. Graham,   76401      4 rooms, 4 pb             Dinner or tea by reserv.
817-965-6885  Fax: 817-965-7555   Visa, MC, *Rated*,  •   Country hideaway
800-711-7283                C-ltd/S-ltd/P-no/H-yes    queen and full beds
Bill & Paula Oxford                                  3rd night 50% off
All year

*Charming 1898 Queen Anne home owned exclusively by the Oxford family, featuring*
*antiques, family pictures & memorabilia. Clawfoot tubs, porch w/rockers, gazebo &*
*gardens.*

TYLER ———————————————————————————————————————

**Mary's Attic**            $$-B&B                    Continental plus bkfst.
417 S. College,   75702     5 rooms, 3 pb             Stocked refrigerator
903-592-5181  Fax: 903-592-3846   AmEx, MC, Visa,     Antique shop next door
Mary Mirsky                 C-ltd/S-no/P-no/H-no
All year

*The completely restored 1920 bungalow and annex garage apartment are located on the*
*brick streets in the historical district of Tyler. American and English antiques.*

**Rosevine Inn B&B**        $$-B&B                    Full breakfast
415 S. Vine,   75702        7 rooms, 7 pb             Comp. wine, cheese tray
903-592-2221  Fax: 903-593-9500   *Rated*,  •         Sitting room, library
Bert & Rebecca Powell       C-ltd/S-no/P-no/H-no      spa, outdoor hot tub
All year                    French                    courtyard, gameroom

*Original bed and breakfast in the rose capital of the world. Pleasant accommodations*
*with delicious breakfast. Friendly hosts make you feel at home. **5th stay is free.***

**Seasons B&B Inn, The**    $$$-B&B                   Full breakfast
313 E. Charnwood,   75701   4 rooms, 3 pb             Afternoon tea
903-533-0803                Visa, MC, AmEx, Disc.,    Library, sitting room
Jim & Myra Brown            C-ltd/S-no/P-no/H-no      TV room, veranda sitting
All year                                             family friendly facility

*Colonial home near downtown Tyler, antique shopping. Rooms decorated in 4 seasons*
*theme; wall art/painting in each room. Original curly pine woodwork. Gourmet break-*
*fast.*

WACO ————————————————————————————————————————

**Judge Baylor House, The** $$-B&B                    Full breakfast
908 Speight,   76706        4 rooms, 4 pb             Aftn. tea, snacks
817-756-0273  Fax: 817-756-0711   MC, Visa, *Rated*,  •   Sitting room, library
Bruce & Dorothy Dyer        C-ltd/S-no/P-no/H-ltd
All year

*Decorated with antiques & Texas Hill Country art. Quiet & comfortable bedrooms. Near*
*Baylor University and IH-35. Easy to find.*

WAXAHACHIE ────────────────────────────────────

**Bonnynook Inn, The**
414 W. Main St.,   75165
214-938-7207  Fax: 214-937-7700
800-486-5936
Vaughn & Bonnie Franks
All year

$$$-B&B
5 rooms, 5 pb
Most CC, *Rated*, •
C-yes/S-yes/P-no/H-no

Full gourmet breakfast
Dinner
Picnic basket, snacks
whirlpool tubs in 2 rms
patio, piano, antiques

*1887 Victorian home, located near Square in a historic national district. Each room is a different experience. Plants & fresh flowers, country garden. **10% off weekdays.***

─────────────────────────────────────────────────

**Chaska House B&B, The**
716 West Main St.,   75165
214-937-3390  800-931-3390
Louis & Linda Brown
All year

$$$-B&B
6 rooms, 6 pb
Visa, MC, AmEx,
*Rated*, •
C-ltd/S-ltd/P-no/H-no

Full Southern breakfast
Aft. tea, comp. wine
Lib., antiques, verandah
tree shaded gardens,
bikes, health facilities

*"Victorian Splendor"-(TX Highways). House beautiful cover. Elegantly romantic National Register mansion near historic square, shopping, dining. **2 couples 10% off.***

WEATHERFORD ───────────────────────────────────

**Victorian House B&B**
P.O. Box 1571,   76086
1105 Palo Pinto
817-596-8295  800-687-1660
Candice Dyer
All year

$$$-B&B
10 rooms, 10 pb
Visa, MC, AmEx, •
C-ltd/S-no/P-no/H-ltd

Full hot breakfast
Snacks
Sitting room
25" stereo TVs

*10,000 Sq.Ft. 3 story Victorian mansion situated on 3 landscaped acres. Home is 100 years old, totally restored with TV's & phones in all rooms. Many historic homes in area. **Midweek disc't.***

WIMBERLEY ─────────────────────────────────────

**Blair House**
100 Spoke Hill Rd.,   78676
512-847-1111  Fax: 512-847-8820
Jonnie Stansbury
All year

$$$$-B&B
7 rooms, 7 pb
Most CC, •
C-ltd/S-no/P-no/H-yes
Spanish

Full breakfast
Comp. wine & dessert
Dinner on Saturday (fee)
sitting room, library
sauna

*Chef-owned country inn offering spa services on 85 acres of Texas Hill Country. Just 1.4 miles from charming Wimberley. **15% off, Sun.–Thurs.***

─────────────────────────────────────────────────

**Homestead, The**
P.O. Box 1034,   78076
Ranch Rd.12/County Rd.316
512-847-8788  Fax: 512-847-8842
800-918-8788
Clark A. Aylsworth
All year

$$$-B&B
8 rooms, 8 pb
•
C-yes/S-yes/P-ltd/H-ltd

Continental plus bkfst.
Hot tubs
6.5 acres and room for
55 guests for reunions

*Eight fully equipped cottages located directly on Cypress Creek and each able to accommodate groups of 6 to 8 adults. **3rd night 50% off, ltd.***

─────────────────────────────────────────────────

**Old Oaks Ranch B&B**
P.O. Box 912,   78676
601 Old Oaks Ranch Rd.
512-847-9374  Fax: 512-847-9374
Susan & Bill Holt
All year

$$-B&B
3 rooms, 3 pb
MC, Visa, *Rated*, •
S-no/P-no/H-no

Continental plus bkfst.
Full breakfast (Sunday)
Sitting room
one 2-bedroom cottage
Two 1-bedroom cottages

*Quiet, country inn furnished with Victorian antiques. Hiking. Cows, geese, wild birds, deer. Picturesque. Close to resort area. Golf & tennis available. **10% off Mon.–Thurs.***

WIMBERLEY ———————————————————————————————

| **Southwind B&B** | $$-B&B | Full breakfast |
|---|---|---|
| 2701 FM 3237,  78676 | 3 rooms, 3 pb | Sitting room, hot tub |
| 512-847-5277  800-508-5277 | • | library, porch |
| Carrie Watson | C-ltd/S-no/P-no/H-no | two cabins w/fireplace |
| All year | Spanish | |

*25 scenic hill country acres; hearty southwestern breakfasts; homemade bread and muffins. Cabins have whirlpools, kitchens and porches. **Stay 7 nights, 8th night free.***

WINNSBORO ———————————————————————————————

| **Thee Hubbell House** | $$-B&B | Full breakfast |
|---|---|---|
| 307 W. Elm St.,  75494 | 12 rooms, 12 pb | Continental bkfst. |
| 903-342-5629 Fax: 903-342-6627 | AmEx, MC, Visa, | Sitting room, library |
| 800-227-0639 | *Rated*, • | veranda, gallery, garden |
| Dan & Laurel Hubbell | C-ltd/S-ltd/P-ltd/H-ltd | Jacuzzi, antique shoppe |
| All year | | |

*1888 historic Georgian home, restored and furnished in period antiques. Massage by appointment. Plantation or continental breakfast. Centrally located to other tourist areas. **Honeymoon packages.***

# More Inns ...

| | |
|---|---|
| Abilene | Bolin's Prairie House B&B, 508 Mulberry St., 79601,  915-675-5855 |
| Austin | Aunt Dolly's Attic B&B, 12023 Rotherham Dr., 78753,  512-837-5320 |
| Austin | Trails End B&B, 12223 Trails End Rd.#7, 78641,  512-267-2901 |
| Austin | Woodburn House B&B, 4401 Ave. D, 78751,  512-458-4335 |
| Azle | Where the Red Rooster Crow, 409 Chaparrel Rd. W., 76020,  817-444-4018 |
| Bastrop | Pfeiffer House, 1802 Main St., 78602,  512-321-2100 |
| Beeville | Nueces Inn, P.O. Box 29, 78104,  713-362-0868 |
| Bellville | High Cotton Inn, 214 S. Live Oak, 77418,  800-321-9796 |
| Brenham | Secrets Bed & Breakfst, Pecan St., 78006 |
| Buchanan Dam | Mystic Cove B&B, RR 1, Box 309B, 78609,  512-793-6642 |
| Burnet | Williams Point, 16 Lakeside Dr., 78611,  512-756-2074 |
| Calvert | Our House, P.O. Box 113, 77837,  409-364-2909 |
| Canyon Lake | Aunt Nora's, 120 Naked Indian Trail, 78132,  210-905-3989 |
| Center | John C. Rogers House, 416 Shebyville, 75935,  409-598-3971 |
| Center | Pine Colony Inn, 500 Shelbyville St., 75935,  409-598-7700 |
| Chappell Hill | Browning Plantation, Rt. 1, Box 8, 77426,  409-836-6144 |
| Chireno | Gingerbread House, Gingerbread St., Box 94, 75937,  409-362-2365 |
| Cleburne | Anglin Queen Anne, 723 N. Anglin, 76031,  817-645-5555 |
| Cleburne | Cleburne House, 201 N. Anglin, 76031,  817-641-0085 |
| Cleburne | Georges Creek Inn B&B, The, Rte 9, Box 440, 76031,  817-798-2348 |
| Columbus | Magnolia Oaks, 634 Spring St., 78934,  409-732-2726 |
| Crosbyton | Smith House, 306 W. Aspen, 79322,  806-675-2178 |
| Dallas | B & G, 15869 Nedra Way, 75248,  214-386-4323 |
| Dallas | Hotel St. Germain, 2516 Maple Ave., 75201,  214-871-2516 |
| Dallas | Inn on Fairmount, P.O. Box 190244, 75219,  214-522-2800 |
| Dallas | McKay House B&B Inn, 9659 Broken Bow Rd., 75238,  214-665-7322 |
| Doss | Hill Top Cafe & Guesthouse, 10661 N. U.S. Hwy. 87, 78618,  512-997-8922 |
| Eagle Lake | Farris 1912, 201 N. McCarty, 77434,  409-234-2546 |
| Edom | Red Rooster Square, Route 3, Box 3387, 75756,  214-852-6774 |
| El Paso | Bergmann Inn, 10009 Trinidad Dr., 79925,  915-599-1398 |
| El Paso | Gardner Hotel, 311 E. Franklin Ave., 79901,  915-532-3661 |
| El Paso | Sunset Heights B&B Inn, 717 W. Yandell Ave., 79902,  915-544-1743 |
| Ennis | Raphael House, 500 W. Ennis Ave., 75119,  214-875-1555 |
| Floydada | Lamplighter Inn, 102 S. 5th, 79235,  806-983-3035 |
| Fort Davis | Hotel Limpia, The, Box 822, 79734,  915-426-3237 |
| Fort Davis | Old Texas Inn B&B, P.O. Box 785, 79734 |
| Fort Worth | Coloney, The, 2611 Glendale Ave., 76106,  817-624-1981 |
| Fort Worth | Miss Molly's Hotel B&B, 109-1/2 W. Exchange Ave, 76106,  817-626-1522 |
| Fort Worth | Stockyards Hotel, Main & Exchange Sts., 76106,  817-625-6427 |
| Fredericksburg | Austin Street Retreat, The, 231 W. Main, 78624 |
| Fredericksburg | Country Cottage Inn, 249 E. Main, 78624,  210-997-8549 |
| Fredericksburg | Crooks' Log Cabin, 231 W. Main, 78624,  210-997-5612 |
| Fredericksburg | Herb Haus @ Fredericksburg, 402 Whitney, 78624,  210-997-8615 |
| Fredericksburg | J Bar K Ranch B&B, HC 10, Box 53-A, 78624,  210-669-2471 |
| Fredericksburg | John Walter Complex, The, 231 W. Main St., 78624,  210-997-5612 |
| Fredericksburg | Palo Alto Creek Farm, Rt. 4 Box 92, 78624,  210-997-0088 |
| Fredericksburg | Pedernales School House, 231 W. Main St., 78624,  210-997-5612 |
| Fredericksburg | River Bend Herb Farm, 231 W. Main, 78624,  210-997-5612 |

| | |
|---|---|
| Fredericksburg | Settler's Crossing, 231 W. Main St., 78624, 210-997-5612 |
| Fredericksburg | Victorian Lace Gastehaus, 231 W. Main, 78624, 210-997-5612 |
| Galveston | 1887 Coppersmith Inn, The, 1914 Avenue M, 77550, 409-763-7004 |
| Galveston | Key Largo, 5400 Seawall Blvd., 77550, 800-833-0120 |
| Galveston | La Quinta Inn, 1402 Seawall Blvd., 77550, 800-531-5900 |
| Galveston | Michael's-A B&B Inn, 1715 - 35th St., 77550, 409-763-3760 |
| Galveston | Queen Anne B&B, 1915 Sealy Ave., 77550, 409-763-7088 |
| Galveston | Tremont House, 2300 Ship's Mechanic Rd, 77550, 800-874-2300 |
| Galveston | Trube Castle Inn, 1627 Sealy Ave., 77550, 409-765-4396 |
| Galveston | Victorian Inn, 511 - 17th St., 77550, 409-762-3235 |
| Garland | Catnap Creek B&B, 417 Glen Canyon Dr., 75040, 214-530-0819 |
| Georgetown | Harper-Chessher Hist. Inn, 1309 College St., 78626, 512-863-4057 |
| Georgetown | Historic Page House, 1000 Leander Rd., 78628, 512-863-8979 |
| Glen Rose | Lodge at Fossil Rim, The, P.O. Box 2189, 76043, 817-897-7452 |
| Glen Rose | Popejoy Haus B&B, P.O. Box 2023, 76043 |
| Granbury | Dabney House, 106 S. Jones, 76048, 817-579-1260 |
| Granbury | Doyle House, The, 205 W. Doyle, 76048, 817-573-6492 |
| Granbury | Nutt House Hotel & Dining, 121 E. Bridge St., 76048, 817-573-5612 |
| Hillsboro | Farlton House of 1895, 211 N. Pleasant St., 76645, 817-582-7216 |
| Hillsboro | Tarlton House, 211 N. Pleasant St., 76645, 817-582-7216 |
| Houston | Barbara's B&B, 215 Glenwood Dr., 77007 |
| Houston | La Colombe d'Or, 3410 Montrose Blvd., 77226, 713-524-7999 |
| Houston | Lovett Inn, The, 501 Lovett Blvd., 77006, 713-522-5224 |
| Houston | Oaks Cottage B&B, The, 1118 So. Shepherd Dr., 77019 |
| Houston | Robin's Nest, 4104 Greeley St, 77006, 713-528-5821 |
| Houston | Sara's B&B Inn, 941 Heights Blvd., 77008, 713-868-1130 |
| Houston | Woodlake House, 2100 Tanglewilde, #371, 77063 |
| Hunstville | Blue Bonnet B&B, 1215 Avenue G #4, 77340, 409-295-2072 |
| Hunt | Joy Spring Ranch B&B, Route 1, Box 174-A, 78024, 512-238-4531 |
| Huntsville | Whistler B&B, The, 906 Avenue M., 77340, 409-295-2834 |
| Ingram | River Oaks Lodge, HCR 78 Box 231-A, 78025 |
| Itasca | Park House of 1908 B&B Inn, 206 N. Wesley, 76055, 817-687-2515 |
| Jefferson | Captain's Castle, 403 E Walker, 75657, 903-665-2330 |
| Jefferson | Excelsior House, 211 W. Austin St., 75657, 214-665-2513 |
| Jefferson | Gingerbread House, 601 E. Jefferson, 75657, 214-665-8994 |
| Jefferson | Magnolias Inn, 209 E. Broadway, 75657, 214-665-2754 |
| Jefferson | McKay House B&B Inn, 306 E. Delta St., 75238, 214-348-1929 |
| Jefferson | Pride House, 409 Broadway, 75657, 903-665-2675 |
| Jefferson | Roseville Manor, 217 West Lafayette, 75657, 800-665-7273 |
| Jefferson | Stillwater Inn, 203 E. Broadway, 75657, 214-665-8415 |
| Jefferson | William Clark House, 201 W. Henderson, 75657, 214-665-8880 |
| Karnack | Mimosa Hall, Route 1, Box 635, 75661, 214-679-3632 |
| Kemah | Captain's Quarters, 701 Bay Ave., 77565, 713-334-4141 |
| Kyle | Inn Above Onion Creek, The, 4444 FM 150 W., 78640 |
| Lago Vista | Mary Jane Robinson, P.O. Box 4529, 78645 |
| Leander | Trails End B&B, 12223 Trails End Rd. #7, 78641, 512-267-2901 |
| Ledbetter | Granny's Hse c/o Ledbetter, P.O. Box 212, 78946, 409-249-3066 |
| Ledbetter | Ledbetter B&B, P.O. Box 212, 78946, 409-249-3066 |
| Llano | Badu House, 601 Bessemer, 78643, 915-247-4304 |
| Llano | Fraser House Inn, 207 E. Main, 78643 |
| Marfa | Fort Russell Inn, U.S. 67, 79843 |
| Marshall | Weisman-Hirsch-Beil Home, 313 S. Washington, 75670, 214-938-5504 |
| Martindale | Forget-Me-Not River Inn, P.O. Box 396, 78643, 512-357-6385 |
| Mineola | Munzesheimer Manor, 202 N. Newsom, 75773, 903-569-6634 |
| Nacogdoches | Haden Edwards Inn, 106 N. Lanana, 75961, 409-564-9999 |
| Nacogdoches | Moundstreet B&B, 408 N. Mound, 75961, 409-569-2211 |
| New Braunfels | Gruene Mansion Inn, 1275 Gruene Rd., 78130, 512-629-2641 |
| New Braunfels | Hill Country Haven, 227 S. Academy St., 78130, 512-629-6727 |
| New Braunfels | Hotel Faust, 240 S. Seguin, 78130, 512-625-7791 |
| New Braunfels | River Haus B&B, 817 E. Zipp Rd., 78130, 210-625-6411 |
| New Braunfels | Rose Garden, The, 195 S. Academy, 78130, 210-625-3296 |
| New Braunfels | Waldrip Haus, 1620 Hueco Spring Loop, 78132, 800-299-8372 |
| New Braunfels | White House, The, 217 Mittman Cr., 78130, 210-629-9354 |
| Paint Rock | Lipan Ranch, Rt 1 Box 21C, 76866, 915-468-2571 |
| Palacios | Moonlight Bay B&B, 506 S. Bay Blvd., 77465, 512-972-3408 |
| Pharr | San Juan Hotel, P.O. Box 731, 78577 |
| Plano | Hermitage, The, P.O. Box 866036, 75086, 214-618-2000 |
| Port Aransas | Tarpon Inn, P.O. Box 8, 78373 |
| Port Isabel | Queen Isabel Inn, 300 Garcia St., 78578 |
| Post | Hotel Garza B&B, 302 E. Main, 79356, 806-495-3962 |
| Rio Grande | La Borde House, 601 E. Main St., 78582, 512-487-5101 |
| Rio Medina | Haby Settlement Inn, The, HC Box 35A, 78066, 512-538-2441 |
| Romayor | Chain-O-Lakes, P.O. Box 218, 77368, 713-592-2150 |
| Round Rock | St. Charles B&B, 8 Chisholm Trail, 78681, 512-244-6850 |
| Royse City | Country Lake B&B, Blockdale Dr., 95189, 214-636-2600 |
| Salado | Rose Mansion, The, P.O. Box 500, 76571, 817-947-8200 |
| San Antonio | Belle Of Monte Vista, 505 Belknap Pl., 78212 |
| San Antonio | Bonner Garden B&B, 145 E. Argarita, 78212, 210-733-4222 |

| San Antonio | Chabot Reed Carriage House, 403 Madison, 78204,  210-734-4243 |
| San Antonio | Gatlin Guesthouse, 123 Cedar St., 78210 |
| San Antonio | Pancoast Carriage House, 102 Turner St., 78204,  210-225-4045 |
| San Antonio | Terrell Castle B&B, 950 E. Grayston St., 78206 |
| San Antonio | Victorian Lady Inn, The,  421 Howard St., 78212 |
| San Augustine | Captain Downs House, 301 E. Main St., 75972,  409-275-5305 |
| San Marcos | Aquarena Springs Inn, P.O. Box 2330, 78666,  512-396-8900 |
| San Marcos | Lonesome Dove B&B, 407 Oakwood Loop, 78666 |
| Seabrook | B&B on the Bay, 7629 Olympia Dr.Houston, 77586,  713-861-9492 |
| Seguin | Weinert House B&B, 1207 N. Austin, 78155 |
| Terlingua | Lajitas on the Rio Grande, Box 400, 79852,  915-424-3471 |
| Texarkana | Main House, 3419 Main St., 75503,  903-793-5027 |
| Turkey | Hotel Turkey, Box 37, 79261,  806-423-1151 |
| Tyler | Charnwood Hill Inn, 223 E. Charnwood, 75701,  903-587-3980 |
| Tyler | Woldert-Spence Manor, The,  611 West Woldert St., 75702,  903-533-9057 |
| Uvalde | Casa De Leona B&B, P.O. Box 1829, 78802,  210-278-8550 |
| Village Mills | Big Thicket Guest House, Box 91, 77663,  409-834-2875 |
| Waxahachie | Rose of Sharon B&B Inn, 205 Bryson, 75165,  214-938-8833 |
| Weatherford | St. Botolph Inn, 808 S. Lamar St., 76086,  817-594-1455 |
| Weslaco | Rio Grande B&B, P.O. Box 16, 78596,  512-968-9646 |
| Wichita Falls | Guest House B&B, 2209 Miramar St., 76308 |
| Wimberley | Dobie House, Rt. 1, Box 12, 78676,  800-460-3909 |

# Utah

## GLENDALE

**Eagle's Nest B&B**
P.O. Box 160,  84729
500 W. Lydia's Canyon Rd.
801-648-2200  Fax: 801-648-2221
800-293-6378
Shanoan & Dearborn Clark
All year

$$-B&B
4 rooms, 4 pb
Visa, MC, *Rated*,  •
C-yes/S-no/P-no/H-no

Full breakfast
Snacks, comp. wine
Sitting room, library
hot tubs
13 acres to roam

*Stay as our friends but be pampered like royalty. Enjoy our sumptuous breakfast, unique furnishings, and three spectacular National Parks. 3rd night 50% off.*

**Smith Hotel**
P.O. Box 106,  84729
Highway 89
801-648-2156
Shirley Phelan
April–October

$$-B&B
7 rooms, 7 pb
MC, Visa,
C-ltd/S-no/P-no/H-no

Continental plus bkfst.
Sitting room
screened porch

*Historic 1927 hotel; lovely view of nearby bluffs from the guest porch. Located in beautiful Long Valley between Zion and Bryce Canyon National Parks. 3rd night $10 off.*

## HUNTSVILLE

**Jackson Fork Inn**
7345 East 900 South,  84317
801-745-0051  800-255-0672
Vicki Petersen
All year

$$-B&B
8 rooms, 8 pb
AmEx, MC, Visa,  •
C-yes/S-no/P-no/H-no

Continental breakfast
Restaurant
Hot tubs, skiing, golf
fishing, water sports
jacuzzis in some rooms

*Old dairy barn renovated into a restaurant & inn. Quiet getaway without phones. Close to ski slopes, two lakes, hunting, fishing, golf, snowmobiles. 3 nights+ reduced rate.*

MOAB ─────────────────────────────────────

**Mayor's House B&B**
505 Rose Tree Ln., 84532
801-259-6015  Fax: 801-259-3019
Tom & Gay Stocks
All year

$$-B&B
6 rooms, 2 pb
Visa, MC, *Rated*, •
C-ltd/S-no/P-no/H-no

Full breakfast
Afternoon tea, snacks
Swimming pool, hot tubs
library, sitting room
locked bike storage

*Southwest contemporary oasis. Nestled in heart of canyonlands. Scenic view from pool to patio. Native born Mayor Tom with his wife Gay will make you feel right at home. **10% disc't, 3 night minimum.***

─────────────────────────────────────

**Pack Creek Ranch**
P.O. Box 1270, 84532
La Sal Pass Rd.
801-259-5505  Fax: 801-259-8879
Ken & Jane Sleight   All year

$$$-AP
10 rooms, 10 pb
Most CC, *Rated*, •
C-yes/S-yes/P-yes/H-no

Full breakfast
All meals included
Bar service, hot tubs
sauna, swimming pool
trail rides & pack trips

*Cozy log cabins on old homestead site. Quiet country setting w/open spaces. Good food, great hiking. Close to canyonlands & Arches National Parks. **Family & winter rates, ask.***

─────────────────────────────────────

**Sunflower Hill B&B Inn**
185 N. 300 East, 84532
801-259-2974  Fax: 801-259-2470
Aaron & Kim Robison
All year

$$-B&B
11 rooms, 11 pb
Visa, MC, *Rated*, •
C-ltd/S-no/P-no

Full breakfast
Sitting room, library
laundry room, hot tub
gardens, patio, BBQ

*Inviting country retreat furnished with antiques, hand painting and stenciling. Serene setting with lush flower gardens. Healthy, homemade breakfast.*

PARK CITY ─────────────────────────────────

**1904 Imperial Hotel B&B**
P.O. Box 1628, 84060
221 Main St.
801-649-1904  Fax: 801-645-7421
800-669-8824
Jae Kane      All year

$$-B&B
10 rooms, 10 pb
Most CC, *Rated*, •
C-yes/S-no/P-no/H-no

Full breakfast
Snacks, coffee shop
Pub & art gallery
jacuzzi & ski lockers
hot tub

*Superbly restored 1904 hotel in heart of Park City. Private baths with large Roman tubs, phone, cable TV & HBO. On National Register of Historic Homes. Near all activities.*

─────────────────────────────────────

**Blue Church Lodge, The**
P.O. Box 1720, 84060
424 Park Ave.
801-649-8009  Fax: 801-649-0686
800-626-5467
Nancy Schmidt
Open ski season

$$$-B&B
11 rooms, 11 pb
MC, Visa, •
C-yes/S-yes/P-ltd/H-no

Continental breakfast
Hot tubs, gameroom
kitchens, fireplaces
ski lockers, sitting rm.

*Elegantly designed condos with antique country charm, 1-4 bedrooms. Listed on National Register Historic Places. Walk to Main Street and town lift.*

─────────────────────────────────────

**Old Miners' Lodge B&B, The**
P.O. Box 2639, 84060
615 Woodside Ave.
801-645-8068  Fax: 801-645-7420
800-648-8068
Susan Wynne/Nancy McLaughlin
All year

$$-B&B
12 rooms, 10 pb
Most CC, *Rated*, •
C-yes/S-no/P-no/H-no

Full country breakfast
Evening refreshments
Organ, fireplace
sitting room, library
hot tub, games

*An original miner's lodge—antique-filled rooms, feather beds, full breakfast, complimentary refreshments and fine hospitality; an unforgettable experience!*

*Alpine Cottages & Saltair, Salt Lake City, UT*

## SALT LAKE CITY

**Alpine Cottages & Saltair**
1645 900E,  84102
801-533-8184  Fax: 801-595-0332
800-733-8184
Jan Bartlett, Nancy Saxton
All year

$$$-B&B
7 rooms, 4 pb
Most CC, *Rated*,  •
C-ltd/S-ltd/P-no/H-no
Some French

Full breakfast
Snacks, comp. wine
Sitting room, A/C
hot tubs, fresh flowers
robes, down comforters

*Classy Victorian on the Nat'l Register of Historic Places. Antiques and charm complement queen size beds, Amish quilts and period lamps.* **3rd night 50%.**

---

**Anton Boxrud B&B Inn**
57 South 600 East,  84102
801-363-8035  Fax: 801-596-1316
800-524-5511
Jane E. Johnson
All year

$$-B&B
6 rooms, 3 pb
MC, Visa, *Rated*,  •
C-ltd/S-no/P-no/H-no

Full breakfast
Hot tubs (winter)
sitting room

*The interior of this "Grand Old Home" is replete with beveled and stain-glass windows, burled woodwork, hardwood floors and pocked doors. Come be pampered.*

---

**Wildflowers, a B&B Inn**
936 E. 1700 S.,  84105
801-466-0600  Fax: 801-466-4728
800-569-0009
Cill Sparks & Jeri Parker
All year

$$-B&B
5 rooms, 5 pb
Visa, MC, AmEx,
*Rated*,
S-no/P-no/H-no
French

Full breakfast
Restaurant nearby
Sitting room, library
reading room, deck
stained glass windows

*Nat'l Historic 1891 Victorian offering delights of past and comforts of the present. Wildflower gardens, close to park/downtown/ski resorts.* **Free bottle of wine 3rd night.**

## SANDY

**Mountain Hollow B&B Inn**
10209 S. Dimple Dell Rd,
  84092
801-942-3428 Fax: 801-943-7229
800-757-3428
Doug & Kathy Larson
All year

$$-B&B
9 rooms,
MC, Visa *Rated*, •
C-ltd/S-no/P-no/H-no

Continental plus buffet
Sitting room, library
jacuzzi, videos
game room, hot tub

*Mountain hideaway, antiques, stream, spa, recreation room, movies, room TVs, cathedral living room, relaxing atmosphere, close to downtown and skiing.* **10% off stay, ltd.**

## ST. GEORGE

**Greene Gate Village Inn**
76 W. Tabernacle,  84770
801-628-6999  800-634-6999
John Greene & Barbara
Greene
All year

$$-B&B
12 rooms, 9 pb
MC, Visa, *Rated*, •
C-yes/S-no/P-yes/H-yes

Full breakfast
Lunch, Dinner
Soft drinks on arrival
sitting room, hot tubs
tennis courts, pool

*Restored original pioneer home in a unique village close to downtown but in a quiet neighborhood. Close to Zion, Grand Canyon.* **3rd night free.**

---

**Seven Wives Inn**
217 N. 100 West,  84770
801-628-3737  800-600-3737
The Curtises
All year

$$-B&B
12 rooms, 12 pb
Most CC, *Rated*, •
C-yes/S-no/P-no/H-ltd

Full gourmet breakfast
Complimentary fruit
Bicycles, hot tub, pool
sitting room, organ
golf & tennis nearby

*1870s pioneer home on National Register, furnished in antiques. Heart of St. George, close to national parks. Honeymoon suite with whirlpool tub room.* **Business special.**

---

## More Inns . . .

| | |
|---|---|
| Blanding | Old Hotel B&B, The,  118 East 300 South St., 84511,  801-678-2388 |
| Bluff | Bluff B&B, P.O. Box 158, 84512,  801-672-2220 |
| Bluff | Calabre B&B,  P.O. Box 85, 84512,  801-672-2252 |
| Boulder | Boulder Mountain Lodge,  P.O. Box 1397, 84716,  800-556-3446 |
| Cedar City | Paxman Summerhouse B&B,  170 North 400 West, 84720,  801-586-3755 |
| Cedar City | Willow Glen Inn B&B,  3308 N. Bulldog Rd., 84720,  801-586-3275 |
| Duck Creek | Meadeau View Lodge,  P.O. Box 1331, 84762,  801-682-2495 |
| Ephraim | Ephraim Homestead,  135 W. 100 N., 84627,  801-283-6367 |
| Escalante | Rainbow Country B&B,  P.O. Box 333, 84726,  801-826-4567 |
| Garden City | Inn Of The Three Bears,  135 S. Bear Lake Blvd., 84028,  801-946-8590 |
| Glendale | Homeplace, The,  P.O. Box 41, 200 Main, 84729,  801-648-2194 |
| Hemefer | Dearden's B&B,  202 West 100 North, 84033 |
| Hurricane | Pah Temple Hot Springs,  825 N. 800 E. 35-4, 84737,  801-635-2879 |
| Kamas | Patricia's Country Manor,  P.O. Box 849, 84036 |
| Kanab | Nine Gables Inn,  106 W. 100 North, 84741,  801-644-5079 |
| La Verkin | Zion Overlook B&B, P.O. Box 852, 84745,  801-877-1061 |
| Liberty | Vue De Valhalla,  2787 Nordic Valley Rd, 84310 |
| Loa | Road Creek Inn,  P.O. Box 310, 84747,  801-836-2485 |
| Logan | Center Street B&B Inn,  169 E. Center St., 84321,  801-752-3443 |
| Manti | Manti House Inn,  401 N. Main St, 84642,  801-835-0161 |
| Manti | Yardley B&B Inn,  190 W. 200 S., 84642,  801-835-1861 |
| Midway | Homestead Resort, The,  P.O. Box 99, 84049,  801-654-1102 |
| Midway | Inn On The Creek,  375 Rainbow Ln., 84049,  801-654-0892 |
| Moab | Canyon Country B&B,  590 North 500 West, 84532,  801-259-5262 |
| Moab | Castle Valley Inn,  CVSR Box 2602, 84532,  801-259-6012 |
| Moab | Cedar Breaks Condos B&B,  Center & 4th East, 84532,  801-259-7830 |
| Moab | Rose Tree B&B,  505 Rose Tree Ln., 84532,  801-259-6015 |
| Moab | Sandi's B&B,  450 Walker St., 84532,  801-259-6359 |
| Moab | Slick Rock Inn,  286 South 400 East, 84532,  801-259-2266 |
| Monroe | Peterson's B&B,  P.O. Box 142, 84754,  801-527-4830 |
| Monticello | Grist Mill Inn, The,  P.O. Box 156, 84535 |
| Nephi | Whitmore Mansion B&B, The,  P.O. Box 73, 84648,  801-623-2047 |
| Park City | 505 Woodside, B&B Place,  P.O. Box 2446, 84060,  801-649-4841 |
| Park City | Snowed Inn,  3770 N. Hwy 224, 84060,  801-649-5713 |
| Park City | Star Hotel B&B,  P.O. Box 777, 84060,  801-649-8333 |
| Park City | Washington School Inn,  P.O. Box 536, 84060,  801-649-3800 |

| | |
|---|---|
| Provo | Sundance, P.O. Box 837, 84601,  801-225-4100 |
| Richfield | Old Church B&B, The,  180 W. 400 S., 84701,  801-896-6705 |
| Rockville | Blue House B&B, The,  125 East Main, 84763,  801-772-3912 |
| Rockville | Handcart House B&B,  P.O. Box 630146, 84763,  801-772-3867 |
| Salt Lake City | Anniversary Inn,  678 E. South Temple, 84102,  801-363-4900 |
| Salt Lake City | Brigham Street Inn,  1135 E. South Temple, 84102,  801-364-4461 |
| Salt Lake City | City Creek Park B&B,  128 E. 2nd Ave., 84103,  810-533-0770 |
| Salt Lake City | Dave's Cozy Cabin Inn, 2293 East 6200 South, 84121,  801-278-6136 |
| Salt Lake City | Log Cabin on the Hill B&B,  2275 East 6200 South, 84121 |
| Salt Lake City | Spruces B&B, 6151 S. 900 East, 84121,  801-268-8762 |
| Sandy | Alta Hills Farm,  10852 S. 20th E. Sandy, 84092,  801-571-1712 |
| Sandy | Quail Hills Guesthouse,  3744 E. N.Little Cttnwd, 84092,  801-942-2858 |
| Spanish Fork | Escalante B&B,  733 North Main St., 84660,  801-798-6652 |
| Springdale | Harvest House, P.O. Box 125, 84767,  801-772-3880 |
| Springdale | O'Toole's Under the Eaves,  POB 29, 980 Zion Park, 84767,  801-772-3457 |
| Springdale | Under the Eaves House,  P.O. Box 29, Zion Park, 84767 |
| Springdale | Zion House B&B,  Box 323, 84767,  801-772-3281 |
| St. George | Maurice Mulberry Inn B&B,  194 S. 600 E., 84770,  801-673-7383 |
| Sterling | Cedar Crest B&B, P.O. Box T, 84665,  801-835-6352 |
| Toquerville | Your Inn Toquerville, P.O. Box 276, 84774,  801-635-9964 |
| Torrey | Skyridge, A B&B,  P.O. Box 750220, 84775,  801-425-3222 |
| Tropic | Bryce Point B&B,  P.O. Box 96, 84776,  801-679-8629 |

# Vermont

## ALBURG

**Thomas Mott Homestead B&B**
Rt 2 Box 149-B, Blue Rock Rd.,  05440
802-796-3736 Fax: 802-796-3736
800-348-0843
Patrick J. Schallert, Sr.
All year

$$-B&B
5 rooms, 5 pb
Major CC, *Rated*, •
C-ltd/S-no/P-no/H-no

Full breakfast menu
Afternoon tea, snacks
Sitting room, library
tennis court nearby
Swim at Lake Champlain

*75 foot private boatdock; swimming; canoeing; snorkleing; quilting decor; hand feed hundreds of quail; bike & hike; R&R; four seasons of charm.* **Comp. Ben & Jerry's ice cream.**

## ANDOVER

**Inn at Highview**
R.R. #1, Box 201A, East Hill Rd.,  05143
802-875-2724 Fax: 802-875-4021
Greg Bohan & Sal Massaro
All year, exc. 2 wk. May

$$$-B&B
8 rooms, 8 pb
Visa, MC, •
C-yes/S-no/P-ltd/H-no
Italian, Spanish

Full breakfast
Dinner - Sat. only
Sitting room, library
sauna, pool, hiking
cross-country trails - 72
acres

*Vermont of your dreams. Secluded elegance; breathtaking views. 8 luxurious rooms with private baths, fabulous food. Tennis/golf nearby.* **3rd night 50% off.**

## ARLINGTON

**Arlington Inn, The**
P.O. Box 369,  05250
Main Street
802-375-6532 Fax: 802-375-6534
800-443-9442
Mark & Deborah Gagnon
All year

$$-B&B
13 rooms, 13 pb
Most CC, *Rated*, •
C-ltd/S-yes
French

Full breakfast
Lunch (summer/fall)
Cookies and cider
Restaurant, bar
sitting rm; tennis court

*Antique-filled rooms in one of Vermont's finest Greek revival homes. Winner of 1988 Travel Holiday Dining Award & Taste of Vermont Award.* **Free dessert with dinner.**

## ARLINGTON

**Hill Farm Inn**
RR 2, Box 2015,   05250
Hill Farm Rd, Sunderland
802-375-2269 Fax: 802-375-9918
800-882-2545
George & Joanne Hardy
All year

$$-B&B
13 rooms, 8 pb
Most CC, *Rated*, •
C-yes/S-no/P-ltd/H-no

Full country breakfast
Dinner 7 nights a week
Sitt. rm., piano, garden
fireplace, fruit baskets
homemade jam/each guest

*1790 & 1830 farmhouses, an inn since 1905. Pleasant mountain views, hearty home cooking. Fish, canoe the Battenkill, hike country roads.* **Free 1/2 pint Vermont maple syrup.**

## BENNINGTON

**Molly Stark Inn**
1067 E. Main St.,   05201
802-442-9631 Fax: 802-442-5224
800-356-3076
The Fendlers   All year

$$-B&B
7 rooms, 7 pb
Most CC, *Rated*, •
C-ltd/S-no/P-no/H-no

Full gourmet breakfast
Champagne dinner avail.
Den with woodstove, TV
hardwood floors, antique
quilts, claw foot tubs

*Charming 1860 Victorian, incl. private cottage w/jacuzzi. Decorated with country American, antiques, classical music playing. Champagne/dinner package.* **3rd night 50%.**

**South Shire Inn**
124 Elm St.,   05201
802-447-3839
Kristina & Tim Mast  All year

$$$-B&B
9 rooms, 9 pb
AmEx, MC, Visa,
C-ltd

Full breakfast
Sitting room, porch
large library, piano
corporate rates

*Elegant historic Victorian mansion furnished with antiques and canopy beds. Large rooms and luxury suites. 7 with fireplaces; 4 with jacuzzis & fireplaces. All rooms have private baths, A/C. Romantic!*

## BRANDON

**Churchill House Inn**
RD #3, Box 3265,   05733
Route 73 East
802-247-3078 Fax: 802-247-6851
800-838-3301
The Jackson Family
Closed Nov. & Apr.

$$$$-MAP
8 rooms, 8 pb
MC, Visa, •
C-ltd/S-no/P-no/H-no

Full breakfast
Dinner included, bar
Swimming pool, golf
library, piano, fishing
biking, hiking, skiing

*Century-old farmhouse on the edge of Green Mountain Nat'l Forest. Delicious home cooking, inn-to-inn adventures. Some rooms w/whirlpool.* **Free bike rental w/multi-day stay.**

## BROOKFIELD

**Green Trails Inn**
By the Floating Bridge,
05036
802-276-3412 Fax: 802-276-3412
800-243-3412
Sue and Mark Erwin  All year

$$-B&B/MAP
14 rooms, 8 pb
*Rated*, •
C-ltd/S-no/P-no/H-no

Full breakfast
MAP in winter
Sitting room w/fireplace
Suites w/frplc./jacuzzi
swimming, biking, hiking

*Nat'l. Register of Historic Places. 17 acre country estate. Relax & be pampered in comfortable elegance. Antique clock collection & clockmaker in residence.* **3rd nite, 50%, ltd.**

## BURLINGTON

**Howden Cottage B&B**
32 N. Champlain St.,   05401
802-864-7198
Bruce M. Howden
All year

$-B&B
3 rooms, 2 pb
MC, Visa,
S-no/P-no/H-no

Continental breakfast
Breakfast Solarium
Sitting room
sinks in rooms
suite w/private bath

*Howden Cottage offers cozy lodging and warm hospitality in the atmosphere of a private home. Owned and operated by a local artist, Bruce M. Howden. Reservations, please!*

LARGEST CITY in VERMONT

CHARLOTTE

**Inn at Charlotte**
32 State Park Rd.,   05445
802-425-2934  800-425-2934
Letty Ellinger
All year

$$$-B&B
6 rooms, 6 pb
MC, Visa,
C-ltd/S-no/P-no/H-no
Philippine (Tagalog)

Full breakfast
Picnic lunch basket
Dinner on adv. request
comp. wine, appetizers
tennis courts, pool

*Beautiful courtyard/flower gardens. Spacious rooms w/country furniture. Breakfast poolside. Picnic baskets & dinner available on request.* **10% disc't on 3+ nights, weekdays.**

CHELSEA

**Shire Inn**
P.O. Box 37,   05038
Main St.
802-685-3031
Jay & Karen Keller
All year

$$$-B&B/MAP
6 rooms, 6 pb
MC, Visa, *Rated*, •
C-ltd/S-no/P-no/H-no

Full breakfast
Dinner by reservation
Sitting room & porch
fireplaces in guestrooms
bicycles, cross-country
skiing

*Elegant country atmosphere; antique furnishings. Gracious candlelight dining. On White River. Romantic getaway. 23 acres of nature trails, games.* **3rd night 50% off.**

CHESTER

**Chester House B&B Inn**
P.O. Box 708,   05143
Main St., Village Green
802-875-2205
Irene & Norm Wright
All year

$$-B&B
4 rooms, 4 pb
*Rated*, •
C-ltd/S-yes

Full breakfast
Sitting room, library
jacuzzi
fireplaces in rooms

*A southern Vermont B&B inn of extraordinary charm & hospitality. Beautifully restored, antique-furnished c.1780 home in the Nat'l Register of Historic Places.* **4+night discount.**

**Henry Farm Inn**
P.O. Box 646,   05143
Green Mountain Trnpk
802-875-2674  Fax: 802-875-2674
800-723-8213
Barbara Bowman
All year

$$-B&B
7 rooms, 7 pb
*Rated*, •
C-yes/S-ltd/P-no/H-ltd

Full breakfast
Tea, coffee, cookies
Sitting room
library
pond, hiking

*1750s farmhouse in charming country setting in the glorious Green Mountains. Full country breakfast each morning. Extensive grounds available for your pleasure.* **3rd night 50%.**

**Hugging Bear Inn &
Shoppe**
Main St.,   05143
802-875-2412  Fax: 802-875-3823
800-325-0519
Georgette Thomas    All year

$$-B&B
6 rooms, 6 pb
Most CC, *Rated*,
C-yes/S-no/P-no/H-no

Full breakfast
Afternoon bev., snacks
Sitting room, library
bikes, den-games, toys
10% shoppe discount

*Elegant Victorian in National Historic District, on the Village Green, thousands of Teddy Bears throughout, Extensive Teddy Bear shop. We are a family inn. FUN!*

**Madrigal Inn, The**
61 Williams River Rd.,   05143
802-463-1339  Fax: 802-463-1339
800-854-2208
Raymond & Nancy Dressler
All year

$$$-B&B/MAP
11 rooms, 11 pb
Most CC, *Rated*, •
C-yes/S-no/P-ltd/H-yes

Full breakfast
Dinner by reservation
Aft. tea, snacks
arts & craft center
sitting room, library

*Beauty inside & out. Romantic guest rooms w/baths. 60 acres mountain/meadow landscape. Warm hospitality. cross-country skiing trails. Arts & crafts workshop/classes.* **10% off bill, ask.**

## CHESTER

**Stone Hearth Inn, The**
RR1, Box 117B, Route 11
West, 05143
802-875-2525
Janet & Don Strohmeyer
All year

$$-B&B
10 rooms, 10 pb
*Rated*, •
C-yes/S-ltd/P-no/H-ltd
Fr., Dutch, Flem., Ger.

Full breakfast
Dinner (by reserv. only)
Lunch, wine cellar, pub
game room, library
pianos, whirlpool spas

*Lovingly restored country inn built in 1810—beams, fireplaces, wide pine floors, attached barn. Family atmosphere. **10% disc't (mdwk) when you mention Lanier's Guide.***

## CHITTENDEN

**Tulip Tree Inn**
Chittenden Dam Rd., 05737
802-483-6213 800-707-0017
Ed & Rosemary McDowell
Exc. Apr, Nov to Thksgvg

$$$-MAP
8 rooms, 8 pb
MC, Visa, *Rated*, •
C-ltd/S-no/P-no/H-no
German

Full breakfast
Dinner included
Full bar & wine cellar
sitting room, library
some rooms w/jacuzzis

*Small, antique-filled country inn, hidden away in the Green Mountains. Gracious dining, homemade breads and desserts, wine list. New room decor. One of Uncle Ben's 10 best.*

## CRAFTSBURY

**Craftsbury Inn**
P.O. Box 36, 05826
Main St.
802-586-2848 800-336-2848
Blake & Rebecca Gleason
Exc. November & April

$$$-B&B
10 rooms, 6 pb
MC, Visa,
C-yes/S-ltd/P-no/H-no

Full breakfast
Dinner, bar
Sitting room, piano
lake swimming

*Authentic Vermont Inn located in a quiet and picturesque hill town. Renowned dining, cross-country skiing. Redecorated rooms with quilts. **10% discount Mon-Thur except holiday weeks, fall foliage.***

## CUTTINGSVILLE

**Buckmaster Inn B&B**
RR1, Box118, Shrewsbury,
Lincoln Hill Rd., 05738
802-492-3485
Sam & Grace Husselman
All year

$$-B&B
3 rooms, 1 pb
C-yes/S-ltd/P-no/H-ltd
Dutch

Full breakfast
Comp. tea & cookies
Sitting room, fireplace
porches, library, organ
bicyles, sports acreage

*1801 historic stagecoach stop with spacious rooms, charm of family heirlooms in Green Mountains. Nature paradise, relaxing atmosphere. Dining on large porch in Summer.*

## DANBY

**Quail's Nest B&B, The**
P.O. Box 221, 05739
Main St.
802-293-5099 Fax: 802-293-6300
Gregory & Nancy Diaz
All year

$$-B&B
5 rooms, 3 pb
MC, Visa, *Rated*, •
C-ltd/S-no/P-no/H-no

Full breakfast
Comp. tea & snacks
Sitting room w/fireplace
library, horseshoes
deck & garden, bicycles

*Nestled among the Green Mountains in a quiet Vermont village; home-baked breakfasts followed by relaxing country fun! Conference facility. Diets upon request.*

**Silas Griffith Inn**
RR 1, Box 66F, S. Main St.,
05739
802-293-5567 800-545-1509
Paul & Lois Dansereau
All year

$$-B&B
17 rooms, 14 pb
AmEx, MC, Visa,
*Rated*, •
C-yes/S-no

Full breakfast
Restaurant, bar, dinner
Aftn. beverages, cookies
sitting room, library
pool, conference 50 ppl.

*Lovingly restored Victorian mansion and carriage house. Relax in antique-filled rooms; enjoy a quiet 19th-century village. Spectacular Green Mountain views.*

## DORSET

| | | |
|---|---|---|
| **Barrows House** | $$$$-MAP | Full breakfast |
| Route 30,   05251 | 28 rooms, 28 pb | Bar, dinner |
| 802-867-4455  Fax: 802-867-0132 | Most CC, *Rated*, • | Playroom for children |
| 800-639-1620 | C-yes/S-ltd/P-ltd/H-ltd | tennis courts, bicycles |
| Jim/Linda McGinnis  All yr | | sitt. room, piano, sauna |

*Eight buildings in picturesque Dorset, close to hiking, fishing, golf, horseback riding, shopping, cross country ski, shopping.* **Nov.–May, midweek discount.**

| | | |
|---|---|---|
| **Cornucopia of Dorset** | B&B | Full unique breakfast |
| P.O. Box 307,   05251 | 5 rooms, 5 pb | Afternoon tea, snacks |
| Route 30 | Visa, MC, AmEx, | Complimentary champagne |
| 802-867-5751 | *Rated*, | sitting room, library |
| Linda & Bill Ley   All year | P-no/H-no | bikes/tennis/pool nearby |

*Five gracious accommodations. Gourmet breakfasts, simple elegance, unmatched amenities/service. Selected a Romantic Hideaway by Discerning Traveler. 10 mins. to Manchester.*

## ENOSBURG FALLS

| | | |
|---|---|---|
| **Berkson Farms** | $$-B&B | Full breakfast |
| RR 1, Box 850,   05450 | 4 rooms, 1 pb | Special menus by arrang. |
| Rt. 108 W. Berkshire Rd. | C-yes/S-no/P-yes/H-no | Sitting room, bicycles |
| 802-933-2522 | | working dairy farm |
| Bob & Connie Fletcher | | farm animals, near golf |
| All year | | |

*Homey 150-year-old farmhouse on working dairy farm. Relax on 600 acres surrounded by animals, nature and warm hospitality.* **Discounts to Shelburne Farms.**

## FAIR HAVEN

| | | |
|---|---|---|
| **Fair Haven Inn B&B** | $$-B&B | Full breakfast |
| P.O. Box 70,   05743 | 3 rooms, 3 pb | Lunch, dinner (fee) |
| 18 Main St. | Visa, MC, AmEx, | Restaurant |
| 802-265-4907  Fax: 802-265-8814 | C-ltd/S-no/P-no/H-no | sitting room, library |
| 800-325-7074 | | fitness center |
| Joan & Peter Lemnotis | | |
| All year | | |

*Charming, tastefully furnished. Adjacent restaurant (fine dining) and Taverna. Located between Killington, VT and Lake George, NY. A great getaway.* **3rd night, 50% (no holiday, foliage).**

| | | |
|---|---|---|
| **Maplewood Inn** | $$-B&B | Continental plus buffet |
| RR 1, Box 4460,   05743 | 5 rooms, 5 pb | Comp. wine, tea, coffee |
| Route 22A South | Most CC, *Rated*, • | BYOB tavern, chocolates |
| 802-265-8039  Fax: 802-265-8210 | C-ltd/S-ltd | sitting room, toiletries |
| 800-253-7729 | | library, TV & A/C in rms |
| The Bairds   All year | | |

*Romantic, elegantly appointed, suites & many common areas. Firepl, bicycles, antiques. In lakes region close to everything. We pamper you! Meeting rooms.* **3rd night 50% ltd.**

## FAIRFAX

| | | |
|---|---|---|
| **Inn at Buck Hollow Farm** | $$-B&B | Full breakfast |
| RR 1, Box 680,  05454 | 4 rooms, | Beer & wine |
| 802-849-2400 Fax: 802-849-9744 | MC, Visa, *Rated*, • | Sun room, jacuzzi, pool, |
| Brad Schwartz | C-yes/S-no/P-no/H-no | hot tub/spa, play area |
| All year | | cross-country skiing, |
| | | antique shop |

*Our intimate inn features canopy beds, antique decor, beamed ceilings, heated pool, fireplace, jacuzzi and 400 spectacular acres. Satellite TV in rooms, A/C.* **Canadian $ accepted Nov .1–June 30.**

---

**FAIRLEE** ——————————————————————————————————————————————

| | | |
|---|---|---|
| **Silver Maple Lodge/Cottage** | $$-B&B | Continental breakfast |
| RR 1, Box 8,  05045 | 17 rooms, 9 pb | Sitting room, fireplaces |
| S. Main St. | MC, Visa, *Rated*, • | picnic area, cottages |
| 802-333-4326  800-666-1946 | C-yes/S-yes/P-no/H-ltd | bicycle & canoe rental |
| Scott & Sharon Wright | | |
| All year | | |

*Quaint country inn located in scenic resort area; convenient to antique shops, fishing, golf, swimming, tennis & winter skiing. Ballooning pkgs. avail.* **3rd night 50% off.**

**GAYSVILLE** ——————————————————————————————————————————————

| | | |
|---|---|---|
| **Cobble House Inn** | $$$-B&B | Full breakfast |
| P.O. Box 49,  05746 | 6 rooms, 6 pb | Romantic restaurant |
| Childrens Camp Rd. | MC, Visa, *Rated*, | Afternoon hors d'oeuvres |
| 802-234-5458 | C-ltd/S-no/P-no/H-ltd | 2 sitting rooms, river |
| Beau & Phil Benson | | swimming, cross-country |
| All year | | skiing |

*Victorian mansion, 1864. Mountain views on the White River; country breakfasts; gourmet dinners; antique furnishings; private baths. Golf tours arranged. Room w/fireplace.*

| | | |
|---|---|---|
| **Laolke Lodge** | $$-MAP | Full breakfast |
| P.O. Box 107,  05746 | 5 rooms, | Evening meal |
| Laury Hill Road | C-yes/S-yes/P-ltd/H-no | Sitting room, piano |
| 802-234-9205 | | pool, color TV, tennis |
| Ms. Olive Pratt | | river swimming, tubing |
| All year | | |

*Family-style vacations in modern, rustic log cabin. Home cooking. Near skiing, horseback riding, fishing, hunting, boating, and other Vermont attractions.* **3rd night 50% off.**

**GOSHEN** ——————————————————————————————————————————————

| | | |
|---|---|---|
| **Blueberry Hill** | $$$-MAP | Full breakfast |
| RFD 3,  05733 | 8 rooms, 8 pb | Dinner, tea |
| 802-247-6735  Fax: 802-247-3983 | MC, Visa, *Rated*, • | Sitting room |
| 800-448-0707 | C-yes/S-ltd/P-no/H-yes | swimming pond |
| Tony Clark, Shari Brown | French, Spanish | 75km cross-country ski trails |
| 2/15–3/31; 6/1–10/31 | | |

*1800 charming inn, gourmet cooking, dining by candlelight. Relax in an atmosphere of elegance and leisure. Fishing, swimming, hiking, cross-country skiing.* **10% off room.**

**GRAFTON** ——————————————————————————————————————————————

| | | |
|---|---|---|
| **Old Tavern at Grafton, The** | $$$-B&B/MAP | Continental breakfast |
| Main St.,  05146 | , | Restaurant, bar |
| 802-843-2231  800-843-1801 | MC, Visa, Check | Lunch, dinner available |
| Tom List, Jr. | *Rated*, • | meetings up to 55 |
| Exc. Dec 24-25 & April | C-ltd/S-ltd/P-ltd/H-yes | weddings up to 155 |
| | French, Sp., Ger., Dut. | |

*Village inn in tiny, picture-perfect Grafton. A virtual museum of antiquity with elegant yet comfortable rooms. 30 miles cross-country ski center with snowmaking.*

**GREENSBORO** ——————————————————————————————————————————————

| | | |
|---|---|---|
| **Highland Lodge** | $$$-MAP | Full breakfast |
| RR1, Box 1790,  05841 | 21 rooms, 21 pb | Lunch, dinner |
| Caspian Lake Rd. | MC, Visa, • | Sitting rooms, library |
| 802-533-2647  Fax: 802-533-7494 | C-yes/S-yes/P-no/H-yes | tennis, beach, lawn game |
| David & Wilhelmina Smith | Dutch | golf, lake, ski trails |
| 12/19–3/23; 5/29–10/12 | | |

*A most comfortable, extremely clean, nicely furnished family resort with rooms & cottages. Lakeside beach & 30 miles of packed cross-country ski trails.* **Special mid-week rates.**

## HANCOCK

**Sweet Onion Inn**
P.O. Box 66,  05748
Route 100
802-767-3734 Fax: 802-767-9227
Pat Merit   All year

$$-MAP
6 rooms, 4 pb
Most CC, *Rated*,  •
C-ltd/S-no/P-no

Full breakfast
Dinner, vegetarian
Nature
skiing, hiking
biking, swimming

*1820s Inn serving exclusively vegetarian meals. Peaceful country setting in Green Mountains. Herb shop and bike rental on property. Enjoy hiking, biking, swimming, skiing.* **Free packed lunch, ltd.**

## HARTFORD

**House of Seven Gables**
P.O. Box 526,  05047
221 Main St.
802-295-1200 Fax: 802-295-1200
800-947-1200
Lani & Kathy Janisse
All year

$$$-B&B
8 rooms, 2 pb
AmEx, MC, Visa,  •
C-yes/S-no/P-yes/H-no

Full breakfast
Snacks
Game room w/pool table
deck and pool
fitness room

*Victorian charm & hospitality; sunny porches or conversation by the fireplace. Unique guestrooms with antique furnishings. Some overlook White River. Pampered tranquillity!*

## HYDE PARK

**Fitch Hill Inn**
RFD 1, Box 1879,  05655
Fitch Hill Rd.
802-888-3834  800-639-2903
R. Pugliese & S. Corklin
All year

$$-B&B/MAP
6 rooms, 6 pb
*Rated*,  •
C-ltd/S-no/P-ltd/H-no
Spanish, some French

Full gourmet breakfast
Lunch, dinner on request
Complimentary wine, tea
sitting rm., lib., bikes
2-bedroom ste. w/firplc.

*18th-century farmhouse near Stowe and Northeast Kingdom. Extensive views of mountains, country antique decor, home cooking, informal atmosphere.* **Ask about specials.**

## JERICHO

**Homeplace B&B**
P.O. Box 96,  05465
90 Old Pump Rd.,Essex Jt.
802-899-4694 Fax: 802-899-2986
Hans & Mariot Huessy
All year

$$-B&B
4 rooms,
*Rated*,  •
C-ltd/S-no/P-no/H-no
German

Full breakfast
Comp. wine, beer, juice
Sitting room, library
Gardens, trails, tennis
nearby, ceiling fans

*Quiet spot in a 100-acre wood, 1.5 miles from Jericho. Farm animals welcome you to their sprawling home. European antiques, Vermont craftwork and charm.* **6th night free.**

## KILLINGTON

**Cortina Inn**
HC 34, Box 33,  05751
802-773-3333  800-451-6108
Robert & Breda Harnish
All year

$$$-B&B/MAP
97 rooms, 97 pb
Visa, MC, Disc. *Rated*,
•
C-yes/S-yes/P-yes/H-yes
Sp., German, French

Full breakfast
Restaurant, bar
8 tennis courts, pool
hot tubs, ice skating
sleigh rides, health spa

*The area's most luxurious inn. Indoor pool, fitness center, game room, ice skating, award-winning cuisine. The amenities of a resort hotel, the hospitality of a country inn.*

**Mountain Meadows Lodge**
RR 1 Box 4080,  05751
Thundering Brook Rd.
802-775-1010  800-370-4567
The Stevens Family
Ex. 4/15-6/1;10/15-11/21

$$$-B&B
18 rooms, 18 pb
MC, Visa, *Rated*,  •
C-yes/S-ltd/P-no/H-ltd

Full breakfast
Dinner (fee)
Coffee, tea
sitting room, pool
mountain getaway pkgs

*A casual, friendly family lodge in a beautiful secluded mountain and lake setting. Complete cross-country ski center. Converted 1856 farmhouse and barn.*

## KILLINGTON

**Vermont Inn, The**
H.C. 34, Box 37J Rt 4, Cream Hill Rd.,  05751
802-775-0708 Fax: 802-773-2440
800-541-7795
Megan & Greg Smith
Memorial Day–April 15

$$-B&B
16 rooms, 16 pb
AmEx, MC, Visa,
*Rated*, •
C-ltd/S-no/P-no/H-ltd
French, Spanish

Full Country breakfast
MAP available, bar
Pool, sauna, whirpool
tennis, fireplace rooms
meeting room

*Award-winning cuisine; fireside dining (winter), spectacular mountain views, secluded romantic stream. Rooms w/frplcs. available. Minutes to Killington and Pico ski area.*

## LAND GROVE

**Meadowbrook Inn**
RR1 Box 145,  05148
Rt. 11 E.
802-824-6444 Fax: 802-824-4335
800-498-6445
Tony & Madeline Rundella
Closed April & Novemer

$$$-B&B/MAP
6 rooms, 6 pb
Most CC,
C-ltd/S-no/P-no/H-no

Full breakfast
Dinner, snacks
Restaurant, bar service
sitting room, fireplaces
whirlpool, cross-country
skiing

*Quiet country inn nestled in the Green Mountain National Forest. Soft, antique filled rooms. Candlelight dinning with fireplaces and views.* **3rd night 50%.**

## LONDONDERRY

**Blue Gentian Lodge**
Box 29 RR #1, Magic Mountain Rd.,  05148
802-824-5908 Fax: 802-824-3531
800-456-2405
The Alberti Family    All year

$$-EP
14 rooms, 14 pb
C-yes/S-yes/P-ltd/H-no

Full breakfast
Dinner
Sitting room, game rooms
swimming pool, walking
distance to ski area

*Mountain vista from secluded pool over pine-fringed pond. In the winter walk to ski lifts of Magic Mountain. Fine homemade meals, lounge with fireplace, game rooms.*

**Highland House, The**
RR#1 Box 107, Route 100,  05148
802-824-3019
Laurie & Michael Gayda
Exc. April, Thanksgiving

$$$-B&B
17 rooms, 15 pb
AmEx, MC, Visa,
*Rated*,
C-ltd/S-ltd/P-no/H-yes

Full breakfast
Dinner Wed-Sun
Tea (winter), sitting rm
pool, tennis court
cross country skiing

*An 1842 country inn with swimming pool and tennis court. Set on 32 acres. Classic, candlelight dining. Located in the heart of the Green Mountains.*

## LUDLOW

**Andrie Rose Inn, The**
13 Pleasant St.,  05149
802-228-4846 Fax: 802-228-7910
800-223-4846
The Fishers    All year

$$-B&B/MAP
21 rooms, 21 pb
AmEx, MC, Visa,
*Rated*, •
C-ltd/S-no/P-no/H-no

Full breakfast buffet
5-course cndlght. dinner
Comp. cheese/fruit/bread
down comforters, bar
hot tubs, bicycles

*Elegant c.1829 country village. Okemo Ski Mountain. Luxury suites with custom made oversized whirlpool tubs in bedroom across from the fireplace, the ultimate in romance.*

**Black River Inn**
100 Main St., Route #103,  05149
802-228-5585
Nancy & Darwin Thomas
All year

$$$-B&B/MAP
10 rooms, 8 pb
AmEx, MC, Visa,
*Rated*, •
C-ltd/S-yes/P-no/H-no

Full breakfast
Dinner on wkends. (fee)
Full beverage service
TV-game room, jacuzzi
sitting room, suite

*Charming 1835 country inn w/antiques, feather pillows, down comforters, brandy at bedside. Near skiing, swimming, golf, fishing, biking.* **4th night 50% off, 5th night free.**

## LUDLOW

| **Combes Family Inn, The** | $$$-B&B/MAP | Full breakfast |
| 953 E. Lake Rd.,   05149 | 11 rooms, 11 pb | Dinner |
| 802-228-8799  800-822-8799 | AmEx, MC, Visa, | Sitting room, piano |
| Ruth B. Combes | *Rated*,  • | bicycles |
| All year exc. 4/15–5/15 | C-yes/S-ltd/P-ltd/H-yes | |
| | French | |

*The Combes Family Inn is a century-old farmhouse located on a quiet country back road. Queen size beds.* **10% off stay (not for travel agent).**

| **Echo Lake Inn** | $$$-MAP | Full breakfast |
| P.O. Box 154,   05149 | 25 rooms, 13 pb | Dinner from menu, bar |
| Route 100 North | Most CC, *Rated*,  • | Swimming, tennis, steam |
| 802-228-8602 Fax: 802-228-3075 | C-ltd/S-ltd/P-no/H-no | hiking, sitting room, |
| 800-356-6844 | | 6-person jacuzzi, pool |
| Yvonne & John & Pardiem | | |
| All year exc. April | | |

*Serene setting in Vermont's central lakes region. Casual gourmet dining in 1840 historic inn. Skiing, horseback riding & golf nearby.* **Free bottle of wine with 2-night stay.**

| **Jewell Brook Inn** | $$-B&B | Full buffet breakfast |
| 82 Andover St., Rt. 100, | 10 rooms, | Snacks |
| 05149 | Visa, MC, AmEx, | Sitting room |
| 802-228-8926  800-681-4855 | C-yes/S-no/P-no/H-no | library |
| Cathy Kubic & John Murray | | |
| All year | | |

*Relax by the pond in summer or a crackling fire in winter in our Tavern Room. 10 comfortably appointed rooms.* **Special mid-week packages available.**

## LUDLOW VILLAGE

| **Governor's Inn, The** | $$$-B&B/MAP | Full 5-course breakfast |
| 86 Main St.,   05149 | 8 rooms, 8 pb | 6-course dinner, bar |
| 802-228-8830  800-Governor | AmEx, MC, Visa, | Restaurant, picnic lunch |
| Deedy & Charles Marble | *Rated*,  • | Culinary Magic Cooking |
| All year exc. April | C-ltd/S-no/P-no/H-no | School, library |

*Stylish, romantic, Victorian inn c.1890. Furnished with family antiques. Beautiful fireplaces. Generous hospitality; quiet town. 1987 INN OF THE YEAR!.* **Inquire about discount.**

## LYNDONVILLE

| **Wildflower Inn** | $$-B&B | Full breakfast |
| Darling Hill Rd., 05851 | 16 rooms, 12 pb | Afternoon tea & snacks |
| 802-626-8310 Fax: 802-626-3039 | MC, Visa, *Rated*,  • | Library, small conf. fac |
| 800-627-8310 | C-yes/S-ltd/P-no/H-ltd | pool, hot tub, sauna |
| Jim & Mary O'Reilly | Nepali | tennis & basketball cts. |
| All year | | |

*Delightful family inn on 500-acre farm with working dairy operations. Homemade breads and snacks. Warm hospitality. Horse-drawn sleigh rides. Near Burke Mountain skiing.*

## MANCHESTER CENTER

| **Brook-n-Hearth** | $$-B&B | Full breakfast |
| P.O. Box 508,   05255 | 3 rooms, 3 pb | Gas BBQ grill, sodas |
| Star Routes 11 & 30 | AmEx, Visa, MC, Disc., | Sitting room, VCR, piano |
| 802-362-3604 Fax: 802-362-4694 | C-ltd/S-ltd/P-no/H-no | A/C in all rooms |
| Larry & Terry Greene | | library, swimming pool |
| Except early Nov & May | | |

*Cozy early American decor, close to everything. Wooded pastoral setting, lawn games, walking and cross-country ski trails by a brook.* **20% off after two nights, ltd.**

MANCHESTER CENTER ─────────────────────

| | | |
|---|---|---|
| **Manchester Highlands Inn** | $$$-B&B | Full breakfast |
| P.O. Box 1754,  05255 | 15 rooms, 15 pb | Dinner by arrangement |
| Highland Ave. | AmEx, MC, Visa, | Sitting rm., bar, snacks |
| 802-362-4565 Fax: 802-362-4028 | *Rated*, • | 7 rooms with canopy beds |
| 800-743-4565 | C-ltd/S-yes/P-no/H-no | carriage house remodeled |
| Patricia & Robert Eichorn | | |
| Exc. midweek Apr & Nov | | |

*Romantic Victorian inn, charming rooms. Resident cat. Homemade country breakfast-in-bed. Tennis, hiking, skiing, antiquing. Manchester's best-kept secret!.* **10% off midweek,ltd**

MANCHESTER VILLAGE ─────────────────────

| | | |
|---|---|---|
| **1811 House** | $$$-B&B | Full breakfast |
| Rt. 7A, Route 7A,  05254 | 14 rooms, 14 pb | Complimentary sherry |
| 802-362-1811 Fax: 802-362-2443 | Most CC, *Rated*, • | Sitting room, library |
| 800-432-1811 | C-ltd/S-ltd/P-no/H-no | canopy beds, fireplaces |
| B. & M. Duff, J. & E. Parker | | gardens, pond, mtn. view |
| All year | | |

*Unequaled charm in a Revolutionary War-era building furnished with English & American antiques. Walk to golf, tennis, swimming; near sailing, hiking, skiing. Central A/C.*

| | | |
|---|---|---|
| **Inn at Manchester, The** | $$$-B&B | Full breakfast |
| Route 7A, Box 41,  05254 | 18 rooms, 18 pb | Comp. wine, aftn. tea |
| 802-362-1793 Fax: 802-362-3218 | Most CC, *Rated*, • | Sitt rm, library, frplc. |
| 800-273-1793 | C-ltd/S-no/P-no/H-no | piano, swimming pool |
| The Rosenbergs   All year | | 3 lounges, porch, A/C |

*Beautiful, restored Victorian mansion. On Nat'l Registry of Hist. Places. Golf, tennis, shopping, antiquing nearby.* **Special packages, summer & winter.**

| | | |
|---|---|---|
| **Reluctant Panther Inn, The** | $$$$-MAP | Full breakfast |
| Box 678,  05254 | 13 rooms, 13 pb | Dinner included |
| 1 West Rd. Off Rt. 7A | AmEx, MC, Visa, | Wine upon arrival |
| 802-362-2568 Fax: 802-362-2586 | *Rated*, • | sitting room |
| 800-822-2331 | C-ltd/S-ltd/P-no/H-no | conference facilities |
| Maye & Robert Bachofen | | |
| Mem Day-Oct, 12/10–4/10 | | |

*Enhance your romance with select lodging and elegant dining. Unusually decorated rooms for adults; 8 with fireplaces.* **Comp. bottle of wine upon arrival.**

| | | |
|---|---|---|
| **Village Country Inn** | $$$$-MAP | Full breakfast |
| P.O. Box 408,  05254 | 34 rooms, 34 pb | Candlelight dinner incl. |
| Route 7A | MC, Visa, *Rated*, • | Tavern, sitting room |
| 802-362-1792 Fax: 802-362-7238 | C-ltd/S-yes/P-no/H-ltd | fireplaces in common rms |
| 800-370-0300 | | tennis court, pool |
| Anne & Jay Degen   All year | | |

*"A French Auberge" located in the heart of the Green Mountains. Beautiful country French decor, antiques, baskets & flower, formal gardens, gracious rooms & 13 special suites. 4 new luxury accom.*

MCINDOE FALLS ─────────────────────

| | | |
|---|---|---|
| **McIndoe Falls Inne** | $-B&B | Full breakfast |
| Rt 5,  05050 | 9 rooms, 1 pb | Afternoon tea |
| 802-633-2240 Fax: 802-633-2230 | C-yes/S-ltd/P-yes | Lunch, dinner (fee) |
| 800-782-9462 | | tennis courts, guides to |
| LaBorie Family   All year | | fishing, hiking, skiing |

*A treasure hidden in the "Northeast Kingdon" of Vermont. Family run for 25 yrs. in this small Scottish settled village. We can guide you in whatever is your pleasure.* **3rd night, 50%.**

## MENDON

**Red Clover Inn**
RR 2, Woodward Rd.,   05701
802-775-2290 Fax: 802-773-0594
800-752-0571
Sue & Harris Zuckerman
Mem.day-Ap

$$$-MAP
12 rooms, 12 pb
Visa, MC, *Rated*, •
C-ltd/S-no/P-ltd/H-no

Full country breakfast
Dinner included, bar
Sitting room, piano
pool, fireside dining
rms. w/frplc, whirlpool

*Beautiful country inn nestled in a hidden mountain valley. Wonderful meals served in warm, gracious atmosphere. Minutes to Killington & Pico. **3rd night 50%.***

## MIDDLEBURY

**Brookside Meadows B&B**
RD 3, Box 2460,   05753
Painter Rd.
802-388-6429 Fax: 802-388-1706
800-442-9887
Linda & Roger Cole
All year

$$$-B&B
6 rooms, 6 pb
*Rated*, •
C-ltd/S-ltd/P-ltd/H-ltd

Full breakfast
Comp. wine
Sitting room, piano
2 bedroom suite w/bath,
woodstove, quiet A/C

*In a quiet meadow setting at base of Green Mnts. & in a beautiful New England small college town. Close to Lake Champlain & Shelburne Museum. **20% disc't on 3rd night, ltd, mention Lanier Guide.***

**Middlebury Inn, The**
Rt. 7, P.O. Box 798,   05753
14 Courthouse Square
802-388-4961 Fax: 802-388-4563
800-842-4666
Frank & Jane Emanuel
All year

$$$-EP
75 rooms,
MC, Visa, *Rated*, •
C-yes/S-ltd/P-ltd/H-yes

Continental breakfast
Restaurant, bar
Afternoon tea, A/C, TV
sitting room, library
private bath, bath phone

*Elegant 1827 historic landmark. Distinctively decorated rooms. Gracious dining. Walk to college, unique shops, historic sites; near Shelburn Museum & VT Teddy Bear Factory.*

## MILTON

**Wright's Bay, 1820**
81 Eagle Mtn. Harbor Rd,
05468
802-893-6717 Fax: 802-524-0084
Bette Wood
All year

$$-B&B
7 rooms, 4 pb
Visa, MC, AmEx,
C-yes/S-no/P-no/H-yes

Continental plus bkfst.
Sitting room
tennis court, cottages
private beach

*Private guest suite in 1820 farmhouse. Cottages on Lake Champlain. Private beach, tennis, biking, in country setting.*

## MONTPELIER

**Betsy's B&B**
74 East State St.,   05602
802-229-0466 Fax: 802-229-5412
Jon & Betsy Anderson
All year

$$-B&B
8 rooms, 8 pb
Visa, MC, AmEx,
*Rated*, •
C-yes/S-no/P-no/H-no
Spanish (some)

Full breakfast
Snacks (fruits)
Sitting room, hot tubs
exercise room

*Lavishly furnished, moderately priced Victorian B&B near great bookstores, gift shops, restaurants. Award-winning restoration & landscaping. **15% off stay, ltd.***

## NEWFANE

**Four Columns Inn, The**
P.O. Box 278,　05345
230 West Street
802-365-7713　Fax: 802-365-0022
800-787-6633
Pam & Gorty Baldwin
All year

$$$-EP/MAP
15 rooms, 15 pb
AmEx, MC, Visa,
*Rated*, •
C-yes/S-no/P-yes/H-no
French

Full breakfast
Restaurant, bar
Afternoon tea
sitting room
pool, hiking trails

*The Four Columns Inn has the only 4-Diamond restaurant rated by AAA in Vermont. And the Inn is just as fine! No smoking inn. Vegetarian items available.* **3rd nite 50%, mention at booking.**

## NORTH HERO ISLAND

**Charlie's Northland Lodge**
U.S. Rt. 2, RR Box 88,　05474
N. Hero
802-372-8822　Fax: 802-372-5215
Dorice & Charlie Clark
All year

$$-B&B
2 rooms,
Visa, MC, Disc., •
C-ltd/S-no/P-no/H-no

Continental plus
Complimentary wine
Sitting room, bicycles
lake, sailing, canoeing
fishing

*Early 1800 guest house in quiet island village on Lake Champlain. 2 guest rooms furnished with country antiques share a modern bath, private entrance & guest parlor.*

## ORWELL

**Historic Brookside Farms**
P.O. Box 36,　05760
Route 22A
802-948-2727　Fax: 802-948-2015
J & M Korda & family
All year

$$$-B&B
6 rooms, 2 pb
*Rated*, •
C-yes/S-yes/P-no/H-yes
Fr., Sp., Ger., It.

Full country breakfast
Lunch, dinner, wine
Sitting room, library
music room, antique shop
cross-country skiing, skating

*Enjoy country elegance in our National Register Greek revival mansion, set on 300 acres and furnished in period antiques. Antique shop on premises.* **3rd night 50% off, ltd.**

## PERKINSVILLE

**Inn at Weathersfield, The**
Rte. 106, P.O. Box 165,　05151
802-263-9217　Fax: 802-263-9219
800-477-4828
The Carters　All year

$$$$-MAP
12 rooms, 12 pb
Most CC, *Rated*, •
C-ltd/S-no/P-no/H-yes
German

Full breakfast
High tea & dinner incl.
Snacks, comp. wine
restaurant, bar service
sitt. rm., lib., sauna

*The perfect balance between peaceful seclusion and access to all that is Vermont. Simply Romantic! Romantic haven for adults.* **Super saver honeymoon packages.**

## PERU

**Johnny Seesaw's**
Rt. 11, Box 68,　05152
802-824-5533　Fax: 802-824-5533
800-424-CSAW　Gary Okun
All year exc. April–May

$$-B&B/MAP
30 rooms, 27 pb
MC, Visa, *Rated*, •
C-yes/S-yes/P-yes/H-ltd

Full breakfast
Dinner (MAP winter)
Afternoon tea, full bar
tennis, swimming pool
library, sitting room

*Unique country lodge, rooms w/private baths, cottages w/king beds & fireplaces, licensed pub, full dining room. Color TVs, phones in all rooms.* **3rd night 50%, ltd.**

---

**Wiley Inn, The**
P.O. Box 37,　05152
Route 11
802-824-6600　Fax: 802-824-4195
Judy & Jerry Goodman
All year

$$-B&B
16 rooms, 8 pb
Visa, MC, AmEx, •
C-yes/S-no/P-no/H-no

Continental plus bkfst.
Restaurant, bar service
Afternoon tea
sitting room, library
swimming pool

*Romantic rooms for couples, spacious family suites. Summer/fall: enjoy new pool, hot tub, playground & trout ponds. Winter: Ski Bromley, Stratton, Okemo & cross-country nearby.* **3rd night 50% off.**

## POULTNEY

**Lake St. Catherine Inn**
P.O. Box 129,   05764
Cones Point Rd.
802-287-9347 Fax: 802-287-9347
800-626-LSCI
Patricia & Raymond Endlich
May–October

$$-MAP
35 rooms, 35 pb
*Rated*, •
C-yes/S-yes/P-no/H-yes

Full breakfast
5-course dinner, bar
Priv. dock, rowboats
free use of sailboats,
paddleboats & canoes

*Rural country inn among tall pines on the shores of Lake St. Catherine. Swimming, boating, fishing & country dining. 3-bedrm cottage avail. Rates inc. gratuities. Family rates*

## PROCTORSVILLE

**Golden Stage Inn**
P.O. Box 218,   05153
1 Depot St.
802-226-7744 Fax: 802-226-7882
800-253-8226
Micki Smith & Paul Darnauer
Exc. April & November

$$$-MAP
10 rooms, 6 pb
MC, Visa, Disc.,*Rated*,
•
C-ltd/S-yes/P-no/H-yes
Swiss, German, French

Full breakfast
Pub room, bear/wine lic.
Sitting room, pool
flower gardens
newly renovated

*Country inn on 4 acres, Swiss specialties, sumptuous desserts, own baking, vegetable garden, flowers, library, hiking, biking, skiing nearby. $25 gift cert. for reservation.*

**Whitney Brook B&B**
RR1, Box 28,   05153
20 Mile Stream, Cavendish
802-226-7460
Ellen & Jim Parrish    All year

$$-B&B
4 rooms, 2 pb
Most CC,
C-ltd/S-no/P-no/H-no

Full breakfast
Afternoon tea
Sitting room, library

*Restored 1870 country farmhouse, private and quiet, fine dining nearby, centrally located for touring, shopping, hiking, biking, swimming or just relax near the brook.*

## PUTNEY

**Hickory Ridge House**
RFD 3, Box 1410,   05346
Hickory Ridge Rd.
802-387-5709
Jacquie Walker/Steve
Anderson    All year

$$-B&B
7 rooms, 3 pb
MC, Visa,
C-ltd/S-no/P-no/H-yes
French, German,
Russian

Full breakfast
Mulled cider in winter
Coffee, tea, cocoa
listed in National Reg.
of Historic Places

*Gracious 1808 brick Federal with six fireplaces, rolling meadows, woods to explore on foot or skis. Our own breads, eggs, jams & honey for breakfast. 10% off single occup. ltd*

**Putney Inn, The**
PO Box 181, Depot Rd.,
05346
802-387-5517  800-653-5517
Randi Ziter
All year

$$$-B&B/MAP
25 rooms, 25 pb
Most CC, *Rated*, •
C-yes/S-yes/P-yes/H-yes

Hearty country breakfast
Restaurant - all meals
Afternoon tea, snacks
bar service, canoeing
hiking, sitting room

*Charming 1790s farmhouse with luxury of privacy. Lodging in adjacent building to hand-hewn, post-and-beam dining room. Exceptional food. 3rd night 50%.*

## QUECHEE

**Parker House Inn**
16 Main St.,   05059
802-295-6077 Fax: 802-296-6696
Walt & Barbara Forrester
All year

$$$-B&B
7 rooms, 7 pb
Visa, MC, *Rated*,
C-yes/S-no/P-no/H-no

Full breakfast
Restaurant, bar service
Comp. dessert w/dinner
sitting room, library
bicycles

*The Parker House Inn is a classic 19th-century Vermont inn, each room charming w/ Victorian furnishings. Dine on American cuisine. Golf course priviledges. 3rd night 50% off.*

## RIPTON

| **Chipman Inn, The** | $$$-B&B | Full breakfast |
|---|---|---|
| Route 125,  05766 | 9 rooms, 9 pb | Dinner available |
| 802-388-2390 Fax: 802-388-2390 | Visa, MC, AmEx, | Bar service |
| 800-890-2390 | *Rated*, | sitting room |
| Joyce Henderson & Bill | C-ltd/S-ltd/P-no/H-no | candlelit dining room |
| Pierce | French, Arabic, Swahili | |
| Closed Apr. & Nov. | | |

*Beautiful 1828 inn in a Green Mountain village. Fine dining for guests. Skiing, country walking & sightseeing. Warm hospitality.*

## ROCHESTER

| **Liberty Hill Farm** | $$$-MAP | Full breakfast |
|---|---|---|
| RR1 Box 158,  05767 | 5 rooms, | Dinner included |
| Liberty Hill Rd. | C-yes/S-yes/P-no/H-no | Sitting room, fishing |
| 802-767-3926 | | bicycles, babysitting |
| Bob & Beth Kennett | | cribs, highchairs |
| All year | | |

*Family dairy farm in Green Mtns. bounded by National Forest & White River. Hiking, cross-country skiing from house. Major ski areas nearby. Farm breakfasts & Farm activities.*

## ROYALTON

| **Fox Stand Inn &** | $$-B&B | Full breakfast |
|---|---|---|
| **Restaurant** | 5 rooms, | Lunch, dinner |
| RR1 Box 108F, Route 14, | MC, Visa, *Rated*, | Licensed restaurant |
| 05068 | C-ltd/S-yes/P-no/H-no | river swimming |
| 802-763-8437 | | tavern |
| Jean & Gary Curley  All year | | |

*Restored 1818 handsome brick building, family-owned and operated inn. Economical rates include full breakfast. Fishing, golf, cross-country skiing nearby.*

## RUTLAND

| **Inn at Rutland, The** | $-B&B | Full breakfast |
|---|---|---|
| 70 N. Main St., Rt. 7,  05701 | 10 rooms, 10 pb | TV room, library, bikes |
| 802-773-0575 Fax: 802-775-3506 | Most CC, *Rated*, • | adjoining rms. conf. fac |
| 800-808-0575 | C-yes/S-no/P-no/H-no | 3 ski areas nearby |
| Bob & Tanya Liberman | Russian | |
| All year | | |

*Victorian city inn with views of mountains and valleys. Many great restaurants in walking distance. Close to all Vermont attractions! . 3rd. night 50% off.*

## SPRINGFIELD

| **Hartness House Inn** | $$$-EP | Lunch, dinner M-F |
|---|---|---|
| 30 Orchard St.,  05156 | , | Sitting room, tennis |
| 802-885-2115 | Most CC, *Rated*, | sauna, swimming pool |
| Eileen Gennette-Coughlin | C-yes/S-yes/P-yes/H-no | nature trails, bar |
| All year | German | |

*A 1903 historic landmark built by Governor James Hartness. Nightly tours of underground museum & operating Turret Equatorial Tracking Telescope. 3rd night free.*

## STOWE

| **Andersen Lodge—Austrian** | $$-B&B | Full breakfast |
|---|---|---|
| 3430 Mountain Rd.,  05672 | 17 rooms, 16 pb | Piano, game room, spa |
| 802-253-7336  800-336-7336 | Most CC, *Rated*, • | Jacuzzi, tennis court |
| Dietmar & Getrude Heiss | C-yes/S-yes/P-ltd/H-no | heated pool, golf nearby |
| | German, French | |

*Set in relaxing surroundings with lovely view of mountains. Trout fishing, horseback riding, mountain hiking. Owners and hosts of Austrian background. Austrian chef.*

STOWE ───────────────────────────────

**Brass Lantern Inn**
717 Maple St., Route 100 N,
  05672
802-253-2229 Fax: 802-253-7425
800-729-2980
Andy Aldrich
All year

$$-B&B
9 rooms, 9 pb
Most CC, *Rated*, •
C-yes/S-no/P-no/H-no

Full country breakfast
Afternoon tea, snacks
Bar, gourmet shop nearby
sitting room with piano
library, fireplaces, A/C

*1800s farmhouse and carriage barn, antiques, handmade quilts, stenciled walls, whirlpool baths. 1989 award-winning restoration by innkeepers.* **Midweek discount rates, ltd.**

───────────────────────────────

**Butternut Inn at Stowe**
2309 Mountain Rd.,  05672
802-253-4277  800-3-BUTTER
The Wimberley's
6/15–10/20, 12/18–4/20

$$$-B&B/MAP
18 rooms, 18 pb
MC, Visa, *Rated*, •
C-ltd/S-no/P-no/H-no

Full country breakfast
Dinner (winter)
Comp. sherry, aftn. tea
sitting room, piano
sunroom, courtyard, pool

*"Award Winning" non-smoking inn. 8 acres landscaped gardens, pond, walking trails & pool. 5 day pkg., hospitality, charm & warmth of home emphasized. Honeymoon/anniversary pkgs.* **Seasonal specials, ask.**

───────────────────────────────

**Fiddler's Green Inn**
4859 Mountain Rd., Route
108,  05672
802-253-8124  800-882-5346
Bud McKeon
All year

$-B&B/MAP
7 rooms, 6 pb
AmEx, MC, Visa, •
C-ltd/S-yes/P-no/H-no

Full breakfast (fee)
Dinner in ski season
beverages & snacks
guest living room
tennis & golf nearby

*Cozy New England inn situated on Vermont babbling brook. Hearty country breakfast. Hiking in Green Mountains or cross-country skiing from our doorstep. Near golf & antiquing.*

───────────────────────────────

**Gables Inn, The**
1457 Mountain Rd.,  05672
802-253-7730 Fax: 802-253-8989
800–GABLES1
Sol & Lynn Baumrind
All year

$$-B&B/MAP
19 rooms, 19 pb
•
C-yes/S-no/P-no/H-ltd

Full breakfast
Sitting room, fireplace
piano, swimming pool
hot tub, jacuzzis, A/C

*Classic country inn-antiques, wide plank floors, panoramic view. Breakfast on lawn/ porch (summer). Near golf, hiking, skiing, tennis, bicycling.* **4th night free in summer.**

───────────────────────────────

**Green Mountain Inn**
P.O. Box 60,  05672
Main St.
802-253-7301  800-253-7302
Patti Clark
All year

$$$-EP
62 rooms, 62 pb
AmEx, MC, Visa,
*Rated*, •
C-yes/S-ltd/P-ltd
French

Restaurant, bar
Lunch, dinner, snacks
full service health club
pool, massage, aerobics

*Beautifully renovated 1833 inn listed in the Register of Historic Places. Antique furnished with every modern convenience. Heart of Stowe Village.* **3rd night 50%, ltd.**

───────────────────────────────

**Guest House Chris.**
**Horman**
4583 Mountain Rd.,  05672
802-253-4846  800-821-7891
Jim & Christel Horman
Nov 15–Ap; Jun–end Oct

$$-B&B
8 rooms, 8 pb
MC, Visa, *Rated*, •
C-ltd/S-yes/P-no/H-no
German

Full breakfast
Complimentary tea
Sitting room
swimming pool
2 bicycles

*Quiet, charming European guest house. Large comfortable double rooms, private bathrooms and cozy guest living room. Near Mount Mansfield skiing.* **10% off 3 nights or longer.**

## STOWE

**Siebeness Inn, The**
3681 Mountain Rd., 05672
802-253-8942 Fax: 802-253-9232
800-426-9001
Sue & Nils Andersen
All year

$$-B&B
10 rooms, 10 pb
Most CC, *Rated*, •
C-yes/S-no/P-no/H-no

Full breakfast
Comp. beverages & snacks
Lounge, hot tub
pool, cross-country skiing
golf & tennis nearby

*Charming country inn, newly renovated with antiques and quilts. Outstanding food served with mountain view. Cross-country skiing from door. Some rooms with fireplace & Jacuzzi.* **Surprise gift.**

---

**Ski Inn**
Route 108, Mountain Rd.,
  05672
802-253-4050
Mrs. Larry Heyer    All year

$-B&B/MAP
10 rooms, 5 pb
•
C-ltd/S-yes/P-ltd/H-no
some French

Continental breakfast
Full breakfast (winter)
Dinner (winter MAP)

*This comfortable inn, noted for good food and good conversation, is a great gathering place for interesting people. MAP available in the winter.* **cross-country and downhill ski packages.**

---

**Walk About Creek Lodge**
199 Edson Hill Rd., 05672
802-253-7354 Fax: 802-253-8429
800-426-6697
Joni & Hutch    All year

$$-B&B
20 rooms, 18 pb
MC, Visa, AmEx,
*Rated*,
C-yes/S-ltd/P-ltd/H-ltd

Full breakfast
Restaurant, bar service
Sitting room, library
tennis court, hot tubs
swimming pool

*Experience Australian hospitality at our classic mountain lodge, nestled on 5 wooded acres. Relax by the fieldstone fireplaces in our living areas or "down under" in the Billabong Pub.* **Call for pkgs.**

---

**Ye Olde England Inne**
433 Mountain Rd., 05672
802-253-7064 Fax: 802-253-8944
800-477-3771
Christopher & Linda Francis
All year

$$$-B&B
23 rooms, 23 pb
MC, Visa, *Rated*, •
C-yes/S-yes/P-ltd/H-no
French, Arabic

Full gourmet breakfast
Dinner, Aftn. tea
Library, piano, pool
pub, banquet center
polo & gliding packages

*Classic English luxury, Laura Ashley rms./cottages. 4 posters, frplcs. & jacuzzis. Gourmet dining in Copperfield's. Mr. Pickwick's Polo Pub. Awarded chef.* **Comp. afternoon tea.**

## VERGENNES

**Strong House Inn**
RD #1, Box 1003, 05491
82 W. Main St.
802-877-3337 Fax: 802-877-2599
Mary & Hugh Bargiel
All year

$$-B&B
8 rooms, 8 pb
AmEx, MC, Visa,
*Rated*, •
C-ltd/S-ltd/P-ltd/H-ltd

Full country breakfast
Dinner with notice
Aftn. beverage & snack
sitting room w/fireplace
piano, A/C, catering

*Comfortably elegant lodging in a tastefully decorated historic home. Wonderful breakfasts. Convenient to Middlebury, Burlington, Lake Champlain. Suites w/cable & living room.*

## WAITSFIELD

**1824 House Inn**
Route 100, Box 159, 05673
802-496-7555 Fax: 802-496-7559
800-426-3986
Lawrence & Susan McKay
All year

$$-B&B
6 rooms, 6 pb
Visa, MC, Disc, *Rated*,
•
C-ltd/S-no/P-no/H-no
Spanish

Full gourmet breakfast
Comp. sherry, tea
Library, swimming hole
alpine & cross-country
skiing,
near tennis/golf/riding

*A special place on the Mad River—6 splendid rooms to enrapture ... scrumptious breakfasts, fireplaces, hot tub. Featured in Travel & Leisure.* **Midweek discounts, ltd.**

WAITSFIELD ─────────────────────────────

| **Hyde Away Inn** | $-B&B | Continental plus bkfst. |
| RR 1, Box 65,  05673 | 12 rooms, 4 pb | Rest./bar, dinner (fee) |
| Route 17 | Visa, MC, AmEx,  • | Sitting room, library |
| 802-496-2322 Fax: 802-496-7012 | C-yes/S-ltd/P-ltd/H-no | volleyball, horseshoes |
| 800-777-HYDE | | |
| Bruce & Margaret Hyde | | |
| All year | | |

*Inn, restaurant & tavern with comfortable, casual "unpretentious" atmosphere. Minutes from skiing, hiking, golfing, bicycling. Children and families welcome.*

| **Inn at Round Barn Farm** | $$$-B&B | Full breakfast |
| RR 1, Box 247,  05673 | 9 rooms, 7 pb | Comp. wine, tea, snacks |
| East Warren Rd. | AmEx, MC, Visa, | Sitting room, library |
| 802-496-2276 Fax: 802-496-8832 | *Rated*,  • | bicycles, 60-ft lap pool |
| J. & D. Simko, A. DeFreest | C-ltd/S-no/P-no/H-no | cross-country ski center/ |
| All year | Hungarian | rentals |

*Sugarbush landmark; 85 acres for quiet walks, gourmet picnics, Bach, Mozart & simple pleasures of unspoiled VT. Romantic retreats package. Concert tickets*

| **Lareau Farm Country Inn** | $$-B&B | Full breakfast |
| Box 563,  05673 | 14 rooms, 11 pb | Apres-ski hors d'oeuvres |
| Route 100 | MC, Visa *Rated*,  • | Dinner, wine/beer (fee) |
| 802-496-4949  800-833-0766 | C-yes/S-ltd/P-no/H-no | sitting room, fireplace |
| Dan & Susan Easley | | porches, picnic lunches |
| All year | | |

*Picturesque Vermont farmhouse, now an inn, nestled in a picturesque meadow beside the Mad River, our 150-year-old farmhouse is minutes from skiing and shopping. Sleigh rides.*

| **Millbrook Inn** | $$-B&B/MAP | Full breakfast from menu |
| RD Box 62,  05673 | 7 rooms, 7 pb | Full dinner from rest. |
| Route 17 | AmEx, MC, Visa, | Comp. refreshments |
| 802-496-2405 Fax: 802-496-9735 | C-ltd/S-no/P-ltd/H-ltd | 3 sitting rooms, piano |
| 800-477-2809 | | vegetarian dining menu |
| Joan & Thom Gorman | | |
| All year exc. April-May | | |

*Charming hand-stenciled guest rooms with handmade quilts, country gourmet dining, vegetarian choices, in our small candlelit restaurant, friendly, unhurried atmosphere.*

| **Valley Inn, The** | $$-B&B/MAP | Full breakfast |
| Route 100, RR 1, Box 8, | 20 rooms, 20 pb | Dinner included (MAP) |
|   05673 | AmEx, MC, Visa, | Sitting room, sauna |
| 802-496-3450  800-638-8466 | *Rated*,  • | group-tour packages |
| Bill & Millie Stinson | C-yes/S-no/P-no/H-yes | soaring packages |
| All year | French | |

*An Austrian-style inn near Sugarbush & Mad River Ski Areas. Winter sports paradise, outstanding summer antiquing, golf & gliding. **Bottle of wine—honeymooners & anniversary.***

| **Waitsfield Inn, The** | $$-MAP/B&B | Full breakfast |
| Rt. 100, Box 969,  05673 | 14 rooms, 14 pb | Apres ski snacks & cider |
| 802-496-3979 Fax: 802-496-3970 | Most CC, *Rated*,  • | Sitting room |
| 800-758-3801 | C-yes/S-no/P-no/H-no | fireplaces |
| Steve & Ruth Lacey | | down comforters |
| Exc. Nov, Apr 15—Mem Dy | | |

*A romantic and restful inn w/wonderfully comfortable guest rooms, two especially cozy fireside lounges. Quaint village location. **3rd night 50% off, ltd.***

## WARREN

**Beaver Pond Farm Inn**
RD Box 306, 05674
Golf Course Rd.
802-583-2861 Fax: 802-583-2860
Betty & Bob Hansen
All year exc. May

$$-B&B
6 rooms, 4 pb
AmEx, MC, Visa, •
C-ltd/S-yes/P-no/H-no
French

Full breakfast
Comp. sherry, brandy
Sitting room, library
weddings, Thanksg. pkg.
hiking, swimming, skiing

*Beautifully restored Vermont farmhouse adjacent to golf course. Spectacular views from spacious deck; hearty breakfasts. Summer golf/winter skiing packages.*

**Sugartree, A Country Inn**
RR 1, Box 38, 05674
Sugarbush Access Rd.
802-583-3211 Fax: 802-583-3203
800-666-8907
Frank & Kathy Partsch
All year

$$$-B&B
10 rooms, 10 pb
Most CC, *Rated*, •
C-ltd/S-no/P-no/H-yes

Full country breakfast
Afternoon snacks
Living room w/fireplace
In-room phones, brass
antique, or canopy beds

*Beautifully decorated with unique country flair and antiques. Enchanting gazebo amid flower gardens. Breathtaking views of ski slopes or fall foliage.* **3rd night free, ltd.**

**West Hill House B&B Inn**
RR1, Box 292, 05674
West Hill Rd.
802-496-7162 Fax: 802-496-6443
800-898-1427
Dorry Kyle & Eric Brattstrom
All year

$$$-B&B
7 rooms, 7 pb
Visa, MC, AmEx, •
C-ltd/S-no/P-no/H-ltd

Full breakfast
Aftn. tea, snacks, wine
Dinner by request
sitting room, library
guest fax, TV, frplcs.

*Relax, romance, refresh. Comfortably elegant 1850s farmhouse on quiet lane. Near everything quintessentially Vermont. Ski, hike, golf, restaurants, quaint village.*

## WATERBURY

**Inn at Blush Hill**
RR 1, Box 1266, 05676
Blush Hill Rd.
802-244-7529
Fax: 802-244-7314
800-736-7522
Pamela & Gary Gosselin
All year

$$-B&B
6 rooms, 5 pb
Most CC, *Rated*, •
C-ltd/S-ltd/P-no/H-ltd

Full gourmet breakfast
Afternoon tea
Library, piano
lawn games, swim/boating
1 room Jacuzzi bathtub

*Cozy, 1790s brick farmhouse, near 9-hole golf course, 15 min. to Sugarbush, Bolton, Stowe. Canopy queen bdrm., views, frplcs. Close to Ben & Jerry's.* **3rd night 50% Sun-Fri, Nov-June, except holidays.**

**Thatcher Brook Inn**
P.O. Box 490, 05676
Route 100 North
802-244-5911 Fax: 802-244-1294
800-292-5911
Kelly & Peter Varty
All year

$$-B&B
24 rooms, 24 pb
AmEx, MC, Visa,
*Rated*, •
C-yes/S-ltd/P-no/H-yes
French

Full country breakfast
Dinner packages (fee)
Restaurant, pub, library
whirlpools, fireplaces
bicycles, gazebo porches

*Beautifully restored 1899 country Victorian mansion. Centrally located between renowned resorts of Stowe and Sugarbush. Exquisite lodging & dining.* **50% off 3rd night, ltd.**

## WATERBURY, STOWE

| **Grunberg Haus B&B &** | $$-B&B | Full musical breakfast |
|---|---|---|
| **Cabins** | 10 rooms, 5 pb | Dinner, comp. wine |
| RR 2, Box 1595-LG, Route 100 | Most CC, *Rated*, • | Self-serve pub, piano |
| South,   05676 | C-ltd/S-no/P-no/H-no | tennis court, jacuzzi |
| 802-244-7726  800-800-7760 | | sauna, flock of chickens |
| Chris Sellers, Mark Frohman | | |
| All year | | |

*We offer lodging in beautiful guestrooms, secluded cabins and a spectacular carriage house suite with many special features.* **10% off 4 or more nights.**

## WEST ARLINGTON

| **Four Winds Country Inn** | $$-B&B | Full breakfast |
|---|---|---|
| River Rd., Box 3580,   05250 | 5 rooms, 3 pb | Sitting room, library |
| 802-375-6734 | *Rated*, • | surrounded by 50 acres |
| Ursula Stratmann | C-yes/S-no/P-ltd/H-no | of protected land |
| May 1 - November | German | |

*Former Norman Rockwell Homestead, bordering the famous Battenkill River - country retreat on back road, ideal for fishing, bicycling, canoeing.*

## WEST DOVER

| **Austin Hill Inn** | $$$-B&B | Full gourmet breakfast |
|---|---|---|
| P.O. Box 859,   05356 | 12 rooms, 12 pb | Dinner, bar service |
| Route 100 | AmEx, MC, Visa, | Afternoon tea, snacks |
| 802-464-5281 | *Rated*, • | sitting room, library |
| Fax: 802-464-1229 | C-ltd/S-ltd/P-no/H-no | heated pool, bikes |
| 800-332RELAX | | |
| Robbie Sweeney | | |
| All year | | |

*Casual elegance, gracious service; antiques, wine list, fine dining. Welcoming wine & cheese. Murder mystery & quilting weekends. Comfort a priority.* **3rd night, 50%, ltd.**

| **Deerhill Inn** | $$$-B&B | Full breakfast |
|---|---|---|
| P.O. Box 136,   05356 | 17 rooms, 17 pb | Restaurant, bar, snacks |
| Valley View Rd. | Most CC, *Rated*, | Tennis, swimming pool |
| 802-464-3100  Fax: 802-464-5474 | C-yes/S-ltd/P-no/H-ltd | sitting room, fireplaces |
| 800-993-3379 | | library, spa days pkg. |
| Michael & Linda Anelli | | |
| All year | | |

*Romantic, relaxed hillside get-away with panoramic mountain views, fireplaces, antiques, art, and acclaimed restaurant. No pomp ... just circumstance. Call for special packages*

| **Doveberry Inn &** | $$-B&B | Full breakfast |
|---|---|---|
| **Restaurant** | 8 rooms, 8 pb | Aftn. tea, dinner (fee) |
| P.O. Box 1736,   05356 | Visa MC, AmEx, | Restaurant, bar service |
| Rt. 100 | *Rated*, • | sitting room, library |
| 802-464-5652  Fax: 802-464-6229 | C-ltd/S-no/P-no/H-no | ideal for family reunion |
| 800-722-3204 | | |
| Christine & Michael Fayette | | |
| Memorial Day-Mid April | | |

*Charming rooms in quaint country inn. Hearty, full breakfast, close to great skiing, mountain biking, golf—an inn for every season!*

WEST DOVER —————————————————————————

| **Mountaineer Inn** | $$-MAP | Full breakfast |
| P.O. Box 140,  05356 | 27 rooms, 27 pb | Dinner |
| Handle Road | MC, Visa, AmEx, | Sitting room, library |
| 802-464-5404 Fax: 802-464-3145 | *Rated*, • | sauna, heated pool, TV |
| 800-684-4637 | C-ltd/S-ltd/P-no/H-no | pool table, ping pong |
| Royal & Ned Wilson  All year | | |

*Charming inn at the base of Mount Snow. Year round activities and events. Newly decorated guest rooms. Spacious lounges w/frplcs. Excellent meals. 5th night free bottle wine.*

| **Shield Inn** | $$$-B&B/MAP | Full country breakfast |
| P.O. Box 366,   05356 | 12 rooms, 12 pb | Dinner (winter), tea |
| Route 100 | MC, Visa, *Rated*, • | Sitting rms. w/cable TV |
| 802-464-3984 Fax: 802-464-5322 | C-ltd/S-no/P-no/H-no | fireplaces, whirpools |
| Phyllis & Lou Isaacson | | near tennis/pool/skiing |
| All year | | |

*Romantic, relaxing country inn, close to skiing/golf/lakes. 8 woodburning fireplaces, 6 jacuzzis, Steinway Grand piano. Jazz & chamber music concerts. 7th night free.*

| **Weathervane Lodge** | $$-B&B | Full breakfast |
| 57 Dorr Fitch Rd., 05356 | 10 rooms, 5 pb | Comp. beverages, snacks |
| 802-464-5426 | C-yes/S-yes/P-no/H-no | BYOB bar, sitting room |
| Liz & Ernie Chabot | French | lounge, piano, fireplc's |
| All year | | Bike & walking trails |

*Mountainous area country inn with spacious grounds. Colonial antiques, lounge. cross-country skiing, tennis, golf, swimming. All things for children. 3rd night 50% off, ltd.*

| **West Dover Inn** | $$$-B&B | Full breakfast |
| Rt. 100, P.O. Box 1208,  05356 | 12 rooms, 12 pb | Gourmet dinner |
| 802-464-5207 Fax: 802-464-2173 | AmEx, MC, Visa, | Full bar, fine wines |
| Greg Gramas & Monique | *Rated*, • | sitting room, library |
| Phelan | C-ltd/S-ltd/P-no/H-no | 4 fireplace suites |
| All year exc. late May | | |

*Country elegant guest rooms feature antiques & hand-sewn quilts. Hearty breakfasts, memorable dinners. Ski & golf packages. The area's original country inn-operating continuously since 1846.*

WESTON —————————————————————————

| **Colonial House, The** | $$-B&B | Full breakfast |
| 287 Route 100,  05161 | 15 rooms, 9 pb | Dinner |
| 802-824-6286 Fax: 802-824-3934 | MC, Visa, *Rated*, | Tea, coffee, baked goods |
| 800-639-5033 | C-yes/S-ltd/P-ltd/H-ltd | sitting room |
| Betty & John Nunnikhoven | | |
| All year | | |

*Your country cousins are waiting with a warm welcome, old-fashioned meals and a relaxing living room for you while you visit the attractions of southern Vermont.*

WILDER —————————————————————————

| **Stonecrest Farm B&B** | $$$-B&B | Full breakfast |
| P.O. Box 504,  05088 | 6 rooms, 6 pb | Snacks, comp. wine |
| 119 Christian St. | MC, Visa, • | Sitting room, |
| 802-296-2425 Fax: 802-295-1135 | C-ltd/S-no/P-no/H-no | inn-to-inn canoe trips |
| 800-730-2425 | Some German, French | down comforters |
| Gail Sanderson   All year | | |

*Country setting 3.5 mi. from Dartmouth College. Gracious 1810 home offers antiques, terraces. All outdoor activities. 7th nite free; newlywed champagne pkg., corporate rates.*

WILLIAMSTOWN ───────────────────────────

**Autumn Crest Inn**
Box 1540, RFD 1, Clark Rd.,
   05679
802-433-6627  800-639-6627
Richard Casson
All year

$$$-B&B/MAP
18 rooms, 18 pb
AmEx, MC, Visa,
*Rated*, •
C-ltd/S-ltd/P-yes/H-yes

Full breakfast
Dinner, restaurant, bar
Equestrian center, hike
swimming pond, library
cross-country skiing

*Central Vermont's best kept secret. Outstanding romantic dinners. Inn over 180 years old, magnificently restored. New equestrian center, 46 acres.* **10% disc't with 2 nites stay.**

WILMINGTON ───────────────────────────

**Nutmeg Inn**
P.O. Box 818,   05363
Route 9W, Molly Stark Trail
802-464-3351  Fax: 802-464-7331
David & Pat Cerchio
All year

$$$-B&B
14 rooms, 14 pb
Most CC, *Rated*, •
C-ltd/S-no/P-no/H-no

Full breakfast from menu
Dinner (fee), aftn. tea
Sitting room, piano, TVs
rooms & suites w/frplc.
Central A/C, whirlpool

*"Charming and cozy" early American farmhouse with informal homelike atmosphere. Spotless guest rooms—delicious "country-style" meals. Enjoy complimentary afternoon tea/coffee.*

**Red Shutter Inn, The**
P.O. Box 636,   05363
41 W. Main St.
802-464-3763  800-845-7548
Renee & Tad Lyon
Exc. early Nov & April

$$$-B&B
9 rooms, 9 pb
MC, Visa, *Rated*,
C-ltd/S-no

Full breakfast
Restaurant, bar service
Snacks, al fresco dining
fireplaces, guest suites
whirlpool bath, packages

*Hillside inn & renovated Carriage House at village edge w/candlelight dining. Fireplace suites. Golf, hike, ski amid mountains & valleys.* **Midwk discounts available, ask.**

**Trail's End, A Country Inn**
5 Trail's End Lane,   05363
802-464-2727  800-859-2585
Bill & Mary Kilburn
Closed Mid April-Mid May

$$$-B&B
15 rooms, 15 pb
MC, Visa, AmEx,
*Rated*,
C-ltd/S-ltd/P-no/H-no

Full breakfast (menu)
Afternoon refreshments
Heated outdoor pool
fireplace/jacuzzi suites
clay tennis court, crib

*Described as "irresistibly romantic" by Best Places to Kiss in New England. Fireplace suites w/canopy beds and whirlpool tubs. Warm hospitality and attention to detail.*

**White House of
Wilmington**
PO Box 757, Route 9,   05363
802-464-2135  Fax: 802-464-
5222 800-541-2135
Robert Grinold   All year

$$$-MAP
12 rooms, 12 pb
Most CC *Rated*, •
C-ltd/S-yes/P-no/H-no
French

Full breakfast
Dinner (incl.), bar
Sitting room, piano
hot tub, sauna/whirlpool
indoor & outdoor pools

*"One of the most romantic inns..." N.Y. Times. Turn-of-the-century mansion, elegant accommodations, fireplaces. Cross-country skiing. Downhill skiing & golf packages. AAA 2 diamonds.*

WINDSOR ───────────────────────────

**Juniper Hill Inn**
RR 1, Box 79,   05089
Juniper Hill Rd.
802-674-5273  800-359-2541
•
Robert & Susanne Pearl
Closed April

$$$-B&B
16 rooms, 16 pb
MC, Visa, Disc. *Rated*,
•
C-ltd/S-no

Full breakfast
Dinner by reservation
Mid-week discounts
hiking, skiing, snowshoe
canoe & bicycle packages

*A stately 28-room mansion on 14 private acres. Rooms with romantic fireplaces available. Antiques, museums, covered bridges in summer; relaxing in winter.* **Seasonal discounts.**

*Kedron Valley Inn, Woodstock, VT*

## WOODSTOCK

**Canterbury House B&B, The**
43 Pleasant St.,   05091
802-457-3077
800-390-3077
Fred & Celeste Holden
All year

$$$-B&B
8 rooms, 8 pb
Visa, MC, AmEx,
*Rated*, •
C-ltd/S-no/P-no/H-yes

Full gourmet breakfast
Lunch, dinner, tea
Sitting room, library
fishing & golf equipment
bicycles, golf, skiing

*Village townhouse beautifully decorated with fine antiques and comfortable reproductions. Close to fine dining, shopping, skiing, golf, hiking.* **AARP-10%-3rd night 10%.**

---

**Charleston House, The**
21 Pleasant St.,   05091
802-457-3843
Bill & Barb Hough
All year

$$$-B&B
7 rooms, 7 pb
AmEx, MC, Visa,
*Rated*, •
C-ltd/S-no/P-no/H-no

Full breakfast
Afternoon tea, snacks
Sitting room, library
bicycles, Luxury rooms
w/fireplace, jacuzzi, TV

*Classic home in historic village. Listed in National Register. All private baths. One large family room. Two blocks to center village.* **Off-season packages.**

---

**Kedron Valley Inn**
Route 106, South Woodstock,
   05071
802-457-1473
Fax: 802-457-4469
 800-836-1193
Max & Merrily Comins
All year

$$$-B&B/MAP
29 rooms, 29 pb
Most CC, *Rated*, •
C-yes/S-yes/P-yes/H-yes
French, Spanish

Full country breakfast
Contem. American cuisine
Sitting room, swim pond
piano, TV's, quilts
A/C in some rooms

*Distinguished country 1822 inn. Wine list won Award of Excellence (Wine Spectator). Canopy beds, fireplaces in 14 rooms. "Adults only" beach. 1991 INN OF THE YEAR!*

## WOODSTOCK

| | | |
|---|---|---|
| **Lincoln Inn, The** | $$$-B&B | Full breakfast |
| Rt. 4, W., 05091 | 6 rooms, 6 pb | Aftn. tea, comp. wine |
| 802-457-3312 Fax: 802-457-5808 | Visa, MC, *Rated*, | Snacks, restaurant |
| Kurt & Lori Hildbrand | C-yes/S-no/P-no/H-yes | bar service |
| All year | German, French | sitting room, library |

*Lovingly restored farmhouse nestled on 6 acres of lovely grounds.* **Complimentary bottle of wine.**

| | | |
|---|---|---|
| **Woodstocker B&B, The** | $$$-B&B | Full buffet breakfast |
| 61 River St., Route 4, 05091 | 9 rooms, 9 pb | Afternoon tea, snacks |
| 802-457-3896 Fax: 802-457-3897 | MC, Visa, *Rated*, • | Sitting room |
| Tom & Nancy Blackford | C-yes/S-no/P-no/H-no | hot tub |
| All year | | |

*Charming 1830s cape in the village. Walking distance to shops, restaurants & galleries. Near hiking, cross-country and downhill skiing and golf. Full buffet breakfast & afternoon refreshments.*

# More Inns ...

| | |
|---|---|
| Dorset | Little Lodge at Dorset, P.O. Box 673, 05251, 802-867-4040 |
| Dorset | Marble West Inn, P.O. Box 847, 05251, 802-867-4155 |
| Dorset | Village Auberge, P.O. Box 970, 05251, 802-867-5715 |
| East Burke | Garrison Inn, The, P.O. Box 177, 05832, 802-626-8329 |
| East Burke | Nutmegger, The, Box 73, Mountain Rd., 05832 |
| East Burke | Old Cutter Inn, Burke Mt. Access Rd., 05832, 802-626-5152 |
| East Dorset | Christmas Tree B&B, Benedict Rd., 05253, 802-362-4889 |
| East Dover | Cooper Hill Inn, Cooper Hill Rd., Box 14, 05341, 802-348-6333 |
| East Fairfield | Whispering Pines, 05448, 802-827-3827 |
| East Hardwick | Brick House, Box 128, 05836, 802-472-5512 |
| East Haven | Hansel & Gretel Haus, Box 95, Town Hwy 34, 05837, 802-467-8884 |
| East Middlebury | October Pumpkin B&B, Route 125 E., Box 226, 05740 |
| East Middlebury | Robert Frost Mountain B&B, Box 246, 05740 |
| East Middlebury | Waybury Inn, Route 125, 05740, 802-388-4015 |
| Fairfield | Hillside View Farm, South Rd., 05455 |
| Fairlee | Aloha Manor, Lake Morey, 05045, 802-333-4478 |
| Grafton | Eaglebrook of Grafton, Main St., 05146 |
| Grafton | Farmhouse 'Round the Bend, P.O. Box 57, 05146, 802-843-2515 |
| Grafton | Hayes House, 05146, 802-843-2461 |
| Guildhall | Guildhall Inn B&B, P.O. Box 129, 05905, 802-676-3720 |
| Hardwick | Carolyn's Bed & Breakfast, 15 Church St., 05843 |
| Hardwick | Kahagon at Nichols Pond, Box 728, 05843, 802-472-6446 |
| Highgate Springs | Tyler Place-Lake Champlain, P.O. Box 45, 05460, 802-868-3301 |
| Jamaica | Three Mountain Inn, Box 180, Main St. Rt.30, 05343, 802-874-4140 |
| Jay | Jay Village Inn, Route 242, Mountain Rd, 05859, 802-988-2643 |
| Jay | Village Inn, Rt. 242, 05859, 802-988-2643 |
| Jay | Woodshed Lodge, 05859, 802-988-4444 |
| Jeffersonville | Smuggler's Notch Inn, The, P.O. Box 280, 05464, 802-644-2412 |
| Jeffersonville | Windridge Inn B&B, Main St., Rt. 15 & 108, 05464, 802-644-8281 |
| Jericho | Henry M. Field B&B, R.R. 2 Box 395, 05465, 802-899-3984 |
| Jericho | Milliken's, RD 2, Box 397, 05465, 802-899-3993 |
| Jericho | Minterhaus B&B, P.O. Box 226, 05465, 802-899-3990 |
| Killington | Grey Bonnet Inn, RT 100N, 05751, 802-775-2537 |
| Killington | Inn at Long Trail, The, P.O. Box 267, 05751, 802-775-7181 |
| Killington | Snowed Inn, Box 2336, Rd. 1, 05751, 802-422-3407 |
| Londonderry | Village Inn, RFD Landgrove, 05148, 802-824-6673 |
| Lower Waterford | Rabbit Hill Inn, Route 18, 05848, 802-748-5168 |
| Ludlow | Fletcher Manor B&B, One Elm St., 05149, 802-228-3548 |
| Ludlow | Jewell Brook Inn, 82 Andover St., Rt. 10, 05149 |
| Ludlow | Okemo Inn, The, RFD#1, Box 133, 05149, 802-228-8834 |
| Ludlow | Winchester Inn, 53 Main St., 05149, 802-228-3841 |
| Manchester | Battenkill Inn, The, P.O. Box 948, 05254, 802-362-4213 |
| Manchester | Inn at Ormsby Hill, The, RR2, Box 3264, 05255, 802-362-1163 |
| Manchester | Inn at Willow Pond, P.O. Box 1429, Route 7, 05255, 802-362-4733 |
| Manchester | Purple Passion, P.O. Box 678, 05254, 800-822-2331 |
| Manchester | Wilburton Inn, The, P.O. Box 468, 05254, 802-362-2500 |
| Middlebury | A Point of View, South Munger St., 05753 |
| Middlebury | Swift House Inn, 25 Stewart Lane, Rt. 7, 05753, 802-388-9925 |
| Montgomery | Black Lantern Inn, Route 118, 05470, 802-326-4507 |
| Montgomery | Inn on Trout River, Box 76, Main St., 05471, 800-338-7049 |
| Montgomery | Phineas Swann, P.O. Box 43, 05471, 802-326-4306 |
| Montpelier | Inn at Montpelier, 147 Main St., 05602, 802-223-2727 |
| Morgan | Nunts Hideaway, Route 111, 05872, 802-895-4432 |
| Morgan | Seymour Lake Lodge, Route 111, 05853, 802-895-2752 |
| Mount Holly | Austria Haus, Box 2, Austria Haus Rd., 05758, 802-259-2441 |
| Mount Holly | Hortonville Inn, Box 14, 05758 |
| Mount Holly | Hound's Folly, Box 591, 05758, 802-259-2718 |
| Mount Snow | Inn at Quail Run, The, HCR 63, Box 28-Smith Rd, 05363, 800-343-7227 |
| New Haven | Horn Farnsworth B&B, RR 1, Box 170A, 05472 |
| Newbury | A Century Past, P.O. Box 186, Route 5, 05051, 802-866-3358 |
| Newfane | West River Lodge, RR 1, Box 693, 05345, 802-365-7745 |
| North Hero | North Hero House, P.O. Box 106, Route 2, 05474, 802-372-8237 |
| North Thetford | Stone House Inn, Box 47, Route 5, 05054, 802-333-9124 |
| North Troy | Rose Apple Acres Farm, RR 1, Box 300, 05859, 802-988-4300 |
| Northfield | Northfield Inn, 27 Highland Ave., 05663, 802-485-8558 |
| Northfield Falls | Four Bridges Inn, P.O. Box 117, School St, 05664, 802-485-8995 |
| Norwich | Norwich Inn, The, P.O. Box 908, 05055, 802-649-1143 |
| Orleans | Valley House Inn, 4 Memorial Square, 05860, 802-754-6665 |
| Perkinsville | Gwendolyn's, Route 106, P.O. Box 225, 05151, 802-263-5248 |
| Pittsfield | Swiss Farm Lodge, P.O. Box 630, 05762, 802-748-8341 |
| Pittsford | Fox Bros. Farm, Corn Hill Rd., 05763, 802-483-2870 |
| Plainfield | Yankees' Northview B&B, RD #2, Box 1000, 05667, 802-454-7191 |
| Plymouth | Hawk Inn & Mountain Resort, P.O. Box 64, 05056, 800-685-4295 |

*Seven Wives Inn, St. George, VT*

| | |
|---|---|
| Plymouth | Salt Ash Inn, Jct. Rts. 100 & 100A, 05056, 802-672-3748 |
| Plymouth | Snowy Owl Lodge, HCR 70, Rt 100A, Box106, 05056, 802-672-5018 |
| Post Mills | Lake House Inn, Route 244, P.O. Box 65, 05058, 802-333-4025 |
| Poultney | Stonebridge Inn, The, 3 Beaman St., 05764, 802-287-9849 |
| Proctorsville | Okemo Lantern Lodge, P.O. Box 247, 05153, 802-226-7770 |
| Putney | Mapleton Farm B&B, RD 2, Box 510, 05346, 802-257-5252 |
| Putney | Misty Meadow, RD 1, Box 458, 05346 |
| Quechee | Quechee B&B, P.O. Box 80, 05059, 802-295-1776 |
| Quechee | Quechee Inn-Marshland Farm, P.O. Box BB, 05059, 802-295-3133 |
| Randolph | Foggy Bottom Farm B&B, Rt. 12, 05060, 802-728-9201 |
| Randolph | Three Stallion Inn, RD #2 Stock Farm Rd., 05060, 802-728-5575 |
| Reading | Peeping Cow B&B, The, Route 106, P.O. Box 178, 05062, 802-484-5036 |
| Readsboro | Old Coach Inn, RR 1 Box 260, 05350, 802-423-5394 |
| Richmond | Black Bear Inn, The, P.O. Box 26, 05477, 802-434-2126 |
| Rochester | New Homestead, 05767, 802-767-4751 |
| Rutland | Hillcrest Guest House, RR 1, Box 4459, 05701, 802-775-1670 |
| Saxtons River | Inn at Saxtons River, The, P.O. Box 448, 05154, 802-869-2110 |
| Saxtons River | Red Barn Guest House, Hatfield Ln., 05154 |
| Shelburne | Inn at Shelburne Farms, Shelburne Farms, 05482, 802-985-8498 |
| Shoreham Village | Shoreham Inn, Route 74W, Main St., 05770, 802-897-5081 |
| South Londonderry | Londonderry Inn, Box 301-12, Rt. 100, 05155, 802-824-5226 |
| South Newfane | Inn at South Newfane, Dover Rd., 05351, 802-348-7191 |
| South Strafford | Watercours Way, Route 132, 05070, 802-765-4314 |
| South Wallingford | Green Mountain Tea Room, RR 1, Box 400, Route 7, 05773, 802-446-2611 |
| St. Albans | Bellevue, 9 Parsons Ln., 05478, 802-527-1115 |
| St. Johnsbury | Echo Ledge Farm Inn, P.O. Box 77, Route 2, 05838, 802-748-4750 |
| Stockbridge | Stockbridge Inn B&B, The, P.O. Box 45, Rt. 100 N, 05772, 802-746-8165 |
| Stowe | 1860 House B&B Inn, The, P.O. Box 276, 05672, 802-253-7351 |
| Stowe | Baas' Gastehaus, Edson Hill, RR1, Box 22, 05672 |
| Stowe | Bittersweet Inn, RR 2, Box 2900, 05672 |
| Stowe | Edson Hill Manor, 1500 Edson Hill Rd., 05672, 802-253-7371 |
| Stowe | Fontain B&B, Route 100, Box 2480, 05672, 802-253-9285 |
| Stowe | Foxfire Inn, RR2, Box 2180, 05672, 802-253-4887 |
| Stowe | Golden Kitz Lodge, 1965 Mountain Rd., 05672, 802-253-4217 |
| Stowe | Grey Fox Inn, 05672, 802-253-8921 |
| Stowe | Hob Knob Inn, Mountain Rd., 05672, 802-253-8549 |
| Stowe | Innsburck Inn, RR1, Box 1570, 05672, 802-253-8582 |
| Stowe | Raspberry Patch B&B, The, 606 Randolph Rd., 05672, 802-253-4145 |
| Stowe | Scandinavia Inn & Chalet, 05672, 802-253-8555 |
| Stowe | Stowe-Away Lodge, Mountain Rd., Box 1360, 05672, 802-253-7574 |
| Stowe | Stowehof Inn, P.O. Box 1108, 05672, 802-253-9722 |
| Stowe | Sun & Ski Motor Inn, Mountain Rd., 05672, 802-253-7159 |
| Stowe | Ten Acres Lodge, 14 Barrows Rd., 05672, 802-253-7638 |
| Stowe | Timberholm Inn, 452 Cottage Club Rd., 05672, 802-253-7603 |
| Swanton | Heron House B&B, RR 2, Box 174-2, 05488, 802-868-7433 |
| Taftsville | Maitland-Swan House, The, P.O. Box 72, School St., 05073, 800-959-1404 |
| Thetford Hill | Fahrenbrae Hilltop Retreat, Box 129, 05074, 802-785-4304 |
| Townsend | Boardman House B&B, P.O. Box 112, 05353, 802-365-4086 |
| Townsend | Townsend Country Inn, RR 1, Box 3100, 05353, 800-569-1907 |
| Underhill Center | Mansfield View Guest House, P.O. Box 114, 05490, 802-899-4793 |
| Vergennes | Emersons' Guest House, 82 Main St., 05491, 802-877-3293 |
| Waitsfield | Inn @ Slide Brook Meadows, RR1, Box 125, 05673 |
| Waitsfield | Battleground, The, Route 17, 05673 |
| Waitsfield | Inn at the Mad River Barn, P.O. Box 88, 05673, 802-496-3310 |
| Waitsfield | Knoll Farm Country Inn, RFD 1, Box 179, 05673, 802-496-3939 |
| Waitsfield | Mountain View Inn, Route 17, RFD Box 69, 05673, 802-496-2426 |
| Waitsfield | Old Tymes Inn, Route 100, P.O. Box 165, 05673 |
| Waitsfield | Snuggery Inn, Box 65, RR#1, 05673, 802-496-2322 |
| Waitsfield | Tucker Hill Lodge, RD 1, Box 147 (Rt. 17), 05673, 802-496-3983 |
| Wallingford | Victorian Inn, The, 9 N. Main St., 05773, 802-446-2099 |
| Wallingford | White Rocks Inn, RR1, Box 297, 05773, 802-446-2077 |
| Warren | Pitcher Inn, P.O. Box 408, 05674 |
| Warren | Sugarbush Inn, Access Rd., 05674 |
| Waterbury Center | Black Locust Inn, The, RR 1, Box 715, 05677, 802-244-7490 |
| West Arlington | Inn on Covered Bridge Gree, RD 1, Box 3550, 05250 |
| West Dover | Gray Ghost Inn, The, Rt. 100 N, P.O. Box 938, 05356, 802-464-2474 |
| West Dover | Inn at Sawmill Farm, Box 8 (#100), 05356, 802-464-8131 |
| West Dover | Snow Den Inn & Gallery, Route 100, Box 625, 05356, 802-464-9355 |
| West Dover | Waldwinkel Inn, 05356, 802-464-5281 |
| West Townshend | Windham Hill Inn, RR 1, Box 44, 05359, 802-874-4080 |
| Weston | Darling Family Inn, The, 815 Route 100, 05161, 802-824-3223 |
| Weston | Inn at Weston, P.O. Box 56, 05161, 802-824-5804 |
| Williston | Partridge Hill, P.O. Box 52, 05495, 802-878-4741 |

*The Blue Church
Lodge, Park City, VT*

| | |
|---|---|
| Wilmington | Brook Bound Building, Coldbrook Rd., 05363,  802-464-3511 |
| Wilmington | Darcroft's Schoolhouse, Rt. 100, 05363,  802-464-2631 |
| Wilmington | Hermitage Inn & Brookbound, P.O. Box 457, 05363,  802-464-3511 |
| Wilmington | Misty Mountain Lodge, 05356,  802-464-3961 |
| Wilmington | Nordic Hills Lodge, 34 Look Road, 05356,  802-464-5130 |
| Wilmington | On the Rocks Lodge, 05363,  802-464-8364 |
| Wolcott | Golden Maple Inn, P.O. Box 35, 05680,  802-888-6614 |
| Woodstock | Applebutter Inn B&B, P.O. Box 24, 05091 |
| Woodstock | Carriage House, 15 Route 4 West, 05091,  802-457-4322 |
| Woodstock | Deer Brook Inn, HCR 68, Box 443, Rt. 4, 05091,  802-672-3713 |
| Woodstock | Jackson House at Woodstock, Route 4 West, 05091,  802-457-2065 |
| Woodstock | Thomas Hill Farm B&B, Rose Hill, 05091,  802-457-1067 |
| Woodstock | Three Church Street B&B, 3 Church St., 05091,  802-457-1925 |
| Woodstock | Village Inn of Woodstock, 41 Pleasant St., 05091,  802-457-1255 |
| Woodstock | Winslow House, 38, Route 4 West, 05091,  802-457-1820 |
| Woodstock | Woodstock Inn & Resort, 14 The Green, 05091,  800-448-7900 |

# Virginia

## ABINGDON

**River Garden B&B**
19080 N. Fork River Rd.,
 24210
540-676-0335  800-952-4296
Bill Crump & Carol
Schoenheur
All year

$$-B&B
4 rooms, 4 pb
•
C-ltd/S-no/P-ltd/H-yes

Full breakfast
Afternoon tea - request
Library, sitting room
rec. room, covered deck
full private baths

*Located in country, private entrances for rooms, antique & period furniture, covered deck facing river, gift shop, delightful host & hostess!*

## AMHERST

**Dulwich Manor B&B Inn**
Rte 5, Box 173A,  24521
804-946-7207
Bob & Judy Reilly
All year

$$-B&B
6 rooms, 4 pb
*Rated*,  •
C-yes/S-ltd/P-no/H-no

Full breakfast
Afternoon tea/request
Complimentary wine
bar service, study w/TV
whirlpool, A/C in rooms

*English style manor, Blue Ridge Mt. views, beautifully appointed, sumptuous breakfast. Surrounded by natural and historic beauty. Outdoor hot tub, cribs, rollaways.*

## ASHLAND

**Henry Clay Inn, The**
114 N. Railroad Ave.,  23005
804-798-3100 Fax: 804-752-7555
800-343-4565
Martin/Kostenbauder/
Houston
All year

$$$-B&B
15 rooms, 15 pb
Visa, MC, AmEx,
*Rated*,  •
C-yes/S-no/P-no/H-yes

Continental plus bkfst.
Lunch & dinner available
Restaurant
snacks
sitting room

*Southern charm—frplcs., front porch w/rocking chairs, period-furnished rooms, rest., art/ gift galleries. Good for receptions, reunions, corporate meetings. **3rd night 50%, ltd.***

BASYE ──────────────────────────

| **Sky Chalet Mountain Lodge** | $-B&B | Continental breakfast |
|---|---|---|
| P.O. Box 300,  22810 | 10 rooms, 10 pb | Delivered to your room |
| Rt. 263 West | Most CC, *Rated*, • | Restaurant, pub |
| 540-856-2147 Fax: 540-856-2436 | C-yes/S-yes/P-yes/H-no | next to 4 season resort |
| Ken & Mona Seay | | trail to skiing, views |
| All year | | |

*Swiss-style mountaintop lodge hideaway in Shenendoah Valley of Virginia; spectacular mountain views; scrumptious dining; comfortable lodging; cozy pub.* **3rd night 50%; ask about restaurant disc't.**

BELLE HAVEN ──────────────────────────

| **Bayview Waterfront** | $$$-B&B | Full breakfast |
|---|---|---|
| 35350 Copes Dr.,  23306 | 2 rooms, 2 pb | Sitting room, library |
| 757-442-6963 800-442-6966 | • | bikes, tennis |
| Wayne & Mary Will | C-yes/S-no/P-no/H-no | swimming pool |
| Browning | | |
| All year | | |

*Old eastern share home with many antiques and family heirlooms, fireplaces, beautiful water views, gracious rooms*

BLACKSBURG ──────────────────────────

| **Clay Corner Inn** | $$-B&B | Continental plus bkfst. |
|---|---|---|
| 401 Clay St. SW,  24060 | 8 rooms, 8 pb | Heated pool, A/C |
| 540-953-2604 Fax: 540-951-0541 | MC, Visa, AmEx, • | walking trail |
| John & Joanne Anderson | C-ltd/S-no/P-no/H-no | |
| All year | | |

*Main house & two guest houses. Cable TV & phones in every room. Healthy breakfast served inside or out on covered deck. One block to Virginia Tech, walking trail, tennis and downtown.*

BOYCE ──────────────────────────

| **River House, The** | $$$-B&B | Full breakfast |
|---|---|---|
| Route 1, Box 135,  22620 | 5 rooms, 5 pb | Fruit, beverages/liqueur |
| 540-837-1476 Fax: 540-837-2399 | MC, Visa, *Rated*, • | Sitting room, library |
| 800-838-1476 | C-ltd/S-yes/P-yes/H-yes | phone in rm., Fax, modem |
| Cornelia S. Niemann | French | special comedy weekends |
| All year | | |

*1780 Fieldstone rural getaway, convenient to scenic, historical, rec. areas, superb rests. Houseparties; small workshops; family reunions. Brunch served.* **3rd nite 50% off.**

CAPE CHARLES ──────────────────────────

| **Bay Avenue Sunset B&B** | $$-B&B | Full breakfast |
|---|---|---|
| 108 Bay Avenue,  23310 | 4 rooms, 4 pb | Afternoon tea, snacks |
| 757-331-2424 Fax: 757-331-4877 | Visa, MC, *Rated*, • | Sitting room, harbor |
| 888-4-BAYAVE | C-ltd/S-ltd/P-no/H-no | bikes, seasonal hot tub |
| Al Longo & Joyce Tribble | | golf, fishing, beach |
| All year | | |

*Waterfront escape on Chesapeake Bay. Beautiful sunsets, breezy porch, central A/C, walking tour. Your home away from home. Relax, unwind.* **3rd night 25% off.**

| **Wilson-Lee House B&B** | $$$-B&B | Full breakfast |
|---|---|---|
| 403 Tazewell Ave.,  23310 | 6 rooms, 6 pb | Afternoon tea |
| 757-331-1954 Fax: 757-331-8133 | Visa, MC, • | Sitting room |
| David Phillips, Leon Parham | C-ltd/S-no/P-no/H-no | bikes, tennis court |
| All year | | 5 min. walk to beach |

*Experience the charm of a bygone era on Virginia's eastern shore in one of historic Cape Charles' finest homes. Gracious hospitality awaits you at Wilson-Lee House.* **3rd night 50%.**

### CASTLETON

**Blue Knoll Farm B&B**
110 Gore Rd.,   22716
540-937-5234
Mary & Gil Carlson
All year

$$$-B&B
4 rooms, 4 pb
Visa, MC,
C-ltd/S-ltd/P-no/H-ltd

Full breakfast
Comp. fruit/snacks/bev.
Sitting room, porches
one room with jacuzzi
antique woodstove, pond

*Charming 19th-century farmhouse in the foothills of Blue Ridge Mountains. 65 miles west of Washington, D.C., near Skyline Dr. and 5 star inn at Little Washington Restaurant.*

### CHAMPLAIN

**Linden House B&B**
P.O. Box 23,   22438
Rt. 17 South
804-443-1170   Fax: 804-443-0107
800-622-1202
Ken & Sandra Pounsberry
All year

$$$-B&B
8 rooms, 5 pb
Visa, MC, *Rated*, •
C-ltd/S-ltd/P-no/H-yes

Full breakfast
Dinner, snacks
Bicycles, sitting room
jacuzzi, steam shower
gazebo, porches

*Linden House offers a beautifully decorated and properly landscaped plantation home with 204 acres. Close to winery, golf and river cruise.* **3rd night 50% off.**

### CHARLES CITY

**Edgewood Plantation**
4800 John Tyler Hwy.,   23030
804-829-2962   Fax: 804-829-2962
800-296-3343
Juilian & Dot Boulware
All year

$$$-B&B
8 rooms, 8 pb
MC, Visa, *Rated*, •
C-ltd/S-yes

Full breakfast
Comp. refreshments
Tea room, shops
formal gardens, gazebos
hot tubs, pool, fishing

*Sweetness, romance, uniqueness & charm. Pre-Civil War 1849 historical house. Business facility.* **Comp. refreshment/dessert tickets to nearby plantations/taverns.**

---

**North Bend Plantation B&B**
12200 Weyanoke Rd., Route 1, Box 13A,   23030
804-829-5176   Fax: 804-829-6828
800-841-1749
The Coplands   All year

$$$-B&B
4 rooms, 4 pb
*Rated*, •
C-ltd
some French

Full country breakfast
Comp. desserts @ tavern
Discount tickets James
River Plantation, enjoy
Croquet, swimming, bikes

*Virginia Historic Landmark circa 1819 in James River Plantation area. Close to Williamsburg. 250 acres of peaceful farmland. Weddings, receptions.* **20% off 3rd night.**

### CHARLOTTESVILLE

**200 South Street Inn**
200 South St.,   22902
804-979-0200   Fax: 804-979-4403
800-964-7008
Brendan Clancy
All year

$$$-B&B
20 rooms, 20 pb
AmEx, MC, Visa,
*Rated*, •
C-yes/S-yes/P-no/H-yes
French

Continental plus bkfst.
Lunch M-F, dinner wkends
Restaurant, comp. wine
sitting room, fireplaces
library, whirlpool tubs

*Restored residences in downtown historic district near landmarks, shops, restaurants. Room options include whirlpool tubs, fireplaces, canopy beds.* **10% discount.**

---

**Clifton - The Country Inn**
1296 Clifton Inn Dr.,   22901
804-971-1800   Fax: 804-971-7098
888-971-1800
Craig Hartman
All year

$$$$-B&B
14 rooms, 14 pb
Most CC, *Rated*, •
C-yes/S-no/P-no/H-yes

Full breakfast
Dinner (fee), aft. tea
Comp. sodas & cookies
restaurant, weddings
private lake fishing

*Virginia hospitality and Chef Craig Hartman's "Universal Cuisine." Fireplace in every room, swimming, tennis. One of "Country Inns" 12 Best. An award winning wine list.*

CHARLOTTESVILLE ────────────────────────────

**Inn at Monticello, The**
445 Maple View Ct., 1188
Scottsville Rd., 22902
804-979-3593 Fax: 804-296-1344
Carol & Larry Engel
All year except X-mas

$$$-B&B
5 rooms, 5 pb
MC, Visa, *Rated*, •
C-ltd/S-no/P-no/H-no
some French

Full gourmet breakfast
Comp. local beer & wine
Sitting room, hammock
covered porch, croquet
tennis court nearby

*19th century manor, perfectly located 2 miles from Thomas Jefferson's beloved "Monticello."Antiques, canopy beds, fireplaces. Golf, tennis, canoeing, wine-tasting nearby.* **Comp. glass of VA wine.**

---

**Palmer Country Manor**
Rt. 2, Box 1390, 22963
804-589-1300 Fax: 804-589-1300
800-253-4306
Gregory & Kathleen Palmer
All year

$$$-MAP
12 rooms, 10 pb
Most CC, *Rated*, •
C-yes/S-yes/P-no/H-no

Full country breakfast
Dinner incl., snacks
Restaurant
sitting room, library
pool, bicycles, trails

*A country estate on 180 acres. Cottages feature a living area w/fireplace, full bath & deck. Deluxe rooms with Jacuzzi tubs. Swimming pool, hiking trails, fishing pond, balloon rides.* **3rd night, 50%.**

---

**Silver Thatch Inn**
3001 Hollymead Dr., 22911
804-978-4686 Fax: 804-973-6156
Rita & Vince Scoffone
All year except Xmas

$$$-B&B
7 rooms, 7 pb
Most CC, *Rated*, •
C-ltd/S-no/P-no/H-no

Continental plus bkfst.
Dinner, comp. wine
Restaurant, bar service
swimming pool

*Circa 1780 historic Southern inn with romantic lodging rooms and full evening dining. Located in one of Virginia's prettiest towns.*

CHATHAM ────────────────────────────

**Eldon, The Inn at Chatham**
1037 Chalk Level Rd., Rt1,
Box 2543, 24531
804-432-0935
Joy & Bob Lemm
All year

$$-B&B
4 rooms, 3 pb
Visa, MC, •
C-ltd/S-ltd/P-no/H-ltd

Full breakfast
Dinner (fee), restaurant
Library, swimming pool
croquet, bocce, winery
nearby, antiquing

*Historic 1835 plantation home. Queen canopy beds, antiques, 13 wooded acres, country setting, orchard, formal garden. Intimate gourmet restaurant.* **Free split of wine.**

---

**Sims-Mitchell House B&B**
P.O. Box 429, 24531
242 Whittle St., S.W.
804-432-0595 Fax: 804-432-0596
800-967-2867
Henry & Patricia Mitchell
All year

$$-B&B/MAP
2 rooms, 2 pb
MC, Visa, AmEx, •
C-yes/S-no/P-no/H-no

Continental plus bkfst.
Private entrances
2 2-bedroom suites
sitting room

*Historic 1870 home w/family atmosphere. Spacious guest suites in raised English basement, adjacent cottage. Serene, charming Victorian town.*

CHINCOTEAGUE ────────────────────────────

**Garden & The Sea Inn**
P.O. Box 275, 23415
4188 Nelson, New Church
804-824-0672  800-824-0672
Tom & Sara Baker
April 1—October 31

$$-B&B
6 rooms, 6 pb
Most CC, *Rated*, •
C-ltd/S-ltd/P-no/H-no
French

Continental plus bkfst.
Dinner, afternoon tea
Comp. wine, restaurant
sitting room, beach near
outdoor patio/garden

*Near Chincoteague & Assateague—elegant, European-style inn with French gourmet restaurant. Luxurious rooms, beautiful beach nearby.*

CHINCOTEAGUE ─────────────────────────────────────────

| | | |
|---|---|---|
| **Miss Molly's Inn** | $$-B&B | Full breakfast |
| 4141 Main St.,   23336 | 7 rooms, 5 pb | English afternoon tea |
| 757-336-6686 | Visa, MC, Disc, *Rated*, | Sitting room |
| 800-221-5620 | • | no smoking! |
| David & Barbara Wiedenheft | C-ltd/S-no | vegetarian bkfst. avail |
| March - New Years | French, Dutch, German | |

*A charming Victorian "painted lady" overlooking the Bay. Marguerite Henry stayed here while writing her classic "Misty of Chincoteague." World-famous scones served at teatime.* **Midweek senior discounts.**

| | | |
|---|---|---|
| **Watson House B&B, The** | $$-B&B | Full breakfast |
| 4240 Main St.,   23336 | 8 rooms, 8 pb | Afternoon tea |
| 804-336-1564 Fax: 804-336-5776 | MC, Visa, *Rateed*, • | Bicycles, beach nearby |
| 800-336-6787 | C-ltd/S-ltd/P-no/H-no | beach chairs & towels |
| The Derricksons & The | | wildlife, whirlpool tubs |
| Sneads | | |
| March–November | | |

*Beautifully restored Victorian. Furnished w/antiques. View of Chincoteague Bay and beach nearby. 2 family cottages. AAA - 3 diamond.* **Mid-week specials available.**

CLARKSVILLE ─────────────────────────────────────────

| | | |
|---|---|---|
| **Needmoor Inn** | $$-B&B | Full gourmet breakfast |
| 801 Virginia Ave.,   23927 | 4 rooms, 3 pb | Aftn. tea, snacks |
| 804-374-2866 | *Rated*, • | Comp. wine, bicycles |
| Carl & Avonda Sweely | C-yes/S-ltd/P-ltd/H-no | library, airport pickup |
| All year | | herb garden, facials |

*Heartfelt hospitality in the heart of Virginia's Lake Country. 1889 homestead amid 1.5 acres of fruit trees. Walk to Kerr Lake. Sailing lessons, all water recreational activities.*

CLUSTER SPRINGS ─────────────────────────────────────

| | | |
|---|---|---|
| **Oak Grove Plantation B&B** | $$-B&B | Full gourmet breakfast |
| P.O. Box 45,   24535 | 3 rooms, | Dinner |
| 1245 Cluster Springs Rd. | *Rated*, • | Sitting room, library |
| 804-575-7137 | C-yes/S-no/P-no/H-no | bicycles |
| Pickett Craddock | Spanish | wildflower walks |
| May–September | | |

*Come enjoy our antebellum country home built by our ancestors in 1820. 400 acres w/ trails, creeks and wildlife. Children welcome; midwk. childcare package.* **3rd night 50%.**

COVINGTON ───────────────────────────────────────────

| | | |
|---|---|---|
| **Milton Hall B&B Inn** | $$-B&B | Full breakfast |
| 207 Thorny Ln.,   24426 | 6 rooms, 6 pb | Box lunch |
| 540-965-0196 | MC, Visa, *Rated*, • | Bar service, comp. wine |
| John & Vera Eckert | C-yes/S-yes/P-yes/H-no | afternoon tea, sitting |
| All year | | room, library, patio |

*English country manor c.1874 set on 44 wooded acres w/gardens. This Historic Landmark adjoins Nat'l Forest, mountains, lakes, springs. Near hunting, fishing. Crib/rollaway available.* **3rd nite 50% off.**

CULPEPER ────────────────────────────────────────────

| | | |
|---|---|---|
| **Fountain Hall B&B** | $$$-B&B | Continental plus bkfst. |
| 609 S. East St.,   22701 | 6 rooms, 6 pb | Complimentary beverages |
| 540-825-8200 Fax: 540-825-7716 | Most CC, *Rated*, • | 3 sitting rooms, books |
| 800-298-4748 | C-yes/S-no/P-no/H-yes | fireplaces, VCR, porches |
| Steve & Kathi Walker  All yr | | golf nearby, bicycles |

*Gracious accomm. for business & leisure. Centrally located in historic Culpepper, between Washington, D.C., Charlottesville & Skyline Dr. Golf pkgs. Dinner pkg. w/Prince Michel.* **$15 disc't on 2nd nite.**

EXMORE —————————————————————————————

**Gladstone House B&B, The**
P.O. Box 296,   23350
12108 Lincoln Ave.
804-442-4614 Fax: 804-442-4678
800-262-4837
Pat & Al Egan
All year

$$-B&B
2 rooms, 2 pb
Visa, MC, AmEx,
*Rated*, •
C-ltd/S-no/P-no/H-no

Full breakfast
Afternoon tea, snacks
Sitting room
bicycles
library

*Step back in time in an elegant brick Georgian home. Small town atmosphere. Four-course breakfast. Vegetarian breakfast available. Coffee at your bedroom door.*

FAIRFAX ————————————————————————————

**Bailiwick Inn**
4023 Chain Bridge Rd.,
   22030
703-691-2266  Fax: 703-934-2112
800-366-7666
Bob & Annette Bradley
All year

$$$$-B&B
14 rooms, 14 pb
Visa, MC, AmEx,
*Rated*, •
C-yes/S-no/P-no/H-yes

Full breakfast
Restaurant, aftn. tea
Sitting room
dinner available at
restaurant for a fee

*Built in 1800; rooms are elegantly furnished with antiques, featuring fireplaces, Jacuzzi, full breakfast and afternoon tea. Candlelight dinners, weddings and special events.*

FREDERICKSBURG ——————————————————————

**Fredericksburg Colonial**
1707 Princess Anne St.,
   22401
540-371-5666
Jim Crisp
All year

$$-B&B
32 rooms, 32 pb
MC, Visa, *Rated*, •
C-yes/S-yes/P-yes/H-yes

Continental breakfast
Conference room avail.
honeymoon/anniversary
Colonial Suites

*Furnished in Victorian decor. Enjoy our antiques, prints, & museum. Located in historic district. Antique shops, restaurants nearby. **Mention ad, 20% disc't/mid-week disc't 35%.***

**La Vista Plantation**
4420 Guinea Station Rd.,
   22408
540-898-8444 Fax: 540-898-9414
800-529-2823
Michele & Edward Schiesser
All year

$$$-B&B
2 rooms, 2 pb
MC, Visa, *Rated*, •
C-yes/S-no/P-ltd/H-no

Full breakfast
Comp. soda and juice
Sitting room, library
bicycles, A/C, kitchen
TV, phone, wicker furn.

*Lovely 1838 classical revival country home on 10 acres outside historic Fredericksburg. Antiques; private fireplaces; old trees; pond. **7th night free, children under 12 free.***

**Rennaisance Manor B&B**
2247 Courthouse Rd.,   22554
540-720-3785 Fax: 540-720-3785
800-720-3784
Deneen Bernard & JoAnn
Houser
All year

$$-B&B
6 rooms, 4 pb
*Rated*, •
C-yes/S-no/P-no/H-no

Continental plus bkfst.
Aftn. tea, comp. sherry
Library, fireplaces
art gallery, rose garden
formal garden, gazebo

*Resembles Mount Vernon in architecture & decor. 8 miles to Historic Fredericksburg, 40 miles to Richmond or Washington D.C. Will pick up from nearby Marina or commuter rail.*

FRONT ROYAL ───────────────────────────────────

**Chester House Inn**
43 Chester St., 22630
540-635-3937
Fax: 540-636-8695
800-621-0441
Bill & Ann Wilson
All year

$$-B&B
6 rooms, 4 pb
MC, Visa, *Rated*, •
C-ltd/S-ltd/P-no/H-no

Continental plus bkfst.
Comp. wine, snacks
Living & dining room
lawns, garden, TV parlor
Carriage House

*Quiet, elegant home reminiscent of a bygone era amidst formal boxwood garden and shade trees. Golf, tennis, horseback riding, hiking, canoeing nearby.* **Comp. wine & snacks.**

---

**Killahevlin**
1401 North Royal Ave.,
  22630
540-636-7335 Fax: 540-636-8694
800-847-6132
Susan & John Lang
All year

$$$-B&B
8 rooms, 8 pb
MC, Visa, *Rated*, •
C-ltd/S-no/P-no/H-no

Full breakfast
Afternoon tea, snacks
Comp. wine/beer, scenic
sitting room, hot tubs
gazebos, screened porch

*Historic Edwardian mansion. Civil War encampment hill. Mountain views, working fireplaces, jacuzzi tubs. Prepare to be pampered. Private Irish pub for guests.* **Comp. champagne.**

---

**Woodward House-Manor Grade**
413 S. Royal Ave., 22630
703-635-7010  800-635-7011
Joan & Bob Kaye
Exc. 2 weeks in Jan

$$-B&B
9 rooms, 9 pb
MC, Visa, •
C-yes/S-ltd/P-no/H-ltd

Full breakfast
Complimentary beverages
Sitting room, bicycles
conf. room, FAX, copying
fitness studio

*Three blocks from Skyline Drive; parklike setting; heart of history land. Located atop a hill with a view of the countryside. 80 minutes to Washington, D.C.* **3rd night 10% disc't.**

GORDONSVILLE ───────────────────────────────────

**Sleepy Hollow Farm B&B**
16280 Blue Ridge Turnpk,
  22942
540-832-5555 Fax: 540-832-2515
800-215-4804
B. Allison & D.A. Comer
All year

$$-B&B
7 rooms, 6 pb
MC, Visa, *Rated*, •
C-yes/S-yes/P-ltd/H-no
Spanish, French

Full breakfast
Comp. wine, beverages
Sitting room, conf. room
croquet field, gazebo
pond fishing & swimming

*Old farmhouse & cottage w/whirlpool furnished in antiques, accessories. One bdrm w/ fireplace & Jacuzzi. In beautiful countryside, near James Madison's Montpelier.* **3rd night 50%, ltd.**

---

**Tivoli**
9171 Tivoli Dr., 22942
540-832-2225
Fax: 540-832-3691
800-840-2225
Phil & Susie Audibert
All year

$$$-B&B
4 rooms, 4 pb
Visa, MC, •
C-ltd/S-ltd/P-no/H-no
French, Spanish

Full breakfast
Comp. wine, bar service
Sitting room, library
235 acres—farm & trails
Ideal for weddings

*Elegant Victorian mansion offers spectacular views, peace, quiet, history, hospitality, antiques, fireplaces in every bedroom, and big country breakfasts.*

## LEXINGTON

**A B&B at Llewellyn Lodge**
603 S. Main St., 24450
540-463-3235 Fax: 540-464-3122
800-882-1145
John & Ellen Roberts
All year

$$-B&B
6 rooms, 6 pb
Most CC, *Rated*, •
C-ltd/S-yes/P-no/H-no

Full breakfast
Complimentary beverages
Sitting room
tennis/pool/golf nearby
hiking, fly-fishing,

*Charming half-century-old colonial with a warm friendly atmosphere, where guests can relax in this historic Shenandoah town. Gourmet breakfast. 2-night minimum in May & Oct.* **Golf packages.**

---

**Applewood Inn**
P.O. Box 1348, 24450
Rt. 678
540-463-1962  800-463-1902
Linda & Christian Best
Closed January

$$$-B&B
4 rooms, 4 pb
C-ltd/S-no/P-no/H-ltd
German

Full breakfast
Hot cider, beverages
Fridge, pantry
sitting room, porches
hot tub, pool, hiking

*Spectacular solar home on 35 acres. Mountain views. Close to historic Lexington. Adjacent 900 acre Rockbridge Hunt. Heart healthy breakfasts. For the nature lover.* **3rd night 50%, ltd.**

---

**Brierley Hill B&B/Inn**
Rt. 2 Box 21A, Borden Road,
  24450
540-464-8421 Fax: 540-464-8925
800-422-4925
Barry & Carole Speton
All year

$$-B&B/MAP
6 rooms, 6 pb
Visa, MC, *Rated*, •
C-ltd/S-no/P-no

Full breakfast
Dinner (fee), aftn. tea
Hiking, canoeing
horseback riding
packages available

*English country house atmosphere. Candlelight dinners available. Magnificent views of Blue Ridge Mountains and Shenandoah Valley.* **3rd night 50% midweek.**

---

**Lavender Hill Farm B&B**
Rt. 1, Box 515, 24450
Big Spring Rd.
540-464-5877  800-446-4240
Colin & Cindy Smith
All year

$$-B&B
3 rooms, 3 pb
Visa, MC, Disc. *Rated*,
•
C-yes/S-no/P-no/H-no

Full breakfast
Dinner - avail. to guest
Sitting room, A/C
horseback riding, hikes
fishing, birding, biking

*English country charm and outstanding food await you. Quiet country setting on working farm located near historic Lexington in the Shenandoah Valley.*

## LINCOLN

**Springdale Country Inn**
Box 80, 22078
703-338-1832  800-388-1832
Nancy & Roger Fones
All year

$$$-B&B
10 rooms, 6 pb
Visa, MC, •
C-ltd/S-no/P-no/H-yes

Full breakfast
Lunch & dinner avail.
Afternoon tea, snacks
Comp. wine, bar service
sitt. rm, library, A/C

*Pristine restoration of historic Quaker boarding school, circa 1832. Babbling brook, walking bridges, wildflower meadow, terraced gardens.* **Discount if booking all rooms.**

## LOCUST DALE

**Inn at Meander Plantation**
HCR 5, Box 460A, 22948
540-672-4912  800-385-4936
S. & B. Blanchard, S. Thomas
All year

$$$-B&B
5 rooms, 5 pb
Visa, MC *Rated*, •
C-ltd/S-no/P-ltd/H-no

Full gourmet breakfast
Lunch & Dinner - arrang.
Hot air balloon rides
sitt. rm, library, piano
horseback riding, A/C

*Historic, elegantly furnished grand 1776 Colonial manor on 80 majestic acres w/spectacular views. Romantic, relaxing getaway. Genuine hospitality.* **Free bottle of wine** .

## LURAY

**Woodruff House B&B, The**
330 Mechanic St., 22835
703-743-1494
Lucas & Deborah Woodruff
All year

$$$-MAP
6 rooms, 6 pb
Visa, MC, Disc. *Rated*,
•
C-ltd/S-ltd/P-no/H-no

Full gourmet breakfast
Aftn. tea, snacks, bar
Bicycles, hot tubs
library

*Shenandoah Valley 1882 fairytale Victorian. Chef prepared gourmet dinners, breakfast. Morning coffee to your door. Relax in romantic garden spa.* **Free bottle of wine 3rd night.**

## LYNCHBURG

**Federal Crest Inn B&B**
1101 Federal St., 24504
804-845-6155 Fax: 804-845-1445
800-818-6155
Ann & Phil Ripley
All year

$$$-B&B
5 rooms, 4 pb
Most CC, •
C-ltd/S-no/P-no/H-no

Full breakfast
Afternoon tea, snacks
Comp. wine, sitting room
library, bicycles
'50s cafe w/60" tv

*Romantic and elegant! Unique 1909 spacious mansion with BR fireplace, AC, jacuzzi, antiques. Theater on the 3rd floor. Near Appomattox, golf, wineries, mountains.* **50% off, ltd.**

**Madison House B&B, The**
413 Madison St., 24504
804-528-1503  800-828-6422
Irene & Dale Smith
All year

$$$-B&B
4 rooms, 4 pb
Visa, MC, AmEx,
*Rated*, •
S-no/P-no/H-no

Full breakfast
Afternoon tea w/scones
Full bar (ABC licence)
TV with cable-all rooms
civil war library

*Lynchburg's finest Victorian B&B, 1880 antique-filled elegant mansion. Breakfast at your convenience. Music room, private phone in guestrooms.* **Free cival war packet.**

## MATHEWS

**Ravenswood Inn**
P.O. Box 1430, 23109
Poplar Grove Ln.
804-725-7272
Sally Preston & Ricky
Durham
Mid-Feb—early Dec

$$-B&B
5 rooms, 5 pb
•
C-ltd/S-ltd/P-no/H-no
Spanish

Full gourmet breakfast
Comp. wine at sunset
Living room, library
sailboats, bicycles
hot tub

*Excellent waterfront location for unwinding, bicycling and enjoying the pleasures of the Chesapeake Bay (tide water area).*

## MIDDLEBURG

**Welbourne**
22314 Welbourne Farm Ln,
  20117
540-687-3201
Nat & Sherry Morison
All year

$$$-B&B
10 rooms, 10 pb
C-yes/S-yes/P-yes/H-ltd
French

Full breakfast
Complimentary wine
Piano
sitting room

*Antebellum home occupied by the same family for seven generations. In heart of Virginia's fox-hunting country. Virginia historic landmark. "Faded elegance."*

## MIDDLETOWN

**Wayside Inn, The**
7783 Main St., 22645
540-869-1797 Fax: 540-869-6038
Mr. Jan Garis
All year

$$$-EP
22 rooms, 22 pb
Most CC, *Rated*, •
C-yes/S-yes/P-no/H-yes

Full breakfast
Lunch, dinner appetizers
Bar serv., entertainment
sitting room, piano
retreat facilities

*In Shenandoah Valley, offering Civil War history with southern cooking. Rooms are decorated in different historic styles with antiques for sale.* **Restaurant discount.**

## MILLBORO

**Fort Lewis Lodge**
HCR 3, Box 21A,   24460
540-925-2314 Fax: 540-925-2352
John and Caryl Cowden
April–October

$$$$-MAP
15 rooms, 11 pb
MC, Visa, *Rated*,
C-yes/S-ltd/P-no/H-no

Full breakfast, dinner
Bar service
Sitting room, bicycles
swimming hole at river
horse, golf nearby

*At the heart of 3200-acre mountain farm; hand-hewn log cabins. Complete privacy, homecooking, outdoor activities. Brings out Huck Finn in everybody. AAA rated three diamonds.*

## MOLLUSK

**Guesthouse on the Water**
Route 354, Box 70,   22517
804-462-5995
Pam & Walt Smith
All year

$$$-B&B
6 rooms, 6 pb
C-ltd/S-ltd/P-no

Continental breakfast
Kitchens
Sitting room, library
veranda, pool, beach
docks, boating, bicycles

*Waterfront guesthouses on 13 acres. Privacy & tranquillity w/pool, dock, private beach. Beautiful sunsets & birdwatcher's paradise. Fishing & crabbing.*

## MOUNT JACKSON

**Widow Kip's Country Inn**
355 Orchard Dr.,   22842
540-477-2400   800-478-8714
Betty Luse
All year

$$-B&B
7 rooms, 7 pb
*Rated*, •
C-ltd/S-no/P-yes/H-ltd

Full breakfast
Complimentary sherry
Fireplaces, pool, golf
ski, battlefields, BBQ
caverns, bicycles

*1830 gracious colonial romantic getaway on 7 acres overlooking Shenandoah. Betty Luse innkeeper since 1991.* **Pay for 2 nights, stay for 3!, ltd.**

## NEW MARKET

**A Touch of Country**
9329 Congress St.,   22844
540-740-8030
Dawn Kasow & Jean
Schoellig
All year

$$-B&B
6 rooms, 6 pb
MC, Visa, •
C-ltd/S-ltd/P-no/H-no

Full breakfast
Comp. beverages
Sitting room with TV

*A comfortable 1870s restored home decorated with antiques, collectibles, and a country flavor. Located in the beautiful Shenandoah Valley.*

## NORFOLK

**Page House Inn**
323 Fairfax Ave.,   23507
804-625-5033 Fax: 804-623-9451
800-599-7659
Stephanie & Ezio
DiBelardino
All year

$$$-B&B
6 rooms, 6 pb
Visa, MC, *Rated*, •
C-ltd/S-no/P-no/H-no
Italian

Continental plus bkfst.
Afternoon tea, snacks
In-room telephone & TV
fax service
refrigerator in rooms

*Award-winning restoration. Elegantly appointed. "Year's best inn buy," Country Inns Magazine. .What's best in Norfolk," Travel Holiday.* **10% disc't w/2 night stay.**

## NORTH GARDEN

**Inn at the Crossroads, The**
5010 Plank Rd.,   22959
804-979-6452
John & Maureen Deis
All year

$$$-B&B
6 rooms, 6 pb
Visa, MC, *Rated*, •
C-ltd/S-no/P-no/H-no

Full breakfast
Aftn. tea, snacks
Sitting room, library

*Historic inn on 4 acres with panormic mountain views only 9 miles from Charlottesville. Country breakfast served in the Keeping Room.*

## ORANGE

**Hidden Inn**
249 Caroline St.,  22960
540-672-3625 Fax: 540-672-5029
Barbara & Ray Lonick
All year

$$$-B&B
10 rooms, 10 pb
MC, Visa, *Rated*, •
C-ltd/S-no/P-no/H-no

Full country breakfast
Afternoon tea
Dinner by reservation
sitting room, jacuzzi
A/C, fireplaces

*Comfortably furnished country inn tucked away in rural community. Convenient to D.C., Charlottesville, Blue Ridge Mountains. Super breakfasts!*

## PETERSBURG

**Mayfield Inn**
P.O. Box 2265,  23804
3348 W. Washington St.
804-861-6775 Fax: 804-863-1971
800-538-2381
Cherry Turner
All year

$$-B&B
4 rooms, 4 pb
MC, Visa, •
C-yes/S-ltd/P-no/H-no

Full breakfast
Afternoon tea
Two sitting rooms
swimming pool, weddings
large suite available

*A 1750 house, completely and very beautifully restored, set on four tranquil acres. Close to historic Petersburg and battlefields.* **10% off for stay of over 2 days.**

## PROVIDENCE FORGE

**Jasmine Plantation B&B**
4500 N. Courthouse,  23140
804-966-9836 Fax: 804-966-5679
800-NEW-KENT
Joyce & Howard Vogt
All year

$$-B&B
6 rooms, 5 pb
Visa, MC, AmEx, •
C-ltd/S-no/P-no/H-no

Full breakfast
Snacks
Sitting room, common
areas, bird watching
walking trails

*Country at its best! Full "skip-lunch" country breakfast. Antique filled 1750s home on 47 acres. Convenient I-64 Williamsburg James River Plantations.* **Comp. dessert at local restaurants.**

## PULASKI

**Count Pulaski B&B &
Garden**
821 N. Jefferson Ave.,  24301
  800-980-1163
Flo Stevenson
All year

$$-B&B
3 rooms, 3 pb
Visa, MC, *Rated*, •
C-ltd/S-no/P-no/H-no

Full breakfast
Guest beverage center
Hiking/biking trail
indoor bike storage

*Gracious historic home in quiet neighborhood. Easy to find. King/queen beds, private baths, ceiling fans, A/C, fireplaces. Family antiques & collections from living & traveling abroad.*

## ROCKVILLE

**Woodlawn B&B**
2211 Wiltshire Rd.,  23146
804-749-3373
M. Ann Nuckols    All year

$$-B&B
2 rooms, 2 pb
C-ltd/S-no/P-no/H-no

Full breakfast
Sitting room, bikes
screened porch
open porch

*Circa 1813 farmhouse surrounded by 40 acres in a rural setting and furnished with antiques; bedrooms with fireplaces have double beds. Located 20 miles west of Richmond.*

## SCOTTSVILLE

**Chester B&B**
243 James River Rd.,  24590
804-286-3960
Jean & Craig Stratton
All year

$$$-B&B
5 rooms, 5 pb
Visa, MC, *Rated*, •
C-ltd/S-no/P-no/H-no

Full breakfast
Dinner available
Aftn. tea, comp. wine
sitting room, library
bicycles, weddings

*Historic 1847 Greek Revival Mansion; 7 acres of tree-shaded lawns; furnished with antiques and Orientals. Featured on 1991 Historic Virginia Garden Week.*

SCOTTSVILLE ———————————————

**High Meadows Inn**
Route 4, Box 6,  24590
High Meadows Lane
804-286-2218 Fax: 804-286-2124
800-232-1832
Peter Sushka, Mary Jae
Abbitt   All year

$$$-B&B/MAP
12 rooms, 12 pb
*Rated*,  •
C-yes/S-ltd/P-ltd/H-no
French

Full breakfast
Candlelight dining
Nightly winetasting
library, hot tub, pond
gazebo, bikes, vineyard

*Enchanting historical landmark south of Charlottesville. Large, tastefully appointed rooms; fireplaces; period antiques. Private 50 acres for walking & picnics. **3rd night 50%.***

SMITH MOUNTAIN LAKE ———————————————

**Manor at Taylor's Store**
Route 1, Box 533,  24184
540-721-3951 Fax: 540-724-5243
800-722-9984
Lee & Mary Lynn Tucker
All year

$$$-B&B
10 rooms, 8 pb
MC, Visa *Rated*,  •
C-ltd/S-no/P-no/H-ltd

Full breakfast
Lunch & Dinner (fee)
Snacks, sitting room
library, hot tubs, pool
fishing, canoeing

*Historic 120 acre estate, luxurious accommodations in either elegant Manor House or hand-hewn log home. A recreational paradise!*

SMITHFIELD ———————————————

**Isle of Wight Inn**
1607 S. Church St.,  23430
757-357-3176  800-357-3245
Bob/Sylvia Harts, J. Madrigal
All year

$$-B&B
12 rooms, 12 pb
AmEx, MC, Visa,
*Rated*,  •
C-yes/S-ltd/P-no/H-yes

Full breakfast
Snacks, tea, soft drinks
Sitting room
jacuzzi, walking tour
golf and fishing nearby

*Luxurious inn & antique shop. Famous for Smithfield hams & homes dating from 1750. Saint Lukes church, 1632. Near Colonial Williamsburg & Jamestown. **50% off 3rd night, ltd***

SPERRYVILLE ———————————————

**Apple Hill Farm B&B**
117 Old Hollow Rd.,  22740
540-987-9454 Fax: 540-987-3139
800-326-4583
Wayne & Dot Waller
All year

$$$-B&B
4 rooms, 4 pb
•
C-ltd/S-ltd/P-no/H-no

Gourmet full breakfast
Lunch baskets, ask
Bar service, snacks
Sitting room
fireplaces

*Peaceful setting, over 20 acres of woods, pastures, river frontage, secluded. Balconies w/ views, hiking, horseback riding, wineries, antiquing. **15% off 3rd. night, ask.***

**Conyers House Inn & Stable**
3131 Slate Mills Rd.,  22740
540-987-8025 Fax: 540-987-8709
Sandra & Norman Brown
All year

$$$-B&B
9 rooms, 9 pb
*Rated*,  •
C-ltd/S-ltd/P-ltd/H-ltd
Fr., Ger., It., Arabic

Hearty gourmet breakfast
Comp. wine & cake
Candlelight dinner
fireplaces, wood stoves
piano, porches, horses

*18th-century former country store graciously furnished with antiques. Hiking, foxhunting & trail rides. Candlelit dinner by reservation. **Free "tacking up" lesson with horses.***

STAUNTON ———————————————

**Frederick House**
P.O. Box 1387,  24401
28 N. New St., 24401
540-885-4220  800-334-5575
Joe & Evy Harman
All year

$$-B&B
14 rooms, 14 pb
Most CC, *Rated*,  •
C-yes/S-no/P-no/H-no

Full breakfast
Vegetarian bkfst. avail.
Sitting room, library
conference facilities
Nat'l Reg. listing

*The oldest city west of the Blue Ridge Mountains of Virginia, historic Staunton is Woodrow Wilson birthplace. Shops and restaurants. Extended stays welcome.*

*The Sampson Eagon Inn, Staunton, VA*

## STAUNTON

**Sampson Eagon Inn, The**
238 East Beverley St.,  24401
540-886-8200
Fax: 540-886-8200
800-597-9722
Frank & Laura Mattingly
All year

$$$-B&B
5 rooms, 5 pb
Visa, MC, AmEx,
*Rated*,  •
C-ltd/S-ltd/P-no/H-ltd

Full breakfast
Comp. snacks/beverages
Sitting area with TV/VCR
video library, In-room
phones, porch with swing

*An elegant alternative in-town historic lodging. Spacious rooms, antiques, complemented by gracious personal service. Walk to restaurants.*

**Thornrose House-Gypsy Hill**
531 Thornrose Ave.,  24401
540-885-7026 Fax: 540-885-6458
800-861-4338
Suzanne & Otis Huston
All year

$$-B&B
5 rooms, 5 pb
*Rated*,
C-ltd/S-ltd/P-no/H-no

Full breakfast
Afternoon tea
Sitting room
tennis, golf across St.
swimming pool across St.

*Stately Georgian residence with A/C and private baths in all guestrooms. In historic Victorian town. Adjacent 300 acre park offers golf, tennis swimming.*

## STEELE'S TAVERN

**Sugar Tree Inn**
Highway 56,  24476
540-377-2197 Fax: 540-377-6776
800-377-2197
Sarah & Hal Davis
April 1-Dec 1

$$$-B&B
11 rooms, 11 pb
Most CC *Rated*,  •
C-ltd/S-ltd/P-no/H-yes

Full breakfast
Dinner by resv., pub
Sitting room, biking
library, porches, rocker
creek & waterfall

*Mountain inn nestled in a forest just off the Blue Ridge Parkway. Fireplaces in every room; some whirlpools, VCRs. Premium suites have A/C. Forty-mile sunset from front porch rockers.*

SYRIA ────────────

**Graves' Mountain Lodge**
Rte. 670,   22743
540-923-4231  Fax: 540-923-4312
Jim & Rachel Graves
Spring, Summer & Fall

$$-AP
47 rooms,
C-yes/S-ltd/P-ltd

Full breakfast
Lunch, dinner included
Tennis court
swimming pool, fishing
hiking, horseback riding

*Rustic, charming inn located in shadow of Blue Ridge Mtns. 3 abundant meals/day in Lodge. Activities range from fishing to horseback riding to relaxing. Dogwood cottage sleeps up to 9.*

TREVILIANS ────────────

**Prospect Hill Plantation**
2887 Poindexter Rd.,  23093
540-967-0844  Fax: 540-967-0102
800-277-0844
The Sheehan Family
All year

$$$$-B&B/MAP
13 rooms, 13 pb
MC, Visa, *Rated*, •
C-ltd/S-yes/P-no/H-no

Full breakfast in bed
Dinner, afternoon tea
Comp. wine or cider
library, fireplaces
jacuzzi, pool

*1732 plantation. 5 bedrooms w/fireplaces in manor house & 8 w/fireplaces in outlying dependencies. 15 miles to Charlottesville. Continental dining, peace & quiet countryside.*

TROUTVILLE ────────────

**WoodsEdge Guest Cottage**
2800 Ridge Trail,  24175
540-473-2992
Ferrel & Fred Phillips
All year

$$-B&B
1 rooms, 1 pb
MC, Visa,
C-yes/S-no/P-no/H-no

Continental plus bkfst.
Housekeeping cottage
full kitchen, sitt. rm.
accommodates families

*On fourteen private acres overlooking the Alleghany Mountains. Delightfully furnished with antiques. Porch w/rocking chairs. Scenic golf course adjacent. **3rd night 50% off.***

WARM SPRINGS ────────────

**Anderson Cottage B&B**
Old Germantown Rd.,   24484
540-839-2975
Jean Randolph Bruns
Mar-Nov

$$-B&B
5 rooms, 4 pb
•
C-ltd/S-no/P-ltd/H-no

Full breakfast
Sitting room, library
parlors, porches, yard
croquet, badminton

*Rambling old home in village. Walk to Warm Springs pools. Near Garth Newel Chamber Music Center. Restaurants nearby. Kitchen cottages available year-round.*

WARRENTON ────────────

**Black Horse Inn, The**
8393 Meetze Rd.,  20187
540-349-4020  Fax: 540-349-4242
800-297-2630
Lynn Pirozzoli
All year

$$$-B&B
7 rooms, 7 pb
Visa, MC, AmEx,
C-ltd/S-ltd/P-no/H-yes

Full breakfast
Aftn. tea, snacks
Comp. wine, bar service
sitting room, library
bikes, rooms w/Jacuzzis

*Historic estate in the heart of hunt country, 45 minutes from Washington D.C. Elegant rooms, scenic views, fireplaces, Jacuzzis, bountiful breakfasts and teas.*

WASHINGTON ────────────

**Caledonia Farm - 1812**
47 Dearing Rd.,  22627
540-675-3693  Fax: 540-675-3693
800-BNB-1812
Phil Irwin
All year

$$$-B&B
4 rooms, 2 pb
Most CC, •
C-ltd/S-ltd/P-no/H-no
German, Danish

Full breakfast from menu
Aftn. tea, snacks, wine
Sitting room, library
bikes, hot tub
porch views

*National Register stone home/cattle farm adjacent to Shenandoah National Park mountains. Skyline Drive views, history, recreation, hospitality, fireplaces, spa, hayride. **Ask for midweek incentives.***

## WASHINGTON

| **Fairlea Farm B&B** | $$-B&B | Hearty country breakfast |
|---|---|---|
| P.O. Box 124, 22747 | 4 rooms, 4 pb | Complimentary drinks |
| 636 Mt. Salem Ave. | • | Sitting room w/fireplace |
| 540-675-3679 Fax: 540-675-1064 | C-ltd/S-ltd/P-no/H-no | hiking, horses, shops |
| Walter and Susan Longyear | French | near Civil War battlflds |
| All year | | |

*Spectacular mountain views, a 5-min. stroll to The Inn at Little Washington. Warm hospitality & sumptuous breakfast in fieldstone manor house.* **2nd night, 50% off, midweek.**

| **Foster-Harris House, The** | $$$-B&B | Full breakfast |
|---|---|---|
| P.O. Box 333, 22747 | 4 rooms, 4 pb | Comp. sweets & beverages |
| 189 Main St. | Visa, MC, *Rated*, • | Sitting room, queen beds |
| 540-675-3757 800-666-0153 | C-ltd/S-no/P-no/H-no | fireplace stove |
| Phyllis Marriott All year | | whirlpool, sunroom |

*Restored Victorian (circa 1900) house in historic "Little" Washington, Virginia. Antiques, fresh flowers, mountain views, 3 blocks from 5-star restaurant.* **3rd nite $10.00 off.**

| **Gay Street Inn** | $$$-B&B | Full breakfast |
|---|---|---|
| P.O. Box 237, 22747 | 4 rooms, 4 pb | Picnic lunch, aftn. tea |
| Gay Street | MC, Visa, AmEx, | Comp. drinks & snacks |
| 540-675-3288 | *Rated*, • | sitting room, library |
| Donna Dalton & Robin Kevis | C-yes/S-ltd/P-yes/H-yes | 1 suite w/kitchen, bath |
| All year | German | |

*In Blue Ridge Mtns.—historic country town. 1850s farm house w/friendly, relaxing atmosphere. Furnished w/period New England furniture. Bedroom w/fireplace.* **25% off 2nd night, restrictions.**

| **Heritage House B&B** | $$$$-B&B | Full gourmet breakfast |
|---|---|---|
| P.O. Box 427, 22747 | 4 rooms, 4 pb | Comp. beverages & snacks |
| 291 Main St. | MC, Visa, *Rated*, • | Parlor with fireplace |
| 540-675-3207 | C-ltd/S-no/P-no/H-yes | walk to restaurant |
| Jean Scott All year | | "British Room" |

*AAA 3-Diamond 1837 house in quaint historic village. Craft shops, art galleries and finest dining; nearby golf, tennis, biking, horses, hiking and vineyards.*

## WHITE POST

| **L'Auberge Provencale** | $$$$-B&B | Full gourmet breakfast |
|---|---|---|
| P.O. Box 119, 22663 | 10 rooms, 10 pb | Dinner, bar service |
| Rt.1, Box 203, Boyce | Most CC, *Rated*, • | Refreshments, flowers |
| 540-837-1375 Fax: 540-837-2004 | C-ltd/S-yes/P-no/H-no | library, sitting room |
| 800-638-1702 | French | bicycles, gardens |
| Alain & Celeste Borel | | |
| Exc. Jan—mid-Feb | | |

*Master chef from France presents nationally acclaimed cuisine. Extensive wine list. Elegant accommodations with fireplaces, private entrances.* **Special goodies in room.**

## WILLIAMSBURG

| **Applewood Colonial B&B** | $$$-B&B | Full breakfast |
|---|---|---|
| 605 Richmond Rd., 23185 | 4 rooms, 4 pb | Afternoon refreshments |
| 575-229-0205 Fax: 757-229-9405 | MC, Visa, *Rated*, • | Sitting room |
| 800-899-2753 | C-yes | fireplaces |
| Jan Brown | | 2 rooms with extra beds |
| All year | | |

*Elegant and comfortable colonial decor. Fireplaces, antiques, apple collection. Walking distance to colonial Williamsburg & College of William & Mary. Parties, reunions, weddings (3 churches nearby).*

*Colonial Capital B&B, Williamsburg, VA*

## WILLIAMSBURG

**Candlewick B&B**
800 Jamestown Rd., 23185
757-253-8693  800-418-4949
Mary & Bernie Peters
All year

$$$-B&B
3 rooms, 3 pb
Visa, MC, •
C-yes/S-no/P-no/H-no
German

Full breakfast
Afternoon tea, snacks
Sitting room
bicycles

*Candlewick compliments colonial Williambsurg w/its wonderful antiques, king & queen canopy beds & private baths. Come down in the morning to the keeping room for a wonderful candlelit breakfast.*

---

**Cedars B&B, The**
616 Jamestown Rd., 23185
757-229-3591  800-296-3591
Carol, Jim & Brona Malecha
All year

$$$-B&B
9 rooms, 9 pb
Visa, MC, *Rated*, •
C-yes/S-no/P-no/H-no

Full gourmet breakfast
Afternoon tea
Fireplaces in parlor and
cottage, off st. parking
A/C, cottage w/2 suites

*Brick Georgian colonial house across the street from William & Mary; 10 min. walk to colonial Williamsburg. Antiques and canopy beds.* **Off season rates, Jan 2–Mid March.**

---

**Colonial Capital B&B**
501 Richmond Rd., 23185
757-229-0233  Fax: 757-253-7667
800-776-0570
Barbara & Phil Craig
All year

$$$-B&B
5 rooms, 5 pb
Most CC, *Rated*, •
C-ltd/S-ltd/P-no/H-no

Full gourmet breakfast
Afternoon tea & wine
Parlor, books, solarium
games, videos, bicycles
free on premise parking

*Antique-furnished Colonial Revival (c.1926) only three blocks from Historic Area. Cozy canopied beds & remote control ceiling fans. Colonial garden. Business fac. available.*

---

**Colonial Gardens B&B**
1109 Jamestown Rd., 23185
757-220-8087  Fax: 757-253-1495
800-886-9715
Scottie & Wilmot Phillips
All year

$$$-B&B
3 rooms, 3 pb
Visa, MC, *Rated*,
S-no/P-no/H-no

Full breakfast
Afternoon teas
Sitting room, library
attention to detail
suites accom. guests

*Country estate setting. In-town location. Williamsburg elegance. Beautifully decorated w/ heirloom antiques. Spacious suites. Plantation breakfast.* **Mid-winter discounts, ask.**

WILLIAMSBURG ─────────────────────────────

**For Cant Hill Guest Home**
4 Canterbury Ln., 23185
757-229-6623
Martha & Hugh Easler
All year

$$-B&B
2 rooms, 2 pb
Visa, MC, •
C-ltd/S-no/P-no/H-no
Spanish, some German

Continental plus bkfst.
Restaurant
Candy in rooms
bikes, tennis court

*City hideaway/furnished in antiques and tradition. Bountiful continental breakfast. Short distance to historic Williamsburg and college. Visitor assistance offered. **Wine for honeymoon/anniversary.***

**Fox & Grape B&B**
701 Monumental Ave., 23185
804-229-6914 800-292-3699
Pat & Bob Orendorff
All year

$$$-B&B
4 rooms, 4 pb
Visa, MC. Disc., •
C-yes/S-no/P-no/H-no

Continental plus bkfst.
Sitting room, rooms have
antiques, counted cross
stitch, quilts, folk art

*This lovely two story colonial with wrap-around porch with rockers and a swing, a perfect place to enjoy your favorite book or plan your days activities*

**Governor's Trace B&B**
303 Capitol Landing Rd.,
23185
757-229-7552 800-303-7552
Sue & Dick Lake
All year

$$$-B&B
3 rooms, 3 pb
Visa, MC, *Rated*, •
S-no/P-no/H-no

Full breakfast
Sitting room, library
tennis/swimming nearby
2 fireplaces

*"Closest inn to the historic district ... vies for the most romantic (in Williamsburg)" - Washington Post. Linger over a candlelit breakfast in the privacy of your own room.*

**Homestay B&B, The**
517 Richmond Rd., 23185
804-229-7468 800-836-7468
Barbara & Jim Thomassen
All year

$$$-B&B
3 rooms, 3 pb
Visa, MC, *Rated*, •
C-ltd/S-no/P-no/H-no

Full breakfast
Sitting room
bicycles

*Cozy and convenient — lovely colonial revival home furnished with turn-of-the century family antiques and country charm. Near Historic Area.*

**Indian Springs B&B**
330 Indian Springs Rd.,
23185
757-220-0726 800-262-9165
Kelly & Paul Supplee
All year

$$$-B&B
4 rooms, 4 pb
MC, Visa, *Rated*, •
C-yes/S-no/P-no/H-yes

Full breakfast
Afternoon tea, snacks
Restaurant nearby
sitting room, library
game room, veranda

*Short walk to historic district, William & Mary College. Fam.-operated restaurant nearby. Seasonal snack served in Carriage House. Cottage & suites avail. **10% off 5+ nights.***

**Legacy of Williamsburg B&B**
930 Jamestown Rd., 23185
804-220-0524 Fax: 804-220-2211
800-962-4722
Mary Ann Gist
All year

$$$-B&B
4 rooms, 4 pb
MC, Visa, *Rated*,
C-ltd/S-no

Full breakfast
Billiards, phones, TV
Six fireplaces, library
18th Century antiques

*Voted best 18th Century B&B-style inn in Williamsburg. Romantic, quaint. Tall poster canopy beds. It will be the highlight of your vacation. The legacy. Highest ratings by AAA.*

WILLIAMSBURG

**Liberty Rose B&B**
1022 Jamestown Rd.,   23185
757-253-1260  800-545-1825
Brad & Sandi Hirz
All year

$$$-B&B
4 rooms, 4 pb
MC, Visa, *Rated*,  •
C-ltd

Full breakfast
Comp. bev., chocolates
Sitting room, gift shop
Suite w/many amenities
TVs, VCRs, movies in rms

*"Williamsburg's most romantic B&B." Charming home renovated in perfect detail. Courtyards, gardens, an acre of magnificent trees. First choice for honeymooners.*

---

**Marl Inn B&B**
P.O. Box 572,   23690
220 Church St.
757-898-3859 Fax: 757-898-3587
800-799-6207
Eugene C. Marlin    All year

$$$-B&B
4 rooms, 4 pb
Visa, MC, *Rated*,  •
C-ltd/S-no/P-ltd/H-no

Continental plus bkfst.
Sitting room, library
bicycles

*Marl Inn is located in the historic district of the restored town. Bicycles with helmets are offered guests to visit battleground, museums, and Revolutionary reception centers.*

---

**Newport House B&B**
710 South Henry St.,   23185
757-229-1775 Fax: 757-229-6408
John & Cathy Millar
All year

$$$-B&B
2 rooms, 2 pb
*Rated*,  •
C-yes/S-no/P-no/H-no
French

Full breakfast
Sitting room
Library, harpischord
Ballroom for receptions

*Designed in 1756. Completely furnished in period. 5-minute walk from historic area. Colonial dancing every Tuesday evening. VA B&B Assoc. and ABBA member.*

---

**Piney Grove at Southall**
P.O. Box 1359,   23187
16920 Southall Plantation
804-829-2480 Fax: 804-829-2480
The Gordineer Family
All year

$$$-B&B
4 rooms, 4 pb
*Rated*,  •
C-yes/S-ltd/P-no/H-no
German

Plantation breakfast
Picnic lunches (request)
Comp. wine, mint juleps
sitting room, library
swimming pool

*Elegant accommodations and gracious hospitality at secluded National Registry property located just west of Williamsburg among the James River Plantations.*

---

**Primrose Cottage B&B**
706 Richmond Rd.,   23185
757-229-6421  Fax: 757-259-0717
800-522-1901
Inge Curtis
All year

$$$-B&B
4 rooms, 4 pb
Visa, MC, *Rated*,  •
C-ltd/S-no/P-no/H-no
German

Full breakfast
Sitting room
garden
cable TV

*Cozy Cape Cod style home decorated with antiques and family treasures. Short walk to colonial Williamsburg. Award-winning garden. Elegant breakfast. **Restaurant discounts.***

---

**Williamsburg Manor B&B**
600 Richmond Rd.,   23185
757-220-8011 Fax: 757-220-0245
800-422-8011
Laura Reeves
All year

$$-B&B
5 rooms, 5 pb
*Rated*,  •
C-ltd/S-no/P-no/H-no

Full breakfast
Dinner by reservation
Sitting room, library
fireplace, TV, A/C
catering/floral service

*1927 restored Georgian brick colonial. Walk to historic area. Award-winning chef; 5-course dinner featuring regional Virginia cuisine ($35 pp). Near College of Wm. & Mary.*

| | | |
|---|---|---|
| **Williamsburg Sampler B&B** | $$$-B&B | Full "Skip-lunch" bkfst. |
| 922 Jamestown Rd., 23185 | 4 rooms, 4 pb | 18th Cty. carriage house |
| 575-253-0398 Fax: 757-253-2669 | *Rated*, • | Antiques/pewter/samplers |
| 800-722-1169 | C-ltd/S-no/P-no/H-no | suites/fireplaces/Tavern |
| Helen & Ike Sisane   All year | | |

*Williamsburg's finest plantation style colonial home. Richly furnished. Guests have included descendants of Charles Dickens, Louisa May Alcott & John Quincy Adams. **Discount to attractions/restaurants.***

## WINTERGREEN

| | | |
|---|---|---|
| **Trillium House** | $$$-B&B | Full breakfast |
| P.O. Box 280/Nellysford, | 12 rooms, 12 pb | Afternoon tea, bar |
| Wintergreen Dr., 22958 | MC, Visa, *Rated*, • | Dinner Fri & Sat |
| 804-325-9126 Fax: 804-325-1099 | C-ltd/S-ltd/P-no/H-yes | sitting room, library |
| 800-325-9126 | | near tennis, pool, golf |
| Betty & Ed Dinwiddie | | |
| All year | | |

*One of the newer country inns, built in '83 to meet today's standards while keeping yesterday's charm. Mountain country with trees & birds can be seen from breakfast table.*

## WOODSTOCK

| | | |
|---|---|---|
| **Azalea House B&B** | $$-B&B | Full breakfast |
| 551 S. Main St., 22664 | 4 rooms, 4 pb | Refreshments |
| 540-459-3500 | AmEx, MC, Visa, | Sitting room |
| Margaret & Price McDonald | C-ltd/S-no/P-no/H-no | parlor, TV |
| All year | | |

*Attractive, comfortable rooms with mountain viewing. Located in the rolling hills of the Shenandoah Valley. Nearby restaurants, vineyards, caverns, hiking. **3rd night & restaurant discounts.***

| | | |
|---|---|---|
| **Inn at Narrow Passage** | $$$-B&B | Full breakfast |
| P.O. Box 608, 22664 | 12 rooms, 12 pb | Sitting room, conf. fac. |
| U.S.11 South | MC, Visa, *Rated*, • | fireplace, swimming |
| 540-459-8000 Fax: 540-459-8001 | C-ltd/S-ltd/P-no/H-yes | fishing, rafting |
| 800-459-8002 | | |
| Ellen & Ed Markel, Jr. | | |
| All year | | |

*Historic 1740 log inn on the Shenandoah River. Fireplaces, colonial charm, close to vineyards. Civil War sites, hiking, fishing and caverns. AAA 3 diamond rating.*

## YORKTOWN

| | | |
|---|---|---|
| **York River Inn B&B** | $$$-B&B | Full breakfast |
| 209 Ambler St., 23690 | 3 rooms, 3 pb | Aftn. tea, snacks |
| 757-887-8800  800-884-7003 | Visa, MC, | Comp. wine, bar service |
| William W. Cole | C-ltd/S-no/P-no/H-no | sitting room, library |
| All year | | |

*Riverfront location in historic town, outstanding accommodations & amenities, & sumptuous breakfast combine with well traveled innkeepers for a delightful visit.*

# More Inns ...

| | |
|---|---|
| Abingdon | Cabin on the River, P.O. Box 1202, 24210 |
| Abingdon | Lone Willow Inn, 337 Valley St., 24210 |
| Abingdon | Martha Washington Inn, 150 W. Main St., 24210,  800-533-1014 |
| Abingdon | Summerfield Inn, 101 E. Valley St., 24210,  703-628-5905 |

| | |
|---|---|
| Afton | Looking Glass House, Route 3 Box 183, 22920, 703-456-6844 |
| Alberta | Englewood, RR 1, Box 141, 23821, 804-949-0111 |
| Aldie | Little River Inn, P.O. Box 116, Rt. 50, 22001, 703-327-6742 |
| Alexandria | Black Shutter Inn, 6204 Redwood Ln., 22310 |
| Alexandria | Morrison House, 116 S. Alfred St., 22314, 703-838-8000 |
| Alta Vista | Castle to Country House, 1010 Main St., 24517 |
| Amherst | Fairview B&B, RR 4 Box 117, 24521 |
| Amissville | Bunree, P.O. Box 53, 22002, 703-937-4133 |
| Arlington | Bluestone Inn, 2101 Crystal Plaza #246, 22202 |
| Arlington | Crystal B&B, 2620 S. Fern St., 22202, 703-548-7652 |
| Arlington | Memory House, 6404 N. Washington Blvd, 22205, 703-534-4607 |
| Bedford | Peaks of Otter Lodge, P.O. Box 489, 24523, 703-586-1081 |
| Bentonville | Gooney Manor, 5865 Gooney Manor Loop, 22610 |
| Blacksburg | Brush Mountain Inn B&B, 3030 Mt. Tabor Rd., 24060, 540-951-7530 |
| Blacksburg | Sycamore Tree B&B, P.O. Box 10937, 24062, 703-381-1597 |
| Blacksburg | Twin Porches B&B, 318 Clay St. SW, 24060 |
| Blackstone | Epes House B&B, 210 College Ave., 23824 |
| Bland | Willow Bend Farm B&B, RR 1, Box 235, 24315, 703-688-3719 |
| Boston | Thistle Hill B&B Inn, 5541 Sperryville Pike, 22713, 540-987-9142 |
| Bowling Green | Old Mansion B&B, Box 845, 22427 |
| Bristol | Glencarin Manor, 224 Old Abingdon Hwy., 24201 |
| Broadnox | Sherwood Manor Inn, Box 236 Pleasant Grove, 23920 |
| Buchanan | Berkley House, The, Route 2, Box 220A, 24066, 703-254-2548 |
| Burkeville | Hyde Park Farm, Route 2, Box 38, 23922, 804-645-8431 |
| Cape Charles | Cape Charles House, 645 Tazwell Ave., 23310 |
| Cape Charles | Nottingham Ridge, 28184 Nottingham Ridge, 23310, 804-331-1010 |
| Cape Charles | Picketts Harbor, Box 87AA, 23310, 804-331-2212 |
| Capron | Sandy Hill Farm B&B, 11307 Rivers Mill Rd., 23829, 804-658-4381 |
| Charles City | Belle Air Plantation, 11800 John Tyler Hghwy., 23030, 804-829-2431 |
| Charles City | Berkeley Plantation, 12602 Harrison Landing, 23030, 804-829-6018 |
| Charles City | Coach House Tavern, 12602 Harrison Landing, 23030 |
| Charles City | Evelynton Plantation, 6701 John Tyler Highway, 23030, 804-829-5075 |
| Charles City | Indian Fields Tavern, 9220 John Tyler Highway, 23030, 804-829-5004 |
| Charles City | Piney Grove at Southall's, 16920 Southall Plant., 23030, 804-829-2480 |
| Charles City | Red Hill, 7500 John Tyler M. Hwy., 23030, 804-829-6045 |
| Charles City | Sherwood Forest Plantation, 14501 John Tyler Hghwy., 23030, 804-829-5377 |
| Charles City | Shirley Plantation, 501 Shirley Plantation, 23030, 804-829-5121 |
| Charles City | Westover, 7000 Westover Rd., 23030, 804-829-2882 |
| Charlottesville | 1817 Antique Inn, 1211 W. Main St., 22903, 804-979-7353 |
| Charlottesville | Carrsbrook, 313 Goucester Rd., 22901 |
| Charlottesville | Guesthouses B&B Inc., P.O. Box 5737, 22905, 804-979-7264 |
| Charlottesville | Inn at the Crossroads, The, RR 692, North Garden, 22959, 804-979-6452 |
| Charlottesville | Oxbridge Inn, 316—14th St. NW, 22903 |
| Charlottesville | Slave Quarters, 611 Preston Place, 22903, 804-979-7264 |
| Chatham | House of Laird B&B, P.O. Box 1131, 24531, 804-432-2523 |
| Chilhowie | Clarkcrest B&B, Star Route Box 60, 24319 |
| Chincoteague | Island Manor House, 4160 Main St., 23336, 804-336-5436 |
| Chincoteague | Main Street House, P.O. Box 126, 23336, 804-336-6030 |
| Chincoteague | Victorian Inn, 6185 Clark St., 23336, 804-336-1161 |
| Chincoteague | Year of the Horse Inn, 3583 Main St., 23336, 804-336-3221 |
| Christiansburg | Evergreen Bell-Capozzi, 201 G Main St., 24073 |
| Christiansburg | Oaks, The, 311 E. Main St., 24073, 703-381-1500 |
| Churchville | Buckhorn Inn, E Star Route, Box 139, 24421, 703-337-6900 |
| Clarksville | Kinderton Manor, RR 1, Box 19A, 23927, 804-374-4439 |
| Clarksville | Noreen's Nest, P.O. Box 356, 23927, 804-374-0603 |
| Clifton Forge | Firmstone Manor B&B, RR 1, Box 257, 24422, 703-862-0892 |
| Columbia | Upper Byrd Farm B&B, 6452 River Rd. W., 23038, 804-842-2240 |
| Culpeper | Hazel River Inn, 11227 Eggbornsville Rd., 22701 |
| Dabneys | Bare Castle Farm B&B, Box 122A, 23102 |
| Daleville | Baileywick Farm B&B, 1250 Roanoke Rd., 24083, 703-992-2022 |
| Deltaville | River Place-at-Deltaville, P.O. Box 616, 23043 |
| Draper | Claytor Lake Homestead Inn, P.O. Box 7, 24324, 703-980-6777 |
| Dublin | Bell's B&B, P.O. Box 405, 24084, 800-437-0575 |
| Edinburg | Mary's Country Inn, Rt. 2, Box 4, 22824, 703-984-8286 |
| Emporia | Little's B&B, 105 Goodwyn St., 23847, 804-634-2590 |
| Exmore | Martha's Inn B&B, 12224 Lincoln Ave., 23350 |
| Farmville | Linden B&B, RR 3 Box 400, 23901 |
| Flint Hill | School House, The, P.O. Box 31, 22627, 703-675-3030 |
| Flint Hill | Stone House Hollow, P.O. Box 2090, 22627, 703-675-3279 |
| Floyd | Brookfield Inn, P.O. Box 341, 24091, 703-763-3363 |
| Fredericksburg | Kenmore Inn, The, 1200 Princess Anne St., 22401, 703-371-7622 |
| Fredericksburg | Mary Josephine Ball B&B, 1203 Prince Edward St., 22401 |

*Inn at the Crossroads,
North Garden, VA*

| | |
|---|---|
| Fredericksburg | McGrath House, 225 Princess Anne St., 22401, 703-371-4363 |
| Fredericksburg | Richard Johnston Inn, 711 Caroline St., 22401, 540-899-7606 |
| Fredericksburg | Selby House B&B, 226 Princess Anne St., 22401, 540-373-7037 |
| Fredericksburg | Spooner House, The, 1300 Caroline St., 22401, 703-371-1267 |
| Ft. Belvoir | New Dawn Farm, 10100 Belvoir Dr., 22060, 703-799-1695 |
| Gloucester | Airville Plantation, RR 3, Box 1193, 23061, 800-296-5758 |
| Gordonsville | Norfields Farm B&B, RR 1, Box 477, 22942, 703-832-5939 |
| Gordonsville | Rabbit Run B&B, 305 N. High St., 22942 |
| Gordonsville | Rocklands, 17439 Rocklands Dr., 22942 |
| Goshen | Hummingbird Inn, The, P.O. Box 147, 24439, 540-997-9065 |
| Hardyville | Rivers Rise B&B, P.O. Box 18, 23070 |
| Harrisonburg | Inn at Keezletown Road,The, P.O. Box 341, 22801, 703-234-0644 |
| Harrisonburg | Joshua Wilton House Inn, 412 S. Main St., 22801, 703-434-4464 |
| Harrisonburg | Kingsway B&B, 3581 Singers Glen Rd., 22801, 703-867-9696 |
| Hillsville | Bray's Manor B&B Inn, P.O. Box 385, 24343, 703-728-7901 |
| Hot Springs | King's Victorian Inn, RR 2, Box 622, 24445, 703-839-3134 |
| Hot Springs | Vine Cottage Inn, P.O. Box 918, Rt. 220, 24445, 540-839-2422 |
| Independence | River View B&B, P.O. Box 686, 24348, 800-841-6628 |
| Lancaster | Inn at Levelfields, P.O. Box 216, 22503, 804-435-6887 |
| Leesburg | Fleetwood Farm B&B, Route 1, Box 306-A, 22075, 703-327-4325 |
| Leesburg | Laurel Brigade Inn, 20 W. Market St., 22075, 703-777-1010 |
| Leesburg | Leesburg Colonial Inn, 21 S. King St., 22075, 800-392-1332 |
| Leesburg | Norris House Inn, The, 108 Loudoun St. SW, 22075, 703-777-1806 |
| Lexington | Alexander-Withrow House, 3 W. Washington, 24450, 703-463-2044 |
| Lexington | Asherowe, 314 S. Jefferson St., 24450, 703-463-4219 |
| Lexington | Fassifern B&B, Route 5, Box 87, 24450, 703-463-1013 |
| Lexington | Historic Country Inns, 11 N. Main St., 24450, 703-463-2044 |
| Lexington | Inn at Union Run, Union Run Rd., 24450 |
| Lexington | Maple Hall, 11 No. Main St., 24450 |
| Lexington | McCampbell Inn, 11 N. Main St., 24450, 703-463-2044 |
| Lexington | Seven Hills Inn, 408 S. Main St., 24450 |
| Louisa | Ginger Hill B&B, Rt. 5 Box 33E, 23093 |
| Luray | Ruffner House Inn, The, Box 620, Route 4, 22835, 703-743-7855 |
| Luray | Spring Farm B&B, 13 Wallace Ave., 22835, 703-743-4701 |
| Lynchburg | Lynchburg Mansion Inn, 405 Madison St., 24504, 804-528-5400 |
| Madison | Olive Mill Bed & Breakfast, Route 231, Banco, 22711, 703-923-4664 |
| Madison | Shenandoah Springs, HC 6, Box 122, 22727, 703-923-4300 |
| Madison | Winridge B&B, RR 1, Box 362, 24572, 804-384-7220 |
| Manassas | Sunrise Hill Farm B&B, 5590 Old Farm Lane, 22110, 703-754-8309 |
| Mathews | Riverfront House B&B, P.O. Box 310, Rt. 14 E., 23109, 804-725-9975 |
| McGaheysville | Shenandoah Valley Farm, Route 1, Box 142, 22840, 703-289-5402 |
| McLean | Evans Farm Inn, 1696 Chain Bridge Rd. , 22101, 703-356-8000 |
| Meadows of Dan | Spangler B&B, Route 2, Box 108, 24120, 703-952-2454 |
| Middleburg | Middleburg Country Inn, P.O. Box 2065, 22117, 703-687-6082 |
| Middleburg | Poor House Farm B&B, P.O. Box 1316, 22117 |
| Middleburg | Red Fox Inn & Tavern, P.O. Box 385, 22117, 703-687-6301 |
| Mineral | Littlepage Inn, 15701 Monrovia Rd., 23117, 800-248-1803 |
| Monroe | St. Moor House, RR 1, Box 136, 24574, 804-929-8228 |
| Monterey | Highland Inn, P.O. Box 40, 24465, 540-468-2143 |
| Montross | Montross Inn & Restaurant, P.O. Box 908, 22520, 804-493-9097 |
| Mount Crawford | Pumpkin House Inn, Ltd., Route 2, Box 155, 22841, 703-434-6963 |
| Natural Bridge | Burger's Country Inn, RR 2, Box 564, 24578, 703-291-2464 |
| Nellysford | Acorn Inn, P.O. Box 431, 22958 |
| Nellysford | Mark Addy, The, RR 1 Box 375, 22958 |
| Nellysford | Meander Inn, The, P.O. Box 443, 22958, 804-361-1121 |
| Nellysford | Sunset Hill, Route 1, Box 375, 22958, 804-361-1101 |
| Nellysford | Upland Manor, Route 1, Box 375, 22958, 804-361-1101 |
| New Market | Cross Roads Inn B&B, 9222 John Sevier Rd., 22844 |
| New Market | Red Shutter Farmhouse, RR 1, Box 376, 22844, 703-740-4281 |
| Norfolk | B&B Larchmont, 1112 Buckingham Ave., 23508, 804-489-8449 |
| Occoquan | Rockledge Mansion 1758, 410 Mill St., 22125, 703-690-3377 |
| Onancock | 76 Market St. B&B, 76 Market St., 23417 |
| Onancock | Colonial Manor Inn, 84 Market St., 23417, 804-787-3521 |
| Onancock | Spinning Wheel B&B, The, 31 North St, 23417, 804-787-7311 |
| Orange | Holladay House, 155 W. Main, 22960, 800-358-4422 |
| Orange | Shadows B&B Inn, Route 1, Box 535, 22960, 703-672-5057 |
| Orange | Willow Grove Inn, 9478 James Madison Hwy, 22960, 800-949-1778 |
| Paeonian Spring | Cornerstone B&B, RR 1, Box 82C, 22129, 703-882-3722 |
| Palmyra | Danscot House, P.O. Box 157, 22963, 804-589-1977 |

*Williamsburg Sampler B&B, Williamsburg, VA*

| | |
|---|---|
| Pamplin | Sleepy Lamb B&B, HcR 1, Box 34, 23958,  804-248-6289 |
| Paris | Ashby Inn & Restaurant,  692 Federal St., 22130,  540-592-3900 |
| Penn Laird | Hearth n' Holly Inn,  RR 2 Box 325, 22846 |
| Petersburg | High Street Inn,  405 High St., 23803,  804-733-0505 |
| Port Hayward | Inn at Tab's Creek Landing,  P.O. Box 219, 23138,  804-725-5136 |
| Pratts | Colvin Hall B&B,  HC 3, Box 30G, 22731,  703-948-6211 |
| Pungoteague | Evergreen Inn,  P.O. Box 102, 23422,  804-442-3375 |
| Raphine | Oak Spring Farm & Vineyard,  RR 1, Box 356, 24472,  703-377-2398 |
| Reedville | Cedar Grove B&B Inn,  Rt. 1, Box 2535, 22539,  804-453-3915 |
| Reedville | Elizabeth House B&B,  P.O. Box 163, 22539,  804-453-7016 |
| Richmond | Abbie Hill Guest Lodging,  P.O. Box 4503, 23220 |
| Richmond | Catlin-Abbott House, The,  2304 East Broad St., 23223 |
| Richmond | Emmanuel Hutzler House,  2036 Monument Ave., 23220,  804-355-4885 |
| Richmond | Linden Row,  First & Franklin Sts., 23219 |
| Richmond | Mr. Patrick Henry's Inn,  2300 E. Broad St., 23223,  804-644-1322 |
| Richmond | West-Bocock House,  1107 Grove Ave., 23220,  804-358-6174 |
| Richmond | William Catlin House, The,  2304 E. Broad St., 23223,  804-780-3746 |
| Roanoke | Grandin Hall c/o T. Turner,  1007 Dominion Bank Bldg, 24011 |
| Roanoke | Mary Bladon House B&B, The,  381 Washington Ave. SW, 24016,  540-344-5361 |
| Rocky Mount | Claiborne House, The,  119 Claiborne Ave., 24151,  703-483-4616 |
| Salem | Old Manse B&B, The,  530 E Main St., 24153 |
| Smith Mt. Lake | Holland-Duncan House,  Route 5, Box 681, 24121,  703-721-8510 |
| Smithfield | Four Square Plantation,  13357 Four Square Rd., 23430 |
| Smithfield | Smithfield Station Inn,  P.O. Box 486, 23431,  804-357-7700 |
| Sperryville | Belle Meade B&B,  353 F.T. Valley Rd., 22740 |
| Spotsylvania | Roxbury Mill B&B,  6908 Roxbury Mill Rd., 22553,  540-582-6611 |
| Stanardsville | Edgewood Farm B&B,  RR 2, Box 303, 22973,  804-985-3782 |
| Stanley | Jordan Hollow Farm Inn,  Route 2, Box 375, 22851,  703-778-2285 |
| Stanley | Milton House,  P.O. Box 366, Main St., 22851,  703-778-3451 |
| Staunton | Ashton Country House,  1205 Middlebrook Rd., 24401,  703-885-7819 |
| Staunton | Belle Grae Inn,  515 W. Frederick St., 24401,  703-886-5151 |
| Staunton | Hilltop House,  1810 Springhill Rd., 24401,  703-886-0042 |
| Staunton | Kenwood,  235 E. Beverly St., 24401,  703-886-0524 |
| Strasburg | Hotel Strasburg,  201 S. Holliday St., 22657,  540-465-9191 |
| Surrey | Seward House Inn,  P.O. Box 352, 23883,  804-294-3810 |
| Surrey | Surrey House,  23883,  804-294-3191 |
| Troutdale | Fox Hill Inn,  16 S., P.O. Box 88, 24378,  703-677-3313 |
| Upperville | 1763 Inn,  Rt. 1 Box 19 D, 22176,  703-592-3848 |
| Urbanna | Atherston Hall B&B,  250 Prince George St., 23175,  804-758-2809 |
| Urbanna | Duck Farm Inn, The,  P.O. Box 787, 23175,  804-758-5685 |
| Urbanna | Hewick Plantation,  P.O. Box 82, 23175,  804-758-4214 |
| Vesuvius | Sugar Tree Inn,  P.O. Box 548, Hwy 56, 24483,  703-377-2197 |
| Virginia Beach | Angie's Guest Cottage,  302 - 24th St., 23451,  804-428-4690 |
| Virginia Beach | Barclay Cottage,  400 16th St., 23451,  804-422-1956 |
| Wachapreague | Hart's Harbor House B&B,  P.O. Box 182, 23480,  804-787-4848 |
| Warm Springs | Hidden Valley B&B,  P.O. Box 53, 24484 |
| Warm Springs | Inn at Gristmill Square,  Box 359, Route 645, 24484,  703-839-2231 |
| Warm Springs | Meadow Lane Lodge,  Route 1, Box 110, 24484,  703-839-5959 |
| Warm Springs | Three Hills Inn,  P.O. Box 99, 24484,  703-839-5381 |
| Washington | Inn at Little Washington,  Box 300, Middle & Main , 22747,  703-675-3800 |
| Washington | Sunset Hills Farm,  R.R. 1 Box 562, 22747 |
| Washington | Sycamore Hill House,  Route 1, Box 978, 22747,  703-675-3046 |
| Waynesboro | Iris Inn,  191 Chinquapin Dr., 22980,  703-943-1991 |
| Weyers Cave | Inn at Keezletown Rd., The,  Rt. 1 Box 14, 24486,  703-234-0644 |
| Williamsburg | Blue Bird Haven B&B,  8691 Barhamsville Rd., 23168,  804-566-0177 |
| Williamsburg | Greenwoode Inn, The,  104 Woodmont Pl., 23188,  804-566-8800 |
| Williamsburg | Holland's Lodge,  601 Richmond Rd., 23185,  804-253-6476 |
| Williamsburg | Magnolia Manor,  700 Richmond Rd., 23185 |
| Williamsburg | War Hill Inn,  4560 Long Hill Rd., 23188 |
| Williamsburg | Wood's Guest Home,  1208 Stewart Dr., 23185,  804-229-3376 |
| Wolftown | Tax Hollow Inn,  P.O. Box 213, 22748 |
| Woodstock | Country Fare,  402 N. Main St., 22664,  703-459-4828 |
| Woodstock | River'd Inn, The,  1972 Artz Rd., 22664,  540-459-5369 |
| Woolwine | Mountain Rose B&B,  RR 1, Box 280, 24185,  703-930-1057 |

# Washington

ABERDEEN, COSMOPOLIS ───────────────────────────────

| | | |
|---|---|---|
| **Cooney Mansion B&B** | $$-B&B | Full breakfast |
| P.O. Box 54,  98537 | 8 rooms, 5 pb | Afternoon tea |
| 1705 Fifth St. | Most CC, *Rated*, | Sitting room, library |
| 360-533-0602 | C-ltd/S-no/P-no/H-no | bicycles, tennis court |
| Judi & Jim Lohr | | hot tub, sauna, golf |
| All year | | |

*Historic Regis. Arts & Crafts style lumber baron's retreat (orig. furniture) exudes warmth & relaxation. Enjoy rose garden & Mill Creek Park.* **10% discount on 3+ nights, ltd.**

ANACORTES ───────────────────────────────

| | | |
|---|---|---|
| **Albatross B&B** | $$$-B&B | Full breakfast |
| 5708 Kingsway W., Fidalgo | 4 rooms, 4 pb | Restaurant 1 block away |
| Island,  98221 | MC, Visa, *Rated*, ● | King & queen beds |
| 360-293-0677  800-622-8864 | C-ltd/S-ltd/P-ltd/H-yes | library, travel videos |
| Barbie & Ken | Spanish, some French | antiques, 46' sailboat |
| All year | | |

*Cape Cod-style house near marina, Washington Park & Sunset Beach. Large deck w/ view. Charter boats, fine fishing, crabbing.* **Summer special, flight & sailboat tour two nights.**

| | | |
|---|---|---|
| **Channel House** | $$-B&B | Full breakfast |
| 2902 Oakes Ave.,  98221 | 6 rooms, 6 pb | Coffee/tea/cocoa/cookies |
| 360-293-9382 Fax: 360-299-9208 | MC, Visa, *Rated*, ● | Sitting room, library |
| 800-238-4353 | C-ltd/S-no/P-no/H-no | outdoor hot tub, views |
| Dennis & Patricia McIntyre | | bicycle rentals |
| All year | | |

*Gateway to the San Juan Islands. Victorian-style mansion, built in 1902; all antiques throughout. All rooms view San Juans and Puget Sound. Separate Rose Cottage. Wonderful views of the water.*

| | | |
|---|---|---|
| **Hasty Pudding House B&B** | $$-B&B | Full breakfast |
| 1312 8th St.,  98221 | 4 rooms, 3 pb | Sitting room, fireplace |
| 360-293-5773  800-368-5588 | Most CC, *Rated*, ● | |
| Mike & Melinda Hasty | C-ltd/S-no/P-no/H-no | |
| All year | | |

*Romantic 1913 Craftsman home. Antique decor. Walk to restaurants, park, shops and marina. Luscious breakfast served in our charming dining room.* **10% off Sunday-Thursday.**

ASHFORD ───────────────────────────────

| | | |
|---|---|---|
| **Hershey Homestead, The** | $$$-EP | Comp. snacks/beverages |
| 33514 Mt. Tahema Canyon, | 6 rooms, 3 pb | Sitt. room/hot tub/sauna |
| 98304 | Visa, MC, | 2 guest houses for 14 |
| 360-569-2897 Fax: 360-569-2897 | S-no/P-no/H-no | fully equipped kitchens |
| Debby | | |
| All year | | |

*Historical Homestead close to the Nat'l Park. Modern facilities w/old-fashioned charm on Hershey Creek. Cozy firepalces. & splendid views.* **Pass to Mt. Rainier Nat'l Park.**

ASHFORD

| **Mountain Meadows Inn B&B** | $$-B&B | Full country breakfast |
|---|---|---|
| P.O. Box 291, 98304 | 6 rooms, 6 pb | Tea, coffee, s'mores |
| 28912 SR 706 E | Visa, MC, *Rated*, • | Natural history library |
| 360-569-2788 | C-ltd/S-ltd/P-no/H-ltd | rooms with kitchens |
| The Latimers   All year | | 6 mi. to Mt. Rainier Prk |

*11 acres with cedar groves, hiking trails, meadows. Native American basketry exhibits. Birdwatching. Nearby Mt. Rainier Natl. Park. Two guesthouses w/kitchenettes. Family rates*

BAINBRIDGE ISLAND

| **Bombay House B&B** | $$-B&B | Continental plus bkfst. |
|---|---|---|
| 8490 NE Beck Rd., 98110 | 5 rooms, 3 pb | Complimentary tea/wine |
| 206-842-3926 800-598-3926 | AmEx, *Rated*, • | Sitting room |
| Bunny Cameron & Roger | C-ltd/S-yes/P-no/H-no | piano |
| Kanchuk   All year | | library |

*Comfortable country atmosphere near shore. Furnished w/antiques. Fresh flowers & romantic atmosphere. Near fishing, boating, golf, tennis, park. **2nd night 25% off, Sun.–Thur.***

BELLINGHAM

| **North Garden Inn** | $-B&B | Full breakfast |
|---|---|---|
| 1014 N. Garden, 98225 | 10 rooms, 8 pb | Complimentary tea |
| 360-671-7828 800-922-6414 | Visa, MC. Disc. *Rated*, | 2 sitting rooms |
| Barb & Frank DeFreytas | • | |
| All year | C-ltd    /    French | |

*North Garden Inn is a Queen Anne Victorian with a sweeping view of Bellingham Bay and the San Juan Islands.*

| **Schnauzer Crossing B&B Inn** | $$$-B&B | Full breakfast |
|---|---|---|
| 4421 Lakeway Dr., 98226 | 3 rooms, 3 pb | Sitting room, library |
| 360-733-0055 Fax: 360-734-2808 | MC, Visa, *Rated*, | lake view, outdoor spa |
| 800-562-2808 | C-yes/S-no/P-ltd | new cottage added 1991 |
| Vermont & Donna McAllister | Some Fr., Sp., Ger. | |
| All year | | |

*A luxury bed & breakfast set amidst tall evergreens overlooking Lake Whatcom. Master suite with Jacuzzi. Cottage has fireplace, VCR, private deck, Jacuzzi, skylights.*

BREMERTON

| **Willcox House Country Inn** | $$$-B&B | Full breakfast |
|---|---|---|
| 2390 Tekiu Rd. NW, 98312 | 5 rooms, 5 pb | Lunch, dinner (fee) |
| 360-830-4492 Fax: 360-830-0506 | MC, Visa, *Rated*, • | Comp. wine and cheese |
| 800-725-9477 | C-ltd/S-no/P-no/H-no | library, game room |
| Cecilia & Phillip Hughes | | with pool table |
| All year | | |

*Secluded 1930s estate on Hood Canal; quiet relaxation in an elegant, historic mansion with landscaped grounds, private pier and beach. Vegetarian dining available with advance notice.*

CAMANO ISLAND

| **Inn at Barnum Point** | $$$-B&B | Breakfast/Full brunch |
|---|---|---|
| 464 So. Barnum Rd., 98292 | 2 rooms, 2 pb | Complimentary beverages |
| 360-387-2256 Fax: 360-387-2256 | Visa, MC, Disc. *Rated*, | Sitting room |
| 800-910-2256 | C-yes/S-no/P-no/H-no | library |
| Carolin Dilorenzo   All year | | |

*On the beach, spectacular sea and mountain view. Spacious rooms with private bath, fireplaces. Near golf, State Park, migrating birds. **3rd Night 50% off.***

*Inn at Barnum Point, Camano Island, WA*

---

**CATHLAMET**

**Bradley-Country Keeper B&B**
P.O. Box 35,   98612
61 Main St.
360-795-3030  800-551-1691
Barbara & Tony West
All year

$$$-B&B
4 rooms,
MC, Visa, *Rated*,
C-ltd/S-no/P-no/H-no

Full breakfast
Comp. wine
Tea & coffee
sitting room, library
near golf, tennis & pool

*Stately 1907 home overlooks scenic Columbia River & Puget Island. Candlelit breakfasts in dining room. Historic area. Marina, ferry, game reserve nearby.* **3+ nites 10% off.**

---

**Gallery B&B, The**
Little Cape Horn,   98612
360-425-7395  Fax:360-425-1351
Carolyn & Eric Feasey
All year

$$$-B&B
4 rooms, 2 pb
AmEx, *Rated*,
C-ltd/S-no/P-ltd/H-no

Full breakfast-ltd.
Comp. cookies
Sitting room
hot tub, beach
windsurfing, fishing

*Very private country elegance. Contemporary home on private beach. Breakfast served overlooking fascinating ship channel of Columbia River.* **3rd night 50%.**

**DEER HARBOR ON ORCAS IS.**

**Palmer's Chart House**
P.O. Box 51,   98243
360-376-4231
Don & Majean Palmer
All year

$$-B&B
2 rooms, 2 pb
•
C-ltd/S-ltd/P-no/H-no
Spanish

Full breakfast
Library, private deck
travel slide shows
flower beds, gardens

*Quiet, intimate and informal atmosphere. Your hosts know how to pamper you. Fishing, hiking, golf, biking nearby. Day sails and overnight sails on racing-cruising sloop.*

**EASTSOUND**

**Outlook Inn on Orcas Isle**
P.O. Box 210,   98245
Main St.
360-376-2200  Fax:360-376-2256
888-OUT-LOOK
Jeanine or Jody    All year

$-EP
29 rooms, 11 pb
AmEx, MC, Visa,
*Rated*, •
C-yes/S-yes/P-no/H-no

Dining facilites
Year round food facil.
Luxury suites
some private phones
whirlpool baths

*Lovely turn-of-the-century inn completely refurbished, full of memorabilia. Home-style dining. Perfect island hideaway.* **50% off room rate winter season.**

## EASTSOUND

**Turtleback Farm Inn**
Route 1, Box 650, 98245
Crow Valley Rd
360-376-4914 Fax: 360-376-5329
William & Susan Fletcher
All year

$$$-B&B
7 rooms, 7 pb
MC, Visa, *Rated*, •
C-ltd/S-no/P-no/H-yes

Full breakfast
Comp. tea & coffee
Bar, comp. sherry
games, living room
fireplace

*Romantic pastoral retreat on Orcas Island. Outdoor adventures—80 acres of meadows, forests and ponds. Furnished with fine antiques. Quiet comfort and warm hospitality.*

## EASTSOUND, ORCAS ISLAND

**Kangaroo House B&B**
P.O. Box 334, 98245
5 N. Beach Rd.
360-376-2175 Fax: 360-376-2175
Jan & Mike Russillo
All year

$$-B&B
5 rooms,
MC, Visa, *Rated*, •
C-yes/S-ltd/P-no/H-no

Full breakfast
Comp. beverages & snacks
Vegy dining on request
fireplace, sitting room
hot tub in garden

*Small country inn; stone fireplace in sitting room; gourmet breakfast in sunny dining room. Furnished in antiques. Close to town and beach.* **Special winter rates.**

## FREELAND

**Cliff Hse./Sea Cliff Cott.**
5440 Windmill Rd., 98249
360-321-1566
Peggy Moore, Walter O'Toole
All year

$$$$-B&B
4 rooms, 4 pb
S-no/P-no/H-no

Continental plus bkfst.
Complimentary wine
Hot tub, fireplace
sitting room, VHS
piano, stereo

*A stunningly beautiful house, for one couple. Complete privacy in this forested hideaway with miles of beach. Award-winning Sea Cliff Cottage with French country decor.*

## FRIDAY HARBOR

**San Juan Inn**
P.O. Box 776, 98250
50 Spring St. West
360-378-2070 Fax: 360-378-6437
800-742-8210
Annette O. Metzger
All year

$$$-B&B
7 rooms, 2 pb
Visa, MC, Disc. *Rated*,
•
C-ltd/S-no/P-ltd/H-no
Danish, Swedish,
German

Continental plus bkfst.
Living room with TV/VCR
Garden suite w/Jacuzzi
extra large suite avail.

*The oldest, continually operating inn of the San Juan Islands. "We are not the best because we're the oldest, we are the oldest because we are the best!"*

**Tucker House B&B**
260 "B" St., 98250
360-378-2783 Fax: 360-378-6437
800-965-0123
Skip & Annette Metzger
All year

$$$-B&B
5 rooms, 3 pb
Most CC, *Rated*, •
C-ltd/S-no/P-ltd/H-ltd
Dan./Swed./Nor./Ger./
Fr.

Full breakfast
Kitchens
Hot tub
children welcome in
cottage, park nearby

*A Victorian home and cottages surrounded by flowers & picket fence in a small Washington port with marinas, gift shops, and gourmet restaurants.* **10% off total stay for 5+ days.**

## KIRKLAND

**Shumway Mansion**
11410 - 99th Place NE, 98033
206-823-2303 Fax: 206-822-0421
Harris & Blakemore Families
All year

$$-B&B
8 rooms, 8 pb
MC, Visa, *Rated*, •
C-ltd/S-no/P-no/H-ltd

Full breakfast buffet
Evening snack, drinks
Sitting room, piano
athletic club privileges
weddings, receptions

*Four-story mansion circa 1910. Beautiful views of lake and bay. Delicious breakfasts and afternoon treats. Walk to beach, shops, galleries. Conferences up to 60 people with catering.*

*The White Swan Guest House, Mt. Vernon, WA*

## LA CONNER

**Katy's Inn**
P.O. Box 869, 98257
503 S. Third St.
360-466-3366
800-914-7767
Bruce & Kathie Hubbard
All year

$$-B&B
5 rooms, 3 pb
Most CC, *Rated*, •
C-ltd/S-ltd/P-no/H-no

Full breakfast
Evening dessert
Sitting room, library
rocking chairs on porch
near boating, fishing

*Charming 1876 Victorian w/lovely antiques. Extensive library, delicious breakfast. Rooms open onto veranda overlooking historic village.* **Oct 15–Mar 15 midwk. 2nd night 1/2 off.**

## LA CONNER, MT. VERNON

**White Swan Guest House**
1388 Moore Rd., 98273
360-445-6805
Peter Goldfarb
All year

$$$-B&B
3 rooms,
*Rated*, •
C-ltd/S-no/P-no/H-no

Continental plus/country
Cookies
Sitting room
library, outdoor patio
garden cottage sleeps 5

*A "storybook" Victorian farmhouse 6 miles from historic waterfront village La Conner. 1 hr. north of Seattle. English gardens. A perfect romantic getaway. Choc. chip cookies.*

## LANGLEY

**Eagles Nest Inn B&B**
3236 E. Saratoga Rd., 98260
360-221-5331
Fax: 360-221-5331
Joanne & Jerry Lechner
All year

$$$-B&B
4 rooms, 4 pb
Visa, MC, Disc, *Rated*, •
C-ltd/S-no

Full gourmet breakfast
Comp. bar, tea, coffee
Library, sitt. rm., TV
fireplace, woodstove
video library, hot tub

*Casual elegance w/native art, in country setting on Whidbey Island 2 miles to seaside village of Langley. View of Saratoga Passage. AAA rates 3 diamonds. Comp. choc. cookies.*

## LANGLEY

| **Island Tyme B&B Inn** | $$$-B&B | Full breakfast |
|---|---|---|
| 4940 S. Bayview Rd., 98260 | 5 rooms, 5 pb | Snacks |
| 360-221-5078 800-898-8963 | Visa, MC, AmEx, | Sitting room, library |
| Lyn & Phil Fauth | *Rated*, • | jacuzzis |
| All year | C-yes/S-ltd/P-ltd/H-yes | fireplaces in rooms |

*Light a fire, soak in your jacuzzi, savor your gourmet breakfast at our Victorian B&B, close to Langley, Whidbey Island.*

| **Log Castle B&B** | $$$-B&B | Full breakfast |
|---|---|---|
| 3273 E. Saratoga Rd., 98260 | 4 rooms, 4 pb | Cider, homemade cookies |
| 360-221-5483 | MC, Visa, • | Sitting room, guest |
| Phil & Karen Holdsworth | C-ltd/S-no/P-no/H-no | canoe & rowboat, beach |
| All year | | fishing, hiking, birding |

*Unique waterfront log lodge on Whidbey Island. Turret bedrooms, secluded beach, fantastic view of mountains, 50 miles north of Seattle.*

| **Lone Lake Cottage & Bkfst.** | $$$-B&B | Continental plus bkfst. |
|---|---|---|
| 5206 S. Bayview Rd., 98260 | 3 rooms, 3 pb | All rooms w/jacuzzis |
| 360-321-5325 | MC, Visa, | private beach, bikes |
| Dolores Renfrew | S-no/P-no/H-no | canoes, 14' sailboat |
| All year | | |

*Whidbey's "Shangri-la"! Romantic, lovely cottages, one a 40-foot house boat. Fireplaces, kitchens, beautiful beach. Boat and canoe rides. Excellent fishing and biking.*

## LEAVENWORTH

| **Haus Rohrbach Pension** | $$-B&B | Full breakfast |
|---|---|---|
| 12882 Ranger Rd., 98826 | 12 rooms, 8 pb | Desserts offered |
| 509-548-7024 | Most CC, *Rated*, • | Sitting room |
| Robert & Kathryn Harrild | C-yes/S-no/P-no/H-no | swimming pool |
| All year | | hot tub |

*One-of-a-kind, European-style country inn, unequaled in the Pacific Northwest. Alpine-setting pool and hot tub. Year-round outdoor activities. Suites w/fireplace and whirlpool.* **10% disc't, Sun.–Thurs.**

| **Pine River Ranch** | $$$-B&B | Full breakfast |
|---|---|---|
| 19668 Highway 207, 98826 | 8 rooms, 6 pb | Snacks, kitchenette |
| 509-763-3959 800-669-3877 | MC, Visa, *Rated*, • | Sitting room, hot tubs |
| Michael & Mary Ann Zenk | C-ltd/S-no/P-no/H-yes | restaurant nearby, suite |
| All year | | hike, bike, fish, ski |

*Upon arrival, this spacious mountain ranch with wonderfully detailed rooms embraces you. You've made the right choice. 2 Jacuzzi suites w/view.* **3rd night 30% off or 4th night free.**

| **Run of the River** | $$$-B&B | Full breakfast |
|---|---|---|
| P.O. Box 285, 98826 | 6 rooms, 6 pb | Afternoon tea, snacks |
| 9308 E. Leavenworth Rd. | Visa, MC, AmEx, Disc., | Sitting rm., library |
| 509-548-7171 Fax: 509-548-7547 | • | hot tub |
| 800-288-6491 | S-no/P-no/H-yes | comp. mountain bicycles |
| The Turners All year | Spanish | |

*The quintessential Northwest Log B&B Inn. From your log porch swing, view the Icicle River, surrounding bird refuge & The Cascade Peaks, appropriately named The Enchantments!*

### LONG BEACH

**Boreas B&B**
P.O. Box 1344,   98631
607 North Blvd.
360-642-8069 Fax: 360-642-8069
888-642-8069
Susie Goldsmith & Bill
Verner   All year

$$-B&B
4 rooms, 2 pb
Visa, MC, *Rated*,  •
C-yes/S-no/P-no/H-no

Full breakfast
Afternoon tea, snacks
Sitting room, library
bicycles, hot tubs
decks, reunions/weddings

*Artistically remodeled 1920s beach home. Oceanview bedrooms, spacious living rooms with fireplace. Enclosed sundeck with hot tub. Walk to boardwalk, shopping & restaurants.* **Free bottle of wine.**

### LOPEZ ISLAND

**Inn at Swifts Bay**
Route 2, Box 3402,   98261
360-468-3636 Fax: 360-468-3637
R. Hermann & C. Brandmeir
All year

$$-B&B
5 rooms, 3 pb
MC, Visa, *Rated*,  •
Portuguese, Ger., Sp.

Full breakfast
Comp. sherry, min. water
Sitt. rm., video library
hot tub, bike rentals
excercise studio w/sauna

*English country comfort in the San Juan Islands. Private separate beach. Delightful breakfasts. Bald eagles, Orca whales. Pastoral, restful. Fully equipped waterfront cabin.*

### LUMMI ISLAND

**Willows Inn, The**
2579 West Shore Dr.,   98262
360-758-2620
Victoria & Gary Flynn
All year

$$$-B&B
7 rooms, 7 pb
MC, Visa,
C-ltd/S-no/P-no/H-ltd

Full breakfast
Aftn. tea, beer, wine &
Cheese, pub w/billiards
darts, cable TV
honeymoon cottage

*On the sunset side of the island, this established inn commands a sweeping view of the other San Juan islands. Offering B&B June thru Sept. and self catering year around.*

### MAZAMA

**Mazama Country Inn**
HCR 74 Box B-9, 42 Lost River
Rd.,   98833
509-996-2681 Fax: 509-996-2646
George Turner   All year

$$-EP/AP
14 rooms, 14 pb
Visa, MC,  •
C-ltd/S-no/P-no/H-no

Full breakfast
EP in the summer
Bicycles, hot hubs
sauna, sitting room
horseback riding

*Secluded year-round country inn with huge stone fireplace in dining room. Hiking, mountain-biking, horseback riding, cross-country ski trails abound.* **Call for our special summer rates.**

### MOUNT VERNON

**Ridgeway B&B**
1292 McLean Rd., P.O. Box
475,   98273
La Conner
360-428-8068 Fax: 360-428-8880
800-428-8068
Louise & John Kelly   All year

$$-B&B
7 rooms, 4 pb
Most CC, *Rated*,  •
C-ltd/S-no/P-no/H-no

Full farm-style bkfst.
Sitting room
2 acres of lawn, flowers
and orchard

*A great getaway for all seasons! Historic Dutch Colonial farmhouse & cottage nestled in the heart of the Skagit Valley. Evening homemade dessert.* **Additional nights, 50%, ltd.**

### OLYMPIA

**Harbinger Inn B&B**
1136 East Bay Dr.,   98506
360-754-0389
Marisa & Terrell Williams
All year

$$-B&B
6 rooms, 6 pb
AmEx, MC, Visa,
*Rated*,
C-ltd/S-no/P-no/H-no

Continental plus bkfst.
Complimentary wine
Sitting room
library, birdwatching
queen bed suite avail.

*Restored turn-of-the-century home with beautiful water view; period furnishings. Conveniently located for boating, bicycling, business and entertainment.*

## OLYMPIA

| **Puget View Guest House** | $$$-B&B | Continental plus bkfst. |
|---|---|---|
| 7924 - 61st Ave. NE,  98516 | 2 rooms, 1 pb | BBQ, canoe available |
| 360-459-1676 | MC, Visa, *Rated*, • | Private dining area/deck |
| Dick & Barbara Yunker | C-yes/S-yes/P-ltd/H-no | books, games |
| All year | | 100-acre park next door |

*Charming waterfront guest cottage suite next to host's log home. Breakfast to your cottage. Peaceful. Picturesque. A "NW Best Places" since 1984. Puget Sound 5 min. off I-5.*

## ORCAS

| **WindSong B&B** | $$$-MAP | Full breakfast |
|---|---|---|
| P.O. Box 32,  98280 | 4 rooms, 4 pb | Snacks, diner |
| Deer Harbor Rd. | Visa, MC, *Rated*, • | Sitting room, library |
| 360-376-2500 Fax: 360-376-4453 | C-ltd/S-no/P-no/H-no | hot tubs |
| Sam & Kim Haines | | |
| All year | | |

*A comfortably elegant adult hide-away featuring a pampering environment on one of the most spectacular islands in the Northwest.*

## PORT ANGELES

| **Domaine Madeleine B&B** | $$$-B&B | Full breakfast |
|---|---|---|
| 146 Wildflower Ln.,  98362 | 4 rooms, 4 pb | Aft. tea, snacks |
| 360-457-4174 | MC, Visa, *Rated*, | Sitting room, library |
| Madeleine & John Chambers | C-ltd/S-no/P-no/H-no | jacuzzi, lawn games |
| All year | Fr., Sp., Farsi., Ger. | |

*Serene waterfront estate with panoramic views—Monet garden replica, unique European/Asian antiques, fireplaces, Jacuzzi, whales and eagles. **3rd night 20% off, off-season.***

| **Tudor Inn B&B** | $$$-B&B | Full breakfast |
|---|---|---|
| 1108 S. Oak,  98362 | 5 rooms, 5 pb | Afternoon tea |
| 360-452-3138 | Most CC, *Rated*, • | Sitting room, library |
| Jane & Jerry Glass | C-ltd/S-no/P-no/H-no | TV/VCR & fireplace in |
| All year | | sitting area |

*The design of the inn is English Tudor, built in 1910 when the sumptuous use of wood was taken for granted. It has been tastefully restored to retain the rustic charm of the Tudor era.*

## PORT TOWNSEND

| **Ann Starrett Mansion B&B** | $$-B&B | Full breakfast |
|---|---|---|
| 704 Clay St.,  98368 | 10 rooms, 10 pb | Comp. sherry, tea |
| 360-385-3205 Fax: 360-385-2976 | MC, Visa, *Rated*, • | Sitting room |
| 800-321-0644 | C-ltd/S-yes/P-no/H-ltd | honeymoon cottage |
| Edel and Bob Sokol | | jacuzzi, hot tub |
| All year | | |

*Award winning, full-service, Victorian inn. Internationally renowned for classic Victorian architecture, frescoed ceilings & three-tiered spiral staircase. **3rd nite 50%, ltd.***

| **Bishop Victorian Suites** | $$$-B&B | Continental breakfast |
|---|---|---|
| 714 Washington St.,  98368 | 12 rooms, 12 pb | Coffee, tea |
| 360-385-6122  800-824-4738 | AmEx, MC, Visa, | Sitting rm., parking lot |
| Joe & Cindy Finnie | *Rated*, | conference facilities |
| All year | C-yes/S-yes/P-yes/H-no | small kitchens-each room |

*Downtown, Victorian-era hotel; beautifully restored. Gracious suites. Mountain and water views. Walk to Port Townsend, Washington's historic Victorian seaport.*

PORT TOWNSEND ──────────────────────────────

| **Holly Hill House** | $$$-B&B | Full breakfast |
|---|---|---|
| 611 Polk, 98368 | 5 rooms, 5 pb | Champagne & chocolates |
| 360-385-5619  800-435-1454 | MC, Visa, *Rated*, | Library, sitting room |
| Lynne Sterling | C-ltd/S-no/P-no/H-no | extensive gardens |
| All year | | 1 suite king size bed |

*Beautifully maintained 1872 Victorian home, in historic uptown. Walking distance to downtown. Bountiful breakfast. Enjoy Victorian waterfront community.* **Free bottle of wine when you mention B&B Guide.**

| **James House, The** | $$-B&B | Full breakfast |
|---|---|---|
| 1238 Washington St., 98368 | 13 rooms, 11 pb | Comp. sherry & cookies |
| 360-385-1238 Fax: 360-385-5756 | MC, Visa, *Rated*, | Sitting parlors |
| 800-385-1238 | C-ltd/S-no/P-no/H-ltd | player piano, fireplaces |
| Carol McGough | | porch with swing, garden |
| All year | | |

*1889 Queen Anne Victorian mansion featuring unsurpassed water and mountain views, period antiques. First B&B in the Northwest, still the finest. Bungalow w/fireplace, jacuzzi*

| **Old Consulate Inn** | $$$-B&B | Full breakfast - banquet |
|---|---|---|
| 313 Walker @ Washington, | 8 rooms, 8 pb | Afternoon tea, snacks |
| 98368 | Visa, MC, AmEx, | Comp. wine, sitting room |
| 360-385-6753 Fax: 360-385-2097 | *Rated*, • | library, tennis, hot tub |
| 800-300-6753 | C-ltd/S-no/P-no/H-no | billiard and game room |
| Rob & Joanna Jackson | | |
| All year | | |

*Award winning Founding Family Mansion-on-the-Bluff. Romantic retreat offering warm hospitality, comfortable elegance, evening cordials! King beds.* **2nd night discount, ltd.**

| **Palace Hotel, The** | $$-B&B | Continental plus |
|---|---|---|
| 1004 Water St., 98368 | 15 rooms, 12 pb | Lunch, dinner, restaurant |
| 360-385-0773 Fax: 360-385-0780 | Most CC, *Rated*, • | Confrence facilities, |
| 800-962-0741 | H-no | bkfst. delivered to room |
| Andrew and Loni Bremner | | full restaurant |
| All year | | |

*Beautifully resotred hotel in the heart of downtown Port Townsend. Complimentary continental plus breakfast & off-street parking.* **20$ off of rack rates, ltd.**

| **Ravenscroft Inn** | B&B | Full breakfast |
|---|---|---|
| 533 Quincy St., 98368 | 8 rooms, 8 pb | Afternoon tea, snacks |
| 360-385-2784 Fax: 360-385-6724 | Most CC, *Rated*, | Sherry |
| 800-782-2691 | C-ltd/S-no/P-no/H-no | Sitting room, library |
| Leah Hammer | | |
| All year | | |

*A visit to the Ravenscroft Inn, relaxing in gracious surroundings, a distant cry of gulls; time traveling to another era.* **3rd night 50%, mid-week, Oct.–May, ltd.**

| **Swan Hotel, The** | $$$-EP |
|---|---|
| 222 Monroe St., 98368 | 9 rooms, 9 pb |
| 360-385-1718  800-776-1718 | Visa, MC, AmEx, |
| All year | C-yes/S-no/P-no/H-yes |

*A waterfront hotel which includes 4, 1 bedroom suites, 2 story penthouse and 4 charming cottages. All are equipped with TVs & kitchen facilities. Close to everything.*

## QUILCENE

**Quilcene Hotel**
P.O. Box 129,  89376
11 Quilcene Ave.
360-765-3447 Fax: 360-765-3447
800-570-0529
George & Reta Miller
All year

$-B&B
9 rooms, 1 pb
•
C-yes/S-no/P-no/H-no

Continental breakfast
Sitting room, library
family friendly facility
book exchange, sun room

*Friendly, simple, country atmosphere. Clean, quiet environment. Hiking trails, restaurants, antique shops nearby.*

## ROSLYN

**Roslyn B&B**
P.O. Box 736,  98005
109 Arizona St.
206-453-1356 Fax: 206-688-5688
Joyce & Dale Widner
All year

$$-B&B
3 rooms, 3 pb
Visa, MC, AmEx,
C-ltd/S-ltd/P-ltd/H-no

Full gourmet breakfast
Snacks
Sitting room, large
living room, dining room
3 outside decks

*Spectacular mountain scenery surround this turn-of-the-century mining town that time has bypassed. Fishing, hiking, skiing and relaxing await you. $25.00 off, ask.*

## SEATTLE

**B.D. Williams House B&B**
1505 - 4th Ave. N.,  98109
206-285-0810 Fax: 206-285-8526
800-880-0810
Williams Family Susan Dovey
All year

$$$-B&B
5 rooms, 3 pb
Most CC, *Rated*,
C-yes/S-ltd/P-no/H-no

Full breakfast
Coffee, tea, cookies
Sitting room, piano
play area inside/outside
gardens nice most of yr.

*Views of Seattle, Puget Sound, mountains. One of Seattle's oldest neighborhoods. Very close to Seattle activities, parks, lakes. 10% off-season discount for 5+ night stay.*

---

**Bacon Mansion**
959 Broadway East,  98102
206-329-1864 Fax: 206-860-9025
800-240-1864
Daryl King
All year

$$-B&B
10 rooms, 8 pb
AmEx, MC, Visa,
*Rated*,
C-ltd/S-no/P-no/H-no

Continental plus bkfst.
Sitting room
library, conference rm.
exercise facility

*One of Capitol Hill's gracious mansions circa 1909. Luxury antique-filled rooms, hand-carved woodwork. Carriage House also available.*

---

**Beech Tree Manor**
1405 Queen Anne Ave. N.,
 98109
206-281-7037 Fax: 206-284-2350
Virginia Lucero
All year

$$-B&B
6 rooms, 3 pb
MC, Visa, *Rated*, •
C-ltd/S-no/P-yes/H-no

Full breakfast
Sitting room, library
antique linen shop
porch with wicker chairs

*1904 mansion, near City Center, English decor; scrumptious breakfasts; original art in all rooms; luxuriously comfortable.*

---

**Capital Hill House**
2215-E Prospect Ave.,  98112
206-322-1752 Fax: 206-322-3809
Katie & Joanne Godmintz
All year

$$$-B&B
3 rooms, 1 pb
*Rated*, •
C-yes/S-ltd/P-no/H-no

Full breakfast
Sitt. rm., 2 person tubs
garden, patio, frplc.
sports activities nearby

*Old World charm is the hallmark of this classic brick house built in 1923. Guest rooms provide elegance unmatched by modern accommodations. Covered patio, beautiful garden.*

SEATTLE ────────────────────────────────────────────────

**Challenger Tugboat**
1001 Fairview Ave. N., 98109
206-340-1201 Fax: 206-621-9208
Jerry & Buff Brown
All year

$$-B&B
14 rooms, 4 pb
*Rated*, •
C-ltd/S-yes/P-no/H-yes

Full breakfast
Soft drinks
Sitting room, library
bicycles, fireplace
small boats

*On board a fully functional, exceptionally clean, restored tugboat. Near downtown Seattle. Closed circuit TV. Carpeted throughout. Nautical antiques.*

---

**Chambered Nautilus B&B Inn**
5005 22nd Ave. N.E., 98105
206-522-2536
Steve Poole & Joyce Schulte
All year

$$$-B&B
6 rooms, 4 pb
Most CC, *Rated*, •
C-ltd/S-ltd/P-no/H-no
French

Full gourmet breakfast
Afternoon tea & cookies
Sitting room with phone
desks in rooms
Fireplaces, conferences

*"Seattle's Finest." Gracious historic in-city retreat near downtown & Univ. of WA. Nat'l Award-winning family-style bkfasts. **3rd weeknight free, Nov.15–March.15, ltd.***

---

**Chelsea Station on the Pk.**
4915 Linden Ave. N, 98103
206-547-6077 Fax: 206-632-5107
800-400-6077
J. Griffin, K. Carbonneau
All year

$$-B&B
7 rooms, 7 pb
Most CC, *Rated*, •
C-ltd/S-no/P-no/H-no

Full hearty breakfast
Tea/fresh-baked cookies
Sitt. rm./jigsaw puzzles
neighborhood strolls
all rooms with phones

*Nestled bet. Fremont neighborhood & Woodland Pk., min. north of downtown. Enjoy warm & casual mood of Chelsea Station-a place to refresh your spirit. **7 nites for price of 6.***

---

**Hill House B&B**
1113 E. John St., 98102
206-720-7161 Fax: 206-323-0772
800-720-7161
Ken Hayes & Eric Lagasca
All year

$$-B&B
5 rooms,
Most CC, *Rated*,
C-ltd/S-no/P-no/H-no
Filipino

Full breakfast
Sitting room
Sitting room
library
CD collection

*1903 Victorian home in historic Capitol Hill. Walk to shops and restaurants on Broadway, near all downtown attractions.*

---

**Mildred's B&B Inn**
1202 - 15th Ave. E., 98112
206-325-6072 Fax: 206-860-5907
Mildred & Melodee Sarver
All year

$$$-B&B
3 rooms, 3 pb
•
C-yes/S-ltd/P-no/H-no

Full breakfast
Afternoon tea or coffee
Sitting room, fireplace
library, veranda
grand piano

*1890 Victorian. Wraparound veranda, lace curtains, red carpets. City location near bus, electric trolley, park, art museum, flower conservatory. Play area across the street.*

---

**Pioneer Square Hotel**
77 Yesler Way, 98104
206-340-1234 Fax: 206-467-0707
800-800-5514
Jo Thompson
All year

$$$-B&B
75 rooms, 75 pb
Most CC, *Rated*, •
C-yes/S-ltd/P-no/H-yes
Spanish, Swedish

Continental plus bkfst.
Lunch/dinner (fee)
Snacks, bar service
restaurant
sitting room, library

*Small luxury boutique accommodation in downtown Seattle's waterfront Pioneer Square Historic District. Near ferry terminals, nightlife, shopping. **Internet & Lanier Guide rates.***

# Washington   533

## SEATTLE

**Prince of Wales B&B**
133 13th Ave. E.,   98102
206-325-9692 Fax: 206-322-6402
800-327-9692
Carol Norton   All year

$$$-B&B
4 rooms, 4 pb
Most CC, *Rated*,
C-ltd/S-no/P-no/H-no

Full breakfast, low fat
Morning coffee to room
Sitting room
fireplaces, garden
attic suite, prvt. deck

*Downtown 1.5 miles away; on bus line; walk to convention center; turn-of-the-century ambiance; panoramic views of city skyline, sound and mtns. **10% off 7+ nights.***

**Shafer Baillie Mansion B&B**
907 14th Ave. E.,   98112
206-322-4654 Fax: 206-329-4654
800-922-4654
Erv, Chris, Gary, Rick
All year

$$$-B&B
13 rooms, 8 pb
AmEx, MC, Visa,
*Rated*, •
C-yes/S-no/P-no/H-no

Continental plus bkfst.
Fax, phones, sitting rm.
tennis & pool nearby
downtown: 5 min. library

*15,000-square-foot brick mansion on Seattle's "Millionaire's Row."Gourmet breakfast; 12 suites/rooms. Television, refrigerator and antiques in all rooms. **10% off 7+ nights.***

**Villa Heidelberg**
4845 45th Ave., S.W.,   98116
206-938-3658 Fax: 206-935-7077
800-671-2942
The Thompsons   All year

$$-B&B
5 rooms,
AmEx, MC, Visa,
*Rated*,
C-ltd/S-ltd/P-no/H-no

Full breakfast
Sitting room
New king suite w/views
and private bath

*1909 Craftsman country home just minutes from the airport and downtown Seattle. Two blocks to shops, bus and restaurants. Sweeping views of Puget Sound & Olympic Mountains.*

## SEATTLE, FREELAND

**Seaside Cottage**
P.O. Box 970,   98249
213 E. Sandpiper Rd.
360-331-8455 Fax: 360-331-8636
Cliff & Virginia Lindsey
All year

$$-B&B
2 rooms, 2 pb
Discover,
C-yes/S-ltd/P-no/H-ltd

Full breakfast setup
Beach, biking paradise
golf, kites, lounges
7 nights for price of 6

*Your own private cottage or garden suite. Sandy beach, great views and close to passing large ships. Close to Seattle! Breakfast set-up in cottage only, not in garden suite.*

## SEAVIEW

**Shelburne Inn**
P.O. Box 250,   98644
4415 Pacific Way
206-642-2442 Fax: 206-642-8904
800-INN-1896
L. Anderson, D. Campiche
All year

$$$-B&B
16 rooms, 13 pb
MC, Visa, *Rated*, •
C-ltd/S-yes/P-no/H-yes
French, German, Port.

Full country breakfast
Restaurant, pub
Lobby with fireplace
organ
2 suites

*The oldest surviving Victorian hotel in Washington state, with the time-honored tradition of superb service, decor and distinguished cuisine.*

## SEQUIM

**Brigadoon B&B**
62 Balmoral Ct.,   98382
360-683-2255 Fax: 360-681-5285
800-397-2256
Larry & Marilyn Cross
All year

$$$-B&B
3 rooms, 3 pb
C-ltd/S-no/P-no/H-no

Full breakfast
Afternoon tea
Sitting room
hot tubs

*A wonderful, peaceful Craftsman country home with many antiques and collections to enjoy. Gourmet breakfasts, banks of flowers, singing birds.*

## SEQUIM

| **Greywolf Inn** | $$-B&B | Full breakfast, 4-course |
| 395 Keeler Rd., 98382 | 6 rooms, 6 pb | Complimentary champagne |
| 360-683-5889 Fax: 360-683-1487 | AmEx, MC, Visa, | Fireplace, patio, decks |
| 800-914-WOLF | *Rated*, • | Japanese hot tub, gazebo |
| Peggy & Bill Melang | C-ltd/S-ltd/P-no/H-no | gardens & woodswalk |
| All year | | |

*Enjoy fine food & good cheer in this splendid little inn. The perfect starting point for light adventure on the Olympic Peninsula or sailing to Victoria, BC.* **3rd night, 50%.**

| **Margie's Inn on the Bay** | $$-B&B | Full breakfast |
| 120 Forrest Rd, 98382 | 6 rooms, 6 pb | Complimentary sherry |
| 360-683-7011 Fax: 360-683-7011 | MC, Visa, *Rated*, • | Sitting room |
| 800-730-7011 | C-ltd/S-no/P-no/H-yes | tennis courts |
| Margie Vorhies | | VCR, TV, boats |
| March–October | | |

*Country hideaway: large modern ranch-style home on the water. Full breakfast. Golf, fish, hike. Close to John Wayne marina.* **3rd night 50%, Oct 15–May 15.**

## SNOHOMISH

| **Countryman's** | $$-B&B | Full breakfast |
| 119 Cedar Ave, 98290 | 3 rooms, 3 pb | Afternoon tea |
| 206-568-9622 800-700-9622 | MC, Visa, • | Sitting room |
| Larry & Sandy Countryman | C-yes/S-no/P-yes/H-no | bicycles |
| All year | German | |

*1896 Queen Anne Victorian in National Historic district. One block from 300 antique dealers. The inn with the extras. Complimentary Historic home tour.*

## SOUTH CLE ELUM

| **Moore House Country Inn** | $-B&B | Full breakfast |
| P.O. Box 629, 98943 | 12 rooms, 6 pb | Lunch, dinner |
| 526 Marie St. | AmEx, MC, Visa, | Sitting room, hot tub |
| 509-674-5939 800-22-TWAIN | *Rated*, • | honeymoon suite w/jacuz. |
| Eric & Cindy Sherwood | C-yes/S-ltd/P-no/H-no | 2 genuine caboose suites |
| All year | | |

*Old railroad hotel adjacent to Iron Horse State Park. Mountain location makes four seasons of activities possible from our doorstep. Group dinners, receptions, weddings.*

## SPOKANE

| **Angelica's Mansion B&B** | $$$-B&B | Full breakfast |
| W. 1321 Ninth Ave., 99204 | 4 rooms, 3 pb | Afternoon tea |
| 508-624-5598 | Visa, MC, Disc., • | Sitting room, library |
| Lynda & Dan Tortarolo | C-ltd/S-no/P-no/H-no | sunroom, verandah |
| All year | | pergola |

*Romantic 1907 craftsman mansion. Elegant atmosphere. Peaceful setting. Enjoy our collection of angels. Private breakfast on verandah. Close to everything.*

| **Fotheringham House** | $$-B&B | Full breakfast |
| 2128 W. Second Ave., 99204 | 4 rooms, 1 pb | Comp. beverages |
| 509-838-1891 Fax: 509-838-1807 | Visa, MC, *Rated*, • | Living room, library |
| Jackie & Graham Johnson | C-ltd/S-no/P-no/H-no | nearby golf, tennis |
| All year | | and park |

*Victorian home located in historic Spokane District. Antique furnishings, queen beds, park across street. Next to restaurant in Victorian mansion. 3 rooms share 2 full baths.*

## SPOKANE

| **Marianna Stoltz House** | $$-B&B | Full breakfast |
| 427 E. Indiana Ave., 99207 | 4 rooms, 2 pb | Veranda, cable T.V. |
| 509-483-4316 Fax: 509-483-6773 | Most CC, *Rated*, • | guest refrigerators |
| 800-978-6587 | C-ltd/S-no/P-no/H-no | bathrobes in rooms |
| Phyllis Maguire | | |
| All year | | |

*Antique quilts, lace curtains, oriental rugs. Delicious breakfasts. Friendly hosts await you in our centrally located 1908 historic B&B. Close to Gonzaga Univ. 3rd night 50%.*

## SUNNYSIDE

| **Sunnyside Inn B&B** | $$-B&B | Full breakfast |
| 800 Edison Ave., 98944 | 8 rooms, 8 pb | Snacks, hot tubs |
| 509-839-5557 Fax: 509-839-3520 | AmEx, MC, Visa, • | Sitting room, Jacuzzi |
| 800-221-4195 | C-yes/S-no/P-no/H-no | near tennis, golf, and |
| Karen & Donavon Vlieger | | over 20 wineries. |
| All year | | |

*Eight luxurious rooms, all with private baths, 7 with private jacuzzi tubs. In the heart of Washington wine country. 3rd night 50% off.*

## TACOMA

| **Chinaberry Hill B&B** | $$$-B&B | Full breakfast |
| 302 Tacoma Ave. N., 98403 | 4 rooms, 4 pb | Comp. drinks & snacks |
| 206-272-1282 Fax: 206-272-1335 | Visa, MC, AmEx, | Sitting room, library |
| Cecil & Yarrow Wayman | *Rated*, • | hot tub in 2 rooms |
| All year | C-yes/S-ltd/P-no/H-no | period library |

*1889 Victorian & cottage on Historic Register. Bay views, private Jacuzzis, fireplaces, antiques, local memorabilia. Wraparound porch overlooks Puget Sound. 7th consecutive night free.*

| **Commencement Bay B&B** | $$$-B&B | Full breakfast |
| 3312 N. Union Ave., 98407 | 3 rooms, 3 pb | Afternoon tea, snacks |
| 206-752-8175 Fax: 206-759-4025 | Most CC, *Rated*, • | Weight room, library |
| Sharon & Bill Kaufmann | C-ltd/S-ltd/P-no/H-no | bikes, hot tubs, TV/VCR |
| All year | Some Spanish | weight room, office area |

*Elegantly decorated colonial home overlooking scenic Tacoma (30 miles from Seattle). View of Bay & mountains from rooms. Secluded hot tub in garden. Discount for frequent stay.*

## VASHON ISLAND, SEATTLE

| **Swallow's Nest Cottages** | $$-EP | Breakfast by arrangement |
| 6030 SW 248th St., Maury | 6 rooms, 6 pb | Cottages have kitchens |
| Island, 98070 | Most CC, *Rated*, • | Swing under cherry tree |
| 206-463-2646 800-ANY-NEST | C-yes/S-no/P-ltd/H-ltd | some hot tubs/fireplaces |
| Bob Keller & Robin Hughes | | golf, boating nearby |
| All year | | |

*Ride ferry boat to country cottages in 3 separate Vashon Island locations: 1) on bluffs w/ spectacular views, 2) across the street from yacht harbor, 3) across from Country Club. $10 off activity pkg.*

## WALLA WALLA

| **Green Gables Inn** | $$$-B&B | Full breakfast |
| 922 Bonsella, 99362 | 6 rooms, 6 pb | Snacks |
| 509-525-5501 | Most CC, *Rated*, | Sitting room, library |
| Jim & Margaret Buchan | C-ltd/S-no/P-no/H-no | tandem bicycles |
| All year | | Family Carriage House |

*Historic, award-winning 1909 mansion in Whitman College campus area of stately homes on tree-lined streets. Expect to be pampered!*

*The Swallow's Nest, Vashon Island, Seattle, WA*

## WHIDBEY ISLAND

**Guest House Cottages**
3366 S. Hwy. 525, Greenbank, 98253
360-678-3115  Fax: 360-321-0631
Mary Jane & Don Creger
All year

$$$$-B&B
7 rooms, 7 pb
Most CC, *Rated*,
S-no/P-no/H-ltd

Continental plus bkfst.
Exercise room, pool, spa
retreat & honeymoon spot
rated 4 diamond by AAA

*Wildflower suite has private entrance. Luxury log mansion for 2 ($285/night). Private cottages w/personal jacuzzis, fireplace, kitchens, TV/VCR.* **10th night free.**

## More Inns . . .

| | |
|---|---|
| Acme | River Valley B&B, Box 158, 98220, 206-595-2686 |
| Anacortes | A Burrow's Bay B&B, 4911 MacBeth Dr., 98221, 206-293-4792 |
| Anacortes | Dutch Treat House, 1220 31st St., 98221, 206-293-8154 |
| Anacortes | Old Brook Inn, 530 Old Brook Ln., 98221, 206-293-4768 |
| Anacortes | Sunset Beach B&B, 100 Sunset Beach, 98211 |
| Anderson Island | Inn at Burg's Landing, The, 8808 Villa Beach Rd., 98303, 206-884-9185 |
| Ashford | Alexander's Country Inn, Hwy. 706, 98304, 206-569-2300 |
| Ashford | Ashford Mansion, Box G, 98304, 206-569-2739 |
| Ashford | Growly Bear B&B, 37311 SR 706, 98304, 206-569-2339 |
| Ashford | Jasmer's Guest House, 30005 SR 706 E, 98304, 206-569-2682 |
| Auburn | Blomeen House B&B, 324 B St. N.E., 98002, 206-939-3088 |
| Bainbridge Island | Bainbridge House B&B, 11301 Logg Rd., N.E., 98110, 206-842-1599 |
| Bainbridge Island | Beach Cottage, 5831 Ward Ave., NE, 98110, 206-842-6081 |
| Bainbridge Island | Rose Cottage, 11744 Olympic Terrace, 98110, 206-842-6248 |
| Bainbridge Island | West Blakeay Inn, The, 8494 Odd Fellows Rd., 98110 |
| Belfair | North Bay Inn B&B, East 2520 Hwy 302, 98528, 206-275-5378 |
| Bellevue | Bellevue B&B, 830 - 100th Ave. SE, 98004, 206-453-1048 |
| Bellevue | Bridle Trails B&B, 2750 122 Place, NE, 98005, 206-861-0700 |
| Bellevue | Petersen B&B, 10228 S.E. 8th St., 98004, 206-454-9334 |
| Bellingham | Anderson Creek Lodge, 5602 Mission Rd., 98226, 206-966-2126 |
| Bellingham | Bellingham's DeCann House, 2610 Eldridge Ave., 98225 |
| Bellingham | Castle, The, 1103 - 15th, 98225, 206-676-0974 |
| Bellingham | Circle F, 2399 Mt. Baker Hwy, 98226, 206-733-2509 |
| Bellingham | De Cann House B&B, 2610 Eldridge Ave, 98225, 206-734-9172 |
| Bellingham | Loganita By the Sea, 2863 Seaview Cir., 98225, 206-758-2651 |
| Bellingham | Loganita, Villa By The Sea, 2825 W. Shore Dr., 98262, 206-758-2651 |
| Bellingham | Secret Garden, 1807 Lakeway Dr., 98226, 206-671-7850 |
| Bingen | Grand Old House, P.O. Box 667, Hwy. 14, 98605, 509-493-2838 |
| Bow | Alice Bay B&B, 982 Scott Rd., 98232 |
| Carnation | Idyl Inn on the River, 4548 Tolt River Rd., 98014, 206-333-4262 |

| | |
|---|---|
| Carson | Carson Hot Springs Hotel, P.O. Box 370, 98610, 509-427-8292 |
| Cashmere | Cashmere Country Inn, 5801 Pioneer Dr., 98815, 509-782-4212 |
| Cathlamet | Cathlamet Hotel, 67-69 Main St, 98612, 800-446-0454 |
| Cathlamet | Country Keeper B&B Inn,The, 61 Main St., 98612, 206-795-3030 |
| Chelan | Brick House Inn, 304 Wapato Ave., 98816 |
| Chelan | Mary Kay's Whaley Mansion, Route 1, Box 693, 98816, 509-682-5735 |
| Chelan | North Cascades Lodge, P.O. Box W, 98816, 509-682-4711 |
| Chimacum | Summer House, 2603 Center Rd., 98325, 206-732-4017 |
| Clinton | Beach House, 7338 S. Maxwelton Rd., 98236, 206-321-4335 |
| Clinton | Home by the Sea, 2388 E Sunlight Beach R, 98236, 206-221-2964 |
| Clinton | Kittleson Cove B&B, P.O. Box 396, 98236, 206-221-2734 |
| Concrete | Cascade Mountain Inn, 3840 Pioneer Ln., 98237, 206-826-4333 |
| Coulee City | Main Stay, The, 110 W. Main, 99115, 509-632-5687 |
| Coupeville | Captain Whidbey Inn, The, 2072 W. Capt. Whidbey, 98239, 206-678-4097 |
| Coupeville | Colonel Crockett Farm Inn, 1012 S. Fort Casey Rd., 98239, 206-678-3711 |
| Coupeville | Fort Casey Inn, 1124 S. Engle Rd., 98239, 206-678-8792 |
| Coupeville | Inn at Penn Cove, The, P.O. Box 85, 98239, 360-678-8000 |
| Coupeville | Victorian House, 602 N. Main St., 98239, 206-678-5305 |
| Darrington | Hemlock Hills B&B, P.O. Box 491, 98241, 206-436-1274 |
| Deer Harbor | Deep Meadow Farm B&B, P.O. Box 321, 98243, 360-376-5866 |
| Deer Park | Love's Victorian B&B, 31317 N. Cedar Rd., 99006, 509-276-6939 |
| Eastsound | Rosario Resort Hotel, 98245, 206-376-2222 |
| Edmonds | Aardvark House, 7219 Lake Ballinger Way, 98026, 206-778-7866 |
| Edmonds | Driftwood Lane B&B, 724 Driftwood Lane, 98020, 206-776-2686 |
| Edmonds | Harrison House, 210 Sunset Ave., 98020, 206-776-4748 |
| Edmonds | Heather House, 1011 "B" Ave., 98020, 206-778-7233 |
| Edmonds | Hudgrens Haven, 9313 - 190th, SW, 98020, 206-776-2202 |
| Edmonds | Maple Tree, The, 18313 Olympic View Dr., 98020, 206-774-8420 |
| Ellensburg | Treehouse B&B, The, 1414 North Cora St., 98926, 509-925-4620 |
| Enumclaw | Homestead B&B, The, 2510 Griffin Ave., 98022, 206-825-7816 |
| Enumclaw | Stillmeadow B&B, 46225 - 284th Ave..S.E., 98022, 206-825-6381 |
| Enumclaw | White Rose Inn, 1610 Griffin Ave., 98022, 206-825-7194 |
| Ferndale | Anderson House B&B, 4461 Sucia Dr., 98248, 206-384-3450 |
| Forks | Manitou Lodge, P.O. Box 600, 98331, 206-374-6295 |
| Forks | Miller Tree Inn, P.O. Box 953, 98331, 206-374-6806 |
| Fox Island | Island Escape B&B, 210 Island Blvd., 98333, 206-549-2044 |
| Friday Harbor | Argyle House, P.O. Box 2569, 98250, 360-378-4084 |
| Friday Harbor | Blair House B&B, 345 Blair Ave., 98250, 206-378-5907 |
| Friday Harbor | Duffy House B&B Inn, 760 Pear Point Rd., 98250, 360-378-5604 |
| Friday Harbor | Hillside House, 365 Carter Ave., 98250, 206-378-4730 |
| Friday Harbor | Mariella Inn & Cottages, 630 Turn Point Rd., 98250, 206-378-6868 |
| Friday Harbor | Meadows, The, 1980 Cattle Point Rd., 98250, 206-378-4004 |
| Friday Harbor | Moon & Sixpence, 3021 Beaverton Valley, 98250, 206-378-4138 |
| Friday Harbor | Olympic Lights, 4531A Cattle Point Rd., 98250, 206-378-3186 |
| Friday Harbor | Roche Harbor Resort, P.O. Box 4001, 98250, 206-378-2155 |
| Friday Harbor | States Inn, 2039 W. Valley Rd., 98250, 360-378-6240 |
| Friday Harbor | Tower House, 1230 Little Rd., 98250, 206-378-5464 |
| Friday Harbor | Trumpeter Inn, 420 Trumpeter Inn, 98250, 800-826-7926 |
| Friday Harbor | Westwinds Bed & Breakfast, 4909 N. Hannah Hghlnds, 98250, 206-378-5283 |
| Garfield | R.C. McCroskey House, Box 95, 99130, 509-635-1459 |
| Gig Harbor | Olde Glencove Hotel, 9418 Glencove Rd., 98335, 206-884-2835 |
| Glenwood | Flying L Ranch Inn, 25 Flying L Ln., 98619, 509-364-3488 |
| Goose Prairie | Hopkinson House, The, 8391 Bumping River Rd., 98929, 509-454-9431 |
| Hamilton | Smith House B&B, 307 Maple St., 98255, 206-826-4214 |
| Ilwaco | Chick-a-Dee Inn, P.O. Box 922, 98624, 360-642-8686 |
| Issaquah | Mountain & Planes B&B, 100 Big Bear Pl NW, 98027, 206-392-8068 |
| La Conner | Heron in La Conner, Box 716, 117 Maple St., 98257, 206-466-4626 |
| La Conner | La Conner Country Inn, P.O. Box 573, 98257, 206-466-3101 |
| La Conner | Rainbow Inn B&B, P.O. Box 15, 98257, 206-466-4578 |
| Langley | Blue House Inn & B&B, 513 Anthes, 98260, 360-221-8392 |
| Langley | Country Cottage of Langley, 215 - 6th St., 98260, 360-221-8709 |
| Langley | Cristy's Country Inn, 2891 E. Meinhold Rd., 98260, 360-321-1815 |
| Langley | Garden Path Inn, The, 111 First St., Box 575, 98260, 360-321-5121 |
| Langley | Inn at Langley, P.O. Box 835, 98260, 360-221-3033 |
| Langley | Orchard, 619 3rd St., 98260, 360-221-7880 |
| Langley | Villa Isola B&B Inn, 5489 S. Coles Rd., 98260, 360-221-5052 |
| Langley | Whidbey Inn, The, P.O. Box 156, 98260, 360-221-7115 |
| Leavenworth | Bavarian Meadows B&B, 11097 Eagle Creek Rd., 98826, 509-548-4449 |
| Leavenworth | Bosch Garten B&B, 9846 Dye Rd., 98826, 509-548-6900 |
| Leavenworth | Cougar Inn, 23379 Hwy. 207, 98826, 509-763-3354 |
| Leavenworth | Edel Haus Pension, 320 Ninth St., 98826, 509-548-4412 |
| Leavenworth | Hotel Europa, 833 Front St., 98826, 509-548-5221 |
| Leavenworth | Old Brick Silo B&B, 9028 E. Leavenworth Rd., 98826, 509-548-4772 |
| Leavenworth | Phippen's B&B, 10285 Ski Hill Dr., 98826, 800-666-9806 |
| Long Beach | Scandinavian Gardens Inn, Rt. 1, Box 36, 98631, 206-642-8877 |
| Longmire | National Park Inn, 98398, 206-569-2565 |
| Lopez | Betty's Place, P.O. Box 86, 98261, 206-468-2470 |
| Lopez Island | Edenwild Inn, P.O. Box 271, 98261, 206-468-3238 |

| | |
|---|---|
| Lopez Island | MacKaye Harbor Inn, Route 1, Box 1940, 98261, 206-468-2253 |
| Lummi Island | West Shore Farm B&B, 2781 W. Shore Dr., 98262, 206-758-2600 |
| Lynden | Century House B&B, 401 S. B.C. Ave., 98264, 206-354-2439 |
| Maple Valley | Maple Valley B&B, 20020 S.E. 228th, 98038, 206-432-1409 |
| Mazama | Lost River Bess' B&B, 98 Lost River Rd., 98833, 509-996-2457 |
| Mercer Island | Duck-In B&B, 4118 100th Ave., SE, 98040, 206-232-2554 |
| Mercer Island | Mole House Bed & Breakfast, 3308 W. Mercer Way, 98040 |
| Montesano | Abel House B&B Inn, The, 117 Fleet St., So., 98563, 206-249-6002 |
| Montesano | Sylvan Haus B&B, 417 Wilder Hill Ln., 98563, 206-249-3453 |
| Morton | St. Helens Manorhouse, 7476 Hwy 12, 98356, 206-498-5243 |
| Nordland | Ecologic Place, 10 Beach Dr., 98358, 206-385-3077 |
| North Bend | Apple Tree Inn, 43317 SE N. Bend Way, 98045, 206-888-3572 |
| North Bend | Hillwood Gardens B&B, 41812 S. E. 142nd St., 98045, 206-888-0799 |
| North Bend | Twin Peaks B&B, 13308 409th Ave., SE, 98045, 206-888-4083 |
| Oak Harbor | Elfreeda's Place B&B, 5140 Anglers Haven Dr, 98277 |
| Oak Harbor | North Island B&B, 1589 NW Beach Rd., 98277, 206-675-7080 |
| Oakesdale | Hanford Castle, The, Box 23, 99158, 509-285-4120 |
| Olalla | Olalla Orchard B&B, 12530 Orchard Ave. S.E., 98359, 206-857-5915 |
| Olga | Sand Dollar Inn, Star Route Box 10, 98279, 206-376-5696 |
| Olympia | Britt's Place, 4301 Waldrick Rd., S.E., 98501, 206-264-2764 |
| Orcas | Orcas Hotel, P.O. Box 155, 98280, 206-376-4300 |
| Orcas Island | Spring Bay in Olga, P.O. Box 97, 98279, 206-376-5531 |
| Pateros | Amy's Manor B&B, P.O. Box 411, 98846, 509-923-2334 |
| Pateros | French House B&B, 206 W. Warren, 98846, 509-923-2626 |
| Port Angeles | Anniken's B&B, 214 East Whidbey Ave., 98362, 206-457-6177 |
| Port Angeles | Lake Crescent Lodge, Star Route 1, 98362, 206-928-3211 |
| Port Angeles | Log Cabin Resort, 6540 E. Beach Rd., 98362 |
| Port Angeles | Our House B&B, 218 Whidbey Ave., 98362, 800-882-9051 |
| Port Angeles | Sol Duc Hot Springs Resort, P.O. Box 2169, 98362 |
| Port of Friday | Wharfside B&B, P.O. Box 1212, 98250, 206-378-5661 |
| Port Orchard | "Reflections" - A B&B Inn, 3878 Reflection Ln., E, 98366, 360-871-5582 |
| Port Orchard | Ogle's B&B, 1307 Dogwood Hill S.W., 98366, 206-876-9170 |
| Port Townsend | Arcadia Country Inn, 1891 S. Jacob Miller Rd, 98368, 206-385-5245 |
| Port Townsend | Chanticleer Inn, 1208 Franklin St., 98368 |
| Port Townsend | English Inn, The, 718 "F" St., 98368, 206-385-5302 |
| Port Townsend | Heritage House B&B Inn, 305 Pierce St., 98368, 206-385-6800 |
| Port Townsend | Irish Acres, P.O. Box 466, 98368, 206-385-4485 |
| Port Townsend | Lincoln Inn, The, 538 Lincoln St., 98368, 206-385-6677 |
| Port Townsend | Lizzie's Victorian B&B, 731 Pierce St., 98368, 360-385-4168 |
| Port Townsend | Manresa Castle Hotel, P.O. Box 564, 98368, 206-385-5750 |
| Port Townsend | Quimper Inn, 1306 Franklin St., 98368, 360-385-1060 |
| Port Townsend | Water Street Hotel, Quincy Street Dock, 98368, 206-385-5467 |
| Poulsbo | Manor Farm Inn, 26069 Big Valley Rd., 98370, 206-779-4628 |
| Poulsbo | Solliden Guest House, 17128 Lemolo Shore Dr., 98370, 206-779-3969 |
| Quinault | Lake Quinault Lodge, P.O Box 7, S. Shore Rd., 98575, 206-288-2571 |
| Randle | Hampton House B&B, 409 Silverbrook Rd, 98377 |
| Redmond | Cottage Creek Manor, 12525 Avondale Rd., 98052, 206-881-5606 |
| Richland | Shirlin Inn, The, 105 Patton St., 99352, 509-375-0720 |
| Ritzville | Portico Victorian B&B, The, 502 S. Adams St., 99169, 509-659-0800 |
| Roche Harbor | Hotel de Haro/Resort, 4950 Tarte Mem. Dr., 98250, 206-378-2155 |
| Seabeck | Summer Song B&B, P.O. Box 82, 98380, 206-830-5089 |
| Seabeck | Walton House, 12340 Seabeck Hwy NW, 98380, 206-830-4498 |
| Seattle | Capitol Hill Inn, 1713 Belmont Ave., 98122, 206-323-1955 |
| Seattle | Dibble House B&B, 7301 Dibble Ave. N.W., 98117, 206-783-0320 |
| Seattle | Gaslight Inn, 1727 15th Ave., 98122, 206-325-3654 |
| Seattle | Hainsworth House, 2657 37th Ave. SW, 98126 |
| Seattle | Pensione Nichols, 1923 First Ave., 98101, 206-441-7125 |
| Seattle | Queen Anne Hill B&B, 1835 7th West, 98119, 206-284-9779 |
| Seattle | Roberta's B&B, 1147 Sixteenth Ave East, 98112, 206-329-3326 |
| Seattle | Salisbury House, 750 16th Ave. East, 98112, 206-328-8682 |
| Seattle | Seattle B&B, 2442 N.W. Market #300, 98107, 206-783-2169 |
| Seattle | Seattle Guest Cottage, 2442 NW Market St. #300, 98107, 206-783-2169 |
| Seaview | Gumm's B&B Inn, P.O. Box 447, 98644, 206-642-8887 |
| Sequim | Granny Sandy's Orchard B&B, 405 W. Spruce, 98382, 206-683-5748 |
| Sequim | Groveland Cottage, 4861 Sequim, 98382, 360-683-3565 |
| Shelton | Twin River Ranch B&B, E 5730 Hwy 3, 98584, 206-426-1023 |
| Silverdale | Dennis Fulton B&B, 16609 Olympic View Rd., 98383, 206-692-4648 |
| Snohomish | Carleton House B&B, 416 Ave. D, 98290, 206-568-4211 |

*The Palace Hotel, Port Townsend, WA*

| Snohomish | Country Manner B&B, 1120 First St., 98290, 206-568-8254 |
| Snohomish | Eddy's B&B, 425 9th St., 98290, 206-568-7081 |
| Spokane | Blakely Estate B&B, E. 7710 Hodin Dr., 99212, 509-926-9426 |
| Spokane | Hillside House, E. 1729 18th Ave., 99203, 509-534-1426 |
| Spokane | Town & Country Cottage B&B, N7620 Fox Point Dr., 99208, 509-466-7559 |
| Spokane | Waverly Place B&B, W. 709 Waverly Place, 99205, 509-328-1856 |
| Stehekin | Silver Bay Inn, P.O. Box 43, 98852, 509-682-2212 |
| Tacoma | Inge's Place, 6809 Lake Grove SW, 98499, 206-584-4514 |
| Tacoma | Keenan House, 2610 N. Warner, 98407, 206-752-0702 |
| Tacoma | Sally's Bear Tree Cottage, 6019 West 64th St., 98467, 206-475-3144 |
| Tacoma | Villa, The, 705 N. 5th St., 98403, 206-572-1157 |
| Tonasket | Orchard Country Inn, Box 634, 98855, 509-486-1923 |
| Trout Lake | Mio Amore Pensione, P.O. Box 208, 98650, 509-395-2264 |
| Usk | River Bend Inn, Route 2 Box 943, 99180, 509-445-1476 |
| Vashon Island | Maury Garden Cottage, 22705 Deppman Rd.,S.W., 98070, 206-463-3034 |
| Vashon Island | Old Tjomsland House, P.O. Box 913, 98070, 206-463-5275 |
| Walla Walla | Stone Creek Inn, 720 Bryant Ave., 99362, 509-529-8120 |
| Waterville | Tower House B&B, P.O. Box 129, 98858, 509-745-8320 |
| White Salmon | Inn of the White Salmon, P.O. Box 1549, 98672, 509-493-2335 |
| White Salmon | Llama Ranch B&B, 1980 Hwy 141, 98672, 509-395-2786 |
| White Salmon | Orchard Hill Inn, 199 Oak Ridge Rd., 98672, 509-493-3024 |
| Woodinville | Bear Creek Inn, 19520 N.E. 144th Place, 98072, 206-881-2978 |
| Yakima | '37 House, 4002 Englewood Ave., 98908, 509-965-5537 |
| Yakima | Irish House B&B, 210 S. 28th Ave., 98902, 509-453-5474 |

# West Virginia

## BERKELEY SPRINGS

**Highlawn Inn**
304 Market St., 25411
304-258-5700  800-CALL WVA
Sandra M. Kauffman
All year

$$$-B&B
5 rooms, 5 pb
MC, Visa, *Rated*,
S-yes/P-no/H-ltd

Full country breakfast
Dinner by reservation
Catering, weddings
TV, veranda, porch swing
golf, tennis, hiking

*Restored Victorian; luxurious touches, solitude & antiques in quiet mountain town. Minutes to famous mineral baths. Winter Victorian escape packages. **Free bottle of WV wine.***

## CHARLES TOWN

**Gilbert House of Middleway**
P.O. Box 1104, 25414
Rt. 1, Box 160, Middleway
304-725-0637
Bernard F. Heiler
All year

$$$-B&B
3 rooms, 3 pb
Most CC, *Rated*, •
C-ltd/S-ltd/P-no/H-ltd
German, Spanish

Full gourmet breakfast
Comp. tea, wine, snacks
Sitting room, library
piano, fireplaces
A/C, bridal suite

*Near Harper's Ferry. HABS listed, 18th-century stone house on original settlers' trail into Shenandoah Valley. Antiques, art treasures, village ghost. **3rd night 40% off, ltd.***

## DURBIN

**Cheat Mountain Club**
PO Box 28, 26264
Rt. 250, Cheat Bridge
304-456-4627  Fax: 304-456-3192
Gladys Boehmer
All year

$$$$-AP
10 rooms, 1 pb
Visa, MC, •
C-yes/S-yes/P-no/H-no

All meals included
Snacks, bar service
Sitting room, sports rm.
family room w/fireplace
bike & X-C ski rentals

*Located on Shaver's Fork River, one of the finest trout streams in WV. Bordered by the million acre Monongahela Nat'l. Forest. A perfect setting for family or business retreats. Guide service.*

## ELKINS

| Retreat, The | $$-B&B | Full breakfast |
|---|---|---|
| 214 Harpertown Rd., 26241 | 8 rooms, | Monongahela Nat'l Forest |
| 304-636-2960 | Visa, MC, | walk to tennis, pool, |
| Leslie Gordon | C-yes/S-no/P-no/H-no | festival and downtown |
| All year | | |

*Gracious turn-of-the-century home surrounded by oaks, hemlock & rhododendron groves. Near Monongahela Nat'l Forest & unspoiled wilderness. 50% off 3rd night.*

| Tunnel Mountain B&B | $$-B&B | Full breakfast |
|---|---|---|
| Route 1, Box 59-1, 26241 | 3 rooms, 3 pb | Restaurant nearby |
| 304-636-1684 | *Rated*, | Sitting room w/fireplace |
| Anne & Paul Beardslee | C-ltd/S-ltd/P-no/H-no | patio, wooded paths, A/C |
| All year | | scenic views, cable TV |

*Romantic country fieldstone B&B nestled in the scenic West Virginia. Mountains next to National Forest and recreational areas. Antiques, fireplaces, warm hospitality.*

## HILLSBORO

| Current B&B, The | $-B&B | Full breakfast |
|---|---|---|
| HC 64, Box 135, 24946 | 5 rooms, 1 pb | Snacks |
| 304-653-4722 | MC, Visa, | Complimentary wine |
| Leslee McCarty | C-yes/S-no/P-yes/H-no | hot tub on outdoor deck |
| All year | Spanish | |

*Peaceful farm retreat on Greenbrier River Trail. Outdoor hot tub, antique-filled rooms near thousands of acres of national forests and state parks.*

## HUTTONSVILLE

| Hutton House B&B | $$-B&B | Full gourmet breakfast |
|---|---|---|
| Rts. 219/250, Box 88, 26273 | 7 rooms, 7 pb | Lunch, dinner, Aftn. tea |
| 304-335-6701 800-234-6701 | MC, Visa, *Rated*, • | Snacks, Comp. wine |
| Loretta Murray & Dean | C-yes/S-no/P-no/H-no | sitting room |
| Ahren | | |
| All year | | |

*Historic Queen Anne mansion conveniently located near cultural & outdoor attractions. Meticulous restoration yet kitchen-friendly atmosphere.*

## MOOREFIELD

| McMechen House Inn B&B | $$-B&B | Full breakfast |
|---|---|---|
| 109 N. Main St., 26836 | 7 rooms, 5 pb | Restaurant (seasonal) |
| 304-538-7173 Fax: 304-538-7841 | Visa, MC, AmEx, | Antique & gift shop |
| 800-298-2466 | *Rated*, | sitting room, A/C |
| Robert & Linda Curtis | C-yes/S-no/P-no/H-no | cable TV, weddings |

*Surrounded by majestic mountains & natural beauty. Built in 1853, furnished in distinctive decor and period antiques. Emphasis on hospitality. 3rd night 50%.*

## ROMNEY

| Hampshire House 1884 | $$-B&B/MAP/AP | Full breakfast |
|---|---|---|
| 165 N. Grafton St., 26707 | 7 rooms, 6 pb | Lunch, dinner |
| 304-822-7171 | Most CC, *Rated*, • | Comp. wine, snacks |
| Jane & Scott Simmons | C-ltd/S-no/P-no/H-no | sitting room, library |
| All year | | bikes, near tennis, pool |

*Completely renovated 1884 home. Period furniture, lamps, fireplaces. Gourmet dining. Quiet. Therapeutic massage available. 3rd night 50% off except October.*

## SHEPHERDSTOWN

| **Thomas Shepherd Inn** | $$$-B&B | Full breakfast |
| P.O. Box 1162,  25443 | 7 rooms, 7 pb | Sherry, coffee, tea |
| 300 W. German St. at Duke | AmEx, MC, Visa, | Living room w/fireplace |
| 304-876-3715 Fax: 304-876-1386 | *Rated*, | bikes, picnics, central |
| Margaret Perry | C-ltd/S-ltd/P-no/H-no | A/C, VCR, film library |
| All year | | |

*1868 restored stately home in quaint, historic Civil War town. Period antiques, very special breakfasts, fireside beverage, excellent restaurants.* **3rd night 50% off.**

## WHEELING

| **Eckhart House, The** | $$-B&B | Continental plus bkfst. |
| 810 Main St.,  26003 | 2 rooms, 2 pb | Guest parlor, gift shop |
| 304-232-5439 Fax: 304-232-5439 | Visa, MC, AmEx, Disc., | near fine restaurants, |
| Joe & Gretchen Figaretti | • | theatres & attractions |
| All year | C-yes/S-no/P-no/H-no | |

*Magnificently restored 1892 grande Victorian featuring original stained glass, fretwork, mantles and chandeliers. Conviently located in Old Town, adjacent to downtown.*

# More Inns ...

| | |
|---|---|
| Aurora | Cabin Lodge,  Box 355, Route 50, 26705,  304-735-3563 |
| Berkeley Springs | Country Inn, The,  207 S. Washington St., 25411,  304-258-2210 |
| Berkeley Springs | Folkestone B&B,  Route 2, Box 404, 25411,  304-258-3743 |
| Berkeley Springs | Manor,  P.O. Box 342, 25411,  304-258-1552 |
| Berkeley Springs | Maria's Garden & Inn, 201 Independence St., 25411,  304-258-2021 |
| Bramwell | Three Oaks & a Quilt,  Duhring St., 24715 |
| Cass | Shay Inn,  Box 46, 24927 |
| Charles Town | Carriage Inn, The,  417 E. Washington St., 25414,  304-728-8003 |
| Charles Town | Cottonwood Inn, The,  Rt. 2, Box 61-S, 25414,  304-725-3371 |
| Charles Town | Hillbrook Inn,  Route 2, Box 152, 25414,  304-725-4223 |
| Charles Town | Washington House Inn,  216 S. George St., 25414,  304-725-7923 |
| Charleston | Histroic Charleston B&B,  114 Elizabeth St., 25311,  304-345-8156 |
| Chloe | Pennbrooke Farm B&B,  Granny-she Run, 25235,  304-655-7367 |
| Davis | Bright Morning,  Route 32, William Ave., 26260,  304-259-2719 |
| Davis | Twisted Thistle B&B,  P.O Box 480, Fourth St., 26260,  304-259-5389 |
| Elkins | Cheat River Lodge,  Route 1, Box 116, 26241,  304-636-2301 |
| Elkins | Lincoln Crest B&B,  P. O. Box 408, 26241 |
| Elkins | Post House, The,  306 Robert E. Lee Ave., 26241,  304-636-1792 |
| Gerrardstown | Prospect Hill B&B,  P.O. Box 135, 25420,  304-229-3346 |
| Greenbrier County | Oak Knoll B&B,  Crawley, 24931,  304-392-6903 |
| Harpers Ferry | Fillmore Street B&B,  Box 34, 25245,  301-337-8633 |
| Helvetia | Beekeeper Inn,  26224,  304-924-6435 |
| Huttonsville | Cardinal Inn B&B, The,  Rte 1 -Box 1, Route 219, 26273,  304-335-6149 |
| Huttonsville | Richard's Country Inn,  U.S. 219 Rt. 1 Box11-A1, 26273,  304-335-6659 |
| Jane Lew | West Fork Inn,  Route 2, Box 212, 26378,  304-745-4893 |
| Lewisburg | General Lewis Inn,  301 E. Washington St., 24901,  304-645-2600 |
| Lewisburg | Lynn's Inn B&B,  Rt. 4 Box 40, 24901 |
| Lewisburg | Minnie Manor,  403 E. Washington St., 24901 |
| Lost Creek | Crawford's Country Corner,  Box 112, 26385,  304-745-3017 |
| Lost River | Guest House,  Low-Gap, 26811,  304-897-5707 |
| Martinsburg | Aspen Hall Inn,  405 Boyd Ave., 25401,  304-263-4385 |
| Martinsburg | Boydsville Inn,  609 So. Queen St., 25401 |
| Mathias | Valley View Farm,  Route 1, Box 467, 26812,  304-897-5229 |
| Middleway | Daniel Fry House B&B, The,  Rt 1, Box 152, 25430 |
| Moorefield | Hickory Hill Farm,  Route 1, Box 355, 26836,  304-538-2511 |
| Morgantown | Maxwell B&B,  Route 12, Box 197, 26505,  304-594-3041 |
| Orlando | Kilmarnock Farms,  Route 1 Box 91, 26412,  304-452-8319 |
| Shepherdstown | Bavarian Inn & Lodge,  Route 1, Box 30, 25443,  304-876-2551 |
| Shepherdstown | Little Inn,  P.O. Box 219, 25443,  304-876-2208 |
| Shepherdstown | Mecklenberg Inn,  P.O. Box 127, 25443,  304-876-2126 |
| Shepherdstown | Shang-Ra-La B&B,  Route 1, Box 156, 25443,  304-876-2391 |
| Sinks Grove | Morgan Orchard,  Route 2, Box 114, 24976,  304-772-3638 |
| Sistersville | Cobblestone-on-the-Ohio,  103 Charles St., 26175,  304-652-1206 |
| Sistersville | Wells Inn,  316 Charles St., 26175,  304-652-3111 |
| Slatyfork | Elk River Touring Center,  26291,  304-572-3771 |
| Valley Head | Nakiska Chalet B&B,  HC 73, Box 24, 26294,  304-339-6309 |
| Wheeling | Stratford Springs Inn,  355 Oglebay Dr., 26003,  304-233-5100 |
| White Sulphur Springs | James Wylie House B&B,  208 E. Main St., 24986,  304-536-9444 |
| Winona | Garvey House B&B,  P.O. Box 98, 25942,  304-574-3235 |

*Pinehaven B&B, Baraboo, WI*

# Wisconsin

## BARABOO

**Pinehaven B&B**
E. 13083 Hwy. 33,  53913
608-356-3489
Lyle & Marge Getschman
All year

$$-B&B
4 rooms, 4 pb
MC, Visa, *Rated*,
C-ltd/S-no/P-no/H-no

Full breakfast
Fishing, rowing
Guest cottage, gazebo
sitting room

*Beautiful view of bluffs private lake. Tranquil setting. Take a stroll, fish, admire the Belgian draft horses. Relax. Acres to roam. Farm tours, country walks. **3rd night 50%.***

## DE PERE

**James Street Inn**
201 James St.,  54115
414-337-0111  Fax: 414-337-6135
Kevin C. Flatley
All year

$$$-B&B
30 rooms, 30 pb
*Rated*, •
C-yes/S-ltd/P-no/H-yes

Continental plus bkfst.
Afternoon tea, snacks
Comp. wine, bar service
sitting room, fireplaces
private decks, whirlpool

*A country inn hidden just outside of Green Bay. Built on the foundation of a c.1858 mill, the river literally flows beneath it!*

## DELAVAN

**Lakeside Manor Inn**
1809 S. Shore Dr.,  53115
414-728-5354  Fax: 414-728-2043
Mary & George Jorndt
All year

$$$-B&B
6 rooms, 3 pb
Visa, MC, *Rated*, •
C-ltd/S-no/P-no/H-yes

Cont. wkdays/full wkends
Cocktail hr/wine-snacks
Sitt rm, fishing, TV/VCR
Private pier & beach
full fam. cottage, porch

*On Delavan Lake shore, a picturesque Victorian inn nestled in Geneva Lakes recreation area. Relaxed lakefront lifestyle has attracted discriminating guests for over a century. **25% off 2nd night.***

## EAGLE

**Eagle Centre House B&B**
W370, S9590 Hwy 67,   53119
414-363-4700
Riene Wells & Dean Herriges
All year exc. Christmas

$$$-B&B
5 rooms, 5 pb
AmEx, MC, Visa,
*Rated*, •
C-ltd/S-no/P-no/H-no

Full breakfast
Comp. wine, cider, etc.
Parlor, tap room
air-conditioning
hiking, riding, skiing

*Greek Revival Inn features period antiques. In scenic Kettle Moraine Forest. Half mile from "Old World Wisconsin" Historic Site. Near Milwaukee.* **Multiple night discount.**

## EAGLE RIVER

**Brennan Manor-Olde World**
1079 Everett Rd.,   54521
715-479-7353    All year

$$$-B&B
4 rooms, 4 pb
•
C-ltd/P-no/H-ltd

Full breakfast
Afternoon tea
Sitting room
bikes

*English Tudor mansion on the lake. Large rooms with private baths. Antiques, quilts. Candlelight breakfast. A wonderful getaway—boating, hiking & skiing close by.*

## ELLISON BAY

**Griff Inn, The**
11976 Mink River Rd.,   54210
414-854-4306
Laurie & Jim Roberts
All year

$$$-B&B
7 rooms, 7 pb
*Rated*,
C-ltd/S-no/P-no/H-no

Full country breakfast
Lnch & dinner by request
Evening popcorn/beverage
gathering rooms, library
tennis court, skiing

*New England-style country inn on Door County Peninsula, since 1910. Handmade quilts on antique beds. cross-country ski from our door trail. On five lovely acres.* **3rd night 50%.**

## EPHRAIM

**Eagle Harbor Inn**
PO Box 588, 9914 Water St.,
   54211
414-854-2121  Fax: 414-854-2121
800-324-5427
Nedd & Natalie Neddersen
All year

$$$-B&B
21 rooms, 21 pb
MC, Visa, *Rated*, •
C-ltd/P-no/H-yes

Full gourmet breakfast
Afternoon refreshments
Indoor pool with current
cottages have TV & grill
200 yds to sandy beach

*An intimate New England-styled country inn. Antique-filled, period wallpapers. Close to boating, beaches, golf course, parks. 12 private cottages. Queen-size or double beds.*

**Hillside Hotel of Ephraim**
P.O. Box 17,   54211
9980 Hwy 42
414-854-2417  Fax: 414-854-4604
800-423-7023
K&D McNeil & Family
May–October, Jan–Feb

$$$-B&B/MAP
12 rooms,
Visa, MC, Disc. *Rated*,
C-ltd/S-no/P-no/H-no

Full specialty breakfast
6-course gourmet dinner
Full rest, aftn. tea
featherbeds, ceiling fan
private beach, mooring

*Country-Victorian hotel in resort w/harbor view, original furnishings, spectacular views; near galleries, shops. Deluxe cottages w/whirlpool baths. Queen beds available.*

## FISH CREEK

**Thorp House Inn & Cottages**
P.O. Box 490,   54212
4135 Bluff Rd.
414-868-2444
C. & S. Falck-Pedersen
All year

$$-B&B
10 rooms, 10 pb
*Rated*,
C-ltd/S-no
Norwegian

Continental plus bkfst.
Sitting room w/fireplace
library, bicycles
winter cross-country skiing

*Antique-filled historic home backed by wooded bluff, overlooking bay. Walk to beach, park, shops, restaurants. Kids O.K. in cottages, 5 w/fireplace, 4 w/whirlpool.* **Off season cottage specials.**

## EPHRAIM

| | | |
|---|---|---|
| **Whistling Swan, The** | $$$-B&B | Continental plus bkfst. |
| P.O. Box 193,  54212 | 7 rooms, 7 pb | Afternoon tea, snacks |
| 4192 Main St. | Most CC, *Rated*, | Sitting room, library |
| 414-868-3442  Fax: 414-868-1703 | C-yes/S-no/P-no/H-no | wicker filled porch |
| Laurie & Jim Roberts | | |
| All year | | |

*A meticulously renovated country inn with 100 years of intriguing history . . . an elegantly appointed room or suite in Door County, Wisconsin.*

| | | |
|---|---|---|
| **White Gull Inn** | $$$-B&B | Full breakfast |
| Box 160,  54212 | 16 rooms, 9 pb | Lunch, dinner |
| 4225 Main St. | C-yes/S-yes/P-no/H-ltd | Bicycles |
| 414-868-3517 | | entertainment |
| Andy & Jon Coulson | | piano |
| All year | | |

*Situated between the bluff and the bay in Fish Creek on Wisconsin's Door Peninsula; charming turn-of-the-century inn.*

## GREEN BAY

| | | |
|---|---|---|
| **Astor House B&B, The** | $$$-B&B | Continental breakfast |
| 637 S. Monroe Ave.,  54301 | 5 rooms, 5 pb | Complimentary wine |
| 414-432-3585 | Visa, MC, AmEx, Disc., | Hot tubs, sitting room |
| Doug Landwehr | • | gas fireplaces, phone |
| All year | C-ltd/S-no/P-no/H-no | cable TV, stereo, VCR |

*Welcome to Green Bay's historic Astor Neighborhood. Five decorative motifs & in-room amenities indulge our guests, including whirlpool and fireplaces.* **3rd night $20 off, ltd.**

## HARTLAND

| | | |
|---|---|---|
| **Monches Mill House** | $$-B&B | Continental plus bkfst. |
| W301 N9430 Hwy E,  53029 | 4 rooms, 2 pb | Sitting room |
| 414-966-7546 | C-yes/S-yes/P-yes/H-yes | hot tub, bikes |
| Elaine D. Taylor | French | tennis, canoeing, hiking |
| May—December | | |

*House built in 1842, located on the bank of the mill pond, furnished in antiques, choice of patio, porch or gallery for breakfast enjoyment.*

## HUDSON

| | | |
|---|---|---|
| **Jefferson-Day House** | $$$-B&B | Four course breakfast |
| 1109 - 3rd St.,  54016 | 3 rooms, 3 pb | Snacks |
| 715-386-7111 | *Rated*, • | Special diets avail. |
| Tom and Sue Tyler | C-yes/H-yes | sitting room, library |
| All year | Spanish | 3 room suite sleeps 5 |

*1857 home blocks away from beautiful St. Croix River. Skiing nearby. 15 min. from St. Paul/Minneapolis. Antique collections.* **Free bottle of wine.**

## LAKE GENEVA

| | | |
|---|---|---|
| **Eleven Gables on the Lake** | $$$-B&B | Full breakfast-wkends |
| 493 Wrigley Dr.,  53147 | 12 rooms, 12 pb | Continental plus-midweek |
| 414-248-8393  Fax: 414-248-6096 | Most CC, *Rated*, | Pvt. pier, swim, fish |
| 800-362-0395 | C-ltd/S-ltd/P-no/H-ltd | hiking, bike rental |
| A. Fasel Milliette | | courtesy phone, Fax |
| All year | | |

*Lakeside historic inn. Romantic bedrooms, bridal chamber, family "country cottages." Fireplaces, down quilts, wet bars, TVs, balconies. Prime location.* **3rd night 50%, ltd.**

## LAKE GENEVA

**Geneva Inn, The**
N-2009 State Rd. 120,  53147
414-248-5680  Fax: 414-248-5685
800-441-5881
Richard B. Treptow
All year

$$$$-B&B
37 rooms, 37 pb
Most CC,
C-yes/S-yes/P-no/H-yes
German, French,
Spanish

Continental plus bkfst.
Restaurant, lunch/dinner
Turndown cognac & choc.
whirlpools, fitness room
atrium, lake swimming

*A relaxing retreat on the shores of Lake Geneva. Deluxe accommodations touched w/ English charm. Restaurant & lounge. Banquet/meeting facilities; marina.* **Seasonal & pkg rates.**

**T.C. Smith Historic Inn**
865 Main St.,  53147
414-248-1097  Fax: 414-248-1672
800-423-0233
Marks Family
All year

$$$-B&B
8 rooms, 8 pb
Most CC, *Rated*, •
C-yes/S-yes/P-yes/H-no

Full breakfast
Afternoon tea, snacks
Sitting room, library
fireplaces, whirlpools
A/C, TV, fireplaces

*Relax by fireplaces to experience romance & warmth of Grand Victorian era in downtown lakeview mansion of 1845. Honeymoon suite w/lighted whirlpool. On National Register.* **Midweek 3rd night discount.**

## LODI

**Victorian Treasure B&B Inn**
115 Prairie St.,  53555
608-592-5199  Fax: 608-592-7147
800-859-5199
Todd & Kimberly Seidl
All year

$$-B&B
8 rooms, 8 pb
MC, Visa, *Rated*, •
C-yes/S-no/P-no/H-no

Full breakfast
Aftn. tea, snacks, wine
Whirlpools, fireplaces
Canopy beds, library
porches, parlors

*Luxurious, romantic Victorian accommodations between Madison & Dells. Meticulous rooms, thoughtful amenities, fussy innkeepers. 4 miles off of I90/94.* **3rd weeknight free.**

## MADISON

**Annie's B&B**
2117 Sheridan Dr.,  53704
608-244-2224  Fax: 608-242-9611
Anne & Lawrence Stuart
All year

$$$-B&B
4 rooms, 2 pb
AmEx, MC, Visa,
*Rated*,
S-ltd/P-ltd/H-no

Full breakfast
Library, whirlpool, A/C
tennis, nature trails
swimming, cross-country
skiing

*Beautiful country garden setting in the city, w/romantic gazebo. Full recreation fac., 10 min to downtown & campus. Woodland whirlpool room for 2 avail.* **4th weeknight free.**

**Arbor House Environmental**
3402 Monroe St.,  53711
608-238-2981  Fax: 608-238-1175
John & Cathie Imes
All year

$$$-B&B
8 rooms, 7 pb
MC, Visa, AmEx,
*Rated*,
C-yes/S-no/P-no/H-yes

Full breakfast
Hiking, biking, cable
cross-country skiing
National design award

*Historic landmark across from UW Arboretum has an enviromental emphasis. Minutes from the Capitol & UW campus. Complimentary canoeing & Gehl's iced cappuccino.* *Corporate rates*

**Collins House B&B**
704 E. Gorham St.,  53703
608-255-4230
Barb & Mike Pratzel
All year

$$$-B&B
5 rooms, 5 pb
MC, Visa, *Rated*,
C-yes/S-ltd/P-yes/H-no

Full breakfast
Comp. chocolate truffles
Sitting room w/fireplace
library, movies on video
whirlpools, frplc., deck

*Restored prairie school style. Overlooks Lake Mendota, near university and state capitol. Elegant rooms, wonderful gourmet breakfasts and pastries.*

*Arbor House Environmental Inn, Madison, WI*

## MADISON

**Mansion Hill Inn**
424 N. Pinckney St.,  53703
608-255-3999  Fax: 608-255-2217
800-798-9070
Janna Wojtal
All year

$$$-B&B
11 rooms, 11 pb
AmEx, MC, Visa,
*Rated*, •
C-ltd/S-yes/P-no/H-no

Continental plus bkfst.
Afternoon tea, snacks
Comp. wine, bar service
sitting room, hot tubs
sauna, steam showers

*Victorian elegance abounds in our antique-filled guest rooms. Fireplaces, private baths with whirlpools, valet service. We await your pleasure.* **3rd night 50% off.**

## MILWAUKEE

**Crane House, The**
346 E. Wilson St.,  53207
414-483-1512
P. Tirrito & S. Skavroneck
All year

$$-B&B
4 rooms,
Visa, MC, Disc.,
C-yes/S-ltd/P-no/H-no

Full breakfast
Sitting room, library
airport pick-up

*Beautiful perennial garden with pond. Sumptuous breakfast and homemade bedtime treats. Friendly, eclectic, comfortable atmosphere. Close to downtown and airport.*

## OSCEOLA

**St. Croix River Inn**
305 River St.,  54020
715-294-4248  800-645-8820
Bev Johnson
All year

$$$-B&B
7 rooms, 7 pb
AmEx, MC, Visa,
*Rated*, •
C-ltd/S-ltd/P-no/H-no

Full breakfast wkends.
Continental bkfast midwk
Sitting rooms, spa
jacuzzis in all suites
seven suites, fishing

*Elegantly furnished suites—some with fireplaces, all with jacuzzis. Overlooking the beautiful St. Croix River. Skiing, fishing and sightseeing nearby.* **3rd night 50%.**

## PORT WASHINGTON

**Port Washington Inn**
308 W. Washington St.,  53074
414-284-5583
Rita & Dave Nelson
All year

$$$-B&B
4 rooms, 4 pb
Visa, MC, AmEx,
C-ltd/S-no/P-no/H-no

Full breakfast
Afternoon tea
Sitting room, library
Lake Michigan & marina
5 block away

*Distictive inn, 4-5 blocks from restaurants and lake. Homemade breads and cookies, fresh flowers, terry robes. Serenity, elegance, comfort.*

## PORTAGE

**Breese Waye B&B**
816 Macfarlane Rd., 53901
608-742-5281
Jack & Dianne O'Connor
All year

$$-B&B
4 rooms, 3 pb
*Rated*,
C-ltd/S-no/P-no/H-no

Full breakfast weekends
Continental plus wkdays.
Breakfast in bed, tea on
arrival, sitting room
tennis & pool nearby

*Circa 1880 Victorian home furnished in antiques—an historic masterpiece. Summer breakfast served in Florida Room, winter breakfast in formal dining room. **3rd. night 50% off.***

## REEDSBURG

**Parkview B&B**
211 N. Park St., 53959
608-524-4333
Tom & Donna Hofmann
All year

$$-B&B
4 rooms, 2 pb
Visa, MC, AmEx, •
C-ltd/S-no/P-no/H-no

Full breakfast
Snacks, wake-up coffee
Sitting room
playhouse on property
park across the street

*1895 Victorian home with comfortable antiques, across from City Park. Wisconsin Dells, Baraboo, Spring Green, bike trails, state park nearby. **3rd night, 10% off total bill.***

## SPARTA

**Franklin Victorian, The**
220 E. Franklin St., 54656
608-269-3894 800-845-8767
Lloyd & Jane Larson
All year

$$-B&B
4 rooms, 2 pb
*Rated*,
C-ltd/S-no/P-no/H-no

Full 3-course breakfast
Afternoon tea, snacks
Sitting room
library
canoe rental

*Relax in quiet, gracious comfort—spacious rooms, fine woods. Delectable breakfasts. Surrounding area abounds with beauty. Recreation all four seasons. Near famous bike trail.*

## STEVENS POINT

**Dreams of Yesteryear B&B**
1100 Brawley St., 54481
715-341-4525 Fax: 715-344-3047
Bonnie & Bill Maher
All year

$$-B&B
7 rooms, 6 pb
Visa, MC, •
C-ltd/S-no/P-no/H-no

Full breakfast
Afternoon tea, snacks
Sitting room, library
tennis court, hot tub
Bike, pool, 2 3-room sts

*Victorian restoration featured in Victorian Homes Magazine. Its truly the kind of place Victorian Dreams are made of. House is A/C. **5% discount 3+ nights.***

## STURGEON BAY

**Inn at Cedar Crossing**
336 Louisiana St., 54235
414-743-4200 Fax: 414-743-4422
Terry Wulf
All year

$$$-B&B
9 rooms, 9 pb
Most CC, *Rated*,
C-ltd/S-no/P-no/H-no

Continental plus bkfst.
Restaurant, pub
Comp. beverages, cookies
dining rms., sitting rm.
Whirlpool in some rooms

*Elegant 1884 inn situated in historic district near shops, restaurants, museum, beaches. Elegant romantic antique decor, fireplaces, whirlpools. 6 rooms have frplcs. Rated "Top 25 Restaurants."*

## WHITE LAKE

**Wolf River Lodge**
Star Route Hwys 55 & 64,
54491
715-882-2182
Joan Jesse
All year

$$-B&B/AP
10 rooms, 3 pb
Most CC, •
C-yes/S-ltd/P-no/H-no

Full breakfast
Restaurant, bar
Sitt. rm., bikes, canoes
hot tubs, cross-country skis
2 bedroom guesthouse

*Comfortable north woods rustic log building overlooking the whitewater Wolf River. Handmade quilts, braided rugs, antique-filled rooms. Huge stone fireplace. Loft sleeps 8. **3rd night 50%.***

# More Inns . . .

| | |
|---|---|
| Albany | Albany Guest House, 405 S. Mill St., 53502, 608-862-3636 |
| Albany | Oak Hill Manor, 401 E. Main St., 53502, 608-862-1400 |
| Albany | Sugar river Inn, P.O. Box 39, 53502, 608-862-1248 |
| Algoma | Amberwood Inn, N7136 Hwy. 42, 54201, 414-487-3471 |
| Algoma | King Olaf's Pub & Inn, Hwy 42, 54201, 414-487-2090 |
| Alma | Gallery House, 215 N. Main St., Box 55, 54610, 608-685-4975 |
| Alma | Laue House, B&B Inn, P.O. Box 176, 54610, 608-685-4923 |
| Appleton | Queen Anne B&B, The, 837 E. College Ave., 54911, 414-739-7966 |
| Avoca | Prairie Rose B&B, 107 S. Second St., 53506, 608-532-6878 |

T.C.Smith Historic Inn,
Lake Geneva, WI

| | |
|---|---|
| Baileys Harbor | Potter's Door Inn, The, 9528 Highway 57, 54202, 414-839-2003 |
| Baldwin | Kaleidoscope Inn, 800-11th Ave., 54002, 715-684-4575 |
| Baraboo | Baraboo's Gollmar Guest, 422 3rd St., 53913, 608-356-9432 |
| Baraboo | Clark House, The, 320 Walnut St., 53913, 608-356-2191 |
| Baraboo | Frantiques Showplace, 704 Ash St., 53913, 608-356-5273 |
| Baraboo | Gollmar Mansion Inn, 422 - 3rd St., 53913, 608-356-9432 |
| Baraboo | Victorian Rose, 423 Third Ave., 53913, 608-356-7828 |
| Barnes | Sunset Resort B&B Lodge, HCR 61, Box 6325, 54873, 715-795-2449 |
| Bay View | Victorian B&B, 346 E. Wilson, 53207 |
| Bayfield | Apple Tree Inn, Rt. 1, Box 251, 54814, 715-779-5572 |
| Bayfield | Baywood Place B&B, The, 20 N. 3rd St., 54814, 715-779-3690 |
| Bayfield | Cooper Hill House, P.O. Box 1288, 54814, 715-779-5060 |
| Bayfield | Greunke's Inn, 17 Rittenhouse, 54814, 715-779-5480 |
| Bayfield | Lakeside Lodging, Route 1, Box 253, 54814, 715-779-5545 |
| Bayfield | Morning Glory B&B, 119 S. 6th St., 54814, 715-779-5621 |
| Bayfield | Old Rittenhouse Inn, The, P.O. Box 584, 54814, 715-779-5111 |
| Bayfield | Pinehurst Inn @ Pike's Cr., Rt. 1, Box 222, 54814, 715-779-3676 |
| Bayfield | Thimbleberry Inn B&B, 15021 Pageant Rd., 54814, 715-779-5757 |
| Belleville | Abendruh B&B Swisstyle, 7019 Gehin Rd., 53508, 608-424-3808 |
| Belleville | Cameo Rose B&B, 1090 Henry & Severson, 53508, 608-424-6340 |
| Brantwood | Palmquist Farm, River Rd., 54513, 715-564-2558 |
| Burlington | Hillcrest B&B Inn, 540 Storle Ave., 53105, 414-763-4706 |
| Cambridge | Night Heron Books & B&B, 315 E. Water St., 53523, 608-423-4141 |
| Campbellsport | Kettlebrook Farm, Inc., W. 541 Hwy. SS, 53010, 414-533-5387 |
| Campbellsport | Mielke-Mauk House B&B, The, W977 County Hwy. F, 53010, 414-533-8602 |
| Campbellsport | Newcastle Pines, N. 1499 Hwy. 45, 53010, 414-533-5252 |
| Cascade | Timberlake Inn, 311 Madison Ave., 53011, 414-528-8481 |
| Cashton | Convent House, Route 1, Box 160, 54619, 608-823-7906 |
| Cassville | Geiger House, 401 Denniston, 53806, 608-725-5419 |
| Cassville | River View B&B, 117 Front St., 53806, 608-725-5895 |
| Cedarburg | Birdsong B&B, N46W5455, 53012, 414-622-3770 |
| Cedarburg | Stagecoach Inn B&B, W61 N520 Washington Ave, 53012, 414-375-0208 |
| Cedarburg | Washington House Inn, W65 N394 Westlawn Ave., 53012, 414-375-3550 |
| Chetek | Annandale Inn, 569 18th St., 54728, 715-837-1974 |
| Chetek | Canoe Bay Inn & Cottages, W16065 Hogback Rd., 54728, 800-568-1995 |
| Chetek | Ruthies B&B, 120 Banks, 54728, 715-924-2407 |
| Chetek | Trails End B&B, 641 Ten Mile Lake Dr., 54728, 715-924-2641 |
| Chilton | East Shore Inn, N2577 Lake Shore Dr., 53014, 414-849-4230 |
| Cochrane | Rosewood B&B, The, 203 S. Main St., 54622, 608-248-2940 |
| Colfax | ClearView Hills B&B, Route 2, Box 87, 54730, 715-235-7180 |
| Colfax | Son Ne Vale Farm B&B, Route 1, Box 132, 54730, 715-962-4342 |
| Columbus | By the Okeag, 446 Wisconsin St., 53925, 414-623-3007 |
| Columbus | Dering House, The, 251 W. James St., 53925, 414-623-2015 |
| Columbus | Maple Leaf Inn B&B, 219 N. Ludington St., 53925, 414-623-5166 |
| Coon Valley | Old Parsonage, 508 Central Ave., 54623, 608-452-3833 |
| Cornell | House in the Woods, 200 N. Riverside Dr., 54732, 715-239-6511 |
| Cornucopia | Village Inn, The, P.O. Box 127, 54827, 715-742-3941 |
| Crandon | Courthouse Square B&B, 210 E. Polk St., 54520, 715-478-2549 |
| Cross Plains | Enchanted Valley Garden, 554 Enchanted Valley Rd, 53528, 608-798-4554 |
| Cross Plains | Past & Present Inn, The, 2034 Main St., 53528, 608-798-4441 |
| Cumberland | Rectory B&B, The, 1575 Second Ave., 54829, 715-822-3151 |
| Curtiss | Thompson's Inn, Cty Hwy E, P.O. Box 128, 54422, 715-223-6041 |
| DePere | Birch Creek Inn, 2263 Birch Creek Rd., 54115, 414-336-7575 |
| Downsville | Creamery, Box 22, 54735, 715-664-8354 |
| Durand | Ryan House, Rt. 2, Box 28, 54736, 715-672-8563 |
| Eagle River | Inn at Pinewood, The, P.O. Box 549, 54521, 715-479-4414 |
| East Troy | Greystone Farms B&B, N. 9391 Adams Rd., 53120, 414-495-8485 |
| East Troy | Mitten Farm B&B, W2454 Hwy. J, 53120, 414-642-5530 |

| | |
|---|---|
| East Troy | Pine Ridge B&B, 1152 Scout Rd., 53120, 414-594-3269 |
| Eau Claire | Apple Tree Inn, P.O. Box 677, 54702, 715-836-9599 |
| Eau Claire | Fanny Hill Inn, 3919 Crescent Ave., 54703, 715-836-8184 |
| Eau Claire | Westlin Winds, 3508 Halsey St., 54701, 715-832-1110 |
| Egg Harbor | Country Gardens B&B, 6421 Hwy. 42, 54209, 414-743-7434 |
| Ellison Bay | Country Woods B&B, 520 Europe Lake Rd., 54210, 414-854-5706 |
| Elroy | Waarvik's Century Farm, N. 4621 County Rd. H, 53929, 608-462-8595 |
| Endeavor | Neenah Creek Inn & Pottery, W7956 Neenah Rd., 53930, 608-587-2229 |
| Ephraim | Ephraim Inn, P.O. Box 247, 54211, 414-854-4515 |
| Ephraim | French Country Inn, 3052 Spruce Ln, Box 129, 54211, 414-854-4001 |
| Fennimore | Gazebo B&B, 825 12th St., 53809, 608-822-3928 |
| Fish Creek | Proud Mary, P.O. Box 193, 54212, 414-868-3442 |
| Fort Atkinson | Lamp Post Inn, 408 South Main St., 53538, 414-563-6561 |
| Frederic | Gandy Dancer B&B, The, P.O. Box 563, 54837, 715-327-8750 |
| Galesville | Clark House B&B, The, 624 W. Ridge Ave., 54630, 608-582-4190 |
| Gay Mills | Miss Molly's B&B, S. Gay St.,P.O. Box 254, 54631, 608-735-4433 |
| Glen Haven | Parson's Inn B&B, Rock School Rd., 53810, 608-794-2491 |
| Green Lake | McConnell Inn, 497 S. Lawson Dr.,Box 6, 54941, 414-294-6430 |
| Green Lake | Oakwood Lodge, 365 Lake St., 54941, 414-294-6580 |
| Green Lake | Strawberry Hill, Route 1, Box 524-D, 54941, 414-294-3450 |
| Hammond | Summit Farm B&B, 1622 110th Ave., 54015, 715-796-2617 |
| Hartford | Jordan House, 81 S. Main St., 53027, 414-673-5643 |
| Hayward | Edgewater Inn B&B, Rt. 1, Box 1293, 54843, 715-462-9412 |
| Hayward | Lumberman's Mansion Inn, P.O. Box 885, 54843, 715-634-3012 |
| Hayward | Mustard Seed B&B, The, 205 California, 54843, 715-634-2908 |
| Hayward | Spider Lake Lodge, Rt. 1, Box 1335, 54843, 800-653-9472 |
| Hazel Green | De Winters of Hazel Green, 22nd at Main St., 53811, 608-854-2768 |
| Hazel Green | Wisconsin House Stagecoach, 2105 E. Main, 53811, 608-854-2233 |
| Hazelhurst | Hazelhurst Inn, 6941 Hwy 51, 54531, 715-356-6571 |
| Hillsboro | Mascione's Hidden Valley, Route 2, Box 74, 54634, 608-489-3443 |
| Hollandale | Old Granary Inn, The, 1760 Sandy Rock Rd., 53544, 608-967-2140 |
| Honey Creek | Honey Creek Acres, N6360 Valley View Rd, 53138, 414-763-7591 |
| Houlton | Shady Ridge Farm, 410 Highland View, 54082, 715-549-6258 |
| Hudson | Phipps Inn, 1005 3rd St., 54016, 715-386-0800 |
| Iola | Iris Inn, 385 N. Main St., 54945, 715-445-4848 |
| Iola | Taylor House B&B, 210 E. Iola St., 54945, 715-445-2204 |
| Kansasville | Linen & Lace B&B, 26060 Washington Ave., 53139, 414-534-4966 |
| Kendall | Dusk to Dawn, P.O. Box 191, Rt. 1, 54638, 608-463-7547 |
| Kenosha | Manor House, The, 6536 - 3rd Ave., 53140, 414-658-0014 |
| Kewaskum | Country Ridge Inn B&B, 4134 Ridge Rd., 53040, 414-626-4853 |
| Kewaunee | Chelsea Rose, 908 Milwaukee St., 54216, 414-388-2012 |
| Kewaunee | Duvall House, 815 Milwaukee St., 54216, 414-388-0501 |
| Kewaunee | Gables, The, 821 Dodge St., 54216 |
| Kiel | River Terrace B&B, 521 River Terrace, 53042, 414-894-2032 |
| La Farge | Trillium, Route 2, Box 121, 54639, 608-625-4492 |
| La Pointe | Chateau Madeleine, P.O. Box 27, 54850, 715-747-2463 |
| La Pointe | Woods manor, 165 Front St., Box 7, 54850, 715-747-3102 |
| Lac du Flambeau | Ty-Bach, 3104 Simpson Ln., 54538, 715-588-7851 |
| LaCrosse | Martindale House B&B, The, 237 S. 10th St., 54601, 608-782-4224 |
| Lake Delton | Swallow's Nest B&B, The, P.O. Box 418, 53940, 608-254-6900 |
| Lake Geneva | Elizabethian Inn, 463 Wrigley Dr., 53147, 414-248-9131 |
| Lake Geneva | Pederson Victorian B&B, 1782 Highway 120 N., 53147, 414-248-9110 |
| Lake Geneva | Red House Inn B&B, 512 Wells St., 53147, 414-248-1009 |
| Lake Geneva | William's B&B, 830 Williams St., 53147, 414-248-1169 |
| Lake Mills | Bayberry Inn, 265 S. Main St., 53551, 414-648-3654 |
| Laona | Laona Hostel, P.O. Box 325, 54541, 800-669-2615 |
| Lewis | Seven Pines Lodge, P.O. Box 137, 54851, 715-653-2323 |
| Livingston | Oak Hill Farm, 9850 Highway 80, 53554, 608-943-6006 |
| Lodi | Prairie Garden B&B, W13172 Hwy. 188, 53555 |
| Loganville | Shanahan's, S. 7979 Hwy. 23, 53943, 608-727-2507 |
| Lomira | White Shutters, The, W265 County Trunk H., 53048, 414-269-4056 |
| Madison | Canterbury Inn, 315 W. Gorham, 53703, 608-258-8899 |
| Madison | Lake House On Monona, The, 4027 Monona Dr., 53716, 608-222-4601 |
| Madison | Livingston, The, 752 E Gorham St., 53703 |
| Madison | Stadium House B&B, 810 Oakland Ave., 53711 |
| Madison | University Heights B&B, 1812 Van Hise Ave., 53705 |
| Maiden Rock | Eagle Cove B&B, W4387 120th Ave., 54750, 800-467-0279 |
| Maiden Rock | Harrisburg Inn B&B, P.O. Box 15, 54750, 715-448-4500 |
| Manawa | Ferg Haus Inn, N8599 Ferg Rd., 54949, 414-596-2946 |
| Manawa | Gage's Gardens & Gables, 539 Depot St., 54949, 414-596-3643 |
| Manawa | Victorian Acres B&B, Box 304, 54949, 414-596-3643 |
| Manitowoc | Arbor Manor B&B, 1304 Michigan Ave., 54220, 414-684-6095 |
| Manitowoc | Holmestead, The, 702 Park St., 54220, 414-692-0434 |
| Manitowoc | Jarvis House B&B, 635 N. 7th St., 54220, 414-682-2103 |
| Manitowoc | Mahloch's Cozy B&B, 2104 Madson Rd., 54220, 414-775-4404 |
| Marinette | Lauerman Guest House Inn, 1975 Riverside Ave., 54143 |
| Mauston | Edward's Estates, N4775 22nd Ave., 53948, 608-847-5246 |
| Medford | Stan & Dorothy Slachetka, W6219 Mulberry Ln., 54451 |

| | |
|---|---|
| Menomonee Falls | Dorshel's B&B Guest House, W140 N7616 Lilly Rd., 53051, 414-255-7866 |
| Menomonee Falls | Hitching Post B&B, N88 W16954, 53051, 414-255-1496 |
| Menomonie | Bolo Country Inn, 207 Pine Ave., 54751, 715-235-5596 |
| Menomonie | Cedar Trail Guest House, Rt 4, Box 175, 54751 |
| Mequon | American Country Farm B&B, 12112 N. Wauwatosa Rd., 53092, 414-242-0194 |
| Mequon | Sonnenhof Inn, 13907 N Port Washington, 53092, 414-375-4294 |
| Merrill | Brick House B&B, The, 108 S. Cleveland St., 54452, 715-536-3230 |
| Merrill | Candlewick Inn, 700 W. Main St., 54452, 715-536-7744 |
| Merrimac | Grandpa's Gate B&B, E13841 Lower DL, 53561, 608-493-2755 |
| Middleton | Middleton Beach Inn B&B, 2303 Middlton Beach Rd., 53562, 608-831-6446 |
| Milton | Chase-on-the-Hill, 3928 N. Highway 26, 53563, 608-868-6646 |
| Milwaukee | Guest House of 819, 819 N. Cass St., 53202 |
| Milwaukee | Ogden House, 2237 N. Lake Dr., 53202, 414-272-2740 |
| Milwaukee | Pfister Hotel, 424 E. Wisconsin Ave., 53202, 414-273-8222 |
| Mineral Point | Chesterfield Inn, 20 Commerce St., 53565, 608-987-3682 |
| Mineral Point | Duke House B&B, 618 Maiden St., 53565, 608-987-2821 |
| Mineral Point | Knudson's Guest House, 415 Ridge St., 53565, 608-987-2733 |
| Mineral Point | Wilson House Inn, 110 Dodge St., 53565, 608-987-3600 |
| Mineral Point | Wm. A. Jones House, 215 Ridge St., Hwy 1, 53565, 608-987-2337 |
| Minocqua | Whitehaven B&B, 1077 Hwy. F, 54548, 715-356-9097 |
| Monroe | Victorian Garden B&B, 1720-16th St., 53566, 608-328-1720 |
| Mount Horeb | H.B. Dahle House, 403 N. 4th St., 53572, 608-437-8894 |
| New Auburn | Jacks Lake B&B, 30497 Chippewa Trail, 54757, 715-967-2730 |
| New Glarus | Jeanne-Marie's B&B, 318 10th Ave., 53574, 608-527-5059 |
| New Glarus | Zentner Haus, N. 8588 Zentner Rd., 53574, 608-527-2121 |
| New Holstein | Krupp Farm Homestead, W. 1982 Kiel Rd., 53061, 414-782-5421 |
| Newton | Rambling Hills Tree Farm, 8825 Willever Ln., 53063, 414-726-4388 |
| Norwalk | Lonesome Jake's Ranch, Route 2, Box 108A, 54648, 608-823-7585 |
| Oconomowoc | Inn at Pine Terrace, 351 Lisbon Rd., 53066, 414-567-7463 |
| Oconomowoc | Victorian Belle, The, 520 W. Wisconsin Ave., 53066, 414-567-2520 |
| Ogema | Timm's Hill B&B, N 2036 County Rd. C, 54459, 715-767-5288 |
| Onalaska | Lumber Baron Inn, 421 2nd Ave. North, 54650, 608-781-8938 |
| Ontario | Inn at Wildcat Mountain, P.O. Box 112, 54651, 608-337-4352 |
| Osceola | Pleasant Lake Inn, Rt2, Box 42B, 2208-60th, 54020, 715-294-2545 |
| Oxford | Halfway House B&B, Route 2, Box 80, 53952, 608-586-5489 |
| Phelps | Limberlost Inn, 2483 Hwy 17, 54554, 715-545-2685 |
| Phillips | East Highland B&B, W4342 Hwy. D, 54555, 715-339-3492 |
| Plain | Bettinger House B&B, 855 Wachter Ave., 53577, 608-546-2951 |
| Plain | Kraemer House B&B Inn, The, 1190 Spruce St., 53577, 608-546-3161 |
| Platteville | Cunningham House, 110 Market St., 53818, 608-348-5532 |
| Plymouth | 52 Stafford (Irish House), P.O. Box 217, 53073, 414-893-0552 |
| Plymouth | B. L. Nutt Inn, 632 E. Main St., 53073, 414-892-8566 |
| Plymouth | Spring Farm, N. 4502 County Rd. S., 53073, 414-892-2101 |
| Plymouth | Tulip House Spring Farm, N4502 County Rd. S., 53073, 414-892-2101 |
| Plymouth | Yankee Hill B&B, 315 Collins St., 53073 |
| Port Washington | Grand Inn, 832 W. Grand Ave., 53074, 414-284-6719 |
| Port Washington | Inn at Old Twelve Hundred, 806 W. Grand Ave., 53074, 414-268-1200 |
| Portage | Country Aire B&B, N. 4452 County U, 53901, 608-742-5716 |
| Portage | Inn at Grady's Farm B&B, W10928 Hwy 33, 53901, 608-742-3627 |
| Poynette | Jamieson House, 407 N. Franklin St., 53955, 608-635-4100 |
| Prairie du Chien | Neumann House B&B, 121 N. Michigan St., 53821, 608-326-8104 |
| Prescott | Oak Street Inn, 506 Oak St., 54021, 715-262-4110 |
| Princeton | Gray Lion Inn, The, 115 Harvard, 54968, 414-295-4101 |
| Racine | Lochnaiar Inn, 1121 Lake Ave., 53403, 414-633-3300 |
| Racine | Mansards on the Lake, The, 827 Lake Ave., 53403, 414-632-1135 |
| Rhinelander | Cranberry Hill Inn, 209 East Frederick St, 54501, 715-369-3504 |
| Richland Center | Lamb's Inn Dairy Farm B&B, Rt. 2, Box 144, 53581, 608-585-4301 |
| Richland Center | Littledale, Rt. 1, Box 74, Hwy ZZ, 53581, 608-647-7118 |
| Richland Center | Mansion, 323 S. Central, 53581, 608-647-2808 |
| River Falls | Knollwood House, N. 8257 950th St., 54022, 715-425-1040 |
| Sister Bay | White Apron, The, 414 Maple Dr., 54234, 414-854-5107 |
| Soldiers Grove | Old Oak Inn & Acorn Lodge, Hwy 131 South, Box 1500, 54655, 608-624-5217 |
| Sparta | Just-N-Trails B&B/Farm, Route 1, Box 274, 54656, 608-269-4522 |
| Spring Green | Hill Street B&B, 353 Hill St., 53588, 608-588-7751 |
| Springbrook | Stout Trout B&B, The, Rte.1, Box 1630, 54875, 715-466-2790 |
| St. Croix Falls | Amberwood B&B, 320 McKenney St, 54024, 715-483-9355 |
| St. Germain | St. Germain B&B, P.O. Box 6, 54558, 715-479-8007 |
| St. Germain | Stonehouse B&B, 7855 Lost Lake Dr. N., 54558, 715-542-3733 |
| Star Lake | Whip-Poor-Will Inn, P.O. Box 64, 54561, 715-542-3600 |
| Stevens Point | Birdhouse, The, 1890 Red Pine Ln., 54481, 715-341-0084 |
| Stevens Point | Marcyanna's B&B, 440 N. Old Wausau Rd., 54481, 715-341-9922 |
| Stevens Point | Victorian Swan on Water, 1716 Water St., 54481, 715-345-0595 |
| Stone Lake | Lakehouse, The, P.O. Box 177, 54876, 715-865-2811 |
| Stone Lake | New Mountain B7b, Rt.1, Box 73C, 54876, 715-865-2486 |
| Stoughton | Stokstad's B&B, 305 Hwy 51, 53589, 608-884-4941 |
| Strum | Lake House, RR 2, Box 217, 54770, 715-695-3223 |
| Sturgeon Bay | Bay Shore Inn, 4205 Bay Shore Dr., 54235, 414-743-4551 |
| Sturgeon Bay | Gandt's Haus und Hof, 2962 Lake Forest Park, 54235, 414-743-1238 |

| | | |
|---|---|---|
| Sturgeon Bay | Gray Goose B&B, The, 4258 Bay Shore Dr., 54235,   414-743-9100 | |
| Sturgeon Bay | Nautical Inn, 234 Kentucky St., 54235 | |
| Sturgeon Bay | Scofield House B&B, 908 Michigan St., 54235 | |
| Sturgeon Bay | White Lace Inn, 16 N. 5th Ave., 54235,   414-743-1105 | |
| Two Rivers | Abba's Inn B&B, 2822 Lincoln Ave., 54241,   414-793-1727 | |
| Two Rivers | Red Forest B&B, 1421 - 25th St., 54241,   414-793-1794 | |
| Verona | Beat Road Farm B&B, 2401 Beat Rd., 53593,   608-437-6500 | |
| Verona | Riley Bed-n-Breakfast Inn, 8205 Klevenville-Riley, 53593,   608-845-9150 | |
| Viola | Inn at Elk Run, The, S4125 Country Hwy SS, 54664,   800-729-7313 | |
| Viroqua | Eckhart-Dyson House, 217 East Jefferson, 54665,   608-637-8644 | |
| Viroqua | Serendipity Farm, Route 3 Box 162, 54665,   608-637-7708 | |
| Viroqua | Viroqua Heritage Inn B&B, 220 E. Jefferson St., 54665,   608-637-3306 | |
| Watertown | Brandt Quirk Manor, 410 S. Fourth St., 53094,   414-261-7917 | |
| Watertown | Karlshuegel Inn B&B, 749 N.Church St, Hwy 26, 53094,   414-261-3980 | |
| Waukesha | Joanie's B&B, 615 E. Newhall Ave., 53186,   414-542-5698 | |
| Waupaca | Crystal River B&B, E1369 Rural Rd., 54980,   715-258-5333 | |
| Waupun | Rose Ivy Inn, 228 S. Watertown St., 53963,   414-324-2127 | |
| Wausau | Rosenberry Inn, 511 Franklin St., 54401,   715-842-5733 | |
| West Salem | Wolfway Farm, Rural Route 1, Box 18, 54669,   608-486-2686 | |
| Westfield | Martha's Ethnic B&B, 226 2nd St., 53964,   608-296-3361 | |
| White Sulphur Sprgs | James Wylie House B&B, 208 E. Main St., 24986,   304-536-9444 | |
| Whitewater | Greene House Country Inn, W5666 US Hwy. 12, 53190,   414-495-8771 | |
| Whitewater | Victoria on Main B&B, 622 West Main St., 53190,   414-473-8400 | |
| Wilmot | Foxmoor B&B, Fox River Rd., 53192,   414-862-6161 | |
| Wilton | Dorset Ridge Guest House, Rt. 1, Box 205, 54670,   608-463-7375 | |
| Wilton | Rice's Whispering Pines, R #2, Box 225, 54670,   608-435-6531 | |
| Wisconsin Dells | Bennett House, 825 Oak St., 53965 | |
| Wisconsin Dells | Historic Bennett House, 825 Oak St., 53965,   608-254-2500 | |
| Wisconsin Dells | Sherman House, 930 River Rd., Box 397, 53965,   608-253-2721 | |
| Wisconsin Dells | Thunder Valley, W. 15344 Waubeek Rd., 53965,   608-254-4145 | |
| Wisconsin Rapids | Nash House, 1020 Oak St., 54494,   715-424-2001 | |

# Wyoming

## BIG HORN

**Blue Barn B&B**
P.O. Box 416,  82833
304 Hwy. 335
307-672-2381  Fax: 307-672-2381
Carol Seidler Mavrakis
All year

$$-B&B
3 rooms, 3 pb
Visa, MC, *Rated*,
C-yes/S-no/P-yes/H-yes
French

Full breakfast
Snacks
Sitting room, library
hot tubs, horse and pet
boarding available, ask!

*Rustically elegant 80-year old dairy barn at foot of Big Horn Mountains. Bountiful breakfasts, hot tub, fly-fishing instruction and pet & horse boarding available.*

**Spahn's Big Horn Mountain**
PO Box 579, 70 Upper
Hideaway Ln.,  82833
307-674-8150
R. & B. Spahn, Heather &
Eric
All year

$$-B&B
3 rooms, 3 pb
*Rated*,  •
C-yes/S-ltd/P-yes/H-no

Full breakfast
Lunch, dinner available
Library, sitting room
hot tub, baby-sitting
fishing

*Secluded handcrafted log lodge on a high, pine-forested mountainside. Hundred-mile vista, hiking trails, deer and moose. Close to Interstate 90 and Sheridan.*

CASPER —————————————————————————————

**Durbin Street Inn B&B**
843 S. Durbin St.,   82601
307-577-5774  Fax: 307-266-5441
Don & Sherry Frigon
All year

$$-B&B
5 rooms, 1 pb
Most CC, *Rated*,  •
C-ltd/S-ltd/P-no/H-no

Full breakfast
Sitting room, deck
Library, patio, robes
Fireplaces

*City charm close to everything - just minutes to mountains and wide open spaces. Located in historic residential district. Seasonal rates May 15-September 15.*

CHEYENNE, LARAMIE ————————————————————

**A. Drummond's Ranch B&B**
399 Happy Jack Rd.,   82007
307-634-6042  Fax: 307-634-6042
Taydie Drummond   All year

$$-B&B
4 rooms, 2 pb
*Rated*,  •
C-ltd/S-no/P-yes/H-no
French

Full breakfast
Lunch, dinner, snacks
Sitting room, library
hot tubs, riding arena
carriage house suite

*Quiet retreat by state park. Relax, cross-country ski, fish, hike, mtn. bike, rock climb, bring horse, magnificent view. Customized "llama & adventure" packages.* **3rd night 25% off.**

CODY ———————————————————————————————

**Cody Guest Houses**
1401 Rumsey Ave.,   82414
307-587-6000  Fax: 307-587-8048
800-587-6560
Kathy & Daren Singer
All year

$$-B&B
13 rooms, 13 pb
Most CC, *Rated*,  •
C-ltd/S-no/P-no/H-ltd

Continental breakfast
Dinner (fee), snacks
Sitting room, library
bicycles, hot tubs,
BBQ grills, yard

*Private, historic lodging. 8 unique fully furnished homes (1-4 bdrm.) featuring authentic western-Victorian antiques. Family reunion complex. Romantic honeymoon suite.*

**Lockhart B&B Inn**
109 W. Yellowstone Ave., U.S.
14, 16, 20,   82414
307-587-6074  Fax: 307-587-8644
800-377-7255
Cindy Baldwin    All year

$$$-B&B
7 rooms, 7 pb
Most CC, *Rated*,  •
C-yes/S-ltd/P-no/H-no

All-you-can-eat breakfst
Comp. brandy, coffee
Elegant "Tea"lunch (fee)
sitting room
phones, cable TV

*Historic home of famous western author Caroline Lockhart—featuring antiques, old-style comfort & hearty breakfast. Western hospitality.* **Free bottle of champagne on 3rd night.**

**Trout Creek Inn**
U.S. Hwy.14,16,20,West, 3656
N. Fork Hwy.,   82414
307-587-6288
Bert & Norma Sowerwine
All year

$$$-B&B
21 rooms, 21 pb
Most CC, *Rated*,
C-yes/S-ltd/P-yes/H-yes
Spanish, some German

Continental breakfast
All-you-can-eat (fee)
Swimming pool, hiking
fishing, sitting room
large picnic area

*Clean, quiet, comfortable mountain ranch. Breakfast in bed or on lawn table in God's big dining room. On-site restaurant. Large meeting room for family reunions, etc.* **Ltd. discount—ask.**

JACKSON —————————————————————————————

**Huff House Inn B&B, The**
Box 1189,   83001
240 E. Deloney
307-733-4164  Fax: 307-739-9091
Jackie & Weldon Richardson
All year

$$$-B&B
9 rooms, 9 pb
Visa, MC, Disc.,  •
C-yes/S-no/P-no/H-no

Full breakfast
Family friendly facility
sitting room, library
hot tubs

*Historic house one and one-half blocks east of the town square, on the quiet side of town. Furnished with antiques and original art.*

## JACKSON

**Wildflower Inn, The**
P.O. Box 11000,  83002
3725 N. Teton Village Rd.
307-733-4710 Fax: 307-739-0914
Ken, Sherrie & Jessica Jern
All year

$$$$-B&B
5 rooms, 5 pb
MC, Visa, *Rated*, •
C-yes/S-no/P-no/H-no

Full breakfast
Comp. wine, tea, coffee
Sitting room, deck
library, hot tubs, pond
solarium, wild ducks

*Lovely log home situated on 3 acres of aspens, cottonwoods, and—of course—wildflowers. 5 sunny guest rooms, some with private decks. Near racquet club, golf club, ski area.*

## JACKSON HOLE

**Alpine House, The**
P.O. Box 20245,  83001
285 N. Glenwood St.
307-739-1570 Fax: 307-734-2850
800-753-1421
The Johnstones    All year

$$$-B&B
7 rooms, 7 pb
Visa, MC, *Rated*, •
C-yes/S-no/P-no/H-yes

Full breakfast
Sitting room, library
balconies

*New timberframe lodge in downtown Jackson Hole; heated floors, simple antiques, down comforters, private balconies; hosts former Olympic skiers.* **Adventure winter packages.**

**Painted Porch, The**
P.O. Box 3965,  83001
3755 N. Moose-Wilson Rd.
307-733-1981
Martha & Matt MacEachern
All year

$$$-B&B
4 rooms, 4 pb
Visa, MC,
C-ltd/S-no/P-no/H-no
Spanish

Full breakfast
Sitting room, library
porches, decks

*Country elegance abounds at our 1901 farmhouse nestled in 3 and a half acres of Aspen and Pine trees at the base of the Tetons where wide open hospitality reins.*

## LARAMIE

**Annie Moore's Guest House**
819 University Ave.,  82070
307-721-4177  800-552-8992
Ann Acuff & Joe Bundy
All year

$$-B&B
6 rooms,
Most CC *Rated*,
C-ltd/S-no/P-no/H-no

Continental plus bkfst.
Comp. juice, coffee, tea
Sitting room
sun deck, Florida room
cat named "Archina"

*Beautifully renovated post-Victorian Queen Anne. Cheerful parlor and second-story sun deck. Close to university, museums, downtown. Rocky Mountain recreational delight.*

## PINEDALE

**Window on the Winds B&B**
P.O. Box 996,  82941
10151 Hwy 191
307-367-2600 Fax: 307-367-2395
Leanne McClain    All year

$$-B&B
4 rooms,
Visa, MC, Disc. *Rated*,
•
C-yes/S-no/P-yes/H-no

Full breakfast
Lunch, dinner, snacks
Grand room with mountain
views, Sunroom w/hot tub

*Rustic log home decorated in Western and Plains Indian decor, lodgepole pine queen beds, with breathtaking mountain views, and the hosts are archaeologists. Vegetarian dinners.* **Winter packages.**

## SARATOGA

**Wolf Hotel**
P.O. Box 1298,  82331
101 E. Bridge St.
307-326-5525
Doug & Kathleen Campbell
All year

$-EP
9 rooms, 9 pb
Most CC, *Rated*,
C-yes/S-ltd/P-no/H-no

Breakfast, lunch, dinner
Luxury suite, Restaurant
TV in 5 rooms, bar
blue ribbon trout stream

*Hotel built in 1893 as a stage stop. Listed in National Register. Blue Ribbon fishing, golf, hot springs nearby. Dining room (AAA approved) & lounge redone in Victorian style.*

SHELL ————————————————————————————

| **Snow Shoe Lodge** | $$$-B&B | Full breakfast, dinner |
|---|---|---|
| Box 215, 82441 | 5 rooms, 3 pb | Lunch (fee), comp. wine |
| Rd. 17, Hwy. 14 | Visa, • | Bar service, library |
| 307-765-2669 | C-yes/S-no/P-no/H-yes | sitting room, hot tubs |
| Diana & Martin Mayland | German | snowmobile & ATV tours |
| June 15-April 30 | | |

*Country log lodge tucked in scenic Big Horn Mountains provides fantastic food, fishing, wildlife, hiking, photography, snowmobiling and ranch recreation.* **10% disc't, ltd.**

WILSON, JACKSON HOLE ————————————————————————————

| **Teton Tree House** | $$$-B&B | heart healthy full bkfst |
|---|---|---|
| P.O. Box 550, 83014 | 6 rooms, 6 pb | Comp. wine, beer, juice |
| 6175 Heck of a Hill Rd. | Most CC, *Rated*, • | Sitting room, fireplace |
| 307-733-3233 Fax: 307-733-0713 | C-yes/S-no/P-no/H-no | library, hot tub |
| Denny & Chris Becker | | slide shows, boating |
| All year | | |

*Helpful longtime mountain and river guides offer a rustic but elegant 4-story open-beam home on a forested, wildflower-covered mountainside.* **7th night free Jan./Apr./Nov.**

# More Inns . . .

| | |
|---|---|
| Alpine | Nordic Inn, Box 14, 82922 |
| Buffalo | Cloud Peak Inn, 590 N. Burritt Ave., 82834, 307-684-5794 |
| Buffalo | Paradise Guest Ranch, P.O. Box 790, 82834, 307-684-7876 |
| Buffalo | South Fork Inn, Box 834, 82834 |
| Casper | Bessemer Bend B&B, 6905 Speas Rd., 82604, 307-265-6819 |
| Cheyenne | Adventurer's Country B&B, 3803 I-80 E. Service Rd, 82009, 307-632-4087 |
| Cheyenne | Bit-O-Wyo Ranch B&B, 470 Happy Jack Rd., 82009, 307-638-8340 |
| Cheyenne | Howdy Pardner B&B, 1920 Tranquility Rd., 82009, 307-634-6493 |
| Cheyenne | Porch Swing B&B, 712 E. 20th St., 82001, 307-778-7182 |
| Cheyenne | Rainsford Inn, 219 E. 18th St., 82001, 307-638-2337 |
| Cheyenne | Storyteller Pueblo B&B, 5201 Ogden Rd., 82009, 307-634-7036 |
| Cheyenne | Willard's B&B, 518 Dartmouth Ln., 82009 |
| Cheyenne | Windy Hills Guest House, 393 Happy Jack Rd., 82007, 307-632-6423 |
| Clearmont | R.B.L. Bison Ranch, 4355 U.S. Hwy. 14-16 E., 82835, 307-758-4387 |
| Cody | Buffalo Bill's Cody House, 101 Robertson St., 82414 |
| Cody | Goff Creek Lodge, P.O. Box 155, 82414, 307-587-3753 |
| Cody | Hidden Valley Ranch, 153 Rd., 6MF, S. Fork R, 82414, 307-587-5090 |
| Cody | Parson's Pillow B&B, 1202 14th St., 82414, 307-587-2382 |
| Cody | Shoshone Lodge Resort, P.O. Box 790BB, 82414, 307-587-4044 |
| Cody | Wind Chimes Cottage B&B, 1501 Beck Ave., 82414, 307-527-5310 |
| Douglas | Akers Ranch B&B, 81 Inez Rd., 82633, 307-358-3741 |
| Douglas | Carriage House B&B, 1031 Steinle Rd. |
| Douglas | Cheyenne River Ranch, 1031 Steinle Rd., 82633, 307-358-2380 |
| Douglas | Deer Forks Ranch, 1200 Poison Lake Rd., 82633, 307-358-2033 |
| Douglas | Two Creek Ranch, 800 Esterbrook Rd., 82633, 307-358-3467 |
| Douglas | Wagonhound Ranch, 1061 Poison Lake Rd., 82633, 307-358-5439 |
| Dubois | Jakey's Fork B&B, Box 635, 82513, 307-455-2769 |
| Dubois | Sunshine & Shadows B&B, P.O. Box 828, 82513, 307-455-3279 |
| Encampment | Grand & Sierra B&B, Box 312, 82325, 307-327-5200 |
| Encampment | Lorraine's B&B Lodge, Box 312, 82325, 307-327-5200 |
| Encampment | Rustic Mountain Lodge, Star Route 49, 82325, 307-327-5539 |
| Evanston | Pine Gables B&B, 1049 Center St., 82930, 307-789-2069 |
| Gillette | Skybow Castle Ranch, P.O. Box 2739, 82717 |
| Glenrock | Hotel Higgins, P.O. Box 741, 82637, 307-436-9212 |
| Glenrock | Opal's B&B, Box 219, 82637, 307-436-2626 |
| Golden | TA Guest Ranch, 1930 Mt. Zion Drive, 80401, 307-684-7002 |
| Guernsey | Annette's White House, 239 S. Dakota St., 82214, 307-836-2148 |
| Hulett | Diamond L Ranch, P.O. Box 70, 82720, 307-467-5236 |
| Jackson | H.C. Richards B&B, P.O. Box 2606, 83001, 307-733-6704 |
| Jackson | Rusty Parrot Lodge, P.O. Box 1657, 83001, 307-733-2000 |
| Jackson | Spring Creek Ranch, Box 3154, 83001, 307-733-8833 |
| Jackson | Sundance Inn, 135 W. Broadway, 83001, 307-733-3444 |
| Jackson Hole | Powderhorn Ranch, P.O. Box 7400, 83001, 307-733-3845 |
| Jackson Hole | Sassy Moose Inn, The, 3859 Miles Rd., HC 362, 83001, 307-733-1277 |
| Jackson Hole | Teton View B&B, P.O. Box 652, 83014, 307-733-7954 |
| Lander | Country Fare B&B, 904 Main St., 82520, 307-332-9604 |
| Lander | Edna's B&B, 53 North Fork Rd., 82520, 307-332-3175 |
| Lander | Outlaw B&B, The, 2411 Squaw Creek Rd., 82520 |

| | |
|---|---|
| Lander | Piece of Cake B&B, P.O. Box 866, 82520, 307-332-7608 |
| Lander | Whispering Winds B&B, 695 Canyon Rd., 82520, 307-332-9735 |
| Laramie | Inn on Ivinson, 719 Ivinson, 82070, 307-745-8939 |
| Laramie | V-Bar Guest Ranch, 2091 State Hwy 130, 82070, 307-745-7036 |
| Lusk | Sage & Cactus Village, SR 1, Box 158, 82225, 307-663-7653 |
| Lusk | Wyoming Whale Ranch, Box 115, 82225, 307-334-3598 |
| Manderson | Harmony Ranch Cottage, P. O. Box 25, 182 Hwy31, 82432, 307-568-2514 |
| Moran | Box K Ranch, Box 110, 83013, 307-543-2407 |
| Moran | Inn at Buffalo Fork, The, P. O. Box 311, 93013, 307-543-2010 |
| Newcastle | 4W Ranch Recreation, 1162 Lynch Rd., 82701, 307-746-2815 |
| Newcastle | Horton House B&B, 17 South Summit, 82701, 307-746-4366 |
| Parkman | Double Rafter Ranch, 521 Pass Creek Rd., 82838, 307-655-9362 |
| Pinedale | Fort William Recreat. Area, P.O. Box 1081, 82941, 307-367-6353 |
| Pinedale | Pole Creek Ranch B&B, P.O. Box 278, 82941, 307-367-4433 |
| Powell | Bar X Ranch, 109 Rd 8 WC, Clark, 82435, 307-645-3231 |
| Powell | I Can Rest Ranch, 1041 Lane 11, Rt. 3, 82435, 307-754-4178 |
| Ranchester | Masters Ranch, Z Bar O Ranch, 82839, 307-655-2386 |
| Rawlins | Ferris Mansion B&B, 607 W. Maple, 82301, 307-324-3961 |
| Rawlins | Lamont Inn, Lander Rt. Box 9, 82301, 307-324-7602 |
| Recluse | Cow Camp, 931 Beason Rd., 82725 |
| Riverton | Cottonwood Ranch B&B, 951 Missouri Valley Rd., 82501, 307-856-3064 |
| Rock River | Dodge Creek Ranch, 402 Tunnel Rd., 82083, 307-322-2345 |
| Rock Springs | Sha Hol Dee B&B, 116 Pilot Butte Ave., 82901, 307-362-7131 |
| Saratoga | Brooksong B&B Home, Star Rt. Box 9L, 82331, 307-326-8744 |
| Saratoga | Hood House B&B, 214 N. 3rd. St., 82331, 307-326-8901 |
| Savery | Savery Creek Thoroughbred, Ranch, Box 24, 82332, 307-383-7840 |
| Savery | Y L Hideaway Holiday, P.O. Box 24, 82332, 307-383-7840 |
| Shell | Clucas Ranch B&B, 1710 Hwy. 14, 82441, 307-765-2946 |
| Shell | Mayland Ranch Recreation, Box 215, 82441 |
| Shell | Trappers Rest B&B, P.O. Box 166, 82441 |
| Story | Piney Creek Inn B&B, 11 Skylark Lane, 82842, 307-683-2338 |
| Ten Sleep | Horned Toad B&B, The, Box 403, 82442, 307-366-2747 |
| Thermopolis | Broadway Inn B&B, 342 Broadway, 82443 |
| Wapiti | Elephant Head Lodge, 1170 Yellowstone Pk Hwy, 82450, 307-587-3980 |
| Wapiti | Mountain Shadows Ranch, Box 110BB, 82450, 307-587-2143 |
| Wheatland | Blackbird Inn, 1101 11th St., 82201, 307-322-4540 |
| Wilson | Heck of A Hill Homestead, P.O. Box 105, 83014, 307-733-8023 |
| Wilson | Moose Meadows B&B, 1225 Green Lane, 83014, 307-733-9510 |

# Puerto Rico

## SAN GERMAN ───────────────────────

**Hotel y Parador Oasis**
PO Box 144, Calle Luna #72,
  00753
809-892-1175
All year

$$-B&B
,
AmEx, MC, Visa, •
C-yes/S-no/P-yes/H-no
Spanish, English, French

Full breakfast
AP & MAP available
Afternoon tea, snacks
wine, restaurant, bar
swimming pool, jacuzzi

*Relax in the friendly atmosphere of this 200-year-old Spanish mansion. Close to beaches, historical sites, and the world famous Phosphorescent Bay.*

## SAN JUAN ───────────────────────

**El Canario Inn**
1317 Ashford Ave., Condado,
  00907
787-722-3861  Fax: 787-722-0391
800-533-2649
Marcos Santana
All year

$$-B&B
25 rooms, 25 pb
AmEx, MC, Visa,
*Rated*, •
C-yes/S-yes/P-no/H-no
English, Spanish

Continental breakfast
Swimming pool, jacuzzi
patios, rooms with A/C
cable TV, phones, wicker

*In heart of Condado, near beach, casinos, boutiques and fine restaurants. Freshwater jacuzzi pool, tropical patio and sun deck for sun, fun, and relaxation.*

## UTUADO

**Parador Casa Grande**
P.O. Box 616,  00641
Rd. 612 Km. 0.3 Caonillas
787-894-3939
Fax: 787-894-3939
800-866-8644
Mr. Jose Pabon
All year

$$-B&B
20 rooms, 20 pb
*Rated*,  •
C-ltd/S-ltd/P-no/H-no
Spanish

Full breakfast
Lunch, dinner (fee)
Restaurant, bar service
swimming pool
family friendly facility

*The fresh mountain air of La Cordillera Central surrounds this centuries old coffee plantation, restored for the pleasure of guests. **3rd. night, 50% off.***

## VIEQUES

**New Dawn Caribbean Retreat**
P.O. Box 1512,  00765
Rt. 995, Barrio Pilon
809-741-0495
Gail Burchard
All year

$$
6 rooms,
•
C-yes/P-no/H-ltd
Some Spanish

Full breakfast (fee)
Restaurant, bar service
Sitting room, library
bicycles, tent sites
great for family reunion

*A quiet, relaxing place "off the beaten path" offering private rooms, dorm & tent sites. Accessible to remote beaches, Phosphorescent Bay & tropical rain forest.*

## More Inns . . .

| | |
|---|---|
| Adjuntas | Hotel Monte Rio, H St., 00601 |
| Carolina | Duffys', The, Ave. Isla Verde #9, 00979,  809-726-1415 |
| Ceiba | Ceiba Country Inn, P.O. Box 1067, 00735,  809-885-0471 |
| Condado | El Prado Inn, 1350 Luchetti St., 00907,  809-728-5526 |
| Condado | Wind Chimes, 53 Calle Taft, 00911,  809-727-4153 |
| Culebra | Posada La Hamaca, 68 Castelar St., 00645,  809-742-3516 |
| Culebra Island | Casa Llave, P.O. Box 60, 00775,  809-742-3559 |
| Culebra Island | Villa Boheme, P.O. Box 218, 00645,  809-742-3508 |
| Humacao | Palmas del Mar,  P.O. Box 2020, 00661,  809-852-6000 |
| Isla Verde | La Casa Mathiesen,  14 Calle Uno, Villamar, 00913,  809-727-3223 |
| Isla Verde | La Playa, 6 Amapola, 00630,  809-791-1115 |
| Luguillo | Parador Martorell, Inc., P.O. Box 384, 00773,  809-889-2710 |
| Maricao | La Hacienda Juanita B&B, P.O. Box 777, 00606,  809-838-2550 |
| Ocean Park | Beach House, 1957 Italia, 00913,  809-727-5482 |
| Ocean Park | Buena Vista by-the-Sea,  2218 Gen.Del Valle, 00913,  809-726-2796 |
| Ocean Park | Safari on the Beach, Yardley Place #2, 00911,  809-726-0445 |
| Old San Juan | Galeria San Juan, Blvd. del Valle 204-206, 00901 |
| Patillas | Hotel Caribe Playa, HC 764 Buzon 8490, 00723,  809-839-6339 |
| Rincon | Horned Dorset Primavera Ho, Apartado 1132, 00743,  809-823-4030 |
| San Juan | Arcade Inn Guest House, 8 Taft St. - Condado, 00911,  809-725-0668 |
| San Juan | Casa San Jose, 61 Calle de San Fran., 00901,  809-723-1212 |
| San Juan | El Canario by the Sea, 4 Condado Ave., 00907,  809-722-8640 |
| San Juan | Green Isle Inn, 36 Cale Uno - Villamar, 00913,  809-726-4330 |
| San Juan | Hotel del Caribe, 954 Ponce de Leon Ave., 00907 |
| San Juan | Jewel's by the Sea,  Seaview 1125-Condado, 00907,  809-725-5313 |
| San Juan | L'habitation Beach,  1957 Calle Italia, 00911,  809-727-2499 |
| San Juan | La Condesa Inn-Guest House, 2071 Cacique St., 00911,  809-727-3698 |
| San Juan | Ocean Walk Guest House, 1 Atlantic Pl.,Ocean Pk, 00911,  809-728-0855 |
| San Juan | San Antonio Guest House, 1 Tapia, Ocean Park, 00752,  914-727-3302 |
| Santurce | Hosteria del Mar,  1 Tapia St. Ocean Park, 00911,  787-727-3302 |
| Vieques | Bananas Guesthouse, P.O. Box 1300 Esperanza, 00765,  809-741-8700 |
| Vieques | La Casa del Frances, Box 458, Esperanza, 00765,  809-741-3751 |

# Virgin Islands

## CHRISTIANSTED, ST. CROIX

| **Breakfast Club, The** | $$-B&B | Full gourmet breakfast |
| 18 Queen Cross St.,  00820 | 9 rooms, 9 pb | Bar service |
| 809-773-7383 Fax: 809-773-8642 | Visa, MC, | Sitting room, library |
| Toby & Barb Chapin | C-yes/S-yes/P-no/H-no | hot tubs |
| All year | | |

*Six blocks from downtown Christiansted. Private kitchens, baths. Harbor island views from deck, rooms. Tax included. Groups inquire about villa.*

## ST. THOMAS

| **Danish Chalet Inn** | $$-B&B | Continental breakfast |
| P.O. Box 4319,  00803 | 15 rooms, 6 pb | Bar service ($1 drinks) |
| 9E Gamble Nordsidevej | MC, Visa, *Rated*, • | Sitting room, library |
| 809-774-5764  Fax: 809-777-4886 | S-yes/P-no/H-no | spa, jacuzzi, sun deck |
| 800-635-1531 | English | beach towels, games |
| Frank & Mary Davis | | |
| All year | | |

*Family inn overlooking Charlotte Amalie harbor, 5 min. to town, duty-free shops, restaurants. Cool breezes, honor bar, sun deck, jacuzzi. Beach-15 min.* **7th night free, ltd.**

| **Galleon House Hotel** | $-B&B | Continental plus bkfst. |
| P.O. Box 6577,  00804 | 14 rooms, 13 pb | Refrigerators |
| 31 Kongens Gade | *Rated*, • | A/C in rooms, pool |
| 809-774-6952  Fax: 809-774-6952 | C-yes/S-yes/P-no/H-no | snorkel gear |
| 800-524-2052 | | veranda, beach towels |
| Donna & John Slone | | |
| December–April | | |

*Visit historical Danish town. Superb view of harbor with city charm close to everything. Duty-free shopping, beach activities in 85-degree weather.*

| **Heritage Manor** | $$-B&B/EP | Continental breakfast |
| P.O. Box 90,  00804 | 8 rooms, 4 pb | Comp. wine upon check-in |
| 1A Snegle Gade | Most CC, • | Bar service, pool |
| 809-774-3003  Fax: 809-776-9585 | C-ltd | English high tea on req. |
| 800-828-0757 | | courtyard |
| Ken & Ann Brasher | | |
| All year | | |

*Beautifully restored manor offers European country charm and simple elegance. Tastefully decorated rooms. Walk to duty-free shops, fine restaurants, sunset cruises, ferries.*

| **Island View Guest House** | $$-B&B | Continental, full avail. |
| P.O. Box 1903,  00803 | 15 rooms, 13 pb | 38 seat dining room |
| 11-1C Contant | *Rated*, • | Hors d'oeuvres (Friday) |
| 809-774-4270  Fax: 809-774-6167 | C-ltd/S-yes/P-no/H-no | sandwiches, bar, gallery |
| 800-524-2023 | | swimming pool |
| Barbara Cooper | | |
| All year | | |

*Overlooking St. Thomas harbor, honor bar and freshwater pool. Spectacular harbor view from all rooms. Convenient to town and airport.* **10% discount direct booking—5-7 night stay.**

## ST. THOMAS

**Mafolie Hotel**
P.O. Box 1506, 00804
809-774-2790 Fax: 809-774-4091
800-225-7035
Tony & Lyn Eden
All year

$$-B&B
23 rooms, 23 pb
Visa, MC, AmEx, •
C-yes/S-yes/P-no/H-no
Spanish, French

Continental breakfast
Lunch & dinner available
Restaurant, bar service
snacks, swimming pool
A/C, Cable TV, Fax serv.

*800 feet above town & harbor, world-famous view. 10 mins. from everything. Family owned & operated. Recent total renovation. Free daily beach shuttle & use of beach towels. Add 10% service, 8% tax.*

## More Inns ...

| | |
|---|---|
| Christiansted | Club Comanche Hotel, 1 Strand St., 00820, 809-773-0210 |
| Christiansted | Pink Fancy Hotel, 27 Prince St., 00820, 809-773-8460 |
| St. Croix | Anchor Inn, 58-A King St, 00820, 809-773-4000 |
| St. Croix | Cane Bay Plantation, P.O. Box %, 00850, 809-778-0410 |
| St. Croix | Lodge Hotel, 43-A Queen Cross, 00820, 809-773-1535 |
| St. Croix | Sprat Hall Plantation, P.O. Box 695, 00840, 809-772-0305 |
| St. Croix | Waves at Cane Bay, P.O. Box 1749, 00850, 809-778-1805 |
| St. John | Cruz Inn, Box 566, Cruz Bay, 00830, 809-776-7688 |
| St. John | Estate Zootenvaal, Hurricane Hole, 00830, 809-776-6321 |
| St. John | Gallows Point, Box 58, 00830, 809-776-6434 |
| St. John | Hotel 1829, P.O. Box 1567, 00801, 809-774-1829 |
| St. John | Intimate Inn of St. John, P.O. Box 432, Cruz Bay, 00830, 809-776-6133 |
| St. John | Pavilions & Pools Hotel, Route 6, 00802, 800-524-2001 |
| St. John | Raintree Inn, Box 566, 00830, 809-776-7449 |
| St. John | Villa Bougainvillea, P.O. Box 349, 00830, 809-776-6420 |
| St. Thomas | Admiral's Inn, Villa Olga, 00802 |
| St. Thomas | Blue Beard's Castle, P.O. Box 7480, 00801, 809-774-1600 |
| St. Thomas | Bunkers' Hill View House, 9 Commandant Bade, 00801, 809-774-8056 |
| St. Thomas | Hotel 1829, 30 Kongens Gade, 00801, 809-774-1829 |
| St. Thomas | Inn at Mandahl, P.O. Box 2483, 00803, 809-775-2100 |
| St. Thomas | Miller Manor Guest House, 27 & 28 Princesse Gade, 00801, 809-774-1535 |
| St. Thomas | Villa Elaine, 66 Water Island, 00802, 809-774-0290 |
| St. Thomas | Villa Santana, Denmark Hill, 00802, 809-776-1311 |

# Alberta

## BANFF

**Pension Tannenhof B&B Inn**
P.O. Box 1914, 121 Cave Ave.,
T0L 0C0
403-762-4636 Fax: 403-762-5660
Herbert & Fannye Riedinger
All year

$$-B&B
15 rooms, 7 pb
Visa, MC,
S-no/P-no/H-no
German, Spanish

Full breakfast
BBQ
Sitting room, library
rms. w/color, cable TV
sauna, tennis nearby

*Featuring woodburning fireplace, CCTV, homey-yet elegant atmosphere. Recreational facilities nearby, OLD BBQ-made from petrified Dinosaur bones!*

## HINTON

**Black Cat Guest Ranch**
P.O. Box 6267L, T7V 1X6
403-865-3084 Fax: 403-865-1924
Amber Hayward
All year

$$-B&B
16 rooms, 16 pb
MC, Visa, •
C-yes/S-yes/P-no/H-no

Full breakfast
Complimentary lunch
Sitting room, piano
adult oriented, trails
patio, outdoor hot tub

*A year-round lodge facing the front range of the Rockies, featuring trail rides and hiking in summer, cross-country skiing in winter.*

# More Inns . . .

| | |
|---|---|
| Airdale | Golden Rod B&B, Box 9, Site 3, R.R. 1, T4B 2A3,   403-948-5341 |
| Alix | Connie's Country Cocoon,  Box 65, T0C 0B0,  403-747-2217 |
| Athabasca | Our Log Cabin,  Box 1402, T0G 0B0,   403-675-3381 |
| Banff | Blue Mountain Lodge, P.O. Box 2763, T0L 0C0,  403-762-5134 |
| Banff | Holiday Lodge, 311 Marten St., Box 904, T0L 0C0,  403-762-3648 |
| Banff | Kananaskis Guest Ranch,  P.O. Box 964, T0L 0C0 |
| Bentley | Crazee Akerz Farm,  RR #1, T0C 0J0,  403-843-6444 |
| Bindloss | Haas' B&B, T0J 0H0,  403-379-2267 |
| Blairmore | Bedside Manor B&B,  Box 1088, T0K 0E0,   403-628-3954 |
| Bragg Creek | Four Point Crossing B&B, P.O. Box 847, T0L 0K0 |
| Bragg Creek | M&M Ranch, Box 707, T0L 0K0 |
| Brooks | Douglas Country Inn, Box 463, T0J 0J0,  403-362-2873 |
| Calgary | Barb's B&B, 1308 Carlyle Rd. SW, T2V 2T8 |
| Calgary | Brink B&B,  79 Sinclair Crescent SW, T2W 0M1,  403-255-4523 |
| Calgary | Harrison's B&B Home,  6016 Thornburn Dr. NW, T2K 3P7,  403-274-7281 |
| Calgary | Lions Park, 1331-15 Street NW, T2N 1B7,  403-282-2728 |
| Calgary | Lucille's B&B, 739 Blackthorn Rd NE, T2K 4Y2,  403-275-1613 |
| Calgary | Midtown B&B,  707 Royal Ave SW, T2S 0G3,  403-245-4446 |
| Calgary | Robin's Nest, The,  Box 2, Site 7, RR 8, T2J 2T9 |
| Calgary | Russells' B&B,  2806 Linden Dr. SW, T3E 6C2,  403-249-8675 |
| Calgary | Scenic Waters B&B,  Box 33, Site 20, RR 2, T2P 2G5,  403-286-4348 |
| Calgary | Turgeon's,  4903 Viceroy Dr. NW, T3A 0V2,  403-288-0494 |
| Canmore | Bird's Nest, Box 2227, 1005-15th St, T0L 0M0,  403-678-2294 |
| Canmore | By-the-Brook B&B,  Box 373, T0L 0M0,   403-678-4566 |
| Canmore | Cougar Creek Inn B&B,  P.O. Box 1162, T0L 0M0,  403-678-4751 |
| Canmore | Georgetown Inn, The,  P.O. Box 3327, T0L 0M0,  403-678-3439 |
| Canmore | Haus Alpenrose B&B, 629 - 9th St., Box 723, T0L 0M0,  403-678-4134 |
| Canmore | Kiska House,  P.O. Box 397, T0L 0M0,  403-678-4041 |
| Canmore | Spring Creek B&B, Box 172, T0L 0M0,  403-678-6726 |
| Caroline | Burlou Ranch, Box 106, T0M 0MC,  403-722-2409 |
| Carstairs | Gray Fox Ranch B&B,  R.R. 2, T0M 0N0,  403-337-3192 |
| Carstairs | Temarest B&B,  R.R.1, T0M 0N0,  403-337-3069 |
| Claresholm | Lane's B&B,  Box 974, T0L 0T0 |
| Cochrane | Angle Acres, Box 531, T0L 0W0,  403-932-5550 |
| Cochrane | Bluebird Acres B&B,  RR1, T0L 0W0 |
| Cochrane | Burke's B&B, R.R. 1, T0L 0W0,  403-932-4354 |
| Cochrane | Timber Trail B&B,  Box 1313, T0L 0W0,  403-932-4995 |
| Cold Lake | Harbour House,  615 Lakeshore Dr.,  T0A 0V2,  403-639-2337 |
| Cremona | B&B Wild Rose Country,  Box 233, T0M 0R0 |
| Cremona | Spruce Hollow B&B, Box 233, T0M 0R0,  403-637-2277 |
| Didsbury | Ausen Hus B&B, The,  R.R. 2, T0M 0W0,  403-335-4736 |
| Didsbury | Pengary House B&B, 1610-15th Ave.,Box 1224, T0M 0W0,  403-335-8353 |
| Didsbury | Westway Hide-A-Away B&B, Box 544, T0M 0W0,  403-335-4929 |
| Drumheller | Pattersons' B&B, Box 1027, T0J 0Y0,  403-533-2203 |
| Drumheller | Riverside Inn Crawford's,  501 Riverside Dr. W, T0J 0Y3,  403-823-4746 |
| Drumheller | Taste the Past,  281-2nd St.W., Box 2305, T0J 0Y0,  403-823-5889 |
| Edmonton | Brookside B&B,  14328 - 56 Ave., T6H 0Y5 |
| Edmonton | Edmonton Hostel,  10422 - 91st St., T0L 0M0,  403-429-0140 |
| Edmonton | McKernan Heritage B&B,  11023-81 Ave., T6G 0S3,  403-482-1096 |
| Edmonton | Zieper's, 31 Patricia Cres., T5R 5N7,  403-487-2973 |
| Evansburg | Rustic Ridge Ranch, Box 389, T0E 0T0,  403-727-2042 |
| Ft. Saskatchewan | Birdwood B&B, R.R. 2, T8L 2N8,  403-998-0082 |
| Granum | Dimm's Ranch B&B,  Box 228, T0L 1A0 |
| Granum | Willow Lane Ranch, Box 114, T0L 1A0,  403-687-2284 |
| High River | Kentucky Ranch,  RR #2, T0L 1B0 |
| Lake Louise | Post Hotel Lake Louise, Box 69, T0L 1E0 |
| Lancombe | Mathis B&B, 5712 - 50th Ave., T0C 1S0,  403-782-4082 |
| Lancombe | Sunset Country B&B,  R.R. 2, T0C 1S0,  403-885-4691 |
| Ma-Me-O Beach | Ma-Me-O Beach B&B,  Box 7, T0C 1X0,  403-586-2031 |
| Markerville | Aspen Acres,  R.R. 1, T0M 1M0,  403-728-3364 |
| Millarville | Hilltop B&B,  RR #1, T0L 1K0 |
| Millet | Broadview Farm,  RR #2, T0C 1Z0,  403-387-4963 |
| Nanton | Broadway Farm B&B, Box 294, T0L 1R0 |
| Nanton | Squire Ranch, The,  RR #1, T0L 1R0 |
| Nanton | Timber Ridge Homestead,  Box 94, T0L 1R0,  403-646-5683 |
| Okotoks | Welcome Acres B&B, Box 7, Site 2, RR 1, T0L 1T0 |
| Okotoks | Wildflower Country House,  Box 8, Site 1, R.R.2, T0L 1T0 |
| Olds | Roost, The, 5629-49th Ave S,Bx 3458, T0M 1P0,  403-556-7998 |
| Pincher Creek | Allison House, Box 1351, T0K 1W0 |
| Pincher Creek | Castle Haus Inn, General Delivery, T0K 1W0 |
| Pincher Creek | Cow Creek Ranch,  Box 522, T0K 1W0 |
| Pincher Creek | Storey Brook Farm, Box 2740, T9K 1W0,  403-627-2841 |
| Ponoka | Woods' Westerm Warmth (The, Box 4235, Hwy. 2A North, T4J 1R6,  403-783-5123 |
| Red Deer | Country Home B&B, R.R. 1, Site 7, T4N 5E1,  403-347-0356 |
| Red Deer | Dutchess Manor Spa & Guest,  4813 54 Street, T4N 2G5,  403-346-7776 |
| Red Deer | McIntosh Tea House B&B, 4631 - 50 St., T4N 1X1,  403-346-1622 |

| | |
|---|---|
| Rocky Mt. House | Inn Town B&B, 5316-55 St., T0M 1T4, 403-845-2616 |
| Rosalind | Rosalind's B&B, General Delivery, T0B 3Y0, 403-375-3943 |
| Sedgewick | Ms. Mona's B&B, Box 504, T0B 4C0, 403-384-3936 |
| Seebe | Rafter Six Ranch Resort, T0L 1X0, 403-673-3622 |
| Spruce Grove | Country Guest House, P.O. Box 4264, T7X 3B4, 403-962-0829 |
| Sylvan Lake | Kozy Corner B&B, 4504 44 St., T0M 1Z0 |
| Sylvan Lake | Swiss Alpine B&B, 4731 50th St., T0M 1Z0, 403-887-4151 |
| Three Hills | Cream Coulee B&B, Box 1118, T0M 2A0, 403-443-7808 |
| Trochu | St. Ann Ranch Trading Co., Box 249, T0M 2C0, 403-442-3924 |
| Turner Valley | Rose's Rest B&B, 221 John St., T0L 2A0 |
| Wainwright | MacKenzie House, 1018-4th Ave, Box 2648, T0B 4P0, 403-842-5867 |

# British Columbia

## CAMPBELL RIVER

**April Point Lodge**
Box 1, 900 April Pt. Rd,
Quadra Island,  V9W 4Z9
604-285-2222  Fax: 604-285-2411
888-334-3474
The Peterson Family
April 15–October 15

$$-EP
36 rooms, 36 pb
Most CC, *Rated*,  •
C-yes/S-yes/P-ltd/H-ltd
Fr., Rus., Ger., Jap.

Full breakfast
Restaurant, bar
Sitting room, piano
entertainment (summer)
saltwater pool, fishing

*Personal service is our pride. More than one staff member per guest. Saltwater pool, many languages spoken. From one to five bedroom deluxe guest houses. Fishing resort.*

## FORT STEELE

**Wild Horse Farm B&B**
Box 7, Hwy 93/95,  V0B 1N0
250-426-6000
Bob & Orma Termuende
May–October

$$-B&B
3 rooms, 3 pb
•
C-ltd/S-ltd/P-ltd/H-no

Full breakfast
Sitting room, antiques
player piano
games table

*Spacious early 1900s log-faced country manor nestled in the Rocky Mountains; extensive lawns, gardens, trees on grounds. Across from Fort Steele Historic Park.*

## HORNBY ISLAND

**Sea Breeze Lodge**
5205 Fowler Rd., Big Tree 3-2,
V0R 1Z0
604-335-2321
The Bishops
All year; AP 6/15–9/15

$$$$-AP
11 rooms, 11 pb
Visa, MC, *Rated*,
C-yes/S-no/P-no/H-ltd
Spanish

Full breakfast
Lunch & dinner also incl
Sitting room, piano
grass tennis courts
hot tub, fishing guide

*Sea Breeze Lodge—mentioned in 1983 edition of West World. Near the ocean. Homemade breads & desserts. Off-season cottages set for housekeeping. Some fireplaces.*

## MAYNE ISLAND

**Oceanwood Country Inn**
630 Dinner Bay Rd., V0N 2J0
604-539-5074  Fax: 604-539-3002
Marilyn & Jonathan Chilvers
Mar 1 - Nov 30

$$$-B&B
12 rooms, 12 pb
Vica, MC, *Rated*,  •
C-ltd/S-ltd/P-no/H-ltd
French

Full breakfast
Dinner (fee), aftn. tea
Bar service, library
sitting room, bikes
hot tubs, sauna, tennis

*Waterfront island retreat; English country house atmosphere; award-winning cuisine; luxurious rooms with fireplace, whirlpool, private deck; ferry from Vancouver or Victoria.*

*Oceanwood Country Inn, Mayne Island, BC*

MILL BAY
**Pine Lodge Farm B&B**
3191 Mutter Rd.,   V0R 2P0
604-743-4083
Clifford & Barb Clarke
April 1- Oct 10

$$-B&B
7 rooms, 7 pb
•
C-ltd/S-ltd/P-no/H-no

Full farm breakfast
Sitting room
antique sales

*Our lodge is on a 30-acre farm with panoramic ocean views. Each room is furnished with exquisite antiques and stained glass windows. Museum open to public. Antique sales.*

NEW WESTMINSTER

**Henley House B&B**
1025 8th Ave.,   V3M 2R5
604-526-3919  Fax: 604-526-3913
Anne O'Shaughnessy/Ross
Hood
All year

$$-B&B
2 rooms, 0 pb
Visa, MC,
C-ltd/S-ltd/P-no/H-no

Full breakfast
Afternoon tea
Sitting room, library
tennis court, hot tubs

*1925 character home in garden setting. Antique furnishings, every amenity, warm hospitality.*

NORTH VANCOUVER

**Norgate Parkhouse B&B**
1226 Silverwood Cnt.,   V7P
1J3
604-986-5069 Fax: 604-986-8810
Vicki Tyndall
All year

$$-B&B
3 rooms,
Visa, MC, •
C-ltd/S-no/P-no/H-no

Full breakfast
Sitting room, TV
fireplace
in-room phones

*Home contains intriguing items from around the world. Lush west coast gardens. Relaxing, restorative atmosphere. 12 minutes from Vancouver centre.*

**Sue's Victorian
GuestHouse**
152 E. 3rd,   V7L 1E6
604-985-1523  800-776-1811
Gail Fowler & Sue Chalmers
All year

$$-EP
3 rooms, 1 pb
S-no/P-no/H-no
English

Guests have a fridge
Color TV/video in rms.
ceiling fan, local phone
limited use of kitchen

*Restored 1904 home, four blocks from harbour, centrally located for transportation, shopping, restaurants and tourist attractions. **7th night free & off-season monthly rates.***

POWELL RIVER ———————————————

**Beacon B&B** | $$-B&B | Full breakfast
3750 Marine Ave., V8A 2H8 | 3 rooms, 2 pb | Packed lunch available
604-485-5563 Fax: 604-485-9450 | MC, *Rated*, | Comp. coffee/cold drinks
Shirley & Roger Randall | C-ltd/S-ltd/P-no/H-ltd | sitting room, library
All year | | hot tub, TV, massage

*Panoramic ocean view & spectacular sunsets. B.C. paradise for canoeing, kayaking, mtn. trekking. Fish, golf, hike. "Our specialty is relaxation." Rejuvenating bodywork available.* **Day 4 10% off, ltd.**

SALT SPRING ISLE, GANGES ———————————————

**Cranberry Ridge B&B** | $$-B&B | Full breakfast
269 Don Ore Dr., V8K 2H5 | 3 rooms, 3 pb | 4-6 person hot tub
250-537-4854 Fax: 250-537-4243 | MC, Visa, *Rated*, • | large sun deck, sitt. rm
Gloria Callison & Roger Lutz | S-no/P-no/H-no | magnificent views
All year

*3 large rooms w/private powder rooms and private entrances, 1 w/fireplace. Fantastic views. Great Canadian hospitality. Full home-cooked breakfast with homebaked goods.*

SOOKE ———————————————

**Ocean Wilderness Country** | $$$-B&B | Full breakfast
109 West Coast Rd., RR# 2, | 9 rooms, 9 pb | Dinner by arrangement
VOS 1N0 | MC, Visa, *Rated*, • | Snacks, bar fridge
250-646-2116 Fax: 250-646-2317 | C-ltd/S-no/P-yes/H-yes | sitting room, hot tubs
800-323-2116 | | beach party buffet
Marion Rolston
All year

*5 wooded acres w/beach; whales, seals; hot tubs in romantic rooms w/canopied beds. Honeymoon? Birthday? Plant a Douglas Fir "Memory Tree."* **5% senior disc't. Winter specials.**

**Sooke Harbour House** | $$$$-B&B | Full breakfast
1528 Whiffen Spit Rd., RR #4, | 15 rooms, 15 pb | Light buffet lunch incl.
VOS 1N0 | Most CC, *Rated*, • | Dinner, bar, entertnmnt.
604-642-3421 Fax: 604-642-6988 | C-yes/S-ltd/P-ltd/H-yes | sitting room, piano
800-889-9688 | French | jacuzzi, bikes, hot tubs
Sinclair & Frederique Philip
All year

*Romantic, relaxing, magical, memorable. Gourmet restaurant serves local sea & land bounty. Golf nearby. Romance packages & midweek, off-season rates*

VANCOUVER ———————————————

**Albion Guest House** | $-B&B | Full breakfast
592 West 19th Ave., V5Z | 4 rooms, 2 pb | Snacks, comp. wine
1W6 | Visa, MC, AmEx, | Sitting room, hot tubs
604-873-2287 Fax: 604-879-5682 | *Rated*, • | picnic lunch service
Howard Ehrilch | C-yes/S-ltd/P-no/H-no | diets by request, bikes
All year | French

*A country retreat in the city offering individualized attention to guests; enjoy our scrumptious breakfasts and relaxing hot tub.* **5 plus nights 10% off.**

**Beautiful B&B** | $$-B&B | Cont. plus/full bkfst.
428 W. 40 Ave., V5Y 2R4 | • | Restaurant nearby
604-327-1102 Fax: 604-327-2299 | C-ltd/S-no/P-no/H-no | Sitting room, piano
The Sandersons | French | Japanese garden, pool
All year | | waterfall, tennis nearby

*Gorgeous colonial home; antiques, fresh flowers, views. Great central location near Q.E. park, shopping, fine restaurants. Easy bus access to downtown. Relax in elegance!*

## VANCOUVER

**Catherine B&B**
658 E. 29 Ave., V5V 2R9
604-875-8968 Fax: 604-877-1786
800-463-9933
Catherine Vong
All year

$-B&B
12 rooms, 6 pb
Most CC, •
C-yes/S-no/P-no/H-no
Chinese

Full breakfast
Library
view of mountains & city

*Downtown convenience at affordable rates, close to buses, airport, ferry. Safe & quiet neighborhood, close to Queen Elizabeth Park. Weekly & monthly rates.* **Pay for 6 nights, 7th is free.**

---

**Columbia Cottage, The**
205 W. 14th Ave.,  V5Y 1X2
604-874-5327 Fax: 604-879-4547
S. Sulzberger, A. Smith
All year

$$$-B&B
5 rooms, 5 pb
Visa, MC, *Rated*,
C-ltd/S-no/P-no/H-no

Full gourmet breakfast
Afternoon tea, sherry
Chocolates, cookies
sitting room
robes & slippers

*Let us spoil you! Quiet country garden w/serene fish pond. Five-min. drive from Vancouver centre. Resident chef offers varied gourmet breakfasts.* **Business/long-stay disc'ts.**

---

**Johnson Heritage House B&B**
2278 W. 34th Ave.,  V6M 1G6
604-266-4175 Fax: 604-266-4175
Sandy & Ron Johnson
All year

$$-B&B
3 rooms, 1 pb
Cash or cheque, •
C-ltd/S-no/P-no/H-no
Some French

Full breakfast
Front & back decks, TV
library, sitting room
rock garden, VCR

*A restored character home in one of Vancouver's finest neighborhoods. Brass beds & carousel horses, antique decor. 2-night minimum May–Nov.* **7th night free, Oct.–March.**

---

**Kenya Court Guest House**
2230 Cornwall Ave.,  V6K 1B5
604-738-7085
Dr. & Mrs. H. R. Williams
All year

$$$-B&B
5 rooms, 5 pb
Personal Checks OK,
C-ltd/S-no/P-no/H-no
Italian, French, German

Full breakfast
Complimentary tea/coffee
Sitting room, library
tennis courts, solarium
salt water swimming pool

*Ocean-front heritage guest house overlooking Kitsiland Beach, mountains, English Bay. Gourmet bkfst. served in solarium w/panoramic view. Minutes to downtown, Granville Isl.*

---

**Manor Guest House, The**
345 W. 13th Ave.,  V5Y 1W2
604-876-8494 Fax: 604-876-5763
Brenda Yablon
All year

$$-B&B
9 rooms, 5 pb
Visa, •
C-ltd/S-ltd/P-no/H-no
French, German

Full vegetarian bkfst.
Galley kitchen use
parlor/music room
English garden, decks

*An Edwardian heritage manor. Convenient to everything. Spacious rooms, fine breakfasts & helpful hosts make your stay memorable. Top-floor suite sleeps six.*

---

**Shaughnessy Village B&B**
1125 West 12th Ave.,  V6H 3Z3
604-736-5511 Fax: 604-737-1321
Dave Rivers
All year

$$-B&B/MAP/AP
15 rooms, 15 pb
Visa, MC, •
C-ltd/S-yes/P-no/H-yes
Fr., Ger., Jap., Chi.

Full breakfast
Bar serv.,lunch, dinner
Gym, billiards, library
crazy putt golf, sauna
swimming, tennis nearby

*Our resort-style residence accommodates "B&B" visitors in a friendly & beautiful nautical atmosphere in theme rooms," like cruise ship cabins."* **Free videos, health club/tan bed.**

*Abigail's Hotel, Victoria, BC*

## VANCOUVER

| | | |
|---|---|---|
| **West End Guest House** | $$$-B&B | Full breakfast |
| 1362 Haro St.,  V6E 1G2 | 7 rooms, 7 pb | Bedside sherry (5-7pm) |
| 604-681-2889 Fax: 604-688-8812 | MC, Visa, *Rated*, • | Sitting room with TV |
| Evan Penner | C-ltd/S-no/P-no/H-no | parking, library, piano |
| All year | English, French | room phones, bicycles |

*Walk to Stanley Park, beaches; enjoy quiet ambiance of our comfortable historic inn. Popular w/romantic couples. Fireplace, antiques, robes. 1 room w/gas frplc. Turndown w/snack.* **10% off 5+nights.**

| | | |
|---|---|---|
| **Windsor Guest House** | $-B&B | Continental plus bkfst. |
| 325 West 11 Ave., V5Y 1T3 | 10 rooms, 5 pb | Afternoon tea |
| 604-872-3060 Fax: 604-873-1147 | Visa, MC, AmEx, • | Sitting room |
| Paul Findlay | C-ltd/S-no/P-no/H-no | |
| All year | Spanish | |

*Victorian style heritage home, c.1895. Central location in residential area near all attractions, shopping, restaurants. Friendly, attentive hosts.*

## VICTORIA

| | | |
|---|---|---|
| **Abigail's Hotel** | $$$-B&B | Full gourmet breakfast |
| 906 McClure St.,  V8V 3E7 | 16 rooms, 16 pb | Afternoon refreshments |
| 604-388-5363 Fax: 604-388-7787 | AmEx, MC, Visa | Social hour, library |
| 800-561-6565 | *Rated*, • | sitting room |
| Daniel & Frauke Behune | C-ltd/S-no/P-no/H-no | Jacuzzi in some rooms |
| All year | | |

*Luxuriously updated 1930 classic Tudor building. Private Jacuzzi tubs, frplcs., goose-down comforters. Walk to downtown. First-class smiling hospitality.* **Comp. honeymoon pkg. w/2 night stay.**

VICTORIA ───────────────

**An Ocean View B&B**
715 Suffolk St., V9A 3J5
250-386-7730
Yvette & Ralf
All year

$$-B&B
6 rooms, 6 pb
Visa, MC, AmEx, •
C-ltd/S-no/P-no/H-no
German, French,
Spanish

Full buffet breakfast
Bar, refrig., microwave
Garden patios, TV
1 block to ocean walkway
old town with attraction

*"Your holiday home." Modern, bright mediterranean home overlooks scenic Victoria harbour, ocean & snow-capped Olympic Mnts. Guests have access to magnificent views from sundeck/lounge, dining room.*

---

**Battery Street Guesthouse**
670 Battery St, V8V 1E5
604-385-4632
Pamela Verduyn
All year

$-B&B
6 rooms, 2 pb
C-ltd/S-no/P-no/H-no
Dutch

Full breakfast
Sitting room
walk to park and ocean

*Comfortable guest house (1898) in downtown Victoria. Centrally located; walk to town, sites, Beacon Hill Park, ocean. Ample breakfast.*

---

**Beaconsfield Inn**
998 Humboldt St., V8V 2Z8
250-384-4044 Fax: 250-384-4052
Con & Judi Sollid
All year

$$$$-B&B
9 rooms, 9 pb
AmEx, MC, Visa,
*Rated*, •
S-no/P-no/H-no

Full gourmet breakfast
Comp. sherry, aft. tea
Social hour, sun room
library, piano, bicycles
6 rms. w/jacuzzi & frplc

*Award-winning restoration of an English mansion. Walk to downtown. Antiques—rich textures, velvets, leather, warm woods. Full breakfast served in dining room & sunroom.*

---

**Blue Castle**
1009 Glen Forest Way, RR 1,
V9B 5T7
604-478-2800 Fax: 604-478-2800
Valerie & Gerry Walther
All year

$$-B&B
3 rooms, 3 pb
AmEx,
C-ltd/S-no/P-no/H-no
German

Full breakfast
Afternoon tea
Sitting room
bikes, private balcony
large wrap-around deck

*A beautiful Victorian style home on a treed hilltop w/panoramic views of mountains & water. Famous honeymoon suite comes w/extra large en-suite & clawfooted bath tub for 2.* **Off season & 3+ nite discount.**

---

**Cadboro Bay B&B**
3844 Hobbs St., V8N 4C4
604-477-6558 Fax: 604-477-4727
Rene Barr
All year

$-B&B
3 rooms, 1 pb
Visa, •
C-yes/S-no/P-no/H-no

Full gourmet breakfast
Afternoon tea
Sitting room
tennis court
family park nearby

*Modern home near University of Victoria. Gourmet breakfasts. Separate cottage in quiet, secluded garden with patio. 15 minutes from downtown.* **Complimentary tea and coffee.**

---

**Dashwood Seaside Manor**
One Cook St., V8W 3W6
604-385-5517 Fax: 604-385-1760
800-667-5517
All year

$$-B&B
14 rooms,
AmEx, MC, Visa,
*Rated*, •
C-yes/S-no/P-yes/H-no

Full breakfast
Complimentary wine
Sitting room, library
Jacuzzis in 2 suites
tennis court nearby

*Victoria's only seaside B&B inn. 1912 Edwardian mansion, adjacent park, near town. 14 suites, each your own home w/fabulous views.* **Champagne included with special occasions.**

## VICTORIA

**Elk Lake Lodge B&B**
5259 Patricia Bay Hwy.,
Route 17,  V8Y 1S8
604-658-8879 Fax: 604-658-8879
800-811-5188
Marty & Ivan Musar
Open May 1 - October 15

$-B&B
5 rooms, 5 pb
MC, Visa, *Rated*,  •
C-ltd/S-no/P-ltd/H-no

Full breakfast
Afternoon tea, coffee
Library and TV
large lounge
hot tub on patio

*Formerly a unique 1910 monastery and church. Antique furnishings with bedrooms and living room overlooking Elk Lake. Ten min. from the city center, ferries.*

---

**Marion's B&B**
1730 Taylor St.,  V8R 3E9
250-592-3070
Marion Simms
All year

$$-B&B
3 rooms,
*Rated*,
C-yes/S-no/P-no/H-no

Full breakfast
Evening tea, snacks
Sitting room
jacuzzi

*Comfortable, friendly accommodation, 5 min. from beautiful downtown Victoria. Delightful linens & handmade quilts dress beds. Full home-cooked breakfast. **7th night free, ltd.***

---

**Markham House B&B**
1853 Connie Rd., R.R. #2,
V9B 5B4
604-642-7542 Fax: 604-642-7538
Lyall & Sally Markham
Easter to September

$$$-B&B
4 rooms, 4 pb
MC, Visa,  •
C-ltd/S-ltd/P-no/H-no

Full breakfast
Afternoon tea
Complimentary wine
sitting room
private cottage w/frplc.

*Romantic self contained cottage on the edge of woods, private hot tub, woodstove and BBQ. Fishing charters arranged, breakfast prepared for dietary needs. **3rd night 50%.***

---

**Oak Bay Guest House**
1052 Newport Ave., Oak Bay,
V8S 5E3
250-598-3812 Fax: 250-598-0369
800-575-3812
Karl & Jackie Morris
All year

$$$-B&B
11 rooms, 11 pb
MC, Visa, AmEx,
*Rated*,
S-no/P-no/H-no
French

Full breakfast
Comp. tea & coffee
Sitting room
library, beach walks,
bike riding

*Charming, peaceful historic home furnished w/antiques, beautiful gardnes, elegant neighborhood, scenic walks, beaches, golf, minutes drive to Inner Harbor. **Low, off-season rates.***

---

**Olde England Inn, The**
429 Lampson St.,  V9A 5Y9
604-388-4353 Fax: 604-382-8311
Lord Cyril G. Lane
All year

$$$
60 rooms, 60 pb
Most CC, *Rated*,  •
C-yes/P-no/H-ltd

Full breakfast
Lunch & dinner available
Restaurant
afternoon tea, museums
Shakespearean replicas

*A charming, romantic inn and restaurant furnished with authentic antiques. Step back in time as you stroll along the lane of this recreated English village.*

---

**Pitcairn House B&B**
1119 Ormond St.,  V8V 4J9
604-384-7078  800-789-5566
Paul & Diana McCarthy
Jan 20-Nov 20

$$-B&B
3 rooms, 1 pb
Visa, MC,
C-ltd/S-no/P-no/H-no
French

Full English breakfast
Snacks
Sitting room
harbour, art gallery
children's cot available

*Victorian Heritage Home furnished in genuine antiques, located downtown, hearty breakfast served in cozy dining room or beautiful English garden. **Restaurant discounts.***

## VICTORIA

**Portage Inlet House, B&B**
993 Portage Rd., V8Z 1K9
604-479-4594 Fax: 604-479-4548
Jim & Pat Baillie
All year

$-B&B
4 rooms, 3 pb
MC, Visa, •
C-yes/S-ltd/P-no/H-yes

Full English breakfast
Organically grown food
Private entrances
garden, water views
"honeymoon" cottage

*Acre of waterfront, 3 miles from city centre, located at mouth of salmon stream. Organic food; hearty breakfast. Ducks, swans, eagles, heron and other wildlife on property.*

**Prior House B&B Inn**
620 St. Charles St., V8S 3N7
604-592-8847 Fax: 604-592-8223
Candis & Ted Cooperrider
All year

$$$-B&B
6 rooms, 6 pb
MC, Visa, *Rated*,
C-ltd/S-no/P-no/H-no

Full breakfast
Afternoon high tea
Comp. wine
sitting room
library

*Grand English manor built for king's representative. Fireplaces, antiques, ocean vistas and gardens. Recapture romance in elegant beauty.* **3rd night 50% off Jan. & Feb.**

**Scholefield House**
731 Vancouver St., V8V 3V4
250-385-2025 Fax: 250-383-3036
800-661-1623
Tana & George Dineen
All year

$$$-B&B
3 rooms, 3 pb
Visa, MC, •
C-ltd/S-no/P-no/H-no

Full gourmet breakfast
Comp. sherry, tea/coffee
Sitting room, library
close to Inner Harbour

*Authentically restored Victorian home, antiques; short stroll to Inner Harbour, shops & restaurants; scrumptious breakfasts featuring herbs & flowers.* **10% off additional nights.**

**Sonia's B&B by the Sea**
175 Bushby St., V8S 1B5
604-385-2700 Fax: 604-763-7443
800-667-4489
Sonia & Brian McMillan
April–September

$$-B&B
4 rooms, 4 pb
*Rated*,
C-ltd/S-no/P-no/H-no

Full breakfast
Tea & coffee
Sitting room
3 rooms-2 queen, 1 king
all have private baths

*Sonia offers marvelous stories, quality lodgings at a good value. Her breakfasts are as bountiful as the hospitality. Innkeeper born and raised in Victoria, can suggest sites.*

**Sunnymeade House Inn**
1002 Fenn Ave., V8Y 1P3
604-658-1414 Fax: 604-658-1414
Capt. Jack & Nancy
Thompson
All year

$$-B&B
5 rooms, 1 pb
MC, Visa, *Rated*, •
C-ltd/S-no/P-no

Full breakfast
Restaurant, bar
Afternoon tea, candy
sitting room, flowers
garden, tennis courts

*Village by the Sea. Country-style inn w/beautiful decor. Honeymoon suite. Walk to shops, restaurants, beach; 15 minutes to Butchart Gardens and Ferry. Golf course nearby.*

**Swallow Hill Farm B&B**
4910 William Head Rd., RR#1,
V9B 5T7
250-474-4042 Fax: 250-474-4042
Gini & Peter Walsh
All year

$$-B&B
2 rooms, 2 pb
MC, Visa, AmEx,
*Rated*, •
C-ltd/S-no/P-no/H-no

Full farm breakfast
Comp. tea/coffee
Sitting room, bicycles
books & games, picnics
working farm, free sauna

*Apple Farm with spectacular ocean & mountain sunrise views. 2 separate suites, private baths, queen & twin beds. Inspected and approved home.*

## VICTORIA

**Top O' Triangle Mtn. B&B**
3442 Karger Terrace,   V9C
3K5
250-478-7853  Fax: 250-478-2245
Henry & Pat Hansen
All year

$-B&B
3 rooms, 3 pb
Visa, MC, •
C-yes/S-ltd/P-no/H-ltd
Danish

Full breakfast
Kettle, hot/cold drinks
Sitting room
great views
near parks, golf, city

*We are best known for our panoramic view, great food and hospitality. Clean comfortable accommodations. Close to city, parks, golf.* **Oct. 15–May 15 all rooms $39.**

---

**Wellington B&B**
66 Wellington Ave.,   V8V 4H5
250-383-5976  Fax: 250-383-5976
Inge Ranzinger
All year

$$-B&B
4 rooms, 4 pb
MC, *Rated*, •
C-ltd/S-no/P-no/H-no
German, Spanish

Full breakfast
Refrigerator, ice
Sitting room, library
sun porch, sun deck
tennis court nearby

*A touch of class! Quiet street, close to ocean, park and downtown. Beautifully designed bright rooms with queen & king beds & fireplaces. One room available long-term.* **3rd nite free, ltd.**

---

**Wooded Acres B&B**
4907 Rocky Point Rd, RR#2,
V9B 5B4
250-478-8172  250-474-8959
Elva & Skip Kennedy
All year

$$$-B&B
2 rooms, 2 pb
•
S-no/P-no/H-no

Full country breakfast
Comp. champagne, tea,
Coffee, hot tubs
sitting room, library
beaches, trails, fishing

*Acreage in the countryside of Victoria. Cosy log home is decorated w/antiques. Perfect for honeymoon & special occasions. Relax in your own private hot tub.* **4th night 50% off.**

## WEST VANCOUVER

**Chickadee Tree B&B**
1395 3rd St., V7S 1H8
604-925-1989  Fax: 604-925-1989
Herb & Lois Walker
All year

$$-B&B
3 rooms, 3 pb
C-ltd/S-ltd/P-no/H-ltd

Full breakfast
In-suite coffee makers
Hot tubs, sauna
swimming pool, jacuzzi
fireplace, kitchen

*Secluded, woodsy, award winning! Two suites/cozy cottage, private entrances/baths/balconies/gazebo. Close to Stanley Park/downtown/beaches/ferries/reatuarants/shops.*

---

**Creekside B&B**
1515 Palmerston Ave.,   V7V
4S9
604-926-1861  Fax: 604-926-7545
604-328-9400
John Boden & Donna
Hawrelko
All year

$$$-B&B
2 rooms, 2 pb
MC, Visa, •
C-ltd/S-no/P-no/H-no
Ukrainian

Full gourmet breakfast
Complimentary wine/snack
Color TV, fireplace
2 person jacuzzi tubs
stocked fridge in rooms

*Private, woodsy creekside hideaway. Close to parks, skiing, beaches & ocean. Honeymoon suite available. 2 day minimum.* **Comp. wine & snacks, restaurant & entertainment coupons.**

---

**Lighthouse Retreat B&B**
4875 Water Ln.,   V7W 1K4
604-926-5959  Fax: 604-926-5755
Hanna & Ron Pankow
All year

$$-B&B
2 rooms, 2 pb
•
C-ltd/S-ltd/P-no/H-no
German

Full breakfast
Afternoon tea
Sitting room, library

*Peaceful, elegant rooms with canopy beds. Secluded patios, fragrant garden. Close to nature trails, seashore paths. Downtown is a short drive away.*

## WHISTLER

| **Alta Vista Chalet B&B** | $$$-B&B | Full breakfast |
| 3229 Archibald Way, V0N 1B3 | 8 rooms, 6 pb | Dinner (fee), Aftn. tea |
| 604-932-9400 Fax: 604-932-4933 | Most CC, *Rated*, • | Sitting room, library |
| Tim & Yvonne Manville | C-yes/S-no/P-no/H-no | hot tubs, sauna |
| All year | French | daily maid service |

*Alpine chalet, 2 kms south of the village ski slopes overlooking Alta Lake and valley trail. Quiet and comfortable. AAA & Tourism B.C. approved*

| **Golden Dreams B&B** | $-B&B | Full breakfast |
| 6412 Easy St., V0N 1B6 | 3 rooms, 1 pb | Comp. sherry, snacks |
| Fax: 604-932-7055800-668-7055 | MC, Visa, • | Full guest kitchen |
| Ann Spence | C-yes/S-no/P-no/H-no | fireside lounge, TV, VCR |
| All year | | outdoor hot tub |

*Just 1 mile to ski lifts! Nutritious vegetarian breakfast, large garden deck with BBQ. Bike rental on-site, ski rental discounts. With condo locations, you can walk to ski lifts, restaurants, shops.*

## More Inns . . .

| | |
|---|---|
| Abbotsford | Shamrock & Shillelagh B&B, 34745 Arden Dr., V2S 2X9, 604-850-5085 |
| Alberta | Douglas Country Inn, Box 463, Brooks, E0A 1Z0, 403-362-2873 |
| Atlin | Nolan House, Box 135, V0B 1A0, 604-651-7585 |
| Black Creek | Country Comfort, 8214 Island Hwy, Box 3, V0R 1C0, 604-337-5273 |
| Brentwood Bay | Brentwood Bay/Verdier B&B, Box 403, V0S 1A0, 604-652-2012 |
| Burnaby | Patterson Guest House, 7106 18th Ave., V3N 1H1 |
| Campbell River | Arbour's Guest House, 375 Murphy St., V9W 1Y8, 604-287-9873 |
| Campbell River | Haida Inn, 1342 Island Hwy, V9W 2E1, 604-287-7402 |
| Campbell River | Pier House B&B, 670 Island Hwy., V9W 2C3, 604-287-2943 |
| Campbell River | Willow Point Guest House, 2460 South Island Hwy, V9W 1C6, 604-923-1086 |
| Chemainus | Pacific Shores Inn, Box 958, V0R 1K0, 604-246-4987 |
| Clearwater | Omas House, 229 Schmidt, B 4074,RR2, V0E 1N0, 604-674-3467 |
| Courtenay | Greystone Manor, RR 6, Site 684/C2, V9N 8H9, 604-338-1422 |
| Cowichan Bay | Blackberry Inn, The, RR1, Box 29, V0R 1N0 |
| Cranbrook | Cranberry House B&B, 321 Cranbrook St. N., V1C 3R4, 604-489-6216 |
| Cranbrook | Glen Flora Castle House, 324-10th Ave S, V1C 2N6, 604-426-7930 |
| Crawford Bay | Wedgwood Manor Country Inn, P.O. Box 135, V0B 1E0, 604-227-9233 |
| Creston | Rising Sun Guest Ranch, 3246 Riverview Rd, V0B 1G0, 604-428-4886 |
| Denman Island | Denman Island Guest House, Box 9, Denman Rd., V0R 1T0, 604-335-2688 |
| Denman Island | Sea Canery Guest House B&B, P.O. Box 31, V0R 1T0 |
| Duncan | Country Gardens B&B, 1665 Grant Rd., RR 5, V9L 4T6, 604-748-5865 |
| Duncan | Fairburn Farm, RR 7, V9L 4W4, 604-746-4637 |
| Duncan | Grove Hall Estate B&B, 6159 Lakes Rd., V9L 4J6, 604-746-6152 |
| Dunster | Hidden Lake Lodge, Hidden Lake Rd, Gen Del, V0J 1J0, 604-968-4327 |
| Eagle Creek | Bradshaw's Minac Lodge, On Canim Lake, V0K 1L0, 604-397-2416 |
| East Kelowna | Kel Kar Acres, 3950 Borland Dr.Box 158, V0H 1G0 |
| Fort St. John | Bickfords's B&B, S16, C-33, RR1, V1J 4M6, 604-785-4546 |
| Gabriola Island | Surf Lodge Ltd., RR1, Site 1, V0R 1X0, 604-247-9231 |
| Galiano Island | Hummingbird Inn, Sturdies Bay Rd., V0N 1P0, 604-539-5472 |
| Galiano Island | La Berengerie, Montague Harbor Bl., V0N 1P0, 604-539-5392 |
| Galiano Island | Woodstone Country Inn, RR#1, Georgeson Bay Rd., V0N 1P0, 604-539-2022 |
| Ganges | Applecroft B&B, RR3, 551 Upper Ganges, V0S 1E0, 604-537-5605 |
| Ganges | Armand Heights B&B, Box 341, V0S 1E0, 604-653-9989 |
| Ganges | Beach House B&B Inn, 930 Sunset Dr., RR 1, V0S 1E0, 604-537-2879 |
| Ganges | Old Farmhouse, 1077 North End Rd, RR4, V0S 1E0, 604-537-4113 |
| Gibsons | Dianne Verzyl, RR 2 S 46 C10, V0N 1V0 |
| Gibsons | Ocean View Cottage B&B, RR 2, Site 46, C10, V0N 1V0, 604-886-7943 |
| Gibsons | Swn-y-mor B&B, 488 Veteran,S47,C53,RR2, V0N 1V0, 604-886-8777 |
| Golden | Columbia Valley Lodge, Box 2669, V0A 1H0, 604-348-2508 |
| Golden | Kinbasket Lake Resort, Box 2366, V0A 1H0, 604-344-6693 |
| Halfmoon Bay | Lord Jim's Resort Hotel, RR 1, Ole's Cove Rd., V0N 1Y0, 604-885-7038 |
| Invermere | Larch Point Lake Retreat, Box 2005, V0A 1K0, 604-342-9650 |
| Invermere | Primrose Manor B&B, Box 2937, 1512-9th Ave, V0A 1K0, 604-342-9664 |
| Kamloops | Imeson's B&B, 492 Sentinel Court, V2E 2G6, 604-374-0841 |
| Kamloops | Park Place B&B, 730 Yates Rd., V2B 6C9 |
| Kamloops | Sunset B&B, 2667 Sunset Drive, V2C 4K4, 604-372-2458 |
| Kelowna | Crawford View B&B, 810 Crawford,RR6,S8,C13, V1Y 8R3, 604-784-1140 |
| Kelowna | Gables Country Inn, 2405 Bering Rd/Box 1153, V1Y 7P8, 604-768-4468 |
| Kelowna | Kel Kar Acres B&B, 3950 Borland Dr, Bx 158, V0H 1G0, 604-763-9333 |
| Kelowna | Poplar Point, 345 Herbert Heights Rd., V1Y 1Y4 |

| | |
|---|---|
| Kelowna | View to Remember B&B, 1090 Trevor Dr., V1Z 2J8,   604-769-4028 |
| Kleena Kleene | Chilanko Lodge & Resort,  Gen. Delivery, Hwy 20, V0L 1M0,   604-Kleena K |
| Ladner | Primrose Hill Guest House, 4919-48th Ave., V4K 1V4,   604-940-8867 |
| Ladner | River Run Cottage & Rest., 4551 River Road West, V4K 1R9,   604-946-7778 |
| Ladysmith | Aneverly-By-The-Sea B&B, 3012 Yellow Point, RR3, V0R 2E0,   604-722-3349 |
| Ladysmith | Manana Lodge, Box 9 RR 1, V0R 2E0,   604-245-2312 |
| Ladysmith | Yellow Point Lodge, RR 3, V0R 2E0,   604-245-7422 |
| Malahat | Aerie, The,  P.O. Box 108, V0R 2L0,   604-743-7115 |
| Mansons Landing | Linnaea Farm, Box 112, V0P 1K0 |
| Mayne Island | Fernhill Lodge, Box 140, V0N 2J0,   604-539-2544 |
| Mayne Island | Gingerbread House,  Campbell Bay Rd., V0N 2J0,   604-539-3133 |
| Mill Bay | Billion $ View B&B, 610 Shorewood Rd., RR#1, V0R 2P0,   604-743-2387 |
| N. Pender Island | Hummingbird Hollow B&B, 36125 Galleon Way, V0N 2M0,   604-629-6392 |
| N. Vancouver | Deep Cove B&B, 2590 Shelley Rd., V7H 1J9,   604-929-3932 |
| Nanaimo | Mountain View Farm, 2437 East Wellington Rd, V9R 5K3,   604-753-6920 |
| Nanoose Bay | Lookout at Schooner Cove, Box 71 Blueback Dr. RR2, V0R 2R0,   604-468-9796 |
| Nanoose Bay | Oceanside B&B,  Box 26, RR2, Blueback, V0R 2R0,   604-468-9241 |
| Naramata | Wild Rose Stables,  RR #1 Site 4 Comp 5, V0H 1N0 |
| Nelson | Ark B&B, 304 Carbonate St., V1L 4P2,   604-352-0114 |
| Nelson | Heritage Inn, 422 Vernon St., V1L 5P4,   604-352-5331 |
| Nelson | Willow Point Lodge, RR 1, V1L 5P4,   604-825-9411 |
| New Westminster | Dutch-Canadian B&B, 201 East 7th Ave, V3L 4H5,   604-521-7404 |
| New Westminster | Kelly House B&B, 230-3rd St., V3L 2R6,   604-522-6564 |
| North Delta | B&B for Visitors,  10356 Skagit Dr., V4C 2K9,   604-588-8866 |
| North Delta | Delta View B&B, 8036 Modesto Drive, V4C 4B1,   604-594-2797 |
| North Vancouver | B&B at Laburnum Cottage, 1388 Terrace Ave., V7R 1B4,   604-988-4877 |
| North Vancouver | Grand Manor,  1617 Grand Blvd., V7L 3Y2 |
| North Vancouver | Helen's B&B,  302 E. 5th St., V7L 1L1,   604-985-4869 |
| North Vancouver | Mountain Valley B&B, 4374 Ruth Cr., V7K 2M9,   604-986-8457 |
| North Vancouver | Nelsons', The,  470 West St. James Rd., V7N 2P5,   604-985-1178 |
| North Vancouver | Poole's B&B,  421 West St. James Rd, V7N 2P6,   604-987-4594 |
| North Vancouver | Sheehan's B&B, 864 East 14th St., V7L 2P6,   604-988-7264 |
| North Vancouver | Thom's Bed & Breakfast, 615 W. 23rd St., V7M 2C2,   604-986-2168 |
| Oliver | Fritzville, 34032 Hwy. 97 S. RR #1, V0H 1T0 |
| Oliver | Mirror Lake Guesthouse B&B, Box 425, V0H 1T0,   604-495-7959 |
| Osoyoos | Haynes Point Lakeside, 3619 - 87th St., V0H 1V0,   604-495-7443 |
| Parksville | Eagle Watch, 810 Sunray Close, V9P 1A6,   604-248-4899 |
| Parksville | Homestyle B&B,  17 Sylvan Cr., V9P 1H1,   604-248-6872 |
| Parksville | Marina View B&B, 895 Glenhale Cr, V9P 1Z7,   604-248-9308 |
| Parksville | Parksville B&B,  19 Jenkins Place, V9P 1G4,   604-248-6846 |
| Parson | Dunphy's B&B, Box 22, V0A 1H0,   604-348-2394 |
| Parson | Taliesin Guest House B&B, Box 101, V0A 1L0,   604-348-2247 |
| Pender Island | Corbett House B&B,  Corbett Rd., V0N 2M0,   604-629-6305 |
| Penticton | Apex Ranch, P.O. Box 426, V2A 6K6 |
| Penticton | Paradise Cove B&B, Box 699, V2A 6P1,   250-496-5896 |
| Port Alberni | Lake Woods B&B,  Site 339, C5, RR3, V9Y 7L7,   604-723-2310 |
| Port Hardy | Hamilton B&B, Box 1926, 9415 Mayor's, V0N 2P0,   604-949-6638 |
| Port Renfrew | Feathered Paddle B&B,  7 Queesto Dr., V0S 1K0,   604-647-5433 |
| Powell River | Cedar Lodge Resort, C-8 Malaspina Rd, RR3, V8A 4Z3,   604-483-4414 |
| Powell River | Herondell B&B, RR1, Black Point #29, V8A 4Z2,   604-487-9526 |
| Powell River | Ocean View B&B, 4024 Dorval Ave., V8A 3G2,   604-485-6880 |
| Prince George | Park Place B&B, 1689 Birch St., V2L 1B3,   604-563-6326 |
| Prince Rupert | Eagle Bluff, 100 Cow Bay Rd., V8J 1A2,   604-627-4955 |
| Prince Rupert | Rose's B&B, 943-1st Ave. W, V8J 1B4,   604-624-5539 |
| Pt. Clements | Swans Keep, Box 431, 197 Bayview Dr, V0T 1R0,   604-557-2048 |
| Quadra Isle | Joha House, Box 668,Quathiaski Cove, V0P 1N0,   604-285-2247 |
| Qualicum Beach | Blue Willow B&B, 524 Quatna Rd., V9K 1B4,   604-752-9052 |
| Qualicum Beach | Quatna Manor, 512 Quatna Rd., V9K 1B4,   604-752-6685 |
| Queen Charlotte | Miller's B&B, Box 421, 602-1st Ave, V0T 1S0,   604-559-8686 |
| Queen Charlotte | Spruce Point B&B, 609-6th Ave, Box 735, V0T 1S0,   604-559-8234 |
| Quilchena | Quilchena Hotel,  V0E 2R0,   604-378-2611 |
| Render Island | Cliffside Inn on the Sea,  Genl. Delivery, V0N 2M0 |
| Revelstoke | L&R Nelles Ranch,  Hwy 23, Box 430, V0E 2S0,   604-837-3800 |
| Revelstoke | Piano Keep,  Box 1893, 815 MacKenzie, V0E 2S0,   604-837-2120 |
| Revelstoke | Smokey Bear Campground B&B, Box 1125, V0E 2S0,   604-837-9573 |
| Richmond | Blueberry Farm Guest House, 10731 Blundell Rd., V6Y 1L2,   604-278-6745 |
| Richmond | McKay's, 7180 Blundell Rd., V6Y 1J4,   604-278-8928 |
| Richmond | Rita's B&B, 6100 Canim Place, V7C 2N2,   604-274-1808 |
| Rossland | Heritage Hill B&B, Box 381,1345 Spokane St, V0G 1Y0,   604-362-9697 |
| Rossland | Ram's Head Inn,  Red Mt Ski Area Box 636, V0G 1Y0,   604-362-9577 |
| Saanichton | Wintercott Country House,  1950 Nicholas Rd., V8M 1X8,   604-652-2177 |
| Salmon Arm | Claire's B&B,  2930-5th Ave SE, V1E 2H1,   604-832-2421 |
| Salmon Arm | Silver Creek Guest House,  6280 - 30th Ave. SW, V1E 4M1,   604-832-8870 |
| Salt Spring Island | Pauper's Perch B&B,  225 Armand Way, V8K 2B6,   604-653-2030 |
| Salt Spring Island | Weston Lake Inn, 813 Beaver Point Rd., V8K 1X9,   604-653-4311 |
| Saltspring Isle | Precious Meadows Farm B&B,  177 Vesuvius Bay, RR1, V0S 1E0,   604-537-5995 |
| Saturna Island | Breezy Bay B&B,  Box 40, V0N 2Y0,   604-539-2937 |
| Sidney | Camelon House,  1865 Landsend Rd, RR3, V8L 3X9,   604-656-9848 |

| | |
|---|---|
| Sidney | Courtyard by the Sea, The, 380 Moses Pt. Rd., V8L 4R4 |
| Sidney | Grahams Cedar House B&B, 1825 Landsend Rd., RR3, V8L 5J2,   604-655-3699 |
| Sidney | Sidney by the Sea, 2512 Rothesay Ave., V8L 2B8,   604-656-5767 |
| Smithers | Driftwood Lodge, C11, S53, RR2, V0J 2N0,   604-847-5016 |
| Smithers | Ptarmigan B&B, Box 2439, Willow Rd., V0S 2N0,   604-847-9508 |
| Sointala | John Gamble B&B,  Box 300, V0N 3E0 |
| Sointula | Wayward Wind Lodge, Box 300, V0N 3E0,  604-973-6307 |
| Sooke | B&B by the Sea, 6007 Sooke Rd., RR1, V0S 1N0,  604-642-5136 |
| Sooke | Tideview, 1597 Dufour Rd., RR4, V0S 1N0 |
| Sorrento | Evergreens B&B, Box 117, Vimy Rd., V0E 2W0,  604-675-2568 |
| Summerland | Heritage House, 11919 Jubilee, Box 326, V0H 1Z0,  604-494-0039 |
| Summerland | Veto's Vineyard, 9402 Front Beach Rd., V0H 1Z0 |
| Surrey | Hirsch's Place, 10336-145 A St., V3R 3S1, 604-588-3326 |
| Tofino | Chesterman's Beach B&B, 1345 Chestermans, Bx 72, V0R 2Z0,   604-725-3726 |
| Tofino | Clayoquot Lodge, P.O. Box 188, V0R 2Z0,  604-725-3284 |
| Ucluelet | B&B at Burley's, 1078 Helen Rd., Box 550, V0R 3A0,  604-726-4444 |
| Ucluelet | Henry's House, 1375 Helen Rd., Box 827, V0R 3A0,  604-726-7086 |
| Vancouver | An English Garden B&B, 4390 Frances St., V5C 2R3 |
| Vancouver | Diana's Luxury B&B, 1019 E. 38th Ave., V5W 1J4,  604-321-2855 |
| Vancouver | English Bay Inn, 1968 Comox St., V6G 1R4,  604-683-8002 |
| Vancouver | Green Gables B&B, 628 Union St., V6A 2B9,  604-253-6230 |
| Vancouver | Nelson House, 977 Broughton St., V6G 2A4,  604-684-9793 |
| Vancouver | On-Line B&B, 3732 18th Ave. W., V6S 1B2 |
| Vancouver | Peloquin's Pacific Pad, 426 West 22nd Ave, V5Y 2G5,  604-874-4529 |
| Vancouver | Penny Farthing Inn, 2855 W. 6th Ave., V6K 1X2,  604-739-9002 |
| Vancouver | Tall Cedars B&B, 720 Robinson St., V5J 4G1,  604-936-6016 |
| Vancouver | Wittmann's B&B, 4550 NW, Marine Dr., V6R 1B8,  604-224-2177 |
| Vernon | "The Cabin", 7603 Westkal Rd., V1B 1Y4,  604-542-3021 |
| Vernon | Eagle's View B&B, 350 Stepping Stones,RR7, V1T 7Z3,  604-545-4708 |
| Vernon | Five Junipers, 3704 - 24th Ave., V1T 1L9,  604-549-3615 |
| Vernon | Gisela's Bed & Breakfast, 3907 17th Ave., V1T 6Z1,  604-542-5977 |
| Vernon | Swan Lake View,  RR #5, S-6, C-66, V1T 6L8 |
| Victoria | A View to Sea, 626 Fernhill Rd., V9A 4Y9 |
| Victoria | Ambleside B&B, 1121 Faithful St., V8V 2R5,  604-383-9948 |
| Victoria | Arundel Manor B&B, 980 Arundel Dr., V9A 2C3,  604-385-5442 |
| Victoria | At Craig House, 52 San Jose Ave., V8V 2C2,  604-383-0339 |
| Victoria | Bay Breeze Manor, 3930 Telegraph Bay Road, V8N 4H7,  604-721-1855 |
| Victoria | Camelot B&B, 934A Fowl Bay Rd., V8H 4H8,  604-592-8589 |
| Victoria | Captain's Palace, 309 Belleville St., V8V 1X2,  604-388-9191 |
| Victoria | Cherry Bank Hotel, 825 Burdetl Ave., V8W 1B3 |
| Victoria | Craigmyle B&B, 1037 Craigdorroch Rd., V8S 2A5,  604-595-5411 |
| Victoria | Dunroamin, 616 Avalon Rd., V8V 1N8,  604-383-4106 |
| Victoria | Emilie's Bed & Breakfast, 1570 Rockland Ave., V8S 1W5,  604-598-8881 |
| Victoria | Glen Meadows B&B, 3130 Glen Lake Rd., V9B 4B7 |
| Victoria | Glyn House,  154 Robertson St., V8S 3X1 |
| Victoria | Gracefield Manor B&B, 3816 Duke Rd., RR4, V9B 5T8,  604-478-2459 |
| Victoria | Graham's Cedar House B&B, 1825 Landsend Rd., V8L 5J2,  604-655-3699 |
| Victoria | Gregory's Guest House, 5373 Patricia Bay Hwy., V8Y 1S9,  604-658-8404 |
| Victoria | Heritage House B&B, 3808 Heritage Ln., V8Z 7A7,  604-479-0892 |
| Victoria | Hibernia B&B, 747 Helvetia Crescent, V8Y 1M1,  604-658-5519 |
| Victoria | Holland House Inn, 595 Michigan St., V8V 1S7,  604-384-6644 |
| Victoria | Humboldt House, 867 Humboldt St., V8V 2Z6,  604-384-8422 |
| Victoria | Inn on St. Andrews, 231 St. Andrews St., V8V 2N1,  604-384-8613 |
| Victoria | Lilac House B&B, 252 Memorial Cres., V8S 3J2,  604-389-0252 |
| Victoria | Maridou House, 116 Elbert St., V86 3H7,  604-360-0747 |
| Victoria | Our Home on the Hill B&B, 546 Delora Dr., V9C 3R8,  604-474-4507 |
| Victoria | Oxford Castle Inn, 133 George Rd., East, V9A 1L1,  604-388-6431 |
| Victoria | Rose Cottage B&B, 3059 Washington Ave, V9A 1P9,  604-381-5985 |
| Victoria | Sea Rose Guest House, 1250 Dallas Rd., V8V 1C4,  604-381-7932 |
| Victoria | Sealake House B&B, 5152 Santa Clara Ave., V84 1W4,  604-658-5208 |
| Victoria | Vacationer B&B, 1143 Leonard St., V8V 2S3,  604-382-9469 |
| Victoria | Whyte House, 155 Randall St., V8V 2E3,  604-389-1598 |
| West Vancouver | Beachside B&B, 4208 Evergreen Ave., V7V 1H1,  604-922-7773 |
| West Vancouver | Ellen's B&B, 1437 Lawson Ave., V7T 2E9,  604-922-9749 |
| West Vancouver | Marisol, 2463 Ottawa Ave., V7V 2T2,  604-926-3992 |
| West Vancouver | Park Royal Hotel, 540 Clyde Ave., V7T 2J7,  604-932-1924 |
| Westbank | Lakeview Mansion, 3858 Harding Rd., V0H 2A0,  604-768-2205 |
| Westminster | Welcome B&B, 325 Pine St., V3L 2T1,  604-526-0978 |
| Whistler | Chalet Luise,  Box 352, V0N 1B0,  604-932-4187 |
| Whistler | Durlocher Hof, P.O. Box 1125, V0N 1B0,  604-932-1924 |
| Whistler | Edelweiss Pension, Bx 850,7162 Nancy Green, V0N 1B0,  604-932-3641 |
| Whistler | Haus Stephanie, 7473 Ambassador, B 1460, V0W 1B0,  604-932-5547 |
| Whistler | Swiss Cottage, P.O. Box 1209, V0N 1B0,  604-932-6062 |
| Whistler | Whistler B&B Inns, P.O. Box 850, V0N 1B0,  604-932-3282 |
| White Rock | Hall's B&B, 14778 Thrift Ave., V4B 2J5,  604-535-1225 |
| White Rock | Odins' B&B, 15319 Marine Dr., V4B 1C7,  604-531-9674 |
| White Rock | Sunset Ridge, 1347 Everall St., V4A 3S7,  604-538-1244 |
| Windermere | Younk's B&B, Box 52, V0B 2L0,  604-342-6295 |

# Manitoba

## More Inns ...

| | |
|---|---|
| Boissevain | Dueck's Cedar Chalet, Box 362, R0K 0E0 |
| Boissevain | Ernie & Tina Dyck, Box 1001, R0K 0E0, 204-534-2563 |
| Brandon | Casa Maley, 1605 Victoria Ave., R7A 1C1, 204-728-0812 |
| Brandon | Gwenmar Guest House, Box 59, RR3, R7A 5Y3, 204-728-7339 |
| Dauphin Beach | Bide Awhile, Box 414, R7N 2V2 |
| Deloraine | Prairie Haven Farms, RR2, R0M 0M0, 204-747-2612 |
| Elkhorn | Windyhill Farm, Box 248, R0M 0N0, 204-845-2101 |
| Hecla | Solmundson Gesta Hus, Box 76, R0C 1K0, 204-279-2088 |
| Morris | Deerbank Farm, Box 23, RR 2, R0G 1K0, 204-746-8395 |
| Richer | Geppetto's, Box 2A, RR #1, R0E 1S0 |
| Riding Mountain | Lamp Post, The, Box 27, R0J 1T0, 204-967-2501 |
| Rossburn | Woodland Hills Ranch, Box 520, R0J 1V0, 204-859-2663 |
| Treherne | Beulah Land, Box 26, R0G 2V0, 204-723-2828 |
| Winnipeg | Algeo's B&B, 183 Larchdale Cres., R2G 0A3, 204-334-7633 |
| Winnipeg | Bannerman East, 99 Bannerman Ave., R2W 0T1, 204-589-6449 |
| Winnipeg | Belanger's B&B, 291 Oakwood Ave., R3L 1E8 |
| Winnipeg | Casa Chestnut, 209 Chestnut St., R3G 1R8, 204-775-9708 |
| Winnipeg | Chestnut House, 209 Chestnut St., R36 1R8, 204-772-9788 |
| Winnipeg | Edna O'Hara, 242 Amherst St., R3J 1Y6, 204-888-6848 |
| Winnipeg | Ellie's B&B, 77 Middle Gate, R3C 2C5 |
| Winnipeg | Fillion's B&B, 45 Abingdon Rd., R2J 3S7 |
| Winnipeg | Hawchuk's B&B, 22 Everette Pl., R2V 4E8, 204-339-7005 |
| Winnipeg | Hillman's B&B, 701 Sherburn St., R3G 2L1 |
| Winnipeg | Irish's B&B, 12-341 Westwood Dr., R3K 1G4 |
| Winnipeg | Lobreau's B&B, 137 Woodlawn Ave, R2M 2P5 |
| Winnipeg | Nancy & Geoff Tidmarch, 330 Waverly St., R3M 3L3, 204-284-3689 |
| Winnipeg | Narvey's B&B, 564 Waverley St., R3M 3L5 |
| Winnipeg | Paul & Trudy Johnson, 455 Wallasey St., R3J 3C5, 204-837-3368 |
| Winnipeg | Preweda's B&B, 13 Nichol Ave., R2M 1Y6 |
| Winnipeg | Selci's B&B, 31 Carlyle Bay, R3K 0H2 |
| Winnipeg | Southern Rose Guest House, 533 Sprague St., R3G 2R9 |
| Winnipeg | Thomas & Marie Wiebe, 25 Valley View Dr., R2Y 0R5, 204-888-0910 |
| Winnipeg | Voyageur House, 268 Notre Dame St., R2H 0C6 |
| Winnipeg | West Gate Manor B&B, 71 West Gate, R3C 2C9, 204-772-9788 |
| Winnipeg | Wiebe's B&B, 281 Wallasey St., R3J 3C2 |
| Winnipeg | Zonneveld's B&B, 144 Yale Ave., R3M 0L7 |

# New Brunswick

## SACKVILLE —————————————————————————————

**Marshlands Inn**
Box 1440, 59 Bridge St.,  E0A
3C0
506-536-0170 Fax: 506-536-0721
800-561-1266
R. Peter & Diane Weedon
February–December

$$$-EP
25 rooms, 15 pb
AmEx, MC, Visa,
*Rated*, •
C-yes/S-yes/P-ltd/H-yes
French

Full breakfast (fee)
Luncheon, dinner, bar
Sitting room, antiques
piano, cordon bleu chef
adjoining rooms, gardens

*Elegant Victorian house surrounded by trees & gardens. Adjacent Hanson House built 1980s. All furnished w/antiques. Museum on grounds. **10% off bookings made via e-mail, ltd.***

## ST. ANDREWS BY-THE-SEA

| | | |
|---|---|---|
| **Pansy Patch** | $$$-B&B | Full breakfast |
| 59 Carleton St.,   E0G 2X0 | 9 rooms, 9 pb | Aftn. tea, snacks |
| 506-529-3834 | Visa, MC, *Rated*, • | Lunch/dinner, restaurant |
| Michael H. O'Connor | C-yes/S-no/P-no/H-no | sitting room, library |
| All year | Japanese on request | bikes, hot tubs, sauna |

*"Most photographed home in New Brunswick," designated Canadian Heritage Property. Canadian-class warmth & hospitality. Resort amenities. Fine dining.* **10% disc't 3+ nights; 10% disc't dining, ltd.**

## More Inns ...

| | |
|---|---|
| Albert | Florentine Manor, RR 2, E0A 1A0,  506-882-2271 |
| Albert County | Broadleaf Farms, Holewell Hill, E0A 1Z0,  506-882-2349 |
| Alma | Cleveland Place, North Main St, E0A 1B0,  506-887-2213 |
| Bathurst | Ingle-Neuk Lodge B&B, RR 3 Box 1180, E2A 4G8,  506-546-5758 |
| Beresford | Poplars—Les Peupliers, RR1 Site 11 Box 16, E0B 1H0,  506-546-5271 |
| Cambridge Narrows | Evengreen Manor B&B, Lakeview Rd, E0E 1B0,  506-488-2614 |
| Campbellton | Aylesford Inn B&B, 8 MacMillan Ave., E3N 1E9,  506-759-7672 |
| Campobello | Owen House, The, Welshpool, E0G 3H0,  506-752-2977 |
| Campobello | Welshpool House B&B, Welshpool Rd, Welshpool, E0G 3H0,  506-752-2040 |
| Cape Pele | Ocean Retreat, RR1, S23, Box 5, E0A 1J0,  506-577-6070 |
| Cape Tormentine | Hilltop B&B, Main Street, E0A 1H0,  506-538-7747 |
| Caraquet | Dugas Tourist Home, 683 Blvd., St. Pierre, E0B 1K0 |
| Centreville | Reid Farms Tourist Home, Knoxford Rd., E0J 1H0,  506-276-4787 |
| Cody's | Norwood Farms, Cambridge Narrows, RR1, E0E 1E0,  506-488-2681 |
| Deer Island | West Isles World, Lords Cove, Box 209, E0G 2J0,  506-747-2946 |
| Fredericton | Back Porch B&B, 266 Northumberland St., E3B 3J6,  506-454-6875 |
| Fredericton | Appelot B&B, RR4, E3B 4X5,  506-472-6115 |
| Fredericton | Brookmount Tourist Home, 4 Brookmount St, E3B 6L1,  506-457-9783 |
| Fredericton | Carriage House Inn B&B, 230 University Ave., E3B 4H7,  506-452-9924 |
| Fredericton | Victoriana Rose B&B, 193 Church St., E3B 4E1,  506-454-0994 |
| Grand Bay | Phyl's B&B, 8 Beverly Hills, Box 31, E0G 1W0,  506-738-2337 |
| Grand Falls | Cote's B&B, Box 2526, E0J 1M0,  506-473-1415 |
| Grand Falls | Maple B&B, 142 Main St., Box 1587, E0J 1M0,  506-473-1763 |
| Grand Falls | Old Farm House, RR 1, E0J 1M0,  506-473-2867 |
| Grand Manan | Compass Rose, North Head, E0G 2M0,  506-662-8570 |
| Grand Manan | Cross Tree Guest House, Seal Cove, E0G 3B0,  506-662-8263 |
| Grand Manan | Ferry Wharf Inn, North Head, E0G 2M0,  506-662-8588 |
| Grand Manan | Fundy Folly Guest House, Box 187, North Head, E0G 2M0,  506-662-3731 |
| Grand Manan | Grand Harbour Inn, Box 73, Grand Harbour, E0G 1X0,  506-662-8681 |
| Grand Manan | Manan Island Inn & Spa, P.O. Box 15, E0G 2M0,  506-662-8624 |
| Grand Manan | Rosalie's B&B, Seal Cove, E0G 3B0,  506-662-3344 |
| Grand Manan | Shorecrest Lodge, North Head, E0G 2M0,  506-662-3216 |
| Hampstead | Eveleigh Hotel, Evandale, RR1, E0G 1Y0,  506-425-9993 |
| Hartland | Campbell's B&B, RR1, E0J 1N0,  506-375-4775 |
| Hartland | Woodsview II B&B, RR 5, E0J 1N0,  506-375-4637 |
| Harvey Station | Magaguadavic River B&B, RR4, E0H 1H0,  506-366-2124 |
| Hopewell Cape | Dutch Treat Farm, RR 1, Shepody, E0A 1Y0,  506-882-2552 |
| Keswick Ridge | Hawks Nest B&B, 150 Rocky Rd., E0H 1N0,  506-363-3645 |
| Lower Jemseg | Oakley House, E0E 1S0,  506-488-3113 |
| Mactaquac | Mactaquac B&B, Mactaquac RR1, E0H 1N0,  506-363-3630 |
| Moncton | Bonaccord House, 250 Bonaccord St., E1C 5M6,  506-388-1535 |
| Moncton | McCarthy B&B, 82 Peter St., E1A 3W5,  506-383-9152 |
| Moncton | Park View B&B, 254 Cameron St., E1C 5Z3,  506-382-4504 |
| Mouth of Keswick | Colonial Country Inn B&B, RR3, E0H 1N0,  506-363-4137 |
| Nackawic | Hilltop B&B, RR3, E0H 1P0,  506-272-2012 |
| Nelson | Governor's Mansion, Main St., E0C 1T0,  506-622-3036 |
| New Mills | Heron Country Inn, S13, Box 10 Charlo, E0B 1M0,  506-237-5306 |
| Plaster Rock | Kingfisher Lodge, RR 1, E0J 1W0 |
| Plaster Rock | Northern Wilderness Lodge, Box 571, E0J 1W0,  506-356-8327 |
| Queens Co. | Gunter's Family Farm, White's Cover, E0E 1S0,  506-488-2037 |
| Riverside | Cailswick Babbling Brook, Albert Co., Route 114, E0A 2R0,  506-882-2079 |
| Rothesay | Shadow Lawn Inn, P.O. Box 41, E0G 5A3,  506-847-7539 |
| Sackville | Different Drummer, The, Box 188, E0A 3C0,  506-536-1291 |
| St. Andrews | Chamcook Forest Lodge B&B, RR2 Chamcook, E0G 2X0,  506-529-4778 |
| St. Andrews | Marcia's Garden Corner, 364 Montague St., E0G 2X0,  506-529-4453 |
| St. Andrews | Puff'Inn, P.O. Box 135, E0G 2X0,  506-529-4491 |
| St. Andrews | Shady Maples, 132 Sophia St., E0G 2X0,  506-529-4426 |
| St. Andrews | Shiretown Inn, Town Square, E0G 2X0,  506-529-8877 |
| St. George | Bonny River House B&B, Bonny River, RR3, E0G 2Y0,  506-755-2248 |
| St. Stephen | A Touch of Country, 61 Pleasant St., E3L 1A6,  506-466-5056 |
| St. Stephen | Bay's Edge, RR3, E3L 2Y1,  506-466-5401 |

| St. Stephen | Blair House, 38 Prince William,B 112, E3L 2W9, 506-466-2233 |
| Sussex | Andersons Holiday Farm, Sussex RR 2, E0E 1P0, 506-433-3786 |
| Sussex | Dutch Valley Heritage Inn, RR4, E0E 1P0, 506-433-1339 |
| Sussex | Stark's Hillside B&B, RR #4 Waterford, E0E 1P0, 506-433-3764 |
| Tracadie | Chez Prime B&B, RR 3, S. 32, Losier St., E0C 2B0, 506-395-6884 |
| Westfield | Blossoms B&B, RR1, E0G 3J0, 506-757-2962 |
| York Co. | Larsen's Log Lodge, RR1Millville, E0H 1M0, 506-463-2731 |

# Newfoundland

## ST. JOHN'S

**A Gower Street House B&B**  $-B&B  Continental plus bkfst.
180 Gower St., A1C 1P9  14 rooms, 12 pb  Afternoon tea, snacks
709-754-0047 Fax: 709-754-0047  *Rated*, •  Sitting room, library
800-563-3959  C-ltd/S-ltd/P-ltd/H-no  Jacuzzi
Leonard Clarke  Russian, Bulgarian

*Spacious rooms, spectacular views, center of downtown within 2 blocks of major hotels, restaurants, theatres, cathedrals, harbour, Signal Hill, tours.*

## More Inns . . .

| Boyd's Cove | Thoms Hospitality House, A0G 1G0, 709-656-3301 |
| Cape Onion | Tickle Inn at Cape Onion, RR1, Box 62, A0K 4J0, 709-452-4321 |
| Clarenville | Islandview Hospitality Hom, 128 Memorial Dr., A0E 1J0, 709-466-2062 |
| Clarenville | Station House, The, 107-111 Memorial Dr. N, A0E 1J0, 709-466-2036 |
| Corner Brook | Bide A Nite B&B, 11 Wellington St., A2H 5H3, 709-634-7578 |
| Corner Brook | Brake's Hospitality Home, 25 Cooper's Rd., A2H 3Y8, 709-785-2077 |
| Corner Brook | Humber Gallery Hospitality, Box 2242, RR1, A2H 2N2, 709-634-2660 |
| Cow Head | J & J Hospitality Home, Box 107, A0K 2A0, 709-243-2521 |
| Eastport | Sharoz Inn, The, Box 115, 5 Burden's Rd., A0G 1Z0, 709-677-3539 |
| Fogo | Payne's Hospitality Home, Box 201, A0G 2B0, 709-266-2359 |
| Fortune | Eldon House, 56 Eldon House, A0E 1P0, 709-832-0442 |
| Fortune Bay | Olde Oven Inn, English Harbour West, A0H 1M0, 709-888-3456 |
| Grand Bank | Thorndyke Heritage Home, P.O. Box 501, A0E 1W0, 709-832-0820 |
| Gunners Cove | Valhalla Lodge, A0K 2X0, 709-632-2018 |
| Lewisporte | Chaulk's Tourist Home, P.O. Box 339, A0J 3A0, 709-535-6305 |
| Lewisporte | Northgate B&B, 92 Main St., A0G 3A0, 709-535-2258 |
| Port-aux-Basques | Caribou B&B, Box 53, 30 Grand Bay Rd, A0N 1K0, 709-695-3408 |
| Port-aux-Choix | Jean-Marie Guest Home, Box 286, 8 Harbourview, A0K 4C0, 709-861-3023 |
| Roberts Arm | Lake Crescent Inn, P.O. Box 69, A0J 1R0, 709-652-3067 |
| Roberts Arm | Starkes B&B, Box 146, A0J 1R0, 709-652-3310 |
| South Branch | Muises Toursit Home, A0N 2B0, 709-955-2471 |
| Sprindale | Indian River Brook B&B, Springdale Junct. B 664, A0J 1T0, 709-673-3886 |
| St. Barbe | Toope's Hospitality House, A0K 1M0, 709-877-2413 |
| St. John's | Fort William B&B, 5 Gower St., A1C 1MA, 709-726-3161 |
| St. Mary's Bay | Whalen's Hospitality House, Box 46, Branch, A0B 1E0, 709-338-2506 |
| Steady Brook | Huxter's B&B, 2 Forest Dr., Box 170, A2H 2N2, 709-634-5644 |
| Traytown | Janes' Toursit Home, General Delivery, A0G 4K0, 709-533-2221 |
| Trinity | Village Inn, A0C 2S0, 709-464-3269 |
| Woody Point | Victorian Manor Hospitalit, Gros Morne Ntl Pk, B 16, A0K 1P0, 709-453-2485 |

# Northwest Territories

## More Inns . . .

| Hay River | Harbour House, Box 54, 1 Lakeshore Dr., X0E 0R0, 403-874-2233 |
| Yellowknife | Arctic House B&B, 20 Hearne Hill, Box 927, X1A 2N7, 403-873-6238 |
| Yellowknife | Captain Ron's B&B, #8, Lessard Dr., X1A 2G5, 403-873-3746 |
| Yellowknife | Eric & Eva's B&B, Box 2262, X1A 2P7, 403-873-5779 |

*Sterns Mansion B&B Inn, Dartmouth, NS*

# Nova Scotia

## ANNAPOLIS ROYAL

**Garrison House Inn**
P.O. Box 108, 350 St. George
St.,  B0S 1A0
902-532-5750 Fax: 902-532-5501
Patrick & Anna Redgrave
May 15–October

$-EP
7 rooms, 5 pb
MC, Visa, AmEx,
C-yes/S-ltd/P-no/H-no
French

Full breakfast (fee)
Intimate 16 seat pub
Licensed dining room
Picnic lunches
sitting room, bicycles

*Restored 1854 Heritage House—early Canadian antiques, hooked rugs, quilts and folk art treasures. Dining room specializes in local seafood and produce. **3rd night 50% off.***

## DARTMOUTH

**Sterns Mansion B&B Inn**
17 Tulip St.,  B3A 2S5
902-465-7414  Fax: 902-466-2152
800-565-3885
Bill de Molitor
All year

$$-B&B
5 rooms, 5 pb
Visa, MC, AmEx,
*Rated*,  •
C-ltd/S-no/P-no/H-no

Full breakfast
Afternoon tea, snacks
Comp. sherry in rooms
swimming & golf nearby
honeymoon suites

*Century old home w/antique bdrm. settings. Hardwood floors, brass chandeliers, honeymoon suites w/priv. jacuzzi spa. Near Casino, ferry & bridge. **$20 restaurant gift certif.***

## HALIFAX

**Halliburton House Inn**
5184 Morris St.,  B3J 1B3
902-420-0658 Fax: 902-423-2324
Robert Pretty
All year

$$$-B&B
30 rooms, 26 pb
*Rated*,  •
C-yes/S-yes/P-no/H-no
French

Continental plus bkfst.
Restaurant - lunch
Dinner, Afternoon tea
bar service, library
sitting room, courtyard

*Experience the pleasure of stepping into the past by visiting this 4-star heritage property in heart of Halifax. **Free use of private dining room with advance booking.***

## MAHONE BAY

| Bayview Pines Country Inn | $$-B&B | Continental breakfast |
|---|---|---|
| RR #2, 678 Oakland Rd | 13 rooms, 11 pb | Dinner, afternoon tea |
| Indian PT1, B0J 2E0 | Visa, MC, | Sitting room, library |
| 902-624-9970 Fax: 902-624-9970 | S-no/P-ltd/H-no | hot tubs, barn, TV |
| 800-565-0000 | German | licenced restaurant |
| Adolf & Elisabeth Sturany | | |
| May 1 - October 31 | | |

*Charming old farmhouse and converted barn surrounded by pasture and woodlands. All rooms have a view of the bay. Two housekeeping units available. Viennese cuisine.*

## MIDDLETON

| Fairfield Farm Inn | $-B&B | Full choice breakfast |
|---|---|---|
| P.O. Box 1287, 10 Main St. (Rt. | 5 rooms, 5 pb | Afternoon tea |
| 1 West), B0S 1P0 | Most CC, *Rated*, • | Sitting room, library |
| 902-825-6689 Fax: 902-825-6689 | C-ltd/S-no/P-no/H-no | video library, quest |
| 800-237-9896 | | kitchen/laundry, A/C |
| Richard & Shae Griffith | | |

*1886 Victorian farmhouse, furnished in period antiques. 110 acre property in Middleton. Walking distance to museums, restaurants & boutiques.* **Museum passes, 2 or more nights.**

# More Inns ...

| | |
|---|---|
| Amherst | Amherst Shore Country Inn, RR #2, B4H 3X9, 902-667-4800 |
| Amherst | Keillor Homestead, RR6, B4H 3Y4, 902-667-5513 |
| Annapolis Royal | Bread and Roses, P.O. Box 177, B0S 1A0, 902-532-5727 |
| Annapolis Royal | Milford House, RR #4, South Milford, B0S 1A0, 902-532-2617 |
| Annapolis Royal | Poplars B&B, 124 Victoria St, Box 27, B0S 1A0, 902-532-7936 |
| Annapolis Royal | Queen Anne Inn, P.O. Box 218 A, B0S 1A0, 902-532-7850 |
| Annapolis Royal | Sea Haven Guest House, RR2, B0S 1A0, 902-638-8881 |
| Annapolis Royal | St. George House B&B, 548 Upper St. George St, B0S 1A0, 902-532-5286 |
| Antigonish | Old Manse Inn, 5 Tigo Park, B2G 1L7, 902-863-5696 |
| Antigonish | Porter's B&B, Romquet Station, RR7, B2G 2L4, 902-386-2196 |
| Antigonish | Sanhaven Farms B&B, Clydesdale Rd., RR2, B2G 2K9, 902-863-3234 |
| Baddeck | An Seanne Mhanse, RR2, B0E 1B0, 902-295-2538 |
| Baddeck | Scalladh Aluinn, Box 59, Shore Rd., B0E 1B0, 902-295-2807 |
| Baddeck | Telegraph House, Box 8, B0E 1B0, 902-295-9988 |
| Barton | Barton House, The, Box 33, B0W 1H0, 902-245-6695 |
| Bear River | Lovett Lodge Inn, P.O. Box 119, B0S 1B0, 902-467-3917 |
| Bedford | South Shore Country Inn, 15 Shore Dr., B4A 2G9, 902-677-2042 |
| Berwick | Fundy Trail Farms, RR5, B0P 1E0, 902-538-9481 |
| Bridgetown | Chesley House B&B, 304 Granville St,Bx 134, B0S 1C0, 902-665-2904 |
| Broad Cove | Lighthouse, The, Route 331, B0J 2H0 |
| Brookfield | Bidia B&B, Middle Stewiacke, RR3, B0N 1C0, 902-673-2016 |
| Canning | 1850 House, Box 22, Main St., B0P 1H0, 902-582-3052 |
| Canning | Farmhouse Inn, The, P.O. Box 38, B0P 1H0, 902-582-7900 |
| Cape Breton | Heart of Hart's T. H., N.E. Margaree, B0E 2H0, 902-248-2765 |
| Cape Breton | Markland, The, Cabot Trail, Dingwall, B0C 1G0, 902-383-2246 |
| Cape Breton | Riverside Inn, Margaree Hrb., B0E 2B0, 902-235-2002 |
| Cape North | Oakwood Manor, Box 19, Dingwall, B0C 1G0, 902-383-2317 |
| Central Port Mouton | Sea-View B&B, Box 32, B0T 1T0, 902-683-2217 |
| Chester | Casa Blanca Guest House, Box 70, 123 Duke St, B0J 1J0, 902-275-3385 |
| Chester | Mecklenburgh Inn, The, 78 Queen St., B0J 1J0, 902-275-4638 |
| Church Point | Golf Course View B&B, Box 217 B, RR1, B0W 1M0, 902-769-2065 |
| Collingwood | Cobequid Hills Country Inn, B0M 1E0, 902-686-3381 |
| Dartmouth | Boutiliers B&B, 5 Boutiliers Grove, B2X 2V9, 902-435-4094 |
| Dartmouth | Martin House, Cabot Street., B2Y 3P5, 902-469-1896 |
| Debert | Ellen Eisses, RR #1, B0M 1G0 |
| Digby | Admiral's Landing, The, Box 657, 115 Montague, B0V 1A0, 902-245-2247 |
| Digby | Westways, The, Box 1576, B0V 1A0, 902-245-5071 |
| East Bay | Big Pond B&B, RR1, B0A 1H0, 902-828-2476 |
| Granville Ferry | Nightingale's Landing B&B, P.O. Box 30, B0S 1K0, 902-532-7615 |
| Granville Ferry | Shining Tides, RR #2, B0S 1K0, 902-532-2770 |
| Guysborough County | Liscombe Lodge, Liscomb Mills, B0J 2A0, 902-779-2307 |
| Halifax | Fresh Start B&B, 2720 Gottingen St., B3K 3C7, 902-453-6616 |
| Halifax | Queen Street Inn, 1266 Queen St., B3J 2H4, 902-422-9828 |
| Hebron | Manor Inn, P.O. Box 56, R.R. 1, B0W 1X0, 902-742-2487 |

| | |
|---|---|
| Inverness | Taylor's B&B, Margaree Harbour, B0E 2B0,  902-235-2652 |
| Iona | Highland Heights Inn, Box 19, B0A 1L0,  902-622-2360 |
| Kingston | Hagen's Hacienda, 350 Brookside Dr, B0P 1R0,  902-765-8897 |
| Liverpool | Hopkins House, 120 Main St., B0T 1K0,  902-354-5484 |
| Louisbourg | Greta Cross B&B, 81 Peperell St., B0A 1M0,  902-733-2833 |
| Louisbourg | MacLeod's B&B and Cottage, RR1, B0A 1M0,  902-733-2456 |
| Louisbourg | Manse, The,  17 Strathcona St., B0A 1M0,  902-733-3155 |
| Louisbourg | Peck Tourist Home B&B,  RR1, B0A 1M0,  902-733-2649 |
| Lunenburg | Blue Rocks Road B&B,  RR #1, B0J 2C0,  902-634-3426 |
| Lunenburg | Boscawen Inn, P.O. Box 1343, B0J 2C0,  902-634-3325 |
| Lunenburg | Snug Harbour B&B,  9 King St., Box 1390, B0J 2C0,  902-634-9146 |
| Luwenburg | South Shore Country Inn,  Broad Cove, B0J 2H0,  902-677-2042 |
| Mabou | Cape Breton Island Farm,  RR 2, B0E 1X0,  902-945-2077 |
| Mahone Bay | Sou'Wester Inn,  Box 146, 788 Main Stree, B0J 2E0,  902-624-9296 |
| Maitland | Cobequid Inn, The,  RR1, B0N 1T0,  902-261-2841 |
| Maitland | Foley House Inn, P.O. Box 86, B0N 1T0,  902-261-2844 |
| Margaree Valley | Brown's Bruaich na H'Aibhn, Box 88, B0E 2C0,  902-248-2935 |
| Masstown | Shady Maple Inn],  RR1, Debert, B0M 1G0,  902-662-3565 |
| Middleton | Morse Century Farm B&B,  Box 220, B0S 1P0,  902-825-4600 |
| Middleton | Victorian Inn B&B,  145 Commercial St., B0S 1P0,  902-825-6464 |
| Mosquodoboit | Seaview Fisherman's Home,  RR1, B0J 2L0,  902-889-2561 |
| Musquodoboit | Camelot,  Box 31, Rt. 7, B0J 2L0,  902-889-2198 |
| New Glasgow | Highland View,  RR2, B2H 5C5,  902-752-8862 |
| North Sydney | Annfield Tourist Manor,  RR 3, Bras D'or, B0C 1B0,  902-736-8770 |
| Plympton | Westway Inn, B0W 2R0,  902-837-4097 |
| Port Clyde | MacLaren Inn, B0W 2S0,  902-637-3296 |
| Port Hood | Haus Treuburg,  Box 92, B0E 2W0,  902-787-2116 |
| Port Williams | Planter's Barracks Inn,  Starr's Point Rd., B0P 1T0 |
| Pugwash | Blue Heron Inn, The,  Box 405, B0K 1L0,  902-243-2900 |
| Queens County | River View Lodge,  Box 93, Greenfield, B0J 2H0 |
| Riverport | Barrett's B&B,  RR1, Rose Bay, B0J 2W0,  902-766-4655 |
| Shelbourne | Cooper's Inn,  36 Dock St., Box 959, B0T 1W0 |
| Shelbourne | Toddle In B&B,  Box 837, B0T 1W0 |
| Smith's Cove | Harborview Inn, P.O. Box 35, B0S 1S0,  902-245-5686 |
| Stellarton | MacDonalds B&B,  Box 831, 292 S Foord St, B0K 1S0,  902-752-7751 |
| Stewiacke | Cloverdale Inn,  RR2, B0N 2J0,  902-673-3313 |
| Sydney | Markland Coastal Resort,  21 Haig St., B1S 2Y1,  902-564-5226 |
| Sydney Mines | Gowrie House Country Inn,  139 Shore Rd., B1V 1A6,  902-544-1050 |
| Truro | Blue House Inn,  43 Dominion St., B2N 3P2,  902-895-4150 |
| Truro | Johnson's B&B,  1702 Salmon River Rd., B2N 5B2,  902-895-4797 |
| Truro | Old Farm House,  195 Truro Heights, RR1, B2N 5A9,  902-895-3671 |
| Upper Stewiacke | Lansdowne Lodge, B0N 2P0,  902-671-2749 |
| Wallace | Senator Guest Manor,  Route 6, Sunrise Trail, B0K 1Y0,  902-257-2417 |
| Westville | Stoneycombe Lodge,  Alma, RR3, B0K 2A0,  902-396-3954 |
| Weymouth | Gilbert's Cove Farm,  RR 3, B0W 3T0,  902-837-4505 |
| Windsor | Clockmaker's Inn B&B,  1399 King St., B0W 3T0,  902-798-5265 |
| Wolfville | Blomidon Inn, P.O. Box 839, B0P 1X0,  902-542-2291 |
| Wolfville | Gingerbread House Inn, P.O. Box 819, BP0 1X0,  902-542-1458 |
| Wolfville | Tattingstone Inn,  434 Main St., B0P 1X0 |
| Wolfville | Victoria's Historic Inn,  Box 819, 416 Main St., B0P 1X0,  902-542-5744 |
| Yarmouth | Churchill Mansion Inn,  RR 1, B5A 4A5,  902-649-2818 |
| Yarmouth | Vaughn Lake B&B,  RR1, Tusket, Box 88, B0W 3M0,  902-648-3122 |
| Yarmouth | Whittaker's B&B,  RR5, Box 1238, B5A 4A9,  902-742-7649 |

# Ontario

## BARRIE ───────────────────────────────

| | | |
|---|---|---|
| **Cozy Corner** | $-B&B | Full breakfast |
| 2 Morton Cresent,  L4N 7T3 | 3 rooms, 1 pb | Continental plus bkfst |
| 705-739-0157 | Visa,  • | Sitting room, Jacuzzi |
| Charita & Harry Kirby | C-ltd/S-no/P-no/H-no | we'll pick you up at |
| All year | German, Spanish | the airport |

*Enjoy elegant retreat surrounded by Muskoka Lakes, Georgian Bay. Quality bedding, A/C. European theme gourmet bkfsts. Different country daily. **Free laundry serv. w/3 nite stay.***

## COBOURG/GORE'S LANDING

| | | |
|---|---|---|
| **Victoria Inn, The** | $$-B&B | Full breakfast |
| 5316 Harwood Rd., K0K 2E0 | 9 rooms, 9 pb | Lunch, dinner, bar |
| 905-342-3261 Fax: 905-342-2798 | AmEx, MC, Visa, | Sitting room, piano |
| 888-221-1131 | C-yes/S-yes/P-no/H-yes | boat rental |
| Donna & Donald Cane | | swimming pool |
| Mid-May–mid-October | | |

*Lakefront estate on 2 acres of lawn, overlooks 3 islands. Specializing in local meat, fish & vegetables. Close to fishing, skiing, antiques, artisan studios, concerts, golf, tennis & curling.*

## GODERICH

| | | |
|---|---|---|
| **Colborne B&B** | $$-B&B | Full breakfast |
| 72 Colborne St., N7A 2V9 | 4 rooms, 4 pb | Afternoon tea |
| 519-524-7400 Fax: 519-524-4943 | C-ltd/S-no/P-no/H-no | Sitting room with |
| Kathryn Darby | French | fireplace, bikes |
| All year | | enclosed porch |

*Centraly located, walking distance to beaches, shopping, etc. One twin, one double, two king. Kings have fireplaces and whirlpool tubs.*

## HAMILTON

| | | |
|---|---|---|
| **Inchbury Street B&B** | $$-B&B | Full breakfast |
| 87 Inchbury St., L8R 3B7 | 2 rooms, | Snacks, comp. cold drink |
| 905-522-3520 Fax: 905-522-5216 | Visa, | Sitting room, TV/VCR |
| 800-792-8765 | C-yes/S-ltd/P-no/H-no | phones, bikes |
| All year | German, French | |

*Quiet enclave next to Dundurn Castle. Walk to downtown. Turn-of-the-century house is also an art gallery. E-mail access and fax receiving for business travelers.* **7th night free.**

## NIAGARA-ON-THE-LAKE

| | | |
|---|---|---|
| **Hernder's Country Home B&B** | $-B&B | Full breakfast |
| 753 Line 3, RR2, L0S 1J0 | 3 rooms, 3 pb | Sitting room |
| 905-468-3192 | MC, *Rated*, | bicycles, hot tubs |
| Pat & Art Hernder | C-ltd/S-no/P-no/H-no | gazebo |
| All year | | |

*Spacious colonial home on a vineyard in heart of wine country. Minutes to Shaw Theatres and Niagara's many attractions.*

| | | |
|---|---|---|
| **Stone Haven B&B** | $-EP | Full breakfast |
| 1936 Niagra Stone Rd., R.R. | 2 rooms, 1 pb | Continental plus bkfst. |
| #3, L0S 1J0 | C-ltd/S-no/P-no/H-no | Sitting room |
| 905-468-4565 | German | |
| Hannah Krauck & Rudy Bartel | | |
| All year | | |

*Warm hospitality awaits you. Minutes from Shaw Festival, wineries, golf, bicycling, and quaint shops. Central air conditioning with ample parking.*

## OTTAWA

| | | |
|---|---|---|
| **Albert House Inn** | $$-B&B | Full English breakfast |
| 478 Albert St., K1R 5B5 | 17 rooms, 17 pb | Tea, coffee, juices |
| 613-236-4479 Fax: 613-237-9078 | AmEx, MC, Visa, | Sitting room |
| 800-267-1982 | *Rated*, • | color cable TV in rooms |
| John & Cathy Delroy | C-ltd/S-yes/P-no/H-no | telephones |
| All year | French, English | |

*Fine restored Victorian residence designed by Thomas Seaton Scott in post-Confederate period. Complimentary breakfast, parking. New queen room sith double jacuzzi available.*

OTTAWA ———————————————————————————————————

| **Auberge des Arts B&B** | $$-B&B | Full breakfast |
|---|---|---|
| 104 Guigues Ave., K1N 5H7 | 3 rooms, 1 pb | Afternoon tea, snacks |
| 613-562-0909 Fax: 613-562-0909 | Most CC, • | Bicycles |
| Chantal Patenaude | C-ltd/S-no/P-no/H-no | balcony |
| All year | French, Spanish | bus/train/airport pickup |

*In the heart of the city; close to all sites and attractions. Homey, cozy & quiet. Homemade breakfast. **4th night, 50%.***

---

| **Blue Spruces** | $$-B&B | Full breakfast |
|---|---|---|
| 187 Glebe Ave., K1S 2C6 | 3 rooms, 3 pb | Afternoon tea |
| 613-236-8521 Fax: 613-231-3730 | Visa, MC, *Rated*, | Sitting room |
| Patricia & John Hunter | C-ltd/S-no/P-no/H-no | central air-conditioning |
| All year | French | vegetarian dining |

*Elegant Edwardian home with antiques in downtown Ottawa. Home-cooked breakfasts. We enjoy talking with guests & helping them find memorable parts of Ottawa to explore.*

---

| **Bye-The-Way** | $-B&B | Full breakfast |
|---|---|---|
| 310 First Ave., K1S 2G8 | 4 rooms, 2 pb | Sitting room |
| 613-232-6840 Fax: 613-232-6840 | Visa, MC, • | bicycles, suite avail. |
| Krystyna or Rafael | C-ltd/S-no/P-no/H-no | close to attractions |
| | French, Polish | |

*Modern home, comfortable and close to everything. Sumtuous breakfast served in lovely dining room. Congenial hosts can help with sightseeing.*

---

| **Gasthaus Switzerland Inn** | $$-B&B | Full Swiss breakfast |
|---|---|---|
| 89 Daly Ave., K1N 6E6 | 22 rooms, 22 pb | Sitting room, TV room |
| 613-237-0335 Fax: 613-267-8788 | MC, Visa, *Rated*, • | air-conditioned |
| 800-267-8782 | C-ltd/S-no/P-no/H-no | barbecue, garden |
| Sabina & Josef Sauter | German, Serb., French | |
| All year | | |

*Warm Swiss atmosphere in Canada's beautiful capital. Clean, cozy rooms; close to tourist attractions; free parking. Warm, clean & cheery!*

---

| **Haydon House** | $$-B&B | Continental plus bkfst. |
|---|---|---|
| 18 Queen Elizabeth Dr., K2P 1C6 | 3 rooms, 1 pb | Afternoon tea |
| 613-230-2697 | *Rated*, | Sitting room, piano |
| Mary & Andy Haydon | C-yes/S-yes/P-ltd/H-no | TV with VHR |
| All year | French | bike & hiking trips |

*Downtown Victorian home, embellished with Canadian pine decor in tranquil residential district beside historic Rideau Canal and scenic parkway."Some spoiling" for special occ.*

TORONTO ———————————————————————————————————

| **Beaconsfield B&B** | $$-B&B | Full breakfast |
|---|---|---|
| 38 Beaconsfield Ave., M6J 3H9 | 3 rooms, 1 pb | Unique, eclectic decor |
| 416-535-3338 Fax: 416-535-3338 | Checks accepted, | |
| Katya & Bernie McLoughlin | C-ltd/S-ltd/P-ltd/H-no | |
| All year | Spanish, Some Fr. & Ger. | |

*Artist/actress couple's unconventional, colorful 1882 Victorian home full of fun & sun, art & heart. Located in quiet neighborhood, short trolley ride to major sites, theatres. Information galore.*

TORONTO

**Palmerston Inn B&B, The**
322 Palmerston Blvd., M6G 2N6
416-920-7842  Fax: 416-960-9529
416-964-2566
Judy Carr    All year

$$-B&B
8 rooms, 3 pb
MC, Visa, *Rated*,  •
C-yes/S-no/P-no/H-no
German, French

Full breakfast
Deck, garden, park
TV lounge, phones
ceiling fans in all rms.

*In charming downtown residential area. Close to Eaton Centre. Nearby public transportation to downtown. Friendly Old World atmosphere. Some rooms have fireplaces. **Nov-Mar 10% discount.***

**Terrace House B&B**
52 Austin Terrace, M5R 1Y6
416-535-1493  Fax: 416-535-9616
S. Charbonneau
All year

$$-B&B
3 rooms, 1 pb
C-ltd/S-no/P-no/H-no
French

Full breakfast
Sitting room, library
A/C guest rooms
close to shopping, sites

*Gourmet breakfast served in our dining room. Artwork and crafts from many trips decorate this, your home away from home.*

# More Inns . . .

| | |
|---|---|
| Almonte | Mount Blow Farm B&B, RR #2, K0A 1A0 |
| Almonte | Squirrels, The, Box 729, K0A 1A0 |
| Almonte | Tackaberry's Grant, RR #2, K0A 1A0, 613-256-1481 |
| Alton | Cataract Inn, 1490 Cataract St., RR#2, L0N 1A0, 519-927-3033 |
| Arden | Puff Ball Villa, RR2, K0H 1B0, 613-335-2243 |
| Arva | Robsons Rolling Ridge Farm, RR1, N0M 1C0, 519-555-0896 |
| Baden | Northridge Farm B&B, RR 2, N0B 1G0, 519-634-8595 |
| Balderson | Woodrow Farm, RR #1, K0G 1A0, 613-267-1493 |
| Baldwin | Baldwin Mill B&B, 24357 Highway 48, L0E 1R0, 416-722-5743 |
| Bancroft | Bancroft B&B, 4 Sherbourne N, Box 327, K0L 1C0, 613-332-1538 |
| Bancroft | Beechmount Studio B&B, RR2, K0L 1C0, 613-332-2329 |
| Bayfield | Little Inn of Bayfield, Main St., N0M 1G0, 519-565-2611 |
| Baysville | Burton's B&B, Box 70, Bay Street, P9B 1A0, 705-767-3616 |
| Bloomfield | Cornelius White House B&B, 8 Wellington St., K0K 1G0, 613-393-2282 |
| Bloomfield | Shirwill Farm, RR2, K0K 1G0, 613-399-2884 |
| Bracebridge | Bourdages B&B, RR3, P1L 1X1, 705-645-3711 |
| Bracebridge | Century House B&B, 155 Dill St., P1L 1E5, 705-645-9903 |
| Bracebridge | Holiday House Inn, P.O. Box 1139, P0B 1C0, 705-645-2245 |
| Bracebridge | Riverview B&B, 420 Beaumont Dr., RR4, P1L 1X2, 705-645-4022 |
| Braeside | Glenroy Farm, RR 1, K0A 1G0, 613-432-6248 |
| Brampton | Creditview B&B, 7650 Creditview Rd., L6V 3N2, 416-451-6271 |
| Bridgeport | Bedrock B&B, 518 Bridgeport Rd., N2K 1N7, 519-578-1746 |
| Brighton | Applecrest House, 61 Simpson St, Box 1106, K0K 1H0, 613-475-0538 |
| Brighton | Main Street B&B, Box 431, 96 Main St, K0K 1H0, 613-475-0351 |
| Brinston | Westergreen Farm, RR2, K0E 1C0, 613-652-4241 |
| Brockville | Brockville B&B, 331 King St. W, K6V 3S5, 613-345-4600 |
| Bruce Mines | Beacon Inn B&B, Box 293, 5 Mitchell St, P0R 1C0, 705-785-9950 |
| Bruce Mines | Lake Forest Farm, RR1, P0R 1C0, 705-785-3510 |
| Cambridge | Langdon Hall, R.R. 33, N3H 4R8 |
| Campbellford | Linden House, 91 Doxsee Ave., South, K0L 1L0, 705-653-4406 |
| Cargill | Cornerbrook Farms, RR2, N0G 1J0, 519-366-2629 |
| Carleton Place | Blue Gables, 192 Henry St., K7C 1B1 |
| Carleton Place | Hudson House B&B, 7 Lorne St., K7C 2J9, 613-257-8547 |
| Carp | White Trillium B&B, 3681 Vaughan Side. RR 2, K0A 1L0 |
| Casselman | Casselmann Country B&B, 18 Racine Rd., RR4, K0A 1M0, 613-764-5607 |
| Cayuga | Broecheler Inn, RR4, N0A 1A0, 416-772-5362 |
| Chaffeys Lock | Alford's B&B, Box 17, K0G 1C0, 613-359-1173 |
| Chalk River | Cedar Lodge Guest House, 10 Ottawa St., K0J 1J0, 613-589-2810 |
| Cherry Valley | Bell's B&B, RR1, K0K 1P0, 613-476-2257 |
| Clarksburg | Grape Grange, Box 39, Marsh St., N0H 1J0, 519-599-2601 |
| Clinton | Godley's, Box 316, N0M 1L0, 519-524-2438 |
| Cloyne | Myers Cave Lodge, RR2, Myers Cave, K0H 1K0, 613-336-9122 |
| Cobden | Cobden B&B, P.O. Box 4, K0J 1K0, 613-646-2643 |
| Cobourg | Northumberland Heights Inn, RR 5, K9A 4J8, 905-372-7500 |
| Cobourg | Victoria View, 216 Church St., K9A 3V9, 416-372-3437 |
| Colborne | Maples, The, Box 743, 119 King St E, K0K 1S0, 416-355-2059 |
| Courtice | Betts' B&B, 71 Pinedale Cres, L1E 1C7, 416-723-3975 |
| Deep River | Settlers Inn, RR1, K0J 1P0, 613-584-2721 |
| Dobbinton | Hatties's Hideaway, RR2, N0H 1L0, 519-363-6543 |

| | |
|---|---|
| Drayton | McIssac's, The, P.O. Box 263, N0G 1P0, 519-638-2190 |
| Dundas | Glenwood B&B, 42 Osler Dr., L9H 4B1, 416-627-5096 |
| Durham | Forest Edge B&B, Forest Edge, RR3, N0G 1R0, 519-369-5661 |
| Dutton | Dunwich Farm B&B, RR 1, N0L 1J0, 519-762-3006 |
| Eagle Lake | Sir Sam's Inn, Eagle Lake P.O., K0M 1M0, 705-754-2188 |
| Eganville | Verch's B&B, RR2, K0J 1T0, 613-628-6901 |
| Elmira | Birdland B&B, 1 Grey Owl Dr., N3B 1S2, 519-669-1900 |
| Elmira | Evergreens, The, RR 1, N3B 2Z1, 519-669-2471 |
| Elmira | Plaid Blanket B&B, The, 17 William Street, N3B 1P1, 519-669-5361 |
| Elmira | Teddy Bear B&B Inn, RR #1, N3B 2Z1, 519-669-2379 |
| Elmvale | Homestead B&B, The, 40 Amelia St., L0L 1P0, 705-322-1334 |
| Elmvale | Watson's, RR2, L0L 1P0, 705-322-2419 |
| Elora | Ann's B&B, 130 Moir St, N0B 1S0, 519-846-0848 |
| Elora | Elora Mill Inn, 77 Mill St. W., Box 218, N0B 1S0 |
| Elora | Ethel's B&B, 231 Queen St N, Box 33, N0B 1S0, 519-846-9763 |
| Elora | Speers' Home, Box 310, Geddes St, N0B 1S0, 519-846-9744 |
| Fergus | 4-Eleven, 411 St. Andrew St. E., N1M 1R4, 519-843-5107 |
| Fergus | Breadalbane Inn, The, 487 Saint Andrew St. W, N1M 1P2, 519-843-4770 |
| Frankville | Gibbons', RR1, K0E 1H0, 613-275-2893 |
| Gananoque | Britton House B&B, 110 Clarence St, K7G 2C1, 613-382-4361 |
| Gananoque | Victoria Rose Inn, The, 279 King St. West, K7G 2G7, 613-382-3368 |
| Goderich | Inn At The Port, The, RR 3, N7A 3X9, 519-529-7986 |
| Goderich | Kathi's Guesthouse, RR 4, N7A 3Y1, 519-524-8587 |
| Goderich | La Brassine, RR 2, N7A 3X8, 519-524-6300 |
| Goderich | Maison Tanguay, 46 Nelson St. W., N7A 2M3, 519-524-1930 |
| Goderich | Quidi Vidi Manor B&B, RR2, N7A 3X8, 519-524-9481 |
| Goderich | Twin Porches, 55 Nelson St E, N7A 1R7, 519-524-5505 |
| Grafton | Griffindale Farm B&B, RR1, K0K 2G0, 416-349-2940 |
| Grafton | Ste. Anne's Inn, RR1, K0K 2G0, 416-349-2493 |
| Grand Bend | Barbara's Naturally B&B, 12 Ontario St, N0M 1T0, 519-238-8489 |
| Gravenhurst | Allen's B&B, Box 2276, 581 David St, P0C 1G0, 705-687-7368 |
| Gravenhurst | Cunningham's B&B, 175 Clairmont, Box 574, P0C 1G0, 705-687-4511 |
| Haliburton | All-Hart B&B, RR2, So. Kashagawigamog, K0M 1S0, 705-457-5272 |
| Hanover | Ayr-Wyn Farms, RR3, N4N 3B9, 519-364-1540 |
| Hanover | Lonesome Pines, 192 - 12th Ave., N4N 3B9, 519-364-2982 |
| Harriston | Country Place, The, RR1, N0G 1Z0, 519-323-1008 |
| Harriston | Maitland Manor, RR 2, N0G 1Z0, 519-338-3487 |
| Hearst | Rejeanne's B&B, 45A Houle St, Box 862, P0L 1N0, 705-362-4442 |
| Heidelberg | Evergreen Lawns, 64 Hilltop Ct., N0B 1Y0, 519-699-4453 |
| Honey Harbour | Elk's Hide-a-Way, The, Box 222, P0E 1E0, 705-756-2993 |
| Hunta | Country Haven B&B, General Delivery, P0L 1P0, 705-272-6802 |
| Huntsville | Falcon Lodge, RR1 Falcon Rd., P0A 1K0, 705-789-2603 |
| Jordan | Travelers Home, RR1, L0R 1S0, 416-562-5656 |
| Kagawong | Bridal Veil B&B, Box 10, 42 Main St, P0P 1J0, 705-282-3300 |
| Kagawong | Park's Folly Bayview B&B, Box 8, P0P 1J0, 705-282-2791 |
| Kawkestone | Simocoe-Side Country B&B, RR2, Lakeshore Rd, L0L 1T0, 705-487-7191 |
| Kenora | Heritage Place, Longbow Lake, P0X 1H0, 807-548-4380 |
| Kimberley | Lamont Guest Home, N0C 1G0, 519-599-5905 |
| Kincardine | Aurel & Marj Armstrong B&B, RR4, N2Z 2X5, 519-395-3301 |
| Kincardine | Hanks Heritage House, 776 Princes St., N2Z 1Z5, 519-396-7991 |
| Kingston | Chart House, 90 Yonge St, K7M 1E6, 613-546-9026 |
| Kingston | Kelly House, 35 Wellington St, K7L 3B9, 613-548-4796 |
| Kingston | North Nook, The, 23 Morley St, K7M 2M4, 613-549-4061 |
| Kitchener | Austrian Home, 90 Franklin St. N., N2A 1X9, 519-893-4056 |
| Kitchener | Driftwood Home, 202 Driftwood Dr., N2N 1X6, 519-745-8010 |
| Kitchener | Roots & Wings, 11 Sunbridge Crescent, N2K 1T4, 519-743-4557 |
| Kitchener | Why Not B&B, 34 Amherest Dr., N2P 1C9, 519-748-4577 |
| Kleinburg | Humber House, 10555 Islington Ave, L0J 1C0, 416-893-9108 |
| Lakefield | Killeen's, The, RR3, 1964 Selwyn Rd., K0L 2H0, 705-652-6369 |
| Lakefield | Windmere B&B, Selwyn, RR 3, K0L 2H0, 705-652-6290 |
| Lanark | Linden Meadow Farm, RR #1, K0G 1K0 |
| Lanark | Red Eagle Guest House, The, RR #3, K0G 1K0 |
| Lancaster | B&B Macpine Farms, Box 51, K0C 1N0, 613-347-2003 |
| Lancaster | MacPine Farm's B&B, Box 51, K0C 1N0, 613-347-2003 |
| Lansdowne | Hart Country Estate, RR #4, K0E 1L0, 613-659-2873 |
| Lansdowne | Ivy Lea Inn, 1000 Isl. Pkwy., K0E 1L0, 613-659-2329 |
| Leamington | Home Suite Home B&B, 115 Erie St. S., N8H 3B5, 519-326-7169 |
| Lindsay | Yellow Shutters B&B, 31 Cambridge St N, K9V 4C6, 705-324-8158 |
| Lion's Head | Bear Walk B&B, RR4, N0H 1W0, 519-793-4506 |
| Lion's Head | Cat's Pajamas, The, 64 Main Street, N0H 1W0, 519-793-3767 |
| Lion's Head | Steinwald, RR4, N0H 1W0, 519-795-7894 |
| Little Current | Pearl's B&B, 11 Dupont St, P0P 1K0, 705-368-2920 |
| London | Annigan's B&B, 194 Elmwood Ave. E, N6C 1K2, 519-439-9196 |
| London | Eileen's B&B, 433 Hyde Park Rd, N6H 3R9, 519-471-1107 |
| London | Ferndale West, 53 Lonfbow Rd., N6G 1Y5, 519-471-8038 |
| London | Lambert House B&B, 231 Cathcart St., N6C 3M8, 519-672-8996 |
| London | Overdale B&B, 1 Normandy Gardens, N6H 4A9, 519-641-0236 |
| London | Rose House, The, 526 Dufferin Ave., N6B 2A2, 519-433-9978 |

| | |
|---|---|
| London | Serena's Place, 720 Headley Dr, N6H 3V6, 519-471-6228 |
| Lucknow | Perennial Pleasures B&B, P.O. Box 304, N0G 2H0, 519-528-3601 |
| Lunenburg | Country Farm B&B, RR1, K0C 1R0, 613-534-2063 |
| Manitoulin Island | Mindemoya Lake View Farm, Mindemoya, P0P 1S0, 705-377-5714 |
| Manotick | Long Island B&B, 5607 Island Park Drive, K4M 1J3, 613-692-2042 |
| Markdale | Cozy Nook B&B, RR7, N0C 1H0, 519-924-2063 |
| Maynooth | Bea's B&B House, Box 133, K0L 2S0, 613-338-2239 |
| McDonald's Corners | Mcdonald's Corners B&B, Box 81, K0G 1M0 |
| McKellar | Inn at Manitou, The, McKellar Center Rd., P0G 1C0, 416-967-3466 |
| Meaford | Cheshire Cat, The, 32 Nelson St., Box 1809, N0H 1Y0, 519-538-3487 |
| Merrickville | Sam Jakes Inn, P.O. Box 580, K0G 1N0, 613-269-3711 |
| Midland | Calvert's, 476 Yonge Street E, L4R 2C3, 705-526-0306 |
| Millbank | Honeybrook Farm, RR 1, N0K 1L0, 519-595-4604 |
| Millbrook | Westmascott House, 60 King St W, Box 386, L0A 1G0, 705-932-2957 |
| Miller Lake | Camariche, Dyer's Bay R., RR1, N0H 1Z0, 519-795-7699 |
| Miller Lake | Craglee B&B, Dyer's Bay, RR1, N0H 1Z0, 519-795-7887 |
| Miller Lake | Pinnell's B&B, N0H 1Z0, 519-795-7869 |
| Milverton | Country Garden, RR 1, N0K 1M0, 519-595-4495 |
| Milverton | Country Parsonage Inn B&B, 22 Pacific Ave., N0K 1M0, 519-595-8556 |
| Milverton | Top Of The Morning, Llana Heights, N0K 1M0, 519-595-8987 |
| Minden | Hunter Creek Inn, Box 765, K0M 2K0, 705-286-3194 |
| Minden | Minden House, P.O. Box 789, K0M 2K0, 705-286-3263 |
| Minden | Stone House, The, RR2, K0M 2K0, 705-286-1250 |
| Mississauga | B&B by the Creek, 1716 Lincolnshire Blvd., K0M 2K0, 416-891-0337 |
| Mississauga | Dillimore Residence B&B, 2110 Varency Dr, L5K 1C3, 416-822-3540 |
| Mitchell | Pinewood Country Inn B&B, RR2, N0K 1N0, 519-348-8760 |
| Mitchell | Town & Country B&B, 84 Frank St., N0K 1N0, 519-348-8051 |
| Mitchell | Victoria's Country Garden, 153 Ontario Rd., N0K 1N0, 519-348-9756 |
| Moonbeam | Moonbeam B&B, 15 Paquette, Box 42, P0L 1V0, 705-367-2777 |
| Mountain | Lilac Bower, RR1, K0E 1S0, 613-989-5347 |
| Napanee | Fairview House B&B, P.O. Box 114, K7R 3S5, 613-354-5142 |
| New Hamburg | Glenalby Dairy Farms, RR 1, N0B 2G0, 519-625-8353 |
| New Hamburg | Station House, The, 216 Steinman St., N0B 2G0, 519-662-2957 |
| New Hamburg | Waterlot Inn, 17 Huron St., N0B 2G0, 519-662-2020 |
| New Hamburg | White Birches, The, 331 Bleams Rd. W., N0B 2G0, 519-662-2390 |
| Newboro | Sterling Lodge, K0G 1P0, 613-272-2435 |
| Newton | Country Charm, RR 1, N0K 1R0, 519-595-8789 |
| Niagara Falls | A Rose & Kangaroo Guest Hs, 5239 River Rd, L2E 3G9, 416-374-6999 |
| Niagara Falls | Bedham Hall B&B, 4835 River Rd, L2E 3GH, 416-374-8515 |
| Niagara Falls | Glen Mhor House, 5381 River Rd, L2E 3H1, 416-354-2600 |
| Niagara Falls | Gorgeview Guest House, 5087 River Rd., L2E 3G7 |
| Niagara Falls | Gretna Green Tourist Home, 5077 River Rd, L2E 3G7, 416-357-2081 |
| Niagara-On-The-Lake | Angel Inn, Est. 1828, 224 Regent St., L0S 1J0, 416-468-3411 |
| Niagara-On-The-Lake | Kiely House Inn, The, P.O. Box 1642, L0S 1J0, 905-468-4588 |
| Niagara-On-The-Lake | Moffat Inn, 60 Picton St., Box 578, L0S 1J0, 416-468-4116 |
| Niagara-On-The-Lake | Old Bank House, 10 Front St., Box 1708, L0S 1J0 905-468-7136 |
| Niagara-on-the-Lake | Hiebert's Guest House, Box 1371, 275 John St, L0S 1J0, 416-468-3687 |
| Niagara-on-the-Lake | Leighton House B&B, 16 Front St, Box 245, L0S 1J0, 416-468-3789 |
| Niagara-on-the-Lake | Oban Inn, 160 Front St., L0S 1J0, 416-468-2165 |
| Niagara-on-the-Lake | Turner House, The, PO Box 1509, 293 Regent, L0S 1J0, 905-468-4440 |
| Niagara-on-the-Lake | Wiens's B&B, 189 William St, L0S 1J0, 416-468-2091 |
| Nobel | Maple Roch Farm B&B, RR #1, P0G 1G0, 705-342-9662 |
| Norland | Moore Lake Inn, RR1, K0M 2L0, 705-454-1753 |
| Normandale | Union Hotel B&B, Main St., Box 38, RR 1, N0E 1W0, 519-426-5568 |
| North Augusta | Gosford Place B&B, 8809 Gosford Rd. RR1, K0G 1R0, 613-926-2164 |
| North Bay | Burak's, 653 Lakeshore Dr, P1A 2G1, 705-472-4734 |
| North Bay | Grand View House on Lake, 1177 Premier Rd, P1A 2J3, 705-474-5531 |
| North Gower | Carsonby Manor, RR3, K0A 2T0, 613-489-3219 |
| Norwich | Willi-Joy Farm, RR #3, N0J 1P0, 519-424-2113 |
| Oakville | Oakville Hideaway, 1306 Napier Cr, L6H 2A4, 416-844-5513 |
| Ontario | B&B By the Lake, 30 Elm Park, N0A 1N0, 519-583-1010 |
| Ottawa | A1 Leclerc's Residence, 253-McLeod St., K2P 1A1, 613-234-7577 |
| Ottawa | Acacia Guest House, 125 Acacia Ave., K1M 0R2, 613-747-6996 |
| Ottawa | Auberge Ambiance, 330 Nepean, K1R 5G6, 613-563-0421 |
| Ottawa | Auberge McGee's Inn, 185 Daly Ave., K1N 6E8, 613-237-6089 |
| Ottawa | Auberge 'The King Edward', 525 King Edward Ave., K1N 7N3, 613-565-6700 |
| Ottawa | Australis Guest House, 35 Marlborough Ave., K1N 8E6, 613-235-8461 |
| Ottawa | Beatrice Lyon Guest House, 479 Slater St., K1R 5C2, 613-236-3904 |

*Colborne B&B, Goderich, ON*

| | |
|---|---|
| Ottawa | Cartier House Inn, 46 Cartier St., K0G 1N0, 613-236-4667 |
| Ottawa | Doral Inn Hotel, 486 Albert St., K1R 5B5, 613-230-8055 |
| Ottawa | Echo Bank House, 700 Echo Drive, K1S 1P3 |
| Ottawa | Flora House, 282 Flora St., K1R 5S3, 613-230-2152 |
| Ottawa | Foisy House B&B, 188 St. Andrew St, K1N 5G4, 613-562-1287 |
| Ottawa | Gilmour Guest House, 661 Gilmour St, K1N 5L9, 613-234-7572 |
| Ottawa | Gwen's Guest Home, 2071 Riverside Dr., K1H 7X2, 613-737-4129 |
| Ottawa | Henrietta Walkers B&B, 203 York St, K1N 5T7, 613-232-3286 |
| Ottawa | King Edwards, 525 King Edwards Ave., K1N 7N3 |
| Ottawa | L'Auberge du Marche, 87 Guigues Ave, K1N 5H8, 613-235-7697 |
| Ottawa | Le Gite Park Ave B&B, 54 Park Ave., K2P 1B2, 613-230-9131 |
| Ottawa | Ottawa House B&B, 264 Stewart, K1N 6K4, 613-789-4433 |
| Ottawa | Rideau View Inn, 177 Frank St., K2P 0X4, 613-236-9309 |
| Ottawa | Robert's B&B, 488 Cooper St, K1R 5H9, 613-563-0161 |
| Owen Sound | Moses Sunset Farms B&B, RR 6, N4K 5N8, 519-371-4559 |
| Oxford Station | Graham's Pightie, Bishops Mills, RR2, K0G 1T0, 613-258-3753 |
| Pakenham | Gillanderry Farms B&B, RR #4, K0A 2X0 |
| Pakenham | Kia Ora Guest House, RR #1, K0A 2X0 |
| Pakenham | Stonebridge B&B, RR #4, K0A 2X0 |
| Palmer Rapids | Wingle Inn, RR2, K0J 2E0, 613-758-2072 |
| Parry Sound | Evergreen B&B, P.O. Box 223, P2A 2X3, 705-389-3554 |
| Parry Sound | Jantje Manor B&B, 43 Church St., P2A 1A3, 705-746-5399 |
| Parry Sound | Makin House B&B, The, Box 92, RR #3, P2A 2W9, 705-732-2994 |
| Parry Sound | Otter Lake B&B, RR #2, P2A 2W8, 705-378-2812 |
| Parry Sound | Quilt Patch B&B, RR #2, P2A 2W8, 705-378-5279 |
| Parry Sound | Stone's Bay View B&B, 15 Oak Ave., P2A 1A3, 705-746-5585 |
| Penetanguishene | Penetanguishene Area B&B, C.P. 1270, L0K 1P0 |
| Perth | Perth Manor Heritage Inn, 23 Drummond St. West, K7H 2J6, 613-264-0050 |
| Peterborough | Elizabeth Davidson House, 520 Dickson St, K9H 3K1, 705-749-6960 |
| Peterborough | King Bethune Guest House, 270 King St., K9J 252, 705-743-4101 |
| Petrolia | Rebecca's B&B, P.O. Box 1028, N0N 1R0, 519-882-0118 |
| Picton | Ginkgo Tree Place, 352 Main St. E, Bx 3117, K0K 2T0, 613-476-7275 |
| Picton | Lloyd's Place B&B, RR4, K0K 2T0, 613-476-4041 |
| Picton | Poplars, The, RR2, K0K 2T0, 613-476-3513 |
| Picton | Travellers' Tales, RR4, County Road 8, K0K 2T0, 613-476-1885 |
| Picton | Wilhome Farmhouse B&B, RR1, K0K 2T0, 613-393-5630 |
| Picton | Woodville Farm, RR2, K0K 2T0, 613-476-5462 |
| Plattsville | Albion, The, P.O. Box 37, N0J 1S0, 519-684-7434 |
| Port Carling | Sherwood Inn, Box 400, Lake Joseph, P0B 1J0, 705-765-3131 |
| Port Dover | Crabapple Creek, RR2, N0A 1N2, 519-583-2509 |
| Port Dover | Historic Port of Call, Box 106, 602 Main St, N0A 1N0, 519-583-1642 |
| Port Elgin | Gowanlock Farm, RR2, N0H 2C0, 519-389-5256 |
| Port Rowan | Bayview B&B, 45 Wolven St, N0E 1M0, 519-586-3413 |
| Port Stanley | Mitchell House, 493 George St, N0L 2A0, 519-782-4707 |
| Port Stanley | Spruce Grove Farm, RR 1, N0L 2A0, 519-769-2245 |
| Port Stanley | Windjammer B&B, 324 Smith St, Box 852, N0L 2A0, 519-782-4173 |
| Portland-On-The-Rideau | Gallagher House, Box 99, West Water St., K0G 1V0, 613-272-2895 |
| Providence Bay | Wilson's, P0P 1T0, 705-377-4575 |
| Puslinch | Fera's, RR2, N0B 2J0, 519-821-0647 |
| Red Bay | Haven on the Bay B&B, RR1, Mar, N0H 1X0, 519-534-4002 |
| Renfrew | Margaret's Guest House, 510 Raglan St. S., K7V 4A4, 613-432-3897 |
| Renfrew | Stretch & Yawn, RR3, Golf Course Rd, K7V 3Z6, 613-432-8163 |
| Richards Landing | Anchorage, The, RR1, P0R 1J0, 705-246-2221 |
| Ripley | Messengers B&B, RR4, N0G 2R0, 519-395-2815 |
| Rockport | Houseboat Amaryllis B&B, Box C-10, K0E 1V0, 613-659-3513 |
| Rodney | A Touch of Home, 184 Furnival Rd, N0L 2C0, 519-785-0823 |
| Rosseau | Giggling Otter Inn, 4 Oak St., P0C 1J0, 705-732-1354 |
| Sauble Beach | Jackson's B&B, Box 24, RR2, N0H 1P0, 519-422-3073 |
| Sault Ste. Marie | Hillsview B&B, 406 Old Garden River Rd, P6B 5A8, 705-759-8819 |
| Sault Ste. Marie | Top o'the Hill B&B, 40 Bross Rd, P6C 5S4, 705-253-9041 |
| Severn Bridge | Severn River Inn, Box 100, P0E 1N0, 705-689-6333 |
| Sheguiandah | Island Oaks B&B, Hwy. #6, Manitoulin Is., P0P 1W0, 705-368-2220 |
| Sioux Narrows | Yellowbird Lodge, P.O. Box 297, P0X 1N0, 807-226-5279 |
| South Mountain | Turn of the Century, The, RR #1, K0E 1W0, 613-989-3220 |
| Southampton | Chantry House Inn, 118 High St., N0H 2L0, 519-797-2646 |
| Southampton | Crescent Manor, 48 Albert St. N., N0H 2L0, 519-797-5637 |
| Southampton | Hollingborne House, 48 Grey St. N., N0H 2L0, 519-797-3202 |
| Sparta | Loma Linda B&B, RR1, N0L 2H0, 519-773-3335 |
| St. Clements | River House, P.O. Box 212, N0B 2M0, 519-699-4430 |
| St. Jacobs | Jakobstettel Guest House, 16 Isabella St., N0B 2N0, 519-664-2208 |
| Stratford | Avonview Manor B&B, 63 Avon Street, N5A 5N5, 519-273-4603 |
| Stratford | Awhile on the Nile, 77 Nile Street, N5A 4C6, 519-271-7934 |
| Stratford | Burnside Guest Home, 139 William St., N5A 4X9, 519-271-7076 |
| Stratford | Cedar Springs, RR1, N5A 6S2, 519-625-8182 |
| Stratford | Deacon House B&B, 101 Brunswick St, N5A 3L9, 519-273-2052 |
| Stratford | Dunn-Drae-Homes B&B, 150 Douglas St., N5A 5P6, 519-273-0619 |
| Stratford | Eighteen Waterloo B&B, 18 Waterloo St N, N5A 5H5, 519-271-9653 |
| Stratford | Rutledge House, 127 Birmingham St, N5A 2T1, 519-273-2394 |

| | |
|---|---|
| Stratford | Shrewsbury Manor, 30 Shrewsbury St., N5A 2V5, 519-271-8520 |
| Stratford | Stone Maiden Inn, 123 Church St., N5A 2R3, 519-271-7129 |
| Sutton West | Baldwin Gristmill, The, 24357 Hwy. 48, RR 1, L0E 1R0, 416-722-5743 |
| Tara | Diebel's B&B, Box 122, 93 Mill St, N0H 2N0, 519-934-2556 |
| Tavistock | Butternut Tree B&B, The, P.O. Box 52, N0B 2R0, 519-655-3207 |
| Tehkummah | Happy Acres B&B, RR1, P0P 2C0, 705-859-3453 |
| Thunder Bay | Unicorn Inn & Restaurant, RR# 1, South Gillies, P0T 2V0, 807-475-4200 |
| Tillsonburg | English Robin B&B, 19 Robin Rd, N4G 4N5, 519-842-8605 |
| Tobermory | Hidden Valley Lodge, RR2, N0H 2R0, 519-596-2322 |
| Toronto | At Craig House B&B, 78 Spruce Hill Rd., M4E 3G3, 416-698-3916 |
| Toronto | At-Home-In-The-Beach, 237 Lee Ave., M4E 2P4, 416-690-9688 |
| Toronto | Bonnevue Manor B&B Place, 33 Beaty Ave., M6K 3B3, 416-536-1455 |
| Toronto | Catnaps 1892 Downtown, 246 Sherbourne St., M5A 2S1, 416-968-2323 |
| Toronto | Craig House B&B, 78 Spruce Hill Rd, M4E 3G3, 416-698-3916 |
| Toronto | English Corner, 114 Bernard Ave., M5R 1S3 |
| Toronto | Karabanow Tourist Home, 9 Spadina Rd., M5R 2S9, 416-923-4004 |
| Toronto | Orchard View B&B, 92 Orchard View Blvd., M4R 1C2, 416-488-6826 |
| Trenton | Smithrim House, The, 272 Dufferin Ave, K8V 5G2, 613-394-5001 |
| Union | Great Lakes Farms Guest, RR1, N0L 2L0, 519-633-2390 |
| Union | Home Place B&B, The, RR1, N0L 2L0, 519-782-3846 |
| Union | Mulberry Lane, Box 75, N0L 2L0, 519-633-1554 |
| Uxbridge | Barton's B&B, 23 Church St, Box 343, L0C 1K0, 416-852-5197 |
| Uxbridge | Woodlawn, 739 Reid Rd, RR4, L9P 1R4, 416-852-7944 |
| Violet Hill | Mrs. Mitchell's, L0N 1S0, 819-925-3672 |
| Vittoria | Karges' B&B, Box 38, RR1, N0E 1W0, 519-426-5568 |
| Vittoria | Union Hotel B&B, The, P.O. Box 38, N0E 1W0, 519-426-5568 |
| Walkerton | Silver Creek B&B, 17 Yonge St S, N0G 2V0, 519-881-0252 |
| Wallenstein | Roewood Farm, RR 3, N0B 2S0, 519-698-2278 |
| Walton | Mitchell's B&B, RR3, N0K 1Z0, 519-887-6697 |
| Warsaw | McMullen's, K0L 3A0, 705-652-3024 |
| Waterford | Kerr's, 150 Main St S, N0E 1Y0, 519-443-5165 |
| Waterloo | Willowbrae Farm, RR 1, N2J 4G8, 519-664-2634 |
| Welland | Schafrick's, 27 Eastdale Cres, L3B 1E6, 416-732-3170 |
| Wellesley | Firella Creek Farm, RR 2, N0B 2T0, 519-656-2974 |
| Wellesley | Paradise Farm, RR 3, N0B 2T0, 519-699-4871 |
| Wellington | Chelsea House, 236 Main St, Box 535, K0K 3L0, 613-399-2407 |
| Wellington | Tara Hall B&B, Box 623, 146 Main St, K0K 3L0, 613-399-2801 |
| Westport | Cove, The, General Delivery, K0G 1X0, 613-273-3636 |
| Westport | Herlehy Homestead B&B, RR #1, K0G 1X0 |
| Westport | Kilpatrick House, RR #1, K0G 1X0 |
| Westport | Spring Street B&B, Spring Street, K0G 1X0, 613-273-5427 |
| Westport | Stepping Stone B&B Inn, RR #2, K0G 1X0, 613-273-3806 |
| Wiarton | Bruce Gables B&B, 410 Berford St, Box 448, N0H 2T0, 519-534-0429 |
| Wiarton | Hillcrest B&B, 394 Gould St., N0H 2T0, 519-534-2262 |
| Wiarton | Maplehurst, 277 Frank St., N0H 2T0, 519-534-1210 |
| Wiarton | McIvor House, RR4, N0H 2T0, 519-534-1769 |
| Wiarton | Vickers' B&B, Box 298, RR4, N0H 2T0, 519-534-3504 |
| Wilberforce | House in the Village, Box 63, K0L 3C0, 705-448-3161 |
| Willowdale | Al's Place, 22 Lescon Rd, M2J 2G6, 416-493-0936 |
| Winchester | Harkhaven Farm, RR1, K0C 2K0, 613-774-3418 |
| Windermere | Windermere House, P0B 1P0, 705-769-3611 |
| Woodlawn | On-The-Ottawa, 4958 Opeonga Rd, Bx 126, K0A 3M0, 613-832-2166 |
| Young's Point | Old Bridge Inn, K0L 3G0, 705-652-8507 |
| Zurich | Brentwood On The Beach, RR 2, N0M 2T0, 519-236-7137 |

# Prince Edward Island

## CHARLOTTETOWN

**Dundee Arms Mgmt. Inc.**
200 Pownal St., C1A 3W8
902-892-2496 Fax: 902-368-8532
800-565-7105
Terry Grandy    All year

$-EP
6 rooms, 6 pb
Most CC, •
S-yes/P-no/H-no
French

Continental bkfst., ltd.
Luncheon, dinner, pub

*A gracious Victorian Inn furnished in antiques. Famous for fine dining, charming atmosphere, and warm hospitality.* **10% discount on dinner entrees in our Griffon Room; 10% discount on accommodations.**

## CHARLOTTETOWN RR3

**Woodmere B&B**
Linden Rd. - Marshfield,
C1A 7J7
902-628-1783  Fax: 902-628-1783
800-747-1783
Doris Wood
All year

$$-B&B
4 rooms, 4 pb
Visa, MC, *Rated*,
C-ltd/S-no/P-no/H-no

Full breakfast
Snacks, lobster suppers
Sitting room, T.V.
beaches, race horses
rose garden, golf,

*Spacious rooms w/view of countryside each w/private bath, individually controlled heat, attractive interior w/queen or extra large twin beds.* **7th night free.**

## MURRAY RIVER

**Bayberry Cliff Inn**
RR 4, Little Sands,  C0A 1W0
902-962-3395  Fax: 902-962-3395
Nancy & Don Perkins
May 15–September

$-B&B
4 rooms, 4 pb
MC, Visa, *Rated*, •
C-ltd
Spanish

Full breakfast
Dinner by reservation
Library, craft shop
sitting room, breezeway
cliff to shore

*Two remodeled post & beam barns; antiques, marine paintings. 8 minutes to W.I.'s ferry. Perfect for honeymooners.* **10% discount to repeat guests the following year or next visit.**

# More Inns ...

| | |
|---|---|
| Alberry Plains | Stewart's B&B, Vernon P.O., C0A 2E0 |
| Bay Fortune | Inn at Bay Fortune, The,  Souris RR #4, C0A 2B0,  902-687-3745 |
| Belfast | Lazydays Farm B&B, RR1, C0A 1A0,  902-659-2267 |
| Belfast | Linden Lodge, RR 3, C0A 1A0,  902-659-2716 |
| Birch Hill | MacLean's B&B, Richmond RR #1, C0B 1Y0 |
| Bonshaw | Churchill Farm T.H.,  RR3, C0A 1C0,  902-675-2481 |
| Bonshaw | Strathgartney Country Inn,  RR #3, C0A 1C0,  902-675-4711 |
| Borden | Goodwin's Tourist Home B&B,  RR #1, C0B 1X0,  902-855-2849 |
| Borden | Rest Awhile Inn,  186 Howland St., Bx 133, C0B 1X0,  902-855-2254 |
| Brackley Beach | Linden Lane B&B, Brittain Shore Rd., C0A 2H0,  902-672-3091 |
| Brackley Beach | Shaw's Hotel & Cottages,  C0A 2H0,  902-672-2022 |
| Brooklyn | Redcliffe Farm B&B, RR1, Montague, C0A 1R0,  902-838-2476 |
| Cape Traverse | Glenhaven B&B,  Borden RR #1, C0B 1X0 |
| Cardigan | Roseneath B&B,  RR #6, C0A 1G0,  902-838-4590 |
| Carleton Siding | Carleton Cove Farm B&B, Albany RR #2, C0B 1A0 |
| Carleton Siding | MacCullum B&B,  Borden P.O., C0B 1X0 |
| Cavendish | Kindred Spirits Cntry Inn,  Hunter River RR #2, C0A 1N0 |
| Cavendish | MacLure B&B,  RR #2 Hunter River, C0A 1N0 |
| Cavendish | Shining Waters Lodge,  Hunter River RR2, C0A 1N0 |
| Charlottetown | Allix's B&B,  11 Johnson Av., C1A 3H7,  902-892-2643 |
| Charlottetown | An Island Rose B&B,  285 Kinlock Rd., RR1, C1A 7J6,  902-569-5030 |
| Charlottetown | Anchors Aweigh B&B,  45 Queen Elizabeth Dr., C1A 3A8,  902-892-4319 |
| Charlottetown | Anne's Ocean View Haven,  Box 2044, Kinlock Rd., C1A 7N7,  902-569-4644 |
| Charlottetown | Barachois Inn,  P.O. Box 1022, C1A 7M4,  902-963-2194 |
| Charlottetown | Court B&B,  68 Hutchinson Ct, C1A 8H7,  902-894-5871 |
| Charlottetown | Dutchess of Kent Inn,  218 Kent St., C1A 1P2,  902-566-5826 |
| Charlottetown | Elmwood,  P.O. Box 3128, C1A 7N8,  902-368-3310 |
| Charlottetown | Jean's B&B,  13 Kirkcaldy Dr., C1E 1G2 |
| Charlottetown | Jolliffe's,  Box 162, C1A 7K4,  902-658-2503 |
| Charlottetown | Just Folks B&B,  RR 5, C1A 7J8,  902-569-2089 |
| Charlottetown | MacInnes B&B,  80 Euston St., C1A 1W2 |
| Charlottetown | Maple B&B,  28 Maple Ave., C1A 6E3,  902-894-4488 |
| Charlottetown | Pope Avenue B&B,  9 Pope Ave., C1A 6N4,  902-875-3229 |
| Charlottetown | Rosevale Farm B&B,  Marshfield, RR 3, C1A 7J7,  902-894-7821 |
| Charlottetown | West Ridge Toursit Home,  249 Westridge Cr, C1A 9A6,  902-566-9128 |
| Cornwall | Chez Nous,  Route 248, RR4, C0A 1H0,  902-566-2779 |
| Cornwall | Obanlea Farm Tourist Home,  RR 4 North River PO,  C0A 1H0,  902-566-3067 |
| Cornwall | On-the-Bay B&B,  P.O. Box 272, C0A 1H0 |
| Cornwall | Strait View Farm B&B, Rice Pt., RR 2, C0A 1H0,  902-675-2071 |
| Corwan | Chez-Nous B&B,  Ferry Rd., RR 4, C0A 1H0,  902-566-2779 |
| Coxehead | Stanhope by the Sea,  Route 25, C01 1P0,  902-672-2047 |
| Darnley | Fralor Farm Tourist Home,  RR 1, Kensington, C0B 1M0,  902-836-5300 |
| Earnscliffe | Esther's Farm Home B&B,  RR3, Vernon, C0A 2E0,  902-651-2415 |
| Ellerslie | Burleigh's B&B, RR2, C0B 1J0,  902-831-2288 |
| Fortune Bridge | Empty Nest B&B, The,  Souris RR #4, C0A 2B0 |
| Frenchford | Miller's Farm B&B, Carlottetown RR3, C1A 7J7 |

| | |
|---|---|
| Hampton | Myers Hilltop Farm B&B, Crapaud RR #1, C0A 1J0 |
| Harrington | Harrington Inn B&B, Winsloe, RR1, C0A 2H0, 902-672-2788 |
| Harrington | Wilbert's B&B, Winsloe RR #1, C0A 2H0 |
| Hunter River | Country House Inn, The, RR2, C0A 1N0, 902-963-2055 |
| Kensington | Beach Point View Inn, RR 5, C0B 1M0, 902-836-5260 |
| Kensington | Blakeney's B&B, 15 MacLean Ave., Box 17, C0B 1M0, 902-836-3254 |
| Kensington | Blue Heron Toursit Home, RR6, C0B 1M0, 902-886-2319 |
| Kensington | Murphy's Sea View B&B, Route 20, C0B 1M0, 902-836-5456 |
| Kensington | Sherwood Acres Guest Home, RR 1, C0B 1M0, 902-836-5430 |
| Kensington | Woodington's Country Inn, Sea View, RR 2, C0B 1M0, 902-836-5518 |
| Knutsford | Smallman's B&B, O'Leary RR1, C0B 1V0, 902-859-3469 |
| Little Pond | Little Pond Country Store, Souris RR #4, C0A 2B0 |
| Little York | Dalvay By The Sea Hotel, P.O. Box 8, C0A IP0, 902-672-2048 |
| Margate | Thompson Tourist House, Kensington, RR6, C0B 1M0, 902-836-4160 |
| Mill River | Thomas Bed & Breakfast, O'Leary RR 3, C0B 1V0, 902-859-3209 |
| Miscouche | Carr's Corner Farm Tourist, Route 12, C0B 1T0, 902-436-6287 |
| Montague | Boudreault's Tourist B&B, RR #2, C0A 1R0, 962-838-2560 |
| Montague | Brydon's B&B, Heatherdale RR 1, C0A 1R0, 902-838-4747 |
| Montague | Countryman B&B, The, Chestnut St., C0A 1R0 |
| Montague | Partridges' B&B, Panmure Island, RR2, C0A 1R0, 902-838-4687 |
| Montague | Pines B&B, The, P.O. Box 486, C0A 1R0 |
| Montague | Pleasant View B&B, Box 89, C0A 1R0 |
| Morell | Kelly's Bed & Breakfast, Box 68, C0A 1S0, 902-961-2389 |
| Morell | Village Bed & Breakfast, Box 71, C0A 1S0, 902-961-2394 |
| Murray Harbour | Harbourview B&B, RR 1, C0A 1V0, 902-962-2565 |
| Murray Harbour N. | Lady Catherine's B&B, Montague RR #4, C0A 1R0, 902-962-3426 |
| Nine Mile Creek | Laine Acres B&B, Cornwall RR2, C0A 1H0, 902-675-2402 |
| North Bedeque | Meadowside Farm B&B, Summerside RR #3, C1N 4J9 |
| North Bedeque | Wright's Bed & Breakfast, Summerside RR#, C1N 4J9 |
| Priest Pond | Sand Dune B&B, Souris RR #2, C0A 2B0 |
| Richmond | Mom's B&B, P.O. Box 13, C0B 1Y0 |
| Rusticoville | Whiffletree Inn, Hunter River RR #3, C0A 1N0 |
| Souris | Matthew House Inn, The, 15 Breakwater St., C0A 2B0, 902-687-3461 |
| Spring Valley | Green Valley B&B, Box 714, Kensington, C0B 1M0, 902-836-5667 |
| St. Patrick's | Carriage Hill B&B, Hunter River RR #1, C0A 1N0, 902-964-2253 |
| St. Peter's Bay | Needles & Haystacks B&B, RR2, C0A 2A0, 902-583-2928 |
| St. Peters Bay | MacCallum's B&B, Route 2, C0A 2A0, 902-961-2957 |
| Stanley Bridge | Gulf Breeze, C0A 1E0, 902-886-2678 |
| Summerside | Arbor Inn, The, 380 MacEwen Rd., C1N 4X8, 902-436-6847 |
| Summerside | Blue Heron Country B&B, North Bedeque, RR3, C1N 4J9, 902-436-4843 |
| Summerside | Dyment B&B, Wilmot Valley, RR3, C1N 4J9, 902-436-9893 |
| Summerside | Silver Fox Inn, 61 Granville St., C1N 2Z3, 902-436-4033 |
| Summerside | Smallman's B&B, 329 Poplar Ave., C1N 2B7 |
| Summerville | VanDykes' B&B, Montague RR #3, C0A 1R0 |
| Tignish | Harbour Lights T. H., RR #2, C0B 2B0, 902-882-2479 |
| Tyne Valley | Doctor's Inn B&B, C0B 2C0, 902-831-2164 |
| Tyne Valley | West Island Inn, Box 24, C0B 2C0, 902-831-2495 |
| Vernon | MacLeod's Farm B&B, UIGG, Vernon P.O., C0A 2E0, 902-651-2303 |
| Vernon Bridge | Dunvegan Farm B&B, RR 2 Uigg, C0A 2E0 |
| Vernon Bridge | Enman's Farm B&B, P.O. RR 2 Vernon Bridge, C0A 2E0, 902-651-2427 |
| Vernon Bridge | Smith's Farm B&B, Millview P.O., C0A 2E0 |
| Vernon River | Lea's B&B, C0A 2E0, 902-651-2501 |
| Victoria | Victoria Village Inn, C0A 2G0, 902-658-2288 |
| Wilmot Valley | Dyment Bed & Breakfast, Summerside RR#, C1N 4J9, 902-436-9893 |
| Winsloe | Windsong Farm B&B, Brackley Beach, Rt. 6, C1E 1Z3, 902-672-2874 |
| Wood Islands West | Baba's House Guests B&B, Belle River RR #1, C0A 1B0 |
| York | Amber Lights B&B, P.O. Box 14, Route 26, C0A 1P0, 902-894-5868 |
| York | Vessey's B&B, Highway 25, off Hway 2, C0A 1P0, 902-629-1312 |

# Province of Quebec

GEORGEVILLE ───────────────────────────────

**Auberge Georgeville**
71, Chemin Channel, J0B 1T0
819-843-8683 Fax: 819-843-5045
Steven/Megan Seline Beyrouty
All year

$$$-MAP
12 rooms, 8 pb
Visa, MC,
C-ltd/S-ltd/P-no/H-no
French

Full breakfast
Dinner, afternoon tea
Restaurant, bar service
sitting room, library
bikes, walk to lake

*An 1889 Victorian Inn, award winning dining, 5 minute stroll to lake; golf and theater nearby. Complimentary touring bicycles, afternoon tea, antiques, croquet, skating.* **Comp. cocktail before dinner.**

MONTREAL ───────────────────────────────

**Auberge De La Fontaine**
1301 Rachel East, H2J 2K1
514-597-0166 Fax: 514-597-0496
800-597-0597
Celine Boudreau
All year

$$$-B&B
21 rooms, 21 pb
AmEx, MC, Visa,
*Rated*, •
C-yes/S-yes/P-no/H-yes
French

Continental plus, buffet
Afternoon tea
Whirlpool in some rooms
suite w/view of park and
priv terrace w/whirlpool

*Facing Parc La Fontaine (84 acres), located near downtown area. A charming inn where you are welcomed as friends. Public transportation nearby.* **Special packages.**

**Downtown B&B & Apartments**
3523 Jeanne-Mance, H2X 2K2
514-845-0431
Bruno Bernard
All year

$$-B&B
7 rooms, 4 pb
Visa, MC, AmEx, •
C-ltd/S-yes/P-no/H-no
French

Full breakfast
Fully equipped apts.
color TV, A/C, sauna
inside pool

*In the heart of downtown; TV and radio, access to a different kitchen for guests. Also, beautiful apartments, all furnished for short or long stays, ltd. parking available.*

**Montreal Oasis**
3000 Chemin de Breslay, H3Y 2G7
514-935-2312 Fax: 514-935-3154
Lena Blondel
All year

$$-B&B
4 rooms, 1 pb
C-ltd/S-no/P-no/H-no
Swed., Fr., Ger., Sp.

Full gourmet breakfast

*Spacious house in downtown's chic and safe West End. Gourmet, 3-course breakfast, world-travelled Swedish hostess, African art and Siamese cat.*

MONTREAL S, BOUCHERVILLE ─────────────────

**Le Relais des Iles Percees**
85 des Iles Percees, J4B 2P1
514-655-3342 Fax: 514-655-3342
Colette & Raymond Leblanc
All year

$-B&B
3 rooms, 3 pb
•
C-yes/S-no/P-no/H-no
French, English

Full breakfast
Afternoon tea, snacks
Sitting room, library
family friendly facility
bicycles, near golf

*Near the main touristic attractions of Montreal (15 minutes). Surrounded by golf courses and bicycle paths.*

## NEW CARLISLE

**Bay View Manor**
P.O. Box 21, 395-337 Route 132
Bona.E., G0C 1Z0
418-752-2725  418-752-6718
Helen Sawyer
All year

$-B&B
6 rooms, 2 pb
*Rated*,
C-yes/P-no
French

Full breakfast
Lunch, dinner
Sitting room, library
tennis courts, pool
near golf, cottage avail

*Seaside country haven, yet on a main highway. Fresh farm produce. August Folk Festival.
Quilts, handicrafts and home-baking on sale. Cottage at $250 per week also available.*

## POINTE-AU-PIC

**L'Eau Berge**
20 Bellevue Blvd., Case
Postale 152, G0T 1M0
418-665-3003  Fax: 418-665-3003
Claudette Dessureault
Closed Nov-Jan

B&B
7 rooms, 2 pb
Visa, MC, *Rated*, •
C-yes/S-ltd/P-no/H-no
French

Full buffet breakfast
Restaurant nearby
Sitting room
bikes, tennis nearby
family friendly facility

*Ancestral Eau Berge house facing the river and welcomes you with its unique decor.
Rooms are particularly comfortable and inviting.*

## QUEBEC CITY

**Chateau de la Terrasse**
6 Terrasse Dufferin, G1R
4N5
418-694-9472  Fax: 418-694-0055
Christiane-Marie Bes
February–November

$$-EP
18 rooms, 18 pb
C-yes/S-yes/P-no/H-no
French, English

Continental (fee)
Breakfast served in room
Some rooms with A/C

*Located inside the walls of Old Quebec, on the boardwalk. Front rooms overlook St.
Lawrence River.*

## QUEBEC CITY, VIEUX

**Hotel Marie-Rollet**
81, Rue Ste-Anne, G1R 3X4
418-694-9271
G. Giroux & D. Chouinard
All year

$$-EP
10 rooms, 10 pb
Visa, *Rated*, •
C-yes/S-yes/P-no/H-no
French

$2.00 rebate on bkfst.
Nearby restuarant
Fireplaces, A/C
rooftop terrace
w/garden view

*Built in 1876 by the Ursulines, the Marie-Rollet captivates with its warm woodwork,
tranquility & serenity. Conveniently located.* **Free bottle of wine for special occasions.**

## ST-MARC-SUR-RICHELIEU

**Auberge Handfield Inn**
555 Chemin du Prince, J0L
2E0
514-584-2226  Fax: 514-584-3650
Conrad Handfield
All year

$$-EP
53 rooms, 53 pb
Most CC, *Rated*, •
C-yes/S-yes/P-no/H-yes
French

Full breakfast (fee)
Restaurant, bar service
Afternoon tea, snacks
pool, horseback riding
tennis courts, marina

*Country inn on the River Sibe. Ancestral house, 165 years old. Rooms decorated with
antiques. Marina available for traveling sailors. Sugaring-off parties, spa, health club*

## ST. PETRONILLE

**Auberge La Goeliche**
22 Chemin du Quai, G0A
4C0
418-828-2248  Fax: 418-828-2745
Andree Marchand
All year

$$-B&B
18 rooms, 16 pb
AmEx, MC, Visa, •
C-yes/S-yes/P-no/H-yes
French, Spanish

Continental plus bkfst.
Restaurant, bar service
Sitting room, art shop
pool

*Overhanging the St. Lawrence River, this castle-like inn offers a breathtaking view of
Quebec City, which is only distant by a 15 minute drive.*

# More Inns ...

| | |
|---|---|
| Ayer's Cliff | Auberge Ripplecove Inn, 700 Ripple Cove Rd., J0B 1C0,   819-838-4296 |
| Ayer's Cliff | Lauzier's, Chemin Audet, RR1, J0B 1C0,   819-838-4433 |
| Aylmer | La Rajotiere, 14 rue Principale, J9H 3K8,   819-685-0650 |
| Aylmer | Maison des Lilas, 36 rue Court, J9H 4L7,   819-684-6821 |
| Baie d'Urfe | Ecles, The, 20799 Lakeshore Rd., H9X 1S1,   514-457-3986 |
| Baie Saint Paul | La Maison Otis, 23 R. St. Jean Baptiste, G0A 1B0,   418-435-2255 |
| Baie St-Paule | La Muse, 39, St-Jean-Baptiste, G0A 1B0,   418-435-6939 |
| Beloeil | Hostellerie Rive Gauche, 1810 boul. Richelieu, J3G 4S4,   514-467-4650 |
| Boisbriand | L'Anse du Patrimoine, 488 Grande Cote, J7E 4H4,   514-437-6918 |
| Buckingham | Auberge Sejour, RR3, J8L 2W8,   819-986-9219 |
| Cap-A-L'aigh | La Pinsonniere, 124 St. Raphael, G0T 1B0,   418-665-4431 |
| Cap-a-l'Aigle | Villeneuve's B&B, 215 Rue St. Raphael, G0T 1B0,   418-665-2288 |
| Cap-Chat | Au Crepuscule, 239 Notre Dame Ouest, G0J 1E0,   418-786-5751 |
| Charlevoix | La Pinsonniere, G0T 1B0,   800-677-3524 |
| Coin du Banc-Perce | Auberge Le Coin Du Banc, Route 132, G0C 2L0,   418-645-2907 |
| Comte de Mantane | Auberge La Martre,  La Martre, G0E 2H0,   418-288-5533 |
| Dunham | Domaine Paradis des Fruits, 519 Road 202, J0E 1M0,   514-295-2667 |
| Dunham | Maplewood,  Malenfant Rd., J0E 1M0,   514-295-2519 |
| Franklin Ctr | Bagnell Hall Manor,  1965 Grimshaw Rd., J0S 1E0,   514-827-2415 |
| Franklin Ctr | Hillspring Farm, 1019 Rt 202, J0S 1E0,   514-827-2565 |
| Gaspe | Gite de la Baie, 270 Montee Wakeham,1413, G0C 1R0,   418-368-2149 |
| Georgeville | Georgeville Country Inn, CP P.O. Box 17, J0B 1T0,   819-843-8683 |
| Havelock | Stoneboro Farm, 164 Rte 202, J0S 1E0,   514-826-0196 |
| Howick | Hazelbrae Farm, 1650 English River Rd., J0S 1G0,   514-825-2390 |
| Hudson | Riversmead B&B,  Main Rd., Box 1063, J0P 1H0 |
| Hudson | Willow Place Inn, 208 Main St., J0P 1A0,   514-458-7006 |
| Hudson Heights | Rowland's B&B, 76 Oakland Ave., J0P 1J0,   514-458-5893 |
| Huntington | Leduc, 1128CH Riviere de Guerr, J0S 1M0,   514-264-6533 |
| Ile d'Orleans | Chez les Dumas, 1415 Chemin Royal, St. , G0A 3Z0,   418-828-9442 |
| Ile d'Orleans | La Vieille Maison Fradet, 1584 Royal, St. Laurent, G0A 3Z0,   418-828-9501 |
| Ile d'Orleans | Pilot's Lookout, The,  170 Ch Marie-Carreau, G0A 3W0,   418-829-2613 |
| Isle d'Orleans | Les Tanaudes, 3616 Royale, Ste Famile, G0A 3P0,   418-829-2894 |
| Joliette | Le Manoir sous les Pins, 239 Rang Ste Julie, NDP, J6E 7Y8,   514-759-8741 |
| Kamouraska | Gite du Passant B&B, 81 Ave. Morel, G0L 1M0,   418-492-2921 |
| Knowlton | Auberge Laketree, RR 2, Stage Coach Rd., J0E 1V0,   514-243-6604 |
| L'Islet-Sur-Mer | La Marguerite, 88 Des Pionniers, CP101, G0R 2B0,   418-247-5454 |
| La Baleine | Les Eglantiers, 40 Principale St., G0A 2A0,   418-438-2500 |
| Lac Carre | La Rocaille B&B,  Box 47, J0T 1J0,   819-688-2852 |
| Lac Nominingue | Le "Provincialat", 2292 Sacre-Coeur, J0W 1R0,   819-278-4928 |
| Lac Superieur | Chalet Caribou Lodge,  J0T 1P0,   819-688-5201 |
| Laval | Gite du Passant, 7 rue Jerome, H7C 2G7,   514-661-3215 |
| Lery | Raymond's, 32 Chemin du Lac, J6N 1A1,   514-692-6438 |
| Maria | Gite du Vieux Bouc, 140 Rang 2, G0C 1Y0,   418-759-3248 |
| Matane | Maison sur le Fleuve, 2112 Matane sur Mer, G4W 3M6,   418-562-2019 |
| Mont Tremblant | Chateau Beauvallon, 616 Montee Ryan, Box138, J0T 1Z0,   819-425-7275 |
| Montmagny | Le Tandem, 39 St. Jean Baptiste, G5V 3B6,   418-248-7132 |
| Montreal | Allaire's, 10840 Avenue d'Auteuil, H3L 2K8,   514-382-4807 |
| Montreal | Antonio Costa, 101 Northview, H4X 1C9,   514-486-6910 |
| Montreal | Armor Inn, 151 Sherbrooke E., H2X 1C7,   514-285-0140 |
| Montreal | B&B de Chez-Nous, 3717 Ste-Famille, H2X 2L7,   514-845-7711 |
| Montreal | Chex Alexis, 3445 Ave St. Andre, H2L 3V4,   514-598-0898 |
| Montreal | La Maison de Grand-Pre, 4660 Rue de Grand-Pre, H2T 2H7,   514-843-6458 |
| Montreal | Le Breton, 1609 St-Hubert St., H2L 3Z1,   514-524-7273 |
| Montreal | Manoir Ambrose, 3422 Stanley St., H3A 1R8,   514-288-6922 |
| North Hatley | Cedar Gables B&B,  Box 355, J0B 2C0,   819-842-4120 |
| North Hatley | Hatley Inn,  P.O. Box 330, J0B 2C0,   819-842-2451 |
| North Hatley | Hovey Manor (Manoir Hovey), 575 Hovey Rd., J0B 2C0,   819-842-2421 |
| Notre Dame de Montauban | Beau-lieu Inn, The,  974 Road Rousseau, G0X 1N0,   418-336-2619 |
| Notre-Dame-de-Pierrevill | Maison du Lac, 63 Ch Coulee, J0G 1G0,   514-568-5041 |
| Perce, Gaspe Peninsula | Hotel la Normandie,  P.O. Box 129, G0G 2L0,   418-782-2112 |
| Pointe-a-la-Croix | Savoie's, 72 rue Interprovincial, G0C 1L0,   418-788-2084 |
| Pointe-au-Pic | Auberge Donohue, 145 Principale, CP 211, G0T 1M0,   418-665-4377 |
| Portneuf | Edale Place, Edale Pl., G0A 2Y0,   418-286-3168 |
| Portneuf | France Beaulieu House, 211 Chemin dela Travers, G0A 2Y0,   418-336-2724 |
| Prevost | Gite de Campagne, 1028 Principale, J0R 1T0,   514-224-7631 |
| Quebec | Gite du Passant B&B, 324, 21E Rue, G1L 1Y7,   418-648-8168 |
| Quebec City | Au Chateau Fleur de Lis, 15 Ave. Ste. Genevieve, G1R 4A8,   418-694-1884 |
| Quebec City | Auberge De La Chouette, 71 Rue D'Auteuil, G1K 5Y4,   418-694-0232 |
| Quebec City | Battlefields B&B, 820 Eymard Ave., G1S 4A1,   418-681-6804 |
| Quebec City | Hayden's Wexford House, 450 rue Champlain, G1K 4J3,   418-524-0525 |

*Auberge
Georgeville,
Georgeville,
PQ*

| Quebec City | Manoir Ste Genevieve, 13 Ave. Ste-Genevieve, G1R 4A7, 418-694-1666 |
| Quyon | Memory Lane Farm, RR #1, J0X 2V0, 819-458-2479 |
| Sillery | B&B Bienvenue a Quebec, 1067 Maguire, G1T 1Y3, 418-681-3212 |
| Sillery | Fernlea, 2156 Rue Dickson, G1T 1C9, 418-683-3847 |
| Sillery | Fleet's, 1080 Holland Ave., G1S 3T3, 418-688-0794 |
| St-Bruno-de-Montarville | Gite St-Bruno, 1959 Montarville, J3V 3V8, 514-653-2149 |
| St-Germain-de-Grantham | Le Madawaska B&B, 644 Rte 239, J0C 1K0, 819-395-4318 |
| St-Jerome | L'Etape, 430 Melancon, J7Z 4K4, 514-438-1043 |
| St-Severe | Au Bourgainvillier, 83 Rue Principale, G0X 3B0, 819-264-5653 |
| St. Anne des Mont | Gite du Mont Albert, Case Postale 1150, G0E 2G0, 418-763-2288 |
| St. Antoine de Tilly | Auberge Manoir de Tilly, 3854 Chemin de Tilly, G0S 2C0, 418-886-2407 |
| St. Lambert | Montreal B&B, 144 Edison Ave., J4R 2P5, 514-672-4133 |
| St. Laurent | Maison sous les Arbres, 145 Chemin Royal, G0A 3Z0, 418-828-9442 |
| St. Roch Des Aulnaies | Pelletier House, 334 de la Seigneurie, G0R 4E0, 418-354-2450 |
| St. Sauveur Des Monts | Auberge St-Denis, 61, St-Denis, CP 1229, J0R 1R0, 514-227-4766 |
| St.-Marc-Sur-Richelieu | Hostellerie Les Trois Till, 290 rue Richelieu, J0L 2E0, 514-584-2231 |
| Ste-Adele | L'Auberge Bonne Nuit Bonjo, 1980 Blvd Ste-Adele, J0R 1L0, 514-229-7500 |
| Ste-Foy | Accueil Ste-Foy Quebec, 2834 Fontaine, G1V 2H8, 418-653-4345 |
| Ste-Foy | Saint-Aubin's, 3045 rue de la Seine, G1W 1H8, 418-658-0685 |
| Ste.-Agathe | Auberge Du Lac Des Sables, 230 St. Venant, C.P.213, J8C 2A3, 819-326-7016 |
| Sutton | Auberge Schweizer, 357 Schweizer Rd., J0E 2K0, 514-538-2129 |
| Sutton | Pine Gable B&B, 45 Main St. S, Box 219, J0E 2K0, 514-538-1525 |
| Sutton | Willow House, 30 Western Ave, Box 906, J0E 2K0, 514-538-0035 |
| Tadoussac | Maison Clauphi, 188 des Pionniers, G0T 2A0, 418-235-4303 |
| Thurso | Steiner Family, 266 Montee Steiner, J0X 3B0, 819-985-2359 |
| Val David | Auberge du Vieux Foyer, 3167 Doncaster, J0T 2N0, 819-322-2686 |
| Val David | Parker's Lodge, 1340 Lac Paquin, J0T 2N0, 819-322-2026 |
| Vieux | Au Petit Hotel, 3 Ruelle des Ursulines, G1R 3Y6, 418-694-0965 |
| Wakefield | Les Trois Erables, 260 River Rd, J0X 3G0, 819-459-1118 |
| Waterloo | Perras, 1552 RR 1, J0E 1N0, 514-539-2983 |
| Wolf Lake | Serendipity, P.O. Box 30, J0X 3K0, 819-456-2316 |

# Saskatchewan

## SASKATOON

**Brighton House B&B**
1308 5th Ave. No., S7K 2S2
306-664-3278 Fax: 306-664-6822
Barb Clay & Lynne Fontaine
All year

$-B&B
4 rooms, 2 pb
Visa, *Rated*,
C-yes/S-ltd/P-no/H-ltd

Continental plus bkfst.
Afternoon tea, snacks
Library, sitting room
bikes, hot tubs
theatres, museum, river

*Welcome to Brighton House! A gracious character home with the warmth of country. Our home is furnished with antiques. Close to the city's main arteries.* **Comp. old-fashioned ice cream making.**

## More Inns ...

| Allan | Moldenhauer's Farm, Box 214, S0K 0C0, 306-257-3578 |
| Balcarres | Ellis Farm, Box 84, S0G 0C0, 306-334-2238 |
| Blaine Lake | Vereshagin's Country Place, Box 89, S0J 0J0, 306-497-2782 |
| Borden | Sargent's Holiday Farm, Box 204, S0K 0N0, 306-997-2230 |
| Flaxcombe | Merry MacKays B&B, Box 83, S0L 1E0, 306-463-3519 |
| Grenfell | Bonshaw House, Box 67, S0G 2B0, 306-697-2654 |
| Gull | Wounded Knee, Box 527, S0N 1A0, 306-672-3651 |
| Gull Lake | Magee's Farm, Box 654, S0N 1A0 |
| Ile-a-la-Crosse | Rainbow Ridge, Box 238, S0M 1C0, 306-833-2590 |
| Meota | Lakeside Leisure Farm, P.O. Box 1, S0M 1X0, 306-892-2145 |
| Meskanaw | Silent Hollow Farms, Box 25, S0K 2W0, 306-864-3728 |
| Paradise Hill | Little Butte Farm, Box 95, S0M 2G0, 306-344-4811 |
| Percival | Pipestone View Ranch, General Delivery, S0G 3Y0, 306-735-2858 |
| Qu'Appelle | Bluenose Country Vacation, Box 173, S0G 4A0, 306-699-2328 |
| Ravenscrag | Spring Valley Guest Ranch, Box 10, S0N 2C0, 305-295-4124 |
| Regina | B & J's B&B, 2066 Ottawa St., S4P 1P8, 306-522-4575 |
| Regina | Turgeon International Hse, 2310 McIntyre St., S4P 2S2, 306-522-4200 |
| Tisdale | Prairie Acres B&B, Box 1658, S0E 1T0, 306-873-2272 |
| Truax | Dee Bar One, Box 51, S0H 4A0, 306-868-4614 |
| Watrous | West Wind - The Graf House, Monitou Beach, S0K 4T0, 306-946-3821 |
| Wawota | Pleasant Vista Angus Farm, Box 194, S0G 5A0, 306-739-2915 |
| Wolsely | Banbury House, The, S0G 5A0, 306-698-2239 |

# Yukon Territory

## More Inns . . .

| | |
|---|---|
| Dawson City | Partridge Creek Farm, Mail Bag 450, Y0B 1G0 |
| Dawson City | White Ram Manor, Box 302, Y0B 1G0, 403-993-5772 |
| Whitehorse | Baker's Bed & Breakfast, 84 - 11th Ave., Y1A 4J2, 403-633-2308 |
| Whitehorse | Blue Gables B&B, 506 Steele St., Y1A 2C9, 403-668-2840 |
| Whitehorse | Klondike House, 39 Donjek Rd., Y1A 3V5, 403-667-4315 |

# Australia

## ADELAIDE

**Leabrook Lodge B&B**
314 Kensington Rd.,
Leabrook, SA 5068
08-8331-7619
Fax: 08-8364-4955
Barbara Carter
All year

65 Australian$ B&B
4 rooms/suites, 4 pb
Visa, MC, *Rated*, •
C-ltd/S-ltd/P-no/H-no
English

Full breakfast
Dinner by request
Lounge, television
library, Q-size beds
near tourist attractions
Airport: Adelaide

*Stone bungalow, lock-up garage, adjacent to bus. By Adelaide & tourist attractions. Excellent restaurants & bush walks. Double rooms have ensuites, singles-indiv. bathrooms.*

## ADELAIDE, NORWOOD

**Laurel Villa B&B**
101 Kensington Rd., SA 5067
08-332-7388
Fax: 08-31-5902
Marian L. Crisp
All year

70 Australian$ B&B
3 rooms/suites,
•
C-ltd/S-no/P-no/H-yes
English, American

Continental plus bkfst.
Full breakfast (fee)
Sitting room
coffee/tea makings
Airport: Adelaide
International

*Historic Victorian stone villa, comfortably furnished in style of period. 5 minute by bus to City Centre. Close to cosmopolitan dining/shopping. Convenient to everything.*

## BYRON BAY

**Taylors Country Guest House**
McGettingans Ln. 2481
066-847-436
Fax: 066-847-526
Ross Skinner
All year

160 Australian$ B&B
6 rooms/suites, 6 pb
Most CC, *Rated*,
C-ltd/S-no/P-no/H-no
English, Dutch

Full breakfast
Dinner, restaurant, tea
Sitting room, library
bicycles, swimming pool
Airport: Coolangatta

*The quintessential country guesthouse- warm Australian hospitality set amid Hinterland scenery. Small and exclusive with great expectations quietly met!*

## CAIRNS, NORTH QUEENSLAND

**Draper House**
461 Draper St., QLD, 4870
070-617-352    Fax: 070-617-352
Marilyn Ware
All year

55 NZ$
6 rooms/suites,
Meal plan: B&B
•
C-ltd/S-no/P-no/H-yes
Japanese, Italian, Eng.

Continental plus bkfst
Full bkfst. avail. (fee)
Restaurant, bar service
swimming pool, bicycles
barbeque, laundry room
Airport: Cairns

*Enjoy the quaint old "Parsonage," just 2 kms to city. Lush tropical garden, pool. Airport shuttle bus to our door (fee)* **Free day on Barrier Reef for 7 nights stay.**

COOLUM BEACH, YAROOMABA────────────────────────────

| | | |
|---|---|---|
| **Coolum Dreams B&B** | 110 Australian$ | Dinner by arrangement |
| 28 Warran Rd., QLD 4573 | 3 rooms/suites, | Tea, sitting room, garden |
| 011-074-46-3868 | *Rated*, | comp. wine, beer, champ. |
| Fax: 011-074-46-3868 | English | Tropical gardens |
| Wendy and | | Airport: Brisbane |
| Ken Budd | | |

*Queensland beachside home-Sunshine Coast. 1 1/2 hours N of Brisbane. Near famous Noosa holiday resort, tourist attractions & Hyatt Regency golfing resort. **Midweek special.***

MALENY────────────────────────────────────────────

| | | |
|---|---|---|
| **Maleny Lodge Guest House** | 116-140 Australian$ B&B | Full breakfast |
| 58 Maple St., QLD 4552 | 6 rooms/suites, 6 pb | Dinner, Restaurant (fee) |
| 011-610-749-42370 | Most CC, *Rated*, • | Sitting room, library |
| Fax: 011-610-749-43407 | C-ltd/S-no/P-no/H-yes | swimming pool |
| Peter and Lorraine Duffy | English | Airport: Brisbane |
| All year | | |

*Traditional Queensland hospitality in this historic Queenslander, furnished with Australian antiques. Situated in the small township of Maleny, 100 kms north of Brisbane.*

SYDNEY-POTTS POINT─────────────────────────────────

| | | |
|---|---|---|
| **Victoria Court Sydney** | 99 Australian$ B&B | Continental breakfast |
| 122 Victoria St., NSW 2011 | 25 rooms/suites, 25 pb | Sitting room |
| 011-61-2-9357-3200 | Most CC | library |
| Fax: 011-61-2-9357-7606 | • | Airport: Sydney |
| Marilyn & Denis | C-ltd/S-yes/P-no/H-no | International |
| McGufficke | English, Fr., Ger., Sp. | |
| All year | | |

*1880's Boutique Hotel in elegant Victorian terrace house. Central, quiet location. Within minutes of Opera House and Harbour. Affordable rates from 99.00 and up.*

TANUNDA────────────────────────────────────────────

| | | |
|---|---|---|
| **Lawley Farm** | 115 Australian$ B&B | Full breakfast |
| Krondorf Rd., SA 5352 | 6 rooms/suites, 6 pb | Hot tubs, picnic baskets |
| 011-61 085-63-2141 | Most CC, *Rated*, • | games room, 2 nights or |
| Fax: 011-61 085-63-2141 | C-yes/S-no/P-no/H-yes | more: complimentary wine |
| Sancha & Bruce Withers | English | Airport: Adelaide |
| All year | | |

*Restored settler's farm - enjoy the ambience and tranquility. Hot tub spa, spacious gardens. Close to excellent restaurants, antique shops, wineries, walks.*

| | | |
|---|---|---|
| **Stonewell Cottage** | 120-135 Australian$ B&B | Full breakfast |
| Stonewell Rd., SA 5352 | Most CC | Complimentary wine |
| 011-61 085-63-2019 | • | Rowing & fishing |
| Fax: 011-610-856-32019 | C-ltd/S-no/P-no/H-yes | feed friendly ducks |
| John & Yvonne Pfeiffer | English, German | Airport: Adelaide |
| All year | | |

*Picket fenced stone cottages nestled within picturesque vineyard & lakeside setting. Enjoy private spas, cozy wood fires, fishing, rowing, country walks. 5 minutes from towns*

THREDBO VALLEY————————————————————————————————

**Bernti's Emu Ground**
Off Westons Rd., Jindabyne,
NSW 2627
61-800-500105
Fax: 61-64-561669
Tricia Hechher
All year

130 Australian$ B&B/
MAP
6 rooms/suites, 3 pb
Visa, MC, AmEx
•
C-yes/S-no/P-no/H-yes
English

Full breakfast
Lunch, dinner, tea, wine
Sitting room, library
bicycles
comp. bottle of wine
Airport: Canberra

*Gourmet guesthouse, off the beaten track. Edge of Kosciusko National Park. For those who love Emu's, Kangaroos, and friendly fireplace chats.* **Bottle of premium local wine.**

THREDBO VILLAGE————————————————————————————

**Bernti's Mountain Inn**
4 Mowamba Place,
NSW 2630
61-64-576332
Fax: 61-64-561669
61-500105
Tricia Hecher
All year

110 Australian$ B&B/
MAP
30 rooms/suites, 30 pb
Visa, MC, AmEx
•
C-yes/S-no/P-no/H-no
English

Full breakfast, AP avail.
Restaurant, bar
Pool, spa, sauna, bicycle
alpine slide, horseriding
comp. bottle of wine
Airport: Canberra

*In the heart of Thredbo, a unique mountain inn specializing in personal service and gourmet food. Winner High Country Cuisine Award 1995.* **Bottle of premium local wine.**

# Austria

HEILIGENBLUT, CARINTHIA————————————————————————

**Haus Senger**
Hof 23  A-9844
0482-42-215
Fax: 04824/2215-9
Senger FamilyJuly-Oct

460 Austrian$ B&B
16 rooms/suites, 16 pb
Visa, MC
C-yes/S-no/P-yes/H-no
English, Italian, German

Continental breakfast
Dinner, restaurant, tea
Sitting room, Sauna
Airport: Salzburg

*A small family run house right on the bottom of the highest mountain in Austria - The Grossglockner. Chaletstyle, stunning view, rooms and suites, hospitality of owners.*

INNSBRUCK, TYROL————————————————————————————

**Gasthof Hotel Weisses Kreuz**
Herzog-Friedrich Strasse
31  6020
0512-59-479
Fax: 0512-59-479-90
Josef Ortner
All year

1,020 Austrian$ B&B
39 rooms/suites, 30 pb
Visa, MC, AmEx,
*Rated*, •
C-yes/S-ltd/P-yes/H-ltd
English, French, Italian

Breakfast buffet
Welcome drink
Sitting room
Airport: Munich

*Typical Austrian inn since 1465, situated in Innsbruck's gothic town. Cozy familiar atmosphere, wooden ceilings, old furniture & friendly service. Mozart stayed here once.*

## OSTERREIGH, HOLLENSTEIN/YBBS

**Gasthot und Alpenbad**
**Staudach**
Walcherbauer 5  3343
0744-52-62
Fax: 07445-262
Helga Zedka
All year

Rates: Inquire B&B
C-yes/S-yes/P-yes
English, German,
French

Continental Breakfast
Full breakfast (fee)
Bicycles, tennis court
pool avail. July & August
Airport: Vienna and Linz

*Sightseeing trips around the hills. Regional and international food, beverages. Skiing in winter by arrangement. Own swimming bath, tennis court. Steam bath in Hollenstein.*

## SALZBURG

**Steakhaus in Landgasthof**
**Fieg**
Fuschl Nr. 60, 5330 Fuschi
Am See  A-5330
0043-06-226/231
Gunter & Maria Fieg
All year

250-320 Austrian$ B&B/
MAP
15 rooms/suites, 15 pb
C-yes/S-yes/P-
yesGerman, English

Continental plus bkfst.
Restaurant (fee)
Sitting room
bicycles
sauna
Airport: Salzburg

*Onlu 20 kilometers to Salzburg. 6 lakes around 20 kilometers. Trekking paradise. Near the places from "Sound of Music." **Welcome drink.***

## SALZBURG, OBERALM

**Schloss Haunsperg**
Hammetstr. 32  A5411
6245-80-662
Fax: 6245-85680
Fam. Von Gernerth
All year

1900 Austrian$ B&B
8 rooms/suites, 8 pb
Most CC
●
C-yes/S-yes/P-yes/H-no
Enlgish, Italian, German

Full breakfast
Snacks,complimentary wine
Sitting room
library, bicycles
tennis court
Airport: Munic, Salzburg

*Our gracious 14 century country manor house offers 8 superbly appointed double rooms and suites with period furniture for 2-5 people. **3rd night 50% off.***

## VIENNA

**Hotel Kaiserin Elisabeth**
Weihburggasse 3  1010
0143-15-152-60
Fax: 0143-15-152-67
All year

2,300 Austrian$ B&B
64 rooms/suites, 63 pb
●
C-yes/S-yes/P-yes/H-yes
English, French, Italian

Full breakfast
Aftn. tea, snacks
Bar service, sitting room
Airport: Vienna

*Traditional hotel located in the heart of Vienna, next to St. Stephan Cathedral, the famous pedestrian area and the subway stop. Rooms are individually furnished & decorated.*

**Minu**
Alserstr.43 3rd Floor  1080
0043-14-056-196
Fax: 0043-1-407-1090
All year

800 Austrian$
10 rooms/suites, 10 pb
Most CC, *Rated*, ●
C-yes/S-yes/P-yes/H-yes
Eng, It, Fr, Sp

Restaurants nearby
Airport: Vienna
International

*Family friendly facility atmosphere, You would feel at home even if you are miles away from home.*

## WACHAU

**Hotel Scholss Durnstein**
Durnstein  A 3601
+4327-11-212
Fax: +43-2711-351
Hans & Rosemarie Thiery
April-October

2500-3100 Austrian$
B&B/MAP
38 rooms/suites, 38 pb
Most CC, *Rated*,
C-yes/S-yes/H-yes
English, French, Italian

Full breakfast
Restaurant (fee)
Bar service, sitting room
library, bicycles
sauna, swimming pool
Airport: Vienna

*Built in 1630, Renaissance castle converted into a hotel of great style. Magnificent position in the most picturesque section of the Danube.*

# Belgium

BRUGGS, FLANDERS ────────────────────────────────────

**The Aragon**
Naaldenstraat 24  B-8000
32-50 333533
Fax: 32-50 342805
Lue & Hedwig Van Laere
Feb 15-Jan 4

3,500-3,950 Belgium$
B&B
18 rooms/suites, 18 pb
Most CC, *Rated*, •
C-yes/S-yes/P-yes/H-no
Eng., Ger., Fr., Spanish

Full breakfast, buffet
Afternoon tea
Sitting room, library
bicycles - present guide
receive free bottle wine
Airport: Brussels

*Most attractive family-run hotel with 4-Star facilities. Oak beamed breakfast room and individually decorated rooms, all ensuite. Situated in the Medieval City Center.*

---

**The Egmond**
Minnewater I5  B-8000
32-50-341445
Fax: 32-50-342940
Kris Van Lagre
Feb 15-Nov 30

3,200-3,600 Belgium$
B&B
8 rooms/suites, 8 pb
*Rated*, •
C-yes/S-yes/P-no/H-no
Eng., Ger., Fr., Dutch

Full breakfast buffet
Afternoon tea
Sitting room
bicycles—all rooms have
garden/park view
Airport: Brussels

*This charming manor house kept the romantic interior. 18th century fireplaces, beamed ceilings. Rooms are ensuite & individually decorated. Setting next to "The Lake of Love."*

---

**De Orangerie**
Kartuizerinnenstraat 10  8000
50-34-16-49
Fax: 50-33-30-16
Mrs. Beatrice Geeraert
All year

7.950 Belgium$ B&B
19 rooms/suites, 19 pb
Most CC, *Rated*, •
C-yes/S-no/P-yes/H-yes
Dutch, Fr., Eng., German

Continental plus bkfst.
Afternoon tea, bar serv.
Sitting room
sauna and swimming pool
in annex
Airport: Brussels

*City centre located, overlooking the canal. 15th century convent fully renovated. Antique furnishings in all personalized decorated rooms and public rooms. **3rd night 50% off.***

---

**Hotel Adornes**
St. Annarei 26  8000
050-34-13-36
Fax: 050-34-20-85
Nathalie Standaert
Feb 12-Dec 31

2,700-3,500 Belgium$
B&B
20 rooms/suites, 20 pb
Most CC, *Rated*,
C-yes/S-yes/P-yes/H-yes
French, Flemish, Ger,
Eng

Buffet breakfast
Afternoon tea
Bar service
sitting room
bicycles
Airport: Brussels

*Charming family-run hotel where everyone feels at home. Several rooms overlooking canal. Splendid buffet breakfast. Free bicycles & parking facilities. **Special offers, inquire.***

---

**Hotel Bryghia**
Oosterlingenplein 4  8000
32-50-33-8059
Fax: 32-50-34-1430
Herman Cools
Closed 3 Jan-18 Feb

3,950 Belgium$ B&B
18 rooms/suites, 18 pb
Visa, MC, AmEx,
*Rated*, •
C-yes/S-yes/P-yes/H-no
English, Fr., Ger., Dutch

Full breakfast
Afternoon tea, snacks
Bar service, sitting room
bicycles
Airport: Brussells
International

*The hotel dates from 15th century, handsomely restored, overlooking picturesque canal. Located in very heart of Bruges. Medieval city. **Welcome drink on arrival.***

LISOGNE, PR. NAPMUR

| | | |
|---|---|---|
| **Hotel du Moulin de Lisogne** | 2,800-3,500 Belgium$ | Full breakfast |
| Rue de la Lisonnette, 5500 | B&B | Restaurant (fee) |
| Dinant 5500 | 10 rooms/suites, 10 pb | Bar service, sitting room |
| 082-226-380 | • | bicycles, trout fishing |
| Fax: 082-222-147 | C-yes/S-yes/P-yes/H-no | tennis court, kayaking |
| The Blondiaux | Dutch, Fr,Eng, | Airport: Bruxelles, |
| Feb 10-Dec 10 | Nederlands | Luxembourg |

*The inn is sitting in the most beautiful country of Belgium. Along the little river: La Leffe" (famous Belgian bar). The rooms are very quiet.* **3rd night 50%.**

# Caribbean, B.V.I.

ROAD TOWN, TORTOLA

| | | |
|---|---|---|
| **Fort Recovery Estates Villas** | 125-185 US$ B&B | Continental plus bkfst. |
| Box 239 | 17 rooms/suites, 17 pb | Dinner (fee) |
| 809-495-4354 | Most CC, *Rated*, • | Sitting room, library |
| Fax: 809-495-4036 | C-yes/S-yes/P- | swimming pool |
| 800-367-8455 | noEnglish, Spanish | private beach |
| Pamelah Jills Jacobson | | Airport: Beef Is.,San |
| All year | | Juan,St.Tho. |

*Luxury 1-4 bedroom Caribbean seaside villas. Private beach. AC, TV, Kitchen, maid. Yoga & massages available.* **7 nights stay includes one welcome dinner & snorkel trip 1 person.**

WEST END, TORTOLA

| | | |
|---|---|---|
| **Sebastian's on the Beach Hotel** | 85-190 US$ EP | Restaurant (fee) |
| Little Apple Bay | 26 rooms/suites, 26 pb | Lunch, Dinner available |
| P.O. Box 6219, Freehold, NJ, | Most CC | Bar service |
| USA, 07728 | • | gift store, commissary |
| 809-495-4212 | C-yes/S-yes/P-yes/H-no | watersports, beach |
| Fax: 809-495-4466 | English, German | Airport: Beef Is.via St.Th./ |
| B. Hochberg, U. Miloleiczik | | S.Juan |
| All year | | |

*Intimate beachfront hideaway with deluxe accommodations; award-winning restaurant. Complimentary sample of Sebastian's famous rum; ocean-lovers paradise.* **4th night free.**

# Caribbean, B.W.I

GRAND TURK, TURK & CAICOS

| | | |
|---|---|---|
| **Salt Raker Inn** | 75 US$ MAP | Full breakfast (fee) |
| P.O. Box 1 | 13 rooms/suites, 13 pb | Lunch, dinner, restaurant |
| 809-946-2260 | Most CC | Bar service, library |
| Fax: 809-946-2817 | • | bicycles, scuba diving |
| Jenny Smith | C-yes/S-yes/P-no/H-yes | Airport: Grand Turk |
| All year | English, French | |

*Quiet, intimate oceanfront inn within a historic Bermudian house.* **10% discount on room rates.**

VIRGIN GORDA————————————————————————————————

**Olde Yard Inn**
The Valley
809-495-5544
Fax: 809-495-5986
Carol Kaufman
All year

100 English$ MAP
14 rooms/suites, 14 pb
Visa, MC, AmEx,
*Rated*, •
C-yes/S-yes/P-no/H-yes
English, French, Spanish

Full breakfast (fee)
Lunch, dinner, restaurant
Bar service, sitting room
library, tennis, pool
health club, Jacuzzi
Airport: Virgin Gorda,
Tortola

*14 charming rooms on hillside amidst tropical gardens, facing sea w/gourmet restaurant, acclaimed library. Romance & serenity abound. Concierge service. Comp. bottle of wine.*

NEWCASTLE, NEVIS————————————————————————————

**Yamseed Inn**
St. Kitts
809-469-9361
Fax: 809-469-9375
Sybil S. Siegfried
All year

100 US$ B&B
4 rooms/suites, 4 pb
C-yes/S-yes/P-no/H-yes
English

Full breakfast (no meat)
Dine in gallery
Sitting room
library, lovely views
on the beach
Airport: St. Kitts

*Lovely home and gardens; on the beach. Large airy bedrooms each with baths. Wonderful breakfast on the gallery. Patio overlooking the breathtaking view of St. Kitts.*

# Caribbean, D.W.I.

SABA, D.W.I.————————————————————————————————

**Captain's Quarters**
Windwardside
599-462201
Fax: 599-462377
Calvin Holm
All year

135-170 US$ B&B
12 rooms/suites, 12 pb
Most CC
•
C-yes/S-yes/P-yes/H-no
English, Dutch, Spanish

Full American breakfast
Restaurant (fee)
Sitting room, library
swimming pool, comp.
upgrade if available
Airport: SAB, SXM

*Charming cliffside Victorian Inn featuring antique/4-poster beds and sweeping ocean/ mountain views-only minutes from rainforest, scuba, hiking and "gingerbread" villages.*

SIMPSON BAY, ST. MARTEEN, D.W.I.——————————————————

**Horny Toad Guesthouse**
2 Vlaun's Dr.
011-599-5-54323
Fax: 011-599-5-53316
800-417-9361
Betty & Earle Vaughan
All year

180 US$ EP
8 rooms/suites, 8 pb
*Rated*, •
C-ltd/S-yes/P-no/H-ltd
English

Food shopping service
Family friendly facility
car rental available
Airport: Juliana

*The Horny Toad is described as "a small and special place" and "one of the best bets on the island." We're inclined to agree & would love the opportunity to prove it to you.*

# Caribbean, F.W.I.

TRINITE, MARTINIQUE

**Saint Aubin Hotel**
P.O. Box 52  97220
011-19-596-69-34-77
Fax: 011-19-596-69-41-14
Foret Guy
All year

450-580 French$ B&B
15 rooms/suites, 15 pb
Most CC, *Rated*, •
C-yes/S-ltd/P-no/H-ltd
French, English

Continental breakfast
Dinner, afternoon tea
Bar service
swimming pool
Airport: Lamentin

*Gingerbread-laden, pink Victorian perched on a hill overlooking the Atlantic. An informal flower garden, wide grassy lawn, swimming pool with cabana included.* **6th night free.**

# Caribbean, W.I.

BLANCHISSEUSE, TRINIDAD

**Blanchisseuse Laguna Mar**
65 1/2 Mile Marker, Paria
Main Rd  99999
809-628-3731
Fax: 809-628-3737
G. Franz, B. Zollna
All year

16 US$ Inquire
6 rooms/suites, 6 pb
Visa, MC, *Rated*, •
C-yes/S-yes/P-no/H-no
English, German

Breakfast (fee)
Restaurant-all meals
Peaceful co-existence of
humans with nature
oceanfront property
Airport: Piarco Airport

*Nature lovers paradise. Sea & river bathing. Birds, butterflies, turtles, waterfalls, hiking trails. Zollna house in Port of Spain.*

ENGLISH HARBOUR, ANTIGUA

**Admiral's Inn**
Nelson's Dockyard
809-460-1027/1153
Fax: 809-460-1534
Miss Ethelyn Philip
Oct 15-Sept 1

78 US$ EP
14 rooms/suites, 14 pb
Visa, MC, AmEx
•
C-yes/S-yes/P-no/H-no
English

MAP 2 meals (fee)
Restaurant, bar, snacks
Sitting room
transportation to beaches
Airport: V.C. Bird

*Cozy Inn, lovely historic Georgian brick building, in Nelson's Dockyard, a yachting center. Terrace restaurant overlooking the water. Free welcome cocktail. Flowers in room.*

**Copper and Lumber Store Hotel**
Nelson's Dockyard
809-460-1058
Fax: 809-460-1529
Alan L. Jeyes
All year

195 US$ EP
14 rooms/suites, 14 pb
Visa, MC, AmEx,
*Rated*, •
C-yes/S-yes/P-no/H-no
English, French

Continental breakfast
Lunch, dinner, restaurant
Bar service, sitting room
library, bicycles, tennis
Airport: V.C. Bird
International

*Historical inn furnished with Georgian antiques. A luxurious blend of gracious living and fascinating naval history.* **May 6–Dec. 15; stay 2 nights & 3rd night free.**

## MARAVAL, TRINIDAD, TOBAGO

**Monique's Guest House**
114 Saddle Rd.
809-628-3334
Fax: 809-622-3232
Michael & Monica
Charbonne
All year

50 US$ EP
20 rooms/suites, 20 pb
Most CC, *Rated*, •
C-yes/S-ltd/P-no/H-yes
English

Full breakfast
Lunch, dinner, restaurant
Bar service, sitting room
Airport: Piarco International

*Though small, our product compares with multinational hotels. Combined with personalized attention, and a homey atmosphere, we are "a unique mix."*

---

**Zollna House**
12 Ramlogan Terrace, La
Seiva
809-628-3731
Fax: 809-628-3737
G. Franz, B. Zollna
All year

50 US$ B&B
6 rooms/suites, 1 pb
Visa, MC
•
C-ltd/S-yes/P-no/H-no
English, German

Full or Continental (fee)
Dinner available
Airport: Piarco Airport

*Suburban. City and mountain-valley views. Five minutes from Queens Park, Savannah. Guidance "What,""See,""Do" in Trinidad.*

## PORT ANTONIO, JAMAICA

**Hotel Mocking Bird Hill**
P.O. Box 254
809-993-7267
Fax: 809-993-7133
Barbara Walker, Shireen Aga
All year

95 US$ Inquire
10 rooms/suites, 3 pb
Most CC
•
S-yes/H-ltd
German, English,
French

Restaurant (fee)
All meals available
Bar service, library
sitting room, art gallery
private massages, hikes
Airport: Kingston

*Split-level, air villa surrounded by rich tropical vegetation. A magnificent view of the mountains and the coast. **14 nights price of 13.***

## WESTMORELAND, JAMAICA

**Charela Inn**
Norman Manley Blvd., Negril
809-957-4648
Fax: 809-957-4414
Daniel & Sylvie Grizzle
All year

140 US$ MAP(fee)
39 rooms/suites, 39 pb
Visa, MC, *Rated*, •
C-yes/S-yes/P-no/H-yes
French, German

Full breakfast (fee)
Lunch, dinner, restaurant
Bar service, sitting room
library, swimming pool
Airport: Sangster's
International

*A quiet, intimate hideaway on Negril beach, for singles, couples, and families. Set amidst lush tropical gardens, gourmet Jamaican/French cuisine is served.*

# Costa Rica

## QUEPOS

**La Mariposa**
Manuel Antonio Beach, P.O.
Box 4
506-777-0456
Fax: 506-777-0050
800-223-6510
La Mariposa
Open All year

160 US$ B&B
18 rooms/suites, 18 pb
Visa, MC, *Rated*, •
C-ltd/S-yes/P-no/H-no
English, Spanish, French

Buffet Breakfast
Restaurant (fee)
Swimming pool
hot tubs in six units
sitting room, library
Airport: Quepos

*Picturesque Colonial-style Inn set on remote bluff w/breathtaking 360 degree view-Pacific Ocean. Courtesy, calm, comfort, cuisine, and character-criteria used here.* ***Specials.***

SANTA BARBARA/HEREDIA————————————————————————

| | | |
|---|---|---|
| **Finca Rosa Blanca Country Inn** | 125 US$ B&B | Full breakfast |
| Apdo. 41-3009 | 8 rooms/suites, 8 pb | Restaurant, bar (fee) |
| P.O. Box 25216, Miami, FL | Visa, AmEx, *Rated*, • | Waterfall swimming pool |
| 33102, USA | C-yes/S-no/P-no/H-no | recreation room, library |
| 011-506-269-9392 | Eng., Sp., It., Fr., Dan. | barbeque, country quiet |
| Fax: 011-506-269-9555 | | Airport: Juan Sta. Maria, San |
| Glen and Teri Jampol | | Jose |
| All year | | |

*Famous country hideaway, extraordinary architecture. Six suites, two villas filled with original art. Waterfall pool, 15 minutes from International Airport.*

# England, U.K.

AMBLESIDE, CUMBRIA————————————————————————

| | | |
|---|---|---|
| **Rothay Manor Hotel** | 118 English$ B&B | Full breakfast |
| Rothay Bridge  LA22 0EH | 18 rooms/suites, 18 pb | Lunch, dinner, restaurant |
| 015-394-33605 | Most CC, *Rated*, • | Bar service, sitting room |
| Fax: 015-394-33607 | C-yes/S-yes/P-no/H-yes | free use of leisure club |
| Nigel and Stephen Nixon | English | nearby |
| Closed January | | Airport: Manchester |

*Situated in the heart of the Lake District, this Regency country-house hotel has an international reputation for cuisine, comfort, and relaxed atmosphere.*

BATH, AVON————————————————————————

| | | |
|---|---|---|
| **Bailbrook Lodge Hotel** | 55 English$ MAP | Full breakfast |
| 35/37 London Rd. West  BA1 | 12 rooms/suites, 12 pb | Bar, Restaurant (fee) |
| 7HZ | Visa, MC, AmEx, | Historic houses & famous |
| 01-225-85-9090 | *Rated*, • | villages nearby |
| Fax: 01-225-85-9090 | C-yes/S-yes/P-noEnglish | Airport: Bristol, Heathrow |
| Mrs. K.M. Addison | | |
| All year | | |

*Splendid Georgian hotel close to world heritage City Bath. Beautiful countryside. Traditional decorations, rooms with all facilities; some four-poster beds.* **3rd night 50% off.**

| | | |
|---|---|---|
| **Gainsborough Hotel** | 52 English$ B&B | Full breakfast |
| Weston Lane  BA1 4AB | 16 rooms/suites, 12 pb | Coffee/tea sets in room |
| 012-253-11380 | Visa, MC, AmEx, | Bar service, sitting room |
| Fax: 012-254-47411 | *Rated*, • | color TV, hairdryers |
| Richard Warwick Smith | C-yes/S-ltd/P-no/H-no | Airport: Bristol, Heathrow |
| | English, French, | |
| | German | |

*Country house hotel situated on grounds near the Botanical Gardens and city. The Hotel provides a relaxing and friendly environment for guests. Private car park, warm welcome.*

## BATH, AVON

**Haydon House**
9 Bloomfield Park  BA2 2BY
012-253-4431-31
Fax: 012-253-4431-31
Gordon & Magdalene
Ashman/Marr
All year

55 English$ B&B
5 rooms/suites, 5 pb
Visa, MC, AmEx,
*Rated*, •
C-ltd/S-no/P-no/H-no
English, French,
German

Full breakfast
Afternoon tea, comp. wine
Sitting room, library
Airport: London Heathrow,
Gatwick

*An oasis of elegance and tranquillity bursting with hospitality. Renowned for superb accommodation and wonderful breakfasts. 3 nights for the price of one with limits.*

---

**Highways House**
143 Wells Rd.  BA2 3AL
012-254-21238
Fax: 012-254-81169
David & Davina James
Closed Christmas

52 English$ B&B
7 rooms/suites, 7 pb
Visa, MC, *Rated*, •
S-yes/P-no/H-ltd
English, Welsh

Full English breakfast
Lunch, dinner, restaurant
Bar service, sitting room
library, tennis court
hospitality tray each rm.
Airport: Bristol

*Come and stay in our beautiful Victorian home. Enjoy a choice of breakfasts before exploring the beauty of Bath. Hot tubs, sauna, swimming pool, bicycles. RAC acclaimed.*

---

**Meadowland**
36 Bloomfield Park  BA2 2BX
01-2253-11079
Fax: 01-4523-04507
Catherine K. Andrew
All year

55-65 English$ B&B/EP
3 rooms/suites, 3 pb
Visa, MC
•
C-ltd/S-no/P-no/H-no
English, French

Full breakfast
Catered to special diets
Sitting room
quiet secluded grounds
color TV with remote
Airport: London Heathrow

*One of the top bed & breakfasts in England. Beautiful accommodations in a substantial, welcoming, family home. Quiet, secure and private.* **Fifth night free October–March.**

---

**Paradise House**
86-88 Holloway  BA2 4PX
012-253-17723
Fax: 012-254-82005
David & Janet Cutting
All year

65 English$ B&B
8 rooms/suites, 8 pb
Visa, MC, AmEx,
*Rated*,
C-yes/S-yes/P-no/H-ltd
English, German,
French

Full breakfast
Sitting room, library
croquet, boules
Airport: Bristol, Heathrow

*Elegant Georgian house on a quiet street, only 5 minutes walk from Bath centre. Lovely garden with panoramic city views.* **3 nights or more 10% reduction.**

---

**Villa Magdala Hotel**
Henrietta Rd.  BA2 6LX
01225-466-329
Fax: 01225-483-207
Alison Williams
All year

50 English$ B&B
17 rooms/suites, 17 pb
Visa, MC, AmEx,
*Rated*, •
C-yes/S-ltd/P-no/H-no
English

Full breakfast
Continental breakfast
Family friendly facility
Airport: Bristol, Heathrow

*Relax in our elegant Victorian town house just minutes from the Roman Baths. The Villa Magdala enjoys a tranquil setting with ample parking.*

---

**Wentworth House**
106 Bloomfield Rd.  BA2 2AP
012-253-39193
Fax: 012-253-10460
Geoff & Avril Kitching
All year

50 English$ B&B
18 rooms/suites, 18 pb
Visa, MC, AmEx,
*Rated*, •
C-ltd/P-no/H-no
English

Full breakfast
Dinner
Bar service, sitting room
swimming pool
Airport: Bristol

*Victorian Mansion set in grounds in quiet part of city, large free car park & views. Licensed lounge. Golf/walks closeby. Bath the complete Georgian City. 3 nights 10% disc't.*

## BATH, SOMERSET

| | | |
|---|---|---|
| **Brompton House** | 60 English$ B&B | Full breakfast |
| St. Johns Road  BA2 6PT | 18 rooms/suites, 18 pb | Complimenatary wine |
| +44-01-225-42-0972 | Most CC, *Rated*, | Bar service, sitting rm. |
| Fax: +44-01-225-42-0505 | C-yes/S-no/P-no/H-no | residential license |
| David, Sue, Belinda, Tim | English, some French | Airport: Heathrow, Bristol |
| Selby | | |
| Closed Xmas, New Yr. | | |

*Charming Georgian Rectory 1777. Beautiful gardens. Minutes walk to city centre. In suite rooms all facilities. Delicious breakfast. No smoking.* **3rd night 50% off.**

## BELFORD, NORTHUMBERLAND

| | | |
|---|---|---|
| **Waren House Hotel** | 110 English$ B&B | Full breakfast |
| Waren Mill  NE70 7EE | 7 rooms/suites, 7 pb | Dinner, restaurant |
| 016-682-14581 | Most CC, *Rated*, • | Bar service, sitting room |
| Fax: 016-682-14484 | C-ltd/S-no/P-yes/H-no | library, hot tubs |
| Anita & Peter Laverack | English | seven acres of land |
| All year | | Airport: Newcastle/ |
| | | Edinburah |

*Traditional country house hotel, rural setting. On coast overlooking Holy Island, excellent food, superb accommodations. 250 plus bin wine list. Special discount available.*

## BETHERSDEN, CO. KENT

| | | |
|---|---|---|
| **Little Hodgeham** | 52 English$ B&B | Full breakfast |
| Smarden Rd., Near | 3 rooms/suites, | Restaurant (fee) |
| Ashford  TN26 3HE | *Rated*, | Bar service, library |
| 0233-850323 | C-yes/S-yes/P-yes/H-no | sitting room |
| Miss Erica Wallace | Danish, It., French | Airport: Gatwick |
| Mid March-Sept 1 | | |

*A Picture postcard cottage, 500 year's old, rose-clad, beamed. Lovely gardens, pond, pool. Dinner party nightly.* **Special room offers, please ask us about it.**

## BLANCHLAND, CO.DURHAM

| | | |
|---|---|---|
| **Lord Crewe Arms Hotel** | 105 English$ B&B | Full breakfast |
| Near Consett  DH8 9SP | 20 rooms/suites, 20 pb | Restaurant (fee) |
| 01434-675251 | Most CC, *Rated*, • | Bar service |
| Fax: 01434-675331 | C-yes/S-yes/P-yes/H-no | sitting room |
| Alec Todd | English | library |
| All year | | Airport: Newcastle |

*One of England's oldest inns set in one of England's prettiest villages. Excellent facilities, outstanding antiques and a renowned restaurant.* **50% off third nights stay.**

## BLEDINGTON, OXFORDSHIRE

| | | |
|---|---|---|
| **Kings Head Inn &** | 60 English$ B&B | Full breakfast |
| **Restaurant** | 12 rooms/suites, 12 pb | Lunch, dinner, restaurant |
| The Green  OX7 6HD | Most CC, *Rated*, | Bar service, sitting room |
| 016-086-58365 | C-yes/S-ltd/H-no | horse riding, quad biking |
| Fax: 016-086-58902 | French, Spanish, English | fishing, golf nearby |
| Michael & Annette Royce | | Airport: Heathrow, |
| | | Birmingham |

*Fifteenth century inn located in the heart of Cotswolds on village green. Complete brook and ducks. Retains olde world charm. Award winning restaurant.*

## BRADFORD-ON-AVON, WILTSHIRE

| | | |
|---|---|---|
| **Widbrook Grange** | 75-85 English$ B&B | Full breakfast |
| Trowbridge Rd., | 20 rooms/suites, 19 pb | Restaurant (fee) |
| Widbrook  BA15 1UH | Most CC | Bar service |
| 01225-863173 | • | swimming pool |
| Fax: 01225-862890 | C-yes/S-yes/P-no/H-yes | indoor gymnasium |
| John & Pauline Price | English | Airport: Bristol |
| All year | | |

*Elegant Georgian house and courtyard rooms. Exquisitely decorated-furnished with antiques. Several four-poster beds. Emphasis on peaceful relaxation.*

| | | |
|---|---|---|
| **Woolley Grange Hotel** | 99 English$ B&B | Full breakfast |
| Woolley Green  BA15 1TX | 22 rooms/suites, 20 pb | Restaurant (fee) |
| 012-258-64705 | Most CC, *Rated*, • | Bar service, sitting room |
| Fax: 012-258-64059 | C-yes/S-yes/P-yes | library, bicycles |
| Nigel & Heather Chapman | English, French, | swimming pool |
| All year | German | Airport: Heathrow |

*"Family Hotel of the Year." Woolley Grange is a Jacobean stone manor house only 8 miles from Bath. Tennis, croquet, swimming pool.*

## BROADWAY, WORCESTERSHIRE

| | | |
|---|---|---|
| **Leasow House** | 52 English$ B&B | Full breakfast |
| Laverton Meadows  WR12 | 7 rooms/suites, 7 pb | Tea & coffee facility |
| 7NA | Visa, MC, AmEx, | Library, color TV |
| 013-865-84526 | *Rated*, • | direct dial telephones |
| Fax: 013-865-84596 | C-yes/S-ltd/H-yes | reduced children's rate |
| Mrs. Barbara Meekings | English | Airport: Heathrow |
| All year | | |

*Sixteenth century Cotswald farm house in quiet countryside close to Broadway. Ideally situated for touring Stratford, Oxford, and Cotswalds. 10% discount 3 nights or more.*

## CARLISLE

| | | |
|---|---|---|
| **Holmhead Guest House** | 46 English$ B&B | Full breakfast |
| Hadrian's Wall, | 4 rooms/suites, 4 pb | Dinner, wine, restaurant |
| Greenhead  CA6 7HY | Most CC, *Rated*, | Sitting room, library |
| 016-977-47402 | C-ltd/S-ltd/P-ltd/H-ltd | golf, horse riding |
| Fax: 016-977-47402 | Norwegian, English | self guided tours |
| Brian & Pauline Staff | | Airport: Newcastle |
| Closed Xmas, New Yr. | | |

*On world heritage site, built from the stones of Hadrians Wall. Several museums & excavations nearby. Gourmet breakfasts. Services of tour guide for spectacular walks.*

## CHELTENHAM, GLOUCESTERSHIRE

| | | |
|---|---|---|
| **Hollington House Hotel** | 48-60 English$ B&B | Full breakfast |
| 115 Hales Road  GL52 6ST | 9 rooms/suites, 8 pb | Dinner (fee), bar service |
| 01242-256652 | Most CC, *Rated*, • | Sitting room, library |
| Fax: 01242-570280 | C-yes/S-no/P-no/H-no | large garden suitable for |
| Juergen & Annette Berg | German, French, Malay | croquet, on site parking |
| All year | | Airport: Birmingham, LTTR |
| | | (London) |

*Victorian house, spacious ensuite bedrooms. Excellent breakfasts, dinners. 700 yards from London Road, 40 minutes to High Street. **Free bottle wine with dinner for two.***

## CUMBRIA

**Aynsome Manor Hotel**
Cartmel, North Grange-over-
Sands LA11 6HH
015-395-36653
Fax: 015-395-36016
Christopher and Andrea
VarleyFebruary-Dec

84 English$ MAP
12 rooms/suites, 12 pb
Visa, MC, AmEx,
*Rated*, •
C-ltd/S-ltd/P-yes
English

Full breakfast
Lunch, dinner, restaurant
Bar service, sitting room
library
Airport: Manchester

*Family-run 17th century manor house situated in the historic village of Cartmel, within Lake District National Park. Excellent food, recommended by English Tourist Board.*

## CUMBRIA, THE LAKE DISTRICT

**New House Farm**
Lorton,
Cockermouth  CA139UU
01900-85404
Fax: 01900-85404
Hazel & John Hatch
All year

60 English$ B&B
3 rooms/suites, 3 pb
*Rated*, •
C-ltd/S-no/P-yes/H-no
English

Full breakfast
Lunch, dinner, aftn. tea
Sitting room
very personal service
bicycles
Airport: Newcastle,
Manchester

*New House Farm is in one of the most spectacular settings, surrounded by high fells with lakes close by. We offer a truly quiet & peaceful place.*

## DREWSTEIGNTON, DEVON

**Hunts Tor**
EX6 6QW
016-472-81228
Chris & Sue Harrison
March-November

60 English$ B&B
4 rooms/suites, 4 pb
*Rated*,
C-ltd/S-ltd/P-yes/H-no
French, English

Full breakfast
Dinner, restaurant
Bar service, sitting room
Good food guide
Airport: Exeter

*Seventeenth century house in idyllic thatched village in Dartmoor National Park. Gourmet candlelit dinners, luxurious bedrooms, some with sitting rooms.*

## EVESHAM, CO. WORCESTERSHIRE

**Evesham Hotel**
Cooper's Lane, off
Waterside  WR11 6DA
013-867-65566
Fax: 013-867-65443
The Jenkinson Family
All year

80 English$ B&B
40 rooms/suites, 40 pb
Most CC, *Rated*, •
C-yes/S-yes/P-yes/H-no
English, American

Full breakfast
Lunch, dinner, restaurant
Bar service, sitting room
swimming indoor pool
Airport: Birmingham

*Modernized 1540/Georgian mansion house in suburban location. Good for Stratford, Cotswolds, Warwick. Informal, efficient, Smilingly, and idiosyncratically run.*

## HYDE PARK, LONDON

**Barry House Hotel**
12 Sussex Place  W2 2TP
44-171-723-0994
Fax: 33-171-723-9775
Mr. & Mrs. Bhasin
All year

60 English$ B&B
18 rooms/suites, 14 pb
Most CC, *Rated*, •
C-yes/S-yes/P-no/H-no
English

Full breakfast
Tea and coffee facilities
Family Friendly Facility
in-room TV, telephone
Airport: Heathrow

*We believe in family-like care. This is a family run Bed & Breakfast in central London close to most major attractions.*

LINCOLN, LINCOLNSHIRE——————————————————————

| | | |
|---|---|---|
| **D'isney Place Hotel** | 68 English$ B&B | Full breakfast |
| Eastgate  LN2 4AA | 17 rooms/suites, 17 pb | Continental breakfast |
| 015-225-38881 | Most CC, *Rated*, | Airport: Birmingham |
| Fax: 015-225-11321 | C-yes/S-ltd/P-yes/H-yes | |
| Judy Payne | French, English | |
| All year | | |

*D'isney Place is near the cathedral in the heart of Old Lincoln. Towelling robes and fresh milk in your room. Special discounts for week-end breaks*

LONDON——————————————————————————

| | | |
|---|---|---|
| **22 Jermyn Street** | 180 English$ Inquire | Continental or full (fee) |
| 22 Jermyn St., St. | 18 rooms/suites, 18 pb | Lunch, dinner (fee) |
| James  SW1Y 6HL | Most CC, *Rated*, • | Complimentary wine,snacks |
| 44-171-734-2353 | C-yes/S-yes/P-yes/H-yes | CD Rom library, bicycles |
| Fax: 44-171-734-0750 | Eng., Fr., It., Dutch | near health/sports club |
| Henry Togna, Annette Foster | | Airport: Heathrow |
| All year | | |

*Luxurious award winning townhouse in the heart of London, ideal for theatre. Let Henry and Annette take care of you!.* **Complimentary bottle of champagne on arrival.**

MARLBOROUGH, WILTSHIRE ———————————————————

| | | |
|---|---|---|
| **The Old Vicarage,** | 60 English$ | Full breakfast |
| **Eastcourt** | 3 rooms/suites, 3pb | Afternoon tea |
| Burbage,  SN8 3AG | Meal plan: B&B | Sitting room, hot tubs |
| 016-728-10495     Fax: 016-728- | Most CC | shooting and riding can |
| 10663 | C-ltd/S-no/P-no/H-no | be arranged |
| Jane Cornelius & Robert | French, English | Airport: Heathrow |
| Hector | | |
| All year | | |

*19th century home in 2 acres of ground in the heart of Wiltshire. Centrally heated. Near Stonehenge & Savernake Forest where deer & pheasants are a common sight.*

MELKSHAM, WILTSHIRE————————————————————

| | | |
|---|---|---|
| **Sandridge Park** | 40 English$ B&B | Full breakfast |
| Sandridge Hill  SN12 7QU | 4 rooms/suites, 4 pb | Dinner |
| 012-257-06897 | Visa, MC | Sitting room, library |
| Fax: 012-257-02838 | • | Airport: Heathrow |
| Annette Hoogeweegen | C-ltd/S-yes/P-no/H-no | |
| Closed Christmas | French, German, Dutch | |

*Early Victorian mansion, beautifully decorated. Set on thirty acres of land, full of birds and wildlife. Once the house of Eisenhower*

NETTLETON, CHIPPENHAM, WILTSHIRE———————————————

| | | |
|---|---|---|
| **Fosse Farmhouse Country** | 80 English$ B&B | Full breakfast |
| **Hotel** | 6 rooms/suites, 6 pb | Lunch, dinner, restaurant |
| Nettleton Shrub  SN14 7NJ | Visa, MC, AmEx, | Bar service, sitting room |
| 012-497-82286 | *Rated*, | antiques for sale |
| Fax: 012-497-83066 | C-yes/S-yes/P-yes/H-no | Rated 3 Crowns E.T.B. |
| Ms. Caron Lois Cooper | French, Japanese, | Airport: Heathrow |
| All year | English | |

*Beautiful 300-year old cotswold stone farmhouse. Antique fixtures & fittings throughout. Good home cooking & classes. Log fires, candlelit dinners. Friendly, caring hosts.*

*Sampson's Farm, Newton Abbot, Devon, U.K.*

## NEWTON ABBOT, DEVON

| | | |
|---|---|---|
| **Sampsons Farm** | 35 English$ MAP | Full breakfast |
| **Restaurant** | 5 rooms/suites, 2 pb | Lunch, dinner, restaurant |
| Preston TQ12 3PP | Visa, MC, AmEx | Bar service, sitting room |
| 016-265-4913 | C-yes/S-yes/P-no/H-yes | historic importance house |
| Fax: 016-265-4913 | English | magnificent walks |
| Nigel Bell | | Airport: Heathrow |
| All year | | |

*14th century Devon thatched long house, oak panelling, screening, great fireplaces. Superb food & service, situated in small hamlet on river Teign. Restaurant 15% discount.*

## NORTH YORKSHIRE

| | | |
|---|---|---|
| **Ashfield House Hotel** | 48 English$ MAP | Full breakfast |
| Ashfield, Village | 7 rooms/suites, 7 pb | Restaurant (fee) |
| Grassington BD23 5AE | Visa, *Rated*, | Aftn. tea, sitting room |
| 01756-752584 | C-ltd/S-no/P-no/H-no | Yorkshire National Park |
| Linda & Keith Harrison | French, English | Airport: Leeds/Bradford/ |
| Feb to Dec | | Manchester |

*Small 17th century hotel central to cobbled village in Yorkshire Dales National Park. Home away from home comforts, informal & friendly. Private car park, walled rear garden.*

## NR. SIDMOUTH, DEVON

| | | |
|---|---|---|
| **Southern Cross** | 40 English$ | Clotted-cream teas |
| Newton Poppleford | English | Near sailing, fishing, |
| 011-44-1395-568439 | | golf, horse riding |
| John Blaymires/Angela | | antique shops, pubs |
| Karande | | |
| All year | | |

*17th-century cottage filled with exposed beams, furniture of the period, leaded pane windows. Newton Poppleford village is 4 miles from Sidmouth, a famous Devon resort.*

## PAINSWICK, GLOUCESTERSHIRE

| | | |
|---|---|---|
| **Painswick Hotel** | 88 English$ B&B | Full breakfast |
| Kemps Lane GL6 6YB | 20 rooms/suites, 20 pb | Lunch, dinner, restaurant |
| 0452-812160 | Visa, MC, AmEx, | Bar service, sitting room |
| Fax: 014-528-12160 | *Rated*, ● | library, bicycles |
| Somerset & Helene Moore | C-yes/S-ltd/P-yes/H-no | Airport: Birmingham |
| All year | French, Spanish, English | |

*Village center, 18th century stonebuilt former old rectory. Antiques, quiet, stunning views, walking. Award winning food. Friendly welcome high in Cotswold Hills.*

## PAR, CO. CORNWALL

**Nanscawen House**
Prideaux Rd., St.
Blazey  PL24 2SR
017-2681-4488
Fax: 017-2681-4488
Keith & Janet Martin
Closed Christmas

68 English$ B&B
3 rooms/suites, 3 pb
Visa, MC, *Rated*,
C-ltd/S-no/P-no/H-no
English

Full English breakfast
Bar service, aftn. tea
Sitting room
hot tubs
swimming pool
Airport: London, Bristol

*Granite-built Georgian house beautifully set in Luxulyan Valley. Luxurious rooms, each with spa bath. South facing garden of five acres.*

## PENRITH, CO.CUMBRIA

**Mill Hotel**
Mungrisdale  CA11 OXR
01-7687-79659
Richard & Eleanor Quinlan
Feb-Nov

110 English$ MAP
9 rooms/suites, 7 pb
*Rated*,
C-yes/S-yes/P-yes/H-no
English

Full breakfast
Restaurant (fee)
Bar service, library
sitting room
two acres of grounds
Airport: Manchester

*Lovely setting on two acres of grounds with Millrace waterfall & trout stream. Offers attractive accommodations, warm friendly service & imaginative cooking.*

## PENZANCE, CORNWALL

**Abbey Hotel**
Abbey St.  TR18 4AR
01-736-66906
Fax: 01-736-51163
Jean & Michael Cox
Closed 2 wks.at Xmas

85-130 English$ B&B/
MAP
7 rooms/suites, 7 pb
Most CC, *Rated*,
C-yes/S-yes/P-yes/H-no
English

Full English Breakfast
Dinner (fee), Aftn. tea
Near quaint old harbours,
Minack cliff-top theatre,
Lands End & other sites
Airport: Exeter

*Built in 1660, formerly a private home. Overlooks the harbour, bay out to St. Micheals Mount. Medieval walled garden, antiques.* **Winter break November to March 25% off.**

---

**Carnson House Hotel**
East Terrace  TR18 2TD
01736-65589
Trish and Richard Hilder
All year

38 English$ B&B
8 rooms/suites, 2 pb
Most CC, *Rated*, •
C-ltd/S-no/P-no/H-no
English, French,
German

Full breakfast
Bar service, sitting room
library
Airport: London, Bristol

*Small, comfortable, granite town house; central location near all transportation. Super food, friendly service. Excursions and carhire available.*

---

**Woodstock Guest House**
29 Morrab Rd.  TR18 4EZ
017-3636-9049
J. & C. Hopkins
All year

24 English$ EP
7 rooms/suites, 3 pb
Most CC, *Rated*,
C-yes/S-no/P-
yesFrench, English

Full breakfast
Airport: Plymouth, Land's
End

*Victorian guest house situated centrally in Penzance. Offering the best of English breakfasts to travellers visiting Penzance and the Land's End peninsula.*

## RYE, EAST SUSSEX

**Little Orchard House**
West Street  TN31 7ES
017-972-23831
Sara Brinkhurst
All year

60 English$ B&B
3 rooms/suites, 3 pb
Visa, MC
C-ltd/S-yes/P-no/H-no
English

Full breakfast
Complimentary wine
Sitting room, library
garden for guest use
Winter houseparties
Airport: Gatwick

*Elegant Georgian townhouse in medieval Rye. Antique furnishings, quiet central location, generous country breakfasts. Relaxed country house. Atmosphere is excellent.*

## SOUTHAMPTON, HAMPSHIRE

| | | |
|---|---|---|
| **Hunters Lodge Hotel** | 52 English$ B&B | Full breakfast |
| 25 Landguard Rd., | 18 rooms/suites, 18 pb | Lunch, dinner, snacks |
| Shirley  SO1 55DL | Most CC, *Rated*, • | Bar service, sitting room |
| 017-032-27919 | C-yes/S-yes/P-yes/H-ltd | library |
| Fax: 017-032-30913 | English | Airport: Eastleish, Heathrow |
| Mr. Steven George Dugdale | | |
| Closed Christmas | | |

*Friendly run family hotel, whose aim is to give good service at a reasonable price. Close to rail airport and the Jenny's Ports.*

## STRATFORD-UPON-AVON

| | | |
|---|---|---|
| **Victoria Spa Lodge Guest House** | 50 English$ B&B | Full breakfast |
| | 7 rooms/suites, 7 pb | Country setting by canal |
| Bishopton Lane  CV37 9QY | Most CC, *Rated*, | Grade II listed building |
| 017-892-67985 | C-yes/S-no/P-no/H-no | having Royal Coat of Arms |
| Fax: 017-892-04728 | French, English | Airport: Birmingham |
| Paul and D'reen Tozer | | |
| All year | | |

*Attractive & very comfortable home. Walks along tow-paths to Stratford & other villages. Once home to Sir Barry Jackson (founder of B'ham Rep:) & cartoonist Bruce Bairnsfather*

## THIRSK, YORKSHIRE

| | | |
|---|---|---|
| **Thornborough House Farm** | 29 English$ B&B | Full breakfast |
| South Kilvington  YO7 2NP | 3 rooms/suites, 3 pb | Dinner |
| 018-455-22103 | Visa, MC, *Rated*, | Sitting room |
| Fax: 018-455-22103 | C-yes/S-ltd/P-yes/H-no | Airport: Manchester |
| David & Tess Williamson | English | |
| All year | | |

*A warm welcome awaits you in our 200 year old farmhouse home. Good home cooking & comfortable rooms - near Thirsk where James Herriot the veterinarian practiced.*

## TIVERTON, CO. DEVON

| | | |
|---|---|---|
| **Little Holwell** | 16-19 English$ B&B/ | Full breakfast |
| Collipriest  EX16 4PT | MAP | Dinner available (fee) |
| 01884-257590 | 3 rooms/suites, 1 pb | Sitting room |
| Fax: 01884-257590 | Visa, MC, *Rated*, | welcome cup of tea |
| Mrs. Ruth Hill-King | C-ltd/S-no/P-no/H-no | peace and quiet |
| Closed Christmass | English | Airport: Heathrow, Gatwick |

*"Olde World" house set in rolling hills. Quiet location, ideal touring centre, a warm welcome awaits you.* **3–4 night breaks, weekly reductions.**

## TROWBRIDGE, CO. WILTSHIRE

| | | |
|---|---|---|
| **Old Manor Hotel** | 50-80 English$ B&B/ | Full breakfast |
| Trowle  BA14 9BL | MAP | Restaurant (fee) |
| 01225-777393 | 14 rooms/suites, 14 pb | Bar service, library |
| Fax: 01225-765443 | Most CC, *Rated*, • | sitting room |
| Barry & Diane Humphrey | C-yes/S-yes/P-no/H-yes | bicycles |
| All year | English | Airport: Bristol |

*500 year old farmstead hotel. Romantic bedrooms, all ensuite. Licensed restaurant. Quiet, south Bath. Good touring area, Cotswolds, Stonehenge.* **Nov. 1–March 31, free wine/champagne.**

## WILTSHIRE

| **The White Hart** | Rates: Inquire | Restaurant (fee) |
|---|---|---|
| Ford, near | 6 rooms/suites, 6 pb | Wide selection-real beer |
| Chippenham  SN14 8RP | English | Excellent golf courses |
| 01249-782213 | | skid pan instruction |
| Chris & Jenny Phillips | | interesting sites nearby |
| All year | | Airport: Heathrow |

*Built in 1553, constructed of stone, situated alongside the Bybrook River. Dine on terrace, contemplate nature. Can accommodate small business conferences.*

## WINDERMERE, CUMBRIA

| **The Archway** | 48 English$ B&B | Full breakfast |
|---|---|---|
| 13 College Rd.  LA23 1BU | 4 rooms/suites, 4 pb | Continental plus bkfst. |
| 015-394-45613 | Most CC, *Rated*, | Bar service, library |
| Anthony & Aurea | C-ltd/S-no/P-no/H-no | sitting soom |
| Greenhalgh   All year | English, some French | Airport: Manchester |

*Civilized Victorian guest house (exclusively non-smoking). Antiques, interesting paintings and prints. Good boks, fresh flowers. Goumet home cooking, home-baked bread.*

| **Holbeck Ghyll Country House** | 130 English$ MAP | Full breakfast |
|---|---|---|
| Holbeck Lane  LA23 1LU | 14 rooms/suites, 13 pb | Dinner, tea, lunch |
| 015-394-32375 | Most CC, *Rated*, • | Bar service, sitting room |
| Fax: 015-394-34743 | C-yes/S-ltd/P-yes/H-no | tennis court |
| David & Patricia Nicholson | French, English | 7 acres, health spa |
| All year | | Airport: Manchester |

*19th century hunting lodge, breathtaking views across Lake Windermere. Oak-panelling, stained glass, log fires, luxury hotel, peaceful setting. Romantic, outstanding & modest.*

| **Windermere Guest House** | 22 English$ B&B | Full breakfast |
|---|---|---|
| Prince's Rd.  LA23 2DD | 7 rooms/suites, 7 pb | Sitting room |
| 015-394-43907 | Visa, *Rated*, • | Airport: Manchester |
| Fax: 015-394-43907 | C-yes/S-no/P-yes/H-no | |
| Mr. Neil Cox | English | |
| All year | | |

*A Victorian stone house. Between Windermere and Bowness. Quiet yet convenient. All rooms tastefully furnished, some have poster beds. Friendly service. Tours arranged.*

## WINDLESHAM, SURREY

| **The Hedges** | 390 English$ B&B | Full breakfast |
|---|---|---|
| Church Road  GU206BH | English | Gourmet dinners available |
| 011-44-1276-471251 | | Private transportation |
| Mr. & Mrs. Peter Braithwaite | | escorted sightseeing |
| | | sports arrangements |
| | | Airport: Heathrow/Gatwick |

*Don't want to rent a car? Couple in Surrey, luxury B&B, gourmet dinners, will personally drive you anywhere including to & from airport. Can accommodate two couples at a time.*

## YETMINSTER, SHERBORNE

| **Manor Farmhouse** | 50 English$ B&B/MAP | Full breakfast |
|---|---|---|
| High Street, Dorset  DT9 6LF | 4 rooms/suites, 4 pb | Dinner-bookings required |
| 01-935-872247 | Visa, MC, *Rated*, | Restaurant |
| Ann & Jack Partridge | C-ltd/S-no/P-no/H-yes | sitting room |
| All year | English | library |
| | | Airport: Bristol-Heathrow-Gatwick |

*Historic 17th century farmhouse in village setting, family ambience. Good center for exploring midwest. Ann offers historic & geographic knowledge of Dorset. 7 nights for 6*

## YORK

| | | |
|---|---|---|
| **Byron House Hotel** | 55 English$ B&B | Full breakfast |
| The Mount  YO2 2DD | 10 rooms/suites, 7 pb | Dinner |
| 019-046-32525 | Most CC, *Rated*, • | Bar service, sitting room |
| Fax: 019-046-38904 | C-yes/S-yes/P-no/H-no | family friendly facility |
| Dick & Jean Tyson | English | Airport: Manchester |
| Closed Christmas | | |

*Late Georgian property circa 1830. Spacious comfortable double rooms, easy walking distance from city center. Excellent food, and friendly personal service.*

## YORK, NORTH YORKSHIRE

| | | |
|---|---|---|
| **Curzon Lodge & Stable** | 52 English$ B&B | Full English breakfast |
| **Cottages** | 10 rooms/suites, 10 pb | Restaurants nearby |
| 23 Tadcaster Rd., | Visa, MC, *Rated*, | Complimentary sherry |
| Dringhouses  YO2 2QG | C-yes/S-ltd/P-no/H-no | sitting room, car park |
| 019-047-03157 | English | bus service-city centre |
| Richard & Wendy Wood | | Airport: Manchester |
| All year | | |

*Delightful 17th century 'listed' house & former stables in conservation area close to Historic center. Many antiques. Cottage style bedrooms all en-suite. Parking in grounds.*

# Fiji, Pacific Islands

## SUVA

| | | |
|---|---|---|
| **Homestay Suva** | 85 US$ Inquire | Full breakfast |
| 265 Princes Road  2259 | 4 rooms/suites, 4 pb | Tea, snacks, dinner, wine |
| 011-679-370-395 | • | Sitting room |
| Fax: 011-679-370-947 | C-ltd/S-no/P-no/H-yes | swimming pool |
| Bruce & Lesley Phillips | English | newly opened B&B |
| All year | | Airport: Nadi |

*Our restored colonial home has panoramic views of Suva Bay. Full breakfast on shaded decks. **Fruit basket on arrival, wine with dinner, daily newspaper.***

# France

## ALOXE-CORTON, BURGUNDY

| | | |
|---|---|---|
| **Hotel Clarion** | 650 French$ B&B | Full breakfast |
|  21420 | 10 rooms/suites, 10 pb | Afternoon tea, comp. wine |
| 33-03-80-26-46-70 | Visa, MC, *Rated*, | Bar service, sitting room |
| Fax: 33-03-80-26-47-16 | C-yes/S-yes/P-yes/H-yes | library, bicycles |
| Christian Voarick    All year | English, German, Dutch | Airport: Paris, Lyon |

*Mansion House dated 1679 - art deco furnished, opening to large garden & vineyards, excellent breakfast. Very quiet, perfectly situated for wine & Burgundy lovers. **Free wine.***

ARLES, PROVENCE——————————————————————————————

| | | |
|---|---|---|
| **Grand Hotel Nord Pinus** | 760 French$ B&B | Continental-full (ask) |
| Place du Forum  13200 | 22 rooms/suites, 22 pb | Restuarant (fee) |
| 33-90-93-44-44 | Most CC | Bar service |
| Fax: 33-90-93-34-00 | • | sitting room |
| Mrs. Ann Jgou | C-yes/S-yes/P-yes/H-yes | near sea, horseriding |
| All year | Eng., Ger., It., Spanish | Airport: Marseille, Nimes |

*Charming hotel, center of town. Surrounding area offers golf courses, tennis courts, horseriding. In July the Festival of Photographie International, bullfights.*

BANNEGON——————————————————————————————————

| | | |
|---|---|---|
| **Auberge du Moulin de** | 350 French$ | Continental breakfast |
| **Chameron**  18210 | 13 rooms/suites, 13 pb | Restaurant (fee) |
| 48-61-83-80 | Visa, MC, AmEx | Bar serv., swimming pool |
| Fax: 48-61-84-92 | C-yes/S-yes/P-yes/H-no | summer meals outside |
| Mr. & Mrs. Candore | French, English, | Airport: Paris |
| March-November | German | |

*Dining rooms in the old mill. Collection of machinery & tools used by millers kept intact. Bedrooms in separate annex overlooking garden. Ground floor rooms private terrace.*

BAYEUX, NORMANDIE——————————————————————————————

| | | |
|---|---|---|
| **Hotel d'Argouges** | 280 French$ B&B(fee) | Continental breakfast |
| 21 rue Saint-Patrice  14400 | 25 rooms/suites, 25 pb | Full bkfst. on request |
| 02-31-92-88-86 | Visa, MC, AmEx, | Minibar in room, terrace |
| Fax: 02-31-92-69-16 | *Rated*, • | garden, sitting room |
| Mr. Auregan | C-yes/S-yes/P-yes/H-no | Airport: CAEN |
| All year | English, French | |

*In the heart of Bayeux, a mansion of the 18th century. Rooms specially decorated. Quiet, small park and flower gardens.* **Stay 3 nights, one night free.**

BRANTOME, DORDOGNE——————————————————————————————

| | | |
|---|---|---|
| **Vue de l'Abbaye** | 250 French$ EP | Morning coffee/tea |
| 3 Place d'Albret  24310 | 4 rooms/suites, 4 pb | Dining nearby |
| 53-05-70-01 | • | Bicycles |
| Fax: 53-05-70-01 | C-yes/S-yes/P-yes/H-no | swimming pool nearby |
| Mme. R.M. Davies | French, English | tennis court |
| All year | | Airport: Bordeaux |

*Situated in a small square of a charming Medieval/Renaissance town. Facilities for canoeing, bicycling, hiking, tennis, golf, swimming, as well as sightseeing.*

CARSAC-AILLAC, DORDOGNE——————————————————————————

| | | |
|---|---|---|
| **Le Relais du Touron** | 265 French$ B&B | Breakfast (fee 36FF) |
| 24200 | 12 rooms/suites, 12 pb | Dinner, restaurant, wine |
| 33-53-28-16-70 | Visa, MC | Afternoon tea, pool |
| Fax: 33-53-28-52-51 | • | TV lounge, fishing |
| Claudine Carlier | C-yes/S-yes/P-yes/H-ltd | Rooms from 265 to 375 FF |
| April-November | English, Italian, Arabic | Airport: Bordeaux |

*Le Relais du Touron offers a friendly atmosphere, plus good regional and traditional cooking. Set in a large park. Near castles & golf.* **Free bottle of wine.**

CHAMONIX-MONT-BLANC ───────────────────────────────

| **Hotel Albert 1er** | 640-1070 French$ | Restaurant (fee) |
|---|---|---|
| 119 Impasse du | Inquire | Bar service |
| Montenvers 74402 | 30 rooms/suites, 30 pb | Sitting room, library |
| 50-53-05-09 | Most CC | sauna, mini golf |
| Fax: 50-55-95-48 | • | swimming pool, skiing |
| Pierre & Martine Carrier | C-yes/S-yes/P-yes | Airport: Geneva |
| Inquire about season | English, German, | |
| | Spanish | |

*A small family hotel which combines Alpine charm and modern comfort, with a famous restaurant.*

CONDOM ───────────────────────────────────────

| **Hotel des Trois Lys** | 440 French$ EP | Full breakfast (fee) |
|---|---|---|
| 38 rue Gambetta 32100 | 10 rooms/suites, 10 pb | Lunch, dinner |
| 62-28-33-33 | Visa, MC, AmEx | Bar service, sitting room |
| Fax: 62-28-41-85 | • | tennis courts, pool |
| Jeannette Manet | C-yes/S-yes/P-yes/H-yes | new restaurant |
| Closed February | English, Spanish, Italian | Airport: Toulouse |

*The Hotel is a marvellous mixture of tradition and modernization. It is the perfect balance between the architectural style of the 18th century, and the comfort of the 20th.*

GANGES ────────────────────────────────────────

| **Chateau de Madieres** | 650 French$ EP | Continental bkfst. (fee) |
|---|---|---|
| Madieres 34190 | 10 rooms/suites, 10 pb | Lunch, dinner, restaurant |
| 67-73-84-03 | Visa, MC, AmEx, | Bar service, sitting room |
| Fax: 67-73-55-71 | *Rated*, | library, swimming pool |
| Bernard and Francoise | C-yes/S-yes/P-yes/H-ltd | Airport: Montpellier |
| Brucy | English, German, | |
| March-November | French | |

*Behind its superbly austere walls, this fourteenth century chateau harbors absolute charm: intimate guest rooms, vaulted restaurant and patios, library.* **Free bottle of wine.**

HUSSEREN-LES-CHATEAUX, ALSACE ────────────────────────

| **Hotel Husseren-les-** | 350 French$ B&B | Full breakfast |
|---|---|---|
| **Chateaux** | 38 rooms/suites, 38 pb | Lunch, dinner, restaurant |
| Rue du Schlossberg 68420 | Most CC, *Rated*, • | Bar service, sitting room |
| 89-49-22-93 | C-yes/S-yes/P-yes/H-yes | library, tennis, sauna |
| Fax: 89-49-24-84 | Eng., Ger., Fr., Dan. | Airport: Mulhouse/Bale |
| Karin & Lucas De Jong | | |
| All year | | |

*Situated in an elevated position on the foothills of the Vosges Mtns., this brand new hotel provides panoramic views over the vineyards and picturesque villages.*

LA BAUME DE TRANSIT ──────────────────────────────

| **Domaine de St-Luc** | 270 French$ B&B/MAP | Continental plus bkfst. |
|---|---|---|
| 26790 | 5 rooms/suites, | Dinner available |
| 75-98-11-51 | C-ltd/S-no/P-no/H-yes | Countryside setting, |
| Fax: 75-98-19-22 | English, French | peace and tranquility |
| Ludovic & Eliane Cornillon | | near wineries |
| All year | | Airport: Marignane |

*An old farmhouse of XVIII Century. Full countryside, flowered courtyard. Excellent cook using provincial vegetables, served with the wines of the Domaine.* **Free bottle of wine.**

## LA GRISOLIERE

| | | |
|---|---|---|
| **La Bastide de Moustiers** | 700 French$ EP | Breakfast & lunch (fee) |
| 59 Avenue Raymond | 7 rooms/suites, 7 pb | Heated pool, private car |
| Poincare' 75116 | French | park, mtn. bike rental |
| 1-47-27-12-27 | | |
| Fax: 1-47-27-31-22 | | |
| Dominique Potier | | |

*Formerly the property of a master-potter, La Bastide with its seven bedrooms, each named after Provencial themes, combines refinement, comfort and simplicity.*

## LA JAILLE-YVON

| | | |
|---|---|---|
| **Chateau du Plessis** | 750 French$ | Continental plus bkfst. |
| 49220 | 8 rooms/suites, 8 pb | Restaurant (fee) |
| 33-02-41-95-12-75 | Visa, MC, AmEx, | Sitting room, library |
| Fax: 33-02-41-95-14-41 | *Rated*, • | bicycles, croquet |
| Mme. & M. Paul Benoist | C-yes/S-yes/P-no/H-no | Airport: Nantes |
| Jan. 4-Nov. 11 | English, Spanish, French | |

*Aristocratic country home, one of France's most exceptional private chateau-hotels. Elegant furnishings, lush grounds, country fresh cuisine (reservations). **Free bottle wine.***

## LES BAUX-DE-PROVENCE

| | | |
|---|---|---|
| **Hotel La Benvengudo** | 530 French$ B&B(fee) | Full breakfast (fee) |
| D 78  13520 | 20 rooms/suites, 20 pb | Restaurant, tea, snacks |
| 90-54-32-54 | Visa, MC, AmEx, | Bar service,swimming pool |
| Fax: 90-54-42-58 | *Rated*, | tennis court, library |
| Beaupied family | C-yes/S-yes/P-yes/H-yes | golf courses nearby |
| Feb 1 - Nov 1 | English, German, Italian | Airport: Marseille |

*L'Auberge is tucked away along the valley. Converted 19th century farmhouse, all rooms furnished with antiques. Very quiet, A/C. Mediterranean style cuisine - very fresh.*

## MAREUIL, DORDOONE

| | | |
|---|---|---|
| **Chateau de Vieux-Mareuil** | 130-290 French$ B&B/ | Continental plus bkfst. |
| Route D'Angouleme- | MAP | Restaurant (fee) |
| Perigueux 23340  24340 | 14 rooms/suites, 14 pb | Bar service, sitting room |
| 53-60-77-15 | Most CC, *Rated*, • | library, bicycles |
| Fax: 53-56-4933 | C-yes/S-yes/H-ltd | swimming pool |
| A.AlbertInquire | English, Ger, It, Spanish | Airport: Bordeaux |

*XIV and XV century castle. Beautifully restored. Set amidst extensive grounds in a charming rural setting of wooded hills and fields. Relax in silence.*

## MEURSAULT

| | | |
|---|---|---|
| **Hotel Les Magnolias** | 380-750 French$ | Continental breakfast |
| 8 Rue Pierre Joigneaux  21190 | 12 rooms/suites, 12 pb | Afternoon tea |
| 03-80-21-23-23 | Most CC, *Rated*, • | Bar service, sitting room |
| Fax: 03-80-21-29-10 | C-yes/S-ltd/P-no/H-yes | library |
| Toni Delarue | English, German, | Airport: Lyon, Paris, Dijon |
| March-November | French | |

*Hotel Les Magnolias is situated in a peaceful wine growing village in the heart of Burgundy. It dates from the 18th century. Each room has its own style and character.*

## NOVES

| | | |
|---|---|---|
| **Auberge de Noves** | 1150 French$ BB/EP/ | Restaurant (fee) |
| Dom.du Deves,Rte.de | MAP | Bar service,lunch,dinner |
| Chateaurenard  13550 | 23 rooms/suites, 23 pb | Swimming pool, bicycles |
| 90-94-19-21 | Visa, MC, AmEx, | tennis court, terraces |
| Fax: 90-94-47-76 | *Rated*, • | sitting room, gardens |
| Famille Lalleman    All year | C-yes/S-yes/P-yes/H-yes | Airport: Marseille, Provence |

*3 generation 19th century manor house. Generous breakfasts, relax by pool, panoramic valley view. Light Provencal flavours by candlelight under the stars. **Aperitifs; cafes.***

ORNAISONS, NARBONNE, LANGUEDOC────────────────────

| | | |
|---|---|---|
| **Le Relais du Val D'Orbieu** | 500 French$ B&B | Continental breakfast |
| Route Departemantape | 20 rooms/suites, 20 pb | Restaurant (fee, lunch, |
| 24  11200 | Most CC, *Rated*, • | Bar service, sitting room |
| 33-68-27-10-27 | C-yes/S-yes/P-yes/H-ltd | library, bicycles, pool |
| Fax: 33-68-27-52-44 | English, Spanish, French | Airport: Toulouse, |
| Agnes & Jean-Pierre | | Montpellier |
| Gonzalvez    All year | | |

*Facing the picturesque Montagne Noire, Le Relais sits in an atmosphere of calm. Delicious breakfasts are served, filled with fresh fruit & pasteries.* **3rd night 50% off.**

PARIS──────────────────────────────────────

| | | |
|---|---|---|
| **Hotel de Banville** | 635 French$ EP | Full breakfast |
| 166 Boulevard | 40 rooms/suites, 40 pb | Afternoon tea, snacks |
| Berthier  75017 | Visa, MC, AmEx, | Bar service, sitting room |
| 01-42-67-70-16 | *Rated*, • | library |
| Fax: 014-44-042-77 | C-yes/S-yes/P-yes/H-no | Airport: Roissy, Charles de |
| Marianne Lambert | English, Dutch, Spanish | Gaulle |
| All year | | |

*Warm French atmosphere near Etoile and Champs Elysees. Individuality and seduction in each of the 40 rooms. A tasteful selection of fabrics and paintings.* **Welcome cocktail.**

| | | |
|---|---|---|
| **Hotel Des Deux Iles** | 720-830 French$ B&B | Continental Breakfast |
| 59 Rue Saint Louis En | 17 rooms/suites, 17 pb | Afternoon tea |
| L'Ile  75004 | Most CC | Sitting room |
| 43-26-13-35 | C-yes/S-yes/P-yes/H-no | air conditioning |
| Fax: 43-29-60-25 | French, English, Spanish | cable TV |
| Roland Buffat | | |
| All year | | |

*A converted townhouse of the 17th century; imaginative country-style decor. Centrally located and close to most monuments. Easy access by private & public transportation.*

| | | |
|---|---|---|
| **Hotel des Tuileries** | 750 French$ B&B | Continental plus bkfst. |
| 10, Rue Saint- | 26 rooms/suites, 26 pb | Afternoon tea |
| Hyacinthe  75001 | Most CC | Sitting room, room serv. |
| 1-42-61-04-17 | • | air-conditioned rooms |
| Fax: 1-49-27-91-56 | C-yes/S-yes/P-yes/H-no | Airport: Orly, Charles de |
| Poulle-Vidal Family | English, Sp., It., Dutch | Gaulle |
| All year | | |

*Eighteenth century residence. Privileged location next to the Tuileries, Louvre, Orsay Museums, and Place Vendome.* **Complimentary bottle of champagne.**

| | | |
|---|---|---|
| **Hotel Eber** | 610 French$ B&B | Continental breakfast |
| 18 rue Leon Jost  75017 | 18 rooms/suites, 18 pb | Lunch, dinner, aftn. tea |
| 1-46-22-60-70 | Most CC, *Rated*, • | Bar service |
| Fax: 1-47-63-01-01 | C-yes/S-yes/P-no/H-no | family room |
| Jean-Marc Eber | English, German, | 20% discount on August |
| All year | French | Airport: Charles de Gaulle, |
| | | Orly |

*The turn-of-the-century house in a residential Paris area, near Champs Elysees, & the Parc Monceau. Breakfast is wonderful, including an array of teas.* **Discounts, inquire.**

## PARIS

**Hotel le Clos Medicis**
56 Rue Monsieur le
Prince 75006
1-43-29-10-80
Fax: 143-54-26-90
All year

792 French$ B&B
38 rooms/suites, 38 pb
Most CC, *Rated*, •
C-yes/S-yes/P-yes/H-yes
English, Italian, Spanish

Buffet breakfast
Afternoon tea, comp. wine
Bar service, sitting room
fireplaces, garden
Airport: Roissy Charles
Gaulle

*Formerly private residence dating to 1860. Magnificent provencal style house. Attractive garden & lounge with open fire. Elegant surroundings. **3rd night 50% or free breakfast.***

---

**Hotel Solferino**
91 Rue de Lille 75007
1-47-05-85-54
Fax: 1-45-55-51-16
Closed Christmas

460 French$ B&B
33 rooms/suites, 27 pb
Most CC
C-yes/S-yes/P-yes/H-no
French, English

Continental plus bkfst.
Afternoon tea
Sitting room
Near La Siene
Airport: CDG/ORLY

*Simple elegant rooms done in fresh colours. Charming lounge, sky-lit breakfast room. Relaxing; pleasantly antiquated.*

---

**Le Relais-Hotel du Vieus**
rue Git-le-Cour 75006
011-33-1-43-54-41-66
Fax: 011-33-1-43-26-99-15

1070 French$ B&B
English

Continental breakfast
In Latin quarter
ancient streets are still
narrow and winding

*The building dates back to 1480. Rooms open onto a courtyard where you can sit in a window overlooking rooftops. Private baths and delicious continental breakfasts.*

## PAULHIAC, AQUITAINE

**L'Ormeraie**
47150  GL52 6ST
53-36-45-96
Fax: 533-645-96
Michel de L'Ormeraie
April-September

Rates: Inquire B&B
5 rooms/suites, 5 pb
Most CC
C-yes/S-yes/P-yes/H-no
English

Continental plus bkfst.
Comp. wine 3rd night
Sitting room, library
bicycles
tennis, swimming pool

*In an unspoiled part of the countryside. Seventeenth century residence, old personalities. Pool, homemade breakfast outside in beautiful surroundings.*

## PROVENCE

**Le Mas d'Aigret**
Les Baux de Provence  13520
33-90-54-33-54
Fax: 33-9054-3354
Pip Phillips, Frederic Laloy
Feb 25-Jan 5

500-950 French$ Inquire
16 rooms/suites, 16 pb
Most CC, *Rated*,
C-yes/S-yes/P-yes/H-no
English, French

Continental plus bkfst.
Restaurant (fee)
Bar service
sitting room, library
swimming pool
Airport: Marseille

*This charming 350 year old farmhouse offers magnificent views of the Camargne and Mediterranean. A family run business with a wonderfully relaxed and friendly atmosphere.*

## SAINT-CIRQ LAPOPIE

**Hotel De La Pelissaria**
46330
65-31-25-14
Fax: 65-30-25-52
April 1-November 15

400 French$ MAP
10 rooms/suites, 10 pb
Visa, MC
•
C-yes/S-yes/P-yes
English, French Italian

Continental breakfast
Restaurant, bar service
Complimentary wine, tea
sitt. rm., swimming pool
Airport: Toulouse

*13th century house in a medieval village ("The first village of France" - say the "Beaux-Arts") with the river Lot just beyond.*

## SAINT-DIDIER

**Hotel Pen'Roc**
La Peiniere  35220
02-99-00-33-02
Fax: 02-99-62-30-89
Mireille et Joseph Froc
All year

534 French$ B&B
33 rooms/suites, 33 pb
Visa, MC, AmEx,
*Rated*, •
C-yes/S-yes/P-yes/H-yes
French, English

Full breakfast
Aftn.tea, restaurant(fee)
Bar, sauna, swimming pool
bicycles, sitting room
Airport: Rennes

*At only 12 km from Vitre, hospitality awaits you in the heart of the countryside. The ideal stopover for relaxation and culinary delights. **10% off restaurant meal only.***

## SOMMIERES, LANGUEDOC

**Auberge du Pont Romain**
2 Avenue Emile
Jamais  30250
04-66-80-00-58
Fax: 04-66-80-31-52
Monique & Bernard Michel
March 16-Jan 14

450 French$ B&B
18 rooms/suites, 14 pb
Most CC
•
C-yes/S-yes/P-yes/H-yes
French, English, Spanish

Full breakfast
Lunch, dinner, restaurant
Bar service, bicycles
swimming pool warmed up
in May & October
Airport: Montpellier

*17th century house ideal location for excursions to Camargue, the sea, Cevennes, Nimes, Montpellier. Guest rooms open to a peaceful park. Near tennis, golf, bull races.*

## ST-GERMAIN-EN-LAYE

**Cazaudehore La Forestiere**
1 avenue du President-
Kennedy  78100
34-51-93-80
Fax: 397-373-88
Cazaudehore Family
All year

950 French$ EP
30 rooms/suites, 30 pb
Visa, MC, AmEx,
*Rated*, •
C-yes/S-no/P-yes/H-no
English, French

Lunch, dinner, restaurant
Bar service, sitting room
tennis court
Airport: Roissy

*All bedrooms are different, each expresses an atmosphere. Some have shades of saffron, mixed with hard blue and thunder green. Terrasse with beautiful array of roses.*

## ST-MARTIN-VALMEROUX

**Hostellerie de la Maronne**
Le Theil  15140
71-69-20-33
Fax: 71-69-28-22
Alain and Lalasoa DeCock
January-May

Rates: Inquire
25 rooms/suites, 25 pb
Visa, AmEx
•
C-yes/S-yes/P-yes/H-yes
English, Spanish, French

Continental bkfst. (fee)
Lunch, dinner, restaurant
Bar service, sitting room
bicycles, tennis, pool
new improved rooms
Airport: Clermont Ferrand

*A house dating from 19th century. Very peaceful valley. Close to castles, churches, walks, river. Heart of volcanic area. Complimentary bottle of wine.*

## STRASBOURG

**Hotel Cathedrale**
12 Place De La
Cathedrale  67000
03-88-22-12-12
Fax: 03-88-23-28-00
Edith Beckers
All year

Rates: Inquire
40 rooms/suites, 29 pb
Most CC
•
C-yes/S-yes/P-yes/H-yes
English, German

Continental bkfst. (fee)
Room, bar service (fee)
Near shops, museum
theater, boating nearby
Airport: Strasbourg,
Entzheim

*Charming hotel in city center, entirely renovated, historical area. Room with beaufiful view of the Cathedral. Elegant bar, buffet breakfast, porter.*

## STRASBOURG, ALSACE

**Hotel du Dragon**
2 rue de l'Ecarlate 67000
33-88-35-79-80
Fax: 33-88-25-78-95
Pierre Iannarelli
All year

565 French$ B&B
32 rooms/suites, 32 pb
Most CC, *Rated*, •
C-yes/S-ltd/H-yes
English, Sp., It., Ger.

Continental breakfast
Afternoon tea
Bar service, sitting room
court yard in front
Airport: Strasbourg SXB

*Down a quiet street of the old part of town, a 17th century house converted into a very modern, cool, contemporary decorated hotel. Special holiday rates available*

## VAR, LES ADRETS DE L'ESTEREL

**Domaine du Grand Jas**
Baisse de Donat 83600
33-04-94-40-97-76
Fax: 33-04-94-40-97-80
Pamela & Olivier Demacon

105-210 French$ AP
3 rooms/suites, 3 pb
Visa, *Rated*, •
C-yes/S-yes/P-yes/H-yes
English, French

Continental plus bkfst.
Restaurant (fee)
Sitting room, library
bikes, tennis court
swimming pool
Airport: Nice International

*Hidden in the heart of the Esterel Mountains between Provence & the French Riviera. Prestigious accomodations, great service & facilities. Mosaic pool overlooks bay.*

## VERVINS, PICARDIE

**La Tour du Roy**
45 rue de General
Leclerc 02140
33-03-23-98-00
Fax: 33-0323-9800-72
Annie Desvignes
All year

450-800 French$ Inquire
18 rooms/suites, 18 pb
Most CC
•
C-yes/S-yes/P-yes/H-yes
English

Restaurant (fee)
Lunch, dinner, snacks
Bar service
sitting room
Airport: Paris, Bruxelles

*A Manor house where Henry IV's ascension to the throne was announced. Stained-glass windows, rooms overlooking terraces, park or landscaped square. **Free glass champagne.***

## VEZELAY, BURGUNDY

**Residence Hotel Le Pontot**
Place du Pontot 89450
03-86-33-24-40
Fax: 03-86-33-3005
Christian Abadie
Easter-Nov 1

1050 French$ EP
10 rooms/suites, 10 pb
Most CC, *Rated*, •
C-yes/S-yes/P-yes/H-no
English, French

Continental plus (fee)
Afternoon tea
Bar service, sitting room
walled flower garden
Airport: Orly

*Glamorous 15th century mansion in medieval Burgundian village. Breakfast in flowered garden. Vineyards, chateaux, abbays near for visiting. Helicopter landing on premises.*

## VILLERS-COTTERETS-PICARDY L'AISNE

**Hotel Le Regent**
26 rue du General
Mangin 02600
03-23-96-01-46
Fax: 03-23-96-37-57
Michele Thiebaut
All year

Rates: Inquire B&B
17 rooms/suites, 17 pb
Most CC, *Rated*,
C-yes/S-yes/P-yes/H-yes
French, English

Snacks
Sitting room
hot tubs
Airport: Charles De Gaulle

*This eighteenth century house represents the charm of "before" and the comfort of "today.S*

# Germany

## HINTERZARTEN, BADEN

| | | |
|---|---|---|
| **Sassenhof** | 92-106 German$ B&B | Full breakfast |
| Adlerweg 17  79856 | 22 rooms/suites, 22 pb | Afternoon tea, comp. wine |
| 07652-15-15 | C-yes/S-yes/P- | 5 sitting rooms, library |
| Fax: 07652-484 | ltdEnglish, Spanish, | bicycles, sauna, pool |
| I. Pfeiffer | German | Airport: Zurich |
| Closed Nov-Dec | | |

*In the center of our charming village, between meadows & absolutely quiet. Excellent breakfast with buffet. Flowers and herb tea in winter garden. 4th night 50% off.*

## KRONBERG, HESSEN

| | | |
|---|---|---|
| **Schlosshotel Kronberg** | 480-700 German$ | Restaurant (fee) |
| Hainstrasse 25  61476 | 58 rooms/suites, 58 pb | Lunch, dinner, snacks |
| 06-173-70101 | Most CC | Bar service |
| Fax: 06-173-701267 | • | library |
| All year | C-yes/S-yes/P-yes/H-yes | golf paradise |
| | German, English, | Airport: Frankfurt |
| | French | |

*Combines atmosphere, luxury with unique architecture. Large old park, beautiful gardens. Close to Frankfurt. Golf paradise. **Fruits, mineral water, souvenir, fresh flowers.***

## MARKTHEIDENFELD, BAVARIA

| | | |
|---|---|---|
| **Hotel Anker** | 170 German$ B&B | Full breakfast |
| Obertorstrasse 6  97828 | 39 rooms/suites, 39 pb | Lunch, dinner, restaurant |
| +49-9391/6004-0 | Most CC, *Rated*, • | Bar service, sitting room |
| Fax: +49-9391/6004-77 | C-yes/S-ltd/H-yes | library, tennis, bicycles |
| Deppisch Family | English, French, Dutch | Airport: Frankfurt |
| All year | | |

*Charming hotel in ancient city, well-furnished, pretty salons around a lovely courtyard-garden. Family house atmosphere and lavish bathroom facilities. Excellent restaurant.*

## OFFENBURG

| | | |
|---|---|---|
| **Hotel Sonne** | 98-190 German$ | Full breakfast |
| Hauptstrasse 94  77652 | 34 rooms/suites, 27 pb | Restaurant (fee) |
| 0781-7-10-39 | Visa, MC, AmEx | Starting point for |
| Fax: 078-171-033 | C-yes/S-yes/P-yes/H-no | excursions to Baden-Baden |
| All year | English, French, | Airport: Strasburg |
| | German | |

*One of the oldest hotels in Germany. Rooms are furnished with antique furnitures of the 19th century. Center of Offenburg next to baroque townhall.*

## PFRONTEN, BAYERS

| | | |
|---|---|---|
| **Berghotel Schlossanger** | 160 German$ B&B | Full breakfast |
| **Alp** | 30 rooms/suites, 30 pb | Restaurant (fee), lunch |
| Am Schlossanger 1  87459 | Visa, MC, AmEx | Sitting room, sauna |
| 08-363-1381 | • | swimming pool |
| Fax: 083-631-6667 | C-yes/S-yes/H-no | Airport: Munich, Stuttgaut |
| Schlachter & Ebert Family | English, French, | |
| | German | |

*The chalet is built amid open fields, full of wooden beams & local folk ornaments. A comfortable room & excellent breakfast awaits you. **Welcome drink upon arrival.***

RUDESHEIM-ASSMANNS-HAUSEN ──────────────────────────

| | | |
|---|---|---|
| **Krone Assmannshausen** | 180-250 German$ | Full breakfast |
| Rheinuferstrasse 10  65385 | 65 rooms/suites, 65 pb | Lunch, dinner, restaurant |
| 067-224-030 | Most CC | Bar service, sitting room |
| Fax: 067-223-049 | • | hot tubs, sauna, pool |
| Hufnagel-Ullrich Family | C-yes/S-yes/P-yes/H-no | Airport: Rhein-Main, |
| | Eng., Fr., Sp., It., Dut. | Frankfurt |

*This B&B stands on the Rhine as if painted there, small towers, spires & wooden balconies create impression of a castle. Oldest part of building is over 450 years old.*

# Guatemala

ANTIGUA ──────────────────────────────────────

| | | |
|---|---|---|
| **Posada del Angel** | 97 US$ B&B | Full breakfast |
| 4a Avenida Sur #24 "A" | 4 rooms/suites, 4 pb | Snacks, comp. wine |
| 011-502-9-320-260800-934-0065 | Visa, MC, AmEx, | Golf, horseback riding |
| Mary Sue Morris | *Rated*, • | mtn. bikes, tennis, pool |
| All year | C-ltd/S-ltd/P-no/H-no | comp. glass of wine |
| | English, Spanish | Airport: Guatemala |
| | | International |

*Romantic, elegant, comfortable Spanish Colonial Inn. Fireplaces & cable TV in each room. Perfect spring climate, beautiful vistas, centrally located. 10% discount per month.*

# Hungary

BUDAPEST ───────────────────────────────────────

| | | |
|---|---|---|
| **Beatrix Panzio** | 100 Hung$ B&B | Full breakfast |
| Szeher ut. 3  1021 | 12 rooms/suites, 12 pb | Afternoon tea, snacks |
| 361-275-0550 | • | Bar service, sitting room |
| Fax: 361-176-3730 | C-yes/S-yes/P-yes/H-no | sauna |
| Martinecz Gyorgy | English, French, | Airport: Budapest, Ferlhegy |
| All year | German | |

*A cozy house located in the green belt of Budapest. Winner of the "Guest house of the Year" award by the Association of Guest Houses in Budapest. Free bottle of champagne*

# Ireland

BALLYMOTE, CO. SLIGO ─────────────────────────────

| | | |
|---|---|---|
| **Temple House** | 80 Irish$ B&B/MAP | Full breakfast |
| 071-83329 | 5 rooms/suites, 4 pb | Dinner, tea, snacks |
| Fax: 071-83808 | Most CC, *Rated*, • | Sitting room |
| Deb & Sandy Perceval | C-yes/S-yes/P-no/H-no | tennis court, hot tubs |
| Closed Dec 1-Easter | French | baby sitting |
| | | Airport: Dublin/Shannon |

*Family owned Georgian mansion on 1000 acres overlooking 13th century castle. Sheep farm, canopy beds, boats. Featured in Bon Appetit.*

**BANTRY BAY, CO CORK** ─────────────────────────────────

| | | |
|---|---|---|
| **Ballylickey Manor House** | 90 Irish$ B&B | Full breakfast |
| Ballylickey | 12 rooms/suites, 12 pb | Lunch, dinner, aftn. tea |
| 353-27-50071 | Visa, MC, AmEx, | Bar service, sitting room |
| Fax: 353-27-50124 | *Rated*, • | library, swimming pool |
| Mr. & Mrs. Graves | C-yes/S-yes/P-no/H-no | Airport: Cork |
| March-November | French, Spanish, | |
| | German | |

*Ballylickey overlooks beautiful Bantry Bay, in the midst of magnificent scenery and within easy reach of Killarney. A wide variety of sports and leisures are offered nearby.*

**BANTRY, COUNTY CORK** ─────────────────────────────────

| | | |
|---|---|---|
| **Bantry House** | 50-60 Irish$ MAP | Full breakfast |
| Bantry | 9 rooms/suites, 9 pb | Bar, restaurant (fee) |
| 027-50047 | Most CC, *Rated*, • | Sitting room, library |
| Fax: 027-50795 | C-yesEng., Fr., Ger., Sp. | billiard room |
| Mr. & Mrs. E. Shelswell-White | | tour of house |
| March-October | | Airport: Cork |

*Stately home, 18th century, open to public—but residents have private wing.* **10% off for 5 nights or more.**

**BUSHMILLS, CO ANTRIM** ─────────────────────────────────

| | | |
|---|---|---|
| **Auberge de Seneirl** | 39-74 Irish$ B&B | Full Irish breakfast |
| 28 Ballyclough Rd.  BT57 8UZ | 6 rooms/suites, 6 pb | Dinner, restaurant (fee) |
| 012657-41536 | Most CC | Sauna, swimming pool |
| Fax: 01265-823910 | C-yes/S-no/P-yes/H-ltd | one suite incl. sitting |
| M. & Barbara Defres | French, English | room & jacuzzi bath |
| All year | | Airport: Belfast International |

*Restored & enlarged country school. Award winning French restaurant & luxury accommodation with leisure facilities. Secluded country site near Bush River.* **3rd night free.**

**CLONES, CO MONAGHAN** ─────────────────────────────────

| | | |
|---|---|---|
| **Hilton Park** | 90-111 Irish$ Inquire | Full breakfast |
| Scothouse | 6 rooms/suites, 6 pb | Tea, bar, dinner (fee) |
| 353-47-56007 | Most CC, *Rated*, • | Sitting room |
| Fax: 353-47-56003 | C-yes/S-yes/P-no/H-no | library |
| Lucy & Johnny Madden | English | bicycles |
| April - September | | Airport: Dublin, Belfast |

*Beautiful lakeside setting in private parkland. Extensive gardens, views. Antique furnishings, famous cuisine.* **15% discount for 3 or more nights.**

**CO. DONEGAL** ─────────────────────────────────

| | | |
|---|---|---|
| **Ardnamona House** | 35 Irish$ B&B | Full breakfast |
| Louch Eske | 6 rooms/suites, 6 pb | Dinner (fee) |
| 073-22650 | Most CC, *Rated*, • | Boating, fishing, walking |
| Fax: 073-228-19 | C-yes/P-yes/H-no | trails, sitting room |
| Kieran & Amabel Clarke | French, Rus., some Ger. | Airport: Belfast |
| Feb. to Christmas | | |

*Victorian manor described in Lewis' Topographical Pictionary 1837 as a very picturesque domain in rural Ireland with int'l. collection Rhododendroms.* **Free bottle wine.**

## CONNEMARA, CO GALWAY

**Zetland Country House Hotel**
Cashel Bay
095-311-11
Fax: 095-311-17
John & Mona Prendergast
Easter-November

105 Irish$ B&B
20 rooms/suites, 20 pb
Visa, MC, AmEx,
*Rated*, •
C-yes/S-yes/P-no/H-yes
French, Italian, English

Full breakfast
Dinner, restaurant, tea
Bar service, sitting room
library, bicycles, tennis
Airport: Shannon

*This is a gracious manor house situated in lovely gardens overlooking the sea. It is furnished with antiques and soft color tones, and offers warm service. Fresh seafood.*

## COUNTY CORK, SO. IRELAND

**Muskerry House**
Foute N22, Farranes
011-353-21-336-469
Fax: 011-353-21-336-469
Plaice Family

50 Irish$ B&B
6 rooms/suites, 6 pb
English

Full Irish breakfast
Agricultural musuem
television in room

*Set in woodland, comfort and care from family-run establishment. Enlightening tours of Ireland's farming past along with agricultural museum are on grounds.*

## ENNISCORTHY, CO WEXFORD

**Ballinkeele House**
Ballymurn
053-38105
Fax: 053-38468
John & Margaret Maher
March 1-November 6

60-75 Irish$ B&B/MAP
5 rooms/suites, 5 pb
Most CC, *Rated*, •
C-yes/S-no/P-no/H-no
English, min. Gr., French

Full breakfast
Dinner available (fee)
Advance booking advisable
sitting room
tennis court
Airport: Dublin

*All-weather tennis court avail. Work off hostess home-cooked breakfasts (& dinners-by arrangement). Wellingtons for walking, full-size table snookers.* **10% off accom. 3rd day.**

## LEENANE, COUNTY GALWAY

**Delphi Lodge**
00353-9542211
Fax: 00353-9542296
Peter Mantle
Closed Xmas, New Yr.

30 Irish$ B&B
11 rooms/suites, 11 pb
Visa, MC, *Rated*, •
C-ltd/S-yes/P-no/H-yes
French, English

Full breakfast
Lunch, dinner, aftn. tea
Sitting room, library
fly fishing for salmon
Airport: Shannon

*Beautiful country house in spectacular setting, surrounded by mountains, overlooking lake in remote valley. Elegant but informal house party atmosphere. Superb food-wine list.*

## MOUNTRATH, CO. LAOIS

**Roundwood House**
0502-32120
Fax: 0502-32711
Frank & Rosemarie Kennan
All year

70 Irish$ B&B
10 rooms/suites, 10 pb
Most CC, *Rated*, •
C-yes/S-yes/P-yes/H-no
English, Spanish

Full continental bkfst.
Dinner available
Bar service, sitting room
library
hot tubs
Airport: Dublin/Shannon

*Beautiful Palladian villa surrounded by its own woods. A piece of warm and welcoming history.* **Third night 50% off by request.**

## NEWMARKET-ON-FERGUS, CO. CLARE

| **Thomond House** | 160-179 Irish$ BB/EP/ | Full breakfast |
|---|---|---|
| Dromoland | MAP | Dinner by arrangement |
| 061-368-304 | 7 rooms/suites, 7 pb | Golf, Fishing, Tennis |
| Fax: 061-368-285 | Most CC, *Rated*, • | Riding, Clay shooting |
| Helen Inchiquin | C-yes/S-yes/H-yes | deer stalking, 4X4 course |
| All year | English, min. French | Airport: Shannon |

*Luxurious and Charming. We offer superb hospitality, delicious food. 10 mins. from Shannon Airport. Golf 5 mins; tennis, swimming, shooting and magnificent walks.*

## YOUGHAL, CO CORK

| **Ballymakeigh House** | 50 Irish$ MAP | Full breakfast |
|---|---|---|
| Killeagh | 6 rooms/suites, 6 pb | Restaurant (fee) |
| 024-95184 | Visa, *Rated*, • | Tennis court, bicycles |
| Fax: 024-95379 | C-yes/S-yes/P-yes/H-no | library, sitting room |
| Margaret Browne | English | Airport: Cork |
| Feb-Dec | | |

*Superb food, fine wines, delightful ambience. "Guesthouse, Housewife, and National Breakfast of the year awards" awarded. Near Blarney and Jameson Heritage Park.*

# Israel

## JERUSALEM

| **Mount of Olives Hotel** | 40 US$ | Restaurant (fee) |
|---|---|---|
| 53 Mount of Olives Rd.  91190 | 61 rooms/suites, 61 pb | Lunch, dinner, snacks |
| +972 (2) 284877 | Visa, MC, AmEx, | Bar service, sitting room |
| Fax: +972 (2) 894427 | *Rated*, • | best view of Jerusalem |
| Ibrahim Dawud | C-yes/S-yes/P-no/H-no | Airport: Tel Aviv-Ben Gurion |
| All year | Eng., Fr., Arabic, | |
| | Hebrew | |

*A family hotel situated at the summit of the Mount of Olives, next to the Chapel of Ascension. Ideal for Pilgrims. **Stay six nights, seventh night free.***

# Italy

## 53040 RADICOFAMI, SIENA

| **Locanda Agrit. La** | 105.000 Italian$ MAP/AP | Full breakfast |
|---|---|---|
| **Palazzina** | 10 rooms/suites, 10 pb | Restaurant (fee), bar |
| Loc. Le Vigne  53040 | Visa, AmEx, *Rated*, • | Afternoon tea, snacks |
| 2 | C-yes/S-yes/P-ltd/H-ltd | pool, complimentary wine |
| 39-578-55771 | English, French, Italian | classical music concert |
| Fax: 39-578-55585 | | Airport: Roma, Piza |
| Sig. Innocenti | | |
| March 20-Nov 10 | | |

*The villa sits centre stage of the magnificent Tuscan countryside, vineyards, woods and olive groves. Most of the food and wine is grown on the farm. Hospitality is legendary.*

## ALTOMONTE

| **Hotel Barbieri** | 120.000 Italian$ | Breakfast to request |
| Via San Nicola, 30  87042 | 24 rooms/suites, 24 pb | Restaurant (fee) |
| 0981-948072 | Most CC, *Rated*, • | Bicycles, tennis court |
| Fax: 0981-948073 | C-yes/S-yes/P-yes/H-no | bar, sitting room |
| Sig. Barbieri | Italian, French | swimming pool |
| All year | | Airport: Lamezie Terme |

*Open all year. Ideal place to enjoy historical/cultural attractions-medieval town of Alto-*
*monte. Cuisine personally supervised. Guided mushroom searching & bird-watching.*

## ANAGNI

| **Villa La Floridiana** | 160.000 Italian$ B&B | Continental breakfast |
| Via Casilina, km. 63.700, | 9 rooms/suites, 9 pb | Lunch, Dinner (fee) |
| FR  03012 | Most CC | Bar service |
| 077-576-9960-1 | C-yes/S-yesFrench, ltd. | train to Rome or |
| Fax: 077-576-9960-1 | English | car rentals available |
| Sigra. Camerini | | Airport: Fiu Micino |
| Closed August 10-31 | | |

*Near the ancient towns of Anagni, Roma, Fumone, etc. Picturesque countryside, 19th*
*century hotel country house offers quiet times, beautiful gardens, food from the orchard.*

## BRIXEN, BRESSANONE, TYROL

| **Hotel Dominik** | 220.000 Italian$ B&B | Comp. wine, lunch, dinner |
| Via Terzo di Sotto 13  39042 | 29 rooms/suites, 29 pb | Afternoon tea & snacks |
| 39-472-830-144 | • | hot tub, sauna, pool |
| Fax: 39-472-836-554 | C-yes/S-yes/P-yes | Airport: Verona |
| Dominik Demetz | English, Italian, German | |
| Easter-Jan 8 | | |

*Relais & Chateaux tradition of hospitality. Excellent cuisine/wines. Quiet location in 1000*
*year old town. Indoor pool, gardens, elevator, promenades, excursions to Dolomites.*

## BURIANO-MONTECATINI VAL DI CECINA

| **Hotel Buriano** | 60.000 Italian$ | Continental, full (fee) |
| Castello, 10  56040 | 7 rooms/suites, 5 pb | Snacks, comp. wine |
| 058-837-295 | *Rated*, | Sitting room |
| Fax: 058-837-295 | C-yes/S-yes/P-yes/H-no | library |
| Elga Schlubach-Giudici | Fr., It., Eng., German | deer farm |
| March-September | | Airport: Pisa, Florence |

*Located in the "sticks" with beautiful views of the countryside. Seaside 35 kms away.*
*Little chapel and meditation room avilable (Christian).*

## CANNERO RIVIERA, VERBANIA

| **Hotel Cannero** | Rates: Inquire B&B | Full breakfast |
| Lungo Lago 2, (VB) Lake | 40 rooms/suites, 40 pb | Lunch, dinner, restaurant |
| Maggiore, VB  28051 | Most CC | Library, bicycles, tennis |
| +39-323-78-80-46 | C-yes/S-ltd/P-yes/H-yes | swimming pool |
| Fax: +39-323-78-80-48 | English, Fr., Ger., It. | Airport: Milano Malpensa |
| M.C. Gallinotto | | |
| March-November | | |

*This charming Hotel Cannero is particularly well placed in this lovely setting just across*
*the promenade from the edge of the lake. **Free drink special.***

## CARLOFORTE DI SANPIETRO, SARDEGNA

| | | |
|---|---|---|
| **Albergo Paola e Maggio** | 64 US$ Inquire | Continental plus bkfst. |
| Localita Tacca Rossa  09014 | 20 rooms/suites, 20 pb | Restaurant (fee) |
| 0781-850098 | Most CC, *Rated*, • | Bar service |
| Fax: 0781-850104 | C-yes/S-yes/P-no/H-no | oceanview from terrace |
| M. Vittoire Ferraro | Italian | private garden |
| May-October | | Airport: Cagliari, Elmas |

*Comfortable rooms with seaview, country location. Local cooking, private garden with local Mediterranean flora. Private park. Italian breakfast served.*

## CASTELLINA IN CHIANTI

| | | |
|---|---|---|
| **Tenuta di Ricavo-Romantik** | 240.000 Italian$ B&B | Continental breakfast |
| **Hotel** | 23 rooms/suites, 23 pb | Restaurant (fee) |
| Localita Ricavo, 4  53011 | Visa, MC | Bar service, sitting room |
| 0577-740-221 | • | library |
| Fax: 0577-741-014 | C-ltd/S-yes/P-no/H-ltd | bicycles, gym |
| Family Lobrano-Scotoni | English, It., Ger., Fr. | Airport: Florence/Pisa |
| All year | | |

*Amidst beauty and quietness of unspoiled nature. Extremely central, in heart of Chianti Hills. Lovingly restored historic hamlet. Long tradition of individual hospitality.*

## CASTIGLION, FLORENTINO

| | | |
|---|---|---|
| **Montanina** | Inquire B&B | Full breakfast |
| Valuberti 17/18  52143 | 2 rooms/suites, 2 pb | Vegetable/herb garden |
| Fax: 011-39-575-659-462 | English | Phone, TV |
| Signora Alda Fantina | | outside gazebo |
| | | covered terrace |

*Stone cottage tucked into the heart of Tuscany. Amid lush orchards and farmland yet, 30 minutes from Florence, Siena, Assissi, Lake Trasimeno.*

## CHIAVERANO D'IVREA, TORINO

| | | |
|---|---|---|
| **Castello San Giuseppe** | 175-270.000 Italian$ | Complimentary breakfast |
| Locality Castello San | B&B/MAP | Restaurant (fee) |
| Giuseppe  10010 | 14 rooms/suites, 14 pb | Bar service |
| 0125-42-43-70 | Most CC | Sauna at 3 km |
| Fax: 0125-64-12-78 | • | swimming pool |
| Naghiero Pasquale, B. Renata | C-yes/S-yes/P-ltdEng., | Airport: Torino, Milano |
| All year | Fr., Ger., Spanish | |

*A Convent in 1600, a Castle under Emperor "Napoleon" in 1800. Recently restructured and converted into a charming hotel with all the comforts.*

## CORTINA D'AMPEZZO

| | | |
|---|---|---|
| **Hotel Menardi** | 260.000 Italian$ Inquire | Buffet breakfast |
| Via Majon No. 110  32043 | 50 rooms/suites, 50 pb | Restaurant, bar (fee) |
| 0436-2400 | Visa, MC | Sitting room |
| Fax: 0436-862183 | • | bicycles |
| The Menardi Family | C-yes/S-yes/P-no/H-no | hot tubs |
| Inquire about season | English, German, | Airport: Venice |
| | French | |

*From the turn of the century: an ancient house, a family. Today: the same house & family. Relaxed atmosphere, rich vegetation, comfortable, modern. Beauty of the Dolomites.*

## COURMAYEUR LA SAXE, AOSTE

**Meuble Emile Rey**
Via Trou Des Romains
14  11013
39-165-844044
Fax: 39-165-846497
Donatella & Auro Bucci
Dec-Apr, June-Sept

120.000 Italian$ B&B
10 rooms/suites, 10 pb
Visa, MC, *Rated*, •
C-yes/S-yes/P-no/H-no
Italian, French, English

Buffet Breakfast
Restaurant (fee)
Sitting room
Minivan service to ski
slopes, night clubs
Airport: Geneva

*A very peaceful and sunny house which belonged to the Italian Kings favorite Alpine guide, Emile Rey. A 19th century historic site close to ski slopes. **Free bottle wine.***

## FERRARA, FE

**Ripagrande Hotel**
Via Ripagrande N. 21  44100
532-76-52-50
Fax: 532-76-43-77
Arch. Lanfranco Viola
All year

280.000 Italian$ B&B
40 rooms/suites, 40 pb
*Rated*, •
C-yes/S-yes/P-yes/H-no
Italian, Dutch,
French,GB

Buffet breakfast
Local, regional cuisine
Bar service, sitting room
courtyards, bicycles
children's playground
Airport: Marconi Bologna

*Renaissance palace of Ferrara, grand entrance, marble staircase, wooden ceilings. Classical style decor. Quiet, refined atmosphere. **Free fruit in room, free bicycle use.***

## FIRENZE, TOSCANA

**Salvadonica-Borgo Agritur. del Chianti**
Via Grevigiana, 82-Mercatale
V.P.  50024
55-821-8039
Fax: 55-821-8043
Baccetti Piero
May-November

150-160.000 Italian$ B&B
15 rooms/suites, 15 pb
Most CC, *Rated*, •
C-yes/S-yes/P-no/H-yes
English, German,
French

Full breakfast
Bar service, snacks
Bicycles,library, bocce
tennis, football field
swimming pool
Airport: Florence, Pisa

*Nestled in the midst of the vineyards that grow the grapes destined to become Chianti classico wine, Salvadonica offers its visitors a hearty taste of real Tuscan style.*

## FLORENCE

**Hotel Monna Lisa**
Via Borgo Pinti 27  50121
55-247-9751
Fax: 55-247-9755
Agostina Cona
All year

240.000 Italian$ B&B
30 rooms/suites, 30 pb
Most CC, *Rated*, •
C-yes/S-yes/P-yes/H-yes
English, Fr, Ger, Spanish

Buffet breakfast
Afternoon tea
Bar service
sitting room
library
Airport: Florence, Pisa

*An elegant Renaissance Palace furnished with fine antique furniture suitable for a pleasant stay, in a delightful atmosphere.*

## FORTE DEI MARMI, LUCCA

**Hotel Tirreno**
Viale Morin 7  55042
584-787444
Fax: 584-787137
Beralle Family
Easter to Sept 30

Rates: Inquire Inquire
59 rooms/suites, 58 pb
Most CC, *Rated*, •
C-yes/S-yes/P-no/H-yes
English, German,
French

Full breakfast
Restaurant (fee)
Bar servoce
sitting room
family friendly facility
Airport: Pisa

*Award winning family-run hotel has two buildings. One, modern with a view of the sea; the other, an 1870s villa in the park. The kitchen is personally overseen by the family.*

## GARLENDA

**La Meridiana**
Via ai Castelli, 11  17033
018-258-0271
Fax: 018-258-0150
Sig. & Sigra. Segre
March-Dec

280.000 Italian$
34 rooms/suites,
Most CC
P-yes/H-yes
Italian

Breakfast (fee)
Lunch, Dinner
Minibar, Pool, Tennis
Bike, Sauna, Parking

*Perfect place for a wonderfull getaway. Romantic settings with delightful restaurants all nearby. Also great entertainment in local neighborhood. An unforgattable place.*

## GUBBIO, PG

**Hotel Bosone Palace**
Via 20 Settembre,
No.22  06024
+39-75-9220688
Fax: +39-75-9220552
Roberto Menichetti
All year

125.000 Italian$ B&B
30 rooms/suites, 30 pb
Most CC, *Rated*, •
C-yes/S-yes/P-yes/H-yes
English, French, Italian

Complimentary breakfast
Restaurant, bar (fee)
Sitting room
forest trekking nearby
modern facilities
Airport: Rome

*13th century place in medieval heart of Gubbio. All modern facilities. Renaissance frescoed suites and breakfast room. **Free bottle of wine.***

## LEVANTO, SP

**Hotel Nazionale**
Via Jacopo Da Levanto
20  19015
0187-808102
Fax: 0187-800901
Angela Lagomarsino
March-November

160.000 Italian$ B&B
32 rooms/suites, 32 pb
Most CC, *Rated*, •
C-yes/S-yes/P-yes/H-no
English, German,
French

Full breakfast (fee)
Restaurant (all meals)
Bar service, aftn. tea
sitting room, parking
comp. wine after 3 nites
Airport: Genova

*Friendly family-run hotel, situated near town, beach, train, boats & "Cinque Terre," a delightful restaurant offering regional cooking. Room rates reflect 1996 fees. Inquire.*

## LIPARI, MESSINA

**Hotel Villa Augustus**
Vico Ausonia, 16  98055
090-9811-233
Fax: 090-9811-233
Mr. D'Albora Augusto
March 1-October 31

60-95.000 Italian$
35 rooms/suites, 35 pb
Most CC
•
C-yes/S-yes/P-yes/H-yes
Italian, English, French

Continental plus bkfst.
Restaurant (fee)
Color TV, terrace,
Bar service, sitting room
library, car parking
Airport: Catania/Reggio
Calabria

*Situated 100 meters from the sea & main harbour & 2 km from the white beaches. Arched gateway leads to garden. Elegant setting; all the amenities. **10% off guide readers, ltd.***

## MARATEA, POLENZA

**Villa Cheta Elite**
Loc. Acquafredda  85041
973-878134
Fax: 973-878135
Lamberto Aquadro
All year

150.000 Italian$ Inquire
17 rooms/suites, 17 pb
Most CC, *Rated*, •
C-yes/S-yes/P-yes/H-no
Dutch, English, Italian

Full breakfast
Restaurant
Bar service
sitting room
tennis court in vicinity
Airport: Naples

*Splendid Liberty-style villa views the sea, beach close. Refined, efficient hospitality. Restaurant features local products. History, art, culture. **Free bottle of wine.***

MENAGGIO, COMO ─────────────────────────────────

| | | |
|---|---|---|
| **Grand Hotel Menaggio** | 195-300.000 Italian$ | Continental breakfast |
| Via IV Novembre 69  22017 | Inquire | Restaurant (fee) |
| 0344-30640 | 56 rooms/suites, 56 pb | Bar service |
| Fax: 0344-30619 | Most CC | swimming pool |
| March-October | • | Airport: Milano |
| | C-yes/S-yes/P-yes/H-yes | |
| | English, French, | |
| | German | |

*Completely restored in 1988. Rooms have TV, radio, phones & Minibar. Hotel looks directly over blue waters of Lake Como. Heated pool, boutique. Golfing, boating, nearby.*

MONTECATINI V.C., PISA ─────────────────────────

| | | |
|---|---|---|
| **Il Frassinello** | 130.000 Italian$ B&B | Continental breakfast |
| Via Della Miniera 22  56040 | 7 rooms/suites, 5 pb | Snacks, comp. wine |
| 0588-30080 | *Rated*, | Sitting room |
| Fax: 0588-30080 | C-yes/S-yes/P-yes/H-no | library |
| Elga Schlubach-Giudici | Fr., It., Eng., German | deer farm |
| Easter-end October | | Airport: Pisa, Florence |

*Located in the countryside with beautiful views; seaside 35 kms away. Little chapel and christian meditation room available.*

MONTEFALCO, PG ──────────────────────────────────

| | | |
|---|---|---|
| **Hotel Villa Pambuffetti** | 135.000 Italian$ B&B | Buffet breakfast |
| Via della Vittoria, 20  06036 | 15 rooms/suites, 15 pb | Dinner available |
| 0742-379417 | Most CC, *Rated*, • | Minibar, Safe |
| Fax: 0742-379245 | C-yes/S-yes/P-no/H-yes | Parking |
| Angelucci Alessandra | English, French, | swimming pool |
| All year | German | Airport: Fiumicino |

*Family country house in the hilltop town of Montefalco. Famous for its 13th century Frescoes, centuries-old park with a swimming pool. Cumbrian cuisine and wines.*

MONTEVETTOLINI, PISTOIA ─────────────────────────

| | | |
|---|---|---|
| **Villa Lucia** | 150 US$ B&B/MAP | Continental plus bkfst. |
| Via dei Bronzoli, 144  15015 | 10 rooms/suites, 10 pb | Other meals on request |
| 572-628-817 | • | Sitting room, library |
| Fax: 572-628-817 | C-yes/S-yes/P-no/H-no | swimming pool, bicycles |
| Lucia Ann Vallera | English, Italian, Fr, Sp | golf nearby, clubs avail. |
| Closed winter | | Airport: Pisa/Florence |

*Among 14 acres of olive groves. 500 year old farmhouse furnished in antiques teaches one the art of living today while exploring treasures of yesterday.*

ORTA SAN GIULIO ─────────────────────────────────

| | | |
|---|---|---|
| **Hotel San Rocco &** | 240.000 Italian$ B&B | Restaurant (fee) |
| **Restaurant** | 74 rooms/suites, 74 pb | Lunch, dinner, bar |
| Via Gippini 11  28016 | Most CC | Sitting room |
| 0322-9177 | • | tennis court |
| Fax: 0322-911964 | C-yes/S-yes/P-no/H-no | sauna, swimming pool |
| Open all year | French, English, | Airport: Milano Malpensa |
| | German | |

*A converted convent located on the romantic Lake Orta and facing the island of San Giulio. Absolute tranquility, refined restaurant. Local and international cuisine.*

PENANGO, ASTI

| | | |
|---|---|---|
| **Locanda del Sant'Uffizio** | 300.000 Italian$ B&B | Full breakfast |
| Frazione Cioccaro  14030 | 43 rooms/suites, 43 pb | Lunch, dinner, restaurant |
| 0141-916292 | Visa, MC, *Rated*, | Bar service, sitting room |
| Fax: 014-1916068 | C-yes/S-yes/P-yes/H-ltd | bicycles, tennis, pool |
| Beppe and Carla Firato | English, Italian | Airport: Milano Malpensa |
| Closed 10-20 Aug. | | |

*Countryside XVIth century Benedictine convent furnished in genuine antiques, surrounded by wineyards. Gourmet dinner & buffet with homemade jams & typical salami & cheeses.*

POMPONESCO, MANTOVA

| | | |
|---|---|---|
| **Il Leone** | 130.000 Italian$ B&B | Continental breakfast |
| Piazza 4 Martiri 2  46030 | 8 rooms/suites, 8 pb | Restaurant, lunch, dinner |
| 0375-86077/86145 | Most CC | Bar service, sitting room |
| Fax: 0375-86770 | • | swimming pool |
| Mori's Family | C-yes/S-yes/P-yes/H-no | very good cellar |
| Closed January | English, German, | Airport: Bologna |
| | French | |

*Beautiful old building with beamed ceilings. Romantic dining area with gracious Italian service provided by family-run establishment. Double room & breakfast 145.000 Italian$.*

PORTOFERRAIO, ISLAND OF ELBA

| | | |
|---|---|---|
| **Hotel Villa Ottone** | 115.000 Italian$ MAP | Full breakfast (fee) |
| Loc. Ottone  57037 | 70 rooms/suites, 70 pb | Lunch, dinner, aftn. tea |
| 0565-933042 | Visa, MC | Bar service, sitting room |
| Fax: 056-593-3257 | • | bicycles, tennis, pool |
| Mario | C-yes/S-yes/P-no/H-yes | piano bar |
| May-September | English, French, | Airport: Pisa |
| | German | |

*Wonderful position on the seashore facing Portoferraio. Dreamlike sunsets, large garden with ancient and exotic plants, private beach, and children's playground.*

REGIONE TRENTINO-ALTO ADIGE

| | | |
|---|---|---|
| **Hotel Accademia** | 150-245.000 Italian$ BB/ | Buffet breakfast |
| Vicolo Colico, 4/6  38100 | EP/MAP | Restaurant (fee) |
| 39-461-233600 | 42 rooms/suites, 42 pb | Bar service |
| Fax: 39-461-231074 | Most CC | sitting room |
| Franca & Giovanna Fambri | • | spec. 2 night wkend. stay |
| All year | C-yes/S-yes/P-yes/H-yes | Airport: Verona Villafranca |
| | English, French, | |
| | German | |

*Medieval house completely restored. Located in historic center close to main cathedral S.Maria Maggiore Council church museums. All rooms have TV, Air Conditioning, minibar.*

ROMA, LADISPOLI

| | | |
|---|---|---|
| **La Posta Vecchia** | Rates: Inquire B&B | Continental breakfast |
| Loc. Palo Laziale  00055 | 17 rooms/suites, 13 pb | Restaurant (fee) |
| 06-9949501 | Most CC, *Rated*, • | Sitting room, library |
| Fax: 06-9949507 | C-yes/S-ltd/P-no/H-no | bicycles, swimming pool |
| Harry C.M. Saio | Eng., Ger., Fr., Italian | ocean/garden/park view |
| April-November | | Airport: Fiumicino |

*Villa XVII century. Furnished in genuine antiques. Private Roman Museum. Small private beach. **Special: upgrade room when possible.***

ROME————————————————————————————————————

| **Hotel Locarno** | 250.000 Italian$ B&B | Full breakfast |
| Via della Penna, 22  00186 | 43 rooms/suites, 43 pb | Afternoon tea, snacks |
| 063-610-841 | Most CC, *Rated*, • | Bar service, library |
| Fax: 063-215-249 | C-yes/S-yes/P-no/H-ltd | sitting room, bicycles |
| Sigra. Celli | English, Spanish | garden, roof garden |
| All year | | Airport: Leonardo da Vinci |

*Located in the very heart of Rome - Liberty style - original antiques. Panoramic 360 degree view St. Peters Chapel, etc. Spanish steps. Breakfast served until noon.*

| **Hotel Piazza di Spagna** | 230-280.000 Italian$ B&B | Continental plus bkfst. |
| Via Mario de'Fiori, 61  00187 | 16 rooms/suites, 16 pb | Afternoon tea, snacks |
| 6-6793-061 | Most CC, *Rated*, • | Bar service |
| Fax: 6-6790-654 | C-yes/S-yes/P-ltd/H-no | sitting room |
| Mariani Roberto | English, French, Spanish | Airport: Fiumicino |
| All year | | |

*Originally built in early 1800's. Rooms completely refurnished, classical Italian atmosphere with all modern comforts. Some Jacuzzi-tub rooms.* **Low season, 3rd nite 50% off.**

| **Hotel Villa del Parco** | Rates: Inquire B&B | Continental plus bkfst. |
| Via Nomentana, 110  00161 | 25 rooms/suites, 25 pb | Snacks, bar service |
| 6-4423-7773 | Most CC | Minibar, Parking |
| Fax: 6-4423-7572 | • | sitting room |
| Elisabetta Bernardini | C-yes/S-yes/P-yes/H-ltd | library |
| All year | English, French, German | Airport: Leonardo Da Vinci |

*Villa from the late 19th Century. Green surroundings, quiet area close to historical town center. Excellent service creates a refined and pleasant atmosphere.* **Weekend rates.**

SAN GIMIGNANO, SIENA————————————————————

| **Relais Santa Chiara Hotel** | 195-295.000 Italian$ B&B | Full breakfast |
| Via Matteotti, 15  53037 | 40 rooms/suites, 40 pb | Lunch, aftn. tea, snacks |
| 577-940701 | Most CC, *Rated*, • | Bar service, sitting room |
| Fax: 577-942096 | C-yes/S-yes/P-no/H-yes | tennis/golf nearby, pool |
| Monica Verdiani,Thom. | English, It., Ger., Fr. | Airport: Rome, Florence |
| Arsulich | | |
| All year | | |

*500 yards from historic center-medieval hill town of San Gimignano. Impeccable surroundings, service - maintains the style of classical Tuscany.* **3+ nights, free bottle wine.**

SIENA, CASOLE D'ELSA ——————————————————

| **Podere Capretto** | 110.000 Italian$ B&B | Continental plus bkfst. |
| Podere Capretto 53031 | 7 rooms/suites, 7 pb | Sitting room |
| 0577-948550 | C-yes/S-yes/P-yes/H-no | family friendly facility |
| Fax: 0577-948550 | Fr, Eng, It, Sp, D, Heb. | Airport: Florence |
| Patrizia, Margaret, Nikolaos | | |

*Tuscan farmhouse w/spectacular views of valleys & medieval hilltop village of Casole d'Elsa. Central, between famous Tuscan places; Florence, Siena, Volterra, San Gimigniano.*

# 630    Italy

## SIENA, TUSCANY

| | | |
|---|---|---|
| **Albergo Villa** | 200.000 Italian$ B&B | Full breakfast |
| **Scacciapensieri** | 32 rooms/suites, 32 pb | MAP available (fee) |
| Strada Di Scacciapensieri | Visa, MC, AmEx, | Bar service, tennis |
| 10 53100 | *Rated*, • | swimming pool, bicycles |
| 577-41-441 | C-yes/S-yes/P-yes/H-yes | Airport: Florence, Pisa, |
| Fax: 577-27-0854 | Ital., Eng., Ger., French | Rome |
| Family Nardi | | |
| March-December | | |

*19th century villa overlooking Medieval walls of Siena. Large park & gardens. Small, peaceful hotel. Dine on terraces. Lovely view from pool of Tuscan Hills and countryside.*

## SO. TYROL - DOLOMITES

| | | |
|---|---|---|
| **Cavallino D'oro** | 80-190.000 Italian$ BB/ | Full breakfast |
| Piazza Kraus-39040 | EP/MAP | Restaurant (fee) |
| Castelrotto  39040 | 20 rooms/suites, 20 pb | Bar service, sitting room |
| 0471-706337 | Most CC, *Rated*, • | bicycles |
| Fax: 0471-707172 | C-yes/S-yes/P-no/H-no | romantic atmosphre |
| Goldenes-Rossl | Most languages spoken | Airport: Munich, Milano |
| All year | | |

*In the village square of Kastelruth you will discover a 600-year tradition of hospitality. Goldenes Rossl has been carefully renovated and is famous for its restaurant.*

## SPELLO

| | | |
|---|---|---|
| **Hotel Palazzo Bocci** | 220.000 Italian$ B&B | Buffet Breakfast |
| via Cavour, 17, PG  06038 | 23 rooms/suites, 23 pb | Restaurant, Bar (fee) |
| 074-230-1021 | Visa, MC, AmEx, | Sitting room, open garden |
| Fax: 074-230-1464 | *Rated*, • | near golf, tennis, pool |
| Sig. Fabrizio Buono | C-yes/S-yes/P-no/H-yes | comp. bottle of Spumante |
| All year | English, French, | Airport: S. Egidio |
| | German | |

*The Palazzo Bocci, converted in 1992 from an 18th Century palazzo, retains the character of the historic building with frescoed ceilings and some walls. **7 nights 1 night free.***

## SPOLETO

| | | |
|---|---|---|
| **Palazzo Dragoni** | 200-300.000 Italian$ B&B | Continental plus bkfst. |
| Via del Duomo, 13, PG  06049 | 15 rooms/suites, 15 pb | Afternoon tea |
| 743-22-2220 | Most CC | Bar service |
| Fax: 743-22-2225 | • | sitting room |
| Erminia Diotallevi | C-yes/S-yes/P- | library |
| All year | yesItalian, | Airport: Roma |
| | Francese,Tedesco | |

*In the historical centre of Spoleto next to the Cathedral. Built in XIV century and considered a "Historic Residence."Furnished in original style, available for conferences.*

## TAI DI CADORE, BELLUNO

| | | |
|---|---|---|
| **Villa Marinotti** | 150-180.000 Italian$ | Full breakfast |
| Via Manzago, 21  I-32040 | 6 rooms/suites, 6 pb | Complimentary wine, tea |
| 435-32231 | AmEx | Bar service |
| Fax: 435-33335 | • | sitting room |
| Aurelia, Roberta & Giorgio | C-yes/S-yes/P-yes/H-ltd | tennis court |
| All year | English, French, Italian | Airport: Venice |

*Very convenient location to visit the Dolonites and (100 kilometers to Venice), at low cost. During July and August restaurant open for dinner.*

## TAORMINA, ME

**Romantik Hotel Villa**
**Ducale**
Via Leonardo da Vinci,
60  98039
942-28153
Fax: 942-28710
Andrea & Rosy Quartucci
All year

250.000 Italian$ B&B
12 rooms/suites, 12 pb
Most CC
•
C-yes/S-yes/P-yes
English, French,
German

Continental plus bkfst.
Afternoon tea, snacks
Bar service, library
sitting room
hot tubs
Airport: Catania

*Rooms individually decorated antique style, hand-painted furniture, modern comfort. Unique view of Mediterranean & volcano. 10 min. to famous Greek-Roman Medieval old town.*

## VALLE D'AOSTA, BREUIL CERVINIA

**Les Neiges d'Antan**
11027 Fraz Perreres  11021
0166-948775
Fax: 0166-948852
La Famiglia Bich
All year

210.000 Italian$ AP/MAP
28 rooms/suites, 28 pb
*Rated*,
C-yes/S-yes/P-yes/H-ltd
It., Eng., Fr., German

Continental plus bkfst.
Restaurant (fee)
Sittin room, library
cross country ski track
boules, fireplace
Airport: Milan, Turin, Genv

*Chalet in tranquil mountain valley. Warm family atmosphere, excellent cuisine and wine cellar. 1996 Best Italian Breakfast Award, skiing and mountaineering.*

## VARENNA, COMO

**Hotel du Lac**
Via del Prestino 4  22050
0341-830238
Fax: 034-183-1081
Laura Pellizzari
March-December

180.000 Italian$ MAP
18 rooms/suites, 18 pb
Most CC
•
C-yes/S-yes/P-yes/H-yes
English, French,
German

Continental breakfast
Lunch, dinner, restaurant
Bar service, sitting room
people may swim in lake
free garage 1st. night
Airport: Linate-Milano

*Ancient villa with a deeply romantic atmosphere. Meals are served on the terrace overlooking the lake, far from traffic. Free place in the garage 1st night.*

## VICCHIO, FIRENZE

**Villa Campestri**
Via Di Campestri  50039
39-55-8490107
Fax: 39-55-8490108
Paolo
March 15-December 31

220.000 Italian$
23 rooms/suites, 23 pb
Visa, MC, AmEx,
*Rated*, •
C-yes/S-yes/P-no/H-no
English, German

Continental breakfast
Restaurant, bar (fee)
Horses, riding school
swimming pool, bicycles
meeting rooms, color TV
Airport: Florence

*History, tradition, beauty, and nature. Oasis surrounded by rolling meadows, forests, vineyards, olive trees. Near golf. Clients love peace, culture, good food.* **Welcome drink.**

# Liechtenstein

## VADUZ

**Park-Hotel Sonnenhof**
Mareestrasse 29, Principality
of  9490
75-232-11-92
Fax: 75-232-00-53
Family Emit Real
Feb 15-Dec 22, 1997

320-430 Swiss$ AP
29 rooms/suites, 29 pb
*Rated*, •
C-yes/S-yes/P-yes/H-ltd
Eng., Ger., Fr., It., Sp.

Buffet Breakfast
Restaurant (fee)
Bar service, library
sitting room, sauna
swimming pool
Airport: Zurich/Kloten

*Enjoy relaxation and warm atmosphere of a family-owned hotel overlooking Vaduz and its medieval castle. Nearby golf course.*

# Mexico

## AJIJIC, JALISCO

**La Nueva Posada**
Donato Guerra #9  45920
376-61344
Fax: 376-61444
Michael E. Jensen
All year

49 US$ B&B
16 rooms/suites, 16 pb
Visa, MC, AmEx,
*Rated*, •
C-yes/S-yes/P-yes/H-yes
Spanish, English, Danish

Full breakfast
Restaurant (fee)
Swimming pool
library
on lakeshore
Airport: Guadalajara

*Enchanting, elegant yet affordable hacienda style inn on lakeshore. Internationally acclaimed, fine cuisine, homestyle breakfast, family operated. Half hour to airport.*

## CUERNAVACA, MORELOS

**Las Mananitas**
Ricardo Linares 107  62000
73-14-14-66
Fax: 73-18-36-72
Ruben Cerda V.
Open all year

99 US$ EP
22 rooms/suites, 22 pb
AmEx, *Rated*, •
C-yes/S-yes/P-no/H-yes
Spanish, English, French

Full breakfast (fee)
Restaurant, lunch, dinner
Bar service
swimming pool
sitting room
Airport: Mexico City

*Although located downtown, this inn is set amid a lush tropical garden. Member of the prestigious Relais & Chateaux and one of the finest places to stay/dine in all Mexico.*

## SAN JOSE DEL CABO

**Huerta Verde**
Las Animas Altas, BCS  23400
7674 Reed St., Aruada CO
80003
303-431-5162
Fax: 303-431-4455

85-135 US$ B&B
8 rooms/suites, 8 pb
Visa, MC, *Rated*, •
C-ltd/S-yes/P-no/H-no
Spanish, English

Full breakfast
Lunch, dinner, snacks
Bar service, pool, golf
For those who seek . . . to
leave the crowds behind . . .
Airport: Los Cabos

*A charming, secluded and tropical desert paradise terraced in the hillside overlooking the orchards of Las Animas, Santa Rosa and the City of San Jose del Cabo.*

**Maxey's at Shipwreck**
East Cape, BCS  23400
P.O. Box 432, Bolinas, CA
94924
415-868-0827
Janie
Dec-June

40-60 US$ B&B
1 room/suites,
C-yes/P-yes
English, Spanish

Continental plus bkfst.
Lunch, dinner, snacks
Beach, snorkeling
desert hiking
great fishing
Airport: Los Cabos

*Rustic beach hideaway, 12 miles to nearest town. Great desert & ocean views. Hiking, snorkeling, surfing. Goumet meal by dedicated cook upon request. A truly great experience.*

## SAN MIGUEL ALLENDE

**Hacienda de las Flores**
Hospicio 16, GTO  37700
415-21808
Fax: 415-21859
A. Franyutti, C. Finkelstein
All year

39-105 US$ B&B
11 rooms/suites, 11 pb
*Rated*, •
C-yes/S-yes/P-yes/H-ltd
English, French

Full breakfast
Meals on contract
Sitting room
swimming pool
tennis, golf nearby
Airport: Silao, GTO

*Located only 2 blocks from downtown. Colonial style with TV, electric blankets, beautiful gardens & a pool. Connections to golf, tennis, horseback riding. Great cultural city.*

## SAN MIGUEL DE ALLENDE

**Hotel Villa Jacaranda**
Aldama 53, GTO 37700
011-52-415-21015
Fax: 011-52-415-20883
Don & Gloria Fenton
All year

85-120 US$ B&B/EP
15 rooms/suites, 15 pb
Most CC, *Rated*, •
C-yes/S-yes/P-yes/H-ltd
Spanish, English

Breakfast by arrangement
Restaurant (fee), bar
Tennis courts, golf
salon/theater
10 person jacuzzi
Airport: Leon Int'l.

*Two cobblestoned streets from Mexico's loveliest colonial square. The worlds best year-round climate. Free use of golf course, tennis courts. Free "Gourmet Magazine Margarita."*

**Mi Casa B&B**
Canal 58, Apdo. 496,
GTO 37700
415-22492
Fax: 415-24382
Carmen McDaniel
All year

65 US$ B&B
2 rooms/suites, 2 pb
*Rated*, •
C-yes/S-yes/P-yes/H-no
Spanish, English

Full breakfast
Bar service
Sitting room
laundry
Airport: Silao, Guanajuato

*Mi Casa, a National Historical Monument, serves a hearty (and attractive) home-cooked breakfast and provides all softs of shopping, dining & sightseeing.*

# Netherlands

## AMSTERDAM, HOLLAND

**Canal House Hotel**
Keizersgracht 148  1015 CX
020-622-5182
Fax: 020-624-1317
Len & Jane Irwin
All year

225 Netherlands$ B&B
26 rooms/suites, 26 pb
Visa, MC, AmEx,
*Rated*, •
C-ltd/S-yes/P-no/H-no
English, Dutch

Full Dutch breakfast
Boiled eggs
Bar service
period antiques
Airport: Schipol

*On quiet residential canal in Centrum. Five minutes to Anne Frank and Dam. Antique decor, no TV, illuminated garden, telephones and fax, very nice.*

**Hotel Piet Hein**
Vossiusstraat 53
20-662-7205
Fax: 20-662-1526
Mr. C. Breider
All year

145-185 Netherlands$
B&B
41 rooms/suites, 41 pb
Most CC
•
C-yes/S-yes/P-no/H-no
Dutch, Eng., Fr., German

Dutch breakfast buffet
Bar service
Sitting room
near museums
Airport: Schiphot

*Family owned, near museums, shopping, bars, restaurants, park and casino. Easy access by train, bus, tram, taxi. Hotel with personal touch.*

**Toro Hotel**
Koningslaan 64  1075 AG
31-20-673-72-23
Fax: 31-20-675-00-31
J. Plooy and M.G. Plooy-Cok
All year

200 Netherlands$ B&B
22 rooms/suites, 22 pb
Most CC, *Rated*, •
C-yes/S-yes/P-no/H-ltd
Dutch, Eng., Ger., Fr.,Sp

Full breakfast
Bar service, sitting room
and terrace
Airport: Schiphol

*Peaceful location, completely rebuilt mansion, near the center & museum, own garden borders canal of park. Furnished in genuine antiques. Parking in front of hotel.*

EDAM, N-H ────────────────────────────────────

**Hotel-Restaurant De Fortuna**
Spuistraat 3  1135 AV
0299-3716-71
Fax: 0299-3714-69
Nicholas B. Dekker
All year

165 Netherlands$
26 rooms/suites, 24 pb
Visa, MC, AmEx
•
C-yes/S-yes/H-yes
English, German, Dutch

Full breakfast
Restaurant, bar service
Sitting room, bicycles
hot tubs, gardens
Airport: Schiphol

*Hotel consists of 5 beautifully restored houses dating back to the 17th century. Centrally located to many fascinating, well known attractions.* **10% discount on room rates.**

# New Zealand

AKAROA, CANTERBURY ────────────────────────────

**Lavaud House**
83 Rue Lavaud
03-304-7121
Fax: 033-047-121
Francis & Frances Gallagher
All year

80-90 NZ$ B&B
4 rooms/suites, 2 pb
*Rated*, •
C-ltd/S-no/P-no/H-no
English

Continental breakfast
Afternoon tea
Sitting room, piano
large garden w/furniture
TV in all rooms
Airport: Christchurch

*Elegant historic 2-story home. Overlooks main beach. Large garden. Antique furniture, comfortable. Near golf-course & restaraunts. One and a quarter hrs. from Christchurch.*

AUCKLAND ────────────────────────────────────

**Bavaria B&B Hotel**
83 Valley Rd., Mt. Eden
09-638-9641
Fax: 096-389-665
Rudi Schmidt & Ulrike
Stephan
All year

99 NZ$ B&B
11 rooms/suites, 11 pb
Most CC
•
C-yes/S-no/P-no/H-no
English, German,
French

Full breakfast
Afternoon tea
Sitting room
all rooms have private
telephones
Airport: Auckland
International

*Generous, airy rooms all with private facilities in immaculately restored villa. First class service and very welcoming.*

**Birchwood Country Heritage Inn**
Clevedon-Takanini
Rd,Clevedon RD3
09-2928-729
Fax: 09-2928-555
Ann and Mike Davies
All year

135 NZ$ B&B
3 rooms/suites, 2 pb
Most CC, *Rated*, •
C-ltd/S-no/P-no/H-no
English

Full breakfast
Restaurant (fee)
Sitting room, library
tennis court
swimming pool
Airport: Auckland
International

*Enjoy the romance and intimacy of the lovingly restored 1887 farmhouse. Rambling gardens, delicious food, warm hospitality.* **Complimentary afternoon tea, coffee, wine, nibbles.**

**Chalet Chevron**
14 Brighton Rd., Parnell
64-9-309-0290
Fax: 64-9-373-5754
Fae & David England
All year

98-110 NZ$ B&B
13 rooms/suites, 13 pb
Most CC
•
C-yes/S-no/P-no/H-yes
English

Full breakfast
Afternoon tea
Sitting room
family friendly facility
Airport: Auckland
International

*True New Zealand hospitality in small Tudor-style hotel. Beautiful harbour views. Handy to city, restaurants, shopping, beaches, and islands.*

## AUCKLAND

| **Clevedon Maritime Marina Resort** | 100-130 NZ$ | Full breakfast |
|---|---|---|
| North Rd. Clevedon | 3 rooms/suites, 1pb | Afternoon tea |
| 64-9-292-8572 Fax: 64-9-292-8039 | Meal plan: B&B | Bar service, bicycles |
| | Visa | hot tubs, sauna, Jet ski |
| | C-yes/S-no/P-no/H-yes | golf near, swimming pool |
| The Balemis   All year | English | Airport: Auckland |

*Clevedon Maritime Marina Resort is a unique combination of a stately country home, maritime resort and on-site relaxation. Dingy, Golf course, Jet ski, model sailing yachts. Host speaks Dutch as a first language.*

| **Karin's Garden Villa & Cottage** | 115 NZ$ B&B | Continental plus bkfst. |
|---|---|---|
| 14 Sinclair St., Devonport 9 | 4 rooms/suites, 3 pb | Afternoon tea, dinner |
| 09-445-8689 | Most CC | Comp. wine, sitting room |
| Fax: 09-445-8689 | • | library, bicycles |
| Karin, Stefan, Tina | C-yes/S-no/P-no/H-no | Airport: Auckland |
| All year | English, German, French | |

*Charming Victorian villa with separate cottage overlooking large lawns. Private entrances. Close to golf, beach, downtown Auckland. Airport shuttle service. **3rd night 25% off.***

| **Peace & Plenty Inn** | 180-210 NZ$ B&B | Full breakfast |
|---|---|---|
| 6 Flagstaff Terr., Devonport | 4 rooms/suites, 4 pb | Afternoon tea, comp. wine |
| 064-944-52925 | Visa, MC, AmEx | Sitting room, bicycles |
| Fax: 064-944-52901 | • | beach across the road |
| Carol and Bruce Hyland | C-yes/S-no/P-no/H-no | Airport: Auckland |
| All year | English | International |

*Romantic luxury; historic waterfront home. Restaurants, shopping, ferry to city, steps away. Antiques, flowers, elegance, comfort, gourmet breakfasts; personal service.*

## AUCKLAND, AVONDALE

| **Kodesh Christian Community** | 35 NZ$ B&B | Continental plus bkfst. |
|---|---|---|
| 31 c Cradock Street | 3 rooms/suites, | Sitting room |
| 09-8285-672   Fax: 09-8285-684 | *Rated*, | library |
| | C-yes/S-no/P-no/H-no | Airport: Auckland |
| Gayle or Sue   All year | English | International |

*Kodesh is a residential ecumenical christian community. Modern facilities in a quiet location. 8 minutes by car from downtown Auckland.*

## AUCKLAND, FREEMAN'S BAY

| **Freeman's B&B** | 75-95 NZ$ B&B | Continental plus bkfst. |
|---|---|---|
| 65 Wellington St. | 12 rooms/suites, 4 pb | Comp. tea, coffee, choc. |
| 65-9-376-5046 | Most CC | Family friendly facility |
| Fax: 65-9-376-4052 | • | sitting room |
| El & Lyn Whyman | C-yes/S-no/P-no/H-no | Airport: Auckland |
| All year | English | International |

*Quiet, friendly, central city. 24 hour shuttle to and from airport. TV lounge, conservatory, garden, guest laundry, luggage storage. **Discounts available, please inquire.***

## AUCKLAND, REMUERA

| **Sedgwick Kent Lodge** | 140 NZ$ B&B | Full breakfast |
|---|---|---|
| 65 Lucerne Rd. | 4 rooms/suites, 2 pb | Dinner, tea, snacks |
| 09-524-5219 | Visa, MC, AmEx, | Bar service, sitting room |
| Louisa & Cliff Hobson-Corry | *Rated*, • | library, hot tubs |
| All year | C-ltd/S-no/P-no/H-yes | Airport: Auckland |
| | English | |

*Edwardian heritage home conveniently situated near suburb Remuera. Garden setting, magnificent views. Gourmet breakfasts, and dinners. **Bottle NZ wine 3rd night.***

AUCKLAND, WAIHEKE ISLAND ────────────────────────

| | | |
|---|---|---|
| **Gulf Haven** | 75-150 NZ$ B&B | Continental plus bkfst. |
| 49 Great Barrier Road, Encl. | 4 rooms/suites, 4 pb | Dinner, wine (fee) |
| Bay | Most CC | Sitting room, library |
| 09-372-6629 | • | rock pools to explore |
| Fax: 09-372-7174 | C-ltd/S-no/P-no/H-no | dramatic views, scenery |
| Alan Ramsbottom, Lou | English | Airport: Auckland |
| Baucke | | International |
| All year | | |

*2 acre garden setting overlooking ocean with own seashore. Breakfast on the deck. Relaxed island life only 35 minutes from downtown Auckland. 2 guestrooms, 2 studios (extra).*

AUCKLAND, WAIMAUKU ────────────────────────

| | | |
|---|---|---|
| **Skovholm Country Lodge** | 130 NZ$ B&B | Full breakfast |
| 78 Hinau Rd. 1250 | 4 rooms/suites, 2 pb | Afternoon tea, snacks |
| 09-411-8326 | MC, *Rated*, • | Sitting room, hot tub |
| Fax: 09-411-8326 | C-yes/S-no/P-no/H-no | comp. sherry in evening |
| Helge & Kathie Kristiansen | English, Danish | Airport: Auckland |
| All year | | |

*Luxurious B&B delightfully hidden in native bush and country garden setting close to beach, wineries, golf, restaurants. Half an hour from Central Auckland.*

BLENHEIM ────────────────────────

| | | |
|---|---|---|
| **Chardonnay Lodge** | 75 NZ$ B&B | Continental plus bkfst |
| Rapaura Road, RD 2 | 4 rooms/suites, 4 pb | Near gourmet restaurants |
| 64-3-570-5194 | Visa, *Rated*, • | Swimming pool, hot tub |
| Fax: 64-3-573-5194 | C-ltd/S-no/P-yes/H-ltd | bicycles, tennis, library |
| Allan & Jan Graham | English | Airport: Woodbourne |
| All year | | |

*Centered in heart of gourmet wine area, friendly relaxed atmosphere. A base for golfing, fishing, tramping. Vintage cars, aeroplanes nearby.* **10% discount over three nights.**

BLENHEIM, MARLBOROUGH ────────────────────────

| | | |
|---|---|---|
| **Stonehaven Vineyard** | 95-110 NZ$ B&B | Continental plus bkfst. |
| 445A Rapaura Road, Road | 3 rooms/suites, 3 pb | Dinner available |
| 3 Y321 | • | Sitting room |
| 3-572-9730 | C-ltd/S-no/P-no/H-no | library, hot tubs |
| Fax: 3-572-9730 | English | swimming pool |
| David & Jocelyn Wilson | | Airport: Blenheim via |
| All year | | Wellington |

*Spacious modern stone and cedar home set in gardens and vineyard in New Zealand's prime wine region. Interesting breakfasts served poolside.* **Rates reduced after 2nd night.**

CHRISTCHURCH ────────────────────────

| | | |
|---|---|---|
| **Cashmere House** | 190 NZ$ B&B | Full breakfast |
| 141 Hackthorne Rd. CHCH 2 | 5 rooms/suites, 5 pb | Afternoon tea, comp. wine |
| 03-332-7864 | Visa, MC, *Rated*, • | Sitting room, library |
| Fax: 033-327-864 | C-ltd/S-no/P-no/H-no | bicycles |
| Birgit & Monty Claxton | Swedish, German, | Airport: Christchurch |
| All year | French | |

*Stylish hillside mansion furnished with antiques and collectables. Library, full sized billiard table, classic cars, one acre garden. Extensive views of city, & coastline.*

*KleynBos, Christchurch, New Zealand*

## CHRISTCHURCH

**Eliza's Manor House**
82 Bealey Ave.
03-366-8584
Fax: 03-366-4946
Roz & John Smith
All year

85-145 NZ$ B&B
12 rooms/suites, 10 pb
Most CC
C-yes/S-no/P-no/H-no
English

Continental buffet
Afternoon tea, snacks
Bar service, sitt. room
A big welcome awaits you
kind, friendly staff
Airport: Christchurch

*Incredibly beautifully restored 1860 mansion. Very comfortable, garden setting. Short level walk to everything. A big welcome awaits you. **Winter rates $20 less 6/1-11/1.***

---

**Home-Lea Guest House**
195 Bealey Ave.
03-379-9977
Fax: 033-799-977
Sylvia & Merv Smith
All year

75 NZ$ B&B
5 rooms/suites, 2 pb
Visa, MC, *Rated*, •
S-no/P-no/H-no
English

Continental breakfast
Afternoon tea
Sitting room
Airport: Christchurch

*Charming character home close to city center. Secluded garden, cozy fire in winter. Complimentary home-baked cookies, tea, coffee. Very homey atmosphere.*

## CHRISTCHURCH 2, S. ISLAND

**KleynBos B&B Homestay**
59 Ngaio Street, (St. Martins)
64-3332-2896
Fax: 64-3332-9789
G. De Kleyne, Hans Van den
Bos
All year

50-80 NZ$ B&B
3 rooms/suites, 3 pb
•
C-yes/S-ltd/P-no/H-no
English

Continental plus bkfst.
Free coffee, tea
Off street parking
sitting room, garden
restaurants nearby
Airport: Christchurst

*Exclusive family home, charming wooden decor, tranquil street. City and shops nearby. Good beds, excellent value for money. Complimentary wine on arrival. **Specials, ask!***

## CHRISTCHURCH R.D.2, CANTERBURY

| **Pear Drop Inn-Orchard** | 70 NZ$ Inquire | Continental/full bkfst. |
|---|---|---|
| **Farmstay** | 3 rooms/suites, 2 pb | Lunch, dinner, tea (fee) |
| Highway 75 | Visa, MC, *Rated*, • | Sitting room, library |
| 03-3296-778 | C-yes/S-no/P-no/H-no | large garden, BBQ |
| Fax: 03-3296-778 | English, min. French | hot tubs |
| Brenda Crocker    All year | | Airport: Christchurch |

*Unique personalized holidays. Learn English or art while you stay in Canterbury. Home produce, home cooking. Warm, friendly, homey atmosphere. **Special rates-inquire!***

## COLLINGWOOD, GOLDEN BAY

| **Collingwood Homestay** | 125 NZ$ AP | Full breakfast |
|---|---|---|
| Elizabeth St. 7171 | 3 rooms/suites, 3 pb | Lunch, dinner, tea, wine |
| 03-5248079 | Visa, MC, *Rated*, • | Sitting room, library |
| Fax: 03-5248979 | C-ltd/S-no/P-no/H-no | squash court |
| Adrian & Maggie Veenvliet | English, Dutch, German | tennis court |
| All year | | Airport: Nelson |

*Elegant country hideaway, at the entrances of Abel Tasman and Kahurangi National Parks and Bird Sanctuary of Farewell Spit.*

## DUNEDIN

| **Lisburn House** | 175 NZ$ B&B | Full breakfast |
|---|---|---|
| 15 Lisburn Ave. Caversham | 3 rooms/suites, 3 pb | Afternoon tea, comp. wine |
| 034-558-888 | Visa, MC, *Rated*, • | Sitting room, library |
| Fax: 034-558-888 | C-ltd/S-no/P-no/H-no | historic home |
| The Forbes    All year | English | Airport: Dunedin |

*One of Dunedin's finest remaining examples of 19th century architecture. Open fires, 4 poster beds, fresh flowers, great breakfasts and private facilities.*

## DUNEDIN, OTAGO

| **Pine Heights Retreat** | 80 NZ$ B&B | Full breakfast |
|---|---|---|
| **Homestay** | 2 rooms/suites, 1 pb | Dinner available |
| 431 Pine Hill Road | Most CC | Complimentary wine |
| 03-473-9558 | • | sitting room |
| Fax: 03-473-0247 | C-yes/S-yes/P-no/H-no | Airport: Dudedin |
| Eli & Lindsay Imlay | English, Scandinavian | |

*Comfortable, homey, with tranquil rural views. Only 5 km from central city. Hospitable Kiwi hosts. Relaxed stay assured.*

## FAIRLIE, S. CANTERBURY

| **Kimbell Park Homestead** | 157 NZ$ B&B/MAP | Full, Continental (fee) |
|---|---|---|
| R.D. 17 | 2 rooms/suites, 2 pb | Lunch, dinner (fee) |
| 03-685-8170 | Visa, MC | Sitting room, gardens |
| Fax: 03-685-8170 | • | library |
| Shirley & Robin Sinclaie | C-yes/S-no/P-noEnglish | trout fishing nearby |
| All year | | Airport: Christchurch |

*Early colonial homestead; charming gardens, native birds, farm animals. Outlook to mountains, beautiful in winter, 2 local ski fields. Near Adventure Playground of Queenstown.*

## FEATHERSON

| **Waituna Homestead &** | 80-240 NZ$ Inquire | Full breakfast |
|---|---|---|
| **Cottage** | 5 rooms/suites, 5 pb | Lunch, dinner (fee) |
| East West Access Road, RD 3 | Most CC | Golf putting |
| 64-06-3077-743 | • | sitting room, library |
| Fax: 64-06-3077-753 | C-ltd/S-ltd/P-no/H-no | bicycles, Petanque court |
| The Luttrells    All year | English | Airport: Wellington |

*Waituna, a country hideaway, original artworks, handpainted wallpapers. Enjoy traditional farm food, award winning wines - The Real New Zealand. **Comp. pre-dinner drinks, wine.***

GERALDINE, S ISLAND

| | | |
|---|---|---|
| **Scotsdale** | 30 NZ$ B&B | Full breakfast |
| Peel Forest & Coopers Ck., 22 | 4 rooms/suites, | Dinner available (fee) |
| RD | English | Fruit trees, garden |
| 011-64-03-6963-874 | | native bush preserve near |
| Aylene & Alex Stalker | | peaceful |

*Rarely can one find anywhere so peaceful or welcoming. Rooms look out on 5,000-foot Mt. Peel. Good stopping off point between Christchurch and Mt. Cook. Rakaia Gorge nearby.*

GREYMOUTH

| | | |
|---|---|---|
| **Oak Lodge** | 130 NZ$ | Full breakfast |
| Coal Creek, State Highway 6 | 3 rooms/suites, | Dinner available |
| 03-768-6832 | *Rated*, | Tennis court |
| Fax: 03-768-4362 | English | hot tubs, swimming pool |
| Roy & Zelda Angerson | | extensive gardens |
| All year | | Airport: CH.CH. |
| | | International |

*Set in rural surroundings 3 km north of Greymouth. Furnished with antique furniture. Centrally situated to visit Paparoa National Park. Great fishing rivers nearby.*

HARI HARI, WESTLAND

| | | |
|---|---|---|
| **Wapiti Park Homestead** | 100-135 NZ$ B&B | Full breakfast |
| State Highway 6 | 5 rooms/suites, 3 pb | Lunch, dinner (fee) |
| 64-3753-3074 | Visa, MC | Sitting room, games room |
| Fax: 64-3753-3074 | • | bicycles, afternoon tea |
| Bev & Grant Muir | C-yes/S-no/P-no/H-yes | guided tours hunting |
| All year | English | Airport: Christchurch |

*Luxurious, spacious, colonial style country lodge/retreat offering traditional hospitality, superb comfort, memorable cuisine on working Rocky Mtn. elk ranch. 3rd nite 25% off*

HASTINGS, HAWKES BAY

| | | |
|---|---|---|
| **Providencia** | 160-185 NZ$ B&B | Full breakfast |
| Middle Rd., R.D. 2 | 3 rooms/suites, 2 pb | Lunch, dinner, aftn. tea |
| 068-772-300 | Visa, MC, AmEx, | Bar service, sitting room |
| Fax: 068-772-300 | *Rated*, | library, 6 acre garden |
| Janet and Raul | C-ltd/S-no/P-yes/H-yes | free bottle of wine |
| Maddison-Mejia | English, Spanish | Airport: Napier |
| All year | | |

*Historical country house set in vineyards and clean, green farmland. Attention to detail. Superb regional food and wine. Great fly fishing.*

HILLSBOROUGH, AUCKLAND

| | | |
|---|---|---|
| **Te Tapere, Homestay B&B** | 85 NZ$ B&B | Continental Breakfast |
| 8 Bluff Terrace 4 | 2 rooms/suites, 2 pb | Sitting room |
| 09-625-5848 | Visa, MC, *Rated*, | Airport: Auckland Int'l. |
| Fax: 09-625-2088 | C-ltd/S-no/P-no/H-no | |
| Jean & John Sandiford | English | |
| November-May | | |

*Sunny Waterside location. Modern home. Ensuite bathrooms. 15 minutes to airport or inner city. Meet & greet service and sightseeing at moderate charges. **2+ nights, $80.00.***

HOPE, NELSON ─────────────────────────────

| **Sunview Country** | 80-95 NZ$ B&B | Full breakfast |
| **Homestay** | 5 rooms/suites, 2 pb | Dinner by arrangement-fee |
| Hill Street South | • | Afternoon tea |
| P.O. Box 3001, Richmond, | C-yes/S-no/P-no/H-yes | sitting room |
| Nelson. NZ | English | swimming pool |
| 03-544-7584 | | Airport: Wellington/ |
| Fax: 03-544-7286 | | Christchurch |
| Noeline & Carl Arnold | | |
| All year | | |

*Subtropical orchard property with panoramic views of plains, sea and mountain ranges. Wine and pottery trails and craft shops nearby.*

HUNTERVILLE ─────────────────────────────

| **Otamaire, A Rural Retreat** | Rates: Inquire EP | Self catering |
| RD 2 | 7 rooms/suites, 3 pb | Meals avail. on request |
| 06-322-8027 | C-yes/S-yes/P-yes/H-no | Grass tennis court |
| Fax: 06-322-8027 | English | river swimming, horses |
| David & Vicky Duncan | | Native Bush walks |
| All year | | Airport: Palmerston North |

*This elegant country home and its extensive garden is a self catering option in lovely rural surroundings 15 minutes off State Highway 1 at Hunterville.*

KAIKOURA ─────────────────────────────

| **The Old Convent** | 60 NZ$ B&B | Continental plus bkfst. |
| Mt. Fyffe & Mill Rd. | 7 rooms/suites, 3 pb | Comp. tea/coffee/biscuits |
| 03-319-6603 | Visa, MC | Sitting room, library |
| Fax: 03-319-5107 | • | bicycles |
| Steve, Liz & Peter Tongue | C-yes/S-ltd/P-yes/H-no | Airport: Christchurch |
| All year | English | |

*Get in the habit, stay at the Old Convent, none can compare! Former convent situated three minute drive from the town in two acres of gardens and paddocks.*

KERIKERI ─────────────────────────────

| **Kilerman Orchard, Farm** | 100 NZ$ B&B/MAP | Full breakfast |
| **Stay** | 2 rooms/suites, 2 pb | Dinner (fee) |
| State Highway 10  0470 | Visa, MC, *Rated*, | Snacks,complimentary wine |
| 9-407-8582 | C-ltd/S-no/P-no/H-no | sitting room |
| Fax: 9-407-8317 | English | Airport: Auckland |
| Heather & Bruce Manson | | |
| All year | | |

*Contemporary home located on 45 acres of orchard and pasture. Handy to famous Bay of Islands. Quiet location, genuine hospitality.*

KERIKERY, BAY OF ISLANDS ─────────────────────

| **Aspley House** | 120-180 NZ$ Inquire | Continental plus bkfst. |
| Waimate N., RD 3 | 2 rooms/suites, 2 pb | Restaurant (fee) |
| 09-4059-509 | *Rated*, • | Swimming pool |
| Frank & Joy Atkinson | S-no/P-no/H-yes | sitting room, library |
| All year | English, min. Italian | historic area |
| | | Airport: Kerikeri |

*3 kms west of S.H. 10 at Puketona Junction, 10 mins.to Paihia-Bay of Islands, 10 min. to Kerikeri Airport. Attractive country colonial home. **Complimentary wine with dinner.***

MANAPOURI————————————————————————

| | | |
|---|---|---|
| **Murrells Grand View** | 160-180 NZ$ B&B | Full breakfast |
| **House** | 4 rooms/suites, 4 pb | Dinner (fee), tea |
| 7 Murrell Ave.  9660 | Visa, MC, *Rated*, • | Sitting room, library |
| 03-249-6642 | C-ltd/S-no/P-no/H-no | complimentary wine |
| Fax: 03-249-6642 | English | tours available |
| Jack & Klaske Murrell | | Airport: Queenstown |
| All year | | |

*Built for overseas visitors in 1889 by Jack's grandparents, we host comfortable, old fashioned hospitality. Large secluded grounds. Excellent views, and good coffee.*

NELSON————————————————————————————

| | | |
|---|---|---|
| **California House Inn** | 140 NZ$ B&B | Full breakfast |
| 29 Collingwood St.  7001 | 4 rooms/suites, 4 pb | Comp. wine, aftn. tea |
| 64-3-548-4173 | Visa, MC | Sitting room, library |
| Fax: 64-3-548-4173 | • | Airport: Nelson |
| Neil & Shelley Johnstone | C-ltd/S-no/P-no/H-no | |
| All year | English, French | |

*Historic villa offering character accommodations. Spacious bedrooms, private bathrooms, sunny verandahs overlooking gardens. Home-baked Californian breakfasts.*

NELSON, BRIGHTWATER ——————————————————————

| | | |
|---|---|---|
| **Pepper Tree Place** | 65 NZ$ B&B | Full breakfast |
| 126 Lord Rutherford | 3 rooms/suites, | Afternoon tea, snacks |
| Rd.South | *Rated*, • | Television room |
| 03-542-3280 | C-ltd/S-no/P-no/H-no | sitting room |
| Fax: 03-542-3280 | English | family friendly facility |
| Andrew and Charlotte | | Airport: Nelson |
| All year | | |

*Friendly, relaxed peaceful environment. Comfortable home on 1/2 acre garden. Semi-rural setting close to town. "Country" breakfast, homemade bread/muffins.*

NELSON, RICHMOND ——————————————————————

| | | |
|---|---|---|
| **Mapledurham Heritage Inn** | 150-165 NZ$ B&B | Full breakfast |
| 8 Edward St. | 3 rooms/suites, 3 pb | Dinner, aftn. tea, snacks |
| 64-3-544-4210 | Visa, MC, *Rated*, • | Sitting room, library |
| Fax: 64-3-544-4210 | C-ltd/S-no/P-yes/H-no | bicycles, hot tub |
| Giles and Deborah Grigg | English | complimentary wine |
| All year | | Airport: Nelson |

*An elegantly restored villa set in peaceful gardens. Expect every comfort, delicious food and warm hospitality. Gateway to Nelson province. Boules, cricket, croquet.*

OPOTIKI, BAY OF PLENTY——————————————————

| | | |
|---|---|---|
| **Capeview Cottages** | 150 NZ$ B&B | Meals on request |
| P.O. Box 69, Tablelands | 2 rooms/suites, 2 pb | Bottle wine after 2 nts. |
| Rd.  3092 | Visa, MC | Golf, fish, jet boat tour |
| +64-7-315-7877 | • | helicopter volcano trip |
| Fax: +64-7-315-8055 | C-yes/S-no/P-no/H-no | Airport: Whakatane |
| Kathleen and Brian Young | English | |
| All year | | |

*Luxury country cottage, fabulous views of sea & mtns. 2 dbl. bdrms., luxury kitchen, priv. hot-tub, peaceful setting. Free Kiwi chocolates. **Free bottle NZ wine 2nd nite stay.***

## OTUREHUA, CENTRAL OTAGO

| **Carngham Homestay** | 45-75 NZ$ Inquire | Full breakfast |
|---|---|---|
| Ida Valley Rd. | 3 rooms/suites, | Other meals avail. (fee) |
| 03-444-5846 | *Rated*, | Sitting room, tennis |
| Fax: 03-444-5859 | C-yes/S-no/P-yes/H-yes | farm visits, local sight- |
| Annette & Neville Butterfield | English | seeing, 4WD tours avail. |
| All year | | Airport: Dunedin |

*Rural tranquility, historic sites, country cuisine and hospitality in a majestic rugged landscape. Guided fishing and hunting trips by arrangement.*

## PAUANUI BEACH, THAMES

| **Pauanui Pacific Holidays** | 95-110 NZ$ B&B | Full breakfast |
|---|---|---|
| 7 Brodie Lane, off Dunlop Dr. | 4 rooms/suites, 4 pb | Restaurant (fee) |
| 07-864-8933 | Most CC | Sitting room, bicycles |
| Fax: 07-864-8253 | C-ltd/S-no/P-no/H-no | tennis court, hot tubs |
| Kevin & Kay Flooks | English | swimming pool |
| All year | | Airport: Auckland, Hamilton |

*Pauanui is a unique holiday resort on the Corommandel Peninsula surrounded by beautiful beaches. Our 4 units have private facilities. We are a 4 minute walk to Pacific Ocean.*

## PICTON, MARLBOROUGH

| **The Gables** | 85 NZ$ B&B | Full breakfast |
|---|---|---|
| 20 Waikawa Rd. | 4 rooms/suites, 4 pb | Afternoon tea, snacks |
| 064-03-573-6772 | Most CC, *Rated*, • | Sitting room, laundry |
| Fax: 064-03-573-8860 | C-yes/S-no/P-no/H-no | complimentary wine |
| The Smiths        All year | English | Airport: Wellington |

*Richard and Ann offer you genuine kiwi hospitality. Centrally located 1920s home with delicious breakfasts, queen beds, private bathrooms. Restaurants nearby.*

## PORIRUA, WELLINGTON

| **Braebyre Rural Homestay** | 85 NZ$ B&B | Full breakfast |
|---|---|---|
| Flightys Rd., Pauatahanui | 3 rooms/suites, 1 pb | Dinner (fee), aftn. tea |
| 04-235-9311 | *Rated*, • | Recreational fac. nearby |
| Fax: 04-235-9345 | C-yes/S-no/P-yes/H-ltd | Tour Mohair goat farm |
| Jenny & Randall Shaw | English | Airport: Wellington |
| All year | | |

*Experience Kiwi friendliness and rural tranquility in spacious home on Mohair Goat Farm. Close to Wellington's attractions. Complimentary wine, hot tub, sitting room, snacks.*

## QUEENSTOWN

| **Melbourne Motor Lodge & Guest House** | 78-106 NZ$ B&B/EP | Continental plus bkfst. |
|---|---|---|
| 35 Melbourne St. | 33 rooms/suites, 23 pb | Kitchen units/Restaurant |
| 03-442-8431 | Most CC, *Rated*, • | Garden patio/lake views |
| Fax: 03-442-7466 | C-yes/S-yes/P-no/H-yes | helicopters, rafts, jet |
| C. Lewis, T. Robinson | English | boats and more nearby |
| All year | | Airport: Queenstown |

*A popular choice for tramper & holidaymaker alike. 3 minutes to town; airport shuttle and ski bus at front gate. Cozy and comfortable year round destination.* **Discount avail.**

| **Stable, The** | 100-120 NZ$ B&B | Full breakfast |
|---|---|---|
| 17 Brisbane St. | 3 rooms/suites, 2 pb | Dinner by arrangement |
| 3-442-9251 | Visa, MC | Library |
| Fax: 3-442-8293 | • | golf course nearby |
| Isobel & Gordon McIntyre | C-ltd/S-ltd/P-no/H-yes | near/tennis/bowling green |
| All year | English | Airport: Queenstown |

*Historic stone building in a quiet location. Close to lake, park, beach. Town center only minutes walking distance. Welsh ponies*

QUEENSTOWN, OTAGO———————————————————————————

**Bush Creek Health Retreat**
Bowen St.  9197
03-442-7260
Fax: 03-442-6816
Ileen Mutch
All year

45 NZ$ B&B
4 rooms/suites, 2 pb
*Rated*, •
C-yes/S-no/P-no/H-no
English

Continental plus bkfst.
Afternoon tea, snacks
Sitting room, library
sundecks, gazebos
1-2 km from town
Airport: Christchurch

*Revitalize your energies, heavenly sounds of native birds & cascading waterfall. Secluded 3 acres of gorgeous garden. Organically grown orchard fresh foods.* **3rd night 50% off.**

ROTORUA———————————————————————————————

**Te Ana Farmstay**
Poutakataka Rd., Ngakuru,
RD 1
073-332-720
Fax: 073-332-720
Heather & Brian Oberer
All year

45-75 NZ$ B&B/MAP
4 rooms/suites, 3 pb
•
C-yes/S-no/P-noEnglish

Full breakfast
Dinner by arrangement
Sitting room
library
family friendly facility
Airport: Rotorua, Auckland
Int'l.

*Idyllic country setting. Spacious garden. 569 acre dairy, beef, sheep and deer farm bounded by lake. Scrumptious breakfasts, 3 course gourmet dinners.*

**Waiteti Lakeside Lodge**
2 Arnold St., Ngongotaha
07-357-2311
Fax: 07-357-2311
Brian & Val Blewett
All year

95 NZ$ B&B
4 rooms/suites, 2 pb
Visa, MC
C-ltd/S-no/P-no/H-no
English

Full breakfast
Tea, coffee
Sitt. rm., lib., TV, pool
pool table, spa, canoes
Airport: Auckland

*Situated on the edge of Lake Rotorua and the Waiteti Stream, there are spectacular panoramic views. 10 minutes from all Rotorua attractions. Charter boat, fly fishing, jetty.*

ROTORUA, AUKLAND————————————————————————————

**Peppertree Farm Homestay**
25 Cookson Rd., R.D. 4
07-345-3718
Fax: 07-345-3718
Deane & Elma Balme
All year

75-135 NZ$ Inquire
3 rooms/suites, 2 pb
*Rated*, •
C-ltd/S-no/P-yes/H-yes
English

Continental/Full bkfst.
Lunch, dinner (fee)
Tea, snacks, comp. wine
sitting room
family friendly facility
Airport: Rotorua

*Great lake views, easy lake access. Ten minutes to Rotorua City. Attractive garden. Meals comprised of all locally grown products.* **Pre-dinner drinks & comp. wine with dinner.**

ROTORUA, BAY OF PLENTY————————————————————————

**Deer Pine Lodge**
Jackson Road, Kaharoa, PO
Box 22
P.O. Box 22, Ngangotaha,
Rotorua, NZ
07-332-3458
Fax: 07-332-3458
John & Betty Insch
All year

90 NZ$ B&B
10 rooms/suites, 6 pb
*Rated*, •
C-yes/S-yes/P-no/H-no
English

Full breakfast
Lunch, dinner, dining rm.
Fully contained units
all private facilities
Airport: Auckland

*Deer farm with panoramic views of Lake Roturua from our own private balcony. Free tour of deer farm. Ten miles from Rotorua City Centre.* **Third night 20% discount.**

## ROTORUA, BAY OF PLENTY

| **Tresco International B&B** | 75 NZ$ B&B | Full breakfast |
| 3 Toko St. 07 | 7 rooms/suites, 0 pb | Sitting room, library |
| 07-348-9611 | Visa, MC | hot tub, laundry fac. |
| Fax: 073-489-611 | • | Airport: Rototua |
| Gay Scott-Fenton/Barrie | C-ltd/S-no/P-no/H-no | |
| Fenton | English | |
| All year | | |

*Quiet warm home style hospitality with hot spa, laundry/drying room, close to city centre, restaurants, museum, lake, golf courses. Thermal heating. 15% off for three nights.*

## STRATFORD, TARANAKI

| **Stallard Farm B&B** | 60 NZ$ B&B | Full breakfast |
| 3514 State Highway 3 | 4 rooms/suites, 3 pb | Dinner (inquire) |
| 06-765-8324 | Most CC, *Rated*, | Cooking facilities |
| Fax: 06-765-8324 | C-yes/S-yes/P-no/H-yes | pool table, TV in rooms |
| Cora & Billie Anne | English | garden walks |
| All year | | Airport: New Plymouth |

*Olde English "Upstairs Downstairs" antique hideaway. Close to town, Mt. Egmont National Park. Extensive gardens, river. Relaxed gracious country comfort. **Farm visit in season.***

## TAIRUA, VIA THAMES

| **Hornsea House** | 40-70 NZ$ B&B | Full breakfast |
| 297 Main Rd. | 2 rooms/suites, | Afternoon tea |
| 64-07-8648-536 | • | Family friendly facility |
| Fax: 64-07-8648-536 | C-yes/S-no/P-no/H-no | near golf, croquet |
| Doreen & Derek Cory-Wright | English | Airport: Auckland |
| All year | | International |

*Comfortable historic family homestead. Farmstyle breakfast. Old established garden and bush. Adjacent golf, bowls, croquet. Near surf; safe beaches.*

## TAUPO

| **Delmont Lodge** | 90-130 NZ$ B&B | Full breakfast |
| 115 Shepherd Rd. | 3 rooms/suites, 3 pb | Lunch, dinner, aftn. tea |
| 07-378-3304 | Most CC, *Rated*, • | Sitting room |
| Fax: 07-378-3322 | C-yes/S-no/P-no/H-no | sun porch |
| Jenny Delmont | English | Airport: Taupo |
| All year | | |

*Beside entrance to Lake Taupo's Botanical Gardens, Delmont Lodge sits on half an acre of beautiful gardens & mature trees. Gardeners dream. **Free bottle of wine 3rd night stay.***

| **Riverway Cottages** | 70 NZ$ B&B | Continental plus bkfst. |
| 16 Peehi Manini, Waitahanui | 2 rooms/suites, 1 pb | Dinner by arrangement |
| RD 2 | *Rated*, | Sitting room, library |
| 07-3788-822 | C-yes/P-no/H-no | Fish |
| John & Joyce Johnson | English | All year/wild trout |
| All year | | tackle & waders provided |
| | | Airport: Auckland - Taupo |

*100 yards from Waitahanui River. 200 yards to Lake Taupo. You fish for wild trout with John as your guide. Fishing All year.*

## TAURANGA, BAY OF PLENTY

**Baumgarten Lodge**
322 Oropi Rd., RD 3  3021
64-7-5432799
Fax: 64-7-5432799
The Limachers
All year

65 NZ$ B&B
3 rooms/suites, 1 pb
C-yes/S-no/P-no/H-no
English, German

Full breakfast
Dinner available (fee)
Sitting room, hot tubs
swimming pool, near golf,
rafting, fishing, treks
Airport: Auckland

*Peaceful semi-rural, minutes from city centre and tourist attractions. Avocado orchard, setting lawns. Gardens, swimming pool, spa, 9 pin bowling alley.*

## TE ANAU, SOUTHLAND

**Shakespeare House**
10 Dusky St.  9681
03-249-7349
Fax: 032-497-629
Margaret & Jeff Henderson
All year

112 NZ$ B&B
8 rooms/suites, 8 pb
Most CC
•
C-yes/S-no/P-yes/H-yes
English

Full breakfast
Dinner by arrangement
Courtesy car
relaxed conservatory area
Airport: Queenstown

*Helpful and friendly hospitality. King size beds. Can arrange Milford and Doubtful Sound trips. Quiet area, within walking distance of lake, shops and attractions.*

## THAMES

**Wharfedale Farmstay**
R.D. I
07-8688-929
Fax: 07-8688-926
Chris & Rosemary Burks
All year

100-110 NZ$ B&B
2 rooms/suites, 2 pb
*Rated*, •
C-ltd/S-no/P-no/H-yes
English

Full breakfast
Dinner by arrangement
Complimentary wine, tea
sitting room, tennis
swimming in private river
Airport: Auckland

*Set in tranquil native forest, cottage gardens, old roses & herbs. River walks, swimming. Dairy goats & produce. English Edwardian antiques.* **20% off 3rd night.**

## THORNDON, WELLINGTON

**Tinakori Lodge B&B**
182 Tinakori Rd.
04-473-3478
Fax: 044-725-554
Mel & John Ainsworth
All year

88 NZ$ B&B
9 rooms/suites, 3 pb
Most CC, *Rated*, •
C-ltd/S-no/P-no/H-no
English

Full breakfast
Comp. tea & coffee
Sitting room
library, bicycles, sauna
Airport: Wellington

*Situated in historic Thorndon. Comfortable furnished 1870s house. Short walk to the Goverment Center and city which features a selection of fine restaurants. TV in rooms.*

## TIMARU, S. ISLAND

**Mountain View**
Talbots Road, Kingsdown, No
1 RD
03-6881070
Fax: 03-6881070
The Bells
All year

60 NZ$ Inquire
3 rooms/suites, 2 pb
•
C-yes/S-no/P-no/H-no
English

Continental - Full (fee)
Afternoon tea, comp. wine
Sundeck
conservatory
gardens
Airport: Christchurch

*Rural homestay 3 kms from city. Warm Kiwi hospitality. Few Deer and sheep. Tranquil garden overlooking farmland. Mountain day trips to lakes and ski-fields.*

## TURANGI

| | | |
|---|---|---|
| **Raukawa Lodge** | 70 NZ$ B&B | Full breakfast |
| State Hwy 1, P.O. Box 195 | 2 rooms/suites, | Lunch, dinner |
| 073-867-637 | C-yes/S-no/P-no/H-no | Sitting room |
| Fax: 073-867-637 | English, French | complimentary wine |
| John & Sarah Sage | | games room, boat |
| All year | | Airport: Auckland |

*Home away from home midway between Auckland and Wellington. Close to New Zealand's famed trout rivers, lake Taupo, Mt. Raupehu, and geothermal wonderland. 20% off 3rd night.*

## TURANGI, LAKE TAUPO

| | | |
|---|---|---|
| **Braxmere Fishing Lodge** | 90 NZ$ B&B | Continental breakfast |
| 88 Waihi Rd., P.O. Box 11 | 12 rooms/suites, | Dinner 22.00 NZ$ |
| Takaanu | Visa, MC, AmEx | Hot tubs |
| 07-386-8011 | • | conference center |
| Fax: 07-386-7513 | C-yes/S-yes/P-yes/H-ltd | |
| Brian Jones | English | |
| All year | | |

*Lakeside hide-away. Thermal pools, fishing guide available, boats, wharf, 30 minutes to snowfields. New Zealands best kept secret. **3rd night 50% off.***

## WELLINGTON

| | | |
|---|---|---|
| **Waitohu Lodge B&B** | 75 NZ$ B&B/MAP | Continental plus bkfst. |
| **Country Homestay** | 3 rooms/suites, 2 pb | Dinner (fee) |
| 294 State Highway 1 Otaki | • | Hot tub, library |
| N. 6471 | C-yes/S-ltd/P-ltd/H-no | sitting room-books, games |
| 06-364-5389 | English | secure off-street parking |
| Fax: 64-6-364-5350 | | Airport: Wellington, |
| Keith & Mary Oldham | | Palmerston |
| All year | | |

*"Quality Award" accommodation in country garden setting. Close to Tararua Forest Park, one hour drive to Wellington City and Picton Ferry. Gateway to the Kapiti Coast.*

## WESTLAND

| | | |
|---|---|---|
| **The Breakers** | 80 NZ$ B&B | Full breakfast |
| Nine Mile Creek - Rapahoe | 3 rooms/suites, 1 pb | Dinner (fee) |
| 037-627-743 | *Rated*, • | Afternoon tea, snacks |
| Fax: 037-627-743 | C-ltd/S-no/P-noEnglish | sitting room |
| Ib & Tony Pupich | | family friendly facility |
| All year | | Airport: Christchurch |

*Absolute beachfront overlooking Tasman Sea. Two acres of native trees and garden. Wonderful sunset and views from all rooms.*

## WHANGAREI

| | | |
|---|---|---|
| **Riviera** | 75-90 NZ$ B&B/EP | Full breakfast |
| 1909A Ngunguru Rd. R.D. | 2 rooms/suites, 2 pb | Dinner by arrangment(fee) |
| 3 0121 | Visa, MC | Sitting room, library |
| 09-434-3916 | • | tennis court |
| Fax: 09-434-3918 | C-ltd/S-no/P-no/H-no | golf,tennis, swim-nearby |
| Jo La Krapes | English | Airport: Auckland |
| Sept 1-May 30 | | |

*Situated bet. Auckland & Bay of Islands. Scuba dive the world famous Poor Knights Islands. House specialty-sourdough pancakes. **Advance booking—1st night meal free/ Complimentary drink.***

## WHITIANGA

| | | |
|---|---|---|
| **Spellbound Homestay B&B** | 50 NZ$ B&B/MAP | Continental plus bkfst. |
| 77 Grange, Hahei Beach, RD | 4 rooms/suites, 4 pb | Dinner by arrangement |
| 1 | Visa, MC | Snacks |
| 64-7866-3543 | • | superb beaches |
| Fax: 64-7866-3003 | C-ltd/S-no/P-no/H-no | fishing |
| Barbara & Alan Lucas | English | Airport: Auckland |
| All year | | |

*Informal, relaxed accommodation in our modern home with panoramic views. Our region offers superb beaches, bush walking, fishing, spectacular scenery.*

## WHITIANGA, MERCURY BAY

| | | |
|---|---|---|
| **Cosy Cat Cottage** | 80 NZ$ B&B | Continental plus bkfst. |
| 41, South Highway | 3 rooms/suites, 3 pb | A-la-carte bkfst. avail. |
| 64-7-8664488 | Visa, MC, *Rated*, • | Sitting room, library |
| Fax: 64-7-8664488 | C-ltd/S-no/P-ltd/H-no | shaded verandah seating |
| Gordon & Janet Pearce | English | Airport: Auckland |
| All year | | |

*Picturesque two story cottage filled with feline memorabilia. Delicious a-la-carte breakfasts. Friendly helpful service. Meet our Tonkinese cats.*

# Portugal

## ESTREMOZ

| | | |
|---|---|---|
| **Monte Dos Pensamentos** | 11,000 Portugese$ B&B | Full breakfast |
| Estrada Da Estacao Do | 4 rooms/suites, 4 pb | MAP, AP available (fee) |
| Ameixial  7100 Estremoz | *Rated*, • | Lunch, dinner, tea, wine |
| 351-68-22375 | C-yes/S-yes/P-yes/H-yes | swimming pool, bicyles |
| Fax: 351-68-332409 | English, French, Spanish | Airport: Lisbon |
| Cristovas Leitas | | |
| All year | | |

*Beautiful house of XIX Century, 2 km from Estremoz. Ideal places to visit nearby are Alentejo, like Borba, Vila Vicosa, Evoramonte, Evora and Monsaraz. Ideal to rest, also.*

## SINTRA

| | | |
|---|---|---|
| **Quinta Sao Thiago** | 18-28,000 Portugese$ | Continental plus bkfst. |
| Estrada de Monserrate  2710 | B&B | Other meals - inquire |
| 01-923-2923 | 10 rooms/suites, 8 pb | Bar service, library |
| Fax: 01-923-4329 | *Rated*, • | tennis court, sitting rm. |
| Maria Teresa Braddell | C-yes/S-yes/P-yes/H-yes | swimming pool, dancing |
| All year | English, French, Spanish | Airport: Lisbon |

*Riding, golf courses near. Lapped by the sea, many beaches within easy reach. Near many palaces, celebrated monuments. Once inhabited by monks. **Free drink of choice on arrival.***

## SINTRA, LISBON

| | | |
|---|---|---|
| **Quinta da Capela** | 24,000 Portugese$ B&B | Buffet breakfast |
| Estrada Velha de | 10 rooms/suites, 10 pb | Dinner, tea, snacks, wine |
| Monserate  2710 | Most CC, *Rated*, • | Bar service, library |
| 01-929-01-70 | C-yes/S-yes/P-yes/H-yes | sitting room |
| Fax: 01-929-34-25 | English, German, | sauna, swimming pool |
| Arturo D. Pereira | French | Airport: Lisbon |
| All year | | |

*30 minutes from Lisbon, surrounded by Sintra hills. Spectacular views, botannical gardens, lush vegetation, ancient castles, historical monuments. Beaches 10 minutes away.*

# Scotland, U.K.

**Tigh-an-Eilean Hotel**
Shieldaig by
Strathcarron  IV54 8XN
01520-755251
Fax: 01520-755321
Callum Stewart
Mid April-October

87 English$ B&B
11 rooms/suites, 11 pb
Visa, MC, AmEx,
*Rated*, •
C-yes/S-ltd/P-yes/H-no
English, French,
German

Full breakfast
Lunch, dinner, aftn. tea
Bar service, sitting room
Airport: Inverness

ARGYLL—————————————————————————————

**Argyll Hotel**
Isle of Iona  PA76 6SJ
01681-700334
Fax: 01681-700510
Mrs. Fiona M. Menzies
Easter-October

78 English$ B&B
17 rooms/suites, 15 pb
Visa, MC
•
C-yes/S-ltd/P-yes/H-no
French, English

Full breakfast
Lunch, dinner, restaurant
Bar service, vegetarian
22 party conference room
Airport: Glasgow

*Friendly hotel lying on the seashore. Cozy lounges, spacious dining room, plant-filled sunlounge. Freshly prepared food w/local ingredients. Free bottle of wine on 3rd night.*

DUMFRIES—————————————————————————————

**Comlongon Castle**
Clarencefield  DG14 4NA
0044-0138-7870-283
Fax: 0044-0128-7870-266
Simon & Phillip Ptolomey
All year

85 English$ B&B
11 rooms/suites, 11 pb
Visa, MC, AmEx,
*Rated*, •
C-yes/S-ltd/P-no/H-no
English

Full breakfast
Dinner, restaurant (fee)
Bar service
sitting room
Airport: Glasgow

*Medieval castle, S.W. Scotland, four course dinner by candle light. Over 300 weeding ceremonies took place in castle in last 12 months. 3 nights 10% discount on B&B rate.*

DUNBARTONSHIRE—————————————————————————

**Kirkton House**
Darleith Rd.  G82 5EZ
013-898-41951
Fax: 013-898-41868
Stewart and Gillian
Macdonald
Closed Christmas

30 English$ B&B
6 rooms/suites, 6 pb
Visa, MC, AmEx,
*Rated*, •
C-yes/S-yes/P-yes/H-ltd
English, French, Dutch

Full breakfast
Dinner, snacks
Sitting room, library
resid. drinks licence
easy drive to Glasgow
Airport: Glasgow

*Converted 18/19th century farm in tranquil rural position, commanding panoramic views of the River Clyde. Informal and relaxing ambience. Wine and dine by oil lamplight.*

DUNOON, ARGYLL————————————————————————

**Enmore House**
Marine Parade  PA23 8HH
013-697-02230
Fax: 013-697-02148
David & Angela Wilson
All year

70 English$ B&B
10 rooms/suites, 10 pb
Visa, MC, AmEx,
*Rated*, •
C-yes/S-yes/P-
yesFrench, English

Full breakfast
Lunch, dinner, restaurant
Bar service, sitting room
water bed & jacuzzi
Airport: Glasgow

*Award winning hotel for both Cuisine, Hospitality and Service. Just one hour from Glasgow airport via ferry. Three golf courses within 10 minutes drive.*

## INVERNESS, INVERNESS-SHIRE

**Old Royal Guest House**
10 Union Street  IV1 1PL
01463-230551
Fax: 01463-711916
Jim & Geraldine Reid
Feb-Nov

40-60.00 English$ B&B
14 rooms/suites, 5 pb
Visa, MC, *Rated*,
C-yes/S-yes/P-no/H-no
English

Full breakfast
Airport: Inverness

*Ideal location for rail travellers. Just opposite the train station. Comfortable home away from home atmosphere.*

## ISLE OF SKYE, HIGHLAND

**Kinloch House**
Sleat  IV 43 8QY
1471-833214
Fax: 1471-833277
Lord and Lady MacDonald
March-November

80-170 English$ B&B
10 rooms/suites, 10 pb
Most CC, *Rated*, •
C-yes/S-yes/P-yes/H-no
English

Full breakfast
Restaurant (fee), tea
Sitting room
library
Airport: Inverness

*Home of Lord and Lady MacDonald, Kinloch has achieved an enviable reputation for everything excellent over the past 23 years.*

## KNIPOCH, STRATHCLYDE

**Knipoch Hotel**
Argyll, by Oban  PA34 4QT
018-523-16251
Fax: 018-523-16249
The Craig Family
Mid Feb-Nov

130 English$ B&B
17 rooms/suites, 17 pb
Most CC, *Rated*, •
C-yes/S-yes/P-no/H-no
English, Danish

Full breakfast (fee)
Restaurant, bar service
Afternoon tea, snacks
sitting room
Airport: Glasgow

*Luxurious country house hotel, family-run. Six miles south of Oban on Loch Feochan. Awards for cuisine, 360 bin wine list, well stocked bar.*

## PENICUIK

**Kykeneuk Cottage**
Peebles Road
011-44-19-68-675-885
Mrs. Celia Hobbs

21 English$
1 room/suites, 1 pb
English

Full breakfast
Alpine garden and pond
panoramic views
color TV, ample storage

*Explore Edinburgh & surrounding areas. Day trips to Farne Islands, Holy Island, and Lindisfarne. Charming cottage offers panoramic view of Pentland Hills and Moorfoot hills.*

## STIRLINESHIRE

**Culcreuch Castle &**
**Country Park**
Fintry, L.Lomond,
Stirline,Tross.  G63 0LW
44-1360-860555
Fax: 44-1360-860556
Laird A. Haslam of Gulcreuch
All year

70 English$ B&B
8 rooms/suites, 8 pb
Most CC, *Rated*, •
C-yes/S-ltd/P-no/H-no
English

Full breakfast
Bar, restaurant (fee)
Golf, fish, water sports
hot tub, library, nature
Airport: Glasgow, Edinburgh

*700-year-old romantic castle, seat of Galbraith Clan, set in spectacular scenery yet only 45 minutes drive from Glasgow/Edinburgh airports. **Special offers, please inquire.***

# South Africa

SOMERSET, WESTERN CAPE————————————————————————

| | | |
|---|---|---|
| **Villa Louise** | 60 US$ MAP | Full breakfast |
| 43 Firmont and Goedehoop | 5 rooms/suites, 5 pb | Dinner, aftn. tea, snacks |
| St. 7130 | Visa, MC, AmEx | Bar service, sitting room |
| 27-2485-216-30 | • | library, bicycles, pool |
| Fax: 27-2485-216-48 | C-yes/S-ltd/P-no/H-no | pick-up at airport |
| Christian-Edmee Voarick | Eng., Ger., It., Fr., Dut | Airport: Capetown |
| All year | | |

*Art deco and Malaysian furnished, gourmet breakfast and dinner served in garden, orchard, or pool. Magnificent views onto ocean and Cape of Good Hope. Close to wine region.*

# Spain

ALHAURIN EL GRANDE, MALAGA————————————————————

| | | |
|---|---|---|
| **Finca la Mota** | 9,000 Spanish$ B&B | Full breakfast |
| Carretera de Mijas 29120 | 13 rooms/suites, 9 pb | Lunch, dinner, restaurant |
| 952-49-09-01 | Most CC, *Rated*, • | Bar serv., sitt. rm. pool |
| Fax: 952-594-120 | C-yes/S-yes/P-yes/H-yes | tennis, golf 1 Km |
| Arun and Jean Narang | English, Spanish, French | Beach 15 Km, Horse-riding |
| All year | | Airport: Malaga |

*Three-hundred year old Andalucian farmhouse inn, decorated in rustic style and surrounded by agricultural land. Informal, family atmosphere. Children very welcome.*

ALLES, ASTURIAS————————————————————————————

| | | |
|---|---|---|
| **La Tahona de Besnes** | 6,000 Spanish$ B&B/EP | Restaurant (fee) |
| Besnes 33578 | 13 rooms/suites, 13 pb | Lunch, dinner, snacks |
| 9-8-54157-49 | Most CC, *Rated*, | Bar service |
| Fax: 9-4272-3402 | C-yes/S-yes/P-no/H-ltd | bicycles |
| Lorenzo & Sarah Nilsson | Spanish, English | sitting room |
| All year | | Airport: Madrid (Oviedo) |

*Charmingly restored stone bakery offering rustic hideaway. Outdoor activities All year. Cozy restaurant specializing in local cuisine. **Free bottle wine with dinner.***

ARCOS DE LA FRA, CADIZ————————————————————————

| | | |
|---|---|---|
| **Hacienda El Santiscal** | 2,750 Spanish$ Inquire | Continental/Full Bkfst. |
| Avenida del Santiscal No. | 12 rooms/suites, 12 pb | Restaurant (fee) |
| 129  11638 | Most CC, *Rated*, • | Sitting room, library |
| 956-708-313 | S-yes/H-no | swimming pool, nautical |
| Fax: 956-708-268 | Eng., Fr., Arabic, | sports, cultural visits |
| Pagvi Gallardo Carrasco | German | Airport: Jerez/Seville/ |
| All year | | Gibralter |

*Many activities abound here. Riding, nautical sports, cultural awareness, swimming, hiking. Full bar & restaurant provides all amenities. **Complimentary bottle of wine in room.***

## COZORLA, JAEN

**Hotel Noguera de la Sierpe**
Coto Rios, Parque de
Cazorla 23478
953-71-30-21
Fax: 953-71-31-09
Lucia Franco Molina
All year

8.500 Spanish$ Inquire
43 rooms/suites, 43 pb
Most CC
•
C-yes/S-yes/P-yes/H-yes
English, Spanish

Continental/Full Bkfst.
Restaurant (fee)
Sitting room, bicycles
swimming pool, horses
fishing, private lake
Airport: Granada-Malaga

*Enjoy peace and quiet in Parque Natural de Cazorla Ysegura. Deer, mountain goats, wild boar inhabit protected area. Extensive hotel grounds, private lake, riding stable, pool.*

## CUENCA

**Posada de San Jose**
Julian Romero 4  16001
969-211-300
Fax: 969-230-365
Jennifer and Antonio
Cortinas   All year

4,500 Spanish$
30 rooms/suites, 21 pb
Most CC, *Rated*, •
C-yes/S-yes/P-no/H-no
English, French, Spanish

Continental breakfast
Afternoon tea, snacks
Bar service, sitting room
terrace and garden
Airport: Madrid

*The Posada de San Jose is situated in the heart of the old historic quarter of Cuenca, in a 17th century building. Its' old portal tempts you to admire the views.*

## LOJA, GRANADA

**Hotel La Bobadilla**
Finca La Bobadilla APDO
144  18300
07-34-58-321861
Fax: 07-34-58-321810
Barcelo Hotels   All year

34,800 Spanish$ Inquire
60 rooms/suites, 60 pb
•
C-yes/S-yes/P-yes/H-yes
Spanish, English, Ger, Fr

Full breakfast
Restaurant (fee)
Bar service, sitting room
library, bicycles, tennis
sauna, swimming pool
Airport: Granada, Malaga

*La Bobadilla is an Andalusian village surrounded by a forest of Holm-Oaks and olives which offer haute cuisine in both restaurants. Each of the 60 different rooms are unique.*

## MALAGA

**Molino del Santo**
Bda Estacion S/N, 29370
Benaojan
95-216-7151
Fax: 95-216-7327
Pauline Elkin   Feb 23-Dec 10

6-11,000 Spanish$ EP
12 rooms/suites, 12 pb
Most CC, *Rated*, •
C-yes/S-yes/H-ltd
Spanish, English, French

Continental & full (fee)
Restaurant - all meals
Bar service, sitting room
library, great walking
bicycles, swimming pool
Airport: Malaga, Sevilla

*Delightful converted watermill alongside a mountain stream in stunning countryside. Peaceful and quiet. Exceptionally helpful staff. 10 km from Ronda.*

## SANLUCAR DE BARRAMEDA, CADIZ

**Posada de Palacio**
Calle Caballeros 11  11540
956-36-48-40
Fax: 956-36-50-60
March-October

8,000 Spanish$ B&B
13 rooms/suites, 13 pb
Most CC
•
C-yes/S-yes/P-yes/H-ltd
English, Ger., Sp., Fr.

Continental bkfst. (fee)
Afternoon tea
Bar service, sitting room
comp. bottle of wine
Airport: Jerez, Seville

*Eighteenth century house in the antique area of Sanlucar.*

## SEGOVIA

**Hotel R. Los Linajes**
Dr. Velasco 9  40003
021-460-475
Fax: 021-460-479
Miguel Borrequero Rubeu
All year

8,200 Spanish$ B&B
55 rooms/suites, 55 pb
Most CC
•
C-yes/S-no/P-no/H-yes
English, French, Spanish

Continental breakfast
Lunch, dinner
Bar service, sitting room
Free bottle of wine
convention & wedding room
Airport: Madrid

*Situated in the historic neighborhood of San Esteban, inside the walled compound of Segovia, we conserve antique facades of the Eleventh century. 10% over room price*

# Switzerland

CH-7524-ZUOZ————————————————————————————————

| **Hotel Klarer** | 140 Swiss$ B&B | Continental Breakfast |
|---|---|---|
| 7524 | 14 rooms/suites, 2 pb | Restaurant (fee) |
| 081-854-1321 | Most CC | Complimentary wine |
| Fax: 081-854-1214 | • | snacks, sitting room |
| June 10-Dec 4 | C-yes/P-yes/H-no | Airport: Kloten |
| | English, Dutch, Italian | |

GSTAAD, BERNE————————————————————————————————

| **Hotel Le Grand Chalet** | 340 Swiss$ B&B | Full breakfast |
|---|---|---|
| Neueretstrasse 3780 | 23 rooms/suites, 23 pb | Lunch, dinner, restaurant |
| 033-748-3252 | Most CC, *Rated*, • | Bar service, sitting room |
| Fax: 033-744-4415 | C-yes/S-yes/P-yes/H-yes | library, sauna, pool |
| Franz Rosskogler | Eng., Ger., Fr., It. | Airport: Geneva |
| Closed Nov, Mar, May | | |

*Cozy hotel, very quiet, with the most beautiful view in Gstaad. Highly rated restaurant - high standard of service. Golf nearby*

ST-MORITZ, GR————————————————————————————————

| **Hotel Eden** | 180-290 Swiss$ B&B | Full breakfast |
|---|---|---|
| Via Veglia 12  7500 | 35 rooms/suites, 35 pb | Afternoon tea, snacks |
| 081-833-6161 | *Rated*, • | Bar service, sitting room |
| Fax: 081-833-9191 | C-yes/S-yes/P-yes/H-yes | library, bicycles |
| H. and P. Jehle-Degiacomi | English, It., Fr., Sp. | Airport: Zurich, Milan |
| June-Oct, Dec-April | | |

*Central & quiet situation, walk to mountain railway, bus & trains. Wood panneled 19thc breakfast room w/open fireplace.* **Free welcome drink upon presentation of travel book.**

VEYTAUX-MONTREUX, VAUD————————————————————————————————

| **Hotel Masson** | 170 Swiss$ B&B | Full breakfast (fee) |
|---|---|---|
| 5 rue Bonivard  1820 | 30 rooms/suites, 30 pb | Lunch, dinner, aftn. tea |
| 021-963-81-61 | Most CC, *Rated*, • | Sitting room, library |
| Fax: 021-963-81-66 | C-yes/S-yes/P-yes/H-no | direct dial phone, safe |
| Mrs. Anne-Marie Sevegrand | French, Ger., Eng., It. | comp. wine after 3 nights |
| March-October | | Airport: Geneva |

*Our hotel is situated in quiet surroundings, next to the lake, Chillon castle, and the mountains. We serve a very copious breakfast w/cheese, meat, homemade bread & jams.*

ZERMATT, VS————————————————————————————————

| **Hotel Antares** | 130 Swiss$ B&B | Buffet breakfast |
|---|---|---|
| Schluhmatte  3920 | 36 rooms/suites, 36 pb | Lunch, dinner, restaurant |
| 027-967-3664 | Most CC, *Rated*, • | Bar service, sitting room |
| Fax: 027-967-5236 | C-yes/S-yes/P-yesEng., | sauna, steam bath |
| Schnidrigs-Holenstein Family | Fr., Ger., It. | Airport: Geneva |
| All year | | |

*Attractive hotel in a peaceful location with lovely views of the Matterhorn; gourmet meals served in the restaurant or on the sunny terrace.*

ZURICH ─────────────────────────────

| | | |
|---|---|---|
| **Hotel Tiefenau** | Rates: Inquire B&B | Full breakfast |
| Steinwiesstrasse 8-10  8032 | 30 rooms/suites, 30 pb | Garden w/restaurant, bar |
| 41-1-251-2409 | Most CC, *Rated*, • | Sitt. rm., own parking |
| Fax: 41-1-251-2476 | C-yes/S-yes/P-yes/H-no | coffee shop, specialties |
| Beat R. Blumer | Eng., Fr., Ger., Sp., Chi | hotel shuttle to airport |
| All year | | Airport: Zurich |

*A complimentary welcome fruit plate awaits you in your room. Member of the Swiss Hotel Association and TOP International Hotels. Welcome cocktail in restaurant with dinner.*

# Wales, U.K.

CARDIFF, GLAMORGAN ─────────────────────────

| | | |
|---|---|---|
| **Egerton Grey Country House** | 90 English$ B&B | Full breakfast |
| | 10 rooms/suites, 10 pb | Lunch, dinner, restaurant |
| Porthkerry near Cardiff  CF62 | Most CC, *Rated*, • | Bar service, sitting room |
| 3BZ | C-yes/S-yes/P-yes/H-no | library, tennis, hot tubs |
| 01446-711666 | French, German, Welsh | Airport: Cardiff |
| Fax: 01446-711690 | | |
| Anthony Pitkin | | |
| All year | | |

*Beautiful old rectory on 7 acres of lush gardens. Outstanding views of coast. "The definitive country house hotel for South Wales." Winner of many awards cuisine & comfort.*

| | | |
|---|---|---|
| **Sant-Y-Nyll House** | 25 English$ B&B | Dinner, aftn. tea, snacks |
| St. Brides-Super-Ely  CF5 6EZ | 6 rooms/suites, 1 pb | Bar service, sitting room |
| 014-467-60209 | AmEx, *Rated*, • | Airport: Cardiff |
| Fax: 014-467-60209 | C-yes/S-yes/P-yes/H-no | |
| Paul & Monica Renwick | French, Danish, Swedish | |
| All year | | |

*Georgian country house set in vale of Glamorgan, spectacular views, 6 acre garden, 15 mins. from Cardiff city centre. Beautifully furnished rooms. 3rd night 20% off.*

CONWY, GWYNEDD ─────────────────────────

| | | |
|---|---|---|
| **The Old Rectory** | 74 English$ MAP | Full breakfast |
| Llansanffraid Glan | 6 rooms/suites, 5 pb | Dinner, restaurant |
| Conwy  LL28 5LG | Most CC, *Rated*, • | Bar service, sitting room |
| 014-925-80611 | C-ltd/S-ltd/H-no | library |
| Fax: 014-925-84555 | English | Airport: Manchester |
| Michael and Wendy Vaughan | | |
| February-Dec | | |

*This is the only inn in Wales to have an award from Michelin for accommodation and cuisine. Welcoming friendly hosts. Children under 9 months or over 5 years old.*

MERTHYR TYDFIL, MID. GLAMORGAN ──────────────────

| | | |
|---|---|---|
| **Tregenna Hotel** | 53 English$ B&B | Full Welsh/British Bkfst. |
| Park Terrace  CF47 8RF | 24 rooms/suites, 24 pb | Restaurant (fee) |
| 1685-723627 | Most CC, *Rated*, • | Bar service |
| Fax: 1685-721951 | C-yes/S-yes/P-yes/H-yes | Sitting room |
| Michael & Kathleen Hurley | Italian, Filipino, French | Airport: L.H.R. |
| All year | | |

*Family run. Twenty four tastefully furnished bedrooms. Super traditional food prepared daily. Highly regarded locally. Details faxed or mailed inmediately.*

PORTMEIRION, GWYNEDD

| | | |
|---|---|---|
| **Hotel Portmeirion** | 100 English$ EP | Restaurant (fee) |
| The Village Hotel | 37 rooms/suites, 37 pb | All meals served |
| Portmeirion  LL48 6ET | Most CC, *Rated*, • | Bar service, sitting room |
| 44-1766-770228 | C-yes/S-no/P-no/H-no | library, tennis court |
| Fax: 44-1766-771331 | Eng., It., French, Welch | swimming pool |
| R. Llywelyn | | Airport: Manchester |
| All year | | |

*Private fantasy village on Welsh coast. Top quality accommodation, good foof & wine. 70 acres of gardens, gateway to North Wales.*

POWYS

| | | |
|---|---|---|
| **Gliffaes Country House** | 70 English$ B&B | Full breakfast |
| **Hotel** | 22 rooms/suites, 22 pb | Lunch, dinner, restaurant |
| Crickhowell  NP8 1RH | Most CC, *Rated*, | Bar service, sitting room |
| 018-747-30371 | C-yes/S-ltd/P-yes/H-no | tennis, croquet, fishing |
| Fax: 018-747-30463 | Spanish, French, English | Airport: Cardiff, London, |
| Nick and Peta Brabner | | Heathrow |
| All year | | |

*This 1885 Italian gem set in stunning surroundings has delicious food, spacious sitting rooms and sun room and a warm welcome. Putting, birdwatching.*

# Reservation Service Organizations

These are businesses through which you can reserve a room in thousands of private homes. In many cases, rooms in homes are available where there may not be an inn. Also, guest houses are quite inexpensive. RSOs operate in different ways. Some represent a single city or state. Others cover the entire country. Some require a small membership fee. Others sell a list of their host homes. Many will attempt to match you with just the type of accommodations you're seeking and you may pay the RSO directly for your lodging.

## ALASKA

| | | |
|---|---|---|
| **Alaska Private Lodgings** | 907-258-1717 | Brochure Free |
| P.O. Box 200047 | Fax: 907-258-6613 | Alaska |
| Anchorage, AK  99520 | Mercy Dennis | 9am - 7pm M-S |
| | $$ | Winter varies |
| | • Deposit 1 night | 100 Houses |
| | Visa, MC, AmEx | |
| | German, French, Spanish | |

## ARIZONA

| | | |
|---|---|---|
| **B&B Southwest** | 602-947-9704   800-762-9704 | Free brochure |
| 2916 N. 70th St. | J. Cummings & J. Peterson | AZ, NM, South CA |
| Scottsdale, AZ  85251 | $ | 7am-7pm Mon-Sat |
| | Deposit 1 night | 35 Houses |
| | Visa, MC, AmEx | |

| | | |
|---|---|---|
| **Advance Reservations Inn AZ** | 800-333-9776 | Brochure Free |
| P.O. Box 13603 | Fax: 602-790-2399 | Arizona |
| Tucson, AZ  85711 | William A. Janssen, Sr. | 8am-8pm weekdays |
| | $$ | 1pm-5pm Sat-Sun |
| | • Deposit 50% 4+ days | 82 Houses |
| | Listing $3 SASE | |

## CALIFORNIA

| | | |
|---|---|---|
| **Eye Openers B&B Reserv.** | 213-684-4428   818-797-2055 | California |
| P.O. Box 694 | Fax: 818-798-3640 | 9am-5pm M-F |
| Altadena, CA  91003 | Ruth Judkins, Betty Cox | 100 Houses |
| | $ | |
| | • Deposit 1 night | |
| | Visa, MC | |
| | Listing $2 SASE | |
| | Sp, Fr, Ger, Hun,Rus,Heb | |

| | | |
|---|---|---|
| **Mendocino Coast Accomm.** | 707-937-1913 | Free brochure |
| P.O. Box 1034 | Fax: 707-937-4236 | California |
| Mendocino, CA  95460 | Flo Jones | 9am-6pm M_F |
| | $$ | Sat & Sun 10-5 |
| | 50% when booking | 40 Houses |
| | Visa, MC | |

| | | |
|---|---|---|
| **B&B International** | 415-696-1690   800-872-4500 | Free brochure |
| P.O. Box 282910 | Fax: 415-696-1699 | Cal., Nevada |
| San Francisco, CA  94128 | Sharene Klein | 9:00-4:00 Mon-Fri |
| | $$ | 350 Houses |
| | • Deposit 25% | |
| | Visa, MC, AmEx | |
| | Fr, Ger, It, Ch, Jap, Sp | |

**B&B San Francisco**
P.O. Box 420009
San Francisco, CA 94142

415-947-1913
Fax: 415-921-BBSF
Susan & Richard Kreibich
bbsf@linex
•
Deposit 1 night
Visa, MC, AmEx
Sample list $2

Free brochure
California
9:30am-5pm M-F
100 Houses

---

**Megan's Friends Reserv.**
1776 Royal Way
San Luis Obispo, CA 93405

805-544-4406
Fax: 805-546-8642
Joyce Segar
$$
• Deposit 20% + $10

Free brochure
California
1-9pm M-Sat.
15 Houses

---

**Wine Country Victorian**
400 Meadowood Lane
St. Helena, CA 94574

707-963-0852
Janet Strong
$$$
Deposit 2 nights

Free brochure
Napa Valley, CA

## CONNECTICUT

**Bed & Breakfast, Ltd.**
P.O. Box 216
New Haven, CT 06513

203-469-3260
Jack M. Argenio
$$
Deposit 20%
Travelers checks
French, Spanish, German

Free broch. SASE
CT, MA, RI
4-9:pm M-F
anytime Summ/wknd
125 Houses

---

**Covered Bridge B&B Reserv.**
**Serv.**
P.O. Box 447, 69 Maple Ave.
Norfolk, CT 06058

860-542-5944  800-488-5690
Hank & Diane Tremblay
$$
• Deposit 50%
Visa, MC, AmEx
Booklet $5
French

Free broch. SASE
CT, MA, NY, RI
10am - 6pm 7 days
70 Houses

---

**Nutmeg B&B Agency**
P.O. Box 1117
West Hartford, CT 06127

203-236-6698  800-727-7592
Michelle Souza
$$
• Ccard for deposit
Visa, MC, AmEx
Booklet $5

Free brochure
Connecticut
9:30am-5pm M-F
also ans. machine
100 Houses

## DELAWARE

**B&B of Delaware**
3650 Silverside Rd., Box 177
Wilmington, DE 19810

302-479-9500  800-233-4689
Millie Alford
$$
• Deposit 20%
Visa/MC/AmEx/Disc
Booklet $1

Brochure $2
DE, MD, PA, VA
9am-5pm M-F
also ans. machine
25 Houses

## DISTRICT OF COLUMBIA

**B&B League/Sweet Dreams &**
**Toast**
P.O. Box 9490
Washington, DC 20016

202-363-7767
Millie Groobey
$$
Deposit $25
Visa/MC/AmEx/DC

Free brochure
Washington, D.C.,
9am-5pm M-Th
9am-1pm F
70 Houses

## GEORGIA

**Bed & Breakfast Atlanta**
1801 Piedmont NE, Suite 208
Atlanta, GA 30324

404-875-0525  800-967-3224
Paula N. Gris
$$$
• Deposit 1 night
Most CC
Heb, Fr, Ger, Yid

Brochure SASE
GA, Metro Atla.
9am-6pm M-F
answering machine
140 Houses

## HAWAII

| | | |
|---|---|---|
| **Pacific-Hawaii B&B** | 808-486-8838  800-999-6026 | Brochure free |
| 99-1661 Aiea Heights Dr. | Fax: 808-487-1228 | Hawaiian Islands |
| Aiea, HI  96701 | Doris Epp Reichert | 24 hours, daily |
| | $ | 400 Houses |
| | Deposit 20% (B&B) | |
| | Visa, MC | |
| | Full dep. (homes) | |
| | German, Sp, Filip, Jap | |

| | | |
|---|---|---|
| **B&B Honolulu (Statewide)** | 808-595-7533  800-288-4666 | Free brochure |
| 3242 Kaohinani Dr. | Fax: 808-595-2030 | Hawaiian Islands |
| Honolulu, HI  96817 | Gene Bridges | 8am-5pm M-F |
| | $ | 8am-12noon Sat |
| | • Dep. 3 days or 50% | 350 Houses |
| | Visa, MC | |

| | | |
|---|---|---|
| **All Islands B&B** | 800-542-0344  808-263-2342 | Free brochure |
| 823 Kainui Dr. | Fax: 808-263-0308 | Hawaii |
| Kailua, Oahu, HI  96734 | Ann Carlin | 8am-5pm Mon-Fri. |
| | $ | 700 Houses |
| | • Deposit 20% | |
| | Visa, MC, AmEx | |

## KENTUCKY

| | | |
|---|---|---|
| **Bluegrass B&B** | 606-873-3208 | Free brochure |
| 2964 McCracken Pike | Elizabeth Pratt | Kentucky |
| Versailles, KY  40383 | $$ | 9am-4pm Mon-Fri |
| | Deposit 35% | 10am-2pm Sat. |
| | Ccard for deposit | 20 Houses |

## LOUISIANA

| | | |
|---|---|---|
| **New Orleans B&B & Accomm.** | 504-838-0071  888-240-0070 | Most CC |
| P.O. Box 8163 | Fax: 504-838-0140 | New Orleans |
| New Orleans, LA  70182 | Sarah Margaret Brown | |
| | $$ | |

## MARYLAND

| | | |
|---|---|---|
| **Amanda's B&B Reserv. Serv.** | 410-225-0001 | 175 Houses |
| 1428 Park Ave. | Fax: 410-728-8957 | |
| Baltimore, MD  21217 | Betsy Grater | |
| | $$ | |
| | Deposit 1 night | |
| | Visa, MC, AmEx | |
| | Listing $3 | |
| | French, German, It, Arab | |

| | | |
|---|---|---|
| **B&B of Maryland** | 410-269-6232  800-736-4667 | Free brochure |
| P.O. Box 2277 | Fax: 410-263-4841 | Maryland, London |
| Annapolis, MD  21404 | G. Page & R. Zuchelli | 9am-5pm Mon-Fri |
| | $$ | $5 brochure |
| | • Deposit 1 night | Maryland, PA, DE |
| | Visa, MC, AmEx | 8:30-5:30pm M-F |
| | Directory $5 | 8:30am-noon Sat |
| | | 200 Houses |

## MASSACHUSETTS

| | | |
|---|---|---|
| **A B&B Agency of Boston** | 617-720-3540  800-248-9262 | Free brochure |
| 47 Commercial Wharf | Ferne Mintz | MA, Camb., Boston |
| Boston, MA  02110 | $$ | 9am-9pm 7 days |
| | • Deposit 30% | also ans. machine |
| | Visa, MC, AmEx | 150 Houses |
| | Fr, Sp, Ger, Arab, It | |

**B&B Associates Bay Colony**
P.O. Box 57166, Babson Park
Boston, MA   02157

617-449-5302   800-347-5088
A. Kardasis, M. Mitchell
$$$
• Deposit 1 night
Visa, MC, AmEx
Directory $6
Fr,Ger,It,Nor,Sp,Gr,Rus

Free broch. SASE
Massachusetts
9:30am-5pm M-F
150 Houses

---

**Host Homes of Boston**
P.O. Box 117, Waban Branch
Boston, MA   02168

617-244-1308
Fax: 617-244-5156
Marcia Whittington
$$
Deposit 1 night
Visa, MC, AmEx
Fr,Ger,Sp,Gr,Jap,Rus

Free broch. SASE
MA, Bost. Cape Cd
9am-noon and
1:30pm-4:30pm M-F
50 Houses

---

**Greater Boston Hospitality**
P.O. Box 1142
Brookline, MA   02146

617-277-5430
K. Simpson & L. Simonelli
$$
• Deposit 1 night
Visa, MC, AmEx
Sp, Fr, Heb, Ger, It,Pol

Brochure SASE
Massachusetts
8:30am-5:30pm M-F
9am-1pm Sat.
100 Houses

---

**Orleans B&B Associates**
P.O. Box 1312
Orleans, MA   02653

508-255-3824   800-541-6226
Gilles & Susanne Thibault
$$
Deposit 2 nights
Most CC

Free brochure
Cape Cod
9am-9pm M-F
also ans. mach.
65 Houses

---

**Golden Slumber Accomm.**
640 Revere Beach Blvd.
Revere, MA   02151

617-289-1053   800-892-3231
Leah Schmidt
$$
• Deposit 33%
Visa, MC

Free brochure
MA, Cape Cod
9am-9pm M-F
9am-6pm Sat-Sun
45 Houses

---

**B&B Cape Cod**
P.O. Box 341
West Hyannisport, MA   02672

508-775-2772   800-686-5252
Fax: 508-775-2884
Clark E. Diehl
$$
Deposit 25%
Most CC

Brochure SASE
MA/Cape Cd/Islnds
9am-6pm daily
also ans. machine
100 Houses

## MISSISSIPPI

**B&B Mississippi; Lincoln, Ltd.**
P.O. Box 3479, 2303 23rd Ave
Meridian, MS   39303

601-482-5483   800-633-MISS
Fax: 601-693-7447
Barbara Lincoln Hall
$$
• Deposit 1 night
Visa, MC, AmEx
$3.50 Directory

French, German
Free Brochure
MS, AL, TN, LA
9:30am-4:30pm M-F
also ans. machine
300 Houses

## MISSOURI

**Ozark Mountain Country B&B**
P.O. Box 295
Branson, MO   65615

800-695-1546   417-334-4720
Fax: 417-335-8134
Kay Cameron
$
• Deposit 1 night
Visa, MC, AmEx

Free broch. SASE
SW MO, NW AR
10am-5pm daily
7-10pm daily
126 Houses

---

**B&B Kansas City RSO**
P.O. Box 14781
Lenexa, MO   66285

913-888-3636
Edwina T. Monroe
$$
• Deposit 20%
Visa, MC, AmEx

Missouri, Kansas
8:30am - 9:30pm
also ans. machine
35 Houses

## MONTANA

**B&B Western Adventure**
P.O. Box 4308
Bozeman, MT 59715

406-585-0557 800-522-7097
Fax: 406-585-2869
Paula Deigert
$$
• Deposit 1 night
Visa, MC, AmEx
Directory $5

Free broch. SASE
SD/MT/ID/WY
9am-4pm summer
9am-1pm winter
80 Houses

## NEW JERSEY

**B&B Adventures**
2310 Central Ave., Suite 132
N. Wildwood, NJ 08260

609-522-4000 800-992-2632
Fax: 609-522-6125
P. DiFilippo & D Buscham
$$
• Full deposit
Most CreCards
Free broch. SASE
Sp,Fr,It,Ge,Ar,Sw,Yi,Lux

Directory $5
NY, NJ, PA, FL
9am - 5pm M-F
120 Houses

**B&B of Princeton**
P.O. Box 571
Princeton, NJ 08542

609-924-3189
Fax: 609-921-6271
John W. Hurley, Jr.
$$
Deposit 1 night

Listing SASE
Princeton, NJ
24 hours, daily
10 Houses

## NEW YORK

**Elaine's B&B Selections**
4987 Kingston Rd.
Elbridge, NY 13060

315-689-2082
Ms. Elaine Samuels
$$
Deposit 1 night
Visa, MC
Catalogue $3

List SASE
Central NY/W MA
10am-7pm daily
45 Houses

**At Home in New York**
P.O. Box 407
New York, NY 10185

212-956-3125
Fax: 212-247-3294
Lois H. Rooke
$$
• Deposit 25%
Visa, MC, AmEx
French, Spanish, German

Free brochure
NY, Nat./Internat
9am-5pm Mon-Fri
9am-12pm Sat-Sun

**Abode Bed & Breakfast, Ltd.**
P.O. Box 20022
New York, NY 10021

212-472-2000 800-835-8880
Shelli Leifer
$$$
Deposit 25%
AmEx
2 nights minimun

Free brochure
NY: Manh/Pk Slope
9am-5pm Mon-Fri
11am-2pm Sat
100 Houses

**B&B Network of New York**
134 W. 32nd St, Ste 602
New York, NY 10001

212-645-8134 800-900-8134
Leslie Goldberg
$$
• Deposit 25%

Free brochure
New York
8am-6pm Mon-Fri
200 Houses

**Bed & Breakfast (& Books)**
35 West 92nd St.
New York, NY 10025

212-865-8740
Judith Goldberg
$$
• Deposit 25%
French, German

Free list SASE
New York City
10am-5pm, Mon-Fri
40 Houses

**Urban Ventures, Inc.**
38 W. 32nd. St., #1412
New York, NY 10001

212-594-5650
Fax: 212-947-9320
Mary McAulay
$$
• Deposit $50
Most CC

Free list SASE
NYC/No. NJ
8am-5pm Mon-Fri
600 Houses

## NORTH CAROLINA

**Asheville Accomm.**
137 Beverly Rd.
Asheville, NC   28805

704-251-9055   800-770-9055
Ellen McKenna
$$
Deposit 1 night
Most CC

Free brochure
W. North Carolina
9:30am-7:30pm M-F
9:00am-12:00 Sat
40 Houses

## OHIO

**Private Lodgings, Inc.**
P.O. Box 18590
Cleveland, OH   44118

216-321-3213
Jean Stanley
$
Deposit 1 night
German, French, Yidish

Free brochure
Ohio
10am-5pm M-F
75 Houses

## OREGON

**Northwest Bed & Breakfast**
1067 Hanover Court S.
Salem, OR   97302

503-243-7616   503-370-9033
Fax: 503-316-9118
David & Betty Hickerson
$$
Deposit in full
Most CC
Free brochure
Fr,Ger,It,Sp,Du,Heb,Arab

Directory $7.95
Northwest, HI, CA
8am-5pm daily
400 Houses

## PENNSYLVANIA

**A B&B Connection**
P.O. Box 21
Devon, PA   19333

610-687-3565   800-448-3619
Fax: 610-995-9524
M.A. Hamilton & P. Gregg
$
Deposit 1 night
Visa, MC, AmEx

Free sample dir.
Philadephia &
Mon.-Fri. 9am-7pm
Sat. 9am-5pm
110 Houses

**Rest & Repast B&B Service**
P.O. Box 126
Pine Grove Mills, PA   16868

814-238-1484   814-861-6566
Linda C. Feltman
$
Deposit $50

Free broch. SASE
Central PA
8:30-11:30am M-F
40 Houses

**Assoc. B&B Phili, Valley Forge**
P.O. Box 562
Valley Forge, PA   19481

610-783-7838   800-344-0123
C. Williams, Fax:783-7783
$
● Deposit 1 night
Most CC
Directory $3
Spanish, French

Free brochure
SE Penna.
10am-9pm 7 days
130 Houses

## RHODE ISLAND

**Anna's Victorian Connection**
5 Fowler Ave.
Newport, RI   02840

401-849-2489   800-884-4288
Fax: 401-847-7309
Susan Collis White
●
Deposit 50%
Most CC

French
Free brochure
RI, S.MA
9am-5pm daily
200 Houses

## SOUTH CAROLINA

**Historic Charleston B&B**
57 Broad St.
Charleston, SC   29401

803-722-6606   800-743-3583
Jo Bacon        $$
Deposit 1 night
Visa, MC, Checks
Reservation Fee
French, Spanish

Free broch. SASE
Charleston, SC
9am-5pm M-F
60 Houses

## TENNESSEE

**B&B – About Tennessee**
P.O. Box 110227
Nashville, TN   37222

615-331-5244   800-458-2421
Fredda Odom        $$
● Deposit 1 night
Most CC
Spanish, French, German

Brochure $4
TN/Nat./Internat
9am-5pm M-F
also ans. machine
90 Houses

## TEXAS

**Sand Dollar Hospitality**
3605 Mendenhall Dr.
Corpus Christi, TX   78415

512-853-1222
Patricia Hirsbrunner
$$
• Deposit 33%
Visa, MC
French

Free brochure
Texas
9am-7pm M-Sat
also ans. mach.
11 Houses

---

**Gasthaus Schmidt Reserv.**
**Serv.**
231 West Main St.
Fredericksburg, TX   78624

210-997-5612
Donna Mittel
$$
• Deposit 1 night
Visa/MC/Disc.
Booklet $4

Free brochure
Fredericksburg,TX
9am-8pm M-F
11am-5pm Sat-Sun
100 Houses

## VIRGINIA

**Blue Ridge B&B**
Route 2, Box 3895
Berryville, VA   22611

540-955-1246  800-296-1246
Fax: 540-955-4240
Rita Z. Duncan
$
• Full deposit
Visa, MC
Ch,Sp,ASL,Fr,Ger,It,Arab

Free broch. SASE
VA, WV, MD, PA
9am-2pm M-F
9am-noon Sat
60 Houses

---

**Guesthouses B&B, Inc.**
P.O. Box 5737
Charlottesville, VA   22903

804-979-7264
Fax: 804-293-7791
Mary Hill Caperton
$$
• Deposit 25%
Ccard for deposit
2 nights minimun
French, German

List $1 SASE
Central Virginia
Noon-5pm Mon-Fri
also ans. mach.
60 Houses

## WASHINGTON

**A Pacific Reservation Serv.**
P.O. Box 46894
Seattle, WA   98146

206-439-7677
Greg & Sharon Kaminski
$
Deposit required
Visa, MC, AmEx

Brochure $5
Washington, OR
9am-6pm M-F

---

**Greater Tacoma B&B Reserv.**
3312 N. Union Ave.
Tacoma, WA   98407

206-759-4088
Fax: 206-759-4025
Sharon Kaufman
$$
• Deposit 1 night
Visa, MC, AmEx

Free brochure
Tacoma, BC
9am-9pm 7 days
30 Houses

## BRITISH COLUMBIA

**Old English B&B Registry**
1226 Silverwood Crescent
North Vancouver, BC   V7P 1J3

604-986-5069
Fax: 604-986-8810
Vicki Tyndall
$$
• Deposit or CrCd
Visa, MC

Free brochure
British Columbia
10am-5pm Mon-Fri
also ans. machine
35 Houses

---

**All Seasons B&B Agency, Inc.**
9858 Fifth St., Suite 101
Sidney, BC   V8L 2X7

250-655-7173
Fax: 250-655-7193
Kate Catterill
$$
• Deposit 20%
Visa, MC
Booklet $6
French, German

Free brochure
British Columbia
9am-5pm daily
60 Houses

| | | |
|---|---|---|
| **AAA Bed & Breakfast**<br>658 E. 29th Ave.<br>Vancouver, BC   V5V 2R9 | 604-872-0938   800-463-9933<br>Fax: 604-877-1786<br>Catherine Vong<br>$$<br>• Deposit 1 night<br>Visa, MC, AmEx<br>English, French, Chinese | Free brochure<br>British Columbia<br>9am-6pm 7 days<br>200 Houses |
| **Town & Country B&B Registry**<br>P.O. Box 74542, 2803 W4th Ave.<br>Vancouver, BC   V6K 1K2 | 604-731-5942<br>Helen Burich<br>$$<br>Deposit 1 night<br>Visa, MC<br>French, German, Spanish | British Columbia<br>9am-4:30pm Mon-Fr<br>evening & wkends<br>35 Houses |
| **AA Accommodations West B&B**<br>660 Jones Terrace<br>Victoria, BC   V8Z 2L7 | 604-479-1986<br>Fax: 604-479-9999<br>M. Doreen Wensley<br>$$<br>• Visa, MC, AmEx<br>Fr,Ger,Sp,Wel,Dan,Jap,Cz | Free brochure<br>BC, Vanc. Isl.<br>7am-10pm daily<br>80 Houses |

ONTARIO————

| | | |
|---|---|---|
| **Niagara Regional/On The Lake**<br>4917 River Rd.<br>Niagara Falls, ON   L2E 3G5 | 905-358-8988<br>Luciana Bertoechi<br>$$<br>Deposit $25<br>Most CC<br>Ger, Pol, Ukr, Fr | Free brochure<br>Ont/Niag. Pen.<br>10am-1pm, 3-8pm<br>35 Houses |
| **B&B Homes of Toronto**<br>Box 46093, College Park PO<br>Toronto, ON   M5B 2L8 | 416-363-6362<br>Katya McLoughlin<br>• | 18 Houses |
| **Downtown Toronto B&B Asso.**<br>P.O. Box 190 Station B<br>Toronto, ON   M5T 2W1 | 416-368-1420<br>Fax: 416-368-1653<br>Linda Lippa<br>$$<br>Deposit 50%<br>Spanish, Italian, French | Free brochure<br>Ontario<br>8:30-7pm Daily<br>24hr. ans. mach.<br>25 Houses |
| **Toronto Bed & Breakfast Inc.**<br>Box 269, 253 College St<br>Toronto, ON   M5T 1R5 | 416-588-8800   416-690-1407<br>Fax: 416-977-2601<br>Marcia Getgood<br>$$<br>Deposit 1 night<br>Visa/MC/AmEx/JCB<br>Fr,Ger,It,Pol,Uk,Jap,Swe | Free brochure<br>Ontario<br>9-noon, 2-7pm M-F<br>25 Houses |

PROVINCE OF QUEBEC————

| | | |
|---|---|---|
| **A Bed & Breakfast**<br>3458 Laval Ave.<br>Montreal, PQ   H2X 3C8 | 514-289-9749   800-267-5180<br>Fax: 514-287-7386<br>Bob Finkelstein<br>$$<br>• Deposit 1 night<br>Visa, MC, AmEx<br>Fr,Ger,Sp,Ch,Viet,Pol | Free brochure<br>Montreal, Quebec<br>8am-7pm every day<br>80 Houses |

## More RSOs ...

**Alaska**————

| | |
|---|---|
| Anchorage | Accommodations Alaska Style, 3605 Arctic Blvd Box173, AK   99503   907-278-8800 |
| Anchorage | Sourdough Bed & Breakfast, 339-BW Cardigan Cl., AK   99503 |
| Fairbanks | Fairbanks B&B, 902 Kellum St., AK   99701   907-452-4967 |
| Juneau | Alaska B&B Assoc., 369 S. Franklin, AK   99801   907-586-2959 |
| Ketchikan | Ketchikan B&B, P.O. Box 7735, AK   99801   907-225-3860 |
| Kodiak | Kodiak B&B, 308 Cope St., AK   99615   907-486-5367 |

## Arizona

| | |
|---|---|
| Scottsdale | B&B Inn Arizona, 23623 N. Scottsdale Rd., AZ 85255  602-860-9338 |
| Scottsdale | Valley o' the Sun B&B, P.O. Box 2214, AZ 85252  602-941-1281 |
| Tempe | Mi Casa Su Casa, P.O. Box 950, AZ 85280  602-990-0682 |
| Tucson | Florence A. Ejrup RSO, 941 W. Calle Dadivoso, AZ 85704 |
| Tucson | Inter-Bed, 5708 N. Via Lozana, AZ 85715  602-323-4045 |

## Arkansas

| | |
|---|---|
| Calico Rock | Arkansas Ozarks B&B Reserv., HC 61, Box 72, AR 72519  501-297-8764 |
| Eureka Springs | B&B Reservation Serv., 11 Singleton, AR 72632  501-253-9111 |

## California

| | |
|---|---|
| Berkeley | Unique Housing, 81 Plaza Dr., CA 94705  415-658-3494 |
| Cambria | Bed & Breakfast Homestay, P.O. Box 326, CA 93428  805-927-4613 |
| Columbia | Pilots International B&B, P.O. Box 1847, CA 95310 |
| Leucadia | B&B Hospitality, 823 La Mirada Ave., CA 92024  619-436-6850 |
| Long Beach | B&B of L.A. & Kids Welcome, 3924 E. 14th. St., CA 90804  310-498-0552 |
| Mendocino | Paradise Vacation Rentals, 45005 Ukiah St, Box 208, CA 95460 |
| Mendocino | S.S. Seafoam Lodge, P.O. Box 68, CA 95456  707-937-1827 |
| Nevada City | Historic Inns Assoc., 116 Nevada St., CA 95959  916-477-6634 |
| Pebble Beach | B&B/Monterey Peninsula, P.O. 1193, CA 93953  408-372-7425 |
| Saint Helena | Bed & Breakfast Almanac, P.O. Box 295, CA 94574  707-963-0852 |
| San Anselmo | B&B Exchange of Marin, 45 Entrata Ave., CA 94960  415-485-1971 |
| San Francisco | American Family Inn-B&B SF, P.O. Box 349, CA 94101  415-931-3083 |
| San Jose | Place to Stay, 14497 New Jersey, CA 95124 |
| Santa Rosa | Wine Country B&B, P.O. Box 3211, CA 95403  707-578-1661 |
| Sunnyvale | Reservations Plus, 1141 Merrimac Dr., CA 94807 |
| Tarzana | Calif. Houseguests Int'l., P.O. Box 643, CA 91356  818-344-7878 |
| Whittier | CoHost, America's B&B, P.O. Box 9302, CA 90608  319-699-8427 |

## Colorado

| | |
|---|---|
| Colorado Springs | B&B Central Information, P.O. Box 38279, CO 80937 |
| Denver | B&B Cambridge Club, 1550 Sherman St., CO 80903 |
| Vail | B&B Reserv. Serv. Agency, 2488 Garmisch Dr., CO 81657  970-476-0792 |

## Connecticut

| | |
|---|---|
| Groton | Nautilus B&B, 133 Phoenix Dr., CT 06340  203-448-1538 |
| Sharon | Alexander's B&B Res. Serv., P.O. Box 1182, CT 06069  203-364-0505 |
| Stamford | Resort Villas Int'l, 30 Spring St., CT 06901  203-965-0260 |
| West Simsbury | Four Seasons Int'l B&B, 11 Bridlepath Rd., CT 06092  203-651-3045 |

## District Of Columbia

| | |
|---|---|
| Washington | B&B Accommodations, Ltd., P.O. Box 12011, DC 20005  202-328-3510 |

## Florida

| | |
|---|---|
| Key West | Key West Reservation Serv., 628 Fleming St., FL 33041  800-327-4831 |
| Orlando | Magic B&B, 8328 Curry Ford Rd., FL 32822  407-277-6602 |
| Saint Pete Beach | B&B Homestays of Fl., 8690 Gulf Blvd., FL 33706  813-360-1753 |
| St. Augustine | RSVP B&B Referral, P.O. Box 3603, FL 32085 |
| West Palm Beach | Open House B&B Registry, 3215 Spruce Ave., FL 33407  407-842-5190 |
| Winter Park | A & A B&B of Florida, P.O. Box 1316, FL 32790  305-628-3233 |

## Georgia

| | |
|---|---|
| Atlanta | Georgia B&B (RSO), 2472 Lauderdale Dr., GA 30345  404-493-1930 |
| Bloomingdale | Miss Pitty Pats, 6 Mesa Ave., GA 31302  800-748-6822 |
| Savannah | Savannah Area Visitors, 222 W. Oglethorpe Ave., GA 31499  912-944-0444 |
| Thomasville | Quail Country B&B, Ltd., 1104 Old Monticello Rd., GA 31792  912-226-7218 |

## Hawaii

| | |
|---|---|
| Kailua | Affordable Paradise B&B, 226 Pouli Rd., HI 96734  808-262-7865 |
| Kailua, Kona | Three Bears' Hawaii RSO, 72-1001 Puukala St., HI 96740  800-765-0480 |
| Kapaa, Kauai | Bed & Breakfast Hawaii, P.O. Box 449, HI 96746  808-822-7771 |
| Puunene | B&B Maui Style, P.O. Box 98, HI 96753  808-879-7865 |

## Idaho

| | |
|---|---|
| Boise | Bed & Breakfast of Idaho, 109 W. Idaho St., ID 83702  208-336-5174 |

## Illinois

| | |
|---|---|
| Chicago | B&B/Chicago Inc., P.O. Box 14088, IL 60614  312-951-0085 |
| Chicago | Heritage B&B, 75 E. Wacker Dr., IL 60601  312-857-0800 |
| Hoffman Estates | B&B Midwest Reserv., P.O. Box 95503, IL 60195  812-378-5855 |

## Indiana

| | |
|---|---|
| Goshen | Indiana B&B Association, P.O. Box 1127, IN 46526 |
| Nappanee | Indiana Amish Country B&B, 1600 W. Market St., IN 46550  219-773-4188 |
| Nashville | Tammy Galm B&B, P.O. Box 546, IN 47448 |
| Redkey | InnServ Nationwide Res., Route 1, Box 68, IN 47373  317-369-2245 |

## Kentucky

| | |
|---|---|
| Independence | Ohio Valley B&B, Inc., 6876 Taylor Mill Rd., KY 41051  606-356-7865 |

## Louisiana
| | |
|---|---|
| Baton Rouge | Southern Comfort B&B Res., 2856 Hundred Oaks, LA  70808  504-346-1928 |
| Metairie | New Orleans B&B Accomm., 671 Rosa Ave., LA  70005  504-838-0071 |
| New Orleans | Bed & Breakfast, Inc., 1021 Moss St., LA  70152  504-488-4640 |
| New Orleans | French Quarter Reserv. Serv., 940 Royal St., LA  70116  504-523-1246 |
| New Orleans | New Orleans Bed, Bath & Breakfast, P.O. Box 52466, LA  70152  504-897-3867 |

## Maryland
| | |
|---|---|
| Annapolis | B&B of Maryland, P.O. Box 2277, MD  21404  410-269-6232 |
| Annapolis | Green Street B&B, 161 Green St., MD  21401 |

## Massachusetts
| | |
|---|---|
| Boston | Rawlins Plantation, 111 Charles St., MA  02114  617-367-8959 |
| Cambridge | B&B Cambridge & Gtr Boston, P.O. Box 665, MA  02140  617-576-1492 |
| Cambridge | Battina's B&B, P.O. Box 585, MA  02238 |
| Dennis | B&B Accom. by Guest House, P.O. Box 8, MA  02360 |
| Hingham | Yankee B&B of New England, 8 Brewster Rd., MA  02043  617-749-5007 |
| Nantucket | Nantucket Accomm., Box 426, MA  02554 |
| Newtonville | B&B Reservations N. Shore, P.O. Box 35, MA  02160  617-964-1606 |
| Oak Bluffs | Dukes County Reserv. Serv., P.O. Box 2370, MA  02557 |
| Orleans | House Guests Cape Cod, P.O. Box 1881, MA  02653  800-666-HOST |
| Osterville | Destination New England, P.O. Box 1173, MA  02655  508-428-5600 |
| South Egremont | Bed & Breakfast USA, P.O. Box 418, MA  01258  800-255-7213 |
| Vineyard Haven | Martha's Vineyard Reserv., P.O. Box 1769, MA  02568 |
| Waltham | New England B&B, P.O. Box 1426, MA  02154  617-244-2112 |
| Williamsburg | Berkshire B&B Homes, P.O. Box 211, MA  01096  413-268-7244 |
| Winchester | Dave & Betty Harvey, 7 Warren St., MA  01890  617-729-3171 |

## Michigan
| | |
|---|---|
| Frankenmuth | Frankenmuth Area B&B, 337 Trinklein St., MI  48734  517-652-8897 |
| Willianston | Capital B&B, 5150 Corey Rd., MI  48895  517-468-3434 |

## Minnesota
| | |
|---|---|
| Duluth | Nisbet Plantation Inn, 613 Missabe Building, MN  55802  218-722-5059 |
| Minneapolis | Uptown Lake District B&B, 2301 Bryant Ave., MN  55405  612-872-7884 |
| Saint Paul | B&B Registry Ltd., P.O. Box 8174, MN  55108  612-646-4238 |

## Mississippi
| | |
|---|---|
| Natchez | Natchez Pilgrimage Tours, 200 State St., MS  39120  601-446-6631 |
| Natchez | Natchez Reserv., 243 John R. Junkin Dr., MS  39120  800-824-0355 |

## Missouri
| | |
|---|---|
| Independence | Truman Country B&B, 424 N. Pleasant, MO  64050  816-254-6657 |
| Lexington | Lexington B&B, 115 N. 18th St., MO  64067 |

## Nebraska
| | |
|---|---|
| Gothenburg | Swede Hospitality B&B, 1617 Avenue A, NE  69138  308-537-2680 |
| West Point | B&B of the Midwest, 230 S. Maple, NE  68788  402-372-5904 |

## New Hampshire
| | |
|---|---|
| Guilford | New Hampshire B&B, 128 S. Hoop Pole Rd., NH  06437  203-457-0042 |
| North Conway | Country Inn White Mnt., P.O. Box 2025, NH  03860  800-562-1300 |

## New Jersey
| | |
|---|---|
| Sea Isle | Cape Associates, 340 46th Place, NJ  08243 |
| Summit | Wesley K. & Sarah K. Burton, 10 Hillcrest Ave., NJ  07901  201-467-1407 |

## New Mexico
| | |
|---|---|
| Santa Fe | B&B of New Mexico, P.O. Box 2805, NM  87504  505-982-3332 |

## New York
| | |
|---|---|
| Buffalo | B&B of Niagara Frontier, 440 LeBrun Rd., NY  14226 |
| Croton-on-Hudson | Bed & Breakfast USA, Ltd., 129 Grand St., NY  10520  914-271-6228 |
| East Hampton | Lodgings Plus B&B, Box 279, 319 Gerald Dr., NY  11937  212-858-9589 |
| Franklinville | B&B Western New York, 40 Maple Ave., NY  14737  716-676-5704 |
| Herkimer | B&B Leatherstocking Assoc., P.O. Box 53, NY  13350  315-733-0040 |
| Hicksville | Mid-Island B&B Res. Serv., 518 Mid-Island Plaza, NY  11801  516-931-1234 |
| Ithaca | Finger Lakes B&B Assoc., Box 6576, NY  14851 |
| Macedon | B&B Reservation Serv., 162 Hook Rd., NY  14502  315-986-4536 |
| Mumford | Apple Reservation Serv., P.O. Box 335, NY  14511  716-538-9685 |
| New York | At Home in New York, P.O. Box 407, NY  10185  212-956-3125 |
| New York | B&B in Manhattan, P.O. Box 533, NY  10150  212-472-2528 |
| New York | City Lights B&B, Ltd., P.O. Box 20355, NY  10028  212-737-7049 |
| New York | Mallory Factor Inc., 275 7th Ave., NY  10001  212-989-0000 |
| New York | New World B&B, 150 5th Ave., NY  10011  212-675-5600 |
| New York | US Virgin Isl. Gov't Trvl., 1270 Ave. of the Americas, NY  10020 |
| Northport | Island B&B Registry, 5 Exeter Court, NY  11768  516-757-7398 |
| Pearl River | B&B Res. Ser. of Gtr. NY, P O Box 1015, NY  10965  914-735-4857 |
| Peconic | Host Homes of N Fork, Box 333, NY  11958  516-765-5762 |

| Port Jefferson | A Reasonable Alternative, 117 Spring St. Ste 100, NY   11777   516-928-4034 |
| Rhinebeck | Tobin's B&B Guide, Rd. 2, Box 64, NY   12572 |
| Scottsville | Adventures B&B Reservation Serv., P.O. Box 83, NY   14456   716-889-7190 |
| Spencertown | B&B of Columbia County, Box 122, NY   12165   518-392-2358 |
| Syracuse | B&B of Central New York, 4336 Fay Rd., NY   13204 |
| Tonawanda | International B&B Club, Inc., P.O. Box 98, NY   14151   716-874-8797 |
| Vernon | B&B Connection NY, RD 1, Box 325, NY   13476   315-824-4888 |

## North Carolina
| Everetts | B&B in the Albemarle, P.O. Box 248, NC   27825   919-792-4584 |

## North Dakota
| Regent | Old West B&B Reserv. Serv., Box 211, ND   58650 |

## Ohio
| Columbus | Columbus B&B, 769 S. 3rd St., OH   43206   614-443-3680 |
| Powell | Buckeye B&B, P.O. Box 130, OH   43065   614-548-4555 |

## Oregon
| Ashland | Ashland's B&B Network, P.O. Box 1051, OR   97520   503-482-BEDS |
| Ashland | Inn Formation, PO Box 1376, OR   97520 |
| Ashland | Southern Oregon Res. Ctr., PO Box 477, OR   97520 |
| Bend | Bend Bed & Breakfast, 19838 Ponderosa Dr., OR   97702   503-388-3007 |
| Myrtle Creek | Country Host Registry, 901 NW Chadwick Ln., OR   97457   503-863-5168 |

## Pennsylvania
| Elizabethtown | B&B-Lancaster Harrisburg, 463 N. Market St., PA   17022   717-367-9408 |
| Harrisburg | Pennsylvania Travel Council, 902 N. Second St., PA   17102   717-232-8880 |
| Kennett Square | B&B of Chester County, P.O. Box 825, PA   19348   215-444-1367 |
| Lancaster | Nissly's Olde Home Inns, 624-632 W.Chestnut St., PA   17603   717-392-2311 |
| Mountville | B&B Lancaster County, 407 E Main St, PA   17554   717-285-7200 |
| Philadelphia | B&B Center City, 1804 Pine St., PA   19103   215-735-1137 |
| West Chester | Abby's Agency & Guesthouse, P.O. Box 2137, PA   19380   800-950-9130 |

## Rhode Island
| Newport | B&B International, 21 Dearborn St., RI   02840 |
| Newport | B&B Registry-Castlekeep, 44 Everett St., RI   02840 |
| Newport | Bed & Breakfast, 33 Russell Ave., RI   02840   401-846-5408 |
| Saunderstown | At Home in New England, Box 25, RI   02874 |

## South Carolina
| Mount Pleasant | Charleston East B&B League, 1031 Tall Pine Rd., SC   29464   803-884-8208 |

## South Dakota
| Philip | Old West & Badlands B&B Assoc., HCR 02, Box 100A, SD   57567   605-859-2120 |

## Tennesee

## Tennessee
| Hampshire | Natchez Trace B&B RSO Serv., P.O. Box 193, TN   38461   615-285-2777 |
| Jonesborough | Jonesborough B&B, P.O. Box 722, TN   37659   615-753-9223 |
| Memphis | B&B in Memphis, 172 Kimbrough Pl., TN   38104   901-726-5920 |

## Texas
| Austin | B&B Society of Austin, 1702 Gaywood Cove, TX   78704 |
| Dallas | B&B Texas Style, 4224 W. Red Bird Ln., TX   75237   214-298-8586 |
| Galveston | Bed & Breakfast-Galveston, 1805 Broadway, TX   77550 |
| Houston | B&B Society of Texas, 1200 Southmore Ave., TX   77004   713-523-1114 |
| Richardson | NRSO, P.O. Box 850653, TX   75085 |
| San Antonio | B&B Hosts of San Antonio, 307 Beauregard, TX   78204   210-824-8036 |
| Wimberley | B&B of Wimberley Texas, P.O. Box 589, TX   78676   512-847-9666 |

## Utah
| Park City | Bed & Breakfast Inns of Utah, P.O. Box 3066, Dept. I, UT   84060   801-645-8068 |

## Vermont
| East Fairfield | Vermont B&B, P.O. Box 1, VT   05448   802-827-3827 |
| Guilford | B&B Inns of New England, 128 S. Hoop Pole Rd., VT   06437   203-457-0042 |
| Saint Albans | American B&B—New England, Box 983, VT   05478 |

## Virginia
| Richmond | B&B on the Hill, 2304 E. Broad St., VA   23223   804-780-3746 |
| Richmond | Bensonhouse Reservation Serv., 2036 Monument Ave., VA   23220   804-353-6900 |
| Roanoke | B&B of Roanoke Valley, 1708 Arlington Rd., VA   24015 |

## Washington
| Bellingham | B&B Guild—Whatcom County, 2610 Eldridge Ave., WA   98225   206-676-4560 |
| Bellingham | B&B Service (BABS), 445 W. Lake Samish Dr., WA   98227   206-733-8642 |
| Langley | Whidbey Island B&B Assoc., P.O. Box 259, WA   98260   206-321-6272 |
| Mercer Island | Travellers' B&B, P.O. Box 492, WA   98040   206-232-2345 |
| Seattle | West Coast B&B, 11304 20th Place S.W., WA   98146 |

| Tacoma | INNterlodging Co-op Serv., P.O. Box 7044, WA   98407   206-756-0343 |

## Wisconsin

| Algoma | B&B Guest Homes, Route 2, 698 County U, WI   54201   414-743-9742 |
| Milwaukee | B&B of Milwaukee, 823 N. 2nd. St., WI   53203   414-277-8066 |

## Virgin Islands

| Frederiksted | The Prince Street Inn, 402 Prince St., VI   00840   809-772-9550 |

## Jamaica

| Negril, Westmoreland | Native Son Villas, Norman Manley Blvd., 201-467-1407 |

## Alberta

| Banff | Banff/Jasper Central Res., 204 Caribou, Box 1628, AB   T0L 0C0 |
| Calgary | AAA Bed West, 207-35A St. S.W., AB   T3C 1P6 |
| Duinheller | Big Country B&B Agency, P.O. Box 1027, AB   T0J 0Y0 |
| Edmonton | Alberta Hostelling, 10926 - 88th Ave., AB   T6G 0Z1   403-433-7798 |

## British Columbia

| Burnaby | Born Free B&B of B.C. Ltd., 4390 Frances St., BC   V5C 2R3   604-298-8815 |
| Burnaby | Home Away From Home B&B, 1441 Howard Ave., BC   V5B 3S2   604-294-1760 |
| North Vancouver | Canada-West Accomm., P.O. Box 86607, BC   V7L 4L2   604-929-1424 |
| Vancouver | A B & C B&B Agency, 4390 Frances St., BC   V5C 2R3   604-298-8815 |
| Vancouver | Alberta & Pacific B&B Reserv., P.O. Box 15477, M.P.O., BC   V6B 5B2   604-944-1793 |
| Vancouver | Westways Accomm. Registry, P.O. Box 48950, BC   V7X 1A8 |
| Victoria | Traveller's B&B, 1840 Midgard Ave., BC   V8P 2Y9   604-477-3069 |
| Victoria | VIP Bed & Breakfast, 1786 Teakwood Rd., BC   V8N 1E2   604-477-5604 |

## New Brunswick

| Frederick | New Brunswick Tourism, P.O. Box 12345, NB   E3B 5C3 |

## New Foundland

| Saint John's | Tourist Services Div., Box 2061, NF   A1C 5R8 |

## Ontario

| Alma | Ontario Vacation Farms Assoc., Box 1111, ON   N0B 1A0   519-846-9788 |
| Beachburg | Beachburg & Area B&B Assoc., Box 146, ON   K0J 1C0   613-582-3585 |
| Brighton | Brighton Area B&B Assoc., 61 Simpson St., ON   K0K 1H0   613-475-0538 |
| Burlington | Bed & Breakfast Burlington, 5435 Stratton Rd., ON   L7L 2Z1   416-637-0329 |
| Calabogie | South Renfrew County B&B, c/o B.Collins, Box 67, ON   K0J 1H0   613-752-2201 |
| Cardinal | Eastern Ontario Cntry B&B, c/o Roduner Farm RR1, ON   K0E 1E0   613-657-4830 |
| Fergus | Fergus/Elora B&B Assoc., 550 Saint Andrew St. E., ON   N1M 1R6   519-843-2747 |
| Hamilton | Hamilton-Wentworth B&B, 61 E 43rd St., ON   L8T 3B7   416-648-0461 |
| Hawkestone | Simcoe-Side Country B&B, RR 2, Lakeshore Rd., ON   L0L 1T0   705-487-7191 |
| Kingston | Kingston Area B&B, P.O. Box 37, ON   K7M 4V6   613-542-0214 |
| Leamington | Point Pelee B&B RSO, 115 Erie St. S., ON   N8H 3B5   519-326-7169 |
| London | Serena's Place, 720 Headley Dr., ON   N6H 3V6   519-471-6228 |
| Millbank | SW Ontario Countryside Vac., RR #1, ON   N0K 1L0   519-595-4604 |
| Morrisburg | Upper Canada B&B, P.O. Box 247, ON   K0C 1X0 |
| Ottawa | Capital B&B Assoc., 2071 Riverside Dr., ON   K1H 7X2   613-737-4129 |
| Ottawa | Ottawa B&B Assoc., 488 Cooper St., ON   K1R 5H9   613-563-0161 |
| Parry Sound | Parry Sound & District B&B, P.O. Box 71, ON   P2A 2X2   705-342-9266 |
| Pelee Island | Pelee Island B&B Assoc., c/o Lynn Tiessen, ON   N0R 1M0   519-724-2068 |
| Penetanguishene | Penetanguishene Area B&B, C.P. 1270, 63 rue Main, ON   L0K 1P0   705-549-3116 |
| Peterborough | B&B Registry of Peterborough, P.O. Box 2264, ON   K9J 7Y8 |
| Port Elgin | Grey Bruce B&B Assoc., 435 Wellington, ON   N0H 2T0   519-832-5520 |
| Port Stanley | Port Stanley & Sparta Area, 324 Smith St. Box 852, ON   N0L 2A0   519-782-4173 |
| Stratford | Stratford B&B Two, 208 Church St., ON   N5A 2R6   519-273-4840 |
| Toronto | Metropolitan B&B Registry, 615 Mt. Pleasant, ON   M4S 3C5   416-964-2566 |
| Wellington | Prince Edward County B&B, 299 Main St., ON   K0K 3L0   613-399-2569 |

## Prince Edward Island

| Charlottetown | Quality Services, P.O. Box 940, PE   C1A 7MJ   902-368-4446 |
| Kensington | Kensington Area Tourist, RR 1, PE   C0B 1M0   902-436-6847 |

## Province Of Quebec

| Montreal | Mont–Royal Chez Soi, Inc., 5151 Cote-St.-Antoine, PQ   H4A 1P1 |
| Montreal | Montreal Oasis B&B, 3000 Chemin de Bresley Rd., PQ   H3Y 2G7   514-935-2313 |
| Montreal | Relais Montreal Hospitalite, 3977 Ave. Laval, PQ   H2W 2H9   514-287-9635 |
| Quebec | B&B Bonjour Qubec, 450 Rue Champlain, PQ   G1K 4J3   418-524-0524 |
| Quebec | Bonjour Quebec B&B, 450 Rue Champlain, PQ   G1K 4J3   418-524-0524 |
| Quebec | Tourism Quebec, CP 20 000, PQ   G1K 7X2 |
| St-Foy | Gite Quebec, 3729 Ave. le Corbusier, PQ   G1W 4R8   418-651-1860 |

## Saskatchewan

| Blaine Lake | Saskatchewan Country Vac., Box 89, SA   S0J 0J0   306-497-2782 |

## Yukon

| Dawson City | Northern Network of B&B's, Box 954, 451 Craig St., YU   Y0B 1G0   403-993-5644 |
| Whitehorse | Tourism Yukon, Box 2703, YU   Y1A 2C6 |

# B&B Inns with Special Features

## Antiques

Many of the inns we list are graced by antiques. These inns have put a special emphasis on antiques and period decor.

**Foxglove B&B**
Helena, AR
**Inn San Francisco**
San Francisco, CA
**Queen Anne Inn**
New London, CT
**Kalorama Guest House**
Washington, DC
**Cedar House Inn**
St. Augustine, FL
**King-Keith House B&B**
Atlanta, GA
**Lion & The Lamb**
Vinton, IA
**Cornerstone**
Middletown, IN
**Cottage House**
Council Grove, KS
**Lafitte Guest House**
New Orleans, LA
**Black Friar Inn**
Bar Harbor, ME

**Gibson's Lodgings**
Annapolis, MD
**Cranberry Inn**
Chatham, MA
**Goshorn House B&B**
Douglas, MI
**Bluebird B&B**
Gerald, MO
**Glynn House**
Ashland, NH
**Queen Victoria**
Cape May, NJ
**Camas de Santa Fe**
Santa Fe, NM
**Cromwell Manor Inn**
Cornwall, NY
**Cedar Crest**
Asheville, NC
**Sather House B&B**
Bend, OR
**Old Appleford Inn**
Gettysburg, PA

**Dundee Arms Mgmt**
Charlottetown, PE
**Flag Quarters**
Newport, RI
**Maison Du Pre**
Charleston, SC
**Noble Inns**
San Antonio, TX
**Seven Wives Inn**
St. George, UT
**Governor's Inn**
Ludlow Village, VT
**Holly Hill House**
Port Townsend, WA
**Eckhart House**
Wheeling, WV
**Oak Bay Guest House**
Victoria, BC
**Sterns Mansion**
Dartmouth, NS
**Brighton House B&B**
Saskatoon, SK

## Gourmet

An excellent meal can add a lot to your stay. The inns listed here are particularly celebrated for their fine cuisine.

**B&B at Saddle Rock**
Sedona, AZ
**Painted Lady B&B**
Benicia, CA
**Abigail's B&B**
Sacramento, CA
**Hammons House Inn**
Sonora, CA
**Country House Inn**
Templeton, CA
**Mary Lawrence Inn**
Gunnison, CO
**Veranda**
Senoia/Atlanta, GA
**Checkerberry Inn**
Goshen, IN
**Kylemere House 1818**
Kennebunkport, ME

**Betsy's B&B**
Baltimore, MD
**Addison Choate Inn**
Rockport, MA
**Hidden Pond B&B**
Fennville, MI
**Thorwood Historic**
Hastings, MN
**Perry Street**
Cape May, NJ
**Maplecrest B&B**
Rome, NY
**Black Mountain**
Black Mountain, NC
**Lawnridge House**
Grants Pass, OR
**Carriage Corner**
Intercourse, PA

**Page House Inn**
Norfolk, VA
**Prospect Hill**
Trevilians, VA
**Jefferson-Day**
Hudson, WI
**T.C. Smith Historic**
Lake Geneva, WI
**Gilbert House**
Charles Town, WV
**Portage Inlet House**
Victoria, BC
**Wooded Acres B&B**
Victoria, BC

## Architecture

These inns are noted for their unusual and fine architecture.

**Crescent Cottage Inn**
Eureka Springs, AR
**Old Monterey Inn**
Monterey, CA
**Allaire Timbers Inn**
Breckenridge, CO
**Adams Inn**
Washington, DC
**Blue Parrot Inn**
Key West, FL
**Captain Gear**
Galena, IL
**Jeweled Turret Inn**
Belfast, ME
**Diamond District**
Lynn, MA

**Inn at the Pass**
Pass Christian, MS
**Bellevue B&B**
Cape Girardeau, MO
**Voss Inn**
Bozeman, MT
**Hitching Post**
Center Ossipee, NH
**New Brighton Inn**
Ocean City, NJ
**La Hacienda Grande**
Bernalillo, NM
**Book & Blanket**
Jay, NY
**Harmony House Inn**
New Bern, NC

**Olde World B&B**
Dover, OH
**King's Cottage**
Lancaster, PA
**Adams Hilborne**
Chattanooga, TN
**Oxford House**
Stephenville, TX
**Brierley Hill**
Lexington, VA
**Ann Starrett Mansion**
Port Townsend, WA
**Mansion Hill Inn**
Madison, WI
**Markham House B&B**
Victoria, BC

## Comfort

Old-fashioned comfort and friendly staff are important to every lodging. These inns have these qualities in abundance.

**Swan House South**
Seldovia, AK
**Lodge at Sedona**
Sedona, AZ
**Intermountain B&B**
Vail, CO
**Inn at Chester**
Chester, CT
**Kenwood Inn**
St. Augustine, FL
**Kula Cottage**
Kula, Maui, HI
**Wheaton Inn**
Wheaton, IL
**1874 Stonehouse**
Cottonwood Falls, KS

**Hearthside B&B**
Bar Harbor, ME
**Village Green Inn**
Falmouth, MA
**Preston Place**
St. Louis, MO
**Mountain Valley**
Conway, NH
**Normandy Inn**
Spring Lake, NJ
**Galisteo Inn**
Galisteo, NM
**Dartmouth House**
Rochester, NY
**Haywood House**
Waynesville, NC

**Tyee Lodge**
Newport, OR
**Brustman House**
Myrtle Beach, SC
**Brackenridge House**
San Antonio, TX
**Guest House C. Horman**
Stowe, VT
**Pension Tannenhof**
Banff, AB
**Top O' Triangle Mtn**
Victoria, BC
**Palmerston Inn B&B**
Toronto, ON
**Mafolie Hotel**
St. Thomas, VI

## Conference

Small conferences can be very productive when held in the inns listed, all of which have the facilities you need and the quiet and opportunity, too, for the followship you require.

**Briar Patch Inn**
Sedona, AZ
**Homestead Inn**
Greenwich, CT
**Morrison-Clark Inn**
Washington, DC
**Gaslight Inn**
Atlanta, GA
**Poor Farm B&B**
Mount Carmel, IL
**Grant Street Inn**
Bloomington, IN
**Licking Riverside**
Covington, KY

**Stone Manor**
Middletown, MD
**Fairview Inn**
Jackson, MS
**Haus Bavaria**
Incline Village, NV
**Whitneys' Inn**
Jackson, NH
**Parrot Mill**
Chatham, NJ
**Nantahala Village**
Bryson City, NC
**Harrison House**
Guthrie, OK

**John Palmer House**
Portland, OR
**New Dawn Caribbean**
Vieques, PR
**John Rutledge House**
Charleston, SC
**Gilded Thistle**
Galveston, TX
**Pack Creek Ranch**
Moab, UT
**Commencement Bay**
Tacoma, WA
**Manor Guest House**
Vancouver, BC

## Decor

Distinctive decor and unusual architecture are always a pleasure. Enjoy them in these inns.

**Lynx Creek Farm**
Prescott, AZ
**Old World Inn**
Napa, CA
**Eagle Cliff B&B**
Estes Park, CO
**Chimney Crest Manor**
Bristol, CT
**Honeymoon Mansion**
New Albany, IN
**A Little Dream**
Camden, ME
**Union Square House**
Baltimore, MD

**Kemah Guest House**
Saugatuck, MI
**Red Gables B&B**
Lake City, MN
**Walnut Street Inn**
Springfield, MO
**Gingerbread House**
Cape May, NJ
**Polly's Adobe**
Santa Fe, NM
**Addison Rose**
Addison, NY
**Shield House Inns**
Clinton, NC

**Plum Tree**
Portland, OR
**Maplewood Inn**
Fair Haven, VT
**Sugar Tree Inn**
Steele's Tavern, VA
**Hampshire House 1884**
Romney, WV
**Huff House Inn**
Jackson, WY
**Olde England Inn**
Victoria, BC
**Island View**
St. Thomas, VI

## Farm Vacation

The inns listed below are working farms.

**Reedley Country Inn B&B**
Reedley, CA
**Conejos River Guest Ranch**
Conejos, CO
**Hedrick's B&B Inn**
Nickerson, KS
**Thistle Hill B&B**
WaKeeney, KS
**Four Columns B&B**
Sherburn, MN
**Agape Farm B&B**
Corinth, NY
**Spring Creek Llama Ranch**
Newberg, OR

**Meadow Spring Farm B&B**
Kennett Square, PA
**Cedar Hill Farm**
Mount Joy, PA
**Whitehall Inn, The**
New Hope, PA
**Barley Sheaf Farm**
New Hope, Holicong, PA
**Kaltenbach's B&B**
Wellsboro, PA
**Lenape Springs Farm**
Westchester, PA
**Ponda-Rowland B&B Inn**
Wilkes-Barre, PA
**Skoglund Farm**
Canova, SD

**Lakeside Farm B&B**
Webster, SD
**Rockinghorse B&B**
Whitewood, SD
**Berkson Farms**
Enosburg Falls, VT
**Liberty Hill Farm**
Rochester, VT
**Caledonia Farm - 1812**
Washington, VA
**Piney Grove at Southall**
Williamsburg, VA
**Snow Shoe Lodge**
Shell, WY
**Bayview Pines Country Inn**
Mahone Bay, NS

## Fishing

Nothing like a good catch. These inns are near the haunts of the really big ones. Fishing over, head back to the inn and tell tales to fellow enthusiasts.

**Glacier Bear**
Anchorage, AK
**Shenandoah Inn**
Basalt, CO
**Harbour Inne**
Mystic, CT
**Captain's Quarters**
Daytona Beach, FL
**Black Walnut Point**
Tilghman Island, MD
**Edgartown Inn**
Edgartown, MA
**Lindgren's B&B**
Lutsen, MN
**Country Goose Inn**
Olive Branch, MS

**Lone Mountain Ranch**
Big Sky, MT
**Inn at Crystal Lake**
Eaton Center, NH
**Beaverkill Valley**
Lew Beach, NY
**Delamar Inn**
Beaufort, NC
**Columbia Gorge**
Hood River, OR
**White Rose B&B**
Narragansett, RI
**Laurel Hill**
McClellanville, SC
**Willow Springs Cabins**
Rapid City, SD

**Big Spring Inn**
Greeneville, TN
**Wiley Inn**
Peru, VT
**Edgewood Plantation**
Charles City, VA
**Katy's Inn**
La Conner, WA
**Blue Barn B&B**
Big Horn, WY
**Black Cat Ranch**
Hinton, AB
**April Point Lodge**
Campbell River, BC

## Gardens

Ah, to while away an hour in a lovely garden. What could be more relaxing? These inns are renowned for their lush gardens.

**Catalina Park**
Tucson, AZ
**Happy Landing**
Carmel, CA
**Clark Cottage**
Pomfret Center, CT
**Merlinn Guesthouse**
Key West, FL
**Kaia Ranch B&B**
Hana, Maui, HI
**Magnolia Place**
Red Bud, IL
**Slattery House**
Shreveport, LA
**Thurston House**
Searsport, ME

**Inn on Cove Hill**
Rockport, MA
**Cedar Rose Inn**
Alexandria, MN
**Cedar Grove Mansion**
Vicksburg, MS
**Timbers B&B**
Ronan, MT
**Deer Run Ranch**
Carson City, NV
**Notchland Inn**
Hart's Location, NH
**Red Maple Farm**
Princeton, NJ
**Westchester House**
Saratoga Springs, NY

**Mousetrap Inn**
Ashland, OR
**1790 House-B&B**
Georgetown, SC
**Olde English Tudor**
Gatlinburg, TN
**Bonnynook Inn**
Waxahachie, TX
**Trail's End**
Wilmington, VT
**Primrose Cottage**
Williamsburg, VA
**Capital Hill House**
Seattle, WA
**Lighthouse Retreat**
West Vancouver, BC

## Golf

Tee off, walk and relax, then head back to your cozy inn. What could be nicer?

**Canyon Villa B&B**
Sedona, AZ
**Cliff Cottage**
Eureka Springs, AR
**Palm Hotel B&B**
Jamestown, CA
**Ice Palace Inn**
Leadville, CO
**Hoyt House B&B**
Amelia Island, FL
**Hale 'Aha**
Princeville, HI
**Hummingbird Haven**
Tama, IA
**Robert Morris**
Oxford, MD

**Augustus Snow**
Harwich Port, MA
**Pentwater Inn**
Pentwater, MI
**Mrs. B's Historic Inn**
Lanesboro, MN
**Willows Inn**
Red Lodge, MT
**Platte Valley**
North Bend, NE
**Homestead Inn**
Sugar Hill, NH
**Murphin Ridge**
West Union, OH
**Abed & Breakfast**
Corvallis, OR

**Steiger House**
Mercersburg, PA
**Old Oaks Ranch**
Wimberley, TX
**Wildflowers**
Salt Lake City, UT
**Highland Lodge**
Greensboro, VT
**Cooney Mansion**
Aberdeen, WA
**Highlawn Inn**
Berkeley Springs, WV
**Shaughnessy Village**
Vancouver, BC
**Bay View Manor**
New Carlisle, PQ

## Low Price

The following lodgings are particularly noted for modest pricing. It is possible to obtain a room for $40 or less.

**Anderson House Inn**
Heber Springs, AR
**Gualala Hotel**
Gualala, CA
**Endaba Wilderness**
Pagosa Springs, CO
**Open Gates B&B**
Darien, GA
**Sherwood Inn**
New Haven, KY
**Bass Harbor**
Bass Harbor, ME
**Ship's Knees Inn**
East Orleans, MA

**Evelo's B&B**
Minneapolis, MN
**Hostetler House**
Glendive, MT
**Village House**
Jackson, NH
**House by the Sea**
Ocean Grove, NJ
**Red House Country Inn**
Burdett, NY
**B&B at Laurel Ridge**
Siler City, NC
**Custer Mansion**
Custer, SD

**Clardy's Guest House**
Murfreesboro, TN
**Grunberg Haus B&B**
Waterbury, Stowe, VT
**Sky Chalet Lodge**
Basye, VA
**Wolf Hotel**
Saratoga, WY
**Windsor Guest House**
Vancouver, BC
**Fairfield Farm Inn**
Middleton, NS
**Blue Spruces**
Ottawa, ON

# Historic

Inns situated in historic buildings or locales hold a special appeal for many people. The following is a sampling.

**Serenity House B&B**
Mayer, AZ
**Wildflower B&B**
Mountain View, AR
**Meadow Creek Ranch**
Mariposa, CA
**Sonoma Hotel**
Sonoma, CA
**Haus Berlin B&B**
Denver, CO
**Red Brook Inn**
Mystic, CT
**French Renaissance**
Plainfield, CT
**Darley Manor Inn**
Wilmington, DE
**Brigham Gardens**
Miami Beach, FL
**Gram's Place B&B**
Tampa, FL
**Shellmont B&B**
Atlanta, GA
**1810 West Inn**
Thomson, GA
**Cool Breeze Estate**
Evansville, IN
**Phillip W. Smith B&B**
Richmond, IN
**Inn at the Park**
Wichita, KS
**Columbine B&B**
Louisville, KY
**Degas House**
New Orleans, LA
**Soniat House Hotel**
New Orleans, LA
**Lincoln House**
Dennysville, ME
**Jonas Green House**
Annapolis, MD
**White Swan Tavern**
Chestertown, MD
**Inn at Walnut Bottom**
Cumberland, MD
**Honeysuckle Hill**
Cape Cod, W.
Barnstable, MA

**Ashley Inn**
Marthas Vyards/
Edgartown, MA
**Chicago Pike Inn**
Coldwater, MI
**Horse & Carriage B&B**
Jonesville, MI
**Oak Square**
Port Gibson, MS
**Lafayette House**
St. Louis, MO
**Washington House**
Washington, MO
**Commercial Hotel**
Verdigre, NE
**Farm by the River**
North Conway, NH
**Three Rivers House**
North Woodstock, NH
**Woodleigh House**
Cape May, NJ
**Laughing Horse Inn**
Taos, NM
**Mill House Inn**
East Hampton, NY
**Veranda House B&B**
Rhinebeck, NY
**Reed House**
Asheville, NC
**King's Arms Colonial Inn**
New Bern, NC
**Cobbler Shop B&B Inn**
Zoar, OH
**Doubleday Inn**
Gettysburg, PA
**Aaron Burr House Inn**
New Hope, PA
**Wedgewood Inn**
New Hope, PA
**Bellevue House**
Newport, RI
**Cookie Jar B&B**
Wyoming, RI
**Ann Harper's**
Charleston, SC
**Pettigru Place B&B**
Greenville, SC
**Villa Theresa**
Hot Springs, SD

**Hale Springs Inn**
Rogersville, TN
**Little Greenbrier**
Sevierville, TN
**Arrowhill**
Talbott, TN
**McCallum House**
Austin, TX
**Rose Cottage**
Fredericksburg, TX
**Beckmann Inn**
San Antonio, TX
**Blue Church Lodge**
Park City, UT
**Thomas Mott Homestead**
Alburg, VT
**West Dover Inn**
West Dover, VT
**Charleston House**
Woodstock, VT
**North Bend Plantation**
Charles City, VA
**Madison House B&B**
Lynchburg, VA
**Newport House B&B**
Williamsburg, VA
**Harbinger Inn B&B**
Olympia, WA
**Whistling Swan**
Fish Creek, WI
**Arbor House**
Madison, WI
**Dreams of Yesteryear**
Stevens Point, WI
**Eckhart House**
Wheeling, WV
**Durbin Street Inn**
Casper, WY
**Painted Porch**
Jackson Hole, WY
**Annie Moore's Guest House**
Laramie, WY
**Pitcairn House B&B**
Victoria, BC
**Heritage Manor**
St. Thomas, VI

## Luxury

These establishments are famed for their luxurious appointments and special attention to creature comforts and style.

**Lynx Creek Farm**
Prescott, AZ
**Old World Inn**
Napa, CA
**Eagle Cliff B&B**
Estes Park, CO
**Chimney Crest Manor**
Bristol, CT
**Honeymoon Mansion**
New Albany, IN
**A Little Dream**
Camden, ME
**Union Square House**
Baltimore, MD
**Simmons Homestead Inn**
Hyannis Port, MA

**Kemah Guest House**
Saugatuck, MI
**Red Gables B&B**
Lake City, MN
**Walnut Street Inn**
Springfield, MO
**Gingerbread House**
Cape May, NJ
**Polly's Adobe**
Santa Fe, NM
**Addison Rose**
Addison, NY
**Shield House Inns**
Clinton, NC
**Plum Tree**
Portland, OR

**Colonel's Lady**
Gatlinburg, TN
**Maplewood Inn**
Fair Haven, VT
**Sugar Tree Inn**
Steele's Tavern, VA
**White Swan**
La Conner, Mt. Vernon,
WA
**Hampshire House 1884**
Romney, WV
**Huff House Inn**
Jackson, WY
**Olde England Inn**
Victoria, BC
**Island View**
St. Thomas, VI

## Nature

Nature lovers, alert! Whether your fancy is ornithology or whale watching, these inns will speak to your heart.

**Fox Creek B&B**
Fairbanks, AK
**A Puffin's B&B**
Gustavus, AK
**Homestead**
Ahwahnee, CA
**Howard Creek**
Westport, CA
**Boulders Inn**
New Preston, CT
**Mansion House**
St. Petersburg, FL
**Aloha Pualani**
Kihei, Maui, HI

**B&B at Sills Inn**
Versailles, KY
**Oakland House**
Brooksville, ME
**Sea Breeze Inn**
Hyannis, MA
**Cameron's Crag**
Point Lookout, MO
**Good Medicine Lodge**
Whitefish, MT
**Henry Ludlam Inn**
Woodbine, NJ
**All Tucked Inn**
Westport, NY

**InnTowne Inn**
Newport, RI
**Red Horse Inn**
Landrum, SC
**Calico Inn**
Sevierville, TN
**Crystal River Inn**
San Marcos, TX
**Four Columns Inn**
Newfane, VT
**Trillium House**
Wintergreen, VA
**Lakeside Manor Inn**
Delavan, WI

## Outstanding

The following inns are some which, due to attention to detail, amenities and ambiance, are truly outstanding.

**Graham B&B Inn**
Sedona, AZ
**Dairy Hollow House**
Eureka Springs, AR
**Williams House B&B**
Hot Springs, AR
**Carter House**
Eureka, CA
**Bishopsgate Inn**
East Haddam, CT
**Manor House**
Norfolk, CT
**White Barn Inn**
Kennebunkport, ME

**Captain's House Inn**
Chatham, MA
**Rock Ledge Manor**
Rye, NH
**Abbey B&B**
Cape May, NJ
**Barnard-Good House**
Cape May, NJ
**Adelphi Hotel**
Saratoga Springs, NY
**Coachaus Inn**
Allentown, PA
**Inn at Turkey Hill**
Bloomsburg, PA

**1661 Inn**
Block Island, RI
**Admiral Benbow**
Newport, RI
**Battery Carriage Inn**
Charleston, SC
**Planters Inn**
Charleston, SC
**Black River Inn**
Ludlow, VT
**Liberty Rose B&B**
Williamsburg, VA
**Beacon B&B**
Powell River, BC

# Romance

Ah, romance! These inns offer a hideaway, a peaceful space in which to be together and let the world go by.

**Victoria, A Country Inn**
Anniston, AL

**Ghost City Inn B&B**
Sedona, AZ

**Vintage Comfort B&B**
Hot Springs, AR

**Casa Cody B&B**
Palm Springs, CA

**Room @ the Inn**
Colorado Springs, CO

**Red Crags B&B**
Manitou Springs, CO

**Bee and Thistle Inn**
Old Lyme, CT

**Josephine's French Inn**
Seaside, FL

**Pathway Inn**
Americus, GA

**Isle of View**
Metropolis, IL

**Cornstalk Hotel**
New Orleans, LA

**Graycote Inn**
Bar Harbor, ME

**Montague Inn**
Saginaw, MI

**Mockingbird Inn B&B**
Tupelo, MS

**Garth Woodside Mansion**
Hannibal, MO

**Inn on Newfound Lake**
Bridgewater, NH

**Cabernet Inn**
North Conway, NH

**Bay Head Sands B&B**
Bay Head, NJ

**Mooring**
Cape May, NJ

**Cabbage Rose Inn**
Flemington, NJ

**T.R.H. Smith Mansion**
Las Cruces, NM

**Dunshee's B&B**
Santa Fe, NM

**La Tienda Inn**
Santa Fe, NM

**Hacienda Del Sol**
Taos, NM

**La Posada de Taos**
Taos, NM

**Touchstone B&B**
Taos, NM

**Friends Lake Inn**
Chestertown, NY

**Greenville Arms 1889**
Greenville, NY

**Saratoga Rose Inn**
Hadley, NY

**Oliver Loud's Inn**
Pittsford, NY

**Woods Edge B&B**
Rochester, NY

**Apple Tree B&B**
Saratoga Spr, NY

**Ivy Terrace B&B Inn**
Saluda, NC

**Colonel Ludlow Inn**
Winston, NC

**Oceancrest House B&B**
Brookings, OR

**Country House**
Eugene, OR

**Edwin K B&B**
Florence, OR

**Pelican's Perch**
Garibaldi, OR

**Floras Lake House**
Langlois, OR

**Falcon's Crest Inn**
Mt Hood Area, OR

**Cliff House**
Waldport, OR

**Spring House**
Airville, PA

**Reynolds Mansion**
Bellefonte, PA

**Gateway Lodge**
Cooksburg, PA

**Gardens of Eden B&B**
Lancaster, PA

**Noble House**
Marietta, PA

**Hollileif B&B**
New Hope, PA

**Candlelight Inn B&B**
Ronks, PA

**Brinley Victorian Inn**
Newport, RI

**Historic Jacob Hill**
Pawtucket, RI

**Villa, The**
Westerly, RI

**Litchfield Plantation**
Pawleys Island, SC

**Durham House B&B Inn**
Houston, TX

**Eagle's Nest B&B**
Glendale, UT

**Madrigal Inn**
Chester, VT

**Combes Family Inn**
Ludlow, VT

**Village Country Inn**
Manchester, VT

**Inn at Weathersfield**
Perkinsville, VT

**Ye Olde England Inne**
Stowe, VT

**Inn at Blush Hill**
Waterbury, VT

**Deerhill Inn**
West Dover, VT

**Silver Thatch Inn**
Charlottesville, VA

**Ravenswood Inn**
Mathews, VA

**Guesthouse on the Water**
Mollusk, VA

**Widow Kip's Country Inn**
Mount Jackson, VA

**L'Auberge Provencale**
White Post, VA

**Colonial Gardens B&B**
Williamsburg, VA

**Turtleback Farm Inn**
Eastsound, WA

**Angelica's Mansion**
Spokane, WA

**Guest House Cottages**
Whidbey Island, WA

**Eleven Gables**
Lake Geneva, WI

**Victorian Treasure**
Lodi, WI

**St. Croix River Inn**
Osceola, WI

**West End Guest House**
Vancouver, BC

## Skiing

These inns share a proximity to downhill or cross-country skiing. Nothing like coming back from an exhilarating day at the slopes to a warm, cozy fire.

**Pearson's Pond**
Juneau, AK

**River Ranch Lodge**
Tahoe City, CA

**Snow Queen Victorian**
Aspen, CO

**Rose & Thistle**
Barkhamsted, CT

**Idaho Country Inn**
Sun Valley, ID

**Swift River Inn**
Cummington, MA

**Dream Catcher B&B**
Grand Marais, MN

**Ellis River House**
Jackson, NH

**Historic Taos Inn**
Taos, NM

**Habersham Country Inn**
Canandaigua, NY

**Mt. Ashland Inn**
Ashland, OR

**Welsh Run Inn B&B**
Greencastle, PA

**Pine Rest Cabins**
Hill City, SD

**1904 Imperial Hotel**
Park City, UT

**Blueberry Hill**
Goshen, VT

**Weathervane Lodge**
West Dover, VT

**Colonial House**
Weston, VT

**Canterbury House B&B**
Woodstock, VT

**Mazama Country Inn**
Mazama, WA

**Cheat Mountain Club**
Durbin, WV

**A. Drummond's Ranch**
Cheyenne, WY

**Alta Vista Chalet**
Whistler, BC

## Spas

Hot mineral waters are nature's own relaxant. These inns are close to, or are, spas!

**Alaska Ocean View**
Sitka, AK

**Singleton House**
Eureka Springs, AR

**Agate Cove Inn**
Mendocino, CA

**Goodbread B&B**
St. Marys, GA

**York Harbor Inn**
York Harbor, ME

**Down to Earth Lifestyles**
Parkville, MO

**Tuc'Me Inn B&B**
Wolfeboro, NH

**El Paradero**
Santa Fe, NM

**Ramble Brook House**
Phoenicia, NY

**Pines Country Inn**
Pisgah Forest, NC

**White Oak Inn**
Danville, OH

**General Hooker's B&B**
Portland, OR

**White Cloud Inn**
Newfoundland, PA

**Southwind B&B**
Wimberley, TX

**Sweet Onion Inn**
Hancock, VT

**Gladstone House B&B**
Exmore, VA

**Willcox House**
Bremerton, WA

**Kangaroo House B&B**
Eastsound, WA

**Chelsea Station**
Seattle, WA

**Thomas Shepherd Inn**
Shepherdstown, WV

**Window on the Winds**
Pinedale, WY

## Vegetarian

These inns can prepare a vegetarian diet for their guests.

**Alaska Ocean View**
Sitka, AK

**Singleton House**
Eureka Springs, AR

**Agate Cove Inn**
Mendocino, CA

**Goodbread B&B**
St. Marys, GA

**York Harbor Inn**
York Harbor, ME

**Down to Earth Lifestyles**
Parkville, MO

**Tuc'Me Inn B&B**
Wolfeboro, NH

**El Paradero**
Santa Fe, NM

**Ramble Brook House**
Phoenicia, NY

**Pines Country Inn**
Pisgah Forest, NC

**White Oak Inn**
Danville, OH

**General Hooker's B&B**
Portland, OR

**White Cloud Inn**
Newfoundland, PA

**Southwind B&B**
Wimberley, TX

**Sweet Onion Inn**
Hancock, VT

**Gladstone House B&B**
Exmore, VA

**Willcox House**
Bremerton, WA

**Kangaroo House B&B**
Eastsound, WA

**Chelsea Station**
Seattle, WA

**Thomas Shepherd Inn**
Shepherdstown, WV

**Window on the Winds**
Pinedale, WY

# VOTE

## FOR YOUR CHOICE OF
## INN OF THE YEAR

Did you find your stay at a Bed & Breakfast, Inn or Guesthouse listed in this Guide particularly enjoyable? Use the form below, or just drop us a note, and we'll add your vote for the "Inn of the Year." The winning entry will be featured in the next edition of **The Complete Guide to Bed & Breakfasts, Inns and Guesthouses in the U.S., Canada, and Worldwide.**

Please base your decision on:

- Helpfulness of Innkeeper
- Quality of Service
- Cleanliness
- Amenities
- Decor
- Food

Look for the winning Inn in the next Updated & Revised edition of **The Complete Guide to Bed & Breakfasts, Inns and Guesthouses in the U.S., Canada, and Worldwide.**

To the editors of **The Complete Guide to Bed & Breakfasts**:

I cast my vote for "Inn of the Year" for:

Name of Inn _____

Address _____

_____

Phone _____

Reasons _____

_____

I would also like to (please check one)

___ Recommend a new inn ___ Comment ___ Critique ___ Suggest

Name of Inn _____

Address _____

_____

Phone _____

Comment _____

_____

Please send your entries to:
**The Complete Guide to Bed & Breakfast Inns**
**Drawer D**
**Petaluma, CA 94953**

## Subscribe To
# THE COMPLETE GUIDE'S GAZETTE
### Newsletter for B&Bs, Inns, Guest Houses and Small Hotels

To get all the latest on the North American inn scene, events, tips and news, send $95 U.S.$ for your subscription to this informative newsletter. Inns that subscribe to the Gazette have first priority to a full listing in this guide. Don't forget to include your name and address with your order. Send your order to:

The Complete Guide's Gazette
Drawer D
Petaluma, CA 94953

# ON BECOMING AN INNKEEPER

Do you dream of being an innkeeper, meeting and making friends with interesting guests and regaling them with your own special brand of hospitality? Make no mistake, innkeeping is hard work, but can be very rewarding.

We have prepared a packet of information on resources for prospective innkeepers which we will send to you *free of charge*.

Many people prefer to buy an established inn. If you are interested in buying an inn you may wish to contact the editor of this guide regarding information we have on inns for sale. To receive the resource packet or information on inns for sale, please **send your request and a legal size, stamped, self-addressed envelope to:**

The Complete Guide to Bed & Breakfasts, Inns & Guesthouses
Drawer D
Petaluma, CA 94953

# *Lanier Travel Guides*
# In Book Stores Everywhere!

Lanier Travel Guides have set the standard for the industry:

**"All necessary information about facilities, prices, pets, children, amenities, credit cards and the like. Like France's Michelin . . ."—*New York Times*.**

**"Provides a wealth of the kinds of information needed to make a wise choice."—*American Council on Consumer Interest*.**

## Golf Courses
## The Complete Guide

It's about time for a definitive directory and travel guide for the nation's 30 million avid golf players, 7 million of whom make golf vacations an annual event. This comprehensive and updated guide includes over 14,000 golf courses in the United States that are open to the public. Complete details, greens fees, and information on the clubhouse facilities is augmented by a description of each of the golf courses' best features. A beautiful gift and companion to *Golf Resorts—The Complete Guide*. Introduction by Arthur Jack Snyder.

## Golf Resorts International

A wish book and travel guide for the wandering golfer. This guide, written in much the same spirit as the best-selling *Elegant Small Hotels,* reviews the creme de la creme of golf resorts all over the world. Beautifully illustrated, it includes all pertinent details regarding hotel facilities and amenities. Wonderful narrative on each hotel's special charm, superb cuisine and most importantly, those fabulous golf courses. Written from a golfer's viewpoint, it looks at the challenges and pitfalls of each course. For the non-golfer, there is ample information about other activities available in the area, such as on-site health spas, nearby shopping, and more.
Introduction by John Stirling.

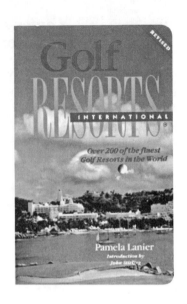

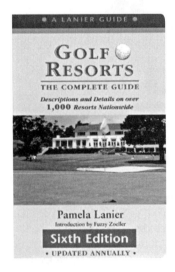

## Golf Resorts —The Complete Guide

The first ever comprehensive and recently updated guide to over 1,000 golf resorts coast to coast. Includes complete details of each resort facility and golf course particulars. "The Complete Guide to Golf Resorts is a wonderful golf destination guide."
—LPGA
Introduction by Fuzzy Zoeller.

## Elegant Small Hotels
### —A Connoiseur's Guide

This selective guide for discriminating travelers describes over 200 of America's finest hotels characterized by exquisite rooms, fine dining, and perfect service par excellence. Introduction by Peter Duchin. "Elegant Small Hotels makes a seductive volume for window shopping."
— *Chicago Sun Times.*

## All-Suite Hotel Guide
### —The Definitive Directory

The only guide to the all suite hotel industry features over 1,200 hotels nationwide and abroad. There is a special bonus list of temporary office facilities. A perfect choice for business travelers and much appreciated by families who enjoy the additional privacy provided by two rooms.

## Condo Vacations
### —The Complete Guide

The popularity of Condo vacations has grown exponentially. In this national guide, details are provided on over 3,000 Condo resorts in an easy to read format with valuable descriptive write-ups. The perfect vacation option for families and a great money saver!

### Elegant Hotels of the Pacific Rim

Over 140 exquisite hotels and resorts located in the burgeoning Pacific Rim. Especially chosen for their inspired architecture, luxurious ambiance and personal service *par excellence*. A must for the globe trotter!

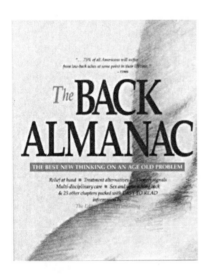

### The Back Almanac
### *The Best New Thinking on an Age-Old Problem*

*by Lanier Publishing*

Just in the nick of time for the 4 out of 5 Americans suffering with back pain, a practical guide to back pain prevention and care. Delightfully illustrated. Internationally acknowledged experts offer the latest thinking on causes, treatment, and pain-free life, including Danger Signals, Sex and Back Pain, and What If Nothing Works? Resource guide lists back schools, pain centers and specialty items.

Revised

"The editors have amassed a wealth of easy-to-find easy-to-read information..." —HEALTHLINE

## AVAILABLE IN BOOK STORES EVERYWHERE